A MANU
OF
MERCANTILE LAW
(INCLUDING INDUSTRIAL LAW)

M.C. SHUKLA

B.A., B.Com. (Birmingham), Barrister-at-Law
Retired Professor of Commerce, and Director of Correspondence
Courses, University of Delhi

For Blanche Shukla Trust

S. CHAND
PUBLISHING
empowering minds

S. CHAND & COMPANY PVT. LTD.
(AN ISO 9001 : 2008 COMPANY)
RAM NAGAR, NEW DELHI-110 055

S. CHAND & COMPANY PVT. LTD.

(An ISO 9001 : 2008 Company)

Head Office: 7361, RAM NAGAR, NEW DELHI - 110 055
Phone: 23672080-81-82, 9899107446, 9911310888 Fax: 91-11-23677446
Shop at: **schandgroup.com**; e-mail: **info@schandgroup.com**

Branches :

AHMEDABAD : 1st Floor, Heritage, Near Gujarat Vidhyapeeth, Ashram Road, **Ahmedabad** - 380 014, Ph: 27541965, 27542369, ahmedabad@schandgroup.com

BENGALURU : No. 6, Ahuja Chambers, 1st Cross, Kumara Krupa Road, **Bengaluru** - 560 001, Ph: 22268048, 22354008, bangalore@schandgroup.com

BHOPAL : Bajaj Tower, Plot No. 2&3, Lala Lajpat Rai Colony, Raisen Road, **Bhopal** - 462 011, Ph: 4274723, 4209587. bhopal@schandgroup.com

CHANDIGARH : S.C.O. 2419-20, First Floor, Sector - 22-C (Near Aroma Hotel), **Chandigarh** -160 022, Ph: 2725443, 2725446, chandigarh@schandgroup.com

CHENNAI : No.1, Whites Road, Opposite Express Avenue, Royapettah, **Chennai** - 600014 Ph. 28410027, 28410058, chennai@schandgroup.com

COIMBATORE : 1790, Trichy Road, LGB Colony, Ramanathapuram, **Coimbatore** - 6410045, Ph: 2323620, 4217136 coimbatore@schandgroup.com **(Marketing Office)**

CUTTACK : 1st Floor, Bhartia Tower, Badambadi, **Cuttack** - 753 009, Ph: 2332580; 2332581, cuttack@schandgroup.com

DEHRADUN : 1st Floor, 20, New Road, Near Dwarka Store, **Dehradun** - 248 001, Ph: 2711101, 2710861, dehradun@schandgroup.com

GUWAHATI : Dilip Commercial (Ist floor), M.N. Road, Pan Bazar, **Guwahati** - 781 001, Ph: 2738811, 2735640 guwahati@schandgroup.com

HALDWANI : Bhatt Colony, Talli Bamori, Mukhani, **Haldwani** -263139 **(Marketing Office)** Mob. 09452294584

HYDERABAD : Padma Plaza, H.No. 3-4-630, Opp. Ratna College, Narayanaguda, **Hyderabad** - 500 029, Ph: 27550194, 27550195, hyderabad@schandgroup.com

JAIPUR : 1st Floor, Nand Plaza, Hawa Sadak, Ajmer Road, **Jaipur** - 302 006, Ph: 2219175, 2219176, jaipur@schandgroup.com

JALANDHAR : Mai Hiran Gate, **Jalandhar** - 144 008, Ph: 2401630, 5000630, jalandhar@schandgroup.com

KOCHI : Kachapilly Square, Mullassery Canal Road, Ernakulam, **Kochi** - 682 011, Ph: 2378740, 2378207-08, cochin@schandgroup.com

KOLKATA : 285/J, Bipin Bihari Ganguli Street, **Kolkata** - 700 012, Ph: 22367459, 22373914, kolkata@schandgroup.com

LUCKNOW : Mahabeer Market, 25 Gwynne Road, Aminabad, **Lucknow** - 226 018, Ph: 4076971, 4026791, 4065646, 4027188, lucknow@schandgroup.com

MUMBAI : Blackie House, IInd Floor, 103/5, Walchand Hirachand Marg, Opp. G.P.O., **Mumbai** - 400 001, Ph: 22690881, 22610885, mumbai@schandgroup.com

NAGPUR : Karnal Bagh, Near Model Mill Chowk, **Nagpur** - 440 032, Ph: 2720523, 2777666 nagpur@schandgroup.com

PATNA : 104, Citicentre Ashok, Mahima Palace, Govind Mitra Road, **Patna** - 800 004, Ph: 2300489, 2302100, patna@schandgroup.com

PUNE : Sadguru Enclave, Ground floor, Survey No. 114/3, Plot no. 8 Alandi Road Vishrantwadi **Pune** – 411015 Ph: 64017298 pune@schandgroup.com

RAIPUR : Kailash Residency, Plot No. 4B, Bottle House Road, Shankar Nagar, **Raipur** - 492 007, Ph: 2443142, Mb. : 09981200834, raipur@schandgroup.com **(Marketing Office)**

RANCHI : Shanti Deep Tower, Opp.Hotel Maharaja, Radium Road, **Ranchi**-834001 Mob. 09430246440 ranchi@schandgroup.com

SILIGURI : 122, Raja Ram Mohan Roy Road, East Vivekanandapally, P.O., Siliguri, **Siliguri**-734001, Dist., Jalpaiguri, (W.B.) Ph. 0353-2520750 **(Marketing Office)** siliguri@schandgroup.com

VISAKHAPATNAM : No. 49-54-15/53/8, Plot No. 7, 1st Floor, Opp. Radhakrishna Towers, Seethammadhara North Extn., **Visakhapatnam** - 530 013, Ph-2782609 (M) 09440100555, visakhapatnam@schandgroup.com **(Marketing Office)**

First Edition 1948
Subsequent Editions and Reprints 1952, 55, 57, 59, 61, 64, 65, 66, 68, 70, 73, 74, 77, 78, 79, 83, 86, 88, 92, 94, 96, 98. 2000. 2002, 2007, 2008 (Twice), 2009 (Twice), Reprint 2010
Enlarged Edition 2014

ISBN: 978-81-219-0241-0   **Code : 1007A 022**

PRINTED IN INDIA
By Nirja Publishers & Printers Pvt. Ltd., 54/3/2, Jindal Paddy Compound, Kashipur Road, Rudrapur-263153, Uttarakhand and published by S. Chand & Company Pvt. Ltd., 7361, Ram Nagar, New Delhi -110 055.

To
the Memory
of My Wife
Blanche Sheila Shukla

PREFACE TO THE THIRTEENTH EDITION

The developments during the period since the publication of the last edition have been such that this thirteenth edition has involved the most substantial revisions. Among statutory changes, those with the most significant and immediate impact, flow from the Companies (Amendment) Act, 1988 and various Notifications issued by the Central Government from time to time, and some of the labour laws, more particularly, Factories Act, Workmen's Compensation Act, Industrial Disputes Act and Payment of Wages Act.

These amendments and case law developments have necessitated thorough and extensive re-writing and updating. Case law has been updated to January, 1991.

The chapters on Contracts and Negotiable Instruments have been considerably strengthened with revised and additional material based upon fresh case law. Apart from these particular areas, where there has been any change in the law, I have revised chapters dealing with other branches of Mercantile or Business Law. These revisions, I believe, will bring still greater clarity to some of the more difficult parts of the book. Great effort has been made to further modernise the book, in the hope that it will prove much more helpful to those for whom it is meant.

In the end, I must continue to offer my grateful thanks to my late wife Blanche Sheila Shukla, for her unflagging assistance and advice at every stage of the publication of the first eleven editions. The dedication of this book to her memory and the transfer of royalties therefrom to a Trust created in her memory is but an inadequate expression of my indebtedness to her.

NEW DELHI.   **M.C. SHUKLA**

PREFACE TO THE FIRST EDITION

The addition of yet another book to the large number of works on Mercantile Law demands, if not apology, certainly an excuse. The excuse for the production of this volume is that it covers the whole teeming ground in a manner differing from the usual textbook, by giving in One volume, a thorough, lucid and easily understandable explana-tion of the various principles of that branch of law which has to deal with mercantile transactions and mercantile community.

The book is intended primarily as a textbook for Pass and Honours students preparing for the various University and Professional Examinations in Mercantile Law, but it cannot fail to be useful to businessmen who have from time to time to deal with several branches of the subject. My aim is to explain the provisions of the different enactments, and in doing so, I have dealth with the law, subject by subject, grouping together the sections of the respective Acts so as to make them simple and logical to the student, convenient to the businessman and interesting to the casual reader who may care to use it as a reference. Even lawyers and practitioners will find the book of practical use inasmuch as it contains in a handy volume the whole range of Mercantile Law, supported by citation of both English and Indian cases and references to the relevant sections of the various Acts. Where controversial points occur, I have based the exposition on the general consensus of standard authoritative opinion of leading writers, and the considered judgments of the Courts. At places I have allowed myself the freedom of expressing my own opinion, with due deference, of course, to the authorities. To facilitate the work of recapitulation, at the time of examination, a summary is given at the end of each chapter. To meet the needs of students preparing for the various examinations held by several British Professional Societies, English, law is explained fully under separate heads. In short, the present work presents the subject from the composite view-point of the student, the businessman, the lawyer and the layman. A maximum range of illustration has been used to illuminate the subject-matter.

I am under considerable obligation to various well-known and monumental legal treatises and take this opportunity to acknowledge the assistance I have derived from them in the preparation of the book.

To thank my wife is but to inadequately express my indebtedness to her, for in the midst of day-to-day lecture work the completion of the book would have been impossible without her unflagging assistance and advice at every stage of its production.

July 1948
Delhi

M.C. SHUKLA

CONTENTS

Nature and Sources of Mercantile Law

PART A

LAW AND SOCIETY

Some knowledge of law is necessary to a greater or lesser extent for all persons. The truth of this statement is obvious, because life of each member of society must proceed to a large extent in conformity with recognised rules and principles of social conduct. Indeed, an individual is confronted almost daily with situations that demand legal information for correct action. Just as a game of football or hockey could not be played satisfactorily without rules to govern the players, so life in general and the business world in particular could not continue without law to regulate the conduct of people and to protect their property and contract rights. Without rules the athletic contest would soon become a brawl. Without law life and business would soon become a matter of the survival not only of the fittest but also of the most ruthless. Without law, our rights would not be secure because we would not know whether rights existing today would be respected tomorrow.

What is Law? Law in its legal sense, as distinguished from other uses of the term, means those rules and principles that govern and regulate social conduct and the observance of which can be enforced in courts. It operates to regulate the actions of persons in respect to one another and in respect to the entire social group or society.

Law is either Public Law or Private Law. *Public Law* concerns the public as a whole and is divided into three classes — Constitutional Law, Administrative Law and Criminal Law.

Private Law pertains to individuals. It is separated into such special fields as contracts, agencies, sales, surety-ships, negotiable instruments, etc. These areas generally are the ones that pertain to business and are termed as Business Law or Commercial Law or Mercantile Law. Our immediate concern is with this branch of law. *Mercantile Law* may be defined as that branch of law which deals with the rights and obligations of mercantile persons arising out of mercantile transactions in respect of mercantile property. An individual, a partnership or a company, carrying on business, is a mercantile person. This law, in turn is founded on the law of contract. The present book deals with the various segments of mercantile or business law as well as some sections of industrial law.

SOURCES OF MERCANTILE LAW

Indian Mercantile Law is, in the main, an adaptation of the English law, it is incorporated in a number of Acts, which follow to a considerable extent the English Mercantile Law with some reservations and modifications necessitated by the peculiar conditions obtaining in India. To ascertain the sources of Indian Mercantile Law we have, therefore, to trace the sources of the English Mercantile Law. The sources of English Mercantile Law are: (1) The Common Law; (2) Equity; (3) The Law Merchant; and (4) The Statute Law.

THE COMMON LAW

The first source of the law is the customary conduct of community life. Group life creates customs, and when these customs become stabilized to the extent that each member of the society is justified in assuming that every other member of society will respect them and will act in conformity with them, it can be said that rules of conduct have been formulated. When these rules of conduct have received the recognition of the community in general and have become formally expressed in judicial decisions, the 'Law' is made. The court, by its decision, lays down a principle, based upon a custom or convenience, and thus creates a precedent which will be controlling in similar future controversies. Thus the Common Law consists of principles based on immemorial custom and enforced by the courts. It is traditionally **unwritten** law, developed in English courts during the period beginning with the thirteenth century and extending into the eighteenth century, and brought to this country by the British rulers of India. It is to be found in some thousands of volumes of reported cases and is common to the whole realm.

EQUITY

In early times the administration of the law was not altogether free from abuses of the grossest kind. The King's officers were sometimes corrupt and partial. In extreme cases the poor subjects had to seek redress of their wrongs by petition to the King, who was the ultimate fountain of justice. Originally the king heard these petitions, but later he began to refer them to his Council. The foremost officer of the King's Council was the Chancellor, who was in the early days generally an ecclesiastic and, therefore, referred to as "Keeper of the King's Conscience." It was, therefore, a natural development that after the middle of the 14th century, all "matters of grace" were addressed directly to the Chancellor. One more cause led to the development of equity. A common-law action was begun by the issue of a writ of summons out of the King's Chancellery or Chancery. The Chancellor and his clerks issued an appropriate writ after hearing the plaintiff and the subsequent proceedings in relation to the suit were determined by the Common Law Judges. In course of time the writs issued from the Chancery became classified and rigid, as is the custom in judicial procedure. But while legal procedure was stiffening, civilization was progressing, society was becoming more and more complex and new relationships between persons were growing up. Who was to supply remedies for new grievances? The common law was too stereotyped to do this. So it came about that there was no writ suitable to meet the case presented to the Chancery by way of petition or complaint, it was then open to the Chancellor, if he found that the common law was deficient, to issue his own **subpoena**—a direction to attend under penalty in case of disobedience—and reserve the case for hearing by the King-in-Council. It was out of this reservation that the jurisdiction of the Court of Chancery arose. From being an office for the issue of common-law writs, it became a court for the hearing of special classes of cases. The rules applied by the Chancery in the exercise of this jurisdiction became known as' 'Equity". Equity in a number of cases mitigated the rigour of the common law in order to carry out the real intentions of the parties.

Equity also developed new remedies. The common law courts only awarded damages, and were without the remedy of injunction to prevent the commission of a tort and had no machinery to compel the specific performance of a contract. The power of the courts of equity to compel personal obedience enabled them to invent these and other much useful remedies. After a time the principles and procedure of equity became virtually as fixed as those of common law. The quality of English law, and the conflicts between law and equity were burdensome, and were put an end to by the Judicature Acts of 1873-75, which enacted that, where the rules of law and equity conflict, equity shall prevail. At the same time one Supreme-Court was constituted with separate Divisions for common law work (King's Bench Division) and equity or chancery work (Chancery Division). But either division can give whatever remedy is most appropriate. In India also, equity empowers Courts to deal with harsh cases where the ordinary law fails to provide any remedy.

THE LAW MERCHANT

The Law Merchant was an independent body of customs and usages governing commercial transactions of the merchants and traders of the Middle Ages, which have been ratified by the decisions of the Courts of Law. The Common Law of England became fixed at a time when little or no attention was paid to trading. Hence, among traders there sprang up a number of customs and usages which were necessary for the conduct of business. During this period the body of commercial usages was practically uniform throughout Europe. In its earliest stages, therefore, the Law Merchant was a kind of private international law administered by tribunals consisting principally of the merchants themselves.

Virtually it fell into two branches, the Law Merchant properly so-called, the Law of Fair and Market, and the Maritime or Sea Law, which early came under the dominion of Admiralty Courts staffed by civilians (lawyers trained to Roman Law) in all the countries of Europe. For many years the English Courts refused to recognise these customs and usages; but a change took place when the administration of law fell into the hands of lawyers who were not irrevocably tied down to ancient ideas. After the beginning of the 17th century the King's Courts began to give effect to the rules of the Law Merchant, the special merchants tribunals dwindled into insignificance and gradually died out. The first great judge to exercise his influence in the recognition of these customs and usages was Lord Holt, but his work was overshadowed by the labours of Lord Mansfield, who was Lord Chief Justice from 1756 to 1787. To Lord Mansfield, Mercantile Law owes more than to many generations of England's legislators. The Law Merchant has, since his time, been regarded as part of the Common Law and is consequently judicially noticed so that a custom once established in Court requires a Statute to alter it. In *Goodwin v. Roberts* (1875), L. R. 10 E.X. Cockburn, C J. observed:' 'The Law Merchant is neither more nor less than the usages of merchants and traders in the different departments of trade, ratified by the decisions of Courts of Law, which upon such usages being proved before them, have adopted them as settled law with a view to the interests of trade and the public convenience, the Court proceeding herein on the well-known principle of law that, with reference to transactions in the different departments of trade, Courts of law, in giving effect to the contracts and dealings of the parties, will assume that the latter have dealing with one another on the footing of any custom or usage prevailing generally in the particular department. By this process, what before was usage only, unsanctioned by legal decision, has become engrafted upon, or incorporated into, the Common Law, and may thus be said to form part of it"

The Law Merchant, or **lex mercatoria**, is the origin of much of the law relating to negotiable instruments, trade marks, partnerships, contracts of affreightment and insurance. In India, the Law Merchant is codified, and the Courts are left only with the task of interpreting the language of the Acts. But where some principles of the Law Merchant (Indian trade customs and usages) are not covered by those Acts, the Indian Courts generally apply the English Law on the subject.

THE STATUTE LAW

The Statute Law means Acts of Parliament. These are the most efficient and the most usual way of bringing about changes in the law today. The authority of the Parliament is supreme, and subject to natural limitations and those laid down by the Constitution, it can pass any law it pleases, and is not bound by its previous Acts. It is also within the power of Parliament to nullify the decisions of the Courts of Law. The Statute Law, therefore, ranks in priority to Common Law and Equity. But while Parliament is supreme in legislation, the Courts of Law are the interpreters of the meaning of the Acts of Parliament. Acts of the Indian Legislature based mainly on the English Mercantile Law form by far the most important source of Indian Mercantile Law. Where there are no Acts relating to certain matters or where Acts are ambiguous, the Common Law of England is applied.

CHAPTER

1

Contracts

PART 1 - A
NATURE AND KINDS OF CONTRACTS

INTRODUCTION

The law of contracts forms the oldest branch of the law relating to business or to commercial transactions. In one form or another it has existed from the beginning of organised society. Just as the safety of person and of property depends upon the rules of criminal law, so the security and stability of the business world are dependent upon the law of contracts. Indeed the basis of trade and commerce today is the enforceability of promises. It would be impossible to plan ahead if we did not have the assurance that agreements once made would be binding. An essential part of enterprise in our economic system is that the rights created by promises are protected and enforced. It is with the enforceability of these promises that the law of contracts is concerned. Furthermore the law of contracts furnishes the foundation for the other branches of commercial or mercantile law. In fact the law of contracts affects every one of us; for every one of us enters into contracts day after day. In every purchase that one makes, or a loan of book that one makes to a friend of his, or a ride that one takes in a bus, in all these and many other transactions of daily life he enters into contracts. For these reasons the study of the general principles of contract law naturally precedes the specialised fields of contracts.

In business transactions, where promises are very often made at one time and the performance is to follow later, the parties have two alternatives open to them. They may either rely upon one another's honour to ensure performance, or else there should be a legally enforceable obligation to perform the agreement. Reliance upon honour alone is insufficient protection. Legal, means of enforcing promises has, therefore, been developed in civilised societies. Legally enforceable promises are termed contracts. Promises that do not meet the requirements of a contract is the most common means of rendering a promise enforceable. The object and function of the law of contract is to see that, as far as it is possible, expectations created by promises of the parties are fulfilled and obligations prescribed by the agreement of the parties are enforced. The contract is, indeed, a cement that holds our economic system together. For this reason the sanctify of contract has always been made an objective of social control and individual liberty.

DEFINITION OF CONTRACT

In the broadest sense, a contract is an exchange of promises by two or more persons, resulting in an obligation to do and refrain from doing a particular act, which obligation is recognised and enforced by law. In creating a legal obligation contract gives a right to one person and casts a corresponding duty on another person. On account of the presence of rights and obligations, the law gives a remedy for the breach of promise and recognises its due performance as a duty. Hence a contract is sometimes defined as "an agreement creating an obligation," which means a binding agreement. Our Contract

Act [S.2(h)] defines a contract as ''an agreement enforceable by law." This definition[1] naturally resolves itself into two distinct parts. First, there must be an **agreement** Secondly, such an agreement must be **enforceable by law.** It will be so enforceable if it is coupled with obligation. Therefore, a contract is a combination of the two ideas of agreement and obligation. An agreement is necessarily the outcome of consenting minds, or there is **consensus ad idem**—consent to the matter. An obligation is the legal duty to do or abstain from doing what one has promised to do or abstain from doing. A contractual obligation arises from a bargain between the parties to the agreement, who are called the **Promisor** and the **Promisee.** In most commercial contracts each party is both a promisor and promisee; that is to say, the contract is formed by mutual promises. If A promises to deliver B a bag of wheat in a week's time for ₹ 100, payable in a fortnight, A is promisor as to delivery, and B is promisor as to payment, while B is promisee of the delivery of the bag of wheat and A is promisee as regards the money to be paid.

It follows from the foregoing discussion that where parties have made a binding contract, they have created rights and obligations between themselves. The contractual rights and obligations are correlative. For example, A agrees with B to sell his car for ₹ 20,000 to B. In this example, the following rights and obligations have been created:

(i) A is under an obligation to deliver the car to B: B has a correlative right to receive the car.

(ii) B is under an obligation to pay ₹ 20,000 to A: A has a correlative right to receive the ₹ 20,000.

All obligations, however, are not contractual in nature. For instance the obligations resulting from the following are not contractual, namely:—

1. Torts or civil wrongs;
2. Quasi-contracts:
3. Judgments of courts—Contracts of Record;
4. Relationship between husband and wife, trustee and beneficiary—status obligations.

As the law of contracts excludes from its purview all such obligations, and agreements of social nature and hence is not enforceable by law. Salmond observes: "The Law of Contracts is not the whole law of agreements, nor is it the whole law of obligations. It is the law of those agreements which create obligations, and those obligations which have their source in agreements." Also, agreement is the genus of which contract is the species; and, therefore, all contracts are agreements, but all agreements are not contracts. Only those agreements which are enforceable by law are contracts. Thus, legally enforceable promises are termed contracts. Promises that do not meet the requirements of a contract are not enforceable. Hence, the making of a contract is the most common means of rendering a promise enforceable. But to be a valid contract it must fulfil certain requirements or possess certain essential elements. We shall deal with these essentials in the following pages, after narrating the different kinds of contracts.

KINDS OF CONTRACTS

Contracts may be classified in terms of their form, or in terms of their enforceability, or the way they are created.

---

1. Our definition follows Pollock's definition which is: "Every agreement and promise enforceable at law is a contract" Salmond defines a contract as "an agreement creating and defining obligations between the parties." Anson says: "A contract is an agreement enforceable at law made between two or more persons, by which rights are acquired by one or more to acts or forbearances on the part of the other or others." Leak observes: "An agreement as the source of a legal contract imports that one party shall be bound to some performance which the other shall have a legal right to enforce." Williston's definition is: "A promise or set of promises, for the breach of which the law gives a remedy, or the performance of which the law in some other way recognizes as a duty."

FORMAL AND SIMPLE CONTRACTS

Contracts are classified in terms of their form as (1) contracts under seal, (2) contracts of record, and (3) simple or parol contracts. The first two classes are known as formal contracts, their validity or legal force being based upon form alone. When the terms of an obligation are written or .printed upon paper or parchment and are signed, sealed, and delivered, the obligation constitutes a **contract under seal**. An instrument of this nature is technically known as a deed or a **common-law specialty.**

An obligation imposed by the judgement of a court and entered upon its records is often called a **contract of record.**

It cannot accurately be described as a contract, however, because it is really not based upon an agreement of the parties. One form of contract of record is in fact a contract. This kind exists when one acknowledges before a competent court that he is bound or obligated to pay a certain sum unless specified thing is done or not done. For example, a party who has been arrested may be released on his promise to appear in court and may bind himself to pay a certain sum in the event that he fails to do so. An obligation of this kind is known as a **recognisance.**

All contracts other than contracts of record and contracts under seal are called **simple** or **parol contracts**, whether they are in writing or merely oral. A parol or simple contract, whether oral or in writing, must be supported by 'consideration.'

Formal contracts or contracts under seal, recognised under the English law, do not find any place in the Indian law. The simple or parol contract supported by consideration is the type of contract largely recognised under the Indian Contract Act. Form alone does not allow to dispense with consideration under the Indian Act. But S.25(l) of the Act makes provision for a kind of contract which to some extent resembles the formal contract or specialty of English law, and is enforceable, if it satisfies four conditions, namely,— (1) the contract must be in writing, (2) it must be registered according to the law of registration of documents, (3) it must be between parties standing in near relation to each other, and (4) it should proceed out of a natural love and affection between the parties.

EXPRESS AND IMPLIED CONTRACTS

Simple contracts may be classified in terms of the way in which they are created as (1) express contracts, and (2) implied contracts.

An Express Contract is one in which the parties have made an oral or written declaration of their intentions and of the terms of the transaction. In other words, an express contract is one, the terms of which are stated in words, spoken or written.

An Implied Contract is one in which the evidence of the agreement is not shown by words, written or spoken, but by acts and conduct of the parties. Such a contract arises when one person, without being requested to do so, renders services under circumstances indicating that he expects to be paid for them, and the other person, knowing such circumstances, accepts the benefit of those services. An implied contract cannot arise when there is an existing express contract on the same subject. Thus, *contracts in which the manifestation of assent is purely acts rather than words are termed implied contracts.*

Under certain conditions the law creates and enforces legal rights and obligations when no real contract, express or implied, exists. These obligations are known as *quasi-contracts.* A quasi or constructive contract rests upon the equitable principle that a person shall not be allowed to enrich himself unjustly at the expense of another. In truth, however, it is not a contract at all. Duty, and not a promise or agreement or intention of the person sought to be charged, defines it. We shall have more to say about it at a later stage.

VALID, VOIDABLE, VOID AND UNENFORCEABLE CONTRACTS

Contracts may be classified also in terms of their enforceability or validity as (1) valid contracts,

(2) voidable contracts, (3) void contracts or void agreements, and (4) unenforceable contracts.

A **Valid Contract** is an agreement which is binding and enforceable. It has all the essential elements to be stated and discussed later.

A **Voidable Contract** is an agreement that is binding and enforceable but, because of the lack of one or more of the essentials of a valid contract, it may be repudiated by the aggrieved party at his option. If the party having the right to avoid his obligation does not exercise the right within a reasonable time, the agreement is binding and enforceable.

A **Void Contract** is really not a contract at all. The term means an agreement which is without any legal effect. Thus an agreement by a minor is void under the Indian law.

An **Unenforceable Contract** is one which, though perfectly valid in all other respects, lacks some technical requirement needed to make it enforceable, e.g., some necessary written evidence. Such a contract will not be enforced by the courts unless and until the defect is rectified. Thus contracts for the sale of land or any interest therein must be evidenced in writing, signed by the defendant, before they can be the subject of a successful action at law.

But such unenforceable contracts are not void, and therefore if they have been performed and property has been transferred the court will not intervene to set the agreement aside. Thus, if A really agrees to buy B's house and pays a deposit to B, then later changes his mind and refuses to sign a written contract to purchase the house, B will be unable to sue A for damages or performance of the contract but will be able to keep A's deposit, and the court will not assist A to recover it.

EXECUTED AND EXECUTORY CONTRACTS

Contracts may be classified in terms of the extent to which they have been performed or carried out as (1) executed contracts, and (2) executory contracts.

An **executed contract** is one that has been completely performed. In other words, an executed contract is one under the terms of which nothing remains to be done by either party. A contract may be executed at once, (i.e., at the time the contract is made), as in the case of a cash sale; or it may become executed in the future by its terms being carried out in due time.

An **executory contract** is composed of undertaking in which one or both parties are under an obligation to do or not to do certain things. In other words, under the terms of the contract something remains to be done. For example, if an electric supply company agrees to furnish electricity to another party for a specified period of time at a stipulated price the contract is executory. If the entire price is paid in advance, the contract is still deemed executory; although, strictly speaking, it is executed on one side and executory on the other.

BILATERAL AND UNILATERAL CONTRACTS

An agreement may originate in one of the several ways. **First,** there may be. an offer of a promise and a simple assent. This is possible only when the promise is under seal or of record, in which case it is binding because of its form alone. This way or mode of making contract is applicable in English law and not in Indian law. **Second way** in which there may be an offer of an act for a promise, as when a public omnibus by running on its route makes an offer of its services for the promise of the one entering to pay his fare. **Third,** there may be an offer of a promise for an act, as one promises to pay a specified sum for the performance of an act, such as the returning of lost goods. **Fourth,** an agreement may originate in an offer of a promise for a promise, as when one person offers to pay ₹ 100 in return for the promise of another to paint his car. The first three methods result in **Unilateral** contracts, because in each instance there is an obligation to perform on the part of only one party. The fourth or last method creates a **Bilateral** contract, in that there is an obligation on the part of both to do or to refrain from doing a particular thing. In the case of a **unilateral** or **one-sided** contract, one party to the contract has performed his part even at the time of its formation and an obligation is outstanding only against the other. In the **bilateral** or **two-sided** contract, at the time of its formation there are two outstanding obligations, one on either party to the contract, e.g., *A* promises to paint a picture in one month in return for which *B* promises to pay ₹ 100. Here, there are two promises and each party is a promisor in respect of one promise and a promisee in respect of the other, and as such each can hold the other liable for the breach of his promise.

It follows from the above distinction between executed and executory contracts and between unilateral and bilateral contracts that a **contract is a contract from the time it is made and not from the time its performance is due.** Thus, the fact that in an executory contract, both the parties have to perform their parts of the contract does not affect the validity of the contract. It was stated in *Sahab Ram* v. *Ram Niwas* (1953) I All. 494 (F.B.), that the fact that the agreement has not been executed or performed does not mean that the agreement was not entered into. Similarly, there may be cases in which performance of a contract is postponed or deferred. Thus, where *A* agrees to supply 100 quintals of wheat three months after the date of contract, the performance will become due three months after the date of the contract but the contract will be a contract on the date when the offer is accepted and other conditions of a valid contract are complied with.

In the following sections of this chapter are discussed the foregoing types or classes of contracts, starting with a valid contract and its essentials.

ESSENTIALS OF A VALID CONTRACT

In order to be an enforceable contract, there must be (1) an agreement, (2) based upon the genuine assent of the parties, (3) supported by consideration, (4) made for a lawful object, (5) between competent parties. These requirements of valid contract may be analysed into the following elements, all of which must be present:

1. Proposal or offer by one party and acceptance of the proposal or offer by another party, resulting in an **agreement—Consensus ad-idem;**
2. An intention to create legal relationship or an intent to have legal consequences;
3. Genuine; (i.e., free and real) consent between the parties (i.e., not marred by mistake, undue influence, coercion, fraud or misrepresentation);
4. The parties to the contract are capable of contracting;
5. The object contracted for is legal and is not opposed to public policy;
6. There are at least two persons to make the contract;
7. The agreement is supported by lawful consideration (or, under English law, proper form is used);
8. The agreement is capable of being performed.
9. The terms of the contract are certain.

PART 1-B
THE AGREEMENT

A contract is a legally binding agreement. This agreement results when one person, the offeror or **promisor**, makes a proposal or offer and the person to whom the offer is made, the **offeree** or **promisee**, accepts it. For an agreement to arise, there must be two or more parties to the transaction. As it is imperative that there be a concurrence of at least two minds, it is impossible for one person to make an agreement with himself. To illustrate, when a person in his official capacity, a Managing Director of a company, makes a promise to himself, as an individual, no agreement is formed by an acceptance in the latter capacity. Plurality of persons is an essential characteristic of an agreement These persons must come to an understanding with a view to creating a right in one party and a corresponding duty on the other. The Contract Act [S. 2(e)] defines an agreement as "every promise and every set of promises, forming the consideration for each other."

CONSENSUS AD IDEM OR MEETING OF MINDS

To constitute an agreement or a contract there must be a meeting of the minds of the parties and both must agree to the same thing in the same sense. This means the will of the parties must meet, or there must be *consensus ad idem*. For example, *A*, a painter, agrees to paint the house of *B* and *B* agrees to pay *A* the sum of ₹ 2,000 upon the satisfactory completion of the work. In this case, there is a meeting of the minds of *A* and *B* on the subject of what is to be done and at what price. Generally speaking, it is true that the minds of the parties must meet, but it is not literally or universally true; for in a few peculiar situations the law finds an agreement even though the minds of the parties have not in fact met. For example, an auctineer may say, ''Who will pay ₹ 100 for this beautiful vase?'' If a person in the crowd present there raises his hand while looking at the auctioneer, his action is regarded by the law as an offer to pay ₹ 100 and, if the auctioneer then brings down his hammer and says. "Sold f   o   r ₹ 100," there is an acceptance and a binding contract. The man who raised his hand cannot be allowed to say that when he raised it, he did not mean to make an offer but was merely stretching his arm. What was in his mind is immaterial because it was reasonable for the auctioneer to assume that the man's motion was an offer. The real test, therefore, is not whether the minds of the parties met but whether under the circumstances one party was reasonably entitled to believe that there was an offer and the other to believe that there was an acceptance.

When we say that there must be a meeting of the minds of the parties, we are not thinking of the subjective thing known as meeting of the minds, but the objective thing— manifestation of mutual assent. Therefore, it is not the meeting of the minds, but the expression of mutual and final assent that is necessary to complete a binding agreement. The reason for the rule is that the inner intention of parties to a conversation cannot be taken to bind the parties, but it is what is said or done. Innermost thoughts of a parties are known only to him, and the other party can depend upon what is said or done. Thus, if *A* signs an agreement to purchase a certain gold watch for ₹ 1,000 from B, the agreement is binding, although *A* later testifies that he never actually intended to buy it. By his conduct he led *B*, as a reasonable man, to think that he would buy it. Such conduct is all that the law requires. To repeat, the phrase 'meeting of the minds' does not mean that the parties must have arrived at a common mental state touching the matter in hand. The standard by which their conduct is judged and their rights are limited is not internal but external. In the absence of fraud or incapacity, the question is: what did the parties say and do? In other words, there is an agreement when the parties lead each other reasonably to believe that they are of the same mind about a given transaction; they have come to the point of agreement and the offer and acceptance have coincided. This is because *consensus ad idem* is the bedrock of contractual jurisprudence.

OFFER OR PROPOSAL

One of the early steps in the formation of a contract lies in arriving at an agreement between the contracting parties by means of offer and acceptance. One party makes a definite proposal to the other, and that other accepts it in its entirety. In its general terms, an offer or proposal is a statement by the offeror of what he will give in return for some act or promise of the offeree. Section 2 (a) of the Contract Act defines an offer or proposal as follows: "When one person signifies to another his willingness to do or to abstain from doing anything, with a view to obtaining the assent of that other to such act or abstinence, he is said to make a proposal." In simple words, an offer is a proposal by one person, whereby he expresses his willingness to enter into a contractual obligation in return for a promise, or act, or forbearance. Note the offer consists of two parts: (1) a promise by the offeror, coupled with (2) a request addressed to the offeree for something in return. The promise that the offeror makes is not binding upon him until the offeree unconditionally assents to the terms contained in the offer. For example, *A* offers ₹ 5 to B if he would mow his lawn. The promise to pay ₹ 5 is binding as soon as B promises to mow the lawn. Until then *A* is free to withdraw his offer.

REQUIREMENTS OF AN OFFER

A valid offer must meet the tests of (1) contractual intention, (2) definiteness, and (3) communication to the offeree,

(1) Contractual Intention—To Constitute an offer, the offeror must intend to create a legal obligation. When there is a lack of such intention on his part, it makes no difference whether the offeree takes any action concerning the offer. Parties are free to make their own agreement, and if they agree that the breach of either party will not give rise to legal rights, there is no contract, even though the offer and acceptance have been reduced to writing. Hence, an offer must contemplate to give rise to legal consequences and be capable of creating legal relations. The following are the examples of a lack of contractual intention on the part of the offeror.

(a) **Social Invitations**—Ordinary invitations to social affairs are not offers in the eyes of the law, because the idea of bargain is absent in such cases and there is no intention to create a legal relationship. An agreement between two persons to go together to pictures, or for a walk does not create a legal obligation on their part to abide by it, as it relates to social matters.

A invited *B* to dinner at his house on a specified date. On the stated date, *A* forgot all about the dinner and his invitation to *B*. When *B* arrived at *A*'s residence *A* was not there and no dinner was ready. This agreement did not give rise to a legally binding agreement, and *B* could not enforce it or claim compensation for expense and inconvenience.

Agreement between a husband and wife who are living in friendly intercourse are not contracts but only domestic arrangements.

In *Balfour* v. *Balfour* (1919) 2 K.B. 571, the husband promised to pay £30 to his wife every month. On his failure to pay, the wife sued him for the recovery of the amount *Held,* she could not recover as the agreement did not create any legal relationship. Warrington, L. J. observed: "... There is no contract here. These people never intended to make a bargain which could be enforced in law. The husband expressed his intention to make this payment, and he promised to make it, and was bound in honour to continue it so long as he was in a position to do so. The wife, on the other hand, made no bargain at all."

In the words of Danckwert LJ in *Jones* v. *Padavattan* (1969) I WLR 328, the *Balfour* "principle applies to dealings between other relations, such as father and son, daughter and mother".

But in *Williams* v. *Williams* (1957) I WLR 148, a wife deserted her husband. He entered into an agreement by which he promised to pay her 30 shillings a week if she would maintain herself and undertake not to pledge his credit He fell in arrear with the payments, and the wife sued him. He pleaded in defence want of consideration. *Held,* there was consideration and the husband was liable to pay.

Also in *Merrit* v. *Merrit* (1970) I WLR 1211, an agreement to transfer to the wife the beneficial ownership of the matrimonial home made at the time of separation was held to be binding.

However, even in business matters parties may wish to rely on each other's good faith and honour and not on the courts. Thus, for example, in *Rose and Frank Co.* v. *J.R.. Crompton* (1923) 2 K.B.261, an agreement contained the following clause: "This arrangement is not entered into as formal legal agreement and shall not be subject to a legal jurisdiction in the law courts." *Held,* the document did not constitute a binding contract as there was no intention to create legal relations.

(b) **Offers made in Jest or Excitement**—A person may make a proposal or statement in a jest without any thought or intention of creating a binding obligation. A proposal made in jest, cannot be expected by the offeree as a reasonable man, to have been made with the intention of making a contract. Also, a person, labouring under the stress of great emotion or excitement, may make a statement that cannot be treated as an offer on account of the fact that it would be obvious to a reasonable man that a legal relation is not contemplated/Promises held out over loudspeakers are often claptrap of politics. Also, as pointed out by Chandrachud, J. later (C.J.) in *Banwarilal* v. *Sukhdarshan Dayal* (1973) 1 S.C.294,' 'microphones have not yet acquired notriety as carriers of binding representations. In the instant case, the announcement was, if at all, a puffing up of property for sale". In this case, in an auction sale of plots of land, a loudspeaker was spelling out the terms of the sale. One of the statements made was that a plot of certain dimension would be reserved for *Dharamshala*, but the plot was sold for private purposes. In an action to restrain the sale of the plot, it was held that the statement was not binding.

(c) **Invitation to Negotiate**—The first statement made by one of the two persons is not necessarily an offer. In many cases there may be preliminary discussion or an invitation by one party to the other to negotiate or talk business. If *A* asks *B*, "Do you want to buy this car of mine?" he is not making an offer but is inviting an offer from *B*. If *B* then says, "I will pay you ₹ 3,000 for the car," he is making an offer that A can accept or reject. On the other hand, after *A*'s invitation, *B* may continue the preliminary negotiations by saying, "What do you want for it?" If A then replies, "I will sell it to you for ₹ 8,000," A makes an offer.

A offered to buy *M*'s bungalow for ₹ 6,000 and *M*'s agent in India cabled to *M* in England: "Have had offer Rupees Six thousand for immediate possession", To this the agent received a reply by cable:' 'Won't accept less than ten thousand". On inquiry by A the agent replied:" I received yesterday a cable from Col. *M* regarding your offer which reads as follows: "Won't accept less than rupees ten thousand". *A* accepted the price of ₹ 10,000 and confirmed it by letter to the agent. But *M* sold the bungalow for a higher price to another. *A* sued for specific performance of the contract. The Supreme Court held that a mere statement of the lowest price at which the vender will sell contains no implied contract to sell at the price to the person making the inquiry. There was no offer by *M* and the whole transaction was still at the negotiation stage (*Macpherson* v. *Apanna*(1941) S.C.184.)

(d) **Invitation to offer**—Ordinarily, marked prices of goods, do not constitute an offer so as to compel the tradesman to sell those goods at the marked prices. Similarly, advertising is not held as offers. Advertisements are generally assumed to constitute "invitations to trade" rather than offers. The trader merely indicates that he is willing to consider an offer made by a buyer on these terms. In other words, he is inviting an offer and not making one. Also, a circular inviting tenders for sale or purchase does not amount to an offer, but only an invitation to offer and unless an offer is accepted no contract is made. Again, an announcement that a person will sell his property at public auction to the highest bidder is a mere declaration of intention to hold an auction at which bids will be received. *A* bid is an offer which is accepted when the hammer falls, and until the acceptance of the bid is signified in some manner neither party assumes any legal obligation to the other. At any time before the highest bid is accepted, the bidder may withdraw his offer to purchase or the auctioneer his offer to sell. The owner's offer to sell is made at the time through the auctioneer, and not when he advertises the auction sale.[2]

A merchant advertises that on a certain day he will sell his goods at bargain prices; but no one imagines that the prospective buyer, who visits the store and is denied the right to buy, has an action for damages against the merchant. He merely offers to buy, and if his offer is refused, he has no remedy, although he may have lost a bargain, and have incurred expenses and lost time in visiting the store. The analogy between such a transaction and an auction is at least close. *In view of the various points discussed above an offer must be distinguished from a mere quotation or an invitation to offer.*

(2) **Definite offer**—An offer must be definite and certain. If it is indefinite, loose or vague or if an essential provision is lacking, it cannot be accepted. The reason is that the courts cannot tell what the parties are to do. Thus an offer to conduct a business for such time as should be profitable is too vague

---

2. Executive Engineer v. Mohan Prasad Sahu, 1990 ori. 26.

to be considered a valid offer, as it does not consist of a definite promise to be bound. Where *A*, who has bought a horse from B, promises to buy another if the first one proves lucky, and refuses to buy the second horse, cannot enforce the promise, it being loose and vague.

(3) **Communication of the offer**—An offer must be communicated to the offeree. Until an offer is made known to the offeree, he does not know what he has to accept. An offer becomes effective only when it has been communicated to the offeree. The mere desire to enter into an agreement, which remains hidden in the recesses of one's mind, can never constitute an offer. Lord Lindlay says: "A state of mind not communicated cannot be regarded in dealings between man and man." The writing of a letter embodying a definite proposition will also prove futile unless the letter is posted and reaches the offeree. Again, an offer must be communicated by the offeror or his duly authorised agent. If the offeree learns of the offeror's intention from some outside source, no offer results. An offer to the public may be made through the newspapers, but it is not effective so far as a particular individual is concerned until he learns that the offer has been made. To the existence of a contract there must be mutual assent—offer and consent to the offer. Without that there is no contract. How can there be consent or assent to that of which the party has never heard. Where *A*, without knowing that a reward is offered for the arrest of a particular criminal, apprehends the criminal, he cannot recover the reward if he learns of the reward after apprehending the criminal. He had no knowledge of the offer and could not be taken to have accepted it.

In *Lalman Shukla* v. *Gauri Dutt,* 11, A.L.J. 489, G sent L, his servant, in search of his missing nephew. Subsequently, G announced a reward for information relating to the boy. L, before seeing the announcement, had traced the boy and informed G. Later, on reading the notice of reward, L claimed it. His suit was dismissed on the ground that he could not accept the offer unless he had knowledge of it.

STANDARD FORM CONTRACTS AND TICKETS

In recent times large corporations have found it useful to adopt, as the basis of their transactions, standard forms instead of drawing up a separate contract with each individual. These standard forms contain the terms and conditions of the contract, including several conditions in fine print which restrict and often exclude liability under the contract. Similarly, transport tickets by air, sea or rail are issued "subject to special rules". These forms and tickets containing exempting clauses are required to be accepted by the offeree *in toto* without any change or modification. Accordingly, the offeree either accepts the document as a whole or refuses to do so; there is no scope for discussion. Such contracts are termed as *contracts of adhesion,* as the conditions are fixed by one of the parties in advance and are accepted or adhered to by the other. As the offeree, being the weaker party, often signs the document presented by the offeror, without reading the fine print, the large company is in a position to take advantage of the exclusionary clauses.

The rule of law, as laid down in *L. Estrange* v. *Graucob Ltd.,* (1934) 2 K.B. 394, is *if the document is signed by the offeree he is bound by all the conditions in the document* signed even if he has not read them.

In that case, Mrs. L signed an agreement without reading it under which she purchased a cigarette vending machine. The agreement excluded liability of the vendor for all kinds of defects in the machine. The machine was totally defective. In a suit by her in respect of the defective machine, it was held that the clause was binding on her, although the vendor made no attempt to read the document to her or call her attention to the clause and she had not read the document.

But the offeree will not be bound if he can prove —
(a) that he signed the document under a fundamental mistake as to its nature (not merely as to its contents), as for example, where a person is induced to sign a negotiable instrument on the mistaken assumption that it is merely a guarantee:
(b) that he was induced to sign as a result of a fraud or misrepresentation by the offeror, or the offeror's agent: *Curtis* v. *Chemical Cleaning & Dyeing Co. Ltd.* (1951) 1 K.B.805. In this case the plaintiff took a wedding dress, with beads and sequins, to the defendant's shop for cleaning. She was asked to sign a receipt which contained the following clause: "The company is not liable for damage howsoever arising". The plaintiff asked what the effect of the document was, and the assistant told her that it exempted the company from liability in certain ways, and particularly that in her case she would have to take the risk of damage to beads and sequins. Thereupon the plaintiff signed the document without reading it. The dress was returned stained, and the plaintiff sued for damages. The company relied on the exemption clause. *Held,* The company could not rely on the clause because the assistant had misrepresented the effect of the document so that the plaintiff was merely running the risk of damage to the beads and sequins.

If the document is unsigned, as in the case of Tickets and Receipts, the offeree is bound by all the terms in the document or annexed to it if—
(a) a reasonable man would assume the document to be contractual, e.g. not merely a receipt for money. A document is contractual if it embodies the contract, and the person to whom it is delivered should know that it is supposed to contain certain conditions: *Chapelton* v. *Barry U.D.C.*(1940) 1 K.B.532.

In this case, *C* took a deck-chair at a beach from a pile under a notice, "Hire of Chairs-2d". Later an attendant came round to collect the money and *C* paid him, receiving in return a ticket which said on it, "The Council will not be liable for any accident or damage arising from hire of chair". *C* put the ticket in his pocket without reading it, thinking it was merely a receipt. The chair collapsed and he was injured, and sued the Council. *Held,* the clause was not binding on *C*. The board by the chairs stating—"Hire of Chairs -2d", did not limit or exempt the Council from liability, and it was unreasonable to communicate conditions by means of a mere receipt.

(b) Reasonable care was taken by the offeror to bring the terms of the offer to his attention, e.g. by a notice "for conditions see Company's rules and regulations" clearly displayed on the face of the ticket.

If the notice given is reasonable the contract is binding whether the offeree reads the conditions or not or even whether the offeree is illiterate and unable to read them, or even when the notice is in a language that he does not understand. It is his duty to ask for the translation, and if he does not do so, he will be presumed to know the conditions and be bound by them?[3]

Three cases will clarify the situation:
(i) In *Henderson v. Stevenson* (1875) 2 H.L.S.C. 470, a passenger bought a steamer ticket on the face of which were these words only: "Dublin to Whitehaven", on the back were printed certain conditions one of which excluded the liability of the company for loss, injury or delay to the passenger or his luggage. The passenger never looked at the back of the ticket, and no one told him to do so, and the front of the ticket bore no reference to the back. The vessel was wrecked and the passenger's luggage was lost. His claim for damages was upheld by the House of Lords in spite of the exemption clauses. It was stated that the passenger could not be said to have accepted a term which he has not seen, of which he knew nothing, and so there was no sufficient communication of the exceptional terms contained on the back of the ticket.

---

3. Mackilligan v. Compagnie de Messageries Maritime (1867) 6 Cal. 227

The result would have been different if words like' *'For conditions see back "*had been printed on the face of the ticket to draw the passenger's attention to the exemption terms.

(ii) In *Parker* v. *South Easternn Rail Co.* (1877) CPD 416, a handbag deposited in the cloakroom of a railway company was lost, and the owner claimed £24-10S., being its value. The railway company's defence was a condition exempting it from liability for articles exceeding £10 in value unless extra charge was paid. The words "see back" were printed on the face of the ticket. A notice to the same effect was also hung up in the cloak-room. The holder of the ticket admitted knowledge of the printed matter on the ticket, but denied having read it. His suit was dismissed. The railway company had given notice of the special condition, and the holder of the ticket must suffer for his carelessness.

(iii) In *Richardson* v. *Rawntree* (1894) A.C.217, *R* booked her passage on a ship and received a ticket folded so that no writing was visible until it was opened. *Held, R* was not bound by the condition which limited the shipowner's liability for loss to £50.

It is, however, essential that the notice of the terms is contemporaneous with the making of the contract. The notice of the terms exempting a party from liability should be given before or at the time of the contract A subsequent notice will amount to a modification of the original contract and will not bind the other party unless he has assented thereto.

In *Olley* v. *Marlborough Court Ltd.*- (1949) 1 K.B.532,O and his wife registered at a hotel and paid for a week's board and residence in advance. They went up to the bedroom allotted to them. On one of the walls of the room was a notice excluding the hotel's liability for articles lost. They locked the room and went out after handing over the key at the counter. On return later to their room they found their furs missing. Olley was held entitled to recover damages for the loss of the furs. He made his contract when he signed the visitors' register, and the hotel could not rely on the exclusionary notice since it was not brought to his attention at the time of making the contract

But the Court may infer notice from previous dealings between the parties. In the above case, if Olley and his wife had stayed before at the hotel, they would have known of the limiting notice and would have been bound by it.

Sometimes the exemption clauses are so unreasonable that the court will not allow their operation even if the other party had notice of them. A term is said to be unreasonable if it would defeat the very purpose of the contract or if it is repugnant to public policy.

(i) In *Lilly White* v. *Mannuswamy*, 1966 Mad. 13, a laundry receipt contained a condition that the customer would be entitled to claim only 15 per cent of the market price or value of the article in case of loss. The plaintiffs new sari was lost. The court held that the laundry could not take advantage of the limiting term and should pay the full value of the sari. It was observed by the Court that the term would place a premium upon dishonesty in as much as it would enable the cleaner to purchase new garments at 15 per cent their price and that would not be in public interest.

(ii) In *M. Siddalingappa* v. *T. Nataraj*, 1970 Mys.154, the laundry receipt contained a condition that only 8 per cent of the cost of a garment would be payable in case of loss. The condition was held to be unreasonable and full value was required to be paid to the owner of the garment. As pointed out by Lord Denning L.J. "There is the vigilance of the common law which, while allowing freedom of contract, watches to see that it is not abused".

It is also important to remember that exemption clauses are construed strictly, so that where the words are capable of bearing wider as well as narrower construction the narrower construction would be preferred and against the party who has inserted the exemption clause *"contraproferentem"*

Liability in Tort

Even where an exemption clause is exhaustive enough to exclude all kinds of liability under the contract it may not exclude liability in tort. Thus, in *White* v. *John Warwick & Co.,* (1953) 1 WLR 1285, the plaintiff hired a cycle from the defendants. The defendants agreed to maintain the cycle in working order and a clause in the agreement provided: "nothing in this agreement shall render the owners liable for any personal injuries......" While the plaintiff was riding the cycle the saddle tilted and he was thrown and injured. It was held that although the clause exempted the defendants from their liability in contract, it did not exempt them from liability in negligence (under law of torts).

AN OFFER MAY BE GENERAL OR SPECIFIC

An offeror may make an offer to a particular person because he wants only that person to do what he has in mind. When it is addressed to a particular person the offer is called a Specific Offer, and it can be accepted only by that person. The offeror may, on the other hand, make the offer to the public at large because he does not care by whom something is done so long as it is done. Such an offer is called a General Offer, but it cannot form the foundation of a contract until it has been accepted by an ascertained person. Offers made by advertisement are the commonest form of general offers made to the general public. For example, when a reward is offered to the public for the return of lost property, the offeror does not care who returns the property. Anyone who, after having read about the reward, returns the property is deemed to have accepted the offer by conduct and is entitled to get the reward. The leading case on the subject of general offer is *Carllil* v. *Carbolic Smoke Ball Co.* (1893) 1 Q.B. 256.

In this case, the Company offered by advertisement a reward of £100 to anyone who contracted influenza after using their Smoke Ball for a fortnight according to printed directions. Mrs. Carllil, on the faith of the advertisement, bought a Smoke Ball and used it as directed, but was attacked by influenza. She sued for the advertised reward. The court decreed the suit on the ground that the advertisement was not a mere statement of an intention to give reward but a definite promise, and although the offer was not made to any particular person but to the whole world, it was capable of being accepted by one or more persons who accepted by conduct or performance of conditions. In such a case acceptance and performance go together, and no communication of acceptance is necessary.

DURATION OF OFFER

An offer that has been communicated properly continues as such until it lapses, or until it is revoked, rejected, or accepted. The offeror is considered to be continually renewing the offer until one of the above takes place.

(1) Offer lapses after stipulated or reasonable time.—An offer does not remain open indefinitely, although the offeror fails to withdraw it. If the offer stipulates the period during which it is to continue, it automatically lapses at the end of that period. An attempted acceptance after that date could only amount to a new offer being made by the offeree of the original offer. An offer which provides for no time limit remains open for a reasonable time—a reasonable time being such period as a reasonable person might conclude was intended.

(*i*) In *Head* v. *Diggon,* 3 *M.* and R. 97, a seller on Thursday offered wool to a buyer, and gave him three days in which to accept. The buyer accepted the offer on Monday but the seller, after waiting for three days, had sold the wool. It was held that the offer had lapsed by Monday morning by its express terms, and the seller was not bound.

(*ii*) In *Ramsgate Hotel Co.* v. *Montefiore* (1866) 1 Ex. 109, *M* applied for shares in June, but the allotment was not made till November. *Held,* that the offer to take shares had lapsed, as the reasonable time had passed since the making of the offer, and *M* was not bound to take the shares.

(2) An offer lapses by the death or insanity of the offeror or the offeree before acceptance.— If the offeror dies before acceptance, there is no offer to accept, and if the acceptance is made it becomes infructuous. "A dead man can no more continue to offer than he could begin to offer." In the same manner, the offeree's death without accepting the offer puts an end to the offer, and his heirs or executors cannot accept for him. But if the acceptance is made in ignorance of the death or insanity of the offeror, there would be a valid contract. In English law, the death or insanity of the offeror or offeree causes an offer to lapse even though the other party has no notice of the death.

S owned certain debentures of a company. *K* offered to buy them. *S* died without accepting the offer. His administrator accepted the offer and sued *K* for damages when he refused to perform the contract. *Held,* the death of *S* terminated the offer to buy, and his administrator after *S*'s death could not accept.

(3) An offer lapses by subsequent illegality—If the performance of the contract becomes illegal after the offer is made, it lapses. Thus if an offer is made to sell alcoholic liquors but a law prohibiting the sale of liquors is enacted before the offer is accepted, the offer is terminated.

(4) An offer lapses by not being accepted in the mode prescribed, or if no mode is prescribed, in some usual and reasonable manner—According to English law, once the offer has lapsed on this account, there cannot be a further acceptance, unless the offeror agrees thereto. In Indian law, if the offer prescribes the manner in which it is to be accepted and the acceptance is not made in such a manner, the proposer or offeror may, within a reasonable time after the acceptance is communicated to him, insist that his offer shall be accepted in the prescribed manner and not otherwise. If he fails to do so, he accepts the acceptance as made.

(5) A conditional offer lapses when the condition is not accepted by the offeree. *Pipraich Sugar Mills Ltd. v. Its Mazdoor Union,* 1957 S.C. 95.

(6) An offer lapses by rejection of offer by the offeree—If the offeree rejects the offfer by distinct refusal, he cannot revive the offer by attempting to accept it, unless the offeror renews the proposal.

(7) An offer lapses by counter-offer by the offeree, as it amounts to rejection of the offer. If *A* makes an offer to B to sell his car for ₹ 5,000 and *B*, instead of accepting the offer, makes an offer to buy it for ₹ 4,000, the original offer by *A* is terminated, *B* in effect saying, "I refuse your offer, but in its place, I make a different offer." Such an offer by the offeree is known as a **counter-offer**. In substance, the counter-offer presupposes a rejection of the original offer. If the original offeror, who is now the offeree, accepts the counter-offer, a binding contract results.

Where, however, the offeree does not make a counter-offer, but only desires to know if the offer does not lapse and may be accepted at any time before it is withdrawn. In *Stevenson* v. *Mclean,*[4] Lush J. says: "If there is nothing specific by way of offer or rejection but a mere inquiry, it should be answered and not treated as rejection of the offer. For example, *A* offered to sell his house to B on an instalment payment basis, but also asked *B* to make a cash offer. *B* made a cash offer which A rejected. B then accepted the instalment payment basis. *A* refused to perform the contract and *B* sued him. *A* claimed there was no contract. *Held, B* was entitled to the decree, as under the circumstances, the making of the cash offer was not a counter-offer, so as to reject the instalment payment basis. When *B* accepted that offer after his cash proposal was rejected, a legal contract was created because the offer was still in existence and could be accepted (*Quinn* v. *February,* 252 Mich. 526).

(8) Revocation of the offer by the offeror—Ordinarily, the offeror can revoke his offer before it is accepted. If he does so, the offeree cannot create a contract by accepting the revoked offer. Thus, the bidder at an auction sale may withdraw (revoke) his bid (offer) before it is accepted by the auctioneer by using any of the customary methods, e.g., fall of hammer. The auctioneer thereafter accepts the revoked offer (withdrawn bid). An offer may be revoked by the offeror before its acceptance, even though he had originally agreed to hold it open for a definite period of time. So long as it is a mere offer, it can be withdrawn whenever the offeror desires. The rule applies even though the offer expressly stipulates that it may not be withdrawn without the consent of the other party. Thus, if the offeror

---

4. (1880) 5 Q.B. D. 346 at p. 350.

agrees to keep his offer open for a specified time, he may nevertheless revoke it before the expiration of that time, unless (*i*) the offer has in the meantime been accepted before notice of revocation has reached the offeree, or (*ii*) there is consideration for keeping the offer open, e.g., option contract

(*i*) In *Cooke* v. *Oxley* (1790) 3 T.R. 653, A offered to sell 266 hogshead of tobacco at a certain price and promised to keep it open for acceptance by *B* till 4 p.m. of that day. Before that time *A* sold them to *C*. *B* accepted before 4 p.m., but after the revocation by *A*. It was held that the offer was already revoked.

(*ii*) In *Dickinson* v. *Dodds* (1876) 2 Ch. D. 463, *A* agreed to sell property to *B* by a written document which stated:' 'This offer to be left over until Friday 9 a.m." On the Thursday A made a contract to sell the property to *C*. *B* heard of this from *X*, and on Friday, at 7 a.m. he delivered to A an acceptance of his offer. *Held,* B could not accept *A*'s offer after he knew it had been revoked by the sale of the property to *C*.

Communication of Revocation.—A revocation of an offer must be communicated or made known to the person to whom the offer was made. Until it is communicated to the offeree, he has reason to believe that there is still an offer which he may accept, and he may rely on this belief and accept the offer. A letter or telegram revoking an offer made to a particular offeree is effective and a revocation against the person who makes it when it is put into course of transmission, (i.e., when the telegram is handed in at the telegraph office or the letter is posted) and as against the offeree when the revocation comes to his knowledge, (i.e., he receives the telegram or letter).

Revocation of a general offer can be made by giving the same publicity as was given to the original offer itself. For example, an offer of a reward that is made to the general public by advertisement in a newspaper may be revoked in the same manner. As a result, a member of the public cannot recover the amount of the reward by thereafter performing the act for which the reward was originally offered, even though he has not seen the revocation. Let us assume that on April 15, *A* offered a reward of ₹ 500 by means of an advertisement in all the English language daily newspapers published in Delhi to be paid to any one who may find and deliver him his lost dog. On April 25, *A* caused to be published in the same newspapers an advertisement withdrawing his offer of reward. On April 30, *B*, who had read the notice of the reward but not the notice of the withdrawal of the offer, found the dog and delivered it to *A*. His claim of the reward will not be upheld, as the offer had been withdrawn by *A* through the same channel in which it was made before B had found the dog. The same notoriety was given to the revocation that was given to the offer, and it did not matter that he had not read the revocation in the papers. The offer of the reward not having been made to him directly, but by means of a published notice,' he should have known that it could be revoked in the manner in which it was made.

NOTE: An offer for shares or debentures in a public company made by application in pursuance of a prospectus cannot be revoked until after the expiration of the 5th day after the time of the opening of the subscription lists: *Companies Act,* 1956, Sec.72(5).

TENDERS

A tender is an offer and may be either (*a*) a definite or specific offer to supply goods or services, or (*b*) a standing offer.

Tender as a definite offer: Where tenders are invited for the supply of specified goods or services, each tender submitted is an offer. The party inviting the tenders can accept any tender he chooses, and thus bring about a binding contract. For example, if *A* company requires a thousand tonnes of coal and invites tenders for the supply of this quantity, and accepts *B*'s tender there is a contract between *A* company and *B*. The terms of the Contract are that *B* shall supply and the *A* company shall accept and pay for one thousand tonnes of coal.

Tender as a standing offer. Where tenders are invited to supply goods or services *as and when* *demanded,* a trader who submits a tender is making a standing or continuing offer. The "acceptance" of such a tender does not convert the standing offer into a binding contract, for a contract of sale implies that the buyer has agreed to accept the goods. For example, where A invites tenders for the supply during the coming year of coal not exceeding 1,000 tonnes at the agreed price when A from time to time demands a precise quantity. A tender by B to supply coal as and when demanded by A amounts to a standing offer and cannot be accepted generally so as to form a binding contract; it is accepted from time to time whenever an order is given for any quantity within the maximum quantity stated in the tender. An "acceptance" of such a tender merely amounts to an intimation that the offer will be considered to remain open during the period specified. Thus where a standing offer has been made, there is a separate acceptance each time an order is placed and, accordingly, a distinct contract is made on each occasion with respect to the quantity ordered, resulting in a series of contracts.[5]

With regard to further supply, the offer may be revoked by notice to the offeree just as the tenderor has the right to revoke his tender as to future orders, so also the acceptor of the tender has the right to refuse to place any orders. Contract results only when an order has been placed, and once an order is placed it must be executed.

ACCEPTANCE

An agreement consists of an offer by one party and its acceptance by the person or persons to whom it is made. **Acceptance** is the manifestation by the offeree of his assent to the terms of the offer. Mathematically stated, Offer and Acceptance = Contract. The acceptance must be absolute and unconditional. It must accept just what is offered. No particular form of words or mode of expression is required for an acceptance. Any expression of an intention to agree is sufficient An acceptance may be indicated, for example, by saying ."Yes", or by an informal "O.K. "by a mere affirmative nod of the head, or in the case of an offer of a unilateral contract, by performing the act called for.

Who can accept.—An offer may be accepted only by the person to whom it is made. If anyone else attempts to accept it, no contract with that person arises. Thus, if a person intends to contract with B. A cannot give himself any right under the offer to B.

In *Boulton* v. *Jones* (1857) 157 E.R. 232, A sold his business to his manager without disclosing the fact to his customers. On the afternoon of the day on which the sale was carried through a customer (Jones), who had a running account, sent an order for some goods addressed to the vendor of the business by name. The new owner of the business executed the order without disclosing that the business had changed hands. It was held that he could not recover the price, as there was no contract.

If the offer is directed not to a specified individual but to the public at large, it may be accepted by any member of the public at large who has knowledge of the existence of the offer. *Carllil* v. *Smoke Ball Co.*[6] (*supra*) is the leading case on the point

Modes of Acceptance.—To make a concluded contract, the acceptance must be unequivocal, unconditional and without any variance of any sort between it and the proposal.[7] A binding contract can only occur when the offer made is met by an acceptance which corresponds with the offer made in every particular. If, therefore, the acceptance does not conform to the terms of the offer in all respects, or contains any new terms or conditions, it becomes a counter-offer and thus rejects the original offer. For example, where an offer was to buy fully paid up shares and partly paid shares were

---

5.   The Bengal Coal Co. v. Homiwadia & Co ; (1899) 24 Bom. 97 ; Jaravia Mall v. Geogopal Dass (1922) 43 MLT 132; Secy, of State v. Madho Ram (1923) 10 lah. 493.
6.   (1893) 1 Q.B. 256.
7.   Life Ins. Corporation of India v. Raja Vasiraddy K. Kawha, 1984 SC 1014.

allotted, there was no acceptance and so no binding agreement.

An absolute and unqualified assent by which acceptance is made may be shown by the acceptor saying "Yes" to the person making the offer, or by doing the act requested in the offer, or by taking benefit or service offered by the offeror.

Where the acceptance is not by conduct, the assent must be actually expressed. Like an offer, it must be communicated. The act of making up one's mind is not sufficient, for a mere mental act of assent will not be treated as a communication. A mental determination not indicated by speech, or put in course of indication by act to the other party, is not an acceptance.

In *Bhagwandas* v. *Girdhari Lal*, 1966 s.c 543, Shah J. (afterwards CJ.) observed: "An agreement does not result from a mere state of mind; intent to accept an offer or even a mental resolve to accept an offer does not give rise to a contract. There must be ..... some external manifestasion of that intent by speech, writing or other act"

In *Brogden* v. *Metropolitan Rly. Co.* (1877) A.C. 666, a draft agreement relating to the supply of coal was sent to the manager of a railway company for his acceptance. The manager wrote the word "approved" and put the draft in a drawer intending to send it to the company's solicitors for formal contract being drawn up. By an oversight, the document remained in the drawer and was never completed. *Held*, this mental act did not amount to acceptance and so did not complete the contract.

While communication of an acceptance is essential, it is open to the offeree to waive it. But in law, silence does not give consent; although nodding one's head intimates acceptance. As the offeror cannot force the offeree to speak, mere silence in most cases does not amount to acceptance. Ordinarily, the offeror cannot frame his offer in such a sway as to make the silence or inaction of the offeree operate as an acceptance. For example, when a seller writes to another with whom he has not had any prior dealing that "unless notified to the contrary" he will send to that person certain quantity of goods to be paid for at specified prices, there is no acceptance if the offeree ignores the offer and does nothing. The silence of the person receiving the letter was not intended by him as an acceptance, and the seller as a reasonable man should not have believed that it was so intended. It was stated in *Gopi* v. *Raghu*, 1949 Pat. 522 that when the offeror says that acceptance will be presumed if no reply is received, absence of reply cannot mean acceptance of the offer. Mere silence is not assent or acceptance. In the case of prior dealings between parties, the offeree may have a duty to reject an offer expressly, and his silence may be regarded as an acceptance. For instance, A subscribed to the **Daily News** for one year. After the expiration of his subscription, the newspaper company continued to send him the paper by mail for 5 years. A continued to use the paper but he failed to pay any of the bills sent to him. He would be liable to pay on the ground that his continued use of the newspaper was an acceptance of the offer made by sending him the newspapers.[8]

If the offeror makes an offer of a unilateral contract, communication of acceptance is ordinarily not required. In such a case, the offeror calls for a completed or accomplished act. If that act is performed, the offer is accepted without any further action by way of notifying the offeror. As a practical matter there will eventually be some notice to the offeror because the offeree who has performed the act will ask the offeror to carry out his promise. It should be noted that the offer is accepted only by the completion of the performance requested. Accordingly, if A offers B ₹ 100 to paint A's house, and after B has finished nine-tenths of the work, A says to B: "Stop, I withdraw my offer, "there is no contract, but B can recover from A the reasonable value of the services he has rendered. The basis of A's liability here is not contract, but quasi-contract, to prevent an unjust enrichment at the expense of B.

---

8. See Ranji Dayawala & Sons P. Ltd. v. Invest Import, 1981 s.c. 2085.

There may be acceptance by taking benefit or enjoying the service offered. A bus driver offers to carry passengers from New Delhi to Kashmere Gate for 30 P. *A* gets into the bus at the Plaza stop and is taken to Kashmere Gate. *A* has taken the benefit or enjoyed the service offered and has thereby agreed to pay the contract price for the ride.

An acceptance should always be accepted in the manner required by the offer. If the offeror specifies that the acceptance must be written, an oral acceptance is ineffective. If the acceptance is required to be given by a specified date, a late acceptance has no effect. If the offer says, "Please wire reply" and the reply is sent by post, that is no compliance with the offer unless the offeror chooses to accept it as such. Remember, Sec. 7(2) of our Contract Act imposes the duty on the offeror to intimate to the offeree that the acceptance is not according to the prescribed manner, and if he keeps quiet, he is deemed to have accepted the acceptance as made.

An acceptance must be made before the offer lapses or is revoked. We have already considered this in connection with the lapse or revocation of an offer. In English law, the moment a person expresses his acceptance of an offer, that moment the contract is concluded, and such an acceptance becomes irrevocable, whether it is made orally or through the post. In Indian law, the position is different as regards contract through post.

CONTRACTS THROUGH POST

In English law, the letter of acceptance is effective and the contract comes into being at the moment the letter is dropped into the mail box, properly addressed and bearing sufficient postage, even if the letter is not received by the offeror. The Indian Law on the point is contained in Sections 4 and 5 of the Contract Act and is summarised as follows:

1. An offer or proposal is made when the letter containing the offer is delivered to the offeree.
2. As regards acceptance the Indian Law has two principles:

(a) Once the letter of acceptance properly addressed and stamped is posted the acceptance is made and binds the offeror, as he is deemed to have received the acceptance at the moment when it is dispatched so as to be "out of the power of the acceptor" and it becomes a promise on which the acceptor can sue even if the letter never reaches the offeror; but

(b) an acceptance binds the acceptor only when it reaches the offeror. This is done to give an opportunity to the acceptor to revoke his acceptance, which is not permitted in English law. As a result of this rule, the acceptor gets the double advantage that, once he posts the letter, he is free from the responsibility and also gets an opportunity to revoke the acceptance.

Regarding revocation the position is like this. An offer may be revoked by an express notice at any time before it is accepted. Therefore, the offer must be revoked before the letter of acceptance is posted. An acceptance, in English law, cannot be revoked, so that once the letter of acceptance is properly posted the contract is concluded. In Indian law, the acceptor can revoke his acceptance any time before the letter of acceptance reaches the offeror. If the revocation telegram arrives before or at the same time with the letter of acceptance, the revocation is absolute.

CONTRACTS OVER THE TELEPHONE

The law with regard to contracts over the telephone is the same both in England and India. The rule in England, as laid down in *Entores Ltd.* v. *Miles Far Eastern Corporation* (1955) 2 All. E.R. 493, is that in Telex[9] or telephonic communications the parties are to all intents and purposes in each other's presence and where a contract is negotiated by such instantaneous communications, there is no binding contract until the notice of the acceptance is received by the offeror. Explaining the necessity

---

9.   Telex is an equipment with the help of which messages can be despatched by a teleprinter operated like a typewriter in one country and almost instantaneously received and typed in another.

of applying the rule that acceptance is incomplete until received by the offeror in cases of contracts concluded during the course of conversation over the telephone, Denning, L.J. observed:

"Now take a case where two people make a contract by telephone. Suppose, for instance, that I make an offer to a man by telephone, and, in the middle of his reply, the line goes "dead" so that I do not hear his words of acceptance. There is no contract at that moment. The other man may not know the precise moment when the line failed. But he will know that the telephone conversation was abruptly broken off, because people usually say something to signify the end of the conversation. If he wishes to make a contract he must therefore get through again so as to make sure that I heard. Suppose next that the line does not go dead, but it is nevertheless so indistinct that I do not catch what he says and I ask him to repeat it. He then repeats it and I hear his acceptance. The contract is made, not on the first time when I do not hear, but only the second time when I do hear. If he does not repeat it, there is no contract. The contract is only complete when I have his answer accepting the offer."

It will be noticed that contracts by instantaneous communication such as telephone or Telex are not treated in the same way as contracts by postal communication. The contracts over the telephone are regarded the same in principle as those negotiated by the parties in the actual presence of each other.

The same rule has been applied in India, because the Indian Contract Act, which is not exhaustive, does not provide for contracts over the telephone; and it is an established rule that when any matter cannot be brought within particular provisions of the Contract Act, it would be permissible to apply English principles in dealing with the matter (*Kanhaiyalal* v. *Dineshwarchandra* 1959 M.P. 234).[10] In this case, Dixit, J., in applying the principles of the English law, observed:

"Now, when the parties negotiate a contract orally in the presence of each other or over telephone and one of them makes an oral offer to the other, it is plain that an oral acceptance is expected, and the acceptor must ensure that his acceptance is audible, heard and understood by the offeror. The acceptance in such a case must be by such words which have the effect of communicating it. If the words of acceptance are inaudible and have not been heard or understood by the offeror, then the acceptance is incomplete and no contract would be formed until the acceptor repeats his acceptance so that offeror can hear it.... the provisions of S. 4 of the Contract Act with regard to the completion of the communication of acceptance, which are meant for contracts through the post, have no applicability where parties negotiate a contract in the presence of each other or over telephone. The object of Sections 4 and 6 is to fix the point of time at which either party negotiating the contract is precluded from changing his mind. When the parties negotiate a contract face to face or over telephone, no question of revocation can possibly arise for in such instantaneous communications a definite offer is made and accepted at one and the same time."

It will be interesting to quote Sir William Anson who sums up the position humorously as follows:[11] "Acceptance is to offer what a lighted match is to a train of gunpowder. It produces something which cannot be recalled or undone. But the powder may have lain till it has become damp, or the man who laid the train may remove it before the match is applied. So an offer may lapse for want of acceptance, or be revoked before acceptance. Acceptance converts the offer into a promise, and then it is too late to remove." This means that as soon as a lighted match is brought in contact with a train of gunpowder, the gunpowder explodes. Gunpowder by itself is inert; it is the lighted match which causes the gunpowder to explode. Similarly, an offer from the offeror does not by itself create any legal relationship between the offeror and the offeree; offer by itself is inert. But as soon as the offer is accepted by the offeree; a legal relationship is established between the parties; the offer is converted into a promise which imposes an obligation on the offeror. Offer is thus compared to gunpowder and acceptance to lighted match; and an offer, when accepted, explodes into a contract and cannot be revoked.

---

10.   See also Bhagwandass v. Girdharilal & Co., 1966 S.C. 543.

11.   Law of Contract, p. 40.

Cross offers. No contract arises from cross offers. It means that when two parties make identical offers to each other, without knowledge of each other's offer, there is no completed agreement, for there cannot be acceptance. For this reason it is well said that two manifestations of willingness to make the same bargain do not constitute a contract unless one is made with reference to the other. An offeree, therefore, cannot accept an offer unless its terms have been communicated to him by the offeror." In *Tinn v. Hoffman & Co.* (1873) 29 LJ. 272. *A*'s offer to sell 800 tons of iron at 69S per ton crossed *B*'s offer to buy 800 tons at 69S per ton. *Held,* there was no contract, as they were merely counter-offers not accepted yet.

An agreement to agree in the future is not a contract, because unless all the material terms of the contract are agreed there is no binding obligation. It was stated by Maugham LJ. In *Foley* v. *Classique Ltd.* (1934) 2 K.B. 2 at p. 13: "It is indisputable that unless all the material terms of the contract are agreed there is no binding obligation. An agreement to agree in the future is not a contract; nor is there a contract if a material term is neither settled nor implied by law and the document contains no machinery for ascertaining it." It was also stated in *Hajee* v. *Murugesa,* 1958, Kerr. 195 that a contract to enter into a contract is not a valid contract.

> ## PART 1-C
> ## CONSIDERATION

The Need for Consideration.—Contracts result only when one promise is made in exchange for something in return. The something in return is what we mean by consideration. The requirement of consideration stems from the policy of extending the arm of the law to the enforcement of mutual promises of parties. We know from our study of offer and acceptance that a mere promise is not enforceable. There must be an offer, which is a promise conditional upon the making of a certain promise by the other party, and the offer must be accepted by a return promise. For example, a mere promise to make a gift, although presumably creating a moral obligation, is not enforceable at law, as the person to whom the promise of a gift is given does not give anything in return. To be enforceable a promise must be purchased, or the consideration be bargained for or given in exchange for the promise.

The requirement of consideration limits the enforcement of promises to those in which each of the parties has bargained to give or surrender something. The fact that each party has agreed to give or surrender something, suggests that the parties have devoted some reflection to the matter and that they seriously desire the promises to have legal consequences. Thus it is said that the justification for the doctrine of consideration is that it provides at least some objective guarantee of deliberation, a certain protection against hasty and ill-considered contracts. Consideration is an aid in determining that promises are worthy of enforcement. Some degree of reciprocity and mutuality of undertaking is requisite before promises will be enforced; and the doctrine of consideration is the most important test of the enforceability of executory promises.

The Trinity.—In order that a contract may arise, three things must concur: first, the offer; second, the acceptance; and third, the consideration. Mutual assent, we have seen, takes place by offer and acceptance; but to have mutual assent, there must be something to be assented and agreed to on each side. That something is **consideration.** Hence, consideration to its essential nature is an aspect merely of the fundamental notion of bargain, other aspects of which are offer and acceptance. *Consideration, offer and acceptance are an indivisible trinity, facets of one identical notion which is that of bargain.*

Definition of Consideration—Sir Frederick Pollock has defined consideration as "the price for which a promise is bought (i.e., as *quid pro quo*)." In *Currie* v. *Misa* (1875) 10 Ex. 153, Lush J., defined consideration as "some right, interest, profit, or benefit accruing to one party for some forbearance, detriment, loss or responsibility given, suffered, or undertaken by the other."

Section 2(d) of the Indian Contract Act, 1872, defines consideration thus: "When, at the desire of the promisor, the promisee or any other person has done or abstained from doing, or does or abstains from doing or promises to do or to abstain from doing something, such act or abstinence or promise is called a consideration for the promise."

In simple terms, consideration means the element of exchange in a bargain, and in order to satisfy the requirements of law consideration must be an act or forbearance of some value in the eye of the law; the promisee must suffer a legal detriment. It may take the form of money, goods, services, a promise to marry, a promise to forbear from suing the promise, etc. It is the giving up by the promisee of a legal right; the refraining from doing what he has the legal right to do, or the doing of what he has the legal right not to do. So, a benefit to the promisor or a detriment to the promisee is a sufficient consideration for a contract. It was stated in *Fazaluddin Mandal v. Panchanan Das,* 1957 Cal. 92, A single consideration may support more than one promise and may move from the promisee or any other person. Reciprocity is not necessarily as essential ingredient for consideration, which can as well be an act done or forbearance made in return for a unilateral promise. Consideration as stated earlier, is the price or a return for a promise— a *quid pro quo* something given or taken as equivalent to another. It is some value received as inducement for the promise. Thus, the doctrine of consideration is that a promise will be enforced only when it has been paid for or purchased either by a promise, an act, or a forbearance.

Forbearance means refraining from doing an act. In other words, the promisor may desire to buy the inaction of the other party of his promise not to act. Examples of forbearance as good consideration are: forbearance to exercise a legal right, e.g., if at the instance of the debtor the creditor forbears to sue there is sufficiency of consideration. Forbearance to sue for ejectment is good consideration for an agreement to pay enhanced rent *(Lakshmi Chand v. Niadar Mal.* 1961 All, 495). A promise in writing to pay a time-barred debt is good consideration. Forbearance to sue on an old contract, or a fresh contract is a good consideration for dispensing with the performance of a prior contract *(Bhoori v. Thakur Gulab Singh,* 1958 Raj. 10).

It should, however, be noted that promise and the consideration must purport to be the motive each for the other, in whole or at least in part. It is not enough that the promise induces the detriment or the detriment induces promise if the other half is wanting. If *A* promises *B* to make him a gift of substantial wealth, consideration is lacking though *B* has renounced other opportunities for betterment in the faith that the promise will be kept. There is no mutuality, as each party is not doing or agreeing to do something. Such situations usually arise in cases relating to subscriptions for charity, where promises are gratuitous.

In Abdul Aziz v. *Masum Ali* (1914)36 All. 268, a person had verbally promised to the secretary of the Mosque Committee to subscribe ₹500 for the rebuilding of a Mosque. On a suit by the secretary to enforce this simple promise it was held that the promise was not enforceable for there was no consideration in the sense of benefit to the promisor or detriment to the promisee. It was said, "the person who made the promise gained nothing in return for the promise made, and the secretary of the Committee to whom the promise was made suffered no detriment in getting the promise from subscriber," and the suit was dismissed.

But a promise, though gratuitous, would be enforceable if on the faith of the promise, the promisee suffers a detriment or undertakes a liability. This is based upon what is called the doctrine of "promissory estoppel", which is applied to avoid the harsh results of allowing the promisor in such a case to repudiate, when the promisee has acted in reliance upon the promise. Here the person makes a donative promise without expecting an equivalent.

In *Kedarnath* v. *Gori Mahomed* (1886) 14 Cal. 64, the defendant had agreed to subscribe ₹ 100 towards the construction of a Town Hall at Howrah. The secretary, on the faith of the promise, called for plans and entrusted the work to contractors and undertook liability to pay them. *Held,* though the promise was to subscribe to a charitable institution and there was no benefit to the promisor, yet it was supported by consideration in that the secretary suffered a detriment in having undertaken a liability to the contractors on the faith of promise made by the defendant.

KINDS OF CONSIDERATION

A consideration may be: (a) Executory or future, (b) Executed or present, or (c) Past.

(a) **Executory consideration** means that it takes the form of a promise to be performed in the future. It is the price promised by one party in return for the other party's promise, e.g. an engagement to marry someone, or a promise to deliver goods or to render services at a future date.

(b) **Executed or present consideration** means consideration which takes place simultaneously with the promise. The act constituting the consideration is wholly or completely performed. If A buys a book from a book-seller and pays the price and the book-seller delivers the book to A there and then, the consideration in this case is executed or present, since it is performed simultaneously by both the parties.

(c) **Past consideration** means a past act or forbearance, that is, one which took place and is complete before the promise is made. If A does B a good turn in 1974, and in 1975 B makes a promise to A to supply him with certain goods in consideration of this act, A will be able to enforce B's promise, as in Indian law, past consideration is also good consideration. But in English law, past consideration is no consideration, and in the above example, A will be unable in English law to enforce B's promise.

But even in English law, there are exceptions to the rule that past consideration is no consideration, namely:

 (i) When services are rendered at the express or implied request of the promisor in circumstances which raise an implication of a promise to pay.
 (ii) When a time-barred debt is acknowledged in writing.
(iii) Under S.27 of Bill of Exchange Act, 1882, past consideration will support a bill of exchange.

RULES GOVERNING CONSIDERATION

(a) **A simple contract, whether oral or in writing, must be supported by consideration**, otherwise it will be normally void. A contract without consideration is a gratuity, or, in the words of Salmond, "a promise without consideration is a gift; one made for a consideration is a bargain". Hence, "bargain without consideration is a contradiction in terms and cannot exist."

(b) **In Indian law, consideration must move at the desire of the promisor.** The promisor must desire the act or forbearance. The act performed at the desire of third party cannot be consideration. But the promisor need not necessarily derive any benefit from the contract. The benefit may be intended for a third party. Under Sec. 2(d), all that is necessary is that the desire of the promisor and the action of the promisee should have a connection (*Gopal Co.* v. *Firm Hazarilal,* 1963 M.P. 37). Again, for consideration to be present, it is essential that what is done must have been done at the desire of the promisor, and not voluntarily. If A notices B's house being on fire and rushes voluntarily to B's help, there is no consideration. If, however, A goes to B's help at B's desire, there is good consideration.

(c) **In Indian law, consideration may move from the promisee or any other person.** Thus, in Indian law, a stranger to consideration may maintain a suit. In *Chinnaya Rav* v. *Ramayya* (1881) 4 Mad. 137, *A*, an old lady, by a deed of gift, made over certain property to her daughter with a direction that the daughter should pay an annuity to *A*'s brother as had been done by *A*. By an agreement of even date between the daughter of *A* and the brother of *A*, the daughter promised to pay the annuity. The daughter, however, did not pay the annuity as promised. *A*'s brother sued the daughter. It was held that the consideration moved from *A*, the donor of the estate, though not from her brother. That was sufficient consideration for the daughter's promise to *A*'s brother, because the consideration in India need not move from the promisee, but can move from any other person. Similarly, in *Samuel* v. *Ananthanatha* (1883) 6 Mad. 351, the administratrix of an estate agreed to pay *S* his share of the estate, if *S* would give a promissory note for portion of a barred debt claimed by *A* from her. *S* executed a promissory note in favour of *A*, gave it to the administratrix, and received his share of the estate. *A* sued *S* on the promissory note and it was held that there was consideration for the same. Hence, in Indian law, a stranger to the consideration can *sue* to enforce the contract, though a stranger to the contract cannot sue.

But the stranger to consideration cannot be a minor, for a minor cannot contract. An agreement for service, entered into by a father on behalf of his minor daughter, is not enforceable at law, as it is without any consideration and therefore void (*Raj Rani v. Prem Adib* (1949) 51 Bom. L.R. 256). In this case the defendant Prem Adib had agreed with the father of Raj Rani (the plaintiff), who was a minor, to employ her as an artist in the defendant's concern called the Prem Pictures for a year at a salary of ₹ 9,500 to be paid in 12 equal monthly instalments. As the plaintiff was a minor, her father had entered into this agreement on her behalf and for her benefit. According to the conditions of this agreement the plaintiff attended all rehearsals at the studio, and attended in the taking of the picture which was being produced by the defendant. She was paid her first monthly instalment also. The defendant then terminated her services. She sued for damages for the breach of the agreement. It was held that as she was a minor at the date of the agreement made on her behalf by her father her agreement was void for want of consideration. Her promise to serve supplied no consideration for the promise made by the defendant to the plantiff's father regarding the employment of the plaintiff as an artist in his studio. Therefore the contract between the plaintiffs father and the defendant was void being without any consideration moving from the promisee (the father of the minor plaintiff); and the plaintiff's promise to serve with the defendant did not constitute any lawful promise or valid consideration in law, as it was void under section 11 of the Contract Act.

It was also held in this case that a contract of marriage entered into on behalf of a minor by her or his parent, for the benefit of the minor, stands on a different footing. So also a contract of apprenticeship stands on a different footing. Both these contracts (viz., contract of marriage and the contract of apprenticeship) can be enforced when made by the parent or guardian of the minor. But a contract of personal service is different; the mere fact that the contract of service is for the benefit of the minor does not entitle the minor to sue on the contract.

Under English law, however, a stanger to the consideration cannot sue to enforce the contract. The person to whom the promise is made (the promisee) must furnish the consideration. As a result, the person seeking to enforce a simple contract in court must prove that he himself has given consideration in return for the promise he is seeking to enforce. For example, *A*, *B*, and *C* enter into an agreement under which *A* promises to do certain work for *B* if *B* will pay £50 to *C*. If *A* does the work, he can sue *B* on the promise; but *C* cannot sue, for he gave no consideration to *B*.[12] The underlying assumption in English law is that a contract is a bargain. If a person furnishes no consideration, he takes no part in the bargain; if he takes no part in a bargain, he takes no part in a contract.

(d) **Though, in Indian law, a stranger to the consideration can sue, yet both in English law and Indian law, a stranger to a contract cannot, as a rule, sue on it**, even though it is made for his benefit.[13] The basis of this rule is that a contract is a private relationship between the parties who make it, and no other person can acquire rights or incur liabilities under it. This rule is usually designated as the doctrine of *Privity of contract.*

Privity of Contract—In general third parties cannot sue for the carrying out of promises made by the parties to a contract

---

12. Price v. Easton (1833) 4 B & Ad. 433; Tweddle v. Atkinson, (1861) 1 B & S 393.

13. Dunlop v. Selfridges (1915) A.C. 847; State of Bihar v. Charanjit Lal 1960 Pat 139.

(i) *Dunlop Tyre Co.* v. *Selfridges Ltd.* **(1915)** A.C. 847, is the leading case on this point. Dunlops supplied tyres to a wholesaler, *D*, on condition that any retailer to whom *D* resupplied the tyres should promise *D* not to sell them to the public below Dunlop's list price. *D* supplied tyres to Selfridges upon this condition, 'but nevertheless Selfridges sold them below the list price. *Held,* there was a contract between Selfridges and *D*, and a contract between Dunlops and *D*, but no contract between Dunlops and Selfridges. Therefore, Dunlops could not obtain damages from Selfridges. [14]

(ii) In *Shankar* v. *Umbabhai* **(1915)**37 Bom. 471, *A* effected a policy of insurance on his own life, and the policy was expressed to be for the benefit of his wife. The wife was held not entitled to sue the insurance company, as she was not a party to the contract of assurance. She could have sued if the policy had been assigned in writing to her by the assured, or a trust had been created by the assured.

Exceptions to the Doctrine of Privity. There are, however, exceptions to the rule of privity of contract recognised both by the English law and the Indian law, under which a person who is not a party to a contract can sue on it. The exceptions to the rule are:

(i) *Constructive trust.* If the right of the third party does not arise out of contract but out of a trust, the *cestui que trust* or the beneficiary has a right of action *(Des Raj* v. *Rabi Ram,* 1957 J & K 10). The stranger should, however, be clearly designated as a beneficiary *(Sivarama Konar* v. *Thiruvadinadu Pillai* 1957 Travancore 189). Thus, if *A* and *B* agree to confer a benefit on *C*, *B* would be regarded as a constructive trustee for *C* of the benefit of the contract. *C* would then be entitled to sue *B* (and join *A* as co-defendant).

In *Amirullah* v. *Central Government* 1959 All. L.J. 271, it was pointed out that the addressee of an insured article is the beneficiary under the contract between the sender and the Central Government who is liable for compensation under Sec. 33, Post Offices Act, for non-delivery. A trust of movable property is deemed to be declared by the sender from the fact that he addressed the insured cover as deliverable to the addressee. A constuctive trust having been created in favour of the addressee, he is entitled to have the benefit as against the trustee, the Central Government through the Post Office, and sue it.

Similarly, persons not parties to transactions like partition or family arrangements conferring benefits on them become beneficiaries. Such transactions are in the nature of trusts. [15]

In *Khwaja Muhammed* v. *Hussaini Begum* (1910) 32 All. 410, a Muslim lady *H* sued her father-in-law *K* to recover ₹ 15,000 being the arrears of allowance called *Kharcha-i- Pandan*—betel box expenses, i.e. "Pin money" payable to her by *K* under an agreement made between *K* and her father prior to and in consideration of her marriage to *K*'s son *D*. Both *H* and *D* were minors at the time of the marriage. The Privy Council held the promise to be enforceable by *H* and declared the suit rejecting the contention on behalf of *K* that *H* could not sue as she was no party to agreement.

(ii) *Agency.* A principal, even if concealed, may sue on a contract made by an agent. Thus, where *A* is secretly acting as agent for *P*, *P* can intervene to enforce the contract between *T* and *A*. [16]

(iii) *Charge in favour of a person.* When a charge in favour of a person has been created on specific immovable property, such charge is enforceable at the instance of the person beneficially interested, though he may not be a party to the document creating the charge.

(iv) *Family settlements.* The fourth exception arises in cases of family arrangements or marriage settlements or otherwise when a charge is created (as above) on specific immovable property intended

---

14. This case has been confirmed by the House of Lords in Midland Silicones Ltd v. Scruttous Ltd. (1962) A.C. 446. See also M.C. Chacko v. The Slate Bank of Travancore, 1970S.C 504.

15. Kamminini Veeramma v. Komminini Appaya, 1966 Andh. W.R. 476.

16. This exception is perhaps more apparent than real, because in fact the principal is the contracting party who has merely acted through the instrumentality of the agent.

to benefit a third person or where provision is made for the marriage expenses of female members (*Saiyed Sajad Ali Khan* v. *Mst. Badshah Begum,* 1936 Qudh 385; *Rakhmabai* v. *Govind* (1904) 6 Bom. L. R. 421). In expenses provided in a partition between brothers.

(v) *Fund in hand of a party.* Where a fund is created in the hands of one of the contracting parties in favour of a third party, it may be possible to give the latter a remedy in quasi-contract on the grounds' that to allow the contracting party to keep the fund would be to allow unjust enrichment Thus, if *A* admits to *C* that he had received money from *B* for payment to *C*, then *C* can successfully recover the amount from *A*.[17]

In *Shamia* v. *Joory* (1958) 1 Q.B. 448, the defendant was an Iraqi merchant having a business in England, and he employed the plaintiffs brother as an agent in Baghdad. At the end of 1952 the defendant admitted that he owed his agent £1,300. The defendant was requested to pay £500 of this as a gift to the plaintiff, who was at that time a student in England. He agreed to do this, and the agent wrote to the plaintiff, his brother, informing him of the defendant's promise. The defendant confirmed this and informed the plaintiff that he would send the money to him. On the defendant's failure to pay, the plaintiff sued him to recover £500 as money had and received to his use (an action in quasi-contract), and it was held that he must-succeed.

(vi) *Assignment. The* assignee of a debt or an actionable claim may, if the assignment is legal assignment, sue the original debtor.

(e) The fifth rule governing consideration is *that there must be mutuality, i.e.,* each party must do or agree to do something. A gratuitous promise, as in the case of a subscription for charity, is not enforceable.

(f) **Consideration need not be adequate, but must have some value, however slight.** It is up to the parties to fix their own prices. For example, where *A* voluntarily agreed to sell his motor car for ₹ 500 to *B*, it became a valid contract despite the inadequacy of the consideration. The parties are presumed to be capable of appreciating their own interests and reaching of their own equilibrium, and the law, as a general rule, leaves people to make their own bargains, and does not concern itself with the adequacy of consideration. If a person, voluntarily chooses to make an extravagant promise for an inadequate consideration it is his own affair. Thus, it was said in *Haig* v. *Brooks* (1839) that the courts do not exist to repair bad bargains, and though consideration must be present, the parties themselves must attend to its value. But the value must be of an economic character, and mere natural affection of itself is not enough. Nevertheless, acts or omissions even of a trivial nature may be sufficient to support a contract (*Chappell* v. *Nestle* (1960) A.C. 87).

However, where the consideration embodied in a deal is woefully inadequate,, it may raise a suspicion of fraud, coercion or undue influence on the part of the person gaining the advantage. Because of the rule of inadequacy of consideration being no bar to a valid contract, it has been said that "in many cases, the doctrine of consideration is a mere technicality irreconcilable either with business expediency or common sense."

(g) **Consideration must be competent.** Though the consideration need not be adequate to the promise, it must be competent, real and not illusory, impossible, uncertain, vague or ambiguous. Consideration must be real, though it may be nominal. A son's vague promise to "stop being a nuisance" to his father is no consideration.

(h) **Consideration must be lawful,** e.g., not some illegal act, such as paying someone to commit a crime. If the consideration is unlawful, the contract is void and unenforceable.

(i) **Consideration must be something more than the promisee is already bound to do for the promisor.** Thus, an agreement to perform an existing obligation made with the person to whom the

---

17. Lily v. Hays (1886) 111 E.R. 1272; Joan Chandra Mukherjee v. Manoranjan Mitra. 1948 Cal 251.

obligation is already owed, is not made for consideration. For instance, discharge of a public duty imposed by law is not consideration; nor is the performance of a contractual duty already owed to the defendant. But performance by *A* of an existing duty owed to *B* will suffice to support a promise by *C* to *A*. Thus, *A* was engaged to marry *B*, and *C* promised *A* an annuity of £150 in consideration of his marrying *B*. On his marriage with *B*, it was held that the fulfilment of *A*'s contract with *B* was consideration to support *C*'s promise to pay the annuity (*Shadwell* v. *Shadwell* (1860) 3 L.T. 628).

NO CONSIDERATION NECESSARY

The general rule is that an agreement made without consideration is void. But Section 25 of the Act lays down three exceptions which make a promise without consideration valid and binding. Thus, an agreement without consideration is valid—

1. if it is expressed in writing and registered if so required by the law relating to registration of documents and is made out of natural love and affection between parties standing in a near relation to each other; or
2. if it is made to compensate a person who has already done something voluntarily for the promisor, or done something which the promisor was legally compellable to do; or
3. if it is a promise in writing and signed by the person to be charged therewith, or by his agent, to pay a debt barred by the law of limitation.

These exceptions are based on principles of equity. In the first and the third instances the promises having been evidenced by writing it would amount to hardship if they were not recognised by the Courts. Thus, a registered agreement between a Mohammedan husband and his wife to pay his earnings to her is a valid contract, as it is in writing, is registered, is between parties standing in near relation, and is for love and affection [*Poonoo Bibi* v. *Fyaz Buksh* (1874) 15 Bom. L.R. 57]. So is a registered agreement whereby an elder brother, on account of natural love and affection, promised to pay the debts of his younger brother [*Venkataswamy* v. *Rangaswamy* (1903) 13 M.L.J. 428). But nearness of relation does not necessarily import natural love and affection. Thus, where a Hindu husband by a registered document, after referring to quarrels and disagreement between himself and his wife, promised to pay his wife a sum of money for her maintenance and separate residence, it was held that the promise was unenforceable [*Rajhikhy Dabee* v. *Bhootnath* (1990) 4 C.W.N. 488]. Agreements simpliciter are not required to be registered. Thus, in *Lalit Mohan Datta* v. *Basudeb Datta*, 1976 Cal. 430, an. agreement was executed by the sons in favour of their father in consideration of the great regard they had for their father, but the agreement was not registered. *Held*, the agreement being a simpliciter agreement did not require registration and was valid and enforceable. Also the rule which insists on the presence of consideration for every agreement does not affect gifts. Explanation I provides: "Nothing shall affect the validity, as between the donor and donee, of any gift actually made."

ACCORD AND SATISFACTION

Under Indian law, the parties to the contract can agree that their respective performances may not be enforced, or the promisee may waive or remit the performance by the promisor. Section 63 of the Contract Act provides: "Every promisee may dispense with or remit, wholly or in part, the performance of the promise made to him or may extend the time for such performance, or may accept instead of it any satisfaction which he thinks fit." Thus, if *A* owes *B* ₹ 1,000, and *B* tells *A* that he will take ₹ 800 in full satisfaction of the debt, *A* will be discharged from his obligation if he pays ₹ 800 to *B* and *B* cannot sue *A* for the balance of ₹ 200.

But under English law such waiver or remission is not binding unless consideration is given for it. So, under English law, in the above example, *A* will remain liable to pay the balance of ₹ 200. Where *A* has performed his part of the contract, but *B* has not, *A* may release *B* from his obligations under the contract, but only if the release is under seal or if *A* receives valuable consideration for forgoing his rights. Such an agreement, where there is the necessary consideration, is *called Accord and Satisfaction.*

Accord and Satisfaction has been judicially defined as follows:[18]

"Accord and Satisfaction is the purchase of a release from an obligation, whether arising under contract or tort, by means of any valuable consideration, not being the actual performance of the obligation itself. The accord is the agreement by which the obligation is discharged. The satisfaction is the consideration which makes the agreement operative."

The rule that payment of a smaller sum of money is not discharge of liability to pay a larger sum, even though the creditor agrees to take it in full discharge is an ancient one and an early example of it was found in *Pinnel's* case (1602) as approved by the House of Lords in *Foakes* v. *Beer* (1884) 9 App. Cas. 605. The practical effect of the rule, however, has been considerably reduced by the following facts:

(i) Payment of a smaller sum at the creditor's request before the due date is good consideration for a promise to forgo the balance, for it is a benefit to the creditor to be paid before he was entitled to payment, and a corresponding detriment to the debtor to pay early.

(ii) When the creditor agrees to take something different in kind, *e.g.,* a chattel, the debt is discharged by substituted performance.

(iii) Where there is a dispute as to the sum owed, if the creditor accepts less than he thinks is owed to him, the debt will be discharged.

(iv) If the debtor makes an arrangement with his creditors to compound his debts, *e.g.,* by paying 80 p. in the £, he is satisfying a debt for a larger sum by the payment of a smaller sum. Nevertheless, it is a good discharge, the consideration being the agreement by the creditors with each other and the debtor not to insist on their full rights? [19]

(v) Payment of a smaller sum by a third party operates as a good discharge. [20]

(vi) Forbearance to sue at the request of the debtor will be good consideration.[21]

It may be reiterated that the doctrine of Accord and Satisfaction does not apply in India, nor does the doctrine of Consideration as extended to the discharge of contracts, because of S.63 of the Contract Act, 1872.

PART 1-D
FLAWS IN CONTRACTS

VOID AND VOIDABLE CONTRACTS

We have already seen that a contract is always based on agreement. But an apparent agreement is not always a real agreement. One party may have deceived the other party, or in some other way there be no genuine consent. The parties may be labouring under a mistake, or one or both parties may be incapable of making a contract. In all such cases there is no real agreement and where there is no real agreement the law has three remedies. *First,* the contract may be treated as of no effect, and it will then be known as a **void contract**. *Secondly,* the law may give the party aggrieved the option of getting out of his bargain, and the contract is then known as **voidable**. *Lastly,* the party at fault may be compelled to pay damages to the other.

---

18. British Russian Gazette, Ltd. v. Associated Newspapers. Ltd. (1933) 2 K.B. 616.

19. Good v. Cheeseman (1831)2B. & Ad. 328.

20. Welby v. Drake (1825) 1 C. & P 557.

21. Combe v. Combe (1951) 2 K.B. 215.

A *void* contract is without legal effect. Such a contract is a nullity and no right is acquired under or through it, and is void *ab initio*. Technically, the words 'void contract' are a contradiction in terms. A void contract is not a contract at all. It is a legal nullity, a legal cipher. But despite semantic inconsistency in using the words 'void contracts,' they provide a useful label for describing the situation that arises when a contract is claimed but in fact does not exist. For example, a contract with or by a minor is void and also where it is made by parties who are labouring under a mistake of fact material to the contract.

A *voidable* contract lies in a middle zone between valid and void contracts. A contract is voidable when it is enforceable by law at the option of one party but not at the opinion of the other. It is an agreement that is binding and enforceable, but because of the lack of free consent of one of the parties, it may be rejected by the aggrieved party if he so desires. Thus, the party aggrieved and so enjoying the option may either elect to be bound by the contract or to repudiate it. When the contract is so repudiated it becomes void, but until it is so disowned it continues to be valid. Hence, the difference between void and voidable contracts is significant. A voidable contract is valid if action is not taken to avoid it. A void contract is and remains a legal cipher, it is non-existent.

FLAWS IN CAPACITY TO CONTRACT

Broadly speaking, every person is presumed by law to be competent to enter into contract and if any one claims exemption from liability on the ground of incapacity to contract he must strictly prove such capacity. Section 11 of the Indian Contract Act provides: "Every person is competent to contract who is of the age of majority according to the law to which he is subject, and who is of sound mind and is not disqualified from contracting by any law to which he is subject". This Section by stating the law in the positive enables us to consider the incapacity to contract. Incapacity to contract may arise out of (*a*) Mental deficiency, or (*b*) Status. Infants or minors, lunatics, idiots and drunken persons fall under (*a*) and Foreign Ambassadors or Sovereigns, etc., alien enemies, professional people, corporations and married women fall under (*b*).

MINORS

In Indian law, the Majority Act 1875, Section 3, declares that every person domiciled in India shall be deemed to have attained his majority when he shall have completed his age of 18 years, and not before. In case, however, a guardian has been appointed to the minor under the Guardianship of the Court of Wards, the age of majority is extended to the date when he completes his age of 21 years. Infancy is said to be a disability, but in practice it is really protection granted by the Law Courts. It has been rightly observed: "The law protects their (infants') persons; preserves their rights and estates, excuseth their laches, and assists them in their pleadings; the Judges are their Counsellors, the Jury are their servants and Law is their guardian."

MINORS IN INDIAN LAW

Sections 10,11 and 68 of the Indian Contract Act deal with the matter of capacity of the contracting parties. Section 11 lays down the rule: "Every person is competent to contract who is of the age of majority according to the law to which he is subject..." If we convert this into a negative proposition, it will read thus: no person is competent to contract who is not of the age of majority, etc.... This clearly shows that a minor is not competent to contract.

The Privy Council's categorical declaration in *Mohori Bibi* v. *Dharamodas Ghose* (1903) 30 Cal. 539, makes it absolutely clear that a minor's contract under the Indian law is absolutely void and therefore there is no possibility or question of ratification by the minor on coming of age. In *Mohori Bibi's* case, the minor had executed a mortgage for the sum of ₹ 20,000 out of which the lender had paid the minor only about ₹ 8,000. The minor then filed a suit for setting aside the mortgage. It was contended that as the contract was voidable and the minor was now repudiating it the amount of ₹ 8,000 actually paid to the minor must be refunded under Section 65 of the Indian Contract Act. The Privy Council pointed out that as the minor's contract was absolutely void no question of refunding money could arise in these circumstances.

The present position of the law in India regarding minor's capacity to contract may be stated thus:

1. A minor's contract is altogether void in law, and a minor therefore cannot bind himself by a contract. There is, however, nothing in the Contract Act which prevents a minor from becoming a promisee. A minor is incapable of making an instrument but is not incapable of becoming a payee or endorsee.[22] A duly executed transfer by way of sale or mortgage[23] in favour of a minor who has paid the consideration money is not void, and it is enforceable by him or any other person on his behalf The reason for this rule is that incapacity means, incapacity to bind oneself by a contract or be bound by a contract. **All those contracts to which a person incompetent to contract is a party are void, as against him, but he can derive benefit under them.** Minority is a personal privilege and only the minor can take advantage of it; the other party is bound. The rule of mutuality does not apply to minors.

2. The incapacity of minor in India is so important that even if a minor does not take the plea of minority it is the duty of the court to protect him and give effect to the statutory prohibition.[24]

3. Since the contract is *void ab initio,* the minor need not sue to set it aside,[25] nor can the minor ratify it on attaining the age of majority.

4. If the minor has obtained any benefit, such as money on a mortgage, he cannot be asked to refund, nor can his mortgaged property be made liable to pay.

5. A minor purchaser of property is entitled to a decree for possession of the property purchased from the vendor.[26] If he is dispossessed of such property by a third party, the minor can sue successfully his vendor for refund of the purchase money. If a minor supplies goods to a major person, he can sue for a decree for the price of the goods.[27]

6. A minor can always plead infancy and is not stopped to do so even where he had procured a loan or entered into some other contract by falsely representing that he was of full age, when in reality he was a minor.[28] The rule of estoppel does not apply to a minor on the ground that if it applied it would give a handle to dishonest traders to, obtain false declaration in writing from the minor that he was a major at the time of entering into the contract. But it may be noted here that where the loan was obtained by fraudulent representation by the minor or some property was sold by him and these transactions are set aside the court may direct the minor to restore the property to the other party,[29] for "Minors can have no privilege to cheat men." If a minor fraudulently overstates his age and takes delivery of a motor car after executing a promissory note in favour of the trader for its price, the minor is not estopped from pleading minority and can escape liability under the promissory note. But the Court on equitable considerations will order the minor to return to the trader the car, if it is still with him. But the trader cannot sue on the pronote for the price, or damages.

However, where the minor invokes the aid of the Court for the cancellation of his contract the

---

22. Goekda Latcharao v. Vishwanadham Bhowayya, 1956 Andhra 182.

23. Ragava v. Srinivas (1917) 40 Mad. 308 (F.B.).

24. TeJawahir v. Mauva, 1241.C. 436.

25. TeLalit v. Nagendra, 1940 Cal. 589.

26. TeCollector of Mecrut v. Hardian, 1945 All. 155.

27. TeAbdul Gaffar v. Piare Lal (1935)16 Lah. 1.

28. TeGadigappa v. Balangowda, 1931 Bom. 561 (KB.); Khangul v. Lakha Singh (1928) 9 Lah 701.

29. TeMohd. Said v.BishambharNath (1923) 45 All. 645.

Court may grant relief subject to the condition that he shall restore all benefits obtained by him under the contract, or make suitable compensation to the other party. For example, in *Jagannath Singh* v. *Lalta Prasad* (1909)31 All 21, a minor was allowed to recover possession of property sold by him only subject to the condition that he restored the consideration. In *Khan Gul* v. *Lakha Singh,* 1928 Lah 609, Sir Shadilal C.J. of Lahore High Court ordered the minor to refund ₹ 17,500 which he had taken in advance for the sale of land when he refused to complete the contract.

And now Section 33 of the Specific Relief Act, 1963, recognises the principle of restitution in such cases and provides: "(1) when a void or voidable contract has been cancelled at the instance of a party thereto, the Court may require him to restore such benefits as he has received under the contract and to make any compensation to the other party which justice may require. (2) Where a defendant successfully resists any suit on the ground that the contract, by reason of his being incompetent, is void against him, he may be required to restore the benefits, if any, obtained by him under the contract but only to the extent to which he or his estate has benefited thereby.

But the Court will not compel any restitution by a minor even when he is a plaintiff, where the other party was aware of the infancy so that he was not deceived. (*Bhim Mandal* v. *Mangaram Corain,* 1961 Pat 21.).

7. A minor's estate is liable for necessaries supplied to him or his wife according to his status in life. Therefore, a tradesman who supplies necessaries can always recover under Section 68 of the Contract Act which provides for liability in respect of necessaries supplied to a person incapable of entering into a contract. It must be noted here that for necessaries supplied to a minor, it is only his property that is liable, not the minor himself personally. In English law, an infant is personally liable for necessaries supplied. Thus in India if a minor has been supplied with necessaries and he fails to pay and owns no property, the tradesman will lose the price of necessaries. As in English law necessaries must be according to the position and status in life of the minor, and must be things which the minor actually needs. Therefore, it is not enough to show that the articles supplied were of the kind which a person of his position and station may reasonably require for ordinary use; they will not be necessaries if he is already supplied with things of that kind. The onus is on the supplier to make sure that the minor actually needs the articles at the time of sale and delivery. Objects of mere luxury are not necessaries nor objects which, though of real use, are excessively costly. For example, buttons are normally used in men's clothing, but pearl or diamond buttons are not necessaries.[30] The following have been held as **"necessaries"** in India. Costs incurred in successfully defending a suit on behalf of a minor in which his property was in jeopardy.[31] Costs incurred in defending him in a prosecution.[32] A loan to minor to save his property from sale in execution of a decree.[33] Money advanced to a Hindu minor to meet his marriage expenses.[34]

It is important to note in this connection that "necessaries" must have been supplied to the minor for *his benefit.* The liability of the minor's estate rests on this factor and not because it is *ex contract.* The relief to be given does not depend on any contract. The liability of minor's estate is independent of any contract and is purely statutory consequent on the provisions of S. 68.

Position of Minor's Parents.—A contract with a minor does not give the creditor any rights against the minor's parents, whether the contract is for necessaries or not. The moral obligation of a father, for instance, to provide for his child does not impose on him any liability to pay the debts incurred by the child. The only case where a parent may be liable is when the child is contracting as an agent for the parent.

---

30. Johnstone v. Marks (1887) 19 Q.B: 609; Jogan Ram v. Mahadeo Pd. (1909)36 CaL 768.

31. Ryder v.Womkwell (1868) R.L.4Ex.32.

32. TeWatkins v. Dhunnoo Baboo (1881) 7 Cal. 140; Palaram v. Ayub Khan (1926) 49 All 52.

33. TeSham Charan Mal v. Chowdhry Lebya Singh (1894) 21 Cal. 872.

34. Kidar Nath v. Ajudhia (1883) P.R. No. 185.

IDIOTS AND LUNATICS

Contracts other than those for necessaries by idiots[35] and lunatics are void. An insane person can make a valid contract during lucid intervals.

DRUNKEN PERSONS

Drunkenness is on the same footing as lunacy. A contract by a drunken person is altogether void. It must be remembered that partial or ordinary drunkenness is not sufficient to avoid a contract. It must be clearly shown that, at the time of contracting, the person, pleading drunkenness, was so intoxicated as to be temporarily deprived of reason and so could not give valid consent to the contract. Illustraiton (b) to Section 12 of the Indian Contract Act reads: "A sane man who is delirious from fever or who is so drunk that he cannot understand the terms of a contract or form a rational judgment as to its effects on his interest cannot contract while such delirium or drunkenness lasts." This illustration clearly shows that in India a contract by a drunken person is void and not voidable. Drunken persons are liable for necessaries supplied.

ALIEN ENEMIES

A person who is not an Indian is an alien. An alien may be either an alien friend or an alien enemy. An alien friend or a foreigner whose Sovereign or State is at peace with the Union of India, has usually the full contractual capacity of a natural-born Indian subject, except that He cannot acquire property in an Indian ship, nor can he be employed as Master or any other Chief Officer of such a ship. On the declaration of war between his country and the Union of India he becomes an alien enemy, and the following rules will apply to him: (1) During the subsistence of the war, an alien enemy cannot contract with an Indian citizen nor can he sue in an Indian Court, except by licence from the Central Government, in case he is permitted to stay on Indian territory. (2) Contracts made before the war between an alien enemy and an Indian citizen are either dissolved, as being against public policy, particularly if their performance would involve inter-course with or help to the enemy, or suspended for the duration of the war and revived after the war is over, provided they have not already become time barred. It may be noted that for the purposes of *evil* rights "an Indian citizen or the subject of a neutral State who is voluntarily resident or who is carrying on business in hostile territory is to be treated as an alien enemy.

FOREIGN SOVEREIGNS AND AMBASSADORS

Foreign Sovereigns and accredited representatives of a foreign State or Ambassadors enjoy a special privilege in that they cannot be sued in our Courts, but they can, if they choose, enter into contracts and then enforce these contracts in our Courts. This immunity of a Sovereign continues even if he engages in trade. But an ex-king is not entitled to the privilege and can thus be sued against in our Courts. In India, under S. 86 of the Civil Procedure Code, in order to sue rulers of foreign States, Ambassadors and Envoys, previous sanction of the Central Government must be obtained.

PROFESSIONAL PERSONS

The only class of professional persons who suffer a handicap in the matter of capacity to contract is that of Barristers practising in England. They are not allowed to enter into any contract relating to their profession or to sue for their fees or to be sued. Their fees are deemed to be debts of honour from the solicitors to them. In India, since the passing of the Bar Councils Act of 1927, a Barrister who is in the position of an Advocate with liberty both to act and plead, has a right to contract and to sue for

---

35. Inder Singh v. Permeshwari Singh, 1957 Pat 491.

his fees. A decision of the Full Bench of the Allahabad High Court has recognised the right of a Barrister enrolled as an Advocate of an Indian High Court to sue his client for his fees.[36]

CORPORATIONS

A corporation is an artificial person created by the process of law. It exists only in contemplation of law and has no physical shade or form. Therefore it can only contract through human agents. Its contractual capacity is determined by its constitution. The contractual capacity of a statutory corporation is expressly defined by the statute creating it. The contractual capacity of a company registered under the Companies Act is determined by the objects clause of its memorandum of association. Any act done in excess of the powers given in the memorandum is *ultra vires* and void.

MARRIED WOMEN

A woman, married or single, in Indian law is under no disability as regards entering into contracts. Thus, a Hindu, or Muslim or a Christian wife can enter into contracts and bind her property. Under English law, married women used to be under certain disabilities in regard to the making of contracts and the holding of property. Formerly, therefore, a husband was responsible for his wife's contracts but since 1935 this disability no longer arises. A married woman now has full contractual capacity even in English law and can sue and be sued in her own name.

PART 1-E
FLAW IN CONSENT

REALITY OF CONSENT

A contract which is regular in all other respects may still fail because there is no real consent to it by one or both of the parties. There is no *consensus ad idem* or meeting of the minds. Consent may be rendered unreal by mistake, misrepresentation, fraud, coercion or undue influence. When there is no consent at all, as in mutual mistake, there is no contract. This is described by Salmond as *error in consensus,* so that there was not at the relevant time any real agreement or common intention between the parties, or their minds had not met. Error in consensus—a misunderstanding—prevents the existence of any *consensus ad idem* and therefore of any contract. Where there is consent, but no free consent, there is generally a contract voidable at the option of the party whose consent was not free, as in the case of misrepresentation, undue influence or coercion. This is known as *error in causa.* In this case a true contract is constituted by the consent of the parties, but the consent of one of the parties was induced or caused by the supposed existence of a fact which actually did not exist. If he had known the truth he would not have entered into the contract. Such *error* in cause makes the contract voidable at the option of the party whose consent was not free. In a mutual or bilateral mistake of fact the consent is altogether absent or excluded, the minds of the contracting parties fail to meet and the contract is void. Unilateral mistake, undue influence or coercion vitiates consent and the contract is voidable.

MISTAKE

The law believes that contracts are made to be kept; the whole structure of business depends on this, as the businessmen depend on the validity of contracts. Accordingly, the law says most clearly that it will not aid anyone to evade consequences on the plea that he was mistaken. On the other hand, the law also realises that mistakes do occur, and that these mistakes are so fundamental that there is no

---

36. Nihal Chand v. Dilawar Khan (1933) 55 All. 570; 1933 All. 3417 (F.B.)

contract at all. So, if the law recognises mistake in contract, that mistake will render the contract void. Thus is the basic law of mistake in contract.

The general common law rule is that mistake made by one or both parties in making a contract has no effect on the validity of the contract. For example, an error of judgment is not an operative mistake and does not affect the validity of the contract. If A buys an article thinking it is worth ₹ 100, when in fact it is worth only ₹ 50, the contract is good and A must bear the loss if there has been no misrepresentation by the seller. In the words of Anson, "We are not concerned with cases in which a man finds the obligation of a contract more onerous than he intended or is disappointed in the performance which he receives from the other party." This is NOT mistake, but miscalculation, or possibly, error of judgment Similarly, a mistake by one party as to his power to perform the contract is not an operative mistake. Where A agrees to build a house by September 15, and finds he cannot complete the work before November 15, he will be liable to an action for damages.

MISTAKE OF FACT OR VITAL OPERATIVE MISTAKE

Section 20 of the Contract Act provides: "Where both the parties to an agreement are under a mistake as to a matter of fact essential to agreement, the agreement is void." Thus, to be operative (so as to render the contract void) the mistake must be (i) on the part of both the parties, (ii) of fact and not of law or opinion, and (iii) so fundamental as to negative agreement. Therefore, where the parties contracted under a fundamental mistake of fact, die contract would be void. Such a mistake prevents the formation of any contract at all, and the court will declare it void. But as Section 22 provides unilateral mistake of fact will not render the contract voidable.

MISTAKE OF LAW

If there is a mistake of law of land, the contract is binding because everyone is deemed to have knowledge of his own law, and ignorance of law is no excuse— *ignorantia juris hand excusat.* But mistake of foreign law and mistake of private rights are treated as mistakes of fact, and are excusable. The laws of a foreign country require to be proved in Indian courts as ordinary facts, and so a mistake of foreign law makes the contract void: Similarly, if a contract is made in ignorance of private rights, it would be void, *e.g.*, where A buys property which already belongs to him [*Cooper* v. *Phibbs* (1867) L.R.2HX. 1491.

OPERATIVE MISTAKE OF FACT

Operative mistakes may be classified into the following categories:
1. Mistake as to the nature of the contract itself.
2. Unilateral mistake, *i.e.*, mistake made by one party only.
3. Bilateral mistake, where both parties make a mistake, which may be either
   (a) Common Mistake, or (b) Mutual Mistake.

Common Mistake occurs where *both* parties have made the *same* mistake and may also be designated as *identical bilateral mistake. Mutual Mistake* occurs where *both* parties make a *different* mistake and may also be called *non-identical bilateral mistake.* These are clearly differentiated in following paragraphs between themselves and contrasted with *unilateral* mistake.

MISTAKE AS TO NATURE OF CONTRACT

The general rule is that a person who signs an instrument is bound by its terms even if he has not read it (*L'Estrange* v. *Grancob* (1934) 2 K.B. 394). A lady bought an automatic machine from the defendants on terms contained in a document, described as a "Sales Agreement," and including a number of clauses which she signed but did not read. It was held that she was bound by these terms and no question of notice arose. But if a person signs a contract in the mistaken belief that he is signing a document of a different nature, there will be a mistake which avoids the contract. The mistake must be as to the nature of the contract and not merely as to the contents of the document, and also the mistake must be due to either (*a*) the blindness, illiteracy, or senility of the person signing, or (*b*) a trick or fraudulent misrepresentation by the other party as to the nature of the document. In *Foster* v. *Mackinnon* (1869) L.R. 4 C.P. 704, *M*, a senile man of feeble sight, endorsed a bill of exchange for £3,000 thinking it was a guarantee. *Held,* there was no contract and so he was not liable on it. He could plead *non estfctum.* When a lady was induced to sign a deed of exchange and gift on the representation that it was a power of attorney, the document was held to be void, as her mind did not go with her signature.[37] In such cases the person signing will not be liable even if he is negligent.[38]

In this case B was fraudulently induced to sign a guarantee in the belief that it was a proposal for insurance. *Held,* the guarantee was not binding.

UNILATERAL MISTAKE

Unilateral mistake occurs when one of the parties to a contract is mistaken as to some fundamental fact concerning the contract and *the other party knows this.* This latter requirement is important because if *B* does not know that *A* is mistaken, the contract is good.

(i) IDENTITY OF PARTY

The cases of unilateral mistake are mainly concerned with MISTAKE by one party as to the IDENTITY OF THE OTHER PARTY. It is a rule of law that if a person intends to contract with *A*, *B* cannot give himself any rights under it. Here, when a contract is made in which personalities of the contracting parties are or may be of importance, no other person can interpose and adopt the contract. For example, where *M* intends to contract only with *A* but enters into contract with *B*, believing him to be A, the contract is vitiated by mistake, as there is no *Consensus ad idem* [*Boulton* v. *Jones* (1857) 2 H.N. 568].

Remember that mistake as to identity of the person with whom the contract is made will operate to nullify the contract only if:

(*a*) the identity is of material importance to the contract, and

(*b*) the mistake, is known to the other parry, *i.e.*, he knows that it is not intended that he should become a party to the contract but some other person is intended, as it happened in *Cundy* v. *Lindsay* (1878).

In *Cundy* v. *Lindsay* (1878) 3 A.C. 459, one Blenkam by imitating the signature of a reputable firm called Blenkiron & Son, induced Lindsay to supply him with goods on credit, which he afterwards sold to Cundy, an innocent purchaser. Lindsay claimed the recovery of the goods, or their value from Cundy. It was held that the contract between Blenkarn and Lindsay was void for mistake, and that no property passed to Cundy. Cundy was liable to Lindsay for the value of the goods.

In *Philips* v. *Brooks* (1919) 2 K.B. 243, the plaintiff was a jeweller. One North entered his shop and asked to see some jewellery. He chose one ring worth £450 and a pearl necklace, priced £2,250 and offered to buy them. The jeweller accepted the offer. North then offered to pay by cheque. The jeweller accepted the cheque, but said delivery would be delayed until the cheque was cleared. North then said that he was Sir George Bullough, a well-known person, and gave a London address, which the jeweller checked in the directory. Since North had signed the cheque as George Bullough, the jeweller was deceived as to his identity and allowed him to take away the ring. North promptly pledged the ring with Brooks, a pawnbroker, for £350. The cheque was dishonored and the jeweller

---

37. Sarat Chandra v. Kanai Lal. 1921 Cal. 786.

38. Carlisle and Cumberland Banking Co. v. Bragg (1911) 1 K.B. 489; Dulari Devi v. Janardhan Singh, 1990 s.c. 1173.

claimed to recover the ring from Brooks. It was held that the contract was made before the identity became important, therefore it was not void on the ground of mistake. The jeweller intended to contract, and did contract with the person present, whoever he was. The misrepresentation took place at the time of signing the cheque after the contract of sale had been made and the property in the jewellery had passed to the man who had bought it, namely, North. The contract could be avoided on the ground of fraudulent misrepresentation before the ring was pawned, but since at the time the ring was pledged it had not been avoided, the pawn broker got good title.

In *Lake v. Simmons* (1927) A.C. 487, A woman, by falsely representing to a firm of jewellers that she was the wife of a certain Baron, obtained two pearl necklaces on the pretext of showing them to her husband with a view to buying at the agreed price. The woman then sold the necklaces to an innocent buyer. It was held that there was no contract between the jewellers and the woman and therefore the buyer from her must return the necklaces to the jewellers. Though the woman got the physical possession of the necklaces, there was no mental assent, as the jewellers intended to deal not with her but quite a different person, namely, the wife of the Baron.

In *Said* v. *Butt* (1920) 3 K.B. 497, B, the manager director of a theatre, gave instructions that a ticket was not to be sold to S. S knew this, and asked a friend to buy a ticket for him. With this ticket, S went to the theatre, but B refused to allow him to enter. It was held that there was no contract with S, as the theatre company never intended to contract with S. By mere device of an agent he could not constitute himself as the contractor with the theatre owners who had already refused him ticket. In the words of Sir William Anson: ''If a man accepts an offer which is plainly meant for another, or if he becomes party to a contract by falsely representing himself to be another, the contract in either case is void, or to put it more accurately, no contract ever comes into existence. In the first case one party takes advantage of the mistake, in the other creates it''.

(ii) UNILATERAL MISTAKE OF OFFEROR

Where the offeror makes a material mistake in expressing his intention, and the offeree knows, or is deemed to know of the error, the mistake is operative and the contract is void. In *Hartog v. Colin & Shields* (1939) 3 All. E.R. 566, H claimed damages for breach of contract, alleging that C had agreed to sell him 30,000 Argentinian hare skins and had failed to deliver them. C contended that there was a material mistake in the offer and that H was well aware of this mistake when he accepted the offer. The mistake alleged by C was that the skins were offered at certain *prices per pound* instead *of per piece.* In the negotiations preceding the agreement, reference had always been made to prices per piece, and it was also the custom of the trade. *Held,* the contract was void for mistake. H could not reasonably have supposed that the offer expressed C's real intention; H must have known that it was made under a mistake.

In *Webster* v. *Cecil* (1861) 54 E.R, 812, A offered to buy certain property from B for £2000, but B declined the offer. Later B wrote to A offering to sell it for £1,250. This was a mistake for £2,250. A immediately, on receipt of the offer, wrote accepting it; but B realizing that he had mistakenly written £1,250 for £2,250 immediately gave notice to A of the error. *Held,* the contract would not be specifically enforced as A had snapped at an offer he perfectly well knew to be made by mistake.

But if there is a mistake on the part of one party alone, and the other does not, and cannot be deemed to, know of the mistake, the contract is binding. In *Van Praagh* v. *Everidge* (1902) 2 Ch. 266, at a sale of landed properties by auction, E purchased one lot in mistake for another. The price was not extravagant and the mistake was solely due to his own carelessness. *Held,* the contract was binding on E.

BILATERAL MISTAKE

A bilateral mistake, as observed earlier, arises when both parties to a contract are mistaken as regards a fact essential to the contract. They may have made a *common* or *identical mistake;* or a *mutual* or *non-identical* mistake.

Common mistake as to the existence of the subject-matter. Where both parties believe the subject-matter of the contract to be in existence at the time of the contract but in fact it is not in existence, there is operative mistake and the contract is void. If *A* agrees to sell his car to *B*, and unknown to them both the car had at the time of the sale been destroyed by fire, then the contract will be void because A has innocently undertaken an obligation which he cannot possibly fulfil. In *Scott* v. *Coulson* (1903) 2 Ch. 249, G agreed to assign to *H* a policy of assurance upon the life of *L*. *L* had died before the agreement was made. *Held,* no contract on account of common mistake. Again in *Couturier* v. *Hastie (*1857) 8 Exch. 40, there was a contract to buy cargo described as shipped from port *A* to port *B* and believed to be at sea which in fact had got lost earlier unknown to the parties and hence not in existence at the time of the contract. It was held that the contract was void due to the common mistake of parties.

But where the circumstances are such that the seller is deemed to have warranted the existence of the goods, the seller is probably liable to the buyer for breach of contract in the goods are non-existent. In *Mc Rae* v. *Commonwealth Disposals Commission* (1951) Argus L.R. 771; 84 C.L.R. 377, the defendant Commission invited tenders for the purchase of a wrecked oil tanker, and plaintiff's tender of £285 was accepted. After the plaintiffs had spent considerable sums in searching for the tanker it was ascertained that no tanker had been wrecked in the named locality. The Australian High Court held that the contract was not nullified by mistake. A party cannot rely on mutual mistake where the mistake consists of a belief... entertained by him without any reasonable ground and . . . deliberately induced by him in the mind of the other party." The Commission had contracted that there was a tanker and, since there was no such tanker, a breach of contract had been committed." The Court awarded the plaintiffs £3,285 damages.

Common mistake as to a fact fundamental to the agreement. Where the parties have made a contract based on a common misapprehension relating to the fundamental subject-matter of the contract there is 'operative mistake'. This means that the contract actually made is essentially different from the contract the parties intend to make. In *Galloway* v, *Galloway* (1914) 30 T.L.R. 531, *A* and *B*, believing themselves to be married, made a separation agreement in which *A* agreed to pay *B* £1 a week. It was later discovered that they were not validly married. *B* claimed the promised payments. *Held,* the agreement was void, as there was a mistake on their part of fact which was material to the existence of their agreement.

Mutual or non-identical mistake as to the identity of the subject-matter. Where the parties are both mistaken as to a fundamental fact concerning the contract but each party has made a different mistake, there is a mutual or non-identical mistake. Thus, if *A* offers to sell his Ambassador Car, and *B* agrees to buy thinking *A* means his Fiat Car, there is a bilateral mistake which is mutual or non-identical. The contract does not come into existence under such a mistake, because there is no *consensus ad idem. The parties* have negotiated completely at cross-purposes and they were never in agreement. In *Raffles* v. *Wichelhaus* (1864) 2 H. & C. 906, *A* agreed to buy from B a cargo of cotton to arrive "ex-Peerless from Bombay". There were two ships called "Peerless" sailing from Bombay, one arriving in October and the other in December. *A* meant the earlier ship and *B* the latter. *Held,* the contract was void for mistake.

There would be no contract even if the mistake was caused by the negligence of a third party.

In *Henkel* v. *Pape* (1870) 6 Ex. 7, *P* wrote to *H* inquiring the price of rifles and suggested that he might buy as many as fifty. On receipt of a reply he wired "send three rifles". Due to the mistake of the telegraph clerk the message transmitted to *H* was "send the rifles." *H* despatched 50 rifles. *Held,* there was no contract between the parties.

Mistake as to Quality of Subject-matter or Promise. Mistake as to the quality raises difficult question. If the mistake is bilateral and because of the mistake the thing does not possess the quality bargained for the contract is obviously void. But if the mistake is only unilateral difficulty arises. Mere mistake as to quality of the subject-matter of a contract does not invalidate it, but mistake of one party to the promise of the other party as to quality of subject-matter, known to that other party, does invalidate the contract. Such a question generally arises in cases of sale of goods. The principle commonly applicable is *caveat emptor—Let* the buyer beware. There is generally no obligation on a contracting party to enlighten the other party even where he knows or suspects there is a misapprehension. For example, *A* offers to sell a watch to *B*, and *B*, thinking it is a gold watch, offers ₹ 500 for it. *A*, knowing the watch is not gold, accepts *B*'s offer without enlightening him. The contract is binding, provided A made no representation in the matter.

In *Leaf* v. *International Galleries* (1950) 2 K.B. 86, *L* bought from *G* a painting which both mistakenly believed to be by Constable and of great value. Later *L* discovered it was by an unknown artist and comparatively worthless. *Held, L* could not avoid the contract, as his mistake related only to the quality of the subject-matter, and *G* had made no representation. But where a party knowing that the other was labouring under a mistake "snatches a bargain" by hurriedly closing the transaction, this unilateral mistake will enable the party to avoid the contract.

Mistake through non-disclosure in contracts uberrimae fidei. A contract *uberrimae fidei* is a contract of utmost good faith. In such a contract the law imposes a special duty to act with the utmost good faith, *i.e.* to disclose all material information. Failure so to disclose all facts truthfully renders the contract voidable at the option of the other party. Here silence can amount to misrepresentation.

CONTRACTS *UBERRIMAE FIDEI*

Contracts *uberrimae fidei* are—

   (a) **Contracts of insurance of all kinds.** The assured must disclose to the insurer all material facts; and non-disclosure or misstatement will render the contract of insurance void (*Ratan Lal* v. *Metropolitan Co.,* 1959 Pat. 413).

   (b) **Contracts to take shares in a company under a prospectus.** When a company invites the public to subscribe for its shares by means of a prospectus, it is under statutory obligation to disclose truthfully the various matters set out in the Companies Act, 1956. Any person responsible for the non-disclosure of any of these matters is liable in damages. Also, the contract to take shares is voidable where there is a material non-disclosure in the prospectus.

   (c) **Contracts for the sale of land.** The vendor is under a duty to purchaser to show good title to the land he has contracted to sell. He must, therefore, disclose all defects in *title*. This duty does not extend to physical defects in the property itself.

   (d) **Contracts of family arrangements.** When members of a family make agreements or arrangements for the settlement of the family property, each member of the family must make full disclosure of every material fact within his knowledge.

   (e) *Suretyship and partnership contracts.* Contracts of suretyship and contracts of partnership, though often described as contracts *uberrimae fidei,* are not properly so described: they do not require utmost good faith at their formation. In both cases, after the contract has been made there is a duty of utmost good faith on the parties to disclose to each other all material facts coming to light after the making of the contract.

   (f) *A confidential relationship* between the contracting parties gives rise to a duty to disclose material facts. This is really based on the equitable concept of fiduciary relationship.

MISREPRESENTATION

A representation is a statement of fact made by one party to the contract to the other which induces that other to enter into the contract. A misrepresentation is a representation that is untrue. But representation always means a statement of *fact* not a statement of intention or of opinion or of law.

An untrue statement or misrepresentation may be either (i) Innocent, or (ii) Wilful or Deliberate with intent to deceive and is called Fraud.

INNOCENT MISREPRESENTATION

Innocent misrepresentation is a misstatement made innocently and with an honest belief as to its truth. It is sometimes called "Invalidating Misrepresentation". The effect of innocent misrepresentation of fact is that the party misled by it may repudiate the contract and (*i*) raise the misrepresentation as a defence to any action the other party may bring against him, or (*ii*) sue for rescission of the contract and restitution of anything he has transferred to the misrepresenter.

Generally, the injured party cannot get damages for innocent misrepresentation. But in the following exceptional cases he can get damages:

(a) From promoters or directors who make such misrepresentation in a prospectus under Company Law;

(b) Against an agent who commits a breach of warranty of authority;

(c) From a person who (at the Court's discretion) is stopped from denying a statement he has made where (i) he made a positive statement intending that it should be relied on, and (ii) the innocent party did rely on it, and thereby suffered damage.

It should be remembered that in order to avoid a contract on the ground of misrepresentation, it is necessary to prove that (i) there was a representation or assertion, (ii) such representation induced the party aggrieved to enter into contract, (iii) the assertion was of fact (and not of law, as ignorance of law is no excuse); (iv) the statement was not a mere opinion, or hearsay, or commendation (*i.e.* reasonable price) or tradesman's "puff", (v) the statement, which has become or turned out to be untrue, was made with an honest belief in its truth.

In an innocent misrepresentation, the party aggrieved may avoid the agreement, even though the statement was true at the time it was made but became untrue later by reason of change of circumstances (*O'Flanagan's Case* (1936) 1 Ch. 575).

WILFUL MISREPRESENTATION OR FRAUD

Section 17 of the Contract Act defines Fraud as follows; Fraud means and includes any of the following acts committed by a party to a contract, or with his connivance or by his agent, with intent to deceive another party thereto or his agent, or to induce him to enter into the contract:

1. the suggestion as to a fact, of that which is not true, by one who does not believe it to be true;
2. the active concealment of a fact by one having knowledge or belief of the fact;
3. a promise made without any intention of performing it;
4. any other act fitted to deceive;
5. any such act or omission as the law specially declares to be fraudulent.

But mere silence as to facts likely to affect the willingness of a person to enter into a contract is not fraud, unless the circumstances of the case are such that, regard being had to them, it is the duty of the person keeping silence to speak or unless his silence is, in itself, equivalent to speech.

In the words of Lord Herschel in *Derry* v. *Peek* (1889) 14 App. Cas. 337, Fraud is "an untrue statement made knowingly, or without belief in its truth, or recklessly, careless whether it be true or false" with intent to deceive. In simple terms, fraud is false statement or wilful concealment of a material fact with intent to deceive another party. The party deceived or defrauded can avoid the contract and also claim damages.

The essential characteristics of fraud are :

(a) *There must be representation or assertion and it must be false, or there must be active or wilful concealment of a material fact.* We have already considered this point under innocent misrepresentation.

If there is an actual false statement, the case is simple. *A*, intending to deceive *B*, falsely represents that the Television set he is offering for sale is German make, when it is in fact a locally made set. If concealment is alleged mere non-disclosure of material facts, however morally censurable, does not render a contract voidable. Mere silence is not misrepresentation, unless silence is in itself equivalent to speech, or where it is the duty of person keeping silence to speak; as where a fiduciary relation exists between the contracting parties or the contract requires utmost good faith. Disclosure is also essential where part-truth amounts to falsehood. If part only of facts is disclosed, and the undisclosed part so modifies the part disclosed as to render it, by itself, substantially untrue, there is a duty to disclose the full facts. Non-disclosure will amount to fraud. In *R. v. Kylsant* (1932)   1 K.B. 442, a prospectus contained statements which were true, that the company had paid dividends every year between 1921 and 1927. In fact, in each of these years the company had incurred substantial losses, and was only able to pay the specified dividends out of secret reserves. No disclosure was made of these losses. *Held*, the prospectus was false, because it put before intending investors figures which apparently disclosed the existing position of the company, but in fact it hid it, and Lord Kylsant, a director, who knew that it was false was guilty of fraud.[39]

(b) *The representation must be of fact.* The assertion must be of fact and not a mere expression of opinion, or hearsay, or puffery or flourishing description. Thus, if *A*, who is about to sell a horse to *B*, says that the horse is a Beauty and is worth ₹ 1,000, that is *A*'s opinion and *B* is at liberty to reject it. But if in fact he paid only ₹ 500 for it, then *A* has misstated a fact, and if *B* has been induced by that statement to buy the horse, he may rescind the contract on the ground of fraud.

(c) *There must be knowledge of the falsehood of the representation*[40] *or a reckless disregard as to its being true or false.* In a reckless misstatement the person is not sure as to the fact in his own mind; he feels a doubt, yet he represents to the other party, as if he is certain about the truth of the fact represented by him. Such misrepresentation is fraud. Also a promise made without an intention of performing it is fraud. To buy goods with the preconceived idea of getting goods without paying for them is fraud.

(d) *The representation must be made with the object of inducing the party deceived to act upon it.* The assertion must be made with the intention of inducing one to act on the assertion who does so act. This means that there is an inducement in fact and the assertion is one which necessarily influenced and induced the party to act. The party misled must not have exercised his own skill of judgment.

(e) *The representation must in fact deceive* The representation must be acted upon as it was intended to be acted upon so that the party misled is actually deceived. A deceit which does not deceive is not fraud.

(f) *The plaintiff must be thereby damnified.* It is a common saying that "there is no fraud without damage", for an action being one of deceit, and unless the plaintiff has sustained damage or injury, no action will lie. The damage may consist of actual and temporal injury, that is, some loss of money or money's worth, or some tangible detriment capable of assessment.

COERCION

Coercion is defined by section 15 of the Contract Act as "the committing or threatening to commit, any act forbidden by the Indian Penal Code, or the unlawful detaining, or threatening to detain, any property to the prejudice of any person whatever, with the intention of causing any person to enter into an agreement." The doing of any act forbidden by the Indian Penal Code will still be coercion, even though such an act is done in a place where the Penal Code is not in force.

---

39.   Peek v. Gurney (1873) 6 H.L. 377.
40.   Horsfall v. Thomas (1862) 158 E.R. 813.

What is coercion in India is 'duress' under English law, but coercion covers much wider field. *Duress* is limited to actual violence or threats of violence to the person, or imprisonment or the threat of criminal proceedings to the person coerced or those near or dear to him, such as his wife, children or parents. Threats to property are not duress. Coercion, on the other hand, may be against person or property, and the person coerced may *be any person,* not necessarily the party to the contract or his wife, parent or child.

In *Muthiah Chettiar* v. *Karuppan Chetli* (1927) 50 Mad. 786, an agent refused to hand over the account books, bonds etc. of the business to his successor agent unless the principal gave him a release of all liabilities during the term of his agency. The' principal did so but later succeeded in the suit to declare the release deed as vitiated by coercion. In *Keshavji* v. *Harjivan* (1887) Bom.566, a son forged his father's endorsement to promissory notes on the strength of which the bankers advanced monies. When the fraud was known the bankers wanted to launch a prosecution against the son. The father was induced to come to a settlement with the Bank to save the son. The settlement was set aside on the ground of coercion, as the father was not a free agent.

In *Gumming* v. *Ince* L.R. 1 H.L. 200, an old lady was induced to settle property on one of her relatives by the threat of unlawful confinement in a mental home. *Held,* the settlement could be set aside on the ground of duress, i.e., the threat of false imprisonment. In *Kaufman* v. *Gerson* (1904) 1 K.B. 591, K sued G on a contract, made in France, which K had coerced G into making by threats of prosecuting G's husband for a criminal offence which he had committed. *Held,* G was not liable under the contract, as her consent was obtained through coercion. In *Ranganayakamnna* v. *Alwar Setti* (1890) 13 Mad. 214, an adoption by a girl, aged 13, was held not binding, when it had been obtained from her by her husband's relatives by pressure on her by obstructing the removal of her husband's dead body.

It should, however, be noted that mere threat by one person to another to prosecute him does not amount to coercion. There must be a contract made under the threat, and that contract should be one sought to be avoided because of coercion (*Ramchandra* v. *Bank of Kohlapur,* 1952 Bom. 715). It may be repeated that coercion may proceed from any person, and may be directed against any person, even a stranger, and also against goods, e.g., by unlawful detention of goods.

UNDUE INFLUENCE

Undue influence occurs where a party enters into a contract under any kind of influence, mental pressure or persuasion, which prevents him from exercising a free and independent judgment. It makes the contract voidable by the party influenced or whose consent was not free. Section 16 of our Contract Act states that a contract is induced by undue influence where the relations subsisting between the parties are such that one of the parties is in a position to dominate the will of the other and uses that position to obtain an unfair advantage over the other. It further states that a person is deemed to be in a position to dominate the will of another (*i*) where he holds a real or apparent authority over the other, or (*ii*) where he stands in a fiduciary relation to the other; or (*iii*) he makes a contract with a person whose mental capacity is temporarily or permanently affected by reason of age, illness,or mental or bodily distress.

It is clear from this definition that contracts which may be rescinded for undue influence fall into two categories; *Firstly*, those where there is no special relationship between the parties. *Secondly*, those where a special relationship exists. In the first case, undue influence must be proved as a fact, by the party alleging it, in the second it is presumed to exist. In litigation, however, the two classes are not mutually exclusive and a plaintiff may allege both that undue influence be presumed and that it existed in fact *(ReGraig Meneces* v. *Middleton* (1971) Ch.95). It was stated in *Smith* v. *Kay* (1859) 7 H.L.C. 750: "The principle of undue influence applies to every case where the influence is acquired or abused, where confidence is reposed and. betrayed". Undue influence is a kind of "mental coercion", it destroys the free agency of one and constrains him to do which is against his will, and which he would not have done if left to his own judgment and volition, so that his act becomes the act of the one exercising the influence, rather than his own act.

Where no special relationship exists between the contracting parties, the plaintiff (*i.e.* the party influenced) must prove two things: (*i*) that the other party was in a position to dominate his will, (*ii*) that the contract was substantially unfair giving the dominant party unfair advantage.

It was observed in *Bhola Ram v. Piari Devi,* 1962 Pat. 168, undue influence has its origin in coercion or fraud. Domination of the will of a person is a kind of mental coercion and the use of his position by a person who dominates the will of the other to obtain an unfair advantage to himself or to his near relations is a variety of fraud.

In *Karnal Distillery Co. Ltd.* v. *Ladli Prasad,* 1958 Punj 190, confirmed by the Supreme Court in 1963 S.C. 1279, the elder brother was shown to have exercised undue influence over his younger brother in respect of a compromise arrangement, the transaction was held to be voidable at the instance of the younger brother. It was observed that when one member of the family exercises weighty influence in the domestic counsels either from age, from character or from superior position acquired from other circumstances an inference of undue influences has to be drawn. The influence subjugates the other's will to his injury. It is a subtle species of fraud, whereby mastery is obtained over the mind of the victim by insiduous approaches and seductive activities. It was further stated in this case that once the position of dominance is proved to exist, it is deemed to continue till its termination is established. So all transactions during such dominance are vitiated. However, a plea of undue influence can only be raised by a party to the contract and not by a third party,[41] unless there was any connivance between the person using undue influence and the third party benefiting by the contract.

In the second class of cases, undue influence is presumed either because of an exceptional authority one has over the other or he stands in a fiduciary position to the other and owes a duty to give that other a disinterested advice. The possibility that he may put his own interest uppermost is so obvious that he comes under a duty to prove that he has not abused the position [*Allcardv. Skinner* (1887) 36 Ch. D. 145], Whether fiduciary or confidential relationship exists or not, the question is always the same—was undue influence used to procure the contract or gift? But the burden of proof is different If *B* seeks to avoid a contract with *A*, then in the absence of any confidential relationship, the entire onus is on *B* to prove undue influence, but if he shows the existence of such relationship, the onus is on *A* to prove that undue influence was not used. *A* must rebut the presumption of undue influence.

To discharge the onus that he did not employ undue influence, the party must show that the other party to whom he owed the duty in fact acted voluntarily, in the sense that he was free to make an independent and informed estimate of the expediency of the contract or other transaction. The other party received independent advice before he completed the contract. A few examples will illustrate undue influence. *A*, having advanced money to his son *B* during his minority, upon *B*'s becoming major obtained, by misuse of parental influence, a bond from *B* for a greater amount than the sum due in respect of the advance. A employed undue influence. *A*; a man enfeebled *by* disease or age, is induced by *B*'s influence over him as his medical attendant, to agree to pay *B* an unreasonable sum for his professional services. *B* employs undue influence.[42] A Hindu, well advanced in years, with the object of securing benefits to his soul in the next world, gave away his whole property to his Guru or spiritual adviser. There was undue influence. Similarly, where a *cestui que trust* (beneficiary) had no independent advice it was held a gift by him to the trustee of certain shares forming part of the trust fund was void.

---

41. Kotumall v. Nur Mohd. 1931 Sind. 78.
42. Diala Ram v. Sargha, 1927 Lah. 536.

In *Debi Prasad* v.*Chhotey Lal*, All. 438,[43] *D* was the grandson of *C*'s own brother, and attended to the comforts of *C* in his illness, as he was also old, infirm and weak. *C* executed a deed of gift at the behest of *D*. The deed was vitiated by undue influence as it was clearly an unconscionable transaction. *D* was held to have had dominant influence over *C*, a sick, infirm and old man. Undue influence was presumed because of fiduciary relation.

But, as was held by the Supreme Court in *Chandra* v. *Ganga Prasad*, 1967 S.C. 878, there can be no presumption as to undue influence simply because the donor was related to the party and that he was of a weak disposition. What is essential of proof is the dominating will of the donee and if he used that position to obtain an unfair advantage over the donor.

In *Afsar Shaikh* v. *Soleman Bibi*, 1976 S.C. 163, the Supreme Court again emphasised that a general allegation in the plaint that the plaintiff was a simple old man of ninety who had reposed confidence in the defendant is much too insufficient to amount to an averment of undue influence. Merely relying on the other for advice does not amount to being unduly influenced. But if the transaction appears to be unconscionable, then the burden of proving that it was not induced by undue influence is to lie upon the person who was in a position to dominate the will of the other.

A third party contracting with notice of the exercise of undue influence by another is in no better position than if he had exercised undue influence himself. In *Lancashire Loans Ltd.* v. *Black* (1934) 1 K.B. 380, *B*, a married woman, under the undue influence of her mother, who was an extravagant woman, borrowed money on the security of her own property. The daughter did not understand the nature of the transaction, and the only advice she received was from a solicitor acting for the mother and the moneylenders. The moneylenders, therefore, knew all the circumstances between *B* and her mother. *Held*, the moneylenders were in no better position than the mother, and the contract was voidable by the daughter.

UNCONSCIONABLE TRANSACTIONS

When a person, without being fraudulent, forces another to enter into an agreement by making an unconscietious use of his superior power he is said to make an "unconscionable bargain." Such a bargain is voidable. The test is that between two parties on unequal footing one has sought to make an exorbitant profit of the other's distress. Where a person is heavily indebted to another and for a fresh loan is made to agree to *pay* extortionate rate of interest, it will be an unconscionable transaction. Similarly, where an heir to an estate borrowed ₹ 3,700 to enable him to prosecute his claim when he was without even the means of subsistence and gave the lender a decree only for ₹ 3,700 with interest at 20% per annum. [44] Also, where a spendthrift and a drunkard 18 years of age executed a bond in favour of his creditor agreeing to pay compound interest at 2 per cent per annum with monthly rests, it was held the bargain was unconscionable.[45] In the following two cases the bargain was held unconscionable: where a poor Hindu widow borrowed ₹ 1,500 from a moneylender at 100% per annum for the purpose of enabling her to establish her claim for maintenance; and where an illiterate agriculturist heavily indebted to a moneylender sold his land worth thrice the amount of the debt under pressure of payment. It must be remembered that in such cases the moneylender must be "in a position to dominate the will" of the borrower, and the bargain must be unconscionable within the

---

43.   See also Nellie Wapshare v. Pierce Leslie Co., 1960 Mad. 411, and Lakshmi Amma v. T.N. Bhatta, 1970 S.C. 1367; In Tapan Ranjan Das v. Smt. Jolly Das, 1990 Cal. 353, no undue influence by husband.

44.   Chunni Kaur v. Rup Singh (1888) 11 All. 57, confirmed on appeal to P.C. (1893) 20 I.A. 127; 15 All. 342.

45.   Kirpa Ram v. Sami-ud-Din (1903) 25 All. 284.

meaning of clause 3 of Sec. 16. The mere fact that the rate of interest is exorbitant is no ground for relief under this section unless it be shown that the creditor was in a position to dominate the will of the borrower. Nowadays, however, drastic legislation in most of the States has provided greater protection to debtors.

PURDA NISHIN WOMEN

The law throws around a Purda Nishin woman a special cloak of protection, and demands that person who deals with her must show affirmatively and conclusively that the deed was not only executed by, but was explained to, and was really understood by the lady. [46] It must also be proved that no coercion or undue influence was exercised on her, either by the party to the transaction or by a third party, and that she had executed the document of her **free will**. [47] The reason is that the ordinary presumption that a person understands the document to which he has affixed his name does not apply in the case of a **Purda Nishin Woman**[48] But a lady, whether Hindu or Muslim, who is claiming to be **Purda Nishin** must prove **complete seclusion**; and some degree of seclusion is not sufficient to entitle her to get special protection.

PART 1-F
UNLAWFUL AGREEMENTS

A contract may have been made with due observance of legal formalities, and may yet be unenforceable, because it is unlawful. An agreement is unlawful and therefore unenforceable, when the object for which it is made is forbidden by law, or if permitted, would defeat the provisions of law, or, is fraudulent, or involves an injury to the property of another, or in the eyes of the court, is immoral or opposed to public policy, (S.23). In simple words, an agreement may be unlawful because it is:

(a) **Illegal**, *i.e.*, contrary to positive law, being forbidden either by Statute law or Common law;

(b) **Immoral**, *i.e.*, contrary to sound and positive morality as recognised by law; and

(c) **Opposed to Public Policy,** *i.e.*, contrary to the welfare of the State as tending to interfere with civil or judicial administration, or with individual liberty of citizens.

Thus, an agreement will not become a contract or will remain unenforceable, if it is made for an unlawful consideration and with an unlawful object. If both parties contemplate an unlawful manner of performance, the case falls within the rule "that a contract lawful in itself is illegal if it be entered into with the object that the law should be violated" Therefore, if both the parties know of the wrongful or immoral intention, the agreement is void; if the party who is to furnish property or money does not know of it, the contract is voidable at his option, when he discovers the other party's intent. Further, an agreement may be rendered unlawful by its connection with a past as well as with a future unlawful transaction. But a contract will be valid if its object is not to defeat the provision of any law.[49] This leads us to make a distinction between Void and Illegal Contracts.

VOID AND ILLEGAL CONTRACTS

A void contract is one which has no legal effect. An illegal contract like the void contract has no legal effect as between the immediate parties, but has this further effect that transactions collateral to such a contract become tainted with illegality and are, therefore, not enforceable. *A* borrowed ₹ 100 from

46. Bhikary v. S. H. Mohd., 1958 Orissa 62.
47. Ranee Anna Purni v. Swaminatha (1910) 34 Mad. 7.
48. Asghar Ali v. Debroos Banoo Begum (1877) 3 Cal. 324.
49. Balkishan v. Laxman, 1951 Nag. 187.

B in order to bet with C as to the result of a horse race. A contract of betting in respect of horse-racing is void under Section 30 of the Act, and if A loses, C cannot recover from A. But B can recover the sum of ₹ 100 from A, since his transaction with A is only collateral to a void contract and is enforceable. On the other hand, if B had borrowed ₹ 1000 from A to buy a revolver to shoot C, the question whether A can recover from B depends on whether A was aware of the purpose for which the money was borrowed. If A knowing the illegal purpose, had lent the money, he cannot recover, because his loan was an aid to an illegal object of B, and illegal object taints the collateral transaction also.[50] If, on the other hand, A did not know the purpose of the loan, even though B had bought the revolver and shot C, A can recover. All illegal agreements are void, but all void agreements are not illegal. A minor's contract is void but not illegal.

CONSEQUENCES OF AN ILLEGAL CONTRACT

A contract that is illegal as formed and is therefore void *ab initio* is treated by the law as if it had not been made at all. As it is totally void and non-existent, no remedy is available to either party. Hence, parties to an illegal contract cannot get any help or protection from a court of law, because, "no polluted hand shall touch the pure fountain of justice." Thus, in the case of an illegal contract for the sale of goods, the buyer, even though he has paid the price, cannot sue for non-delivery; the, seller who had made delivery cannot recover the price. A servant cannot recover arrears of salary under an illegal contract of employment *(Miller* v. *Karlinski* (1945) 62 T.L.R. 85). Even though the illegal object fails, any money paid under the illegal contract cannot be got back. The effect of this principle is that the plaintiff who founds his cause of action upon an illegal act will not get any assistance from the court, and the defendant, though equally guilty, will benefit.[51] No suit can be filed in respect of an illegal contract. The maxim is *Ex turpi causa non oritur actio*—from an evil (illegal) cause, no action arises. As the court refuses to help either party, the plaintiff appears to be punished and the defendant is helped. But actually the court is neutral and the defendant gets the advantage of the court's neutrality. The maxim is: *in pari delicto potior est conditio defendentis*— "in cases of equal built, more powerful is the condition of the defendant". Similarly, an agreement, the consideration is which is immoral or fraudulent, cannot be enforced at law. *Ex dolo malo non oritur actio*— "No right of action can arise out of what is fraudulent or immoral." To right of action can arise out of what is fraudulent or immoral." To repeat, neither party can recover what he has given to the other under an illegal contract if in order to substantiate his claim he is driven to disclose the illegality *(Chettiar* v. *Chettiar* (1962) A.C. 294). The maxim *in pari delicto potior est conditio defendentis* applies and the defendant can keep what he has been given.

This principle, however, is subject to the following exceptions:

(a) A plaintiff may recover money, goods or land transferred under an illegal contract to the defendant, if he can frame a cause of action entirely independent of the contract. "Any rights which he may have irrespective of his illegal interest will, of course, be recognised and enforced" *(Scott* v. *Brown* (1892) 2 Q.B. 724). Where A has let a house knowingly to a prostitute, he cannot recover the rent from her, but he can sue for ejectment and for possession as the owner of the house, and he does not have to disclose the illegality.[52]

---

50. Fisher v. Bridges (1854) 118 E.R. 1283. There was an illegal contract under which F agreed to sell certain land to B. B paid the purchase price except for £630, and the land was conveyed to him. By a separate deed B promised to pay £630 to F. *Held,* the collateral agreement under seal was tainted with illegality.

51. Virayya v. Subba Rao, 1959 A.P. 647; Ramjanam Bharathi v. D. Kuer, 1959 Pab. 506.

52. See Sita Ram v. Radha Bai, 1968 S.C. 534.

(b) Where the transferor is not *in pari delicto* (equally guilty) with the defendant (*i.e.*, the transferee), *e.g.*, he was induced to enter into the contract by the fraud of the defendant, or where an ignorant man enters into an illegal contract under the influence of a cleverer man. In *Hughes* v. *Liverpool Friendly Society* (1916) 2 K.B. 482, *T* effected five policies with *L. Company*, and then decided not to keep them up. The *L.Company*'s agent fraudulently represented to *H* who had no insurable interest in the lives insured, that if she paid the arrears on the policies and paid the premiums in the future, she would be entitled to the policy, monies. *T* knew nothing of this arrangement. On learning that the policies were illegal, *H* sued to recover the premiums she had paid. *Held, H*, not being *in pario delicto,* succeeded in recovering the monies paid by her.

(c) The third exception to the principle is that a party to a contract, despite its illegality, is allowed to repent in case the contract is still executory. That is to say, where the illegal purpose has not yet been substantially carried into effect, he may recover what he has transferred to the other party.[53]

The next point to note is that the court presumes that a contract is legal, and where a contract is capable of two constructions, the one making it valid and the other void, the first will be adopted. Where a contract is alleged to be illegal, it is for the party so alleging to prove conclusively its illegal character. Where a contract consists of two parts, one part legal and the other illegal, and the legal part is separable from the illegal one, the court will enforce the legal part. If the legal and illegal part cannot be separated the whole contract is unenforceable. Similarly, if part of the consideration for a contract be illegal, that would taint the whole contract.

ILLEGAL AGREEMENTS FORBIDDEN BY LAW

A contract that is expressly or impliedly prohibited by statute, *e.g.*, by Indian Penal Code, or by some other special legislation, or by regulations, or by ordinances is illegal. If there is an express prohibition, the contract is undoubtedly illegal. A sub-lease of a licence for manufacture and sale of country liquor (under the Abkari Act),[54] or of opium (under the Opium Act)[55] was held to be void as the prohibition is for the protection of the public as well as the revenue. A loan granted to the guardian of a minor to enable him to celebrate the minor's marriage in contravention of the Child Marriage Restraint Act is illegal and cannot be recovered.[56] An agreement to pay consideration to a tenant to induce him to vacate premises governed by the Rent Restriction Act is illegal and cannot be enforced.[57] An agreement to withdraw a criminal prosecution for burning a house, on payment of compensation by the accused is void, as it is for an illegal purpose.[58] Where an agreement to sell spindles was entered into without prior permission of the Textile Commissioner as required under the control order issued under the Essential Commodities Act, the agreement being illegal, could not be enforced. For similar reasons, the buyer who had paid advance would not be able to recover it.[59] The principle underlying all these and similar cases is: "You cannot make a trade of a felony."

Where the statute does not prohibit a contract but imposes penalties merely to protect revenue, the contract in violation of the terms of the statute is not illegal. A statute may require a trader to take out

53. See M/s Anand Prakash Om Prakash v. M/s Oswal Trading Agency, 1976 Delhi 24.
54. Devi Prasad v.Rup Ram (188)10A11.577.
55. Raghunath v. Nathu (1894) 19 Bom. 626.
56. Srinivas v. Raja Ram Mohan (1951) 2 M.L.J. 264.
57. Mohanchana v. Mahindra, 1955 Cal. 442.
58. Shivram Darshne v, Visvanath, 1956.
59. Universal Plast Ltd. v. Santosh Kumar Gupta 1985 Del. 383; See also Naveen Chandra v. 6th Addle. Distt. & Session Judge, 1983 All. 116.

a licence; or to furnish certain particulars. If he fails to do this, the contract he has made is not prohibited and is in no sense tainted with illegality. A tobacconist had failed to take out a licence as required by law under a penalty of £200. He was held entitled to recover the price of tobacco delivered, for the object of the legislation was to impose penalty for failure to take out a licence for the purposes of the revenue and not to prohibit a contract.[60] Also, it has been held in India that where the holder of licence for collecting tolls, sub-leased it in violation of the terms of the, licence,[61] and where the licence of a right to cut grass from a forest, assigned it to another,[62] when the licence provided a penalty for doing so, the transactions were not void though they might expose the wrongdoer to the stipulated penalty.

IMMORAL AGREEMENTS

A contract is illegal for immorality:

(a) where the consideration is an act of sexual immorality, *e.g.* an agreement for future illicit co-habitation,[63] or a settlement in consideration of concubinage.[64] An agreement between husband and wife for future separation is bad, though one for immediate separation is enforceable;[65]

(b) where the purpose of the contract is the furtherance of sexual immorality, and both parties know this. If a landlord knowingly lets out his premises for immoral purposes, *e.g.*, for running a brothel, he cannot recover any rent. In *Pearce* v. *Brookes* (1866) L.R. 1 Exch, 213, A let a cab on hire to B a prostitute, knowing that it was to be used for immoral purposes, *i.e.*, soliciting. *Held, A* could not recover the hire.

WAGERING CONTRACTS

Meaning of a Wager. A Wager is a promise to pay money or transfer property upon the determination or ascertainment of an uncertain event, *e.g.*, a horse race, or a football match. In *Carlill* v. *Carbolic Smoke Ball Co.* (1892) 2 Q.B. 484, Hawkins, J., gave the following definition of a wagering contract which later received the unqualified approval of the Court of Appeal in *Ellesmere* v. *Wallace,* (1929) 2 Ch. 1:

"A *Wagering Contract* is one by which two persons, professing to hold opposite views touching the issue of an uncertain event, mutually agree that, dependent upon the determination of that event, one shall win from the other, and that other shall pay or hand over to him, a sum of money or other stake; *neither of the contracting parties having any other interest in that contract* than the sum or stake he will so win or lose, there being no other real consideration for the making of such contract by either of the parties."

There are several aspects of this definition which must be emphasised. Thus, the following points are essential to make a contract a wagering contract.

1. In *the first place,* there must be a promise to pay money or money's worth.
2. *Secondly,* the promise must be conditional on an event happening.
3. *Thirdly,* the event must be uncertain, either because it has to happen in the future and no one knows whether or not it will happen, or though it has happened, the contracting parties do not know of the result.

---

60. Smith v. Mawhood (1845) M. & W. 452.
61. Bhikanbhai v. Hiralal (1900) 24 Bom. 622.
62. Nazarali v. Babamiya (1946) 40 Bom. 64.
63. Hussain Ali v. Dinabai, 1923 Bom. 135.
64. Suhava Yellapa v. Yamavappa Sabu, 1933 Bom. 209.
65. Brodie v. Brodie (1917) p.271; Wilson v. Wilson (1848).

4. *Fourthly,* one party has to win and the other to lose on the conclusion of the event. Each party must stand either to win or lose under the terms of the contract. But if one party may win but cannot lose, or if he may lose but cannot win, or if he can neither lose nor win, it is not a wagering contract. As was observed by the Supreme Court in *Firm Pratap Chand Nopaji* v, *Firm of Kotrike Venkata Setty & Sons,* 1975 S.C. 1223: " In a wagering contract there has to be mutuality in the sense that the gain of one party would be the loss of the other on the happening of the uncertain event which is the subject-matter of the wager.

5. The last essential feature of a wager is that the stake or bet must be the only interest which the parties have in the contract; and *there must not be any other consideration for the making of the contract by either of the parties.* For example, if *A* lays *B* ten to one in rupees against a particular horse, *B* stands to win ₹ 10, *A* stands to win Re. 1, but neither of them has any other interest whatsoever in the contract.

Wagering contracts are void and not illegal except in Bombay, where they have been declared illegal under the Avoiding Wagers (Amendment) Act, 1861. Therefore, in Bombay, a wagering contract, being illegal, is void not only between the immediate parties, but taints and renders void a contract collateral to it. In the rest of India, wagering contracts are only void, so that a contract collateral to a wagering contract is not void.[66] The winner of a wager cannot sue the loser for his winnings, even though the loser makes a fresh promise to pay. Thus, where *A* bets with *B* and loses; applies to *C* for a loan in order to pay *B*. *C* gives the loan to *A* to enable him to pay *B*. In Bombay, *C* cannot recover his money from A, because this is money paid "under" or "in respect of" a wagering transaction which is illegal there. But in the rest of India such a transaction would be void and not illegal and C could recover from *A*[67]. Money paid to a stakeholder to retain pending the result of a wager can be recovered from the stakeholder by the payer any time before he has handed it over to the winner of the wager, but winner cannot sue the stakeholder for the money.

There is an exception in favour of subscriptions or contributions or agreements to subscribe or contribute for plate or sum of money or prize of the value or amount of ₹ 500 or upwards for the benefit of the winner of any horse race. Games other than horse race are not exempted, so that the same may be wagering and thus void.

Commercial Transactions and Wagers—Wagering Contracts may assume a variety of forms and it may sometimes be difficult to distinguish between genuine commercial transactions and mere Wagering contracts. If two persons *A* and *B* contract for the sale and purchase of 100 bags of wheat at ₹ 400 per bag, to be delivered two months hence, it may be difficult to say whether it is a good commercial transaction with the object of delivering the goods or whether the two merchants are really speculating and wagering upon the prices two months hence, with a view to paying the difference. Where *delivery of goods is intended* to be given and taken it is a valid contract, but where only the *differences are intended* to be paid, it will be a wagering contract and unenforceable. Therefore, in order to constitute a wagering contract, neither party should intend to perform the contract itself, but pay the differences.[68] It is not sufficient if the intention to gamble exists on the part of only one of the contracting parties. A contract will be a wagering contract only if *both* contracting parties at the time of entering into contract had the intention not to take delivery of goods. There must be common intention to wager.[69] A suit will not lie for the recovery of money deposited with a person on account of *Satta* transaction by way of security.

---

66. Gherulal v. Mahadeodas, 1959 S.C. 781 : Soorajmal v. Doongemal, 1959 Raj 27.

67. Ramimadhodas v. Kaushal Kishore (1900) 2 All. 452.

68. Perosha v. Manekjj (1898) 22 Boni. 699.

69. Gherulal Mahadeodas, 1959 S.C. 781: See also Firm of Pratap Chand Nopaji v. Firm of Kotrike Venkata Setty & Sons. 1975 S.C. 1223.

Teji Mandi Transactions or Option Dealings—These transactions are in the nature of speculation pure and simple, and the Stock and Commodity Exchanges provide good facilities to Bulls and Bears to enter into speculation freely. There was a time when it was believed that such transactions were by way of wager and so void under Section 30. But at the present time the presumption is that *Teji Mandi* is not a wagering transaction, and is valid and binding between the parties, unless it is positively proved that both parties intended not to give and take delivery. The English equivalent of the terms *Teji Mandi* is "Option Dealing" and means a right to buy or sell certain goods at a price by a certain date. In Bombay by virtue of Act XXV of 1930, options in cotton are prohibited and declared void. But cross transactions, *i.e.*, forward contracts of sale and purchase which sometimes balance each other when the settlement date comes, are valid because of the *bonafide* intent to do business, even though no delivery may actually have taken place. Option dealings in securities on stock exchanges are now prohibited by the Securities Contracts (Regulation) Act, 1956.

Agreements between Pakka Adatia and his Constituents—A *Pakka Adatia* is not merely the agent of his constituent, and thus a disinterested middleman bringing two principals together, but is a principal. Therefore, a transaction between a *Pakka Adatia* and his Constituent may be by way of wager like any other transaction of the nature of a wager between two contracting parties. As between a *Kalcha Adatia* and his Constituent there cannot be dealings by way of wager, as the relation between them is that of agent and principal and not that of principal and principal as between *Pakka Adatia* and his Constituent.

Lotteries—A wagering contract amounting to lottery is not only void but illegal. A lottery is a game of chance. Therefore an agreement to buy a ticket for lottery is a wagering agreement; and all transactions in connection with a lottery remain illegal even if the Government has authorised the holding of lottery. The only effect of such permission is that the persons conducting the lottery will not be punished.[70] But in *Anraj* v. *Govt. of Tamil Nadu,* 1956 SC 63, has held lotteries, with the prior permission of the Central Govt. as valid so that the winner is entitled to receive the prize.

Crossword Competitions—A Crossword competition is not, in so far as it involves, for a successful solution, a good measure of skill, a wager. But in an English case it has been held that a crossword puzzle in which prizes depend upon correspondence of the competitor's solution with a previously prepared solution kept with the editor of a newspaper, is a lottery and, therefore, a wagering transaction.[71] Prize competitions which are games of skill, e.g., picture puzzles, athletic competitions, etc., are not wagers, but those involving prizes of more than ₹ 1,000 have been declared gambling and so void, by the Prize Competition Act, 1955. Also, if the agreement does not involve loss to either party, it is got a wager. Thus, an agreement to enter into a wrestling contest, in which the winner was to be rewarded by the whole of the sale proceeds of tickets and the party failing to turn up on that day would have to forfeit ₹ 500 was held not to be a wagering contract.[72]

Contracts of Insurance are not wagering agreements even though the payment of money by the insurer may depend upon a future uncertain event. Contracts of insurance differ from wagering agreements as follows:

(a) It is only a person possessing insurable interest that is allowed to insure life or property, and not any person, as in the case of wager. An insurance contract is, therefore, entered into to protect an interest. In a wagering agreement there is no interest to protect.

---

70. Dorabij v. Lance (1918) 42 Bom. 676.

71. Coles v. Odham's Press (1936) 1 K.B. 416; see also J.N. Gupta v. State of West Bengal, 1959 Cal. 141; R.M.D. Chamarbaugwala v. Union of India, 1957 S.C. 628; State of Bombay v. R.M.D. Chamarbaugwala, 1957 S.C. 699.

72. Babasaheb v. Rajaram (1931) 33 Bom. L R. 260.

(b) In the case of fire and marine insurance only the actual loss suffered by the party is paid by the insurer, and not the full amount of the policy.

(c) Even in the case of life insurance, the amount payable on the assured's death is fixed because of the difficulty in estimating the loss caused by the death of the assured in terms of money, but the underlying idea is that of indemnification; not so in a wagering agreement.

(d) Contracts of insurance are regarded as beneficial to the public and are, therefore, encouraged. Wagering agreements do not serve any useful purpose and are considered to be against public policy.

AGREEMENTS OPPOSED TO PUBLIC POLICY

An agreement which tends to prejudice the welfare of the community or the State is said to be contrary to Public Policy and thus unenforceable. Public Policy is that principle of the law which holds that no subject can unlawfully do that which has a tendency to be injurious to the public or against the public good. It is difficult to give a clear cut classification of agreements which are bad on the ground of public policy, for "public policy" is a rather vague and elastic term, and it may vary with different judges. Lord Halsbury observed in *Janson* v. *Drieftein Consolidated Mines Ltd.,* A.C. 484, "that categories of public policy are closed, and that no court can invent a new head of public policy." This view is, however, too rigid; and S. 23 of the Indian Contract Act seems to provide that it is open to the Court to hold that the consideration or object of an agreement is unlawful on the ground that it is opposed to what the Court regards as public policy. In India, therefore, it cannot be affirmed as a matter of law that no Court can invent a new head of public policy but the dictum of Lord Davey in the same case [(1902) A.C. 484] that "public policy is always an unsafe and treacherous ground for legal decision" may be accepted as a sound cautionary maxim in considering the reasons assigned by a judge for his decision. The doctrine should only be invoked in clear cases in which the harm to the public is substantially incontestable, and does not depend upon the idiosyncratic inference of a few judicial minds. In popular language, the contract should be given the benefit of the doubt, and enforced.

In *Gherulal Parakh* v. *Mahadeodas,* 1959, S.C. 781, the doctrine of 'public policy' has been described in the following manner:—

'Public Policy' is a vague and unsatisfactory term, and calculated to lead to uncertainty and error when applied to the decision of legal rights; it is capable of being understood in different senses. Therefore, it is an illusive concept; it has been described— as "untrustworthy guide", "of variable quality", "uncertain one", "unruly horse", etc. The primary duty of a Court is to enforce a promise which the parties have made and to uphold the sanctity of contracts which form the basis of society, but in certain cases, the Court may relieve them of their duty on a rule founded on what is called the public policy. The doctrine of public policy is only a branch of common law and, just like any other branch of common law, it is governed by precedents; the principles have been crystallized under different heads and though it is permissible for the Court to expound and apply them to different situations, the doctrine should only be invoked, in clear and incontestable cases of harm to the public. Though the heads are not closed and though theoretically it may be permissible to evolve a new head under exceptional circumstances of a changing world, it is advisable in the interest of stability of the society not to make any attempt to discover new heads in these days. As is stated by Cheshire and Pifoot, "The judges must expound, not expand, this particular branch of the law" (*i.e.,* public policy).[73]

Some of the commonly accepted grounds of public policy (including those contained in Sections 26-28 of the Indian Contract Act) are dealt with in the following paragraphs:

Trading with enemy—It is a long settled law that an Indian National cannot trade with an alien enemy without the Government's licence. So all trade with the Union's enemies without licence is unlawful. If the performance of a contract made in time of peace is rendered unlawful by the outbreak,

---

73. Law of Contract, (8th Edn), p. 322.

of war the obligation of the contract is suspended or dissolved according as the intention of the parties can or cannot be substantially carried out by postponing the performance till the end of hostilities.

Agreement for stifling Prosecution—Such agreements are a well-known class of those contracts which the Courts refuse to enforce on this ground. The law is "you cannot make a trade of your felony. You cannot convert a crime into a source of profit" If a person has really committed a crime he should be prosecuted, and if found guilty, sentenced. If he is not guilty, the contract is only a blackmail. "No court of law can countenance or give effect to an agreement which attempts to take the administration of law out of the hands of the judges and put it in the hands of private individuals.[74] Where A, Knowing that B has committed an offence, obtains a promise from B, in consideration of not exposing B, there is a case of stifling prosecution. The agreement is void. But an agreement in writing between persons not to resort to a Court of law, but to refer their dispute to arbitration is not opposed to public policy, and is valid.

Agreements to vary the Periods of Limitations—Agreements curtailing or extending the period of limitation prescribed by the Law of Limitation are not enforceable, as the object of such agreement will be to defeat the provisions of the law. Agreements in fraud of insolvency law are illegal and void. Thus, an agreement by a creditor to forbear opposition to the discharge of the insolvent, or an agreement interfering with an equal distribution of the assets will be void. Agreements to the Indemnity Bail are void on the ground of public policy, as the law requires people to stand bail staking their own money on the conduct of the accused. Where A, the accused, pays money to B and requests him to stand bail, A cannot recover back the money, even if the bail is over.[75] Again, if B forfeits his bail on account of A's absconding, B cannot sue and recover the money from A's property either on an express or an implied purpose.[76]

Agreement tending to an abuse of legal process—Maintenance and Champerty—known to English law—are two important types of agreements under this head. Maintenance has been defined as the promotion of litigation in which a person has no interest of his own. Champerty has been defined as a bargain whereby one party is to assist another in recovering property and is to share the proceeds of the action. The difference between Maintenance and Champerty is this: In Champerty the desire is to share in the proceeds of the litigation, in Maintenance, the desire is to stir up litigation. Both of them are illegal and unenforceable in English law. In Indian law, however, Champerty and Maintenance are not illegal and the specific rules of English law against these have not been adopted here. In *Bhagwat Dyal Singh* v. *Debi Dyal Sahu* (1908) 35 I.A.48; 35 Cal.420, Their Lordships of the Privy Council clearly laid it down that an agreement Champertous according to English law was not necessarily void in India; it must be against public policy to render it void here. The .principle is taken to be part of the law of "Justice, equity, and good conscience," and if any agreement tends to go against, these, it would not be enforced. A fair agreement to supply funds to carry on a suit in consideration of having a share of the property, if recovered is *not per se* opposed to public policy. If, however, agreements of this kind are made not with the *bonafide* object of assisting a claim believed to be just and of obtaining reasonable recompense therefore, but for improper objects as for the purpose of gambling in litigation, or of injuring or oppressing others by abetting and encouraging unrighteous suits so as to be contrary to public effect will not be given to them.[77] Where in consideration of the plaintiff agreeing to defray the expenses of prosecuting the defendant's suit to recover a certain property, the defendant agreed to transfer to plaintiff, in one case 55 P. share of the property,[78] in

74. Sudhindra Kumar v. Ganeshchandra 1938 Cal. 840; Eastern Mercantile Bank v. Philip; 1960 Ker, Narsimhraj v. Guru Raju, 1963 S. C. 107.
75. Fateh Singh v. Sauwal Singh (1878) 1 All. 751.
76. Bhupati v. Chowdry (1919) 24C.W.N. 368.
77. Ram Kumar v. Chander Kant (1876) 2 Cal. 233 (P. C), see also 1931 P.C. 100.

another 12 P. share, and in a third 50 P. share, it was held that the agreement was extortionate and inequitable,[79] and the plaintiff was awarded the expenses legitimately incurred by him with interest. Similarly, where the claim was of a simple nature and in fact no suit was necessary to settle it, an agreement to pay ₹ 30,000 to the plaintiff for assisting in recovering the claim was held to be extortionate and inequitable. In *re G., Senior Advocate of the Supreme Court,*[80] *the Supreme Court held that an agreement to render services for the conduct of litigation in consideration of payment of 50 per cent of the amount recovered through Court would be legally enforceable and valid as the rigid English rules of champerty and maintenance do not apply in India.*

Interference with course of Justice—An agreement for the purpose or to the effect of using improper influence of any kind with judges or officers of justice is void.[81] Thus an agreement whereby one person agreed to assist another in carrying out litigation for the purpose of delaying execution of a decree was held to be unenforceable.[82]

RESTRAINT OF PARENTAL RIGHT

According to law the father is the guardian of his minor child, and in the absence of the father, the mother has the right of guardianship. This right cannot the bartered away by any agreement.[83] Thus, where a father having two minor sons agreed to transfer guardianship of those boys in favour of Mrs. Annie Besant and also agreed not to revoke the transfer, but subsequently changed his mind and filed a suit for recovery of the boys and a declaration that he was the rightful guardian, the Court held him to be the rightful and proper guardian and also held that he had the right to revoke his authority and get back the children.[84]

AGREEMENT IN RESTRAINT OF MARRIAGE

The law regards marriage and the married status as the ordinary right of every individual, and so according to Section 26 of the Indian Contract Act every agreement in restraint of the marriage of any person, other than a minor, is void. Therefore in India, there is a prohibition on restraints on marriage, whether partial or complete, so that a contract agreeing not to marry a certain person or class of persons is void. But in English law only an absolute restraint is void, *e.g.,* an agreement to marry no one but the promisee is void.

MARRIAGE BROKERAGE OR BROCAGE CONTRACTS

Agreements to procure marriage for reward are void, as being opposed to public policy. When a *purohit* was promised ₹ 20 in consideration of procuring a second wife for the defendant, the promise was held invalid for where the agreement is by a person to pay money to a stranger hired to procure a wife for him, it is opposed to public policy and void.[85] An agreement to pay money to parent or guardian in consideration of his giving his daughter in marriage is void as, opposed to public policy. The validity of the marriage is not affected, because *Asura* form of marriage is recognised by Hindu Law. So, money, if actually paid cannot be recovered back, and if not paid, a suit therefore would not

78. Kanwar Ram Lal v. Nil Kant (1893) 201. A. 112; Alopi Prasad v. Court of Wards 1938 Lah. 23.
79. Harilal v. Bhailal. 1940 Bom. 145.
80. 1954 S.C. 554
81. Gulabchand v. Kudilal, 1966 S. C. 1734.
82. Nandkishore v. Kunjbechari, 1903 All. 303.
83. Re Caroll (1931) 1 K. B. 307.
84. Giddu Narayanish v. Mrs Annie Besant (1915) 38 Mad. 807 1914 P. C. 41.
85. Vaidyanaihan V. Gangarazu (1890) 17 Mad. 9

lie.[86] In India converse cases are more common, where moneys are promised to be paid by the girl's parent or guardian to the bridegroom or his parents in consideration of marriage. Such contracts are equally illegal. Thus, where a sum of money has been promised, and the marriage takes place, the money cannot be recovered on the promise, as it is illegal. Where the moneys have .been paid they cannot be got back. Where, however, moneys have been paid but no marriage has taken place they could be recovered since the illegal purpose has not been carried out. A promised to pay a sum of ₹ 1,100 to B, the father of the bridegroom, and actually paid ₹ 400. The marriage fell through. The Court held that ₹ 400 were recoverable by A.[87]

Traffic in Pensions—S. 12 of the Pensions Act prohibits traffic in pensions. Therefore, traffic in pensions is opposed to public policy and void.[88]

Sale of Public Offices and Titles—Traffic by way of sale of public offices and appointments obviously militates against public service. An agreement to transfer office from one person to another or to secure an office or honour or title for monetary consideration, is totally bad, because if such an agreement is enforced in law, it will impair the efficiency, and corrupt the administration of the State. An agreement to pay money to a Government servant to induce him to retire before the due time, in order to make room for another, was held to be illegal as amounting to sale of public office and moneys paid were held irrecoverable.[89]

Agreements tending to create monopolies are void as opposed to public policy.[90] Agreements not to bid at an auction sale may be unlawful if made with the object of defrauding a third party.[91] Again an agreement which involves an injury to the properties of other persons is void under S.23 of the Contract Act (*K. Abdul Khadar* v. *Plantation Corpn of Kerala Ltd.,* 1983 Ker.l). But a combination of persons at an auction sale between two persons not to bid each other and to convey half the property to the other if the bid of the one was accepted is *per se* not against public policy (*Sujan Singh* v. *Mohkam Chand,* 1983 P & H 180.

RESTRAINT OF TRADES

It has long been a principle of English Law that it is for the good of the community that everyone should be at liberty to use his skill, where, when, and how he likes. Contracts by which a man fetters his liberty in this direction are presumptively to the detriment of the general good, and the Courts are prepared to treat them as void. Thus, if a father were to bind his son not to enter various specified trades, the contract would be void even if under seal and supported by consideration paid by the father to the son. It was, however, found that in result, this strict rule defeated its own purpose and was, therefore, relaxed. Thus, in **English Law**, though general and total restraints will be bad, reasonable restraint will be enforceable. In other words, if the restraint is limited to such a space, and is only for such a time, as will be reasonably sufficient to carry out the intentions and objects of the parties, it will be enforceable. The character of particular trade may justify a very wide restraint.

In **Indian Law**, a contract in restraint of trade is void. Sec. 27 of Indian Contract Act reads: "Every

86. Baldeodas v. Mahamaya (1911) 16 C.W. N. 447, see also Abbaskhan v. Nurkhan (1920) 1, Lah.. 574, Venkatkrishna v. Venkatchalan (1908) 32 Mad. 185.
87. GDharani v. Kanhji.l 949 Pat. 250; Rajindra v. Roshan, 1950 All. 592.
88. Baldeo Jha v. Ganga Prasad, 1959, Pat 17.
89. GSaminatha v. Muthuswamy (1907) 30 Mad. 530; Karuppin v. Pannuochami 1933 Mad.. 768.
90. Somu Pillai v. the Municipal Council Mayavaram (1905) 28 Mad. 520. Maharajadhiraja Sir Kameshwer Singh v. Yasin Khan 1938 Pat 473. District Board of Jhelum v. Harichand 1934 Lah. 474.
91. Ramlal Misra v. Rajendranath, 1938 Oudh 124; But see (1950) 2 M. L. J. 634.

agreement by which any one is restrained from exercising a lawful profession, trade or business of any kind, is to that extent void." Accordingly, **in India, all agreements in restraint of trade, whether general or partial, qualified or unqualified, are void,** and the fact that the restraint is limited in point of time or place is immaterial. It is, therefore, not open to the Courts in India to enter into any question of reasonableness or otherwise of the restraint. [92] In *Shaikh Kalu* v. *Ramsaran Bhagat* (1909) 13 C.W.N. 388,29 out of 30 makers of combs in the city of Patna agreed with *R* to supply him with combs and not to sell combs to any one else leaving *R* free to reject the goods if he found there was no market for them in Patna Calcutta or elsewhere, the agreement was held void. As between an employer and an employee there can be no agreement whatever in restraint of trade after the term of employment is over. In *Oakes & Co.* v. *Jackson* (1876) 1 Mad. 134, *J* who was an employee of *Oakes & Co.*, agreed not to employ himself in any similar concern within a distance of 800 miles from Madras after leaving the company's service. This restraint was held void.[93] A restraint imposed upon a servant is not valid and is not reasonable even in English law. But an agreement of service by which a person binds himself *during the term of the agreement* not to take service with any one else or directly or indirectly take part in or promote or aid any business in direct competition with that of his employer is not in restraint of a lawful profession, trade or business and is valid.[94] *A* agreed to become assistant for 3 years to *B* who was a doctor practising at Zanzibar. It was agreed that during the term of the agreement A was not to practise on his own account in Zanzibar. At the end of one year, *A* ceased to act as *B*'s assistant and began to practise on his own account It was held that the agreement was valid and *A* could be restrained by an injunction from doing so.[95] But if a servant is wrongfully dismissed by the employer he may treat the dismissal as the repudiation of the contract and is free from the restrictive covenant.[96]

Trade Combinations—It should be remembered in this connection that, while agreements operating as a bar to the exercise of a lawful business are void, agreements merely to restrain freedom of action in detail in the actual exercise of a lawful business are valid. Section 27 is not intended to take away the rights of a trader to regulate his business according to his own discretion and choice. Thus, an agreement between manufacturers or traders not to sell their goods below a certain price, to pool profits and to divide business and profits in certain proportion does not amount to a restraint of trade and is perfectly valid. An agreement in the nature of a trade combination for the purpose of avoiding competition is not necessarily unlawful, even if it damages others.[97] If the agreement was not clearly for the mutual benefit of the parties but was an attempt to create a monopoly, it would be void as against public policy. It was observed in *Vancouver Brewery Co.* v. *V. Breweries* (1934) P.C. 101, that "Liberty of trade is not an asset which the law will permit a person to barter away except in special circumstances."

WHEN A CONTRACT IN RESTRAINT OF TRADE IS VALID

We have noted above that every restraint is bad in law, but certain exceptions to the general rule are recognised and, if a partial and reasonable restraint falls under any of these exceptions the contract will be enforceable. The exceptions are as follows:—

   (a) **Sale of goodwill**—Exception 1 to Section 27 of the Contract Act provides that a seller of

---

92. Khemchand v. Dayaldas, 1942 Sind. 114.

93. See also Brahmputra Tea Co. v. Searth (1985) 11 Cal. 545; Cohen v. Wilkie. (1912) 16 Cal. W. N. 534; Kores v. Kolok (1957) 3 All. E. R. 158, Superintendence Co. of India (P) Ltd. v. Krishan Murgai, 1982 Sc 1717.

94. Charles v. Macdonald (1899) 23 Bom. 103.

95. *Ibid.*

96. Desh Pande v. Arvind Mills (1946) 48 B. L. R. 90; see also Niranjan Golkari v. Century Mills Ltd., 1967 S. C. 1098.

97. Daulat Ram v. Dharam Chand, 1934 Lah 110.

goodwill of a business may agree with the buyer to refrain from carrying on a similar business, within specified limits as to territory and time so long as the buyer or his representative in title carries on a like business, and the restraint appears to the Court reasonable. Thus, a restraint clause in the sale of a right to ply ferries was held to be enforceable as it was a reasonable covenant in a sale of goodwill.[98]

(b) **Partners' agreements**—Section 11 (2) of the Indian Partnership Act permits contracts between partners to provide that a partner shall not carry on any business other than that of the firm while he is a partner.

(c) **Section 36** (2) of the same Act provides that a partner may make an agreement with his partners that on ceasing to be a partner he will not carry on any business similar to that of the firm within a specified period or within specified local limits; and the agreement shall be valid if the restrictions are reasonable.

(d) **Section 54** of the same Act provides that partners may, upon or in anticipation of the dissolution of the firm, make an agreement that some or all of them will not carry on a business similar to that of the firm within a specified period or within specified local limits; and such agreement shall be valid if the restrictions imposed are reasonable.

(e) **Section 53** (3) of the Act provides that a partner may, upon the sale of the goodwill of a firm, make an agreement that such partner will not carry on any business similar to that of the firm within a specified period or within specified local limits; and such agreement shall be valid if the restrictions imposed are reasonable.

RESTRAINT OF PERSONAL FREEDOM

The law generally allows all persons freedom to enter into any contract they please, but at the same time, if the Court finds that the contract unduly restrains individual liberty and virtually amounts to slavery, it will refuse to enforce it. Where a borrower in an agreement with the money-lender, undertook not to change his address nor his employment, not to consent to reduction of salary, not to part with any property, not to incur obligations on credit, not to incur any obligations legal or moral, without first obtaining in each case the money-lender's express permission in writing, it was *held* that the agreement was void as against public policy.[99] Again, where a borrower executed a bond to do work in lieu of interest, and the work was paid for at very low rate the Court held that the agreement was not enforceable, as it virtually amounted to slavery.[100]

VOID AGREEMENTS

All the agreements which are or are declared by the Contract Act to be void are summed up here for the convenience of the reader.

1. Contracts by a minor or a person of unsound mind (Sec. 11).
2. Contract made under a mistake of fact material to the agreement on the part of both the parties (Sec. 20).
3. An agreement of which the consideration or object is unlawful (Sec. 23).
4. If any part of a single consideration for one or more objects, or any one or any part of any one of several considerations for a single object, is unlawful, the agreement is void (Sec. 24).
5. An agreement made without consideration (Subject to 3 exceptions already noted) (Sec. 25).

---

98. Chandra v. Mullick (1921) 48 Cal. 1030. P.C. 167.
99. Harwood v. Miller's T & T Co., (1971) K. B. 305.
100. Rama Sastier v. Ambela Koren 1929 Mad 167.

6. An agreement in restraint of marriage (Sec. 26).

7. An agreement in restraint of trade (Sec. 27).

8. An agreement in restraint of legal proceedings (Sec. 28)

9. Agreements, the meaning of which is not certain, or capable of being made certain (Sec. 29).

10. Agreements by way of wager (Sec. 30).

11. An agreement to enter into an agreement in the future.

12. An agreement to do an act impossible in itself [Sec. 56 (1)].

WHEN CONTRACT BECOMES VOID

An agreement not enforceable by law (as in the above 12 cases) is void *ab initio* [2(g)].

But a contract which ceases to be enforceable by law becomes void when it ceases to be enforceable [2(j)].

A contract becomes void when, by reason of some event which the promisor could not prevent, the performance of the contract becomes impossible. The impossibility must happen after the formation of the contract. *A* and *B* contract to marry each other. Before the time fixed for the marriage, A goes mad. The contract becomes void.

A contract also becomes void by reason of subsequent illegality. *A* in England agrees to supply goods to *B* in Germany. After the formation of the contract war breaks out between England and Germany, and the supply of goods to Germany is prohibited by legislation. The contract becomes void.

A contingent contract to do or not to do anything if an uncertain future event happens becomes void if the event becomes impossible.

Where a contract is voidable at the option of the promisee the contract becomes void when the promisee exercises his option by avoiding the contract.

RESTITUTION

When the contract becomes void, it need not be performed by either party, but where any party has received any benefit under such a contract from the other party he must restore it or make compensation for it to the other party. *A* agrees to sell to *B* after 6 months a certain quantity of gold and receives ₹ 500 as advance. Soon after the agreement, private sales of gold are prohibited by an Act of the legislature. The contract becomes void, but *A* must return the sum of ₹ 500 to *B*.

Restitution is also provided for by Sec. 65 where an agreement is discovered to be void. *A* pays *B* ₹ 500 in consideration of *B*'s promising to marry *C*, *A*'s daughter. *C* is dead at the time of promise. The agreement is discovered to be void, but *B* must pay back ₹ 500.

To sum up, Sec. 64 provides that the party rescinding voidable contract shall, if he has received any benefit thereunder from another party to such contract, restore such benefit, so far as may be, to the person from whom it was received.

Section 65 gives a right of restitution (*i*) when an agreement is discovered to be void, and (*ii*) when a contract becomes void. It should be noted that in the first case the agreement never amounted to a contract because it was void *ab initio*, the fact of its being void being discovered at a later stage. The second part deals with a contract which was enforceable at its inception but becomes void at a later stage.

The section, however, does not apply to a case where the parties are wholly incompetent to contract, *e.g.*, where one of the parties is a minor. The minor cannot be asked to restore the benefit; although where he had misrepresented his age, the court may, on equitable grounds, order for the restoration of the benefit received or pay compensation.[101]

Where benefit cannot be restored, the party may be asked to make compensation for it.

PART1-G
QUASI-CONTRACTS
OR
CERTAIN RELATIONS RESEMBLING THOSE OF CONTRACTS

A contract to be enforceable must have certain essential elements, namely, offer and acceptance, genuine consent, lawful consideration, lawful object, and capacity to contract. But under certain conditions the law creates and enforces legal rights and obligations when no real contract exists. These obligations are known as quasi- contracts. Our Contract Act describes them as certain relations resembling, those of contracts.

A quasi or constructive contract rests upon the equitable principle that a person shall not be allowed to enrich himself unjustly at the expense of another. The maxim is *Nemo debet locuplatari ex liena justua*—"No man must grow rich out of another person's loss". In truth, it is not a contract at all. It is an obligation which the law creates, in the absence of any agreement, when and because the acts of the parties or others have placed in the possession of one person money, or its equivalent, under such circumstances that in equity and good conscience he ought not to retain it, and which *ex aequo bono* (in justice and fairness) belongs to another. Duty, and not a promise or agreement or intention of the person sought to be charged, defines it. It is fictitiously deemed contractual, in order to fit the cause of the action to the contractual remedy" (*Miller* v. *Schloss,* 218 N.Y. 400,113 N.E, 337—An American case).

The following types of quasi-contracts have been dealt with in the Contract Act., Sees. 68-72:—
1. Necessaries supplied to a person incapable of contracting or on his behalf (Sec. 68).
2. Suits for money had and received (Sees. 69 & 72).
3. *Quantum Meruit.*
4. Obligations of a finder of goods (Sec. 71).
5. Obligations of a person enjoying benefit of a non-gratuitous act (Sec. 70).

Necessaries supplied to a person incapable of contracting—We have already seen that contracts by minors, idiots, lunatics, etc., are void, but Sec 68 provides that their estates are liable to reimburse the trader who supplies them with necessaries of life. This is on the basis of quasi-contract.

Suit for money had and received—The right to file a suit for the recovery of money under this head may arise:

(a) Where the plaintiff paid money to the defendant (*i*) under a mistake, (*ii*) in pursuance of a contract the consideration for which has failed, (*iii*) under coercion, oppression, extortion or other such means. A debtor may recover from a creditor the amount of an overpayment made to him if it was made by mistake.

The mistake may be mistake of fact or that of law. The term 'mistake' used in Sec. 72 of the Contract Act has been used without any qualification or limitation whatever and comprises within its scope a mistake of law as well as a mistake of fact. There is no conflict between the provisions of Sec. 72 on the one hand and Sees. 21 and 22 on the other. The true principle is that if one party under a mistake, whether of fact or law, pays to another party money which is not due by contract or otherwise,

---

101. V. Pillai v. A. Chettiar, 1941. Mad 641; B. Verrailah v. Sarraju, 1959 A. P. 100; but see Dyaviah v. Shivamma, 1959 Mys. 188.

that money must be repaid. The mistake lies in thinking that the money paid was due when in fact it was not due, that mistake, if established, entitles the party paying the money, (even if it is a tax paid), to recover back from the party receiving it (*Sales Tax Officer v.* Kanhaya Lal, 1959 S.C. 135.)

In this case, *K* was levied a sales tax on his forward transactions in Billion which he paid. The levy of this tax was declared *ultra vires. K* demanded refund of the amount of the sales tax on the ground that payment was made under a mistake of law. *Held,* that he was entitled to the refund. It was observed that no distinction can be made in respect 'of a tax liability' and any other liability on a plain reading of Sec. 72 of the Act.

It was held in *Shiba* v. *Srish,* 1949 P.C. 297 that money paid under a contract caused by mistake of law cannot be said to have been paid under mistake of law. Thus, although the contract will stand yet the money paid under mistake of law which is not due under the contract or otherwise, can be recovered. (*The Ramanathapuram Market Committee* v. *East India Corporation Ltd.,* 1976 Mad. 323). Moneys to be recovered in respect of consideration which has failed are only recoverable if the whole consideration has failed and not a part of the consideration. If only a part of the consideration has failed, the case must be such that the consideration is a separable part. If an apprentice paid premium to a master and before the relationship had commenced the master died, the money would be recoverable, but not if the relationship had commenced. Where money has been obtained by coercion, oppression, fraud, or extortion the plaintiff can recover it as the money is paid involuntarily. Cases generally arise when money is paid under protest in discharge of an illegal demand, e.g., where a pledgee refused to deliver goods unless extra amount was paid. This extra amount could be recovered. If a person pays money to save his property which has been wrongly attached in execution, he is entitled to recover it. Money paid to avoid prosecution can be recovered. *T* was caught travelling without ticket on a tramcar and paid on demand by the Traffic Supervisor ₹ 5 as penalty to avoid prosecution. *Held,* he could recover. [102] But money paid under compulsion cannot be recovered. Thus, where the Official Assignee in Insolvency paid a creditor under directions of the Court, he cannot recover it on the ground that it was paid by mistake.[103] Excess payment made under the belief that price paid was controlled price can be recovered.[104]

(b) **Payment to third party of money which another is bound to pay**—Cases under this head usually arise where the properties of a person get into the hands of third parties who will not release them unless some amount due from another is paid. It must be remembered that, in order to be able to recover, the plaintiff must have been compelled by law to pay, or the plaintiff himself has interest in payment. Where *A*'s goods are wrongfully attached in order to realise arrears of Government Revenue due by *B*, and *A* pays the amount to save the goods from being sold, he is entitled to recover the amount from *B*. The payment, however, must have been made on behalf of the person who was bound by law to pay it, whether in contract or in tort or by statute.[105]

(c) **Money obtained by the defendant from third parties**—This usually happens where the defendant being the agent of the plaintiff obtains a secret commission of fraudulent payment from a third party. In such cases, the principal has a right to obtain the payment from his own agent as money paid to the use of the plaintiff.

QUANTUM MERUIT

The expression " Quantum Meruit" literally means "as much as earned." It is used where a person claims reasonable remuneration for the services rendered by him when there was no express promise to pay the definite remuneration.[106] The general rule is that where a party to a contract has not fully

---

102. Trikmadas Udeshi v. Bombay Municipal Corporation. 1954 Bom. 427.
103. Official Assignee v. Dayabhoy, 1937 R. Ang. 234.
104. Lakshmanprasad v. Kamal Bai, I960 Mad. 335.
105. Govind v. Gondal State, 1950 P. C. 99.
106. B. N. Rly. v. Raianji, 62 Cal. 175.

performed what the contract demands as a condition of payment, he can bring no action for payment for that which he has done. In *Cutter* v. *Powell* (1795) 101 E.R. 573, a mate was engaged on the terms that he would be paid a lump sum for a complete voyage. He died before the voyage was completed. It was held his representatives could not recover the lump sum, neither could they sue for payment for the services rendered by the deceased. The first claim failed because the deceased had not completed his part, the second could not be made because the existing contract was the only basis for action and it was indivisible and so made full performance a condition precedent to the ship owner's liability. Moreover, the ship-owner did not prevent the completion of the work.

But where one party who has performed part of his contract is prevented by the act of the other from completing his side of the contract, he may sue on a *quantum meruit,* for the value of what he has done. This is not a claim on the contract but is a claim on the quasi-contratual obligation which the law implies in these circumstances.

In *William Lacey (Hounslow)Ltd.* v. *Davis* (1957) All E.R. 712, W. Co. was asked by *D* for tender in connection with a reconstruction scheme, W. Co. was given to understand that it would receive the contract and thereafter did on behalf of *D* a considerable amount of work of calculations for timber and steel requirements which fell right outside the work of a builder. As a result of the estimates and other information provided by W. Co. *D* was able to get increased price for the premises. *D* therefore gave up the idea of rebuilding and sold the premises, and thus failed to give any contract to W. Co, who sued *D* claiming damages for breach and, alternatively, remuneration as on a *quantum meruit* in respect of the work done by it subsequent to the tender. The claim for damages failed, but Barry, J. held that as the builder had done work in a belief (mutual to both parties) that he would get a contract for re-building the premises, a promise by *D* to pay to W. Co. a reasonable remuneration *(quantum meruit)* for its work could be implied.

The claim on a *quantum meruit* also arises—(1) When one party abandons or refuses to perform the contract.

In *Planch* v. *Colburn* (1831) 8 Bing. 14, *P* was engaged by *C* to write a book to be published in instalments in a weekly magazine. After a few numbers had appeared the magazine was abandoned. *Held, P* could recover on *quantum meruit* for the work done under the contract.

(2) When work has been done and accepted under a void contract.

In *Cravan Ellis* v. *Canons, Ltd.* (1936) 2 K.B. 403, *C* was employed as managing director by a company under a written contract. The contract was not binding, because the directors who made it were not qualified. *C* rendered the services and sued for remuneration. *Held,* he could recover on a *quantum meruit.*

A party in default may also sue on a *quantum meruit* for what he has done if the contract is divisible and the other party has had the benefit of the part which has been performed as in *Ritchie* v. *Atkinson* (1808), where a ship-owner recovered pro-rata freight although he had failed to take a complete cargo.

But if the contract is not divisible, the party in default cannot claim the value of what he has done.

In *Sumpter* v. *Hedges* (1898) 1 Q.B. 673, *S*, a builder, agreed with *H* to erect a house for £565. He did work to the value of £333 and then abandoned the contract *H* thereupon completed the contract *Held,* (*i*) S could not recover anything under the original contract because he was only entitled to payment on completion of the work; (*ii*) S could not recover on *quantum meruit* based on *H*'s acceptance of his work, because H had no option but to accept the work, and no fresh contract to pay could be implied from his acceptance.

But where there is a lumpsum or indivisible contract which is completely performed, though badly, the person who has done the work can recover the lump sum, less a deduction for his bad work [*Dakin* v. *Lee* (1916) 1K. B. 566].

In *Hoeing* v. *Isaacs* (1952) 1 All. E.R. 176, *A* agreed to decorate *B*'s flat and to fit a wardrobe and a book case for a lump sum of £750. The work was done, but *B* complained of faulty workmanship, the cost to remedy which being £294. *Held, A* could recover from *B* £750 less £294.

Obligations of Finder of Goods—The liability of a finder of goods belonging to some one else is stated to be the same as that of a bailee (Sec. 71). The responsibility of a bailee is indicated in Sec. 151 which provides that the bailee must take as much care of the goods as a man of ordinary prudence would, under similar circumstances, take of his own goods of like description, quality and value. Thus, so far as the real owner is concerned the finder is the bailee and must try to find out the owner and must not appropriate the property to his own use, and if the owner is traced, must restore it to him. A finder who appropriates such property to his own use when he knows and has means of discovering the owner, or before he has used reasonable means to discover the owner, or has kept the property for an unreasonable time, is guilty of criminal misappropriation of the property under Sec. 403 of Indian Penal Code. The finder is entitled to recover from the owner any expenses he might have incurred in protecting and preserving the property. It is clear, therefore, that finding is not keeping, unless it is reasonably certain that the real owner cannot be found.

Obligations of a person enjoying benefit of non-gratuitous act—Where a person lawfully does something for another person, or delivers anything to him without any intention of doing so gratuitously and the other person accepts and enjoys the benefit thereof the latter must compensate the former or restore to him the thing so delivered (Sec. 70). When one of the two joint tenants pays the whole rent to the landlord, he is entitled to compensation from his co-tenant.[107] And where one of the two mortgagors paid off the mortgage amount to save the property from sale, he was held entitled to compensation from his comortgagor.[108] Where a person managed the estate of his wife and his sister-in-law and believed that he would get remuneration for his services, he was entitled to claim reasonable compensation.[109] Where *S* ploughed the field of *R* with a tractor in the presence of the son of *R* to the satisfaction of *R*, it was held that *S* was entitled to payment as the work was not intended to be gratuitous.[110] If *A*, a tradesman, delivers a bag of wheat by mistake at *B*'s house instead of at *C*'s there is an obligation on the part of *B* to return the bag of wheat to *A* or to pay its value, if it is not possible to return the bag. Here the parties never intended to enter into contract, but the law *implies a contract*. For Sec. 70 to apply two things are essential, viz., (*i*) the act must not have been intended to be gratuitous and (*ii*) the party for whom the act is done must have enjoyed a benefit of it.

The contract found to be void should not be one whose consideration or object is unlawful (*Rakurti Mankyam* v. *Meddi Satyanarayan,* 1972 A.P. 367). It was stated by the Supreme Court in *Pannalal* v. *Deputy Commissioner, Bhandara* (1973) 1 S.C. 639, that the real basis of the liability under Sec. 70 is the fact that the person for whom the work has been done, has accepted the work and has received the benefit thereunder. What Sec. 70 prevents is unjust enrichment. Further, the real basis of a claim under Sec. 70 is not the terms of the contract but the quantum of the benefit actually derived.

PART 1-H
VARIOUS DISCHARGES OF CONTRACT

Modes of discharge or termination of contracts—Contracts may be discharged or terminated by any one of the following modes:—

1. By performance.

---

107. Nirdosh v. Jakarta (1914) 20 Cal. L J. 492.
108. Babu Bhagwati v. Maiyan Murat (1931) 10 Pat 528.
109. Palanivelu v. Neela Vati 1937 P. C. SO. 39 B. L. R. 720.
110. R. Shanker Rao v. Rangoo Bai, 1959 Bom. 519.

2. By consent or agreement.
3. By impossibility.
4. By lapse of time.
5. By operation of law.
6. By breach.

BY PERFORMANCE

The obvious mode of discharge of a contract is by performance, for that is what the contracting parties had contemplated at the time of entering into it. Every person who is bound by an obligation must be ready to perform it at the time when he had promised to perform it (Sec. 37). No difficulties arise where the contract is fully performed, nor are there any serious difficulties when the contract consists of an absolute promise by A made to B for a consideration already received. In this latter case, if A does not fulfil his promise, B can sue him for damages for breach of contract. But between these simple cases lie several more complicated cases arising out of the fact that in several different ways a promise may be conditional and not absolute. From this point of view contracts are of two kinds. Contracts Absolute and Contingent or Conditional.

CONTINGENT CONTRACTS

An absolute contract is one in which the promise has to be performed independently of any contingency or condition. A **Contingent** contract is a contract to do or not to do something, if some event, *collateral to such contract,* does or does not happen (Sec. 31). A contracts to pay B ₹ 10.000 if B's house is burnt. This is a contingent contract—a contract of fire insurance. Quite a good part of commercial business transactions consists of contingent contracts; all contracts of insurance, indemnity and guarantee are contingent contracts. A wager is a contingent agreement, but Sec. 30 prevents it from being a contract. Such contracts are also called "conditional contracts"; but a contract in which performance by one party is conditional upon the performance, or readiness and willingness to perform, by the other, is conditional, but not contingent. If A agrees to deliver 100 bags of wheat and B agrees to pay the price only afterwards, the obligation of B to pay is conditional upon A's delivering the wheat, but this is not a contingent contract, because the event on which B's liability depends is a part of the promise itself (a condition precedent) and not a collateral event Also, if A offers a reward for the recovery of his lost dog, there is not a contingent contract; there is no contract at all unless and until someone, acting on the offer, finds the dog and brings it to A. A contract to pay a man for a piece of work on the terms that he is to have no pay till the work is all done, is not contingent, because the completion of the work is the very thing contracted for, and is not collateral to the contract. Also, a promise amounts to no promise if its operation depends upon the mere will or pleasure of the promisor. If A promises to pay B ₹ 500 *if he so chooses,* or says he will pay for B services whatever he himself thinks reasonable, it is not a contingent contract.

RULES REGARDING CONTINGENT CONTRACTS

The rules as deduced from Secs. 32-36 are given below:

1. Contracts contingent upon the happening of a future uncertain event, cannot be enforced by law unless and until that event has happened. If the event becomes impossible, such contracts become void (Sec. 32).

Illustrations:

(a) A makes a contract to buy B's horse if A survives C. This contract cannot be enforced by law unless and until C dies in A's lifetime.

(b) A contracts to pay B a sum of money when B marries C. C dies without being married to B. The contract becomes void.

2. Contracts contingent upon the non-happening of an uncertain future event, can be enforced when the happening of that event becomes impossible and not before (Sec. 33).

A agrees to pay *B* a sum of money if a certain ship does not return. The ship is sunk. The contract can be enforced when the ship sinks.

3. If a contract is contingent upon how a person will act at an unspecified time, the event shall be considered to become impossible when such person does anything which renders it impossible that he should so act *within* any definite time or otherwise than under further contingencies (Sec. 34).

A agrees to pay *B* ₹ 1,000 if *B* marries *C*. *C* marries *D*. The marriage of *B* to *C* must now be considered impossible although it is possible that *D* may die and that *C* may afterwards marry *B*.

4. Contracts contingent on the happening of an event within a fixed time become void if, at the expiration of the time, such event has not happened or if, before the time fixed, such event becomes impossible (Sec. 35).

A promises to pay E a sum of money if a certain ship returns within a year. The contract may be enforced if the ship returns within the year, and becomes void if the ship is burnt within the year.

5. Contracts contingent upon the non-happening of an event within a fixed time may be enforced by law when the time fixed has expired and such event has not happened, or before the time fixed has expired, if it becomes certain that such event will not happen (Sec.35).

A promises to pay B a sum of money if a certain ship does not return within a year. The contract may be enforced if the ship does not return within the year, or is burnt within the year.

6. Contingent agreements to do or not to do anything if an impossible event, happens, are void, whether the impossibility of the event is known or not to the parties to the agreement at the time when it is made (Sec. 36).

(a) *A* agrees to pay *B*, ₹ 1,000 if two straight lines should enclose a space. The agreement is void.

(b) *A* agrees to pay *B* ₹ 1,000 if *B* will marry *A*'s daughter *C*. *C* was dead at the time of agreement. The agreement is void.

ORDER OF PERFORMANCE OF RECIPROCAL PROMISES

A contract consists of reciprocal promises when one party makes a promise (to do or not to do something in the future) in consideration of a similar promise (to do or not to do something in the future) made by the other party. Reciprocal promises are of three classes: (1) Mutual and Independent; (2) Mutual and Dependent; (3) Mutual and Concurrent.

1. Where each party must perform his promise without waiting for the performance or the readiness to perform of the other, the promise is **Mutual and Independent.** Sec. 52 of the Contract Act deals with this kind and provides: Where the order in which reciprocal promises are to be performed is expressly fixed by the contract, they shall be performed in that order; and, where the order is not expressly fixed by the contract, they shall be performed in that order which the nature of the transaction requires.

(a) *A* and *B* contract that *A* shall build a house for *B* at a fixed price. *A*'s promise to build the house must be performed before *B*'s promise to pay.

(b) If *B* promises to deliver his goods on 15th May and *A* promises to pay the price on 10th May, *A*'s paying the price is independent of *B*'s delivering the goods on the 15th May. *B* can, of course, sue *A* for damages and the payment of price.

2. Where the performance of one party depends on the prior performance of the other party the promise is **Mutual and Dependent.** Sec. 54 provides for this:

When a contract consists of reciprocal promises, such that one of them cannot be performed, or that its performance cannot be claimed till the other has been performed and the promisor of the promise last mentioned fails to perform it, such promisor cannot claim the performance of the reciprocal promise, and must make compensation to the other party to the contract for any loss which such other party may sustain by the non-performance of the contract.

(a) *A* contracts with *B* to construct a building for a fixed price, *B* supplying the necessary timber. *B* fails to supply the timber and the work cannot be executed. *A* need not work and *B* is bound to compensate *A* for the loss caused to *A*.

(b) A promises *B* to sell him 100 bales of cotton, to be delivered next day, and *B* promises *A* to pay for them within a month. *A* does not deliver according to his promise. *B*'s promise to pay need not be performed, and *A* must make compensation.

3. Where each promise has to be performed at the same time, it is a **Mutual** and **Concurrent** promise. Sec. 51 provides: When a contract consists of reciprocal promises to be simultaneously performed, no promisor need perform his promise unless the promisee is ready and willing to perform his reciprocal promise.

A and *B* contract that *A* shall deliver goods to *B* to be paid for by *B* on delivery. Here the promise of each should be performed at the same time, and so *A* need not deliver the goods unless *B* is ready and willing to pay for the goods on delivery; and *B* need not pay for the goods unless *A* is ready and willing to deliver them on payment.

4. When a contract contains reciprocal promises, and one party to the contract prevents the other party from performing his promise, the contract becomes voidable at the option of the party so prevented; and he is entitled to compensation from the other party for any loss which he may sustain in consequence of the non-performance of the contract (Sec. 53).

A and *B* contract that *B* shall execute certain work for *A* for ₹ 1,000. *B* is ready and willing to do the work, but *A* prevents him from doing so. The contract is voidable at the option of *B*; and, if he elects to rescind it, he is entitled to recover from *A* compensation for any loss he has sustained by its non-performance.

Mode of performance—Broadly speaking, a person who is bound to perform a contract must be ready to perform it at the time when he has undertaken to do so. But, under the Indian law, the promisee has to demand performance, unless the promisor has absolutely bound himself to perform even without a request or demand (Sec. 48). Where the time and place are prescribed by the promisee, the performance must be at the specified time and place. If no time and place are mentioned, then the agreement must be performed within a reasonable time (Sec. 50), and with regard to the place the promisor roust ask the promisee where he would like the contract to be performed (Sec. 49). Further, it is essential for the discharge of a contract that the performance must be in strict accordance with the terms of the contract. The promisor has no right to substitute for what he has promised something else which is equally or even more advantageous to the promisee.

APPROPRIATION OF PAYMENTS

It may happen that a debtor owes several debts to the same creditor, and makes payment, the question will arise, as to which of these debts the payment is to be applied. Secs. 59,60,61 contain the answer to this question. Where the debtor has stated that the payment made by him should be appropriated to a particular debt, the creditor must do so (*Wasudeo* v. *Namdeo*, 1951 Nag. 155). But where he does not express his intention, the law will gather his intention from the circumstances attending the payment For example, if the amount paid by the debtor is the exact amount of one of the debts, it must be used to discharge that one. If the creditor asks for the payment of a specific debt, the payment made in response to this demand must be applied to that debt. Where the creditor demands discharge of several debts and the debtor sends a lump sum, the same will have to be applied proportionately to the several debts. But if there is no indication and it cannot be reasonably ascertained from the circumstances in respect of which the payment has to be appropriated then it is open to the creditor to apply the payment to any debt lawfully due from the debtor, irrespective of the question of limitation. But the creditor cannot apply the payment to a disputed debt or an unlawful debt. The creditor is not bound to appropriate the payment immediately; he may wait to the last moment. He may appropriate even during the pendency of the suit concerning the payment (*Uthup* v. *Kathanar,* 1960, Ker. 90). And where neither the debtor nor the creditor has made any appropriation, then according to law, it has to be applied in discharge of the earlier debt in the order of time. Endorsement of payment not stating whether it is towards interest or principal; payment must first be applied towards interest and balance to principal (1950 Fed. C38).[111]

Who can demand performance? The person to demand performance is the party to whom the promise is made, even though the promise is not made for the benefit of the promisee, but for the benefit of some third person. *A* promises *B* to give *C* ₹ 100 in favour of *C*. The banker makes a mistake as to *A*'s balance and refuses payment. The person to whom the Banker is liable is *A* and not *C*. In case of the death of the promisee his legal representatives can demand performance.

Who may perform? In cases involving personal skill, taste, or credit, the promisor must himself perform the contract. The court will enforce the intention of the parties. In all other cases the promisor or his representative may employ a competent person to perform it. *A* promises to paint a picture for *B*. *A* must paint it personally. But where *A* promises to pay *B* a sum of money, *A* may pay the money personally or cause it to be paid to *B* by another.

(i) *Lala Kapur Chand Godha* v. *Mir Nawab Himayatali Khan Azmiah, 1963* S.C. 250. *A,* owing a large amount to *B,* found a friend *C* who offered to pay *B* a lesser sum in full settlement or satisfaction of *B*'s claim on *A*. This was accepted by *B. Held,* the case is covered by Sec. 63 and since the plaintiff had accepted the payment in full discharge he could not sue *A,* the defendant, for the balance in view of Sec. 41.

(ii) *Textile and Yarn (P) Ltd.,* v. *India National Steamship Co. Ltd.,* 1964 Cal. 362. The Calcutta High Court following the rule laid down by the Supreme Court in the aforesaid case held that a consignee after having received compensation for loss from the insurer, cannot again sue the carrier for recovery of the damages for the loss of goods in view of Sec. 41.

But Sec. 41 applies only to executory contracts and the stranger must have fully performed it and not in part (*Chandra Shekhar Hebbar* v. *Vittala Bhandari,* 1966 Mys. 84). Moreover, the payment must be *unconditional* if Sec. 41 is to be attracted.

(iii) *Union of India* v. *Hindustan Aeronautics,* 1968 Mys. L.J. 240, the suit for damages was against the Union of India, the Railway Administration and several insurance companies. The insurance companies (third defendants) settled the claim by paying full amount on the stipulation that the plaintiff would continue to prosecute the suit against the other defendants, viz., the Union of India and the Railway Administration and to pay to the third defendants whatever is recovered from them. *Held,* the settlement being conditional, the plaintiff could continue the suit and Sec. 41 was not attracted.

DEVOLUTION OF JOINT RIGHTS AND LIABILITES

Two or more persons may enter into a joint agreement with one or more persons. For example *A, B* and *C* jointly borrow from *P* a sum of ₹ 3,000 and jointly promise to repay the said amount. In such cases question arises who is liable to pay. The rules on the subject are stated in Secs. 42-45.

1. When two or more persons make a joint promise, the promisee may, in the absence of express agreement to the contrary, compel any one or more of such joint promisors to perform the whole of the promise. In the above example, in case of default, P may realise the entire amount from *A,* or *B,* or

111. See also Srinivasulu v. Kondappa 1960. A. P. 174, and Megh Raj v. Mst. Bayabai. 1970 S. C. 161.

C, or from all or any two of them. A promisor cannot claim the right of being sued only along with his co-promisors.[112] The liability in India is joint and several. If, however, the promisee sues only one or some of the several joint promisors, and obtains a decree against him or them, his claim merges in the decree, and he is precluded from suing the others if he fails to realise the whole of the decretal amount.

The English law is different. Under that law the liability is joint so that all joint promisors must be sued jointly.

2. The joint promisors during their lives must jointly fulfil the promise. After the death of any one of them his legal representative jointly with the survivor or survivors, must fulfil the promise. After the death of the last survivor, the legal representatives of all the original promisors must jointly fulfil the promise. The above rule regarding the devolution of joint liability shall not apply when a contrary intention appears from the contract. It would be noted that though the joint promisors or the legal representatives are required to perform the promise jointly the promisee may compel any one of the joint promisors to perform the promise. That is, as against the promisee, their liability is joint as well as several.

3. If one of the joint promisors is made to perform the whole contract, he can ask for equal contribution from the others. In our example, if *A* is compelled to pay the entire amount of ₹ 3,000, *A* can realise from *B* & *C* ₹ 1,000 each. This rule is also subject to any contrary intention of the parties. If any one of the joint promisors makes default in making contribution the remaining joint promisors must bear the loss arising from such default in equal shares. If *C*, in our example, is compelled to pay one half of his debts, *C* is entitled to receive ₹ 500 from *B*'s estate, and ₹ 1,250 from *A*. But for *B*'s default in paying ₹ 500 out of his contribution, *C* could not have received more than ₹ 1,000 from *A*.

4. In case of a joint promise, if one of the joint promisors is released from his promise, his liability to the promisee ceases but his liability to the other promisors to contribute does not cease.

In English law, as the liability is joint, the question of contribution between joint promisors does not arise for the promisee must sue all the promisors. Also, release of one promisor under English law releases all the promisors.

The rule of contribution does not, even in India, apply as between the principal debtor and his surety, even though as against the creditor they are joint promisors. So a surety can recover from the principal debtor the entire amount paid by him on behalf of the principal debtor, who in his turn cannot ask for any contribution from the surety if the entire amount is recovered from him by the creditor, because by paying his debt he is discharging his own liability.

5. When one person has made a promise to several persons jointly, the right to claim performance rests on all the promisees jointly so long as all of them are alive. When one of the promisees dies the right to claim performance rests with his legal representative jointly with the surviving promisees. When all the promisees are dead, the right to claim performance rests with their legal representatives jointly.

ASSIGNMENT OF CONTRACTS

The Indian Contract Act has no section dealing generally with assignment of contracts. But the following rules have been accepted by courts in India in respect of assignment of contract. Broadly speaking, an obligation under or burden or liability of a contract cannot be assigned; for instance, if *A* owes *B* ₹ 1,000, and *A* transfers his liability to *C*, *i.e.*, asks *C* to pay the sum to *B*, this would not bind *B* and *B* may not consent to this arrangement as he may know nothing of *C*'s solvency. But if *B* consents to accept performance from *C*, there is a substitution of new contract and the old contract disappears and all rights and liabilities under it are extinguished. This is technically called 'Novation'

112. Jainarain Ram v. Surajmall Sagaimall (1949) F. C. R.379; Jodh Singh v. Kesar Singh, 1950. J&K.96.

(Secs. 41, 62). It is, however, open to a party to have the contract performed vicariously by another person provided the contract does not expressly or impliedly contemplate performance only by the promisor. But in such cases, the promisor will continue to be liable under the contract. For if a person employs an agent to do something for him, the agent's act will be taken to be that of the principal. It will be noted that even here it is really not the assignment of burden but the obligation is discharged by a delegated performance. It must be remembered that where the performance of the contract depends on the personal skill or solvency of the contracting party, it cannot be assigned; *e.g.*, where A promises to paint a picture for B, A cannot get it done by another, but must paint it himself (Sec.40).

Though the liability under a contract cannot generally be assigned without the consent of the promisee, the rights and benefits under a contract may be assigned and the assignee can demand performance against the other contracting party (the promisor). But this can be done only subject to all the equities if any, existing as between the original contracting parties. Thus, if A owes B ₹ 1,000 and if B, the creditor, transfers his right to C, C can demand payment from A. But if A can prove that he has already paid, say ₹ 500, to B, C will be bound by that payment and can get only ₹ 500, the balance due. And, if A has already discharged the total debt, C will get nothing. Therefore, in order to protect the rights of innocent third parties, the law requires that the party who gets the transfer, must give notice to the party liable under the contract giving intimation of the transfer and calling upon him for payment. After such notice has been given, any payment to the original party will not bind the assignee. In other words, the debtor can assert no equity against the assignee arising out of the transaction with the assignor after notice of assignment but he may set off a debt existing at the time of notice. Any payments obtained by the assignor after assignment and before notice, should be accounted for to the assigee. A contract for the future delivery of goods cannot be assigned under the Indian Law, because the burden of an executory contract cannot be assigned. Where A agrees to sell goods to B deliverable at a future date, neither the seller nor the buyer can assign the contract before the date fixed for delivery to a third person without the consent of the other so as to entitle the assignee to sue in his own name. There is, however, no objection to a suit being brought by the assignor and assignee as co-plaintiffs for when the suit is by them both there is no question as to which of them is to recover.[113]

An actionable claim (chose in action of the English law) can always be assigned; but assignment to be complete and effectual must be effected by an instrument in writing, and upon the execution of such instrument all the rights and remedies of the assignor vest in the assignee, who may thereupon sue in his own name without making the assignor a party to the suit. It has been held in *Jaffar Mehar Ali* v. *Budge Budge Jute Mills Co.,* (1906) 33 Cal. 702 affirmed on appeal in 34 Cal. 289; and *Hansraj Morar ji* v. *Nashoo Gangaram* (1907) 9 Bom. L.R. 838 that the interest of a buyer of goods in a contract for forward delivery is an actionable claim and may be assigned as such so as to enable the assignee to sue in his own name. There is no definite decision with regard to the seller's right to call for payment of price on delivery of goods but the dicta *in Jaffar Mehar Ali* v. *Budge Budge Jute Mills Co.,* are wide enough to cover the seller's interests, and it is probable that a seller can also assign his interest. But a claim for damages for breach of contract, after breach, is not an actionable claim and cannot, therefore, be assigned.[114] An option to repurchase property sold is *prima facie* assignable, unless it is meant to be personal to the grantee.[115] What is an actionable claim or chose in action? An actionable claim is defined in Sec. 3 of the Transfer of Property Act, 1882 as "a claim to any debt

---

113. Tod v. Lakshmidas (1892) 16 Bom. 441; Jiwan v. Haji Oosman (1903) 6 Bom. L.R. 373.

114. Mahomed v. Chunder (1909) 36 Cal. 34S; Varahaswami v. Ramchandra (1915) 38 Mad 138, 140:18 UC. 520.

115. Vishweshwar Narsabhatta v. Durguppa (1904) Bom. 674; A.I.R. 1904 Bom. 339; 191 I. C. 139.

(except secured debt), or to any beneficial interest not in movable property in the possession, either actual or constructive, of the claimant, whether such debt or beneficial interest be existent, accruing, conditional or contingent." With regard to chose in action. Channel, J., in *Trokintan* v. *Magee* (1902) 2 K.B. 427 (430), says: "A chose in action is a known legal expression used to describe all personal rights of property which can only be claimed or enforced by action, and not by taking physical possession." It means a thing reducible to possession only by an action at law.

DISCHARGE BY TENDER

We have seen that a contract is discharged by performance. But it may sometimes happen that a person who is bound to perform a promise has been ready and willing to perform and has offered to perform his promise at the proper time and place, but the other party will not accept performance. In such a case, the contract is discharged because of the wrongful refusal to accept performance. Tender is called attempted performance, and to discharge, the party tendering it must fulfil all the features of a proper performance.

If the promise is to deliver goods at the premises of the buyer the seller must take the goods of the identical description to the place of the other party during office hours and offer to deliver, there and then, the whole lot of goods which he is bound to deliver under the contract. If it is a promise to pay money then the promisor must go to the creditor, and offer the whole amount to him in such a way that the creditor might take the whole amount due to him. (*Bank of Mysore* v. *Naidu*, 1954 Mys. 168). An offer of money in a locked box would not be a proper tender. Similarly, payment by cheque will not be a proper tender, unless the other party agrees or has asked for payment by cheque.

Section 38 deals with performance by tender and lays down the essential conditions of a valid tender as follow:—

"Where a promisor has made an offer of performance to the promisee, and the offer has not been accepted, the promisor is not responsible for non-performance, nor does he thereby lose his rights under the contract." The section then goes on to state the essential conditions for a valid tender as given below:

ESSENTIALS OF A VALID TENDER

Every tender must fulfil the following conditions:—
1. It must be unconditional.
2. It must be made at a proper time and place.
3. It must be made under circumstances enabling the other party to ascertain that the party by whom it is made is able and willing then and there to do the whole of what he is bound by his promise to do.
4. If the tender relates to delivery of goods, the promisee must have a reasonable opportunity of seeing that the thing offered is the thing which the promisor is bound by his promise to deliver.
5. Tender made to one of several joint promisees has the same effect as a tender to all of them.

DISCHARGE BY MUTUAL AGREEMENT OR CONSENT

By agreement of all parties to the contract, or by waiver or release by the party entitled to performance, a contract may be discharged. The discharge by consent may be expressed or implied; and an expressed consent may be given at the time of the formation of the contract or subsequently. For example, it may be agreed at the time of making the contract that on the happening of an event one or both parties will be absolved from performance. A buyer may be given the option to return the goods sold within a specified period of time, if certain conditions are not fulfilled.

In *Head* v. *Tattersall* (1871) 7 Ex. 7, the contract was for the purchase of a horse on the understanding that the buyer could return the same within two days, if the horse had not been hunted with the

Bicester hounds. The horse was returned within two days as it had not been hunted with the Bicester rounds. The Court held the return valid.

Express consent subsequently to the formation of the contract may be given by waiver, release, abandonment, novation, remission, alteration, rescission, and in English law, by accord and satisfaction. Each one of these methods is dealt with here. Secs. 62 and 63 expressly provide for these methods and are reproduced here:—

"Sec. 62—If the parties to a contract agree to substitute a new contract for it, or to rescind or alter it, the original contract need not be performed."

"Sec. 63—Every promisee may dispense with or remit, wholly or impart, the performance of the promise made to him, or may extend the time for such performance or may accept instead of it any satisfaction which he thinks fit."

NOVATION

Novation occurs when a new contract is substituted for an existing contract, either between the same parties or between different parties, the consideration mutually being the discharge of the old contract

(a) A owes money to B under a contract. It is agreed between A, B, and C that B shall thenceforth accept C as his debtor, instead of A. There is novation. The old debt of A to B is at an end, a new debt from C to B has been contracted.

(b) M insured his life with X Co. The X Co. became amalgamated with the Y Co., and a memorandum was endorsed on M's policy that the Y Co. would be liable for the policy money. *Held,* There was a complete novation and M could recover from the Y Co. [In re: *European Ass. Society* (1876) 3 Ch-D 391].

ALTERATION

Alteration of a contract takes place when one or more of the terms of the contract are changed. Alteration is valid when it is made with the consent of all the parties to the contract. Where, however, an alteration of written contract is made by one party to the contract without the consent of the other party and of a material fact so that the legal effect of the instrument is changed, the contract is discharged and the other party is also discharged from his duties.

RESCISSION

A contract may be rescinded by agreement between the parties at any time before it is discharged by performance or in some other way. For example, a contract for the sale of goods can be discharged by mutual agreement between the buyer and the seller at any time before delivery of the goods or payment of the price.

Rescission may also take place in the following manner. Where a party to a contract fails to perform his obligations, the other party can rescind the contract without prejudice to his rights to receive compensation for breach of contract. In a voidable contract, one of the parties has the option of rescinding the contract.

(i) A promises to deliver certain goods to B on a certain date. Before the date of performance, A and B mutually agree that the contract will not be performed. The parties have rescinded the contract.

(ii) A was induced to enter into an agreement by coercion. He can rescind the contract

REMISSION

Remission is the acceptance of a lesser sum than what was contracted for or a lesser fulfillment of the promise made. Sec. 63 specifically provides for remission of performance or promise. Thus, the law in India is different from that in England. In the latter century, remission must be supported by a fresh consideration. In India, under Sec. 63, a promisee may remit or give up a part of his claim and a promise to do so is binding even though there is no consideration for doing so. (*Hari Chand Madan Gopal* v. *State of Punjab* (1973) 1 S.C. 204).

(i) *A* owes *B* ₹ 5,000. *A* pays to *B* and *B* accepts in full satisfaction ₹ 2,000. The whole debt is discharged.

(ii) *A* owes *B* ₹ 5,000. *C* pays to *B* ₹ 1,000 and *B* accepts them in satisfaction of his claim on *A*. This payment is a discharge of the whole claim.

ACCORD AND SATISFACTION

As we have already seen, these two terms are used in English law and find no place in Indian law. According to English law, a promise to accept less than what is due under an existing contract, is not enforceable, because it is not supported by consideration. But an exception is made where the lesser sum is actually paid or lesser obligation actually performed and accepted by the promisee. In such a case the old contract is discharged by accord and satisfaction. Accord means the promise to accept less than what is due under the old contact. Satisfaction means the payment or the fulfilment of the lesser obligation. An accord is unenforceable; but an accord followed by satisfaction discharges the pre-existing obligation. Accord without satisfaction is not discharge.

(i) *A* owes *B* ₹ 5,000. *B* agrees to accept ₹ 2,000 in full satisfaction of his claim. This promise is unenforceable in English law. But when ₹ 2,000 is actually paid and accepted, there is accord and satisfaction and the original debt is discharged,

(ii) If *A* owes *B* ₹ 1,000 and *B* agrees to take a cheque for ₹ 500 in full settlement, there is an accord. This agreement is unenforceable. As soon as *B* accepts the cheque there is both an accord and satisfaction. If *B* will not accept the cheque when it is offered, the agreement can be enforced by counterclaim when *B* sues for ₹ 1,000.

WAIVER

Waiver means the intentional relinquishment of a right which a person is entitled to. A party may waive his rights under the contract, whereupon the other party is released from his obligations. In the case of an executory contract, (e.g., an agreement to sell and buy), each party may excuse the other from paying for or from buying the goods. In the case of a unilateral promise, the party entitled to performance may waive performance of it. In English law, waiver is possible only by release under a deed.

MERGER

When a superior right and an inferior right coincide and meet in one and the same person, the inferior right vanishes into the superior right. This is known as merger. Thus, merger is where a party to a contract takes a better security than the one he has already. To effect a merger, three conditions must be fulfilled, namely,—(1) the two securities must be different in their legal operation, one higher than the other; (2) the subject-matter must be the same; (3) the parties must be the same. Therefore, there can be no merger when the securities are of equal degree, so that an oral agreement is not merged in a written contract to the same effect.

A man holding property under a lease, buys the property. His rights as a lessee vanish. They are merged into the rights of ownership which he has now acquired.

DISCHARGE BY IMPOSSIBILITY OF PERFORMANCE

The law relating to discharge by impossibility of performance of a contract is laid down in Sec. 56 of the Contract Act Sec. 56 says:

"An agreement to do an act impossible in itself is void. A contract to do an act which, after the contract is made becomes impossible, or, by reason of some event which the promisor could not prevent, unlawful, becomes void when the act becomes impossible or unlawful.

Where one person has promised to do something which he knew, or, with reasonable diligence, might have known, and which the promisee did now know to be impossible or unlawful, such promisor must make compensation to such promisee for any loss which such promisee sustains through the non-performance of the promisor."

This section covers a wide range of cases and lays down certain clear rules. It is clear from the different parts of the section that impossibility is of various kinds. The impossibility may be absolute, *i.e.*, inherent in the nature of the matter promised; or it may exist only relatively to the ability and circumstances of the promisor. The former is objective, (viz., inherent in the nature of the thing to be done) and discharges the contract. The latter is subjective impossibility, *i.e.*, it is due to the inability of the individual promisor to perform his promise, and does not discharge a contractual duty.

The performance may be impossible as a matter of fact; or it may be impossibly by the rules of law. The impossibility may exist at the time of contracting either with or without the knowledge of the parties or it may arise subsequently to the making of the contract, and in the latter case, it may be caused by events beyond the control of the parties or it may be caused by some act of the promisor or promisee. The impossibility may affect the promise or consideration for the promise. These variations in the nature and incidence of the impossibility produce corresponding modifications in its effects.[116] Thus, a contract may be impossible of performance at the time it is made, or it may become impossible or unlawful after it was made. In the first case the contract is void *ab initio*. In the second case it becomes void. This is known as the doctrine of supervening impossibility or supervening illegality.

IMPOSSIBILITY AT THE TIME OF CONTRACT

A contract to perform something that is obviously impossible, *e.g.*, a promise to ride a horse to the moon, is void because there is no consideration for the contract. Here both parties are aware of the impossibility. It may be that at the time of the agreement both parties are ignorant of the impossibility. In such a case also the contract is void on the ground of mistake. In either case the contract is void *ab initio*. In such a case, there is no contract to terminate and the parties are excused from performance (Sec. 56, Para 1). Promises which are manifestly impossible cannot be binding. Impossible promise is no consideration for a contract which fails in its very foundation and is therefore unenforceable. If, however, the promisor alone knows of the impossibility then existing, he is bound to compensate the promisee for any loss he may suffer through non-performance of the promise (Sec. 56, Para 3).

SUBSEQUENT OR SUPERVENING IMPOSSIBILITY

Paragraph 2 of Sec. 56 provides that subsequent or supervening impossibility or illegality will make the contract, void in certain circumstances and the contract will be discharged. Supervening impossibility may occur in many ways, some of which are explained below.

DISCHARGE BY SUPERVENING IMPOSSIBILITY

A contract will be discharged by subsequent or supervening impossibility in any of the following ways:—

(1) **Destruction of Subject-matter**—When there is a contract in respect to a particular subject-matter which is later destroyed without the fault of the parties, the contract is discharged.

---

116. See Leake on Contracts, p. 513.

(i) In *Taylor* v. *Caldwell* (1863) 122 E.R. 299, the leading case on this point, a music hall was agreed to be let out for a series of concerts on certain days. The hall was burnt down before, the date of the first concert. The contract was held to have become void and the owner of the hall was absolved from liability to let the hall as promised. Blackburn J. observed in this case as follows: "In contracts in which the performance depends on the continued existence of a given person or thing, a condition is implied that the impossibility of performance arising from the perishing of the person or thing shall excuse the performance."

(ii) In *Howell* v. *Coupland* (1876) 1 Q.B.D. 258, a person contracted to deliver a part of a specific crop of potatoes. The potatoes were destroyed by blight through no fault of the party. The contract was held to be discharged.

(iii) In *V. L. Narasu* v. *P. D.V. Iyer,* I.L.R. (1953) Mad. 831, a contract was entered into between a producer and a theatre owner to exhibit a picture at the latter's theatre for a particular period and share the profits. The exhibition of the picture had to be stopped, because the building was demolished under the orders of the authorities on account of its being defective and unsafe. The owner had no knowledge of the defective and unsafe nature of the building. *Held,* that the continued existence of the theatre was a fundamental basis of the contract and the demolition discharged the contract.

The destruction of the subject-matter need not be total, as long as it is sufficient to prevent the contract from being carried out.

In *Nickoll & Knight* v. *Ashton. Eldridge & Co.* (1901) 2 K.B. 126, *A* sold to *N* a cargo of cotton seed to be shipped by a specified ship in a named month. Before the time for shipping arrived, the ship was so injured by stranding as to be unable to load by the agreed time. *Held,* the contract was discharged.

If *A* in the above case, had not named the ship on which the cargo was to be loaded in his contract, he would not have been excused from performance by the destruction of the ship on which he had intended, in his own mind, to load the cargo.

(2) **Non-existence of a state of things necessary for performance**—When a contract is entered into on the basis of the continued existence of a certain state of things, the contract is discharged if the state of things changes or ceases to exist. In this case there is no destruction of any property affected by the contract, but the use of that property contemplated by the contract has become impossible.

(i) In *Krell* v. *Henry* (1903) 2 K.B. 740, *H* hired a room from *K* for two days. The room was taken for the purpose, as both parties well knew, of using the room to view the coronation procession of King Edward VII, although the contract contained no reference to the coronation. Owing to the King's illness the procession was abandoned. *Held,* that *H* was excused from paying rent for the room, as the existence of the procession was the basis of the contract, and its cancellation discharged the contract.

(ii) *A & B* contract to marry each other. Before the time fixed for the marriage, *A* goes mad. The contract becomes void [Illustration (B) of Sec. 56].

(3) **Death or personal incapacity**—Where the personal qualification of a party is the basis of the contract, the contract is discharged by the death or physical disablement of that party. In other words the death or illness of a particular person whose action is necessary for the promised performance discharges the duty to render that performance.

(i) In *Robinson* v. *Davison* (1871) L.R. 6 Ex. 269, *R* contracted with *D* that *D* should play the piano at a concert given on a specific day. *D* was ill on the day in question and unable to perform. The contract was discharged and *D*'s illness excused him from performance.

(ii) *A* contracts to act at a theatre for six months in consideration of a sum paid in advance by *B*. On several occasions *A* is too ill to act. The contract to act on these occasions becomes void [Illustration (e) of Sec. 56].

DISCHARGE BY SUPERVENING ILLEGALITY

A contract which is contrary to law at the time of its formation is void. But if, after the making of the contract, owing to an alteration of the law or the act of some person armed with statutory authority the performance of the contract becomes impossible, the contract is discharged. This is so because the performance of the promise is prevented or prohibited by a subsequent change in the law.

(i) In *Baily* v. *De Crespignay* (1869) L.R. 4 Q.B. 180, *D* leased some land to *B* and covenanted that he would not erect any but ornamental buildings upon the adjoining land. A railway company, under statutory powers, took this adjoining land and built a railway station on it. *Held, D* was excused from performance of his covenant, because the railway company's statutory powers had rendered it impossible.

(ii) In *re. Shipton, Anderson & Co.* (1915) 3 K.B. 676, *A* sold to *B* a specific parcel of wheat in a warehouse in Liverpool. Before delivery, the wheat was requisitioned by the Government under statutory power. *Held,* the delivery being now legally impossible, the contract was discharged.

(iii) In *Noorbux* v. *Kalyan,* 1945 Nag. 192, *A* had agreed to transport goods belonging to *B* from one point to another. Subsequent to the contract, *A*'s trucks were requisitioned by the Government under a statutory power. *Held,* the contract was discharged.

On the other hand, if at the time of the making of he contract, compulsory powers are in existence, the exercise of which may affect the contract, a party knowing of those powers cannot rely on the fact that they are subsequently exercised as a defence to his breach of contract.[117] The exercise of the compulsory powers was an event which might have been anticipated and guarded against in the contract . Also, a continuing contract is not discharged by a prohibitive regulation which may be determined or varied and leaves a substantial part of the contract capable of execution. So, where a notification regulating retail prices was issued which did not make the performance of the contract impossible or unlawful, the parties were not discharged. [118] But if a contract to be performed in a foreign country becomes illegal owing to a change in the law of that country, the contract is discharged.[119]

DECLARATION OF WAR

A contract entered into during war with an alien enemy is void *ab initio*. A contract entered into, before the war commenced, between citizens of countries subsequently at war, remains suspended during the pendency of the war, provided it does not involve intercourse with the alien enemy or is not helpful to him or his country. Such a contract will be revived and may be enforced at the end of the war. If a contract entered into before the outbreak of the war amounts to aiding the enemy in the pursuit of war, it would be abrogated or discharged and not merely suspended.[120] It will also be discharged if it cannot remain suspended, e.g., the contract involves the continuous performance of mutual duties.

CASES WHICH ARE NOT COVERED BY THE DOCTRINE OF SUPERVENING IMPOSSIBILITY

Apart from the cases mentioned above, impossibility does not discharge contracts. Therefore,

---

117. Walton Harvey, Ltd., v. Walker and Homfrays, Ltd. (1931) 1 Ch. 274.
118. Sarada Prasad v. Bhutnalh (1941) 2 Cal. 78.; 1942 Cal. 231; The Naihatti Jute Mills Ltd. v. Khyaliram Jagannath, 1968 Sd. C. 522.
119. Ralli v. Compania Naviera (1920) 2 K. B. 287.
120. Esposito v. Bowden, 7 E. & B. 763.
121. Ka Ron Lanong v. State of Assam, 1959 Assam 75.

impossibility of performance is, as a rule, not an excuse from performance.[121] He that agrees to do an act should do it, unless absolutely impossible which may happen in any one of the ways discussed above. It may be stated, as a general rule, that impossibility to perform arising subsequently to the agreement will not, as a rule, discharge the promisor, because when there is a positive contract to do a thing which is not unlawful, the promisor must perform it, or pay damages for not doing it, although the performance becomes unexpectedly burdensome or even impossible on account of unforeseen events. The supervenning event should destroy the contract itself. Merely making the contract difficult cannot attract Sec. 56 (*Ramji Rao* v. *Nittor Nair,* 1967 Ker. L:R. 771). Some of the circumstances in which a contract is not discharged on the ground of supervening impossibility are stated here.

(1) **Difficulty of performance**—The mere fact that performance is more difficult or expensive or less profitable than the parties anticipated does not discharge the duty of performance. Increased or unexpected difficulty and expense do not, as a rule, excuse from performance.

(i) *A* sold to *B* a certain quantity of Finland timber to be delivered between July and September, 1914. No deliveries were made before August when war broke out and transport was disorganised so that *A* could not bring any timber from Finland. *Held, B* was not concerned with the way in which *A* was going to get timber from Finland and therefore the impossibility of getting timber from Finland did not excuse performance [*Blackburn Bobbin Co.* v. *Allen & Sons* (1918) 2 K.B. 467].

(ii) *A* promised to send certain goods from Bombay to Antwerp in September. In August war broke out, and the shipping space was not available except at very high rates. *Held,* the increased freight rates did not excuse performance (40 Bom. 301).

(2) **Commercial impossibility** to perform a contract will not discharge the contract. A contract cannot be said to be impossible of performance because expectation of higher profits is not'realised (*Sachindra* v. *Gopal,* 1949 Cal. 240). A promisor's contractual duty to lay gas mains is not discharged because the outbreak of war makes it expensive to procure the necessary materials.[122]

(3) The principle of supervening impossibility does not extend to the case of a third person on whose work the promisor relied.

(i) In *Ganga Saran* v. *Firm Ram Charan,* 1952 S.C. 9, a contract between the parties provided that "61 bales as noted below are to be given to you by us; we shall go on supplying goods to you of the Victoria Mills as soon as they are supplied to us by the said mill." In a suit for damages for non-delivery of goods the defendants pleaded impossibility and frustration on the ground that the goods were not supplied to them by the mill. *Held,* that the law is contained in Sec. 56 of the Act, and the words "as soon as they are supplied to us by the mill" simply indicated the process of delivery and did not convey the meaning that delivery was contingent on their being supplied by the mills. The case did not fall within the provisions of Sec. 56, as the default was due to the fault of the defendant.

(ii) In *Toolsidas* v. *Venkata,* 25 C.W.N. 26 P.C., a contract regarding the sale of dyes contained a stipulation about the adjustment of prices according to rates published by a syndicate but the war destroyed the syndicate. The contract was not discharged as it was not dependent upon the continuance of the syndicate.

(4) Partial impossibility rarely discharges a promisor beyond the extent of the impossibility. Thus, if the state of things in question is not the sole basis of the contract, so that there will still remain a substantial portion, though not all, of what was contracted for, the contract will not be discharged. In other words, where there are several purposes for which a contract is made, failure of one of the objects does not terminate the contract.

In *H.B. Steamboat Co.* v. *Hutton* (1903) 2 K.B. 683, the Company agreed to let a boat to *H* to view the naval review at the coronation and to cruise round the fleet. Owing to the King's illness the naval

---

122. See M/s.Alopi Prasad v. Union of India, 1960 S. C. 588.

review was cancelled, but the fleet was assembled, and the boat might have been used for the intended cruise. *Held,* the Co. were not discharged from performance as the naval review was not the sole basis of the contract.

(5) Strikes, lockouts and civil disturbances like riots do not terminate contracts unless there is a clause in the contract providing that in such cases the contract is not to be performed or that the time of performance is to be extended.

(i) The lessee of certain salt pans failed to repair them according to the terms of his contract, on the ground of a strike of the workmen. *Held,* strike of workmen is not sufficient reason to excuse performance of a term of the contract (52 Bom. 142).

(ii) In *Jacobs* v. *Credit Lyonnais* (1884) 12 Q.B.D. 589, a contract was entered into between two London merchants for the sale of certain Algerian goods. Owing to riots and civil disturbances in that country, the goods could not be brought *Held,* there was no excuse for non-performance of the contract.

THE DOCTRINE OF FRUSTRATION

The Common law of England started with the harsh doctrine that unless the parties expressly stipulated to the contrary, impossibility was no defence to an action for breach of a contract. In course of time, however, exceptions were introduced to modify the severity of the Doctrine. In English cases, it has been now held that when the common object of a contract can no longer be carried out the court may declare the contract to be at an end. This is known as the Doctrine of Frustration. The doctrine developed in England under the guise of reading implied terms in contracts. The idea was that they could not have intended to stick to a contract the purpose of which has disappeared. Thus, when the performance depends on the continued existence of a given person or thing, a condition is implied that impossibility of performance arising from the perishing of the person or thing shall excuse performance. If the act became impossible subsequently by reason of some event which the promisor could not prevent, the contract is discharged. This is based on the maxim *Les non cogit ad impossibilia*— the law does not compel the impossible. This discharge of a contract rendered impossible of performance by external causes beyond the contemplation of the parties is known as frustration. Frustration, as said above, is a device by which the rule as to absolute contracts are reconciled with a special exception which justice demands. It has become a gloss on the older theory of impossibility which it has greatly developed under the guise of reading ' "implied terms" into contracts.[123] Therefore, as observed by Lord Radcliffe, "frustration occurs whenever the law recognises that without default of either party a contractual obligation has become incapable of being performed because circumstances in which performance is called for would render it a thing radically different from that which was undertaken by the contract. *Non haec in foedera veni*—"It was not this that I promised to do.[124]

Furthermore, under the doctrine of frustration the fundamental assumption underlying the contract becomes impossible. The performance of the contract may not be actually impossible, but if the contract cannot be performed as originally contemplated by the parties, there is frustration. In such a case, there is a frustrating of the object of the contract. Where, for instance, goods were seized as prize and then released and transhipped so that they arrived two years late, the arrival was not such as was contemplated by the parties.[125] The discharge of a contract by reason of frustration follows automatically when the relevant event happens and does not depend on the volition or election of either party.[126] The doctrine applies if the disturbing cause goes to the extent of substantially preventing the performance of the whole contract. Thus, a contract may become frustrated or impossible of

---

123. Darwood v. Q. Ins. Co., 1949 Cal 390.
124. Davis Contractors, Ltd. v. Fareham (1956) A. C. 696.
125. Gourishanker v. Moitra (1921) 26 C. W. N. 573.
126. D. M. and D Ltd. v. James B. D. F. & Co. Ltd. (1944) A. C. 265.

performance by an Act of Legislature, or by operation of law; it may be discharged by a subsequent declaration of war, or by emergency regulations. The frustration of venture may arise through an Act of God or *vis majeur* or by restraints of princes subsequent to the promise. An Act of God or *vis majeur* is ' 'an accident due to natural causes, directly and exclusively, without human intervention and which could not have been avoided by any amount of foresight or care." In *British Movietone News Limited* v. *London and District Cinemas, Limited* (1943) A.C. 2 the House of Lords based the doctrine of frustration on the principle of "Construction." It was said that where the court gathers as a matter of construction that the contract itself contained impliedly or expressly a term, according to which it would stand discharged on the happening of circumstances, the dissolution of the contract would take place under the terms of the contract itself.

The doctrine of frustration has no application to a demise of land [*Matthey* v. *Gurling* (1922) A.C. 180], to a lease of furnished house, or to a building lease for 99 years [*Linghton's Investment Trust* v. *Cricklewood Property Co.* (1943) 2 K.B. 493]. It does not extend to the case of a third person on whose work the promisor relied. Commercial impossibility also does not frustrate a contract. The doctrine does not apply where the event which is said to have frustrated the object of the contract arises from an intentional act or election of a party [*Maritime National Fish, Ltd.* v. *Ocean Trawlers, Ltd.* (1935) A.C. 524 (P.C.)].

INDIAN LAW REGARDING FRUSTRATION

In India, the law is codified and Sec. 56 which deals with this subject provides for discharge of contract by impossibility of performance or frustration. Paras 1 and 2 of Sec. 56 read as follows:

"An agreement to do an act impossible in itself is void."

"A contract to do an act which after the contract is made, becomes impossible, or by reason of some event which the promisor could not prevent, unlawful, becomes void when the act becomes impossible or unlawful..."

It is clear from the language of the section that it departs from the English law to a large extent and lays down positive rules of law which according to English decisions are only matters of construction depending on the intention of parties. There is no question of reading implied terms in contracts. In India frustration of contract is equivalent to supervening impossibility or illegality. The point of frustration raises some difficulties but a recent pronouncement of the Supreme Court has clarified the position.

In *Satyabrat Ghose* v. *Mugneeram Bangur &. Co.,* M & Co., who were the owners of a large tract of land started a scheme for its development for residential purposes and accordingly divided it into a large number of plots for the sale of which they invited offers from intending buyers. The company's plan was to accept a small portion of the price by way of earnest money from the buyers at the time of agreement, construct the roads and drains itself and within one month after their completion call upon the buyers to complete the conveyance by paying one-third of the price at the time of the registration and the balance within 6 years bearing interest at 6 per cent per annum, time being deemed the essence of the contract.

B entered into a contract on those terms with M & Co., on 5-8-1940 and later on assigned the contract to *S*. Shortly prior to that assignment a portion of the land covered by the scheme was requisitioned for military purposes by the Government under the Defence of India Rules, and later the rest of the land was also requisitioned. M & Co. thereupon informed B that the land pertaining to the scheme was taken possession of by the Government and there was no knowing how long the Government would retain possession and that the company could not, therefore, take up the construction of roads and drains during the continuance of the war and possibly for many years after its termination. The company also wrote to *B* to treat the contract as cancelled and take back the earnest money. This letter was handed over by *B* to his assignee *S*, who asserted that the company was bound by the contract and could not resile. *S* filed a suit for declaration that the contract dated 5-8-1940 was subsisting and that *S*, as the assignee of *B*, was entitled to get the conveyance executed and registered by the company on payment of consideration mentioned in the agreement and in the manner and under the conditions specified therein. The company contended that the contract of sale became discharged by frustration as it became impossible of performance by reason of supervening events. On appeal the Supreme Court held that it could not be said that the requisition order vitally affected the contract or made its performance impossible and accordingly the appeal was allowed and the suit was decreed.

The law relating to frustration in India as laid down by the Supreme Court in Saryabrat Ghose's case may be summed up as follows:—

'The Courts in India should look primarily to the law as embodied in Secs. 32 and 56 of the Indian Contract Act. Indeed, the above sections of the Contract Act embrace the Whole of the Indian law on the subject. Sec. 32 applies in cases of contingent contract and Sec. 56 covers the rest. Under either, however, impossibility is the central or dominating idea and the determining factor. "The essential idea upon which the doctrine of frustration is based is that of impossibility of performance of the contract. In fact, impossibility and frustration are often used as interchangeable expressions. The changed circumstances make performance of the contract impossible and the parties are absolved from the further performance of it as they did not promise to an impossibility.[127] **The doctrine of frustration is in reality an aspect or part of the law of discharge of contract by reason of supervening impossibility or illegality of the act agreed to be done and hence comes within the purview** of Sec. 55[128]. To the extent that the Contract Act deals with particular subject, it is exhaustive upon the same and it is not permissible to import the principles of English law 'de hors' those statutory provisions. The decisions of the English Courts possess only a persuasive value and may be helpful in showing how the Courts in England have decided cases under circumstances similar to those which have come before Indian Courts. In deciding cases in India the only doctrine that we have to go by is that of supervening impossibility as laid down in Section 56, taking word impossible in its practical and not literal sense.

Section 56 lays down a rule of positive law and does not leave the matter to be determined according to the intention of the parties. Therefore, in India, the doctrine of frustration is applied not on the ground that parties themselves agreed to an implied term which operated to release them from the performance of the contract. The relief is given by the Court on the ground of subsequent impossibility when it finds that the whole purpose or the basis of a contract was frustrated by the intrusion or occurrence of an unexpected event or change of circumstances which was beyond what was contemplated by the parties at the time when they entered into the agreement. When such an event or change of circumstances occurs which is so fundamental as to be regarded by law as striking at the root of the contract as a whole, it is the Court which can pronounce the contract to be frustrated and at an end.

In applying this rule the Court has to examine the nature and terms of the contract before it and the circumstances under which it was made and to determine whether or not the disturbing element which is alleged to have happened in the particular case has substantially prevented the performance of the contract as a whole. If the answer be in the affirmative, the contract will stand dissolved or discharged by virtue of Sec. 56, as it is well settled that, if and when there is frustration the dissolution of the contract occurs automatically. In ascertaining the meaning of the contract and its application to the

---

127. Satyabrat Ghose v.Mugneeram Bangur & Co., 1954 S.C. 44; M/s. Alopi Prasad v. Union of India, 1960 S.C. 588; Hari Singh v: Dewani Vidyawaiti, 1960 J & K. 91; Union of India v. Kishorilal, 1959 S. C. 1362.

128. See also Ka Ron Lanong v. State of Assam, 1959; Assam 76; M. Bangur v. G. Singh, 1959 Cal576.

actual occurrences, the Court has to decide, not what the parties actually intended, but what as reasonable men they should have intended.[129] The Court personifies for this purpose the reasonable man. In construing the word 'impossible' in Section 56, it should be noted that the word has not been used in the sense of physical or literal impossibility. The performance of an act may not be literally impossible but it may be impracticable and useless from the point of view of the object and purpose which the parties had in view; and if an untoward event or change of circumstances totally upsets the very foundation upon which the parties rested their bargain, it can very well be said that the promisor finds it impossible to do the act which he promised to do.

In *State of Rajasthan* v. *Madanswarup,* 1960 Raj. 138, *M,* an advocate, of Bikaner High Court, was appointed by the Bikaner State to look after its criminal work in the High Court. After merger of Bikaner, its High Court was abolished and a new High Court for the United State of Rajasthan was established at Jodhpur by an Act of Legislature. Thereafter the services of *M* were terminated by the successor State. *M* sued the State of Rajasthan for damages for breach of contract *Held,* that in view of the change of circumstances the contract became virtually impossible and all that could be said was that it was discharged or put an end to and not broken. The doctrine of frustration was, therefore, applicable so that *M* could not found an action for damages on that account.

EFFECT OF SUPERVENING IMPOSSIBILITY OR FRUSTRATION

Sections 56 and 65 of the Indian Contract Act expressly provide for the consequences of impossibility of performance as follows:—

1. When the performance of a contract becomes subsequently impossible or illegal, the contract becomes void—Sec. 56, Para 2.

2. When a contract becomes void, any person who has received an advantage under it must restore it, or make compensation for it to the person from whom he received it.,

The English law on this point is laid down in *Fibrosa, etc.,* v. *Fairbairn, etc.* (1943) A.C. 3 in these words: All sums paid to any party in pursuance of the contract before it is discharged are recoverable. Sums payable cease to be payable.

In this case, English sellers agreed to sell machinery to Polish buyers, part of the price to be paid in advance. The buyers paid £1,000. Performance became impossible, as before delivery was due Germany occupied Poland. *Held,* the contract was discharged by frustration, and the buyers could recover £1,000 paid and were not liable to pay the balance.

3. Where one person has promised to do something which he knew, or with reasonable diligence, might have known, and which the promisee did not know to be impossible or unlawful, such promisor must make compensation to such promisee for any loss which such promisee sustains through the non-performance of the promise— Sec. 56, Para 3.

A contracts to marry B being already married to C, and being forbidden by the law to which he is subject to practise polygamy. A must make compensation to B for any loss caused to her by the non-performance of his promise.

DISCHARGE BY LAPSE OF TIME

The Limitation Act, in some circumstances, affords a good defence to suits for breach of contract, and in fact terminates the contract by depriving the party of his remedy at law. For example, where a

---

129. Joseph C.S. Line Ltd. v. Imperial S. Corp. Ltd. (1942) A. C. 154. See also Mugneeram Bangur & Co. V. Gurcharan, 1959 Cal. 576, which has followed the law as laid down by the Supreme Court in Satyabrat Ghose case, and held that there was no frustration on similar facts as in the Supreme Court case.

debtor has failed to repay the loan on the stipulated date the creditor must file the suit against him within three years of the default If the three years expire and he takes no action, he will be barred from his remedy, and the other party is discharged of his liability to perform. The period of limitation for simple contracts is three years in India and six years in England, and in the case of special contracts it is twelve years.

DISCHARGE BY OPERATION OF LAW

Discharge under this head may take place as follows:

By merger—Where the parties embody the inferior contract in a superior contract. When between the same parties, a new contract is entered into, and a security of a higher degree, or a higher kind is taken, the previous contract merges in the higher security. Where securities of the same kind of degree are taken there is no merger.

By the unauthorised alteration of terms of a written document—Where a party to a contract in writing makes any material alteration without the knowledge and consent of the other, the contract can be avoided by the other party. An alteration even by a stranger will entitle the other party to avoid the contract, but where the alteration is due to mere accident or is not material contract cannot be avoided.

By insolvency—The Insolvency Acts provide for discharge of contracts under particular circumstances. So, where the Insolvency Court passes an order discharging the insolvent this order exonerates or discharges him from liabilities on all debts incurred previous to his adjudication.

DISCHARGE BY BREACH OF CONTRACT

We have seen that contract must be strictly performed according to its terms. But where the promisor has neither performed his contract nor tendered performance and where the performance is not excused by consent, express or implied, or where the performance is defective, there is a breach of the contract by him, which entitles the other party to file a suit. If the contract is unilateral the only remedy for the other party is to claim relief for breach. In the case of a bilateral contract the party not in breach can claim relief for breach and also in certain circumstances is exonerated from liability to perform his part of the contract. The breach of a contract may be (*i*) actual, or (*ii*) constructive or anticipatory. The actual breach may take place (*a*) at the time when performance is due, or (*b*) when actually performing the contract. The constructive on anticipatory breach of contract, i.e., a breach before the time for performance has arrived, may also take place in two ways, namely, (*a*) by the promisor doing an act which makes the performance of his promise impossible or (*b*) by the promisor in some other way showing his intention not to perform his promise.

Actual Breach of Contract at the time when Performance is due—Where a person fails to perform a contract, when performance is due the other party can hold him liable for breach. But, if a party who has failed to perform the contract at the appointed time, subsequently expresses willingness to perform, the question whether he can do so or not would depend upon whether time was of the essence of the contract or not. In all mercantile contracts time is of the essence of the contract and a breach of contract results on failure to perform within the limited time. This is specially so in shipping contracts. In a sale of goods subject to rapid fluctuations of market price, the time of delivery is of the essence. There are other transactions, *e.g.*, contract relating to sale of land in which time is not deemed to be of the essence unless parties specially stipulate to that effect. But the terms of the contract, or the nature of the property sold, will determine whether time was of the essence. In the case of sale of a house to be immediately occupied or sale of a business as a going concern, time will be of the essence. In Indian law, where in a contract time is not of the essence and the party expresses willingness to perform it after the appointed time, the law permits him to do so subject to payment of compensation for failure of due performance. The party accepting performance after the due date is required to give notice while accepting that he intends to claim compensating, otherwise he is deemed to have waived the right to compensation (Sec. 55).

Breach during the Performance of the Contract—Where a party apparently performs the promise but the other party says that it is not a proper performance according to the contract, the question arises whether there is a breach of the contract exonerating the other party from performance of his part of the bargain. If breach is of a condition vital to the contract, the contract is discharged and the other party need not perform his part of the bargain. In the case of sale of goods by description, unless the goods answering to the description are offered, the buyer is not bound to take delivery or to pay for them. But if the breach is only of a collateral term (non-essential condition) this will not exonerate the party from performance of his part of the bargain, but only entitle him to claim damages. Where the buyer has obtained possession of goods and his right of enjoyment is disturbed in any way, he can claim damages caused by the breach of the implied warranty of quiet possession. Where the promisor had made more than one promise, or a divisible promise, his repudiation must either be of the whole contract, or of a part of it which is a condition precedent to the promisee's liability, else the promisee will not be entitled to treat such repudiation as equivalent to the breach of the whole contract.

CONSTRUCTIVE OR ANTICIPATORY BREACH OF CONTRACT

It may sometimes happen that even before the time of performance arrives, the promisor may do some act which makes the performance impossible or may definitely renounce the contract or show his intention not to perform it. Thus where A promised to assign to B within 7 years from the date of promise all his interest in 4 houses for £140, and before the end of the 7 years assigned all his interest to another person, it was *held,* that without waiting for the 7 years to elaspe B could sue for breach of his promise.[130] In another case a courier was engaged in April to accompany his employer on a tour of three months to commence on June 1. On May 11 the employer wrote to the courier that he had changed his mind and declined his services but refused to make him any compensation. On May 22 the courier brought his action for breach of contract, and the defence was that there could be no breach before June 1. It was *held,* that the courier was entitled to treat the letter of May 11, equivalent to breach of contract. It is to be noted that a constructive or anticipating breach of contract does not give rise to a right of action, unless the promisee elects to treat it as equivalent to actual breach. Thus, instead of bringing an immediate action, as in the examples given above, the promisee may treat the conduct, act or notice of the promisor as inoperative, and wait for the time when the contract is to be performed, and then hold the promisor responsible for all the consequences of non-performance. But in that case the promisee keeps the contract alive for the benefit of the promisor as well as his own, he remains liable under it, and enables the promisor not only to complete the contract in spite of previous repudiation, but also to avail himself of any excuse for non-performance which may have come into existence before the time fixed for performance. Thus, in our second example, if the courier had waited till June 1, the employer could withdraw his letter of May 11, and ask the courier to accompany him on tour, or if the performance had become impossible due to some cause, such as the declaration of war, the courier would have lost his remedy and the employer would have been excused from performance. A party putting an end to the contract must restore any advantage he may have received.[131]

LIABILITY OF PARTY PREVENTING PERFORMANCE

When a contract contains reciprocal promises, and one party to the contract prevents the other from performing his promise, the party so prevented can avoid the contract and claim compenation for any loss he may sustain (Sec. 53). Where A and B contract that B shall execute a certain work for A for ₹ 1,000, and B is willing and ready to do the work, but A prevents him from doing so, the contract is voidable at the option of B. If he elects to rescind it, he can recover from A compensation

---

130. Lovelock v. Franklyn (1849) 8 Q.B. 317.
131. Murali v. I Film Co., 1943 P. C. 34.

for any loss which he has suffered by non-performance of the contract. This is based on the principle that one of the contracting parties is exonerated from the performance of a contract when it is prevented by the wrongful act of the other party. No person can take advantage of the non-fulfilment of condition the performance of which has been hindered by himself. Money paid or ornaments given for the benefit of the bride or bridegroom or of both, can be recovered by suit, if the marriage contract is broken (*Dholidas* v. *Fulchand,* 26 Bom. 638). A betrothal is a contract; when it is broken or otherwise becomes void, parties are entitled to the return of the gifts made by them. (*Rajendra* v. *Roshan,* 1950 All. 592).

PART 1-I
REMEDIES FOR BREACH OF CONTRACT

Where there is a breach of contract on the part of one party, the injured party becomes entitled to any one or more of the following reliefs:

1. Rescission of the contract with the result that the injured party is freed from all obligations under the contract;
2. Suit for damages;
3. Suit upon a *quantum meruit;*
4. Suit for specific performance of the contract;
5. Suit for an injunction.

RESCISSION

If one party has broken his contract, the other party may treat the breach as discharge, and refuse to perform his part of the contract. He may also successfully defend an action for non-performance, or an action brought for specific performance. Sec. 75 further entitles him to compensation for any damage he may have sustained through the non-fulfilment of the contract. For instance, *A*, a singer, contracts with *B*, the manager of a theatre, to sing at his theatre for two nights in every week during the next two months, and *B* engages to pay her ₹ 100 for each night's performance. On the sixth night, *A* wilfully absents herself from the theatre, and *B*, in consequence, rescinds the contract *B* is entitled to claim compensation for the damage which he has sustained through the non-fulfilment of the contract.

DAMAGES

Where a contract has been broken, the party who suffers by such breach is entitled, under Sec. 73, to receive from the party who has broken the contract, compensation for any loss or damage caused to him thereby, which naturally arose in the usual course of things from such breach, or which the parties knew, when they made the contract, to be likely to result from the breach of it. But compensation is not to be given for any remote or indirect loss or damage sustained by reason of the breach. Compensation is also available against a party for breach of a quasi-contract. Sec. 73 is based on the leading case of *Hadley* v. *Baxendale* (1854) 9 Ex. 34, the facts of which are as follows:

The plaintiff, an owner of a mill, delivered a broken shaft to the defendant, a common carrier to take to a manufacturer, to copy it and make a new one. The carrier delayed delivery of the shaft beyond a reasonable time, as a result of which the mill was idle for a longer period than should have been necessary. The plaintiff did not make known to the defendant carrier that delay would result in a loss of profits. *Held,* the carrier was not liable for loss of profits during the period of delay. Alderson, B. observed: "When two parties have made a contract, which one of them has broken, the damages which the other party ought to receive in respect of such breach should be either such as may fairly be considered as arising naturally, *i.e.,* according to the usual course of things, from such breach of contract itself, or such as may reasonably be supposed to have been in the contemplation of both the parties at the time the contract was entered into as a probable result of the breach."

The principle enunciated in Sec. 73 is that a party who suffers by the breach of contract is entitled to:—

(a) such damages as naturally arose in the usual course of things, as a result of the breach;

(b) and if he claims special damages for any loss sustained (which would not ordinarily flow from the breach) he must prove that the other party knew at the time of making the contract that the special loss was likely to result from the breach of the contract;

(c) such compensation is not to be given for any remote and indirect loss or damage sustained by reason of the breach;

(d) compensation for quasi-contract as damages is the same as for a contract.

LIQUIDATED DAMAGES AND UNLIQUIDATED DAMAGES

Where there is a breach of contract by one party, the other party is entitled to sue for damages. Therefore, unless the court passes a decree for a specified amount, the claim for damages is merely a right to sue and not a debt or actionable claim. Consequently, this claim can be assigned or transferred, since it is not a debt under the law (*Mirza Javed Murtaza* v. *U.P. Financial Corporation,* 1983 All. 234; *Union of India* v. *Roman Iron Foundry,* 1974 s.c. 1265). The suit may be for liquidated damages or unliquidated damages. *Liquidated damages* are damages agreed upon by the parties in the contract itself to be paid by the party breaking the contract in case of breach. The plaintiff has only to prove the breach of contract, and no proof of loss is required. But liquidated damages must appear to be a genuine pre-estimate of the loss that will be caused to one party if the contract is broken by the other.

Where no damages are fixed by the contract, but the amount of compensation claimed for a breach of contract is left to be assessed by the court, damages claimed are called *unliquidated damages.*

Unliquidated damages may be classified as follows:

(a) Ordinary, General, Compensatory or Substantial damages;

(b) Special damages;

(c) Exemplary, Punitive or Vindictive damages;

(d) Nominal damages;

(e) Contemptuous damages.

ORDINARY OR COMPENSATORY DAMAGES

In deciding a suit for damages, the court has to answer two questions: (*i*) Proximity and remoteness of damage, (*ii*) measure of damages. The judge has to first decide whether or not the damage has resulted from proximate consequences of the breach, for remote consequences are not regarded. Once the court has decided that the damage is sufficiently proximate, it will then turn to the measure of damages, that is, the amount of money that will compensate the plaintiff. The question of remoteness of damage is governed by the maxim (recognised in *Hadley* v. *Baxendale* and Sec. 73 of our Contract Act): *Injure non remota causa, sedproximo spectatur*—"in law, not the remote cause, but the proximate cause is taken notice of". Thus, if the damage or loss suffered by reason of the breach of the contract is *remote* or *indirect* no compensation would be allowed. The aggrieved party, however, would in case of breach of contract, be entitled to recover compensation for damage or loss caused to him thereby, if such loss or damage arose *naturally* and *directly* in the *usual course of things* from such breach, or which the parties to the contract *knew,* at the time of making the contract, to be likely to result from breach of contract The first part of this rule states the case for ordinary damages and the latter concerns with special damages.

In *Hadley* v. *Baxendale,* the common carrier negligently delayed delivery of the broken shaft to the manufacturer who had to copy it and make a new one. On account of the delay by the common carrier the mill remained idle for a longer period than should have been necessary. The plaintiff did not make known to the defendant, the common carrier, that for want of the shaft the mill would remain idle which would result in a loss of profit. The plaintiff was held entitled to recover damages for delay in delivery but not for loss of profits occasioned by the closure of the mill since there was no way the common carrier could have foreseen that the mere absence of a shaft would cause the closure of the mill. The mill-owner could have recovered damages for loss of profits if he had informed the carrier of the likely result of delayed delivery.

The test of remoteness of liability as laid down in this case was reformulated by Asquith, L.J. in *Victoria Laundry Ltd.* v. *Newman Industries Ltd.* (1949) 2 K.B. 528, in the following propositions:

"In cases of breach of contract, the aggrieved party is only entitled to recover such part of the loss actually resulting as was at the time of the contract reasonably foreseeable as liable to result from the breach. What was at that time reasonably so foreseeable depends upon the knowledge then possessed by the parties or, at all events, by the party who commits the breach.

For this purpose knowledge 'possessed' is of two kinds: one imputed, the other actual. Everyone, as a reasonable person, is taken to know the 'ordinary course of things' and consequently what loss is liable to result from a breach of contract in that ordinary course. This is the subject-matter of the 'first rule' in *Hadley* v. *Baxendale.* But to this knowledge, which the contract-breaker is assumed to possess whether he actually possesses it or not, there may have to be added in a particular case knowledge which he actually possesses of special circumstances outside the 'ordinary course of things', of such kind that a breach in those special circumstances would be liable to cause more loss. Such a case attracts the operation of the 'second rule' so as to make additional loss also recoverable.

In *Victoria Laundry Ltd.* v. *Newman Industries Ltd.,* (1949) 2 K.B. 528, the plaintiffs, launderers and dyers, with a view to extending their business and also for the purpose of obtaining certain dyeing contracts of an exceptionally profitable character, bought a boiler from the defendants who undertook to deliver it on 5th June. The boiler, however, was not delivered until the 8th November. The defendants were aware of the nature of plaintiff's business and they were informed in more than one letter before the conclusion of the contract that the plaintiffs were "most anxious" to put the boiler in use "in the shortest possible space of time". In an action for breach of contract, the plaintiffs claimed (1) loss of profit the laundry would have made had the boiler been delivered in time, (2) loss of exceptional profit expected to arise under the valuable dyeing contracts. *Held,* the plaintiffs could recover damages for loss of ordinary profits occasioned by the delay since the defendants knew the laundry would be closed pending delivery of the boiler: but the loss on the valuable contract could not be recovered as the defendants were not informed of this at the time of the contract. This being an extension of the plaintiff's business, it could not be recovered.

In *The Heron 11* (1969) 1 A.C. 350, a ship owner agreed to carry a cargo of sugar belonging to *A* from Constanza to Basrah. He knew that there was a sugar market at Basrah and that *A* was a sugar merchant, but did not know that he intended to sell the cargo immediately on its arrival. Owing to the shipowner's default, the voyage was delayed by at least 9 days, and the sugar fetched a lower price than it would have done had it arrived on time. It was held by the House of Lords that the consequential loss fell to be borne by the shipowner under the first branch of rule laid down by *Hadley* v. *Baxendale.* Although he had no knowledge of special circumstances he could and should at the very least have contemplated that if the ship arrived 9 days late *A* would suffer some financial loss. The criterion for determining remoteness of damage arising from a breach of contract was laid down as: "Whether the probability of its occurrence was within the reasonable contemplation of both parties at the time when the contract was made, having regard to their knowledge at that time."

Measure of damages. The measure of damages is the estimated loss directly and naturally resulting in the ordinary course of events, from the breach of contract.[132] The injured party is to be put in the

---

132. Union of India v. Vasudeo Agarwal, 1960 Pat 87.

same financial position as he would have been if the contract had been performed according to its terms. [133] In the case of sale and purchase, the damages payable would be the difference between the contract price and the market price at the date of the breach. The damages are calculated as on the date of breach and any subsequent change of circumstances tending to an increase or reduction of damage cannot be taken note of. In a contract of sale of shares the buyer broke the contract, and seller sued for damages on the basis of the difference between the contract price and the market rate on the date of the breach. The buyer proved the price of shares subsequently rose and that the seller did not really suffer any damage. But the court *held,* that the damages should be ascertained as on the date of breach and any risk of profit or loss arising from a subsequent increase or decrease is entirely vendor's and has nothing to do with the other party.[134] If, however, at the date of the breach the price of the goods is higher than the contract price and so the seller does not suffer any loss, he will receive only nominal damages.

Damages may also be coined for breach of warranty or condition and such damages will include all damages flowing from the breach. A cow was sold with the condition that it was free from disease. The cow was suffering from foot and mouth disease at the time of sale. Not only did the cow die but it also infected other cows of the buyer. *Held,* damages could be recovered for the entire loss.[135]

SPECIAL DAMAGES

Special damages are those resulting from a breach of contract under some special or peculiar circumstance. If at the time of entering into a contract a person has notice of special circumstances which make special loss the likely result of the breach in the ordinary course of things, then upon his breaking the contract and the special loss following the breach he will be required to make good the special loss. If therefore there be any special damage which is attributable to the wrongful act, then special damages, if proved, will be awarded. Hence, if an unusual damage is likely to be sustained as the result of a breach of contract, its nature should be communicated to the other party before the contract is made so that he contracts subject to the prospective liability. Thus, if in *Hadley* v. *Baxendale,* the mill-owner had told the carrier that delay would result in a loss of profits through stoppage of the mill, he would have recovered damages for such a loss. Similarly, in *Victoria Laundry* v. *Newman Industries,* if the launderer had told the defendants that he was expecting a valuable contract and that delay would result in loss of special profit he would have recovered that, too.

EXEMPLARY OR PUNITIVE DAMAGES

These damages are a sum awarded beyond the pecuniary loss sustained by the injured party. Ordinarily, damages for breach of contract are intended to compensate the plaintiff, not to punish the defendant. The object of exemplary damages is to punish the defendant, and to deter him and others from similar conduct in the future. Award of exemplary damages is made in only two cases: (*i*) Breach of Promise of Marriage cases, (*ii*) where a bank wrongfully dishonours a commercial customer's cheque. In a breach of promise to marry, the amount of the damages will depend upon the extent of injury to the party's feelings. It is really an additional sum known as a *Solatium* awarded to the jilted woman as a solace for her injured feelings. In the case of wrongful dishonour of a cheque of a customer who is a trader the rule is 'the smaller the cheque dishonoured the greater the damage.'

Note: Since the coming into force on January 1, 1971, of the Law Reform (Miscellaneous Provisions) Act, 1970, actions for breach of promise to marry have been abolished in England. In England, therefore, no suit for damages for breach of promise to marry can be filed.

---

133. B. Sunley & Co. Ltd. v. Cunard White Star Ltd. (1940) 1 K. B. 740.

134. Jamal v. Maulla Dawood & Co. (1916) 43 Cal. 193 (P. C); Trojan v. Nagappa 1953 S. C. '   135.

135. Smith v. Green (1876) 1 C.P.D. 92.

NOMINAL DAMAGES

Nominal damages consist of a small sum of money, *e.g.*, a rupee. They are a token award where there has been an infringement of contractual right, but no actual loss has been suffered. These damages are awarded to establish the right to decree for breach of contract.

CONTEMPTUOUS DAMAGES

Damages are said to be contemptuous, when the court finds that a breach has been committed, but that the breach is so insignificant or petty that a reasonable man would not have filed the suit. A rupee or even less may be awarded to mark the court's disapproval of the plaintiff's conduct in bringing the action. The law does not take account of trifling things; and where it does, it awards also something of a contemptuous character. Such damages have been awarded to male plaintiffs in breach of marriage actions.

RULES REGARDING AMOUNT OF DAMAGES

The rules applicable to the awarding of damages may be summarised as follows:

1. Where a party sustains a loss by reason of a breach of contract he is, as far as money can do it, to be placed in the same situation with respect to damages, as if the contract has been performed.

2. Subject to the above rule, the measure of damages is the estimated loss directly and naturally resulting in the ordinary course of events, from the breach of the contract. Ordinarily, therefore, the injured party can recover by way of compensation only the actual loss suffered by him.

3. Remote damages, *i.e.*, damages for remote consequences, or those not naturally arising out of the breach are usually not allowed.

4. The damages should be such as both parties would reasonably assume to be the result of a breach of contract.

The court may allow remote damages, if such damages may reasonably be supposed to have been in the contemplation of both the parties at the time they made the contract.

5. It follows that to recover special damages the special circumstances must be communicated to the other party at the time of the contract.

6. If the parties agree about the amount of the damages for breach of contract, no more than the agreed amount can be recovered.

7. Exemplary damages cannot be awarded for breach of contract, except for breach of promise to marry or against a banker for wrongful dishonour of a cheque.

Note: Under English law, actions for breach of promise of marriage have been abolished with effect from January 1,1971.

8. In a breach of contract for the sale of goods, the damages payable would be the difference between the contract price and the market price at the date the breach takes place.

9. It is the duty of the injured party to minimise the damages by mitigating the loss consequent on the breach. Thus, the plaintiff must take all reasonable steps to mitigate the loss resulting from the breach, and if he fails to do that he will not get any damage resulting from such failure.

10. The fact that damages are difficult to assess does not prevent the injured party from recovering them. The court will always attempt to assess damages, and award them for prospective as well as the actual loss.

In *Chaplin v. Hicks* (1911) 2 K.B. 786, *H* advertised a beauty competition, by which readers of certain newspapers were to select fifty ladies, from whom *H* himself would select twelve and for whom he would provide theatrical engagements. *C* was one of the fifty selected by readers but by *H*'s breach of contract, she was not present when the final selection was made. *Held,* although it was problematical whether she would have been one of the selected twelve, and although it was difficult to assess damages, C was entitled to have damages assessed.

LIQUIDATED DAMAGES AND PENALTY

Where the parties have fixed at the time of the contract the damages that would be payable in case of breach, a question may arise (in English law at least) whether the provision amounts to "liquidated damages" or a "penalty". Courts in England give effect to liquidated damages, but they relieve against penalty. The test of the two is that where the amount fixed is a genuine pre-estimate of the loss in case of breach; it is liquidated damages and will be allowed; and if the amount fixed is without any regard to probable loss, but *in terrerem* as it were, to prevent a party from committing breach of contract, it is a penalty and will not be allowed.[136] In Indian law, there is no such difference between liquidated damages and penalty, as Sec. 74 specifically provides payment of only "reasonable compensation." Sec. 74 reads:

"When a contract has been broken, if a sum is named in the contract as the amount to be, paid in case of such breach *or if the contract contains any other stipulation by way of penalty* the party complaining of the breach is entitled whether or not actual damage or loss is proved to have been caused thereby, to receive from the party who has broken the contract a *reasonable compensation* not exceeding the amount so named or, as the case may be, *the penalty stipulated for.*

Explanation—A stipulation for increased interest from the date of default may be a stipulation by way of penalty[137]....

The party suffering from breach is entitled to get the actual damages he has suffered. With regard to the amount named in the contract, the compensation payable is the reasonable amount up to the stipulated amount whether it is by way of liquidated damages or penalty. *A* contracts with *B* to pay ₹ 1,000 if he fails to repay *B* ₹ 500 on a given day. *A* fails to repay *B* ₹ 500 on that day. *B* is entitled to recover from *A* such compensation, not exceeding ₹ 1,000, as the Court considers reasonable. But where a contract provides for payment in a number of instalments but on the failure to pay any instalment the whole amount is to be paid forthwith, such a stipulation is not a penalty and die contract can be enforced according to its terms.[138]

Payment of Interest—With regard to the payment of interest the following rules have been laid down:—

1. Where a contract provides that the amount should be paid by a particular date and in default, it will be payable with interest, the Court will give effect to the stipulation if the interest is reasonable. Where the interest is exorbitant, the Court will give relief.

2. Where the bond provides that in default of the payment of the principal by a stated date, enhanced interest should be payable, if the enhanced interest is made payable from the date of default and is resonable, it is regarded reasonable compensation and is allowed. But if the enhanced interest is exorbitant, e.g., increase from 12 per cent to 75 per cent, it will be penalty and relief will be granted against it.

3. The Courts do not lean towards compound interest, they do not award in the absence of stipulation, but where there is a stipulation for its payment it is, in the absence of disentitling circumstances, allowed, *i.e.*, it will be allowed only if it is not an enhanced rate.

136. Union of India v. Vasudeo Agarwal, 1960 Pat. 87.
137. See Nageswaraswami v. Viswasundararao (1953) S. C. R. 894, where the Supreme Court did not allow compound interest in place of simple interest as originally fixed in case of breach; Fateh Chand v. Balkishan Das. 1963 S. C. 1405.
138. Tayya v. Gangayya (1927) M. W. N. 597; 53 M. L J.. 562.

SPECIFIC PERFORMANCE

Instead of, or in addition to, awarding damages to the injured party, a decree for specific performance may be granted. Specific performance means the actual carrying out by the parties of their contract, and in proper cases the Court will insist on the parties carrying out their agreement. This remedy, however, is discretionary, and will not be granted in the following cases:—

1. Where monetary compensation is an adequate remedy.
2. Where the Court cannot supervise the execution of the contract, *e.g.*, a building contract.
3. Where the contract is for personal services.
4. Where one of the parties is a minor.

Specific performance is usually granted in contracts connected with, land, *e.g.*, purchase of a particular plot or house, or to take debentures in a company. In the case of sale of goods, it will only be granted in the case of specific goods and is not ordered as a rule unless the goods are unique and cannot easily be purchased in the market, or are of special value to the party suing by reason of personal or family associations.

It is, however, to be noted that the plaintiff who seeks specific performance must, in his turn, perform all the terms of the contract which he ought to have performed at the date of the action *(Pudi Lazarus* v. *Rev. Johnson Edward,* 1976 AP. 243).

INJUNCTION

An injunction is a mode of securing the specific performance of a negative term of the contract. It is an order of the court whereby an individual is required to refrain from the further doing of the act complained of. It may be used to prevent many wrongful acts, *e.g.*, torts, but in the context of contract the remedy will be granted to enforce a negative stipulation in a contract in a case where damages would not be an adequate remedy. Thus, where a party to a contract is doing something which he had promised not to do, the court may, in its discretion, issue an order to the defendant restraining him| from doing what he promised not to do. Its application may be extended to contracts where there is no actual negative stipulation but where one may be inferred. In *Metropolitan Electric Supply Company* v. *Ginder* (1901) 2 Ch. 799, *G* agreed to take the whole electric energy required by his premises from the plaintiffs. *Held,* this was in substance an agreement not to take energy from any other person and it could be enforced by injunction.

In a proper case injunction may be used as an indirect method, of enforcing a contract of personal services, but in that case a *clear negative* stipulation is required. In *Lumley* v. *Wagner* (1852) 1 De G.M. & G. 604, *W* agreed to sing at *L*'s theatre and nowhere else. *W*, in breach of her contract with *L*, entered into a contract to sing for *Z. Held,* although *W* could not be compelled to sing at *L*'s theatre, she could be restrained by injunction from singing for *Z.* Again, in *Warner Bros.* v. *Nelson* (1937) 1 K.B. 209, the defendant, the film actress Bette Davis, had entered into a contract in which she agreed to act *exclusively* for the plaintiffs for 12 months. During the year she contracted to act for *X. Held,* she could be restrained by injunction from acting for *X.*

OPERATION OF CONTRACT

A contract cannot impose liabilities upon one who is not a party to the contract. In *McGruther* v. *Pitcher* (1904) Ch. 306, *A* sold to *B* some rubber heels packed in a box, in the lid of which was a notice that the heels were sold on the express agreement that they were not to be re-sold below certain prices. *Z* bought the heels from *B* with notice of the agreement, but re-sold them below the prices. *Held,* as there was no contract between *A* and *Z, A* could not enforce the agreement.

A contract imposes a duty on third party not to induce others to commit a breach of contract. In *Lumley* v. *Gye* (1853) 2 E ans B 216, *L* engaged *W*, an opera singer, to sing in his theatre for a season, and *G*, knowing of his contract induced *W* to break it and to sing for him. *Held, L* could recover damages from *G*.

INTERPRETATION OF CONTRACT

Construction. It often happens that, because of a difference of opinion, the two parties are in doubt as to their rights and obligations. This is not to say that they are in mistake, which would render the contract void. They are merely in dispute. The contract is still valid, still carries rights and obligations, but the two parties cannot agree on what these rights and obligations are. For example, two parties may contract on a job "to be completed during the summer of the year 1976." One side expects the job to be finished by the end of June, the other contends that in India, August is, still summer, being still quite hot, Only the Court can decide whether, having regard to all the facts, August is summer or not.

In a case like this the law must construe the contract. First the court will seek to discover the intention of the parties. But, as judges are human, the law does not try to give them a superhuman task. It is therefore assumed that "the intentions of the parties are set out in the memorandum to the contract and must be discovered from what is written within the four corners of the contract". If it is written, and is reasonable, the law must, of necessity, assume what is written was intended.[139] Of course, if there is no writing, the court will have to consider evidence of behaviour. But 'construction' is usually confined to "construction of documents," and will be dealt with here on that basis.

Extrinsic evidence. Intention of the parties must be discovered from what is written, not what may be surmised on howsoever probable grounds. Accordingly, extrinsic evidence is not allowed to contradict add to, or vary contractual terms. But it may be used to *explain* the terms, where these are in dispute. This distinction is very important and must be borne in mind at all times.

Parol evidence can be given to prove a trade usage or a local custom. It is legal for courts to add words which have clearly and obviously been omitted in error. It must however, be remembered that the law does not exist to make contracts: it is only there to interpret them. Only when the contract is defective will the law do anything, and then only the minimum needed to give "business efficacy to the contract."

The canons of construction. Because construction cases come before the courts in such large numbers, the courts have laid down a number of canons of construction. The Canons are as follows:

(a) The word or words will be construed according to their plain and ordinary dictionary meaning.

(b) The words will be considered in their context—the context of the document, and of the contract.

(c) The contract must be construed as a whole. In this context, where written words have been inserted, any printed words which contradict them will be deleted. The fact of writing shows second thoughts.

(d) The terms must be construed in such a way as to make the contract effective *Ut res magis valet quam per-eat*—"the thing shall be valid rather than perish". If one construction renders the contract effective, whilst another makes it ineffective, the former shall be adopted. A contract must be interpreted in such a manner as to give it efficacy rather than to invalidate it (*Union of India* v. *Basudev Dutta,* 1976 S.C. 430).

(e) If the contract fails to express the undoubted intentions of the parties, the court will *rectify* it so as to make it express such intentions.

(f) Where a clause is ambiguous, it shall be most strongly construed against the party who inserted it. This is the *contraproferentem* rule—against him who puts forward. It is assumed that the party putting in a clause does so in full knowledge *of all faults*. It is particularly important where large firms have standardized printed forms of contract.

139. See State of Gujarat v. M/s. Variety Body Builders, 1976 S. C, 2108.

(g) Lastly, the *ejus dem generis* rule, under which general terms must be construed against the special terms referred to in the document. In simpler language, general terms which follow special terms are restricted in meaning to sub-groups of the special term. Thus, in "loss through flood, fire, earthquake, *or any other cause, however occasioned"*, the general terms (which are underlined) would be construed as of the same kind as "flood, fire, earthquake" and would not cover theft or piracy.

SUMMARY

A contract is an agreement enforceable by law. A contract will be enforceable at law where there is an intention to create legal obligation.

ESSENTIALS OF VALID CONTRACT

1. Proposal or offer and acceptance of that proposal or offer.
2. An intention to create legal relationship.
3. Free and real consent between the parties.
4. Each party capable of contracting.
5. Contract is for legal object.
6. There are two parties to it.
7. The agreement is supported by lawful consideration.

OFFER AND ACCEPTANCE

Every contract is the result of the acceptance of an offer or proposal.

An offer or proposal is made when, and not until, it is communicated to the other party.

The terms of an offer must be certain and not loose and vague.

An offer must be distinguished from a mere quotation or an invitation to offer.

An offer may be specific or general, but no contract can result until it has been accepted by an ascertained person.

An offer may lapse or be revoked before acceptance.

An offer lapses by rejection or by counter-proposal.

An offer lapses by the death of the offeror or the offeree.

Acceptance of an offer can be made by the person to whom the offer is made by giving absolute and unqualified assent in the mode prescribed by the terms of the offer.

An acceptance must be made before the offer lapses or is terminated.

Like an offer, an acceptance must be communicated.

An acceptance can be revoked before its communication.

Acceptance by post is communicated when the letter of acceptance has reached the offeror.

CONSIDERATION

A contract must be supported by a consideration, unless it is in writing and registered under the Registration Act, and made for natural love and affection between parties standing in near relation to each other, or is a promise to compensate for something done, or is a promise in writing to pay a debt barred by limitation law. Consideration is a technical term used in the sense *of quid pro quo* and must be either a benefit to the promisor or a detriment to the promise or both.

Consideration must move at the desire or request of the promisor, so that an act done at the desire of a third party is not a consideration.

In English law, consideration must move from the promisee. In Indian law, it may proceed from the promisee or any other person, with the result that in India a stranger to a consideration may maintain a suit.

A consideration may be

Executory or future, which means that it takes the form of a promise to be performed in the future, or

Executed or present, in which it is an act of forbearance made or suffered for promise, or

Past, which means a past act or forbearance, *i.e.,* one which is complete before the promise is made. In English law, as a rule, past consideration is no consideration; but in Indian law, past consideration is valid.

A consideration need not be adequate but it must be competent, real and not illusory, illegal, impossible, uncertain or ambiguous.

FLAWS IN CONTRACTS

A contract destitute of legal effect is void.

A void contract is a nullity and no right is acquired under or through it. It is bad *ab initio.*

A contract is voidable when it is enforceable at the option of one party and not at the option of the other. The party aggrieved may elect to be bound by the contract or repudiate it. When the injured party repudiates the contract it becomes void.

A contract is unlawful where the subject-matter is one forbidden by law.

CAPACITY OF PARTIES

In general, every person is presumed by law to be competent to contract, and any one claiming exemption from liability on the ground of incapacity to contract must strictly prove it. Incapacity to contract may arise out of (*a*) mental deficiency or (*b*) status. Minors, lunatics, idiots and drunken persons fall under (*a*) and Foreign Sovereigns; Ambassadors, alien enemies, professional people, corporations and married women under (*b*).

A minor's contract is absolutely void. He is not bound by it, nor can he ratify it on attaining the age of majority. It is void even where the minor misrepresented his age. The property of the minor is, however, liable for necessaries supplied to him according to his station in life provided he was in need of them at the time of sale and delivery. A contract for minor's benefit is valid.

Contracts by idiots and lunatics are void except for necessaries. A lunatic can make a valid contract during lucid intervals. Similarly, a contract by a drunken person does not bind him, but he can make a valid contract when he is sober.

An alien can make binding contracts in India, but on the declaration of war between his country and the Union of India he becomes an alien enemy, and cannot enter into a contract. Contracts made before the war are dissolved if they involve contract with the enemy or they are likely to help the enemy, or they are suspended during the war. Foreign Sovereigns and Ambassadors cannot be sued in our Courts but if they submit themselves to the jurisdiction of our Courts they will be treated as commoners.

A contract by the directors of a company made beyond the powers of the company as stated in the Memorandum of Association is *ultra vires* the company and thus not binding on it, nor can it be ratified at a general meeting of the shareholders.

A married woman can contract in respect of her private property.

FLAW IN CONSENT

Mistake of material fact on the part of both the parties renders the contract void. Mistake of law, however, is not excused.

Mistake of fact may be as to the nature of the transaction, identity of party and the subject-matter. Mistake as to subject-matter may relate to its existence, identity, title of the party, price, quantity or quality.

Misrepresentation is a mis-statement made innocently and with an honest belief as to its truth, and renders the contract voidable at the option of party misled by it.

Fraud or wilful misrepresentation is the representation either by words or conduct that something is true which is not so, so as to deceive another person, either intentionally or with reckless disregard as to the truth or falsehood of the words or conduct The party defrauded either by mis-statement or wilful concealment can avoid the contract and claim damages.

Coercion is doing of anything forbidden by the Indian Penal Code, and a contract made under coercion is voidable.

Undue influence—A contract is said to be induced by undue influence where the relations subsisting between the parties are such that one of the parties is in a position to dominate the will of the other and uses that position to obtain an unfair advantage over the other. A contract made under undue influence is voidable at the option of the party so influenced.

As a rule, undue influence will be presumed between parent and child, guardian and ward, trustee and beneficiary, solicitor and client, doctor and patient, *Guru* and disciple, *Malik* and cultivator.

Unlawful Agreements—An agreement may be unlawful because it is
(a) Illegal, *i.e.*, opposed to positive law, being forbidden either by statute law or common law.
(b) Immoral, *i.e.*, contrary to positive morality as recognised by law.
(c) Opposed to Public Policy, *i.e.*, contrary to the welfare of the State as tending to interfere with civil or judicial administration, or with individual liberty of citizens.
An agreement will not become a contract or will remain unenforceable if it is made for unlawful consideration and with unlawful objects.

VOID AND ILLEGAL CONTRACTS DISTINGUISHED

A void contract is one which has no legal effect. An illegal contract, like the void contract, has no legal effect as between the immediate parties, but has this further effect that transactions collateral to such a contract become tainted with illegality and therefore become unenforceable.

Wagering Contracts—In Bombay Presidency, wagering contracts are unlawful by Statute, and taint collateral transactions rendering them void. In the rest of India wagering contracts are only void, and thus collateral contracts are not affected.

What is a Wager—A wager is a promise to pay money or transfer property upon the happening of an uncertain event. Betting on the results of a horse race, a wrestling match, are examples.

Commercial transactions may amount to wagering contracts if both parties at the time of entering into contract have the intention not to give and take delivery of goods, but only to settle differences. *Teji Mandi* transactions or option dealings are good contracts. Agreements in respect of immoral purposes are not only void but illegal. A transaction collateral to an immoral contract knowingly entered into is equally unenforceable.

Agreements Opposed to Public Policy:—
(a) trade with Indian Union's enemies without the Union's licence is unlawful;
(b) agreements for stifling prosecution and for ousting jurisdiction of courts are unlawful;
(c) agreements curtailing or extending the period of limitation prescribed by law are not enforceable;
(d) agreements in fraud of insolvency law are illegal;
(e) agreements for using improper influence of any kind with judges or officers of justice are void;
(f) agreement in restraint of the marriage of any person other than a minor is void;
(g) agreements to procure marriages for reward are void;

(h) agreements to pay money to parent or guardian in consideration of giving his daughter in marriage is void. Similarly, a promise by the bride's parent to pay money to the bridegroom or his parent is illegal;

(i) traffic by way of sale in public offices and appointments or titles for monetary consideration is illegal;

(j) agreements tending to create monopolies are void;

(k) agreements in restraint of trade are void. Partial restraint is allowed in sale of goodwill.

(l) contracts unduly restraining individual liberty are unenforceable.

Quasi Contracts—In the Indian Contract Act such contracts are described as "certain relations resembling those created by contracts." In certain circumstances the law implies from the conduct of the parties a promise imposing an obligation on one party and conferring a right in favour of the other, although there is no offer or acceptance, no consent, and, in fact, no agreement or promise. The Contract Act deals with the following types *of Quasi contracts:*—

1. A person incapable of contracting is liable for necessaries supplied to him or on his behalf.
2. Suits for money had and received. A right to sue for recovery of money may arise—
   (a) where plaintiff paid money to the defendant;
      (i) by mistake of fact or of law
      (ii) in pursuance of a contract the consideration for which has failed, and
      (iii) under coercion, undue influence, fraud, etc.;
   (b) when plaintiff paid to third party money which another is to pay;
   (c) where defendant obtained money from third parties, *e.g.*, agent making secret profits.
3. *Quantum Meruit*—No claim can be made on an entire and indivisible contract until the entire work is done. Payment can be claimed under *quantum meruit* for part performance if the contract is divisible into parts so that payment for each part can be made.
4. A *finder of goods* lost by another must try to find the owner and must not appropriate the property to his own use. He can recover from the owner expenses incurred in protecting and preserving the property. Finding is not keeping, unless it is reasonably certain that the real owner cannot be found.
5. A person enjoying benefit of non-gratuitous act is under an obligation to compensate the other party.

Discharge of Contract—A contract terminates by—

Performance—Performance means the actual carrying out of all the terms of the contract Performance must be in accordance with the obligations under the contract. In a conditional contract, with condition precedent, performance becomes due only on the happening of the event, certain or uncertain; and with condition subsequent, performance ceases to be due on the happening of some event. Where one party has performed his obligation the other must perform his bargain. Where both promises are outstanding, the order of performance may be—

Mutual and Independent—Where each party must perform his promise independently and neither can say that he did not perform because the other failed to perform his promise.

Dependent—Performance of the one promise depends upon the prior performance of the other. Performance of one is condition precedent to performance of the other.

Mutual and Concurrent—Here the two acts are done at the same time. Promisee alone can demand performance, or if he has died before performance, his legal representative can demand it. Promisor must perform the promise and in case of his death, his legal representatives.

Assignment of Contracts—As a rule, an obligation under contract cannot be assigned. It can never be assigned when performance depends on the personal skill of the promisor. An actionable claim can always be assigned in writing.

Discharge by Tender—Where one party is ready and willing to perform his promise and has offered to do so at the right time and place, but the other party does not accept performance, the contract is discharged by tender or "attempted performance."

Discharge by Covenant or Agreement

Waiver of performance by the promisee or rescission by both will discharge the contract.

Release—Where one party agrees to excuse performance by the other after breach by the latter.

Novation—By agreement between parties that the performance may be carried* out by different parties. A fresh contract is substituted in place of the original one.

Discharge by Implied Consent or Impossibility of Performance—The law does not compel a man to do the impossible thing. Contract is discharged when performance becomes impossible—

  (i) due to destruction of the subject-matter,
 (ii) due to death or incapacity of the promisor in a contract for personal services;
(iii) due to subsequent change of legislation;
(iv) due to non-existence or cessation of a state of affairs the existence or continuance of which formed the basis of the contract;
 (v) due to such an alteration of circumstances as to bring about complete frustration of commercial object.

Discharge by Lapse of Time—Contract is discharged if the suit is not brought by the injured party within the time permitted by the Limitation Act, for breach of promise. For example, if, on the debtor failing to pay a loan on the stipulated date, the creditor does not file a suit within 3 years of the default, the contract is discharged and the creditor is barred from his remedy.

Discharge by Operation or Law may take place—

By Merger, where the parties embody the inferior contract in a superior contract. The lower security merges in the higher security.

By the unauthorised alteration of terms of a written document— Where a material alteration is made by one party the other can avoid the contract.

By insolvency—Where an insolvent is discharged by the Court he is exonerated or discharged from liability on all debts incurred before adjudication.

Discharge by breach—Breach of contract may be Actual or Constructive or Anticipatory.

Actual breach may take place—

(a) **At the time when performance is due,** in which case the other party can sue the defaulter for breach of contract. If party, failing to perform at the appointed time, subsequently expresses willingness to perform, he can do so if time is not of the essence after paying compensation. In mercantile contract time is of the essence.

(b) **During performance of the Contract**—Where a party apparently performs the promise, but the other party says it is not a proper performance, then the other party is exonerated from performance of his part of the bargain, if the breach is of a condition vital to contract.

Constructive or Anticipatory Breach, *i.e.*, breach before performance is due, may take place—
(a) by the promisor doing an act which makes the performance impossible,
(b) by the promisor in some other way showing his intention not to perform his promise.

The promisee may, if he likes, elect the breach as equivalent to actual breach and sue the defaulter, or he may wait till the time of actual performance. In the second case the promisee keeps the contract alive for the benefit of promisor and his own. He remains liable under it, and enables the promisor to perform in spite of previous repudiation and also to avail himself of any excuse for non-performance which may come into existence before time for performance.

Remedies for Breach of Contract:—

Damages— Breach of contract entitles the injured party to file a suit for damages. Damages are the money awarded to a person who has a right to sue for breach of contract.

General or Ordinary Damages will be awarded if actual loss has been suffered from the proximate consequences of the breach. The amount awarded will be compensation to the plaintiff for loss sustained and not punishment of the defendant.

Special Damages are those which result from a breach of contract under some special circumstances. If special loss is likely to be sustained as a result of the breach, this should be communicated to the other party; otherwise special damages will not be awarded.

Exemplary Damages are the exceptions to the rule that damages are not to be in the nature of punishment, but only compensation for the loss sustained.

Exemplary damages will be awarded:—

(a) In suit for breach of promise of marriage, and the amount will depend upon the extent of injury to the lady's feeling;

(b) In suit against bank for wrongfully dishonouring customer's cheque.

The customer, though he has sustained no pecuniary damage, may recover substantial damages for injury to his credit.

Nominal Damages consist of a very small amount of money, *e.g.*, a rupee. Nominal damages are awarded where the plaintiff has proved a breach of contract but has suffered no real damage. Nominal damages are awarded to establish right to decree or to vindicate plaintiff's honour.

Specific Performance— Where for the breach of a contract damages are inadequate remedy, the party at fault may, at the discretion of the Court, be ordered to perform the contract in specie. But specific performance will not be granted—

(a) to enforce a contract for personal service;

(b) in cases where Court cannot supervise performance of contract;

(c) where damages are adequate remedy;

(d) contract contains ambiguous terms;

(e) contract by its nature is revocable;

(f) contract by or on behalf of public company in excess of its power,

(g) contract which can be performed in more than three years;

(h) where subject-matter or major part of such subject-matter of contract has, unknown to both parties, ceased to exist before contract is made.

Injunction— This is another discretionary remedy granted to secure specific performance of negative terms of the contract. Injunction restrains a person from doing or continuing to do something which amounted to breach of contract.

CASES FOR RECAPITULATION

1. An auctioneer advertised in the newspapers that a sale of office furniture would be held at Connaught Circus, New Delhi. A broker with a commission to buy office furniture came down from Bombay to attend the sale, but all the furniture was withdrawn. The broker thereupon sued the auctioneer for his loss of time and expenses. It was *held* that a declaration of the intention to hold auction did not create a binding contract with those who acted upon it; it was only an invitation to offer and so the broker could not recover *(Harris* v. *Nickerson* (1873) L.R. 8 Q.B. 286].

2. An actress was engaged for a provincial tour. The agreement also provided that if the piece came to Delhi she would be engaged at a salary "to be mutually arranged between *us.*" *Held,* no contract. The parties had not agreed on the terms of the contract but had made an agreement to agree in the future *[Loftus* v. *Roberts* (1902) 18 L. T. R. 532].

3. *B* ordered some machinery from J. & Co. Before the company had taken any action on the order, it received a letter from *B* cancelling the order. The company refused to recognise the cancellation and sued *B* for the purchase price. *Held,* B is not liable. An order is merely an offer which must be accepted by the seller before there is a binding contract. Before acceptance the offeror may remove his order (*Owens Co.* v. *Bemis, 22* N.D. 159).

4. On June, 1, 1968, A advertised in a newspaper that he would pay ₹ 100 to any one who would find his lost dog before July 1, 1968. On June 10, *A* advertised in the same newspaper that he had cancelled his offer of June 1. On 15th June, B, who had read the first advertisement, but not the second one, found the lost dog and claimed ₹ 100 from *A*. *Held, B* could not recover, as the offer had been revoked before it was accepted. The revocation was given the same publicity as was the offer of the reward and it did not matter that *B* had not read the second notice cancelling the offer (*Shuey* v. *US* Govt.92 U.S. 73).

5. The defendants advertised in their paper that their city editor would be glad to advise the readers of the paper with reference to investments. The plaintiff wrote for advice and asked for the name of a good stock-broker. The editor recommended a broker who was an undischarged bankrupt, though this fact was not known to the editor. Relying on the recommendation, the plaintiff sent sums of money to the broker for investment and the broker misappropriated them. *Held,* the plaintiff is entitled to recover from the defendants,. The price paid by him for the paper he bought was good consideration and hence there was a contract between him and the defendants [*De la. Bere.* v. *Pearson* (1908) 1 K.B.-280].

6. *M* lost a sum of ₹8,500 to L. & Co. on bets on horse races and on his failure to pay was reported to the Royal Calcutta Turf Club. M subsequently executed in favour of L. & Co. a hundi for ₹ 8,500 in consideration of their withdrawing his name from the Club and thereby preventing his being posted as a defaulter. When L. & Co. demanded payment *M* pleaded that the consideration was unlawful. *Held, M* was liable to pay as the consideration in the shape of L & Co.'s promise to withdraw *M*'s name from the club in order to prevent *M* being posted as a defaulter was legal. A wagering contract is only void and so does not affect the collateral transaction (*Leicester & Co.,* v. *S. P. Mullick,* 1923 Cal. 445).

7. During a strike by the workers in a coal, mine, the police authorities thought it enough to provide a mobile force for the protection of the mine. The colliery manager wanted a stationary guard. It was ultimately agreed to provide the latter at a rate of payment by the company owning the colliery, which involved a sum of £2,200. Subsequently, the company refused liability to pay, pleading absence of consideration. *Held,* that the promise to pay the amount was not without consideration and the company was liable to pay. It was said that the police, no doubt, were bound to accord protection, but they had a discretion as to the form it should take. The undertaking to provide more protection than what they deemed to be necessary was a consideration for the promise to pay the amount [*Glassbrook Bros.* v. *Glamorgan Country Council* (1925) A.C. 270].

8. A minor falsely representing himself to be of age, enters into an agreement to sell his property to *R* and receives from him as price a sum of ₹ 10,000 in advance. Out of this sum the minor purchases a car for ₹ 6,000 and spends the rest on a pleasure trip. After the minor has attained majority, R sues him for the conveyance of the property or in the alternative, for the refund of ₹ 10,000 and damages. *Held,* R cannot succeed in his suit for conveyance of property or refund of the amount. A minor's contract is void and he is not liable under it. Since he falsely misrepresented himself to be of full age the court may, in its discretion, order him to hand over the car to *R* [*R. Leslie Ltd.* v. *Shell* (1914) 3K.B.607].

9. *E*, who was on the staff of a foreign, embassy, was a tenant of *M*'s house. *M* sued him for arrears of rent. *Held,* whether *E* owed the rent or not, no action could be brought against him, as he was protected by diplomatic privilege [*Engelke* v. *Musman* (1928) A.C. 433].

10. The defendants had commenced a periodical publication, called the *Juvenile Library,* and had engaged the plaintiff to write a volume on ancient armour for it. For this he was to receive the sum of £100 on completion. When he had completed part of his volume, the defendants abandoned the publication. The plaintiff sued the defendants for recovery of the amount contracted alternatively by way of (*i*) damages, or (*ii*) a *quantum meruit. Held,* that the plaintiff is entitled to get damages for breach of contract and payment on *quantum meruit* [*Planche* v. *Colburn* (1831) 8 Bing 14].

11. *A,* a Madras doctor, employed another doctor *B,* as an assistant for a period of three years on a salary of ₹ 1,000 per mensem. The agreement between *A* and *B* provided that after the termination of his employment *B* should not practise as a doctor in Madras within a radius of one mile of his dispensary for a period of one year, and if *B* did'so, *B* should pay ₹ 10,000 to *A* as 'liquidated damages.' Immediately after the termination of his employment *B* begins to practise as a doctor next door to *A*'s dispensary. *A* sued *B* for the recovery of ₹ 10,000. *Held, A* could not recover, as the contract was altogether void being in restraint of trade. In Indian Law, a restraint, whether general or partial, qualified or unqualified, is void if it is in the nature of a restraint of trade [*Oakes & Co.* v. *Jackson* (1872) 1 Mad. 134].

12. *A* and *B* were joint proprietors of a hotel. Water connection to the hotel had been taken from the Municipal Board in the name of *A.* Subsequently *B* made an application to the Board for recording his name as tenant jointly with *A* in respect of water rates payable by the hotel. The Board refused to do so, as *B* would not give an undertaking to fulfil certain conditions proposed by the Board. Later on the Board filed a suit for recovery of arrears of water rates against *A* as the promisor and *B* as the beneficiary under the contract *Held, B* is not liable to pay as a beneficiary under the contract, as the Board had refused to recognise *B* as a tenant. The acceptance and enjoyment of the thing delivered or done, which is the basis for the claim under Section 70 of the Contract Act, must be voluntary. In this case the services were rendered against the will of *B* for whose use they were supposed to have been rendered and hence the Board could not recover under Section 70. Also, there was no privity of contract between *B* and the Board [*Jaygopal* v. *J.W.W. Committee.* (1964) Orissa 69].

13. In May. 1936, a building lease was made to the lessees for a term of 99 years. Before any buildings had been erected the war of 1939 broke out and restrictions were imposed by the Government on the supply of building materials. As a result, the lessees were unable to carry out any building on the land covenanted in the lease. In an action against them for the recovery of the rent the lessees pleaded that the lease was frustrated. *Held,* by the House of Lords that the doctrine of frustration, even if it were capable of application to a lease, did not apply in the instant circumstances. The compulsory suspension of building did not strike at the root of the transaction, for when it was imposed the lease still had more than 99 years to run, and therefore, the interruption in the performance was likely to last only for a small fraction of the term [*Cricklewood Property & Investment Trust Ltd.* v. *Leighton's Investment Trust Ltd.* (1945) A.C. 221].

14. *S* entered into a contract with *K* in July, 1952 for the sale of 200 tons of scrap iron at the controlled price of ₹ 70 per ton plus incidental charges. Subsequently in January, 1953, when the controlled price was the same as in July, 1952, *K* agreed to supply the scrap iron to *E* for export. *S,* who had no knowledge of this subsequent contract, failed to supply the scrap and, as a result, *K* could not comply with his contract with *E,* who purchased the necessary scrap iron from the open market and obtained from K ₹ 20,700 being the difference between the contract price and the market price. *K* sues *S* for the recovery of ₹ 20,700 as damages for breach of contract *Held,* by the Supreme Court that *K* was not entitled to claim damages from *S* at an amount equal to difference between the price paid by his vendee, *E* and the price he would have paid to *S* for 200 tons of scrap iron, as he had not entered into the contract with *S* after informing *S* that he was buying for further sale. In fact, he was not entitled to claim any damages, as the price was the same at all times, and if the third party had bought from the uncontrolled sources and paid more, it was not his responsibility (*Karsan Das* v. *Saran Engineering Co.* 1965 S.C. 1981).

15. *L* had entered into an agreement with two of his employees whereby he promised to pay, and did in fact pay, considerable sums to them in compensation for the premature termination of their contracts of service. This payment, however, was strictly unnecessary, for during their employment the two men had been guilty of certain breaches of duty which would have entitled *L* to dismiss them immediately. When *L* discovered this fact, he claimed to avoid the contract and recover the money paid on the ground, *inter alia,* that the employees were bound to disclose to him those breaches of duty. The House of Lords held that *L* could not avoid the contract and recover back the money paid to the two employees, as they were not bound to disclose to him the breaches of duty. Lord Atkin observed: "It is a contract of service which does not fall within the category of contracts *uberrimae fidei* which require disclosure" [*Bell* v. *Lever Bros. Ltd.* (1962) A.C. 161].

16. *X* offered to buy a car from *Y* and to pay by cheque. *Y* refused the offer and the cheque, as she did not know him. *X* then convinced her that he was a well-known person, and being convinced, she accepted his cheque and let him take the car. He sold the car to L and the cheque proved worthless. *Y* filed a suit to recover the car from L. *Held, Y* could recover the car from *L.* The contract between *X* and *Y* was void for mistake, since the mistake occurred during the negotiations and *Y* would not have accepted *X*'s offer if she had not been convinced of his identity. *X* had no title to the car and could give none to *L* (*Ingram* v. *Little* (1861) 1 Q.B. 31).

17. A letter accepting an offer of employment was followed by a further letter withdrawing the acceptance. Both letters were received by the offeror by the same post. *Held,* the acceptance was validly revoked. (*Dunmore* (*Coutess*) v. *Alexander* (1830) 9 Sh. 190).

18. *A* minor purchased certain property from *B,* and sued for possession, *Held,* if the minor has performed his obligations, he is allowed to enforce the obligations against the other party. He was given a decree for possession of the property purchased by him. (*Collector of Meerut* v. *Hardian.* 1945 All. 156).

19. *A*'s suit against *B* for possession of premises and arrears of rent was decreed and in execution *A* obtained an order for attachment of moveables of *B.* Then, in consideration of *B* agreeing not to appeal against the decree. *A* allowed him one month's time to pay the balance of the decretal amount and vacate the premises. *Held,* the undertaking not to appeal against the decree was lawful consideration and the agreement was valid (*Gousmohoddin Gajabur Salteb Bhagwan* v. *Appa Saheb,* 1976 *Karnatak* 90).

20. *A* supplied goods to *B* pursuant to an agreement for the sale of goods entered into between the parties in the black market and the consideration for the promise to supply the goods was to consist of unaccounted funds popularly known as the "black money". It was held that the contract, which is *ex facie* innocuous, could not be said to be tainted with illegality under Sec. 23 of the Contract Act. Sec. 23 makes a contract unlawful of which the consideration or the object is contrary to public policy. The consideration in the instant case could not be said to be contrary to public policy because the corresponding considerations are the payment of money and the delivery of goods. The object of the contract is also not opposed to public policy because the object of the contract was not to consume or generate unaccounted funds or to defraud the revenues. The object obviously was to do business—so far as the seller is concerned, to sell the goods and so far as the buyer is concerned, to buy the goods for further sale-and in the process to make income (*M/s Anand Prakash Om Prakash* v. *M/s Oswal Trading Agency,* 1976 Delhi 74).

21. A firm paid sales tax of more than ₹ 26,000 in respect of sales to consumers outside the State of Bombay and which were, therefore, not liable to any sales tax. The firm had itself collected the tax money from its customers. The amount was ordered to be refunded as the sales tax was paid under a mistake of law (*Trilokchand Motichand* v. *Commr of Sales Tax,* 1970 SC898).

CHAPTER 2

Contracts of Indemnity and Guarantee

The Indian Contract Act (Section 124) defines a contract of Indemnity as "a contract by which one party promises to save the other from·loss caused to him by the conduct of the promisor himself, or by the conduct of any other person". The person who promises or undertakes to indemnify or make good the loss is called indemnifier and the promisee or whose loss is made good is called the indemnified. Where *A* contracts to indemnify *B* against the consequences of any proceedings which *C* may take against *B* in respect of a certain sum of ₹ 200, there is a contract of indemnity. If *B* is ordered to pay to *C* ₹ 200 and costs of suit, *A* shall be required to pay *B* the total amount.[1]

Now, according to the above definition the loss to be made good must be caused either by the conduct of the promisor himself or by the conduct of any other person, and, so if loss is caused by accident or by the conduct of the promisee, it would not apparently amount to a contract of indemnity. If this strict view were accepted the contracts of insurance might have to be excluded. It may be submitted that such a strict application of the definition so as to have excluded contracts of insurance and certain other relations was not intended by the Legislature. The Indian Courts have, therefore, applied the English equitable principles to indemnity for as was stated in a Bombay case by Chagla, J., "...I have already held that Secs. 124, 125, Contract Act, are not exhaustive of the law of indemnity and that the Courts here would apply the same equitable principles that the Courts in England do...."

In English law, a contract of indemnity has been defined as "a promise to save another harmless from loss caused as a result of a transaction entered into at the instance of the promisor." It includes the loss caused by events or accidents which may not or do not depend upon the conduct of any person, or by liability arising from something done by the promisee at the request of the promisor. The English definition is more happily worded and the English law in respect of indemnity has been followed by Indian Courts.

A contract of indemnity may either be express or implied, and the latter may be inferred from the circumstances of a particular case, *e.g.*, acts done by *A* at the request of *B*, or money paid by *A* under compulsion of law in respect of liability imposed on B, or may be based on the obligation caused by the relationship of the parties, *e.g.*, (the obligation of a beneficiary to indemnify his trustee, the relation between auctioneer and client, principal and agent). The promisee (indemnified) in a contract of indemnity, can recover from the promisor (indemnifier) all the damages that he may sustain, and if there has been any suit against the promisee, any cost therein, and any amounts *bonafide* paid in respect of any compromise, provided the promisee had acted as a prudent man and there has been no express direction by the promisor not to compromise (Section 125).

---

1. Gajnan Moreshwar v. Moreshwar, Madan, 1942 Bom. 302.

Since the Contract Act has not stated the time of the commencement of the indemnifier's liability to indemnify and the word "loss" has been used in Section 124, doubt has arisen as to the commencement of the promisor's liability. The High Courts of Lahore,[2] Nagpur,[3] and Bombay[4] have held that the indemnifier does not become liable until the indemnified has incurred an actual loss. But the High Courts of Calcutta,[5] Madras,[6] Allahabad,[7] and Bombay (not following the earlier decision)[8], have decided that the promisee (indemnified) may compel the indemnifier to place him in a position to meet liability that may be cast upon him, without waiting until the promisee (indemnity-holder) has actually discharged it.

It is submitted that the latter view is more correct. We may quote with profit the observation of Chagla, J. in the Bombay case. The learned Judge says: "It is true that under the English Common Law no action could be maintained until actual loss has been incurred. It was very soon realized that an indemnity might be worth very little indeed if the indemnified could not enforce his indemnity till he had actually paid the loss. If a suit was filed against him, he had actually to wait till a judgment was pronounced and it was only after he had satisfied the judgment that he could sue on his indemnity. It is clear that this might under certain circumstances throw an intolerable burden upon the indemnity-holder. He might be in a position to satisfy the judgment and yet he could not avail himself of his indemnity till he had done so. Therefore, the Court of Equity stepped in and mitigated the rigour of the Common Law. The Court of Equity held that if his liability had become absolute then he was entitled either to get the indemnifier to pay off the claim or to pay into Court sufficient money which would constitute a fund for paying off the claim whenever it was made. Sections 124 and 125 Contract Act, are not exhaustive of the law of indemnity and the Courts here would apply the same equitable principles that the Courts in England do. Therefore, if the indemnified had incurred a liability and that liability is absolute, he is entitled to call upon the indemnifier to save him from that liability and pay it off." In *Osman Jamal & Sons* v. *Gopal,*[9] the plaintiff company before having actually made any payment to the vendor in respect of its liability to him was held entitled to recover from the indemnifier under contract of indemnity. "Indemnity is not necessarily given by repayment after payment. Indemnity requires that the party to be indemnified shall never be called upon to pay."

A contract of indemnity, being a species of contract, is subject to all the rules of contract, such as, genuine consent, legality of object, etc., and an indemnity procured by fraud will not be enforced, or where *A* asks *B* to beat *C*, promising to indemnify *B* against the consequences and *B* beats *C* and is fined ₹ 500, *B* cannot recover the amount from A.

PART 2-B
CONTRACT OF GUARANTEE

A person who seeks to borrow money or to undertake some other obligation may be required to pledge some property with the creditor as security. But the creditor may be willing to lend money to a person if he can get some other person to assume personal liability as security for the payment of the

---

2. Sham Sunder v. Chandra Lal 1935 Lah. 974.
3. Ranganath v. Pachusoo 1935 Nag. 147.
4. Sanker Nimbaqi *v.* Lazman Napu 1940 Bom.161.
5. Kamnannath Bhattacharjee v. Nohokumar (1899) 26 Cal. 241.
6. Ramadigalhudayar v. Munamdai Achi (1915) 38 Mad. 791; 251.C 835.
7. Shiamlal v. Abdul Salal 1931 All. 754; Abdul Majid v. Abdul Rashid 1936, All.598.
8. Gajnan Mureshwarv. Mureshwar Madan 1942 Bom. 302.
9. (1919) 56 CaL. 262; Profulla v. Gopee 1946 CaL 159.

loan or for the performance of the promised acts. In this case the creditor gives a loan to the debtor on the combined financial standing of the debtor and some third person, called the surety.

Section 126 of the Contract Act defines a contract of guarantee as: " A contract to perform the promise, or discharge the liability of a third person in case of his default. The person who gives the guarantee is called the 'Surety', the person for whom the guarantee is given is called 'Principal Debtor', and the person to whom the guarantee is given is called 'Creditor.' "In India a guarantee may be either oral or written, although in English law it must be evidenced in writing.

Suretyship is the lending of credit to aid a principal debtor who has not sufficient credit of his own. It follows that in a contract of guarantee there must be three parties, viz., the creditor, the principal debtor and the surety, the debtor being primarily liable to discharge his debt or perform his promise and the surety being secondarily liable.

When A requests B to lend ₹ 5,000 to C and guarantees that C will repay the amount within a stated time, and on C's failing to pay he will himself pay to B, there is a contract of guarantee.

It will be noticed that in a contract of guarantee there are three separate contracts giving rise to a triangular relationship. These are: (i) between the creditor and the debtor, creating the debt; (ii) between the surety and the creditor, creating a liability of surety in case of debtor's default, and (iii) an implied contract between the surety and the debtor that the debtor will indemnify the surety after the latter has paid the creditor on the debtor's default. A guarantee may be given not only in case of a debt, but also where a party wants to buy goods on credit, and for the good conduct of another person. The English definition brings out this more clearly, which says: "A guarantee is a promise made by one person to another to be collaterally answerable for the debt, default or miscarriage of a third person." To constitute a guarantee, however, it is not necessary that the surety must undertake to be personally liable for the default of the principal debtor, it would be sufficient if a person deposits documents of his property by way of security with the creditor.[10]

Fiduciary Relationship.—A contract of guarantee is not, as is the contract of insurance, a *contract uberrimaefidei,* so that neither the creditor nor the principal debtor is under any legal duty to disclose to the guarantor facts which might influence him against entering into the contract. Thus, if A offers to guarantee B's bank account the bank is under no obligation to reveal matters which show that B is a bad risk.[11] But active misrepresentation by the creditor (or the debtor with the creditor's knowledge) will be grounds for rescission. Active concealment will amount to misrepresentation. However, once the contract is made, the creditor owes a duty of the utmost good faith to the guarantor, who is entitled to be discharged if this duty is not observed. Thus the creditor must disclose material facts coming to his knowledge and affecting the surety's risk, but need not disclose *mere suspicions, e.g.,* A guaranteed B's bank account, and B overdrew on the guaranteed account to pay off debts to another creditor.. The bank suspected that A was being defrauded, but did not disclose this. *Held,* the banker was under no duty to do so [*Provincial Bank v. Glanusk* (1913)].

Guarantees in the nature of insurance are *uberrimae fidel e.g.,* "fidelity guarantee" of the conduct and good faith of some third person. In such a guarantee the creditor (e.g., the employer must disclose the material facts about the principal debtor (i.e., the employee), otherwise the surety will be discharged. Thus A gave a fidelity guarantee in respect of L to L's employer, B. B omitted to disclose that L had misappropriated some of B's money and was only being retained in employment in reliance on A's guarantee bond. *Held,* L's former dishonesty should have been disclosed, and A was not liable on his

10. Jagjivandas v. King Kami ton & Co. (1931) 55 Bom. 677:1931 Bom. 337; Re Couley (1938) 2 All E.R. 127.
11. Wythes v. Labouchere (1859)

guarantee.[12] In other kinds of guarantee, the rule is that the creditor need not offer information if the surety has equal opportunity to discover facts about the principal debtor.

DISTINCTION BETWEEN INDEMNITY AND GUARANTEE

(1) In indemnity a promisor is primarily and independently liable to the promisee, and, therefore, there are only two parties. In a guarantee, the liability of .the surety is collateral or secondary, the primary liability being that of the principal debtor; and, hence, here the concurrence of three persons is essential.

(2) In the case of a contract of indemnity it is not necessary for the indemnifier to act at the request of the debtor, whereas in the case of a contract of guarantee it is necessary that the surety should give the guarantee at the request of the debtor.[13]

(3) In the case of guarantee there is an existing debt or duty, the performance of which is guaranteed by the surety, while in the case of indemnity, the possibility or risk of any loss happening is the only contingency against which the indemnifier undertakes to indemnify.[14]

(4) In a contract of guarantee, where the surety discharges the debt payable by the principal debtor to the creditor, the surety, on such payment, is entitled in law to proceed against the principal debtor in his own right, while in the case of indemnity,- the indemnifier cannot sue third parties in his own name, unless there be assignment. He must bring the suit in the name of the indemnified.[15]

(5) The person giving indemnity has some interest in the transaction apart from his indemnity, while the guarantor is totally unconnected with the contract except by means of his promise to pay on debtor's default. In fact, the guarantor must not have any financial interest in the contract.

(6) Rights of indemnity may arise out of express or implied contracts or out of obligations imposed by law, *e.g.*, as between principal and agent, or as between master and servant. The liability of the surety arises only out of contract between him and the creditor. The surety undertakes an obligation at the express or implied request of the principal debtor (*P.N. Bank v. Sri Bikrani Cotton Mills,* 1970 S.C. 1973).

(7) In English law, a contract of guarantee to be actionable, must be evidenced by a memorandum or note as required by section 4 of the Statute of Frauds while a contract of indemnity need not be in writing and an oral promise will be enforceable. But this distinction does not prevail in India, as both the contracts of indemnity as well as guarantee are valid whether they are written or oral.

Like a contract of indemnity, a guarantee must also satisfy all the essential elements of a general contract. There is, however, a special feature to be noted with reference to consideration in a contract of guarantee; the consideration received by the principal debtor is sufficient for the surety. The detriment suffered by *A* lending money to or dealing with *B* at *C*'s request is a sufficient consideration for *C*'s promise to stand surety (Section 127).

Surety and minor debtor. In *Kashiba* v. *Sripat,*[16] the Bombay High Court held that where the principal debtor is a minor and so is not liable, the surety is liable. It was observed that the contract

---

12. London General Omnibus Co. v. Holloway (1912)

13. Brahmayya v. Srinivasan, 1959 Mad. 122.

14. Guild v. Cinrad (1894) 2 Q.B. 885.

15. Periamramnia Marakkayar v. Banias & Co. (1926) 49 Mad. 156: 1926 Mad. 445; Vyavan Chettiar v. Official Assignee (1932) 55 Mad. 949; 139 I.C. 562.

16. Kashiba v. Shripat (1894) 9 Bom. 1697; Sohan Lal v. Puran Singh 1916 Punj. Rec. No. 54, 165; Tikki Lal v. Kanial Chand (1940) Nag. 1632, 1940 Nag. 327; But see Coutts & Co. v. Brown. Lecky (1947) K.B. 104.

between the surety and the creditor is not collateral but independent and the surety is held liable as principal debtor. Later decisions of the Bombay High Court and a recent decision of the Madras High Court have taken the contrary view and the surety is held not liable. In *E.K Nambiar v. M.K. Raman,* 1957 Mad. 164, Rajgopala Ayyangar, *J.* observed: ".... the liability of the surety is only ancillary and can rest only on a valid obligation on the part of the party whose debt or obligation is guaranteed." "As the obligation of a surety is an obligation accessory to that of the principal debtor, it follows that it is of the essence of the obligation that there should be a valid obligation of a principal debtor; consequently if the principal debtor is not obliged, neither is the surety as there can be no accessory obligation without a principal obligation". (Pothier). In the words of Chitty: "In the case of guarantee as distinguished from indemnity, the *sine qua non* is the existence of the liability of the principal debtor. So the surety is not liable if the debt of the principal debtor (minor) is itself void". Hence a surety for a minor debtor is not liable, as a minor cannot be regarded in default. But a discharge of the principal debtor by operation of law does not discharge the surety.[17]

NATURE OF SURETY'S LIABILITY

The liability of a surety is variously described as secondary, accessory or contingent, in the sense that **the surety is liable only on default of the principal debtor.** So, unless the principal debtor has made a default, the surety cannot be called upon to pay, and where the surety becomes insolvent before default by the principal debtor, the creditor cannot prove against surety's assignee in insolvency. But the moment the principal debtor defaults in the payment or where the guarantee was for the conduct of a party and, there is some breach of duty by the party causing damage to the holder of the guarantee, then, immediately, the surety becomes liable, as if he were the principal debtor. It is obvious that the surety has no right to ask the creditor to exhaust his remedy against the principal debtor nor can he demand a notice from the creditor, that the principal debtor has defaulted, for according to law it is the surety's duty to see that the principal debtor pays or performs his obligation.[18] Therefore, **as soon as the time for payment has come and the principal debtor does not or is unable to pay the surety becomes liable to pay.** Thus, the creditor may file a suit against the surety without suing the principal debtor.[19] A suit may also be maintained against the surety for the full amount of the debt where the principal debtor has been adjudged insolvent or has gone into liquidation.[20] Again, where a creditor holds securities from the principal debtor for his debt, the creditor need not first resort to these securities before suing the surety. Of course, a contract may specially provide that the creditor must exhaust his remedies against the principal debtor, or give notice of default or proceed against the securities. And, since the surety is liable only for the guaranteed debt, if the sum or part of the sum has been paid by the principal debtor, the surety cannot be liable for more than the amount remaining unpaid.

Similarly, the surety will not be liable for the cost of fruitless action against the debtor, unless the creditor has given previous notice of his intention to sue. But apart from agreement, the surety will be liable for interest, he is liable for all that the principal debtor would be liable for. Hence, once the liability of the surety arises, it is co-extensive with that of the principal debtor. It will be neither more nor less, although by a special contract it may be made less than the principal debtor's but never greater (Section 128). The law does not treat the principal debtor and surety as one person; therefore,

---

17. Subramanian v. Patchu Rowthar (1914) Mad. 45.
18. Bank of Bihar v. Damodar Prasad, 1969 SC 297.
19. Sankana v. Virupokahapa (1883) 7 Bom. 146; Inayatullah v. Rani 1886 All. W.N. 306; Depat Datt Chaudhri v. Secretary of State 1929 Lah. 393.
20. Jagannath v. Shivanarayan (1940) Bom. 387:1940 Bom. 247.

any admission by the principal debtor or a judgment obtained against the principal debtor will not be enforceable against the surety, without a special agreement to that effect.[21] Similarly any acknowledgment or part payment made by the principal debtor with a view to saving limitation will not be binding upon the surety. Further, it is not open to the creditor to call upon the surety to pay under the contract of guarantee unless the creditor has performed his part of the contract.[22] For this reason the surety is sometimes called a "Favoured debtor." "A surety is undoubtedly and not unjustly, an object of some favour both at law and at equity" (Lord Selborne)

KINDS OF GUARANTEE

A contract of guarantee may be for an existing debt, called "Retrospective" guarantee, or for a future debt termed as "Prospective" guarantee. It may, again, be a "Specific" guarantee, when it is given for a single debt, and comes to an end when the debt guaranteed has been paid, or a' 'Continuing" guarantee, when it extends to a series, of distinct and separable transactions. It is a continuing guarantee where A, in consideration of B.'s discounting, at A's request, bills of exchange of C, guarantees to B, for 12 months, the due payment of all such bills to the extent of ₹ 10,000, or A becomes answerable to C for B's purchases from C for 6 months to the extent of ₹ 1,000. A continuing guarantee can be revoked by the surety as to future transactions, by notice to the creditor; but the surety remains liable for all transactions, previous to the notice of revocation. So, if during the three months B has discounted bills for C to the extent of ₹ 2,000, and A revokes the guarantee, then A will be discharged of all liability to B for any subsequent discount But A is liable to B for ₹ 2,000 on default of C. When a guarantee is continuing it is not exhausted by the first advance or credit up to the pecuniary limit. A guarantees B's overdraft up to ₹ 1,000. If B overdraws up to ₹ 1,000 and then reduces his overdrafts to ₹ 500 and subsequently increases it to ₹ 1,000 again, A is still liable if his guarantee is a continuing one. A guarantee given for an entire consideration, is not continuing and cannot be revoked during the continuation of the consideration, unless a material change occurs in the situation, such as miscarriage of the person whose fidelity is guaranteed. So, a guarantee of the fidelity of a person appointed to a place of trust, e.g., in a bank, is not a continuing guarantee.[23] Nor is a guarantee for the payment by instalments of a certain sum within a definite time.[24]

Again, the guarantee may be for an ascertained debt, e.g., for a loan of ₹ 5,000, or in respect of a floating balance, e.g., a trade debt with a running balance of account not exceeding ₹ 5,000. Further the guarantee may be for the whole amount or for a limited amount. Difficult questions, however, arise in the case of a guarantee for a limited amount, for an important distinction exists as to guarantee limited in amount. A surety may guarantee only a part of the whole debt or he may guarantee the whole debt subject to a limit. For instance, where B owes A ₹ 5,000 and C has stood surety for ₹ 3,000 the question may arise whether C has guaranteed ₹ 3,000 out of ₹ 5,000 subject to a limit of ₹ 3,000. This matter becomes important when B is adjudged insolvent and A wants to prove in B's insolvency and also enforce the liability against C. If C has stood surety only for a part of the debt and if B's estate can pay only 25 Paise dividend in the rupee, then A can get ₹ 3,000, the full guaranteed amount from C and ₹ 500 from B's estate being one-fourth of the balance of ₹ 2,000, which was not guaranteed. Since after paying ₹ 3,000 to A, C can step into his shoes and claim from B's estate, C

21. Exparte Young (1181) 17 Ch. D. 688: Shree Menakshi Mills v. Ratilal Tribnavindas (1941) Bom. 273:1941 Bom. 108. See also 1950 Mad. 79, and 1951 Mad. 48 (F.B.).
22. KaProbodh Kumar v. Gillanders & Co. 1934 Cal. 699; Pratapsingh v. Keshavlal 1935 P.C. 12; Necresalinghum v. Subhoraduda 1939 Mad. 932 and also 1939 Mad. 152.
23. KaSen v. Bank of Bengal (1929) 47 I.A. 164; 58 I.C.I.
24. KaBhagwandas v. Secretary of State 1924 Bom. 465; 961.C. 248.
25. Gray v. Seckhan (1872) Ch. Ap. 690; Philips v. Mitchell (1930) 57 Cal. 764; 1930 Cal. 17.

will get from B's estate ₹ 750, being one-fourth of ₹ 3,000 paid by C to A.[25] If, on the contrary, C has stood surety for the whole debt of ₹ 5,000 subject to a limit of ₹ 3,000, then A can recover from C ₹ 3,000 and from B's estate 25 Paise dividend on the entire amount of ₹ 5,000 i.e., ₹ 1,250, and C will not be entitled to get any dividend, unless A has been fully paid and this can happen only if B's estate declares higher dividend, say 50 Paise in the rupee. For, in that case, B's estate will pay ₹ 2,500 and then C can get half of this amount

Where there is a floating or running balance of account and the guarantee is only of a portion thereof such a contract applies *prima facie* to a part of the debt only.[26] Thus, C guarantees A against trade debts to B contracted by B as a running balance of account to any amount not exceeding ₹ 3,000, and B becomes indebted to A for ₹ 5,000 and then becomes insolvent. If a dividend of 50 Paise in the rupee is declared, A will get ₹ 2,500 from B's estate and only ₹ 500 from C and not the balance of ₹ 2,500 as the guarantee by C was only for ₹ 3000 and that amount A has recovered.[27] If the liability is not for a floating balance, but in respect of a debt already ascertained, *then prima facie* the contract would be construed as security for the whole debt. In such cases, it is a question of construction as to whether the intention was to guarantee the whole debt with a limitation on the liability of the surety or to guarantee part only of the debt. It is, however, open to parties to contract, even in case of a floating balance, that a limited guarantee shall be applicable to the whole debt. In such a case, the creditor can in the event of principal debtor's insolvency, prove for the whole debt without any deduction and the surety cannot stand in the creditor's shoes until creditor has been paid 100 paise in the rupee.

RIGHTS OF THE SURETY

The surety has certain rights against the creditor, the principal debtor and his co-sureties, and such rights include those of exoneration, subrogation, indemnity, and contribution.

RIGHTS AGAINST THE CREDITOR

Right of Exoneration: In the case of fidelity guarantee, the surety can call upon the creditor or the employer to dismiss the employee whose honesty he has guaranteed, in the event of proved dishonesty of the servant. Also, the surety may file a suit for declaration that the principal debtor is the person to pay the amount. In that event the surety is exonerated.

At the time of payment, a surety can ask the creditor to marshal his securities. Thus, where the creditor has got two or more securities from the debtor in respect of the same debt, the surety can compel the creditor to resort to those securities first which are exclusively the creditors, and to that extent he is exonerated.

If the surety learns that the debtor is about to remove his property from the jurisdiction to avoid his creditors, the surety may call upon the creditor to take steps against the principal debtor to enforce his right. If the creditor fails to take action against the principal debtor, the surety is released to the extent he has been harmed.

Right to Securities: On paying off the creditor, the surety steps into his shoes and is entitled to all the securities which the creditor may have against the principal debtor, whether the surety is aware of the existence of such securities or not "It is the duty of the creditor to keep the securities intact; not to give them up or to burden them with further advances". Further, the creditor must hand over to the surety the securities in the same condition as they formerly stood in his hands. If the creditor loses, or, without the consent of the surety, parts with the securities, then the surety is discharged to the extent of the value of the securities.

---

26. Ellis v. Emmanual (1876) Ev. Div. 157.
27. Bardwell v. Lydall (1831) Bing. 489.

Difficulty arises, when the surety has guaranteed only a part of the debt and consequently even when he has paid all that he was liable to pay, the creditor's claim against the principal debtor is not yet fully satisfied. The Bombay High Court held in *Goverdhan Das* v. *The Bank of Bengal* (1851) 15 Bom. 48, that the surety was entitled to the securities only after the creditor has been paid fully even when the surety has paid his guaranteed amount. So, where *A* owed a total debt of ₹ 3,15,000 half of which was secured by a mortgage and the other half guaranteed by *C. C*, on payment of ₹ 1,25,000 claimed that he was entitled to that extent to stand in the place of the creditor and to receive a share of the proceeds of the securities proportioned to the sum which he had paid. But Farran J. held that although the equity between the creditor and the surety is that the creditor shall not do anything to deprive the surety of his right, yet the creditor's right to hold his securities is paramount to the surety's claim upon such securities, which only arises when the creditor's claim against such securities has been satisfied."

However, the Madras High Court has held differently in *Bhushayya* v. *Suryanarayna,* 1944 Mad 195. Krishnaswami Ayyanger, J. held that the sureties who have paid off their obligations were entitled to a proportionate share in the mortgage, even when a part of the creditor's claim against the principal debtor was still unsatisfied. The learned Judge said : "The condition laid down by Section 140 for this right to arise is that the payment by the surety of all that *he* is liable for, and not the payment of all that may be due to the creditor who holds the securities. Where the guaranteed debt is a fraction only of the debt, the surety's right comes into existence immediately on payment of that fraction, for that fraction is, so far as he is concerned, the whole"

Right to Share Reduction : In *Hobson* v. *Bass* (1871) 6 Ch. D. 792, *J* gave a guarantee to *B* in the following words: "I hereby guarantee to the payment of alt goods you may supply to *H*, but so as my liability to you under this or any other guarantee shall not at any time exceed the sum of £ 250". *E* gave a similar guarantee. *B* supplied goods to *H* to the amount of £ 657. *H* became bankrupt *B* proved the whole sum in the insolvency of *H* and then called upon the guarantors who paid him £ 250 each. Subsequently, *B* received from the Receiver a sum of 2 S. 1 d. in the pound on £ 657. It was held that each of the guarantors was entitled to a part of the dividend bearing to the whole the same proportion as £ 250 to £ 657"

Right of Set off : If the creditor sues the surety the surety may have the benefit of the set off, if any, that the principal debtor had against the creditor. He is entitled to use the defences of the debtor against the creditor. If, for example, the creditor owes the debtor something, or has in his hand something belonging to the debtor for which the debtor could have counter-claimed, the surety can also put up that counter-claim. He can claim such a right not only against the creditor, but also against third parties who have derived their title from the creditor.

RIGHT AGAINST THE PRINCIPAL DEBTOR

Right of Subrogation : When the surety has paid the guaranteed debt on the default of the principal debtor, he steps into the shoes of the creditor and will be able to exercise as against the principal debtor all these rights and remedies which could be exercised by the creditor. In other words, the surety is subrogated to all the rights which the creditor had against the principal debtor. In *Amritlal Goverdhan Lallan* v. *State of Travancore,* 1968 SC 1432, the Supreme Court has laid down that the surety will be entitled to every remedy which the "creditor has against the principal debtor, to enforce every security and all means of payment; to stand in place of the creditor, to have the securities transferred to him, though there was no stipulation for that; and to avail himself of all those securities against the debtor. This right of surety stands not merely upon contract, but also upon natural justice........"

Right to Indemnity: In every contract of guarantee there is an implied promise by the principal debtor to indemnify the surety; and the surety is entitled to demand from the principal debtor whatever he has paid under the guarantee. But if he pays any amount which the principal debtor is not liable to pay, he cannot demand indemnification from the principal debtor.

RIGHTS AGAINST CO-SURETIES

Contribution : Sometimes it may happen that one and the same debt has been guaranteed by two or more sureties either jointly or severally. Section 146 provides for a right of contribution between co-sureties. When a surety has paid more than his share of the debt to the creditor or a decree has been passed against him at the suit of the creditor, for more than his share, he has a right of contribution from the co-sureties, who are equally bound to pay with him.

A, *B* and *C* are sureties to *D* for the sum of ₹ 3,000 lent to *E*. *E* makes default in payment. *A*, *B* and *C* are liable, as between themselves, to pay ₹ 1,000 each, and if any one of them has to pay more than ₹ 1,000, he can claim contribution from the other two to reduce his payment to only ₹ 1,000.

If one of the sureties becomes insolvent, the co-sureties shall have to contribute the whole amount equally. Although a surety can file a suit for a declaration against the other co-sureties before he is actually compelled to pay, yet he cannot ask for contribution, unless he has actually paid more than his share. Also all the sureties are entitled to share in the benefit of any security or indemnity which anyone of them has obtained from the principal debtor, and this whether they knew of it or not.[28] Where the creditor releases any of the several sureties, that does not operate as a discharge of his co-sureties. But the released co-surety will remain liable to the others for contribution in the event of default (*Sri Chand* v. *Jagdish Pal Kishanchand* 1966 SC 1427).

It should be noted that the right of contribution is available only when all the sureties guarantee one and the same debt. It cannot be exercised where more persons than one become sureties by distinct and separate obligations for different portions of a debt.[29] Where the co-sureties have agreed to guarantee different sums they are bound under Section 147 to contribute equally up to the maximum of the obligation of each one.

A, *B*, and *C* as sureties for *D*, enter into three several bonds, each in a different penalty, viz., A in the penalty of ₹ 10,000, *B* in that of ₹ 20,000, *C* in that of ₹ 40,000 conditioned for *D*'s duly accounting to *E*, *D* makes default to the extent of ₹ 30,000. *A*, *B* and *C* are each liable to pay ₹ 10,000. But if *D* makes default to the extent of ₹ 40,000, then *A* is liable to pay ₹ 10,000 (his maximum obligation) and *B* and *C* will pay equal shares of the balance, i.e., they will pay ₹ 15,000 each. Again, if *D* makes default to the extent of ₹ 70,000, then *A*, *B*, and *C* will each pay the full penalty of his bond.

The rule in these cases is that subject to the limit fixed by his guarantee, each surety is to contribute equally and not proportionately to the liability undertaken.

DISCHARGE OF SURETY

A surety may be discharged by (*i*) the revocation of the contract of guarantee, (*ii*) by the conduct of the creditor, or (*iii*) by the contract of suretyship being invalid. Each of these main grounds of discharge of surety has further classes. The classification is given in the following chart.

By Revocation of Contract of Guarantee — We have been seen that a contract of guarantee may be either specific or continuing. A specific guarantee, *i.e.*, guarantee relating to one transaction, cannot be revoked if the liability is incurred. Thus, if A lends *B* a certain sum on the guarantee of *C*, then *C* cannot revoke the contract of guarantee. But it can be revoked by notice if the liability has not been incurred. So, where *A* has not yet given the sum to *B*, even though the guarantee has been executed by *C*, *C* may revoke the contract by giving notice to the creditor; and if *A* gives the money to *B* after this

---

28. Sleel v. Dixon (1881)17Ch.D.325.

29. Ceppe v. Tyyan (1823) Turn & Roth 420; 24 R.R. 89.

1. By Revocation	1. Revocation by Surety (Sec. 130)
	2. Death of Surety (Sec.131)
	3. Novation.
2. By conduct of creditor	1. Variation of terms without consent of Surety (Sec.133).
Discharge of Surety	2. Release or Discharge of Principal Debtor without Surety's consent (Sec.134).
	3. Compounding by Creditor with of Principal Debtor without Surety's consent (Sec. 135).
3. By Invalidation of Contract	1. Creditor's act or omission impairing Surety's eventual remedy (Sec.139).
	2. Guarantee obtained by Fraud or Misrepresentation (Sec. 142) or by Concealment (Sec.143).
	3. By failure of Consideration.

notice then *C* will not be liable to pay on *B*'s default Where the guarantee is a continuing one and extends to a series of transactions, it may be revoked by the surety as to future transaction by giving notice to the creditor. The Act contemplates series of distinct and separate transactions to constitute a continuing guarantee which can be revoked by notice. The test adopted by Courts in order to find out whether revocation for the guarantee is entire, supplied at one time; or whether it is fragmentary, supplied from time to time. A guarantee by *C* of payment of monthly rent by *B* in respect of a lease for five years is not revocable, as the guarantee is for five years and the consideration is a lease for 5 years. But, if *A*, in consideration of *B*'s discounting bills of exchange for *C*, guarantees, for six months, the due payment of all such bills to the extent of ₹ 50,000, and *B* discounts bills to the extent of ₹ 20,000, and after this *A* revokes his guarantee, this revocation discharges *A* from all liability to *B* for any subsequent discount. But *A* will remain liable for ₹ 20,000 in case of default by *C*. The guarantee by *A* is nothing more than an offer by him and does not become binding unless accepted by *B* by discounting *C*'s bills. Each discount being a separate transaction, the standing offer can be revoked with regard to future acceptance.

Revocation by Death—As a continuing guarantee can be revoked with respect to future transactions, so does the death of the surety act as revocation and the surety's estate will not be liable for any transactions after his death. For the death of the surety to act as revocation it is not necessary that the creditor must have known of the surety's death. So, if the creditor enters into fresh transactions after the Surety's death without any knowledge of such death, then the deceased surety's estate will not be liable for such transactions. In English law, however, notice of surety's death is essential before the rule will come into operation.

Revocation by Novation—A contract of suretyship may be discharged by novation, *i.e.*, fresh contract being entered into either between the same parties or between other parties, as a consequence of which the original contract of suretyship becomes discharged.

Discharge by Conduct of Creditor —A surety is discharged by the conduct of the creditor. As a surety is liable only for what he has positively undertaken in the guarantee, any alteration made without the surety's consent in the terms of the contract between the principal debtor and the creditor,

30. Narayan v. Markandya, 1959 Bom. 516. See also C. Nambiar v. Raman Nair 1959 Ker. 176; Indian Bank v. Krishnswamy, 1990 Mad. 115.

will discharge the surety as to transactions subsequent to the variation.[30] In *Kahan Singh* v. *Tek Chand,* 1968 J & K 93, where after decrease had been passed against the principal debtor and sureties, the creditor and principal debtor compromised without consulting the sureties, the sureties were held discharged. A surety is bound to the letter of his engagement, and it is incumbent on the creditor to show that the terms of guarantee have been strictly complied with. An alteration without the surety's consent even for his benefit will discharge him, as Lord Westbury said in *Blest* v. *Brown* (1862) 45 E.R. 1225:135 R.R. 181: ":.....you bind him [surety] to the letter of his engagement........ If that engagement be altered [without the surety's consent] in a single line, no matter whether it be altered for his benefit, no matter whether the alteration be innocently made, he has a right to say: 'The contract is no longer that for which I engaged to be surety; you have put an end to the contract that I guaranteed and my obligation therefore is at an end'. A guarantor cannot be held liable beyond the liability undertaken by him or beyond the terms of his contract (*State of Maharashtra* v. *Kaul,* 1967 S.C. 1634). There is, however, one qualification to this general rule that, where a guarantee is for the performance of several distinct debts, duties or obligations, a variation in the nature of one of them will not discharge the surety as to the rest.[31] A contract of repurchase of goods by the seller from the buyer (whose purchases were guaranteed) does not discharge the original contract but the two contracts stand together and, therefore, the surety under the original contract is not discharged. Similarly, a contract of resale to the vendor does not discharge a surety from his original contract. Again, an attempted variation which is inoperative, as being against law applicable as between the creditor and the principal debtor will not discharge the surety. A surety will not be discharged by a variation to which he has assented, but the onus is on the creditor to show that the surety assented to the alteration.

By Release or Discharge of Principal Debtor—A surety will be discharged if the creditor makes a contract with the principal debtor by which the principal debtor is released, or acts or makes an omission which results in the discharge of the principal debtor (Section 134). *A* supplies goods to *B* on the guarantee of *C*. Afterwards *B* becomes embarrassed and contracts with *A* to assign his property to him in consideration of his releasing him from his demands on the goods supplied. Here *B* is released from his debt, and *C* is, in consequence, discharged from his suretyship. Or, again, where *A* contracts with *B* for a fixed price to build a house for *B* within a stated time, *B*, supplying the necessary timber. *C* guarantees *A*'s performance of the contract. *B* omits to supply the timber. *C* is discharged from his suretyship. But if the principal debtor is discharged of his debt by the operation of law, *e.g.,* is discharged in insolvency, this will not operate as a discharge of the surety. And, if the creditor expressly reserves his remedies against the surety, the surety will not be discharged. Also, where there are co-sureties, a release by the creditor of one of them does not discharge the others (*Srichand* v. *Jagdishchand,* 1966 S.C. 1427): neither does it free the surety so released from his responsibility to other sureties (Section 138). But in English law, if the co-sureties are jointly liable, the release of one will discharge the others.

CREDITOR'S OMISSION TO SUE WITHIN LIMITATION PERIOD— WHETHER DISCHARGES SURETY

Where the creditor failed to sue the principal debtor within the period of limitation, thereby, in effect, discharging the principal debtor, opposite views have been taken by the Indian Courts. But the Privy Council ruling confirming the majority view has set at rest the conflict, and the law may be taken as settled now. Accordingly, *omission of the creditor to sue within the period of limitation does not discharge a surety.* Of course, even Section 137 provides that mere forbearance on the part of the creditor to sue the principal debtor or enforce any other remedy against him does not discharge the

---

31. Croyden Gas Co. v. Dickenson (1876) 2 C.P.D. 56; Skillet v. Fletcher (1866-67) L.R.I.C.P. 217 : 2 C.P. 469.

surety. *B* owes to *C* a debt guaranteed by *A*. The debt becomes payable. *C* does not sue *B* for a year after the debt has become payable. A is not discharged from his suretyship. A surety cannot compel the creditor to enforce his rights against the principal debtor.

Compounding by Creditor with Principal Debtor—Where the creditor, without the consent of the surety, makes an arrangement with the principal debtor for composition or promises to give him time or not to sue him, the surety will be discharged (Section 135). This section will apply only where there is a binding contract, though it need necessarily be expressed as even a tacit or implied contract inferred from the acts of the parties, is equally binding as an express one. And, forbearance to sue, exercised in pursuance of an agreement without consideration, would not discharge the surety, as it is nothing more than "forbearance" within Section 137. The acceptance of interest in advance by a creditor without the consent of the surety, operates as an agreement to give time and will discharge the surety, for the creditor cannot sue the principal debtor until the time covered by the payment in advance has expired.[32] A consent decree, made without the surety's consent, for payment by instalments of the sum due from principal debtor discharges the surety as payment by instalments gave time to the debtor.[33] The mere fact of striking a balance between the creditor and principal debtor so as to decide what is due does not discharge the surety for it could not extend the time.[34] And, if the surety has paid part of the debt before the composition, he is as to that not a surety, but a principal creditor and cannot recover it under section 135.[35] It is laid down in Section 136 that where the contract to give time to the principal debtor is made by the creditor with a third person, and not with the principal debtor, the surety is not discharged. *C*, the holder of an overdue bill of exchange drawn by *A* as surety for *B* and accepted by *B*, contracts with *M* to give time to *B*, in consideration of an undertaking by *M* to see the bill paid. *A* is not discharged.

By Creditor's Act or Omission Impairing Surety's Eventual Remedy—If the creditor does any act which is against the rights of the surety, or omits to do any act which his duty to surety requires him to do, and the eventual remedy of the surety himself against the principal debtor is thereby impaired, the surely is discharged (Section 139). Where against the terms of the guarantee the Government allowed the contractor (the principal debtor) to remove felled trees from a forest, the surety was held to be discharged (State of M.P. v. Kaluram, 1967 Sc 1105). Again, *A* puts *M* as apprentice to *B*, and gives a guarantee to *B* for *M*'s fidelity. *B* promises on his part that he will, at least.once a month, see *M* make up the cash. *B* omits to see this done, as promised and *M* embezzles. *A* is not liable to *B* on his guarantee. But mere passive acquiescence by the creditor in irregularities on the part of the principal debtor such as laxity in the time and manner of rendering accounts by a collector of public moneys whose fidelity is guaranteed will not itself discharge the surety. Neither is the surety discharged from liability for the principal debtor's default by saying that default would not have occurred, if the creditor had exercised all powers of superintending the performance of the debtor's duty. For, the employer of a servant whose due performance of work is guaranteed does not contract with the surety that he will use the utmost diligence in checking the servant's work. Likewise, the mere passive inactivity of the creditor to whom a guarantee is given or his neglect to call the principal debtor to account in reasonable time and to enforce payment against him does not discharge the surety. There must be some positive act done to the prejudice of the surety, or such degree of negligence as to imply connivance and amount to fraud.[36] But where the surety bond in respect of a

---

32. Kalir Prasanna v. Ambica Charan (1872) 9 B.L.R. 261: Protab Chundra v. Tour Grander (1878) 4 Cal. 132.
33. National Coal Co. v. Kashitish Bose & Co. 1926 Cal. 818.
34. Devidas v. Sant Mohan Singh 1931 Lah. 627.
35. Bombay Co. Ltd. v. Official Assignee (1921) 44 Mad. 381.
36. Black v. Ottoman Bank (1862) 15 E.R. 573; R.R. 101.

decree in instalments provided that the decree-holder should execute the decree if default was made, and the decree-holder allowed the decree to become time-barred, the surety was discharged.[37] Also, where a person stood surety to a bank for payment of a customer's current account, the act of the bank in allowing such customer to open a separate account in his own name, was held to discharge the surety.[38] Similarly, where one stands surety for several defendants and the decree-holder proceeds[39] against one of them only, the surety will be discharged by virtue of the exoneration of the other defendants. Sec. 139 is similar to Sec. 40 of the Negotiable Instruments Act, 1881, which discharges the indorser from liability in cases where the holder destroys or impairs indorser's remedy against a prior party.

By Invalidation of Contract — A contract of guarantee, like any other contract, may be avoided, because it is either void or voidable. If the debt itself is void for illegality, it cannot be recovered from the guarantor. So, guarantees have been held void given for a secret preference by a bankrupt for compounding a debt. Also, where guarantee is obtained by coercion or undue influence, it would be void. Therefore, a contract of suretyship will be unenforceable and a surety is not liable, if it is void, at the option of the surety, as in the case of mistake or fraud. Sections 142 and 143 read:

"142. Any guarantee which has been obtained by means of misrepresentation made by the creditor, or with his knowledge and assent, concerning a material part of the transaction, is invalid."

"143. Any guarantee which the creditor has obtained by means of keeping silence as to material circumstance is invalid."

Failure of consideration—A surety will be discharged on the failure of consideration. But there must be substantial failure of consideration in order to operate as discharge. Where it was intended that two or more co-sureties should join, but it was discovered that they did not join, then the surety who actually signed under the impression that others were going to join is discharged from his suretyship. This is provided in Section 144.

SUMMARY

Indemnity—Where a person promises to indemnify the other or make good his loss caused to him by the conduct of the promisor or any other person or by accident, there is a contract of indemnity. A contract of insurance is a contract of indemnity.

There are two parties to a contract of indemnity—the indeminifier who promises to make good the loss, and the indemnified, whose loss is made good.

Indian Contract Act is silent on the point of time for indemnifier's liability to indemnify. There is a conflict of opinion of various High Courts. Better view appears to be that where the indemnified has incurred an absolute liability, though not actual loss, he is entitled to call upon the indemnifier to save him from that liability and pay it off.

Guarantee — A contract to perform the promise, or discharge the liability of a third person in case of his default, is called a contract of guarantee or suretyship.

The person who gives the guarantee is called *Surety;* the person for whom the guarantee is given is called the *Principal Debtor,* and the person to whom guarantee is given is called the *Creditor.*

In Indian Law, a guarantee may be oral or in writing. In English Law it must be evidenced by a memorandum.

---

37. Hazari v. Chuni Lal 8 All. 259.

38. Ghuzanvi v. National Bank of India (1916) 20 C.W.N. 562.

39. Sitaramaswamy Sastri v. Basavayya (1921) 601.C. 114; 12 LW. 536.

Indemnity and Guarantee Distinguished

Indemnity	Guarantee
1. Prom is or primarily and independently liable to the promisee.	1. Liability of surety is collateral or secondary, the primary liability being that of the principal debtor.
2. Only two parties are required to contract.	2. Three parties are essential to this contract.
3. Indemnity depends upon the possibility or risk of some loss.	3. In guarantee there is an existing debt or duty performance of which is guaranteed by the surety.
4. Indemnifier cannot sue third parties in his own name, unless there is assignment. He must sue in the name of the indemnified.	4. Surety on payment of debt to the creditor can proceed in his own name against the principal debtor.

Consideration received by the principal debtor is sufficient consideration for a contract of guarantee.

It is obvious that creditor and surety must be competent to contract and so also the principal debtor.

Surety will be liable to pay the creditor on default by principal debtor.

Discharge of principal debtor by operation of law does not discharge the surety.

Nature of Surety's Liability—Surety's liability is secondary. He is liable only on default of the principal debtor. As soon as the time for payment has come and principal debtor does not or is unable to pay, the surety becomes liable to pay. But surety is liable only for the guaranteed debt and only the part remaining unpaid. Surety's liability, once it has arisen, is co-extensive with the principal debtor: it may be made less by special agreement, but never greater than that of the principal debtor.

Kinds of Guarantee

Retrospective Guarantee is for an existing debt.

Prospective Guarantee is for a future debt. It is specific, when it is given for single debt, and continuing, when it extends to a series of distinct and comparable transactions.

Rights of Surety: against creditor in fidelity guarantee. Surety can call upon the creditor or the employer to dismiss the employee, in the event of proved dishonesty of servant. In a loan guarantee he may, before paying, get declaration by Court that the principal debtor is bound to pay.

At the time of payment surety can ask the creditor to marshal his securities.

Surety's Rights: against principal debtor. After paying the debt or performing the duty, the surety stands in the shoes of the creditor and can sue principal debtor for payment. He is surrogated to all the rights which the creditor had against the principal debtor.

Surety's Rights: against co-sureties. When a surety has paid more than his share of the guaranteed debt to the creditor he has a right of contribution from the co-sureties.

Discharge of Surety—A surety may be discharged-
(a) By revocation by the surety, which can be done only in the case of a continuing guarantee in respect of future liability;
(b) by the death of the surety;
(c) by Novation;
(d) by variation of terms of contract without his consent;
(e) on the principal debtor being released or discharged by the creditor without surety's consent;
(f) compounding by creditor with principal debtor without surety's consent;
(g) where creditor's act or omission impaired surety's eventual remedy;
(h) where guarantee was obtained by fraud, misrepresentation or concealment of some fact;
(i) on failure of consideration.

CASES FOR RECAPITULATION

1. *H* and *A* guarantee *C*'s debt with *D*, who had as security three policies on *C*'s life. *H* later on paid off the debt and took an assignment of the policies. In an action for contribution against *A*, it was held that *H* was entitled to contribution from *A*, on bringing into account the value of the policies. [*In re Arcedeckne* (1883) 24 Ch. D.709]. The law on the point is that, before recovering contribution, the guarantor who has paid the debt must bring into account all securities he has received from the creditor in respect of the debt.

2. *C* and *D* go into a shop. *C* says to the shopkeeper—
(*i*) "Let him (*D*) have the goods, I will see you are paid." The contract is one of indemnity;
(*ii*) "Let *D* have the goods, and if he does not pay you, I will." This is a contract of guarantee [*Birkmyr* v. *Darnell* (1704) 1 Salk, 27].

3. *T* bought from *M* a motor car under a hire-purchase agreement by which he was to pay ₹ 1,500 per month. *N* guaranteed these payments. *T* fell into arrears with his instalments, and it was agreed between *T* and *M* that *T* should give a cheque for ₹ 2,500 and pay the rest of the arrears at the end of the month. *Held, N* was discharged from the whole contract, because *M* had agreed to give time to *T*, and the contract was one contract and not a series of monthly contracts [*Midland Motor Showrooms* v. *Newman* (1929)2 K.B. 256].

4. *A* gives a guarantee to *C* for goods to be supplied by *C* to *B*. *C* supplies the goods to *B* in due course. Afterwards *B* becomes financially embarrassed and contracts with all his creditors to assign to them all his property in consideration of their releasing him from their demands. The sale proceeds of the property are just sufficient to pay 80 paise in the rupee. Here *B* is released from his debt by the contract with *C* and as a result of this release *A* is discharged from his suretyship [*Illustration (a)* to Sec. 134].

5. *A* agreed to stand surety for an overdraft allowed by the *T*. Bank to *S*. The Bank required a guarantee in the form which was handed over to *S*. *S* got it filled by *A* for a sum of ₹ 25,000. The *T* bank declined to accept this letter of guarantee. *S* took back the letter and after some time brought it back with the figures so changed as to read ₹ 20,000. The Bank accepted the letter and kept it. In respect of this transaction there was no prior agreement between *A* and the Bank; and the letter of guarantee was given by *A* after the loan of ₹ 20,000 had already been made. On the failure of *S* to repay the loan, the Bank sued *A* upon the letter of guarantee. *A* pleaded discharge from liability on the ground of a material alteration of the instrument. It was held by the Supreme Court that *A* was not discharged from his liability, as there was no material alteration by the creditor. The alteration was made by *S* who was at that time acting as the agent of *A* and who brought the document to the Bank on both occasions. *A* must be deemed to have held *S* out as his agent for this purpose and this created an estoppel against *A*, because the Bank believed that S had the authority. The offer thus remained in its amended form an offer by *A* to the Bank and the Bank by accepting it turned it into a contract of guarantee which was backed by the past consideration on which the offer of *A* was originally based. (*Anirudham* v. *Thomco's Bank,* 1963 S.C. 746).

6. *S* guaranteed the honesty of a servant in the employ of *C*. The servant was guilty of dishonesty in the course of his service, but *C* continued to employ him and did not inform the defendant of what had occurred. Subsequently the servant committed further acts of dishonesty. *C* seeks to recover his loss from *S*. *Held,* S is discharged and *C* cannot recover his loss from him (*Co. op. Commission Shop* v. *Udham Singh,* 1944 Lah. 424).

7. *G* made an offer to *P* that if he would discount bills for *D* he would guarantee the payment of such bills to the extent of ₹ 6,000 during the period of 12 months. Some bills were discounted by *P* and duly paid, but before the 12 months had expired, *G* revoked his offer and notified that he would guarantee no more bills. *P* continued to discount the bills, some of which were not paid by *D*. *P* sued

G on the guarantee. *G* was discharged after revocation from all liability to *P* for any subsequent discount, and is not liable to pay to *P*. [*Illustration* (*a*) to Sec. 130].

8. *A* guarantees *C* against the misconduct of *B* in an office to which he is appointed by *C* and of which the duties are defined by an Act of Parliament. By a subsequent Act, the nature of the office is materially altered. Afterwards *B* misconducts himself. *A* is discharged by the change from future liability under his guarantee, though the misconduct of *B* is in respect of a duty not affected by the later Act [*Illustration* (*b*) to Sec. 133].

9. *A* held partly paid shares in a company and *D* guaranteed the payment of his unpaid calls to the company. The company called upon *A* to pay the calls and, on default being made, forfeited the shares under a power given in the articles, *Held,* the company by forfeiting the shares had deprived *D* of his lien on the shares to which he would have been entitled had he been compelled to pay the calls, and he was, therefore, discharged from his liability as surety under the guarantee [*In re Darwen & Pearce* (1927) 1 Ch. 176].

10. *B* pointed *A* as his agent to collect his rents, and required him to execute a fidelity bond in which *C* was surety. *C* died. In a suit by *B* against *C*'s legal representatives, it was held that *C* could not revoke his liability under the bond during his lifetime, and consequently his death did not release his estate from liability [*Baljour* v. *Crace* (1902) 1 Ch. 733].

11. *K* was appointed the manager of the T.C. Bank and *C* executed an indemnity bond rendering himself liable in the sum of ₹ 4,500 as guarantee for the fidelity of *K* in the performance of his duties as manager. Two years thereafter *K* committed suicide. It was discovered that *K* had misappropriated about ₹ 1,72,350 by falsifying accounts. No scrutiny into cash balance was ever made by directors as required by the provisions of the bye-laws; in fact; the directors had shut their eyes to the fraudulent career of the manager. In a suit by the bank for the recovery of ₹ 4,500, the guaranteed amount, from *C*, it was held that by the conduct of the directors, the guarantor (indemnitor) stood discharged from his obligations under the indemnity bond. It was stated that no employer who secures a fidelity guarantee can tell his guarantor that the guarantor is liable even if an act of infidelity was assisted by the employer himself. A person in whose favour a guarantee is given is bound to a faithful observance of the rights of the surety and to the performance of every duty necessary for the protection of those rights (*Chandrasekharan Pai* v. *Town Co-op. Bank Ltd.,* 1965, Mysore 209).

12. An agreement between the Corporation and M/s Sadhu & Co. contractors required a bank guarantee to be furnished by the contractor for due performance. A guarantee was furnished by Punjab and Sindh Bank. Disputes arose between the Corporation and the contractor and suit was pending in the court. The Corporation demanded payment (₹ 5 lakhs) from the Bank; and the contractor applied for injunction restraining the Bank from releasing the amount. It was held that no injunction could be issued and the Bank must release the amount on demand by the Corporation. The court observed, "The Bank guarantee constitutes an agreement between the Bank and the contractor under which there is an absolute obligation of the Bank to make payment to the Corporation...." (National Project Construction Corporation Ltd. v. M/s Sadhu & Co., 1990 P.H. 300).

CHAPTER 3

Bailment and Pledge

A bailment arises when one person (the bailor) transfers possession of goods to another person (the bailee) on condition that the bailee will restore them to the bailor after the purpose for which they were delivered is accomplished. Bailments may be divided into three main classes -

1. Those for the exclusive benefit of the bailor, *e.g.*, where your neighbour agrees to look after your dog while you are out of station.
2. Those for the exclusive benefit of the bailee, *e.g.*, where you lend your book to a friend.
3. Those for the mutual benefit of both parties, *e.g.*, where you hire furniture against payment of hire charges.

The first two are Gratuitous bailments and the third type is bailment for Hire or Reward, and is the most usual and important.

Section 148 of the Contract Act reads: A bailment is the delivery of goods by some person to another for some purpose, upon a contract that they shall, when the purpose is accomplished, be returned or otherwise disposed of according to the directions of the person delivering them. The person delivering the goods is called the "bailor". The person to whom they are delivered is called the "bailee".

Explanation. If a person already in possession of the goods of another contracts to hold them as a bailee, he thereby becomes the bailee and the owner becomes the bailor, of such goods although they may not have been delivered by way of bailment.

The definition emphasises the following essential features of bailment:

(1) There must be actual or constructive delivery, (2) of goods, (3) by the owner called the bailor, (4) to another person called the bailee, (5) for a specific purpose, (6) on condition that the goods shall be returned in *specie* either in their original or in an altered form or shall be disposed of according to the directions of the bailor.

To constitute a bailment there must be delivery of possession of goods for a specific purpose.

In *Kalia Perumal* v. *Visalakshmi,* 1938 Mad. 32, a lady employed a goldsmith for the purpose of melting old jewellery and making new out of the same. Every evening she used to receive the half made jewels from the goldsmith and put them into a box which was left in a room in the goldsmith's house of which she retained the key. One night the box was stolen. It was held that the goldsmith was not in possession of the jewels, as he had given back to the lady the jewellery bailed to him. As the key to the room was with the lady, there was no re-bailment with the goldsmith. Furthermore, no negligence on the part of the goldsmith was proved. Therefore, the goldsmith was not liable for the loss of the jewellery.

As stated earlier, the delivery of possession may be actual or constructive. It is actual when the bailor hands over to the bailee physical possession of the goods; and it is constructive delivery when there is no change of physical possession, the goods remaining where they are, but something is done which has the effect of putting them in the possession of the bailee. For example, delivery of the railway receipt amounts to delivery of goods (*Morvi Mercantile Bank* v. *Union of India* (1965) S.C. 1954).

Similarly, where a person pledged the projector machinery of his Cinema under an agreement which allowed him to retain the machinery for the use of the Cinema, there was a constructive delivery, or delivery by attornment to the bank (*Bank of Chittor* v. *Narnimbubi*, 1966 AP 163).

Again, although Section 148 speaks of delivery of goods on a contract, bailment can arise even where there is no contract. In *Lasalgaon Merchants' Cooperative Bank Ltd.* v. *Prabhudas Hathibhai*, 1966 Bom. 134, the Bombay High Court has imposed the obligation of a bailee without a contract. In the opinion of the Court, where certain goods belonging to an individual are seized by the Government, the latter becomes the bailee thereof even if there is no suggestion of a contract between the Government and the individual. Similarly, the Supreme Court in *State of Gujarat* v. *Memon Mohammed*, 1967 SC 1885, has recognised bailment without a contract, and held the State liable for damage to goods while in its custody. Certain Motor Vehicles and other goods belonging to the plaintiffs were seized by the State in the exercise of its powers under a Sea Customs Act. The goods, while in the custody of the State, remained totally uncared for and were heavily damaged. In a suit for damages the State contended that it was not liable as a bailee, as there was no contract of bailment Shellat J., observed as follows: "The contention is not sustainable. Bailment is dealt with by the Contract Act in cases where it arises from a contract, but it is not correct to say that there cannot be a bailment without an enforceable contract..... Nor is consent indispensable for such a relationship to arise. A finder of goods of another has been held to be a bailee in certain circumstances".

Since the essence of bailment is the delivery of goods for a stated purpose and their return in specie, it is only the possession that passes from the owner to the other and not the ownership. So, where goods are transferred by the owner to another in consideration of money price, it is a sale, or where the goods are not to be delivered back in specie but their price is paid it is not a bailment Again, **where money is deposited by a customer with a bank in a current, savings bank, or fixed deposit account, and, therefore, there is no obligation to return the identical money but an equivalent of it there is no bailment, but a relationship of creditor and debtor is created** (*Shanti Prasad* v. *Director of Enforcement*, 1962 S.C. 1764.)[1] But if valuables or even coins or notes in a box are deposited for safe custody there is a contract of bailment, for these are to be returned as they are, and not their money value. The point is important for the purposes of limitation, for if the transaction amounts to a loan, the cause of action for recovery commences from the date of the loan, and if it is a bailment from the date of demand for the return. Goods given on hire, or handed over to be turned into something, *e.g.*, gold to be made into ornaments, or left with a warehouseman for safe keeping, or given to a factor for sale, or entrusted to a carrier for conveyance from one place to another, or something left with a friend for use or to be looked after, are all examples of bailment, as also where the Master of the ship leaves the goods in the custody of the Port Trust.[2]

DUTIES OF BAILEE

1. **To take care of goods bailed.**—The first and most important duty of a bailee is to take care of the goods entrusted to him. The Contract Act does not recognise any distinction between a gratuitous bailment and bailment for reward, and lays down uniform standard of care for all types of bailments. Sec. 151 and 152 read:

---

1. Union Bank of India v. K. V. Venugopalan, 1990 Ker. 223—No Banker's lien as no bailment
2. G.E. Shipping Co. v. S.M.S. Saheb & Co., 1919 Mad. 367.

"151. In all cases of bailment the bailee is bound to take as much care of the goods bailed to him as a man of ordinary prudence would, under similar circumstances, take of his own goods of the same bulk, quality and values as the goods bailed."

"152. The bailee, in the absence of any special contract, is not responsible for the loss, destruction or deterioration of the thing bailed if he has taken the amount of care of it described in Section 151."

The degree of care that is expected of a bailee is that of the average prudent man in his own affairs under similar circumstances, and if, in spite of that much care any damage is caused to the goods, the bailee will not be liable. But if he does not take as much care of the goods as a man of ordinary prudence would do of his own goods, in like circumstances, he will be liable for negligence and will be required to make good the loss. Section 152 contemplates enlargement of legal liability by special agreement.

Thus, a bailee may agree to keep the property safe from all perils and answer for accidents or thefts. But, even such a bailee will not be liable in case of loss happening by an Act of God, such as fire or tempest, or by public enemies. The bailee is not an insurer of goods deposited with him.

Section 151 expressly provides for the standard of care expected of a bailee; and the liability cannot be reduced by contract below the limit prescribed by this section. Also, where the master is the bailee, and the servant is either dishonest or negligent in dealing with goods bailed, the master is liable if the goods are lost due to the negligence of the servant (B.C. *Co-op Bank* v. *State*. 1959 M.P. 77).

Not to make any unauthorised use of Goods.—The bailee is under a duty not to use the goods in a manner inconsistent with the terms of the bailment. If he does so, the bailor can terminate the bailment; and if any loss or damage results from the use of goods for a purpose other than the one agreed upon, or in a manner opposed to the one stated, the bailee becomes responsible for such a loss, unless such a use is necessary for its preservation. There is a breach of good faith. *A* lets to *B* his horse for his own riding. *B* cannot drive the horse in his carriage, or lend it to another person for any purpose. If *B* drives the horse in his carriage or lends it to someone else, *A* can terminate the contact; and if the horse is injured, *A* can also claim damages for the injury.

Not to mix Bailor's Goods with his own Goods.—The next duty of the bailee is to keep the goods of the bailor separate from his own. Sections 155, 156 and 157, however, lay down certain circumstances in which intermingling is permitted. The intermixture of goods of the bailor and bailee may take place with the consent of the bailor, or it may be the result of accident, mistake or inadvertence, or it may be wilful or intentional. If the intermixture be with the consent of the bailor, then the bailor and the bailee become joint owners and possess common interest in the goods in proportion to their respective shares. Where the intermixture is made without the consent of the bailor and the goods so mixed are separable or divisible, such as articles of furniture, the parties remain the owners of their respective shares, and so each party can claim proportionate share; but the cost of separation, or any damage as a result of mixture, shall be borne by the bailee. Where the mixture without the consent of the bailor is inseparable or indistinguishable so that the bailor's goods cannot be returned, the bailee is bound to compensate the bailor for the whole of the goods. If *X* deposits a tin of *A* grade ghee with *Y* and *Y* mixes it with his ghee of grade *B*, *Y* must pay the price of *A* grade tin. Where, however, a bailee, by accident or inadvertence, mixed the goods left by bailor with his own goods, or where the mixture is the result of an Act of God or of an unauthorised third party, and the mixture consists of goods of similar kinds and quality, such a mixture belongs to both parties in proportion to their shares, but the cost of separation will be borne by the bailee.

Not to set up Adverse Title.— Generally, the bailee has no right to deny the bailor's title or set up against the bailor his own title or the right of a third party. He will, however, refuse to deliver goods to the bailor if there is an effective pressure of an adverse claim amounting to an actual eviction by a paramount title. This is Common Law rule and is laid down in Section 117 of the Evidence Act, 1872.

To return the Goods.—It is the duty of the bailee to return or deliver the goods, without demand, on the expiry of the time fixed or when the purpose is accomplished. If he does not return or deliver as directed by the bailor, or tender the goods at the proper time, he becomes liable for any loss, destruction or deterioration of the goods even without negligence during the period it is detained. Post Office is a bailee of the articles of the sender. Where goods are delivered to the Post Office for transmission by V.P.P. to a buyer, they must be delivered to the buyer on payment by him of the price. Delivery of the goods by the Post Office without receiving the price will render it liable as a bailee for delivering goods against directions (*Income-lax Commer.* v. *VPM. Rathod & Co.,* 1959 S.C. 1394). If the bailee sells the goods, the bailor can in equity follow the goods or their proceeds, wherever they may be. If the bailor does not take delivery when it is offered at the proper time, the bailee can claim compensation for necessary expenses of and incidental to the safe custody. Where, however, the article bailed or hired does not serve the purpose, the bailee may leave the article where it is and give notice to the bailor that it is unfit for the purpose. Where the goods are lost before the proper time without negligence on the part of the bailee he will not be liable for the loss, and a bailee, who returns the goods in good faith to the bailor who really had no title to the goods, is not responsible to the true owner of the goods.

A bailee is excused from returning the goods to the bailor where the goods were taken away from him by authority of law exercised through regular and valid proceedings [*Jugilal Kamlapat Oil Mill* v. *Union of India,* 1976 S.C.227]. In this case a consignment of oil from Kanpur to Calcutta was accepted by the Railway under Risk Note Z and after the wagon had reached Calcutta with locks and seals intact, the delivery could not be made as the oil was seized by the Food Inspector of Calcutta in pursuance of an order of Health Officer of Calcutta Corporation under S. 419 of the Calcutta Municipal Act and was destroyed under the order of the High Court as the contents were found to be adulterated, The Railway was not liable.

As regards the return of goods bailed by two or more joint owners, the bailee *may* return the goods to any one without the consent of the bailors, provided that there is no contract that delivery must be given to all. It is to be noted that the word used in Section 165 is "may" and not "must" with the effect that no one bailor can compel the bailee to return him the goods. But the bailee may, if he likes, do so. But even where there is a contract asking the bailee to redeliver only to all joint owners, and he returns them to one of the joint owners, no suit can be filed by the others against the bailee joining the one who got the goods and he cannot be a party to a suit, for the breach is occasioned by his act.

In the absence of any contract to the contrary, the bailee must return to the bailor any increase or profits which have accrued from the goods bailed. This usually happens in the case of animals. So, where A leaves a cow in the custody of B to be taken care of, and the cow gets a calf, B is bound to deliver the cow as well as the calf to A, Similarly, new shares allotted in respect of shares that have been pledged are an increase which the pledger is entitled to get.[3] And where a bailee entrusted with some goods for some purpose finds something else hidden in them, such other goods belong to the owner and not to the bailee.

DUTIES OF BAILOR

To disclose Known Facts—The first and foremost duty of the bailor is to disclose the faults in the goods bailed in so far as they are known to him; and if he fails to do that he will be liable to pay such damages to the bailee as may have resulted directly from the faults. A lends a horse, which he knows to be vicious, to B, without disclosing this fact. B, in ignorance of the horse's vicious nature, rides the horse and is thrown off and injured. A is responsible to B for damages sustained. Or, A delivers to B, a carrier, some explosives in a case, but does not warn B. The case is handled without extraordinary care necessary for such articles and explodes. A porter is injured and some other goods are damaged.

---

3. Lucknow Municipal Board v. Abdul Razzaq 1931 Oudh 15.

A is liable for all the resulting damage. In the case of bailment of hire a still greater responsibility is placed on the bailor. He will be liable for all damages as above even if he did not know of the defects. *A* hires a carriage of *B*. The carriage is unsafe, though *B* does not know this. *A* is injured. *B* is responsible to *A* for the injury. It follows from this that a gratuitous lender is not liable for defects in the things lent of which he is not aware. Thus, if the carriage were lent gratuitously. *B* would not be liable under the circumstances.

To bear Extraordinary Expenses—The bailee is, no doubt, required to pay the ordinary and reasonable expenses of the bailment, but for any extraordinary expenses the bailor would be responsible. If a horse is lent for a journey, the expenses of feeding the horse would, of course, be borne by the bailee. But, if the horse becomes sick and expenses have been incurred, the bailor shall have to pay these expenses. The parties can, however, enter into any contract as regards expenses. In the case of bailment without remuneration to the bailee Section 158 provides that all the necessary expenses incurred by the bailee in connection with the bailment must be paid by the bailor.

To indemnify Bailee—The bailor is bound to indemnify the bailee for any cost or loss which the bailee may incur because of the defective title of the bailor to the goods bailed (Section 164). This right to indemnity extends also to a suit by third parties, even after the goods are returned to the bailor or delivered to someone else according to his directions.

Bailee's Lien—Where the goods are bailed for a particular purpose, and the bailee, in due performance of bailment, expends his skill he has a lien on the goods, *i.e.*, the bailee can detain the goods until his charges in respect of labour and skill used are paid by the bailor. But, if the bailee does not complete the work within the agreed time, or a reasonable time, he is not entitled to a lien to the goods. *A* gives a piece of cloth to *B*, a tailor, for making it into a suit. *B* promises to have the suit ready for delivery within a fortnight. *B* has the suit ready for delivery. He has a right to retain the suit until he is paid his dues. But if *B* takes a month to complete the suit, he has no lien. Further, the right of lien arises only where "labour and skill" have been used so as to confer an additional value on the article. So, a person who takes an animal for feeding has no lien, but a veterinary surgeon has. And also the bailee keeping the article to enforce his lien cannot charge for keeping it.

Liens are of two kinds: Particular Lien and General Lien. *A particular lien* is one which is available only against that property in respect of which the skill and labour are used. A *general lien,* on the other hand, is a right to detain any property belonging to the other and in the possession of the person trying to exercise the *lien* in respect of any payment lawfully due to him. A *general lien* is the right to retain the property of another for a general balance of accounts; but a *particular* lien is a right to retain it only for a charge on account of labour employed or expenses bestowed upon the identical property detained. We have so far dealt with the particular lien, and that is the lien to which a bailee is ordinarily entitled. The right of general lien is specifically given by Section 171 only to the Bankers, Factors, Wharfingers, Attorneys of a High Court, and Policy-brokers. These persons are authorised, in the absence of a contract to the contrary, to retain the goods bailed to them as security, for any debt due to them. A banker has a general lien on cash, cheques, bills of exchange and securities deposited with him in his character of a banker for any money due to him as a banker. But, where valuables and securities are deposited for a specific purpose, *e.g.*, for safe custody, the banker has no general lien on them. A factor "is an agent entrusted with the possession of goods for the purpose of sale." If any money is due to him by his principal, he can retain the principal's goods, in exercise of his right of general lien until his dues are paid. This lien, however, applies only to debts due to the factor in that character; it does not extend to debts which arose prior to the commencement of his relation as a factor to his principal. It extends to all his lawful claims against the principal as a factor, whether for advances, or remuneration, or for losses, or liabilities in the course of his employment as a factor. A wharfinger can, as a rule, exercise general lien on goods as regards claims against the owner of the goods. Therefore, he has no lien as against a buyer for charges becoming due from the seller after the wharfinger had notice of the sale.

An attorney (*i.e.* a solicitor) of High Court has a lien on all papers and documents belonging to his client which are in his possession in his professional capacity for his professional fees, but not for ordinary loans and advances. A solicitor who is discharged by his client holds the papers entrusted to him subject to his lien cost, but if he discharges himself he is not entitled to a lien.

RIGHTS OF BAILOR AND BAILEE AGAINST THIRD PARTIES

As the bailee is the person entitled to the possession of the goods bailed, the law (Section 180) vests in him a right to such remedies as the owner would have had, if no bailment had been made. Thus, if a third person wrongfully deprives the bailee of the use or possession of the goods bailed, or causes them any injury, the bailee may file a suit for trespass or conversion or for damages. He can recover from the wrong-doer in this manner even when he is not himself responsible to the bailor for loss and damage to the goods. The section further gives an option to the bailor also to sue for the injury or deprivation caused by the third party. As between the bailor and bailee it is provided that whatever is recovered from the third party by way of relief or compensation, is to be apportioned according to their respective interests. If, for instance, the bailee recovers more than his interest he must account for it to the bailor. It does not matter which of them recovers first or whether one sues or both; a recovery by one will oust the other of his recovery from the third party, for there cannot be a double satisfaction. And the defendant cannot be liable in all or more than the value of the goods, and special damages, if any.

TERMINATION OF BAILMENT

Where the bailee does any act with regard to goods bailed inconsistent with the condition of bailment, *e.g.*, wrongfully uses or disposes of them, the bailor may determine the bailment.

As soon as the period of bailment expires or the, object of the bailment has been achieved, the bailment comes to an end, the bailee must return the goods "without demand" by bailor.

A gratuitous bailment can be terminated by bailor at any time, even before the stated time, subject to the limitation that where such a termination of bailment before the stipulated period causes loss in excess of benefit, the bailor must compensate the bailee.

A gratuitous bailment terminates by the death of either the bailor or the bailee.

FINDER OF LOST GOODS (SECTIONS 168 AND 169)

We have seen under Section 71 that the position of a finder of goods is exactly that of a bailee. It is true that a person who comes by an article is not obliged to take charge of it; but if he does pick it up, he becomes a bailee. The rights of a finder are that he can file a suit against the owner for any reward that might have been offered, and may retain the goods until he receives it. But where the owner has offered no reward, the finder has only a particular lien and can detain the goods until he receives compensation for the trouble and expenses incurred in preserving the property or for finding out the true owner; but he cannot file a suit for the recovery of such compensation. In English law, however, the finder has, in the absence of an offer of reward, no right to any remuneration or lien, as the service is rendered without request.

As against everyone save the true owner, the property in the goods found in a public or *quasi* public place vests in the finder on his taking possession of it. Thus, a person who picks up a purse or a ring, accidentally dropped by a stranger, can keep it as his own as against the whole world, except the true owner. The finder keeps the article in trust for the real owner, and according to common law cannot sell it even if the true owner has not turned up. But in Indian Law, the finder is given a right to sell the property (1) where the owner cannot with reasonable diligence be found, or (2) when found, he refuses to pay the lawful charge of the finder and (*a*) if the thing is in danger of perishing or losing greater part of its value, or (*b*) when the lawful charges of the finder for the preservation of goods and the finding out of the owner amount to two-thirds of the value of this thing.

COMMON CARRIERS AND INN-KEEPERS AS BAILEES

The Contract Act does not deal with carriers and innkeepers, but to complete the subject of bailment, we may consider these here.

Common Carriers: A common carrier is one who undertakes to carry from place to place the goods of all persons *indiscriminately* who are willing to pay his usual or reasonable rates. The liability of common carriers in India is governed by the Common Law in conjunction with the provisions of the Carriers Act 1865. Under Common Law, he is an insurer of goods, but the Carriers Act enables him to limit his common law liability of insuring the goods by special contract in the case of certain goods such as valuables, perishable goods, or explosives, but not so as to get rid of liability for negligence.[4] As regards railways, their liabilities, before 1961, were those of a bailee. But now railways are common carriers subject to the provisions of sections 72 to 78B of the Railways Act, 1890.

Inn-Keepers: The liability of a hotel-keeper is governed by sections 151 and 152 of the Contract Act and is that of an ordinary bailee with regard to the property of the guests.

In *Jan & Son.* v. *Cameron* (1922) 44 All. 735, *C* stayed in a room in a hotel. The hotel-keeper knew that the room was in an insecure condition. While *C* was dining in the dining room, some articles were stolen from his room. It was held that the hotel-keeper was liable as he should have taken reasonable steps to rectify the insecure condition of the room.

PART 3-B
PLEDGE OR PAWN

A pledge or pawn is a special form of mutual benefit bailment by which one person transfers possession of some article to another to secure the payment of debt or the performance of a promise. A pledge is. thus a security device based upon a bailment. The bailor is called the "pawnor" and the bailee the "pawnee." Note, deposit of goods as security for a loan is necessary, and if there is no transfer of possession of goods, no pledge is created. Since pledge is a branch of bailment, the pawnee is bound to take reasonable care of the goods pledged with him. He must not use the goods pledged, and if he does so, he would be responsible for damages and any loss occasioned by such uses.

A pledge is distinguished from other types of bailments by the nature of the lien possessed by the pledgee. The pledge lien gives the pledgee the right to sell the goods in the event of the non-payment of the debt or non-performance of the obligation secured.

PLEDGE, LIEN AND MORTGAGE DISTINGUISHED

A pledge is something between a simple lien and mortgage. In the case of a lien there is no transfer of any interest, the person exercising a lien has only a right to retain the subject-matter of the lien until he is paid. In the case of a mortgage the property passes to the mortgagee; he has an absolute interest in the property subject to a right of redemption by the mortgagor. But, in the case of a pledge, though the deposit of goods is made security for payment of a debt or performance of a promise, the pledgee has only a special property in the pledge, while the general property therein remains in the pledgor and wholly reverts to him on the discharge of the debt or the performance of the promise. On the contrary, the pledgee can sell the goods after notice if the pledgor fails to discharge the debt on the stipulated date. (*J. & K.Bank* v. *Tekchand,* 1959 J.& K. 67; *Narsyyamma* v. *Andhra Bank,* 1960 A.P. 273).

---

4. Orient S.S. Co. v. K.S.S. Co., 1951 Trav. Coch. 1.

RIGHTS OF THE PAWNEE

No property or ownership in the goods pawned passes to the pawnee but be (pawnee) gets a "special property to retain possession even against the true owner until the payment of the debt, interest on the debt, and any other expenses, incurred in respect of the possession or for preservation of the goods" (Section 173). The pawnee must, therefore, deliver the goods to the pawnor on the tender of all that is due and if he persists in retaining the goods thereafter, he will make himself a 'wrong-doer', and his 'special property' is determined and the pawnor can recover the goods. As the pledgee does not transfer ownership, the mere right to retain confers no title to alienate except upon default of payment in accordance with the terms of the contract. Hence, the pawnor cannot, apart from the above circumstance, confer a good title upon a *bonafide* purchaser for value. Further, the articles pledged are security only for the particular debt, unless the parties contract that they shall be security also for any other subsequent debt (Section 174). We have said above that for necessary expenses incurred in the preservation of the pawned goods the pawnee has a right of lien, but if there be any extraordinary expenses ("the cost of curing a pawned horse which meets with an injury by accident"), he has only a right to sue the pawnor for recovery of such extraordinary expenses, and cannot retain the goods for such expenses (Section 175).

Should the pawnor make a default in payment of the debt, or performance of the promise, at the stipulated time, the pawnee may either (*i*) file a suit for the recovery of the amount due to him while retaining the goods pledged as collateral security, or (*ii*) may sue for the sale of the goods and the realisation of the money due to him, or (*iii*) may himself sell the goods pawned, after giving reasonable notice to the pawnor, sue for the deficiency if any, after the sale (Section 176). If the sale of the goods is made in execution of his decree, the pawnee may buy the thing at the sale. But he cannot sell it to himself, and if he were to do so, then it would be treated as wrongful sale and the pawnor will have the right to recover the article on payment of the pawnee's dues according to the terms of the contract. While exercising either of his first rights of suit the pawnee need not give any notice to the pawnor, but if the pawnee wants to sell the goods, he must give reasonable notice of his intention notwithstanding any contract to the contrary.[5] And, should he sell the goods in default of payment, and find the proceeds insufficient to meet his full dues, he may recover the balance from the pawnor, but if there is a surplus, he must pay it over to the pawnor. In this respect, the right of a pledgee or pawnee differs from the right of an unpaid seller, because if there is a surplus, the unpaid seller can retain the surplus. Furthermore, the pawnor can redeem at any time before sale, though the time for payment has expired for the rights of the pawnee depend solely upon possession and he does not own the subject-matter. Hence the rule that tender of the amount due or even the pledge coming to the hands of the pawnor otherwise than for a limited purpose will extinguish all the pawnee's rights in respect of the pledge. Thus, an agreement that the pledge should become irredeemable, if it is not redeemed after a certain time, would be invalid.

RIGHTS OF PLEDGOR

We have seen above that in case of default by the pledgor to repay on the stipulated date, the pledgee may sell the goods after giving the pledgor a reasonable notice. This notice is compulsory in all cases of pledge, even when the instrument of pledge contains an unconditional power of sale. Therefore, if the pledgee makes an unauthorised sale (*i.e.* without giving the notice as required under Section 176), the pledgor has the following courses open to him:

1. to file a suit for redemption of goods by depositing the money, treating the sale as if it had never taken place; or
2. to ask for damages on the ground of conversion.

---

5. Narsavyamma v. Andhra Bank, 1960 A.P. 273, T.S. Kotagi v. Tahsildar, Gadag, 1985 Kant 265.

A pledgor who impugnes the sale by the pledgee cannot sue for a declaration that the sale is contrary to law and does not affect the rights of the pledgor [*Narsayyamma* v. *AndhraBank,* 1960, A.P. 273; *Neckram Dobay* v. *Bank of Bengal* (1892) 19Cal.322].

PLEDGE BY NON-OWNERS

(*i*) **Mercantile Agents**—Hitherto we have assumed that the person creating the pledge is the owner of the goods. But the law permits under certain circumstances a pledge by a person who is not the owner but is in possession of goods. In the first case, a mercantile agent who is, with the consent of the owner, in possession of goods or documents of title of goods may, in the ordinary course of his business as a mercantile agent, pledge the goods, and such a pledge will bind the owner. It will also be a valid pledge even when made by the mercantile agent without the authority of the owner, provided that the pawnee has acted in good faith and did not have at the time of the pledge notice that the pawnor had no authority to pledge the goods. A mercantile agent has been defined by Sec.2(9) of the Indian Sale of Goods Act as a "mercantile agent having in the customary course of business as such agent authority either to sell goods, or to raise money on the security of goods" Thus a commission agent, or a broker may make a valid pledge of the goods, but a person in bare possession cannot do so.[6] Similarly, a person entrusted with goods for a specific purpose cannot pledge the goods. It must be noted that a mercantile agent like an owner can create a pledge by the delivery either of goods or of the document of title to goods (*Morvi Mercantile Bank* v. *Union of India,* 1965 S.C. 1954).

(*ii*) **Seller or buyer in possession after sale**—A seller, left in possession of goods sold, is no more owner of the goods, but a pledge created by him will be valid, provided the pawnee acted in good faith and had no notice of the sale of goods to the buyer. Where B buys goods from A, pays for them, but leaves them in the possession of A, and A then pledges the goods with C who does not know of the sale to B, the pledge is valid. Similarly, where a buyer or a person who has agreed to buy, obtains possession of goods with the seller's consent, before the payment of price, pledges these goods to a pawnee who takes them in good faith and without notice of the seller's right of lien or any other right of the seller, the pledge is valid.

(*iii*) **Pledgor having Limited Interest**— When the pawnor is not the owner of the goods but has a limited interest in the goods which he pawns, *e.g.*, where he is mortgagee or he has a lien with respect to those goods, the pledge will be valid to the extent of such interest. A found a watch on the road and had it repaired, paying ₹ 10 as repairing charges, and then pledged it for ₹ 50. The real owner can recover the watch only on paying ₹ 10 to the pledgee.

(*iv*) **Pledge by Co-owners**—One of the joint owners in sole possession of goods, with the consent of the others, can make a valid pledge.

(*v*) **Pledge by person in possession under voidable contract**—A person may obtain possession under a contract which is voidable at the option of the lawful owner on the ground of fraud, misrepresentation, coercion or undue influence. Possession so obtained is not by free consent, but it is nevertheless possession by consent, and the person in possession may make a valid pledge of the goods provided the contract has not been rescinded at the time of the pledge. But in a case where there is no real consent as where goods have been obtained by means of theft, no pledge can be made. A thief has no title and can give none.

SUMMARY

A "Bailment" is (*i*) the actual or constructive delivery, (*ii*) of goods, (*iii*) by the owner called bailor, (*iv*) to another person called bailee, (*v*) for a specific purpose, (*vi*) on condition that goods shall be returned in specie either in their original or in an altered form, or shall be disposed of according to directions of bailor.

---

6. Visalakshi v. Janopakara, 1942 Mad. 298.

In a bailment, only possession of goods passes to the bailee and ownership remains with the bailor.

Bailment may be —
(a) for the exclusive benefit of the bailor;
(b) for the exclusive benefit of the bailee;
(c) for the mutual benefit of both.

DUTIES OF BAILEE—

1. To take as much care of goods bailed as a man of ordinary prudence would, in similar circumstances, take of his own goods of similar nature.
2. Not to make any unauthorised use of goods.
3. Not to mix his own goods with bailor's goods.
4. Not to set up adverse title.
5. To return the goods in specie.

DUTIES OF BAILOR—

1. To disclose known facts relating to the goods bailed.
2. To bear extraordinary expenses incurred by the bailee in connection with bailment
3. To indemnify the bailee for cost or loss incurred because of the defective title of bailor.
4. Bailee has lien on the goods, *i.e.*, he can retain the goods until his charges in respect of labour and skill used by him with respect to the goods are paid.

TERMINATION OF BAILMENT—

1. The bailor may determine the bailment, where the bailee does any act with regard to goods inconsistent with conditions of bailment.
2. A bailment comes to an end as soon as the period of bailment expires or the object is achieved. Goods must be returned without any demand by bailor.
3. A gratuitous bailment can be terminated by bailor at any time, provided that the termination before the stipulated period does not cause to the bailee a loss greater than the benefit.
4. A gratuitous bailment terminates by the death either of the bailor or the bailee.

Finder of Lost Goods—A finder of goods is a bailee, with all his rights and liabilities, as against the real owner, and an owner as against the rest of the world.

A finder can sell the property found—
1. where the owner cannot with reasonable diligence be found, or
2. when found, he refuses to pay the lawful charges of the finder, and
3. if the thing is in danger of perishing or losing greater part of its value, or when lawful charges of finder for preservation of goods and finding out the owner amount to two-thirds of the value of the thing.

Carrier as Bailee—A common carrier undertakes to carry goods of all persons who are willing to pay his usual or reasonable rates. He further undertakes to carry them safely, and make good all losses, unless they are caused by Act of God or public enemies. Carriers by land, including railways, and carriers by inland navigation, are common carriers. Carriers by sea for hire are not common carriers and they can limit their liability. Railways in India are now common carriers.

Inn-keepers—In India the liability of inn-keepers or hotel-keepers in respect of goods belonging to guests appears to be that of a bailee.

Pledges—A pledge or a pawn is a contract whereby an article is deposited with a lender or promisee as security for the repayment of a loan or performance of a promise. The bailor or depositor is called a Pledger or Pawnor and the bailee or depositee the Pledgee or Pawnee.

Pawnee must take reasonable care of the goods pledged with him. He must not use the goods pledged, and if he does so, he may be liable for any loss caused by user.

Rights of Pawnee—A pawnee gets special property in goods pawned, and he can retain them until payment of the principal, interest and any other expenses. If the debtor fails to pay on the stipulated date, the pawnee.may, after giving due notice, sell the goods pawned, and if there is any deficiency, sue for the balance. Any surplus must be paid over to the debtor.

Pledge by Non-Owner—A mercantile agent in possession of goods with owner's consent can pledge the goods. A seller in possession of goods may pledge to a pawnee who acts in good faith and has no notice of the sale to buyer. Buyer in possession with seller's consent may pledge before paying the price. A person with limited interest in the goods, *e.g.*, mortgagor, a person in possession under voidable contract, may pledge the goods. A thief cannot create a valid pledge of stolen goods, as he has no title and can give none.

CASES FOR RECAPITULATION

1. *A* finds a costly ring and, after making reasonable efforts to discover the owner sells it to *B* who buys without knowledge that *A* was merely a finder. The true owner sues *B* to recover the ring. *Held*, the owner can recover the ring. The mere fact of an innocent and *bonafide* purchase from a person with no title is no answer to the claim of the true owner [*Farquharson Bros.* v. *King and Co.* (1902) A.C. 325].

2. *B* hired from *G* a van and driver for three hours for the purpose of delivering goods to his customers expeditiously. During the journeys, the van driver left the van unattended for an hour in order to have a meal, and the goods were stolen while he was away. An exemption clause in the contract of hire stated '*G* does not hold himself responsible for loss or damage to goods in the van.' *B* sued *G* for the value of the goods and, alternatively, for damages for breach of contract. *Held, G* is liable to pay damages to *B*. The Court of Appeal declared that, even though *G* had effectively excluded his liability in tort, he could not exclude his fundamental duty under the contract to deliver the goods forthwith to their destination. *G* had failed to perform the contract into which he had entered, and was bound to pay damages for this fundamental breach [*Bontex Knitting Works Ltd.* v. *St. John's Garage* (1944) 1 All. E.R.381].

3. *A*, a jeweller, was entrusted with a diamond by *P* with the instructions that *A* should obtain offers for it, and if any such offer was approved by *P*, *A* should sell it to the offerer. Acting contrary to *P*'s instructions, *A* sold the diamond to *S* who bought it in good faith. Thereafter *A* absconded with the price money. In a suit by *P* against *S* to recover the diamond, it was held that *P* could not recover the diamond from *S*, as the sale was made by *A*, as a mercantile agent in the ordinary course of his business, though contrary to *P*'s instructions. (1929) 3 Bom. L.R.

4. A guest, arriving late for dinner at a hotel, saw a number of ladies' coats left in an ante-room which was previously used as a supervised cloak-room. At that time, however, there was no attendant in the room. Nevertheless, she left her mink coat with the other coats. Whilst she was dining, the coat was stolen. It was held that the hotel-owners were liable to pay for the loss.

5. Some cattle belonging to *A* were agisted with *B*. Without any negligence on *B*'s part the cattle were stolen. *B* did not inform the owner or the police immediately, or made any efforts to recover them because he thought that it would be useless to do so. *Held, B* was liable for the loss, unless he could prove that, even if he had reported the loss, the cattle still could not have been recovered [*Coldman* v. *Hill* (1919)1 K.B. 443].

6. *A* gives an electric kettle to *B*, an electric repairer, on condition that the kettle must be returned completely repaired within a fixed period. *A* part only of the work is done within the period. When *A* asks for the return of the kettle, *B* claims to retain it until he is paid due remuneration for the work done by him. *Held, B* cannot refuse to deliver the kettle until payments for part of the work done by

him are made. He has lost his right of lien as he has failed to complete the work within the agreed period and *A* can take it back without payment [*Judah* v. *Emperor* (1925) 53 Cal.174].

7. *H*, the owner of a motor car, agreed with the C.M. Co., that the company would maintain and garage her car for three years, on being paid an annual sum by *H*. *H* was entitled to take the car out of the company's garage as and when she liked. The annual payment being in arrear, the company detained the car in the garage and claimed a lien, *Held*, as *H* was entitled to take the car away as and when she pleased, the company had no lien [*Hatton* v. *Car Maintenance Co., Ltd.* (1915) 1 Ch. 621].

8. Six boxes containing menthol crystals were consigned by *H* to 'self' and entrusted to the railway for carriage from Bombay to Delhi under a railway receipt. *H* borrowed ₹ 20,000 from *M* Bank, executed a promissory note for the amount and endorsed the R/R pertaining to the six boxes in favour of the Bank as security for the loan. The consignment did not reach Delhi and the railway failed to deliver the boxes to the Bank. The Bank, claiming to be the pledgee of the goods, sued the Union of India for the recovery of ₹ 35,000, being the value of the goods, as damages. The Supreme Court held that the Bank is entitled to recover the full amount of ₹ 35,000. The owner of goods can make a valid pledge of them by transferring the railway receipt representing the said goods. The Bank is a pledgee and as such can sue for the value of the goods. Sec. 180 gives the bailee the same remedies against third parties as are available to the owner of the goods. The three transactions, viz., the advancing of loan, the execution of the promissory note and the endorsement of the R/R, together form one transaction. Their combined effect is that the Bank would be in control of the goods till the debt was discharged. Such a transaction is a pledge (*Morvi Mercantile Bank* v. *Union of India*, 1965 S.C. 1954).

9. In *D*'s shop, a customer, *P* put down her coat with a brooch. She forgot to pick it up. One of the assistants of *D* found it and placed it in the drawer. It was weekend and on Monday it was missing. It was held that *D* was liable to *P* as he did not exhibit the ordinary care which a person in his situation (a bailee) would have taken (*Newman* v. *Bourn and Hollings-Worlh* (1915) 31 TLR209).

10. *H*, while serving in the Royal Artillery, was stationed in a house requisitioned by the Government. He accidentally found a brooch in an upstairs room occupied by him. He handed over the brooch to the police, and they, failing in their attempts to discover the rightful owner, delivered it to *P* who was the owner of the house. *P* sold the jewel for £66. *H* sued for the recovery of the brooch or its value, on the ground that he was the finder. *P* contended that he was entitled to it as the owner of the property on which it was found. *P* was never in possession of the house and had no knowledge of the brooch until it was brought to his notice by the police. It was held that *P* had neither *defacto* control nor *animus* of excluding others and as such had no possession. Therefore, *H* was entitled to the brooch or its value since his claim as finder prevailed over all but the rightful owner (*Hannah* v. *Peel* (1945) 2 All. E.R. 288).

11. *G* had loaned his car to his brother, who obtained petrol on credit from *X*. *X* took possession of the car and refused to return it until he was paid. *G* is entitled under Sec. 180 of the Contract Act to sue *X* for unlawfully taking the car from the possession of his brother, the bailee.

12. Certain goods were with the Bank of Bihar. These goods were seized by the State of Bihar for certain liabilities of the pawnor. It was held that the seizure could not deprive the pledgee of his right to realise the amount for which the goods were pledged and, therefore, the State was bound to indemnify him upto the amount which would have been realised from the goods (*Bank of Bihar* v. *State of Bihar*, 1971 SC 1210).

13. The defendant borrowed ₹ 20,000 from the plaintiff on a promissory note and gave his aeroscrapes with about ₹ 35,000 as security for the loan. The plaintiff sued for the repayment of the loan, but was unable to produce the security, having sold it. His suit for the loan was rejected (*Lallan Prasad* v. *Rahmat All*, 1967 SC 1322).

CHAPTER 4

Principle and Agent

So far we have been considering our legal persons as acting entirely by themselves, and as being self-sufficient for their necessary legal actions. In real life we do not always act ourselves. We employ a merchant to distribute our goods, we ask our broker to buy shares, and so on. In fact, much, and under Corporate organisation, all, of the business must be conducted through representatives or agents. In law, a person who acts in place of another is called an *agent,* and the person on whose behalf he acts is called the *principal.*

Agency is a relation based upon an express or implied agreement whereby one person, the **agent**, is authorised to act for another, his **principal**, in transactions with third persons. The idea of relation indicates that the agent is merely a connecting link between the principal and the third party. The acts of the agent bind the principal to third persons or give the principal rights against the third persons. Agency is based upon consent and for that reason, it is called a consensual relation. If consideration is present, the relationship is also contractual.

There are two general rules regarding agency. One, with certain exceptions, whatever a man *sui juris* may lawfully do of himself he may do by another. In other words, a person may, in general, act through an agent The second rule follows from the first: the acts of the agent are the acts of the principal. The maxim is *qui facit per alium facit per se*—he who acts through an agent is himself acting. The agent is clothed with the capacity of the principal.

Who may be a Principal—Any person, if he is competent to act for himself, may act through an agent. A person under a legal or natural disability or incapacity cannot appoint an agent. For example, the appointment by a minor is held void, and if an agent acts for a minor, he will be personally liable to the third party.

Who may be an Agent—Since a contract made by an agent is in law the contract of the principal, it is immaterial whether or not the agent has legal capacity to make a contract for himself. Thus a minor can be agent; the agent is only a connecting link and is not personally bound by his acts performed on behalf of his principal. The law requires the principal and the third party to be competent to contract.

In considering, however, whether the contract of agency itself as between the principal and agent is enforceable, the contractual capacity of the agent becomes important. Where an agent is an adult of sound mind (competent to enter into contract) then, where the agent has misconducted himself in the business of agency, he will be responsible to the principal for damages arising from such misconduct But, if the agent happens to be a person incapable of entering into a contract, *e.g.*, a minor, then the principal cannot hold the agent liable, in case of misconduct or negligence (Sec. 184). For example, where P, a principal, gives A, a minor, a ring worth ₹ 500 and asks him not to sell it on credit or for less than ₹ 450, and *A* sells the ring to *C* on credit for ₹ 350, the transaction will positively bind *P* and *C*, but *P* will have no right to claim damages as against *A* for his misconduct, since the latter happens to be a minor, and the contract with a minor is void. Had *A* been an adult, he would have been liable to *P* for damages sustained by his misconduct.

Capacity to contract must be distinguished from authority to contract. Capacity means power to bind oneself; authority means power to bind another. Capacity is part of the law of status; authority is part of the law of principal and agent. Capacity is usually a question of law; authority is usually a question of fact. Thus, a minor has no capacity to contract, but he may have authority to act as agent.

CREATION OF AGENCY

A contract of agency, like any other contract, may be express or implied; but consideration is not an essential element in this contract. The fact that the principal has consented to be represented by the agent is a sufficient 'determinant' and consideration to support the promise by the agent to act in that capacity. It is of importance to remember in this connection that if no consideration has passed to the agent, he is only a gratuitous agent and is not bound to do the work entrusted to him, although if he begins the work, he must do it to the satisfaction of his principal. Agency may also arise by **estoppel, holding out, necessity or subsequent ratification** by the principal of the act done by the agent. The last type is sometimes called **ex post facto** Agency. The relationship of principal and agent may be created by statute.

Express Agency—The contract of agency, with certain exceptions, as to writing and registration, may be made orally or in writing. In fact in a large number of business dealings agencies are created by word of mouth. The usual form of a written contract of agency is the Power of Attorney, which gives him the authority to act as agency on behalf of the principal in accordance with the terms and conditions mentioned therein. Where an agency is created to transfer or assign immovable property, the power of attorney or authority must also be registered in India, and in England it should be given by Deed. Powers of attorney vary very much in scope, and may be divided into three classes—a general power of attorney, a special power, or a particular power. A general power of attorney authorises the agent to do all things on behalf of the principal, *i.e.*, to act generally in the business of agency. A special power of attorney empowers the agent to perform a single transaction *e.g.*, selling a house or borrowing money on a mortgage. A particular power of attorney is one which authorises an agent to do a single act, e.g., to present a document before the Registrar for registration.

Implied Agency— Implied authority may arise by conduct, situation of parties, or the necessities or circumstances of the case. Implied agency would, therefore, include agency by estoppel, agency by holding out agency of necessity.

Agency by Estoppel—The rule of estoppel may be briefly stated thus: Where a person by his words or conduct has wilfully led another to believe that certain set of circumstances or facts exists, and that other person has acted on that belief, he is estopped or precluded from denying the truth of such statements. In the words of Lord Halsbury, "Estoppel arises when you are precluded from denying the truth of anything which you have represented as a fact although it is not a fact." Thus, where A tells B in the presence and within the hearing of *P* that he (*A*) is *P*'s agent and *P* does not contradict this statement and later on *B* enters into a transaction with *A bonafide* believing that *A* is *P*'s agent, then *P* is bound by this transaction, and in a suit between himself and *B*, cannot be permitted to say that *A* was not his agent even though *A* was not in actual fact his agent. It is, therefore, said, "If you lure a person out on a limb, you cannot saw the limb off."

Agency by Holding Out—This is something more than estoppel. Here, there is some affirmative conduct by *P* indicative of *A* being held out as his agent. Thus, *P* sends his servant *A* asking him to get goods on credit from *C*, and pays the bill. *A* later abuses *P*'s authority and buys goods on credit from *C* for himself. *C* sues *P*. *P* cannot plead that *A* had no authority on the second occasion to purchase on credit. *P* is bound by his prior conduct in holding out that *A* was his agent.

In both agency by estoppel and agency by holding out, although there is no express appointment of the agent by the principal, the agent acquires authority through the principal. Thus, in these circumstances implied or apparent or ostensible agency is as effective as an agency expressly and deliberately created. Appearance and reality are one.

Agency of Necessity—Agency may also arise from the necessities of the case.[1] In certain circumstances, a person who has been entrusted with another's property, may have to incur unauthorised expenses to preserve it. In such a case, although specific authority to act does not exist, the law presumes it. Such an agency is known as agency of necessity. A master of a ship is entitled, in cases of accident and emergency, to enter into a contract which will bind the owners of the ship or cargo, notwithstanding that it transcends his express authority, if it is *bonafide* made in the best interest of the owners concerned. The same power is possessed by a land carrier in respect of perishable goods.

In *Sims & Co.* v. *Midland Rly. Co.* (1913) I K.B.103, a quantity of butter was consigned with the defendant railway company. It was delayed in transit owing to a strike. The goods being perishable the company sold them. The sale was held binding on the owner. The company action was justified by the necessities of the case and it was also not practicable to get instructions from the owner. The doctrine of necessity applies only when there is real emergency, the agent is not in a position to get instructions from the principal and acts *bonafide* in the best interests of the principal.

A deserted wife or one compelled to live apart from the husband (*e.g.*, either ejected or ill-treated by him) and lacking means of support for herself and her children becomes an agent of necessity and can pledge her husband's credit for necessaries, provided she has not been given an adequate allowance. But if she voluntarily leaves, there is no agency of necessity.

Agency by Ratification—If the agent had no authority to contract on behalf of principal or exceed such authority as he had, the contract is not binding on the principal. No one can become the agent of another person except by the will of that person. The principal may, however, afterwards confirm and adopt the contract so made, and this is known as ratification; agency by ratification or by subsequent authority arises. This is also known as *ex post facto* agency or agency arising after the event. The effect of ratification is to render the contract as binding on the principal as if the agent had been properly authorised beforehand. Ratification relates back to the original making of the contract, so that the agency is taken to have come into existence from the moment the agent first acted, and not from the date of principal's ratification. The rule is *Omnis ratihabitio retrotrahituret mandato prior aequiparatur* (every ratification relates back and is equivalent to a previous command or authority). The legal result of ratification is that a present act is recognised as binding retroactively. This is so even if the other party has in the meantime purported to repudiate the transaction. Ratification is tantamount to prior authority, or, ratification is equivalent to an antecedent authority.

In *Bolton Partners* v. *Lambert* (1889) 41 Ch. D. 295, *L* made an offer to *M*, the managing director of a company. *M* accepted the offer on the company's behalf, although he had no authority to do so. *L* then gave notice to the company that he withdrew the offer. The company subsequently ratified *M*'s unauthorised acceptance. *Held,* as the ratification dated back to the time of the acceptance, the withdrawal of the offer was inoperative. An offer once accepted cannot be withdrawn.

But where an agent purports to accept an offer "subject to ratification" the rule of relation back does not apply so that the contract will be deemed to have been made on the date of ratification or approval by the principal and the offer can be withdrawn, before such ratification. In the above case *M*, the agent, had warranted his authority and so the contract was complete and the ratification related back to the time of the acceptance by *M*. In *Watson* v. *Davies* (1931) 1, Ch. 455, the agent had expressly accepted an offer subject to the principal's approval and had thus made his lack of authority

---

1. See Hindustan Ins. Co. v. Jayalakshmanuna, 1959. A.P. 562.

known so that there has been no finality about his acceptance, which had been conditional, and the third party could withdraw his offer before ratification.

A contract can only be ratified under the following conditions:—

1. The agent must avowedly or expressly contract as an agent for a principal in contemplation [*Keighley* v. *Durent* (1901) A.C. 240]. In other words, the act ratified must have been done by the agent not for himself but intending to bind a named or ascertainable principal. So that at the time of the act the third parties know that the agent is acting for a principal [*Imperial Bank of Canada* v. *Mary Begley* (1936) P.C. 193]. The agent must not allow the third party to imagine that he is really the principal.

2. The contract can, therefore, be ratified only by a principal who was named or ascertainable at the time of the contract. If the principal is named, he can ratify the contract even if the agent never intended that he should do so, but wanted to keep the benefit of the contract for himself [*Re Tiedemann* (1899) 2 Q.B. 66].

3. The person ratifying must have been not only in contemplation but he must have also been in existence at the time of the contract. Thus contracts entered into by promoters of a company on its behalf before its incorporation, cannot be ratified by the company after it comes into existence [*Kelner* v. *Baxter* (1966) 2 C.P. 174].[2]

Moreover, the person who ratifies must be the person on whose behalf the agent purported to contract.

4. The principal must have contractual capacity at the date of the contract and at the date of ratification. Thus a minor on whose behalf a contract is made cannot ratify it on attaining majority.

In *Boston Deep Sea Fishing, etc., Ltd.* v. *Farnham* (1957) 3 All. E.R. 204, after the fall of France in 1940, a Fresh trawler, *S.S. Jena,* came to an English port and was managed by the appellant company. In 1945 the French company which owned the trawler purported to ratify the acts of the appellant. *Held,* it was unable to do so because at the time when the acts were done the French company was an alien enemy and therefore not competent principal.

5. The principal must, at the time of ratification, have full knowledge of the material facts or intend to ratify the contract whatever the facts may be (Sec. 198).

6. The principal must ratify the contract as a whole. He cannot ratify in part and repudiate in part. He cannot reject the burdens attached to the transaction and accept only the benefits. Either the contract is accepted in its entirety or rejected. If the principal ratifies part of a contract he is taken to have ratified it *in toto*. A person cannot approbate and reprobate.

7. The ratification must take place within a reasonable time after the contract is made, and, must be of the whole contract.

8. The ratification must be of such acts as the principal had the power to do, *e.g.*, acts of directors which are *ultra vires* the powers of a company cannot be ratified so as to bind the company.

9. Ratification can be made of voidable contracts or even of tortious acts of the agent, but it cannot be made with regard to void or criminal acts. An act which is a legal nullity cannot be ratified.[3]

10. Ratifier must communicate his ratification to the agent.

11. The act of the agent must relate to an existing thing. Thus when the tenancy has ceased there is no meaning in ratifying it.

12. Ratification cannot be made so as to subject a third party to damages, or terminate any right or interest of a third person (Sec. 200).

---

2. Taquiddin v. Gulam Mohd. 1960 A. P. 300
3. Mohd Dilawar Ali v. A.P. Muslim Wakf Board , 1967 A.P. 291.

A not being authorised thereto by *B*, demands on behalf of *B*, the delivery of a chattel, the property of *B*, from *C* who is in possession of it. This demand cannot be ratified by *B*, so as to make *C* liable for damages for his refusal to deliver. Or, *A* holds a lease from *B*, terminable on 3 months' notice. *C*, an unauthorised person, gives notice of termination to *A*. The Notice cannot be ratified by *B*, so as to be binding on *A*.

Agency by Statute—By virtue of Sec.18 of the Partnership Act, 1932, every partner is an agent of the firm and his other partners for the purpose of the business of the firm. Under the Companies Act, in the exercise of their express or implied authority, the directors (the Board of directors) are the agents through whom the company acts and, in order to bind the company, must act collectively as a Board. An individual director is not an agent of the company, unless he has been given authority by the Board to act for the Company.

CLASSES OF AGENTS

Agents are classified in various ways according to the point of view adopted. They may be divided into Mercantile or Commercial Agents, and Non-mercantile or Non-commercial Agents. Another classification, as based upon the extent of their authority, may be made into Special Agents, General Agents, and according to some writers, Universal Agents.

A **special agent** is appointed for a specific purpose or occasion to which his authority is restricted. He has authority only to do that particular act or acts in that particular transaction. If a special agent does anything outside his authority, the principal is not bound by it; and a third party is not entitled to assume that the agent has unlimited powers, but should make due enquiry as to the extent of his authority. **A general agent**, on the other hand, is appointed to do anything within the authority given to him by the principal in all transactions, or in all transactions relating to a specified trade or matter. Third parties may assume that such an agent has power to do all that it is usual for a general agent to do in the business involved; and even where the principal has limited the agent's authority the third party may safely do business with him generally, unless he is aware of the limitation, in which case he is bound by the limitation of the agent's authority. A **universal agent** is said to be one whose authority is unlimited and who can do anything on behalf of his principal. Strictly speaking, there is no such agency, and the so-called universal agent is no other than a general agent with extensive powers. For, there are many acts which cannot be performed by an agent. We do not get married by proxy, nor we paint a picture through an agent. In fact, where the work to be done is obviously personal to a particular individual, no agent can be employed.

MERCANTILE OR COMMERCIAL AGENTS

Factors—A factor is a person to whom goods or bills of lading or other documents of title are consigned for sale by a merchant residing abroad or at a distance from the place of sale. He is entrusted with possession of goods, and usually sells in his own name, without disclosing that of his principal. A factor may sell upon usual terms as to credit, may receive payment of the price, and give valid receipts. He may pledge the goods in his possession. He has *general lien* on the goods in his possession for all charges and expenses, and also an insurable interest in them. He may also warrant the goods he sells.

Brokers—"A broker is one who makes bargains for another, and receives commission (brokerage) for doing so." Thus, a broker is an agent employed to buy and sell goods for compensation known as "brokerage", and differs from a factor in not being entrusted with the possession of goods for sale, and in not having authority to contract in his own name. He makes a trade of finding buyers for those who wish to sell, and sellers for those who wish to buy. When he makes a contract, he enters the terms in his book called the memorandum book and signs it. He then sends out "Bought Note" and "Sold Note" to the buyer and seller respectively. As long as he describes himself as broker, whether with or without the name of his principal, he incurs no personal liability on his contracts. A broker has no lien on the goods, as he has no possession of goods; but on any books and papers of his principal in his possession he has a lien. An insurance broker will have a lien on the policy for his general balance.

Commission Agents—A commission agent ordinarily is a person employed to buy goods in a foreign market. He buys as principal, in the fixed foreign market and ships the goods to his own principal charging a fixed commission on the price paid. He is bound to get the goods as cheap as he reasonably can. He is an agent so far as he is bound to do his best for his principal, and may not make any profit beyond his agreed commission. He is in the position of an independent purchaser so far as his right to the goods is concerned. He cannot pledge his principal's authority without previous sanction. The term 'commission agent' is also used for an agent commissioned to act on behalf of his principal within the country under different circumstances and on different terms. Generally speaking, as pointed out by Viscount Simon L.C. in *Luxor (Eastborne) Ltd.* v. *Cooper,* 1941 A.C. 108 at p.120, such contracts can fall in three classes:

1. The first is the class in which the agent is promised a commission by his principal if he succeeds in introducing to his principal a person who makes an adequate offer usually an offer of not less than the stipulated amount.
2. The second class is of cases in which the property is put into the hands of the agent to dispose of for the owner and the agent accepts the employment and, it may be, expends money and time in endeavouring to carry it out.
3. The third class is of cases where the agent is promised his commission only upon completion of the transaction which he has endeavoured to bring about between the offeror and his principal.

In the cases falling under the first class the only thing which the agent undertakes is to introduce to his principal a person who is ready, willing and prepared to take the property for the stipulated amount. He does not undertake to do anything further and if he performs what he has undertaken to do he earns his commission. In the second class of cases the agent is given full authority to transfer the property after he has found a possible purchaser. He has accepted to expend time and money in carrying out his part of the work and there is a sort of implied term that the principal will not withdraw the authority he has given after the agent has succeeded in finding a possible purchaser. In such cases, if the principal withdraws his instructions after the agent has found a purchaser, the commission will still be payable. In the third class must be put contracts by which a person instructs an agent to arrange for the transfer of a property and promises to pay a sum of money only in case the agent succeeds in getting the transfer completed. The intention is to pay the amount of the consideration of the transfer when it is received by the principal. It is obvious that in this class of cases the commission will be payable only if the agent succeeds in having the transaction completed. Till that event happens he has no claim (*Raja Ram Jaiswal* v. *Ganesh Prashad,* 1959 All. 29).

Del Credere Agents—A Del Credere agent is an agent, who in consideration of an extra remuneration called the Del Credere Commission guarantees to his principal that the third persons with whom he enters into contracts shall perform their obligations. Thus such an agent guarantees to his principal that he will only sell to persons who will pay for what they buy; and if the buyer does not pay, he (Del Credere agent) will pay. The position of a *Pakka adatia* as agent is analogous to that of a *del credere agent.* His legal position like that of a *del credere* agent is partly that of an insurer, and partly that of a surety. He agrees for a special remuneration to find a buyer or seller for his up-country constituent; and if he fails to do so he is liable in damages. But a *Katcha adatia* is merely an agent and does not make himself responsible to the principal for the non-performance of the contract by the third party. He is, however, responsible to the other adatia or shroff who acts on behalf of the other contracting party.

Auctioneers—An auctioneer is an agent who sells goods by auction, i.e., to the highest bidder in public competition. He has no authority to warrant the goods sold and can deliver the goods only on receipt of the price. He is the agent only of the vendor; but in English law, he is also the agent of the buyer for the purpose of signing the memorandum under the English Sale of Goods Act. As he has possession of the goods, he is bound to arrange for their proper storage, and is responsible to the owner for any damage caused through his negligence. He is authorised to receive proceeds of the sale of goods, but on a sale of land to receive only a deposit. He enjoys a lien on the goods for his charges.

Bankers—The relationship between a banker and his customers is ordinarily that of debtor and creditor, but he is an agent of his customer when he buys or sells securities, collects cheques, dividends, bills or promissory notes on behalf of his customer. The banker is an agent in so far as he must pay the customer's cheque when the account is in credit The banker has a general lien on all securities and goods, in respect of the general balance due to him by the customer which has come into the banker's possession in the course of his dealings as banker with his customer and which security and goods have not been left for specific purposes, *e.g.*, safe custody.

INDENTORS

An indentor or indenting agent is one who, for a commission, procures a sale or a purchase on behalf of his principal, with a merchant abroad.

NON-COMMERCIAL AGENTS

Non-commercial agents may be Estate Agents, who are employed to negotiate the sale and purchase, or lease, of immovable property, or House Agents, who are similarly engaged with respect to houses, shops, etc., or Law Agents, whose business it is to look after the legal affairs of their principals. Besides, there are Counsel (Barrister or Advocate), and Attorney and wife.

Counsel (Barrister or Advocate)—According to the practice and traditions of the English Bar, an Advocate or Barrister, accepting a brief is not an agent of the client, and although he undertakes a duty on his client's behalf, he does not enter into any contract with him. As a consequence, the ordinary rule as to limits of an agent's authority does not apply, and a counsel has wide powers as to the mode of conducting the case for his client, and can even compromise it on his client's behalf. The same is the case in India, at least in the three Presidency towns.

Attorney—The English and Indian rule with regard to the attorney is that he can make a reasonable *bonafide* compromise if not specifically prohibited by the client.

Wife—The relationship between husband and wife has sometimes led to difficult questions, as to how far the wife is the agent of the husband. The Full Bench of the Allahabad High Court has laid down the rule in *Girdhari Lal* v. *Crawford* (1887) 9 All. 146 at p. 156, that' 'the liability of a husband for a wife's debt depends on the principles of agency, and the husband can only be liable, when it is shown that he has expressly or impliedly sanctioned what the wife has done. Where the husband has expressly authorised his wife to borrow money or pledge his credit, the position is simple: the husband is liable. The question becomes difficult when a wife is regarded to have implied authority as agent of her husband. Where the husband and wife are living together, the wife is presumed to have implied authority to pledge the husband's credit for necessaries. But the husband may escape liability if he can prove that (*i*) he has expressly forbidden his wife from borrowing money or buying on credit, (*ii*) the goods purchased were not necessaries, (*iii*) he has allowed sufficient funds for purchasing the articles she needed to the knowledge of the tradesman; or (*iv*) the tradesman has been expressly told to give credit to the wife." Where the wife lives apart from the husband, through no fault of hers, and is therefore entitled to claim support or maintenance, she has an implied authority to bind the husband for necessaries of life, if the husband does not provide for her maintenance. But if the wife lives apart of her own will and without any justification, she is not her husband's agent and cannot bind him even for necessaries as the husband is under no obligation to maintain her.

DELEGATION OF AUTHORITY BY AGENT

When the fact of agency is established, it is also established that the agent has some authority, depending upon the type of agency, to act on behalf of the principal and bind him by his acts. The nature and quantum of authority need further discussion but at this stage, it is advisable to state that ordinarily the agent is expected to perform his duties as agent himself personally. *Delegatus non potest delegare*—a delegate cannot further delegate, is the maxim. An agent, being himself a delegate of his principal, cannot pass on that delegated authority to some one else. The reason for this rule is that confidence in a particular person is at the root of the contract of agency. An agent is usually selected in reliance upon some personal qualifications, and it would be unfair, if not injurious to the principal, if the authority to act could be shifted to another. This is particularly true when the agent is appointed for the performance of any task requiring discretion or judgment. But to this general rule there are certain exceptions, when the agent is permitted to delegate his authority. He may appoint sub-agents in the following circumstances:

(1) Where the principal has expressly permitted delegation of such power; (2) where the custom of the trade permits delegation; (3) where the principal knows that the agent intends to delegate his authority; (4) where the nature of the authority is such that a deputy is necessary to complete the business; (5) where the act to be done is purely ministerial and does not involve the exercise of discretion, e.g., clerical or routine work; (6) in an unforeseen emergency, the agent can always delegate.

SUB-AGENT AND SUBSTITUTED AGENT

Where an agent under express or implied authority of delegation, appoints another person to act in the matter of the agency, such other person is called a "sub-agent", if he works under the control of the agent; and a "substituted agent", if the agent walks out of the transaction and the newly appointed agent carries on the business of the agency. The relation of the sub-agent to the original agent is as between themselves, that of agent and principal. As the sub-agent acts under the control of the agent, there is no privity of contract between the principal and the sub-agent, and, therefore, the sub-agent cannot use the principal for any moneys due, although the sub-agent binds the principal, as regards third parties. But the principal and the sub-agent have right to sue only the "agent", who is the immediate contracting party, for anything due to principal from the sub-agent and for remuneration payable to the sub-agent by the principal. To this rule, there is one exception that, if the sub-agent is guilty of fraud or wilful wrong, the principal has a concurrent right to proceed both against the agent and the sub-agent. The privity of contract between the principal and the sub-agent is established in such a case. Where an agent improperly appoints a sub-agent, *i.e.*, appoints without authority to appoint, the principal will not be bound by the acts of the sub-agent, nor can he hold the sub-agent responsible for the latter's fraud or wilful wrong. The acts of the sub-agent will, however, bind the agent, as regards third parties as well as the principal.

The Indian Contract Act makes a distinction between an "ordinary sub-agent" and a person who is put in relation with the principal and called the "substituted agent" or "agent of the principal." The important difference between the two is that in the case of the substitute there is privity of contract between him and the principal so that the principal can sue the substitute for accounts or damages and the substitute can sue the principal for remuneration. The original agent who appointed or named this agent drops altogether from the transaction. Where A instructs B, his solicitor, to sell his property by auction, and to employ an auctioneer for the purpose, and B names C, an auctioneer, to conduct the sale, C is not a sub-agent, but he is A's agent for the conduct of the sale, and will be called a substitute or substituted agent. As the original agent walks out of the transaction, he is required to exercise due diligence and care in choosing the substitute, and if he is negligent in his choice he will be liable for damages to the principal. Diligence here means the diligence which a man of ordinary prudence would exercise in his own affairs.

AGENT, SERVANT OR INDEPENDENT CONTRACTOR

An agent may be either a servant or independent contractor; but every servant or a contractor is not necessarily an agent. The relation between master and servant and that between principal and agent was explained by the Supreme Court in *Lakshminarayan Ram Gopal & Son Ltd.* v. *The Government of Hyderabad,* 1954 S.C. 364.[4] Briefly stated, it is as follows: A principal directs the agent as to what is to be done, while a master has the further right to direct how the work is to be done. A servant acts under the control and supervision of his master and is bound to conform to all reasonable orders given to him in the course of his work. An agent, though bound to exercise his authority in accordance with all lawful instructions of the principal, is not subject in its exercise and the direct control or supervision of the principal. An agent as such is not a servant, but a servant especially in superior service, is generally for some purposes his master's implied agent, the extent of agency depending on the duties or position of the servant. It is for this reason that an agent is sometimes described as a "superior servant." An independent contractor is independent of any control or interference by the employer and uses his own means to produce the result. Thus if the agreement between E and C provides that C is to accomplish a certain result, *e.g.*, to build for E a boat for ₹ 500, and has full control over the manner and methods to be pursued in bringing about the result, (*i.e.*, building the boat) he is deemed an independent contractor and E, who receives the benefit of his services, is in no sense responsible to third parties for his actions.

PART4-B
DUTIES AND RIGHTS OF AGENT

DUTIES OF AN AGENT

1. To carry out the work undertaken according to instructions—If the agent fails to act according to instructions, the ordinary rules of contract will apply and he will become liable for breach. He must act within the scope of the authority conferred upon him and carry out strictly the instructions of the principal. Thus, where the principal instructed the agent to warehouse the goods at a particular place, and the agent warehoused them at another place equally good but cheaper, and the goods were destroyed by fire, it was held that as the agent had not acted according to instructions of the principal, he was liable for the loss, even though he had acted for the benefit of the principal and the loss had ensued without any neglect on his part.

2. To follow the custom in the absence of instructions—Where the principal has not given any express instructions, the agent must follow the custom prevailing in the same kind of business at the place where the agent conducts business, otherwise he will be liable for any loss sustained by the principal (Sec.211).

3. To carry out the work with reasonable care, skill and diligence—What is reasonable care and diligence depends on the circumstances of each case, but generally the agent must at least exercise the same degree of care, skill and diligence as he would exercise about his own affairs. Where, by the nature of his profession, the agent purports to have special skill, then the degree of skill reasonably to be expected from the members of that profession must be shown. Thus a solicitor, who is an agent of his client, may be held liable for not possessing the requisite skill. For example, where he instituted proceedings in a Court having no jurisdiction, or where he started proceedings under a wrong section, and the suit was therefore dismissed, the solicitor was held liable for damages.

4. To communicate with the principal—In cases of difficulty, the agent must communicate with the principal and get his instructions (Sec. 214). Thus, where the goods were consigned by the principal

---

4. See also State of Madras v. J.R.M. Contractors Co. 1959 A.P. 352.

to a place and the agent took them to a different place for sale in order to minimise the loss without communicating and getting principal's instructions, and the loss resulted, the agent was held responsible.

5. Not to make any profit out of his agency other than his agreed or reasonable remuneration— As the agent acts on behalf of his principal, all moneys received by him on the principal's behalf must be paid over to the principal. The agent can, however, deduct all moneys for his remuneration or expenses properly incurred. This duty to pay over moneys includes also the duty to pay over all illegal gratification received by the agent. Where an agent receives some moneys *bonafide,* he will be required to pay over the same to the principal, but he is entitled to his remuneration; but where his acts are not *bonafide,* he will also lose his remuneration. Thus, where *P* directed *A* to sell a shop at the best price obtainable, and *A* sold it to *B* on the understanding that *B* would pay *A* ₹ 200, it was *held* that *A* must pay over ₹ 200 to *P* and forgo his commission. Where the third party is guilty of fraud, the principal may rescind the contract.

6. To keep and render accounts—It is the duty of the agent to keep true and correct accounts of all his transactions and to be always ready to produce them to his principal. In general, he should not mix moneys belonging to his principal with his own money, and in these circumstances the agent is the trustee of the funds in his hands. But, where the terms of the agency permit mixing, the agent may do so, when he will be treated a debtor of the principal. Thus a banker holds his customer's funds as the customer's debtor and is entitled to mix them with his own.

7. Not to deal on his own account—An agent must not deal on his own account in the business of the agency, as no agent is "permitted to put himself in the position where his interest conflicts with his duty." An agent must not become a principal party to the transaction as against his principal. But, if he wants to do so, he must fully disclose to the principal all the facts in respect of the transaction and obtain his consent, before acting on his own account. Thus a broker employed to sell stock, can not himself buy, nor can a broker instructed to buy, become the seller himself, without obtaining a distinct consent to do so. If the agent acts on his own account without obtaining consent and without disclosing all the material information the principal may claim the profits which the agent might have made, or disclaim the losses if the business had ended in a loss; and where there has been an executed contract the principal may obtain rescission of the same without proving fraud on the part of agent. So where a *vakil,* employed to bid for certain properties, purchased the properties himself, it was held that the principal could claim the properties. Or, where an agent, employed to buy grain, delivered his own grain to the principal at a rate higher than the market rate, it was held that he must account for the profit. Again where an agent for sale, purchased the property himself, it was held that the sale was not binding. But, if the agent had, in the above cases, told the principal that he himself was purchasing or selling, and had given the principal free and unbiased use of his own discretion and judgment in the matter, the transaction would be binding.

8. Not to set up adverse title—When the agent has obtained goods or property from the principal as an agent, he is precluded from setting up his own title or setting up the title of third parties to the property.

9. Not to use information obtained in the course of the agency against the principal—Where an agent has obtained any information in the course of agency, the agent must on no account use it against the interest of the principal. If an agent does make use of such information, the principal can stop him from doing so by an injunction.

10. Not to delegate authority—Subject to the six exceptions noted above an agent must not delegate his authority to another person, but perform the work himself.

RIGHTS OF AN AGENT

1. Right to receive remuneration—Where the services rendered by the agent were not voluntary or gratuitous, the agent is entitled to receive the agreed remuneration or if none was agreed, a reasonable remuneration. An agent becomes entitled to receive remuneration as soon as he has done what he had undertaken to do even though the transaction has fallen through either because the principal has failed to carry out his part of the contract or because the third party has backed out. But the agent must show that he has done all that he had agreed to do, before he can claim his remuneration. Thus, commission becomes due to the broker, where he has procured a party who is willing to open negotiation on a reasonable basis and is desirous of entering into a contract with the principal.[5] The agent is entitled to commission, where he has procured orders for the manufacturers, and they are unable to execute them owing to the outbreak of the war. Even where the contract becomes void because of *bonafide* mistake, the Agent will be entitled to remuneration, if he has carried out what he had bargained to do. Where the agent is prevented from earning his remuneration by some wrongful act or default of the principal, the agent can recover by way of damages the actual loss sustained by him which, in cases where he has done everything will be the full amount of remuneration.[6] But where the agent has misconducted himself in the business of the agency, he will not be entitled to his remuneration (Sec. 220). A principal is entitled to have an honest agent and it is only the honest agent who is entitled to any commission.

2. **Right of lien**—Certain classes of agents, *e.g.*, factors, who have the goods and property of their principal in their possession, have a lien on the goods and property in respect of their remuneration and expenses and liabilities incurred. This lien is generally a particular lien confined to claims arising in respect of the particular goods and property. But by special contract, an agent factor may get a general lien extending to all claims arising out of the agency. For the exercise of a lien, the goods must be in actual or constructive possession of the agent, and the possession must have been acquired by the agent without prejudice to any of his duties. Thus, if the goods are in the agent's possession the lien will not be affected even by the subsequent insolvency of the principal. A properly appointed sub-agent also enjoys the right of lien against the principal's goods. But an agent loses his right of lien, where he parts with the possession of the goods. If, however, at the time of parting with the goods he reserves the right of lien or where goods are obtained from him by fraud or other unlawful means, he will not lose his lien.

3. **Right of stoppage in transit**—This right is acquired by the agent in two cases. If he has bought goods on behalf of his principal either with his own money, or by incurring a personal liability for the price, he stands towards the principal in the position of an unpaid seller, and as such possesses the right to stop the goods in transit, if they have been delivered to the carrier for transmission to the principal. Conversely, where an agent (*del credere*) is personally liable to his principal for the price of the goods sold, he may exercise the unpaid seller's right to stop the goods in transit on the insolvency of the buyer.

4. **Right of Indemnification**—As the agent represents the principal, the agent has a right to be indemnified by the principal against all charges, expenses and liabilities properly incurred by him in the course of the agency. Although the right of indemnity covers all liabilities incurred by the agent, yet the damages which the agent can recover from the principal are those which directly, immediately and naturally flow from the execution of the agency. K carried on the business of commission agents. B entered into several forward contracts for the purchase and sale of bullion through K. The transactions proved unprofitable to B and loss aggregated to a sum of ₹ 21,500. The entire amount was paid to third parties by K on behalf of B. *Held, B* must indemnify K, as K had paid the losses for B.[7] Sec. 225 of

5. D.S. Sahni v. Faqir Singh, 1960 J. & K. 6; Raja Ram v. Ganesh Prasad, 1959 AIL 29; Roopji & Sons v. Dyer Meaken, 1930 All. 545; Farid Baksh v. Hergulal Singh, 1936 A.LJ. 1163; Giddys v. Horcfall (1747) 1. A.E.R. 460; E.H. Bennett v. Millet (1948) 2 A.E.R. 929.

6. Abdullah Ahmed v. Animendra K. Mitter (1950) S.C.R., 30

7. Kishanlal v. Bhanwarlal. 1954 S.C,. 500.

the Indian Contract Act gives right to the agent to compensation for injuries sustained by him by neglect or want of skill on the part of the principal. He can also claim against his co-agents on the same grounds. But the principal is entitled to plead contributory negligence or common employment, wherever possible.

> ### PART 4-C
> ### EXTENT OF AGENT'S AUTHORITY AND PRINCIPAL'S RESPONSIBILITY

SCOPE AND EXTENT OF AGENT'S AUTHORITY

When the fact of agency is established, it is not enough to know that he has authority to bind his principal, but we must know the scope and quantum of authority. The need to consider this fact arises because the agent is bound to obey the instructions of the principal, having no right to depart from them even for the principal's benefit. But he has also, what may be called incidental or implied authority. Sec. 188[8] of the Contract Act gives him an implied authority to do all that may be reasonably necessary for doing the act authorised by the principal. On the basis of the section the authority of an agent includes that which is—

1. expressly given by the principal—Express or Declared authority;
2. incidental to the authority that is expressly given by the principal—Incidental or Implied authority;
3. customary for such agent to exercise—Customary authority;
4. an apparent or ostensible authority, which arises by estoppel.

The first three kinds of authority may be classified as Real Authority as distinguished from Apparent or Ostensible Authority.

Express Authority—An authority specifically bestowed by the principal on an agent through written or oral communication is termed express authority. Here the principal tells the agent to perform a certain act.

Incidental or Implied Authority—An agent has implied authority to perform an act reasonably necessary to execute the express authority. To illustrate, if the principal authorises the agent to purchase goods without furnishing funds to pay for them, the agent has implied incidental authority to purchase the goods on credit Similarly, where A is employed to find a purchaser for property he can describe the property and state any circumstances which may affect the value. Again, where A is engaged to recover a debt due to the principal abroad, he can adopt any legal process necessary for the purpose and give a valid receipt for the money received. Also, the secretary of a co-operative society authorised to carry on its business on sound lines is deemed to have implied authority to buy goods on credit.[9] But where A is authorised to find a buyer, he cannot enter into a contract of sale.[10] A station master has no authority to pledge the credit of the railway for medical attendance on a sick passenger.[11]

Agent's Authority in Emergency—An agent has authority to do all such things which may be necessary to protect the principal from loss in an emergency and which he would do to protect his own property under similar circumstances (Section 189). This kind of authority arises only when the agent has no opportunity to contact the principal and request instructions. For example, where owing to delay in transit, butter may be in danger of becoming useless, its sale by the railway for the best

---

8. "Section 188. An agent having an authority to do an act has authority to do every lawful thing which is necessary in order to do such act. An agent having an authority to carry on a business has authority to do every lawful thing necessary for the purpose, or usually done in the course of conducting business."

9. Valapad Co-op. Stores v. Srinivasan Iyer, 1964 Ker. 176.

10. Durga v. Rajendra. 1923Cal.57.

11. Cox v. Midland Countries Rly. Co. (1849) 3 Ex. 268.

price will be justified, as an authority exercised in emergency.

Agent's Authority by Custom—An agent has authority to do any act which, according to the custom or usage of the trade, usually accompanies the transaction for which he is authorised to act as agent. For example, where a salesman is authorised to receive payments for cars sold, he would be deemed to have implied authority to accept a cheque instead of cash in the usual or customary way. But an agent with authority to receive cheques in payments does not have implied authority to cash them.

Apparent Authority—Apparent authority, if it may be called authority, is one which is not real but which the principal by his words or conduct reasonably leads a third party to believe that the agent possesses. If a principal creates an appearance that reasonably leads another to believe that his agent has the authority to make contracts for him, he cannot deny this authority when a third party relies upon this appearance by making a contract with that agent. The result of apparent authority is that a person is bound on a contract he never wished to make. The policy behind apparent authority is similar to that of estoppel. Looking at the reasons from a broader perspective, the policy behind apparent authority is of practical nature. Remember that almost all business is carried on by agents. If business firms could avoid their contracts merely by denying the authority of their agent in a particular case, almost no contract would be enforceable. Business as it is known in the modern world could not be conducted. Because of these pragmatic considerations, the opposite approach is taken. Businessmen are entitled to assume that an agent has the authority that his principal causes him to appear to have. For all these reasons, a contract negotiated by an agent whom the principal has clothed with an appearance of authority may be enforced just as if the agent actually had the real authority he appeared to have. This will be so even if the principal has instructed the agent not to make that very sort of contract.

The reason is obvious. If the principal has clothed his agent with authority to perform certain acts but has given the agent certain secret instructions which limit his authority, the third person is allowed to take the authority of the agent at its face value and is not bound by the secret limitations of which he has no knowledge. If the third person is aware of the limitations, as for example, contained in a written authority, he cannot hold the principal liable for acts of the agent which are in excess of limitations. The purpose of the rule that a principal is bound by apparent authority is to protect innocent parties, and it has no application when the person dealing with the agent has actual knowledge of the agent's powers.

Very often a title or a position automatically gives an agent a measure of apparent authority. A store manager, for example, would have rather broad powers to contract Therefore, naming an agent as General Manager but secretly limiting his authority to an unusual degree will result in his having an area of apparent authority. The apparent authority in this case stems from the title 'general manager'.

It may be observed that the mere assertion by the agent that he has a certain measure of authority does not create apparent authority. The source of the apparent authority must be traceable to some deed or word of the principal. Were this not the case, any one could assume the power to contract for almost any principal, merely by telling third parties that he possessed the authority to do so. This sort of thing is beyond the control of any principal. For this reason, the burden is placed upon the third party to ascertain that there is reasonably convincing evidence, stemming from circumstances, a statement, or an impression that stem from the principal, that the agent does have authority for his act.

RESPONSIBILITIES OF PRINCIPAL TO THIRD PARTIES

The principal is bound by all acts of the agent done within the scope of actual, apparent and ostensible authority. In other words, the principal is liable for acts done by the agent when actually authorised to do those acts, as also for such acts as are necessary for the proper execution of such authority. Again, where a principal gives general authority to conduct any business, he will be bound by every act of the agent incidental to such business, or which falls within the apparent scope of the agent's authority[12] or as it is often called the "ostensible authority" of the agent. We have already dealt with the doctrine of apparent authority, which may be reiterated for purposes of emphasis. When an appearance has been created by the principal that his agent has a certain measure of authority, and relying upon this appearance a third party enters into a contract, the principal will be liable for this apparent authority even if he has instructed the agent not to make that sort of contract. An apparent or ostensible agency is as effective as an agency deliberately created. Appearance arid reality are one. Where *P* authorises *A* to sell goods, but privately instructs him not to sell for credit, and *A* sells them for credit to *C*, who does not know of the limitation, the sale is binding on *P*. Where, however, the agent exceeds the authority granted to him by the principal, the principal may either disown such an act as in excess of the authority or ratify the same.

The principal is liable for misrepresentation or fraud of the agent committed in the course of the employment or within the scope of the employment or within the scope of the agent's apparent authority (Section 238). It is immaterial whether such acts are done for the benefit of the principal or exclusively for the benefit of the agent, and against the principal's interest.

The principal is bound by the admissions made by the agent. For example, where a passenger lost his article by theft and the station master reported to the police that the porter had absconded with the parcel, it was held that the admission made by the station master was binding on the railway, and the company was responsible to pay for the parcel.

The principal is bound by the information obtained by the agent in the course of the business of the principal, on the presumption that the agent has done his duty and 'communicated the information-to the principal, even though, in fact, he has not done so. Knowledge of the agent is said to be the knowledge of the principal: the principal is said to have constructive notice. But to be binding on the principal, the information must be material to the business of the agency and not irrelevant to it. Constructive notice will not be presumed where the agent is guilty of fraud, for it cannot be reasonably expected that the agent would ever communicate his own fraud to the principal.

LIABILITY OF UNDISCLOSED PRINCIPAL

The principal even though his name was kept secret by the agent at the time of the contract is, on being discovered, responsible for the contracts of the agent—It may sometimes happen that an agent discloses the fact that he is an agent but at the same time conceals his principal's name. Here the principal is liable, and not the agent, unless there is a trade custom making the agent liable. But it is essential that the undisclosed principal exists and is, in fact, the principal at the time the contract is made. He cannot be brought into existence as a principal after the contract has been concluded.

CONCEALED PRINCIPAL

The principal is liable to third parties even where the agent is also liable, unless the third parties have elected to sue the agent, or led the principal to believe that the agent alone will be *held* responsible. The law which superadds the liability of an agent does not detract from the liability of the principal. This will happen where an agent conceals not merely the name of the principal but also the fact that there is a principal. In this case, the third parry must necessarily look to the agent for payment or performance, and the agent may sue or be sued on the contract. Careful consideration must be given to the position of the principal: (*i*) when the third party discovers his existence and wants to make use of discovery, and (*ii*) when the principal decides to intervene and assert any rights he may have against the third party. In the first case, when the third party discovers that there is a principal, if he

12. Gayarsilal. v. Sita Charan, 1963 M.P. 164.

has not already obtained judgment against the agent he (third party) may sue either the principal or the agent, or both, and the principal is not released from liability until a clear election has been made by the third party to proceed against the agent alone. If the third party chooses to sue the principal and not the agent he must allow the principal the benefit of all payments made by him to the agent on account of the contract before the agency was disclosed. Secondly, if the principal intervenes and sues the third party, then in the same way the third party is entitled to be placed in the same situation at the time of the disclosure of the real principal as if the agent had been the contracting party. For example, if the third party has made part payment to the agent, he must be allowed the benefit of it. Para 2 of Section 231, however, states that "if the principal discloses himself before the contract is completed, the other contracting party may refuse to fulfil the contract if he can show that, if he had known who was the principal in the contract, or if he had known that the agent was not a principal, he would not have entered into the contract"

It is clear from the three circumstances that the effect of a contract made by an agent varies according to the circumstances under which the agent contracted, *i.e.*, for a disclosed, undisclosed or concealed principal.

PART4-D
PERSONAL LIABILITY OF AGENT TO THIRD PARTY

We have seen above that when an agent contracts as agent on behalf of a principal whom he names to the other party, the agent is merely a connecting link between his principal and the other party, and incurs no personal liability. As we have seen earlier, the essential characteristic of an agent is that he is invested with a legal power to alter his principal's legal relations with third parties; the principal is under the a correlative liability to have his legal relations altered. To this rule, there are certain exceptions. An agent will be personally liable in the following cases:—

When the contract expressly provides—The third party may, when contracting with an agent, stipulate that the agent should make himself personally liable on the contract. If the agent agrees to this stipulation he will be personally liable for any breach of the contract.

When the agent signs a negotiable instrument in his own name without making it clear that he is signing it only as agent, he would be personally liable as the maker of the note, even though he may be described in the body of the note as the agent.

When the agent acts for a foreign principal, it is the agent who is liable, not the principal.

When acting for a concealed principal—The agent would be personally liable where he acts for a concealed principal because the third party could not look to the credit of a principal whose existence is not disclosed, and relies mainly on the credit of the agent. The third party may, however, on discovering the identity of the principal sue the principal also if he so chooses.

When acting for principal who cannot be sued—Where the name of the principal has been disclosed, but no suit can be filed against him, agent will be personally liable as the credit is presumed to have been given to the agent and not to the principal. For example, where an agent acts for a minor or an Ambassador, he will be personally liable (*Union of India* v. *Chinoy Chablani & Co.,* 1976 Cal. 467).

Agent liable for breach of warranty—A person who professes to act as agent, but has no authority from the alleged principal or has exceeded his authority, is liable to an action for breach of warranty of authority at the suit of the party with whom he professed to make the contract [*Cohen* v. *Wright* (1857) 8 E. & B. 647]. The action is based not on the original contract, but on implied promise by the agent that he had authority to make the original contract. For instance, where an agent acts for a non-existing principal, he is personally liable. But before the agent could be *held responsible,* it must first be shown that: (*i*) he had made an untrue representation; (*ii*) the third party had been misled or induced to deal with the agent on the faith of such untrue representation; (*iii*) the principal had repudiated or refused the transaction; (*iv*) loss had occurred to the third party; and (*v*) the untrue representation was one of fact and not one of law. In *Haji Ismail* v. *James Short* (1910) M.L.J. 383, where broker acted upon a wrong telegram due to a mistake on the part of the telegram authorities, it was *held* that the broker was personally liable.

Money paid by mistake or fraud—Where an agent receives money by mistake or fraud from third parties, he can be sued therefor. Similarly, where an agent has paid money by mistake or fraud to third parties, the agent can himself file a suit for the recovery of the amount.

When authority is one "coupled with interest" or where trade-usage or custom makes agent personally liable—Where an agent has an interest in the subject matter of the contract which he signs, his authority is said to be coupled with interest. He is really a principal to the extent of that interest and may sue in his own name or be sued. *A* authorises *B* to sell *A*'s land and out of the sale proceeds to pay himself the debts due to him from *A*. *B*'s authority is coupled with interest. If a factor is authorised to pay himself out of the sale proceeds, or he is authorised to sell at the best possible price and if the proceeds are insufficient to pay him off, to draw on the principal, this gives the factor an interest in the goods. In these cases he becomes personally liable to the extent of his interest.

For his Tort independently of contract or tort arising out of the contract, as where it has been induced by the fraud of the agent, the agent is severally and jointly liable with his principal. In the particular form of agency known as partnership, a partner is both an agent and principal, and as such personally liable.

PART4-E
TERMINATION OF AGENCY

Agency may terminate in the same manner as any other contract, viz., by the operation of law or by the act of parties. In particular, a contract of agency may come to an end—

By performance of the contract of agency—Where the agency is one for a single transaction, the agency terminates when the transaction is completed. For example, an agency for the sale of property ends when the sale is completed and does not continue until payment of the price.

By agreement between the parties—The agency can be terminated at any time and at any stage by the mutual agreement between the principal and the agent.

By expiration of the period fixed for the contract of agency—If the authority is given for a fixed period, the agency comes to an end on the expiry of the period even if the business is not completed.

By the death of the principal or the agent—An agent with a power of attorney to present a document for registration, presented it for registration after the death of the principal, and the Registrar knowing of the death of the principal registered the document. The registration was *held* to be invalid.[13] On the termination of the agency by the death of the principal the agent must, on behalf of the representative of his late principal, take all reasonable steps to protect the interests of the principal entrusted to him (Section 209).

By the insanity of either party—Doubtless it is true an agent need not be a person capable of entering into a contract so that a person can appoint even a lunatic as his agent, if he so desires, but if an agent becomes insane during the agency, the agent's authority terminates as soon as the agent becomes insane. The authority will, of course, terminate on the principal becoming insane, in which case the agent is required to do everything for the protection of the principal's interests.

---

13. Majid-in-Nissa v. Abdur Rahim (1900) 23 All. 233.

By the insolvency of the principal and in some cases that of the agent—The bankruptcy of the principal terminates the agency, and also that of the agent, except in cases where the act which the agent is to do is merely formal.[14]

Where the principal or agent is an incorporated company, by its dissolution. A company, after being dissolved, comes to an end, and its powers as principal or agent terminate thereafter.

By the destruction of the subject-matter—Where the subject-matter in respect of which agency was created has been destroyed, the agency comes to an end. Thus, when the agency was created for the sale of a horse or a house, and the horse dies or the house is destroyed by fire, the agency necessarily comes to an end.[15]

By the renunciation of his employment by the agent—Generally, an agent can, after giving a reasonable notice of his intention, renounce the contract of agency, for a person cannot be compelled to continue as agent against his will. Where an agency is for a fixed period and the agent renounces it without sufficient cause before the time fixed he shall have to compensate the principal.

By revocation by the principal—The principal can revoke the authority of the agent at any time. Where the agent is appointed to do a single act, the authority can be revoked any time before the act is begun. In the case of a continuous agency, notice of revocation is essential to the agent and also to the third parties who have acted on the agency with knowledge of the principal. If reasonable notice is not given the principal will be liable to compensate the agent, and be bound by the acts of the agency with respect to third parties. Notice to the agent is also necessary in the case of agency for a fixed period.

AN AGENCY IS IRREVOCABLE IN THE FOLLOWING CASES

(*i*) Where the agency is one coupled with interest, *i.e.*, one created for effectuating any security or protecting any interest of the agent, it is irrevocable during the existence of such interest.[16] Where a factor has made advances to the principal and is authorised to sell at the best price and recoup the advances made by him, or where the agent is authorised to collect moneys from third parties and pay himself the debt due by the principal, the agencies are those coupled with interest and irrevocable. Even the death or insanity of the principal does not terminate the authority in this case.

(*ii*) When an agent has incurred personal liability the agency becomes irrevocable, for the principal cannot be permitted to withdraw, leaving the agent exposed to risk or liability he has incurred.

(*iii*) When the authority has been partly exercised by the agent it becomes irrevocable, in particular with regard to obligations which arise from acts already done (Section 204).

WHEN TERMINATION OF AGENCY TAKES EFFECT

Termination of agency takes effect or is complete when it becomes known to the agent, and as far as the third parties are concerned, when it becomes known to them (Section 208), and in case of termination by revocation not from the moment revocation is made by the principal but from the time of the knowledge of the agent or the third parties of such revocation. Therefore, if an agent, knowing that his authority has terminated, enters into a contract with a third party who deals with him *bonafide* the contract will be binding on the principal as against the third party.

Sub-Agents—The termination of an agent's authority puts an end also to the authority of the sub-agent appointed by the agent (Section 210). But the authority of a substituted agent will not be affected thereby.

---

14. Re Pollitt (1893) 1 Q.B. 455.

15. French & Co. v. Leesten Shipping Co. (1922) A.C. 451.

16. Ramchandra v. Chinubhai (1943) 45, B.L.R. 1075.

MEANING OF AUTHORITY COUPLED WITH AN INTEREST

An agency is coupled with interest when the agent has an interest in the authority granted to him or when the agent has an interest in the subject-matter with which he is authorised to deal. An agent has an *interest in the authority* when he has given a consideration or has paid for the right to exercise the authority granted to him. To illustrate, if the agent, in return for making a loan of money to the principal, is given as security authority to collect rents due to the principal such authority cannot be revoked by the principal. An agent has an *interest in the subject-matter* when for a consideration he is given an interest in the property with which he is dealing. Hence, when the agent is authorised to sell certain property of the principal, and is given, as security for a debt owed to him by the principal, a lien on such property, his authority to sell cannot be revoked by the principal.

The employment must, in its nature, be such as the authority of the agent cannot be revoked without loss to the agent. The interest must be a substantial interest in the subject-matter of the agency, and not the ordinary interest which a man usually has in getting remuneration for his services. A mere arrangement that the agent's remuneration be paid out of the rents collected by him as such does not give him interest in the property within the meaning of Section 202 of the Contract Act. Thus, an agent who sells cloth and is entitled by an agreement with his principal to retain part of the price of the goods has no interest in the cloth kept with him and is not a person who has an interest in the property which forms the subject-matter of the agreement within the meaning of his section (*Dalchand* v. *Hazarimal,* 1932 Nag. 32). But a vendee retaining a part of the price to pay off encumbrances is an agent with interest of the vendor (*Subba Row* v. *Varadiah,* 1943 Mad. 885). In the words of Willis, C.J. in *Smart* v. *Sanders* 5 C.B. 917, "the authority must have been given by an agreement entered into for sufficient consideration for the purpose of conferring some benefit on the donee of that authority."

SUMMARY

Principal and Agent—A person employed by another to act on behalf of or represent that other in dealings with third parties is called the agent. The person on whose behalf the agent acts is known as the principal.

Generally, what a person can do himself, he can do through an agent. And the acts of the agent are the acts of the principal, for he who acts through an agent is taken to be acting himself. Although the principal and the third party must be competent to contract, an agent need not have capacity to contract, as the agent is only the connecting link between the two parties, and his acts are the acts of the principal. But a minor agent is not liable to the principal for misconduct or negligence. Thus, a minor can be an agent and can effectively bind his principal, but he is not bound to the principal.

A contract of agency like any other contract may be express or implied, but consideration is not an essential element in this contract. The fact that the principal has consented to be represented by the agent is sufficient determinant, and consideration to support the promise by the agent to act in that capacity.

Agency may also arise by estoppel, holding out, necessity, or subsequent ratification by the principal.

In a large number of business dealings, agencies are created by word of mouth or in writing, and are called express agencies. The best example of written contract of agency is a Power of Attorney. A power of attorney may be general, which authorises the agent to do all things on behalf of the principal; or special, which empowers the agent to perform a single transaction.

Implied agency may arise by conduct, situation of the parties, or the necessities or circumstances of the case. An implied agency includes agency by estoppel, agency by holding out, and agency of necessity.

An **agency by estoppel** arises where *A* tells *B* in the presence and within the hearing of *P* that he

(*A*) is *P*'s agent and *P* does not contradict this statement, and *A* contracts on behalf of *P* with *B*, *P* is bound by this transaction, and in a suit between himself and *B* he will be estopped or precluded from saying that *A* was not his agent.

Agency by holding out arises where a person holds out another as his agent and third parties contract with the agent on the faith of the conduct of the principal. The principal is liable.

Agency of necessity may arise in a number of circumstances. A wife is an agent of necessity of her husband and can pledge his credit to buy all necessaries of life according to his station in life. A master of a ship may pledge owner's credit for the purchase of necessities for the voyage. A person may become an agent of necessity in an emergency.

Agency by ratification—*ex post facto*—arises where a person acts on behalf of another without knowledge or assent and afterwards his act is adopted or ratified by the latter. If the act is not ratified, there is no agency and the person acting as agent is personally liable.

Agency may be general or special. They may be mercantile or non-mercantile. A general agent is appointed for general purposes, all matters concerning the type of business on which he is employed. A special agent is appointed for a special or a particular transaction.

Mercantile agents are:

Factor is a person to whom goods or bills of lading or other documents of title are consigned for sale by a merchant residing abroad or at a distant place. He gets the possession of goods and may sell in his own name.

Broker makes bargains for another, and receives commission for so doing. He does not buy or sell in his own name. He is merely a connecting link between his principal and the third party.

Commission Agent is a person employed to buy goods in foreign market as principal and then ship them to his principal, charging a fixed commission.

Del Credere Agent, in consideration of an extra remuneration, guarantees to his principal the performance of the contract by the third party. This agent makes himself liable for the performance of the contract on the default by the third party.

Auctioneer sells goods by auction as an agent of the owner. In English law, he also becomes the agent of the buyer after the sale is made.

Bankers are agents of their customers for collecting cheques, dividend warrants, etc., and for sale and purchase of securities for their customers.

Non-commercial agents are estate agents, law agents, counsel, attorney, pleader and wife.

An agent cannot delegate his authority, as he himself is a delegate. There are a number of exceptions to this general rule.

An agent may delegate his authority in the following cases :—

(*a*) where principal has expressly permitted delegation; (*b*) where trade usage or custom permits delegation; (*c*) where the nature of the authority is such that deputy is necessary to complete the business; (*d*) where acts to be done are purely ministerial, *i.e.*, clerical or routine work; (*e*) where an unforeseen emergency has arisen.

The person to whom authority is delegated is called a sub-agent, who is really an agent of the original agent. He is responsible to the agent and can demand remuneration from him. He will, however, bind the principal to third parties, although there is no contract between him and the principal.

Duties of an agent—(1) To carry out the work undertaken according to instructions. (2) To follow the custom in the absence of instruction. (3) To carry out the work with reasonable care, skill and diligence. (4) To communicate with the principal. (5) Not to make any profit out of his agency other than his remuneration. (6) To keep and render true accounts. (7) Not to deal on his own account.

(8) Not to set up adverse title. (9) Not to use information obtained in the course of the agency against the principal. (10) Not to delegate authority.

Rights of an agent—(1) To receive remuneration for the work done. (2) To exercise lien, where in possession of goods. (3) To stop goods in transit. (4) To claim indemnification for all charges, expenses and liabilities incurred in the course of the agency.

Liability of principal to third parties—(1) The principal is bound by all acts of the agent done within the scope of actual, apparent and ostensible authority. (2) Principal is liable for agent's fraud and misrepresentation during the course of the agency. (3) Principal is bound by the agent's admission. (4) He is bound by the information obtained by the agent in the course of the principal's business. (5) An Undisclosed Principal is, on being discovered, responsible for the contract of the agent. A Concealed Principal is liable even where the agent is also liable, unless the third party has elected to sue the agent, or has led the principal to believe that the agent alone will be responsible.

Agent's personal liabilities to third parties—An agent is personally liable: (1) when the contract expressly provides for his personal liability, (2) agent signs a negotiable instrument without making it clear that he is signing it only as an agent, (3) when the agent acts for a foreign principal, (4) when acting for a concealed principal, (5) when acting for a principal who cannot be sued, (6) when acting for a non-existing principal, (7) where there is a breach of warranty of authority on his part, (8) where he receives money by mistake or fraud from a third party, (9) where authority is one coupled with interest, (10) where trade usage or custom makes agents personally liable, (11) for his torts during the course of the agency, (12) in the particular form of agency known as partnership, each partner is liable as an agent of the others.

Termination of Agency—(1) By performance of the contract of agency. (2) By expiration of the period fixed for the contract. (3) By the death of either the principal or the agent (4) By the insanity of either. (5) By the insolvency of the principal. (6) Where the principal or agent is an incorporated company, by its dissolution. (7) By the destruction of the subject-matter. (8) By mutual agreement between the principal and the agent to terminate the agency. (9) By renunciation of his employment by the agent (10) By revocation by the principal.

Agency is Irrevocable
  (*i*)   Where agency is one coupled with interest;
 (*ii*)   When agent has incurred personal liability;
(*iii*)   When the authority has been partly exercised by the agent

Termination of agency takes effect when it becomes known to the agent, and as far as the third parties are concerned, when it becomes known to them.

The termination of an agent's authority also puts an end to the authority of the sub-agent.

CASES FOR RECAPITULATION

1. *H*, the owner of a restaurant sold the restaurant to *F*, who continued *H* as manager. *W*, who knew nothing of this transaction or of *F*, sold cigars to *H* for use of the restaurant. *H* had been expressly forbidden by *F* to purchase cigars on credit. Being unable to obtain payment from *H*, W sued *F*. *Held, W* is entitled to recover from *F* because (*i*) cigars and cigarettes would usually be dealt in at such a restaurant and *H* was acting within the scope of his apparent or ostensible authority as manager in ordering cigars; (*ii*) *F* could not as against *W*, set up any secret limitation of that authority [*Watteau* v. *Fenwick*(1893) 1 Q.B.346].

2. L owned some cottages and consulted G & Co., solicitors. She was seen by *S*, their managing clerk, who had authority to transact conveyancing business on behalf of his employers. S fraudulently induced *L* to sign deeds, which in fact transferred the cottages to *S*. With the help of the documents S sold the cottages and absconded with the proceeds. *L* sued G & Co., for the recovery of the price of

the property. *Held, G & Co.*, were liable for the fraud of *S*, as the fraud was committed in the course of his employment.

3. *A* instructs *B*, a merchant to buy a ship for him. *B* employs *C*, a ship surveyor of good reputation, to choose a ship for *A*. *C* makes the choice negligently and the ship turns out to the unseaworthy and is lost The surveyor is liable to *A* for the loss of the ship and not *B*. *B* had exercised due care in selecting the agent for his principal [*Illustration* (a) to Section 195].

4. *A*, at the request of a party, *B*, purchased and sent certain goods to *C*. *C* appropriated the goods for himself and wrote to *A* that he would pay him the price in few days. *B* was declared insolvent. *A* sued *C* for the price of the goods. *Held, C* is not liable to pay *A*. *A* was acting as the agent of *B* and could claim only from him. *C*'s letter (in the absence of any proof to the contrary) must be taken to have been written by *C* as *B*'s agent. It did not create any personal liability of *C* [*Khushi Ram v. Mathura Das*, 1917 Lah. 404].

5. *S*, who was a corn factor, was entrusted by Smart with a certain quality of wheat to sell on his behalf. *S* subsequently advanced the sum of £ 3,000 to Smart, which Smart failed to repay. Smart gave orders that the wheat was not to be sold. Notwithstanding this *S* sold it to secure his advance. In an action against him *S* pleaded that the agency was irrevocable. *Held*, the agency was not irrevocable, as the authority had not been given to secure the advance of £ 3,000, since it had been given prior to, and independently of the loan [*Smart v. Sanders* (1848) 5 C.B. 895].

6. *R*, authorised by *K* to buy wheat at a certain price, exceeded his authority and bought at a higher price from *D*. *R* bought in his own name, but intended to buy for *K*. *K* agreed with *R* to take the wheat at the price, but failed to take delivery. *Held, K* was not liable to *D*, as he could not ratify *R*'s contract for *K* and had not disclosed his intention to *D* [*Keighley, Maxsted & Co. v. Durant* (1901) A.C.240].

7. *K* agreed to sell a hotel to *B*, who was acting as agent for a company which was about to be formed. *Held, B* was personally liable on the contract and no subsequent ratification could be made by the company, as at the time of the contract the company was not in existence [*Kelner v. Baxter* (1866) L.R.2 C.P. 174],

8. *M* employed B & Co., as his agents to collect a debt from *X*. To do this B & Co. properly employed *F*, who collected the debt, B & Co. owed *F* money and *F*, not knowing at the time he was employed that B & Co. were agents, claimed to set off the debt against the money owed him by B & Co. *Held*, he was entitled to do so. If an agent acts for a concealed principal, the principal may sue the third party but subject to right of the third party to exercise any defence which may be available to him against the agent before the third party discovered the existence of the principal [*Montagu v. Forwood* (1893)2 Q.B. 350].

9. *A* enters into a contract with *B* for buying *B*'s motor car as agent of *C* and without *C*'s authority. *B* repudiated the contract before *C* comes to know of it *C* subsequently ratified the contract and sued to enforce it. *Held, B* was bound to sell the motor car to *C*, as ratification by *C* related back to the date of the contract made by the agent and repudiation by *B* was ineffective [*Ballon Partners v. Lambert* (1889) 41 Ch. D 295].

10. In *Southern Railway Ltd. v. SM. Krishnan*, 1990 S.C. 673, the agent was allowed to remain in possession of company's premises for carrying on agency business of the company. After termination of agency by the company, the agent has no right to remain in possession of the premises. He is not entitled to interfere with company's business.

11. The conductor of a bus, who had temporarily taken over the wheel in the absence of the bus driver, injured *A*, a passer-by, by his negligent driving. *A* claims damages from the bus company. *Held*, the bus company is not liable to pay damages to *A*. The principal is, no doubt, liable for all torts committed by an agent (or servant) in the course of employment, *i.e.*, where the agent or servant does improperly what he is employed to do properly. But in the present case the driving of the bus by the

conductor could not be regarded as part of the course of employment, since this was not what he was employed to do, and therefore his tort would not make his employer or principal liable. [*Beard* v. *London General Omnibus Co.* (1900) 2 Q.B. 530].

12. A picture dealer in Bombay sends pictures to an agent in Delhi, some being for sale and some for exhibition only. The dealer shortly afterwards revokes the agent's authority either to sell or to exhibit the pictures and directs him to return them. In defiance of these instructions the agent pledges the pictures with a pawn broker. The pawn broker got title to the pictures. The agent was in possession of the pictures with the consent of the owner, and would almost certainly be regarded a mercantile agent This would give him a general authority to pledge the goods in the ordinary course of his business, and the pawn broker would get a good title if he acted in good faith and without knowledge that the owner had withdrawn his instructions [*Moody* v. *Pall Mall Deposit Co.* (1917) 33 T.L.R. 306].

13. *D*, a carrier, discovers that a consignment of tomatoes owned by *E* has deteriorated badly before the destination had been reached. He therefore sells the consignment for what he can get: this is about a third of the market price for good, tomatoes. *E* has now sued *D* for damages. *D* claims he was an agent of necessity. *Held,* that since the tomatoes would have become valueless by the time they reached the destination and the carrier acted *bonafide* in the interest of all concerned, *D* will be entitled to claim that he was agent of necessity provided it was practically impossible for him to obtain fresh instructions from *E*. If it was possible to get instructions, and the carrier failed to do so, he will be liable in damages to *E*. [*Springer v. G.W. Rly.* (1921) 1 K.B. 257].

14. *K* bought a statuette which he later left with *X* to arrange for a photograph of the statuette to be taken and signed by the sculptor's widow. *X* handed the statuette to *S*, who was an auctioneer, with instructions to sell it. *S* gave him an advance. *Held,* *K* was the true owner, *X* was not a mercantile agent under the Factors Act, 1889, and *S* was ordered to deliver the statuette to *K*. *X* was ordered to repay the advance paid by *S* and also to pay all costs. (*Kendrick* v. *Sotheby & Co.* (1967) 117 New L.J. 408).

15. *A* authorised *B* to carry on business on his behalf in any manner he liked. *B* appointed *C* as commission agent to buy and sell bullion on his behalf. Position of *C* vis-a-vis *B* held was of a sub-agent to *A*. As a sub-agent is not answerable to *A* the suit by *A* for accounts against *C* was not maintainable. (*Raghunath Prasad* v. *Firm Sewa Ram Tikka Das,* 1980 All 15).

5

Law of Partnership

Partnership is now governed by the provision of the Partnership Act, 1932, which came into force on October 1,1932, excepting Sec. 69 relating to registration of firms which came into force a year later. This Act repeals Chapter XI (Sec. 239-266) of the Indian Contract Act, 1872, which contained the law relating to partnerships.

The present enactment does not purport to alter in any substantial way the law of partnership, but only to clarify it with a view to avoiding doubts and difficulties, and also for making it uniform with the law in force in England and other parts of the Commonwealth. For this purpose the present Act is mainly based on the English Partnership Act, 1890, and practically codifies the Indian law of partnership, though, as was to be expected, it expressly provides (Sec. 3) that it is a branch of the general law of contracts and that the rest of the provisions of the Contract Act shall continue to apply to partnerships, except so far as they are inconsistent with the express provisions of this Act.

CHANGES INTRODUCED BY THE NEW ACT

REGISTRATION OF FIRMS

One important change brought about by the Act is that every partnership firm should be registered with the Registrar of Firms, in the form of a statement signed by all the partners, and accompanied by a registration fee of ₹ 3, stating—

(1) The name of the firm. (2) The principal place of business of the firm. (3) Names of other places (if any) where the firm carries on business. (4) The date on which each partner joined the firm. (5) The names in full and addresses of the partners. (6) The duration of the firm.

It is also provided that every change in the names and addresses of the partners or place of business should be duly notified to the Registrar. It is to be noted that the Act does not expressly make registration compulsory, nor does it provide penalty for non-registration as does the English law, but it introduces certain disabilities, which make registration necessary at one time or other. In fact, the Act has effectively ensured the registration of firms without making it compulsory. If all the requirements, as stated above, are satisfied, registration cannot be refused on the ground that a firm of the same name had already been registered (*Hiralal Agarwal* v. *The State of Bihar,* 1972 Pat. 507).

EFFECT OF NON-REGISTRATION

As stated above, though registration in India is optional, it becomes indirectly necessary, so that if a firm is not registered the following consequences will ensue:

1. A partner (or a person claiming to be or to have been a partner) cannot bring a suit to enforce a right arising from a contract or conferred by this Act, against the firm or his co-partners unless the firm is registered and the name of the partner suing appears in the Register of Firms as a partner in the Firm.

The only remedy of the partner or partners desiring to bring a suit in such a case will be to ask for dissolution of the firm and accounts or for accounts-if the firm is already dissolved. For example, a partner of an unregistered firm cannot sue his co-partners (the unregistered firm) for damages, for wrongful dismissal or for share of profits, unless he also asks, in the suit, for the dissolution of the firm or for accounts if the firm is already dissolved. A is a partner in a firm and is wrongfully dismissed from the firm by the other partners. A cannot bring a suit asking merely for damages or share in the profits, if his firm is unregistered; but he can bring such a suit by adding in it a prayer for dissolution of the firm, or, if the firm is already dissolved, for accounts of the dissolved firm, and in such a case the suit would be maintainable at law, on the ground that it is a suit substantially for dissolution of the firm or for accounts of a dissolved firm—(*Radhey Shyam* v. *Beni Ram,* 1967 All. 28). However, a reference to arbitration is not covered by Sec. 69(3). Therefore, a reference to arbitration made or entered into by an unregistered firm is valid. The word "proceeding" under Sec. 69(3) does not cover reference to arbitration (*Ghelahbai* v. *Chunilal,* 1941 Rang. 219).[1] Although non-registration of firm does not invalidate arbitration clause in the partnership deed and reference can be made to arbitration under it, the firm cannot move the court under Sec. 20 of the Arbitration under it, the firm cannot move the court under Sec. 20 of the Arbitration Act, 1940, to enforce arbitration (*Smt. Rampa Devi* v. *Bishamber Nath Puri,* 1976 All. 19).

2. An unregistered firm cannot file a suit, or take other legal proceedings, to enforce a right arising from a contract, or to claim a set-off in any suit filed against the firm, until registration of the firm is effected,[2] and the persons suing are shown as partners in the Register of Firms.[3] But an unregistered firm can bring a suit to enforce a right arising otherwise than out of a contract, e.g., for an injunction against a person wrongfully using the name of the firm, or for wrongful infringement of trade mark, trade name, or patent of the firm.

3. As registration is not compulsory, an unregistered firm is not an illegal association.[4]

4. The entries found in the register would be conclusive of the fact, and if subsequent changes or modifications are not noted (as required under Secs. 60-63), they will not be taken into account.

The registration can, however, be effected at any time, so that it is open to the partnership firm on the eve of a suit to ask for registration. Even if a suit has been filed, it would be open to the firm to withdraw the suit, get itself registered and file a fresh suit if it is within time. The same is true where a suit was dismissed merely on the ground of non-registration of the firm. The firm can file another suit within limitation period after registration for doing this, no permission of the court is needed (*M/s Behari Trading Co. etc* v. *M/s Bulhari Trading Co.,* 1983 IMLJ 10). But registration pending the suit does not cure the defect.[5]

The non-registration of a firm does not affect the following rights, namely:
1. The right of the third party to sue the firm or any partner.
2. The right of the partner to sue for dissolution of the firm or for accounts if the firm is already dissolved or for his share of the assets of the dissolved firm.

1. See Jagat Mittar Saigal v. Kailash Chandra Saigal 1983 Del 134 and Jagdish Chandra Gupta v. Kajaria Traders Ltd.196 S.C. 1882.
2. See Govindmal Gianchand v. Kunjbeharilal, 1954 Bom. See also Sudarsanam v. Viswanadham Bros.1955 Andhra 12.
3. V. S. Bahal v. Kanpur & Co. 1956 Punj. 24.
4. Badridas v. Nagarmal, 1959 S. C. 559.
5. Jammu Cold Storage v. K. L. & Sons.1960 J & K. 101; D.N. Singh v. G. Chandra, 1953 Cal. 497; Prithvi Singh v. Hasan Ali, 1951 Bom. 6.

3. The right of an unregistered-firm to bring a suit to enforce a right arising otherwise than out of a contract, *e.g.*, for the injunction against a person wrongfully using the name of the firms or for wrongful infringement of trade mark, or patent of the firm. An application by a partner for reference to arbitration can be made.[6]

4. The power of an Official Assignee or Receiver to realise the property of an insolvent partner.

5. The rights of firms or partners or firms having no place of business in India.

6. A suit or set-off not exceeding ₹100 in amount which is of a nature cognisable by Small Causes Court.

PENALTY FOR A FALSE STATEMENT

The Act also provides that if any information supplied to the Registrar of Firms is false to the knowledge of the person supplying the same, he is liable to a penalty of imprisonment up to three months or fine or both.

> ## PART 5-B
> ## DEFINITION AND NATURE OF PARTNERSHIP

Partnership is defined by the Act (Sec.4) as "the relation between persons who have agreed to share the profits of a business carried on by all or any of them acting for all." The English Act defines it as 'the relation which subsists between persons carrying on business in common with a view of profit." There are five expressions in these definitions which, if studied carefully, will tell us a good deal about partnership, namely:

1. An association of two or more persons.
2. An agreement entered into by all persons concerned.
3. Business.
4. Carried on by all or any of them acting for all.
5. For sharing profits (of the business).

An Association of two or more Persons—It is essential that there must be more than one person to constitute a partnership, as no one can be a partner with himself. The Act (Sec. 41) also provides that when the number of partners in a partnership gets reduced to one whether by death or insolvency, it would cease to be a partnership. The Partnership Act does not say anything about the maximum number of partners, but Sec. 11 of the Companies Act, 1956, lays down the maximum number at 10 for a partnership carrying on banking business and at 20 for a partnership carrying on any other business for gain. Accordingly, *a partnership is illegal if it consists of more than 20 persons, and if it is a banking partnership of more than 10 persons.*[7] Besides, a partnership may be illegal on the same ground as a general contract; namely, when its object is forbidden by law, or is immoral or opposed to public policy, or where it has become illegal by some supervening illegality, *e.g.*, war.

An Agreement or Contract—A partnership can only arise as a result of an agreement or contract, express or implied,[8] between the partners; it does not arise from status. This is an important feature that distinguishes it from various other relations which arise by operation of law and not from agreement. The co-owners, or co-legatees do not simply by reason of their community of interest become partners. Where, for instance, a sole proprietor of a business dies, leaving a number of heirs, who naturally inherit the business, such heirs do not *ipso facto* become partners. Before a partnership can come into

---

6. Mohindra v. Gurdayal, 1951 Pat 196.

7. Badri Prasad v. Nagarmal, 1959 S.C. 559.

8. In re. Kakaria Narasayya, 1953 Mad. 516.

existence there must be an express or implied agreement among the heirs that the business should be continued in common. The agreement must be to carry on business by way of present partnership, and an agreement to carry on business from a future date will not result in partnership until that date arrives.

Business—It is essential that there must be a business for a partnership to exist. Partnership implies business, and where there is no combination to carry on business there is no partnership. The term-"business" is, however, used in the widest sense, and covers all sorts of enterprises. It includes every trade, occupation, or profession. It is not confined to lengthy operation, but may consist of a single adventure or a single undertaking (Sec. 8). Persons may be partners for a single voyage of a ship, or for one performance of a play, or a single contract to build for someone.

Carried on by all or any of them. Mutual Agency—This is a very important ingredient of partnership, as the underlying and fundamental principle which constitutes partnership is the idea of 'Agency'. The other partners are bound by the act of one of them only on the principle of agency. Agency is the foundation of a partner's liability; in fact, the law of partnership is a branch of the general law of agency. Each partner is both an agent and principal for himself and others; a partner embraces the character both of a principal and of an agent. That is to say each partner is an agent binding the other partners who are his principals and each partner is again a principal, who in turn is bound by the acts of the other partners. Thus, an implied agency flows from their relationship as partners with the result that every person who conducts the business of the firm is in doing so deemed in law to be the agent of all the partners (Sec. 18). It is not necessary, however, that every partner must be actively concerned in the conduct of the business. What is essential is that the business is carried on, on behalf of all the partners. So, the fact that partners have agreed that the management of the firm is to rest with one of the partners does not negative the existence of partnership.

Sharing profit—The essence of a partnership is the attempt to make profit in business for the partners. Therefore, a piece of philanthropy, though it may involve a good deal of business, cannot be a partnership. And this principle applies to each individual, as well as the whole body carrying on the undertaking. Thus, if A carries on a business with B and C on terms which exclude A from sharing any profit, A is not a partner, as his carrying on of business is not for profit. Though sharing in the profits of a business is essential, it does not follow that everyone who participates in the profits of a business is necessarily a partner. A manager with a share of profits may claim to be a servant of the firm and not a partner.

"PARTNERS", "FIRM" AND "FIRM NAME"

Persons who have entered into partnership with one another are called individually "partners" and collectively "a firm," and the name under which their business is carried on is called the "firm name" (Sec.4).

In law "a firm" is only a convenient phrase for describing the two or more persons who constitute the partnership, and the firm has no legal existence apart from those persons. It is neither a legal entity, not is it a person as is a corporation; it is a collective name of members of a partnership. For the purposes of "determining legal rights, there is no such thing as a firm known to the law".[9] The rights and obligations of the firm are really the rights and obligations of the individuals composing the firm; and it is difficult to think of the firm apart from the members constituting it.[10] Thus, a firm, not being a legal entity, cannot maintain a suit for libel or slander. After all, libel or slander of the firm is really the

---

9. Per S. R. Das, C. J. in Dulichand v. I. T. Commr. Nagpur 1956 S. C. 354.

10. Kanhayalal v. Devi Dayal, 1936 Lah. 514; Mohd. Abdul Karim & Co. v. Commissioner of Income-tax; Madras (1948) 161. T .R. 412.

libel or slander of the partners. So the partners, not the firm, can file a suit for libel or slander. All partners are not necessarily to join in such a suit. Any one or more of the aggrieved partners may file the suit and the other partners may be joined as *pro forma* defendants (*P.K. Oswall Hosiery Mills* v. *Tilak Chand,* 1969 Punj. 150). But for the purposes of the Indian Income-tax Act it is an entity quite distinct from the partners composing it. Under Sec. 3 of that Act it is assessable as distinct from the individuals composing it.[11]

The language in use in mercantile circles does not tally with this and may easily mislead. It is undoubtedly convenient to speak of the firm's property, debts of the firm, but these are not legal phrases and are countenanced by the Act to a limited extent. The legal position has been expressed thus: "The firm cannot possess property; therefore, it cannot be a debtor or a creditor. The rights which a partner enjoys, and the duties which he owes, are enjoyed against and owed to the other partners, and not to the firm; and if an action between the partners be necessary to enforce such rights and duties, the individual partners, and not the firm, are the parties to the action." Yet the "firm" is often regarded as a "convenient symbol" or "shorthand form" for collectively designating all partners regarded as joint creditors or debtors; and for convenience the firm name may be used for the purpose of suing and being sued, provided that the names of all the partners are disclosed. A firm as such cannot be a member of a partnership, nor can a firm and a Hindu joint family legally constitute a partnership.

Partnership and Firm— 'Partnership' is the relation that exists between persons who have agreed to do business for gain and to share the profits thereof, each person being the agent of the rest of the partners. The 'Firm' does not denote relationship; but it means the partners who carry on the business as agents of each other. The Act also says: Persons who have entered into partnership are called collectively "a firm".

Firm Name—Persons have a right to carry on business under any name and style which they choose to adopt, whether it be a combination of their own several names or the names of others or fancy names, provided they do not violate the rules relating to trade name or goodwill. They must not adopt a name calculated to mislead the public into confusing them with a firm of repute already in existence with a similar name. They must not use words implying the sanction or patronage of the Government, except with the express permission of the Government. A partnership firm cannot use the word "Limited" as part of its name.

FORMATION OF PARTNERSHIP

In a contract of partnership, all the elements required for a valid contract must be present. There must be free consent, consideration, lawful object and the parties must be competent to contract. Thus, an alien friend can enter into partnership, an alien enemy cannot. A person of unsound mind is not competent, not is a minor. Though a minor cannot become a partner in a firm, yet if all the partners agree, he may be admitted to the benefits of partnership.

POSITION AND RIGHT OF A MINOR

Partnership is a relation resulting from contract, and a minor's agreement is altogether void. Accordingly, a minor, being incompetent to contract, cannot become a partner, nor can a partnership be created with a minor as a partner. But he can be admitted to the benefits of an already existing partnership if all the partners agree to admit him.[12] However, even after such admission he does not become one of the group of persons called a firm. He is not personally liable nor is his separate

---

11. Commissioner I.T., W. Bengal v. A.W. Figg. & Co. S.C. 455.
12. Devi Ditta v. Thanmal (1933) 142 I. C.203:1933 Lah. 180. Chotelal v. Raj Mal. 1951 Nag. 449. But see Sahai Bros. v. I.T. Commr. 1958 Pat. 177.

property for the debts of the firm; but his share in the partnership property and profits will be so liable. A minor cannot be adjudged an insolvent even where the adult partners have been so adjudged. Sec. 30 lays down the rights and liabilities of a minor admitted to the benefits of a partnership as follows: (1) A minor cannot become a partner in a firm. (2) A minor may with the consent of all partners, be admitted to the benefits of the partnership. (3) A minor so admitted will be entitled to his agreed share and can inspect books of account of the firm. (4) He will not be personally liable for the debts and obligations of the firm, though his share in property and the profits of the firm will be liable for the same. (5) He can bring a suit for account and for his distributive share when he intends to sever his connections with the firm, but not otherwise. But he has access to the accounts of the firm and can inspect and copy any of them. (6) Within six months of his attaining majority or when he comes to know of his being so admitted (whichever date is later), he has to elect whether he wants to continue his relation and become a full-fledged partner, or sever his connection with the firm. He may *give public notice*[13] of his election to continue or repudiate, but if he fails to give any public notice within the period stated above, he will be deemed to have elected to become a partner in the firm. It is well said: "If he chooses to be inactive, his opportunity passes away; if he chooses to be active the law comes to his assistance." (7) A minor who thus becomes a partner will become *personally liable* for all debts and obligations of the firm incurred *since the date of his admission to the benefits of the partnership.*[14] In this respect the Indian law is different from the English law; according to the English law, a person who does not repudiate would be liable only from the date of his attaining majority and not from the date of original admission. (8) Where the minor on becoming major or obtaining knowledge elects to sever his connections with the firm all his liabilities will cease from the date of the public notice to this effect. (9) Although the rights and liabilities of the minor during the six months after his attaining the age of majority continue to be those of a minor, yet, if he has during this period represented himself to be a partner to a party, he will be liable to that party on the ground of holding out. But if a minor becomes major after dissolution of partnership and fails to exercise his option, he is not liable [*Shiva Gauda* v. *Chandrakant,* 1965 S.C. 212].

CLASSES OF PARTNERS

Extent and Duration of their Liability—A person who deals with a firm, so long as matters proceed smoothly and debts are paid or goods delivered, possibly does not worry as to who the partners are; but as soon as he has a claim against the firm which is not met, he has to look for individuals who may be liable to meet his claim. Further, from a legal point of view there are two aspects of a partnership, one from within and the other from outside. The inside agreement will bind the partners, but may have no effect on outsiders. Therefore, the claimant would like to know who are the partners; and to what extent each is liable. The position of different classes of partners may be examined as follows:—

ACTUAL PARTNER

A person who has by agreement become a partner and who takes active part in the conduct of the partnership business is an actual or ostensible partner. He is the agent of the other partners for the purposes of the business of the partnership. All his acts performed in the ordinary course of the business, so far as third parties are concerned, bind him and the other partners.

---

13. A public notice, as required by Sec. 72, is a notice to the Registrar of Firms, and publication in the local official Gazette and in at least one vernacular newspaper circulating in the district where the firm has its place or principal place of business. This notice is also necessary in matters relating to
    (a) retirement or expulsion of a partner, or
    (b) dissolution of firm.
    In other cases, notice to Registrar of Firms is not necessary.
14. See Bhagilal v. I.T. Commr. 1956 Bom. 411.

PARTNER BY ESTOPPEL OR HOLDING OUT

As observed above, with regard to the partners themselves, a partnership is created by agreement between the partners, and in no other way. But, as regards outsiders the partnership relation may also arise by the conduct of the partners, and this in spite of contrary agreement between themselves. This is said to be on the principle of estoppel or holding out, and the partners are called partners by estoppel or partners by holding out. We have already had examples of this principle in agency. Sec.28(l) of the Partnership Act states that ' *'any one who by words spoken or written or by conduct represents himself, or knowingly permits himself to be represented, to be a partner in a firm is liable as a partner in that firm to any one who has on the faith of any such representation given credit to the firm, whether the person representing himself or represented to be a partner does or does not know that the representation has reached the person so giving credit."*

So, whether a person conducts himself as to lead another to believe him to be a partner, although really he is not and on that belief the other person gives credit, then he is estopped from denying that he is a partner. His mouth is shut by his own conduct, and he is treated as a *partner by estoppel.* Thus, if *A, B* and *C* carry on a-business for profit, but under very special condition as to *C,* that *C* is to contribute neither labour nor money, and not to receive any profits, but to lend to the firm his name as a partner, then *C* will be liable to every outsider who gives credit relying on his being there as partner. Similarly, where a person is held out as a partner by another, and does not disclaim the partnership relation even after knowledge that his name is being used as partner, he will be liable as *partner by holding out* to any one who has given credit on the faith of this representation. Thus, if *A* and *B* hold *C* out to be a partner, they cannot afterwards turn round and deny to a creditor, who has acted on these representations, the fact of *C* being a partner, though *C* himself might not be able to claim to be a partner. Nor can *C,* if he has allowed himself to be represented as a partner, escape a partner's liability. Such a person, not being in fact a partner, will not be entitled to any profit, but he will be liable as partner for the firm's obligations. He is held liable on the principle of holding out, estoppel, representation, ostentation, acquiescence [*Bond* v. *Pittard,* (1838) 3 M. & W. 357; *S.W.F: Product (P) Ltd.* v. *Sohanlal Bagla,* 1964 Cal, 209]. Instances usually arise where a partner having retired from the firm, fails to give public or actual notice of his retirement and if his name is continued to be sued as a partner in the bills, letterheads, etc., of the firm, and if he does not take steps to stop his name being so used, he will be liable to creditors who have lent on the faith of his being still a partner. But, where after the' retirement of one partner another is brought in, the creditor cannot sue all of them. He must either depend upon estoppel or the real facts. Thus where A and B carried on partnership business under an assumed name "Z and Company," *A* retired, but gave no notice of his retirement, *C,* a new partner, joined and the firm continued in its old name "Z and Company". A creditor filed a suit against *A, B* and *C* partners; it was held that he could not do that. He must either proceed against *A* and *B* or against *B* and *C* but never against *A, B* and *C,* as *A* never held himself out to be a partner with *C.*[15]

DORMANT OR SLEEPING PARTNER

A person who is in reality a partner but whose name does not appear in any way as partner, and, therefore, he is not known to outsiders as partner in the firm, is called a dormant, sleeping or secret partner. Such a partner will be liable to third parties who lent to the firm even without knowing of his being a partner but subsequently discovering the fact. The Act says that if an act is binding on the firm, every partner will be liable for it . A dormant partner's liability may be said to rest on his being in the position of an undisclosed principal. So, a party dealing with ostensible partners and intending, at the time, to give credit only to them, may nevertheless proceed against the dormant partner when

---

15. Scarfe v. Jardine (1882) 7 A. C. 345.

discovered. While, as long as he remains a partner, he is liable for the debts of the partnership, his liability ceases immediately on his retirement from or on dissolution of the firm. He is not required, like other known partners, to give notice in order to absolve himself from liability for acts of other partners after he ceases to be a partner. The dormant partner, as a rule, has no duties to perform, and consequently, his insanity will not be a ground for dissolution, but he has the right to have access to books of accounts and to examine and copy them.

NOMINAL PARTNER

A person whose name is used as if he were a member of the firm, but who is really not a member, and, is not entitled to share the profits of the concern, is called a nominal partner. Such a person is not a necessary party to a suit relating to the firm, except in cases of suits on negotiable instruments. But he is liable for all acts of the firm as if he were a real partner.

PARTNER IN PROFITS ONLY

A partner may stipulate with the other partners that he will be entitled to a certain share of the profits only without being liable for the losses. Such a partner may be called a partner in profits only. He will doubtless be liable to third parties for all acts of the firm. Partners of this kind generally have no part in the management of the business.

WORKING PARTNER

It may, at times, be agreed between the partners that one of them shall, because of certain special qualifications, work the business and have control over it. Such a partner is commonly known as a working partner. It may be noted that the fact that the other partners do not take any part in the management of the business does not absolve them of liability to third parties.

SUB-PARTNERS

Where a member of the firm agrees to share the profits derived by him from the partnership with a stranger, there arises a sub-partnership between the contracting member and the stranger. Such stranger is said to be a sub-partner, although he is in no sense a partner in the original firm and has no rights against it nor is he liable for its debts.[16]

INCOMING PARTNERS

A person who is admitted as a partner into an already existing firm either with the consent of all the parties or in accordance with a previous contract between the partners permitting the introduction of a new partner or partners is called a new partner. The incoming partner does not become liable for any act of the firm done before he became a partner, unless he agrees to be liable for obligations incurred before his admission into the firm. Even such an agreement with his co-partners to bear past liabilities only binds the partners *inter se*. It will not entitle the creditors of the firm to hold him liable for debts incurred by the firm before he joined, in spite of the agreement, for there is no privity of contract between the creditors and the incoming partner, and the other partners were not his agents when they acted, nor can there be a presumption of ratification, as ratification can only be of an act done on behalf of the person who ratifies it. As the liability of the incoming partner ordinarily commences from the date when he is admitted as a partner, so in order to hold him liable for the debts incurred by the firm before he became a partner, it must be proved that:—

---

16. Sugar Syndicate v, Commr. I. T. (1957) Andh. p. 332; Deviji v. Maganlal, 1965 S. C. 139.

(*i*) the firm as constituted after his admission assumed the liability to pay the past debts, and

(*ii*) the creditor agreed to accept the new firm as his debtors and to discharge the old partnership from the liability.

The position of a minor who has been admitted to the benefits of the partnerships and who, on attaining the age of majority, becomes a partner, is not the same as that of a new partner. Such minor becomes liable to third parties for all the debts and obligations incurred since the date when he was admitted to the benefits of the partnership and not since the date of his becoming a partner.

RETIRED OR OUTGOING PARTNER

A partner who goes out of a firm in which the remaining partners continue to carry on the business is called a retired or outgoing partner. A partner may retire from a firm (*i*) with the consent of all the other partners, (*ii*) in accordance with an agreement by the partners, or (*iii*) where the partnership is at will by giving notice in writing to all the other partners of his intention to retire [Sec.32 (1)]. A partner, whether active or dormant, who retires from a firm does not thereby cease to be liable for partnership debts or obligations incurred before his retirement. For example, *A*, *B* and *C* are partners. *D* is the creditor of the firm. *A* retires from the firm. *A* still remains liable with *B* and *C* to *D*. If two years after *A*'s retirement the firm becomes insolvent, *A* will still be liable for such debts as were in existence at his retirement and are still undischarged. *A* retiring partner will also be liable to third parties for all transactions of the firm begun but unfinished at the time of his retirement, even though notice of his retirement is given to the third parties. Furthermore, a retiring partner should see that all creditors of the firm have proper notice of retirement, as he may be liable for debts incurred after his retirement, if credit is given to the firm in the belief that he is still a partner. This is another instance of the doctrine of 'holding out'. Thus a duty is cast on the partner who retires from the firm to give public or actual notice of his retirement, and if he fails to give such notice he will be liable for the subsequent acts of the firm to all persons having knowledge of the fact of his being a partner and he will still be liable even though the creditors had never dealt with the firm before his retirement but only subsequent to his retirement.[17]

A retiring partner may, however, be discharged from his liability by the consent of the creditors, and this consent need not be embodied in a formal agreement, but may be left to be inferred as a fact from the course of dealing between the creditors and the firm as newly constituted. This rule is the application of the general rule of the law of contract known as "Novation." When a debt originally payable by one set of partners becomes payable by another set of partners the technical phrase for what has happened is "a novation of the debt". It is a well-settled law that when a creditor of a firm agrees with the continuing partners to their security in discharge of that of the former partners, the outgoing partner is discharged for any liability to pay the debt. But there is not *a priori* presumption to the effect that a creditor who is informed of the retirement of a partner and does nothing is deemed to agree to discharge the latter form liability. Also, the mere fact that a creditor of the firm, after knowledge of the retirement of a partner, has treated the continuing partners as his debtors is not sufficient evidence of 'novation'. Thus, where a creditor has proved his debt in the insolvency of the continuing partners or has received higher rate of interest than before, or has taken additional securities, these facts do not in themselves show that he did not intend to hold the retiring partner liable for the debt. To prove novation, it is essential to show that there was agreement, express or implied, to make the new firm liable in place of the old. Where, after the retirement of a partner, a new partner has been introduced and the reconstituted firm has adopted an old debt and the creditor with knowledge of the facts has treated them as liable to him, the Court will infer that right against the retiring partner was relinquished and the liability of the new partner was accepted in its place along with the liability of the continuing

---

17. Jagat Chandra v. Guony (1925) 30 C. W. N. 11,1920, Bengal National, Bank v. Jogindra nath (1927) Cal. 714.

partners. This is a case of novation by implied agreement, as the old and the reconstituted firm cannot both be liable at once for the same debt.[18]

DEED OF PARTNERSHIP

A partnership is not necessarily created by an agreement in writing. It may be by oral agreement, or agreement may be inferred from the conduct of the parties[19] though the business may involve lakhs of rupees. But the agreement may be contained in an elaborate document called the Deed of Partnership and drafted by a lawyer. The deed must be stamped according to the provisions of the Stamp Act. Broadly, the deed should provide for the following: (1) the nature and place of business, the name of the firm and names of partners; (2) the date at which partnership is to commence and the period of its duration; (3) capital, banking account and who is to sign cheques; (4) how profit and losses are to be shared; (5) management; (6) account; (7) whether firm to continue after the death or insolvency of a partner; (8) arbitration clause.

TEST OF PARTNERSHIP
PARTNERSHIP OR NO PARTNERSHIP

It is often a very difficult matter to determine, in the absence of a definite partnership agreement, whether a partnership does or does not exist. Sec.6 of the Act provides that **"in determining whether a group of persons is or is not a firm, or whether a person is or is not a partner in a firm, regard shall be had to the real relation between the parties, as shown by all relevant facts taken together,"** and not merely on their expressed intention.[20] Individuals cannot create a partnership merely by intending that partnership relation shall exist between them. To create a partnership there must be present the three elements, viz., (1) agreement, (2) agreement to share profits of a business, (3) business carried on by all of them acting for all. This relation may be shown by books of account, correspondence, evidence of employees, etc. In addition to this rule, the section lays down:

The joint use of the property, while not conclusive, is evidence that a partnership exists, if the property is used in common in business for sharing profits. Further, an active participation in the conduct of a joint business venture may, in conjunction with other circumstances, lead to the conclusion that a partnership exists, although even a servant may manage the business and he is not a partner. Also, absence of management does not prevent one from occupying the position of a partner. Also, a joint venture that does not contemplate a quest for mutual profit cannot qualify as a partnership. But, while there can be no partnership without the sharing of profits, a sharing of profits is not a conclusive test that a partnership exists. It is a strong evidence but not conclusive. Therefore, explanation II to Sec. 6 makes it clear that the receipt of a share of profit or of payment contingent or varying with profits does not of itself make the recipient a partner in the business or liable as such.[21] It goes on to specify certain persons who may receive a share of the profits and yet be not partners. These persons are (1) a lender of money; (2) a servant or agent receiving share of profits as his remuneration; (3) the widow or child of a deceased partner receiving annuity; the seller of goodwill of the business. The reason for specifying these persons who may share in the profits is that in each case one of the essential elements of partnership is wanting, namely, the *agency and authority*. The persons carrying on the business cannot be said to be carrying it on, on behalf of the lender, servant, agent, annuitant

---

18. P.D. Shamia v. Phanindra Nath (1931) C. W. N. 593; Scarfe v. Jardine (1882) A, C. 345. 351.

19. Somayya v. Commr. E.P.T. (1956) Hyd, 87.

20. *Ibid.* Cox v. Hickman (1860) 8 H. L C. 268; Manbbaribai v. B. Mills, 1956 Nag. 5; Musa Saheb v. N. K. Mohd. Chouse, 1959 Mad. 1875.

21. Debi Prashad v. Jairam Das. 1952 Punj. 284.

or seller of goodwill, and thus are not agents of the specified persons. Therefore, it is said *that the true test* of partnership is *Agency,* and not sharing of the profits.[22]

The Cloth Dealers' Association, the members of which could buy cloth only from the quota allotted to the Association by the Central Government and the margin of profit was also fixed by the Central Government, is not a partnership merely because its members shared the profits earned by the Association. The doctrine of partnership necessarily involves mutual agency between the parties. If the relationship constituted between the parties in respect of a certain matter does not expressly or by necessary implication involve the right of one party to pledge the other as an agent, there is no partnership (*Bhawahi Lal Lachchi Ram* v. *Badri Lal,* 1964 M.P. 153; see also *Chiman Ram v. Jayantilal,* 1939 Bom.410).

CREDITOR OR PARTNER

A creditor who advances monies on the stipulation that he will have a share in the profits earned by the firm besides a certain rate of interest and further he is to have control over the conduct of the business, does not thereby become a partner, but he is a creditor.[23] Similarly, where a man advances money at a rate of interest varying with the profits, he is only a creditor. *To constitute a partnership there must be a community of benefit and not a conflict of interest as in the case of creditor and debtor.*

PARTNER OR SERVANT

The mere fact that a servant or an agent of a firm is given a share of the profits of the business either in lieu of his remuneration or in addition to it does not make him a partner with his employer or principal. It is a common practice in India to pay a *gomashta* or *munim,* or manager a certain share of profits in the firm, in lieu of or in addition to his salary, in order to encourage industry on his part, and not to make him a partner.

SELLER OF GOODWILL

A person who by way of *bona fide* agreement receives by way of annuity or otherwise, a portion of the profits, in consideration of the sale by him of the goodwill of the business will not by reason only of such receipt become a partner.

There are some other cases which are often confused with partners. Where a retiring partner leaves his property in the firm as loan, but receives a share of profits as interest, he will be a creditor. Similarly, where in a partnership a share of the profits is paid to the widow or child or executor of a deceased partner, the mere fact of the receipt of such share will not make the widow or child a partner in the business.

PARTNERSHIP DISTINGUISHED FROM OTHER ASSOCIATIONS

CO-OWNERSHIP AND PARTNERSHIP

There is a possibility that two co-owners may employ their property in a business and share the profits, and still be not partners. We may distinguish the two. Co-ownership is not always the result of an agreement; it may arise by the operation of law or from status, e.g., co-heirs of a property, persons to whom property is given jointly. Partnership, on the contrary, must arise of an agreement,

22. Cox v. Hickman (1860) H. C. L. 268; Musa Saheb v. Mohd. Ghouse. 1959 Mad. 379; v. Maganlal, 1965 S.C. 139.

23. Mollwo, March & Co. v. Court of Wards (1872) L R. 4 P. C. 436.

express or implied. There is no implied agency between co-owners, which exists in the case of partners. Co-ownership does not necessarily involve community of profit and loss, partnership does. One co-owner can without the consent of the others transfer his rights and interests to strangers, a partner cannot do so without the consent of all the partners. A partner, being an agent of the other partners, has a lien on the partnership property, a co-owner has no such lien on the joint property. A co-owner can demand division of property *in specie* but no partner can ask for division in specie. His only right is to have a share of the profit out of the properties.

COMPANY AND PARTNERSHIP

In a partnership, the members constituting it do not form a whole as distinct from the individuals composing it. The firm has no legal entity and has no rights and obligations separate from the partners. A company, as soon as it is incorporated, say by registration, becomes a legal entity and can sue and be sued as company like any natural person. In the case of partnership, there are rights and obligations as against individual partners, but in the case of a company the rights and obligations are as against the fictitious whole, the company, and not the members composing it. The liability of partners is unlimited, but the shareholders' liability is limited. Further, dissolution of the firm by death of a partner, inability of a partner to transfer his interest so as to substitute another person in his place as partner without the consent of his co-partners, mutual obligations of partners to one another, are some of the other features which distinguish a partnership from an incorporated company.

PARTNERSHIP AND HINDU JOINT FAMILY FIRM

In Hindu law, a business is as heritable as any other property. A joint Hindu family which carries on a trade handed down from its ancestors becomes a trading family. The interest in the trade passes by survivorship to the surviving members, and every member acquires by birth an interest in the profits and assets of the trade. This is not partnership, but a co-parcenery, a relationship, created by Hindu law, and each member is called a co-parcener. A joint family firm is created by the operation of law, whereas a partnership is the result of a contract. In a partnership, the death of a member dissolves the partnership, the death of a co-parcener does not dissolve the joint family firm, in a joint family firm only the *Karta* or manager has an implied authority to borrow and bind other members, in a partnership each partner can do this. In partnership every partner is *personally* liable for the debts and liabilities of the partnership, while in a joint firm, it is only the manager who is personally liable for the firm's debts. The junior adult members are liable only if they are actual contracting parties or if they have by their conduct adopted or ratified the transaction. Minor members of the family are never personally liable, but only liable to the extent of the family property; The partners have a right to demand accounts of the partnership firm, a co-parcener cannot ask for an account of past dealings; his only right is to ask for partition of the assets of the firm. All associations arising by the operation of law or by status, and particularly the Hindu Joint Family Firm are excluded from the operation of the Indian Partnership Act (Sec. 5)

A Hindu Joint family is not a juristic person for all purposes, so that as a joint family it cannot enter into partnership nor can the *Karta* do so on behalf of the joint family. The individual members can, however, enter into partnership with individual members of another Hindu joint family or with other individuals (*Venkideswara Prabhu Ravindranatha Prabhu* v. *Surendranatha Prabhu Sudhalkar Prabhu*, 1985 Ker. 265).

CLUBS

Clubs are not associations for gain and are not therefore partnerships. The members of a club are not liable for each other's acts, but the partners are so liable. No member of a club is liable to a creditor of the club. A member of a club has no transmissible interest so that on his death his heirs cannot claim to inherit any of his rights.

DURATION OF PARTNERSHIP

The parties are at liberty to fix the duration of the partnership or say nothing about it. Where the partners stipulate that they should carry on business for a definite period of time, it is called **partnership for a fixed term**. When the term is over the partnership comes to an end; but if the business is continued after the period originally fixed, the renewed partnership will become a partnership at will, and in the absence of any agreement or any course of dealing varying by implication any term of the original agreement, the mutual rights and duties of the partners remain the same, as far as they are not inconsistent with a partnership at will. Where a partnership is formed for the purpose of carrying on particular adventures or undertakings, it is called a **Particular** Partnership which would presumably last only so long as the business is not completed (Sec. 8). But if the firm proceeds to carry out other undertakings, then, in the absence of agreement to the contrary, the rights and duties of the partners in the new undertakings will continue to be the same as in the original undertaking. It is also open to the partners either to say nothing about the duration or to agree that the business shall be carried on not for any fixed period, but so long as the partners are inclined to carry it on. Such a partnership is called a partnership at will, because it is carried on at the willingness and desire of the partners and is determinable at the will of any of the partners, on his giving notice. Where, however, it is stipulated that the partnership should dissolve by "mutual agreement only," it will not be a partnership at will determinable by notice, for, unless all the partners agree, dissolution will not take place. Such a partnership can be dissolved by court under Sec. 44 of the Act. (See *Iqbalnath Premnath Anand* v. *Rameshwarnath etc.,* 1976, Bom. 405).

PARTNERSHIP PROPERTY

It is open to the partners to agree among themselves as to what is to be treated as the property of the firm, and what is to be the separate property of one or more partners, although employed or used for the purpose of the firm. Therefore, in the absence of any such agreement, express or implied, the property of the firm is deemed to include—

(a) all property, rights and interests which have been brought into the common stock for the purposes of the partnership by the individual partners, whether at the commencement of the business or subsequently added thereto;

(b) those acquired in the course of the business with money belonging to the firm, including secret profit and personal benefit derived by a partner;

(c) the goodwill of the business.

Difficulties, sometimes, arise where a partner has drawn money out of the partnership and acquired immovable and movable properties in his own name. In general such acquisitions by a partner in his sole name, made with the partnership funds, will be treated as the property of the firm. But to ascertain whether the property standing in the name of a partner belongs to him or the firm, recourse should be had to the account books of the firm, which may show how it has been dealt with. If it is credited as part of the capital of that partner, it will be his property; but, if it has been treated as part and parcel of the partnership property in the course of dealing between the partners, it will be deemed to be the property of the firm. Further, any secret profit or personal benefit derived by a partner will be deemed as acquired for the firm and will have to be accounted for and paid to the firm. But the mere fact that certain property is used or employed for the purposes of the firm does not necessarily raise a presumption that it is property of the firm. Thus, where a colliery belonged to A, but it was worked in partnership by A and B, who shared the profits of the venture, the colliery did not become the property of A and B firm, but remained the property of A. But, where a colliery was taken on lease by A and B for the purpose of working it, it would be presumed to be the property of the firm. In the latter case, it would become necessary to see whether the property was treated by the partners as part of the common stock or was merely as ancillary to the carrying on of the partnership business.

GOODWILL

The Act specially provides that goodwill of the firm is partnership property. Lord Macnaughten describes[24] goodwill as "the advantage which is acquired by a business, beyond the mere value of the capital, stock, fund and property employed therein, in consequence of the general public patronage and encouragement which it receives from constant or habitual customers." By Goodwill is meant the approbation of the public as regards the business, an approbation varying with the age, credit and stability of the firm. Says Mr.Justice Warrington,[25] "it is the advantage which a person gets by continuing to carry on and being entitled to represent to the outside world that he is carrying on a business which has been carried on for some time previously." "Goodwill, I apprehend", said Wood V.C.,[26] "must mean every advantage .... that has been acquired by the old firm in carrying on its business, whether connected with the premises in which the business was previously carried on, or with the name of the late firm, or with any other matter carrying with it the benefit of the business," In a recent Bombay case it was stated: [27] "The goodwill of a business is inclusive of positive advantages, such as carrying on the commercial undertaking at a particular place and in a particular name, and also its business connections, its business prestige, and several other intangible advantages which a business may acquire". It is this which constitutes the difference between a business just started, which has no goodwill attached to it, and one which has acquired goodwill by established reputation, and business connections. The goodwill of a firm may have an appreciable value, often it is the very sap and life of a business, without which the business will yield little or no fruit. It is part of the partnership property in which all the partners are jointly interested, and can be sold either separately or along with the other property of the firm [Sec. 55(1)]. Every partner is entitled to have the partnership property used exclusively for the purposes of the partnership.

PART 5-C
RELATIONS OF PARTNERS TO ONE ANOTHER

The relation of partnership comes into existence by an agreement between the partners, and such an agreement may provide for the mutual rights and duties of the partners. It is indeed usual for partners to agree at the time of the formation of partnership about the conduct and management of the business, by providing as to the capital each partner has to contribute, the proportion in which each partner will share the profits, and the rights and duties of the partners in the business. Where, however, partners fail to provide for any of these things, the rules laid down in the Act, and examined below, are applicable.

RIGHTS OF A PARTNER

1. Right to take part in Management [Sec. 12 (a)].—Every partner has a right to take part in the conduct and management of the business. It may be pointed out again that this rule, like most of the following rules, is subject to any contract to the contrary between the partners, and applies only when no agreement regarding conduct of business exists.

2. Right to be consulted [Sec. 12(c)]—Every partner has a right to be consulted and heard in all matters affecting the business of the partnership. Where there is a difference of opinion between the partners, the decision of the majority of the partners will prevail, *but only in ordinary matters of*

---

24. Trego v. Humt (1896) A. C. 7, leading case on the subject

25. Hill v. Fearies (1905) 1 Ch. 466 at 471.

26. Churton v. Douglas (1859) John 176,188.

27. New Gujarat Cotton Mills Ltd., v. Appellate Tribunal, 1957 Bom. 111.

routine, and that too if the majority has acted in perfect good faith and as far as possible every partner has been consulted. *If the partners are equally divided in opinion, those who are against the proposition in dispute will have their way.* That is to say, the particular resolution will not be carried. But, *where the matter is of importance and affects the policy and nature of the business, or relates to an alteration in the partnership constitution, a majority will not be sufficient and unless all the partners agree, no change can be effected.* Thus, in matters affecting the nature of business, even one dissenting partner can prevent any change. To illustrate, there must be unanimity among the partners to change from life assurance business to marine insurance, to select the place of business, to enlarge the business requiring additional capital or to sell the whole business.

3. Right of Access to Accounts [Sec. 12(d)]—Every partner, active or dormant, has a right to free access to all records, books and accounts of the business and also to examine and copy them. The partner is not bound to exercise this right personally but may engage an agent for the purpose, provided that the other partners have no particular objection to that agent. But a minor admitted to the benefits of the partnership has only a right of access to "accounts" and inspect and copy them, but not to "books".

4. Right to Share Profits [Sec. 13(b)]—Every partner is entitled to share in the profits equally, unless different proportions are stipulated. There is no connection between the proportion of capital contributed by the partners and the share in the profits earned, nor will the fact that the work done by the partners is unequal affect the question of their shares. So, in the absence of special agreement, "equality", says Pollock,[28] "is equity, not as being absolutely just, but because it cannot be taken that any particular degree of inequality would be more just." It may be noticed that a minor in the firm has no right to sue for his profits when severing his connection with the firm.

5. Interest on Capital [Sec. 13(c)]—No partner is entitled to interest on the capital subscribed by him unless there is an agreement express or implied or a trade custom to that effect. Again, interest which is allowed by agreement or trade custom, is payable *only out of the profits, if any,* unless agreed to be paid even in the absence of profits. Further, where interest is payable on capital it stops running at the date of dissolution, unless otherwise agreed.[29]

6. Interest on Advances [Sec. 13(d)]—A partner who has contributed more than the share of the capital for the purposes of business is entitled to interest at a rate agreed upon, and where no rate is stipulated for, at six per cent per annum. This interest is payable *out of the partnership property* as an item of expense and not necessarily out of the profits. A partner is not entitled to any interest on undrawn profits left in the business, unless there is an agreement express or implied to that effect.[30]

7. Right to Indemnity [Sec. 13(e)]—A partner is entitled, in the absence of an agreement to the contrary, to be indemnified by the firm for all acts done by him in the course of the partnership business, for all payments made by him in respect of partnership debts or liabilities and expenses and disbursements made in an emergency for protecting the firm from loss, provided he acted as a person of ordinary prudence would have acted in similar circumstances.

8. Joint Owner of Partnership Property (Sec. 14)—Every partner is, as a rule, a joint owner of the partnership property, and in the absence of an agreement providing for the interest of each partner in the property every partner is presumed to have an equal share in it. Every partner is entitled to have the partnership property used exclusively for the purposes of the partnership.

9. Powers in an emergency (Sec.21)—A partner has power to act in an emergency for protecting the firm from loss. But in doing so, he must act as a prudent person would act in his own affairs in

28. Soma Sundaram Chettiar v. Savagan Chettiar (1930) Mad. 505, see Mansha Ram v. Tej Bhan, 1958 Punj. 5
29. Motilal v. Sarup Chand (1936) 38 Bom. L R. 1059.
30. Dinham v. Brandford (1890) Cjh. 519.

similar circumstances. A partner's right to be indemnified by his co-partner for payments made or liabilities incurred in acting for the firm in an emergency is co-extensive with his authority.

10. No New Partner to be introduced [Sec. 31(1)]—Every partner is entitled to prevent the introduction of a new partner into the firm without his consent, unless there is an express contract permitting such introduction.

11. No liability before joining the firm [Sec. 31 (2)]—An incoming partner will not be liable for any debts or liabilities of the firm before he became a partner, excepting by his own consent.

12. Right to retire [Sec. 32(1)]—Every partner has a right to retire, if the contract so provides, failing which, with the consent of other partners, and if the partnership be one at will, at any time on giving notice to the other partner.[31]

13. Right not to be expelled [Sec. 33(1)]—Every partner has a right to continue in the partnership and not to be expelled from it, excepting when there is a clause in the agreement conferring a power of expulsion by majority or any particular partners. But a power of expulsion, where it exists, must be exercised *banafide,* and in good faith and not with any ulterior motive of getting an advantage, *e.g.,* purchasing his interest in the firm at a favourable rate.

14. Right to carry on competing business (Sec. 36)—Every outgoing partner has a right to carry on a competing business, but without using the firm name or soliciting the firm's customers or in any way representing himself as carrying on the business of the firm unless he has been restrained by a reasonable agreement from carrying on a similar business for a specified period of time within specified local limits.[32]

15. Right after retirement to share in profits or interest (Sec. 37)—Where a member of a firm dies or otherwise ceases to be a partner as a result of retirement, expulsion, insanity, or any other cause and the surviving or continuing partners carry on the business with the property of the firm without any final settlement of accounts, viz., without the share of the assets of the outgoing partner being paid over, or without his interest being purchased by the remaining partners, the estate of such deceased partner or the partner himself, as the case may be, is entitled to share in the profit earned with the aid of the assets of such outgoing partner[33] or interest at six per cent per annum at the option of the legal representative of the deceased partner or the outgoing partners. The rule applies to the case of an alien enemy where partnership is dissolved on the outbreak of war, the alien enemy in such case has a right to claim share of profits or interest after the war is over.[34] The option to claim a share of the profits or interest can be exercised only when the accounts of the subsequent business are made. And, as the right is an alternative one, a claim both for share of the subsequent profits as well as interest will not be allowed. Further, once the election has been made, the party will not be allowed to go back on it, nor will he be permitted to claim profits for part of the period and interest for remaining period.[35]

DUTIES OF PARTNERS

The relation of partners is founded on mutual confidence and the law requires that a partner shall act towards the other members of the firm with the utmost good faith. Every partner must use his knowledge and skill for the benefit of the firm. The fundamental duties of partners are contained in

---

31. Anand Prasad v. Bhagwant (1932) All. 926.

32. Mansha Ram v. Tej Bhan, 1958 Punj. 5.

33. Nagarajan v. Robert Hotz. 1954 Punj. 278; Mansha Ram v. Tej Bhan, 1958 Punj.. 5.

34. Hugh Stevenson & Sons v. Aktiengesttechaft Co. (1918) A. C. 239.

35. Vyse v. Foster (1874) 7 H. L. C. 318.

Sec. 9 which reads: "Partners are bound to carry on the business for the firm to the greatest common advantage, to be just and faithful to each other, and to render true accounts and full information of all things affecting the firm to any partner or his legal representative."

1. To work for the greatest common advantage—Every partner is bound to carry on the business of the firm to the greatest common advantage. This is one of the first principles of law of partnership, for, like agency, mutual confidence is the foundation of partnership.

2. To be just and faithful—Every partner must be just and faithful to the other partners. Partnership being a fiduciary relationship, it is the duty of each partner to exercise the utmost good faith and fairness in his dealings with his co-partners. A partner, for instance, must be fair when buying the share of another or when exercising right of expulsion of another partner.

3. To render true accounts—A partner is bound to keep and render true, proper, and correct account of the partnership. He must permit the other partners to inspect such accounts and to take copies of them either by themselves or by their unobjectionable agent at all reasonable times. In addition to submitting statements of accounts, he should be ready to explain them and also hand over to firm all monies of the firm which may have come to his hands, and produce relevant vouchers.

4. To give full information—Utmost good faith between the partners is the rule and one partner must not take advantage of the other. Every partner is an agent of the other partners and as such is bound to communicate full information to them. Thus a partner who acquires any information in the course of the partnership must pass it on to the other partners, so that notice to one partner is taken to be notice to all partners.

5. To indemnify for fraud (Sec. 10)—Every partner is bound to indemnify the firm for any loss caused by his fraud in the conduct of business. The liability of a partner is absolute and no partner can contract himself out of it. If a partner commits a fraud on his copartners, he must indemnify them for any loss caused to them by his fraud.

6. To indemnify for wilful neglect [Sec. 23(f)]—Every partner who is guilty of wilful neglect in the conduct of the business and the firm suffers loss in consequence, is bound to make compensation to the firm and other partners.[36] It is to be noted that the liability here is for wilful neglect or what is also called culpable negligence, and not for failure on the part of a partner to carry out his ordinary duties. Not only that, but the partners can contract themselves out of this liability which they cannot do in the case of fraud.

7. To share losses [Sec. 13(b)]—As in the case of profits, in the absence of an agreement to the contrary, every partner is bound to share the losses equally with the others. If there is an agreement, then in the proportion as the agreement provides.

8. To attend diligently without remuneration [Sec. 12(b), 13(a)]—Every partner is bound to attend diligently to the business of the firm and, in the absence of any agreement to the contrary, he is not entitled to any remuneration whether in the shape of salary, commission or otherwise, on account of his own trouble in conducting the partnership business. Thus, even a managing partner or a partner who does much more work than the others will not get any remuneration. But it is usual for partners to agree, that a certain partner, e.g., managing partner, is to receive in addition to his share a salary or commission for his trouble in conducting the business of the firm. Such an arrangement would ordinarily come to an end on dissolution of the firm. But in exceptional cases where, for instance, one or more partners have additional burden thrown on them owing to the inactivity or idleness or inability of another partner to do his share of the work, such partners would be allowed compensation for such additional services.[37] This rule is based on the duty of a partner to compensate other if he deliberately

---

36. Thomas v. Atherstone (1878) 10 Ch. D. 185.
37. Harris v. Sleep (1897) 2 Ch. 80; Krishnamachari v. Samkaraska (1920) 23 Bom. L R. 1343; 1921 P. C 91.

ceases to do his duty, so that the neglectful partner would be required to pay out of his share to the partner who has to do his work also. In *Gokul* v. *Sashimukhi* (1911) 16 C.W.N. 299, where the partnership was with the *Pardanashin* widow of a diseased partner and surviving partners, remuneration to the active partner was allowed.

9. To hold and use property for the firm (Sec. 15)—In the absence of an agreement to the contrary, every partner is bound to hold and use the partnership property exclusively for the firm. The property of the firm, being the property of all the partners, must be held and used only on account of land for the common benefit of all the partners.

10. To account for private profits [Sec. 16(a) and 60]—The partnership property belongs to all the partners, and so a partner cannot directly or indirectly use the property of the firm for his own private purposes, or try to get any advantage because of his connection with the firm and if any such advantage is derived by him, he must account for the same and pay it to the firm. A partner, like a trustee, cannot make private gain by reason of his membership with the firm. Thus, where a partner in the course of the business has received an information and uses it for any purpose competing with the partnership business, he must pay over any benefit that he may have obtained by the use of such information. Where *T* was common partner in two firms publishing newspapers, he was prevented from conveying information and news of the firm to the other.[38] Further, a partner cannot sell his own property to the firm or purchase the firm's property without making full disclosure. He cannot bargain for a private gain from the customers of the firm. This obligation continues even after dissolution of the firm by the death of a partner, for any profits made by any surviving partner or any representatives of the deceased after dissolution and before winding up belong to the firm. Thus, the liability of a partner to account to the firm extends to any benefit derived by him from any transaction affecting the partnership. The application of the rule is, of course, subject to any agreement between the partners.

11. To account for profits of competing business [Sec. 16(b), 11(2)]—Sec. 12 of the Indian Contract Act provides that an agreement in restraint of trade is void. But Sec. 11(2) of the Partnership Act permits an agreement between partners that a partner shall not carry on business other than the business of the partnership as long as he is partner. In practice, such a clause generally appears in partnership agreements. In the absence of any such arrangements, partners are free to be interested in private business of their own, provided the same does not compete with the business of the partnership. The rule contained in Sec. 16(b) may be stated thus: No partner can carry on any business which is likely to compete with the business of the partnership, except with the consent of the other partners. If a partner, without obtaining the consent of the other partners, carries on a competing business, he must account for the profits of such business to the firm, and must also compensate the firm for any loss sustained by his carrying on such competing business. Not only during the continuance of the firm, but also after dissolution of the firm, and during the winding up, a partner may be prohibited and can be restrained from carrying on a competing business in the name of the firm or using the property of the firm (Sec. 53).

12. To act within authority—Every partner is bound to act within the scope of the actual authority conferred upon him. Where he exceeds his authority, he shall have to compensate the other partners for any ensuing loss, unless they ratify his act.

13. Not to assign his rights [Sec. 29 (1 & 2)]—No partner can assign or transfer his partnership interest to any other person, so as to make him a partner in the business. But a partner may assign the profits and share in the partnership assets. Where such assignment is made, the person in whose favour it is made, would have no right to ask for the accounts or to interfere in the management of the business so long as the business is continuing; he would be entitled only to share the actual profits.

---

38. Glassington v. Thwanes (1823) Sam. and St. 124; Abdul Razak v. M. Din Ahmed. 1959 Cal.660.

Where, however, the partnership is dissolved, he would be entitled to the share of the assets and also to accounts but only from the date of dissolution.

PART 5-D
RELATION OF PARTNERS TO THIRD PARTIES

POWER OF PARTNER TO BIND THE FIRM

Every partner is an agent of the firm for the purposes of the business of the firm (Sec. 18). The law of partnership has often been stated to be a branch of the general law of principal and agent; this section expressly recognises that doctrine. If two or more persons agree to carry on a partnership business and share its profits, each is a principal and each is an agent for the other, and each is bound by the other's contract in carrying on the business, as much as a single principal would be bound by the act of an agent, who was to give the whole profits to his employer. This is the true principle of partner's liability [*Cox* v. *Hickman* (1860) 8 H.L.C. 268]. **A partner, indeed, virtually embraces the character both of a principal and of an agent.** So far as he acts for himself and his own interest in the common concern of the partners he may properly be deemed an agent. The main distinction between him and a mere agent is that he has a community of the partnership; while an agent as such has no interest in either. Since, as between the partners and the outside world (whatever may be their private arrangements between themselves), each partner is an unlimited agent of every other in every matter connected with the partnership business, his acts bind the firm. The general authority of a partner as agent of the firm is variously described as 'ordinary', 'apparent', 'ostensible' or 'implied'. The Indian Partnership Act calls it 'implied authority' of a partner.

IMPLIED AUTHORITY OF A PARTNER

Secs. 19(1) and 22 read together provide that the act of a partner which is done to carry on, in the usual way, business of the kind carried on by the firm, binds the firm, provided the act is done in the firm name, or in any manner expressing or implying an intention to bind the firm. Such an authority of a partner to bind the firm is called his *Implied Authority*. The implied authority of a partner to bind the firm is restricted to acts usually done in the business of the kind carried on by the firm. A partner can no doubt do certain acts in an emergency so as to bind the firm, but these acts do not form part of his implied authority. The words "in the usual way" are put in because as soon as a usual act is done in an unusual way the outsider may well be put on inquiry into the unusual circumstances under which he is being called upon to give credit. It is not unreasonable to expect him to ask whether the partner has authority to act as he is doing. If the outsider chooses to pass what is unusual then he must not seek to charge persons other than the one with whom he is actually dealing. **So, a partner has implied authority to bind the firm by all acts done by him in all matters concerned with the partnership business and which are done in the usual way and are not in their nature beyond the scope of the partnership.**

The question whether a given act has been done in carrying on a business in the way in which it is usually carried on must be determined by the nature of the business, and by the practice of the persons engaged. What is usual for one kind of business may be unusual for another, e.g., it is usual for one member of a firm of bankers to draw, accept or endorse a bill of exchange on behalf of the firm, but it is not usual for one of several solicitors to possess a similar power, for it is no part of ordinary business of a solicitor to draw, accept or endorse bills of exchange. In the case of commercial partnerships (trading firms), every partner has an implied authority to pledge or sell the partnership goods, buy goods on credit for the partnership, borrow money, contract debts and pay debts, on account of the partnership, make, draw, sign, endorse, accept, transfer, negotiate, get discounted negotiable instruments, in the name and on account of the partnership. Where the business is not of commercial nature, *i.e.*, does not involve buying and selling of goods, a partner has no implied authority to borrow, pledge or to make or issue negotiable instruments, though he may sign a cheque. Even in the case of a cheque a partner has no implied authority in a non-trading concern to bind his co-partners by giving a post-dated cheque, for he will in effect be drawing a bill of exchange; and he cannot draw or accept a bill of exchange. Any admission or any representation made by any partner concerning the partnership business is evidence against the firm and will bind it This is again on the principle that every partner charges the partnership by virtue of an agency to act for it. An admission or representation will bind the firm even though made by a partner in fraud of his co-partners. But, of course, if such fraudulent admission is made by the partner in collusion with the other party who seeks to rely on it, it will not bind the firm. Again, it is not within the implied authority of a partner to set-off his own separate debt against a debt due to his firm: and such payment by way of set-off does not bind the firm (*Dalichand Parekh* v. *Mathuradas Ravji,* (1957) 59 Bom. L.R. 1066).

NO IMPLIED AUTHORITY [Sec. 19(2)]

The Act, with a view to avoid litigation and to make the law as definite as possible, has specifically enumerated certain acts which do not, in the absence of any usage or custom of trade to the contrary, fall within the implied authority of a partner stated in Sec. 19(1) above. Sec. 19(2) reads:

"In the absence of any usage or custom of trade to the contrary the implied authority of a partner does not empower him to—

(a) submit a dispute relating to the business of the firm to arbitration,[39]
(b) open a banking account on behalf of the firm in his own name,
(c) compromise or relinquish any claim or portion of a claim by the firm,
(d) withdraw a suit or proceeding filed on half of the firm,
(e) admit any liability in a suit proceeding against the firm,
(f) acquire immovable property on behalf of the firm,
(g) transfer immovable property on behalf of the firm,
(h) enter into a partnership on behalf of the firm."

D holds permanent leasehold right over a colliery and had worked the colliery himself for some time. In 1949, he grated a sub-lease of the colliery to *M*, a partner in a firm having 3 other partners, for a term of 5 years. The colliery was worked and ₹ 57,000 became due to *D*. *D* filed a suit for the recovery of the amount against *M*, the three partners and the firm. The other partners deny liability on the ground that there was no privity of estate between them and *D*. *Held, D* can recover only from *M*; there was no contract between *D* and the firm. It was only between D and M, as M had no implied authority to enter into such a contract (*Devji* v. *Magan Lal, 1965 S.C.* 139).

It is, however, open to the partners by means of an express contract to extend or limit the implied authority, but third parties will be bound by such limitation only when they have notice of such curtailment (Sec. 20).[40]

LIABILITY OF PARTNER FOR ACT OF FIRM

Sec. 25 of the Act lays down the general rule that every partner is liable for all acts of the firm done while he is a partner and that the liability is joint and several. Sec. 2(a) defines an **Act of the Firm** as an "act or omission by all the partners, or by any partner or agent of the firm which gives rise to a right enforceable by or against the firm." It follows that **all partners are liable jointly and severally for all acts or omissions binding on the firm including liabilities arising from contracts as well as torts**. In

---

39. In Calcutta there is a trade usage permitting a partner to refer film's disgutes to arbitration.
40. Saramal v. Puran Chand (1924) 48 Bom. 170,1924 Bom. 260.

order that an act done may be an act of the firm and therefore binding on the firm, it is necessary that the partner or the agent doing the act on behalf of the firm must have done that act **in the name of and on behalf of the firm** and not in his personal capacity; and the **act must have been done in the ordinary course of the business of the firm.** Two important points should be noted in this connection. *First,* that if any act is binding on the firm every partner, whether active or dormant, will be liable for it *Secondly,* to be binding on a partner, the obligation must have been in such a way as to bind the firm. An act done or instrument executed by a partner will bind the firm only if it is done or executed in the firm name or in a manner expressing or implying an intention to bind the firm. That is to say, the partner should not have acted in his individual or personal capacity but as a partner of the firm and as agent of the other partners and in the firm name. The act of a partner must be within the scope of the actual authority of the partner. Thus, if a partner buys on credit *usual* stock-in-trade, all the partners are liable for the debt so incurred. If the purchase does not fall within the business of the firm, it is not an act of the firm and so does not bind the other partners. Where A, B and C carry on the partnership business as cloth merchants, and A orders on credit two cases of Kulu apples on his own initiative, but sends the order on the firm's note paper and in the firm's, name, the order is so clearly not for the purpose of the business of the firm that he alone is liable. A is not an agent of B and C for buying fruit, for the business is actually and also ostensively that of cloth merchants and not that of fruiterers, and a third party cannot reasonably assume authority to buy fruit.

LIABILITY FOR THE WRONGFUL ACTS OF PARTNER

Every partner is liable for the negligence and fraud of the other partners in the course of the management of the business. A partner charges the firm by virtue of an agency to act for it. A principal is liable for the loss or injury caused to any third person by any wrongful act or omission of an agent while acting in the ordinary course of business. A principal is also liable for the tort of his agent if he has expressly directed him to do it. On the same principle the firm is liable for any loss or injury caused to a third party by the wrongful acts or omissions of a partner if they were done by him while acting in the ordinary course of the business of the firm, or with the authority of his co-partners. Where one of the partners bribed the clerk of the plaintiff, who was a competitor in the business, to disclose certain confidential information, which it was the business of the firm to obtain by legitimate means, the firm was held liable.[41]

Fraud—B and C, who carried on business in partnership as wine merchants, were employed by A to purchase wine for him and sell the same on commission. C represented that he had bought the wine, had sold part of it at a profit and paid the proceeds of such supposed sale to A. In fact C had neither bought nor sold any wine, and the transactions of which he rendered accounts to A were fictitious. B was wholly ignorant of C's fraud. In a suit by A against both, it was held that B was liable for the false representation of C.[42]

Negligence—So also, all the partners in a firm are liable to a third party for loss or injury caused to him by the negligent act of a partner acting in the ordinary course of the business. Thus, in *Blyth* v. *Fladgate* (1891) 1 Ch. 337, partners in a firm of solicitors were held liable in damages on the ground of negligence of a partner for failure to discharge the duty entrusted to him. A firm of taxi drivers would be liable for the negligent driving of one of them, and a firm of surgeons for the professional negligence of one of the partners, and a firm of newspaper proprietors for the liability of one of them and so on.

Misappropriation of money (Sec. 27).—Where a partner acting within his apparent authority receives money or property from a third party and misapplies it, or a firm in the course of its business receives

---

41. Hamlyn v. Houston & Co. (1903) K. B. 81.
42. Rapp v. Latham (1819) 2 B & A 795.

money or property from a third party, and the money or property is misapplied by any of the partners while it is in the custody of the firm, the firm is liable to make good the loss (Sec. 27). This is the liability of the partners for misappropriation of money or property belonging to a third party. But if the receipt of money by one partner is not within the scope of his authority, then this receipt cannot be treated as receipt of the firm, and the other partners are not liable, unless money received comes into their possession or under their control.[43]

Failure to Communicate Information (Sec. 24)—Notice to a partner who habitually acts in the business of the firm, of any matter relating to the affairs of the firm operates as notice to the firm; except in the case of fraud on the firm committed by or with the consent of that party (Sec, 24). All the partners are deemed to have received any information obtained by one of them in the course of the partnership business, so that it can be said that **notice to a partner is notice to the firm.** When the partner is a party to a fraud and keeps back the information, the firm will not be imputed with notice.

LIABILITY WHEN CEASES

Every partner is liable for all the obligations of the firm until the date of his severing connection with the firm but his liability will continue to creditors subsequently also, unless there be a fresh contract or what is called **Novation or a tripartite agreement,** by which the creditors agree to accept the liability of the other partners and the incoming partners, if any, and exonerate the retiring partner [Sec. 32(2)]. Further every partner, though he might have retired from the partnership, would still be liable for the acts of the firm, even after retirement, if he has failed to give public notice as required by the Act. Similarly, after dissolution of a firm the liability of partners to third parties for acts of their partners which would otherwise have been binding on all partners, continues until proper notice is given that the firm is dissolved. But the estate of the deceased partner or the insolvent partner will not be liable for such act after the demise or adjudication, even if no notice is given. The partner's liability would also continue even during a winding up for such acts of another partner as may be necessary for purposes of winding up but not for the acts of an insolvent partner [Secs.45(l) and 47].

PART 5-E
DISSOLUTION

The Indian Partnership Act has introduced a distinction between the '**dissolution of partnership**' and '**dissolution of firm**'. Sec. 39 provides that the dissolution of partnership between all the partners of a firm is called the "dissolution of the firm." It follows that a partnership may be dissolved without dissolving the firm. Dissolution of partnership involves a change in the relation of the partners, but it does not end the partnership. For example, where A, B and C were partners in a firm and A died or was adjudged insolvent, the partnership firm would come to an end; but if the partners had agreed that the death, retirement, or insolvency of a partner would not dissolve the firm then on the happening of any of these contingencies, the "partnership" would certainly come to an end although the" firm " or as the Act calls it, a "reconstituted firm" might continue under the same firm name. Legally speaking, where A has gone out, the relationship which subsisted between A, B and C, having broken up and a fresh relationship between B and C, or if D is brought in between B, C and D having been created, there will be new or reconstituted firm. For, the partnership composed of A, B and C is not the same partnership as that between B and C, or between B, C and D. This fact is further emphasised by the Act, and Sec.38 provides to the effect that a continuing guarantee for the liabilities of a firm ceases as soon as there is a change in the constitution of the firm. So the dissolution of a partnership may or may not include the dissolution of the firm,[44] but dissolution of the firm necessarily means the dissolution

---

43. Mara v. Browne (1895)2Ch. 69.

44. See Sundarsanam v. Viswanadham Bros. 1955 Andhra 12.

of the partnership as well. On the dissolution of partnership the business may be carried on by the reconstituted firm, and on the dissolution of the firm all business must be stopped, the assets of the firm realised and distributed among the partners, the jural relation between *all* partners of the firm is discontinued (*Keshavlal Patel* v. *Narandas,* 1968 Guj. 157).

DISSOLUTION OF PARTNERSHIP

It may be repeated that the dissolution of partnership may also involve the dissolution of the firm, (i.e., severance of the partnership relation between all the partners). The dissolution of partnership takes place in any of the following circumstances:—

1. By the expiry of term—Where the partnership is for a fixed term, the firm gets dissolved at the end of the period, unless the partners have made a contract to the contrary [Sec. 42(a)].

2. By the completion of adventure—Where a partnership has been constituted for carrying out a particular adventure, such partnership comes to an end on the completion of the adventure, in the absence of any contrary agreement [Sec. 42(b)].[45]

3. By the death of a partner—A partnership, whether at will or for a fixed period, is dissolved by the death of partner, unless there is a contract to the contrary [Sec. 42(c)].

4. By the insolvency of a partner—Subject to the contract between the partners, a partnership whether for a fixed period or at will, is dissolved by the adjudication of a partner as an insolvent [Sec. 42(d)].

5. By the retirement of a partner—Where a partner retires from the partnership, then also the partnership gets dissolved, but not the firm.[46] If, however, a partnership firm consists of two partners only, then on the retirement of one of the partners, the remaining partner alone cannot constitute a partnership and it ceases to exist, as there cannot be a partnership firm unless there are at least two partners.[47]

In all the cases mentioned above the remaining partners may continue the firm in pursuance of an express or implied contract to that effect. If they do not continue, the dissolution of firm takes place automatically.

Dissolution of Firm—In die following cases there is necessarily a breaking up or extinction of the relationship which subsisted between all the partners of the firm, and closing up of the business:—

1. By mutual consent—A firm may be dissolved where all the partners agree that it should be dissolved. Just as a partnership is formed by the consent of all the partners, similarly a partnership, the firm, gets dissolved by all the partners agreeing to such a dissolution. This is an application of the general rule that a contract may be discharged by mutual agreement.

2. By the insolvency of all the partners but one—We have seen that the insolvency of one or more partners would only dissolve the partnership if the remaining solvent partners are two or more and they agree to continue the business of the firm; yet, if all the partners or all the partners but one become insolvent, there must necessarily be a dissolution of the firm. The dissolution is automatic or compulsory [Sec 41 (a)]. But the insolvency of partnership firm does not *ipso facto* result also in the insolvency of its partners. To make them insolvent it is essential to make them party to the insolvency proceedings of the firm (*Jayantilal Mohanlal* v. *Narain Das & Sons,* 1983 Bom. 226).

3. By business becoming illegal—The firm is in every case dissolved if the business of the partnership is prohibited by law, *i.e.*, the object for which the partnership was formed is unlawful or

---

45. Gherulal Parakh v. Mahadeodas, 1959 S. C. 781.

46. Sundarsanam v. Viswanadham Bros. 1955 A. P. 12. Bishnu Chandra v. Chandrika Prasad 1983 S.C.523.

47. Chunilal v. Ahmad Rowther, 1960 Ker. 156.

becomes illegal as a result of some subsequent events. Here also the dissolution is automatic or compulsory [Sec. 41 (b)]. There is operation of law.

4. By notice of dissolution—Where the partnership is at will, whether originally so or subsequently becoming one by a partnership for a fixed time being continued beyond the stated period, the firm may be dissolved at any time, by any partner giving notice in writing of his intention to dissolve, to all the other partners.[48] The dissolution in such a case takes place from the date mentioned in the notice, or if no date is mentioned from the date of the communication of the notice to the other partners (Sec.43). The notice must not be ambiguous or vague. It must be effected. And a notice once given cannot be withdrawn without the consent of the other partners. But if the partner giving the notice dies while the notice is in the post, the dissolution will be by death and not by notice. The mere filing of a suit for dissolution does not amount to notice of dissolution (*Banarsidas* v. *Kanshi Ram* 1963 S.C. 1165). Also, a transfer of running business does not by itself bring about dissolution of a firm (*Radha Soami Sahha v. Pavan Electric Co.* 1967 All. 9). A firm cannot however, be dissolved by forcible expulsion of a partner in violation of contract of partnership.[49]

DISSOLUTION THROUGH COURT

A partnership for a fixed period, unlike a partnership at will, cannot be dissolved by a notice and where it is not dissolved for any of the reasons mentioned above it would be possible to dissolve it only by a Court of Law at a suit of a partner. The remedy of a suit is open to partners of all kinds of partnerships, but it is of practical importance in the case of a partnership for a fixed period.

The following are the circumstances provided by Sec. 44 in which a firm may be dissolved by the Court:—

1. When a partner becomes of unsound mind—The lunacy or insanity of a partner does not *ipso facto* dissolve the partnership, and the partner's authority to bind the firm continues, and also the lunatic partner's property continues to be liable for Subsequent debts till actual dissolution. Even the acts of a lunatic partner will continue to bind the firm till dissolution is decreed. Therefore, the lunatic himself through his guardian in order to protect his interests, or other partners, having lost his services or to save themselves from the acts of the lunatic, may file a suit for the dissolution of the firm. In either case the Court may order dissolution which will commence from the date of the order of the Court. In the case of insanity of a dormant partner dissolution will not be ordered by the Court, unless a very special case is made out for dissolution.

2. Permanent incapacity of a partner—As partnership proceeds on the assumption that all partners would attend diligently to the partnership business, the firm may be dissolved by theCourt at the instance of any of the co-partners of a partner who becomes *permanently* incapable of performing his duties as a partner, e.g., he becomes blind, paralytic, etc. This rule will not apply to a dormant partner who has not taken an active part in the business and whose incapacity is not likely to affect the partnership business.

3. Misconduct of a partner affecting the business—Where a partner is guilty of misconduct which is likely to affect prejudicially the business of the firm, the Court may dissolve the firm at the instance of any of the other partners. The guilty partner evidently is not entitled to file a suit for dissolution. Where the partnership is at will he can get the firm dissolved by notice. It is not essential that misconduct must be in the actual carrying on of the business, all that is required is that the misconduct must be likely to affect prejudicially the carrying on of the business. Gambling by partner, misapplication of a client's money by a solicitor, issuing of puffing advertisements by a partner in dentist's firm,

---

48. Srikrishan Gupta v. Ram Babu Gupta 1990 All. 171.
49. Ramnarayan v. Kashinath, 1954, Pat. 53.

conviction of a partner for travelling without ticket, have been held to be sufficient misconduct for dissolution of a firm.

4. Persistent disregard of partnership agreement by a partner—Where a partner frequently commits breaches of the partnership agreement and the other partners find it impossible to carry on the partnership business, the Court may dissolve the firm at the instance of any of the other partners. Constant refusal to perform duties or studies, prolonged and continued attention to the affairs of the business by a partner, or continuous quarrels, misappropriation of income and erroneous accounts by a partner are good grounds for dissolution.[50]

5. Transfer of interest or share by a partner—A partner cannot assign away his interest so as to introduce a new partner into the firm. Therefore, where a partner has transferred the *whole* of his interest to a third person or where his share has been attached under a decree or sold under process of law, the other partners may sue for dissolution. The partner at fault, of course, cannot apply for dissolution.

6. Business working at loss—The Court may dissolve a partnership when it is satisfied that the business of the firm cannot be carried on save at a loss. Thus, where the partners find that the business cannot be carried on at a profit which was the motive for the formation of the firm, but must necessarily end in loss, if continued for the stipulated period, or in order to complete the particular adventure, the partners may ask for dissolution through Court.

7. Where just and equitable—As the grounds mentioned above upon which a partner may apply for dissolution are not exhaustive the Act in sub-section (g) permits a partner to seek dissolution on any other ground which would satisfy the Court that dissolution is just and equitable. The sub-section gives a discretion to the Court to dissolve a firm where it appears that a situation contrary to the good faith and essence of agreement between the partners has arisen, or where the substratum of the partnership firm has gone or where there is a complete deadlock, and there is complete destruction of confidence between the partners or they can no longer perform their duties.[51]

WINDING UP

On the dissolution of a firm, whether by an order of the Court or otherwise, it becomes necessary that the affairs of the firm should be wound up, the assets realised, the liabilities paid out and the surplus, if any, distributed to the partners or their representatives according to their respective rights.

Partner's lien—Sec. 46 provides to the same effect and lays down the rule that on dissolution of a firm, for the discharge of the liabilities of a partner *qua* partner, each partner or his representative has a right to have the property of the firm applied in payment of the debts of the firm. With regard to the division of the surplus assets, if any, a partner has a right to have the accounts adjusted and the net assets divided among the partners according to their rights. In other words, he has a right to have whatever may be due from co-partners deducted from what would be otherwise payable to them in respect of their shares. This right of a partner is often called *partner's lien*. But, as pointed out in *Babu v. Gokuldas,* 1930 Mad. 393, affirmed on appeal to the Privy Council (1934) M.W.N. 717, it is merely a convenient mode of referring to the right and the word "lien" in relation to partners is not used in its technical sense.

After dissolution, the rights and obligations of partners continue in all things necessary for the winding up of the business. Thus, after dissolution, the surviving partners have a right to continue the business, in so far as it is necessary for the purpose of winding up, and all the acts done by such

---

50. Bhagwan Ram Kairi v. Radhika Ranjan Das, 1953 Ass. 125.

51. See 1954 Mad. 9 and 1954 V. P. 43.

continuing partners for the purpose of winding up will be binding upon the other partners.[52] This provision has been made to enable the partners to complete all unfinished transactions, and if necessary for winding up, to borrow money or continue business in order to sell the assets. But the authority given here is only for the winding up of the affairs of the firm, and so, though unfinished transactions of the firm may be completed, the continuing partners have no right to enter into fresh contracts or incur fresh liabilities; and no partner can carry on any competing business, and if he does so, the partners can restrain him until the affairs of the firm are fully wound up (*Shadilal* v. *Nagin Chand* (1973) 1 S.C. 185). It will be remembered that the estate of the deceased partner or the insolvent partner is not liable for the acts of the firm, after the demise or adjudication, in spite of the fact that no notice of dissolution is given (Sec. 45 Proviso). In a winding up, however, all the property of the firm will have to be sold and realised.

Goodwill—We have seen that the goodwill of the business is one of the important items in a partnership. It may be sold either separately or along with the other property of the firm. Its valuation will depend upon the facts and circumstances of each case. It was stated in *Page v. Ratliffe* (1896) 75 L.T. 371 that its value may be taken to be equal to three years' net profits. It is open to any of the partners to purchase the goodwill and carry on the business under the firm name.

Restraint of trade by buyer of goodwill—Since ordinarily every partner would have a right to carry on a business competing with that of the buyer of goodwill, provided he does not use the firm name or solicit the old customer or make it appear that he is continuing the old business, it becomes necessary for the buyer of the goodwill in his own interest to impose a reasonable restraint on such partner from carrying on a similar business within specified limits and for a specified period; and such restraint would be binding on the partner (Sec. 55). Further, such a contract in restraint of trade may be made upon or in anticipation of the dissolution of the firm by partners even when goodwill is not sold (Sec.54).[53]

SETTLEMENT OF ACCOUNTS

Usually the "articles of partnership" contain an accounting clause according to which the final accounts between the partners are settled. But in the absence of an agreement between the partners the rules stated in Sec. 48 are to be observed. The mode of settlement of accounts between the partners after dissolution, as dealt with in the section which incorporates the Rule in *Garner* v. *Murray* (1904) 73 L.J. Ch. 66, is as follows:—

(a) Where the firm has suffered losses, or where the capital has dwindled, in either case, the undistributed profits, if any, should first of all be applied to the payment of such loss and to the making up of the deficiency of capital. If the profits prove insufficient, the capital must be applied for the payment of the losses. If even then there is loss, the partners must contribute from their separate property *pro rata,* i.e., in the proportion in which they would be entitled to share the profits if profits had resulted.

(b) The second rule which deals with the distribution of the assets may be stated thus:

The **assets** of the firm, including the original contributions of the partners, and subsequent ones, if made to make up deficiencies of capital, must first be applied on paying the debts of the firm due to third parties. If after paying these liabilities, there be surplus, such surplus should be applied to the payment to each partner of any advance received from him over and above the capital contributed by each. But if the amount is not sufficient to pay up fully the advances, then the advances should be paid rateably. If, however, there remains surplus after payment of these advances, then the surplus is

---

52. Kedar Nath v. Finn Rekh Chand Dasu Ram, 1983 All. 270
53. Krishnarao v. Shanker. 1954 Bom. 532.

to be paid rateably to each partner on account of capital. The residue, if any, is to be divided among all the partners, *pro rota, i.e.,* in the proportion in which they were entitled to share profits. (*Addanki Narayanappa* v. *Bhaskara,* 1966 S.C. 1300). If, however, the assets are not sufficient, and the partners have agreed to share equally the profits and losses but have contributed unequal amounts towards the capital of the firm, then, in the absence of any contrary agreement on the point, the deficiency of capital must be regarded as losses and must be made up by contributions by the partners in equal shares, with the result that the losses finally suffered by the partners will be equal. The contributions by the partners towards the deficiency need not be actual; they may be *notional, i.e.,* by adjustment of the amounts payable to the partners as the distribution of capital. If, in such a case one partner is insolvent and nothing can be recovered from him as his contribution to make up the deficiency, the solvent partners will not be liable to contribute for him.[54] After the partners contribute their share of the deficiency they will be paid rateably the amount due to them by way of return of their capital (Sec. 48; *Garner* v. *Murray*).

1. *A, B* and *C* were partners who had agreed to share equally in the profits and losses of the firm, and had contributed to the capital ₹ 20,000, ₹ 10,000 and ₹ 2,000 respectively, making a total capital of ₹ 32,000. On dissolution it is found that, after paying the debts of the firm and advances made by the partners, the assets are ₹ 14,000, which leave a deficiency of ₹ 18,000. This amount being losses, each partner must contribute ₹ 6,000 to make it up. After this is done the assets then available, ₹ 14,000 + ₹ 18,000 = ₹ 32,000 will be distributed rateably among the partners, so that each will have suffered a loss of ₹ 6,000. In actual practice it will not be necessary for *A* and *B* to pay ₹ 6,000 each in cash but notional adjustment may be made so that *C*, whose capital contribution was only ₹ 2,000 will have to pay ₹ 4,000, and out of the amount of ₹ 14,000 + ₹ 4,000 = ₹ 18,000, *A* will get ₹ 14,000 and *B* ₹ 4,000.

2. Difficulty may arise where one or more of the partners is insolvent and so cannot contribute anything toward the deficiency. Thus in the above case if *C* is insolvent and nothing can be recovered from him the assets will be distributed as follows: *A* and *B* will have in the first place to contribute their share of the deficiency, i.e., ₹ 6,000 each: and the assets then available, ₹ 14,000 + ₹ 6,000 + 6, 000 = ₹ 26,000 will be distributed between *A* and *B* in the proportion of their contribution to the capital, *i.e.,* in the ratio of 2 to 1. *A* will get ₹ 17,333.67 p. and B ₹ 8,666.33 p. and the ultimate result will be that *A* on the whole will have lost ₹ 8,666.33 p. and *B* ₹ 7,333.67 p. This is in accordance with the rule laid down in *Garner* v. *Murray,* a leading case on the subject. The effect of the rule is that in such a case a partner who has contributed a greater part of the capital may lose more than his other partners, otherwise sharing equally with him in the profits and losses of the firm.

3. The same principle will apply if *C* in the case mentioned in illustration 1 above, though not insolvent, fails to contribute his share of the deficiency. Out of the actual amount of ₹ 14,000, *A* will get ₹ 11,333.33 p. and *B* ₹ 2,666.67 p. and the Court will pass a decree for ₹ 2.666.67 p. in favour of *A* against *C* and for ₹ 1,333.33 p. in favour of *B* against *C*.

PAYMENT OF FIRM DEBTS AND PRIVATE DEBTS (SEC.49)

Difficulty sometimes arises when the assets of the firm are insufficient to pay the firm's debts or where the partners themselves have become insolvent or are not otherwise able to pay their private or individual creditors. In such a case there is likely to be a scramble between the partnership creditors and partner's private creditors, and difficult questions may arise as to how to distribute the available funds between them. The Act lays down that the partnership creditors should be first paid out of the partnership assets and similarly private creditors out of the private assets. In both cases, if there be

---

54. Mulchand v. Bhemmal 1948 Sind. 35. See Venkayyamma v. Triupaya, 1955 Mad. 2, where partner has died.

surplus, the other set of creditors will be entitled to share in it. It may be observed that this rule applies only when a question arises as to the order in which the firm debts and separate debts are to be paid from the joint and separate property of partners. It does not, however, entitle a partner to insist that a creditor of the firm must proceed against the assets of the firm before proceeding against the partner individually. All the partners, we have seen, are jointly and severally liable for all the acts of the firm and it is, therefore, open to a creditor of the firm to proceed against the firm (all the partners) or against any one or more of them.

RETURN OF PREMIUM ON PREMATURE DISSOLUTION (SEC. 51)

It may sometimes happen that a person is admitted as a partner into an already established business on the newcomer paying a "premium" to the other partners for their personal use and benefit. The consideration for such premium is not only the creation of a partnership with the newcomer but the continuance of that partnership for the period fixed. Sec. 51, dealing with the question of the return of premium on premature dissolution of the firm, provides to the effect that where a partner has paid a premium on entering into partnership for a fixed term, and the firm is dissolved before the expiry of that term for any reason other than the death of the partner, he (the newcomer) shall be entitled to a refund of the whole or a reasonable portion of the premium, as on a failure of consideration. But he will not be entitled to claim the refund where the dissolution is brought about by his own misconduct or where the partnership is dissolved by agreement and this agreement does not contain any provision for the refund of the premium or any part of it.

There are two points of great importance to be noted in this connection. *First,* the rule stated above applies only to a partnership for fixed term; and does not deal with the case of a partnership at will. *Secondly,* the premium is paid by the incoming partner to the other partner or partners for their personal use and not as a contribution for the firm. In fact, premium has been defined as "a sum of money paid by an incoming partner to the other partner or partners, not by way of contribution to the firm in which the payer is about to acquire an interest, but for personal use and benefit of the other partner or partners" (Strahan). It follows that the refund or repayment is by a partner or partners who had received the premium and not by the firm; it cannot, therefore, be allowed to come in competition with the claims of the creditors of the *firm.*[55]

LIMITED PARTNERSHIP

The Indian law does not recognise Limited Partnership, but, as we have referred to English law also throughout the book, it may not be out of place to describe here the important provisions of the English Limited Partnership Act, 1907.

The object of the Act is to allow some of the partners to be responsible only for the capital actually found by them, thus limiting the liability of those partners and leaving the others fully liable for the debts of the firm. It will be noted the limitation of liability is entirely different in scope, though similar in nature, fo that constituted by the Companies Act. The Act does not create limited partnership in the sense that the Companies Act creates limited companies. The principle of unlimited liability is left untouched for debts as regards partnership, and where one or more partners are responsible to an unlimited extent for the debts of the firm, the Act enables a new class of partners to be added whose liability is limited. So, we may say, that it is an Act for creating partners with limited liability, but not partnerships.

Sec. 4 of the Act contains the important rules, and it reads: "A limited partnership must consist of one or more persons called general partners, who shall be liable for all debts and obligations of the

---

55. Bury v. Alien (1845) 1 Cal. 589; Exparte Broom (1811) 1 Rose 69.

firm." These partners, it will be noticed, are liable as any partners under the general partnership law. The section further provides that the limited partnership must also contain "one or more persons, to be called limited partners, who shall at the time of entering into such partnership contribute a sum or sums of capital, or property valued at a stated amount, and who shall not be liable for the debts and obligations of the firm beyond the amount so contributed." It will be noted that a limited-partner is very much in the position of a fully paid shareholder. On the same analogy his share capital must not be returned to him as long as the partnership continues. Sec. 4 further provides that "a limited partner shall not during the continuance of the partnership draw out or receive back any part of his contribution, and if he does so draw out or receive back any such part he shall be liable for the debts and obligations of the firm up to the amount so drawn out or received back." A limited partner must not take part in the management of the partnership business, and has no power to bind the firm; but he has the right to inspect the books of the firm, and to examine into the state and prospect of the partnership business, and he may advise with his partners thereon. If a limited partner takes part in management he is liable for all debts and obligations of firm incurred while he so takes part in the management as though he were a general partner. A limited partner may, with the consent of the general partners, assign his share in the partnership, and upon such an assignment the assignee becomes a limited partner with all the rights of the assignor.

(a) Every limited partnership must be registered; (b) registration is effected by sending to the Registrar a signed statement containing the following particulars: (i) The firm name, (ii) The general nature of the business. (iii) The principal place of the business, (iv) The full name of each parrtner. (v) The term for which the partnership is entered into, and the date of its commencement, (vi) A statement that the partnership is limited, and the description of every limited partner as such, (vii) The sum contributed by each limited partner and whether paid in cash or how otherwise.[56]

SUMMARY

Partnership is defined as: "the relation between persons who have agreed to share the profits of a business carried on by all or any of them acting for all." The definition contains five elements which make a partnership, namely:
1. partnership results from a contract
2. between two or more persons who
3. agree to carry on business
4. with the object of making and sharing profit;
5. this business is conducted either by all the persons or by any of them acting for all.

The minimum number of persons required to constitute a partnership is two and the maximum number prescribed is 10 in the case of a banking firm and 20 in other cases.

The essence of partnership is the attempt to make profit in business for the partners. Existence of contract, business and the intention to make and share profit must be there.

Persons who enter into partnership with one another are called individually "partners" and collectively "a firm". "Firm" is only a convenient phrase to describe the partners and has no legal recognition or existence apart from those persons.

In a contract of partnership, all the essential elements of a valid contract must be present. A minor cannot become a partner by contract but he may be admitted to the benefits of an already existing partnership by the consent of all partners. Minor so admitted is entitled to his agreed share and can inspect books of account, but he is not personally liable for the debts and obligations of the firm, though his share in the property of the firm and the profits of the firm will be liable. A minor must,

---

56. Adapted from Tillyard, *Commercial Law.*

within six months form his attaining the age of majority, or on coming to know of his being so admitted (whichever date is later), elect whether he wants to continue in the firm or sever his connection with it. He must give a public notice of his intention within this period and if he fails to do so, he will be deemed to have elected to be a full partner. If he elects to continue or fails to repudiate, he will be liable for the firm's debts incurred since the date of his original admission to the partnership.

Partnership is an extension of agency, and every partner is an agent of the other partners, so that the acts of a partner during the course of business of a firm bind all the partners. Partners are of different kinds with different liabilities, namely,—

Actual partner who has by agreement become a partner and takes active part in the conduct of the business. All his acts for the business bind the other partners.

Partners by estoppel or holding out—A person may become a partner by implied contract arising out of the conduct of the parties. Where a person conducts himself so as to lead another to believe him to be a partner, though really he is not one, and on that belief the other person gives credit, then he is estopped from denying that he is a partner. Such a partner is called a partner by estoppel. Similarly, where a person is held out as a partner by another, and does not disclaim the partnership relation, he will be liable as a partner to any one who gives credit on the faith of this representation. He is a partner by holding out.

Dormant or sleeping partner is one who is in reality a partner but whose name does not appear in any way as partner, and who is not known to outsiders as partner. He is liable to third parties who subsequently discover this relationship. His position is similar to that of an undisclosed principal.

Nominal partner is a person whose name is used as if he were a member of the firm, although he is not really a partner and is not entitled to share the profits of the concern. He is, however, liable for acts of the firm.

Partner in profits only is a person who gets a share of the profits and does not share losses. He is liable to outsiders. He takes no part in the management of the business.

Sub-partner—Where a partner in a firm agrees to share with a stranger the profits derived by him from the partnership there arises a sub-partnership between the contracting member and the stranger, and the latter is called a sub-partner. A sub-partner has no rights against the firm, nor is he liable for its debts.

New partner is one who is admitted into an already existing partnership. He does not become liable for debts and obligations of the firm incurred before his joining the firm, unless he agrees to that. The creditors of the firm can, in no case, look to him for payment of past debts.

Retired or outgoing partner—An outgoing partner continues to be liable for obligations incurred before his retirement, and will continue to be liable even for future obligations, if he does not give public or actual notice of his retirement.

Formation of partnership—A partnership may be formed orally or in writing; but where it is reduced to writing, the deed of partnership must be stamped according to the provisions of the Stamp Act.

Test of partnership—To determine whether or not the relation of partnership exists between two or more parties, it is essential to look to the intention of the parties and their contact as it appears from the whole facts of the case. To constitute a partnership, two or more persons must agree to carry on some business in common for sharing profit. Therefore, two co-owners of property held not for carrying on business with the object of making profit do not constitute a partnership. Their relation will only result in co-ownership. The co-owners are not agents *inter se* and one cannot bind the other by his acts.

A creditor of the firm who stipulates to receive interest on the loan in the form of share of profit of the firm, and also to have some control over the conduct of the firm's business does not thereby become a partner.

A servant of the firm getting a share of the profits of the business either in lieu of remuneration or in addition to it is not a partner.

Duration of partnership—A partnership may be for a fixed period, and when the period so fixed for its duration is over, it comes to an end. Where after expiration of fixed period the business is carried on, the partnership will become a partnership at will. Where nothing is said as to the duration of partnership and the partners are free to carry on business as long as they like, it is a partnership at will. It may also be a single adventure or a single undertaking, when it lasts only until the undertaking is completed.

Partnership property—The partners may agree among themselves as to what is to be treated as the property of the firm, and what is to be separate property of one or more partners, although employed for the purposes of the firm. In the absence of any such contract the property of the firm is deemed to include—

(a) all property, rights and interests which have been brought into the common stock for purposes of partnership by the individual partners,

(b) those acquired in the course of the business with money belonging to the firm, and

(c) the goodwill of the business.

Goodwill is the advantage which is acquired by a business beyond the mere value of the capital, stock, fund and property employed therein in consequence of the general public patronage and encouragement which it receives from constant or habitual customers.

RIGHTS OF PARTNERS

1. To take part in the management of the business, unless otherwise stipulated.

2. Every partner has a right to be consulted and heard in all matters affecting the business. In case of difference of opinion, the decision of the majority of partners does not prevail unless the matter is unimportant.

3. Every partner has a right of free access to all records, books and accounts of the business, and also to examine and copy them.

4. Every partner is, in the absence of a contract to the contrary, entitled to equal share in the profits of the business.

5. A partner is entitled, in the absence of contract to the contrary, to be indemnified by the firm for all acts done, for all payments made and for all expenses incurred for and on behalf of the firm.

6. Every partner is, as a rule, a joint owner of the partnership property and each partner is presumed to have equal share in it.

7. Every partner has a right to prevent the introduction of a new partner into the firm without his consent, unless there is an express contract permitting such introduction.

8. Every partner has a right to retire, if the contract so provides, failing which with the consent of other partners, and if the partnership is at will, at any time on notice to the partners.

9. Every partner has a right not to be expelled from the firm.

10. An outgoing partner can carry on competing business without using the firm name or soliciting firm's customers.

Duties of partners:

1. To work for the greatest common advantage.

2. To be just and faithful.

3. To render true accounts.

4. To give full information.

5. To indemnify for fraud and wilful neglect

6. To share losses.

7. To attend diligently without remuneration.

8. To hold and use the partnership property for the firm.

9. To account for profits.
10. To account for profits of competing business.
11. To act within authority.
12. Not to assign his rights.

Relations of partners to third parties

All the partners are jointly and severally liable for all acts done by any partner in the course of business.

Every partner has an implied authority to bind other partners.

An **implied authority** of a partner consists in doing an act to carry on in the usual way the business of the firm provided the act is done in the firm name or in any manner expressing or implying an intention to bind the firm.

A partner has, in the absence of usage or custom of trade, no implied authority to—
(a) submit a dispute relating to the firm to arbitration,
(b) open a banking account on behalf of the firm in his own name,
(c) compromise or relinquish any claim or portion of claim by the firm,
(d) withdraw a suit or proceeding filed on behalf of the firm,
(e) admit any liability in a suit or proceedings against the firm,
(f) acquire immovable property on behalf of the firm,
(g) transfer immovable property belonging to the firm, or
(h) enter into partnership on behalf of the firm.

Every partner is liable for the negligence and fraud of other partners in the course of the management of the business.

All partners are liable for misappropriation by a partner of money or property of a third party received for or lying in the custody of the firm.

All the partners are deemed to have received any information obtained by one of them in the course of partnership business.

Dissolution of partnership—
1. By the expiry of term.
2. By the completion of adventure.
3. By the death of a partner.
4. By the insolvency of a partner.
5. By the retirement of a partner.

Dissolution of firm—
1. By mutual agreement
2. By insolvency of all the partners but one:
3. By business becoming illegal.
4. By notice of dissolution by any partner, where partnership is at will.

Dissolution through Court—
1. When a partner becomes of unsound mind.
2. Where a partner becomes permanently incapable of performing his duties.
3. Where a partner is guilty of misconduct which is likely to affect prejudicially the business of the firm.
4. Where a partner persists in disregarding the partnership agreement
5. Where a partner transfers his share or interest in the partnership to a third person.
6. Where the business cannot be carried on save at a loss.
7. Where the court finds it just and equitable to dissolve the firm.

Settlement of accounts after dissolution—

Payment of losses—Where the firm has suffered losses or where the capital has dwindled, the undistributed profits, if any, should first of all be applied to payment of losses and to making up of deficiency of capital. If profits prove insufficient, the capital must be applied to pay losses. If even then there are losses, the partners must contribute from their separate property *pro rota.*

Distribution of assets—The assets must first fee applied in paying the debts of the firm due to third parties. Any surplus should then be used to pay 'off partners' advances; if any. Any further surplus is to be distributed among partners rateably on account of capital. The residue, if any, should be divided among all partners pro *rota.*

Payment of Firm debts and private debts—Partnership creditors are first paid out of the partnership assets, and similarly private creditors out of the private assets; if there be a surplus, the other set of creditors will be entitled to share in it.

CASES FOR RECAPITULATION

1. Certain iron merchants, being in financial difficulties, assigned their business to trustees for the benefit of their creditors. The trustees carried on the business with the object of paying off the creditors out of the business.. *Held,* the creditors were not partners in the business. The trade was not carried on by or on account of the creditors, but the trade still remained the trade of the debtors. The debtors were still the persons solely interested in the profits, save only that they had mortgaged them to their creditors [*Cox* v. *Hickman* (1860) 8 H.L.C. 268].

2. A firm consisting of *A* and *B* partners and doing export and import business entered into a contract with *C*, the creditor. *C*, in consideration of moneys advanced or to be advanced from time to time by him, was to receive a share of the net profits of the business of the firm and large powers of control over the conduct of the business. But *C* had no power to direct transactions or the course of trade. *Held,* *C*'s powers were powers of control only, given to provide to him largest possible security. This was not sufficient to constitute him a partner with *A* and *B*. [*Mollwo, March & Co.* v. *Court of Wards* (1872)L.R.4419].

3. *A* and *B* purchase a tea shop and incur additional expenses for purchasing utensils, etc., each contributing half of the total expense and the shop is leased out on a daily rent which is divided between them both, *A* and *B* are co-owners and not partners (*Govindan Nair* v. *Nagabhusmanammal,* 1948 Mad. 343].

4. *A*, *B* and *C* carried on a business of profit. *C* contributed neither .labour nor money, and did not receive any profits, but lent his name to the firm. *Held, C* was liable to every outsider who gave credit on his being there as partner [*Waugh* v. *Carver* (1793) 2H.B.I.235].

5. *J* and *W* are in partnership as solicitors. *P* pays £ 1,500 to both of them to be invested on a mortgage of a specified real estate, and they jointly acknowledge receipt of the amount for that purpose. Afterwards *P* hands over another £ 1,500 to *W* alone on his representation that it will be invested on a mortgage of some real estate of F, another client of the firm, such estate not being specially described. *J* dies and afterwards both these sums are fraudulently applied to his own use by *W*. *W* also dies, having paid interest to *P* on both the sums till within a short time before his death. *W*'s estate is declared bankrupt. *Held,* *J*'s estate is liable to make good to P the loss sustained by him on account of *W*'s fraud only to the extent of £ 1,500 (the first 1,500 paid by *P* to both *J* and *W*) and not for the second £ 1,500 paid to *W* alone. The first amount was taken for the purpose of making a specific investment or mortgage which was in the ordinary course of business of a firm of solicitors. The second sum of £ 1,500 was taken by *W* for the general purpose of investing it, as the problem states the money 'will be invested on a mortgage of some real estate of *F*,.... such estate not being specifically described.' To receive money for general purpose investing it is not an act within the scope of the ordinary business of firm of solicitors [*Harman* v. *Johnson* (1853) 2 E. & B. 61].

6. *A, B, C* and *D* enter into a partnership agreement for ten years and *B, C* and *D* are placed in charge of the management of the business. They carry on the business well and make it a successful concern. *A*, in order to resile from the agreement, creates obstructions in the way of *B, C*, and *D* and sues for dissolution. *Held,* he cannot succeed, for the court will not interfere at the suit of a partner who is himself guilty of misconduct (*Manilal* v. *Keshabjipitamber,* 1952 Pat. 33).

7. *M* was a partner in a firm. The firm ordered goods in *M's* lifetime, but delivery was not made until after *M's* death. *Held M's* estate was not-liable for the price of the goods in *M's* lifetime [*Bagel* v. *Miller* (1903) 2 K.B. 212].

8. *A, B & Co.* is a newly constituted firm and commences business without registration. *Y* is indebted to the firm in the sum of ₹ 500 and the firm files a suit against *Y* for the recovery of the said sum and immediately thereafter gets itself registered. *Held,* the suit was not maintainable as the firm was not registered and the subsequent registration was of no avail [*Ram Prasad* v. *Kamla Prasad* (1935) 33 A.L.J. 1243].

9. An unregistered firm sold glass phials worth ₹ 2,700 to *B*, who gave a cheque for the amount on the H.C. Bank, but the cheque was dishonoured. *R*, who was a partner in the firm, demanded money from *B* who paid only ₹ 1,500. In the meantime, the firm was dissolved and the sum of ₹ 1,200, the unpaid balance, was assigned to *R* for realisation. *R* sued *B* for the recovery of the amount. *B* contends that the suit is not maintainable as the firm was not registered. The firm was dissolved before the suit was filed. Section 69(3) makes an exception in favour of a suit for realising the assets of a dissolved firm (*Radhey Shyam* v. *Beni Ram Mool Chand* 1967 All. 28).

10. *B & M* carried on business in partnerships as proprietors and managers of picture houses. The partnership deed prohibited a partner from borrowing money on behalf of the firm. *M* borrowed money from *H*, representing that it was required for partnership purposes. *Held, H* was not entitled to recover the loan from the firm, because it was not a trading firm and *M* had no implied authority to borrow on behalf of the firm. A trading firm is one which depends on buying and selling of goods, and the firm in question did not do so (*Higgins* v. *Beauchamp* (1914) 3 K.B. 1192).

11. *A, B* and *C* as partners bought the property of H consisting of plots of land and shares in a company. The company also owned some other plots of land in the same locality. *B* and there after apart from A purchased the company's other plots of land and made good profits. *A* sued *B* and *C* for the share of the profits so made. *Held, A* was not entitled to a share in the profit so made, as this transaction was not within the scope of the partnership and was not shown to be in rivalry with or in any way injurious to the business of the firm (*Trimble* v. *Godbery* (1906) A.C. 494).

12. Jain Bros. Hosiery, a partnership firm, was allotted woollen yarn quota. The firm was dissolved and *S*, one of the partners, took over the entire business assets of the firm along with goodwill and liabilities. He therefore carried on the business in the same name and continued to obtain the quota. The other (retired) partners claimed one-third share of the quota on the ground that it was not part of goodwill and the remaining partner was drawing on the basis of the basic period when they were partners. *Held,* quota attaches to the owner of a business at the point of time the quota is granted. It is the business at the relevant time which obtains the quota. Quota cannot be an asset of the partnership. Assets are divisible among partners. Quota cannot be divided. Hence the other two retired partners (respondents) have no proprietary claim in the appellant's quota (*Shadilal* v. *Nagin Chand & others,* (1973) 1 S.C. 185).

CHAPTER 6

The Sale of Goods

Not every one who agrees to buy or sell goods is fortunate enough to find that the transaction turns out as he had hoped. In many cases those who are disappointed have to seek the assistance of the law in order to enforce their rights. The law defining those rights is codified in an enactment known as the Indian Sale of Goods Act, 1930, which came into force on July 1, 1930. The Indian Sale of Goods Act follows more or less closely the English enactment.

CONTRACT OF SALE OF GOODS

According to Section 4 of the Act, a contract of sale of goods is a contract whereby the seller (*i*) transfers or (*ii*) agrees to transfer the property in (ownership of) goods to the buyer for a price. A contract of sale may be (1) absolute or (2) conditional according as the parties desire. It may be between one part-owner and another. The term "contract of sale" is a generic term. It includes an actual sale as well as agreement to sell. Where the contract of sale is executed, *i.e.*, the property in goods has passed from the seller to the buyer, it is called a sale; but where the contract is executory, i.e., the transfer of the property in goods is to take place at a future time or subject to some condition thereafter to be fulfilled, it is in an **Agreement to Sell.**

SALE AND AGREEMENT TO SELL DISTINGUISHED[1]

The difference between sale and agreement to sell is of vital importance as the two have different legal effects. The difference between the two may be considered in the form of points of distinction.

1. In a sale, the property in goods sold passes to the buyer so that the seller is no more the owner of the goods, but it is the buyer who owns them; while in an agreement to sell, the ownership does not pass to the buyer at the time of the contract so that the seller continues to be the owner until the agreement to sell becomes an actual sale by the expiry of certain time or the fulfilment of some condition.

2. An agreement to sell is an executory contract, while a sale is an executed contract.

3. An agreement to sell is a contract pure and simple, and thus creates merely *jus in personan,* i.e., gives a right to either buyer or seller against the other for any default in fulfilling his part of the agreement. A sale is contract plus conveyance, and creates *jus in rem,* i.e., gives right to buyer to enjoy goods as against the whole world.

---

1. See Sales Tax Officer v. Budh Prakash,1954 S.C. 459.

4. In a sale, the seller can sue for the price, even though goods are in his possession; but in agreement to sell, his only remedy is to sue for damages if buyer fails to accept and pay for the goods.

5. In an agreement to sell, the seller being still the owner, he can dispose of the goods as he likes and the buyer's remedy for seller's breach is a suit for damages. In a sale, however, seller's breach gives the buyer double remedy; a suit for damages against the seller, and the proprietary remedy in respect of the goods so that if the goods are sold to third parties, he can in many cases sue and recover them as owner from the third parties.

6. If there is an agreement to sell and the goods are destroyed by an accident, the loss, as a rule, falls on the seller, even though the goods are in the possession of the buyer. In a sale, the loss falls on the buyer, even though the goods are with the seller.

7. If, in an agreement to sell, the buyer who has paid the price, finds that the seller has become insolvent, his only remedy would be to claim a rateable dividend. In a sale, however, on the seller becoming insolvent the buyer, as an owner, would be entitled to recover the goods from the official Receiver or Assignee in insolvency.

8. If, in an agreement to sell, the buyer is adjudged as insolvent before he pays for the goods, the seller may refuse to deliver the goods unless paid for, as ownership has not passed to the buyer. In a sale, however, in these circumstances, the seller, in the absence of a lien over the goods, must deliver to the official Receiver or Assignee and will be entitled only to a rateable dividend for the price due.

SALE DISTINGUISHED FROM OTHER TRANSACTIONS

As the transfer of ownership by the buyer for a price paid or payable in money is an essential ingredient of sale, it differs from several other classes of contracts, which resemble sale in some respects. Since the Sale of Goods Act applies only to contracts of sale of goods and to no others, it is expedient to note the points of distinction between sale and other contracts.

SALE AND BAILMENT

In a contract of bailment, goods are delivered by one person to another for a certain purpose on the condition that when that purpose is over the goods will be returned in specie. The ownership does not pass to the bailee. It is only the possession that is given to him. In sale, the delivery of goods is made by the seller to the buyer for a price, and the buyer becomes the owner of the goods and can deal with them as he likes.

SALE AND GIFT

Where goods are transferred by one person to another without any price or other consideration being given in return the transaction is called a gift. In a gift the ownership of the goods passes to the donee *gratis,* and thus the price element is absent; it is not a sale.

SALE, BARTER AND EXCHANGE

It is necessary for sale that goods must be exchanged for a money consideration called the price. Where goods are exchanged for goods, it does not amount to sale but only to barter. If money is exchanged for money, it will be a transaction of exchange and not a sale. But if the consideration consists partly of money and partly of goods, it would be contract of sale. If goods on either side are delivered in an exchange, any balance of money payable may be recovered as on a contract of sale. So also, if the party liable to deliver goods in exchange refuses to do so or is unable to do so, the other party may recover the value of the goods given in exchange.

MORTGAGE, PLEDGE AND HYPOTHECATION OF GOODS

A mortgage of goods is a transfer of interest in goods from a mortgagor to a mortgagee to secure a debt. A pledge is a bailment of goods by one person to another to secure payment of a debt. If the pledger makes default in paying the debt the pledgee may sell the goods after due notice to the pledger. A hypothecation of goods is an equitable charge on goods without possession, but not amounting to a mortgage. All the three are different from sale, for the ownership is not transferred by one party to the other in any of them. The essence of a contract of sale is the transfer of general property in goods for a price. The essence of a contract of mortgage is the transfer of special property in goods from the mortgagor to the mortgagee in order to secure a debt.

SALE AND HIRE-PURCHASE AGREEMENT

A transaction of hire is a kind of bailment which differs form a contract of sale in that, even though the hirer pays money on consideration of the use of goods, yet the ownership continues with the person who gives goods on hire. The hire-purchase contract is a development of modem commercial transactions. Here the owner of goods delivers the goods to a person who agrees to pay certain stipulated periodical payments as hire charges. Though the possession of the goods is with the hirer, the ownership still remains with the original owner. If the payments are made regularly, the hirer gets the option of purchasing the goods on making the full payment. Before this option is exercised, the hirer may return the goods hired. The essence of hire-purchase agreement is that there is no agreement to buy, but only an option is given to the hirer to buy under 'certain conditions' so that the hirer has a right to become the owner after paying regularly the stipulated rent or to return the goods and put an end to hiring. Mere payment of price by instalments does not make it a hire-purchase; it is a sale.

In *KL. Johar & Co.* v. *Deputy Commercial Tax Officer,* 1965 S.C. 1082, Wanchoo J. (afterwards C.J.) said : "The essence of a sale is that the property is transferred from the seller to the buyer for a price whether paid at once or paid later in instalments. On the other hand, a hire-purchase agreement has two aspects. There is first the aspect of bailment of goods subject to the hire-purchase agreement, and there is next an element of sale which fructifies when the option to purchase is exercised by the intending purchaser." Where the hirer does not have the option to return the goods, it will be an agreement to buy even if the price is payable by instalments.

The distinction is of great importance. If the hirer becomes insolvent or fails to pay any instalments, the owner may seize the goods and sue for arrears of instalments upto the time of seizure (as these are treated as hire charges), no benefit being allowed to the hirer for the fact that the owner has resold the goods at a higher price (*Enayatullah* v. *Jalan T. Co.,* 1965 Pat. 214). Since the hirer is not the owner of the goods, but only a bailee, he cannot pass on any title even to innocent and *bonafide* third parties.

SALE AND AGENCY

A transaction of sale must be distinguished from one of agency, for where a retailer obtains goods from a manufacturor or wholesaler, it may become important to know whether he has got them on his own account or as an agent. The significance of the distinction becomes very important in case of loss of the goods or insolvency of either party. Where *A & Co.* were appointed sole agents for three years for the sale of all the bricks of the manufacturers, it was held that the relation was one of vendor and purchaser rather than of agent and principal.

SALE AND SKILL AND LABOUR

In *Lee.* v. *Griffin* (1861) 1 B.& S.272, where the contract was to make false teeth and fit them to the mouth of a person, Blackburn, J., ruled that if the contract results in the transfer of the property in the goods from one person to another, it is. a contract of sale. This statement was considered too sweeping and was not followed in *Robinson* v. *Graves* (1935)1 K.B. 579, where it was held that a contract to paint a portrait was a contract for skill and labour and not a contract for the sale of goods, despite the fact that it was the object of the contract, to transfer the property in the completed portrait. However, much depends upon the circumstances, and a contract for the construction of two ship's propellers was held by the House of Lords to be a contract of sale of good;[2] so too was a contract for the making of a fur coat from selected skins.

SALE AND LABOUR AND MATERIALS

A contract for the supply of goods to be installed or fitted into a building or construction is normally regarded as a contract for labour and materials and not a contract for the sale of goods—in particular with respect to the time when the property in the materials passes to the buyer or client. Here again, much will depend upon the intention of the parties. For instance, the contract may clearly be intended to be for the sale of the materials to be installed afterwards, even by the seller. If the contract is for labour and materials the property will pass when the materials have been installed. If it is a sale, the property passes at the time of the contract. However, too much stress on the distinction should not be laid as in both cases implied conditions apply (*Young & Marten Ltd.* v. *McManus Childs Ltd.* (1969) 1 A.C. 454).

WHAT IS A SALE—ESSENTIAL ELEMENTS OF A SALE[3]

We are now in a better position to lay down the essential elements of a sale. To constitute a sale the following elements must be present:—

1. There must be some goods, the general property in which is transferred from the seller to the buyer.

2. A price in money must be paid or promised to be a paid as a *quid pro quo* on a transfer of property on a sale.

3. The contract of sale is consensual, bilateral and cumulative. There must be a seller and a buyer. Two persons are necessary to complete a sale, as the same person cannot be both seller and buyer. A person cannot buy his own goods, as there is nothing to buy. But where in law, one person has a right to sell another's goods, the owner may himself buy such goods. This may happen where goods are sold under a distress or execution or by a pledgee as, in fact, the buyer and seller are different persons. But the seller in such cases cannot buy, though he is selling the goods of which he is not the owner because of his fiduciary position. A part-owner may, however, sell his share to the part-owner so that a partner can always sell to the other partners. Similarly, a partner can sell goods to his firm. But a club consisting of several members does not sell, when it supplies liquor or meals to a member who pays for them though the transaction resembles a sale. The transaction is a release of the joint interest of the members, and the member is in substance consuming his own property, and the mode of payment is a matter of internal arrangement regulated by the rules of the club and agreed to by the member on his admission.

---

2. Cammell Laird & Co. Ltd v. Manganese Bronz & Brass Co. Ltd. (1934) A.C. 402; State of Madras v. Cannon Dunkerly & Co. (Madras) Ltd., 1958 S.C. 560.

3. State of Bombay v. United Motors (India) Ltd. 1953 S.CJ. 373.

4. There must be a transfer of ownership from the seller to the buyer. The transfer must be of the absolute or general property in the goods sold. In law, a thing may in some cases be said to have in a certain sense two owners, one of whom has the general property and the other a special property in it; and the transfer of the special property is not a sale of the thing. For example where goods are delivered on pawn or pledge, only the special property is transferred to the pawnee, and the general property remains with the pawnor. which he may transfer to a third person subject to the rights of the pawnee. The same rule applies to the case of a bailee.

5. All the essential elements of a valid contract must also be present.

PART 6-B
FORMATION OF A CONTRACT OF SALE

FORMALITIES OF THE CONTRACT (Section 5)

A contract of sale is regulated by the general law of contract, namely, there must be an offer to buy or sell goods and an acceptance of that offer, parties competent to contract, genuine mutual assent, a thing the property in which is transferred or is to be transferred for a money consideration called the price paid or promised to be paid. A contract of sale may be made in any of the following modes: (1) there may be immediate delivery of the goods; (2) there may be immediate payment of price but the delivery to be made at some future date; (3) there may be immediate delivery of goods and also immediate payment of price; (4) it may be agreed that the delivery or payment or both are to be made in particular instalments; or (5) the delivery or payment or both may be given at some future date.

In law, except where specially provided by some law for the time being in force, no formalities are required to constitute a valid contract of sale of goods. A contract of sale may be express or implied from the conduct of the parties, and in case of express contract, it may be oral or in writing or partly in writing and partly by word of mouth. A written offer to sell goods may be accepted verbally or a verbal offer may be accepted in writing. So also goods may be ordered by a letter and may be supplied without further communication.

SUBJECT-MATTER OF CONTRACT OF SALE
GOODS

The subject-matter of the contract of sale is essentially the goods. Section 2(7) in defining goods lays down that "Goods" means every kind of movable property other than actionable claims and money; and includes stocks and shares, growing crops, grass, and things attached to or forming part of the land which are agreed to be severed before sale or under the contract of sale. According to this definition **money** and **actionable claims** are not goods and cannot be bought and sold. **Money** here means current money, i.e., the recognised currency in circulation in the country, but not old and rare coins which may be treated as goods and bought and sold as such. **An actionable claim** is a thing which a person cannot make use of or enjoy, but which can be recovered by him by means of a suit or an action. Thus a debt, due to a man from another is an actionable claim and cannot be sold as goods, although it can be assigned. Since stocks and shares, according to English law, are things in action and not goods, they have been expressly included by the Indian Act in the definition as goods. Goodwill, trademarks, copyrights, patents are all considered goods. Similarly, water, gas, electricity, ships are regarded as goods and can be bought and sold as such.

Goods may be (1) Existing, (2) Future, or (3) Contingent. The Existing Goods may be (*i*) Specific, or (*ii*) Generic, (*iii*) Ascertained or (*iv*) Unascertained.

EXISTING GOODS

Existing goods may be either owned or possessed by the seller at the time of the contract Instances of sale of goods possessed but not owned by the sellers are sales by agents and pledgees. Where the existing goods are the subject-matter of a contract, it is essential that they must be in actual or possible existence, for a present sale can be made only of a subject-matter having actual or possible existence. If, therefore, *A* sells his horse, ship or merchandise to *B*, believing that they exist, when in fact the horse is dead and the ship is actually lost on the high seas and the merchandise is utterly destroyed by fire, no contract will arise. If, however, the things sold be only partially destroyed at the time of the sale, the buyer may either abandon the contract or he may take the thing at a proportional reduction of the price according to the terms of the original bargain. The existing goods may be either specific goods or ascertained goods, or they may be generic goods or unascertained goods. **Specific Goods** means goods identified and agreed upon at the time a contract of sale is made. To be specific, goods must be actually identified or individualised, and not merely identifiable. **Ascertained Goods**, though sometimes used as specific goods, are not always identical with specific goods. The former term is really of wider import. As contrasted with specific goods, "Ascertained Goods" may be intended to cover the case of goods which have become ascertained subsequently to the formation of the contract, although they would not be specific goods as defined by Section 2(4) of the Act. An examination of goods by the buyer does not make them "ascertained."

GENERIC OR UNASCERTAINED GOODS

These are goods which are not specifically identified but are defined only by description. *A* has ten cows. He promises to sell one of them to *B*, pointing it out to *B* at the time of the sale. The contract in this case is a sale of the specific cow. If, on the other hand, *A* merely promises to sell any one of the cows, the contract is for unascertained goods. The cow will become ascertained when *A* makes up his mind as to which one of the ten cows he will sell and *B* consents to buy that cow.

FUTURE GOODS

Sec. 6(1) makes it possible for a person to sell or offer to sell future goods, i.e., goods which he does not own or possess at the time of the contract, but which he will manufacture or produce or acquire after the making of the contract. Future goods are not the same as unascertained goods which form a class of existing goods. *A* contracts on August 1,1977 to sell *B* 25 bales of Broach cotton to be delivered and paid for on October 1,1977. This is a valid contract even though *A* has no cotton bales with him and can acquire them only by purchase in the market. Similarly, a person can make a contract of sale even though the subject-matter of sale is not in existence at all at the time of the contract, provided that it be the natural product, or expected increase of something, to which the seller has a present right. For example, a valid contract of sate may be made of the wine that the vineyard is expected to yield during die coming year, or the wool that may grow on the sheep, or the fruit that may grow on the trees, or the young that may be born of the sheep. So also an expectation depending upon chance may be sold, as where a fisherman agrees to sell the casting of his net, before casting it. But a mere possibility or contingency not dependent on any present right nor resulting from any present property or interest, cannot be made the subject-matter of a present sale, though it may be valid as an executory agreement to sell. It must be remembered, however, that **the present sale of future goods does not amount to sale proper but an agreement to sell the goods.** Though the seller may purport to effect a present sate of future goods, the transaction is only an **agreement to sell**, for a man cannot assign what has no existence, although he can agree to assign property which is to come into existence in the future. Again, only those goods which can be the subject-matter of ownership, i.e., tamed animals, birds in a cage, fish in a pond, or fish caught by the fisherman, can be sold; but wild animals in the jungle, birds in the air, fish in the sea or river, being free and not owned by anyone, cannot be the subject-matter of sale.

CONTINGENT GOODS

Sec. 6(2) is merely a particular instance of sale of future goods and categorically states that there may be contract for the sale of goods the acquisition of which by the seller depends upon a contingency which may or may not happen. As a contract of sale may be either absolute or conditional, a seller may contract unconditionally to sell goods to be afterwards acquired, or he may contract to sell goods 'to arrive', or to agree to sell a crop which is to be sown. The parties are left free to make what bargain they please. They may stipulate (1) that the contract shall be conditional on the part of the seller only, the price being payable in any event; or (2) that the contract shall be absolute on the part of the seller, despite the uncertainty of his being able to acquire the goods, and in such case he will be liable to pay damages if he fails to perform his contract; or (3) that the contract shall be conditional on both sides, and, if the event does not happen, both parties shall be freed from their obligations or (4) the buyer may have to pay in any event, for "a man may buy the chance of obtaining goods."

PERISHING OF GOODS

Where specific goods are the subject-matter of a contract of sale (both actual sale and agreement to sell) and they, without the knowledge of the seller, perish at or before the time of the contract, the contract is void. This is based on the rule that mutual mistake of a fact essential to the contract renders the contract void. The parties are contracting about something which unknown to them has no existence and, therefore, the intention of both of them is completely frustrated. *A* sold to *B* a specific cargo of goods which he honestly believed was on its way from England to India. It turned out, however, that before the day of the bargain, the ship conveying the cargo had foundered and the goods were lost. Neither party was aware of the fact. The agreement was held to be void. Under Sec.7, a contract for the sale of specific goods will also be void if such goods without the knowledge of the seller have become so damaged as no longer to answer to their description in the contract. This is so because the goods have ceased to exist in the commercial sense, *i.e.*, their merchantable character as such has been lost, although they are not physically destroyed. Where cement was spoiled by water and converted practically into stone, or where sugar became *sherbal* and were, thus unsaleable as cement or sugar, they were deemed to have been destroyed in the commercial sense and the contracts were held void. But if the goods, though damaged, still answer to the description, the contract is not void, and the buyer must take the risk as to their quality and condition and pay the price. The section applies also to cases where the seller is irretrievably deprived of the goods as when they have been stolen, or lawfully requisitioned by the Government or have in some other way been lost and cannot be traced.

DESTRUCTION OF PART OF GOODS SOLD

A difficulty is likely to arise where in a contract for the sale of specific goods, only part of the goods is destroyed or damaged. The solution will depend upon whether the contract is entire or divisible. If it is one and indivisible and part only of the goods has perished or damaged, the contract is void. If the contract is divisible, it will not be void, and the part available or in good condition must be accepted by the buyer. In *Borrow* v. *Phillips* (1929)1 K.B. 574, where a contract was made for a parcel containing 700 bags of groundnuts, and 591 bags could be delivered, the remainder having perished for the purpose of the contract (the 109 bags having been stolen), the contract was held to be void, and the buyer could not be compelled to take delivery of the 591 bags.

GOODS PERISHING BEFORE SALE BUT AFTER AGREEMENT TO SELL (SECTION 8)

Where the contract does not amount to sale, but is only agreement to sell, and the goods without any fault of either the seller or the buyer perish or are damaged subsequent to the agreement, but before the risk passes to the buyer by the agreement to sell ripening into sale, the agreement becomes void. This is based on the rule that impossibility of performance, arising after the contract is made, absolves the parties from their obligations. Sec. 7 lays down the rule as to goods perishing before the making of the contract; Sec. 8 lays down the rule as to goods perishing after the agreement to sell but before the sale is effected. Also, under Sec. 7 the contract is void *ab initio,* but under Sec, 8 it is not so, the performance on either side is excused as from the time of the perishing of the goods. Four conditions under Sec. 8 must be fulfilled before the agreement can be avoided, viz.,—(*i*) the contract must not be an agreement to sell and not an actual sale; (*ii*) the loss must be specific; (*iii*) the loss must not be caused by the wrongful act or default of either party, and if either party is at fault, the party in default will be liable; (*iv*) the goods must perish before the risk passes to the buyer, for if the risk has passed to the buyer, he must pay for the goods, though undelivered. *A* had contracted to erect machinery on *B* 's premises for a price to be paid on completion. During the progress of the work the premises and machinery were consumed by an accidental fire. It was held that both parties were excused from further performance, and *A*, having contracted for an entire work for a specific sum could not recover the price of the work actually done.[4]

In cases, where the agreement is avoided, it becomes void at the time of the perishing of the goods, and not before. Consequently, the right of either party previously vested will not be affected. For example, where the price is payable by the buyer at a date prior to the destruction of goods, the seller can sue for the price, if unpaid and, if paid, the buyer cannot recover it.[5]

On a bargain for the purchase of a horse, the horse was delivered to the buyer upon trial for 8 days, the agreed price being £ 40. If found suitable for the intending buyer's purpose, the bargain was then to be absolute. The horse died without fault in either party, within 8 days; it was held in *Elphic* v. *Barense* (1880) 5 C.P.D. 321 that the intending buyer was not liable for the price. The provisions of this Section, like any other implication of law, may be negative or varied by express agreement, or by the usage of a particular trade, as permitted by Sec. 62 of the Act. Thus, by virtue of Sec. 62, a C.I F. contract is saved from the operation of Secs 7 and 8, in as much as such a contract being a contract for the sale of goods, cost, insurance and freight, is in fact 'a contract for the sale of goods, lost or not lost', the performance of which is satisfied by the tender of documents, and is not affected by the loss or damage to the goods sold. It is a sale of documents and not of good. But if before the delivery of documents, war breaks out and such delivery becomes impossible of performance, the contract becomes void under these sections, but under Sec. 56 of the Indian Contract Act, which contains a general provision applying to all the circumstances constituting impossibilities and supervening illegalities avoiding contracts. As regards perishing of part only of the goods agreed to be sold, the same rules as under Sec. 7 will apply.

THE PRICE

PRICE

In respect of sales, the first rule is that no sale can take place without a price. If there, be no valuable consideration to support a voluntary surrender of goods by the real owner to another person, the transaction is a gift, and is not governed by the rules relating to sales (Story on Sales). Sec. 4(1) lays down that to constitute a contract of sale, the transfer or agreement to transfer property in goods must be for a price. Therefore price, which is defined by Sec. 2(10) as the money consideration for a sale of goods, constitutes the essence of a contract of sale. It may be money actually paid or promised to be paid according as the agreement is for a cash or a credit sale; but if other consideration than money be given, it is not a sale. Moreover, the money must be given as the price, *i.e.*, as a *quid pro quo* on a transfer of property on a sale.

---

4. Appleby v. Myers (1867) L.R.C. 651.
5. Blakely v. Muller (1930) 2 K.B. 769

MODES OF FIXING PRICE

The price must either be certain and definite, or must be determinable by some method of calculation or some criterion prescribed by the contract. Sec. 9 suggests five methods of fixing the price, which are given below:

1. The price may be expressly stated in the contract. This is primarily what is intended to be done. The parties are free to fix any price they like, and the Court will not embark on an investigation as to the adequacy of the price. Thus a man may sell at any price he likes, and to undersell his trade rivals he may offer goods at a loss, or a manufacturer may sell goods to a wholesaler on the condition that they shall not be sold at less than a certain price. But that condition does not bind a subsequent buyer even with notice for there is no privity between him and the original seller. In the case, however, of patented goods the sub-buyer may be bound by such a condition, if he has notice of it.

2. The contract may provide for the manner in which the price is to be fixed.[6] The agreement may be to pay as much for the goods as others pay. In such a case, notice must be given to the buyer as to how much others pay. No sale will be made if the price is agreed to be whatever sum the seller be offered by any third party, nor if it is left to be fixed only by one of the contracting parties.

3. Where the price is not expressed in the contract nor is any provision made for its determination, it may be determined by the course of dealing between the parties. Thus, in *Browne* v. *Byrine* (1854) 118 E.R. 1304, a usage to deduct discount in determining the price was implied from the course of dealings.

4. Where nothing is said by the parties regarding price, the law implies, in case the contract is *executed* and the goods sold are accepted that the buyer agrees to pay a reasonable price; and where there is a market price for the goods, that may be a reasonable price.

5. The price may also be left to be fixed by the valuation of a third party, provided he accepts the duty and performs it. But if the third party fails to make the valuation the agreement becomes void. If, in pursuance of the contract, goods have been delivered by the seller and accepted by the buyer, then the buyer is bound to pay a reasonable price. If, however, one of the parties prevents the third party from making the valuation, he would be liable to pay damages to the other contracting party.

MODE OF PAYMENT

The seller is not bound to accept any kind of payment except in the currency unless there is an agreement express or implied to the contrary or unless the seller is estopped from disputing the mode of payment. He is not bound to accept payment by cheque. Also, the price should be in legal tender money.

EARNEST OR DEPOSIT

Sometimes it happens that the buyer pays part of the price in advance as *security* for the *due performance of his part of the contract,* and not as part-payment of purchase money.[7] The money so paid as security is called Earnest or Deposit. If the purchase is carried out, the deposit goes against the purchase-money, and only the balance of the price is required to be paid. But if the sale goes off *through buyer's fault,* the deposit unless otherwise agreed is forfeited to the seller, and where it goes off by the seller's *default* he must return the earnest money. If on the breach of the agreement by the buyer the seller resells the goods, and sues to recover the loss arising on such resale, the deposit, although forfeited, is to be taken into account as diminishing the deficiency.

---

6. See Venkata Malhyya v. Ramaswami & Co. 1964 *S.C.* 818

7. Amamath Nikkuram v. Mohan Singh, 1954 M.B., 134; Thota Sombavya v. Ramananda, 1960 A.P. f5; but see Maula Bux v. Union of India, 1970 S.C. 1955.

ADDITION TO OR DEDUCTION FROM PRICE OF TAX

Sec.64-A, which was added to the Act in 1940 and was amended in 1963, makes provision for the addition to or deduction from a contract price of any increase or decrease or remission in customs, or excise duty, or any tax on the sale or purchase of goods imposed or increased or decreased or remitted after the contract for the sale of goods was made.

PART 6-C
CONDITIONS AND WARRANTIES

CAVEAT EMPTOR

The parties are at liberty to enter into contract with any terms they please. In the case of a sale of goods, the ordinary common law maxim is *Caveat Emptor—let* the buyer beware. That is to say, the buyer gets the goods as they come and takes the risk of their suitability for the purpose. It is no part of the seller's duty to point out the defects in the goods he is selling. By this is not meant that the buyer must 'take chance'; it means that he must 'take care.' If the buyer depends upon his own skill and integrity and the goods turn out to be defective, it is his own fault and he cannot hold the seller responsible. But the buyer may want to be sure of the quality of the goods and may make known to the seller the purpose for which he intends to buy the goods so as to show that he relies on the seller's skill or judgement, and buys them depending on the representations made by the seller. Such representations may rank either as conditions or warranties, and in that case the principle *of Caveat Emptor* will not apply, and the contract will be subject to the condition or warranty.

As the contract of sale is consensual, it may be either absolute or conditional, as the parties please. As a rule, before a contract of sale is concluded, certain statements are made by the parties to each other; it always depends upon the construction of the contract whether any statement made with reference to the goods is a stipulation forming part of the contract or a mere expression of opinion which is no part of the contract. A representation or statement will amount to a stipulation or a promise, if the seller assumes to assert a fact of which the buyer is ignorant; and will be a mere opinion not amounting to a stipulation where the seller merely states an opinion or judgement upon a matter on which he has no special knowledge and on which the buyer may be expected to have an opinion. A mere *commendation* by the seller of goods or his wares does not amount to a stipulation and does not give right of action.

A stipulation in a contract of sale made with reference to goods which are the subject-matter thereof may be either a condition or a warranty. Sec. 12 draws a clear distinction between a condition and a warranty. If stipulation forms the very basis of the contract, or in the words of the Section is *essential to the main purpose of the contract* it is a *Condition.* If, however, the stipulation though not essential to the main purpose of the contract is *collateral to the main purpose of the contract,* i.e., is a subsidiary promise, it is known as a *Warranty.* The effect of a breach of a condition is to give the aggrieved party a right to treat the contract as repudiated; while in the case of a breach of warranty he cannot repudiate the contract but can only claim damages. Thus if the condition is not fulfilled the buyer has a right to repudiate the contract to refuse the goods, and, if he has already paid for them, to recover the price.[8] In the case of a breach of warranty, however, the buyer must accept the goods and claim damages for the breach of warranty. A man buys a particular horse, which is warranted quiet to ride and drive. If the horse turns out to be vicious, the buyer's only remedy is to claim damages. But if instead of buying a particular horse, a man asks a dealer to supply him with a **quiet horse** and the horse turns out to be vicious, the stipulation is a condition and the buyer can reject the horse, or keep

---

8. Antony v. Arappunni Mani, 1960 Ker. 176; Wallis v. Pratt, (1910) 2 K.B. 1003.

the horse and claim damages. He can also get damages for injury, if any, even when he rejects the horse. Of course, the right of rejection must be exercised within a reasonable time.[9]

EXPRESS AND IMPLIED CONDITIONS AND WARRANTIES

Conditions and warranties may be express or implied. An express condition or warranty is one stated definitely in so many words as the basis of the contract. Implied conditions or warranties are those which attach to the contract by operation of law or custom. The law incorporates them into the contract unless the parties agree to the contrary. Implied conditions and warranties are enforced on the ground that the law infers from all the circumstances of the case that the parties intended to add such a stipulation to their contract, but did not put into express words. The existence of an implied condition or warranty may, however, be rebutted by proof of facts which show a contrary intention. The contract of sale being consensual, bilateral and cumulative, and the parties may alter at will the obligation which the law implies from the general nature of the contract. Sec. 62 of the Act recognises the maxims: *Expressum facit cessare tacitum* : What is expressed makes what is implied to cease; and *Modus et conventio vincent legem:* custom and agreement over-rule law.

A sold pigs to *B* and it was mentioned that *B* was to take the pigs sold "with all faults." The pigs were diseased and *B* suffered a heavy loss. *Held,* as it was expressly agreed that the seller was giving no warranty and as he had done nothing to conceal the defect he was relieved from all liability in respect of any defect in the goods [*Ward* v. *Hobbs* (1878) 4 App. Cas. 13].

WAIVER OF CONDITION

Sec. 13, as amended, mentions three cases in which waiver of a condition, or its sinking or descending to the level of a warranty, operates. The first two cases are given, in sub-section (1) and are voluntary, depending on the volition of the buyer namely—(1) where he *may* waive the condition, or (2) he *may* treat the breach of condition as a breach of warranty. The third case which is given in sub-section (2) does not depend on the will of the buyer, but creates an estoppel against him by his conduct and where waiver is comprehensively presumed by law. It arises when the contract is indivisible and the buyer has accepted the goods or part thereof. In these cases the breach of a condition can be treated only as a breach of a warranty; and the buyer can claim compensation for the loss suffered by him by breach of the condition in respect of the goods accepted by him, as he would have a right to in the case of a breach of warranty. The parties are, however, at liberty to contract themselves out of this rule by including a stipulation to that effect in which case the terms of the contract must be strictly adhered to, and will not be affected by these provisions.

THE TIME FACTOR IN BUYING AND SELLING

In general law of contract, where no time is fixed for performance, the contract is required to be performed within a reasonable time. As regards contracts for the sale of goods, stipulations as to time, *except as regards time of payment,* are usually held to be of the essence of the contract. Therefore, if time is specified for delivery of goods or for doing any other act, delivery must be made or act done at the specified time; and if not done, the other party can repudiate the contract. Thus, if *A* agrees to sell and deliver goods to *B* on a certain day, he must deliver them on that day. If he fails to do so, *B* is entitled to put an end to the contract. With regard to the time fixed for payment. Sec. 11 lays down that it is not deemed to be of the essence of the contract, unless it appears from the contract that parties intended that it should be so. Thus, the failure by the buyer to pay on the appointed day does not, as a rule, entitle the seller to treat the contract as repudiated, though he may be entitled to withhold

---

9. Hartley v. Hymans (1920) 3 K.B. 475.

delivery until the price is paid and resell the goods if the buyer does not pay or tender the price within a reasonable time. Consequently, if before such resale the buyer tenders the price, even though it be on a date after the date named in the contract, the seller cannot, in the absence of stipulation to the contrary, treat the contract as at an-end and refuse to allow the buyer to have the goods.

IMPLIED CONDITIONS AND WARRANTIES

We have seen before that even though in a contract of sale definite representations might not have been made, the law implies certain representations as having been made, and those are dealt with in Secs. 14 to 17 of the Act. Such implied representations may amount to conditions or warranties with the effects already noted.

IMPLIED WARRANTIES

As said before, a condition may sink to the level of a warranty in cases in which the buyer is content with his right of damages or is not in a position to reject the goods. The Act also provides for two more implied warranties, namely, (1) implied warranty of quiet possession, and (2) implied warranty against encumbrances.

1. **Implied warranty of quiet possession**—In a contract of sale, unless the circumstances of the contract are such as to show a different intention, there is an implied warranty that the buyer shall have and enjoy quiet possession of the goods. This means that where the buyer has obtained possession of the goods, he has a right to enjoy them, and if the right of possession and enjoyment is in any way disturbed, he is entitled to sue the seller for damages. It is a warranty that the seller shall not, nor shall anybody claiming under a superior title, or under his authority, interfere with the quiet enjoyment of the buyer.

2. **Implied warranty against encumbrances**—The buyer is also entitled to a further warranty that the goods are not subject to any right in favour of a third party, or the buyer's possession *shall not* be disturbed by reason of the existence of encumbrances. In other words, if the buyer is required to, *and does in fact, discharge the amount of the encumbrance,* there is a breach of warranty, and he is 'entitled to damages'. This clause will not apply if such encumbrances are declared to the buyer when the contract is made or he has notice of them. It should be noted that the breach of this warranty occurs only when the buyer discharges the amount of the encumbrance.[10]

IMPLIED CONDITIONS : CONDITION AS TO TITLE TO GOODS

The first implied condition in **EVERY** contract for the sale of goods is that the seller, in an actual sale, has the right to sell the goods and, in an agreement *to* sell he will have it when property is to pass. As a result of this, if the title turns out to be defective, the buyer is entitled to reject the goods. In *Rowland* v. *Divall* (1923) 2 K.B. 500, it was held that a buyer of a motor car who was deprived of the same owing to the seller's want of title was entitled to recover the full price from the seller even though he had used the car for some months, as the consideration had totally failed. But this implied condition as to title may be negatived by an express term, as in Court sales, where only such rights as the judgement-debtor has are sold. Court officer selling in execution debtor's goods gives no implied undertaking as to title.

SALE BY DESCRIPTION

(i) **Goods must correspond with their description**—In a contract of sale by description, there is an implied condition that the goods shall correspond with their description. A sale is essentially by

---

10. Collinge v. Heywood (1839) 9 A. & E. 633.

description where the purchaser has not seen the goods but is relying on the description alone, *e.g.*, a sale of furniture or unascertained goods. But in addition a sale in many cases may still be by description even where the buyer has seen the goods, *e.g.*, ordinary sale in a shop. In *Grant* v. *Australian Knitting Mills Ltd.* (1936) A.C. 85, it was remarked : " ....there is a sale by description even though the buyer is buying something displayed before him on the counter: a thing is sold by description, though it is specific, so long as it is sold not merely as the specific thing, but as a thing corresponding to a description, *e.g.*, woollen undergarments, a hot-water bottle, a second hand reaping machine, to select a few obvious illustrations". The term "sale by description" is wide enough to cover a sale even where no words are spoken at all, as, for example, in a self-service store, at least if there is some label or other description attached to or otherwise indicating the nature of the goods being sold. In fact it is probably true to say that the only case of a sale not being by description occurs where the buyer makes it clear that he is buying a particular thing because of its unique qualities, and that no other will do.

In *Beale* v. *Taylor* (1967) 1 W.L.R. 1193, *T* advertised his car for sale as a "Herald, convertible, white, 1961" and the car was bought by *B* after examination. In fact the car was made of two parts which had been welded together, only one of which was from a 1961 model. The court held that the words "1961 Herald" were part of the contractual description and even though the car was fully examined by the buyer, the sale was by description because the buyer had relied in part on a newspaper advertisement issued by the seller. As the car did not correspond with the description, there was a breach of the implied condition and *B* could reject the car. In *Varley* v. *Whipp* (1900) 1 Q.B. 513, the defendant agreed to buy from the plaintiff a second-hand reaping machine, which was stated to have been new the previous year and hardly used at all. This was a gross misdescription as the machine was old and repaired, and defendant declined to accept it or pay for it. The defendant succeeded because there was a breach of the implied condition, as the machine did not correspond with the description. Now, the defendant could not have relied on the breach of the implied condition of merchantability under Sec. 16(2) as the plaintiff was not a dealer in reaping machines.

It follows that this condition applies both to private sales and sales by dealers of goods sold, whereas the conditions relating to quality or fitness for a particular purpose and merchantable quality apply only to sales made by dealers in goods sold by them and not to private sales. Moreover, if there is a breach of condition as to description, the buyer is entitled to reject the goods even though he suffers no damage therefrom. Also, the duty of the seller is very strict and the goods supplied must strictly conform to the description.

(ii) Condition as to quality or fitness—This condition and those in respect of merchantable quality and wholesomeness discussed below are *Exceptions* to the rule of *Caveat Emptor*. Ordinarily, there is no implied warranty or condition as to the quality or fitness for any particular purpose of goods supplied under a contract of sale. But where the buyer, expressly or by implication, makes known to the seller the particular purpose for which the goods are required, so as to show that the buyer relies on the seller's skill and judgement, and the goods are of the description which is in the course of the seller's business to supply (whether he is the manufacturer or producer or not), there is an implied condition that the goods shall be reasonably fit for such purpose. The rate of *Caveat Emptor* will not apply.

There is no need for the buyer to specify the particular purpose for which the goods are required when they have in the ordinary way only one purpose. Reliance on the seller's skill and judgement will be readily implied even to the extent of saying that the buyer has gone to the seller because he relies on the seller's having selected his stock with skill and judgement. In *Priest* v. *Last* (1903) 2 K.B. 148 C.A., a hot water bottle was bought by the plaintiff, a draper, from a chemist who sold such articles. While being used by his wife, the bottle burst and injured her. *Held,* the seller was responsible for damages. The implied condition as to fitness for the purpose also applies to containers in which the goods are packed [*Geddling* v. *Marsh*, (1920) 1 K.B. 668]. The defendant was manufacturer of mineral waters and he supplied the same to the plaintiff who kept a small general store. The bottles were returnable when empty. One of the bottles was defective, and whilst the plaintiff was putting it back carefully into a crate, it broke and injured her. *Held,* even though the bottles were returnable, they were supplied under a contract of sale. There was an implied condition of fitness for the purpose for which they were supplied, and the defendant was liable in damages. But where mere are special circumstances of which the seller is unaware, the implied condition as to fitness does not apply. In *Griffith* v. *Peter Conway Ltd.* (1939) 1 All. E.R. 685, a woman with abnormally sensitive skin, bought a Harris tweed coat, and got rashes through wearing. She sued the supplier for damages, because the coat was not fit for the purpose for which it was bought. *Held,* she failed because the defendant did not know of plaintiffs abnormality and should not be expected to assume that it existed. Similarly, in *Ingham* v. *Emes* (1955) 2 All. E.R. 740, it was held that where a hair-dye is sold to a customer who is allergic to a particular dye, there is a duty on the part of the customer to disclose known peculiarities.

Where, however, the goods supplied are purchased under a patent or other trade name, there is no implied condition as to their fitness for any particular purpose. So where the buyer wrote and said, "send me your patent smoke-consuming furnace for fitting up my brewery" and it was found that furnace supplied was not fit for the purpose, it was held that the purchase was of a defined and well-known type of furnace and so the sellers were not liable. If, when buying the article under its patent or other trade name, the buyer makes it" clear to the seller that he is relying on the seller's skill and judgement to recommend ah article, it must be reasonably fit for the purpose. In *Baldry* v. *Marshall* (1925)1 K.B. 260, the plaintiff informed the defendants that he wanted a comfortable car suitable for touring. The defendants sold him a Bugati 8-Cylinder model, which did not suit the plaintiffs purpose at all. *Held,* the defendants were liable. Again, if the seller supplies an article of the description in which he usually deals under its patent or other trade name there is an implied condition that it is fit for the purpose. In the sale of a Refrigerator the name of the article itself implies that the seller warrants that the machine is fit for the particular purpose."[11]

It may be noted that even if the proviso does not apply, the seller will frequently be caught by the implied condition of merchantability.

(iii) Implied Condition as to Merchantability—Where goods are bought by description from a seller who deals in goods of that description (whether he is a manufacturer, producer or not), there is an implied condition that the goods shall be of merchantable quality. But, if the buyer has examined the goods, there is no implied condition as regards defects which such examination ought to have revealed. If, however, examination by the buyer does not reveal the defect, and he approves and accepts the goods, but when put to work, the goods are found to be defective, there is a breach of condition of merchantable quality. P bought black yam from D and found it to be damaged by white ants. *Held,* condition as to merchantability was broken. Similarly, where hemp was damaged by sea water, cement turned into stone by sea water, or beer was contaminated with arsenic and dates contaminated with sewage, the condition of merchantability was held to have been broken. But where in a sale of vegetable glue packed in casks, the buyer who came to examine them simply looked at the outside of the casks, and therefore the defect which could have been discovered by examination, was overlooked, it was held that there is no implied condition and the buyer was not entitled to any relief (*Thornett and Fehr* v. *Beers & Son* (1919)1 K.B.486).

The next problem is the meaning of the term merchantable. The House of Lords in *Henry Kendall & Sons* v. *William Lillico & Sons Ltd.*(1969) 2 A.C. 31, stated: "The goods should be in such a state that a buyer, fully acquainted with the facts, and therefore, knowing what hidden defects exist and being limited to their apparent condition would buy them without abatement of the price obtainable for such goods if in reasonable sound order and condition and without special terms". Lord Reid

11. E.V. Evans v. Stella Benjamine 1951 Cal. 740.

added: "What is now meant by 'merchantable quality' is that the goods in the form they were tendered would not have been used by a reasonable man for any purpose for which goods which complied with the description under which these goods were sold would normally be used, and hence were not saleable under that description". Merchantability is a somewhat flexible concept and the buyer is the best judge of what he wants. If the buyer gets exactly what he has ordered it hardly lies in his mouth to say that the goods are unmerchantable. If a new car was sold with a defective clutch the car would be properly said to be unmer-chantable. But if a second-hand car is sold with a defective clutch and the defect proves more serious than anticipated the car will not said to be unmerchantable.

(iv) **Condition as to wholesomeness**—The condition of merchantability includes another condition, namely, that of wholesomeness in the case of sale of provisions or foodstuff. The provisions or food supplied must not only answer the description, but must also be merchantable AND wholesome or sound. In *Frost v.Avlesbury Dairy Co. Ltd.* (1905) 1 K.B. 608, *F* bought milk from *A*. Dairy, and the milk contained typhoid germs. *F*'s wife became infected and died. *A* was liable for damages, because the milk was not fit for human consumption. *C* bought a bun at *M*'s bakery, and broke one of the teeth by biting on a stone present in the bun, *M* was held liable.

It may be reiterated that *the rules as to fitness for purpose and merchantable quality do not apply to private sales* and there is still a fairly wide application of the maxim *caveat emptor.* They apply only to sales made by dealers who normally deal in goods of the type in question. Hence if the seller does not normally deal in goods of the type in question, there is no condition as to fitness nor as to merchantability unless there is a sale by sample which is dealt with below. The only condition in a private sale is that the goods must correspond with the description.

SALE BY SAMPLE

Sec. 17(1) states that a contract of sale is contract for sale by sample where there is a term in the contract, express or implied, to that effect. It is clear from the definition that the mere fact that the seller provides a sample for the buyer's inspection is not enough; to be such a sale there must be either an express provision in the contract to that effect, or there must be evidence that the parties intended the sale to be by sample. But there may be a custom or usage in respect of certain commodities that sale would be by sample, even though the written contract is silent on the point. A sale of tobacco is always considered to be a sale by sample by custom of trade.

IMPLIED CONDITIONS IN SALE BY SAMPLE

There are three implied conditions in a sale by sample—

(i) **Bulk should correspond with sample**—In a sale by sample, the bulk shall correspond with the sample in quality.

(ii) **Buyer to have reasonable opportunity to compare**—In a sale by sample, the buyer shall have a reasonable opportunity of comparing the bulk with the sample. The buyer will not be deemed to have accepted the goods until he had an opportunity to compare the bulk with the sample, and will be able, therefore, to reject the goods, even though they have been delivered, if the bulk does not correspond with the sample.

(iii) **Condition of merchantability as regards latent defects**—The goods must be free from any defects, rendering them unmerchantable, which would be apparent on reasonable examination of the sample. Thus, in regard to the implied condition of merchantability, a right of repudiation exists in the case of defects not discernible by ordinary inspection of a prudent buyer.' 'Worsted Coating" quality equal to sample was sold to tutors. The cloth was found to have a defect in the texture rendering the same unfit for stitching into coats. The seller was held liable, even though the same defect existed in the sample, which was examined and the defect could not be discovered.

In *Godley* v. *Perry* (1960) 1 All E.R. 36, G (aged 6) bought a catapult from *P*, a dealer in toys, and was injured by its defective condition. *Held, G* could recover damages from *P* for breach of the conditions as to fitness for purpose and merchantable quality. Also, *P* could recover damages from his supplier under sale by sample, since he had bought by sample and the defect was not apparent on reasonable examination of the sample.

SALE BY SAMPLE AS WELL AS BY DESCRIPTION

In a sale by sample as well as by description, the goods supplied must correspond both with the sample as well as with the description, and be merchantable. Correspondence with sample alone is not enough. In *Nichol* v. *Godts* (1845) E.R. 426, there was a sale of "foreign refined rape-oil" warranted only equal to sample. The oil tendered was the same as the sample, but it was not "foreign refined rape-oil", being a mixture of it and other oil. It was held that the seller was liable, and the buyer could refuse to accept

Liability of Manufacturer in Negligence—Where the goods are purchased from a retailer, no action can be brought under the Sale of Goods Act by the purchaser against the manufacturer because there is no contract between them into which the warranties and conditions set out in the Act can be implied. However, the buyer may have an action in negligence (under the law of torts) against the manufacturer in respect of physical injuries caused by defects in the goods [*Donoghue* v. *Stevenson* (1932) A.C. 562]. The appellant's friend bought a bottle of ginger beer from a retailer and gave it to her. The respondents were the manufacturers of the ginger beer. The appellant consumed some of the ginger beer and her friend was replenishing the glass when the decomposed remains of a snail came out of the bottle. The bottle was made of dark opaque glass so that the snail could not be seen until most of the contents had been consumed. The appellant became ill and claimed damages from the manufacturers. The House of Lords held that there was negligence on the part of the manufacturers and they were liable in damages.

It is interesting to note that the appellant had no cause of action against the retailer in contract because her friend bought the bottle, so that there was no privity of contract between the retailer and the appellant. Therefore, terms relating to fitness for purpose and merchantable quality, implied into such contracts, did not apply here.

The rule enunciated in the above case has been widened and applies to defective goods generally which cause injury to purchasers. In *Grant* v. *Australian Knitting Mills Ltd.* (1936) A.C. 85, Dr. Grant bought a pair of long woollen underpants from a retailer, the respondents being the manufacturers. The underpants contained an excess of sulphite which was a chemical used in their manufacture. The chemical should have been eliminated before the product was finished, but a quantity was left in the underpants purchased by Dr. Grant. After wearing the pants for a couple of days he developed a rash which turned out to be dermatitis compelling him to spend many months in hospital. He sued the retailers and manufacturers for damages. *Held,* the retailers were liable for breach of implied conditions of fitness for a purpose and merchantable quality. The manufacturers were liable in negligence. This was a latent defect which could not have been discovered by reasonable examination. It should also be noted that the plaintiff has a perfectly normal skin.

Exceptions to Caveat Emptor

Although the exceptions to maxim *Caveat Emptor* have been discussed in connection with implied conditions, they are stated here at one place for the convenience of the reader. Those exceptions are:—

1. Where the buyer makes known to the seller the purpose for which he requires the goods and relies on the representation or Skill and judgement of the seller, there is an implied condition that the goods will be suitable for the said purpose.

2. In a sale by description by a dealer in the goods there is an implied condition that the goods are of merchantable quality.

3. Proof of reasonable usage or custom of trade may also establish an implied condition as to quality or fitness of the goods for a particular purpose.

4. Where the consent of the buyer, in a contract of sale, is obtained by the seller by fraud or where the seller knowingly conceals a defect which could not be discovered on a reasonable examination, the doctrine of Caveat Emptor does not apply.

PART 6-D
PASSING OF PROPERTY OR TRANSFER OF OWNERSHIP

The main purpose of a sale is the transfer of ownership from the seller to the buyer. It is important to know the precise moment of time at which the property in goods passes from the seller to the buyer, because:—

1. the general rule is that **risk follows the property or ownership** whether delivery has been made or not. If the goods are damaged or lost by accident or otherwise, then, subject to certain exceptions, the loss will fall on the owner of the goods at the time they are lost or damaged;

2. when there is a danger of the goods being damaged by the action of third parties, it is the owner who can take action; and

3. in case of the insolvency of either seller or buyer, it is necessary to know whether the goods can be taken over by the Official Assignee or the Official Receiver. The answer will depend upon whether the property in the goods was with the party who has become insolvent "The property" in the goods means ownership of the goods, as distinguished from their possession.

PASSING OF PROPERTY IN SPECIFIC OR ASCERTAINED GOODS

In a sale of specific or ascertained goods the property passes to the buyer at the time when the parties intend it to pass. The intention must be gathered from the terms of the contract, the conduct of the parties, and the circumstances of the case (Sec. 19). Specific goods, as already explained, are goods identified and agreed upon at the time the contract is made. Unless a contrary intention appears the following rules are applicable for ascertaining the intention of the parties:—

1. Where there is an unconditional contract for the sale of specific goods in a deliverable state the property passes to. the buyer when the contract is made. Deliverable state means such a state that the buyer would be bound to take delivery of them. The fact that the time of delivery or the time of payment is postponed does not prevent the property from passing at once. For example, if *A* goes into a shop and buys a radio set, asking the shopkeeper to send it to his house and put it down to his account, and the shopkeeper agrees to do so, the radio set immediately becomes the property of *A*.

2. When there is a contract for the sale of specific goods not in a deliverable state, *i.e.*, the seller has to do something to the goods to put them in a deliverable state, the property does not pass until that tiling is done and the buyer has notice of it. The plaintiffs sold carpeting to the defendants which they were required to lay. The carpet was delivered to the defendant's premises but was stolen before it could be laid. It was held that the carpet was not in a deliverable state, as it had not been laid which was part of the contract and hence the property had not passed to the buyer. (*Phillip Head &. Sons Ltd.* v. *Showfronts Ltd.* (1970) 1 Lloyd's Rep.140).

3. Where there is a sale of specific goods in a deliverable state, but the seller is bound to weigh, measure, test or do something with reference to the goods for the purpose of ascertaining the price, the property does not pass until that thing is done and the buyer has notice of it. [12]

---

12. Union of India v. Dwarkadas, 1959 Pat. 59.

4. In a self-service supermarket where goods are picked up by the customers from the shelves and their prices are paid at the barrier, no contract of sale is made until the price is actually paid and so property in the goods passes only after the price is paid at the barrier (*Lacis* v. *Cashmarts* (1969) 2 W.L.R. 329).

5. When goods are delivered to the buyer on approval or "on sale or return," the property therein passes to the buyer—

(a) when he signifies his approval or acceptance to the seller, or does any other act adopting the transaction;

(b) if he retains the goods, without giving notice of rejection, beyond the time fixed for the return of goods or, if no time is fixed, beyond a reasonable time.

In *Kirkham* v. *Attenborough* (1897) 1 Q.B.201, *K* delivered jewellery to *W* on sale or return. *W* pledged it with *A*. *Held,* the pledge was an act by *W* adopting the transaction, and, therefore, the property in the jewellery passed to him, so that *K* could not recover it from *A*.

'Sale or return' must be distinguished from 'sale for cash only or return', for in the latter case, the property does not pass to the buyer until paid for.

In *Weiner* v. *Gill* (1906) 2 K.B. 574, *A* delivered goods to *B* on the terms that they were to remain his property until settled for or charged (a sale for cash or return basis) the property did not pass to *B* until either of those events had happened. Where *B* pawned the goods with *D*, *A* could recover from *D*, the pawnee.

OWNERSHIP IN UNASCERTAINED GOODS

Sec.18 provides that where goods contracted to be sold are not ascertained or where they are future goods, ownership will not pass to the buyer, unless and until the goods are ascertained. "A contract to sell unascertained goods," says Lord Loreburn, ' 'is not a complete sale but a promise to sell." As to when the goods get ascertained Sec. 23 provides:

(1) Where there is a contract for the sale of unascertained or future goods by description and goods of that description and in a deliverable state are unconditionally appropriated to the contract either by the seller with the assent of the buyer or by the buyer with the assent of the seller, the property in the goods thereupon passes to the buyer. Such assent may be expressed or implied, and may be given either before or after the appropriation is made.

(2) Where, in pursuance of the contract, the seller delivers the goods to the buyer or to a carrier or other bailee (whether named by the buyer or not) for the purpose of transmission to the buyer, and does not reserve the right of disposal, he is deemed to have unconditionally appropriated the goods to the contract".

The appropriation of goods may be made (1) by the buyer with the assent of the seller, or (2) by the seller with the assent of the buyer; (a) by putting the goods in suitable receptacles, or (b) by separating the articles contracted for from the others, or (c) by their delivery by the seller to a carrier without reserving rights of disposal.

APPROPRIATION

The ascertainment of the goods or their appropriation may be made—

(i) **by the buyer with the seller's assent**—Where the goods are in the possession of the buyer, as for example, where the buyer is a warehouseman for the seller in respect of 60 bales of cotton and agrees" to buy. 25 bales out of them, the buyer, *i.e.,* the warehouseman may, with the seller's assent, select 25 out of 60 bales, and when he has done so, the goods (25 bales) become appropriated and the ownership in them passes to the buyer.

(ii) by the seller with the buyer's assent—The more common thing is for the seller to appropriate the goods, but such appropriation must be with the buyer's consent. In the above example, if the bales were lying with the seller and he selected 25 bates out of the lot with the buyer's assent, the ownership of those 25 bales would pass to the buyer as soon as this is done. Therefore, we may say that *the selection of goods by the one party and the adoption of that act by the other converts that which before was a mere agreement to sell into an actual sale.* The assent may be given subsequent to the appropriation or even prior to it.

The seller may appropriate the goods—

(a) by putting the quantity contracted for in suitable receptacles, as for example, filling hogsheads with sugar and then getting the buyer's assent thereto; or putting the oil into bottles or grain in bags, supplied by the buyer;

(b) by separating the articles contracted for from the others, as for instance, in a sale of jute, the marking by the seller of the quality of the goods required by the buyer, or in a sale of oil, setting apart the number of tins contracted for as those meant for the buyer, will transfer property;

(c) by delivery to the carrier or other bailee for transmission to the buyer, without reserving the right of disposal; for example, handing over the goods to the railway administration or a shipping company or a motor transport agency. Where the buyer asks to send the goods by a carrier, the buyer's assent to the appropriation is taken to have been given, and the carrier carries the goods as the buyer's agent But mere delivery to the carrier for transmission does not necessarily pass property to the buyer, for it is quite possible that the seller may deliver the goods to the carrier without intending to part with the ownership of the goods. So, until the railway receipt or bill of lading is made out, it is not possible to say on whose account the goods have been shipped. Where the goods are delivered to the carrier and the R/R or the bill of lading is taken in the name of the seller or his agent, and so the goods are deliverable to the seller or his agent, it is presumed that the seller has reserved the right of disposal; and in such a case the property in goods will not pass to the buyer. But where the documents on delivery of goods to the carriers are made out in the name of the buyer, the presumption is that the seller has made the appropriation and ownership passes to the buyer. But these are only presumptions, for it is open to the seller, having taken R/R or B/L in the buyer's name to send to his own agent with instructions to part with it only on payment of the price, or having taken it in his own name, send it endorsed unconditionally to the buyer.[13] Thus, delivery to the carrier may be *absolutely for the buyer, i.e.,* where no right or control is reserved by the seller. Or, the delivery to the carrier *may be absolutely for the seller,* so that where the B/L is taken in the seller's own name or to his order or in the name of a fictitious person, ownership does not pass to the buyer.

Where the seller of goods draws on the buyer for the price and transmits to the buyer the bill of exchange together with the bill of lading or the railway receipt to secure acceptance or payment of the bill of exchange, the buyer is bound to return the bill of lading or the railway receipt if he does not honour the bill of exchange; and, if he wrongfully retains the bill of lading or the railway receipt, the property in the goods does not pass to him.[14]

In *Mohd. Sltarif v. Off. Liquidator,* 1964 Ker. 135, the buyer had agreed to pay 65% of the price on arrival of the goods and a bill was drawn for that purpose and though the railway receipt was taken in the name of the consignee it was not sent to him but was sent to a bank alongwith the bill for the 65% of the price and the railway receipt was to be received by the consignee after retiring the bill. The consignee obtained delivery of the goods from the railway not by retiring the bill and producing the

13. See Sheo Prasad v. Dominion of India, 1954 All. 747; See also State of Madras v. V.P.V. and Sons. 1959 A.P. 23, M. Balkrishna Rao v. M.D.O. and Sons, 1959 A.P. 30.
14. Sec. 25 (3), amended by the sale of Goods (Amendment) Act, 1963.

railway receipt but by giving a letter of indemnity to the railway. It was held that the property had not passed to the buyer and it was really by a tortious act that he came into possession of the goods. The fact that the railway receipt was taken in the name of the consignee did not show that the property in the goods passed as soon as the goods were appropriated and handed over to the railway.

Before concluding the subject of appropriation, two more essentials may be noted here. The first point is that the appropriation must be of goods answering the description, both as to quality and quantity. *Secondly,* the appropriation must be intentional, *i.e.,* it must be made with intent to appropriate goods to the specific contract; and it must not be due to mere accident or mistake.

F.O.B. CONTRACTS

In the case of a contract for the sale of goods which are to be shipped to a foreign port, a number of conditions are attached by the parties or by custom and practice of merchants. The most usual of such contracts are F.O.B. contracts *i.e.,* "FREE ON BOARD". This means that the property in goods passes to the buyer only after the goods have been loaded on board the ship, and accordingly the risk attaches to the buyer only on shipment of goods which may at that time be specified or unascertained. Therefore, the seller or shipper has to bear all the expenses up to and including shipment of goods on behalf of the buyer.

C.I.F. OR C.F.I. CONTRACTS

In foreign transactions, two things are guarded against, namely: (*i*) the insolvency of the parties, and (*ii*) the perishing of the goods through no fault of either party. In order to protect the interests of both the parties, it is usual to enter into a contract known as the C.I.F. or C.F.I. contract. The three letters C. I. and F. stand for COST, INSURANCE and FREIGHT. Where the buyer orders goods from a merchant abroad, the seller will insure the goods, deliver them to the shipping company and send the B/L and insurance policy together with the invoice and a certificate of origin to a bank and the buyer has to pay the price (which includes cost of goods, premium of insurance and freight), and receive the above documents from the bank. This method protects the seller for the goods continue to be in his ownership until the buyer pays for them and gets the documents and the buyer is equally protected, as he is only called upon to pay against the documents, and the moment he pays he obtains the documents which would enable him to get delivery of the goods, as soon as they arrive. If, in the meantime, the goods are lost at sea; neither will be put to loss, for either the seller or the buyer, whoever is the owner at the time of the loss, can make a claim against the insurer for such loss. The buyer is bound to accept the documents which represent the goods and honour the draft. If after taking delivery he finds that the goods are not according to the contract he may reject the goods and sue for damages.[15]

The incidents of a C.I.F. contract have been authoritatively explained in several decisions, notably *Johnson* v. *Taylor & C.,* 1920 A.C. 144 and *Biddell Bros.* v. *Clemens Horst Co.,* (1911) 1 K.B. 934. In the latter case Hamilton J, as he then was, observed; "A seller under a contract of sale containing the C.I.F. terms *has firstly* to ship at the port of shipment goods of the description contained in the contract; *secondly* to procure a contract of affreightment, under which the goods will be delivered at the destination contemplated by the contract; *thirdly* to arrange for an insurance upon the terms current in the trade which will be available for the benefit of the *buyer, fourthly* to make out an invoice; *and finally* to tender these documents to the buyer so that he may know what freight he has to pay and obtain delivery of the goods, if they arrive, or recover for their loss if they are lost on the voyage. Such terms constitute an agreement that the delivery of the goods, provided they are in conformity with the contract, shall be delivery on board a ship at the port of shipment. It follows that against

---

15. M. Gulamali & Co. v. P.M.S. Md. Yosuf, 1954 Mad. 268; Narayan Swami Chetry v. Sondaranjan & Co., 1958 Mad. 43.

tender of these documents— the bill of lading, invoice, and policy of insurance—which completes delivery in accordance with that agreement, the buyer must be ready and willing to pay the price."[16]

"It will thus appear", observed Chakravarti C.J, in *Joseph Pyke & Son* v. *Kedarnath,* 1959 Cal. 328, "that although the seller is taken to have performed the contract by delivering the shipping documents, it is not delivery of any shipping documents which suffice. The documents must show that the seller has shipped the goods and that the goods he has shipped are of the contract quantity and description. The seller thus does not discharge his obligation by merely presenting to the buyer or making available to him certain pieces of paper with writings as to a contract of a affreightment inscribed on them, but must also deliver the goods covered by the contract, although the delivery is to be to the ship. It is true that after the seller has shipped the goods he is no longer responsible for their safe landing at the port of destination, but he is not responsible, because he has taken out a policy of insurance for the benefit of the buyer and thus made it possible for the buyer to look to the insurer for compensation or reimbursement if the goods failed to be delivered. The fact, however, remains that although a C.I.F. contract is not a contract by the seller that the goods shall arrive at the port of destination, it is nevertheless a contract to ship goods complying with the contract of sale. Indeed, as observed in Chalmers, such a contract is not a contract for the sale of documents but a contract for the sale of insured goods, to be implemented by the delivery of proper documents.[17] After all it is but plain common sense that a person, who purchases goods under a C.I.F contract, does not intend to purchase mere paper and does not expect to get merely some documents, but he intends to purchase and get goods which he may either utilise himself or in which he may trade by disposing of them at a profit. It is a total misconception to think that C.I.F. contracts are altogether divorced from delivery of the goods by them.

"To say that a seller under a C.I.F. contract performs the contract wholly by delivering the shipping documents to the buyer is to state half the truth. The liabilities of the seller do not altogether end with the shipping of the goods and the dispatch or delivery of the shipping documents relating to them. If, after the goods have been landed, the buyer finds them not to conform to the contract, either in regard to quantity or in quality, he is entitled to reject them and repudiate the contract, although he may have previously paid the price. Indeed as has been well explained in the very instructive judgment of Devlin J. in *Kwei Tek Chao.* v. *British Traders & Shippers Ltd.,* (1954) 2 Q.B. 459, a buyer under a C.I.F. contract has two rights, one to reject the documents and the other to reject the goods. The two rights are distinct and, corresponding to them, there are two distinct obligations of the seller, as the learned Judge also points out:

"In a C.I.F. contract the goods are delivered, so far as they are physically delivered, when they are put on board a ship at the port of shipment. The documents are delivered when they are tendered. A buyer who takes delivery from the ship at the port of destination is not taking delivery of the goods under the contract of sale, but merely taking delivery out of his own warehouse, as it were, by the presentation of the document of title to the goods, the Master of the ship having been his bailee ever since he became entitled to the bill of lading."

It is true that it has sometimes been said that a C.I.F. contract is a contract for the sale of documents rather than a sale of goods. That view owes its origin to the observations which Scrutton J., as he then was, made in the case of *Arnhold Karberg &. Co.* v. *Blythe, Green Jourdain & Co.* (1916) 1 K.B. 495, when dealing with it as a Court of first instance. "The key to many of the difficulties arising in C.I.F. contracts," said the learned Judge, "is to keep firmly in mind the cardinal distinction that a C.I.F. sale is not a sale of goods, but a sale of documents relating to goods." That view was dissented from by the

16. See Raj Spinning Mills v. G. King Ltd., 1959 Punj, 45.
17. See Chalmers on Sale of Goods, 13th Edition, pp. 112-113.

Court of Appeal which clarified what the true position in law was. Bankes, L.J., for example, observed that he could not agree with Scrutton J., in the view taken by him, but would himself prefer to look upon C.I.F. contracts as contracts for the sale of goods to be performed by the delivery of documents. Warrington LJ. expressing disagreement with the statement of Scrutton J., observed: "The contracts (C.I.F.) are contracts for the sale and purchase of goods, but they are contracts which may be performed in the particular manner, viz., the delivery of the goods may be effected *first* by placing them, on board a ship, and *secondly* by transferring to the purchaser the shipping documents". In conclusion, Chakravarti CJ. in *Joseph Pyke and Son* v. *Kedarnath,* 1959 Cal. 328, observed: "The delivery of goods is not unnecessary under C.I.F. contracts but the obligation as to delivery is discharged by the delivery of the goods on board a ship instead of directly and at once to the buyer. It cannot be said that a C.I.F. contract is not a contract for the delivery of any article. I have already pointed out that even after the shipping documents have been presented to the buyer and even after he has paid out the invoice price, he still retains the right to examine the goods shipped to him and to reject them, if he finds any deficiency in regard to either quantity or quality. It is thus impossible to see how it can be said that under a C.I.F. contract delivery of the goods to the buyer is not material or is not contemplated." It is, therefore, not correct to say that a C.I.F. sale is not a sale of goods, but a sale of documents relating to goods. It is more correct to say mat it is a contract for the sale of insured goods, lost or not lost, to be implemented by the transfer of proper documents.[18]

C.I.F.C.I. CONTRACTS

Where the order for the supply of goods is placed with a commission agent, he is entitled to charge his commission for the work done and interest for the time during which the price of the goods remains unpaid. Such a contract is known as C.I.F.C.I.— COST, INSURANCE, FREIGHT, COMMISSION, INTEREST.

EX-SHIP CONTRACTS

In the case of contracts where delivery has to be made "Ex-Ship", the ownership in the goods will not pass until actual delivery. It will, therefore, be for the seller to insure the goods to protect his interests. Even if the buyer has paid the price against the documents, the buyer does not thereby acquire an interest in the goods or even an insurable interest therein.

RISK prima facie PASSES WITH OWNERSHIP

As already observed, the question whether property has passed is important, *firstly*, in considering upon whom loss will pass in the event of the destruction of the subject-matter and, *secondly,* in determining their rights of disposal of the goods although the price remains unpaid. The rule in the first case is *res perit domino—the loss falls on the owner.* But it is open to the parties to enter any contract they please so that the risk can be separated from ownership. *A* buys goods of *B* and property has passed to him; but the goods remain in *B*'s warehouse and the price is unpaid. Before delivery a fire burns down the warehouse destroying the goods. *A* must pay *B* the price of the goods, as A was the owner. Furs are ordered' 'on approval" with invoice. They are stolen by burglars. By the custom of the fur trade the goods are at the risk of the person ordering them on approval. The buyer must pay the invoice price. A motor car is deposited for sale with a garage keeper "at owner's risk." It is damaged by the negligence of the garage keeper's servant. The garage keeper is not liable. Under Sec.26 of the present Act the parties are allowed to provide by their agreement that the risk shall pass at some time or on some condition not necessarily simultaneous with the passing of the property.

---

18. Haskell v. Continental Express (1950)'l All. E.R. 1033.

The proviso to Sec.26 lays down that where delivery of the goods has been delayed through the fault of either buyer or seller, the goods are at the risk of the party in fault as regards any loss which might not have occurred but for such fault.

PART 6-E
TRANSFER OF TITLE BY NON-OWNERS

GENERAL RULE AS TO TITLE

The general rule is that only the owner of goods can sell the goods. No one can convey a better title than he himself has. If a person transfers articles not belonging to him, the transferee gets no title. This rule is expressed by the maxim, *"Nemo dat quod non habet"* (no one gives that he has not). This rule protects the true owner, as the buyer from the non-owner does not acquire a better title than what the seller had; and the mere fact of an innocent and *bona fide* purchase from the non-owner is no answer to the claim of the true owner. For example, A, the hirer of goods under a hire-purchase agreement, sells them to B. B, though, acting in good faith, does not acquire the property in the goods as against the owner but, at the most, such interest as the hirer had. There is a sale of horse at a public auction. Unknown to the auctioneer and the buyer, the horse has been stolen. The buyer obtains no title against the true owner.

EXCEPTIONS TO THE GENERAL RULE AS TO TITLE

Sec. 27, while recognising the general rule that the buyer acquires no better title than the seller had, provides for a number of exceptions to it. Under the exceptions to the general rule, therefore, the buyer gets a better title to the goods than the seller himself has. The exceptions are discussed below.

SALE BY MERCANTILE AGENT

The first and most important exception to the general rule is in the case of a *bona fide* buyer of goods with no notice that the seller had an imperfect title to sell the goods, provided that the seller is a "mercantile agent" in possession of either the goods or documents of title to goods, with the consent of the owner and sells the goods in the ordinary course of business as a mercantile agent. Thus, a person who in good faith buys goods of a factor, broker or auctioneer, will get good title to them, even though the seller has exceeded his authority, or authority has been revoked by the true owner before the sale, provided (the buyer) did not have notice of the authority being exceeded or its revocation.

SALE BY A CO-OWNER

A buyer in good faith of one of the several joint owners who is in sole possession of the goods with the permission of his co-owners will get good title to the goods, provided that he had no notice of want of authority to sell. One of several co-owners holding a jewel in his safe custody is a person in such possession as is contemplated in this rule, and a buyer in good faith and with no notice of defective title will get good title to the jewel. (Sec. 28).

SALE BY A PERSON IN POSSESSION UNDER A VOIDABLE CONTRACT

The next exception relates to a person who is in possession of the goods under a contract which is voidable, and who, before the contract is rescinded, sells the same to a buyer who buys in good faith and without notice of the seller's defective title. The buyer in such a case will get good title to the goods. The rule pre-supposes a contract, and does not apply unless there is a contract. Thus it does-not apply to a contract originally void, or where goods are obtained by theft (Sec. 29).

SALE BY SELLER IN POSSESSION AFTER SALE

Where a seller, after having sold the goods, continues to be in possession of the goods, or a document of title to the goods, and again sells them or pledges the same either by himself or through a mercantile agent to a person who acts in good faith and without notice of the previous sale, such a person gets a good title to the goods. It is to be noted that the possession of the seller must be as seller and not as hirer or bailee. (Sec.30).

SALE BY BUYER IN POSSESSION

Where a buyer who having bought or agreed to buy the goods being in possession of the same or of a document of title to the same, with **consent of the seller**, sells or pledges them either by himself or through a mercantile agent, the buyer who acts in good faith and without notice of lien or of any other right of the owner gets a good title. *B* agreed to buy a car and pay for it, if his solicitor approved, and, having obtained possession of the car, sold it to *C*, but the solicitor subsequently disapproved of the transaction. *C*, the *bona fide,* buyer, got good title, for *B* "agreed to buy it". It is to be noted that the consent of the seller for possession of goods by the buyer must be free and real to enable the buyer to give good title to a sub-buyer or a pledgee. If the consent of the seller or his agent is absent, then an innocent buyer or pledgee cannot get any title to the goods.[19] Also, a person who has got merely an *option to* buy as in hire-purchase agreement cannot transfer title to sub-buyer *however bona fide,* for option to buy is not agreement to buy. Thus, where H entered into a hire-purchase agreement with B in relation to a piano on the condition that on paying 12 instalments of ₹ 100 each the piano should be his property, and after 6 instalments, B pawned the piano with M, who took it in good faith; H can take back the piano from *M*.[20] (Sec 30).

In addition to the above expressly provided exceptions, the Indian Sale of Goods Act recognises three more exceptions, as Sec. 27 commences with the words "Subject to the provisions of this Act and of any other law for the time being in force." The three exceptions are as given below.

SUBJECT TO THE PROVISIONS OF SECTION 54(3) OF THE ACT

An unpaid seller can stop the goods in transit or exercise his right of lien; and where such unpaid seller has exercised his right and is in possession of goods (of which ownership has passed to the buyer) he can re-sell these goods. The buyer on such re-sale gets an absolute title to the goods, even though the re-sale may not be justified in the circumstances.

SUBJECT TO THE PROVISIONS OF ANY OTHER LAW

Under Sec.176 of thie Indian Contract Act, a pawnee or pledgee has a right to sell the goods pledged with him, and the buyer gets a better title than what the seller has. Further, Sec. 169 of the same Act provides power for sale to the finder of lost goods. Again, under the Negotiable Instruments Act, a holder in due course may get a better title than what his endorser had. Similarly, under Order 40, Rule 1 of the Civil Procedure Code, Receivers appointed by Court have authority to sell properties. Also, Official Assignees under the Presidency towns Insolvency Act, Official Receivers under Provincial Insolvency Act, Liquidators under Indian Companies Act and Officers *at* Court selling goods in execution under Order 21, Civil Procedure Code, and Executors and Administrators, all these persons are not owners, yet they sell properties belonging to others and convey title to the buyers than they themselves possess.

---

19. Central National Bank v. United Industrial Bank, 1954 S.C. 181.
20. B. Motor Supply Co. v. Cox. (1914)1 K.B. 244.

SALE UNDER THE IMPLIED AUTHORITY OF OWNER, OR TITLE BY ESTOPPEL

The words in the last part of Sec.27 are "unless the owner of the goods is by his conduct precluded from denying the seller's authority to sell." This is really the application of the doctrine of estoppel, as the sale may be made in circumstances which may preclude the owner from disputing the authority of the person who sells. In a contract of sale, estoppel may arise where the owner by any act or omission leads the buyer to believe that the seller has the right to sell. In a sale by an agent within the scope of his apparent authority the buyer gets a better title than what the seller has. The lessee of a public house who allows another to sell the fixtures and fittings as if they are his own, whereby a third person is induced to purchase them *bona fide,* cannot recover them from the purchaser. This is so because, as pointed out by Lord Denman, if "a party who negligently or culpably stands by and allows another to contract on the faith and understanding of a fact which he can contradict, cannot afterwards dispute that fact in an action against the person whom he has himself assisted in deceiving." An owner may also be estopped if he received the sale proceeds with the knowledge that the sale is without authority.

MARKET OVERT

There is another very important exception in English law which has not been recognised in India. According to English law, where a purchase is made in what is called "Market Overt", the buyer is absolutely protected and the ownership passes to him so that the true owner cannot recover from the buyer. A market overt is understood as a sale at certain prescribed places and times in which cases a good title is passed to the buyer in good faith and without notice of the defective title of the seller. The rule of market overt is omitted in India, probably because it is likely to be an incentive to theft, and because "it would be difficult to specify places to which it should be applied."

> ## PART 6-F
> ## PERFORMANCE OF THE CONTRACT OF SALE

DUTIES OF THE SELLER AND BUYER

It is the duty of the seller to deliver the goods and of the buyer to accept and pay for them, in accordance with the terms of the contract of sale (Sec.31). Unless otherwise agreed, payment and delivery are concurrent conditions, that is, they both take place at the same time as in a cash sale over a shop counter (Sec. 32). The seller has the duty of giving delivery according to the contract and according to the rules contained in the Sale of Goods Act, as stated below.

The buyer has the duty to pay for the goods and accept delivery. If he wrongfully refuses to accept delivery, he must pay compensation to the seller.

DELIVERY

Delivery is the voluntary transfer of possession from one person to another. Delivery may be made by doing anything which the parties agree shall be treated as delivery. Delivery to a wharfinger or a carrier is generally regarded as delivery to the buyer.

Delivery may be actual, constructive or *symbolic. Actual* or physical delivery takes place where the goods are handed over by the seller to the buyer or his agent authorised to take possession of the goods. *Constructive delivery* or delivery by attornment takes place when the person in possession of the goods acknowledges that he holds the goods on behalf of and at the disposal of the buyer. For instance, where the seller agrees to hold the goods as bailee for the buyer there is a constructive delivery. Also, where a warehouseman or a carrier who holds the goods as bailee for the seller agrees and acknowledges to hold them for the buyer there is a constructive delivery. Symbolic delivery is made by indicating or giving a symbol. Here the goods themselves are not delivered (probably because they are ponderous or bulky), but the "means of obtaining possession" of goods is delivered, *e.g.*, by delivering the key to the warehouse where the goods are stored or the bill of lading which will entitle the holder to receive the goods on the arrival of the ship.

RULES REGARDING DELIVERY

1. Delivery should have the effect of putting the buyer in possession. Thus, where the wood of fallen tress is sold the mere fact of the buyer cutting them will not amount to taking possession of them until he carts them away. In order to constitute delivery the buyer or his authorised agent must have possession of the goods, *i.e.*, the buyer should be in a position to exercise some degree of control over the goods either directly or through an agent.

2. The seller must deliver the goods according to the contract, and where there is a condition precedent to the performance of the contract, the seller is not bound to deliver, unless the condition precedent is satisfied. Again, unless otherwise agreed, delivery of the goods and payment of the price are concurrent conditions. A contract of sale always involves reciprocal promises, the seller promising to deliver the goods sold and the buyer to accept and pay for him. In the absence of contract to the contrary, they are to be performed simultaneously and each party should be ready and willing to perform his promise before he can call upon the other to perform his. Therefore, unless the sale is on credit, the seller need not be ready and willing to deliver the goods before the price is paid. If the buyer is insolvent or states that he will not accept delivery, this is a strong evidence that he is not ready and willing to pay.

3. Though the seller is bound to deliver the goods according to the contract, yet he need not deliver them unless the buyer applies for delivery (Sec. 35). The rule is not affected by the fact that the goods are to be acquired by the seller and when they are acquired, the seller notifies to the buyer that they are in his possession, it is still the duty of the buyer to apply for delivery. Thus, when the seller gives notice of arrival of the goods, it is the buyer's duty to apply for delivery. The demand by the buyer for delivery of the goods must be made at reasonable hour. On the other hand, it is the duty of the seller to deliver the goods when the buyer applies for delivery, and if the seller fails to do so, he is guilty of a breach of contract.

4. The condition precedent imported in all contracts by this provision of Sec.35, apart form special agreement, to the buyer's duty to claim delivery, may, however, be waived by the seller and is waived by him impliedly where he so incapacitates himself from complying with the demand, by consuming, reselling or otherwise disposing of the goods, as to render the demand idle and useless. Whether it is for the buyer to take possession of the goods or for the seller to send them to the buyer is a question depending in each case or the contract express or implied between the parties [Sec.36(l)].

5. Where the goods at the time of the sale are in the possession of a third person, there is no delivery by the seller to the buyer unless and until such third person acknowledges to the buyer that he holds the goods on his behalf [Sec.36(3)].

6. **Time of Delivery**—As said above, the goods must be delivered as per the terms of the contract. Where the contract uses words like "directly", "immediately", "forthwith", "without loss of time", it has been held that quick delivery is con templated. Where, however, no time is fixed for delivery of the goods, the seller is bound to deliver them within a reasonable time. Delivery must be at a reasonable hour. A contract by a manufacturer to supply some specified goods' 'as soon as possible", means within a reasonable time.

7. **Tender of Delivery**—It is not, however, the duty of the seller to send or carry the goods to the buyer unless the contract so provides. His only duty is to place the goods at the buyer's disposal so that the buyer may remove them. He is to tender the delivery of goods, and if the buyer is not willing to take them, he is excused from performance and can maintain a suit against the buyer. But it is essential that the goods must-be in a deliverable state at the time of delivery or tender thereof.

8. **Place of Delivery**—The place of delivery may be stated in the contract, and where it is so stated, the goods must be delivered at the place during business hours on a working day. Where no place is mentioned, the goods are to be delivered at a place at which they happen to be at the time of the contract of sale, or if the contract is with respect to future goods, at the place at which the goods are manufactured or produced. The buyer in these cases can ask to have the goods made over to him at the seller's place of business and not at his own.

If the seller agrees to deliver the goods to the buyer at a place other than that where they are when sold, the buyer must, in the absence of agreement to the contrary, take the risk of deterioration, necessarily incident to the course of transit.

9. **Cost of Delivery**—The seller has to bear the cost of delivery unless the contract otherwise provides. While the cost of obtaining delivery is said to be the buyer's, the cost of putting the goods into deliverable state must be borne by the seller. In other words, in the absence of an agreement to the contrary, the expenses of and incidental to making delivery of the goods must be borne by the seller, the expenses of and incidental to receiving delivery must be borne by the buyer. Thus, when the contract is for delivery "ex-ship", the seller must do all that is necessary to release the shipowner's lien, and if "from the deck" pay all charges to be paid, such as harbour dues, to enable the goods to be removed from the deck. Where goods are sold "F.O.B.", the seller must bear the expenses of, and up to shipment. In a "C.I.F." contract, the seller is, as between himself and the buyer, chargeable with the amount of the freight and the insurance charges, and the buyer, if he pays any such charges, can claim credit for them. Wharfage charges incurred after shipment and delivery of the shipping documents fall on the buyer.

10. **Duty to Insure Goods Where Goods Delivered to a Carrier**—Where goods are delivered to a carrier or wharfinger, the seller is bound to enter into a reasonable contract on behalf of the buyer with the carrier for the safe transmission of the goods; and if he fails to do so and the goods are destroyed, the buyer may decline to treat delivery to the carrier as delivery to him or claim damages. If the transit be by sea, the seller must inform the buyer in time, so that he may have the goods insured. If the seller fails to do so, the goods would be at seller's risk during transit. This clearly applies to F.O.B, contracts. But, it is open to the parties to contract to the contrary and by usages term may be inferred authorising the seller to send goods at buyer's risk uninsured. If the contract is a C.I.F. contract, the buyer is not bound to take delivery if the seller fails to insure, even though the goods arrive safe (Sec. 39).

11. When the seller is ready and willing to deliver the goods and requests the buyer to take delivery and the buyer is liable to the seller for (*i*) any loss occasioned by his neglect or refusal to take delivery; and (*ii*) a reasonable charge for the care and custody of the goods.

ACCEPTANCE OF GOODS BY BUYER

The buyer has a right to have delivery as per contract, and accept them when they are according to the contract

Acceptance of goods by buyer takes place when the buyer—
1. intimates to the seller that he has accepted the goods; or
2. retains the goods after the lapse of a reasonable time, without intimating *to* the seller that he has rejected them; or
3. does any act to the goods which is inconsistent with the ownership of the seller, e.g., a pledge or resale (Sec. 42).

In *Ruben* v. *Faire* (1949) 1 All. E.R. 215, the plaintiff contracted to sell to the defendant by sample a quantity of "Linatex in 41 ft rolls, 5 ft wide." The defendant asked the plaintiff to send half of this material to *X* to whom he had resold it. The plaintiff did so, and *X* rejected it on the ground that it did not correspond. The plaintiff now sued the defendant for the price, and the defendant pleaded that the plaintiffs breach of condition entitled them to rescind the contract and repudiate all liability under it. It was held that there had been a delivery and the buyer was deemed to have accepted half of the goods and must treat the seller's breach of condition as a breach of warranty. In a suit for price by the seller, he could only counter-claim for damages. By Sec. 42, if the goods are delivered to a sub-purchaser at the request of the buyer, there is a constructive delivery to the buyer, and he has 'accepted' the goods, as he had done an act 'inconsistent with' the seller's ownership of the goods.

When goods are delivered to the buyer which he has not previously examined he is not deemed to have accepted them unless and until he had had reasonable opportunity of examining them. He is entitled to demand of the seller a reasonable opportunity of examining them in order to ascertain whether they are in conformity with the contract (Sec. 41). The buyer may, however, accept them at once, although a reasonable time for making an examination has not elapsed [*Hardy & Co.* v. *Hillerus & Fowler* (1923) 2 K.B.490].

If the seller sends the buyer a larger or smaller quantity of goods than ordered, the buyer may (Sec. 37)—

1. reject the whole;
2. accept the whole;
3. accept the quantity he ordered and reject the rest

The contract was for the sale of 4,000 tons of meal, 2 per cent more or less. The sellers delivered meal greatly in excess of the permitted variation. *Held,* the buyer could reject the whole [*Payne and Routh* v. *Lillico & Sons* (1920) 36 T.L.R. 569].

What the buyer accepts he must pay for at the contract rate. Where the contract is for the sale of "about" so many kilos or tonnes, or so many kilos or tons "more or less"', the seller is allowed a reasonable margin. If, however, he exceeds that margin the buyer cannot be compelled to accept the goods.

If the seller delivers, with the goods ordered, goods of a wrong description the buyer may accept the goods ordered and reject the rest or reject the whole.

If a buyer has a right under his contract to reject goods, he is not bound to return the rejected goods to the seller, but it is sufficient if he intimates to the seller that he refuses to accept them (Sec. 43). A buyer cannot be compelled to take delivery by instalments.

INSTALMENT DELIVERIES

When there is a contract for the sale of goods to be delivered by stated instalments which are to be separately paid for; and either buyer or seller commits a breach of contract, it is a question depending on the terms of the contract and the circumstances of the case whether the breach is a repudiation of the whole contract or a severable breach merely giving a right to claim for damages (Sec.38).

If the breach is of such a kind as to lead to the inference that similar breaches will take place with regard to future deliveries, the contract can be at once repudiated by the injured party. For example, if the buyer fails to pay for one instalment under such circumstances as to suggest that he will not pay for future instalments, or the seller fails to deliver goods of the contract description under similar circumstances the contract can be repudiated.

A sold to *B* 1,500 tons of meat and bone meal of a specified quality, to be shipped 125 tons monthly in equal weekly instalments. After about half the meal was delivered and paid for, *B* discovered that it was not of the contract quality and could have been rejected, and he refused to take further deliveries. *Held B* was entitled to do so, as he was not bound to take the risk of having put upon him further deliveries of goods which did not conform to the contract. [*Robert A. Munro & Co.* v. *Meyer* (1930) 2 K.B. 312].

The tests to be applied *are: first,* the ratio quantitatively which the breach bears to the contract and *secondly,* the degree of probability that such a breach will be repeated.

A bought from *B. Co.* 5,000 tons of steel to be delivered 1,000 tons monthly. After the delivery of two instalments, but before payment was due, a petition was presented to wind up *B. Co.*, and *A* refused to pay unless the sanction of the Court was obtained, being under the erroneous impression that this was necessary. *Held,* the conduct of *A* in so refusing payment did not show an intention to repudiate the contract so as to excuse the liquidator of *B. Co.* from making further deliveries [*Mersey Steel & Iron Co.* v. *Naylor.* (1884) 9A.C.434].

REMEDIAL MEASURES
RIGHTS OF THE UNPAID SELLER

WHO IS AN UNPAID SELLER?

The seller of goods is deemed to be an unpaid seller (*a*) when the whole of the price has not been paid or tendered; or (*b*) when a conditional payment was made by a bill of exchange or other negotiable instrument, and the instrument has been dishonoured (Sec. 45). In simple words, an unpaid seller is one who has sold goods on cash terms and does not include a seller who has sold goods on credit.

An unpaid seller has a two-fold right: One *against the goods,* and the other *against the buyer personally.* The unpaid seller's right can be exercised by any agent of the seller to whom the bill of lading has been endorsed or a consignor or agent who has himself paid, or is directly responsible for the price.

RIGHTS OF UNPAID SELLER AGAINST THE GOODS

An unpaid seller of goods, even though the property in the goods has passed td the buyer, has (*i*) a lien on the goods remaining in his possession; (*ii*) if the buyer is insolvent, a right of stoppage in transit after he has parted with possession of the goods; (*iii*) a limited right of resale (Sec. 46).

LIEN

An unpaid seller in possession of goods sold may exercise his lien on the goods, i.e., keep the goods in his possession, and refuse to deliver them to the buyer until the full payment or tender of the price in cases where (Sec. 47)—

(*a*) the goods have been sold without any stipulation as to credit;
(*b*) the goods have been sold on credit, but the term of credit has expired;
(*c*) the buyer becomes insolvent.

The seller's lien is a *possessory lien, i.e.,* the lien can be exercised only so long as the seller is in possession of the goods. Lien can be exercised for the non-payment of price, not for any other charges. For example, the seller cannot claim lien for godown charges which he had to incur for storing the goods in exercise of his lien for the price. When an unpaid seller has made part delivery of the goods he can exercise lien on the balance of the goods not delivered unless the part of delivery was made in circumstances to show an intention to waive the lien. The lien can be exercised even though the seller has obtained a decree for the price.

TERMINATION OF LIEN

Lien depends on physical possession. Therefore, the unpaid seller loses his lien on the goods—

(*a*) when he delivers them to a carrier or other bailee for the purpose of transmission to the buyer, without reserving the right of disposal of the goods;
(*b*) when the buyer or his agent lawfully obtains possession of the goods;
(*c*) by waiver of his lien (Sec.49).

STOPPAGE IN TRANSIT

The right of stoppage in transit is a right of stopping the goods while they are in transit, *resuming possession* of them and retaining possession until payment of the price. It is available when (Sec. 50)—
  (a) the buyer becomes insolvent; and
  (b) the goods are in transit

The buyer is insolvent if he has ceased to pay his debts in the ordinary course of business, or cannot pay his debts as they become due, whether he has committed an act of insolvency or not [Sec.2(8)].

LIEN AND STOPPAGE IN TRANSIT DISTINGUISHED

The points of difference between an unpaid seller's right of lien and stoppage in transit are: (1) the right to stop goods arises only when the buyer is insolvent, but the right to lien can be exercised even when the buyer is able to pay, but does not pay; (2) lien is available only when the goods are in actual or constructive possession of the seller, but the goods can be stopped in transit when the seller has parted with possession, and the buyer or his agent has not obtained possession, *i.e.*, the goods are in the custody of a "middleman" between the two; (3) when possession is surrendered by the seller, his lien is gone, but his right to stop commences and remains as long as the goods are in transit and before they pass into the possession of the buyer; (4) the right of lien is to retain possession, the right of stoppage is to regain possession. The right of stoppage in transit is, in fact, an extension of the right of lien.

DURATION OF TRANSIT (S.51)

Goods are in transit from the time they are delivered to a carrier or other bailee for the purpose of transmission to the buyer until the buyer takes delivery of them. The goods are still in transit if they are rejected by the buyer. The transit continues so long as the goods are not delivered to the buyer or his agent in this behalf no matter whether they are lying with the carrier or a forwarding agent, awaiting transmission, or are in actual transit, or are lying at the destination.

If goods are ordered to be sent to an intermediate place from which they are to be forwarded to their ultimate destination the transit is at an end if fresh instructions have to be sent to the intermediate place before the goods can be forwarded, but otherwise the goods are still in transit. The transit is at an end in the following cases:—
  (a) If the buyer obtains delivery before the arrival of the goods at their destination.
  (b) If, after the arrival of the goods at their destination, the carrier acknowledges to the buyer that he holds the goods on his behalf, even if a further destination of the goods is indicated by the buyer.
  (c) If the carrier wrongfully refuses to deliver the goods to the buyer.

When goods are delivered to a ship chartered by the buyer, whether they are in possession of the master of the ship as carrier or as agent for the buyer is a question depending on the circumstance of the case.

Where part delivery of the goods has been made to the buyer or his agent in that behalf, the remainder of the goods may be stopped in transit, unless such part delivery has been given in such circumstances as to show an agreement to give up possession of the whole of the goods.

HOW STOPPAGE IN TRANSIT EFFECTED

The right to stop in transit may be exercised either by taking actual possession of the goods or by giving notice of the seller's claim to the carrier or other person having control of the goods (Sec. 52).

The notice may be given either to the principal, whose servant has the custody at such a time as and under such circumstances as he may, by the exercise of reasonable diligence, communicate it to his servant in time to prevent the delivery to the consignee. The notice to the principal will take effect only after the lapse of a time reasonably sufficient for him to communicate with his agent. The notice need not be a written notice, and no particular form is necessary; all that is required is to ask the carrier before the goods have been delivered by him to the buyer or his agent, so that he may prevent delivery. A mere notice to the buyer before the goods come to his possession that the seller wished to exercise the right will not be sufficient. If the carrier, after receiving notice, wrongfully delivers the goods to the buyer, he does so at his own peril. His duty is to re-deliver the goods to the unpaid vendor, though, of course, at the vendor's expense. The setter's right is so strongly maintained that while the goods are in transit and the insolvency of the buyer occurs, the seller may take them by all means not criminal.

EFFECT OF SUB-SALE OR PLEDGE BY BUYER

This right of lien or stoppage in transit is not affected by the buyer selling or pledging the goods or making any disposition of them unless the seller has, by his own conduct, precluded himself from exercising the lien or stoppage in transit by recognising the title of the sub-buyer or the pledgee. This is on the principle that a second buyer cannot stand in a better position than his seller (*i.e.*, the first buyer). *W* sold 80 maunds of barley out of a granary to *A* who sold 60 maunds to *K* before the goods had been ascertained by *W*. *K* paid *A*, obtained a delivery order and presented it to *W*, who expressed willingness to forward the barley on being requested to do so. *Held*, *W*, the unpaid seller, has recognised the title of *K*, the sub-buyer, and therefore was estopped from exercising the lien which he has waived.[21] Similarly, where the sub-buyer produced delivery orders to the seller who endorsed on them that he was willing to give delivery, but after delivery of part of the goods, refused to deliver the rest on the ground that the first buyer had not paid the price; it was held that the seller was estopped. [22] But it must be noted that consent of the seller to the sub-sale is essential; it is not sufficient that the seller simply has notice of the fact of sub-sale. There must be a recognition of the sub-buyer's right to the goods free of the seller's lien so as to evince an intention to renounce the seller's right on the goods.

While the goods are in transit, if the buyer transfers the document of title or pledges the same to a person in good faith and for consideration, then, if the transaction is sale, the right of stoppage is defeated. But, if the transaction is a pledge, the seller's right to stop will be subject to the pledge. But where the pledgee has two securities, the unpaid seller can compel the pledgee to marshal his securities and to resort first to the other security, *i.e.*, he may require the pledgee to satisfy his claim against the buyer first out of any goods or securities in the hands of the pledgee, and if still anything is left unpaid turn to the document of title so pledged [Sec.53(2)].

It should be noted that the exercise by the unpaid seller of his rights of lien or stoppage in transit does not amount to rescission of the contract. He may retain or regain the possession of the goods, but he does not regain the property in them, nor does he thereby cancel the sale. In no proper sense, does he by the stoppage become the owner of the goods. What is then a seller, having retained or regained possession of the goods to do with them if the buyer, after notice to take the goods and pay the price, remains in default? Must he keep them until he can obtain judgement against the buyer and sell them on execution? What if the goods are perishable, *e.g.*, fruit, or expensive to keep, as cattle or horses. Sec. 54 gives him a limited right to re-sell the goods.

---

21. Knights v. Wiffen (1870) 5 Q.B. 660.
22. Ganges Mfg. Co. v. Sourajmul (1880) 3 Cal. 669.

RIGHT OF RE-SALE

The unpaid seller may re-sell—
(i) where the goods are perishable;
(ii) where the right is expressly reserved in the contract;
(iii) where in exercise of right of lien or stoppage in transit seller gives notice to buyer of his intention to re-sell, and the buyer does not pay or tender the price within a reasonable time. .

The right of re-sale is the third right of the unpaid seller, the other two being the rights of lien and stoppage in transit. The transaction under the present right is called re-sale, because there has been already a sale by which the ownership has passed to die buyer.

A further valuable right is given to the unpaid seller, namely, Right to Surplus or Profit. If on a re-sale there is a deficiency between the price due and the amount realised, he will be able to recover this from the buyer. The profit arising on a re-sale belongs to the seller because the re-sale is the result of a breach of contract on the part of the buyer, and such a buyer cannot take advantage of his own wrong and claim the profits.

NOTICE

The seller is bound to give reasonable notice to the buyer that he is going to-re-sell the goods unless the goods are of perishable nature. What is reasonable notice is a question of fact depending, upon the nature of the goods, the distance at which the parties are situated and other circumstances of the case. The notice has been made compulsory for two reasons, *first,* that the buyer may have an opportunity of fulfilling the contract by paying the price even at the last moment before such re-sale. *Secondly,* if the buyer is still unable to pay, he may at least see that on such re-sale the goods fetch a proper price. Therefore, if the re-sale is improperly conducted, although the subsequent buyer will get good title to the goods sold to him, the seller cannot keep the surplus, if there is any; and if there is a deficiency he cannot sue the buyer for it. Where perishable goods were sold after a delay of eight months, the re-sale was held to be improper.

This right of re-sale is, however, optional and the buyer cannot demand re-sale. Thus, where the goods were in the possession of the seller and were destroyed by fire, it was held that the seller was entitled to the price and the buyer could not plead that the loss would not have happened if the seller had re-sold the goods, since the seller was not bound to re-sell. Where the right of ownership should have passed to the buyer, but the goods should have been ascertained or appropriated to the contract before the right of re-sale is exercised. But the parties may provide for re-sale even without appropriation of goods.

RIGHT OF WITHHOLDING DELIVERY

If the property in the goods has passed to the buyer, the unpaid seller has a right of lien as described above. If, however, the property has not passed, the unpaid seller has a right of withholding delivery similar to and co-extensive with his right of lien [Sec. 46(2)].

SUITS FOR BREACH OF CONTRACT

The Seller, in addition to his rights against the goods set out above, has two rights of action **against the buyer personally.**

Suit for price—1. Where the property in the goods has passed to the buyer, the seller is entitled to sue for price, whether the possession is with the buyer or the seller.

2. Where the price is payable on a certain day irrespective of delivery, the seller may sue for the price, if it is not paid on that day, although the property in the goods has not passed.

SUIT FOR DAMAGES FOR NON-ACCEPTANCE

Where the buyer wrongfully neglects or refuses to accept the goods and pay for them, the seller has a right to sue the buyer for damages for non-acceptance. The measure of damages of the loss resulting from the buyer's breach of contract which is, where there is an available market for the goods *prima facie,* the difference between the contract price and the market price. An available market means that the goods can be sold freely because there is an existing demand.

R contracted to buy a "Vanguard" motor-car from *T Ltd.*, who were car dealers. *R* refused to accept delivery. *Held, T Ltd.* were entitled to damages for the loss of their bargain, viz., the profit they would have made, as they had sold one car less than they otherwise would have sold [*Thompson Ltd.* v. *Robinson* (1955) 2 W.L.R. 185].

When the seller is ready and willing to deliver the goods and requests the buyer to take delivery, which the buyer does not do within a reasonable time, the seller may recover from the buyer—

1. any loss occasioned by the buyer's refusal or neglect to take delivery;[23] and
2. a reasonable charge for the care and custody of the goods.

The Buyer has the following rights to sue the seller for breach of contract:

SUIT FOR NON-DELIVERY

Where the seller wrongfully neglects or refuses to deliver the goods to the buyer, the buyer may sue him for damages for non-delivery (Sec. 57). The measure of damages is, as in the case of a suit for non-acceptance, the estimated loss naturally resulting from the breach of contract which *is prima facie,* when there is an available market for the goods, the difference between the contract price and the market price at the time when the goods ought to have been delivered or, if no time for delivery was fixed, from the time of the refusal to deliver.

If the buyer purchased the goods for re-sale and the seller knew of this, the measure of damages will be the difference between the contract price and the re-sale price, if the goods cannot be obtained in the market. If they can be obtained in the market the buyer ought to obtain them there and so fulfil his contract of re-sale, with the result that the damages will be the difference between the market price and the contract price.

Where delivery is delayed, but the goods are ultimately accepted notwithstanding the delay, the measure of damages is the difference between the value of the goods at the time when they ought to have been and the time when they actually were delivered [*Elbinger Actien Gesellschaft* v. *Armstrong* (1874) L.R.9 Q.B. at p. 477].

SUIT FOR RECOVERY OF THE PRICE

If the buyer has paid the price and the goods are not delivered, he can sue the seller for the recovery of the amount paid.

SPECIFIC PERFORMANCE

A buyer can only get his contract specifically performed, *i.e.*, obtain an order of the Court compelling the seller to deliver the goods he has sold, when the goods are specific or ascertained. The remedy is discretionary and will only be granted when damages would not be an adequate remedy. Specific performance will be granted if the goods are of special value or are unique, *e.g.*, a rare book, a picture or a piece of jewellery.

---

23. Ramanathan Chettiar v. National Textile Corpn. Ltd; 1985 Ker. 262.

SUIT FOR BREACH OF CONDITION

On breach of condition the buyer is entitled to reject the goods. But he cannot reject the goods, if—

1. he waives the breach of condition, and elects to treat it as a breach of warranty; or
2. the contract is pot severable and he has accepted the goods or part of them;
3. the contract is for specific goods, and the property has passed to the buyer.

In all these cases, as provided in Sec. 13, the condition sinks or descends to, or is treated as warranty, and the goods cannot be rejected but only a suit for damages can be filed.

L, in 1944, bought from *G* a picture of Salisbury Cathedral said by *G* to be by Constable. In 1949 *L* found it was not by Constable and claimed to rescind the contract and recover the purchase price. *Held,* as the picture had been accepted it could not later be rejected [*Leaf* v. *International Galleries* (1950) 2 K.B. 86].

SUIT FOR BREACH OF WARRANTY

On breach of warranty, the buyer can either:—

(a) set up against the seller the breach of warranty in diminution or extinction of the price; or
(b) sue the seller for damages for breach of warranty (Sec. 59).

The measure of damages for breach of warranty is the estimated loss arising directly and naturally from the breach, which *is prima facie* the difference between the value of the goods as delivered and the value they would have had if the goods had answered to the warranty.

INTEREST

The seller or the buyer may recover interest or special damages in any case where by law interest or special damages may be recoverable. He may also recover the money paid where the consideration for the payment of it has failed.

In the absence of a contract to the contrary, the Court may award interest at such rate as it thinks fit on the amount of the price—

(a) to the seller in a suit by him for the amount of the price—from the date of the tender of the goods or from the date on which the price was payable;
(b) to the buyer in a suit by him for the amount of the price in case of a breach of the contract on the part of the seller—from the date on which the payment was made.

AUCTION SALES

A sale by auction is a public sale, where goods are offered to be taken by the highest bidder. It is a proceeding at which people are invited to compete for the purchase of property by successive offers of advancing sums.

The rules regulating sales by auction are contained in Sec. 64 which reads: "64." In the case of a sale by auction:—

(i) Where goods are put for sale in lots, each lot is *prima facie* deemed to be the subject of separate contract of sale;
(ii) the sale is complete when auctioneer announces its completion by the fall of the hammer or in other customary manner; and, until such announcement is made, any bidder may retract this bid;
(iii) a right to bid may be reserved expressly by or on behalf of the seller and, where such right is expressly so reserved, but not otherwise, the seller or any one person on his behalf may, subject to the provision hereinafter contained, bid at the auction;

(iv) where the sale is not notified to be subject to a right to bid on behalf of the seller, it shall not be lawful for the seller to bid himself or to employ any person to bid at such sale, or the auctioneer knowingly to take any bid from the seller or any such person; and any sale contravening this rule may be treated as fraudulent by the buyer;

(v) the sale may be notified to be subject to a reserved price;

(vi) if the seller makes use of pretended bidding to raise the price, the sale is voidable at the option of the buyer."

This section only deals with the rights and liabilities of the parties to the contract of sale. It has nothing to do with the rights and liabilities of the auctioneer either in relation to his principal or to the buyer.

According to Benjamin sales by auction are of three kinds:—

1. Sale without reserve where the employment of a puffer renders the sale voidable.

2. Sale with a condition that the highest bidder shall be the purchasers, nothing being said about reserve.

3. Sale with a right expressly reserved to bid by or on behalf of the seller.

A sale subject to a reserve price and the reservation of a right to bid are distinct matters.

According to the usual practice a proposed auction is duly advertised and a printed catalogue in the case of goods with conditions of sale is circulated. At the appointed time and place the auctioneer, standing at a desk or rostrum, "puts up" the several lots in turn by inviting bidding from the persons present. He announces the acceptance of the last bid by a tap with his hammer or by any other approved or customary method, *e.g.*, by shouting one, two, three or by saying going, going, gone, and so "knocks down*'" the lot to the person who has made the bid.

An auction "with reserves" is one where an up-set price is fixed below which the auctioneer refuses to sell or reserves to himself the option of buying. An auction is said to be "without reserve" when the goods are to be sold to the highest bidder whether the sum bid be equivalent to the real value or not. It is not necessary that these particular words should be used; that the seller reserves the right. The auctioneer can refuse to deliver the goods to the highest bidder, if he by mistake knocks down the lot for less than the reserve price.

In *Rainbow* v. *Howkins* (1904) 2 K.B.322, the auctioneer by mistake knocked down a lot for less than the reserve. On finding this out he refused to complete the sale or sign the necessary memorandum. It was held that the buyer had no remedy against the auctioneer; and that it was immaterial that he did not know what the actual reserve was.

It may be observed that clauses 3 and 4 of the section prohibit secret bidding or the use of pretended bids, or the employment of "puffers" on behalf of the seller to raise the price at auction. Even when the sale is with reserve or subject to an upset price only, the seller or in his absence only one person acting on his behalf may bid. If more persons than one bid to the knowledge of the seller with a view to enhancing the price the buyer can avoid the contract treating the sale as fraudulent. On the other hand, an agreement among intending bidders not to complete against each other with a view to knocking off the article at a low price (usually called a "knock out" agreement) has been held to be not illegal. The seller can protect himself against too low a bid by fixing a reserve price, below which he will not sell. Puffers, by-bidders, white bonnets, or decoy ducks are the various technical names of the persons who, without having any intention to buy, are employed by the seller to raise the price by fictitious bids, thereby increasing competition among the bidders, while they themselves are secured from risk by a secret understanding 'with the seller, that they shall not be bound by their bids.

A "knock out" is a combination of persons to prevent competition between themselves at an auction by an agreement that only one of their number shall bid and that anything obtained by him shall be afterwards disposed of privately among themselves. Such a combination is not illegal.

"Damping" is the illicit or overt act of dissuading the would-be purchaser from bidding or from raising the price by pointing out defects or by doing some other acts which prevent persons from forming a proper estimate of the price of the goods or by scaring them away by some other device. Damping is illegal and entitles the auctioneer to withdraw the property from the auction.

SUMMARY

A contract of sale of goods is a contract whereby the seller transfers or agrees to transfer the property in goods to the buyer for a price. It includes actual sale and an agreement to sell. In an agreement to sell, the ownership does not pass to the buyer, while in a sale the ownership passes as soon as the contract is made. The essentials of a sale are: (*i*) there must be some goods, (*ii*) they must be exchanged for a money consideration called the price, (*iii*) the buyer and the seller must be two different persons, and (*iv*) property in the goods must pass from the seller to the buyer.

A contract of sale is regulated by the general law of contract, *i.e.*, offer and acceptance, parties competent to contract, mutual assent, subject-matter and money consideration. Goods are of two types, viz., existing goods or future goods. Existing goods are those which are owned and possesses by the seller at the time of contract. Future goods are goods to be manufactured or acquired or produced by the seller after making the contract of sale. Existing goods are either specific or ascertained goods or generic or unascertained goods. Specific goods are goods identified and agreed upon at the time the contract of sale is made. Generic goods are those which are not specifically identified but are defined by description only.

Caveat Emptor—Let the buyer beware. The buyer gets the goods as they come and takes the risk of their suitability for his purpose. It is not the duty, of the seller to point out the defects in the goods. If the buyer depends upon his own skill and integrity and the goods turn out to be defective, it is his own fault and he cannot hold the seller responsible.

Conditions and Warranties—But the purchaser may make known to the seller the particular purpose for which he intends to buy the goods so as to show that he relies on the seller's skill and judgement and the seller makes certain representations with regard to the goods, which representations may rank either as conditions or warranties. Where a condition or warranty appears in a contract of sale, the principle of caveat emptor does not apply.

A condition is a stipulation essential to the main purpose of the contract the breach of which gives rise to aright to treat the contract as repudiated. A warranty is a stipulation collateral to the main purpose of the contract, the breach of which gives rise to claim for damages but not to a right to reject the goods and treat the contract as repudiated.

Conditions and warranties may be express or implied. They are express where they are agreed upon between the buyer and the seller at a time of the contract. The conditions or warranties which are not expressed but are recognised by law are implied conditions and warranties.

Implied warranties are two in number, namely, (i) warranty for quiet possession, and (ii) warraty against encumbrances.

Implied conditions are 8 in number, the first applies to all kinds of sale and 2nd to Sth to sale by description and 6th to 8th apply to sales by sample. General Implied Condition is that the seller has got a title to the goods.

Sale by Description—(i) Goods sold should correspond to description (ii) Goods bought for a particular purpose must be fit and suitable for that purpose, (iii) The goods must be merchantable, (iv) The goods in the nature of provisions must be merchantable and wholesome.

Sale by Sample—(i) Bulk should correspond to sample, (ii) The buyer should have reasonable opportunity of comparing the bulk with sample, (iii) As regards defects which are not apparent on reasonable examination of sample goods must be merchantable.

Passing of Properly—Ascertained Goods. In an unconditional contract for sale of specific goods which are in deliverable state, the property in the goods passesto die buyer as soon as the contract is entered into, even though the payment of the price or the delivery of the goods or both are to take place at a later date. In the case of specific goods which are not in a deliverable state and the seller is bound to do something to the goods to put them into a deliverable state the ownership will not pass to the buyer until the goods are so put and the buyer has notice thereof.

In the case of sale on approval the ownership of the goods passes to the buyer (a) when he signifies his approval or acceptance to the seller or does another act adopting the transaction; (b) if he does not signify his approval or acceptance to the seller, but retains the goods without giving notice of rejection then, if a time has been fixed for the return of the goods, on the expiration of such time and if no time has been fixed, on the expiry of a reasonable time. If buyer rejects the goods he should give notice of rejection to the seller.

Ownership in Unascertained Goods—Where the goods contracted to be sold are not ascertained or where they are future goods, ownership will not pass to the buyer unless and until goods are ascertained.

The ascertainment of goods or their appropriation may be made (i) by the buyer with' the seller's assent, (ii) by the seller with the buyer's assent

The seller may appropriate the, goods (a) by putting the quantity contracted for in suitable receptacles, (b) by separating articles contracted for from others, (c) by delivery to carrier or other bailee for transmission to buyer, without reserving right of disposal.

Risk follows Ownership—The general rule is that the loss falls on the owner. When the property in the goods is transferred by the seller to the buyer, the risk, in general, will fall upon the buyer. But the general rule may be qualified by an express contract between the parties in which case the risk may be separated from ownership.

Transfer of Title by Non-Owners—The general rule of law is that a seller cannot pass a better title to the buyer than he has. To this rule the Sale of Goods Act provides some exceptions, under which buyer gets better title than the seller's. They are:

(i) Sale by a mercantile agent, (ii) sale by a co-owner, (iii) sale by persons in possession under voidable contract, (iv) sale by seller in possession after sale, (v) sale by buyer in possession, (vi) re-sale by an unpaid seller where he exercises his right of lien or stoppage in transit, (vii) sale by a pawnee or pledgee where the loan is not repaid on a stipulated date, (viii) sale by certain persons under special rules of law, such as Receivers, Official Assignees or Receivers, Liquidators, Officials of Court, Executors and Administrators, (ix) under the implied authority of the owner.

Duties of Seller—The first duty of the seller is to deliver the goods. Delivery may be actual, symbolic, or constructive. Where goods are handed over by the seller to the buyer it is an actual delivery. Where goods are incapable of being handed over by one person to another a symbol indicating the title to the goods, e.g., the key of a warehouse containing the goods, may be given, and it will be symbolic delivery. Where delivery is given by attornment, i.e., a formal acknowledgment of the person who is in actual physical possession of the goods that he holds them on behalf and at the disposal of the buyer there is a constructive delivery.

The seller must deliver the goods according to the contract and where there is a condition precedent to the performance of the contract the seller need not deliver unless the condition is satisfied.

Unless otherwise agreed, delivery of the goods and payment of the price are on current conditions. The seller must be ready and willing to deliver the goods to the buyer and the buyer must be ready and willing to pay the price to the seller.

It is not the duty of the seller to send or carry the goods to the buyer unless the contract so provides; his only duty is to place the goods at the buyer's disposal. It is the buyer's duty to demand the delivery and accept it when tendered. But the goods must be in a deliverable state at the time of delivery or tender thereof.

Subject to the contract to the contrary, the goods must be delivered at the place at which they happen to be at the time of the contract of sale, or if the contract is with respect to future goods, at the place at which the goods are manufactured or produced. The seller bears the cost of delivery unless the contract otherwise provides.

Where the goods are delivered to a carrier the seller is bound to enter into a reasonable contract on behalf of the buyer with the carrier for safe transmission of the goods. In a transit by sea the seller must inform the buyer in time so that he may insure the goods.

Rights of Buyer—To have delivery as per contract. To get delivery of the goods of actual quantity contracted for. If the goods offered are in quantity more or less than that contracted for, or if, what is offered is mixed with goods of different description, the buyer has a right, subject to the usage of trade (i) to reject the goods, if less is delivered, (ii) to reject the excess or even the whole, if more is offered, and (iii) if the goods are mixed with others not ordered, to reject the whole or those not according to the contract.

If the contract is an instalment contract, and the terms of the contract permit, the buyer has a right to repudiate the whole contract, for any defect or non-delivery of any instalment and where he has accepted goods, to claim compensation.

Where the buyer has no opportunity to examine the goods beforehand, he has a right to a reasonable opportunity of examination of the goods for delivery.

The buyer has a right to sue for damages for breach of warranty or for non-delivery of the goods, or for interest. He may also sue for specific performance.

Duties of Buyer—To take delivery of the goods and pay for them. Also to pay any incidental charges for the care and custody by the seller if the goods are kept by him on behalf of the buyer.

Duties of Seller—Where the buyer wrongfully neglects or refuses to accept and pay for the goods, the seller has a right to sue for damages for non-acceptance of the goods.

Where property in goods has passed to the buyer, the seller has a right to sue for the price of the goods whether the possession is with the buyer or the seller. Even where ownership has not passed but the buyer has agreed to pay the price on a certain day fixed irrespective of his obtaining delivery of goods the seller may claim the price.

Rights of Unpaid Seller—The unpaid seller has a lien on the goods or any part of them remaining in his possession, or a right of stoppage in transit when the buyer becomes insolvent and the seller has parted with possession to the carrier and in certain circumstances he has the right to resell the goods. An unpaid seller in possession of goods may exercise his lien on the goods and refuse to deliver them to the buyer until the full payment or tender of the price, in case where (i) the goods have been sold without any stipulation as to credit, (ii) the goods have been sold on credit but term of credit has expired, (iii) the buyer becomes insolvent. The unpaid seller may exercise lien even when in possession as bailee for buyer.

The right of stoppage in transit is an extension of the right of lien, but it arises only on the insolvency of die buyer.

The right of stoppage in transit is a right possessed by an unpaid seller who has parted with the goods but the goods have not yet come into the possession of the buyer, to stop the goods in transit with a view to exercising his lien, if the buyer has become insolvent. The unpaid seller may re-sell the goods, (i) where the goods are perishable; (ii) where the right is expressly reserved in the contract; (iii) where in exercise of right of lien or stoppage in transit seller gives notice to the buyer of his intention to re-sell, the buyer does not pay or tender the price within a reasonable time.

CASES FOR RECAPITULATION

1. *L* was shopping in a self-service super market. He picked up a bottle of soft drinks from a shelf. While he was examining it, the bottle exploded in his hand and injured him. He sued the Aerated Drinks Co., which has bottled the drink, to recover damages for breach of condition arising from the sale of food. *Held, L* would not succeed. A warranty or condition does not arise unless there is a sale. No sale occurs when a customer in a self-service super market takes an article from a shelf since he may decide not to buy and pay for it and return it to the shelf. As there was not sale, there was no implied condition (*Lock* v. *Confair's Beverage Co.,* 366 Pa. 158).

2. The plaintiff, a housewife, ordered from the defendants, coal merchants, 'a ton of coalite' and it was duly delivered to her. When part of the consignment was put on fire in an open grate in the plaintiff's house an explosion occurred which caused damage. The plaintiff sued the defendants for damages. *Held,* the defendants were liable to pay damages; for there was a breach of the condition of merchantable quality. The goods were bought by description and defendants dealt in them, and there was an implied condition that 'coalite' was of merchantable quality. The explosion proved the breach of that condition [*Wilson* v. *Rickett, Cockerell & Co.* (1954) 1 All. E.R. 868].

3. On 6th May, *A* entered into a contract for the sale of 814 tins of Kerosene oil to *B*, and received ₹ 1,000 in part payment of the price. The goods were not with the seller at that time but had been dispatched from Calcutta on 25th April. *A* had received the R/R which he endorsed in favour of *B*. The goods never reached the destination, as they were burnt on or about 12th May while in transit. *Held,* the buyer has to bear the loss, as the property in the goods had passed to him and the seller could not be called upon to refund the price (*Shanker Doss* v. *Bhana Ram,* 1926 Lah. 406).

4. *P* sold barley to *B* by sample, delivery to be made at *T* railway station. *B* sold the barley to *X*. The barley was delivered at *T* railway station and *B*, after inspecting a sample of it, sent it on to *X*. *X* rejected it as not being according to sample. *B* seeks to reject the goods. *Held, B* cannot reject the barley. *B*'s action in inspecting a sample and then ordering the barley to be sent to *X* was an acceptance of the goods by him, and he could not afterwards reject the goods [*Perkins* v. *Bell* (1893) 1 Q.B. 193].

5. *B* bought a motor car at an auction sale conducted by *C*, an auctioneer. The car was sold on behalf of *A* who had no title to it, and the owner subsequently recovered it from *B*. *B* sues *C* for the return of the price. *Held, B* cannot recover, as he knew that *C* was an agent and the sale was of specific goods. It was stated that where an auctioneer, disclosing the fact that he is acting as an agent but not disclosing the name of the principal, sells specific goods, he does not warrant the goods or his principal's title to the goods [*Benton* v. *Cambell. Parker & Co. Ltd.* (1925) 2 K.B.410].

6. *A* bought from *B* a shipment of nuts, and *B* sent to *A* the bill of lading. *A* handed the bill of lading to *C* in return for a loan and then became insolvent. *B* attempted to stop the goods in transit, but *C* claimed them. *Held, C* had a good title to the goods, which defeated *B*'s right to stop the goods in transit [*Leask* v. *Scott. Bros.* (1877) 2 Q.B.D.376].

7. A manufacturer contracted to supply 30 tons of apple-juice in accordance with sample to a wine merchant, to be delivered in weekly truck-loads. He crushed the apples, put the juice in casks and kept it pending delivery. After 20 tons had been delivered, no further deliveries were made through the delay of the buyer in breach of the contract notwithstanding requests for delivery instructions from the seller, and ultimately the undelivered juice went putrid and had to be thrown away. *Held,* the juice was assembled by the seller for the purpose of fulfilling the contract and kept ready for delivery as and when the buyer proposed to take; after the delay, therefore, the juice was at the risk of buyer, who must suffer the loss [*Demby Hamilton Co. Ltd.* v. *Barden* (1949) 1 All. E.R.435].

8. *A* agreed to buy from *B* a car and pay ₹ 8,000 for it, if his solicitor approved. *A* took possession of the car and sold it to *C*. The solicitor subsequently disapproved of the transaction. *B* sued *C* for the

recovery of ₹ 8,000. *Held, B* cannot recover the price of the car. *C*, the *bonafide* buyer, got good title, for *A* "agreed to buy it". It was a sale by buyer in possession [*Martin* v. *Whale* (1917) 2 K.B. 480 C.A.].

9. *A*, a jeweller, was entrusted with a diamond by *P* with the instructions that *A* should obtain offers for it, and if any such offer was approved by *P*, *A* should sell it to the offerer. Acting contrary to *P*'s instructions, *A* sold the diamond to *S* who bought it in good faith. Thereafter *A* absconded with the price money. *P* sued to recover the diamond. *Held, P* cannot recover the diamond from *S* as the sale was made by *A*, the jeweller, as a mercantile agent in the ordinary course of his business, though contrary to *P*'s instructions [(1929) 3 Bom. L.R.].

10. *A* bought from *B* a second-hand refrigerator for ₹ 450 and' it was agreed between *A* and *B* that the refrigerator should be put in order at a cost of ₹ 320. *A* took delivery and admitted that its condition was satisfactory. Later, *A* reported to *B* that the refrigerator was not in working order and *B* took away two parts of it for repairs. The full bill for repairs had not, however, been paid and *B* claimed a lien on the two parts for the balance of the original cost of repairs and refused to return the same until he was paid the balance due for the repairs. *Held, B*'s refusal to return the two parts until payment of the balance for the repairs is not justified. He has no right of lien. The contract had been fully performed and the refrigerator was handed over once and the lien had ended. It did not revive when the seller undertook the work of repairing the two parts (*Edaljee* v. *Cafe Johan Bros.* 1943 Nag. 249).

11. *A* ordered a certain quantity of new red chillies and *B* sold to him goods said to answer to those described while they were in transit from Calcutta to Cuddalore. The Contract was c.i.f. and *A* paid for the goods on presentation of shipping documents. The goods were cleared at Cuddalore port by *A*'s clearing agents and railed to him to Alandur where he had his place of business. On inspection, the goods were found to be greatly deteriorated, white in colour and the seeds falling out *A* rejected the goods but retained them as security for the price already paid. *Held,* the contract was for the delivery of new chillies and the buyer could properly reject them as there was a breach of condition on the part of the sellers (*Muthu Kishan* v. *Madhavji Devi Chand,* 1953 Mad. 817). But after, rejection the buyer cannot retain the goods as security for the price already paid or otherwise in satisfaction of his claim for damages arising out of non-delivery. He can only charge the seller, in whom the goods revested after rejection for keeping the goods safely [*Lyton & Baker Ltd.* (1923) 1 K.B.685].

12. The plaintiff, who wished to buy a motor car, approached the defendants, a firm of motor car dealers, and told them that he wished to buy a car suitable for touring purposes. The defendants recommended a Bugatti Car and so he ordered an eight cylinder Bugatti car. The car was supplied with a guarantee which expressly excluded 'any other guarantee or warranty, statutory or otherwise.' The car was unsuitable for touring purposes and the plaintiff repudiated the contract and sued the defendants for recovery of the price. The defendants raised the defence of the exemption clause in the contract. *Held,* the plaintiff was entitled to reject the car and recover the price, as the car was not fit for the purpose for which it was bought; the exemption clause did not apply [*Baldry* v. *Marshall Ltd.* (1925) 1 K.B.260].

13. A contract was made for the sale of some china clay f .o.b. at Fowey. The buyer chartered a ship and gave notice to the sellers who delivered the clay on board at Fowey. The destination of the clay had never been communicated by the buyer to the sellers, but in fact it was carried to Glasgow. No bill of lading was signed and before the ship left the port the sellers heard of the insolvency of the buyer and gave notice stopping the goods. *Held,* the clay being in the possession of the master of the ship only as a carrier the transit was not at an end, and the notice to stop was given in time. It was observed by the Appeal Court that delivery of goods by the seller to the carrier, even though the carrier be nominated and hired by the buyer, its only constructive, not actual delivery to the buyer, inasmuch as the contract with a carrier to carry goods does not make the carrier the agent or servant of the person with whom he contracts. Till the goods are in actual possession of the buyer the transit is not at an end,

and it makes no difference that their ultimate destination has not been communicated by the buyer to seller [*In Exp Rosevear China Clay Co., Re Cock* (1879). 11 Ch D.560].

14. *X* sold copper to *Y* and sent him a bill of lading, endorsed in blank together with a draft for the price. *Y* was insolvent and did not accept the draft but handed the bill of lading to *Z*, in fulfilment of a contract for the sale of copper to him. *Z* paid for the copper and took the bill of lading without notice of *X*'s right as unpaid seller. *X* stopped the copper in transit. *Held*, *Z* can sue the carrier for non-delivery, as the seller had lost his right of stopping the goods in-transit. An unpaid seller's right of stoppage in transit is defeated against a transferee who takes in good faith and for consideration [*Cahn* v. *Pockett's, etc., Co.* (1899) 1 Q.B. 643].

15. *X*, a dealer in cattle food, sold to *Y*, another such dealer, 15,000 tons of meat and bone meal of a specified quality to be shipped 1,250 tons monthly in equal instalments. After about half the meal was delivered and paid for, it was found that it was not of the contract quality, and *Y* refused to take further delivery. *Held*, *Y* was entitled to refuse to take further delivery, as he was not bound to take the risk of having put upon him further deliveries of goods which did not conform to the contract [*Robert A. Munro & Co.* v. *Meyer* (1903) 2 K.B. 312].

16. *A* sells and consigns to *B* goods of the value of ₹ 12,000. *B* assigns the railway receipt to *C* to secure a specific advance of ₹5,000 on the railway receipt. Before the goods reach the destination *B* becomes insolvent being indebted to *C* for ₹ 9,000. *A* gives notice to stop the goods in transit *A* can stop the goods in transit but subject to the pledge of *C*. Since the pledge was to secure a specific advance of ₹ 5,000, *C* can recover that amount from the goods or from *A*. *A* will have to pay ₹ 5,000 to *C* and can rank as creditor of *B* in insolvency, *C* will rank as creditor as to ₹ 4,000.

17. There was a sale by sample of mixed worsted coatings to be in quality and weight equal to the samples. It is found that the goods owing to a latent defect will not stand ordinary wear when made up into coats. The same defect appeared in the sample but could not be detected. *Held*, the buyer can reject the goods as the defects in the cloth were not discoverable by the ordinary inspection [*Drummond* v. *Van Ingen* (1877) 2 App. Ces.248].

18. A firm of confectioners' materials agreed to sell condensed milk in tins of a certain standard to *N* who received the shipping documents and paid the price. The goods arrived bearing a brand which was an infringement of a registered trade mark of another manufacturer and were, therefore, detained by the customs authorities. *Held*, the sellers had broken the implied condition relating to title to the goods. As the sellers had no right to sell these goods, the buyer could get back the price and sue for damages [*Niblett* v. *Confectioners' Material Co. Ltd.* (1921) 3 K.B. 387],

19. *M* made a hire-purchase agreement with *N* for a motor-car of which *N* was described as the owner. *M* paid four of the twelve monthly instalments and then learnt that *X* claimed to be the owner of the car. He nevertheless paid the balance of instalment and exercised his option to purchase. *X* then demanded the car and *M* gave it up to him. *M* then sued *N* to recover the full price and *N*-counter claimed for a reasonable sum as hiring charges for the car during the period it was with *M*. *Held*, *M* was entitled to recover the full price paid by him to *N*, but *N* could not get anything. There was a breach of condition of title treated as a breach of warranty and so *M* could get back the amount paid by him. But *N* could not get anything because there was a total failure of consideration for which, had he been so minded, *M* could have sued in quasi-contract and which prevented *N* from recovering any sum of money whether under the hire-pur-chase contract or by way of *quantum meruit* [*Warman* v. *Southern Countries Car Finance Corp. Ltd.* (1949) 2 K.B. 576].

20. *R* bought a radio set from *B*, the local distributor of HGE Ltd., for ₹ 675 with a one-year guarantee of satisfactory service. The radio set proved defective from the very beginning and had to be repaired by the local distributor twice and once by the manufacturers. But it was not found satisfactory. *R* claims refund of its price. *Held*, *R*'s claim carte under the purview of exception (1) and

(2) of Sec. 16 of the Sale of Goods Act, and he is entitled to refund of the price. The radio was not of merchantable quality nor was it fit for the purpose, *i.e.*, as a radio set (*Ranbir Singh* v. *Hindustan General Electric Corp. Ltd.* 1971 Bom. 97).

21. *H* let a piano on hire to *B* on the following terms: *B* was to pay 10 S.o.d. every month; on payment promptly of 36 monthly instalments the piano should become his property. *B* had the right to terminate the hire any time by returning the piano to *H*. Held by the House of Lords, that *B* was in possession under a hire-purchase agreement and not under an agreement to buy (*Helby* v. *Mathews* (1983) A.C. 471).

22. *M* entered into a contract for supply of tents to Director General of Supplies and Disposals. The goods were to be inspected at premises of the supplier and the same being passed by the Inspector, the goods were to be despatched by railway to the consignee. The term of delivery was F.O.R. place of despatch. One of the consignments of 1500 tents was despatched to the consignee under Railway Receipt. The consignee reported that 224 tents out of the said consignment had not been received at the destination. The consignee deducted the price of 224 tents from the other bills of the consignor. It was held by the Supreme Court that the consignee had no right to deduct the price because as soon as the goods were loaded in the railway wagons at the place of despatch as per the terms of delivery, the property in goods together with risk passed from the seller to the buyer. The consignee was liable to bear the loss and not the seller .(*M/s Marwar Tent Factory* v. *Union of India*, 1990 S.C. 1808).

CHAPTER 7

Insurance

In business, as in private life, there are dangers and risks of every kind. The aim of all insurance is to make provision against such dangers which beset human life and dealing. He who seeks safety, called the insured or assured, pays a certain sum, called the premium, to the insurer or underwriter who, in consideration of this premium, takes upon himself the risk insured against and undertakes to make good to the assured any loss which he may sustain by reason of the named peril.

The risks which may be insured against include fire, the perils of the sea (marine insurance), death (life insurance) and accidents and burglary. In fact, nowadays the happening of practically any event may be insured against at a premium commensurate with the risk involved.

NATURE OF THE CONTRACT OF INSURANCE

The contract of insurance is called an aleatory contract because it depends upon an uncertain event. If such a thing happens, e.g., if the house is burnt down or the ship is stranded, the insurer will pay the value of it. At first sight this would seem to be a wagering transaction, the insurer betting with the assured that his house will not be burnt or his ship will not sink and giving him the odds of its value against the premium. It is because of this uncertainty that Lord Mansfield[1] described insurance as "a contract on speculation." But the modern view is that insurance contracts are not speculative or wagering contracts. Insurance is not merely a gamble on an uncertain future. In reality, a contract of insurance is a perfectly valid contract; for the assured is only indemnified for his loss, and he does not gain by the happening of the event insured against; he does not make a profit of his loss. Moreover, the assured must have an insurable interest in the subject-matter insured; while in a wager no insurable interest is present. Therefore, although it is an aleatory contract, depending upon an uncertain event, it is not a wagering or a speculative contract nor is it merely a gamble on an uncertain event.

FUNDAMENTAL PRINCIPLES OF INSURANCE

Insurance transactions are conducted upon principles which on examination prove simple and almost self-evident, yet they are constantly being invoked, and we must, never lose sight of them. These principles are common to all types of insurance including life assurance, excepting the principle of indemnity which does not apply to life assurance. These principles are (i) good faith, (ii) insurable interest (iii) indemnity, (iv) mitigation of loss, (v) attachment of risk, (vi) causa proximo.

GOOD FAITH

A contract of insurance is a contract uberrimae fidei, a contract based on utmost good faith and if the utmost good faith is not observed by either party the contract may be avoided by the other. Since

---

1. Carter v. Bochm (1765) Sm. L.C. 546.

insurance shifts risks from one party to another, it is essential that there must be the utmost good faith and frankness between the insured and insurer; the whole truth must be told about the subject-matter of insurance and all circum-stances surrounding it, in order that the underwriter may know the extent of his risk and how much he must charge for the insurance of it. The wilful or innocent withholding of any relevant information is a most serious matter, and the underwriter can declare the contract void on discovering it. The obligation to make a full and true disclosure applies to all types of insurance. The duty to disclose continues up to the conclusion of the contract and covers any material alteration in the character of the risk which may take place between proposal and acceptance.[2] Fraud invalidates the insurance, and deprives the party committing it of all his rights arising out of the contract. Concealment or misrepresentation of material facts is fatal to the contract; but in the case of innocent misrepresentation the premium is returnable on the avoidance of the policy. Non-disclosure of a fact of which the assured was ignorant is not fatal to the contract. He need not mention what the insurers know. In India, the doctrine of utmost good faith is subject to the provisions of Sec. 45 of the Insurance Act, 1938.

INSURABLE INTEREST

The second principle is that the assured must have an actual interest called the insurable interest, in the subject-matter of the insurance; either he must own part or whole of it, or he must be in such a position that injury to it would affect him adversely. He must be "so situated with regard to the thing insured that he would have benefit by its existence, loss from its destruction."[3] Any person may be said to have an interest in the subject-matter of insurance who may be injured by the risks to which the subject-matter is exposed, or would but for those risks have a certainty of advantage. To illustrate this point we may take an example from marine insurance. The owner of a ship runs a risk of losing his ship, the charterer of the ship runs a risk of losing his freight, and the owner of the cargo of losing his goods and profit. All these persons are interested because they all run a risk, have something at stake, something to lose by the happening of the peril insured against. *It is the existence of insurable interest in a contract of insurance that differentiates and distinguishes it from a mere wager or a gaming contract.* But it is essential that the insurable interest must be actual and real and not a mere expectation or an anxiety. It must be pecuniary interest; a purely sentimental interest would not be enough. A contract of insurance effected without insurable interest is void.

INDEMNITY

The third fundamental principle is that excepting life assurance and personal accident and sickness insurance, a contract of insurance contained in a fire, marine, burglary or any other policy is a contract of indemnity. This means that the assured in the case of loss against which the policy has been made shall be fully indemnified but never more than fully indemnified. Thus, the insurer does not agree to pay a specific sum on a certain contingency but undertakes to indemnify the insured what he actually loses by the happening of the event upon which the insurer's liability is to arise, and in no case is the insured entitled to make a profit of his loss. If the house is burnt down, the insurer will pay the value of it. At first sight this might appear to be a wagering transaction, the insurer betting with the insured that his house will not be burnt down and giving him the odds of its value against the premium. But so long as the insured is only indemnified for the loss and does not make any gain by the happening of

2. See Vijayakumar v. New Zealand Ins. Co. 1954 Bom.347; Seethamma v. Bombay Life Ass. Co., 1954 Mys. 134; Kolhatkar v. W.I.L.I. Co., 1954 Nag. 325; V.K.S. Selly v. P.L. & G. Ins. Co. 1958 Mys. 53; Rattan Lal v. Metropolitan Ins. Co. 1959 Pat. 413; Looker v. Law Union and Lock Ins. Co. (1928) 1, K.B. 554; Rohni Goswami v. Ocean Accident & Guarantee Corporation Ltd. (1961) 31 Camp. Cas. 17.

3. Lucena v. Crawford (1806) 1 Taunt, 325, per Lawrence J.

the event insured against, the contract is valid. *A contract of insurance, however, ceases to be a contract of indemnity if the insurer promises to pay a fixed sum on the happening of the event insured against whether the assured has suffered any loss or not.* From their very nature contracts of life and accident insurance belong to this class and in their case indemnity is not the governing principle. In these cases, the value of the peril insured against cannot be appraised in money, and therefore, the injury or death cannot really be indemnified. Even contracts of fire or burglary insurance need not necessarily be contracts of indemnity. If the insurer agrees to pay a certain fixed sum irrespective of loss, the contract is not one of indemnity. An insurance was against loss of certain specified articles including a pearl necklace, and the necklace disappeared. The insurer under agreement with the insured gave him some other articles to take its place. The necklace was later found. The Court held that the insured could retain the articles supplied by the insurance company.

MITIGATION OF LOSS

The next essential principle is that, in the event of some mishap to the insured property, the owner (the insured) must act as though he were uninsured, and make every effort to preserve his property. He must take such steps to this end as he considers prudent, and should his property be touched by peril he must do everything in his power to minimise the loss and to save what is left. In a word, he must act as a prudent uninsured person would do in similar circumstances. But it must be remembered in this connection that though a man is bound to do his best for his insurer, he is not bound to do it at his own peril. So, if reasonable effort was made and precaution taken to save the property, the insurer will be liable for all loss resulting from the peril insured against.

RISK MUST ATTACH

The next principle is that a contract of insurance can be enforced only if the risk has attached. If the risk is not run the consideration fails, and therefore the premium received by the insurer must be returned. It is so even where the cause of the risk being not run is the fault, will or pleasure of the assured. The underwriter receives a premium for running the risk of indemnifying the assured, and if he does not run the risk, the consideration for which the premium was put into his hands fails and therefore he must return it.[4] While a policy does not attach till the risk begins, it can equally not attach after the risk is determined one way or other, except in those special insurances where both parties being ignorant of the position of the thing insured, contract to insure it lost or not lost.[5]

CAUSA PROXIMA

The last principle is that in order to make the insurer liable for loss, such loss must have been proximately caused by the peril insured against. "Every loss that clearly and proximately results, whether directly or indirectly, from the event insured against is within the policy."[6] The maxim in *causa proximo non remota spectatur, i.e.,* the proximate and not the remote cause is to be looked to, and if the cause of the loss is a peril insured against the assured can recover. "The question, which is the *causa proximo* of a loss, can only arise where there has been a succession of causes. When a result has been brought about by two causes, you must in.... insurance law, look to the nearest cause, although the result would, no doubt, not have happened without the remote cause."[7] In this case the peril insured against was collision with another ship, resulting in delay and mishandling of cargo of oranges

---

4. Tyrie v. Fletcher (1777) 99 E.R. 1997.
5. Picard, *Elements of Insurance Law,* p. 3.
6. Stanley v. Western Ins. Co. (1886), 3 E.X. at 74, per Kelly, C.B.
7. Pink v. Fleming (1899) 25 Q.B.D.396, per Lord Esher, M.R.

which deteriorated. The Master of the Rolls held that the damage to oranges was not direct result of collision, but of delay and mishandling and as these causes were not insured against the insured could not recover. "The law will not allow the assured to go back in the succession of causes to find out what is the original cause of loss."[8] The last or the effective of the causes is to be looked into and others rejected.

CONTRACT OF INSURANCE ONE FROM YEAR TO YEAR

The general rule is that except in the case of life assurance a contract of insurance is a contract from year to year only, and the insurance automatically comes to an end after the expiry of the year; but it can be continued for a further period, if before the expiry of the year, the insured expresses his intention to continue and pays the premium. A contract of life assurance is not a contract for a year only, but is a continuing contract with a provision that if premium is not paid every year at or about the specified time the contract would lapse. This distinction is of great importance with regard to the duty of disclosure and the operation of conditions subsequent to the assignment of the policy or its proceeds, and days of grace.

PREMIUM

The premium is the price for the risk undertaken by the insurer. It is the consideration for the insurance. The premium need not always be a money payment, although in majority of cases it is so. Any consideration sufficient for a simple contract may become the premium in a contract of insurance. For example, in the case of mutual insurance, it consists of a liability to contribute to the losses of other members of the mutual society.

The rate of premium is based upon the average of losses as compared with profits. All circumstances affecting the risk like locality, the construction and use of the property, are taken into consideration. In life assurance, the premium is calculated on the average rate of mortality and a premium which on that ordinary average will prevent the insurance company from being the loser is charged. Over and above estimates and averages the premium includes an additional sum for office expenses and other charges. The amount of the premium may not always be a fixed sum, for it may be arranged to vary according to the changes in the risk at any time. We have observed before that payment of the premium constitutes, in most cases, a condition precedent to the creation of a binding contract of insurance. Though pre-payment of the premium is not a condition implied in law a precedent to the liability of die insurer, it is the general practice of the insurance companies. In such cases unless the premium has been paid, the contract will not be effective even after an agreement to issue and accept a policy.

DAYS OF GRACE

The days of grace are the days allowed by the insurance company after the expiry of the stipulated period of insurance during which the assured can pay the premium in order to continue or to renew the policy of insurance. If the contract of insurance is only for a year, the days of grace are meant to afford to the assured an additional opportunity of renewing the contract and not of continuing it. So, if the insured has not agreed before the year is over to renew the contract, and the loss happens during the days of grace, the company is not liable. Also in insurances where the insurer reserves the option to renew the risk, the insured is not covered during the days of grace if the renewal premiums remain unpaid, *i.e.* before" it is tendered and accepted. If therefore before the expiration of the year the company gives notice to the insured that unless an increased premium is paid the insurance would not be renewed and if the insurer refuses to pay, the company is not liable on the destruction by fire of the

---

8. *Ibid.*

premises of the assured after the expiration of the year but within the days of grace. In the case of contract of life insurance, on the other hand, the insurers have no option but to continue the policy on the payment of the premium every year, as the policy creates a continuing risk. On the non-payment of the premium the policy merely lapses. If, therefore, death occurs during the days of grace without the payment of the premium, the money due under the policy becomes payable.

RETURN OF PREMIUM

We have seen above that premium is the consideration for the risk run by the insurers, and if the risk insured against is not run, then the consideration fails, the policy does not attach, and as a consequence the premium paid can be recovered from the insurers. The general principle applicable to the claim for the return of premium is that if the insurers have never been on the risk, they cannot be said to have earned the premium. The risk is never run where before the policy comes into force the subject-matter of insurance ceases to exists or where it is wrongly described, or where the assured had never any insurable interest in the subject-matter, or where the policy issued is *ultra vires* the company, or where the policy is void on account of some illegality, or where the policy is void on account of some breach of a condition precedent. But where the insurance is avoided by the insurers on the ground of breach of warranty the premium 'can only be recovered if it is shown that there was breach *ab initio*. Where, however, the risk has begun to run no matter for how short a period, the premium cannot be recovered; and so a breach of condition subsequent is no ground for ordering the return of the premium, as the risk has once attached. Where the value of the interest insured turns out in fact to be less than the amount insured, a proportionate part of the premium must be returned, for the insurers have only been liable to indemnify the assured and in the event of a loss would only have paid the actual value of the subject-matter destroyed. Therefore, the insurance has not really attached in respect of the amount over-insured and a proportionate part of the, premium has never been earned by the insurers. The over-in-surance must be made in good faith otherwise no portion of the premium would be returned. This does not, however, mean that the risk which has begun to run can be apportioned and a proportionate premium returned unless the risk is divisible, and has attached only to some separable part of the subject-matter.

POLICY

The policy is a formal and enforceable stamped document signed and issued by the insurance company embodying the terms of the contract between the parties. Although it is a universal practice of insurance companies to issue policies, yet, except in marine insurance, there is no rule of law requiring the issuing of a policy or its being in any particular form. A policy is only a documentary evidence of a contract of insurance between the parties, and neither law nor custom disfavours oral evidence to prove the terms of the contract of insurance. The existence of a policy, therefore, is not necessary for the validity of a contract of insurance, other than marine insurance. A contract of marine insurance shall not be valid unless it is expressed, in a Sea or Marine Policy.

The articles of association of every insurance company usually provide the mode in which the company is to be bound, and policies must be issued in accordance with the provisions contained therein, before the assured can sue on the insurance. But where there is a clear proof of agreement to insure, the Court will order the company to issue a policy in accordance with such agreement. No company whose business is confined to certain classes of risk, can issue a valid policy not covering such risk. All insurance policies must be stamped. A policy is a unilateral document and the assured is no party to it. It is issued by the insurers and bears the seal of the company, and is signed by certain responsible officers of the company. It does not purport to be signed by or on behalf of the insured. But the assured can enforce his right under it, if he has done everything required of him, and he is also bound by it. If a condition appears for the first time in the policy which was neither contemplated nor agreed upon between the parties, the assured is not bound by the contract, unless he accepts this condition. Delivery of the policy to the assured is not essential to make a binding contract; and the risk will attach where no policy is delivered, if the contract is otherwise complete and the first premium has been paid. When the policy is under the seal of the company, it becomes operative from the time it is formally 'signed', sealed and delivered to the assured or his agent. The policy when issued is the property of the assured even though it may be retained by the insurers for convenience only, for "there is no duty on the part of an insurer to get the policy of insurance into the physical possession of the assured." And mere delivery to die assured does not amount to an acceptance by him of the terms of the contract. Further, as the delivery of the policy is not a necessary condition to the attaching of the risk, similarly, its production is not a condition precedent to the payment of the money due under it. Its non-production may be explained by showing that the policy is lost or it is in the hands of a person who does not part with it.

INTERIM RECEIPT, CERTIFICATE OR COVER NOTE

A cover note or interim certificate is a document which the insurance company, on receiving the proposal, may issue pending the execution of a policy or the final decision of the directors as to acceptance or rejection of the proposal. It acknowledges receipt of premium and forms a binding contract of insurance during the interval between the proposal and the final acceptance or rejection by the insurers. The practice of issuing cover notes is very common in fire, burglary or accident insurance business.

RE-INSURANCE

Every insurance company has a limit to the risk it is willing to undertake in respect of an individual policy. Thus, if an insurance company finds that it has entered into an insurance contract which is an expensive proposition for it or if it wishes to minimise the chances of any possible loss, without, at the same time, giving up the contract, it will re-insure a portion of the risk with some other insurance company or companies. This device is known as re-insurance. Suppose a man wishing to insure his house for ₹ 50,000 goes to an insurance company, which will accept the risk if it is satisfied as to the condition of the property. But if its own limit is probably ₹ 25,000, it will arrange with another company to re-insure or take up so much of the risk as exceeds its limit, i.e., ₹ 25,000, so that if the house is burnt down the original insurers would pay the owner ₹ 50,000, but they would be recouped ₹ 25,000 by the re-insurance office. Re-insurance can be resorted to in all kinds of insurance. Re-insurance is a contract which insures the thing originally insured, and by which an insurer is to be indemnified against any loss which he may sustain by reason of being himself compelled to pay the assured under the original contract of insurance. A contract of insurance creates in the insurers an insurable interest sufficient to support are insurance to the full amount of their liability on the original policy. But a contract of re-insurance is always a contract of indemnity. Hence the re-insurers before paying money must be satisfied that the sum originally insured has been paid by the re-insured.

The re-insurance is subject to the clauses and conditions in the original policy, and is also entitled to any benefits which the original insurance policy is entitled to. If the original contract is altered without the consent or knowledge of the re-insurers, the re-insurers are discharged. As a policy of re-insurance is co-extensive with the original policy, the former cannot remain in force for a period exceeding the duration of the original policy. If, therefore, the original policy lapses or the insurance comes to an end for any other reason the re-insurance policy also ceases to exist automatically from that date. Just as in the case of an insurance so in a re-insurance the parties must show the utmost good faith. If information possessed by re-insured and material to the risk be not communicated to the re-insurer the policy of re-insurance will be void. The re-insured must inform the re-insurer not only all the facts disclosed to him by his assured, but also such facts as he learned subsequent to the original contract. A re-insured being himself an assured, is required not only before, but after the contract comes into force, to act with the greatest good faith. Though misrepresentation or non-disclosure of a material fact by the re-insured will avoid the policy, yet representation as to the nature of the risk will not help the re-insurer who has formed his own judgment of the nature of the risk. Re-insurers are entitled to be subrogated to all the rights of the original insurers including the right of the insured to which the original insurers are subrogated.[9]

DOUBLE INSURANCE

When the same subject-matter is insured with two or more insurers and the total sum insured exceeds the actual value of the subject-matter, it is known as double insurance and it amounts to over-insurance. As stated in Sec. 34 of the Marine Insurance Act, over-insurance and double insurance are valid unless the policy otherwise provides. For example, if A insures his factory worth ₹ 1 lakh with three insurers as: with X for ₹ 40,000, with Y for ₹ 35,000 and with Z for ₹ 50,000, there is double insurance because the aggregate of all the policies exceeds the total value of A's factory. If A insures with X for ₹ 40,000, with Y for ₹ 30,000 and with Z for ₹ 30,000 there is no double insurance.

In case of loss, the assured may claim payment from the insurers in such order as he thinks fit, but he will not get more than his actual loss, as each contract of insurance is a contract of indemnity. The advantage of double insurance is that it protects him against loss in the event of one or more of the insurers becoming insolvent, he can recover up to the value of the policy from the solvent insurer. The insurers as between themselves are liable to contribute to the loss in proportion to the amount for which each one is liable. Note, there is no double insurance in case of life insurance. Human life is priceless and a person can get his life insured with as many insurers as he likes; life insurance is not a contract of indemnity. In India, Life Insurance Corporation of India being the only insurer of life there is no question of double insurance of life.

PART 7-B
SUBROGATION AND CONTRIBUTION IN FIRE AND MARINE INSURANCE

SUBROGATION

As observed before, the essence of fire and marine insurance is indemnity, which means that the assured shall be fully indemnified. He is not to make a "profit of his loss" and it is this rule that gives rise to the doctrine of subrogation. **The right of subrogation is a necessary corollary of the principle of indemnity and is essential for its preservation.** It is inherent in and springs from the principle of indemnity and the basis of the right is justice, equity and good conscience so that the insurer may reduce the extent of his liability within limits.[10] If the assured recovers the full extent of the loss from the insurer and then he gets compensation from third parties in respect of the same loss, the assured would be more than fully indemnified and the whole doctrine of indemnity would be done away with.[11] Subrogation is the substitution of one person in place of another in relation to the claim, its rights, remedies or securities. The doctrine is applicable to both fire and marine insurance, by which, on indemnifying the insured for his loss, "the underwriter is entitled to the advantage of every right of the assured, whether such right consists in contract or in remedy for tort or in any other right." Having satisfied the claim of the assured, the insurers stand in his place; they are subrogated to all his rights, and if he also receives compensation from some other person in respect of the same loss he must pay

---

9. Assicurasioni, etc. v. Empress Ass. Corp. (1907) 2 K.B. 814.

10. Vasudeva v. Caledonian Ins. Co., 1965 Mad. 159.

11. North England Iron Steamship Ins. Asson. v. Armstrong (1879) 30 L.J. Q.B. 81; John Edward & Co. v. Motor Union Ins. Co. (1922) 2 K.B. 249.

over that amount to the insurers. He cannot take with both hands. To illustrate the doctrine, we may give the facts of the case *Castellain* v. *Preston*.[12]

A vendor contracted with a purchaser for the sale of a house which had been insured against fire by the vendor. There was no mention of the insurance in the contract of sale. A fortnight later the house was damaged by fire and the vendor received £ 330 under his policy. Subsequently the purchase was completed and the purchase money agreed upon paid without any deduction of the sum received by the vendor from the insurers. *Held,* in an action by the insurance company against the vendor that the insurers were entitled to recover a sum equal to the insurance money.

In another case, a ship is posted at Lloyd's as "missing" and the underwriter on her hull pays a total loss. If the vessel should subsequently arrive, she is then the property of the underwriter.[13] Or, where goods are jettisoned for the general safety, the under-writer on payment for a total loss of the jettisoned goods, stands in the place of the assured and is entitled to general average compensation for the jettison.[14] The insurers, however, have only the rights which the insured himself has; for, in the words of Lord Cairns, "the right of the underwriters is merely to make such claim for damages as the assured himself could have made and ...it cannot of course be made against the assured himself."

In *Simpson* v. *Thompson,*[15] two ships *A* and *B* belonging to the same owner came into collision. The insurers of the ship *A* indemnified the owner and then sued him as owner of the ship *B* for negligence, claiming the amount they had paid in respect of ship *A*. *Held,* they could not recover, as both vessels were owned by one and the same person, no remedy had been transferred to the underwriter, inasmuch as a person cannot sue himself.

The insurers having contracted to indemnify, they cannot insist on others being sued first, though after having indemnified the assured, the underwriters stand in his place and can enforce whatever rights to contribution or damages the assured was entitled to.[16] The result is that the owner has two remedies and he may avail himself of which he pleases, though he cannot retain the proceeds of both, so as to be repaid the value of his loss twice over.

CONTRIBUTION

Contribution is the right of the insurers to claim from others some payment towards the loss, and arises only where there is double insurance, *i.e.,* where two or more policies have been taken out the total amount whereof exceeds the total value of the loss suffered. Remember, it takes place where different insurers insure the same interest in respect of the same property and the same perils. It resembles the remedies between co-sureties whereby the liability of each may be made proportionate. As the contract of insurance is a contract of indemnity, the assured cannot get more than the actual value of the property or the amount of the loss. The insurer is only entitled to contribution where he has paid the assured. The assured may sue all insurers together, or provided the policy is not subject to average, he may recover the whole amount of damages from one and let that one seek contribution of the amount paid by him in excess of ratable proportion of loss. Ratable proportion is such a proportion of the loss as the amount of the policy or item under which loss occurs bears to the total insurance under the same heading. Thus, if *A* insured his house with *B* company for ₹ 20,000, and with *C* company for ₹ 10,000 and the house is damaged to the extent of ₹ 6,000, *A* may sue *B* company and

---

12. Castellain v. Preston (1883) H.Q.B.D. 38 at p. 38, per Brett L.J.

13. Houstman v. Thomton (1810) Holt N. 242.

14. Dickinson v. Jardine (1866) LR. 3 C.P. 639.

15. (1877)3A.C.279.

16. Dickinson v. Jardine, *Ibid.*

recover the entire sum of ₹ 6,000 from it. *B* company can then sue *C* company for contribution. The loss will be divided ratably as follows:-

$$\text{B Company } \frac{20,000}{30,000} \text{ of } 6,000 = ₹ \, 4,000$$

$$\text{C Company } \frac{10,000}{30,000} \text{ of } 6,000 = ₹ \, 2,000$$

But the interest insured must be the same; if not, the insurers of the person who would have been liable if no insurance whatsoever had -been effected will have to bear the loss. Thus in-

North British and Mercantile Co. v. London, Liverpool and Globe Ins. Co. (1877) 5 Ch. D. 569, goods were burnt whilst in a warehouse. The merchant had insured the goods and the wharfinger had also done so to cover his common Law liability. The merchant's insurers having paid the loss sued the wharfinger's insurers. *Held,* that the merchant's insurers could recover the whole amount of the loss as this was a case of subrogation and not contribution, since each insurer represents his assured and the right of the bailor against the bailee is not to contribution merely, but to complete indemnity.

DISTINCTION BETWEEN SUBROGATION AND CONTRIBUTION

1. Contribution implies more than one contract of insurance each of which under-takes a similar, if not identical, liability in respect of the same subject-matter and the same interest therein. Subrogation does not imply more than one insurance.
2. The object of contribution is to distribute the actual loss in such a way that each bears his proper share. No one insurer is more liable than any other, no more than the whole loss can be recovered. In case of subrogation, the object is substitution of one person in place of another so that the one who is substituted succeeds to the rights and remedies of another person.
3. In contribution, the insurer, after making payment to the assured, recovers the amount that he has paid in excess of his share from other insurers. In subrogation, after satisfying the claim, the insurer stands in the place of the assured. He may recover from a third party who would have been liable to pay had there been no insurance.

"For subrogation to arise, the assured must have concurrent remedies against the person causing the loss and against the insurer. There need not be more than one policy nor need that offer complete indemnity. All that is necessary is that there should be, besides the insurer, another person liable to the insured, or other means of indemnity open to the assured other than and besides recourse to the insured... In subrogation the aim is to shift the loss on him who would have been liable if there had been no insurance; in contribution the aim is to spread the loss equitably amongst the different underwriters who have insured the same interest."[17]

---

17. *Porter's Laws of Insurance,* 8th ed., p. 251.

CHAPTER 8

Marine Insurance

MARINE INSURANCE

The law relating to marine insurance is now found in the Marine Insurance Act, 1963, and references in this section are to that Act, unless the contrary is expressed.

A contract of marine insurance is an agreement whereby the insurer undertakes to indemnify the assured, in the manner and to the extent thereby agreed, against marine losses, that is to say, the losses incidental to marine adventure (Sec. 3). There is a marine adventure when (1) any insurable property is exposed to maritime perils; (2) the earnings or acquisition of any freight, passage money, commission, profit or other pecuniary benefit, or the security for any advances, loans, or disbursements is endangered by the exposure of insurable property to maritime perils; (3) any liability to a third party may be insured by the owner of, or other person interested in or responsible for, insurable property by reason of maritime perils [Sec. 2(d)].

Maritime Perils (sometimes called Perils of the Seas) means the perils consequent on, or incidental to, the navigation of the sea, that is to say, perils of the seas, fire, war perils, pirates, rovers, thieves, captures, seizures, restraints and detainments of princes and peoples, jettisons, barratry and any other perils which are either of the like kind or may be designed by the policy [Sec. 2(e)]. The term "perils of the seas" refers only to fortuitous accidents or casualties of the sea, and does not include the ordinary action of the winds and waves.

THE POLICY

A contract of marine insurance must be embodied in a marine policy which may be executed and issued either at the time of the conclusion of the contract or, as is generally the case, afterwards by initialling of the slip by the insurer or underwriter.(Sec. 24). According to Sec. 25, a marine policy must specify—

1. the name of the assured or of some person who effects the insurance on his behalf;
2. the subject-matter insured and the risk insured against;
3. the voyage, or period of time, or both, as the case may be, covered by the insurance;
4. the sum or sums insured;
5. the name or names of the insurer or insurers.

A marine policy must be signed by or on behalf of the insurer; and where a policy is subscribed by or on behalf of the two or more insurers, each subscription, unless the contrary be expressed, constitutes a distinct contract with the assured. The subject-matter insured must be designated in a marine policy with reasonable certainty.

TYPES OF POLICIES

Marine policies are of different kinds and are known by different names according to the manner of their execution or the risk they cover.

VOYAGE POLICY

Where the contract is to insure the subject-matter "at and from" or from one place to another or others, the policy is called a voyage policy. Where the subject-matter is insured "from" a particular place, the risk attaches only when the ship starts on the voyage insured (i.e., as soon as it leaves the port of commencement) and ends as soon as the ship enters the port of destination. Where the ship is insured "at and from" a particular place, and she is at that place in good safety when the contract is concluded, the risk attaches immediately; and if she be not at that place when the contract is concluded, the risk attaches as soon she arrives there in good safety.

TIME POLICY

Where the contract is to insure the subject-matter for a definite period of time, the policy is called a time policy, e.g., from noon January 1,1976 to noon January 1,1977. No time policy can be made for a period exceeding twelve months, and if it is so made, it shall be invalid (Sec. 27). In a time policy the subject-matter is covered during the period of insurance no matter where the ship is and how many voyages it makes. A contract for both voyage and time may be included in the same policy.

VALUED POLICY

A valued policy is a policy which specifies the agreed value of the subject-matter insured. In the absence of fraud, this value is conclusive as between the insurer and the assured, whether the loss be partial or total; but it is not conclusive in determining whether there has been a constructive total loss (Sec. 29).

UNVALUED POLICY

An unvalued policy is a policy which does not specify the value of the matter insured, but subject to the limit of the sum insured, leaves the insurable value to be subsequently ascertained (Sec. 30). The insurable value is ascertained as follows:—

1. In insurance on ship, the insurable value is the value, at the commencement of the risk, of the ship, including her outfit, provisions and stores for the officers and crew, money advanced for seamen's wages, and other disbursements incurred to make the ship fit for the voyage or adventure contemplated by the policy, plus the charges of insurance upon the whole. In the case of a steamship, the insurable value includes also the machinery, boilers, and coals and engine stores owned by the assured.

2. In insurance on freight, the insurable value is the gross amount of the freight at the risk of the assured, plus the charges of insurance.

3. In insurance on goods or merchandise, the insurable value is the prime cost of the property insured, plus the expenses of and incidental to shipping and the charges of insurance upon the whole.

4. In insurance on any other subject-matter, the insurable value is the amount at the risk of the assured when the policy attaches, plus the charges of insurance (Sec. 18).

FLOATING POLICY

A floating policy is a policy which describes the insurance in general terms, and leaves the name or names of the ship or ships and other particulars to be defined by subsequent declaration. The subsequent declarations may be made by endorsement on the policy, or in any other customary manner, and must be made in order of shipment. They must, in the case of goods, comprise all consignments within the terms of the policy, and the value of the goods, or other property must be honestly stated. If the value is not stated until after notice of loss or arrival, the policy must be treated as an unvalued policy as regards the subject-matter of that declaration (Sec. 31).

WAGER OR HONOUR POLICY

It is a policy in which the assured has no insurable interest or the insurer or underwriter is willing to dispense with the proof of interest. If the property contains such words as "Policy Proof of Interest". — "P.P.I.", or "Interest or No Interest" or "Interest Admitted" or "Without Benefit of Salvage to the Insurer" or any other words to that effect, it is unenforceable at law, being a "Wagering Contract". Although valueless in a Court of law, such policies continue to be common, the assured trusting in the honour of the insurer that payment will be made and indeed these policies enjoy great respect as they are invariably honoured by the underwriters (Sec. 6).

INSURABLE INTEREST

The person who effects an insurance, or issues instructions for effecting it, must have an insurable interest in the subject-matter. It is not, however, the owner alone who may insure but every person having an insurable interest in the marine adventure. By Sec. 7, a person has an insurable interest if he is interested in a marine adventure in consequence of which he may benefit by the safe arrival of insurable property or be prejudiced by its loss, damage or detention. Thus the owners, shippers, agents and others have insurable interest in respect of money advanced. A mortgagee of a vessel has insurable interest to the extent of his mortgage, a bailee in respect of property left in custody and care, and charterers of vessels. An underwriter has an insurable interest in respect of risk underwritten by him, which he may re-insure. The lender of money on bottomry or respondentia in respect of the loan. The master or any member of the crew of a ship has an insurable interest of his wages. The assured has it in the charges of any insurance which he may effect. All persons irrespective of nationality have the right to protect their property by insurance, excepting alien enemies.

The assured must have insurable interest at the time of the loss though he may not have been interested when the insurance was actually effected.

Where a shipper of cargo, having insured it, assigns the policy to a purchaser of the cargo while the ship is at sea, and after this assignment the ship is lost, the assignee will be entitled to recover under the policy, as he has acquired an interest at the time of the loss, though he had no interest in the cargo at the time it was originally shipped and insured. It sometimes happens that the goods of a merchant are exposed to the perils of the sea before he has news of their shipment, or an opportunity of protecting them by insurance. In such a case the subject-matter is insured *"lost or not lost"* when the assured may recover under the policy although he may have acquired interest subsequent to the loss. But if at the time of effecting the insurance the assured knew of the loss and the underwriter did not know, it would amount to concealment and breach of good faith, and the contract would become void. Where neither the underwriter nor the assured has knowledge of the loss, the assured will be entitled to recover for such loss.

INSURABLE VALUE

The Marine Insurance Act, 1963 makes a distinction between Insurable Interest and Insurable value. An insurable interest, as we have seen, is that interest which the law requires a person to have to enable him to effect a valid insurance. Insurable value is the amount of the valuation of the insurable interest for the purpose of insurance. If there is no express valuation in the policy, then, by virtue of Sec. 18, the insurable value of the subject-matter insured is to be ascertained as follows:

1. In an insurance on the ship, the insurable value is the value of the ship at the commencement of the risk. The ship includes her outfit, provisions and stores for the officers and crew, money advanced

for seamen's wages, and other disbursements, if any, made to make the ship seaworthy for the voyage or adventure, plus the insurance charges on the whole. A steamship includes its machinery, boilers and coal and engine stores.

2. In an insurance on the freight, whether paid in advance or not, the insurable value is the gross amount of the freight at the risk of the assured, plus the charges of insurance.

3. In an insurance on the goods and merchandise, the insurable value is the prime cost of the cargo insured, plus the expenses of and incidental to shipping and the charges of insurance upon the whole.

4. In an insurance on any other subject-matter, the insurable value is the amount at the risk of the assured when the policy attaches, plus the charges of insurance.

DISCLOSURE AND REPRESENTATION

A contract of marine insurance, like any other contract of insurance, is one in which the utmost good faith (*uberrimae fidei*) must be observed, and if it is not, the contract is voidable by the insurer. The assured must disclose to the insurer every material circumstance which is known to him, and he is deemed to know everything which he ought to know in the ordinary course of business. A circumstance is material if it would influence the judgment of a prudent insurer in fixing or determining whether to take the risk (Secs. 19 and 20). The following are examples of the concealment of facts, which have been held to be material, entitling the insurer to avoid the contract:—

The fact that the ship had grounded and sprung a leak before the insurance was effected.[1] A merchant, on hearing that a vessel similar to his own was captured, effected an insurance without disclosing this information.[2] The nationality of the assured concealed at a time when his nationality was important.[3] In an insurance on a ship, the fact that the goods carried were insured at a value greatly exceeding their real value.[4]

In every case, however, whether a circumstance is material or not depends on the particular facts. In the absence of inquiry by the insurer, the following circumstances need not be disclosed:—
  (a) those which diminish the risk;
  (b) those which it is superfluous to disclose by reason of any insurer in the ordinary course of his business;
  (c) those as to which the information is waived by the insurer,
  (d) those which it is superfluous to disclosed by reason of any express or implied warranty.

If the insurance is effected by an agent, the agent must disclose to the insurer every fact which the assured himself ought to disclose and also every material circumstance known to the agent. The agent is deemed to know every fact which he ought to know in the ordinary way of business or which ought to have been communicated to him (Sec. 21).

In addition to his duty to make a full disclosure, the assured is under a duty to see that every material representation made during the negotiations for the contract is true. If any material representation be untrue the insurer may avoid the contract (Sec. 22).

The method followed in effecting a contract of marine insurance differs from that adopted in other forms of insurance. In a contract of insurance, other than marine insurance, a proposal form is filled in by the assured and forwarded to the insurance company for its acceptance. Marine business is often done through an insurance broker, who, on receipt of instructions from his principal, prepares a brief

1. Russell v. Thomton (1859), 20 L.J. Ex. 9.
2. De Costa v. Scandert (1817) 2 K.B. 184.
3. Associated Oil Carriers Ltd. v. Union Ins. Socy. of Canton Ltd.
4. Ionides v. Pender (1874), L.R. 9 Q.B. 531 (1917) 2 K.B. 184.

memorandum of the risk, called the "SLIP". This slip is shown by him to an underwriter at Lloyd's or to an "Insurance Company" underwriter. If the risk is accepted the underwriter quotes a rate of premium and if accepted by the broker, it is entered on the slip. The underwriter then "writes his line" (*i.e.* the amount he is willing to underwrite), initials this figure and dates it. Should the underwriter accept only a portion of the value of the slip, the broker takes his slip round to several underwriters until the full value is covered. The slip has no legal value as it is not stamped and also the Marine Insurance Act provides that a contract of Marine Insurance can only be entered into by means of a duly stamped policy. But at Lloyd's, the slip initiated by a member of the organisation will be binding on him under the rules of the Lloyd's. Where a policy has been issued after the slip, the slip may be referred to as regards the date of the contract and the intention of the parties.

Frequently, a *cover note* or an insurance note is issued instead of the slip, as preliminary step to the final preparation of the policy. These documents also do not constitute a contract. But all of these have moral worth, as the code of honour by which the underwriter is bound is very strong, and he would invariably issue a policy or pay the loss occasioned by the peril before the issue of the policy.

A contract of marine insurance is deemed to be concluded when the proposal of the assured is accepted by the insurer, whether the policy be then issued or not; and for the purpose of showing when the proposal was accepted, reference may be made to the slip, covering note or other customary memorandum of the contract, although it be unstamped (Sec. 23).

DOUBLE INSURANCE

Double insurance is where two or more policies are effected by or on behalf of the assured on the same adventure and interest or any part thereof and the sums insured exceed the indemnity allowed by the Act, *e.g.*, if A insured property worth ₹ 10,000 with X for ₹ 7,500 and with Y for ₹ 5,000, there is a double insurance, because the measure of A's indemnity, viz., ₹ 10,000, has been exceeded. If A had insured with X for ₹ 4,500 and with Y for ₹ 5,500 there would be no double insurance [Sec. 34(1)].

Where the assured is over-insured by double insurance he may, unless the policy otherwise provides, claim payment from the insurers in such order as he may think fit, provided he does not recover more than his indemnity. If the policy is a valued policy the assured must give credit as against the valuation for any sum received by him under any other policy without regard to the actual value of the subject-matter insured. If the policy is unvalued, the assured must give credit, as against the full insurable value, for any sum received under any other policy. If the assured receives any sum in excess of the indemnity, he is deemed to hold such sum in trust for the insurers, according to their, right of contribution among themselves [Sec. 34(2)]. As between insurers, each is liable to contribute to the loss in proportion to the amount for which he is liable. If any insurer pays more than his proportion he can sue the others for contribution (Sec. 80).

WARRANTIES

In a contract of marine insurance, there are two kinds of conditions known as "warranties." A warranty, according to Sec. 35 of the Act, is an undertaking by the assured that some condition shall be fulfilled, or that a certain thing shall be or shall bot be done, or whereby he confirms or negatives the existence of a particular state of facts. A warranty may be *express* or *implied*. An express warranty is a condition which is set forth in the policy or attached thereto; and an implied warranty is an essential condition implied by law, though not written in the policy. Strict compliance with these warranties is absolutely essential, for non-compliance with any one of them is fatal to the contract and absolves the underwriter from all liability. But non-compliance with an express warranty is excused when, by reason of a change of circumstances, the warranty ceases to be applicable to the circumstances of the contract, or when compliance with the warranty is rendered unlawful by any subsequent law.

EXPRESS WARRANTY

There can be and, in practice, are express warranties of endless variety, but space will not permit reference to them all. We may consider here, as illustration, the most commonly met with express warranties. One of them is a warranty that the ship will sail on or before a certain date. If the ship had started on her voyage even though it has not as yet quitted the port, the warranty is satisfied, provided she moved with everything ready and with the intention and ability to leave port. The "Free of Capture and Seizure" (F.C. & S.) clause and the "Memorandum" are two of the best known express warranties. F.C. & S. clause reads:

"Warranted free of capture, seizure, arrest, restraint or detainment, and the consequences thereof or of any attempt thereat (piracy excepted), and also from all consequence of hostilities or war-time operations whether before or after declaration of war." When this clause remains in the policy it overrides all the perils stated in the policy to which its terms are opposed. Gold bullion having been "commandeered" by the Transvaal Government whilst in transit from the mine, in anticipation of the outbreak of war which occurred some days subsequently, the gold was held to have been "seized" and underwriter was declared exempt from liability.[5]

The ordinary marine policy contains certain provisions in regard to particular average which are embodied in what is called a "Memorandum." The memorandum reads:" N.B. Corn, fish, salt, fruit, flour, and seed are warranted free from average, unless general, or the ship be stranded—sugar, tobacco, hemp, flex, hides and skins are warranted free from average, under five pounds per cent, and all other goods, also the ship and freight, are warranted free from average, under three pounds per cent unless general, or the ship be stranded." The memorandum provides minimum limit to the underwriters' liability in respect of claims for particular average by exempting him from such claims either absolutely or under certain percentages, unless the ship be *stranded*. It is important, in this connection, to remember that if the ship strands, the underwriter will be liable for all damages to the ship or cargo caused previous to stranding or subsequent to it, even where the stranding is not the direct cause of the damage.

The Marine Insurance Act mentions two forms of express warranties namely, (*i*) a warranty of neutrality, and (*ii*) a warranty of good safety. Sections 38 and 40 specifically deal with these. Where the subject-matter is expressly warranted neutral, it must be so at the commencement of the risk and, so far as the assured can control the matter, the neutral character preserved during the risk. Where the subject-matter insured is war-ranted "well" or "in good safety" on a particular day, it is sufficient if it be safe at any time during that day.

IMPLIED WARRANTIES

These warranties are in the nature of preliminary essential conditions which must be complied with in order to render a contract of marine insurance valid, and their non-compliance is fatal to the contract. These warranties are : (*i*) sea-worthiness, (*ii*) legality of voyage.

SEA-WORTHINESS

In every "voyage" policy the ship must be sea-worthy at the commencement of the voyage, or if the voyage is divisible into distinct stages, at the commencement of each stage. To be sea-worthy a ship must be reasonably fit in all respects to encounter the perils of the voyage she is about to undertake. She must be sound as regards her hull; she must not be overloaded, her cargo must be properly stowed. She must be .fully manned and her officers and crew must be efficient. She must be fit to carry the cargo to the destination contemplated by the policy, *i.e.*, "she must be cargo-worthy". It is to

---

5. Robinson Gold Mining Co. v. Alliance Marine & General Insurance Co. Ltd., (1910) 2 K.B. 919.

be noted that there is no hard and fast standard of sea-worthiness, for it varies with circumstances of each particular case, and each venture must "be considered on its own merits. Thus a ship which is reasonably fit for a voyage from London to Bombay may be totally unfit for a trip to the coast of Labrador unless she has fitting peculiar to a Semi-Arctic voyage. Further, where a voyage is made in distinct stages the ship must be sea-worthy at the commencement of each stage.

In *Bouillin v. Lupton*[6] three steamers which were trading on the River Rhone had been sold for service on the Danube, and were insured for the voyage from Lyons to Gallatz. In order to pass under a number of low bridges on the Rhone, the steamers left Lyons without masts and continued their journey as far as Marseilles, where they were fitted with masts and generally prepared for the voyage to Gallatz. When the vessels entered the Black Sea storm arose, and they all foundered. The underwriter declined to pay on the ground that the steamers were not sea-worthy for the whole voyage when they left Lyons—the place of commencement of the voyage. But the Court held that the warranty had been complied with, for different stages of sea-worthiness were necessary for the different stages of voyage and at the commencement of each stage the ships were properly equipped. In descending the Rhone they were "sea-worthy" for the Rhone; and from Marseilles to Gallatz they were ready for the sea.

This warranty is required to be literally complied with; strictly speaking, even ignorance or innocence will not be an excuse. Where a ship-owner has done everything in his power to make his ship fit for the voyage, and in spite of all care, has failed to discover some latent defect such defect would defeat his object and deprive him of his right to recover for a loss.

In *Quebec Marine Ins. Co. v. Comm. Bank of Canada,*[7] where a ship had been insured for the voyage from Montreal to Halifax, when she sailed there was an undiscovered defect in her boiler, which became visible after some time and became so serious as to necessitate her return to Montreal for repairs. After the repairs she resumed her voyage, but was lost in bad weather. It was held the assured could not recover as ship was not sea-worthy when she originally started on the voyage.

In Time Policies there is no implied warranty of sea-worthiness.

LEGALITY

The second implied warranty is that the venture insured is a lawful one, and that, so far as the assured can control the matter, the adventure shall be carried out in a lawful manner. Therefore, an insurance of an adventure which is illegal according to law, *e.g.,* smuggling, is void. If the adventure is legal one, but the master or crew, without the knowledge of the owner, indulge in smuggling on their own account, there would be no breach of the implied warranty, and the contact will not become void so as to absolve the underwriter of liability. A policy of insurance effected for the purpose of insuring an alien enemy is void, because it is illegal.

However, there is no implied warranty as to the nationality of a ship, or that her nationality shall not be changed during the risk (Sec. 39). In a policy on goods or other movables there is no implied warranty that the goods or movables are sea-worthy (Sec. 42).

THE VOYAGE

The subject-matter may be insured by a voyage policy "from a port" or "at and from" a port. The policy "from" a port only protects the subject-matter of the insurance from the time of sailing from the port, *e.g.,* an insurance "from Bombay to London" only attaches when the ship has actually left the precincts of the port of Bombay, and is on her voyage to London. But an insurance "at and from" a port protects the subject-matter insured whilst at the port of departure previous to the ship's sailing

---

6. (1863) 33 L.J.C.P.37.

7. (1870) LR. 3 P.C. 234.

and also from the time of leaving it, and on her voyage. If the ship is at a port and is insured" at and from" the port, the insurance attaches immediately it is effected and continues to protect her whilst she is making the necessary preparations for the voyage.[8] If a ship is insured for a voyage "at and from" a port which she has not then reached, the insurance commences immediately on her arrival at the port in a reasonably good physical safety. Should the ship arrive at the port so damaged that she cannot lie there in safety until repaired, the policy does not attach.

DEVIATION AND CHANGE OF VOYAGE

The voyage must be accurately described in the policy, and properly performed. The ship must follow the course specified in the policy, or if not specified therein, the usual and customary course. If the ports of call are named, she must take them in order named or, if not named, in the order customary to the voyage, but she can miss out any or all of them. When a ship starts from her port of departure for her port of destination, but proceeds by an unusual or by an improper course, or takes the ports of call by an order different from the one specified or customary, there is a *deviation;* and if the deviation takes place without any lawful excuse, the insurer is discharge from *liability as from the time of deviation,* even though the ship may have regained her route before any loss occurs. On the other hand, the underwrites is liable for any loss from perils insured against which occurs previous to the deviation. Furthermore, the voyage must be commenced and proceeded with or without its unreasonable delay. If the adventure insured is not prosecuted throughout its course with reasonable dispatch, there will be a variation in the risk, and the underwriter will be discharged of liability, as from the time when delay became unreasonable. It should be noted that variation in the risk does not necessarily mean increase in the risk. The only question is whether the risk has been varied.

In *African Merchants Co.* v. *British and Foreign Marine Ins. Co.* a ship was insured "at and from Liverpool to the West and/or South-West coast of Africa, during her stay and trade there, and back to port of discharge in the United Kingdom." The ship arrived at the African coast, discharged her outward cargo there and then loaded her homeward cargo. Instead of sailing on the homeward voyage, which would have been the reasonable thing to do, she stayed a month in Canada Bay, by instructions of the owners, in order that her master and crew could help salving of the cargo of another vessel which had been wrecked there. Whilst there she was driven from her moorings by a heavy storm and became a total loss. This delay was held to be a deviation which had discharged the underwriter from liability.

CHANGE OF VOYAGE

Where the destination is specified in the policy and the ship, after the commencement of risk, sails for another destination, no risk attaches to the policy from the time when the determination to change the voyage became manifest. Where, before the commencement of the voyage the destination is altered, no risk attaches to the policy at any time. Change of voyage differs from deviation in that the policy is void from the moment a change of voyage was *contemplated,* whereas a deviation must become a fact before the validity of the policy is brought into question. Thus, if a vessel originally intended to sail on a voyage from Liverpool to Karachi via the Suez Canal proceeds on a voyage to Calcutta via Cape Town and is lost on the Portuguese Coast, the underwriter is relieved from any liability for the loss, although the vessel, at the time of loss, was on that part of the course common to both voyages. According to the law she was on an entirely different voyage.

Justifiable Deviation— There are certain circumstances in which deviation or delay would be excused, and these are set forth in the Marine Insurance Act. Deviation or delay is excused—

----

8. Palmer v. Marshall (1831) 8 Bing. 76.

1. where authorised by any special term in policy;
2. where caused by circumstances beyond the control of the master and his employer;
3. deviation by the vessal being blown out of her course by violent gales or being ordered during war by the Naval Authorities to deviate from her ordinary course in order to avoid the danger of submarines;
4. where reasonably necessary in order to comply with an express or implied warranty, *e.g.*, delay in making the ship sea-worthy at the commencement of a stage of the voyage;[9]
5. where reasonably necessary for the safety of the ship or subject-matter insured, *e.g.*, putting into port for repair a ship which has been severely damaged by violent weather,
6. for the purpose of saving human life, or aiding a ship in distress where human life be in danger,
7. where reasonably necessary for the purpose of obtaining medical or surgical aid for any person on board the ship. The excuses under clauses 5 and 6 are based on 'the ground of humanity. In the case of (5) it is essential that the danger must be to human life and not to property;
8. where caused by the barratrous conduct of the master or crew, if barratry be one of the perils insured against

When the cause which excuse deviation or delay cease to be operative, the ship must resume her course with reasonable despatch.

With regard to "Time Policies", the exact date and hour of the commencement and termination should always be inserted in the policy, but in the absence of hour, the day will be deemed to begin from and end at midnight.

Name of Vessel—The name of the vessel should be inserted in the policy when once an insurance on cargo has been effected, the vessel cannot be changed without the sanction of the underwriter. But if the original ship meets with disaster during the voyage, the cargo may be transhipped to another vessel for safe conveyance to destination.

Commencement of Risk. On Ship—This has already been dealt with, while discussing an insurance "from" and "at and from" a port.

On Goods or Freight— In the absence of any special clause, the risk on goods and freight commences immediately, and not until, the goods are on board the vessel.

Termination of Risks. On Ship— In the case of insurance on hull, for voyage, the risk continues, after the vessel has arrived at her port of destination, "until she has moored at anchor twenty-four hours in good safety"; for when the ship arrives with cargo the twenty-four hours will begin to run after the ship has been moored at the usual place for the discharge of cargo.

On Goods and Freight— In the absence of any stipulation to the contrary, the risk on goods and freight terminates as soon as the goods are safely "discharged and landed".

Perils—Perils are the risks which the underwriter agrees to take upon himself, and are inserted in the policy. *Perils of the Sea* are all perils, losses, misfortunes of a marine character or a character incident to a ship as such. The following casualties come within the definition of perils of sea, namely, "those happening during the voyage which reasonable skill, diligence and care cannot guard against and those which cannot be foreseen as the necessary or ordinary incidents of voyage," *e.g.*, when a vessel strikes upon a sunken rock in fair weather and sinks; a loss by foundering, owing to a vessel coming into collision with another vessel, even when the collision results from the negligence of the other vessel. They do not protect ordinary "wear and tear" which result from the inevitable action of the winds and waves. The test is that there must be some casualty, something which could not be foreseen as one of the necessary incidents of the adventure. **The purpose of the policy is to secure an indemnity against accidents which may happen, not against events which must happen.**[10]

---

9. Bouillin v. Lupton (1863) 33 L.J.C.P. 37.
10. Xantho's case (1887) VI Asp. M.L.C. 207:12 A.C. 503; Buller and others v. Fishtrs and others, 3, ESP.67.

"Fire" is the next peril, and the underwriter is liable for the loss caused by it. "Men of War, enemies" include all damage or loss sustained owing to the hostile acts of an enemy. "Pirates, Rovers" cover losses caused by marauders plundering indiscriminately for their own ends. The terms include passengers who mutiny, and rioters who attack the ship from the shore. "Thieves are robbers using force or violence not clandestine thieves or pilferers or pickpockets, from amongst the passengers or crew. "Jettison" is the throwing (overboard) of cargo, or the cutting and casting away of masts, spars, rigging or sails to lighten the ship in an emergency. Losses by jettison are recoverable under the policy. But no Jettision of cargo owing to its inherent vice is covered by the policy. For example, the jettison of fruit which has become rotten on account of delay, or of hemp shipped in an improper condition which as a result becomes dangerously heated is not covered.

"Arrests"—This clause refers to political or executive acts and does not cover a loss caused by riots or by ordinary judicial process. Seizure in time of war by enemies or stoppage of vessels belonging to neutral powers suspected of carrying enemy goods, are examples of political, etc., acts.

"F.C. and S." Clause—Free of Capture and Seizure clause is specially inserted under which the underwriter absolves himself from any loss caused by capture or seizure of the vessel.

"Barratry"—Includes every wrongful act wilfully committed by the master or crew in contravention of their duties, thereby causing prejudice to the owner or charterer, and is covered by the policy. Examples of barratry are: wrongfully scuttling a ship, intentionally running her on shore, or setting fire to her.

"All other Perils"—At first sight these words would seem to cover losses from whatever source arising. But it is not so. These words include only those perils which are similar to those which have been enumerated in the policy, i.e., perils or losses *ejusdem generis* with those which have been previously specified.

"Sue and Labour" Clause—This well-known clause is supplemental to, and distinct from the contract of insurance, and enables the .underwriter and the assured to work together with a view to preserving the property, after accident, covered by the policy and to make the best of the bad bargain. Under this clause all expenses incurred by the assured or his agents or servants in mitigation of losses after the casualty has occurred are payable by the underwriter. No expenses incurred for averting the occurrence of peril would be paid under this clause.

"Waiver" Clause—This is really supplementary to the "Sue and Labour" Clause, provided simply to assure that; in the event of a casualty, either party to the contract may take such steps, or incur such expenses, as are contemplated under the Sue and Labour Clause, to minimise a loss, without prejudice to the rights of the assured on the one hand and the underwriter on the other.

"Memorandum" or "N.B." Clause—For its meaning and discussion see page 324 *et. seq. supra.*

"F.P.A." Clause—The Free from Particular Average Clause is, in effect, an extended application of the memorandum. It prevents the assured from recovering in respect of any losses other than the loss incurred by a general average sacrifice. But claims under Sue and Labour Clause will be *maintainable.*

"The Collision" or "Running Down" Clause—This clause really amounts to an additional contract to the contract of insurance itself, whereby the underwriter agrees to pay up to the amount of his policy, three-fourths of any sum which the owner of the ship insured may have to pay to the owner of another ship for damage caused as the result of the collision.

"Inchmaree" Clause—This clause derives its name from a steamer *Incnmaree;* a case in respect of which went up to the House of Lords, whose decision necessitated its insertion in the policy. The said vessel was insured under a time policy in the ordinary form. When the donkey engine was set to work for navigation purposes in order to pump water into the main boiler, a valve, which ought to have been kept open, had been, either accidentally or negligently, closed with result that the water, instead of passing into the boiler, was forced into the air chamber of the donkey-pump and split it. The House of Lords held that this was not a loss covered by an ordinary marine policy, being neither a peril of the sea nor coming within the general words "all other perils, losses, etc." [11] Among other things, this clause covers certain losses caused by (i) the negligence of master, mariners, engineers, pilots, crew; (ii) explosives; (iii) a latent defect in any machinery. But the clause is not to be taken to include any other risk except those mentioned therein.

Continuation Clause—This is very common clause in time policies, the effect of which is to place the shipowner, when the ship is at sea, on the expiration of the policy (which we know cannot be issued for more than a year), and in consideration of a *pro rata* additional premium, in the same position as if he had insured his vessel for the particular voyage in the course of which the policy expired, instead of for a portion only of the time occupied in the prosecution of that voyage.

Re-Insurance Clause—This clause is used in cases of re-insurance, *i.e.*, where an underwriter, who has accepted a risk, re-insures the whole or part of that risk with another underwriter, either because he deems the risk undesirable, or because he has accepted a greater responsibility in respect of a particular risk than he thinks it prudent to retain. The clause reads: "Being a re-insurance subject to the same clauses and conditions as the original policy or policies, and to pay as may be paid thereon"—*i.e.*, on the original policy. In order to be paid on the .reinsurance under this clause two conditions must have been complied with, namely, (i) the loss which has been paid must have been a loss for which the re-insuring underwriter is legally liable; and (ii) it must have been a loss for which the re-insuring underwriter *is,* under the particular terms of the re-insurance policy, also liable.

ASSIGNMENT OF POLICY

A marine policy is assignable by indorsement or in any other custormary manner, and the assignee can sue on it in his own name subject to any defence which would have been available against the person who effected the policy. The assignment may be made either before or after loss, but an assured who has parted with or lost his interest in the subject-matter insured cannot assign.

PART 8-B
LOSSES

CAUSA PROXIMA

Proximate Cause—Before dealing with the kinds of losses and their adjustment, the fundamental principle underlaying the contract of marine insurance may be re-stated and explained for clear understanding. This principle is that the loss for which the underwriter is to be made liable must have been proximately and directly caused by the peril insured against. The principle is most rigorously applied to the contract of marine insurance. An underwriter is not liable for damage to cargo directly caused by rats or vermin; but if it is destroyed by sea water flowing through a hole gnawed by rats in a bathroom pipe, the underwriter will be liable, as the proximate cause of damage is the sea water, and the rats' partiality for lead pipe being the remote cause. In another case, where hides and tobacoo were shipped in the same vessel, and the hides became putrid by reason of sea water during a storm, and the stench from them spoiled the tobacco, the damage thus caused was held as having been proximately caused by perils of the sea. [12] It must be noted that an underwriter is not liable for any loss if it be caused by the wilful act or default of the assured himself. But if loss was occasioned by negligent navigation of the master or carelessness of a seaman, the underwriter would be liable. Furthermore, in the case of goods, the damage must be actual damage to the goods themselves, and not suspicion of, or what is called sentimental damage.

---

11. Thames and M.M. Insurance Co.v. Hamilton Fraser & Co. (1887) 12 A.C. 484.

12. Hamilton v. Pandorf (1887) VI Aps. M.L.C. 212.

The question, which is the *causa proxima* of a loss, can only arise where there has been a succession of causes. When a result has been brought about by two causes, we must, in marine insurance law, look only to the effective or predominant cause although the result would, no doubt, not have happened without the remote cause. 'Proximate' does not mean "the nearest in time". The cause which is truly proximate is that which is proximate in efficiency, which is the effective cause.

KINDS OF LOSSES

A loss may be either Total or Partial. Total loss may be subdivided into two classes: (i) Actual Total Loss, and (ii) Constructive Total Loss. The case of partial loss arises when the subject-matter of the insurance is partially lost. Partial loss is also of two classes; (i) Particular Average, and (ii) General Average.

ACTUAL TOTAL LOSS

An actual total loss occurs when the subject-matter insured is destroyed or so damaged as to cease to be the thing of the kind insured, or where the assured is irretrievably deprived of the subject-matter. From this definition it is clear that besides actual or absolute destruction by a peril insured against, goods are deemed to be totally lost where they are so damaged as to cease to exist in specie, *i.e.*, when they no longer answer to the denomination under which they were insured, or cannot be utilised as the thing insured. The well-known case of *Roux* v. *Salvador*[13] illustrates this point.

A ship with a cargo of hides started on its voyage from Valparaiso to Bordequx. During the voyage it sprang a leak and put into Rio de Janeiro, where it was found that the hides were in a state of incipient putridity as a result of inflowing sea water. If they had been carried to the destination they would have become entirely putrid and valueless as hides, and they were consequently sold at Rio de Janeiro. This was held to be total loss.

In *Dilip Kumar Ghosh* v. *New India Ass. Co. Ltd.,* 1990 Cal. 303, goods were handed over to the shipping company for carriage to a foreign country. The Consignor (Shipper) had done all that he could do regarding the shipment of goods. There was no delay on his part and the cargo had no "inherent vice." The cargo never reached the destination because the ship was abandoned by the crew in sea. The Insurance Company was held liable to pay the amount of insurance covered by the policy.

A ship is posted at Lloyd's as "missing" or is captured and seized by the enemy, it is an actual total loss as it is deemed to be irretrievably lost to the owner even though it is still in existence. So also where the subject-matter is lost to the owner by any decree of the court, foundering at sea in a gale, or sinking after collision, or a vessel which is "missing" are simple instances of actual loss of ship, cargo, and freight.

CONSTRUCTIVE TOTAL LOSS

A constructive total loss occurs (to use the words of the Marine Insurance Act) where the subject-matter insured is reasonably abandoned on account of its actual total loss appearing to be unavoidable, or because it could not be preserved from actual total loss without an expenditure which would exceed its value when the expenditure had been incurred. In particular there is a constructive total loss:—

1. when the assured is deprived of the possession of his ship or goods by a peril insured against, and (a) it is unlikely that he can recover the ship or goods as the case may be, or (b) the cost of recovering the ship or goods, as the case may be, would exceed their value when recovered; or
2. in the case of a damage to the ship, where she is damaged by a peril insured against that the cost of repairing the damage would exceed the value of the ship when repaired; or

---

13. (1836) 3 Bing. N.C.266.

3. in the case of damage to goods, where the cost of repairing the damage and forwarding the goods to their destination would exceed their value on arrival (Sec. 60).

In *Moss* v. *Smith*,[14] Maul, J. explained the doctrine of constructive total loss in these words: "A man may be said to have lost a shilling when he had dropped it into deep water, though it might be possible by some very expensive contrivance, to recover it. The shilling exists, and it could be recovered at a price, but what man would be foolish enough to spend, say two shillings in order to recover one?" The safer course would be to abandon the shilling in the deep water, in which case that shilling would be a constructive total loss.

In *Roux* v. *Salvador*,[15] Lord Abigner observed: The underwriter engages that the object of the insurance shall arrive in safety at its destined termination. If, in the progress of the voyage, it becomes totally destroyed or annihilated or if it be placed by reason of the perils insured against in such a position that it is wholly out of the power of the assured or of the underwriter to procure its arrival, he is bound by the letter of his contract, to pay the sum insured. But then are intermediate cases, (*i.e.*, there may be frustration of adventure), there may be a forcible detention which may last so long as to end in the impossibility of bringing the ship or the goods to their destination. There may be some other peril which renders the ship unnavigable without any reasonable hope of repair, or by which the goods are partly lost, or so damaged, that they are not worth the expense of bringing them, or what remains of them, to their destination. In all these cases or in similar cases if a prudent man, not insured, would decline any further expenses in prosecuting an adventure the termination of which will probably never be successfully accomplished, a party insured may, for his own benefit as well as that of the underwriter, treat the ease as one of a total loss, and demand the full sum insured. But if he elects to do this, and the thing insured, or a portion of it still exists and is vested in him, the very principle of indemnity requires that he should make a cession of all his right to the recovery of it, and that, too within a reasonable time after he receives the intelligence of the accident, that the underwriter may be entitled to all the benefits of what may still be of any value and that he may, if he pleases, take measures at his own cost for realising or increasing the value". The last portion of the above statement refers to "Abandonment" and "Notice of Abandonment."

Abandoment and Notice of Abandoment— Where there is a constructive total loss, the assured may either treat the loss as partial loss or abandon the subject-matter insured to the insurer and treat the loss as if it were an actual total loss; but in the latter case it is essential for him to give with reasonable diligence after the receipt of information about the casualty, notice of abandonment to the insurer, otherwise the loss will be treated only as partial loss. **Abandoment** is the surrendering of the interest of the assured in whatever may remain of the subject-matter insured and all proprietary rights incidental thereto, to the underwriter, and claiming from him a total loss. This cession of right is necessary in order to entitle the underwriter to whatever remains of die property, and enable him, if he so wishes, to take means for the protection of his own interest. There is no special form of notice of abandonment but it must be worded as to give explicit intimation to the underwriter that the assured abandons *unconditionally* to the underwriter his whole interest in the subject-matter insured. It is usual for the word "abandon" to be used in the notice.

If the underwriter accepts the abandonment, he pays the total loss, and realises what he can with the property which has been abandoned to him. But if he declines to accept the abandonment it is then necessary for the assured to issue a writ against the underwriter to recover the loss. The Court will look at the state of facts existing at the time of the writ to determine whether or not a constructive total loss has occurred.

14. (1845) 2 C.B. 94 at p. 103.
15. (1836) 3 Bing N.C. 266.

PARTIAL LOSSES

PARTICULAR AVERAGE

1. A particular average loss is a partial loss of die subject-matter insured caused by a peril insured against, and which is not a general loss.

2. Expenses incurred by or on behalf of the assured for the safety or preservation of the subject-matter insured, other than general average and salvage charges are called particular charges. Particular charges are not included in particular average (Sec. 64).

The damage, in order to be a particular average, must be accidentally and fortuitously caused by a peril insured against and it concerns solely the person interested in the subject-matter insured and the underwriter, and no question of contribution by various parties in the adventure arises, as it is in the case of a General Average loss. These two points are of particular importance, as they are the distinguishing features between particular average and general average. In order to get a clear idea of particular average some imaginary cases may be given as illustration. A ship meets with foul weather, as a result of which she sustains serious damages such as wreckage of her propeller, a severe strain to the hull, the damages so occasioned is a particular average on ship. And if during violence of the weather, sea water gets into the hold and damages the cargo, the damage so occasioned to the cargo is particular average on cargo. Again, if the cargo is, for example, sugar, and half of it becomes *sherbat* by getting dissolved in the sea water, that damage is a particular average on freight. This is so because half of the sugar cannot be delivered at the destination, involving a loss of freight on that half, for the sugar is no more there to be carried to and delivered at the destination.

PARTICULAR AVERAGE ON SHIP

Suppose a ship has suffered a considerable damage in heavy weather. Ordinarily, the owner will repair the ship, and the measure of the underwriter's liability will be the actual cost of repairing the ship, prudently and reasonably incurred, less the deductions "new for old", (*i.e.*, less the improvement resulting from the repair) unless, as is now usual, the policy provides for the full payment of costs. In settling the claim of particular average on ship no regard is paid to insured value of the ship as agreed between, the assured and the underwriter. *It is the reasonable actual outlay for repairs which form the basis of the claim.*

When the total amount of the particular average has been determined, the next question is to ascertain the amount recoverable under the various policies. This is done by apportioning the particular average in the proportion which each underwriter's policy, or subscription bears to the total insured value. The liability of the underwriter on ship is ordinarily limited to the amount of his policy so far as any one accident is concerned. But it may, and often does, happen that a vessel meets with several accidents, in which case the underwriter is liable to pay successive losses, even though the total amount of such successive losses may far exceed the amount of his policy unless there is a contract to the contrary. For example where a ship during the currency of the policy has been damaged, and has been repaired, and is subsequently totally lost, the underwriter will have to pay the total plus the particular average loss. And if the repairs are not made, and the ship is totally lost before the expiration of the risk, then the owner can recover only for a total loss, and not for a particular average damage, since the repairs have never been effected and he has suffered no loss so far as they are concerned. And if in such a case the total loss was not caused by the peril insured against, then the underwriter will not be liable for anything at all.

Where particular average repairs have not been effected and the vessel is not totally lost before the expiry of the policy, the underwriter's liability in respect of the particular average would be ascertained by estimating the cost of repairs. The point may be illustrated by means of an example. A ship insured with underwriter *X* for a voyage sustained particular average damage, and the damage was unrepaired when the policy expired. Immediately on the expiry of *X*'s policy the ship was covered by *Y*'s policy, and before the particular average damage attaching to X's policy had been repaired, the ship was totally lost. It was held that X would pay the estimated cost of repairing the particular average damage, which would he a clear profit to the owner of the ship, whilst Y would pay a total loss.[16]

PARTICULAR AVERAGE ON FREIGHT

Freight is money payable either for the hire of a vessel or for the conveyance of cargo from one port to another. Freight, therefore, suffers any physical damage by perils insured against in the same way as a vessel or goods. To constitute a particular average on freight there must be partial loss in respect of it. Suppose a car go of sugar is shipped from Bombay to London, freight not being prepaid, and during the voyage, and owing to the peril insured against, one half of the sugar is dissolved in sea water. There is loss of one half of the freight, and the underwriter would be liable to one half of the amount for which the freight was insured.

PARTICULAR AVERAGE ON CARGO

A claim for particular average on cargo arises when the cargo has been either partially damaged by the peril insured against, or a portion of the cargo is totally lost. If, for example, out of a shipment of one hundred bales of cotton, twenty arrive at their destination depreciated by sea water to the extent of twenty-five per cent; or 5 bales arrive totally worthless; or all the hundred bales arrive depreciated to the extent of seventy-five per cent or even more, in all these cases the claim is one of particular average on cargo. To arrive at the depreciation of damaged cargo, the sound value of the cargo has first to be found out and then the gross sound value and the gross proceeds are to be compared. This shows the amount of the loss which is usually worked out at so much per cent on the sound value. It is to be noted that the comparison is made between gross values and not between net values. The reason for doing this is to avoid marked fluctuation becoming a factor in the loss and also because by comparing net proceeds, although the actual loss would remain unaltered, the ratio of depreciation would be increased, to the prejudice of the underwriter, because of deduction of ordinary charges from the sound value. An example will make this clear.

		Sound Value	₹ 1,000
		Less Charges	₹ 100
		Net Sound Value	₹ 900
Gross Sound Value	₹ 1,000	Net Sound Value	₹ 900
		Proceeds (at auction)	₹. 500
Gross Proceeds	₹ 500	Less Charges	₹ 100
Loss	₹ 500	Net proceeds	₹ 400

Depreciation 50 per cent.

But depreciation on sound value of ₹ 900 is 55½ per cent.

It is to be observed that there is a fundamental difference between the adjustment of claims for particular average on cargo. In the case of a ship, the reasonable cost of repairs is paid for by the underwriter without regard to the insured value. But in the case of cargo the percentage of depreciation is always applied to the insured value to arrive at the liability of the underwriter. If the insured value is less than the gross sound value, then the underwriter pays proportionately less of the loss, and if the insured value is more than the gross sound value, the underwriter pays proportionately more.

16. Lidgett v. Secretan (1871) 1 Asp. M.LC. 95.

Suppose of sea-damaged bale of cotton

Gross sound value	₹ 100
Gross proceeds	₹ 50
Loss	₹ 50

or a depreciation of 50 per cent.

If the insured value is ₹ 80 the underwriter is liable for 50 per cent of it, or ₹ 40; or if the insured value ₹ 120, the underwriter is liable for 50 per cent of it, or ₹ 60.

GENERAL AVERAGE

The Marine Insurance Act (Sec. 66) provides:

1. A general average loss is a loss caused by or directly consequential on a general average act. It includes a general average expenditure as well as general average sacrifice.

2. There is a general average act where any extraordinary sacrifice or expenditure is voluntarily and reasonably made or incurred in time of peril for the purpose of preserving the property imperilled in the common adventure.

3. Where there is general average loss, the party on whom it falls is entitled, subject to the conditions imposed by maritime law, to ratable contribution from the other parties interested, and such contribution is called a general average contribution.

On analysing the section we get the following essentials of a general average contribution, namely:

1. The common adventure must be in peril.
2. The sacrifice must be voluntary, *i.e.*, it must be the intentional act on the part of man as opposed to an accidental loss by maritime peril.
3. The sacrifice or expenditure must be prudently or reasonably made.
4. The sacrifice or expenditure must be extraordinary in nature.
5. The object of the sacrifice or expenditure must be nothing other or less, than the preservation of the property imperilled in the common adventure. In other words, it must not be for the safety of the ship alone, or of the cargo alone, nor merely for the completion of the adventure.
6. The loss must be direct result of a general average act.

The following sacrifices or expenses may give rise to General Average. Contribution:—

SACRIFICE

Sacrifices of ship— If in time of peril, the master voluntarily destroys any part of the ship, or puts any of her appurtenances or appliances to use for which they were not intended, at the risk of destroying or injuring them, any loss or damages thus caused for the common safety is to be made good by general contribution. The cutting away of masts, spars and sails, the scuttling of a vessel in order to admit water to extinguish a fire are examples of voluntary sacrifices of a ship. The using of a sail in connection with stopping a leak or to cover up hatches broken by shipping on sea during a storm are examples of using the appurtenances for purposes other than those for which they are originally intended. The amount to be made good in general average in respect of sacrifice of any part of the vessel, or her machinery, is measured by the reasonable costs of repairs, less the usual deductions "new for old". Sometimes it may happen that a general average sacrifice follows a particular average damage resulting conjointly in die condemnation of the ship. Suppose, for example, a vessel is very seriously damaged in violent weather, subsequently she gets into another storm, and whilst on her beam ends, the master cuts away her masts and gear in order to right her. On her arrival and port of refuge, she is condemned and sold. In such circumstances in order to arrive at the amount to be allowed in general average, the method to be adopted is to deduct from the value of the vessel the estimated cost of repairing the particular average damage. This would give the value of the vessel immediately preceding the general average sacrifice, and the difference between that value and the sum realised by the sale, is the amount of the general average sacrifice.[17] An example will make this point more clear:

Suppose the sound value of the ship to be	₹ 1,00,000
Deduct estimated cost of repairing particular average sacrifice	₹ 75,000
Value of ship immediately preceding general average sacrifice	₹ 25,000
Amount realised by sale of ship	₹ 2,000
Amount to be made good in general average in respect of sacrifice	₹ 23,000

Sacrifice of Cargo and Freight— Sacrifice of cargo for the common good by jettison, i.e., throwing overboard of cargo, or damage to cargo by pouring water on it to extinguish a fire or the burning of cargo as fuel for the engines to avert loss of ship and cargo gives rise to a claim for general average contribution. When a sacrifice of cargo also involves a loss of freight, it follows that the freight so sacrificed is also made good in general average. In the event of goods having been jettisoned, or otherwise sacrificed, the amount to be allowed in general average is the net value which they would have had on the day of discharge at the port of destination, less the charges which would have been incurred had the goods arrived instead of having been sacrificed, e.g., freight if not prepaid, discount, duty, landing and sale charges.

EXPENDITURE

All extraordinary expenditure properly incurred in time of peril for joint preservation of the common adventure is the subject of general average contribution. Thus, if a ship puts into a port of refuge to repair a general average sacrifice, the cost of entering the port of refuge, the cost of discharging, warehousing, and reloading the cargo, and the cost of leaving the port of refuge, are the subjects of general average, because all the expenditure so incurred is the consequence of a general average act. Where there is a general average loss the party on whom the loss falls is entitled to a ratable contribution from all the other parties who are interested in the adventure. Whatever comes under the head of general average loss must be shared by those who have benefited by the sacrifice or adventure, and the contribution that they make is called a general average contribution.

RAISING FUNDS

The incurring of expenditure at a port of refuge entails the advancing of funds to meet it, and the actual out-of-pocket expenses which have been reasonably incurred for interest and for commission for advancing funds are allowable in average. In the older days forced sale of cargo or loans on *bottomry* or *respondentia* in order to provide funds were fairly common but one seldom hears nowadays of such instances as the cable and the wireless usually enable such provisions to be arranged. For the sake of completeness, however, we may briefly refer to these subjects.

FORCED SALE OF CARGO

The sale of cargo in order to raise funds can be resorted to by the master only when he has failed to obtain money by other means. Where the cargo has been properly and rightly sold at a port of refuge, and it realises more than the net value which it would have realised had it been brought on to the destination instead of being sold, the owner of the goods is entitled to the actual proceeds at the port of refuge.[18] But conversely, if the goods realise less than they would have fetched at the destination,

---

17. Henderson v. Shankland (1896) C. Com. Cas. 333.
18. Richardson v. Nourse (1819) 3 B. & Aid. 237.

then the owner of goods is entitled to their net values as if they had arrived at destination. He is entitled to any profit and is not to suffer any loss.

BOTTOMRY AND 'RESPONDENTIA'

Bottomry is a monetary loan obtained in cases of urgent necessity on the security of the ship and cargo jointly; and *Respondentia* is a loan similarly obtained on the security of the cargo alone, the sum so advanced being repayable to the lender a certain agreed number of days after arrival of the vessel as specified in the document called Bottomry or Respondentia Bond. If the vessel is lost before arrival at destination, the lender loses his money, as it is only payable on condition that the ship and[19]/or cargo arrive.

SALVAGE

Salvage is the reward under maritime law to a salvor for saving, or helping to save, property, at sea, or property and life conjointly. The salvor who saved the property has a possessory lien on it for the reward of his services. But if the property is not in his possession he has what is called a maritime lien, *i.e.*, a claim which he can enforce by legal process in the Court of Admiralty. When he goes to this Court, the remuneration awarded to him is called a Salvage Award. It is to be noted that no salvage will be awarded if the services of the salvor were of no material assistance in salving the vessel. Moreover, the services must have been rendered by third parties, *i.e.* who are strangers to the adventure. These salvage charges are recoverable from the underwriter as partial loss. Salvage, recoverable under maritime law by a salvor independent of contract, should be apportioned over the values on which it was assessed. In recovering from underwriters, where the insured value is less than the contributory value, the amount recoverable is reduced in proportion, in exactly the same manner as in dealing with general average contribution. In *Balmoral Steamship Co.* v. *Marten*[20] a vessel was valued in the policy at and was insured for £ 13,000. Salvage services were rendered to her, and a salvage award was made by the Admiralty Court, the amount being based on a valuation of £ 10,000. It was held that the underwriters were only liable for 30/40ths of the amount so awarded.

If the salvage services were rendered necessary as a consequence of unseaworthiness of the ship, the underwriter on the hull would not be liable for any portion of the remuneration awarded to the salvor.

---

19. *Ibid.*
20. (1902) VII Com. Cas. 292.

CHAPTER 9

Fire Insurance

A fire insurance is a contract to indemnify the insured for destruction of or damage to property caused by fire. The insurer undertakes to pay the amount of the assured's loss not in excess of the maximum amount stated in the policy. It will be noticed that a contract of fire insurance is essentially a contract of indemnity, and not against accident but against loss caused by accident. If a person has insured his house for ₹ 50,000, the insurer is not necessarily liable to pay that amount, although the house may have been totally destroyed by fire; but he will pay the actual loss within the maximum limit of ₹ 50,000. So if the property was over-insured and the actual loss to the insured does not exceed ₹ 40,000, he will get only that amount. Or, if he had under-insured it, he will get the actual loss not exceeding ₹ 50,000, even if the property is totally lost and was worth more than the sum insured. It is because of this rule that a number of insured have complained, though mistakenly, that they were not "put in the same position as they were before the fire."

AVERAGE CLAUSE

It is becoming very common in policies of fire insurance to insert a condition called the average clause, by which the insured is called upon to bear a portion of the loss himself. This condition is called the *pro rota* condition of average. The main object of this clause is to check under-insurance and to encourage full insurance, and above all, to impress on the property-owner the necessity of having his property accurately valued before insurance. Under the average clause, the insurer and insured share the loss in proportion to the risk that each is carrying. The proportion of the loss is ascertained by a rule of three as under, namely, real value of property covered: insured amounts: damage done: damage payable. Thus, if a policy containing average clause is for ₹ 40,000 upon a subject-matter whose value is ₹ 50,000 and the actual loss is ₹ 10,000 the insured will only get 40,000/50,000ths of ₹ 10,000, *i.e.*, ₹ 8,000 and the balance of ₹ 2,000 the insured will bear himself, for he is considered to be his own insurer for ₹ 10,000 the difference between the actual value and insured amount, and bears the-ratable proportion of loss, viz., ₹ 2,000. This condition comes into operation if the assured is under-insured and in the case of partial loss he would be paid in the ratio above mentioned; but if there is a total loss, he is entitled to be paid the full sum insured.

Insurable interest. In the case of fire insurance, the insured must have insurable interest in the subject-matter both at the time of effecting the policy and at the time of the loss.[1]

Insurable Interest in Property—In the case of goods, insurable interest arises on account of (*a*) ownership, (*b*) possession, and (*c*) contract. Ownership may be absolute or limited. It may be legal or equitable. As an example of the latter, a purchaser of property after the contract of sale but before

---

1. Sadler's Co. v. Badcock (1743) 26 E.R. 733; See also Sec.30 Indian Contract Act.

the payment of purchase price has an equitable interest in the property. Persons with a limited interest in the goods may insure not only to the extent of their own interest but also to cover the interest of others in the goods. The most common examples are carriers, wharfingers, mercantile agents, etc. If the party insuring intends to cover the interests of all concerned in the property and not merely his own interest, he may, in the event of a loss, recover the whole amount of such loss, and not only the value of his limited interest. He will, however, hold the amount above the value of his loss, in trust for the person entitled thereto. A person in lawful possession of goods may insure them without instruction from the owners, and even without their knowledge.[2] A commission agent who purchased gold in order to send it to various dealers at different places was held to have insurable interest in the gold.[3] A shareholder has no insurable interest in the property of the company of which he holds shares,[4] nor has a simple creditor of the company.[5] As regards contract, typical instance is provided by the case of bailee and bailor. Bailees have insurable interest in the goods entrusted to them, and can insure the goods to their full value. In case of loss by fire, they will get the amount and after satisfying their own claim, keep the balance in trust for the real owner. An insolvent debtor who is in possession of goods which have vested in the Official Receiver has an insurable interest in the goods found.

Immovable Property—The insurance of buildings may be effected by any one interested in them. The owner can always insure. So may a tenant whether for life, or from year to year, in virtue of his interest in the property. A purchaser of immovable property acquires interest from the date of the execution of the contract of sale but if the policy is effected by the vendor, the purchaser cannot claim any benefit of it. The seller continues to possess interest as long as the price is not paid to him, and can recover under a fire policy if loss accrues before the payment of price. A mortgagor may insure and recover the whole amount of the loss, for he is liable personally for the amount of the mortgage debt, and the loss of the property means a reduction of his total assets. Mortgages, on the other hand, have insurable interest only to the extent of the mortgage debt. A creditor has no insurable interest in the property of the debtor, unless the creditor has a right to proceed against the property of the debtor before he effects an insurance.[6]

THE RISK

The risk in fire policy commences from the moment the cover note,[7] or the deposit receipt, or the interim protection is issued and continues for the term covered by the contract of insurance. It may even date back, if the parties so intend.

In *Indian Trade and Gen. Ins. Co. v. Bhailal,* 1954 Bom. 148, a cover note was issued on 18th June which assured the risk from 15th June and it appeared that, unknown to both parties, the goods had been destroyed by fire on the 16th June, held the insurance company was liable and that no question of mistake under Sec.20 of the Contract Act arose.

A contract of fire insurance is a contract of one year only with option to the parties to continue it for a further period on the payment of the stipulated premium. It is customary to allow certain days of grace in which to renew the policy, and if fire should occur during these days of grace, the insurer would be liable. As has been said before, the days of grace can give protection only if the assured

---

2. Waters v. Monarch Life Ass. Co. (1856) 25 L.J.Q.B. 102.
3. Commercial Union Ass. Co, v. Binjraj Johurmull 1931 Cal. 285; Williams v. Baltic Ins. Asso. Co. of London Ltd.(1924) 2 K.B.282.
4. Macaura v. Northern, Ins.Co. 1925 A.C. 619.
5. Moran, Galloway & Co. v. Uzielli (1905) 2 K.B. 555.
6. Stainbank v. Forming (1851) 11 C. B.151.
7. Indian Trade and General Ins. Co. v. Bhailal, 1954 Bom. 148.

intended to renew the policy. In case no days of grace are allowed, the insured will not be entitled to get anything, if fire occurs after the expiration of the term of policy and before its renewal.

WHAT IS FIRE

The word fire as used in the expression "loss by fire" is to be construed in its popular and literal sense, and means a fire which has *broken bounds*. Therefore, fire which is used for ordinary domestic purposes, or even for manufacturing, is not fire, as long as it is confined within the usual or proper limits. Fire means the production of light and heat by combustion; and unless there is actual *ignition* there is no fire within the meaning of the term in an ordinary policy,[8] heating, unaccompanied by ignition is not fire. "Loss or damage" occasioned by fire means loss or damage either by ignition of the articles consumed, or by ignition of that part of the premises, where the article is. In one case there is loss, in the other case, a damage occasioned by fire.[9] If an actual fire or burning is the proximate cause of the loss, and that fire is accidental or fortuitous in its origin so far as the insured is concerned, then such loss is covered by the policy. The cause of the fire is immaterial, unless it was the deliberate act of the insured. Fire risks do not include damage by explosion, unless the explosion causes actual ignition which spreads into fire.

Fire by spontaneous combustion is usually excepted in fire policies, but in the absence of such exception, it is submitted that it would be covered. Damage from lightning is not included in the fire risk but if lightning causes ignition, the loss would be covered. The same rule applies to loss or damage caused by electricity. Damage which occurs as a result of smoke or of putting out the fire would also be covered by the fire risks. " ....Any loss resulting from apparently necessary and *bona fide* efforts to put out a fire, whether it be by spoiling goods by water, or by throwing articles of furniture out of the window, or even by destroying a neighbouring house by explosion for the purpose of arresting fire; in fact, every loss directly, or if not directly at least consequently resulting from the fire is within the policy.[10] Loss by theft during a fire is covered as a fire risk.[11] Almost every fire policy excludes certain articles, either on account of their special value, or on account of their being liable to danger and destruction. The exceptions may also relate to certain causes for which the insurers are not prepared to accept liability, for example loss or damage caused by earthquake, riot, military power, or civil commotion.[12] Even loss by fire caused by the insured's negligence is covered. In *Harris* v. *Poland* (1941) 1 K.B. 462, *H* hid jewellery in her grate under the coal. Later, having forgotten this, she lit the fire and jewellery was damaged. *Held, H* could recover under a fire policy.

The rate of premium varies according to the degree of hazard or risk involved. Where more than one rate would apply to a risk the figure to be charged is that which will produce the highest net premium. If a godown contains twenty bales of cotton and ten bales of cloth, the rate charged will be the one payable on cotton, which is higher than the one for cloth.

ASSIGNMENT

In English law policy of fire insurance can be assigned only with the consent of the insurer. It is said that a contract of property insurance, whether the event insured against is fire or theft or burglary or accident, is a personal contract, entirely distinct from the subject-matter of insurance, and, therefore, the assignment of the subject-matter does not mean the assignment of the policy of the insurance.

---

8. Everett v. London Ass. Co. (1865) L.J.C.P.299.

9. *Ibid.*

10. Stanley v. Western Ins. Co. (1868) 37 L.J. Ex. 73, at p. 75 per, Kelly, C.B.

11. Levy v. Bailey (1831) 131 E.R. 135; Marsden v. City & County Ass. Co. (1865) 35 L.J.C.P.60.

12. Curtiss & Sons v. Mathews (1918) 2 K.B. 825.

Thus, if property insured against fire is assigned, the assignor of the property, in the event of loss, cannot recover under his policy, because his interest in the property will have ceased; and the assignee of the property will not recover, in case of loss, for he has not acquired any interest in the fire policy. In order that the assignee of the property may take the benefit of the policy of fire insurance, it is essential that the policy should be duly assigned to him at the time of the assignment of property, and the consent of the insurer to hold the assignee assured must be obtained.

Under Indian law the position is the same, but consent of the insurer is not necessary to make a valid assignment of policy; only notice is sufficient. Thus, in India, under Secs. 130 A and 135 A of the Transfer of Property Act, in the absence of any express provision prohibiting assignment, a fire insurance policy may be assigned by writing either by endorsement in the policy or in any other customary manner. But the assured must have insurable interest at the time of assignment and if he parts with or loses his interest in the property insured, an assignment of the policy thereafter by him will be of no effect. Before loss the policy can only be assigned to a person who has acquired some interest in the property, *e.g.*, the purchaser or a mortgagee, or a bailee, or a pledgee; for otherwise the assignee will have no insurable interest in the subject-matter at the date of the loss. Therefore, in India, the law is more clear and simple. By Sec. 135 A of the Transfer of Property Act, all that is required for a valid assignment of a fire policy is that it must be an endorsement or any other writing. Notice to the insurer of the assignment is necessary only to make him liable to the assignee if he pays the money to the assured even after such notice. On a valid assignment the assignee becomes entitled to all the benefits under the contract and can sue the insurer on the contract in his own name.[13] Under Sec. 49 of the Transfer of Property Act, a transferee for consideration of an immovable property insured against fire, is entitled to call upon the transferor to apply any money received by him under a fire policy, to reinstate the property.

PART 9-B
SPECIAL FIRE POLICIES

VALUED POLICY

Under an ordinary fire policy the insurer merely indemnifies the assured. But even contracts of fire insurance need not always be contracts of indemnity. If the insurers agree to pay a certain fixed sum on a fire policy irrespective of the loss, the contract is not one of indemnity. A departure in this direction has been made in the "valued policy" under which the insured can recover a fixed amount, agreed at the issue of the policy without the necessity for any further proof of value at the time of the fire.

RE-INSTATEMENT OR REPLACEMENT POLICY

Lately, insurers have gone a step further to complete the breach of the principle of indemnity in the shape of "replacement" or "reinstatement" policies. A clause is inserted in the policy under which the insured can recover not the value of buildings or plant as depreciated, but the cost of replacement of the property destroyed by new property of the same kind, or the insurers may themselves reinstate the property instead of paying in cash. In both cases we have the example of "new lamps for old."

CONSEQUENTIAL LOSS POLICY

This type of policy is again of recent origin and is also known as Loss of Profits Insurance. Under this type the insured is indemnified for the loss of profits which he sustains through interruption or cessation of his business as a result of fire. The usual policy covers loss of net profit, payment of

---

13. See Gyarsilal v. Sitacharan, 1963 M.P. 164.

standing charges, *i.e.*, debenture, interest, salaries, rates, taxes, etc., and increase in the cost of working, *e.g.*, taking up of temporary premises, having orders completed by other firms at extra cost, extra advertising, etc. Although apparently such compensation appears to go beyond indemnity, yet actually under a properly drafted policy there is hardly any chance of the insured gaining an advantage by the occurrence of a fire. The worst that can happen is that the complete security may tend to make the insured less careful in guarding his property against fire.

CLAIMS

On the happenings of any destruction or damage the insured or any other person on his behalf must forthwith give notice of fire to the insurance company so that they may take prompt steps to safeguard their interests, *e.g.*, in dealing with the salvage, and also judge for themselves the cause and nature of fire and the extent of the loss. This duty on the part of the insured is incorporated in the policy and is usually a condition precedent. In that case failure to give notice may avoid the policy altogether. The assured is further required by the terms of the policy to furnish the insurers within a specified time full particulars of the loss and damage and the proof of the value of the property, and if it is fully destroyed, of its existence. Failure to do so may prove fatal to the claims of the assured, as the delivery of the particulars is a condition precedent to his right to recover the loss.[14] But where the insurers repudiate their liability on the policy before the particulars are due, the assured need not submit any particulars.[15] If the assured prefers a fraudulent claim, he would forfeit all benefits under the policy, whether there is condition to that effect in the policy or not and whether the fraudulent claim is in respect of all or part of the policy.[16] Generally the fraud consists in over-valuation. If over-valuation is due to mistake it is not fraudulent, for valuation is generally a matter of opinion.[17] But in the great majority of cases, the expert assessors retained by the offices are in a position to arrive at a fair valuation satisfactory to both the insured and insurers.

---

14. Mason v. Harvey (1853) 22 L.J. Ex. 336.

15. Re Coleman's Depositories Ltd. and Life & Health Ass. Assoc. (1907) 2. K.B. 798

16. Britton v. Royal Ins. Co. (1866) 4 F.F. 905.

17. Dalby v. Indian & Lond. Life Ass. Co. (1954) 15 C. 365.

CHAPTER 10

Life Insurance

Life assurance may be defined as a contract in which the insurer, in consideration of a certain premium, either in a lump sum or by other periodical payments, agrees to pay to the assured, or to the person for whose benefit the policy is taken, a stated sum of money on the happening of a particular event contingent on the duration of human life. Thus, under a Whole-Life Assurance, the policy money is payable at the death of-the assured, and under an Endowment Policy, the money is payable on the assured's surviving a stated period of years, *e.g.*, on his attaining the age of 55, or at his death should that occur previously.

LIFE ASSURANCE AND OTHER FORMS OF INSURANCE DISTINGUISHED

The distinction between life assurance and marine and fire insurance is based on the principle that the risk insured against in respect of life policies is a certain event and in the case of the other two it is an uncertain event. The distinction is based on the principle that the risk insured against in respect of life policies is a certain event.

Life Assurance differs from the other forms of insurance in the following respects, namely:—

1. In life assurance the event is bound to happen sooner or later, the only uncertainty being the actual time of its occurrence, but in the case of fire, marine or accident, it is not certain that the event insured against will happen at all.

2. Fire, marine and accident insurance are contracts of indemnity. The assured cannot recover the whole of the amount insured if the loss be less than that and in no case can he recover more than the loss suffered by him. The amount recoverable is measured by the extent of the assured's pecuniary loss. In life assurance and personal accident insurance, the sum insured is payable irrespective of any proof of loss and to the full extent of the amount insured. Life assurance is not a contract of indemnity, but in a way it constitutes a form of investment.

3. In a marine or fire policy, the assured is required to have an insurable interest in terms of the policy and such interest should be capable of valuation in terms of money. But in a life policy, the insurable interest is one required by law and such interest cannot be measured in terms of money.

4. In a contract of life assurance insurable interest has only to be proved at the date of the contract and it is not necessary that the assured should have insurable interest at the time when the policy falls due. In marine insurance, the assured must have insurable interest at the time of the loss though he may not have been interested when the insurance was actually effected. In fire insurance, he should have it both at the time of loss and when the policy was effected.

5. A contract of fire or marine insurance is a contract from year to year only, and the insurance automatically comes to an end after the expiry of the year, though it can be renewed for a further

period of one year if the assured expresses his intention to continue the policy and pays the premium. A contract of life assurance is not a contract for a year but is a continuing contract with a provision that if the premium is not paid every year at or about the specified time the contract would lapse.

LIFE INSURANCE IS NOT A CONTRACT OF INDEMNITY

As we have already seen, life insurance is not a contract of indemnity. It stands on a totally different footing from fire and marine insurance. In the leading case *Dalbey* v. *The India and London Life Assurance Co.* (1854) 15 C.B. 365, Parke, B. observed: "The contract commonly called life assurance when properly considered is a mere contract to pay a certain sum of money on the death of a person, in consideration of the due payment of a certain annuity for his life ..... This species of insurance in no way resembles a contract of indemnity."

In this case, the Anchor Co. had issued policies on a life to a total of £ 3,000. They had reinsured £ 1,000 with the India Co. Subsequently the policies for £ 3,000 were surrendered, but the Anchor C. kept up to £ 1,000 policy with the India Co. On the death of the life assured, it was held that the Anchor Co. could recover.

In *Law* v. *London Ind. Life Policy Co.* (1855) 1 K. & J. 223, *L* insured the life of his debtor for ₹ 5,000, the amount of the debt. The debtor paid back the debt in due course. It was held *L* could recover the amount of the policy on the death of the debtor.

It may be further emphasised that, although life insurance may be said to partake of indemnity in the sense that one dependent on the insured may be protected to some extent against loss of that support, yet the policy calls for a specified amount which may be more or less than the value of the anticipated benefits of the continuation of the life. The interest which one has in his own life, or in the life of another, is difficult to estimate in rupees and paise; hence it is said that indemnity finds no place in life insurance.

Another feature of life insurance precludes it from being a contract of indemnity. Life insurance policies (except term policies) increase in value yearly; and therefore life insurance is usually considered as an investment device.

INSURABLE INTEREST

A contract of life assurance requires that the assured must have at the time of the contract an insurable interest in the life upon which the insurance is effected. In a contract of life assurance, unlike other insurance, interest has only to be proved at the date of the contract; and it is not necessary that the assured should have insurable interest at the time when policy falls due. The reason for this rule is that contract of life assurance is not a contract of indemnity.

In the following three cases insurable interest is presumed and no proof is necessary, viz., (*i*) own life, (*ii*) husband in the life of wife, and (*iii*) wife in the life of husband.

PERSON IN HIS OWN LIFE

A person is presumed to have an interest in his own life and every part of it, and can insure for any sum whatsoever, and as often as he pleases. Such interest in a person's own life is incapable of pecuniary valuation, hence there is nothing to prevent him *bona fide* insuring his own life as many times as he likes *for his own benefit,* even though when insuring he intends to assign the policy to another person. But if *ab initio* the insurance is intended *for the benefit of another person only* and that fact is concealed, that insurance is void for the lack of insurable interest

RELATIVES

A wife has an insurable interest in the life of her husband, and a husband has an insurable interest in the life of his wife. These three cases in which insurable interest is not required to be proved but is presumed, form an exception to the general rule that insurable interest in life assurance means pecuniary interest. The interest in these three cases is much higher than the pecuniary interest and is incapable of valuation. Therefore, no other relationship, as such, gives rise to an insurable interest. It must be shown that (a) the person effecting an insurance on the life of another is so related to that other person as to have upon him a claim for support by the person whose life is assured. Mere, natural love and affection is not sufficient to constitute an insurable interest Thus, a father has not necessarily an insurable interest in the life of his child, nor a child in the life of his father. In these cases pecuniary interest must be proved. So, a son has an insurable interest in the life of father who supports him but not in the life of the father dependent on him for support, nor in the life of mother whose funeral expenses he may be called upon to pay. A sister has an insurable interest in the life of a brother who supports her. The fact that a child or other relative was rendering valuable domestic service to the assured and that the loss of service would entail the employment of hired labour does not create an insurable interest.

PERSONS NOT RELATED

A creditor has an insurable interest in the life of his debtor to the extent of the debt; and although the debt may have been repaid since the date of the insurance the creditor can on the dropping of the life of the debtor recover from the insurer the policy money, thus making a profit out of the debt. A creditor can insure the life of his debt of up to the amount of the debt at the time of issue of the policy. The creditor can recover the policy money even though the debt becomes time-barred before the life drops. It is to be noted that although the creditor has insurable interest in the debtor's life he has no insurable interest in the debtor's property. A creditor has also an insurable interest in the life of a surety and the surety has an insurable interest in the life of the principal debtor. Similarly, a joint debtor or joint surety has an insurable interest in the life of another joint debtor or joint surety to the extent of his proportion of the debt. But a promise by the creditor to a debtor with consideration not to require payment of the debt during his life does not give the debtor an insurable interest in the life of the creditor.

An employee has an insurable interest in the life of the employer arising out of contractual obligations to employ him for a stipulated period at fixed salary. An employer may also have an insurable interest in the life of the employee who is bound by the contract to serve for a certain time. A partner has an insurable interest in the life of a copartner to the extent of the capital invested by the latter.

POLICIES

Life assurance, in an attempt to meet the varying wants of the community, has taken on many forms, *First* of all we have **Whole Life Policy**, which matures only at the death, whenever it may occur. *Secondly,* we have **Endowment Policy,** in which the sum insured is payable after the expiration of a certain term of years if the policy-holder is alive, or at his death if he dies previously. This policy combines the essential feature of life assurance (payable on death) with the advantages of a savings bank (as amount is payable after certain period and can be used by the policy-holder himself). *Thirdly,* **Joint Life Policies** are issued under which the sum assured is payable at the death of the first of the two lives. *Lastly,* **Survivorship Policy** is also granted under which the sum assured is payable at the death of the last or survivor of two lives. Similar policies may be issued for three or more lives, and are occasionally of value in business transactions. **A Survivorship Policy** is one under which the sum assured is payable if one person dies before another and in that event only. **Term Assurance** provides for payment only in the event of the life dropping before a certain date or age. This type is frequently adopted as collateral security for a loan. Such a policy provides for a low premium at the outset with a gradual increase, and is thus known as **Ascending Scale Policy**, or with large subsequent interest when it may be converted to whole life or endowment policy and is known as **Convertible Terms Assurance**. These policies are usually for a short period and are also called **Short Term Policies**, There are also Sinking Fund Policies, which are effected by payment of yearly premiums in order to secure a fund at the end of a certain period for the payment of debts in connection with joint stock companies with a redeemable debenture debt. A life policy may be with profit or without profit. A person who holds with-profit policy shares in the profits of the office, but pays a higher rate of premium. A holder of policy without profit does not share in the company, and pays a lower rate of premium.

SURRENDER VALUE

The surrender value of a life policy is the amount which the insurers are prepared to pay in total discharge of the contract, in case the assured wishes to surrender his policy and extinguish his claim upon it. The surrender values are based on the actual premiums paid, and usually the policy is required to have run for two or three years before the surrender value will be allowed. Surrender values increase with each payment of premium. Some companies guarantee a minimum surrender value of 40 per cent of the total premium paid.

LOANS ON POLICIES

Where a policy has a surrender value, it also has a loan value, and assurance companies usually lend 95 per cent of the surrender value, keeping the balance of 5 per cent as margin for a year's arrears of interest. The loan may be repaid at the convenience of the borrower, and in case it is not repaid it keeps alive with interest accumulation, to be deducted from the policy money becoming payable by the insurers either on its final surrender or on its maturity. This is the best investment that an insurance company can make, as there is never any danger of the money being lost.

PAID-UP POLICY VALUE

The paid-up value of a policy is the amount to which the sum assured would be reduced at any time if the assured requested a rearrangement of his contract so that no further premium should be payable. The amount on the paid-up policy is payable on the happening of the event assured against.

PRINCIPLE OF GOOD FAITH AND SEC. 45 OF INSURANCE ACT

The general rule is that in all kinds of insurance the assured must disclose everything which is likely to affect the judgement of the insurer and what is stated must be truthful. Misrepresentation of a material fact or its concealment will entitle the insurer to avoid payment of the claim. In India, Sec. 45 of the Insurance Act 1938, expressly lays down an exception to the rule of utmost good faith, and provides for certain limitations on the power of the insurer to refuse to pay the claim. It states that, after the expiry of two years from the date on which the policy was effected, the insurer cannot challenge it on the ground of misstatement unless he can prove that the misrepresentation, concealment or suppression of facts was fraudulently made by the policy holder and he knew that the statement was false and made it with knowledge and understanding of its falsity. The burden of proof is on the insurer, who must positively prove that the misstatement or concealment was deliberate and made with intent to deceive. Proof of mere constructive fraud is not enough. Mere inaccuracies, or even false statements that are not material cannot be regarded as sufficient to enable the life insurer to avoid his liability under the policy that is of two-year duration (*L.I.C.* v. *Parvathavardbin Ammal*, (1965) 35 Comp. Cas. 23: *L.I.C.* v. *Bibi Padmavati* (1967) 2 Com. L.J. 292 (S.C.);L.I.C. *Janaki Ammal* (1968) 38 Comp. Cas. 278. Sec. 45 is applicable even if the assured had died within two years of the making of the policy (*Vaid Mahesh Chandra Shastri* v. L.I.C. (1968) 38 Comp. Cas. 767 (All.)

ASSIGNMENT OF LIFE INSURANCE POLICY

Life insurance policies are freely assignable as actionable claims. They may be sold, mortgaged, or settled, provided the procedure laid down in Sec. 38 of the Insurance Act, 1938 is followed. Sec.38 lays down as follows:

1. A transfer or assignment of a policy of insurance, whether with or without consideration, may be made by an endorsement upon the policy itself, or by a separate instrument, setting forth the fact of transfer or assignment signed by the transferor or his agent and attested by at least one witness.

2. The transfer or assignment shall be complete and effectual upon the execution of such endorsement duly attested. Except where the transfer or assignment is in favour of the insurer, it shall not be operative as against the insurer and shall not confer upon the transferee or assignee any right to sue for the amount of such policy or the moneys secured thereby, until a notice in writing of the transfer or assignment together with the said endorsement or instrument itself, or a policy of the same certified to be correct, by both the transferor and the transferee, has been delivered to the insurer at his principal place of business.

3. The date on which the notice is delivered to the insurer shall regulate the priority of all claims under a transfer or assignment as between persons interested in the policy. Where there are more instruments than one, transferring or assigning the policy, the priority of the claims under such instruments shall be governed by the order in which the said notices are delivered.

4. On receipt of the notice, the insurer shall record the fact of such transfer or assignment together with the date thereof, and also the name of the transferee or assignee. The insurer shall, on the request of the person who gave the notice or of the transferee or assignee, grant a written acknowledgment of the receipt of such notice on payment of a fee not exceeding one rupee.

5. Subject to the terms and conditions of the transfer or assignment, the insurer shall from the date of the receipt of the notice, recognise the transferee or assignee named in the notice as the only person entitled to the benefit under the policy. The transferee or assignee shall be subject to all liabilities and equities to which the transferor or assignor was subject at the date of the transfer or assignment. The assignee may also institute any proceedings in relation to the policy without the consent of the transferor or assignor, or without making him a party to such proceedings.

6. An assignment in favour of a person made with the condition that it shall be inoperative or that the interest shall pass to some other person on the happening of a specified event during the lifetime of the person whose life is insured, and an assignment in favour of survivor or survivors of a number of persons, shall be valid.

NOMINATION BY THE POLICY-HOLDER

Section 39 makes the following provisions regarding nomination by a policy-holder:

1. The holder of a policy of life insurance on his own life may, when effecting the policy or at any time before the policy matures for payment, nominate a person to whom the amount due thereunder shall be paid after his death.

2. The nomination, in order to be effectual, shall be either incorporated in the text of the policy or endorsed thereon and communicated to the insurer who shall register it.

3. The nomination can be changed or cancelled by the assured any time before the policy matures for payment, and notice thereof given to the insurer. Unless a written notice of such change or cancellation of the nomination is delivered to the insurer, he shall not be liable for any claim under the policy made *bona fide* by him to a nominee registered in the records, or mentioned in the text of the policy.

4. The policy-holder is entitled to receive from the insurer, and the insurer shall furnish, a written acknowledgment of having registered a nomination or a cancellation or change thereof on payment of a fee of one rupee.

5. A transfer or assignment made in accordance with Sec. 38 shall automatically cancel a nomination. But the assignment of a policy to the insurer in consideration of a loan granted by him within the surrender value of the policy, or its re-assignment on repayment of the loan shall not cancel a nomination but shall affect the rights of the nominee only to the extent of the insurer's interest in the policy.

6. Where the policy matures for payment during the lifetime of the person whose life is insured, or where the nominee dies before the policy matures for payment, the policy money shall be payable to the policy-holder or his heirs or legal representatives, as the case may be.

7. Where the nominee survives the policy-holder, the policy money shall be payable to the nominee, and where there is no dispute as to who the heirs are and legal representatives of policy-holder, the production of succession certificate cannot be insisted upon by the Life Insurance Corporation of India (*Arumugam Chellial Paul (Since deceased by Legal Representatives* v. *Life Insurance Corporation of India,* 1990 Bom. 255).

CLAIMS

A person, claiming on the maturity of the policy, must satisfy the insurance company that he is entitled to receive the money on account of his being the owner of such policy, or because the actionable claim is vested in him as legal representative, or as nominee, or as assignee. Primarily, the assured is entitled to get payment but after his death his legal representatives acquire this right.

PROOF OF AGE AND DEATH

On the ripening of a life policy, insurance company requires a satisfactory and reasonable proof of age, if not already given and admitted, and of death of the assured. Death may be proved by direct evidence or by death certificate or by evidence of prolonged absence or other facts from which the fact of death may be properly inferred. The company will, as said above, require a strict proof of age of the assured before satisfying any claim under a life policy. Age can be proved by a certified copy of an entry in the register of births; in the absence of this, an entry in the horoscope, or family Bible, or in any family pedigree, or upon any tombstone or family portrait, etc.[1] The evidence of a person who is older in age than the assured is also considered sufficient. It is incumbent on the assured to give proof of his age during his life-time, and if he does so, the insurance company either writes across the policy the words "age admitted" or issues a certificate stating that the age has been admitted as correct. When this has been done, the legal representatives are not required to give any proof of the age.[2] Once the company has admitted the age, it is precluded from disproving the age as admitted unless it can show that the admission was obtained by fraud.[3] Hence again, the company cannot refuse to pay the claim, if the age turns out to be more than what was given, but it must pay the claim after deducting the amount of the difference of premium between the two ages.

When the money under the policy becomes payable, the company is in the position of a debtor and the nominee, assignee or legal representative is in the position of a creditor. The company does not. hold the money on any trust.[4] If the assured prefers a fraudulent claim, he would forfeit all benefits under the policy, whether there is a condition to that effect in the policy or not.[5] In joint insurance, fraudulent claim of one of the joint assured would equally hit the claim of the other assured.[6]

---

1. Sec. 32, Indian Evidence Act.
2. Sec. 58, Indian Evidence Act.
3. Oriental Govt. Security Life Ass. Co. v. Narasimhachari (1901) 25 Mad. 183.
4. Mathews v. Northern Ins. Co. (1879) 9 Ch. 80.
5. Brittonv.Royl Ins.Co.(1866)4F.&F.905.
6. Guardian Ins Co. v. Rustomji (1936) 162 I.C. 443.

SUICIDE

Suicide implies a wilful and intentional taking of one's own life. Policies of life assurance usually contain a condition by which the liability of the insurer is modified and limited in case of suicide by the assured; and if the condition is broken (*i.e.*, the assured commits suicide) the insurers cease to be liable. But where there is no condition in respect of suicide the liability of the insurer differs in English law from that under the Indian law. Under English law, in the absence of-any express condition to that effect, a policy of life assurance will be avoided when the assured commits suicide while of a sound mind, for his act amounts to a crime, and it would be contrary to public policy to let any one make capital out of his own crimes.[7] But if the assured commits suicide while of unsound mind the policy cannot be avoided. Under the Indian law, a policy cannot be upset on the ground of public policy in case of suicide even of a sane assured.[8]

ACCIDENT INSURANCE

The term "accident" is not easy to define so far as to determine accurately the distinction between an injury or death by accident and an injury or death by natural causes. To understand the meaning of the term, recourse may be had to the decided cases.

Lord Macnaughten defines an accident[9] as "an unlooked-for mishap, or an untoward event which is not expected or designed." In the term accident some "violence, casualty or *vis major* is necessarily involved." It is something unexpected as opposed to something proceeding from natural causes.[10] An injury is accidental where it is the natural consequence of an unexpected cause, or the unexpected consequence of a natural cause. Running over of the assured by a tram is an instance of the former and injuring his spine by lifting a heavy burden in the ordinary course of business is an instance of the latter.[11] If a man stumbles and sprains his ankle, he meets with an accident because he did not intend to stumble, but a man with a weak heart who while running to catch a train, injures it, does not meet with an "accident".[12] If the cause and. the result are both natural, injury cannot be called accidental.[13] Death by sunstroke is not accidental but death by drowning is.

Accident may also happen by the acts of third persons. For the purpose of the accidental policy, it is immaterial whether the acts of the third party are innocent, negligent or even criminal. It is accidental so far as the assured is concerned.[14]

Accident insurance consists of three branches:—

 (*a*) Personal accident insurance, including insurance against sickness;
 (*b*) Property insurance, including burglary, fidelity, insolvency, etc.
 (*c*) Liability insurance, including motor insurance, workmen's compensation insurance, etc.

Personal Accident Insurance—A contract of personal accident insurance is a contract whereby a sum of money is secured to the assured or his legal representative in the event of his disablement or death by accident. It is a contract against injury or death resulting from accident. Personal accident

---

7. Beresford v. Royal Ins. Co. (1936) 54 T.L.R. 789 H.L.

8. Northern India Ins. Co.v. Kanya Lal 1938 Lah.561.

9. Fenton v. Thorley (1903) A.C. at 448.

10. Sinclair v. Maritime Passengers Ass. Co. (1861) 30 L.J.Q.B. 77.

11. Re Etherington & Lancashire & Yorkshire Accident Ins.. Co. (1909) 1 K.B. 591; Theobald v. Rly. Passengers Ass. Co. (1854) 10 Exch. 45.

12. Scarr v. General Accident Ass. Co. Corp. (1905) 1 K.B. 387.

13. *Ibid.*

14. Trim Joint District School Board Management v. Kelly (1914) A.C. 667; Letts v. Excess Ins. Co. (1916) 32T.L.R.361.

insurance is akin to life assurance and is not a contract of indemnity. The insurer usually undertakes to pay specified sums in the event of temporary or permanent disability, whether partial or total. Other sums are agreed to be payable in the event of death, or loss of limb, etc., as the result of an accident. For example, the insurer may agree to pay ₹ 10,000 for the-loss of both eyes, and ₹ 5,000 for the loss of one eye; or ₹ 50,000 for permanent disablement and ₹ 1,000 for temporary disability plus ₹10 per week during the period of disability and so on.

A policy of personal accident insurance generally provides for insurance against the event of bodily injury or death "caused by violent, accidental, external and visible means." Therefore, the injury or death must not only be accidental but also be paused by accidental means. The assured or his legal representative, as the case may be, must show that an accident occurred within the meaning of the policy, and that the injury or death was caused by such accident. As this is not a contract of indemnity, the insurer cannot deduct from the amount payable to the assured any sum received by him from a person responsible for the accident. Neither is the insurer subrogated to the rights of damages that the assured may have against a third party. The existence of the insurance does not affect the amount recoverable from the third parties.[15]

The contract of personal accident insurance is made in the same manner as in the case of life and the fire insurance. The fundamental principles of insurance, such as insurable interest, good faith, apply to this insurance just as they do to any other form of insurance. The doctrine of proximate cause if of particular importance in this contract of insurance. If the accident is the direct or immediate cause of injury or death the insurer is liable. He is also liable if the immediate cause of death or disablement is a part of the train of events set in motion by the accident. But if there are other intervening causes like disease, or physical infirmity, and such other causes have some connection with the accident or injury, the doctrine of proximate cause must be resorted to for determining the liability of the insurer. If the disease is already in existence at the time the accident takes place, and the effect of each is independent of the other, death or disablement by such accident is covered by the policy.[16] If, on the other hand, accident is merely responsible for the exaggeration of the effects of the disease, death or disablement caused under these circumstances is not covered.[17] If, however, the accident brings out a disease which was merely latent in the system, the insurer is responsible.[18] If the accident happens first and the disease follows, death or disablement will be taken to have been caused by accident, as the disease is only a link in the chain of causation.[19]

As is common in all kinds of insurance policies, certain causes are excepted from the operation of the peril. Impersonal accident policies the most important exceptions relate to the conduct or the physical condition of the assured. The policy may provide that if at the time of the accident the assured is occupied or engaged in any occupation, trade or business, involving more danger to his safety of life, the company will not be liable.[20] There may be a clause that if at the time of the accident the assured is under the influence of liquor so much as to upset the working of his intellectual facilities, the insurer will not be liable.

Coupon insurance is almost unknown in India, but in the Western countries, insurance against railway accident is often effected by means of a ticket purchased like a railway ticket at a station. These insurance tickets enable passengers to protect themselves against accident by the payment of a very small sum.

---

15. Bradburn v. Great Western Rly. (1874) 44 L.J. Ex. 9.

16. Smith v. Accident Ins. Co. (1870) L.R. 5 Ex. 302

17. Fitton v. Accident Death Ins. Co. (1864) 17 C.B. 122.

18. Fidelity & Casualty Co. of New York v. Michell (1917) A.C. 592.

19. Mardford v. Accident Ins. Co.(1903) 1 K.B. 584.

20. Cox v. Employers Liability Ass. Corpn. (1916)2 K.B. 629.

Property Insurance—Contract of property insurance is a contract of indemnity,[21] and the principle of subrogation is applicable to it. Proof by the assured of loss is an essential element of property insurance. The policies of insurance against burglary, house-breaking or theft usually provide their own definition of the risk insured against,[22] but in the absence of such definitions, resort must be had to criminal law for the definition. To constitute a loss within the meaning of the policy, it is necessary that a criminal offence falling within the scope of the policy, must have been committed.[23] Further, it must be shown that the property insured has been carried away permanently from the premises. Policies against loss by theft generally cover "theft following upon actual, forcible and violent entry upon the premises."

Articles of special value, or those held in trust, are usually excluded. Also, loss or damage capable of being covered by a different kind of insurance is excluded, *e.g.*, loss by theft following a fire.

A description of the premises containing the property insured is an essential part of the contract, for the risk varies according to the character and locality of the premises,[24] and the risk attaches only whilst the property is in the premises defined in the policy. If the assured parts with the insured property or removes it from the specified locality, the insurance ceases to be effective. The assured is usually required to take all reasonable precautions to protect the insured property. After the loss has taken place, the assured is usually required to notify the police as to the loss.

Fidelity Insurance—In this insurance the insurer undertakes to indemnify the assured (employer), in consideration of certain payments, up to a certain specified amount insured against for loss arising through the fraud, or embezzlement on the part of the employees. This kind of insurance, which is also known as "fidelity guarantee" insurance, is frequently adopted as a precautionary measure in cases where new and untried employees are given positions of trust. The "collective" policy embracing all employees falling within certain categories, or alternatively, the whole staff, has become very common.

Motor Car Insurance—The owner of a motor vehicle may, and usually does, insure his vehicle against any damage that it may suffer. He may also insure against personal accident to himself and other occupants of the car. He may insure his car or may not do so, but he **MUST** now insure in respect of the liability which he may incur to others in consequence of the use of his vehicle. This is known as "Compulsory Insurance of Motor Vehicles against Third Party Risks" which has been provided for in Chapter VIII of the Motor Vehicles Act, 1939.

A policy of motor vehicle insurance, therefore, serves three purposes, in as much as it is an insurance (*i*) on property—the motor vehicle, (*ii*) against personal accident, and (iii) against liability for accidents. The policy covers loss or damage due to accident, theft, fire or self-ignition and wilful damage. The personal accident insurance in a motor accident policy covers two classes of accidents, namely, (*a*) if the accident happens, in connection with the insured vehicle the insured is protected along with the other occupants of the car, (*b*) if 'he accident happens in connection with other vehicles the assured is covered to the extent of all accidents happening while he was travelling in such other vehicles.[25]

The delivery of a certificate of insurance to the assured imposes upon the insurers the duty of satisfying by payment to the third party any judgment subsequently obtained by him against the assured. The effect of this and other provisions in the Act is to compel the insurer to satisfy those claims, notwithstanding that he may be entitled to avoid or cancel the policy.

---

21. Dane v. Mortgage Ins. Corp.(1894) 1 Q.B. 54.

22. Wasserman v. Blackburn (1927)T.L.R. 99; Leizard Bros. v. Brookes (1932)38Ccn..Cas. 48.

23. Re, George & Goldsmiths etc., (1899) 1 Q.B. 595.

24. Person v Commercial Union Ass, Co. (1876) I.A.C. 489.

25. Singh, B.N.: *Insurance Law and Practice*, p. 466.

SUMMARY

A contract of insurance is a contract by which one party, called the insurer or underwriter, undertakes, in consideration of a certain sum, called the premium, to make good to the other party, called the assured, any loss which he may sustain by reason of the peril insured against.

The risks which may be insured against include fire, accident, burglary, the insolvency of a debtor, the perils of the sea (marine insurance) and death (Life assurance)

Fundamental Principles of Insurance

1. A contract of insurance is a contract *uberrimae fidei*—contract based on utmost good faith.

2. The assured must have insurable interest in the subject-matter of the insurance i.e., either he must own part or whole of it or he must be in such a position that injury to it would affect him adversely. By insurable interest is meant pecuniary interest in the subject-matter.

3. Excepting life assurance and personal accident and sickness insurance, a contract of insurance is a contract of indemnity and indemnity only.

4. In the event of some mishap to the insured property, the insured must act as though he were uninsured, and make every effort to preserve the property.

5. A contract of insurance can be enforced only if the risk has attached. If the risk is not run the consideration fails, and, therefore, the premium received by insurer must be returned.

6. The loss must be proximately caused by the peril insured against.

7. Except life assurance, a contract of insurance is a contract from year to year, although it can be renewed if the assured so desires.

Life Assurance—In Life Assurance, the insurer agrees to pay to the assured or to the person for whose benefit the policy is taken a stated sum of money on the happening of a particular event contingent on the duration of human life.

Under a Whole Life Assurance, the policy money is payable at the death of the assured; while under an Endowment Policy money is payable on the assured's surviving a stated period of years, *e.g.*, on his attaining the age of 55, or at his death should that occur previously.

Insurance Interest—1. A person has insurable interest in his life and can insure it for any sum whatsoever, and as often as he likes.

2. A wife has an insurable interest in the life of her husband, husband in the life of his wife.

3. A creditor has an insurable interest in the life of his debtor to the extent of the debt.

4. A person has an insurable interest in his relative if (*a*) he has by such relation an enforceable claim on him, or (*b*) the relative is supported by the assured.

Mere love and affection is not sufficient to constitute insurable interest. Thus, a parent as such has no insurable interest in his child and *vice versa*.

5. An employee has an insurable interest in the life of his employer and *vice versa*.

6. A partner has an insurable interest in the life of a co-partner to the extent of the capital invested by the latter.

Surrender Value—Surrender value of a life policy is the amount which the insurer is prepared to pay in total discharge of the contract, in case the assured wishes to surrender his policy and extinguish his claim on it. The surrender value is based on the actual premium paid, and policy is required to have run for 2 or 3 years before surrender value will be allowed.

Paid-up Policy Value is the amount to which the sum assured would be reduced at any time if the assured requested a re-arrangement of his contract so that no further premium should be payable. The amount on the paid-up policy is payable on the happening of the event assured against.

Life Policies are freely assignable as actionable claims. They may be sold, mortgaged or settled, provided that a written notice to the insurer is given of such assignment, so as to make the assignee's title effective against the insurer. Assignment may be made by the execution of an instrument in writing or by a mere endorsement on the policy.

Claim—A person claiming money on the maturity of the policy must satisfy the insurer that he is entitled to receive the money either (a) as the owner of the policy, or (b) because the actual claim is vested in him as legal representative or as nominee, or as assignee.

On the maturity of the life policy the insurer requires a satisfactory and reasonable proof of age and death of the assured. Death may be proved by direct or indirect evidence.

In the absence of any conditions to the contrary, suicide does not avoid the policy in India.

Fire Insurance—A contract of fire insurance is essentially a contract of indemnity. Subject to the maximum of the amount of the policy the insurer indemnifies the assured for any loss caused by fire within a specified period.

Average Clause—A condition, called the average clause, is usually incorporated in fire policy, by which the insured is called upon to bear a portion of the loss himself, in the case of under-insurance. If a property worth ₹ 5,000 is insured for ₹ 4,000 and suffers a loss of ₹ 1,000 the insured will get 4/5ths of 1,000 i.e., ₹ 800, and the balance of ₹200 will be borne by the assured.

Insurable Interest—In fire insurance, the assured must have insurable interest both at the time of effecting the policy and at the time of the loss. In consequence of this fact a fire policy is not assignable. In the case of goods, insurable interest arises, on account of ownership, possession and contract. The insurance of a building may be effected by anyone interested in it, e.g., owner, tenant, purchaser, mortgagee.

The risk on fire policy commences from the moment the cover note, or the deposit receipt or the interim protection note is issued.

The word 'Fire' is to be construed in its popular and liberal sense, and means a fire which has broken bounds: Actual ignition is essential.

Subrogation—The essence of fire insurance is indemnity, and therefore the assured cannot make a profit of his loss. The rule gives rise to the doctrine of subrogation, which means that on indemnifying the assured, the insurer is entitled to the advantage of every right of the assured. Having satisfied the claim of the assured the insurer stands in his place; he is subrogated to all the rights of the assured.

Contribution—Where a person effects two or more insurances in respect of the same subject-matter and the same perils, he will recover only the actual loss, even though the total amount with different insurers far exceeds the loss. If any insurer pays more than his share of the liability, he can claim contributions from others, so that the liability of each is made proportionate to the risk covered.

Claims—Before his claim will be met the assured is required to cause a notice of fire to be given to the insurer, and also furnish full particulars of the loss and damage and the proof of the value of the property, and if it is totally destroyed, even of its existence at the time of the fire.

Marine Insurance—Marine insurance is a contract of indemnity in which the underwriter agrees to indemnify the assured for loss or damage caused to the subject-matter insured by the perils of the sea.

A contract of marine insurance must be embodied in a marine policy, otherwise the insurance contract will be veid. The marine policy must specify (i) the name of the assured, (ii) the subject-matter insured and the risk insured against, the voyage, or period of time, or both, (iii) the sum insured, and (iv) the name or names of the insurers.

Implied Warranties—There are two implied warranties, namely, seaworthiness and legality of voyage, which must be complied with to render the contract of marine insurance valid.

In every voyage policy the ship must be seaworthy at the commencement of the voyage, or if the voyage is divisible into distinct stages, at the commencement of each stage. To be seaworthy a ship must be reasonably fit in all respects to encounter the perils of the voyage she is about to undertake.

The adventure insured must be a lawful one, and so far as the assured can control the matter, it shall be carried out in a lawful manner.

The ship must follow the-course specified in the policy, or if not specified therein, the usual and customary course. It must not deviate from the voyage without any lawful excuse, and the voyage must commence without unreasonable delay.

Where the destination is specified in the policy, and the ship, after the commencement of the risk, sails for another destination, no risk attaches to the policy from the time when change of voyage is contemplated.

Losses—A loss may be either Total or Partial. Total loss may be actual or constructive, and partial loss may be particular average or general average.

An Actual Total Loss occurs where the subject-matter insured is destroyed, or so damaged as to cease to be a thing of the kind insured or the assured is irretrievably deprived of the subject-matter.

A Constructive Total Loss occurs where the subject-matter insured is reasonably abandoned on account of its actual total loss appearing to be unavoidable, or because it could be preserved from actual total loss without an expenditure which would exceed its value when the expenditure has been incurred. Notice of abandonment must be given to the insurer within a reasonable time.

A Particular Average Loss is a partial loss accidentally and fortuitously caused to the subject-matter by the peril insured against. Particular average loss becomes payable by the underwriter only when it has been actually incurred.

A General Average Loss is a partial loss, which occurs when any extraordinary sacrifice or expenditure is voluntarily and reasonably made or incurred in time of peril for the purpose of preserving the property imperilled in the common adventure.

A sacrifice may be made by destroying any part of the ship, or by throwing overboard any part of the cargo.

Bottomry and Respondentia are monetary loans obtained in cases of urgent necessity and are covered by General Average Loss. Bottomry is a loan obtained on the security of the ship, or ship and cargo jointly, and respondentia is a loan taken on the security of the cargo alone.

Accident Insurance consists of three branches, namely,

(a) Personal Accident Insurance whereby a sum of money is secured to assured or his legal representative in the event of his disablement or death by accident.

(b) Property Insurance, including burglary, fidelity and insolvency. Property insurance covers all loss of property by burglary, theft or house-breaking, or by any other act which is a criminal offence.

In Fidelity-Insurance the insurer undertakes to indemnify the assured (employer) against any loss arising through the fraud or embezzlement on the part of the employees.

(c) Liability Insurance, including motor insurance. Workmen's Compensation insurance, etc., under which the insurer agrees to compensate the assured for his liability which he may incur to others in consequence of the use of his motor vehicle or to his employee under Workmen's Compensation Act.

CASES FOR RECAPITULATION

1. W insured his house against fire. Later, while insane, *W* killed his wife, severely injured his only son, set fire to the house and died in the fire. The son survived and sued the insurers for the loss. *Held,* the son could recover on the fire policy, as the insurer is not relieved of his liability on the fire policy for the insured caused the fire when he was insane (*Karow* v. *The Continental Ins. Co.* 57 Wis. 56).

2. M insured against fire his shop containing stock of merchandise worth ₹ 75,000 for ₹ 20,000 only in order to pay a smaller amount of premium. The policy contained a condition that if the property insured should at the breaking out of any fire be of greater value than the sum insured thereon, the insured should be considered as being his own insurer for the difference and should bear a ratable proportion of the loss accordingly. In a fire the entire stock and furniture worth ₹ 70,000 were burnt to ashes. M claimed the whole insured amount. The insurer pleaded the average clause. *Held,* M can recover the whole amount of ₹ 70,000. The average clause comes into play only if it is proved that the loss sustained by the assured is less than the sum insured. When the loss is much more than the sum insured, the insured can recover the whole amount in spite of the average clause. (*General Ass. Society Ltd. v. Mohd Salim,* 1965 All 561).

3. M was the owner of nearly all the shares and the only substantial creditor of a company carrying on timber business. He insured the timber against fire in his own name. A fire occurred and all the timber was destroyed. He put in a claim under the policy and the insurer refused to pay. It was held that M could not recover the loss as he had no insurable interest. Lord Wrenbury said "... the corporator, even if he holds all the shares, is not the corporation, and neither he nor any creditor of the company has any property, legal or equitable, in the assets of the Corporation." [*Macaura* v. *Northern Assurance Co.*(1925) A.C.619].

4. A effected an insurance on his goods against loss or damage by fire. Afterwards A and his wife quarrelled and she set fire to and destroyed the goods. *Held,* A was entitled to recover under the fire policy as the wife had set fire to the goods without his connivance. The illegal act was not his but of his wife, and he was covered under the policy against loss caused by an illegal act of another [*Midland Ins. Co. v. Smith* (1881) 6 Q.B.D.561].

5. In a case of fire insurance contract the insurer, on receiving information of the insured property having been lost by fire, repudiated his liability *in toto* on the ground that it was a case of intentional arson. The assured brought an action against the insurer for the recovery of his loss. The insurance policy contained a clause to the effect that in case of any difference between the insurer and the assured as to the amount of damage suffered by the loss of property, the same should be referred to arbitration. The insurer pleaded that the suit was prematurely filed, as the dispute had not been referred to arbitration and should be dismissed. *Held,* that the suit was maintainable, as the repudiation of the claim on a ground going to the root of the contract precluded the insurer from pleading the arbitration clause. A party cannot approbate and reprobate at the same time. He cannot claim that the policy is void and yet seek benefit of a condition in that policy by insisting upon arbitration [*Jureidini* v. *National Br. &. Irish Millers Ins. Co.* (1915) A.C 499].

In *Heyman* v. *Darwins* (1941) A.C., the House of Lords seems to have doubted me principle laid down by the House of Lords in Jureidini's case. It is therefore safest for the assured to go to arbitration and sue on the amount awarded by arbitration.

6. Property worth ₹5,000 is insured up to ₹ 1,000. There is an 'average clause' in the policy. Property worth ₹ 1,000 is destroyed by fire. The insured can recover the full amount of ₹ 1,000 on the same principle as explained in case No.2.

7. A's goods in a warehouse are insured. B is the insurer. The goods are burnt A recovers their full value of ₹ 1,000 from B. Then A sues the warehouse-keeper and recovers ₹ 1,000 from him. B claims this amount from A. It was held that B could recover this amount of ₹ 1,000 from A, as this amount makes his receipt in excess of the loss actually sustained by him. He cannot be allowed to make a profit of his loss. As B had made good his loss, A must refund to B the amount of ₹ 1,000 which he recovered from the warehouse-keeper. This problem is based on the *case Darell* v. *Tibhits* (1880) 5 Q.B.D. 560.

8. A ship insured against the perils of the sea was lying at anchor off the shore about to proceed on her voyage. While the boilers were being filled, a valve remained closed, due to the fault of somebody

on board whose duty it was to see that it remained open. Consequently in the operation of pumping, water was forced back, split the air-chamber and disabled the pump. The House of Lords, reversing the judgments of the Courts below, held that this was not a loss covered by an ordinary marine policy, being neither a peril of the sea nor coming within the general words "all other perils, losses, etc." The underwriters were held not liable to pay. [*Thames and Mersey Marine Insurance Co. Ltd.* v. *Hamilton, Fraser & Co.* (1887) 12 A.C. 484], As a result of this case, the *Inchamaree* clause, named after the Steamer *Inchamaree* of this case was brought into general use, extending the liabilities of the underwriter.

9. A ship was valued at, and insured for £6,000, though her real value was £ 9,000. Owing to a collision she was sunk, and the underwriters paid a total loss of £6,000. In due course, the assured recovered from the owners of the wrong doing vessel a sum of £5,700. The assured contended that they were entitled to retain one-third of this sum (the ship's actual value being £ 9,000, and the insured value being £6,000), but it was held that the underwriters were entitled to the whole of this £5,700, £6,000 being the value admitted in the policy. (*North of England Ins. Association* v. *Armstrong*).

10. A ship, which was insured under a time policy, was sent to sea unseaworthy in two respects; her hull was in an unfit state for the voyage and her crew was insufficient The assured knew of the insufficiency of the crew but not of the unfitness of the hull. The ship was lost because of the unfitness of the hull. *Held,* the insurers were liable. In a time policy there is no implied warranty that the ship shall be seaworthy at any stage of the adventure provided the loss is not attributable to the unseaworthiness to which the assured was privy [*Thomas* v. *Tyne and Wear S.S. Freight Ins. Assn.* (1917) 1 K.B. 938].

11. On 15th January, 1968, A assigned his life insurance policy to B for valuable consideration by a separate deed of assignment. On 15th February, 1968 A transferred the same policy by endorsement thereon to C as a gift, and on the same day gave notice of the transfer in favour of C to the Life Insurance Corporation in the prescribed manner enclosing therewith the original deed of assignment. Both B and C claim the amount of the policy on maturity. The Life Insurance Corporation will recognise the claim of C and pay him the policy money. Under Sec. 38 (3) the assignment is complete and effectual but does not confer upon the assignee any right to sue on such policy until notice in writing of the assignment has been given to the corporation and either the endorsement or the instrument has been given to the corporatioa and either the endorsement or the instrument itself or a copy certified to be correct by both the transferor and the transferee have been delivered to the corporation. The date on which the notice in writing is delivered to the corporation shall regulate the priority of all claims under a transfer or assignment as between persons interested in the policy. As notice of assignment in favour of C was given, C would get the policy money. It makes no difference even if both assignments have been made for valuable consideration.

12. A, the holder of a policy of life insurance on his own life, nominates B as the person to whom the policy money is to be paid in the event of his death. Thereafter A secures a loan from the insurer and assigns his policy to the insurer in consideration of the loan. In due course, the loan is repaid and the policy is re-assigned to A. A thereafter dies. Both B and the legal representatives of A claim the amount of the policy. B's claim will succeed as the nomination in his favour was not affected by the assignment to the insurer. Although Sec.39 (4) of the Insurance Act, 1938 provides that a transfer or assignment of a policy made in accordance with the provisions of Sec. 38 of the Act shall automatically cancel a nomination, the proviso to it makes an exception to this rule. An assignment of a policy to the insurer, who bears the risk on the policy at the time of assignment, in consideration of a loan granted by that insurer on the security of the policy within its surrender value or its assignment on repayment of the loan shall not cancel the nomination, but shall affect the rights of the nominee only to the extent of the insurer's interest in the policy.

13. X, a policy-holder in an insurance company nominates Y as his nominee. Before the maturity of

the policy *Y* dies. On the maturity of the policy, *Y*'s heirs claim the policy money from the insurance company. By virtue of Sec. 39(5) of the Insurance Act, 1938 where the nominee dies before the policy matures for payment the amount secured by the policy shall be payable to the policy-holder or his heirs or legal representatives or the holder of a succession certificate, as the case may be. In view of the express provisions of law, the heirs of the nominee will not be entitled to the sum payable under the policy in this case.

14. *A* holder of a marine insurance policy obtains a decree against the insurer in respect of a claim arising out of his policy. Prior to the date of this decree another decree had been passed against the insurer in a suit for arrears of rent filed by the landlord of the premises rented by the insurer. Upon the failure of the insurer to satisfy the decrees, the decree-holders seek to execute their respective decrees by attaching the amount of the statutory deposit made by the insurer with the Reserve Bank under Sec.7 of the Insurance Act. The policy holder's decretal amount can only be paid out of this deposit and the landlord cannot get anything; for the statutory deposit can be utilised only for the payment of policy money due from the insurer and no other claim can be met out of it.

15. *M* is the holder of a policy of life insurance on his own life, and Mrs. *M* is mentioned in the text of the policy as the person who should be paid the amount of the policy in the event of his death. Afterwards *M* nominates by will his brother, *R*, in place of Mrs. *M*. and sends a notice of the change by post to the L.I.C. The letter is lost in transit. Upon the death of M, the corporation pays the policy money to Mrs. *M*. *R* contends the payment. *R*'s contention cannot hold good, as the written notice of change in nomination was not 'delivered' to insurer, as required by the Act, as it was lost in transit. The payment by L.I.C. to Mrs. *M* was *bona fide.*

16. *A*, the holder of policy of life insurance on his own life, assigned it to his wife *B*, on the condition that the benefits under the policy are to revert to him should *B* die during his lifetime. A year later *A* revoked the assignment on the ground that it was conditional. Thereafter *A* died during the lifetime of *B*. Both *B* and *A*'s legal representatives claimed the policy money. *Held,* that the claim of *B* prevailed. Although under Sec. 38 (7) of the Insurance Act it is permissible to make a conditional assignment of life policy, yet the assignor cannot revoke or cancel an assignment once validly made. The policy remained assigned to *B*, and on *A*'s death *B* was entitled to get the policy money (*Bai Lakshmi* v. *Jaswantlal T. Das* 1947 Bom.369).

17. *A* took a loan from the *A*. Bank Limited, and assigned his life policy in its favour. *A* died and the bank claimed the policy money, but the insurer declined to pay. In the meantime, *R*, the legal representative of *A*, redeemed the policy by satisfying the bank's debt, and put in a claim with the insurer for the policy money. The insurer refused to pay *R* on the plea that only the bank, as assignee, was entitled to receive payment. *Held,* the insurer must pay *R* the policy money. The assignment of the policy in favour of the bank was merely by way of security for the loan made by the bank. On the satisfaction of the debt, the assignment terminated, the policy was redeemed and its benefits reverted to the estate of the deceased. These facts entitled *R*, as the legal representative of *A*, to sue the insurer and recover the policy money (*Scottish Union and National Ins. Co. Ltd.* v. *Roushan Jahan Begum,* 1945 Oudh, 152).

18. *A* made a proposal to an insurance company for an insurance on his life for ₹ 50,000. On the proposal form he answered various questions truthfully and disclosed all relevant facts. A few days later, but before the proposal was definitely accepted, *A* was taken ill with pneumonia. Later the company accepted the proposal and the first premium was paid. Two days later *A* died of pneumonia and the company then learned for the first time of his illness. The company was held not liable to pay ₹50,000. *A* contract of insurance is a contract of utmost good faith, and it is the duty of the proposer to disclose all material facts. Also, where a material alteration of the risk arises between the date of the proposal and the issue of the policy, notice must be given to the insurer, otherwise he will be entitled to avoid the contract (*Looker* v. *Law Union and Rock Insurance Co. Ltd.*). Since A's illness is

clearly a material fact within the above definition, and substantially alters the risk, and since no notice of illness was given to the insurance co. before it accepted the proposal, the company can rescind the policy and thereby avoid the liability to pay the ₹ 50,000.

19. The insurers paid the assured the full value of a ship at the time of the loss and subsequently the assured received on agreement from the Canadian Government a certain agreed sum which exceeded that paid by the insurers owing to the devaluation of the pound against the dollar. *Held,* the insurer could not recover from the assured anything more than they had paid under the doctrine of subrogation [*Yorkshire Ins. Co. Ltd.* v. *Nisbet Shipping Co. Ltd.* (1961) 2 All. E.R.487].

CHAPTER

11

The Law of Negotiable Instruments

PART 11-A
INTRODUCTION

The law relating to negotiable instruments is to be found in the Negotiable Instruments Act, 1881, which came into force on 1st March, 1882. The Act operates subject to the provisions of Sections 31 and 32 of the Reserve Bank of India Act, 1934. Section 31 provides that no person in India other than the Reserve Bank of India or the Central Government shall draw, accept, make or issue any bill of exchange, hundi, promissory note or engagement for the payment of money payable to bearer on demand. Section 31 further provides that no one except the Reserve Bank or the Central Government can make or issue a promissory note expressed to be payable to the bearer of the instrument, *whether payable on demand or after a certain time.* Section 32 makes the issuing of such bills or notes punishable with fine which may extend-to the amount of the instrument, and the instrument will be illegal and unenforceable.

The effect of these provisions is that —

   (*a*) a bill of exchange cannot be made payable to the bearer on demand, although it can subsequently become payable to bearer on demand on being indorsed in blank;

   (*b*) a promissory note cannot be made payable to the bearer, no matter whether it is payable on demand or after a certain time.

   (*c*) But a cheque (though a bill of exchange) payable to bearer on demand can be drawn on a person's account with a banker.

MEANING OF NEGOTIABLE INSTRUMENT

By virtue of Sec. 13(a) "Negotiable Instrument" means a promissory note, bill of exchange or cheque payable either to order or to bearer, whether the words "order" or "bearer" appear on the instrument or not. Although the Act mentions only these three instruments, it does not exclude the possibility of adding any other instrument to the list if it satisfies the following two conditions of negotiability, viz:—

   (*i*) that it is by custom of trade transferable by delivery or by endorsement and delivery; and

   (*ii*) that it is capable of being sued upon by the person holding it *pro tempore* (for the time being) in his own name. Thus, documents such as share warrants payable to bearer, debentures payable to bearer, and Dividend Warrants are negotiable. But postal orders, money orders, deposit receipts, share certificates, bills of lading, dock warrants, and I.O.U.S. are not negotiable instruments.

In simple terms, a negotiable instrument is an instrument which entitles a person holding it to a sum of money and which is transferable from person to person by mere delivery like cash. The transferee becomes entitled to the money and also to the right to further transfer it.

It is pertinent to note that negotiable instruments constitute an exception to the general principle of law *nemo dat quod non-habet* (no one can transfer a better title than he himself has). Consequently, a person who takes a negotiable instrument in good faith and for value acquires good title to it, (*i.e.* becomes its owner) even if he takes it from a person who has no title to it (*i.e.* he is a thief or finder). In the words of Willis J, "A negotiable instrument is one the property in which is acquired by every person who takes it *bona fide* and for value, notwithstanding any defect of title in the person from whom he took it."

It follows from this definition that a person taking the instrument *bona fide* and for value gets a good title, and is not affected by defects in the title of his predecessor, and takes it free from any equities, which could be enforced against the original or any intermediate holder. It is essential, for this principle to apply that the instrument must be such that it can be transferred like cash by simple delivery, which is possible only when it is payable to bearer. If it requires something more than mere delivery, e.g., indorsement (being payable to order), it is not negotiable till it is *properly* indorsed. Thus, in the case of an instrument made payable to order, it is imperative that the indorsement is valid, proper or genuine before the instrument is delivered. If it is delivered without indorsement or the indorsement is forged, no title passes to the receiver of the instrument even though he took it *bona fide* and for value, as the instrument is not negotiable.

In *Whistler* v. *Forster* 143 E R 441, G, by means of a fraud, obtained a cheque from F. The cheque was made payable to G or order. G gave the cheque to W in payment of his own debt, but forgot to indorse it. W had no notice of the fraud then, but, before he could get G's indorsement, he was given notice of the fraud. Accordingly, W could not get a good title. It was pointed out by Erle C.J. that "the title to a negotiable instrument payable to order passes by valid indorsement and delivery."

Requirements of Negotiability or Essential Elements of a Negotiable Instrument—To be negotiable an instrument must have the following elements:—

1. It must be in writing, which includes typing, printing, engraving.

2. The instrument must be signed by the maker or drawer.

3. There must be an unconditional promise or order to pay. If the instrument is a promissory note, it must contain an unconditional promise to pay. If the instrument is a bill or cheque, it must contain an unconditional order of command to pay money. If the promise or order is conditional, the instrument is non-negotiable.

4. The instrument must call for payment of a certain sum of money only, and nothing else.

5. The instrument must be payable at a time which is certain to arrive. If it is payable "when convenient", the instrument is not negotiable.

6. In case of a bill or cheque, the drawee must be named or described with reasonable certainty.

7. The instrument must be such or in such a state that it can be transferred like cash by simple delivery. This is possible when it is payable to bearer. If it is payable to order, it becomes negotiable and makes the transferee its owner only when it is *property* indorsed before it is delivered.

A negotiable instrument, therefore, possesses the following special characteristics which distinguish it from an ordinary chattel or chose-in-action:—

(*a*) The property in it passes by mere delivery (when payable to bearer) or by valid indorsement and delivery (when made payable to order.)

(*b*) The holder in due course is not in any way affected by any defect of title of his transferor or any party.

(*c*) The holder in due course can sue on it in his own name without giving notice to the debtor of the fact that he has become holder.

(*d*) Consideration is presumed to have passed, and this presumption cannot be rebutted when the instrument has passed into the hands of a holder in due course.

Our Act provides that an instrument to be negotiable must be payable in any one of the following forms:

(*i*) Pay *A*; (*ii*) Pay *A* or order; (*iii*) Pay to the order of *A*; (*iv*) Pay *A* and *B*; (*v*) Pay *A* or *B*; (*vi*) Pay *A* or bear; (*ii*) Pay bearer.

An instrument made payable in any one of the following forms is not negotiable:

(*i*) Pay *A* only; (*ii*) Pay to *A* and none else; (*iii*) Pay Dhani (owner) or Shah (any respectable bearer of Worth and substance in the market). This last is, however, recognised by custom as negotiable being a *Shahjog hundi;* (*iv*) Promise to pay *A* or bearer; (*v*) Promise to pay bearer. These instruments, though not negotiable, are assignable, but the transferee takes them subject to all equities and liabilities of the transferor.

PRESUMPTIONS AS TO NEGOTIABLE INSTRUMENTS

Since the philosophy underlying the law of negotiable instruments is that business transactions should be facilitated by making available evidences of rights to money that will pass freely from hand to hand, Sec. 118 of the Act provides that until the contrary is proved, the following presumptions shall be made:—

1. that every negotiable instrument was made or drawn, accepted, endorsed and negotiated or transferred for consideration;[1]
2. that it bears the *date* on which it was made or drawn;
3. that every accepted bill was *accepted within a reasonable time* after its date and before its maturity.
4. that every *transfer* of a negotiable instrument was made *before maturity,*
5. that the endorsements appearing on it were made *in the order* in which they appear thereon;
6. where an instrument has been lost or destroyed, that it was duly stamped and the stamp was duly cancelled;
7. that the holder of the instrument is a holder in due course.

But the presumptions are rebuttable. In *Adikanda Behera* v. *Daini Krishna Murthy Patra,* 1983 Orissa 238, a pronote was executed by the defendant and registered. By a subsequent document the plaintiff admitted that the pronote was obtained from the defendant by way of additional security for a loan advanced to certain society. *Held,* there was no independent liability to pay under the pronote.

PART 11-B

PROMISSORY NOTES AND BILLS OF EXCHANGE

PROMISSORY NOTES

A promissory note is an instrument in writing (note being a bank- note or a currency note) containing an unconditional undertaking, signed by the maker, to pay a certain sum of money to, or to the order of, a certain person (Sec. 4). It will be noted that all the requisites of a negotiable instrument are present in this definition, which are reiterated in the following paragraphs. An instrument to be a promissory note must possess the following elements:—

1. It must be in writing—Mere verbal promise to pay will not do. The method of writing is unimportant, but it must be in a medium that cannot be altered easily.

2. It must contain an express promise or clear undertaking to pay—A promise to pay cannot be inferred; it must be express.[2] A mere acknowledgement is not enough.

---

1. Pardhan Purushottam v. Shantilal Purushottam, 1954 Sau. 42; Abdul Shakur v. Kotwaleshar, 1958 All. 54; State of M.P. v. Jauhrilal, 1962 M.P. 348.
2. Keshavji Thackershi v. Narshi Ramji, 1954 Sau. 52

The following are not promissory notes, as there is no promise to pay:

(*a*) "Mr. B.I.O.U. (I owe you) ₹ 500."

(*b*) "I am liable to pay you ₹ 500."

(*c*) "I have taken from you ₹ 100; whenever you ask for it, I have to pay."[3]

Although the promise to pay may be opposed to public policy and unenforceable, once a promissory note is executed the promise to pay is performed because a promissory note amounts in law to payment and what vitiates a promise does not vitiate a payment.

In *C. Iyer v. A. Krishna,* 1954 T.C.231, *A*, the father of a bride, executed a promissory note in favour of her father- in-law in connection with the marriage and in respect of jewels agreed to be paid thereon, it was held that, notwithstanding the original promise being opposed to public policy and so unenforceable, *A* was liable on the pronote. Once a pronote is executed the promise to pay is performed because a promissory note amounts in law to payment and what vitiates a promise does not vitiate a payment.[4]

3. The promise to pay must be unconditional—We have seen before that an instrument, to be negotiable, must contain an unconditional promise or order. So a promise to pay contained in a note must be unconditional. A conditional undertaking destroys the negotiable character of an otherwise negotiable instrument. Therefore, the promise to pay must not depend upon the happening of some outside event. It must be payable absolutely. Although the event upon which the note is payable happens, this fact does not remove the objection; the happening of the event does not cure the defect The rule is *'once non-negotiable, always non-negotiable.'*

A promise to pay 'when able,' or 'when convenient,' or 'as soon as I can,' or 'after my marriage with C,' or 'out of money due to me from *B* as soon as *B* pays it' or 'on *A*'s death provided he leaves me sufficient funds to pay,' is conditional and not binding as a pronote. But **a promise to pay at a particular place or after a specified time or on the happening of an event which must happen is not conditional.** For example, 'I promise to pay *B* ₹ 500 seven days after *C*'s death' is not conditional, for *C* is certain to die some time or the other.

4. The maker must sign the promissory note—The person who draws the instrument and signs it is known as the maker and the person to whom the promise is made is called the payee. The instrument will be complete only when it is signed by the maker even when it is written by him and his name appears in the body of the instrument. Signature may be in any part of the instrument, and may be expressed by thumb-mark or any other mark, if the executant is illiterate. The impression of a printed mark is sufficient signature. The signature may be indicated by a facsimile or by stamping the name.

5. The maker must be a certain person—The note itself must show clearly who is the person engaging himself to pay. Where the promisors are more than one they may bind themselves jointly or jointly and severally but not in the alternative.

6. The payee must be certain—A promissory note must contain a promise to pay to some person or persons ascertained by name or designation or to their order. A promissory note made payable to the maker himself is nullity, but if such a note is endorsed by him, it becomes payable to bearer, and is valid.

7. The sum payable must be certain, and the amount must not be capable of contingent additions or subtractions. Thus, if *A* promises to pay ₹ 500 and all other sums which shall become due to him, or to pay £ 130 and all fines according to rules, the instrument is not a promissory note. But the payment of interest does not make the sum indefinite, if the rate of interest is stated. If the rate is not

---

3. Laxmibai v.Ganesh Raghunath (1901) 25 Bom. 373.

4. See also K. Iyer v. Ammal, 1950 T.C.73; Bherulal v. Ghisulal, 1957 Raj 387.

stated the instrument is not a promissory note. In *Raghunath Prasad* v. *Mangi* Lal, 1960 Raj. 20, and entry in the *bahi* of the plaintiff and signed by the defendant was as follows: "Balance due after understanding the account ₹ 30,167. Whenever Mangi Lal Ji demands the same I shall pay with interest. Raghunath Prasad." *Held,* that the document was not a promissory note, as the sum payable wa,s not certain as no rate of interest was stated. Moreover, a writing on a *bahi* was not intended to be negotiable, and it was not a pronote.

8. Payment must be in legal money of the country—Thus, an agreement to pay money or grain or to deliver 100 tons of iron is not a promissory note.

9. A bank note or a currency note is not a promissory note within the meaning of the section— They are expressly excluded from the definition, as they are treated as money and not merely securities for money. **A promissory note or a draft cannot be made payable to bearer, no matter whether it is payable on demand or after a certain time.**

10. Other matters of form like number, place, date, etc., are usually found given in notes, but they are not essential in law.

The date of a note is not material unless the amount is made payable at a certain time after date. But even in this case the absence of date does not invalidate the note and the date of execution can be independently proved. A stamp is, however, necessary under the Indian Stamp Act,

The following two examples satisfy all the above conditions:—

(*a*) I promise to Pay *B* or order ₹ 500.

(*b*) I acknowledge myself to be indebted to B in ₹ 1,000 to be paid on demand, for value received.

SPECIMEN OF A PROMISSORY NOTE

₹ 500   Delhi

January 4, 1990

On demand [or six months after date] I promise to pay Ram or order the sum of five hundred rupees with interest at 6 per cent per annum until payment

Stamp

Sd/-

Gopal

Gopal is the maker and Ram is the payee.

BILL OF EXCHANGE

A bill of exchange is an instrument in writing containing an unconditional order, signed by the maker, directing a certain person to pay a certain sum of money only to, or to the order of, a certain person or to the bearer of the instrument (Sec. 5). The definition of a bill is very similar to that of a note, and for most purposes the rules which apply to notes are in general applicable to bills. The fundamental requirements and ingredients are the same. But a bill differs from a note in some particulars, it being an order to pay.

DISTINCTION BETWEEN BILL AND NOTE

1. In a note there are only two parties—the maker (debtor) and the payee (creditor). In a bill there are three parties, namely, drawer, drawee and payee; though any two out of the three capacities may be filled by one and the same person. In a bill the drawer is the maker who orders the drawee to pay the bill to a person called the payee or to his order. When the drawee accepts the bill he is called the acceptor.

2. A note cannot be made payable to the maker himself, while in a bill the drawer and payee or drawee and payee may be same person.

3. A note contains an unconditional promise by the maker to pay to the payee or his order; in a bill there is an unconditional order to the drawee to pay according to the drawer's directions.

4. A note is presented for payment without any prior acceptance by the maker. A bill payable after sight must be accepted by the drawee or some one else on his behalf before it can be presented for payment.

5. The liability of the maker of a note is primary and absolute, but the liability of the drawer of a bill is secondary and conditional.

6. The maker of the note stands in immediate relation with the payee, while the maker or drawer of an accepted bill stands in immediate relation with the acceptor and not the payee.

7. Foreign bills must be protested for dishonour when such protest is required to be made by the law of the country where they are drawn but no such protest is necessary in the case of a note.

8. When a bill is dishonoured, due notice of dishonour is to be given by the holder to the drawer and the intermediate indorsers, but no such notice need be given in the case of a note.

DESCRIPTION AND FORMS OF BILLS OF EXCHANGE

A bill of exchange may be an Inland Bill or a Foreign Bill. It was originally a means by which a trader in one country paid a debt in another country without the transmission of coin. If A in Bombay owed money to C in Aden but himself was owed an equal sum of money by B in Aden, A would order B to pay C, the two debts would be cancelled and the same effect would have been produced as if A had sent money to C and B had sent money to A. A's written order to B, sent to C and acceded to (accepted) by B, was the first form of a bill of exchange. A is the drawer, B the drawee who, upon consenting to the arrangement, becomes the acceptor and C is the payee.

INLAND BILLS

The following is a specimen inland trade bill of the simplest type:—

₹1,000.00.   Delhi,

January 5,1990.

Stamp

Three months after date pay R. Patel or order the sum of one thousand rupees only for value received.

To

    Seth B. Mehta,

    101-A.D., Naoroji Road,

    Bombay.   Shiv Ram

Here Shjv Ram is the drawer, R. Patel is the payee, and B. Mehta the drawee who, on testifying his willingness to pay by "accepting" the bill, becomes acceptor.

The acceptance by B. Mehta will be made across the face of the Bill as under:—

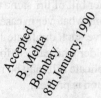

Accepted
B. Mehta
Bombay
8th January, 1990

ACCOMMODATION BILL

All bills are not genuine trade bills, as they are often drawn as a convenient mode of accommodating a friend. Thus Patel may be in want of money and approach his friends Shiv Ram and Mehta who, instead of lending the money directly, propose to draw an "Accommodation Bill" in his favour. Patel promises to reimburse Mehta before the period of three months is up. If the credit of Shiv Ram and Mehta is good, this device enables Patel to get an advance of ₹ 1,000 from his banker at the commercial rate of discount. The real debtor in this case is not Mehta, the acceptor, but Patel the payee who has engaged to find the money for its ultimate payment, and Patel is here the principal debtor and the others merely sureties. This inversion of liability affords a convenient definition of an accommodation bill: "If, as between the original parties to the bill the one who would *prima facie* be principal is in fact, the surety, whether he be drawer, acceptor, or indorser, that bill is an accommodation bill." (Lloyds, p. 27).

FOREIGN BILLS

Stamp

London,

7th January, 1990

Sixty days after sight of the first of Exchange (second and third of same tenor and date unpaid) pay to the order of Messrs. Bird & Co., Bombay, the sum of Rupees Ten Thousand only. Value received.

₹10,000.

Messrs Henry Brown,
Lamington Road,
Bombay.

Bird & Co.

BILLS IN SETS

The foreign bills are generally drawn in sets of three, each of which is called a "Via" and as soon as any one of them is paid the others become inoperative. These bills are drawn in different parts. They are drawn in order to avoid their loss or miscarriage during transit. Each part is sent separately. To minimise the delay the holder can send all the parts on the same day, each part by separate means of conveyance. All these parts form one bill and the drawer must sign and deliver all of them to the payee. The stamp is affixed on one part only and only one part of the whole set is required to be accepted, and when this is done and the accepted part is paid all the other parts are extinguished. Where, however, a person accepts or indorses different parts of the bill in favour of different persons, he and the subsequent indorsers of each part are liable on such part as if it were a separate bill (Sec. 132). But as between the holders in due course of different parts of the same set, he who first acquired title to his part is entitled to the other parts and money represented by the bill (Sec. 133).

RIGHT TO DUPLICATE BILL

Where a bill of exchange has been lost before it was overdue, the person who was the holder of it may apply to the drawer, to give him another bill of the same tenor, giving security to the drawer if required, to indemnify him against all persons whatever in case the bill alleged to have been lost shall be found again. If the drawer refuses to give such duplicate bill he may be compelled to do so by means of a suit (Sec. 45 A). It is only the holder who can ask for a duplicate, and the right is given to the holder also of notes and cheques. A duplicate bill may be required even in the case of destroyed bills, and without any indemnity if destruction is proved.

BANK DRAFT

A demand draft is a bill of exchange drawn by a bank on another bank, or by itself on its own branch, and is a negotiable instrument. It is very nearly allied to a cheque, the difference between it and a cheque consisting largely in three facts. *Firstly,* it can be drawn only by a bank on another bank, and not by a private individual as in the case of cheques. *Secondly,* it cannot so easily be countermanded as a cheque, either by the person purchasing it, or by the bank to which it is presented. *Thirdly,* it cannot be made payable to bearer.[5] Also, when a bank issues a draft on its own branch for the sole object of transmitting the money, a fiduciary relationship may arise between the bank and the purchaser of a demand draft from the bank. (*Tukaram Bapuji Nikam* v. *The Belgaum Bank Ltd;* 1976 Bom. 185).

Thus, a document stating "pay cash or order" is not a cheque, for although drawn on a banker, it is not a bill of exchange within the meaning of Sec. 5 of the Negotiable Instruments Act, 1881. This instrument is not to or to the order of a certain person and it is not' 'to bearer " (*Orbit Mining & Trading Co. Ltd.* v. *Westminster Bank Ltd.* (1962) 3 All. E.R. 565).

PART 11-C
CHEQUES

In the words of Sec. 6 of the Act, a cheque is a bill of exchange drawn on a specified banker, and not expressed to be payable otherwise than on demand. In simple language a cheque is a bill of exchange drawn on a bank payable on demand. Thus, a cheque is a cheque is a bill of exchange drawn on a bank payable on demand. Thus, a cheque is a bill of exchange with two additional qualifications, namely, (*i*) it is always drawn on a bank, and (*ii*) it is always payable on demand. Consequently, all cheques are bills of exchange, but all bills are not cheques. A cheque, being a species of a bill of exchange, must satisfy all the requirements of a bill—it must be signed by the drawer, and must contain an unconditional order on a specified banker to pay a certain sum of money to or to the order of a certain person or to the bearer of the cheque. It does not, however, require acceptance. A cheque is a payment, unless dishonoured the payment becomes effective from the delivery of the cheque and does not wait till it is honoured and money paid.[6]

DISTINCTION BETWEEN BILLS AND CHEQUES

As a general rule, the provisions applicable to bills payable on demand apply to cheques, yet there are a few points of difference between the two, namely—

1. A cheque is always drawn on a banker, while a bill may be drawn on any one, including a banker.

2. A cheque can only be drawn payable on demand, a bill may be drawn payable on demand, or on the expiry of a certain period after date or sight.

3. A bill must be accepted before payment can be demanded, a cheque does not require acceptance and is intended for immediate payment

4. A grace of 3 days is allowed in the case of time bills, while no grace is given in the case of a cheque.

5. The drawer of a bill is discharged, if it is not presented for payment but the drawer of a cheque is discharged only if he suffers any damage by delay in presentment for payment

6. Notice of dishonour of a bill is necessary, but not in the case of a cheque.

7. A cheque being a revocable mandate, the authority may be revoked by counter-manding payment, and is determined by notice of the customer's death or insolvency. This is not so in the case of a bill.

8. A cheque may be crossed, but not a bill.

---

5. Suganchand v. Brahmayya, (1951) 64 M.L.W. 842 (D.B.), see also 1944 P.C. 58,

6. Comn. of Income Tax v. Ogalay Glass Works, 1954 S.C. 429; Damadila v. Parasuram, 1976 S.C. 2229

BANKER AND CUSTOMER

The relationship between a banker and a customer is fundamentally that of debtor (banker) and creditor (customer) and is not fiduciary. When a customer deposits money in.a bank, this money is under the control of the banker and he can deal with it as he pleases, but he has obligations in connection with it. The foremost obligation of the banker is to repay the whole or part of the money so deposited upon presentation of the customer's written authority (*i.e.*, the cheque) during banking hours at the branch where the account is kept. The banker is under obligation to honour a customer's cheques up to the amount of the customer's deposit or alternatively up to the amount of an agreed overdraft. Wrongful dishonour of a customer's cheque will make the banker liable to compensate him for any loss or dun age. But the payee or holder of the cheque has no cause of action against the banker, even if the cheque has been marked good for payment by the drawee banker. This was laid down by the Privy Council in *Bank of Baroda* v. *Punjab National Bank* 1944 P.C.58.

In this case, *G* was indebted to M. on June, 13, *G* gave *M* a cheque for ₹ 2,75,000 on the Bank of Baroda post-dated to 20th June. The cheque was certified by the Manager of the Bank as "marked good for payment on 20-6-39". *M* discounted this cheque with the Punjab National Bank and received ₹ 2,40,000 immediately. On 20.6.39, the Punjab National Bank, as holder in due course, presented the cheque for payment, but the Baroda Bank refused payment as there were annas 7 and pies 3 only in the account of *G*, the drawer of the cheque. The PN Bank sued the Baroda Bank on the plea that by marking the cheque as good for payment the Baroda Bank had accepted the cheque within the meaning of Sec.7 of the Act, and should, therefore, he held liable as acceptor. It was held that the Baroda Bank was not liable, as the certification was not an acceptance of the cheque and the manager had no authority to certify a post-dated cheque.

However, the banker is under *no obligation to pay cheques in parts,* and if a customer with a deposit of ₹ 4,000 draws against it a cheque for ₹ 5,000, the bank is not empowered to pay it as to ₹ 4,000, but should either pay it is full (thus granting an overdraft of ₹ 1,000) or refuse payment altogether.

Again, the relationship between the banker and customer being confidential, the banker must not divulge information concerning the account and affairs of the customer, except where required to do so by law or permitted by the customer himself.

PROTECTION OF PAYING BANKER

Section 85 lays down that when a cheque payable to order purports to be endorsed by or on behalf of the payee, the banker is discharged *by payment in due course.* He can debit the account of the customer with the amount even though the endorsement of the payee turns out subsequently to have been forged, or the agent of the payee without authority endorsed it on behalf of the payee. It would be seen that the payee includes endorsees. This protection is granted because a banker cannot be expected to know the signatures of all the persons in the world. He is only bound to know the signatures of his own customers.

With regard to bearer cheques, the rule is: *Once a bearer cheque always a bearer cheque.* Therefore, where a cheque is *originally* expressed by the drawer himself to be payable to bearer, the banker may ignore any endorsements on the cheque. He will be discharged by payment in due course. But a cheque which becomes bearer by a subsequent endorsement in blank is not covered by this section.

The banker is also protected against forged or unauthorised endorsements on demand drafts drawn by one branch of a bank upon another branch of the same bank (Sec. 85 A). A banker is also discharged from liability on a crossed cheque, if he makes payment in due course, that is to say, the paying banker pays (*i*) to a banker, in accordance with the crossing, (*ii*) in good faith, and (*iii*) without negligence.

LIABILITY OF PAYING BANKER

No statutory protection is available to the paying banker where he pays—
- (*a*) a cheque bearing a forged signature of the drawer; or
- (*b*) a cheque bearing a non-apparent alteration; or
- (*c*) a countermanded cheque.

(a) Payment of forged cheque—A payment of a cheque bearing forged signature of the customer is clearly contrary to the customer's mandate, and the banker must suffer. A forged cheque is a nullity and the amount of any such cheque debited to the customer's account will have to be refunded. The banker has with him the specimen signatures of the customer and the signature on the cheque can be compared with them.

(i) In *Prablut Dayal* v. *Jw la Bank* (1938) All. 634, one of the rules of the bank required customers to keep the cheque book under lock and key, otherwise the bank will not be liable in this connection. The customer left his cheque book in an unlocked box. A cheque was stolen from the cheque bock, the customer's signature was forged and the cheque was presented and duly paid by the bank. The banker was held liable for the loss. No doubt the customer was negligent, but his negligence was not the proximate cause of the loss.

(ii) In *Brewer* v. *Westminster Bank Ltd.* (1952) 2 All. E.R. 650, the managing clerk forged the signature of the customer to a series of cheques and over a period of years drew £ 3,000 from the account, and used it for his own purposes. The forgeries were so skillful that no negligence could be imputed to bank officials. It was held that the bank was liable to pay to the customer the amount, because it paid the cheques without the authority or mandate of the customer.

(iii) In *Babu Lal Agarwala* v. *Stale Bank of Bikaner and Jaipur* 1989 Cal. 92, the cheque was forged. Even if the banker officer is duped by the mechanisation of the forger, the bank cannot debit the account of the customer, as the signatures on the cheque are forged.

However, the banker can recover the whole amount from the forger as money paid under a mistake of fact. (*Imperial Bank of Canada* v. *Bank of Hamilton* (1903) A.C 49).

It is therefore the duty of the customer, when he learns of the forgery of his signature to inform the banker so that the banker may take action against the forger. If the customer fails to inform the banker and the banker loses his remedy against the forger, the customer will be estopped from relying upon the forgery of his signature.

In *Greewood* v. *Martins' Bank Ltd.* (1933) A.C. 51(H.L.), G's wife forged his signature on 40 cheques. Upon his discovery of the forgeries, G did not inform the bank, being persuaded by the wife to say nothing about it. However, later on, when he stated his intention to notify the bank, the wife shot herself. G now claimed that the bank should credit his account with the amounts of the forged cheques. *Held,* the action could not be sustained as his continued silence operated to prevent the bank from taking remedies against the wife. G was estopped from asserting that the signatures to the cheques were forgeries.

The banker is also under a corresponding duty to inform his customer if he ascertains that his signature is being forged.

Again, when a customer has drawn his cheque with reasonable care but even so some dishonest person by using some technique has altered and raised the amount so that the banker, not knowing the forgery, has paid the increased amount, the banker must bear the loss. He cannot charge the customer with the excess amount, as there was no negligence on the part of the customer. This is an ordinary risk of the banking profession and the banker must put up with it. (*Hall* v. *Fuller* (1826) 5 B & C 750).

(b) Payment of cheque bearing a non-apparent alteration—But where the customer has been negligent in drawing the cheque and has left unusual spaces which facilitate interpolation of figures and words and that becomes the cause of forgery, the loss falls on the customer.

In *London Joint Stock Bank Ltd.* v. *Macmillan and Arthur,* (1918) A.C. 777, *M* and *A*, partners, were customers of the bank and entrusted their clerk with the duty of filling in cheques for signature. The clerk presented a cheque to a partner for signature, drawn in favour of the firm or bearer, and made out for £2 0s 0d in figures with no sum written in words. The clerk then easily altered the figures to £120 0s. 0d. and wrote "one hundred and twenty pounds" in words, presenting the cheque to the bank and obtaining £120 in cash. The banker was held by the House of Lords entitled to debit the account of the customer, with the full amount. Lord Finlay, L.C. stated: "The relationship of banker and customer imposes a special duty of care on the customer in drawing cheques. A cheque is a mandate to the banker to pay according to the tenor. The customer must exercise reasonable care to prevent the banker being misled. If he draws a cheque in a manner which facilitates fraud, he is guilty of breach of duty as between himself and the banker....... If the cheque is drawn in such a way as to facilitate or almost to invite an increase in the amount by forgery if the cheque should get into the hands of a dishonest person, forgery is not a remote but a very natural consequence of such negligence. The bank could, therefore, debit Macmillan and Arthur with the full £120 0s 0d.

(c) Payment of Countermanded Cheque—The authority of a banker to pay a cheque drawn on him by his customer is determined by countermanding of payment. Thus, where a customer issues instructions in writing not to honour a cheque, the banker after having received them must not pay it. Payment made after the countermand is not good against the drawer.

However, where the payment of a countermanded cheque actually satisfies a debt due from a customer to his creditor, the customer would make a profit by reason of the restoration rule. For example, if the bank paid a countermanded, cheque which *A*, a customer, had drawn in favour of *B*, to whom *A* owed money, the result of restoration rule would be that *A*'s debt to *B* would be satisfied and *A*'s balance at the bank would have to be restored. To prevent this profit being made the bank, on restoring *A*'s account, is *subrogated* to *B*'s rights against *A*, and can recover from *A* by this means.

WHEN BANKER MUST REFUSE PAYMENT

In the following cases the authority of the banker is determined and he *must* refuse to honour his. customer's cheques—

1. When customer countermands payment—Where a customer issues instructions not to honour a cheque, the banker must not pay it. The effect of a notice countermanding payment of a cheque is the same as if the cheque had never been drawn. A stopped cheque is a piece of waste paper in the hands of payee. Payment made after the countermand is not good against the drawer. The notice to the drawee banker must however, be given in sufficient time.

2. When banker receives notice of customer's death—Notice of customer's death determines the authority of banker to honour cheques, but a payment made before the receipt of notice is valid.

3. When customer has become insolvent—When a customer has been adjudged an insolvent the banker must refuse to pay his cheques.

4. When banker receives notice of customer's insanity—On receipt of a notice that a customer of his has become insane, the banker must not pay the cheque drawn by that customer until the customer recovers from his malady, or an order is made by the Court for payment of the money.

5. When an order of Court prohibits payment—After receiving a Garnishee order or other legal orders attaching or otherwise dealing with customer's money in his custody, the banker should not honour the cheques drawn against customer's account.

6. On notice of assignment—The banker should not honour his customer's cheques after the customer has given notice of assignment of the credit balance of his account.

7. When holder's title is defective—If the banker comes to know of any defect in the title of the party presenting the cheque, he must not pay it.

8. Closing of account—The banker should not after receiving notice from the customer closing the account, pay any cheque of the customer.

In the following cases the duty of the banker is determined and he may dishonour a customer's cheque:—

1. Where the cheque is post-dated and is presented before the ostensible date. The mandate of the customer, to the banker is to pay the cheque on the date it bears and not before, and the refusal before that date does not amount to dishonour. Indeed, a banker honouring a post-dated cheque before due date runs the risk of the cheque being countermanded before date, or another cheque bearing earlier date being presented for payment when funds have dwindled on account of the payment of the post-dated cheque.

2. Where the banker has not sufficient funds of the drawer with him.

3. Where the cheque is of doubtful legality.

4. Where the funds in the hands of the banker are not properly applicable to the payment of the customer's cheques, e.g., funds are subject to lien, or are held in trust and the cheque is drawn in breach of trust.

5. Where a cheque is not duly presented, e.g., presented after banking hours.

6. Where the cheque is irregular, ambiguous or otherwise materially altered.

7. When the cheque is presented at a branch where the customer has no account

8. Where some persons have joint account and the cheque is not signed by all jointly or by the survivors of them.

9. Where the cheque has been allowed to become stale, i.e., it has not been presented within a reasonable time after the date mentioned in it In India six months are reasonable.

PAYMENT IN DUE COURSE

Section 10 provides that in order to constitute a payment of a negotiable instrument as a payment in due course, the following conditions must be fulfilled, viz.,

1. **Payment must be in accordance with the apparent tenor of the instrument**, i.e., according to what appears on the face of the instrument to be the intention of the parties. It is necessary that payment should be made at or after maturity. A payment before maturity is not payment in due course so as to discharge the instrument. For example, a bill payable after sight must not be paid before the lastday of grace.

2. **Payment must be made in good faith and without negligence, and under circumstances which do not afford a reasonable ground for believing that the person to whom it is made is not entitled to receive the amount**—When there are suspicious circumstances and the payer fails to make any enquiry which may bring home the defects, the payment is not in due course. Payment of a cheque bearing forged signature of customer as drawer without the banker exercising due care is not payment in due course,[7] nor is it so where payment is made to a person who the person paying knows is not entitled to receive payment, although the instrument is payable to bearer. Payment of a *Shahjog* hundi without inquiry about the *shah* is not payment in due course.

3. **Payment must be made to the person in possession of the instrument**—A payment cannot be a payment in due course if it is made to a person not entitled to receive it. A thief is not said to be in possession of the instrument as he cannot give a valid discharge.

4. **Payment must be made under circumstances which do not. afford a reasonable ground for believing that he is not entitled to receive payment of the amount mentioned therein**—Before

---

7. Abhu Chettiar v. Hyderabad State Bank (1954) Mad. 1001.

making a payment on a negotiable instrument, the person making such payment should make sure that the person presenting it is the person entitled to receive payment thereon. There must be no suspicion either about the payee or the amount to be paid. Thus, if the drawee of a hundi negligently makes payment to a wrong person, such payment is not payment in due course.[8]

5. **Payment must be made in money only**—Money includes Bank or currency notes. The holder is entitled to be paid in money only, and he cannot be compelled to accept payment in goods or by cheque. He may, however, agree to accept payment by cheque or another bill, in which case this mode will amount to payment in due course.

COLLECTING BANKER

Sec. 131 affords protection to the collecting banker who in good faith and without negligence receives payment of a crossed cheque for a customer, even though the customer's title to the cheque proves defective. In order to obtain protection, the banker must prove that (*i*) the cheque was crossed before it reached his hands, (*ii*) the cheque was presented by or on behalf of the customer and that he received payment for the customer, (*iii*) he acted in good faith and without negligence in collecting the money due on the cheque. Therefore, if he collects an uncrossed cheque or a crossed cheque for a non-customer, he gets no protection in the event of the cheque having a forged indorsement, and is liable to the true owner for wrongful conversion of the funds. The explanation to Sec. 131 extends protection to a collecting banker where he credits his customer's account with the amount of the cheque before receiving payment thereof.

OVER-DUE, STALE, OR OUT-OF-DATE CHEQUES

A cheque becomes statute-barred after three years from its due date of issue. A holder cannot sue on the cheque after that time. Apart from this provision the holder of a cheque is required to present it for payment within a reasonable time, as a cheque is not meant for indefinite circulation. A cheque which has been in circulation for an unreasonably long time, becomes stale and the banker can refuse to pay it. The period for this purpose differs with particular bankers and may vary with special agreement with any particular customer. As a rule, in India and in the Provincial towns in England, the bankers regard a cheque which has been in circulation for more than 6 months as stale. In London, a cheque may remain in circulation for 12 months without becoming stale. Also, if as a result of any delay in presenting a cheque the drawer suffers any loss, as by the failure of the bank, the drawer is discharged from liability to the holder to the extent of the damage. In the case of dividend warrants, the issuing companies usually do not honour them if they are presented more than three months after issue, unless they are subsequently revalidated by the companies concerned. Similarly, the drawee banker may, after getting the stale cheque confirmed by the drawer, honour it.

LIABILITY OF INDORSER

In order to charge an indorser, it is necessary to present the cheque for payment within a reasonable time of its *delivery* by such indorser. *A* indorses and delivers a cheque to *B*, and *B* keeps it for an unreasonable length of time', and then indorses and delivers it to *C*. *C* presents it for payment within a reasonable time after its receipt by him, and it is dishonoured. *C* can enforce payment against *B* but not against *A*, as *qua A* the cheque has become stale.

RIGHTS OF HOLDER AGAINST BANKER

We have observed that a banker is liable to his customer for wrongful dishonour of his cheque and not to the payee or holder of the cheque. The holder has no right to enforce payment from the banker,

---

8. Lalta Prasad v. Charles Campbell, 9 C.W.N. 841.

except in two cases, namely, (*i*) where the holder does not present the cheque within a reasonable time after issue, and as a result the drawer not present the cheque within a reasonable time after issue, and as a result the drawer suffers damage by the failure of the bank, and is therefore discharged[9] then, the holder can prove his debt against the banker in insolvency proceedings. The holder in such case becomes the creditor of the banker in lieu of the drawer and can recover the amount from him [Sec.84 (3)]; and (*ii*) where a banker pays a crossed cheque by mistake over the counter, he is liable to the true owner for any loss occasioned by it (Sec. 129). If the holder has, through banker's mistake, received payment in respect of a cheque counter-manded by the drawer, the banker is not entitled to a refund of the amount from the payee, nor can he debit the customer's account.

CROSSING OF CHEQUES

So far we have dealt with "open cheques" which can be presented by the payee to banker on whom they are drawn arid are paid over the counter. A banker, who pays in due course such cheques whether they are payable to bearer or to order, is discharged provided that in the case of an order cheque it purports to be indorsed by or on behalf of the payee. It is obvious that an open cheque is liable to great risk in the course of circulation. It may be stolen or lost and the finder can get it cashed, unless the drawer has already countermanded payment. In order to avoid the losses incurred by open cheques getting into the hands of wrong parties the custom of crossing was introduced.

A *crossing* is a direction to the paying banker to pay the money generally to a banker or a particular banker, as the case may be, and not to pay to holder across the counter. A banker paying a crossed cheque over the counter does so at his own peril if the party receiving the payment turns out to be not entitled to get payment. The object of crossing is to secure payment to a banker so that it could be traced to the person receiving the amount of the cheque. The crossing is made to warn the banker, but not to stop negotiability of the cheque. To restrain negotiability addition of words ' 'Not Negotiable" or "Account payee only" is necessary. A crossed bearer cheque can be negotiated by delivery and crossed order cheque by indorsement and delivery.

MODES OF CROSSING

There are two types of crossing which may be used on a cheque, namely, (*i*) General and (*ii*) Special. To those two statutory types may be added another mode, *i.e.*, the Restrictive crossing. **Specimen of General Crossing—**

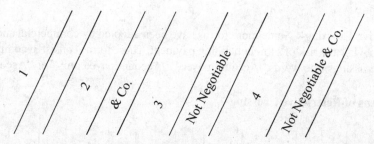

A General Crossing is defined in Sec. 123 thus: where a cheque bears across its face an addition of
 (a) the words "and Company", or any abbreviation thereof between two parallel transverse lines,
 or
 (b) two parallel transverse lines simply, either with or without the words "Not Negotiable";
that addition constitutes a crossing and the cheque is crossed generally.

Two transverse lines on the face of the cheque are essential for general crossing, though not for special crossing. If a cheque is crossed generally, the paying banker shall pay only to a banker.

9. Abdul Majid v. M/s. G. Kalooram, 1954, Orissa 124.

A **Special Crossing** is defined in Sec. 124 thus:

Where a cheque bears across its face an addition of the name of a banker, either with or without the words "not negotiable" that addition constitutes a Crossing and the cheque is crossed specially and to that banker. Thus, a special crossing requires the name of the banker to whom or to whose collecting agent payment of the cheque should be made to be written on the face of the cheque. Transverse lines are not compulsory.

Specimens of Special Crossing—

1	2	3	4
Bank of India	Cental Bank of India / Not Negotiable	Allahabad Bank	Bank of Baroda / Not Negotiable

Double Crossing—Section 127 states that if a paying banker receives a cheque crossed specially to two bankers he must not pay it; however, if one of the bankers named is acting as an agent for collection for the other, the cheque may be paid to the agent bank. Collection through an agent may be resorted to where the banker in whose favour the cheque is specially crossed, is not a member of the clearing house or does not have a branch where the cheque is to be paid. Such crossing may be in the following form:

Indian Commercial Bank
To
Bank of India
As Agent for Collection

Restrictive Crossing—Some more forms have been adopted by commercial and banking usage in order to obviate the risk of a thief obtaining payment. These forms consist in adding to the general or special crossings, the words "Account payee," "Account payee only" or "Account John Smith only".

Specimens of Restrictive Crossing—

1	2	3	4	5	6
A/c Payee	A/c Payee only	A/c Payee / Not Negotiable	Bank of India / A/c Payee only	State Bank of India / A/c John Smit	Not Negotiable / Syndicate Bank / A/c John Smith

Such crossings warn the collecting banker that the proceeds are to be credited only to the account of the payee, or the party named, or his agent. If the collecting banker allows the proceeds of a cheque so crossed to be credited to any other account he may be held guilty of negligence in the event of an action for wrongful conversion of the funds. These words are not addition to the crossing and do not prevent a cheque from being negotiated, but a mere direction to the receiving or collecting banker. They do not affect the paying banker, who is under no duty to ascertain that the cheque is in fact collected for the account of the person named as payee. In the case of a cheque bearing restrictive crossing but not specially crossed to another the paying banker need only see that the cheque bears no other endorsement but that of the payee or the party named in the crossing, and that it is otherwise in order. But where the cheque is also crossed specially, the paying banker must pay only to the bank named in the crossing or to an agent bank, and should also see that no other endorsement appears, and that no misapplication of the funds is apparently taking place.

WHO MAY CROSS A CHEQUE

Sec. 125 provides that—
  (a) A cheque may be crossed generally or specially by the drawer.
  (b) Where a cheque is uncrossed, the holder may cross it generally or specially.
  (c) Where a cheque is crossed generally, the holder may cross it specially.
  (d) Where a cheque is crossed generally or specially, the holder may add the words "not negotiable."
  (e) Where a cheque is crossed specially, the banker to whom it is crossed may again cross it specially to another banker for collection.
  (f) Where an uncrossed cheque or a cheque crossed generally is sent to a banker for collection, he may cross it specially, to himself. But such crossing does not enable the collecting banker to enjoy statutory protection against being sued for conversion.

"NOT NEGOTIABLE" CROSSING

If a cheque is made payable to a payee and to him only, it becomes non-transferable in the strict sense. No one but the payee can give a good discharge for its payment, and no one but the payee can bring an action on the instrument. Where a cheque bears the "Not Negotiable" crossing, it is transferable, but it loses its special feature of negotiability. Such a cheque is like any goods—a stolen pen or a watch—the transferee of which does not get a better title than that of a thief. A cheque crossed with the words "Not Negotiable" is deprived of both the characteristics of negotiability', namely, transferability free from defects, and transferability by endorsement. The transferee gets no better title than that of his transferor. The object of "not negotiable" crossing is to afford protection to the drawer or holder against miscarriage or dishonesty in the course of transit by making it difficult to get the cheque cashed until it reaches its destination. While the words "not negotiable" do not stop transferability of a cheque, they perpetuate the defect in it. When the words "Not-Negotiable" appear on a bill of exchange or a document other than a cheque, their effect is altogether different; they make the bill or the document not only not negotiable but also not transferable.

MARKING OF CHEQUES

Cheques being intended for immediate payment are not in the ordinary course accepted. But in some countries there is a usage to so accept, by marking or certifying cheques as good for payment by the paying banker. In fact, in the U.S.A., Certified or marked cheques are in common use and the practice of certifying has received statutory recognition. Accordingly, the certification of a cheque by the banker is equilvent to acceptance, and the banker is bound to pay and the drawer and indorsers are discharged from liability.

In India also bankers often marked cheques as good at the request of the holder, but now the banks in bur country have, by agreement, stopped this practice. However, since marking is still done in some countries a brief account of the practice is in point. The marking is generally done by the banker writing the words "good for payment" across one corner of the cheque, adding the bank's stamp and initials of the banker'-cashier. Marking may be done by the paying banker at the request of (*a*) the drawer, (*b*) the holder, or (*c*) the collecting banker.

Marking at drawer's instance—Where the cheque is marked at the request of the customer (drawer), the banker' assumes responsibility for payment of the cheque when presented and usually "earmarks" or sets apart sufficient funds from the customer's account to meet the cheque. The customer cannot countermand or stop payment and the banker is entitled to dishonour cheques presented subsequently, should the remainder of the funds be insufficient to meet them.

Marking at holder's instance—Marking of a cheque at the request of the holder does not amount to acceptance of liability on the cheque by the banker. It merely indicates that at the time of marking the banker had sufficient funds of the drawer in his hands. The banker may represent to pay the cheque when eventually presented by reason of insufficiency of funds or payment being stopped by the drawer. Again, a post dated, cheque cannot be marked as good.[10]

Marking at Collecting Bankers' instance—Where a cheque is received by a collecting bank too late for inclusion in the clearing, it may, to safeguard the interests of its customer, may present the cheque for marking by the drawee banker. If the paying banker would have honoured the cheque had it been presented for payment through the clearing on that day, an official of the bank would mark it good. Banking custom demands that such a cheque shall be honoured when presented through the next clearing. The legal position also seems to be the same, as such a marking is treated as constructive payment.

ISSUING A CHEQUE THAT BOUNCES IS AN OFFENCE

A new chapter XVII has been inserted by the 1988 Amendment Act. It is now provided that where any cheque drawn by a person *for the discharge of any liability* is returned by the bank unpaid because of insufficiency of the amount of money standing to the credit of the account on which the cheque was drawn or by reason that exceeds the arrangements by drawer of the cheque with the bankers for that account, the drawer of that cheque shall be deemed to have committed an offence, and shall be punishable with imprisonment up to one year, or with fire upto twice the amount of the cheque, or with both.

However, to constitute the said offence, (*a*) such cheque should have been presented to the bank within a period of 6 months of the date of drawal or within the period of its validity, whichever is earlier; (*b*) the payee or holder in due course of such cheque had made a demand in writing for the payment of the said amount of money from, the drawer within 15 days of the receipt of information by him from the bank regarding the return of the cheque unpaid; and (*c*) the drawer of the cheque had failed to pay the money to the payee or holder in due course of the cheque within 15 days of the written demand for payment. Thereafter, the payee or the holder in due course of the cheque may make a complaint within one month of the date on which the cause of action arises to the court of a Metropolitan Magistrate or a Judicial Magistrate of the First Class.

It should be noted that the offence will be deemed to have been committed if the bounced cheque was drawn *for the discharge of any liability* and not for any other purpose. For example, if a cheque was drawn in favour of the payee as a gift, no offence will he deemed to have been committed, if the said cheque is returned by the bank unpaid.

---

10. Bank of Baroda v. Punjab National Bank (1944) P.C. 53.

PART 11-D

INLAND AND FOREIGN INSTRUMENTS

Instruments may be inland or foreign. A promissory note, bill of exchange or cheque drawn or made in India, and made payable in or drawn upon any person resident in India, is an inland instrument (Sec. 11). Thus, an inland instrument is one which is (*i*) drawn and payable in India, or (*ii*) drawn in India upon some person resident therein, even though it is made payable in a foreign country. But a promissory note to be inland must be drawn and payable in India, as it has no drawee. All instruments which are not inland are deemed to be foreign (Sec. 12); and an instrument is presumed to be inland unless the contrary appears on the face of it. The distinction between the two is important inasmuch as foreign instruments (bills) must be protested for dishonour, if the law of the place of making or drawing them requires such protest; which inland instruments need not be so protested.

Examples or inland bills—The following are inland bills:—
1. A bill drawn in Kanpur on a merchant in Delhi payable in Delhi or in London.
2. A bill drawn in Delhi on a merchant in Paris but made payable or accepted payable in Bombay.
3. A bill drawn in Delhi on a merchant in Bombay and accepted payable in London.
4. The above bills endorsed in Paris.
5. Where a pro-note recited that both parties belonged to India and were temporarily in Singapore, the note was held to be an inland instrument, as it was an instrument drawn on person resident in India (*C. Somayya* v. *E.V. Chinniah Konar,* 1976 Mad.254).

Examples of foreign bills—The following are foreign bills:—
1. A bill drawn in India, on a person resident outside India and made payable outside India, *e.g.*, a bill drawn in Delhi on London payable or accepted pay able in Paris.
2. A bill drawn outside India on a person resident outside India.
3. A bill drawn outside India and made payable in India.
4. A bill drawn outside India and made payable outside India.

Foreign Bills are usually drawn 'in sets' to avoid danger of loss. Each part is separately numbered and sent separately, but all the parts constitute one bill.

USANCES

Continental bills are sometimes drawn at usances—one, two, or more usances. A usance is the time which is fixed by the custom of countries, for payment of bills drawn in one country and made payable in another. The length of a usance varies in different countries. When usance is a month, half usance is always 15 days. The usance has to be proved by the person who pleads it. In India, according to custom, usance Hundis are drawn.

AMBIGUOUS INSTRUMENTS

An instrument, which in form is such that it may either be treated by the holder as a bill or as a note, is an ambiguous instrument (Sec. 17). According to Sec. 5 (2) of the English Bills of Exchange Act, "where in a bill the drawer and the drawee are the same person, or where the drawee is a fictitious person or a person not having the capacity to contract, the holder may treat the instrument, at his option, either as a bill of exchange or as a promissory note. Bills drawn to or to the order of the drawee or by an agent on his principal, or by one branch of a bank on another or by the directors of a company on their cashier, are also ambiguous instruments. A promissory note addressed to a third person may be treated as a bill by such person by accepting it, while a bill not addressed to anyone may be treated as a note. But where the drawer and payee are the same, *e.g.*, where *A* draws a bill payable to *A*'s order, it is not an ambiguous instrument and cannot be treated as a promissory note. Once an instrument has been treated either as a bill or as a note, it cannot be treated differently afterwards. Insufficiency of stamp on such an instrument will not interfere in its being treated as admitted.

INCHOATE INSTRUMENTS

When one person signs and delivers to another a paper stamped in accordance with the law relating to negotiable instruments, then in force in India, and either wholly blank or having written thereon an incomplete negotiable instrument, he thereby gives *prima facie* authority to the holder thereof to make or complete, as the case may be, upon it a negotiable instrument, for any amount specified therein, and not exceeding the amount covered by the stamp. Such an instrument is called an Inchoate Instrument. The person so signing shall be liable upon such instrument, in the capacity in which he signed the same, to any holder in due course for such amount, provided that no person other than a holder in due course shall recover from the person delivering the instrument anything in excess of the amount intended by him to be paid thereon (Sec.20).

The principle of the rule stated in this section is one of estoppel, enabling persons to lend their mercantile credit to others by signing their names on stamped but blank or incomplete papers to be afterwards filled up as completed instruments. By such signatures they bind themselves, as drawers, makers, acceptors, or indorsers. The instrument may be wholly blank or incomplete in any particular, *e.g.*, without any mention of the sum or the name of the payee, the holder may make or complete the instrument as a negotiable instrument. The authority to fill up a blank or incomplete instrument may be exercised by any "holder," and not only the first holder to whom the paper is delivered. Delivery of such paper is essential for the operation of estoppel; for instance where an instrument was placed by the Bank Manager in his drawer, and some one stole it and filled it up for ₹500, no estoppel would arise against him as he never issued the instrument intending it to be used as a negotiable instrument. The section in terms applies to stamped instruments only, but its principle would apply even to cheques which do not require stamp in India, if estoppel is pleaded and proved.

The person signing and delivering the paper is liable both to a "holder" and a "holder in due course." But there is a difference in their respective rights. A holder can recover only what the signer intended to be paid under the instrument, while a holder in due course can recover the whole amount made payable by the instrument provided that it is covered by the stamp, even though the amount authorised was smaller. The power of completing the instrument must be exercised within a reasonable time, even though it may be exercised after the death of the acceptor. But where once the payment is made so as to discharge the instrument, a holder cannot claim on it.[11]

INSTRUMENTS PAYABLE ON DEMAND

The following instruments are payable on demand:—
1. A cheque is always payable on demand (Secs. 6,19).
2. A note or bill expressed payable "on demand", or "at sight" or "on presentment" (Sec. 21).
3. A note or bill in which no time for payment is specified (Sec. 19).

Although the expressions "at sight" and "on presentment" mean "on demand", yet they are distinguishable from the expression "on demand." Instruments payable on demand need not be presented before payment can be demanded, while instruments payable "at sight" or "on presentment" must be presented before payment can be demanded on them. Moreover, in the case of instruments payable on demand or without specification of time of payment the period of limitation (3 years) begins to run from the date of the execution, while in the case of instruments payable at sight the time of 3 years commences from the date of presentment. But where simultaneously with the note payable on demand a period for payment is fixed in a separate written agreement, time begins to run from the expiry of the fixed period. The words "on demand" simply mean that note is payable immediately or at sight and do not imply that a demand must be made. Where a note is made at a certain place and is payable on demand but no place of payment is mentioned therein, it can be sued upon at any place.

---

11. A. Ibrahim v. D. Ramadas, 1954 Mad. 532.

Instrument which are not payable on demand are expressed to be payable at a certain period "after sight," or "after happening of an event" which is certain to happen, though the time of its happening may be uncertain. Thus a bill or note may be made payable, say, 30 days after sight, or 60 days after date, or 90 days after the death of X, and payment can be demanded on presenting it on its maturity. There is, however, one difference in bills and notes payable "at sight." The note has simply to be exhibited to the marker before payment is demanded, while a bill has td be presented for acceptance to the drawee. If the drawee accepts the bill, payment can be demanded after the expiry of the specified period on the maturity of the bill. But if the drawee refuses to accept the bill, payment cannot be demanded until the bill has been noted or protested for non-acceptance.

MATURITY

Maturity is the date on which the payment of an instrument falls due. Every instrument payable at a specified period after date or after sight or after the happening of a certain event is entitled to three days of grace. Such a bill or note matures or falls due on the last day-of grace, and must be presented for payment on that day, and if dishonoured, the suit can be filed on the next day after maturity (Sec. 22). If an instrument is payable by instalments each is entitled to 3 days of grace. Instruments payable on demand become payable at once, and no days of grace are allowed for them. Therefore no days of grace are allowed for cheques, which are always payable on demand. The calculation of time should always be made according to the British calendar, and the term month means a calendar month and not a lunar month.

Where a note or bill is expressed to be payable a stated number of months after sight, or after date, or after certain event, the period of payment terminates on the day of the month which corresponds with the date of the instrument, or with the date of acceptance if the bill be accepted, or presented for sight, or noted or protested for non-acceptance. Where an after-sight bill is accepted for honour the period is to be reckoned from the date of such acceptance, and not from the date of noting for non-acceptance, as is the case in England. If the month in which the period would terminate has no corresponding day, the period shall be held to terminate on the last day of such month (Sec. 23). In all the above cases the day or the date of the instrument or of presentment for acceptance or sight, or on which the event happens, is to be excluded (Sec. 24).

Illustrations:

(*a*) A negotiable instrument dated 29th January, 1985, is made payable at one month after date. The instrument is at maturity on the third day after 28th February, 1990 (*i.e.*, on 3rd March, 1990).

(*b*) A negotiable instrument, dated 30th August, 1990, is made payable three months after date. The instrument is at maturity on 3rd December, 1990.

(*c*) A promissory note or bill of exchange, dated 31st August, 1990, is made payable three months after date. The instrument is at maturity on 3rd December, 1990.

If the day of maturity falls on a public holiday, the instrument is payable the next preceding business day (Sec. 25). Thus, if a bill is at maturity on a Sunday, it will be deemed due on Saturday and not on Monday. In England, a distinction is made between public holidays and Bank holidays. If, therefore, the last day of grace is a public holiday, the bill is payable on the preceding business day, as in India; but when the last day of grace is a Bank holiday, the bill is payable on the succeeding business day.

PARTIES-TO NEGOTIABLE INSTRUMENTS

PARTIES TO BILL OF EXCHANGE

1. The Drawer: the person who draws the bill.
2. The Drawee: the person on whom the bill is drawn.

3. The Acceptor: one who accepts the bill. Generally, the drawee is also the acceptor, but as we have seen, a stranger may accept on behalf of the drawee.

4. The Payee: one to whom the sum stated in the bill is payable. Either the drawer or any other person may be payee.

5. The Holder: is either the original payee or any other person to whom the payee has endorsed the bill. In case of the bearer bill the bearer is the holder.

6. The Indorser: when the holder indorses the bill to any one else he becomes the indorser.

7. The Indorsee: is the person to whom the bill is indorsed.

8. **Drawee in case of need**—Besides the above parties, another person called the "drawee in case of need," may be introduced at the option of the drawer. In English law, he is called "reference in case of need." The name of such a person may be inserted either by the drawer or by any indorser in order that resort may be had to him in case of need, *i.e.*, when the bill is dishonoured by either non-acceptance or non-payment. For example, in the case of bills drawn by English firms on their Indian importers the agent of the drawer's firm in India is often named in the bill as a drawee in case of need. In India a bill must be presented to the drawee in case of need, before it will be deemed to be dishonoured. Under the English law, the holder need not resort to the referee in case of need, if the bill is dishonoured by the drawee. The following is a specimen bill with a drawee in case of need:—

₹ 1,000.00   London, 10th January, 1990.

Three months after date pay to the order of Shiv Lall the sum of one thousand rupees, value received.

To
    Henry Smith,
    Cannaught Place,
    New Delhi.   John Jones
In case of need with
    The Lloyds Bank Ltd., New Delhi.

9. **Acceptor for Honour**—Further, any person may voluntarily become a party to a bill as an acceptor. A person who, on the refusal by the original drawee to accept the bill or to furnish better security when demanded by the notary, accepts the bill in order to safeguard the honour of the drawer or any indorser, is called the acceptor for honour.

PARTIES TO A PROMISSORY NOTE

1. The Maker: the person who makes or executes the note promising to pay the amount stated therein.
2. The Payee: one to whom the note is payable.
3. The Holder: is either the payee or some one to whom he may have indorsed the note.
4. & 5. The indorser, and Indorsee: same as in the case of a bill.

PARTIES TO A CHEQUE

1. The Drawer: the person who draws the cheque.
2. The Drawee: is always the drawer's banker on whom the cheque is drawn.
3, 4, 5, & 6. The Payee, Holder, Indorser and Indorsee: same as in the case of a bill or note.

HOLDER

The word holder is used in respect of negotiable instruments in three grades of meaning—"holder," "holder for value," and "holder in due course." There is a slight difference between the English and the Indian law on the subject.

In English Law, "holder" means a person in whose legal possession the instrument is, or the bearer. If the instrument is a bearer instrument or is indorsed in blank, any person who is in possession of it even though by theft is a holder. A "holder for value" is the holder of a bill for which value has at any time been given, but it is not essential that he should have himself given value. His title depends upon the same grounds as those of a simple holder except that lack of consideration cannot be set up against him save by his immediate transferor, if in fact he did not give value. A "holder in due course" is a holder who has taken a bill complete and regular on the face of it, before it was overdue and without notice of its having been previously dishonoured, and in good faith and for value, and without notice at the time of negotiation to him of any defect in title of the person who negotiated it.

In Indian Law, it is not every person in possession of an instrument who is called a holder. Sec. 8 provides that a person, who is entitled in his own name (*i*) to the possession of the instrument, and (*ii*) to recover or receive its amount from the parties thereto, is a holder. The person may or may not be in possession of the instrument. He is required to be a holder in law (*dejure*) and not necessarily in fact (*de facto*). In order to be entitled to the instrument in his own name, the person must be named therein as the payee, or the indorsee, or he must be the bearer thereof. He must also be entitled to recover its amount from the parties thereto. In Indian law, therefore, a person who has obtained possession of an instrument by theft, or under a forged indorsement, is not a holder, as he is not entitled to recover the amount of the instrument. The heir of a deceased holder or any other person becoming entitled by operation of law is a holder, but not a transferee, under a sale deed. A joint Hindu firm may become the holder of a note if it is made in the firm's collective or business name, and all the adults of the family may join in a suit to recover the debt. But a coparcener who becomes entitled by survivorship to the property cannot sue on an instrument payable to the deceased or his order, as he cannot give a valid and proper discharge to the maker. A beneficiary of a note is not a holder.[12]

HOLDER IN DUE COURSE

In Indian law, a "holder in due course" is (*a*) a person who for consideration obtains possession of a negotiable instrument if payable to bearer, or (*b*) the payee or indorsee thereof, if payable to order, before its maturity, and without having sufficient cause to believe that any defect existed in the title of the person from whom he derived his title (Sec.9). Before a person can claim to be a "holder in due course" he must show that (*i*) he is a holder, *i.e.*, he is in possession of the instrument, if it is payable to bearer, or he is the payee or indorsee, if it is payable to, or in the order of the payee, (*ii*) he became the holder before the amount mentioned in the instrument became payable, *i.e.*, before maturity, (*iii*) he became the holder for valuable consideration, and (*iv*) he became the holder without having sufficient cause to believe that any defect existed in the title of the person from whom he received it, though not of any prior party.[13] Provision in (*iv*) makes a little departure from the English law. Under the latter "a holder for value in good faith without notice" is a holder in good faith, *i.e.*, holder honestly, whether negligently or not. He may take it even 'blunderingly or stupidly.' But in India a person who takes these instruments should not only do so honestly but should take them with reasonable caution and should use reasonable diligence to satisfy himself that they were free from defects of title in order to constitute himself a holder in due course. But this does not mean that he must make full inquiries in every case. If, however, there is anything which excites suspicion that there is something wrong in the transaction, then omission to make inquiries will amount to bad faith.

Negotiable instruments in the course of their currency pass freely from hand to hand according to their face value like current coins. A holder in due course is not only himself protected against all

---

12. Bacha Prasad v. Janaki Rai & others, 1957 Pat. 380.
13. Braja Kishore Dikshit v. Puran Chandra Panda, 1957 Orissa 153.

defects of title of the person from whom he received the instrument as current coin, but also serves as a channel to protect all subsequent holders. A holder in due course can recover the amount of the instrument from all previous parties, although, as a matter of fact, no consideration was paid by some of the previous parties to the instrument or there was a defect of title in the party from whom he took it. *Once an instrument passes through the hands of a holder in due course, it is purged of all defects.* It is like current coin. Whosoever takes it can recover the amount from all parties previous to such holder.

SPECIAL PRIVILEGES OF A HOLDER IN DUE COURSE

A holder in due course enjoys the following privileges under the Act:—

1. A person, who signed and delivered to another a stamped but otherwise inchoate instrument, is estopped from asserting, as against a holder in due course, that the instrument has been filled in accordance with the authority given by him, the stamp being sufficient to cover the amount (Sec. 20).

2. Every prior party to a negotiable instrument, *i.e.*, the maker, or the drawer, the acceptor, and all the intervening indorsers, continue to remain liable to the holders in due course until the instrument is duly satisfied *i.e.*, the payment is made by the maker or acceptor at or after maturity (Sec. 36).

3. Where a bill is drawn payable to drawer's order in fictitious name and indorsed by the same hand as drawer's signature, the acceptor cannot allege as against a holder in due course, that such name was fictitious (Sec. 42).

4. Where an instrument is negotiated to a holder in due course, the other parties to the instrument cannot escape liability on the ground that the delivery of the instrument was conditional or for a special purpose only (Secs 46 & 47).

5. Even though as between the immediate parties to an instrument it was caused by fraud, etc., once the instrument passes through the hands of a holder in due course, it is purged of all defects, and any person acquiring it takes it free of all defects, unless he was himself a party to the fraud (Sec.53).

6. The defences on the part of a person liable on a negotiable instrument that it has been lost, or obtained from him by means of an offence or fraud or unlawful consideration, cannot be set up against a holder in due course (Sec. 58).

7. The law presumes that every holder is a holder in due course, although the presumption is rebuttable (Sec. 118).

8. No maker of a note and no drawer of a bill or cheque and the acceptor of a bill for the honour of the drawer is, in a suit thereon by a holder in due course, permitted to deny the validity of the instrument as originally made or drawn (Sec. 120).

9. No maker of a note and no acceptor of a bill payable to order is, in a suit thereon by a holder in due course, permitted to deny the payee's capacity at the date of the note or the bill to indorse it (Sec. 121).

Capacity of Parties

Capacity to incur liability as a party to a negotiable instrument is co-extensive with capacity to contract. Sec. 26 provides that every person capable of contracting, according to the law to which he is subject, may bind himself and be bound by making, drawing, acceptance, indorsement, delivery and negotiation of a note, bill or cheque. Negatively minors, lunatics, idiots, drunken persons and persons otherwise disqualified by their personal law, do not incur any, liability as parties to negotiable instruments. But the incapacity of one or more of the parties to a negotiable instrument in r.o way diminishes the liabilities of the competent parties thereto.

Minors—A minor is not liable in any way under contracts on negotiable instruments, although the other adult parties are liable. Thus, if a minor makes, draws or indorses a bill, note or cheque, the holder would be entitled to enforce the instrument and receive payment on it against all parties except the minor. Also, where instrument is executed by a minor and an adult, the adult cannot escape liability, not even where the adult is only a surety, for it is only as against the minor that the contract is void. A minor serves as a channel or conduit pipe to pass title or liability, though he cannot originate it. A minor is not bound by a bill or note given by him even for necessaries supplied to him, although the supplier may sue on the original consideration to be reimbursed from minor's property for necessaries supplied. A minor can be a holder though he cannot negotiate. A minor cannot incur liability under a negotiable instrument, but he can acquire rights under it. He can be promisee and, therefore, an instrument can be drawn or made in his favour as payee. He can also become a payee by process of law and enforce payment of the amount of the instrument.

Lunatics, idiots and drunken persons—Bills or notes drawn or made by such persons or any others who for the time being are incapable of forming a rational judgment as to the effects of such bills or notes are not binding on them. Their position is the same as that of minor. A lunatic or a drunken person may, however, bind himself by a negotiable instrument executed by him during a lucid interval or when he is sober. The English law is different, and according to it, unsoundness of mind will not render a contract void, if it was not known to the other party. In order to invalidate a negotiable instrument, it must be shown that the other party was aware of the insanity or the state of drunkenness of the first party.

Insolvents—An insolvent during insolvency cannot accept or indorse a bill, though if he indorses an instrument of which he is payee to a holder in due course the latter can recover from all parties except the insolvent. An insolvent cannot sue on a negotiable instrument, as his property vests in the Official Receiver or Assignee; but if the instrument is executed in his favour after adjudication, he can sue on it unless the Official Receiver intervenes.

Corporations—The rule that capacity to incur liability on negotiable instruments is co-extensive with capacity to contract does not apply to corporations, for part three of Sec.26 reads: "Nothing herein contained shall be deemed to empower a corporation to make, indorse or accept such instrument except in cases in which, under the law for the time being in force, they are so empowered." A corporation being an artificial creation of law, possesses only those rights which the charter of its creation, the Memorandum of Association confers upon it, either expressly or as incidental to its very existence. A non-trading company cannot bind itself by negotiable instruments unless expressly authorised to do so by its memorandum. But a trading company has implied power to bind itself by negotiable instruments.

Agents—A person who is competent to contract may sign a negotiable instrument either himself or through a duly authorised agent. This may be done in one of the two ways: (1) The agent may put his principal's name to the instrument, for it is immaterial as to whose hand holds the pen to put the signature so long as the agent has authority, or (2) the agent may put his own signature by procuration making it clear on the face of the instrument that he signs as an agent for a stated principal. The principal's name must be so disclosed on the instrument that his responsibility is made plain and can be instantly recognised as the document passes from hand to hand. Where an agent simply puts his own signature to an instrument without signifying clearly the capacity in which he signs it, he renders himself personally liable. An agent will also be personally liable if he executes an instrument without or in excess of authority. He can be sued for damages for breach of warranty of authority. In law every partner is an agent of a fellow-partner and of the partnership. Therefore, in a trading firm each partner has *prima facie* authority to bind his co-partners by drawing, accepting or indorsing negotiable instrument, provided that it is signed by him in the name of the firm.

Hindu Joint Family—The *Karta* or Manager of a Hindu Joint Family represents the family in all dealings with the outside world, and has implied authority to borrow money for the family business on a note or bill, and such note or bill will bind all the members of the joint family. The minor members are equally liable with adult members to the extent of their shares. They are not, however, personally liable.

Legal Representative—A person who represents the estate of the deceased or intermeddles therewith is the legal representative of the deceased. A person's heir or body of heirs, executors and administrators are his legal representatives. The legal representative is entitled to the instruments after the death of the holder. An heir of a deceased holder can sue on a pro-note to recover the amount of it to the deceased, as he can give a valid discharge.[14] A legal representative of a deceased person who signs his name to a negotiable instrument is liable personally thereon unless he expressly limits his liability to the extent of the assets received by him as such (Sec. 29). For example, an executor can escape personal liability only by "Sans Recourse" indorsement The legal representative of a deceased person cannot negotiate by mere delivery an instrument payable to order and endorsed by the deceased but not delivered. He must re-indorse and deliver it, taking care to exclude his personal liability thereon.

Liabilities of Parties

1. The drawer of a bill or a cheque is bound in case of dishonour by the drawee or acceptor thereof, to compensate the holder, provided due notice of dishonour has been given to, or received by, the drawer (Sec. 30).

2. The maker of a note, the drawer of a cheque, the drawer of a bill until acceptance, and the acceptor are, in the absence of contract to the contrary, respectively liable on the instrument as principal debtors (Sec. 37).

3. The other parties, i.e., the intermediate indorsers, and the drawer of a bill after acceptance, are liable thereon as sureties for the maker, drawer or acceptor (Sec. 37).

4. As between parties so liable as sureties, each prior party is, in the absence of a contract to the contrary, also liable thereon as a principal debtor in respect of each subsequent party (Sec. 38).

Illustration—A draws a bill payable to his own order on B, who accepts it. A afterwards indorses the bill to C, C to D, D to E. As between E and B, B is the principal debtor, and A, C and D are his sureties. As between E and A, A is the principal debtor and C and D are his sureties. As between E and A, A is the principal debtor and C and D are his sureties. As between E and C, C is the principal debtor and D is his surety.

5. In the absence of a contract to the contrary, the maker of a note and the acceptor before maturity of a bill are bound to pay the amount at maturity according to the apparent tenor of the note or acceptance respectively, i.e., the payment must be to the holder, as payment to any other person is not according to tenor (Sec. 32). [15]

6. The acceptor of a bill at or after maturity must pay the amount thereof to the holder on demand.

7. The drawee of a cheque (paying banker) must pay it when presented for payment, provided the drawer has sufficient funds to his credit with the banker. Refusal to pay without justification will render the banker liable to pay exemplary damages to the drawer (Sec. 31).

8. The engagement of the indorsers is similar to that of the drawer. A person who indorses and delivers a negotiable instrument before maturity without excluding or making conditional his liability, is bound to every subsequent holder, in case of dishonour by the drawee, maker or acceptor, to compensate such holder for any loss or damage caused to him by such dishonour, provided due notice of dishonour has been given to, or received by such indorser (Sec. 35).

9. Every indorser after dishonour is liable as upon an instrument payable on demand (Sec. 35).

10. The liability of each party to a subsequent holder in due course continues until the instrument is duly satisfied. Therefore, each prior party is liable to each subsequent party until the liability is extinguished by final payment (Sec. 36).

---

14. Padam Prasad v. Lok Nath, 1964 Punj.497. (F.B.)
15. See Jagjivan Mavji v. R. Meghji. 1954, S.C. 554.

11. An agent who signs or indorses a negotiable instrument without clearly signifying on it that he is signing only on behalf of his principal is personally liable on the instrument (Sec. 28).

12. A legal representative of a deceased person who signs a negotiable instrument is personally liable thereon unless he expressly limits his liability to the extent of the assets by him as such (Sec. 29).

PART 11-E
NEGOTIATION

A negotiable instrument may be transferred by negotiation or assignment Negotiation is the transferring of an instrument (a note, bill or cheque) from one person to another in such a manner as to convey title and to constitute the transferee the holder thereof.[16] When a negotiable instrument is transferred by a negotiation, the rights of the transferee may rise higher than those of the transferor, depending upon the circumstances attending the negotiation. When the transfer is made by assignment, the assignee has only those rights which the assignor possessed and the assignee is subject to all defences existing against the assignor prior to notice of the assignment. Therefore, a person who receives a negotiable instrument either by negotiation or assignment is a holder and is entitled to recover the amount due thereon from parties thereon.

In *Narsingh Panda* v. *N. Narsinha Murty,* 1966 Orissa 194, on March 14,.1959, M executed a promissory note for ₹ 1,000 in favour of *R*, who in turn sold the pro-note to *N* under a separate sale deed dated December 12,1960. *N* sued *M* for the recovery of the amount of the note. *M* pleaded that *N* could not recover as he was not a holder-in due course of the note and that the suit was not maintainable. *Held,* it is true that *N* is not a holder in due course, but he is a holder under Sec. 8 as he is in possession of the note and as an assignee entitled to recover in his own name. A transfer of a pro-note by means of a registered instrument is valid; it is an assignment.

It is clear that, while the Act does not prohibit transfer of negotiable instruments otherwise than by negotiation, transfer by negotiation has manifest advantages, as will be seen from the following:

TRANSFER BY NEGOTIATIONS AND TRANSFER BY ASSIGNMENT DISTINGUISHED

1. "Negotiation" requires mere delivery of a bearer instrument and endorsement and delivery of an Order instrument to effectuate a transfer; "assignment" requires a written document signed by the transferor.

2. Notice of assignment of debt (actionable claim) must be given by the assignee to the debtor in order to complete his title; no such notice is necessary in a transfer by negotiation.

3. On "assignment" the transferee of an actionable claim takes it subject to all the defects in the title of, and subject to all the equities and defences available against the assignor, even though he took the assignment for value and in good faith. In case of "negotiation," the transferee, as holder in due course, takes the instrument free from any defects in the title of the transferor. This feature is the very essence of negotiability. Negotiability eliminates all personal defences between the original parties, thus making negotiable instrument free to pass from person to person as money, fulfilling the purpose for which it was created.

4. Consideration is always presumed in case of negotiable instruments; in case of "assignment," the transferee must prove consideration for the transfer.

IMPORTANCE OF DELIVERY IN NEGOTIATION

"Negotiation" is effected either by mere delivery or by endorsement and delivery. This means that "delivery" is a very important point relating to negotiable instruments, and Sec. 46 emphasises it. It

---

16. Sec. 14 reads: "When a note, bill or cheque is transferred to any person, so as to constitute that person the holder thereof, the instrument is said to be negotiated."

says that the making, acceptance or indorsement of a negotiable instrument is not complete until delivery, actual or constructive, of the instrument. Delivery of the instrument is essential not only for negotiation, but also to create rights under it. Mere execution (by writing and signing) of an instrument does not make it operative.[17] Delivery made voluntarily with the intention of passing the property in instrument to the person to whom it is given is essential.[18]

In *Bank of Van Diemen's Land* v. *Bank of Victoria* (1871) L.R. 3 P.C. 526, *D* drew a bill on *A* and transferred it to *B*. *B* sent the bill to *A* who writes his acceptance on it Afterwards *A* hears that *D*, the drawer, has become bankrupt. *A* cancels his acceptance and returns the dishonoured bill to *B*. This is no acceptance, as *A* never delivered the accepted bill so as to make himself liable on it.

Delivery may be actual or constructive. It may be conditional or for a special purpose. Actual delivery means change of actual possession. A person is in constructive possession when the instrument is in the actual possession of his agent, clerk or servant on his behalf. Where an instrument is delivered conditionally for a special purpose only, the property in it does not pass to the transferee, even though it is indorsed to him. The plea of conditional delivery or for special purpose is available only against parties who take the instrument with notice of the condition or special purpose, but not against a holder in due course who can hold all prior parties liable on it.

A is the holder of a cheque payable to bearer. He hands it over to his banker for collection. The cheque is delivered for a special purpose and not to entitle the banker to further negotiate it.

NEGOTIATION BY MERE DELIVERY

Sec. 47 provides that a bill or cheque payable to bearer is negotiated by mere delivery of the instrument. An instrument is payable to bearer (*i*) where it is made so payable, or (*ii*) where it is originally made payable to bearer or to order, but the only or the last indorsement is in blank. A cheque, if originally drawn payable to bearer remains bearer, even though it is subsequently indorsed in full. The rule is once a bearer cheque always a bearer cheque; or (*iii*) where the payee is fictitious or a non-existing person. These instruments do not require signature of the transferor. The person who takes them is a holder, and can sue in his own name on them. Where a bearer negotiates an instrument by mere delivery, and does not put his signature thereon, he is not liable to any party to the instrument in case the instrument is dishonoured, as he has not lent his credit to it. The transaction is mere sale of the instrument and, therefore, the transferee cannot recover against the transferor upon the instrument nor can he get back the amount paid by him to the transferor on the failure of consideration, if the transferor delivered in good faith.

The transferor by mere delivery only makes an oral sale of the instrument to his transferee, and his obligations are those of a seller of any goods to the buyer only, *i.e.*, towards his immediate transferee and to no other holders. Like a seller of goods, he warrants by implication to his immediate transferee for consideration that—(*i*) the instrument is genuine, unaltered and is what it purports to be on its face. If any signature turns out to be a forgery, or the amount is altered, the transferee can recover his loss from the transferor; (*ii*) the parties to the instrument were competent to contract. If any party turns out to be incompetent the transferor is liable to the transferee on a breach of warranty; (*iii*) he is entitled to transferee instrument; (*iv*) he is not aware of any facts which make the instrument valueless, *e.g.*, insolvency of a party, or discharge of the instrument or its being void. Thus, the transferor by delivery can be compelled to return the purchase money to his immediate transferee if the instrument turns out to be worthless and the consideration wholly fails, but incurs no liability on the instrument.

17. Thrappa v. Umedmalji, 1924 Bom. 205.

18. Bhogi Ram v. Kishorilal, 1928. All. 289.

NEGOTIATION BY INDORSEMENT AND DELIVERY

Instruments payable to a specified person or to the order of a specified person or to a specified person or order are instruments payable to order. Such instruments can be negotiated only by indorsement **AND** delivery. Unless the holder signs his indorsement on the instrument, the transferee does not become a holder. If there are more payees than one, all must indorse it. Where an instrument payable to order is delivered without indorsement it is merely assigned and not negotiated, and the holder thereof is not entitled to the rights of a holder in due course, and he cannot negotiate it to a third person. If an indorsement is declared invalid, the property in the instrument again vests in the payee and he can sue on it without reindorsement from such indorsee. An unconditional indorsement followed by an unconditional delivery transfers immediately to the indorsee the property in the instrument with the right of further negotiation.

INDORSEMENT

When the maker or holder of a negotiable instrument signs the same otherwise than as such maker, for the purpose of negotiation, on the back or face thereof or on a slip of paper annexed thereto, or signs for the same purpose a stamped paper intended to be completed as a negotiable instrument, he is said to indorse the same, and is called the indorser (Sec. 15). The person to whom the instrument is indorsed is called the indorsee. An indorsement is the signature by the maker or holder of a negotiable instrument for the purpose of negotiation. It is usually on the back of the instrument, although it may be even on the face thereof, or if no space is left on the instrument, on a slip of paper attached to it, called 'ALLONGE."

An indorsement can be made by—

1. the holder of the instrument.
2. the maker signing it otherwise than as such maker,
3. every maker, drawer or indorsee or all of several joint makers, drawers, payees or indorsees of the instrument,
4. the payee of an instrument.

A stranger cannot indorse an instrument, and if he does indorse it, no suit can be brought against him. But he may make himself liable as a surety, if he guarantees payment. When a stranger indorses an instrument he is called the **BACKER** and although such an indorsement is void in India and the indorsee cannot sue on the instrument, under Sec. 56 of the English Bills of Exchange Act, a Backer is liable as an indorser to the holder in due course.

CLASSES OF INDORSEMENT

An indorsement may be (a) Blank or General, (b) Special or Full, (c) Restrictive, (d) Partial, or (e) Conditional or Qualified.

BLANK OR GENERAL

An indorsement is said to be blank or general where the indorser merely writes his signature on the back of the instrument, and the instrument so indorsed becomes payable to bearer, even though originally it was payable to order. Thus where a bill is payable to "James Brown or order," and he writes on its back "James Brown", it is an indorsement in blank by James Brown, and the property in the bill can pass by mere delivery, as long as indorsement continues to be in blank. But a holder of an instrument in full, by writing above the indorsees signature a direction to pay the instrument to another person or his order (Sec. 49). The advantage of such a course is that the holder, though he transfers the instrument, does not incur the responsibility of an indorser. A is the holder of a bill indorsed by B, in blank. A writes over B's signature the words "Pay to C or order." A is not liable as an indorser, but the writing operates as an indorsement in full from B to C. (Illustration to Sec.49).

An instrument indorsed in blank in the first instance may be followed by an indorsement in full, in which case it continues to be payable to bearer and negotiable by mere delivery in connection with all parties *prior* to the indorsement in full, and the indorser in full is only liable to the person to whom he indorses it in full or who derives title through indorsement by such persons.[19] In this case, the holder of a bill originally indorsed in blank indorsed it specially to Barber, Walker & Co., who carried on business both as "Barber, Walker & Co.", and "Eastwood & Co." and who indorsed the bill as "Eastwood & Co." The bill was dishonoured on presentation on the ground that it was not indorsed by " Barber, Walker & Co."[20] The Court held that, as the bill was initially indorsed in blank, its negotiability could not be restrained by a special indorsement and the presentment was such as to render the defendant liable to the plaintiff. In another case, *A*, the payee-holder of a bill, indorsed it in blank and delivered it to *B*. *B* also indorsed it in blank and delivered it to *C*. *C* indorsed it in full to *D* or order. *D* without indorsement delivered the bill to *E*. *E* as the bearer against *A*, *B*, the drawer, and acceptor, was entitled to receive payment from them, but he could not proceed against *C* or *D*. *D* could sue *C* as he received the bill from *C* by indorsement in full. If, however, *D* instead of passing the bill to *E* had passed it by a regular indorsement, *E* could claim against all prior parties.

SPECIAL OR FULL.

If the indorser signs his name and adds a direction to pay the amount mentioned in the instrument to, or to the order of a specified person, the indorsement is said to be special or in full. A special indorsement specifies the person to whom or to whose order the bill is to be payable. A bill made payable to James Brown, or James Brown or order, and indorsed "Pay to the order of Henry Smith" would be specially indorsed and Henry Smith may indorse it. A blank indorsement can be turned into a special indorsement by the addition of an order making the bill payable to the transferee.

RESTRICTIVE

An indorsement is restrictive which prohibits or restricts the further negotiation of an instrument, which expresses that it is a mere authority to deal with the instrument as thereby directed and not a complete and unconditional transfer of the ownership thereof. If a bill is indorsed "Pay *C* only" or "Pay *C* for my sue" or "Pay *C* on account of "*B*" or "Pay *C* or order for collection" or "The within must be credited to *C*," it is restrictively indorsed, and cannot be negotiated.

PARTIAL

An indorsement is partial which purports to transfer to the indorsee a part only of the amount payable on the instrument. A partial indorsement does not operate as a negotiation of the instrument. Sec. 56 prohibits an instrument being negotiated for a portion only of the sum at the time due upon it, for a partial indorsement would cause "inconvenience to prior parties, subject them to a plurality of action, and interfere with the free circulation of these instruments." To be valid for the purpose of negotiation, an indorsement must be of the entire instrument, because a personal contract cannot be apportioned. *A* holds a bill for ₹ 1,000 and indorses it thus: "Pay *B* or order ₹500" or "Pay ₹500 to *B* or order, and ₹500 to *C* or order," the indorsement in either case is partial and invalid. But where an instrument has been paid in part, the fact of the part-payment may be indorsed on the instrument, and it may then be negotiated for the residue. For example, a bill may be indorsed thus: "Pay *A* or order ₹500 being the unpaid residue of the bill." Such an indorsement would be valid.

CONDITIONAL OR QUALIFIED

An indorsement is conditional or qualified which limits or negatives the liability of the indorser. It differs from a restrictive indorsement in that the latter places restrictions on the negotiability of an

---

19. Walker v. Macdonald (1848) 2 Ex. 527.
20. Smith v. Clarke (1794) 1 Peake 295.

instrument, while conditional indorsement limits or negatives the liability of the indorser. A drawer of a bill cannot draw it conditionally and a maker of a note cannot make his liability conditional or exclude it. The acceptor of a bill can accept it conditionally but cannot exclude his liability by acceptance. An indorser is entitled to insert by express words in the indorsement a stipulation negativing or limiting his own liability to the holder. This may be done in any of the following ways:—

(a) **By 'Sans Recourse' Indorsement**—Where the indorser makes it clear that he does not incur the liability of an indorser to the indorsee or subsequent holders and they should not look to him in case of dishonour of the instrument, it is a Sans Recourse indorsement. Here the indorser expressly excludes his liability by adding the words "**Sans Recourse**" or "Without recourse." He may indorse thus:— "Pay A or order **Sans Recourse**" or "Pay A without recourse to me" or "Pay A or order at his own risk."

(b) By making his liability depend upon the happening of a specified event which may never happen, e.g., the holder of a bill may indorse it thus: "Pay A or order on the arrival of S.S. Ravensltaw at Bombay" or "Pay A or order on his marrying B." In such cases the indorser will not be liable until the happening of the events, and if the events become impossible and do not happen, his liability is extinguished. The indorsee gets no title to the bill nor can he sue the indorser. But he can sue the prior parties before the happening of the event.

(c) By making the right of an indorsee to receive the amount of the instrument depend upon the specified event, which may never happen. In this case, the indorsee's right being dependent upon the happening of an event he cannot recover the amount either from the indorser or from any prior party until the event has happened.

(d) **By Facultative Indorsement**—Where the indorser extends his own liability by stipulating in the indorsement that he waives presentment or notice of dishonour by the holder. An indorsement "Pay A or order. Notice of dishonour waived" is facultative, and the person who has signed remains liable to A even though no notice of dishonour has been given to him.

(e) **By "Sans Frais" Indorsement**—Where the indorser does not want the indorsee or any other holder to incur any expense on his account on the bill, the indorsement is **sans frais**.

The insertion of a condition in the indorsement does not in any way affect the negotiability of the instrument.

NEGOTIATION BACK

Where an indorser negotiates an instrument and again becomes its holder, the instrument is said to be "negotiated back" to that indorser, and none of the intermediate, irvdorsers are then liable to him. The rule, the object of which is to prevent a circuity of action, is an exception to the general rule that the holder in due course of a negotiable instrument may sue all prior parties to the instrument. Therefore, when a instrument is "negotiated back" to a prior parry, that party is remitted to his former position and comes within the definition of a holder." A, the holder of a bill indorses it to B. B indorses it to C, C to D, D to E and E indorses it again to A. A; being a holder in due course of the bill by second indorsement by E, can recover the amount thereof from B, C, D or E, and himself being a prior party is liable to all of them. Therefore, A having been relegated by the second indorsement to his original position, cannot sue B, C, D and E, for if A were allowed to sue E, E could sue D and D could sue C, and C could sue B, and B could sue A, and this circuity of action the law prohibits. A can, however, further negotiate the bill if he cancels or strikes off the indorsement of B, C, D and E. Such a transaction is called **Taking up of a Bill.** When the indorsements are struck off without the consent of the indorsers, the right of the subsequent indorsee to recover indemnity from them is destroyed and they are discharged. But clause 2 of Sec. 52 provides that where an indorser excludes his liability and afterwards becomes the holder of the instrument, all inter-mediate indorsers are liable to him. So, if A has at the time of first indorsement excluded his liability by the use of the words "without recourse" he is not liable to *B, C, D* or *E*, and if the bill is negotiated back to *A*, then *B, C, D* and *E* are all liable to him and he can recover the amount from all or any of them.

EFFECT OF INDORSEMENT

The effect of indorsement, when Sec. 50 is read subject to Secs. 46 and 52, may be stated thus: An unconditional indorsement of a negotiable instrument followed by its unconditional delivery transfers to the indorsee the property therein, vesting in him the title to the instrument. The indorsee acquires a right to negotiate the instrument to any one he likes and to sue all parties whose names appear on it.

He cannot sue third parties on the original consideration. The nature of the contract which the indorser enters into with his indorsee is very much the same as that of the drawer of the bill. Every indorsement is in the nature of a new bill issued by the indorser in favour of his indorsee. By indorsement the indorser impliedly represents to his immediate indorsee that the instrument will, when presented in due course, be accepted and subsequently paid when it falls due, and if it is not paid at maturity, the indorser will indemnify the indorsee, provided that due notice has been given or received, by him. The indorser cannot deny the signature or capacity to contract of any prior party. But where the holder, without the consent of the indorser, destroys or impairs the indorsees remedy against a prior party, the indorser is discharged from liability to the holder as if the instrument had been paid at maturity (Sec. 40). The effect of an indorsement in blank and delivery of an instrument originally made drawn payable to order is to convert it into one payable to bearer and transferable by mere delivery. The effect of restrictive indorsement is (*i*) to prohibit or exclude further negotiation, (*ii*) to constitute the indorsee an agent of indorser to indorse the instrument, or to receive its contents for him or (*iii*) to constitute the indorsee as agent to receive its contents fotsome other specified person.

Joint payees or indorsees must all indorse to complete the negotiation of the instrument (Sec. 51). Thus, an indorsement made by only one of the two payees is invalid, even if it is made in favour of the other payee. But this does not deprive the creditor (holder of the instrument) of the right to a decree for the amount. He can get the money on the ground that the indorsement amounted to an assignment of a chose-in-action (*Srinivasulu* v. *Kondappa,* 1960 A.P. 174). A non-negotiable promissory note may be assigned by indorsement so as to enable the assignee to sue upon the note in his own name.[21]

NEGOTIATION OF LOST INSTRUMENT OBTAINED BY UNLAWFUL MEANS OR OF UNLAWFUL CONSIDERATION

When a negotiable instrument has been lost or has been obtained from any maker, acceptor or holder thereof by means of an offence or fraud, or for an unlawful consideration, no possessor or indorser, who claims through the person who found or obtained the instrument is entitled to receive the amount due thereon from such maker, acceptor, or holder or from any parry prior to such holder unless such possessor or indorsee is, or some person through whom he claims was, a holder thereof in due course (Sec. 58). The general rule of law is that a person cannot pass better title then he himself possesses. This section embodies the chief difference between the transfer of ordinary goods and negotiation of negotiable instruments. Two sets of circumstances are dealt with here. *Firstly,* the legal position of **a possessor** or an **indorsee** of a negotiable instrument which has been lost, or which has been obtained from any maker, acceptor or holder by means of an offence, or fraud, or unlawful consideration. *Secondly,* the position of a holder in due course under similar circumstances. We shall deal with these conditions separately.

21. Mohd. Khumarali v. Ranga Rao (1901) 24 Mad. 654; Muthar Sahib v. Kadir Sahib (1905) 28 Mad. 544.

LOST INSTRUMENTS

1. The finder of a lost instrument does not acquire any title to it as against the rightful owner, nor can he claim payment from the acceptor of a bill or maker of note or cheque. The rightful owner has a right to recover the instrument from the finder.
2. An acceptor or maker who makes payment in due course on lost bill or note to a finder thereof is discharged from all liability to the rightful owner. But the true owner can recover the money from the finder.
3. Where a bill or note payable to bearer or indorsed in blank is lost and the finder negotiates it to a *bona fide* transferee for value the latter acquires a valid title to it. He can retain the instrument as against the true owner, and also claim payment from parties liable thereon.
4. Where the finder of a lost bill or note payable to order negotiates it by forging the indorsement of the loser to a *bona fide* transferee for value, the latter acquires no title to it for the indorser himself had no title which he could transfer; forgery can corifer no title, and this holder is not a holder in due course.[22]
5. Where a holder has lost a bill, he should give notice of the loss to all parties liable on it, and also a public notice by an advertisement.
6. The holder of a bill, who has lost it must apply to the drawee for payment at maturity, and if the payment is refused, he must give notice of dishonour to all the parties liable on it. If he fails to give notice of dishonour, he will lose his remedy against the drawer and indorsers.

STOLEN INSTRUMENT

A person, who has stolen a negotiable instrument from the true owner, cannot claim payment against any party liable thereon, and the true owner can get back the instrument or the money if he has realised it from the drawee. But if a stolen instrument is negotiated by delivery to a transferee for value without notice of the theft the transferee gets a good title to it not only against the thief but also against all the parties prior to him.

INSTRUMENTS OBTAINED BY FRAUD

Fraud vitiates all transactions. Where an instrument is obtained by fraud of is obtained for the purpose of defrauding any third person, the person defrauding is not entitled to recover anything, as his title is defective; but if such an instrument passes into the hands of a holder in due course, he will acquire good title to the instrument and the plea of fraud will not avail against him. The position is the same where an instrument has been obtained by undue influence or coercion.

INSTRUMENT OBTAINED FOR AN UNLAWFUL CONSIDERATION

The general rule of contracts that every agreement of which the object or con-sideration is unlawful or immoral is void applies to a negotiable instrument for unlawful consideration, e.g., a note in favour of a witness forgiving false evidence, or in part consideration for giving one's daughter in marriage creates no obligation between the parties thereto. But a holder in due course, or a person deriving title through him gets a good title to the instrument.

FORGED INSTRUMENTS

Forgery is the fraudulent making of alteration of a writing to the prejudice of another's right. Forgery with she intention of obtaining title to instrument would include (i) fraudulently writing the name of an existing person; (ii) signing the name of a fictitious person with the intention that it may

---

22. Mercantile Bank of India v. Mascarenhas, 1932 P.C.22

passes that of a real person, or (*iii*) signing one's own name with the intention that the signature may pass as the signature of some other person of the same name. The forged or unauthorised signature is inoperative, and the property in the instrument remains in the person who was the holder at the time when the forged or unauthorised signature was placed on it. Therefore, the holder of a forged instrument cannot enforce payment thereon, nor can he give a valid discharge therefor, and even if he has obtained the payment of the bill, he cannot retain the money. The forged signature does not give to the forger any title whatever. It is not a case of defect of title. There is from the very beginning a complete absence of title and a forged signature is altogether inoperative. A forged instrument has in law no existence whatever. It is a nullity no matter in whose hands it may be. Even if it has during the course of circulation passed through the hands of a holder in due course it is not cured of its defects, because there is no defect of title to cure; there is a complete absence of title.

FORGED INDORSEMENTS

The case of a forged indorsement is slightly different. If an instrument is indorsed in full, it cannot be negotiated except by an indorsement signed by the person to whom or to whose order the instrument is payable, for the indorsee obtains title only through his indorsement. Thus, if an instrument be negotiated by means of a forged indorsement the indorsee acquires no title even though he be a purchaser for value and in good faith, for the indorsement is a nullity. But where the instrument is a bearer instrument or has been indorsed in blank, it can be negotiated by mere delivery, and the holder derives his title independent of the forged indorsement and can claim the amount from any of the parties to the instrument. A bill is indorsed: "Pay *A* or order." *A* indorses it in blank, and it comes into the hands of *B*, who simply delivers it to *C*. *C* forges *B*'s indorsement and transfers it to *D*. Here, *D*, as the holder, does not derives his title through the forged indorsement of *B*, but through he genuine indorsement of *A*, and can claim payment from any of the parties to the instrument in spite of the intervening forged indorsement.

NEGOTIATION OF DISHONOURED AND OVERDUE INSTRUMENT

We have seen before that the holder for value of a negotiable instrument is not affected by any defect in the title of the transferor. But this general rule is subject to two exceptions with respect to instrument acquired with notice of dishonour and after maturity. Sec. 59 lays down that where a negotiable instrument has been dishonoured or has become overdue by the expiry of the day of payment, any person who takes it with notice of dishonour or after maturity, takes it subject to any defect of title attaching to it at the time of dishonour or maturity. The transferee is not a holder in due course, and gets no better title than his transferor.

The case of notes and accommodation bills is different. The proviso to Sec. 59 lays down that a holder for consideration and in good faith of a note or an accommodation bill after maturity is a holder in due course in the same way as a holder before maturity, and can recover the amount from any prior party.

A bill is payable 90 days after date. It is accepted for the accommodation of the drawer. After maturity, (*i.e.*, after expiry of 93 days from the date of the bill) the drawer indorses it to A for value. A can recover the amount of the bill from the acceptor.

DURATION OF NEGOTIABILITY

A bill or note is negotiable *ad infinitum* and can circulate by negotiation until it has been finally discharged by payment or satisfaction by, or on behalf of the acceptor or maker at or after maturity. A payment before maturity is not a payment in due course, and does not stop negotiability.

A bill is said to be **Retired** when it is paid before maturity. The acceptor or maker who receives the instrument after payment but before maturity may re-issue it Negotiability of the instrument stops only when the party ultimately liable thereon pays it.

SURRENDER TO THE DRAWEE NOT NEGOTIATION

It is customary for a holder, when presenting a cheque to the drawee banker or other bill of exchange to the drawee for payment, to write his name across the back of the instrument. Such writing is not an indorsement, and the transfer of the instrument from the holder to the drawee for payment and discharge is not a negotiation. A negotiable instrument, when transferred from one person to another by delivery or indorsement and delivery, is a sale of the instrument, thus enabling it to pass as money. The passing of an instrument from the holder to the drawee, on the other hand, is a surrender of the instrument for discharge, and is not a negotiation. Therefore, no indorsement is necessary to entitle the holder to receive payment. A person signing his name on an instrument before surrender to the drawee has no liability as an indorser, because the drawee does not occupy the position of a holder. The drawee, however, becomes a holder if he purchases the bill before maturity with intention further to negotiate it. In the absence of this situation, the signature upon a bill or cheque before surrender to the drawee for payment merely acts as a receipt for money so far as the drawee is concerned.

PART 11-F
ACCEPTANCE

The drawee, as such, has no liability on any bill addressed to him for acceptance or payment. A refusal to accept or to pay such bill gives the holder no right against him. A bill of exchange of itself does not operate as an assignment of the funds in the hands of the drawee available for the payment thereof, and the drawee is not liable on the bill unless and until he accepts the same. The liability of the acceptor is primary.

The acceptance of a bill is die indication by the drawee of his assent to the order of the drawer. Thus, when the drawee writes on the bill, generally, across the face of the bill the word "accepted" and signs his name underneath he becomes the acceptor of the bill. The acceptance may, however, be made by mere signature of the drawee without the addition of the word "accepted." But an oral acceptance, or the writing of the word "accepted" without the drawee's signature, is not an acceptance. The drawee is not liable on the bill unless the bill is presented to him for acceptance and he actually accepts it and then delivers it over to the holder or gives notice of acceptance to the holder or someone on his behalf. And, where a drawee, having signed his acceptance, change his mind and before delivering it to the holder, obliterates his acceptance, he will not be liable as an acceptor. Where there are more parts of a bill than one the drawee should sign his acceptance only on one part, for if he signs on more than one part and they get into the hands of the several holders in due course, he would be liable to all of them. It is possible to accept an overdue or a dishonoured bill, an incomplete or blank bill, and even before the drawer has signed it or after notice of drawer's death. An acceptance to be valid must be (*i*) written, (*ii*) signed by the drawee or his agent, (*iii*) on the bill, and (*iv*) completed by delivery to the holder or by notice of acceptance to him or some person on his behalf.

An acceptance may be either *general* or *qualified.*

General acceptance—A general acceptance is absolute and assents without any qualification to the order of the drawer. It is according to the apparent tenor of the bill. A general acceptance is signified by the drawee by signing his name on the bill with or without the word "accepted", without adding any condition regarding payment. As a rule, an acceptance must be general.

Qualified acceptance—Where an acceptance is made subject to some condition or qualification, thereby varying in express terms the effect of the bill as drawn, it is a qualified acceptance. The holder of a bill may either refuse to take a qualified acceptance or acquiesce in it. Where he refuses to take it, he can treat the bill as dishonoured by non-acceptance, and sue the drawer accordingly. But if he accepts the qualified acceptance, it binds him and the acceptor, but not the other parties not consenting thereto.

Sec. 86 gives instances of qualified acceptance which are stated below with a few; more which may also be regarded as such. An acceptance is qualified when it is—

1. **Conditional**—An acceptance which makes the payment dependent on the happening of an event therein stated is conditional. Thus, bills "accepted payable when in funds" or "accepted payable on giving bills of lading for Clover per *SS. Amazon*" or "accepted when a cargo consigned to me is sold," are all conditional acceptances.

2. **Partial**—An acceptance which undertakes to pay only a part of the amount of the bill is a partial acceptance, *e.g.*, a bill drawn for ₹ 1,000 is "accepted for ₹ 500 only." In English law, partial acceptance is good to that part.

3. **Qualified as to place**—An acceptance, which undertakes to pay only at a specified place and not elsewhere, or to pay at a place different from the one mentioned in the bill, and not elsewhere, is qualified as to the place of payment. "Accepted payable at the Central Bank only" or "accepted payable at the Central Bank and not elsewhere" is qualified acceptance. But if a bill is "accepted payable at Central Bank" it is a general acceptance, for it is payable at a particular place without stating that it is payable only there or is not payable elsewhere.

4. **Qualified as to time**—An acceptance which makes the payment of the amount of the bill payable at a time different from that mentioned in the order of the drawer. Where a bill is drawn payable 3 months after date and is' 'accepted, payable six months after date" or where a bill in which no time is fixed is accepted payable on a particular date is qualified as to time.

5. **Acceptance for payment in instalments**—In this case a bill is accepted as payable in instalments, *e.g.*, a bill for ₹ 1,000 is "accepted payable in monthly instalments of ₹ 100."

6. **Acceptance by some of the drawees only**—Where the drawees are not partners and only one or some of them accept, the acceptance is qualified. But if the drawees are partners one or more can accept on behalf of all the partners and the acceptance will be general.

Who may accept—A bill of exchange can be accepted only by the following persons, and no other:—

1. The drawee of the bill; *i.e.*, the person directed to pay.
2. All or some of the several drawees, where the bill is addressed to more than one drawee. In order that all the drawees be liable on the bill it must be accepted by them all. A bill accepted by some of the several drawees binds only those who accept it, and not the non-accepting drawees, and the acceptance is a qualified acceptance. If the bill is drawn on a partnership firm, it may be accepted in the firm name or by one partner on behalf of himself, and the other partners provided he has authority to accept.
3. A drawee in case of need, *i.e.*, a person whose name is mentioned in the bill as one whom the payee should resort to in case the real drawee refuses to accept.
4. The agent of any of the persons named above.
5. If no drawee is named in a bill and a person accepts it, he will become acceptor by estoppel.
6. An acceptor for honour, *i.e.*, any person who accepts the bill for the honour of any party already liable on it.
7. The agent of the acceptor for honour.

ACCEPTANCE FOR HONOUR

When a bill of exchange has been noted or protested for non-acceptance or for better security, any person not being a party already liable thereon may, with the consent of the holder, by writing on the bill, accept the same for the honour of any party thereto (Sec. 108). This section provides for acceptance by a stranger to the bill for the honour of any party to it and such acceptance is called "acceptance for honour" or "acceptance supra protest." The acceptance is allowed when the original drawee refuses to accept, or declines to give better security when demanded by the notary. Acceptance for honour is made with the consent of the holder who is not bound to accept the acceptance. If the bill is noted or protested, the holder may treat it as dishonoured. There may be several acceptors for the honour of different parties, but there cannot be acceptors one after another for the honour of the same person, unless the first acceptor for honour has died or become insolvent. This acceptance must be for the whole amount of the bill and must be made before the bill is overdue.

A person desiring to accept for honour must, by writing on the bill under his hand declare that he accepts under protest the protested bill for the honour of the drawer or of a particular indorser whom he names, or generally for whose honour (Sec. 109). Where the acceptance does not express for whose honour it is made it shall be deemed to be made for the honour of the drawer (Sec. 110).

RIGHTS AND LIABILITIES OF ACCEPTOR FOR HONOUR

An acceptor for honour enjoys a slightly better position than an ordinary acceptor. His liability is conditional, as an acceptance for honour is in the nature of a qualified acceptance and amounts to a collateral engagement. He undertakes to pay only when the bill has been duly presented at maturity to the drawee for payment and the drawee has refused to pay and the bill has been noted or protested for non-payment. On acceptance the acceptor for honour takes exactly the same position as the party for whose honour he accepts. His rights and liabilities are the same. Thus he is liable to all parties subsequent to the party for whose honour he accepts to pay in case the drawee fails to pay (Sec. 111).

PAYMENT FOR HONOUR

The general rule of law is that no person by voluntarily paying the debt of another can make himself his creditor. Sec. 113 makes an exception in the case of negotiable instruments. The Section reads: "When a bill of exchange has been noted or protested for non-payment, any person may pay the same for the honour of any party liable to pay the same, provided that the person so paying or his agent in that behalf has previously declared before a notary public the party for whose honour he pays, and that such declaration has been recorded by the notary public." Thus, any person may intervene when a bill has been protested for non-payment after having been duly accepted, and pay supra protest for the honour of any party liable on the bill. When a bill has been paid supra protest it ceases to be negotiable.

A payer for honour, on paying the bill for honour, acquires all the rights of a holder to whom he pays, and is entitled to all the remedies of the holder on the instrument. These remedies are available only against the party for whose honour he pays and all parties prior to such person-; and all parties subsequent to such person are discharged.

PRESENTMENT

Presentment or presentation means presenting a negotiable instrument to the drawee, maker or acceptor thereof for the purpose of getting payment. Presentment is made for two purposes: (*i*) Presentment for acceptance, and (*ii*) Presentment for payment.

PRESENTMENT FOR ACCEPTANCE

It is only bills of exchange that require presentment for acceptance, and even these of certain kinds only. Bills payable on demand or on a fixed date need not be presented. For example, a bill payable 60 days after date or on the happening of a certain event may or may not be presented for acceptance. But the following bills must be presented for acceptance otherwise the parties to the bill will not be liable on it:

1. A bill payable *after sight*. Presentment for acceptance is necessary in order to fix maturity of the bill.

2. A bill in which there is an express stipulation that it should be presented for acceptance before it is presented for payment.

But even in cases where presentment is optional, it is always desirable to get a bill accepted as soon as possible, in order to obtain (*i*) the additional security of the acceptor's name on the bill, or (*ii*) an immediate right of recourse against the drawer and the other parties if the bill is dishonoured by non-acceptance. Presentment for acceptance also helps the drawer, for if acceptance is refused, he may on receiving early notice of dishonour, be able to get his effects out of the hands of the drawee.

Presentment for acceptance to whom—The presentment for acceptance must be made—
1. To the drawee or his duly authorised agent.
2. To all the drawees where there are several drawees, unless they are partners and one has express or implied authority to accept on behalf of all.
3. If the drawee is dead, to his legal representative. A legal representative accepting the bill should expressly limit his liability to the extent the assets come to his hands, otherwise he will be personally liable.
4. If the drawee has been declared an insolvent, to the Official Receiver or Assignee.

Time and Place for Presentment—The following rules maybe stated with regard to time and place of presentment:—
1. All bills must be presented before maturity.
2. Where presentment is obligatory, it must be made within reasonable time or without unreasonable delay.
3. A bill the presentment of which is not necessary may be presented at any time before payment.
4. Where a period for a presentment is specified in a bill, it must be presented within that period.
5. A bill payable after sight must, if no time is specified therein for presentation, be presented within a "reasonable time" after it is drawn.
6. This presentment must be made on a business day within business hours.
7. It should be made at the place of business or residence of the drawee and where a place for presentment is mentioned in the bill, the presentment must be made at that place. A bill which requires presentment at a particular place is called a Domiciled Bill. If the drawee cannot, after reasonable search, be found, the bill is deemed to be dishonoured.

PROOF OF PRESENTMENT

Presentment is deemed to have been made only when the bill is exhibited to the drawee so that he may see the same and judge whether he will accept it or not Mere notice of its existence in the possession of the holder is not sufficient. The drawee can insist on the product ion of the bill and is entitled to 48 hours' time for considering whether or not to accept it (Sec. 63). The holder must prove that the bill was properly presented or a real attempt to present it to the drawee or his agent was made.

EFFECT OF NON-PRESENTMENT

Where presentment for acceptance is compulsory and the holder fails to do so, the drawer, and all the indorsers are discharged from liability to him. He is not entitled to a decree, nor can he base his claim even on the original consideration.

PRESENTMENT WHEN EXCUSED

Where presentment for acceptance is necessary, it is excused and the bill may be treated as dishonoured in the following cases:—
1. Where the drawee cannot after reasonable search be found (Sec. 61).
2. In English Law, where the drawee becomes insolvent, or is dead. But in Indian Law, the bill must be presented to the legal representative of the deceased drawee or to the Official Receiver of the insolvent drawee (Sec. 75).

3. Where the drawee is a fictitious person or one incapable of contracting (Sec. 91).

4. Where although the presentment is irregular, acceptance has been refused on some other ground.

The fact that the holder has reason to believe that the bill on presentment will be dishonoured, does not excuse presentment.

PRESENTMENT FOR PAYMENT

All notes, bills and cheques must be presented for payment to the maker, acceptor, or drawee thereof respectively by on behalf of the holder during the usual hours of business, and if at banker's within banking hours. Where the maker, acceptor or drawee has died, presentment may be made to his legal representative or where he has become insolvent to the Official Receiver or Assignee. On behalf of presentment for payment the parties, other than the maker, acceptor or drawee thereon are not liable to the holder (Sec. 64).

A promissory note, payable at a certain period after sight, must be presented to the maker thereof for sight (if he can, after reasonable search, be found) by a person entitled to demand payment, within a reasonable time after it is made and in business hours on a business day. On default of such presentment no party thereto is liable thereon to the person making such default (Sec. 62).

Where a promissory note is payable on demand and is not payable at a specified place, no presentment is necessary to charge the maker thereof (Exception to Sec. 64).

A note or bill made payable at a specified period after date or sight thereof, must be presented for payment at maturity (Sec. 66). Thus bills and notes must be presented for payment on the day they fall due, and where days of grace are allowed, they must be presented on the last day of grace. An earlier presentment is premature and ineffective.

A note or bill, made, drawn or accepted payable at a specified place must, in order to charge the maker or drawer thereof, be presented for payment at that place (Sec. 69). But a note made payable at any particular town, such as "Poona, Bombay or elsewhere," is not made payable at a specified place, and, therefore, need not be presented for payment.

A note, bill or cheque made, accepted or drawn payable at "specified place and not elsewhere" must, in order to charge any party thereto, be presented for payment at that place (Sec. 68). But an instrument made payable at either of two places may be presented at any one place.

A promissory note payable by instalments must be presented for payment on the 3rd day after the date fixed for payment of each instalment and the note will be deemed to be dishonoured on the non-payment of any instalment (Sec. 67).

A note or bill, not made-payable at a specified place must be presented for payment at the place of business, if any, or at the usual residence, of the maker, drawee or acceptor thereof, as the case may be (Sec. 70). But where the maker, drawee or acceptor has no known place of business or fixed residence and no place is specified in the instrument for presentment for acceptance or payment, such presentment may be made to him in person wherever he can be found (Sec. 71). The holder must exercise due diligence in finding the place of business or residence, and he can make personal presentment only if he fails to find the place after due diligence. Mere inquiry at the house is not sufficient.

In order to charge the drawer, a cheque must be presented at the bank upon which it is drawn before the relation between the drawer and his banker has been altered to the prejudice of the drawer (Sec. 72). Where the holder does not present the cheque within a reasonable time, and in the meantime the relation between the drawer and the banker is altered and the drawer suffers a damage due to delay, the drawer will not be liable if the bank fails to cash the cheque (Sec. 84).

In order to charge any person except the drawer, (*i.e.*, indorsers), a cheque must be presented within a reasonable time after delivery, thereof by such person (Sec. 73).

Delay in presentment for acceptance or payment is excused, if it is caused by circumstances beyond the control of the holder, and not imputable to his default, misconduct or negligence. When the cause of delay ceases to operate, presentment must be made within a reasonable time (Sec. 75A). Delay may arise because of impracticability of transmitting the bill to the place of payment or declaration of statutory moratorium. Also where a hundi is lost and the drawer on demand refuses to supply a duplicate non-presentment is excused.

Presentment for payment excused—Sec. 75 provides that no presentment is necessary and the instrument may be treated as dishonoured in the following cases:—

1. Where the maker, drawer or acceptor actively does something so as to intentionally prevent the presentment of the instrument, *e.g.*, deprives the holder of the instrument and keeps it till after maturity, or misleads the holder, or the drawer refuses to give a duplicate of hundi which is lost.

2. Where his business place is closed during the usual business hours on the due date.

3. Where there is no person to make payment at the place specified for payment.

4. Where he cannot after due search be found.

5. Where there is a promise to pay notwithstanding non-presentment, *e.g.*, where the indorsement of the notary public on the instruments was "endorsers state if drawer does not pay we will pay at request of the manager," it was a sufficient promise to pay by the indorsers.

6. Where the presentment is expressly or impliedly waived by the party entitled to presentment. An express waiver may be made in the instrument, by such words as "presentment waived," or "notwithstanding non-presentment", or other words to the effect. An implied waiver will be inferred from the conduct of the drawee or indorsee. The waiver may be made at any time before maturity. An implied waiver may be inferred when *after maturity* of the instrument any party, (*i*) makes a part-payment on account of the amount due thereon, or (*ii*) promises to pay the amount due thereon in whole or part, or (*iii*) waives his right to take advantage of any default in presentment for payment.

7. Where the drawer could not possibly have suffered any damage by non-present-ment.

8. Where the drawee is a fictitious person, or one incompetent to contract.

9. Where the drawer and the drawee are the same person.

10. Where the bill is dishonoured by non-acceptance.

11. Where presentment has become impossible, for instance, by the declaration of war between the countries of the holder and the drawee or by the country where presentment is to be made being overrun by the enemy.

DISHONOUR

A bill or hundi may be dishonoured either by non-acceptance or by non-payment. Where an instrument is dishonoured, the holder must give notice of dishonour to the drawer or his previous holders if he wants to make them liable. But in certain cases, as stated below, notice need not be given.

DISHONOUR BY NON-ACCEPTANCE

1. When the drawee does not accept it within 48 hours from the time of presentment for acceptance.
2. When presentment for acceptance is excused and the bill remains unaccepted.
3. When the drawee is incompetent to contract.
4. When the drawee is a fictitious person or after reasonable search cannot be found.
5. Where the acceptance is a qualified one or where one or some of several drawees not being partners make default in acceptance, on being duly required to accept. In this case, the holder may at his own risk treat the bill as accepted.

DISHONOUR BY NON-PAYMENT

A promissory note, a bill of exchange or cheque is said to be dishonoured by non-payment when the maker of the note, acceptor of the bill or drawee of the cheque makes default in payment upon being duly required to pay the same (Sec.92). Also, a negotiable instrument is dishonoured by non-payment when presentment for payment is excused and the instrument when overdue remains unpaid (Sec. 76).

A drawee in case of need must accept, or pay a bill when presentment is made. A bill will be dishonoured if the drawee in case of need also refuses to accept or pay after acceptance.

EFFECT OF DISHONOUR

The drawer and all the indorsers of the bill are liable to the holder if the bill is dishonoured, either by non-acceptance or by non-payment, provided that he gives them notice of such dishonour. The drawer is liable only when there is dishonour by non-payment.

NOTICE OF DISHONOUR

When a negotiable instrument is dishonoured either by non-acceptance or by non-payment the holder or some party liable thereon must give notice of dishonour to all other parties whom he seeks to make liable (Sec. 93). Each party receiving notice of dishonour must, in order to render any prior party liable to himself, give notice of dishonour to such party within a reasonable time after he has received it (Sec. 95). Notice of dishonour is so necessary that an omission to give notice discharges all parties other than the maker or acceptor. These parties are discharged not only on the bill or note but also in respect of the original consideration.

Notice of dishonour must be given by the holder, or by a person liable on the instrument. When the holder has given notice of dishonour to any party liable on the bill, and that party has in turn given due notice of dishonour to all prior parties, the holder may in a suit against the drawer take advantage of notice given by that party and treat it as a notice by himself. The agent of any of the above parties may give notice. But a notice by a stranger is a mere nullity for a valid notice can be given only by a person who is liable on the instrument at the time of the notice or by his agent.

Notice of dishonour to the acceptor of a bill or to the maker of a note or the drawee of a cheque is not necessary as they are the principal debtors and primarily liable on the instrument, and they must pay on the due date at the proper place. It is they who dishonour the instrument by non-acceptance or non-payment, and to give them notice is to tell them something which they already know. Notice of dishonour must be given to all parties other than the maker or acceptor or drawee whom the holder wants to be made liable. Notice may also be given to the duly authorised agent of the party. Where the drawee or indorser is dead, the notice may be given to the legal representative of the deceased. Likewise, the notice may be given to the Official Receiver or Assignee where the party has been declared an insolvent. In case of two or more joint drawers or indorsers, notice to one of them will bind all.

Notice may be oral or in writing, but it must be an actual, formal notification. A letter merely demanding payment is not sufficient. It may be given in person, or through a messenger, or by post. Notice by post is more expedient, for if the letter is properly addressed and miscarries or is delayed in transit, the sender is not responsible once he has posted it into the post box.

Notice must be given within a reasonable time of dishonour. As to what is a reasonable time will depend upon the nature of the instrument and the usage of trade in regard to similar instruments (Sec. 105). Where the holder of the instrument and the party to whom notice is given carry on business or live in different places, the notice of dishonour must be posted by the next post if there be one on the day, or on the next day of dishonour. Where the said parties carry on business or live in the same place, it is sufficient if the notice is dispatched so that it reaches its destination on the day next after the day of dishonour (Sec. 106). Any party receiving notice of dishonour, who seeks to enforce his right against a prior party, transmits the notice within a reasonable time if he transmits it within the same time after its receipt as he would have had to give notice if he had been the holder (Sec. 107). Thus, each party is entitled to a clear day for giving notice and one clear day is to be allowed for each step in the communication between parties who are liable on the instrument. But a holder or indorser, who wants to give notice to all parties, cannot claim as many days as there are indorsers. He must give notice to all whom he wants to hold liable within the time in which he is to give notice to his immediate indorser.

NOTICE OF DISHONOUR UNNECESSARY

We have seen above that in a suit against the drawer or indorser on a dishonoured instrument notice of dishonour is a material part of the cause of action. But Sec. 98 enumerates cases in which notice of dishonour can be dispensed with.

No notice of dishonour is necessary—

(a) When it is dispensed with or waived by the party entitled thereto, e.g., where an indorser writes on the instrument such words as "notice of dishonour waived" or where the drawer of the bill informs the holder that the bill will be dishonoured on presentment, or where he tells the holder before maturity that he has no fixed residence, and that he will call in a few days to see if the bill has been paid by the acceptor.

(b) When the drawer has countermanded payment. This is so because he has made it impossible for the holder to obtain payment.

(c) When the party charged could not suffer damage for want of notice, e.g., if at the time when the instrument is drawn there were no funds belonging to the drawer in the hands of the drawee, the drawer suffers no damage, and is not entitled to notice of dishonour. But the burden of proving that the drawer could not suffer damage for want of notice is on the person seeking to excuse himself.

(d) When the party entitled to notice cannot after due search be found.

(e) Where the omission to give notice is caused by unavoidable circumstances, e.g., death or dangerous illness of the holder or his agent, or any other accident.

(f) When the acceptor is also a drawer, e.g., where a firm draws on its branch, or a partner on the partnership. No notice is necessary where the acceptor is one of the drawers.

(g) Where the promissory note is not negotiable. Such a note cannot be indorsed; and if it is indorsed, the indorsee cannot have any claim against the maker or indorser. Therefore, no one is prejudiced for want of notice.

(h) Where the party entitled to notice promises to pay unconditionally the amount due under an instrument after dishonour and with full knowledge of facts.

NOTING

Where a note or bill is dishonoured, the holder is entitled, after giving due notice of dishonour, to sue the drawer and the indorsers. Sec. 99 provides a convenient method of authenticating the fact of the dishonour by means of "Noting." Where a note or bill is dishonoured, the holder may, if he so desires, cause such dishonour to be noted by a notary public on the instrument, or on a paper attached thereto or partly on each. The "Noting" or minute must be recorded by the notary within a reasonable time after dishonour and must contain the fact of dishonour, the date of dishonour, the reason, if any, assigned for such dishonour, or, if the instrument has not been expressly dishonoured, the reason why the holder treats it as dishonoured and the notary's charges (Sec. 99). Noting is not compulsory in the case of an inland bill or note, but foreign bills must be protested, if so required by the law of the place where drawn.

PROTESTING

The protest is the formal notarial certificate attesting the dishonour of the bill, and based upon the noting which has been effected on the dishonour of the bill. After the noting has been made within the specified or reasonable time, the formal protest may be drawn up by the notary at his leisure; and when the protest is drawn up it relates back to the date of noting.

Where the acceptor of a bill has become insolvent, or has suspended payment, or his credit has been publicly impeached, before the maturity of the bill, the holder may have the bill protested for better security. For this purpose, the notary public is employed to demand better security and on its refusal protest may be made within a reasonable time. This is called a "Protest for Better Security." It may be observed that the acceptor is not bound to give such security, nor can the holder sue the drawer, and the indorsers before maturity of the bill in spite of the protest. The advantage of protest for better security, in addition to the fact being placed on record for the information of the drawer and the indorsers, is that it enables the bill to be accepted for honour.

Foreign bills must be protested for dishonour when such protest is required by the law of the place where they are drawn. Foreign promissory notes need not be so protested. Where a bill is required by law to be protested, then instead of a notice of dishonour, notice of protest must be given by the notary public.

CONTENTS OF PROTEST

A protest to be valid, must contain the particulars given below, and the omission of one or more of them will render the protest invalid. The particulars that a protest must contain are:—
1. The instrument itself, or a literal transcript thereof.
2. The names of the parties for and against whom the instrument has been protested.
3. The fact and reasons for dishonour.
4. Place and time of dishonour or refusal to give better security.
5. The signature of the notary public.
6. In the event of an acceptance for honour or of payment for honour, the name of the person by whom, or the person for whom, and the manner in which, such acceptance or payment was offered or effected.

PART 11-G
DISCHARGE OF PARTIES AND INSTRUMENT

The term discharge in relation to negotiable instruments has two meanings, namely, (i) the discharge of the instrument, and (ii) discharge of one or more parties from liability on the instrument.

DISCHARGE OF THE INSTRUMENT

An instrument is said to be discharged when all rights under it are extinguished, it ceases to be negotiable and even a holder in due course does not acquire any rights under it. Such a discharge of the negotiable instrument would take place when the party who is primarily and ultimately liable on the instrument is discharged from liability. A negotiable instrument may be discharged:—
1. By payment in due course;
2. When the principal debtor becomes the holder;
3. By an act that would discharge a simple contract;
4. By renunciation; and
5. By cancellation.

1. **By Payment**—A negotiable instrument is discharged by payment made in due course by or for the primary party or by a person who is accommodated, in case the instrument was made or accepted

for accommodation. Payment in due course means that it must be made at or after the **MATURITY** of the instrument to the Holder in good faith or his agent as agent. A payment by one secondarily liable does not discharge the instrument. The payer holds it to enforce it against prior indorsers and the principal debtor. He may also strike out his and subsequent indorsements and further negotiate the instrument. The right of further negotiation is denied (*a*) when the drawer pays an instrument which is payable to the order of a third person, or (*b*) when an instrument executed or accepted for accommodation is paid by the party for whose accommodation the instrument was executed. This denial is based on the theory that further negotiation would unfairly continue the liability of the payee indorser or of the person who executed or accepted the instrument for the accommodation of the person making the payment.

To complete payment, the principal and interest, if any, must be paid. The person paying the instrument should demand the surrender of the instrument when paid. Payment is a personal defence and is not valid against a holder in due course. Thus, if a maker of a pro-note pays the original payee after the note has been transferred to a holder in due course, the maker is liable for payment to such a holder. The possession by the payer of a receipt for payment is no substitute for the surrender of the instrument.

2. **Debtor as Holder**—When the primary party lawfully becomes the holder of the instrument in his own right at or after maturity, the instrument is discharged. The instrument will not be discharged, (*i*) if the debtor acquires the instrument before maturity, in which case he may negotiate it further in the same way as any other holder could; or (*ii*) if the holder did not acquire it lawfully or in his own right as when he acquired it by fraud or as an agent for another person.

3. **Discharge as Simple Contract**—A negotiable instrument in some instances may be discharged in the same way as a simple contract for the payment of money. Like an ordinary contract the instrument may be discharged by agreement of the parties in the form of a novation, a covenant not to sue, or by rescission or substitution of another instrument or obligation. For example, where the holder of a note agreed to accept a conveyance of a house and certain acts by the maker in payment of the note, the instrument was discharged. The instrument may be discharged by operation of law in the case of insolvency, in the case of lapse of time under the Statute of Limitations. This provision regarding discharge of an instrument in the same way as a simple contract applies only to immediate parties. It cannot be raised as a defence against a holder in due course. In result it will discharge certain parties to the instrument and not the instrument itself, unless expressly agreed.

4. **By Renunciation**—A negotiable instrument is discharged when the holder renounces or gives up his right against all the parties to the instrument. The renunciation must be in writing unless the instrument is also surrendered to the party primarily liable.

5. **By Cancellation**—The party who is entitled to enforce payment of an instrument may surrender it to the party liable thereon with an intent to release him from the obligation. This operates as a discharge of the instrument and is known as cancellation. Cancellation may also take place by physical destruction of the instrument itself made with the intention to terminate liability, or by crossing out signatures on the instrument.

DISCHARGE OF A PARTY OR PARTIES

When any particular party or parties are discharged, the instrument continues to be negotiable and the undischarged parties remain liable on it. For example, the non-presentment of a bill on the due date discharges the indorsers from their liability, but the acceptor remains liable on it.

A party may be discharged from liability in the following ways:—

1. **By cancellation**—Where the holder of a negotiable instrument cancels the name of any party to it with the intention of discharging him from liability, such party and all other persons between the holder and such party are discharged from liability. But a cancellation made unintentionally or by

mistake will not discharge any party. The proper and safe mode of cancellation is to draw a line through the name so as to leave it legible.

In an accommodation bill, where it is drawn for the accommodation of the drawer the cancellation of the name of the acceptor who is the accommodating party discharges the indorser, but not the drawer; and where it is drawn for the accommodation of the payee, the cancellation of drawer's name does not discharge the payee [Sec. 82(a)].

2. **By Release**—Where the holder releases any party to the instrument by any method other than cancellation, the party so released is discharged from liability. Sec. 63 of the Contract Act permits a promisee to remit wholly or in part the performance of the contract [Sec. 82 (b)].

3. **Discharge of Secondary Parties (*i.e.*, indorsers)**—A person secondarily liable on the instrument is discharged also by the discharge of a prior party and by a valid tender of payment made by a prior party.

4. **By Operation of Law**—Discharge from liability takes place by operation of law, *e.g.,* by insolvency of the debtor, or by loss of remedy on expiry of the limitation or by merger of note into the judgement debt or of a lesser security into a higher security.

5. **By allowing drawee more than 48 hours**—If the holder of a bill allows the drawee more than 48 hours, exclusive of public holidays, to consider whether he will accept the same, all previous parties not consenting to such allowance are discharged from liability to the holder (Sec. 83).

6. **By non-presentment of cheque**—Where a cheque is not presented for payment within a reasonable time of its issue, and the bank fails and the drawer suffers actual damage through the delay, he is discharged from liability to the holder to the extent to which such drawer is a creditor of the banker, but no more (Sec. 84).[23]

7. **Cheque payable to order**—Where a cheque payable to order purports to be indorsed by or on behalf of the payee, the banker is discharged by payment in due course, even though the indorsement might turn out to be a forgery. In the case of a cheque originally drawn payable to bearer, the banker is discharged by paying in due course to the bearer thereof, even if any indorsement restricts or excludes further negotiation (Sec. 85).

8. **Drafts by one branch on another**—Where a draft, *i.e.*, an order to pay money, drawn by one office of a bank upon another office of the same bank for a sum of money payable to order on demand, purports to be indorsed by or on behalf of the payee, the bank is discharged by payment in due course (Sec. 85-A).

9. **By taking qualified acceptance**—If the holder of a bill takes a qualified acceptance all the previous parties whose consent is not obtained to such acceptance are discharged from liability, unless on notice being given, they assent to such acceptance (Sec. 86).

10. **By Material Alteration**—Any material alteration of a negotiable instrument renders the same void as against any one who is a party thereto at the time of the alteration and does not consent thereto, unless it was made in order to carry out the common intention of the original parties. Any alteration made by an indorsee discharges his indorser from all liability to him in respect of the consideration thereof (Sec. 87). The section, however, recognises certain cases in which alteration may be allowed. They are: (*i*) the filling in of the blanks in an inchoate instrument (Sec. 20), (*ii*) the conversion of an indorsement in blank into an indorsement in full (Sec. 49), (*iii*), the qualifying or limiting of an acceptance (Sec. 86), and (*iv*) the crossing of a cheque after it has been issued. These are not material alterations and do not render the instrument void.

The rule as to alteration in this section is based upon two grounds, namely, (*a*) that no man is permitted to take chance of committing a fraud without running any risk on its detection, and (*b*) that

---

23. Abdul Majid v. M/s. G. Kalooram 1954 Orissa 124.

by the alteration the identity of the instrument is destroyed. In these cases it is immaterial whether the alteration is beneficial or detrimental to the party charged on the contract, or whether the alteration ultimately involves any change in the rights and liabilities of the parties or not.[24] What is necessary to make the instrument void is that the alteration must be material. A material alteration in the pronote debars the person from recovering the amount of the pronote on the basis of original contract (Suresh Chandra v. Satish Chandra, 1983 All. 81).

WHAT IS MATERIAL ALTERATION?

An alteration is material which in any way alters the operation of the instrument and the liabilities of the parties thereto, whether the change be beneficial or detrimental. An alteration is material which alters the business effect of the instrument if used for any business. Therefore, any change in an instrument which causes it to speak a different' language in legal effect from that which it originally spoke, or which changes the legal identity or character of the instrument either in its terms or the relation of the parties to it is a material alteration.

There is a material alteration where it is an alteration (1) of the date of the instrument, (2) of the sum payable, (3) in the time of payment, (4) of the place of payment, (5) of the rate of interest, (6) by addition of a new party, (7) by tearing an instrument in a material part, (8) in the dates of indorsements, and so on....

There is no material alteration so as to vitiate the instrument in the following cases, namely, (1) correction of a mistake, (2) to carry out the common intention of the parties, (3) an alteration made before the instrument is issued, and (4) made with the consent of the parties.

The alteration affects only those persons who have already become parties at the date of the alteration. Those who take an altered instrument cannot complain. Sec. 88 lays down that an acceptor or indorser of a negotiable instrument is bound by his acceptance or indorsement notwithstanding any previous alteration of the instrument. Further, the holder is not affected by a material alteration made by a stranger without the consent of the holder, and without any fraud or laches on his part. The fact that the change is accidental negatives the possibility of assent.

11. **Discharge by payment of altered instrument**—Where an instrument has been materially altered but does not appear to have been so altered, or where a cheque is presented for payment which does not at the time of presentation appear to be crossed or to have had a crossing which has been obliterated, payment of the amount due on the instrument according to the apparent tenor thereof and in due course discharges the person making the payment (Sec. 89).

12. **Bill in acceptor's hand**—If a bill which has been negotiated is, at or after maturity, held by the acceptor in his own right, all rights of action thereon are extinguished (Sec. 90). This is the final discharge of the bill, and the principle applies to notes as well.

RETIREMENT OF BILLS AND REBATE

An acceptor may make payment of a bill before maturity, and the bill is then said to be **retired,** but it is not discharged and must not be cancelled except by the acceptor when it comes into his hands. A bill accompanied by shipping documents which are to be delivered to the acceptor only on payment of the bill is frequently **retired** by the acceptor before its maturity in order to be able to get possession of the goods. It is customary in such a case to make an allowance of interest on the money to the acceptor for the remainder of the time which the bill has to run, *e.g.*, where a bill due on 15th May is retired on 5th May, interest for 10 days on the amount of the bill will be allowed. The interest allowance is known as **rebate.**

---

24. Rampadarath v. Hari Narain, 1965, Pat 224.

COMPENSATION

Sec. 117 lays down rules for determining the amount of compensation to the holder or an indorser in case the instrument is dishonoured.

Compensation to holder—The holder is entitled to the amount due on the instrument, together with the expenses properly incurred in presenting, noting and protesting it.

Compensation to indorser—The indorser who has paid the amount due on the instrument is entitled to the amount so paid with interest at 6 per cent per annum from the date of payment until tender or realisation thereof together with all expenses caused by the dishonour and payment.

Re-exchange—When the holder or the indorser entitled to claim the amount resides in a country different from that in which the bill was drawn or indorsed, the holder or indorsee is entitled to receive from the drawer or prior indorsers the sum at the current rate of exchange between countries on the date of dishonour. Re-exchange is the measure of damages occasioned by the dishonour of a bill in a country different to that in which it was drawn or indorsed.

Re-draft—The party entitled to compensation may draw a bill payable at sight or on demand upon the party liable to compensate him for the amount due to him together with all expenses properly incurred by him. Such a bill is called a "Re-draft". This re-draft must be accompanied by the instrument dishonoured and the protest, if any. The party who makes payment of a re-draft may draw a similar re-draft on the parties prior to him. If the re-draft is dishonoured, the party on whom it is drawn will have to compensate the drawer, as if the re-draft were an original bill.

Compensation against banker—There is no provision in this Act for determining the compensation payable by a banker who wrongfully dishonours his customer's cheque. In English law, such compensation will include damages to credit and reputation of the drawer, and the court would ordinarily award exemplary damages. The same rule would, however, seem to apply in India.

INTERNATIONAL LAW

In the absence of a contract to the contrary, the liability of the maker, or drawer of a foreign note, bill or cheque is regulated in all essential matters by the law of the place where he made the instrument, and the respective liabilities of the acceptor and indorser by the law of the place where the instrument is made payable (Sec. 134). Where an instrument is made payable in a different place from that in which it is made or indorsed, the law of the place where it is made payable determines what constitutes dishonour and what notice of dishonour is sufficient (Sec. 135). If a negotiable instrument is made, drawn, accepted or indorsed out of India, but in accordance with the law of India, the circumstance that any agreement evidenced by such instrument is invalid according to the law of the country wherein it was entered into does not invalidate any subsequent acceptance or indorsement made thereon in India (Sec. 136). The section provides an exception to the general rule laid above that the *lex loci contractus* (law of the place where the contract is made) determines the form and essential validity of the contract. Therefore, where the first contract of making or drawing is invalidated by want of stamp or some other similar circumstance, the subsequent contracts created by acceptance and indorsement being independent contracts will be valid even though the prior contract was invalid according to the law of the place where it was made provided that it is valid according to the law of India. Where foreign law is different from Indian law and a party to a suit relies on foreign law that party must specifically allege and prove this fact like any other fact; for the court will not take notice of foreign law excepting the English Bill of Exchange Act. Sec. 137 provides that the law of any foreign country regarding negotiable instruments shall be presumed to be the same as that of India unless and until the contrary is proved.

HUNDIS

Hundis are negotiable instruments written in an oriental language. They are sometimes promissory notes, but more often bills of exchange, and subject to local usages. The hundis were in circulation in

India long before the Negotiable Instruments Act, 1881. Traditions as to their use in the court date as far back as 5000 B.C. The word hundi is derived from the Sanskrit word *hund*—to collect. It appears that hundis were originally used for the purpose of collecting debts. Even now they are often employed for the same purpose, although now hundis are used more and more as internal bills of exchange. Hundis are negotiable instruments under the Act, although they are so independently of the provisions of the Act. They are recognised by custom as negotiable, and the Act recognises the custom pertaining to hundis.

There are several varieties of hundis current in the country, but only the more important among them are given below:

Darshni hundi—A darshni hundi is a hundi which is payable at sight. A darshni hundi payable on demand must be presented for payment within a reasonable time after its receipt by the holder. Any loss caused to the drawer by delay in presentment falls on the party at fault

Muddati or Miyadi hundi—A hundi payable after a specified period of time is called a Muddati or Miyadi hundi—the time bill of exchange.

Shah Jog hundi—A shah means a respectable and responsible person, a man of worth, and known in the bazar. A shah jog hundi is payable to or through a shah. A hundi payable to shah is payable on the responsibility of the shah, and if he or the parties through whom he claims became the holder of the hundi through offence or fraud, the drawee can proceed against him for the re-imbursement of the amount. Thus if the hundi turns out to be false, stolen or forged, the shah is bound to refund the amount of the hundi with interest unless he produces the actual drawer or the person who committed the fraud. The drawee to recover money should file a separate suit against the shah.

The words shah jog in a hundi lend to it additional credit and make it of the nature of a cheque generally crossed. But it is payable only to a respectable bearer and only when it is indorsed to the last indorsee—on the shah presenting the hundi. It is neither a bill nor a note; but if attested, it can be sued on either as a bond or a promissory note. A shah jog hundi differs from a bill in two respects, namely, (*i*) the acceptance of the drawee is not generally written across it but the particulars are entered in the drawer's book, and (*ii*) it is not usually presented for acceptance before due date. The shah jog hundi in its inception is a hundi which passes from hand to hand by delivery and requires no indorsement, until it reaches the shah who after making inquiries to secure himself should present it to the drawee for acceptance or payment Although it passes by delivery, it is not similar to the bearer bill. The shah's name must always be indorsed on the hundi at the time of the presentment. It can any time be restricted by being specially indorsed and when so restricted, the hundi ceases to be a hundi. If it is dishonoured, notice of dishonour must be given as in the case of a bill.[25]

The shah does not guarantee the solvency of the drawer, although he guarantees the genuineness of the hundi. A drawee will not pay the hundi unless he has funds in his hands belonging to the drawer, or he is willing to give credit. And he is not bound to pay unless he is satisfied as to the respectability of the shah presenting the hundi, as he has to look to the shah in the event of the hundi turning out to be a forged one.

A shah jog hundi may be darshni or muddati. It may mention the name of the depositor or not, but it is payable only to a shah. It differs from an ordinary hundi inasmuch as (*i*) it need not be presented for acceptance and the acceptance of the drawee is not necessary and need not be written across the hundi, and (*ii*) the holder is relieved from liability if he produces the forger.

Nam Jog hundi—A nam jog hundi, in contradistinction to shah jog hundi, is payable to the person whose name is specified in the body of the hundi. In form both are similar except with the difference that the nam jog has the name of the payee, while the shah jog has the name of the shah inserted

25. Central Bank of India v. Khub Ram, 1960 Punj. 157.

therein. The nam jog hundi is payable to the order of the payee and can be indorsed like a bill of exchange payable to order.

Dhani Jog hundi—In the case of a dhani jog hundi, the amount is payable to a *dhani,* owner, and the words "dhani jog" are inserted in the hundi. The amount of the hundi is, therefore, payable to the owner or holder or bearer. It is indeed a negotiable instrument payable to bearer; where it is indorsed in full, it ceases to be a bearer hundi.

Jokhami hundi—A jokhami hundi is drawn by the consignor of goods on the consignee against the goods shipped on the ship mentioned in the hundi. According to the custom of Hindu merchants the money of the hundi is payable only when and if the goods arrive. The hundi is in the nature of a policy of insurance, but with this difference that the money is paid beforehand, and is to be recovered if the ship arrives safely. The jokhami hundi is drawn with two-fold object, namely, to put the drawer of the hundi in funds, and at the same time to effect an insurance on the goods themselves. The hundi is drawn by the consignor on the consignee and negotiated with the insurer at a price which is less than the amount of the hundi by the amount of the premium of insurance. If the goods arrive safely the insurer may obtain them or their value as stated in the hundi.

The hundi is an authority to the consignee to pay for the goods or deliver them up to the holder, but the holder has no right of action against the consignee and holds the hundi on the credit of the drawer or indorser. As the holder is an insurer, he cannot claim payment if the goods are totally lost, although he is entitled to be paid in full in case of partial loss or damage (particular average loss). If the loss is a general average loss then a rebate is made to the extent of the loss.

Jawabi hundi—Jawabi hundi is used as a means of remittance of money from one place to another via a banker. The nature of the transaction known as jawabi hundi is as follows: A person desirous of making a remittance writes to the payee and delivers the letter to a banker, who either indorses it on to any of the correspondents near the payee's place of residence or negotiates its transfer. On its arrival the letter is forwarded to the payee who attends and gives his receipt in the form of an answer to the letter which is forwarded by the same channel to the drawer of the order.

Zikri Chit—The zikri chit is a letter of protection given to the holder of a hundi by the drawer or any other prior parry when the hundi is dishonoured by non-acceptance or even when the dishonour is feared. It is addressed to some person residing in the town where the hundi is payable, asking him to take up the hundi in case of its dishonour. The addressee of the letter there accepts the hundi for honour and pays it at maturity. According to the custom prevalent among the Marwari shroffs, the zikri chit enables the person to accept for hondur the hundi without being noted or protested. Zikri chits are used throughout the country in connection with Marwari hundis.

Purja—It is a request in writing by the borrower to the lender to pay the amount mentioned therein. It bears a ten paise stamp. The purja is not a bill of exchange, and is not negotiable. Purjas are commonly used for temporary loans.

Finnan Jog hundi—It is a hundi which is payable to order, and **Dekhanhar** is payable to bearer. When a hundi is lost the holder may demand from the drawer a duplicate, which is called a **Peth.** If the duplicate is lost the holder may ask for a triplicate and so on. Each of these subsequent hundis is called a **Per Peth.** When a hundi has been paid and cancelled it is called a **Khokha.**

SUMMARY

A negotiable instrument is one the property in which is acquired by every person who takes it *bona fide* and for value notwithstanding any defect of title in the person from whom he took it. Thus a person taking the instrument *bona fide* and for value gets a good title irrespective of previous defects.

The Negotiable Instruments Act defines the term thus: "A negotiable instrument means a promissory note, bill of exchange or cheque payable either to order or to bearer."

A promissory note is an instrument in writing containing an unconditional undertaking, signed by the maker, to pay a certain sum of money only to, or the order of, a certain person.

A bill of exchange is an instrument in writing containing an unconditional order, signed by the maker, directing a certain person to pay a certain sum of money only to, or to the order of, a certain person or to the bearer of the instrument.

A cheque is a bill of exchange drawn on a specified banker and payable only on demand.

Essentials of notes, bills and cheques—Each of these instruments must be in writing. It must contain a clear and definite **promise to pay,** if it is a note; and imperative and rightful **order for payment,** if it is a bill or cheque. The promise or order must be unconditional, and must be for the payment of money only, and the sum payable must be certain. It must be signed by the maker or drawer.

The chief parts of these instruments are the amount, date, stamp, time for payment, place of payment, designation of payee, signature of maker or drawer and name of drawee.

The date, though a usual and convenient part of every bill and note, is not, in general, essential, and if it is omitted the instrument dates from the day on which it was made. The date of making or drawing is a material part of .the instrument where the amount is payable a certain time after date or is an essential factor in the calculation of interest, and an unauthorised alteration of it will make the instrument void. Mere correction of the date or insertion of date in an inchoate instrument is allowed. A cheque may be drawn on a holiday, or may be ante-dated, post-dated or even undated, although payment can be refused, if it is stale, or until the date mentioned therein has arrived or does not bear a date.

The amount in words and figures must tally and if they differ the amount stated in words shall be taken to be correct.

Stamp—Bills and notes executed in India must be stamped with revenue stamps of adequate amount before or at the time they are signed. Cheques do not require any stamp duty in India.

The time for payment may be either—

(1) On demand; or (2) at sight or on presentation; or (3) a certain time after sight; or (4) a certain time after date; or (5) a certain time after some specified certain event. **A cheque is always payable on demand.**

An instrument expressed to be payable "at sight" or "on presentment" means "on demand." If no time is specified then also the bill or note is payable on demand.

A note or bill expressed to be payable "after sight" must be presented to the maker for sight or to the drawee for acceptance respectively within a reasonable time of its making or drawing.

A note or bill is at **Maturity** on the day on which it falls due. It matures or falls due on the third day after the expiry of the period after it is made payable. These three days are called **days of Grace.** In computing such periods public holidays are excluded, the months and days are reckoned according to British calendar, and if the month in which the period would terminate has no corresponding date the period shall be taken to terminate on the last date of such month.

The place of payment is not ordinarily specified but a drawer may, if he so desires, fix one and if he does so, payment must be made at the place specified. The maker is liable to pay a promissory note at the place specified therein. **Presentment for** acceptance of a bill is necessary when it is made payable at a place other than the place of the drawee. Presentment for payment of a bill or note payable at a specified place is necessary at that place in order to charge the maker, drawer or indorser. Bills and notes made payable at a specified place and not elsewhere must be presented at that place to charge any party thereto.

Instruments which are (*i*) drawn or made in India, and (*ii*) made payable in or drawn upon any person resident in India are **inland instruments,** while others not so drawn or made so payable are

foreign instruments. An instrument which in form is such that it may either be treated by the holder as a bill or as a note, is an **ambiguous instrument.** Once the instrument has been treated either as a bill or as a note it cannot be treated differently afterwards.

An inchoate instrument is one where one person signs and delivers to another a paper stamped according to law of negotiable instruments and either wholly blank or having written thereon an incomplete negotiable instrument, he thereby gives *prima facie* authority to the holder thereof to make or complete upon it a negotiable instrument for any amount covered by the stamp. The signor of such an instrument is liable both to the holder and holder in due course.

Parties—Every person competent to contract may bind himself and be bound by making, drawing, acceptance, indorsement and delivery, and negotiation of a note, bill or cheque. Negatively, persons incompetent to contract do not incur any liability as parties to a negotiable instrument. Thus a minor is not liable, but he can be a holder or payee and can act as a good channel for passing title from one person to another.

The maker and payee are two necessary parties to a note, while there must be at least three parties on the face of a bill or cheque—the drawer, the drawee and the payee—although the same person may fill any two of the positions.

Signature of the maker or drawer is essential to the making or drawing of the instrument. The name may be subscribed by himself or by his agent. The maker of a note and the drawer of a bill until acceptance are principally liable on the note or bill. They must pay the amount on maturity according to the apparent tenor of the instrument or in default they must compensate any party for any loss and damage sustained by such default.

Where a bill is accepted before maturity the acceptor takes the place of the drawee and the drawer becomes surety for the acceptor. Other parties are liable as sureties for the maker, drawer or acceptor, as the case may be, and each party stands as surety to each subsequent party.

The drawee must be named or otherwise indicated in the bill with certainty for the holder has to present the bill for acceptance to the drawee.

A bill may be drawn on one or several drawees or on a company, association or body of individuals. It may be addressed to the drawer himself though in legal operation it will be a note rather than a bill.

A bill drawn on a fictitious person or one incompetent to contract may be treated as dishonoured and the drawer must compensate the holder. The holder has no claim upon the drawee until the latter has accepted the bill.

If the drawee refuses to accept, the contract is broken. The drawee after acceptance is called the acceptor and is then the principal debtor.

The drawee of a cheque is always a banker and he must pay if he has sufficient funds of the drawer in hand properly applicable to the payment of such cheque.

Foreign bills are usually drawn in sets of three, each part containing a condition that it shall continue payable only so long as the others remain unpaid. The method reduces chances of losing. All the parts constitute one bill. Only one part is to be accepted.

The payee must be a certain person. A bill, or a cheque is generally made payable to—

(1) Certain person or persons, (2) the order of a certain person, (3) a certain person or order, (4) a certain person or bearer or (5) bearer. A note cannot be made payable to a person or bearer or to a bearer.

Drawee in case of need—Where in a bill or in any indorsement thereon the name of any person is given to be resorted to in case of need, such a person is called a drawee in case of need. He may accept the bill and pay without previous presentment. The bill is not dishonoured unless it is also dishonoured by a drawee in case of need.

Delivery—The delivery of the note, bill or cheque is necessary in order to complete the making, acceptance or indorsement thereof and to transfer the right of suing thereon. Delivery may be actual or constructive. But it must be made with the intention to pass the property in the instrument. It may be conditional or for a specified purpose only and not absolute. Such a delivery makes the holder a mere bailee, trustee or agent.

Negotiation is such transfer as constitutes the transferee a holder with rights of further negotiation. An instrument is negotiated by mere delivery when it is payable to bearer, and by indorsement and delivery when it is payable to order.

An indorsement may be Blank, Full, Restrictive, Partial or Qualified. An **indorsement in blank** is one where the indorser merely writes his signature on the instrument, and the instrument becomes payable to bearer, even though it was originally payable to order.

A full indorsement is one in which the indorser signs his name and adds the name of the party to whom or to whose order the instrument is to be payable.

A **restrictive indorsement** prohibits or restricts the further negotiability of an instrument.

An **indorsement is partial** which purports to transfer to the indorsee a part only of the amount of the instrument. A partial indorsement does not operate as a negotiation of the instrument.

An indorsement is **conditional** or **qualified** which limits or negatives the liability of the indorser.

Signature by way of indorsement must be on the instrument (generally, on the back) or on a slip of paper attached to it—**Allonge.**

It must be by maker or holder or drawer or payee or indorsee, but not by a stranger. It must be made for the purpose of negotiation and must be completed by delivery.

The **effect of indorsement** is that the indorsee acquires the title to the instrument, and can negotiate it to any party he likes, and may, as holder of the instrument, sue any or all of the prior parties. Every party is liable to all parties subsequent to him. Each prior party is liable as surety to each subsequent party.

The indorser's engagement is like that of a maker that the instrument will be paid when it falls due, and if it is dishonoured he will compensate the holder provided due notice of the dishonour is received by him. He guarantees to all holders in due course the genuineness of the drawer's signature and all previous indorsements.

Holder—A person entitled in his own name to the possession of an instrument (though not necessarily in actual possession of it) and to receive or recover the amount due thereon is a **holder**.

No person can sue on a negotiable instrument in his own name unless his name appears thereon as payee or indorsee or unless the instrument is made payable to bearer and he is the possessor thereof.

But when an instrument is lost, or destroyed, its holder is the person entitled to the possession of the instrument at the time of such loss or destruction.

Holder in due course—A holder in due course is holder who became such for consideration without having sufficient cause to believe that any defect existed in the title of the person from whom he derived his title before maturity. Thus a donee of an instrument may be a holder but cannot be a holder in due course. But unless the contrary is proved a holder is presumed to be a holder in due course.

The title of a holder in due course is free from the equities and other defences which could have been raised by prior parties. Once an instrument passes through the hands of a holder in due course it is purged of all defects. It is like current coin.

Consideration is presumed in respect of the making, drawing, acceptance or indorsement of a negotiable instrument. But this presumption is rebuttable and it can be shown that as between immediate parties to an instrument no consideration ever passed. This plea cannot be set up between prior parties against a holder in due course or any subsequent holder deriving title from him.

Acceptance of bill is the indication by the drawee of his consent to the order of the drawer. This is done by writing his name generally accompanied by the word '' accepted,'' across the face of the bill. The acceptance is complete and binds the drawee only when he delivers the accepted bill to the holder, or gives him notice of such acceptance.

Only the person to whom the bill is addressed can "accept it unless he accepts it supra protest for the honour of a party liable on the bill.

An acceptance may be either general or qualified. A **general acceptance** is absolute and assents without any qualification to the order of the drawer but where, an acceptance is made subject to some condition or qualification, thereby varying in express terms the effect of the bill as drawn, it is a **qualified acceptance**.

The holder of a bill may refuse to take a qualified acceptance or he may acquiesce in it. Where he refuses to take it, the bill is dishonoured by non-acceptance. If he accepts the qualified acceptance, it binds him and the acceptor, but not other parties not consenting thereto.

It is always advisable to present a bill for acceptance, for if acceptance is refused, the parties other than the drawee become immediately liable though the bill has not yet matured.

Presentment must be made:—
(i)   where a bill or note is payable after sight, or
(ii) where a bill is payable at a place other than the place of the drawee,
(iii) when it is expressly stipulated that presentment shall be made.

The holder must present a bill payable after sight for acceptance or negotiate it within reasonable time. The penalty for non-presentment is the discharge of the drawer and prior indorsers. The drawee is entitled to 48 hours for deciding whether he will accept or not.

Presentment is excused in the following cases:—
1. Where the drawee is dead or is insolvent or is a fictitious person or a person incompetent to contract.
2. Where after reasonable search the drawee cannot be found.
3. When although presentment has been irregular, acceptance has been refused on some other ground.

Payment at maturity of the amount due on the note, bill or cheque by or on behalf of the principal party liable to the holder is a discharge of the liability of each and every party to pay the amount. Payment may be made to the holder or his representative.

An instrument payable to bearer whether originally or by indorsement is discharged by payment in due course.

Any person liable to pay and called upon by the holder to pay is, before payment, entitled to have the instrument shown to him and is, on payment, entitled to have it delivered to him and if the instrument is lost or cannot be produced, to be indemnified against any further claims thereon against him.

Presentment for payment is not necessary to charge the principal debtor, but it is essential to charge other parties. But where a place for payment is specified in a note payable on demand and where an instrument is made payable at a specified place and not elsewhere, presentment at that place is necessary to charge even the principal debtor.

Only the holder or his duly authorised agent, or in case of death or insolvency, the legal representative or assignee of the holder can make presentment.

Where a bill has been lost before it is overdue, the holder thereof can compel the drawer to give him a duplicate of the lost bill on his undertaking to furnish security for indemnifying him against all persons in case the bill alleged to have been lost is found again.

Dishonour—A note, bill or cheque is dishonoured by non-payment when the maker of the note, acceptor of the bill or drawee of the cheque makes default in payment on being duly required to pay the same.

Where presentment for payment is excused the instrument is deemed to be dishonoured on the due date for presentment, if it remains unpaid.

Where a drawee in case of need is named in the bill, the bill is not dishonoured until such drawee has also refused payment on proper presentment.

In case of dishonour by non-payment the holder has a right of action against (a) the maker of the note, (b) the acceptor of the bill, (c) the drawer of the bill or cheque if due notice of dishonour has been given, and (d) each of the indorsers of a note, bill or cheque, if due notice has been given.

In case of dishonour by non-acceptance of a bill the holder has a right of action against the drawer and indorsers, if due notice of dishonour has been given.

Notice of dishonour by non-payment or by non-acceptance must be given by the holder or by some party to the instrument who remains liable thereon to all parties to whom he seeks to make severally liable and some of several parties whom he seeks to make jointly liable, except the maker of the note or acceptor of the bill.

Any party receiving notice of dishonour must in order to make any prior party liable to himself transmit the notice to such party. Notice must be given within reasonable time after dishonour and transmitted within reasonable time after its receipt. The notice may be given in writing or it may be oral.

Notice is dispensed with—
1. Where after reasonable search a party cannot be found or notice is impossible.
2. Where it is waived by the party entitled to it.
3. As regards drawer, where the drawer and the drawee are the same person; the drawer is fictitious or incapable of contracting; the drawer himself is the person to whom the bill is presented for payment; or where the drawer has countermanded payment.

Noting and Protest—In addition to giving notice of dishonour, the holder of a dishonoured inland bill, if he so desires, may cause the bill to be noted or protested.

Foreign bills must be protested when such protest is required by the law of the place where they are drawn.

Noting is the minute recorded by the notary public on a dishonoured bill at the time of dishonour. Noting is a convenient method of authenticating the act of dishonour.

Notaries Public are appointed by the State Governments and are officers who take note of anything which may concern the public, attest deeds or writing to make them authentic in another country and so on.

A bill may be protested not only for non-payment or non-acceptance but also for better security. When the acceptor of a bill has become insolvent, or has suspended payment, or his credit has been publicly impeached, before the maturity of the bill, the holder may within reasonable time cause a notary public to demand better security from the acceptor. If the acceptor refuses to furnish better security the notary shall note the facts or certify them as above. This certificate is called protest for better security.

The acceptor is not bound to give such security, but the bill can be accepted for honour.

Acceptance for honour may be made voluntarily by any person to save the credit of some or all the parties to a bill. It must be made after noting or protest and must be made with the consent of the holder by a person not liable on the bill, by a writing on the bill and for the whole amount, for which the bill is drawn and must be made before the bill is overdue.

Payment for honour may be made by anyone for the honour of any party liable on the bill when it has been protested for non-payment.

Cheques—A cheque is a bill of exchange drawn on a banker and payable only on demand.

The banker who is the drawee must pay the cheque of his customer as long as he holds sufficient funds to his credit, and if he wrongfully refuses to pay the cheque, he shall have to compensate the drawer for any loss or damage to his credit. But the payee or holder of the cheque has no cause of action against the banker.

The paying banker is in a privileged position as regards the payment of the customer's cheque. Where a cheque payable to order purports to be indorsed by or on behalf of the payee, the banker is discharged by payment in due course. He is discharged in respect of a bearer cheque by payment to the bearer or holder without indorsement. He can even ignore any indorsement if the cheque is originally made payable to bearer. The rule is "Once a bearer cheque always a bearer cheque."

The collecting banker is protected if he receives payment in good faith and without negligence of a crossed cheque for a customer, even though the customer's title to the cheque proves defective. The protection is given because a crossed cheque can be cashed only through a banker and a banker collecting his customer's crossed cheque acts as his agent.

A cheque may be "open" or "crossed." An open cheque can be presented by the payee to the banker across the counter for payment.

A crossed cheque can be cashed only through a banker, and not across the counter. The object of crossing is to secure payment to a banker so that it may be possible to trace the person receiving payment of the cheque.

The crossing is made to warn the banker and not to stop negotiability of the cheque. To restrain negotiability addition of words "Not negotiable" or "Account payee only" is made.

A cheque may be crossed generally or specially.

Payment of cheques generally crossed may be made through any banker while of one specially crossed only to the banker to whom the cheque is crossed or his agent for collection.

CASES FOR RECAPITULATION

1. *A* lost money playing cards with *B*. *A* gave *B* a promissory note for the amount of the gambling debt. *B* negotiated the note to W Bank Ltd., which received it in good faith and for value. *A* refused to pay the note, and the Bank sued *B* as indorser. *B* defended on the ground that the note was given to pay a wagering debt and was therefore void. It was held that the bank was entitled to recover from *B*, the indorser of the note, because the indorser warrants that the instrument is a valid obligation.

2. *A* bill drawn on *M* in favour of *A* is accepted by *M* through the fraud of *F*. *M* is not liable on the bill to *A*. If the acceptance of the bill is procured by fraud the acceptor is only liable to a holder in due course and not to other holders [*Ayers* v. *Moore* (1940) 1 K.B. 278].

3. *A*, the payee-holder of a bill, endorsed it in blank and delivered it to *B*, *B* also endorsed it in blank and delivered it to *C*. *C* endorsed it in full to *D* or order. *D* without endorsement delivered the bill to *E*. It was held, in a suit by *E*, that *E*, as the bearer against the drawer, acceptor, and the indorsers *A* and *B* is entitled to receive payment from them, but he cannot proceed against *C* or *D*, as he received an order instrument from *D* without endorsement. If, however, *D*, instead of merely handing over the bill to *E*, had passed on to him by regular endorsement, *E* could have claimed payment from all prior parties [*Smith* v. *Clarke* (1794) 1 Peake 295].

4. *A* draws on *B* a bill payable three months after sight. It passes through several hands before *X* becomes its holder. On presentation by *X*, *B* refuses to accept. *X* can recover from all the prior parties except *B*. The drawee is not liable on the bill unless he accepts it and then delivers it over to the holder. The other parties are liable because they guarantee payment.

5. *A* bill is drawn payable to '*A* or order.' *A* loses the bill and *X*, who finds it, forges *A*'s signature and indorses it to *B* who takes it for value and in good faith. *B* acquires no title to the bill, because there was no indorsement in favour of the finder, *X*, he had no title to convey. The forged indorsement

being a nullity can convey no title, and the subsequent holder cannot claim to be a holder in due course [*Mercantile Bank of India* v. *Mascaranhas*, 1932 P.C. 22].

6. *M* draws a cheque in favour of *N*, a minor. *N* endorses it in favour of *P*, who in turn endorses it in favour of *Q*. The cheque is dishonoured by the bank. *N*, being a minor, is not liable on the cheque, so that *P* and *Q* cannot claim from N. P can claim payment from *M*, the drawer and *Q* can claim against *P*, the indorser and *M*, the drawer (Sec. 26).

7. A executes a promissory note in favour of *B* for ₹2,500. *B* receives the amount from *C* and makes an indorsement thus: "Received amount due under this promissory note from *C*", and signs it and hands over the note to *C*. *C* cannot maintain a suit on the promissory note as the writing is not an endorsement and so the instrument is not negotiated to him and he is not a holder in due course. He cannot sue even under Sec.8, as there is no assignment of the instrument either (Secs. 8 and 16).

8. *A* owes *B* ₹ 1,000. *A* makes a promissory note for the amount payable to *B*. *A* dies and the note is afterwards found among his papers and delivered to *B*. *B* sued on the bill. *Held, B*'s suit does not lie, as the pronote was never delivered by *A* to *B*. Until the instrument is delivered after execution it is incomplete and there is no cause of action oh *it.[Bromage* v. *Lloyd* (1847) I Exch. 32].

9. A cheque is drawn 'payable to *B* or order.' It is stolen and *B*'s indorsement is forged. The banker pays the cheque in due course. The banker is discharged and he can debit the account of the customer with the amount of the cheque even though the payee's endorsement is forged. This is so because cheques are a special exception to the general rule that a forged endorsement is no endorsement [*Charles* v.*Blackwell* (1877) 2 C.P.D. 151]. But if the drawer's signature is forged the banker is liable for the amount of the forged cheque, unless the banker can show he took due care to compare the signature with the specimens or unless he can show that the conduct of the customer was immediately connected with the forgery. [Orr v. *Union Bank* (1854) 1 Macq. H.L. 513].

10. *A* is the holder of a bill of exchange made payable to the order of *B*, which contains the following endorsements in blank:—

First endorsement '*B*'.

Second endorsement 'Peter Williams.'

Third endorsement 'Wright & Co.'

Fourth endorsement 'John Rozario.'

This bill *A* puts in suit against John Rozario and strikes out, without John Rozario's consent, the endorsements by Peter Williams and Wright & Co. *Held, A*'s suit against John Rozario is not maintainable. By striking out endorsements by Peter Williams and Wright & Co., *A* has impaired the remedy of John Rozario against them and so John Rozario is discharged from liability on the bill [*Mayar* v. *Judis* (1833) IM & Rob 247].

11. A bill of exchange is accepted payable at *B & Co.*, but is subsequently altered by the holder by erasing the name of *B & Co.* and substituting the name of *E & Co.* The way the problem is worded shows that the endorsement was forged after acceptance and without the knowledge and consent of the acceptor. As such the acceptor is not liable on the bill and can plead that endorsement is a forgery. But if the endorsement had been forged before he accepted the bill, he would be liable under Sec. 41 if he knew or had reason to believe the indorsement to be forged when he accepted it.

12. A draws a cheque on the Imperial Bank for ₹5,000 in favour of *B*. *C* steals the cheque and forges B's signature on it and makes it payable to D who pays consideration for the same and obtains it *bona fide*. D puts the cheque crossed generally into his account with the National Bank who obtains payment of it from the Imperial Bank and credits *D*'s account with the amount. *A* claims to recover the amount of the cheque from *D*, or the Imperial Bank, or the National Bank. *C*, as a thief acquired no title to the cheque, nor could he give any. D did not acquire good title as he received it from a thief. Therefore, *A* can recover the amount from *D*, but not from the Imperial Bank or the National Bank. The National Bank, as a collector of the crossed cheque for a customer and without negligence is protected under Sec. 131 of the Act. The Imperial Bank is not liable as it has simply made payment to

the other banker and at its credit. But if the cheque were uncrossed, then both D and the National Bank would be liable to A. The National Bank would not get the protection of Sec. 131, as it had collected an uncrossed cheque.

13. A draws a bill of exchange payable to the order of B only and C accepts it payable at D Bank. The bill bears the words 'not negotiable.' B indorses the bill to E. The bill being dishonoured on presentation, E sues C thereon. The words 'not negotiable' make the instrument not negotiable. B could not endorse the bill to E and E could not as such derive a good title to the bill. E cannot sue C. The bill was valid between the parties thereto, i.e., A and B only and could not be valid between E and C. E's suit will be dismissed [*Hibernian Bank* v. *Gysin & Hanson* (1938) 1 K.B. 483].

14. A gave R. Co. a promissory note payable "forty-five .... after date." Ten months later the holder of the note filled in the blank space to read "days". The holder then sued A who pleaded that the note was not binding because when delivered it was not complete in that it did not specify whether a payment was to be made forty-five days, weeks, months or years after date. *Held,* R. Co. as original holders had authority to complete the instrument by filling in the blanks so as to make it conform to the true intention of the parties. Although this must be done within a reasonable time, a ten months' delay is not unreasonable between the original parties [*Alien* v. *Rouseville Cooperage Co.,* 157 Va. 355].

15. X and Y, husband and wife, have a joint account in a bank. The account can be operated upon by either of them. The deposits in the account are usually made by X, the husband and withdrawals are usually made by Y, the wife. The banker comes to know that a garnishee order attaching X's money in the bank has been issued by the court. X and Y order the banker to transfer the amount standing in their joint account to current account of Y, the wife, in the same bank. The bank may transfer the amount to the current account of Y, the wife. Joint account moneys cannot be attached under a garnishee order, if the order is in the *sole* name, and here the order relates only to the sole name of X (*Hirschorn* v. *Evans* (1938).

16. A by mistake draws a cheque payable to B, who does not exist. The cheque is negotiated by C by forged endorsement to D, who takes it in good faith and for value. D can enforce payment of the cheque, as he is a bearer of the cheque, and his title does not depend upon the forged endorsement, under which he would have been unable to acquire any right to the cheque. When a cheque is drawn payable to a non-existing person, the cheque may be treated as payable to bearer. The holder of a bearer cheque acquires his title merely from possession of the cheque (See *Bank of England* v. *Vagliano Bros.* 1891-4 All. E.R.93).

17. A sells a radio set to M, a minor who pays for it by his cheque. A endorses the cheque to B, who takes it in good faith and for value. The cheque is dishonoured on presentation. B can enforce payment of the cheque against A, but not against M who is minor, nor can A take any action against M. A minor incurs no liability by drawing, indorsing or accepting a bill of exchange (a cheque is a bill of exchange), even if the bill is given for necessaries. But the holder in due course can enforce it against other parties.

18. Rider signed a document in these terms "In consideration of the loan of £100 from Williamson, 1, Rider, agree to repay Williamson the sum of £100 on, or before, 31st December, 1956." *Held,* this was not a promissory note because the option to pay at an earlier date created an uncertainty or contingency in the time of payment (*Williamson* v. *Rider* 1962) 2 All. E.R.268).

19. B executed a pronote in favour of A in 1967 in consideration of the price of a buffalo purchased in 1966. *Held,* money due prior to the execution of the pro-note was good consideration (*Joseph Mariano Santos Pinto* v. *Aires Concocao Rodrignes,* 1976 Goa 8)[26]

20. An instrument drawn in the form of a cheque but made payable to "cash or order" is not a cheque or a bill of exchange as the payee is not certain. (*Cole* v. *Milsome* (1951) 1 AII ER 311.

---

26. See also Ram Nandan v. Kapil Deo Ramjee, 1951 Sc 455; Shrinivas Pansari v. Prasad Mehra. 1983 Pat. 321.

CHAPTER 12

Law of Insolvency

The Indian insolvency law, like the English law of bankruptcy, is purely the creation of statutes. At present two statutes simultaneously cover the law of insolvency in India, namely, (1) The Presidency Towns Insolvency Act, 1909, which applies to the Presidency Towns of Bombay, Calcutta and Madras, (2) The Provincial Insolvency Act, 1920, which applies to the rest of India. Most of the provisions of the two Acts are similar, and therefore, the principles stated below are applicable both to the Presidency and mofussil towns. Wherever there is a difference on any point it has been separately dealt with.

In essence, there are five points of difference between the two Acts, namely, (1) the constitution of courts, (2) the procedure to be followed from the date of the presentation of the petition to the date of the order of adjudication, (3) the person in whom the debtor's property is to be vested, (4) the doctrine of relation back, and (5) the machinery for investigating the debtor's conduct.[1]

Before dealing with the rules of the law of insolvency in India, it may be observed that the terms "bankruptcy" and "bankrupt" as used in English law, are synonymous with the terms "insolvency" and "insolvent" as they are employed in India. In English law, a bankrupt is a person who has committed an act of bankruptcy and who has been adjudged a bankrupt. Such a person in India would be said to have committed an act of insolvency and to have been adjudged an insolvent.

DEFINITION

The Indian Acts do not define the terms insolvency and insolvent. "Bankruptcy," says Blackstone, "is a proceeding by which, when a debtor cannot pay his debts or discharge his liabilities or the persons to whom he owes money or has incurred liabilities cannot obtain satisfaction of their claims, the State, in certain circumstances, takes possession of his property by an officer appointed for the purpose, and such property is realised and distributed in equal proportions among the persons to whom the debtor owes money or has incurred pecuniary liabilities." An "insolvent" may be defined as a person against whom an order of adjudication has been passed.

OBJECTS OF INSOLVENCY LEGISLATION

Under the survival-of-the-fittest system society could ignore those who became insolvent. However, our society is not willing to do so. It has accordingly provided a system by which the honest debtor can, in substance, pay into court what he has, be relieved of all unpaid debts, and start economic life anew. This system comprises insolvensy laws. Thus, when a person is adjudicated insolvent his assets are taken over by an officer of the court and distributed ratably among his creditors. After the distribution

---

1. Mulla on Insolvency, p. iii.

is complete, the unpaid debts (except certain specified debts) are cancelled and the insolvent is allowed to engage in trade or service without any of his former obligations. The creditors lose a part of their claims, the debtor gets fresh start in life. Says Blackstone in this regard: "The laws of insolvency are made for the benefit of trade and are founded on the principles of humanity as well as justice; and to that end they confer some privileges both on the creditors and the insolvent or debtor."

It follows from the above that the objects of modern insolvency legislation are:
 (a) To secure fair and equal distribution of available property among the creditors;
 (b) To free the debtor from his debts, so that he can make a fresh start as soon as he is discharged by the court;
 (c) To enquire into the reasons for his insolvency, and so to deter people from rashly incurring debts they cannot pay.

From the point of view of the society, the insolvent suffers from certain *disqualifications*. The insolvent is disqualified from being (i) appointed a Magistrate, (ii) elected to any office of a local authority, (iii) elected for sitting or voting as member of any local authority. These disqualifications are removed only (a) if the order of adjudication is annulled, or (b) if he obtains from the Court an order of discharge. In addition to these disqualifications the Companies Act, 1956 provides that an insolvent cannot be director or manager of a company.

WHO MAY BE ADJUDGED INSOLVENT

In general, any person capable of entering into a contract may be adjudged an insolvent. But before he can be adjudged an insolvent, two conditions must be satisfied: (1) he must be a debtor, and (2) he must have committed an "Act of Insolvency", as defined in the Acts.

The term *debtor,* as used in the Insolvency Acts, has a limited meaning and includes persons who are subject to the laws of India. It does not mean the debtor all the world-over. Debtor means a person who has made himself amenable to adjudication but who has not yet been adjudicated.

FOREIGNERS

A foreigner cannot be adjudged insolvent in India unless he commits an act of insolvency in India during his personal residence here. But if he commits an act of insolvency during his residence in India, he can be adjudged insolvent, even though he may absent himself at the time of the petition.

MINORS

In India, a minor, being absolutely incompetent to contract, is not 'debtor' within the meaning of the Acts. Therefore, a minor can never be adjudged insolvent either on his own petition or on the petition of a creditor, even though the debt was contracted in the course of a trade carried on by him, or arose in connection with necessaries supplied to him, as minor is *never personally* liable in India. If a minor is adjudged insolvent the adjudication must be annulled.

LUNATICS

A lunatic cannot commit an act of insolvency involving intention, *e.g.*, transfer his property with intent to defeat his creditors, and cannot, therefore, be adjudged insolvent. But he may, it seems, be adjudged insolvent if he contracted the debt and committed the act of insolvency whilst sane. The question is, however, not yet decided in India and must be regarded as open.

PARTNERS: FIRM

A creditor may present a petition of insolvency against any one partner of the firm without joining the others, or he may present a joint petition against two or more of them. A joint petition can be presented only if each of the partners has jointly or severally committed an act of insolvency. Under Sec. 99 of Pre-t.1. Act an adjudication order can be made again st firms in the firm name, and such an order operates as if it were an order made against each of the partners. The Supreme Court has held in *Mukand Lal* v. *P. Singh,* 1968 S.C. 1182 that similar power exists under the Pro. I. Act also as regards adjudication of firms, as Sec. 79 (2) (c) of that Act provides or rules being made, by the High Court "for the procedure to be followed where the debtor is a firm".

JOINT HINDU FAMILY

The members of a joint Hindu family may be adjudged insolvent on a single petition by a creditor, if they are personally liable on a joint debt and have committed a joint act of insolvency, such as a joint transfer of family property in favour of a creditor by way of fraudulent preference. Where the business.of the family is carried on by the *Karta* or manager and debts are contracted by him in the course of die business, the other members are *not personally* liable for the debts and cannot be adjudged insolvent, nor can they be adjudged insolvent on a decree obtained against them by a creditor for their father's debts. A minor member of a joint Hindu family can in no case be adjudged an insolvent even if he has taken active part in the business.

JOINT DEBTOR

Where a joint debt by two or more persons is not satisfied, the creditor may present a single petition against the joint debtors, provided that some act of insolvency has been committed by each of them, or jointly by all.

COMPANIES

No insolvency petition can be presented against any corporation or association or company registered under any enactment. Thus, a company registered under the Com-panies Act, 1956, cannot be made insolvent; it must be wound up under that Act.

CONVICTS

A convicted felon can be adjudged bankrupt.

DECEASED PERSONS

A deceased person cannot be made insolvent on proceedings instituted after his death. His estate may, however, be administered in insolvency. When a debtor dies after the presentation of the petition the proceedings will, unless the Court otherwise orders, be construed as if he were alive.

ACTS OF INSOLVENCY

We have seen that a person cannot be adjudged insolvent unless he is a "debtor" within the meaning of the inslovency law **AND** has committed an act of insolvency. An act of insolvency is something done or suffered by a debtor which gives the Court jurisdiction *to* make an order of adjudication.

A debtor commits an act of insolvency in each of the following cases, namely:

(a) *If, in India or elsewhere, he makes a transfer of all or substantially all his property to a third person for the benefit of his creditors generally.*

The question under this clause is not that of intention but of the transfer of the bulk of the property; and where the whole or substantially the whole of the debtor's property has been transferred, even though honestly as for the benefit of creditors, it will amount to an act of insolvency. The transfer becomes void if the debtor is adjudged insolvent within 3 months of transfer.

(b) *If, in India or elsewhere, he makes a transfer of his property, or any part thereof with the intent to defraud or delay his creditors.*

This clause relates to transfer of whole or 'any part' of debtor's property made with the intention of defeating or delaying creditors, and the intention is to be inferred from surrounding circumstances. The transfer becomes void upon the passing of the order of adjudication.

(c) *If, in India or elsewhere, he makes any transfer of his property, or any part thereof, which would, under this or any other enactment for the time being in force, be void as a fraudulent preference if he were adjudged an insolvent.*

The word preference means favouring one creditor to the detriment of others. If the transfer is made voluntarily in order to prefer one creditor it is fraudulent preference.

(d) *If with intent to defeat or delay his creditors—*

(i) *he departs from or remains out of India;*

(ii) *he departs from his dwelling house or usual place of business or otherwise absents himself;*

(iii) *he secludes himself so as to deprive his creditors of the means of communicating with him.*

Under this clause it is an essential feature of an act of insolvency that the act should be done with the intent to defeat or delay the creditors generally, and not only a particular creditor. The debtor's intention can be inferred from surrounding circumstances.

(e) **Pro. I. Act:** *If, any of his property has been sold in execution of the decree of any court for the payment of money.*

Pre-t. I. Act: *If, any of his property has been sold or attached for a period of not less than 21 days in execution of the decree of any Court for the payment of money.*

(f) *If he petitions to be adjudged an insolvent.*

(g) *If he gives notice to any of his creditors that he has suspended, or that he is about to suspend, payment of his debt.*

The notice conveying a clear impression that the debtor has no intention to pay his debts may be oral or in writing. Mere service of notice by the Insolvency Court informing the creditors of the date of hearing of debtor's petition cannot amount to notice of suspension of payment.

(h) *If he is imprisoned in execution of the decree of any Court for the payment of money.*

Explanation —The act of an agent may be the act of the principal (even though the agent has no special authority to commit the act).

(i) **In Maharashtra State only:** If, after a creditor has served an "insolvency notice" on him in respect of any decree or order for payment of money, he does not, within the period specified in the notice, pay the decretal amount or give sufficient security for the payment of the same.

PROCEDURE

There are four stages in the process by which a debtor becomes insolvent and ultimately obtains his discharge, namely—

1. presentation of a petition either by the debtor or by the creditor;

2. appointment of an *Interim Receiver* (at the Court's discretion) for the purpose of protecting the property while the debtor's affairs are inquired into and the creditors as a body are given opportunity of expressing their wishes;

3. adjudication, when the debtor is declared insolvent and he is divested of his property which is realised for distribution among his creditors; and

4. discharge when the insolvent is released from all liabilities which could rank against his estate in the insolvency.

PETITION

To proceed against a person in insolvency it is essential that an application by way of petition must be presented to the Insolvency Court. To avoid frivolous petitions which could not but prejudice the mercantile community, it has been provided that the debtor or creditor can present a petition subject only to specified conditions in respect of jurisdiction of the Court and qualifications of the petitioner.[2]

WHO MAY PRESENT PETITION

An insolvency petition may be presented either by the debtor himself or by a creditor. *The petitioning debtor* is the person who can be adjudged an insolvent.

PETITIONING CREDITOR

A creditor is one who can compel the performance of an obligation by another person called the debtor. Therefore, any person who has a right to take legal proceedings for the recovery of a debt may present an insolvency petition against the debtor.

SECURED CREDITOR

A secured creditor does not fall within the meaning of the word creditor as used in the Acts, and as such cannot petition for insolvency. He stands outside the insolvency. But if he intends to present an insolvency petition he must place himself in the position of an unsecured creditor either by giving up his security for the benefit of the general body of creditors, or valuing it and deducting its value from his total dues claiming for the balance as an unsecured creditor.

Jurisdiction—The insolvency petition can be presented only in an Insolvency Court within the jurisdiction of which the debtor originally resident carries on business personally or through an agent or personally works for gain or if he is arrested or imprisoned in execution of a decree of Court for non-payment of money where he is in custody. In the case of a petition by or against a partnership firm, the firms should have earned on business within a year prior to the date of petition within those limits (Sec. II). In the Presidency Towns the insolvency jurisdiction is conferred on the High Courts of Bombay, Calcutta and Madras. In the rest of India governed by the Provincial Insolvency Act the insolvency jurisdiction is primarily conferred on the District Courts, but the State Government may by notification in Official Gazette invest any Court subordinate to a District Court, and such Court including Small Cases Court will have insolvency jurisdiction concurrent with its ordinary jurisdiction. The Court having insolvency jurisdiction shall have full powers to decide all questions of title and priority of any nature whatsoever. The jurisdiction of the Insolvency Court is sufficiently wide to decide all questions that may come before it, and in fact, it is co-extensive with the Civil Court so that it may make a complete distribution of the property. But the Insolvency Court has no jurisdiction of realising debts due to the insolvency. The Court is managing the estate of the insolvent. It has power to inquire into claims against the estate, and not into claims by the estate. Thus an Insolvency Court cannot pass a money decree against a third person.

CONDITIONS OF CREDITORS' PETITION

The conditions which must be fulfilled before a creditor can present an insolvency petition against a debtor are:
1. the debt owing by the debtor to the creditor, or if two or more creditors join in the petition, the aggregate amount of debts owing to such creditors, amounts to ₹ 500 or more, and
2. the debt is a liquidated sum payable either immediately or at some certain future time, and
3. an act of insolvency has been committed by the debtor, and
4. the act of insolvency on which the petition is grounded has occurred within three months before the presentation of the petition.

---

2. Added by Bombay Act XV of 1939.

A creditor can present a petition only if his debt was in existence at the time of the alleged act of insolvency, and also at the time of the presentation of the petition. The debt must continue to exist throughout the hearing of the petition and down to the order of adjudication. The debt must be owing by the debtor personally in his own right and not in any other capacity, *e.g.*, as an executor. The debt must not be less than ₹ 500 at the date of the act of insolvency, but this amount may be due to one or more petitioning creditors. The debt must be a liquidated sum, *i.e.*, a certain and ascertained sum admittedly due, and certainly payable to the person who presents the petition. For example ₹ 500 with or without interest at a certain rate for, a certain time is a definite sum and is a liquidated sum. But a claim for mesne profits or for damages based on tort or breach of contract, is not a liquidated sum.

A creditor's petition must allege the specific act of insolvency on which it is based, and that act of insolvency must have occurred within three calendar months before the presentation of the petition. The three months' period is a condition precedent to the filing of a petition and will not be extended in any case. (*Harnam Singh* v. *Balai Kumar Sinha,* 1975 Pat. 259).

A secured creditor cannot present a petition unless he places himself in the position of an unsecured creditor, either by giving up his security for the benefit of his fellow creditors, or by giving an estimate of the value of his security which may be deducted from his dues and then claiming for the balance as an unsecured creditor.

CONDITIONS OF DEBTOR'S PETITION

A debtor can present an insolvency petition *only if he is unable to pay his debts,* **AND** *any* of the three conditions given below is fulfilled—

(a) his debt amounts to ₹ 500;

(b) he is under arrest or is in prison in execution of a money decree;

(c) there is subsisting an order of attachment against his property in execution of such a decree.

Inability to pay his debt is a condition precedent to the presentation of a debtor's petition. The debtor's petition must allege that he is unable to pay his debts and he must furnish a *prima facie* grounds for his inability to pay. The expression "unable to pay his debt" means that the market value of the realizable assets is less than the total amount of the debts.

An insolvency petition, whether presented by the debtor or by a creditor, cannot be withdrawn without the leave of the Court; and the Court should not allow a withdrawal without giving notice to other parties and unless it is satisfied that it will not be detrimental to other parties. The Court cannot allow withdrawal of the petition after the order of adjudication has been made. When two or more insolvency petitions are presented against the same debtor, or where separate petitions are presented against joint debtors, the Court may consolidate them, on such terms as it thinks fit.

EFFECT OF DEBTOR'S DEATH ON INSOLVENCY PROCEEDINGS

If a debtor by or against whom an insolvency petition has been presented dies, the proceedings in the matter shall, unless the Court otherwise orders, be continued as if he were alive, so far as it may be necessary for the realisation and distribution of the property of the debtor. As a result the death of the debtor does not interfere with the insolvency proceedings; and where the property has vested in the Official Receiver or Assignee after adjudication, the death of the insolvent does not divest the Receiver or Assignee of the property. But if an insolvent dies before obtaining a discharge, he is automatically discharged.

PROCEDURE ON ADMISSION OF PETITION

An insolvency petition on its presentation is treated in the same manner as an ordinary plaint in a civil suit. Where the petition is admitted the Court shall fix a date for its hearing, notice whereof must be given to the other party. There is some difference in the procedure on admission of the petition between the law under the two Indian Acts.

Under the **Pre-t. Act**, where the Court is satisfied with the proofs furnished by the creditors as to the acts of insolvency or as to the debts due to the petitioning creditors, or as to the instability of the debtor to pay his debts, it will pass an order adjudging the debtor an insolvent. The Court may appoint an *interim* Receiver of the property of the debtor to take possession of it pending the petition and before an order of adjudication, if it is satisfied that such an appointment is necessary for the protection of the estate.

Under the **Pro. I. Act**, the Court, when making an order admitting a creditor's petition may arid where the debtor is the petitioner **ordinarily must**, appoint an *interim* Receiver of the property of the debtor or any part thereof. The *interim* Receiver will take immediate possession of the property of the debtor and exercise such powers as conferred by the Court. An Interim Receiver does not enjoy all the powers of an Official Receiver appointed after adjudication. The property does not vest in him unless the Court expressly makes an order to that effect. The Official Receiver or Assignee is appointed for the purpose of realisation of the estate, while an Interim Receiver is appointed for the protection of the estate for the general body of creditors. The Interim Receiver may be appointed by the Court any time before adjudication.

INTERIM ORDER AGAINST DEBTOR

At the time of making an order admitting the petition or at any subsequent time before adjudication the Court may either of its own motion or on the application of any creditor make one or more of the following orders, namely—

1. order the debtor to give reasonable security for his appearance until final orders are made upon the petition and direct that, in default of giving such security, he shall be detained in the civil prison;
2. order the attachment by actual seizure of the whole or any part of the property" in the possession or under the control of the debtor, other than such particulars (not being his books of account) as are exempted by the Civil Procedure Code or by any other enactment from liability to attachment and sale in execution of a decree;
3. order a warrant to issue with or without bail for the arrest of the debtor, and direct either that he is detained in civil prison until the disposal of the petition, or that he be released on such terms as to security as may be reasonable and necessary:

Provided that an order under cl. (2) or cl. (3) shall not be made unless the Court is satisfied that the debtor with intent to defeat or delay his creditors or to avoid any process of the court:

(i) has absconded or has departed from the local limits of the jurisdiction of the Court, or is about to abscond or to depart from such limits or is remaining outside them, or

(ii) has failed to disclose or has concealed, destroyed, transferred or removed from such limits, or is about to conceal, destroy, transfer or remove from such limits, any documents likely to be of use to his creditors in the course of the hearing or any part of his property other than such particulars as aforesaid.

DUTIES OF DEBTOR UNDER P.I. ACT

Sec. 22 of the Act lays down certain duties which the debtor must perform before the order of adjudication, and provides that failure on his part to do so will render him liable to imprisonment which may extend to one year. The debtor must—

(a) as soon as the insolvency petition is admitted produce all his books of account;
(b) at any time thereafter give inventories of his property, lists of his creditors and debtors and of the debts due to arid from him respectively;

(c) submit to such examination in respect of his property or creditors as may be required by the Court;

(d) attend before the Court or Receiver as and when required;

(e) execute such instruments and do all such acts and things in relation to his property as may be required by the Court or Receiver.

These duties are cast upon the debtor when his petition is admitted. Where a creditor is the petitioner, the Court, must not ask the debtor to perform these duties until the petitioning creditor or creditors have established their right to present the petition, as the debtor cannot possibly be aware of the admission of a creditor's petition until notice thereof has been served on him. Where the debtor is under arrest or detention in execution of a money decree, the Court may, either at the time of admitting the petition or at any subsequent time before adjudication, order his release.

HEARING OF THE PETITION

At the hearing of the petition the Court shall require proof (a) that the creditor is entitled to present the petition, and (b) that the debtor has been served with notice of order admitting the petition. In order to be able to present the petition the creditor must prove that (i) there subsists a relationship of creditor and debtor, (ii) the debtor is unable to pay the debt, (iii) the debt is a liquidated sum and amounts to ₹ 500 or more, and (iv) the debtor has committed an act of insolvency within three months of the presentation of the petition. The Court shall also examine the debtor, if he is present, as to his conduct, dealings and property in the presence of such creditors as appear at the hearing. If the Court is not satisfied with any of the above it shall dismiss the petition, and may award compensation up to ₹ 1,000 to the debtor, if the creditor's petition was frivolous or vexatious. The Court may also dismiss the petition if the, debtor satisfies it that he is able to pay his debts. Similar examination of the debtor, called the Public Examination, is held by the Court after the order of adjudication but before discharge under the Pre-t. Act

In the case of a petition by a debtor, he has to furnish a *prima facie* proof that he is entitled to present the petition. For this purpose the debtor must show that he is unable to pay his debts, and either (i) his debts amount to ₹ 500 or (ii) he is under arrest or in prison in execution of a money decree, or (iii) an order of attachment is subsisting against his property. If the debtor has no right to present the petition it shall be dismissed.

ORDER OF ADJUDICATION AND ITS EFFECTS

If the Court is satisfied with the proofs and does not dismiss the petition, it shall make an order of adjudication and shall specify in such order that period within which the debtor must apply for his discharge. The Court may, however, on sufficient cause being shown, extend the period of the application for discharge. The Order of Adjudication is an order whereby the debtor by or against whom an insolvency petition was presented has been legally found by the Court to be unable to pay his debts. The Effect of this order is that (i) the whole of the insolvent's property vests in the Court or a Receiver appointed by the Court, or the Official Assignee (under the Presidency- Towns Act), and becomes divisible among the creditors; (ii) the insolvent is deprived of all power to enter into transactions which will bind his creditors in respect of his property. After adjudication only the Receiver or Assignee can deal with the property, and every transaction by the insolvent is void against the Receiver or Assignee; (iii) the insolvent is disqualified from being appointed to or holding certain offices; (iv) the debtor is released from his liabilities so that no creditor of his can, pending the insolvency proceedings, have any remedy against the property in respect of any debt provable in insolvency or commence any suit or other legal proceedings, except with leave of the Court unless the creditor is a secured creditor who intends to realise his security; (v) the insolvent must help the Receiver or Assignee in the realisation of his property and the distribution of the proceeds amongst his creditors; (vi) any suit pending before a Court may, on proof that an order of adjudication has been made, be stayed by the Court (not the Insolvency Court); (vii) the order will relate back to, and take effect from, the commencement of insolvency. The right of a secured creditor to realise or otherwise to deal with his security is unaffected by the order of adjudication; and he can commence a suit to realise his security without the leave of the Insolvency Court. The Order of Adjudication operates as a statutory transfer to the Official Assignee of all the property of the insolvent in India, whether movable or immovable (*Official Assignee, Bombay* v. *Registrar, Small Causes* 37 I.A. 86). As regards foreign property, the better opinion is that movables will vest in the officer; but immovable property will not so vest, unless foreign law permits it (*Yokohama Specie Bank* v. *Curlenders &. Co.* 43 Cal. L. J. 436).

DOCTRINE OF RELATION BACK

From the above it is clear that until an order of adjudication is made there is no insolvency, and the debtor retains the property. In other words, no vesting takes place until this order; but once the order is made the property vests in the Receiver or Assignee from the date of the commencement of the insolvency and not the order of adjudication. The title of the Receiver or Assignee is by a legal fiction taken to relate back to the commencement of the insolvency which is always some anterior date. The dates of commencement of insolvency, however, differ under the two Acts. Under the Provincial Insolvency Act, an order of adjudication relates back to the date of the presentation of the petition on which it is made, *i.e.*, the insolvency commences with the presentation of the petition, if the order is made : Sec. 28 (7) of the Act reads ; "An order of adjudication shall relate back to, and take effect from, the date of the presentation of the petition on which it is made." The effect of sub-sections (2) and (7) is that the properties of the insolvents wherever they may have been and whoever may have been in possession of them, automatically vest in the Court or the Receiver, if one is appointed by the Court. Under the Presidency-Towns Act, which follows the English Bankruptcy Act, the order of adjudication relates back to the first available act of insolvency and it is from that date the insolvency is deemed to commence. Thus, the title of the Receiver relates back to and commences at the date of the presentation of the insolvency petition, and that of the Assignee at the time of the first available act of insolvency committed within three months before the presentation of the insolvency petition. The effect of the doctrine of relation back is that any charge created by a decree or otherwise or any other transaction in relation to the property after the date of the commencement of the insolvency is not binding on the Receiver or Assignee.

PROTECTION ORDER

A Protection Order means an order by the Court prohibiting the arrest of an insolvent debtor in execution of a decree for the payment of money. A debtor on being adjudged an insolvent may apply to the Court for protection and the Court may in its discretion, make an order for protection of the insolvent from arrest or detention. If he is in prison or under arrest, his release may be ordered. The protection which the Acts extend to an insolvent against arrest or attachment or sale of his property can be enjoyed by him only in respect of provable debts. No protection with regard to debts due to the Union of India can be granted. The Court may order the arrest of an insolvent, if it is satisfied that he has deliberately absconded with intent to avoid any obligations imposed on him.

SPECIAL MANAGER

Sec. 19 of the Presidency-Towns Act provides that if in any case the Court, having regard to the nature of the debtor's estate or business or to the interest of the creditors generally, is of the opinion that a special manager of the estate or business ought to be appointed to assist the Official Assignee, it may appoint a manager thereof accordingly to act for such time as the Court may authorise, and to have such powers of the Official Assignee as may be entrusted to him by the Official Assignee or as the Court may direct. The special manager must furnish security and keep and tender accounts in such manner as the Court may direct, and will receive such remuneration as the Court may determine.

EFFECT OF INSOLVENCY ON ANTECEDENT TRANSATIONS

EXECUTION CREDITOR

Where execution of a decree has been issued against the property of a debtor, no person shall be entitled to the benefit of the execution against the Official Receiver or Assignee except in respect of assets realised in the course of execution by sale or otherwise, under the Provincial Insolvency Act, before the date of the admission of the petition, and under the Presidency-Towns Insolvency Act, before the date of the order of adjudication and before he had notice of the presentation of an insolvency petition. Any creditor or anyone interested may give notice to the executing Court of the admission of the insolvency petition or of the order of adjudication, as the case may be, whereupon the Court must, on application, direct the property, if in the possession of the Court, to be delivered to the Official Receiver or Assignee, but the costs of the execution will be a first charge on the property so delivered. The Provincial Insolvency Act also provides that the costs of the suit in which the decree was made are a first charge on the property so delivered. If, however, the property has been sold in execution of the decree any person who in good faith purchased the property would acquire a good title against the Official Receiver or Assignee. Nothing stated above affects the rights of secured creditors.

AVOIDANCE OF VOLUNTARY TRANSFER

Every transfer of property which is not made, (*i*) before and in consideration of a marriage, or (*ii*) to a purchaser or incumbrancer in good faith and for valuable consideration, shall be void against the Official Receiver or Assignee? if the transferor is adjudged insolvent on a petition presented within two years of the date of the transfer, and under Presidency-Towns Act, within two years after the date of the transfer. The effect of this difference in time in the two Acts is that under the Presidency-Towns Act the transfer must have been made within two years next before the date of the commission of the first available act of insolvency, and under Provincial Insolvency Act, it must have been made within two years next before the presentation of the insolvency petition. In the latter case, a voluntary transfer, if made within two years before the date of the presentation of the insolvency petition, may be avoided, even if the transfer was made more than two years before the date of the order of adjudication. The onus of proving that a particular transaction was not entered into in good faith and for valuable consideration is on the Official Receiver, unless the transferee knew that the transferor was in insolvent circumstances at the time of the transfer.[3]

AVOIDANCE OF FRAUDULENT PREFERENCE

In order to protect the interests of the whole body of creditors, the Acts provide for the avoidance of fraudulent preference by the debtor of some creditors over others. The Acts provide that every transfer by a debtor of his property, every payment made, every obligation incurred and every judicial proceeding affecting his property taken or suffered by him, *is fraudulent* and void as against the Official Receiver or Assignee and shall be annulled by the Court, provided that the following five conditions are fulfilled, namely:—

1. the debtor was at the time of the transfer or payment unable to pay from his own money his debts as they became due;
2. the transfer or payment was made in favour of creditor;
3. the transfer or payment in fact prefers one creditor to another;

---

3. Srikantiah Setty v. A. Basha Saheb & Co., 1958 Mys. 35.

4. the transfer or payment was made with a view to giving such creditor a preference over other creditors; and

5. the debtor has been adjudged insolvent on a petition presented within three months after the date of the transfer of payment.

This rule as to fraudulent preference will not affect the rights of any person who in good faith and for valuable consideration has acquired a title through or under a creditor of the insolvent.

PROTECTED TRANSACTIONS

Subject to the provisions of the Insolvency Acts as to executions, voluntary transfers, and fraudulent preferences, discussed above, nothing in the Acts invalidates in the case of an insolvency:

(a) any payment of money by an insolvent to a creditor;

(b) any payment of money or delivery of property to the insolvent;

(c) any transfer by the insolvent for valuable consideration; or

(d) any contract or dealing by or with the insolvent for valuable consideration;

Provided that (i) any such transaction takes place before the date of the order of adjudication, and (ii) the person who deals with the debtor has not at the time of any such transaction notice of the presentation of any insolvency petition by or against the debtor. It is to be noted that the protection accorded by the Acts extends only to *bona fide* transactions—transactions which are fair and honest.

INSOLVENT'S SCHEDULE

Under Sec. 24 of the Prsidency-Towns Act an insolvent is required to prepare and submit to the Court a schedule verified by affidavit in prescribed form within 30 day of the order on the petition of the debtor or within 30 days of the service of the order passed on the petition of a creditor. If the insolvent fails to prepare the schedule on the prescribed form the Official Assignee may prepare it and the insolvent may be committed to civil prison.

According to Sec. 33 of the Provincial Insolvency Act the Schedule of Creditors is to be framed by the Court on its satisfying itself as to the validity of the claim.

DUTIES OF INSOLVENT

Sec. 3 of the Presidency-Towns Insolvency Act enumerates the duties of the insolvent as follows :—

1. The insolvent must, unless prevented by sickness or other sufficient cause, attend any meeting of his creditors which the Official Assignee may require him to attend and must submit to such examination and give such information as the meeting may require.

2. The insolvent must:—

   (a) give such inventory of his property, such lists of his creditors and debtors, and of the debts to and from them respectively;

   (b) submit to such examination in respect of his property or his creditors;

   (c) wait at such times and places on the Official Assignee or special manager;

   (d) execute such powers-of-attorney, transfers and instruments; and

   (e) generally, do all such acts and things in relation to his property and the distribution of the proceeds amongst his creditors, as may be required by the Official Assignee, special manager or the Court.

3. The insolvent must aid, to the utmost of his power, in the realisation of his property, and the distribution of the proceeds among his creditors.

4. If the insolvent wilfully fails to perform any of the duties mentioned above, he is guilty of Contempt of the Court and liable to be punished for it.

5. He will be guilty of Contempt of the Court if he fails to deliver possession to the Official Assignee of any part of his property which is divisible among his creditors, even after discharge.

Under the Provincial Insolvency Act these duties are provided in two sections. The duties before adjudication are given in Sec. 22 (discussed on page 358), and those after adjudication in Sec. 28, as given below :—

1. The prime duty of the insolvent is to aid the Receiver in the realisation of his property and the distribution of the proceeds among the creditors.
2. He must appear for examination though he may reside more than 200 miles away from the Court-house.
3. He must give all information he can to the Official Receiver and supply him with lists of his properties and liabilities, his creditors and debtors.
4. He must do everything that the Official Receiver may reasonably require of him or the Court may order him to do in relation to his property.
5. If he wilfully fails to perform any of the duties or fails to deliver up possession of any part of his property which is divisible among his creditors, he shall be punishable with imprisonment extending to one year.

PUBLIC EXAMINATION

Under the Presidency-Towns Insolvency Act, the Court fixes a date for holding a public examination of the insolvent. The insolvent must, on the appointed date, attend court and answer all questions put to him by the Court, the Official Assignee and any creditor. The object of the examination is to determine the causes which led to insolvency. The Court may dispense with the holding of the public examination if the insolvent is a lunatic or a *pardanashin* woman or if he or she is suffering from some disease or disablement.

Under the Provincial Insolvency Act the Court must examine the debtor while the petition for adjudication is being heard by the Court During such examination the creditors present may put questions to the debtor.

ANNULMENT OF ADJUDICATION

There are four cases in which an adjudication may be annulled by the Court, namely:—

A. (i) where in the opinion of the Court a debtor ought not to have been adjudged insolvent, or
(ii) where it is proved to the satisfaction of the Court that the debts have been paid in full, or
(iii) where an adjudication is made on a debtor's petition, who did not owe ₹ 500 or more, or
(iv) where an adjudication is made without leave of the Court, when such leave was necessary.

Thus, an adjudication order made against a minor, or against a debtor who was deceased at the time of the petition, may be annulled. It may be annulled where 100 paise in the rupee, together with interest up to the date of payment, have been paid.

B. Where concurrent proceedings are pending in another Court.

A debtor can be adjudged insolvent by two or more Courts, *e.g.*, by the Court of the place where he resides and by the Court of the place where he carries on business. The power to annul is discretionary and if a debtor is adjudged insolvent by two Courts. either Court may annul its **OWN** order of adjudication or stay its proceedings, if the assets can be more conveniently administered by the other Court.

C. Where the Court approves the proposal of the insolvent for a compromise or a scheme of arrangement.

D. Where the insolvent absents himself on the date of the hearing of his application for discharge, or does not apply for his discharge within the period specified by the Court.

Notice of every order annulling adjudication must be published in the Official Gazette and in such other manner as may be prescribed.

EFFECT OF ANNULMENT

The effect of annulment depends on the terms of the order made by the Court while annulling the adjudication. The order varies according to the nature of the case. Where an adjudication is annulled, all sales and dispositions of property and payments duly made, and all acts theretofore done, by the Court or Receiver or Assignee shall be valid; but subject as aforesaid, the property of the insolvent shall vest in such persons as the Court may appoint, or in default of such appointment, shall revert to the debtor to the extent of his right or interest therein on such conditions (if any) as the Court may by an order in writing declare.

In the case of annulment for default to apply for discharge or appear at the hearing of the application for discharge, the Court may recommit the insolvent to custody where he has been released; by the order of the Court, and all processes against his person in force at the time of his release shall be deemed to be in force against him.

COMPOSITION AND SCHEME OF ARRANGEMENT

A debtor who is unable to pay his debts in full may arrange his affairs with his creditors without filing a petition for his own adjudication. Arrangements between debtors and creditors are known as composition agreements. A composition has been defined as an agreement between compounding debtor and all or some of the creditors by which the compounding creditors agree with the debtor and (expressly or impliedly) with each other to accept from the debtor payment of less than the amounts due to them in full satisfaction of their claims. But a debtor cannot settle with his creditors out of Court after he has been adjudged an insolvent. That can be done only by a composition or scheme as provided by the two Acts. Therefore, an insolvent may at any time **after the making of an order of adjudication** submit proposal for a composition in satisfaction of his debts or a proposal for a scheme of arrangement of his affairs whereupon the Court will fix a date for the consideration of the proposal and issue notice to all his creditors to attend the meeting on the date so fixed. If, the proposal being placed before the meeting of creditors, a majority in number and three-fourths in value of the creditors whose debts are proved and who are present in person, or by pleader under the Provincial Insolvency Act, or by proxy or a letter addressed to the Official Assignee under the Presidency-Towns Act, resolve to accept the proposal and the Court approves it, the same is deemed to have been duly accepted by all the creditors. The proposal for composition is not absolutely final. It is really a basis of negotiation with the creditors, and may be amended at the meeting of the creditors at which it is considered, but it must satisfy the Court as calculated to benefit the general body of creditors.

If, in the opinion of the Court, the terms of the proposal are not reasonable or are not calculated to benefit the general body of creditors, the Court must refuse to accept the proposal. The Court in deciding one way or the other will consider the report of the Official Receiver or Assignee and hear any objections which may be made by or on behalf of any creditor. The Court must also refuse to accept the proposal, if the circumstances surrounding the debtor's insolvency are such that it would have no power to grant an unconditional discharge, unless it provides reasonable security for payment of not less, than 40 paise in the rupee on all the unsecured debts against the debtor's estate. Where the Court approves the proposal, the terms must be embodied in the order; and the order of adjudication must be annulled. Thereafter, the debtor will have power to deal with his estate by realising it in ordinary course of business for the purpose of enabling himself to pay the composition.

ANNULMENT OF COMPOSITION

If default is made in the payment of any instalment due in pursuance of the composition or scheme, or it appears to the Court that the composition or scheme cannot proceed without injustice or undue delay, or that the approval of the Court was obtained by fraud, the Court may, if it thinks fit, re-adjudge the debtor insolvent and annul the composition or scheme but without prejudice to the validity of any transfer or payment duly made or of any thing duly done under or in pursuance of the composition or scheme. After such annulment, the creditors can prove for their original debts and not simply what would have been due under the composition. The annulment will also discharge a surety for composition for liability.

DEBTS PROVABLE IN INSOLVENCY

Under both Acts: All debts and liabilities, present or future, certain or contingent, to which the debtor is subject when he is adjudged an insolvent, or to which he may become subject before his discharge by reason of any obligation incurred before the date of such adjudication, are deemed to be debts provable in insolvency. Under the wide words of the Acts all kinds of debts or liabilities of the insolvent can be proved, except those enumerated below.

Examples of provable debts—The following have been held as debts provable in insolvency; (a) damages for breach of contract; (b) damages for breach of trust; (c) annuities for life; (d) a lessor can prove for loss of rent or any other liability in respect of a subsisting lease; (e) an uncalled amount on shares held by the insolvent; (f) the liability of a member of a Co-operative Society in the event of its being dissolved is a debt provable in insolvency; (g) a contingent liability on a contract to indemnify; (h) the balance of a loan under the decree of the court; (i) on the insolvency of a surety, the creditor can prove for the whole amount due, even if since that date he has received sums on account from the principal debtor, or co-surety provided the creditor does not receive in all more than 100 paise in the rupee.

DEBTS NOT PROVABLE

The following debts are not provable under both Acts: (i) debts incapable of being fairly estimated; (ii) demands in the nature of unliquidated damages arising otherwise than by reason of a contract or breach of trust.

In addition to these two debts, according to Sec. 46 (I) of Pre-t. Act, debts or liabilities contracted by an insolvent from a person having notice of the presentation of an insolvent petition by or against a debtor are not provable.

Examples of not provable debts—(a) Claims for damages for a tort; (b) claims for damages in respect of fraud; (c) a debt contracted after presentation of petition but before order of adjudication or after this order; (d) illegal debts and debts against the policy of insolvency law (*e.g.*, agreement to pay for not opposing discharge); (e) debts barred at the commencement of insolvency.

PROOF OF DEBTS

The method of proof, as laid down in Sec. 49 of the Provincial Insolvency Act, is that the creditor must deliver, or send by a registered letter, to the Court, an affidavit verifying the debt. The affidavit must contain particulars of the debt and specify the vouchers, if any, by which they can be substantiated. The Court, after hearing the parties and after considering the report of the Official Receiver, may admit the proof or reject it. The Court will then frame a schedule of creditors containing the names of all those creditors who have proved their debts, and the amount of the respective debts. Any creditor may challenge the validity of a debt set up by another creditor and the Court must decide the question. It cannot delegate to the Official Receiver the power to frame the Schedule, unless the High Court has especially empowered it so to do under Sec. 80. A creditor who has not proved his debt when the schedule was framed may tender proof at any time before the discharge of the insolvent. Also, where a creditor is placed on the schedule in respect of a debt he may prove further debt which he had omitted to prove. A creditor who has failed to prove a provable debt cannot enforce his claim against the insolvent after his discharge. Debts and liabilities not provable in insolvency are not affected by the discharge, and the creditor can sue the discharged insolvent in respect of them.

Under the Presidency-Towns Insolvency Act, the proof in the manner stated above is to be submitted to the Official Assignee, and not to the Court. The Official Assignee is given the powers to admit or reject in writing any proof and claim.

PROOF BY SECURED CREDITORS

A secured creditor has his remedy independently of the Insolvency Court to realise his security, but he can, if he so desires, come in the insolvency proceedings as an unsecured creditor by relinquishing his security or by deducting the value of the security. If he wishes to participate in the benefits of insolvency proceedings he must comply with the requirements of the Acts.

Three courses are open to a secured creditor who wishes to take advantage of the insolvency proceeding, namely :—

  (i) he may enforce and realise his security and then prove for the balance that may still remain due to him; or

 (ii) he may relinquish or surrender the security for the general body of creditors and prove for the whole debt that may be due to him; or

(iii) he may value his security, state the particulars of his security in his proof and then receive a dividend for the balance that may remain due to him after the value so assessed has been deducted subject to the right of the Court or Official Assignee to redeem the security on payment to the creditor of the assessed value.

Where a creditor, after having valued his security, subsequently realises it, i.e., sells the property in order to appropriate the sale proceeds towards the payment of his principal, interest and costs, the net amount realised must be substituted for the amount of any valuation previously made by the creditor, and must be treated as an amended valuation made by the creditor. Where a secured creditor does not comply with the above provisions, he shall be excluded from all shares in any dividend, and in that case, he shall have to be content with his security whether or not it is sufficient for the payment of his debt.

PROOF FOR INTEREST

The general rule in insolvency is that the interest ceases from the date of the order of adjudication, and no proof for interest after that date is admitted, unless the estate is more than sufficient to pay 100 paise in the rupee. In the latter case, the creditors can get interest up-to-date and if there is still any surplus, that goes to the insolvent, "Theory in bankruptcy," says James, L. J. in *Re Savia*,[4] "is to stop all things at the date of bankruptcy, and to divide the wreck of the man's property as it stood at that date." It is provided that:—

  (i) in case of debts where no interest is agreed upon, but there is a due date, interest not exceeding 6 per cent per annum may be proved from the due date to the date of adjudication;

 (ii) in case of debts where no interest is agreed upon and there is no due date, interest not exceeding 6 per cent per annum may be proved from the date of the demand notice to the date of adjudication;

(iii) in case of debts where no interest is agreed upon, interest not exceeding 5 per cent per annum may be proved without prejudice to the right of receiving a higher rate from surplus, if any.

Where the rate of interest agreed upon is excessive, the Court has the power under the Usurious Loans Act, 1918, to reduce it. An insolvent's solvent debtors are not absolved from the liability to pay interest on the ground that the insolvent has filed his petition in insolvency. The interest when collected is distributed among the creditors.

---

4. (1872) L.R. 7 Ch. A.P.P. 760

PART 12-B
INSOLVENT'S PROPERTY

The Insolvency Acts define "Property" as including property over which, or over the profits of which, any person has a disposing power which he may exercise for his own benefit. When the Acts refer to property of insolvent, they always mean such of his property as is divisible amongst his creditors. The property includes not only material objects but also rights over material objects. Thus, in the case of a Hindu father it includes his disposing power over his son's undivided interest. All valuable rights which may be turned into money or whose worth can be assessed in money are property. The word property includes immovable property, movable property, and actionable claims. Though the definition of property is not exhaustive, yet it is comprehensive enough to include money, goods, things in action, land and every description of property whether real or personal, movable or immovable obligations, easements and every description of estate, interest and profits, or contingent, present or future, arising out of or incidental to property and includes any property over which or over the profits of which the insolvent has a disposing power which he may exercise for his benefit. This property vests in the Official Receiver or Assignee and is divisible among the insolvent's creditors.

PROPERTY DIVISIBLE AMONGST CREDITORS

Property of the insolvent which can be divided among his creditors comprises the following particulars, namely :—
1. property which may belong to him at the commencement of the insolvency;
2. property which may be acquired by or devolve on him after the date of the order of adjudication and before his discharge, (i.e., after-acquired property); .
3. the capacity to exercise all such powers in respect of property as might have been exercised by him for his own benefit at the commencement of the insolvency or before his discharge;
4. goods in the possession, order or disposition of the insolvent in his trade or business so that he is the reputed owner thereof.

The following is an enumeration of some of the properties which constitute the properties of the insolvent and vest in the Official Receiver or Assignee: Money in the hands or at the disposal of the insolvent, his personal earnings, and salary, except the amount sufficient for the maintenance, according to his station in life, of the insolvent and his family, secret formulas invented by him, life insurance policies, copy-right, partnership assets in case of firm's insolvency, goodwill, Hindu joint family property, interest, statutory tenancy, occupancy rights, actionable claims, equity of redemption, movable and immovable property of the insolvent, goods in the possession, order or disposition of the insolvent in his trade or business, goods held by commission agent, property under bailment, and a right to sue in respect of a tort or a breach of contract resulting in injury to the estate of the insolvent.

PROPERTY NOT DIVISIBLE AMONG CREDITORS

Property which is not divisible among the creditors of the insolvent falls into two classes, namely:—
1. Property held by the insolvent on trust for any other person or in fiduciary capacity; and
2. Tools of trade, necessary wearing apparel and other similar property.

PROPERTY HELD BY INSOLVENT IN FIDUCIARY CAPACITY

Property held by the insolvent as a trustee under a trust does not pass to the Official Receiver or Assignee and is not divisible among his creditors. Similarly, property held by him as executor or administrator, or in any fiduciary capacity is not divisible. Thus, property in the hands of an insolvent as a bailee, factor, solicitor, broker, auctioneer or cashier is property held by him in fiduciary capacity, and on his being adjudged insolvent, it will belong to the principal, and will not pass to the Official Receiver or Assignee. The position is the same in respect of money held by an agent to collect and remit or by a secretary or treasurer of a society. Also, property in the possession of an insolvent at the time of his insolvency for a specific purpose, for paying his pressing creditors does not belong to the debtor, and does not vest in the Official Receiver or Assignee on the debtor being adjudged an insolvent.

TOOLS OF TRADE, WEARING APPAREL, ETC.

Both the Acts provide that the insolvent is entitled to retain certain property which cannot be divided amongst his creditors. Such property, under the Presidency-Towns Insolvency Act, consists of the tools of trade and the necessary wearing apparel, bedding, cooking vessels, and furniture of himself, his wife and children, to a value, inclusive of tools and apparel and other necessaries as aforesaid, not exceeding ₹ 300 in the whole.

The Provincial Insolvency Act makes a general provision that property (not being books of account) which is exempted by the Code of Civil Procedure, 1908 or by any other enactment for the time being in force from liability to attachment and sale in execution of a decree, is not divisible among the creditors of the insolvent.

Property exempted from attachment and sale under Sec. 60 of the Code includes (*i*) the necessary wearing apparel, cooking vessels, beds, and bedding of the judgement-debtor, his wife and children, and such personal ornaments as, in accordance with the religious usage, cannot be parted with by a woman; (*ii*) tools of artisans and, where the judgment-debtor is an agriculturist, his implements of husbandry, etc; (*iii*) houses and other buildings belonging to an agriculturist and occupied by him as such and for the purpose of agriculture, that is, in order to enable him to cultivate the land. An agriculturist here means a person whose sole means of living is gained by cultivating a small holding.

In addition to the properties specified in the two Acts as stated above, there are some other properties which are not divisible among the insolvent's creditors, namely:—

1. Pension; 2. Provident Fund money; 3. Gratuity payable to a railway servant, 4. *Spes successionis, i.e.,* a bare possibility of succession, such as the chance of an heir-apparent succeeding to an estate, or the chance of a person obtaining a legacy on the death of a relative; and 5. Right of action in respect of a tort or a breach of contract resulting in injuries wholly to the person or feelings of the insolvent.

REPUTED OWNERSHIP

The doctrine of reputed ownership apples only in the case of traders. The provision is made for the protection of the general creditors of a trader against the false credit which might be acquired by his being suffered to have the possession and power of disposition of property as his own, which does not really belong to him. This prevents traders from gaining a delusive credit by a false appearance of substance to mislead those who deal with them. This provision which is known as the Reputed Ownership Clause as contained in the two Acts is similar in effect except as to the time when the clause takes effect Under the Presidency-Towns Act it is provided that **goods** which are at the **commencement of the insolvency** in the possession, order or disposition of the insolvent, in his trade or business by the consent and permission of the true owner, under such circumstances that he is the reputed owner thereof, are divisible among his creditors. The Provincial Insolvency Act lays down that the **goods** which are, **at the date of the presentation of the petition on which the order of adjudication is made**, in the possession, order or disposition of the insolvent in his **trade** or **business**, by the consent and permission of the true owner thereof, are divisible among his creditors. It is clear from these provisions that it is not only the goods of which the insolvent is the true owner which vest in the Official Assignee or Receiver, but also the goods which belong to other people of which the insolvent is the apparent or reputed owner. Thus, if a person buys goods from a trader and pays for them, but leaves the goods in the possession of the seller, and the seller becomes insolvent, the goods will, as a general rule, pass to the Official Assignee or Receiver and will be divisible among his creditors. The buyer is the true owner of the goods, and the insolvent is the apparent or reputed owner thereof. The goods are said to be in the reputed ownership of the insolvent, or in his possession, order or disposition. This is so because the property is held out to the world as that of the trade and will be treated as his own in his insolvency and be divisible among his creditors. By far the largest number of cases of reputed ownership arise in connection with mortgages of goods. The effect of the reputed ownership clause is to transfer to Official Assignee property that does not belong to the insolvent. It is to take one man's property to pay another man's debt. Under the Provincial Insolvency Act, the doctrine of reputed ownership does not apply to goods which have been mortgaged or hypothecated by the insolvent and this is the substantial point of difference between the two Acts. Where goods are mortgaged or hypothecated, the Receiver takes the goods subject to the mortgage or hypothecation.

The doctrine of reputed ownership, as stated above, applies only to goods and chosen-in-action are not "goods" in this connection. And it does not extend to all kinds of goods. It extends only to such goods as are in the possession, order or disposition of the insolvent **in his trade or business**. Goods not used for purposes of the insolvent's trade or business do not pass to the Official Assignee or Receiver. Further, to bring goods within the reputed ownership clause, they must be in the Sole possession and Sole reputed ownership of the insolvent. The clause does not extend to cases in which the insolvent and other persons who are not insolvent are jointly in possession of goods and of which, he and those persons are jointly reputed owners.

AFTER-ACQUIRED PROPERTY

It may happen at times that an insolvent acquires property after adjudication and before discharge. He may carry on business after insolvency, and, in the course of business, he may acquire rights and property. He may also acquire property by inheritance or by way of gifts or under a settlement or a will. He may have personal earning, salary and income from other sources. There is a slight difference in law under the two Acts, and we shall, therefore, deal with it separately.

Under the Presidency-Towns Insolvency Act, the property acquired by the insolvent after adjudication and before discharge vests in the Official Assignee only when he intervenes on behalf of the insolvent's estate. If the Official Assignee does not intervene, and the insolvent transfers the property to another who takes it in good faith and for value, the transferee acquires a good title to it. Further, unless the Official Assignee has intervened, it is competent for the insolvent, his legal representatives and his assigns, to maintain a suit for the recovery of after-acquired property or for any other relief in respect thereof against a stranger, and that the Official Assignee is not a necessary part to such suit. The provision in this Act is based on the English rule of law stated in *Cohen* v. *Mitchell* (1890), Q.B.D. 262 that "until the trustee intervenes, all transactions by a bankrupt after his bankruptcy with any person dealing with him *bona fide* and for value, in respect of his after acquired property, whether with or without the knowledge of the bankruptcy, are valid against the trustee."

The Legislature in drafting Sec. 28(4) of the Provincial Insolvency Act has departed from the above rule probably because in places outside Presidency-Towns fraud was more rampant and that, under the guise of *bona fide* transfer for value, after-acquired property would be transferred *benami* to the prejudice of insolvent's creditors. The section, therefore, provides that all property acquired by the insolvent after adjudication and before discharge shall forthwith vest in the Receiver. The effect of this provision is that all property, whether it is owned by the insolvent at the time of the order of adjudication or it is acquired after such order but before discharge, vests in the Official Receiver as soon as the adjudication order is made. Unlike the Official Assignee, the Receiver is not required to necessarily intervene before the after-acquired property will vest in him.

PERSONAL EARNINGS

Wages and other money earned by the insolvent by his personal labour and exertions constitute his "personal earnings." The personal earnings of an insolvent vest in the Official Assignee or Receiver like any other property except such part of them as is necessary for the maintenance of the insolvent and his family. Thus, the Assignee or Receiver can intervene only if they are more than sufficient for the maintenance of the insolvent and his family. Similarly, as soon as the amount of a provident fund reaches the hands of an undischarged insolvent depositor it becomes the insolvent's property and vests in the Receiver, or the Assignee can intervene with respect to it. The pension of a retired insolvent is also property for the benefit of his creditors as it becomes payable each month.

DISCLAIMER OF ONEROUS PROPERTY BY OFFICIAL ASSIGNEE

Secs. 62-67 of the Presidency-Towns Insolvency Act provide for a disclaimer of onerous property by the Official Assignee. This is necessary to protect him from personal liability in respect of onerous property. Land burdened with onerous covenants, shares or stocks in companies, unprofitable contracts, or any other property, which is unsaleable, or not readily saleable, by reason of its binding the possessor thereof to the performance of any onerous act or to the payment of any sum of money, are different forms of onerous property, and the Official Assignee may disclaim them. He cannot, however, disclaim a contract entered into by the insolvent for the sale of a lease unless he also disclaims the lease itself. The period for disclaiming is twelve months from the date of adjudication or the time when the Official Assignee came to know of such property after adjudication.

EFFECT OF DISCLAIMER

As regards the insolvent and his property, the disclaimer operates to determine, as from the date thereof, his rights, interests and liabilities in or in respect of the property disclaimed. As regards the Official Assignee personally, his liability in respect of the property is determined by the disclaimer as from the date when the property is vested in him. Disclaimer does not affect the rights or liabilities of third parties except so far as is necessary for the purpose of releasing the insolvent and his property and the Official Assignee from liability.

TITLE OF OFFICIAL ASSIGNEE OR RECEIVER

The combined effect of the doctrine of reputed ownership and of the effect of insolvency on antecedent transactions is that the title of the Official Assignee or Official Receiver is superior to that of the insolvent. According to the doctrine of reputed ownership, the Official Assignee or Receiver may claim the goods belonging to persons other than the insolvent lying in the possession of the latter. The result is that as against the Official Assignee or Receiver even the true owner of the goods cannot claim them. But the insolvent could not claim such goods as his own. Secs. 53 and 54 of Pro. I. Act and Secs. 55 and 56 of the Pres-t Act are also illustrations of the superior title of these officials in respect of the insolvent's property. All property belonging to the insolvent vests in them and they alone can deal with it, and not the insolvent. Further, every voluntary transfer not being a transfer made before and in consideration of marriage or made in favour of a purchaser in good faith and for valuable consideration is void against these officials if made within 2 years next before the presentation of the petition. Similarly, a fraudulent preference is void against them. Moreover, an Official Assignee can disclaim onerous property, but the insolvent could not disclaim it.

REALISATION OF PROPERTY

As to the mode of realisation there is some difference under the two Acts. Therefore, each set of provisions will be dealt with separately. The powers and duties of realisation, however, of the Official Assignee and of the Receiver are the same, and they will be treated together.

POSSESSION OF PROPERTY BY OFFICIAL ASSIGNEE

It is the duty of the Official Assignee to take possession as soon as possible of the deeds, books and documents of the insolvent and of all other parts of his property capable of manual delivery. If the insolvent is in possession of any such property, the Official Assignee alone is entitled to possession thereof. If the insolvent has sold his book debts and delivered his books of account to the purchaser, the Official Assignee cannot claim the books. The Official Assignee is the owner of the property which vests in him, and he has all the remedies which are available to an owner. Besides these, he has certain special remedies open to him.

POSSESSION OF PROPERTIES BY OFFICIAL RECEIVER

Sec. 56(3) of the Provincial Insolvency Act provides that where the Court appoints a Receiver, it may remove any person in whose possession or custody any property of the insolvent is from the possession or custody thereof, but this does not authorise the Court to remove from the possession or custody of property any person whom the insolvent has not a present right so to remove. It is to be noted that under this Act the Court alone has the power to remove; the Receiver has no such power, although he can make an application for possession.

Sec. 60 provides that in any area in which a declaration has been made under Sec. 68 of the Civil Procedure Code, no sale of the immovable property of the insolvent paying revenue to the Government or held or let for agricultural purposes can be made. In Punjab even temporary alienation of agricultural land cannot be made, whether the alienee is an agriculturist or otherwise.

POWER OF OFFICIAL ASSIGNEE AND RECEIVER TO REALISE

The Acts lay down that the Official Assignee and Receiver must with all convenient speed realise the property of the insolvent and distribute dividends among the creditors, and for that purpose may, without the leave of the Court—

(a) sell all or any of the property of the insolvent;

(b) give receipts for any money received by him;

He may also, with the leave of the Court, do any of the following things, namely:—

1. carry on the business of the insolvent so far as may be necessary for beneficial winding up of the same;

2. institute, defend or continue any suit or other legal proceedings relating to the property of the insolvent;

3. employ a legal practitioner or other agent to take any proceedings or do any business which may be sanctioned by the Court;

4. accept as the consideration for the sale of any property of the insolvent a sum of money payable at a future time subject to such stipulations as to security and otherwise as the Court thinks fit;

5. mortgage or pledge any part of the property of the insolvent for the purpose of raising money for the payment of his debts;

6. refer any dispute to arbitration and compromise all debts, claims and liabilities on such terms as may be agreed upon;

7. divide in its existing form amongst the creditors, according to its estimated value, any property which, from its peculiar nature or other special circumstances cannot readily or advantageously be sold.

DISTRIBUTION OF PROPERTY

Both the Acts provide that the Official Assignee or Receiver, as the case may be, must begin the distribution of dividends with all convenient speed. Under the Presidency-Towns Insolvency Act the first dividend must be distributed within one year after adjudication unless the Official Assignee satisfies the Court that there is sufficient reason for postponing the declaration to a later date, and the subsequent dividends must be declared and paid at intervals of not more than six months unless there is sufficient reason for further delay. The Official Assignee is also required to publish a notice of his intention to declare a dividend and to notify each creditor mentioned in the insolvent's schedule who has not proved his debt, and when he has declared a dividend, to send to each creditor who has proved, a notice showing the amount of the dividend and the time and manner of its payment. *No such period is fixed and no such declaration and notice are required under the Provincial Insolvency Act.* In the calculation of dividends and their distribution the Official Receiver or Assignee must retain in his hands sufficient assets to meet the claims of creditors residing in places so distant that they have not had sufficient time to tender their proofs and also for claims not yet determined. He must also make provision for any disputed proofs and claims and for the expenses necessary for the administration of the estate. He is not, however, required to hold any money in his hands to meet the possible claim of a secured creditor who has neither realised nor valued his security, though he may have notice of the date. A creditor who has not proved his debt before the declaration of particular dividend does not thereby lose his right in respect thereof. If there are assets available for distribution of that dividend he is entitled to be paid what he may have failed to receive out of those assets before they are applied to the payment of any future dividend, but he cannot disturb the distribution of any dividend already declared before his debt was proved. The Court is not to interfere in case where the creditor comes in late.

FINAL DIVIDEND

Under the Presidency-Towns Insolvency Act the final dividend is to be declared when the Official Assignee has realised all the property of the insolvent or so much thereof as can, *in his opinion* be realised without needlessly protracting the proceeding in insolvency. Under the Provincial Insolvency Act it is to be declared when the Receiver has realised all the property of the insolvent or so much thereof as can, in the *opinion of the Court,* be realised without needlessly protracting the receivership. The Official Assignee cannot declare a final dividend without the leave of the Court but the Receiver can do so without leave of Court except in Madras. Before declaring final dividend the Assignee or Receiver must give notice to persons whose claims have not *been proved* that, if they do not prove their claims to the satisfaction of the Court within the time limited by the notice, he will proceed to make a final dividend without regard to their claims.

The insolvent is entitled to any surplus remaining after payment in full to his creditors with interest. The insolvent may assign the surplus or dispose of it by will to any person even before it is known whether there will be a surplus. Such an assignment is valid against the Official Assignee or Receiver in a second insolvency. But the insolvent or his assignee cannot interfere in the administration of the estate.

COMMITTEE OF INSPECTION

A Committee of Inspection may be appointed from among the creditors who have proved or persons holding general powers-of-attorney from such creditors for the purpose of superintendence and administration of the insolvent's property by the Official Assignee or Receiver.

PRIORITY OF DEBTS

In the distribution of the property of the insolvent, the following debts must be paid in priority to all other debts, namely:—

1. all debts to the Government or any local authority;
2. the salary or wages of any clerk, servant or labourer in respect of the services rendered to the insolvent during four months before the date of the presentation of petition under the Presidency-Town Insolvency Act not exceeding ₹ 300 for each such clerk, and ₹ 100 for each such servant or labourer; and under the Provincial Insolvency Act, the salary or wages not exceeding ₹ 20 in all, of any clerk, servant or labourer. Under the Presidency-Town Insolvency Act, rent due to a

landlord from the insolvent, not exceeding one month's rent, is also among the preferential debts. It is not so under the Provincial Insolvency Act.

The debts mentioned above rank equally between themselves and are to be paid in full unless the assets are insufficient to meet them in which case they abate in equal proportions between themselves. They must be paid at once, subject only to the retention by the Assignee or Receiver of such sums as may be necessary for the expenses of administration or otherwise.

After the preferential debts have been paid in full, all debts entered in the schedule are to be paid rateably according to the amount of such debts respectively and without any prejudice. If there is any surplus after payment of all debts mentioned above it must be applied in payment of interest from the date of the order of adjudication at the rate of 6 per cent per annum on the debts. Any surplus after all such payments must be paid to the insolvent.

ADMINISTRATION OF PARTNERSHIP PROPERTY

In the insolvency of partners, partnership property is applicable in the first instance to the payment of the partnership debts, and the separate estate of each partner is applicable in the first instance to the payment of his separate debts. If there is a surplus from the separate estates of the partners, it is to be dealt with as part of the partnership property; and if there is a surplus of the partnership property, it is to be dealt with as a part of the respective separate estates in proportion to the interest of each partner in the partnership property.

The above rule as to priorities in the case of joint and separate debts is subject to the following exceptions:—

1. Joint creditors may prove against the separate estates of the partners in competition with the separate creditors if there is joint account and no solvent partner.

2. Where a joint creditor is the petitioning creditor in respect of a joint debt against one partner, he may prove in competition with the separate creditors of that partner, and this is so, even where that partner owes him a separate debt which was sufficient to have supported the petition.

3. Where the separate property of a partner has been fraudulently converted by his co-partners to the use of the partnership, the separate estate may prove against the joint estate in competition with the joint creditors; and where property belonging to the partnership has been fraudulently converted by a partner to his own use, the creditors of the firm are entitled to prove against the separate estate in competition with the separate creditors.

4. Where a member of a firm carries on a distinct and separate trade, and a debt becomes due to the firm, in the ordinary course of business between the member and the firm, the firm may prove against the estate of such member in competition with the separate creditors, he may prove against the joint estate in competition with joint creditors.

As regards proof by a partner against a partner, the general rule is that neither a partner, nor a retired partner, nor the representative of a deceased partner, can prove in the insolvency of the continuing or surviving partner in competition with the joint creditors of the firm of which the partner, or retired or deceased partner was a member. This rule applies only if there is actually proved in the insolvency some debt in respect of which the insolvent and the retired or deceased partner were jointly liable.

PART 12-C
OFFICIAL ASSIGNEE, RECEIVER AND OFFICIAL RECEIVER

OFFICIAL ASSIGNEE : HIS APPOINTMENT AND REMOVAL

The Chief Justice of the High Courts of Judicature at Calcutta, Madras and Bombay, may appoint any person as an Official Assignee of insolvent's estates, and may with the concurrence of a majority of the other Judges of the Court, remove him for any sufficient cause. Every Official Assignee must give such security as may be prescribed by the rules. He can administer oaths for the purpose of affidavits, verify proofs, petitions or other proceedings in insolvency. His duties have relation to the conduct of the insolvent as well as to the administration of his estate. In particular it is his duty:—

(a) to investigate the conduct of the insolvent and to report to the Court upon any application for discharge, stating whether there is reason to believe that the insolvent has committed any act which constitutes an offence under the Act or under Sees. 421 to 424 of the Indian Penal Code in connection with his insolvency or which would justify the Court in refusing, suspending or qualifying an order for his discharge;

(b) to make such other report concerning the conduct of the insolvent as the Court may direct or as may be prescribed; and

(c) to take such part and give such assistance in relation to the prosecution of any fraudulent insolvent as the Court may direct or as may be prescribed.

The Official Assignee may sue and be sued by the name of "the Official Assignee of the property of an insolvent," inserting the name of the insolvent. He may by that name hold property of every description, make contracts, enter into any engagements binding on himself and his successors in office, and do all other acts necessary or expedient to be done in the execution of his office. If an Official Assignee is adjudged an insolvent, he thereby vacates his office as such.

In the administration of the property and its distribution, he must have regard to any resolution that may be passed by the creditors at a meeting. This is to be done subject to the directions of the Court. He may summon meetings of the creditors to ascertain their wishes; and it is his duty to summon meetings at such times as the creditors by resolution at any meeting, or the Court, may direct or whenever requested in writing to do so by one-fourth in value of creditors who have proved their claims.

COMMITTEE OF INSPECTION

The Court may, if it thinks fit, authorise the creditors who have proved their claims to appoint from among themselves a committee of inspection for the purpose of superintending the administration of the insolvent's property by the Official Assignee. The committee may meet as often as necessary but must meet at least once in a month. The Official Assignee shall in the administration and distribution of the property of the insolvent have regard to any direction of the committee. He must also consult the committee, if there is one, before applying to the Court for leave to perform his duties and to exercise his powers in which leave is necessary.

If any Official Assignee does not faithfully perform his duties, or if any complaint is made to the Court by any creditor in regard thereto, the Court must enquire into the matter and take such action thereon as may be deemed expedient. He must account to the Court and pay over all monies and deal with all securities in such manner as may be prescribed by the Rules or as the Court directs.

REMUNERATION OF OFFICIAL ASSIGNEE

The Official Assignee is to be paid such remuneration as may be prescribed by rules, and never more than prescribed. The remuneration is in the nature of a commission or percentage on the amount realised by him after payment to secured creditors, or on the amount distributed in dividends, or partly on one and partly on the other, as may be provided by Rules.

OFFICIAL RECEIVER—HIS APPOINTMENT, REMUNERATION, ETC.

Under Sec. 28 (2) of the Provincial Insolvency Act, the property of the insolvent vests, on the making of an order of adjudication, in the Court or in a Receiver appointed by the Court. A receiver may be appointed at the time of the order of adjudication or at any time afterwards. Whatever may be the date of appointment all property acquired by and devolving on the insolvent after adjudication vests in him as from the date of acquisition or devolution. The Receiver may be required to give such security as the Court may think fit to account for what he shall receive in respect of property. Subject to such conditions as may be prescribed by the Rules, the Court may by general or special order fix the amount to be paid as remuneration for the services of the Receiver out of the assets of the insolvent. The payment is made in the same manner as to the Official Assignee.

The primary duties of the Receiver are to take the necessary steps for the discovery of the insolvent's property, to realise the property and to distribute it amongst the creditors. The Receiver may also make a report on the conduct of the insolvent. Where he fails to submit his accounts at such periods and in such form as the Court directs, or fails to pay the balance due from him thereon as the Court directs, or occasions loss to the property by his wilful default or gross negligence, the Court may direct his property to be attached and sold and may apply the proceeds to make good any balance found to be due from him or any loss so occasioned by him. The Receiver may be removed for just cause.

The State Government may appoint the Official Receiver to be the Receiver under the Provincial Insolvency Act with such local limits as it may prescribe. In the absence of any exceptional reasons such as personal disqualifications affecting the Official Receiver he alone shall be appointed Receiver. The Official Receiver has on the appointment as Receiver all the powers of an ordinary Receiver. The Insolvency Court cannot delegate any of its powers to an ordinary Receiver. But to an Official Receiver the Court if so directed by the High.Court under Sec. 80 may delegate all or any of the following powers namely :—

  (i) to frame schedules and to admit or reject proofs of creditors.

  (ii) to make interim orders in any case of urgency, and

 (iii) to hear and determine any unopposed or *ex parte* application.

Subject to the appeal to the Court, any order made or act done by the Official Receiver in the exercise of the said powers will be deemed to be the order or the act of the Court. The Official Receiver has no power to adjudicate upon a claim by a third person to property alleged to belong to the insolvent and claimed by such person as his own. Such a claim can only be tried by the Court under Sec. 4 of the Act.

Where no Receiver is appointed, the Court has all the rights of, and may exercise all the powers conferred, on a Receiver under the Provincial Insolvency Act.

PART 12-D
DISCHARGE OF INSOLVENT

"The intention of the Legislature is that the debtor, on giving up the whole of the property, shall be a free man again, able to earn his livelihood and having the ordinary inducement to industry." An insolvent who has obtained his discharge is *prima facie* freed from the statutory restriction peculiar to undischarged insolvents. However, an insolvent does not stand automatically discharge's; He must apply to the Court and obtain an 'order of discharge. The Acts provide that a debtor may at any time after the order of adjudication apply to the Court for an order of discharge and the Court is required to appoint a day for the hearing of the application. Such a day, under the Presidency-Towns Insolvency Act, must not be before the public examination of the debtor has been concluded. Under the Provincial Insolvency Act the Court is required to specify the time within which the debtor must apply for his discharge. If the insolvent does not apply within the requisite time the adjudication will be annulled by the Court.

Before the application for discharge is heard on the date fixed for this purpose the Official Assignee or Receiver is required to submit his report as to the insolvent's conduct and affairs. This report is, for the purposes of an application for discharge, *prima facie* evidence of the statements therein contained, but it is not conclusive and the Court can look into evidence on which the findings of the report are based. On the day fixed for the hearing, the Court hears the debtor as well as the creditors, and may also hear the Official Assignee or Receiver. The Court will, after hearing the parties, in its discretion grant or refuse to grant conditionally the discharge. The court has almost full discretion to grant or refuse an order of discharge, except insofar as such discretion is limited by the Act. In the exercise of that discretion the Court may either :—

    (a) grant an absolute order of discharge; or

    (b) refuse an order of discharge; or

    (c) suspend the operation of the order of discharge for a specified period; or

    (d) grant an order of discharge subject to any conditions with respect to any earnings or income which may afterwards become due to the insolvent or with respect to his after-acquired property; or

    (e) exercise the above powers of suspending and attaching conditions to an insolvent's discharge under heads (c) and (d) concurrently, that is it may suspend the operation of the order for a specified period and at the same time attach *conditions* to the order for payment out of the future earnings or property of the insolvent.

    The benefit of freedom from restrictions by means of a discharge is intended for an honest debtor who by reason of misfortune incurs loss. The benefit must not be extended to those traders who fail to keep proper accounts or who deal extravagantly and contract debts recklessly without any reasonable prospect of being able to pay them. The limitations placed on the discretion of the Court are two under the Presidency-Towns Insolvency Act and one under the Provincial Insolvency Act.

LIMITATIONS UNDER PRESIDENCY-TOWNS ACT—ABSOLUTE REFUSAL OF DISCHARGE

Under Sec. 39 of this Act the Court **MUST** *absolutely refuse* to discharge an insolvent in the following cases, namely :—

    1. fraudulent concealment of the insolvent's state of affairs by destruction of documents, keeping false books or making false entries;

    2. fraudulently giving undue preference or discharging or concealing debts or making away with property.

    3. fraudulent concealment of property to prevent its distribution amongst creditors;

    4. fraudulently preventing debts from being available for creditors;

    5. fraudulent transfers containing false statements relating to the consideration for the transfers;

    6. dishonest or fraudulent removal or concealment of property.

REFUSAL OF IMMEDIATE UNCONDITIONAL DISCHARGE

The Court **MUST**, under both the Acts, refuse to grant an absolute discharge to take effect immediately on proof of any of the facts, namely—

    1. that the insolvent's assets are not, under the Presidency-Towns Insolvency Act, of a value equal to 25 paise in the rupee, and under the Provincial Insolvency Act, of a value equal to 50 paise in the rupee, on the amount of his unsecured liabilities. But if he shows to the Court that such fact is not due to his misconduct, but has arisen from circumstances for which he cannot justly be held responsible, the Court may grant an absolute discharge;

    2. that the insolvent has omitted to keep such books of account as are usual and proper in the business carried on by him and as sufficiently disclose his business transactions and financial position within three years immediately preceding his insolvency;

    3. that the insolvent has continued to trade after knowing himself to be insolvent, i.e. unable to pay his debts in the ordinary course;

    4. that the insolvent has contracted any debt without having at that time any reasonable or provable ground for expecting to be able to repay it. It is for the insolvent to show that when he contracted

the debt he had reasonable or provable ground for expecting to be able to pay it. It is the contracting of debts which is an offence, and not the obtaining of goods;

5. that the insolvent has failed to account satisfactorily for any loss of assets or for any deficiency of assets to meet his liabilities;

6. that the insolvent has brought on, or contributed to, his insolvency by rash or hazardous speculation, or by unjustifiable extravagance in living, or by gambling, or by culpable neglect of his business affairs;

7. that the insolvent has, within three months preceding the date of the presentation of the petition, when unable to pay his debts as they became due, given an undue preference to any of his creditors;

8. that the insolvent has on any previous occasion been adjudged an insolvent or made a composition or arrangement with his creditors;

9. that the insolvent has concealed or removed his property or any part thereof, or is guilty of any other fraud or fraudulent breach of trust;

Under the Presidency-Town Insolvency Act, also

10. that the insolvent has put any of his creditors to unnecessary expense by a frivolous or vexatious defence to any suit properly brought against him;

11. that the insolvent has within three months preceding the time of presentation of the petition incurred unjustifiable expense by bringing frivolous or vexatious suit.

FAILURE TO APPLY FOR DISCHARGE

An insolvent must apply for the discharge within the prescribed time. If an insolvent does not appear on the day fixed for hearing of his application for discharge or if an insolvent does not apply to the Court for an order of discharge within such time as may be prescribed or fixed under the Presidency-Towns Insolvency Act, the Court may annul the adjudication or make such other order as it may think fit, and under the Provincial Insolvency Act, the Court must annul the order of adjudiction. The debtor where he was released from custody on adjudication may be re-committed to custody and all process against him at the time of release will recommence as if no release was made. In order to protect the creditors the Court will order that the property shall vest in a certain person. The creditors cannot pursue their money under the ordinary civil law. They must recover their dues by dividends to be paid by the person in whom the Court has vested the assets of the debtor.

EFFECT OF ORDER OF DISCHARGE

An order discharging an insolvent releases him from all debts provable in insolvency except those mentioned below, namely—

(a) any debt due to the Government;

(b) any debt or liability incurred by means of any fraud or fraudulent breach of trust to which he was a party;

(c) any debt or liability in respect of which he has obtained forbearance by any fraud to which he was a party;

(d) any liability under an order for maintenance of his wife made under Sec. 488 of the Code of Criminal Procedure, 1898.

An order of discharge does not affect the rights of a secured creditor against the insolvent. It does not put an end to the insolvency proceedings, and the Court has power to give directions as to the distribution of the assets amongst the creditors. It releases the insolvent from all the debts due from him at the time of adjudication and which were provable in his insolvency. It was held in *New Citizen Bank of India Ltd.* v. *K. B. Burnel & Co.* (1954) 24 Comp. Cas. 233, a decretal amount is provable debt. The petitioner bank had obtained a decree to recover a loan against the security of goods. The goods were sold and part only of the amount of the loan was recovered. The respondent was adjudicated insolvent. The bank ought to have ranked and proved in insolvency of the respondent; but the bank did not do so. After the discharge of the insolvent, the bank applied for the execution of the decree. *Held,* as the bank did not prove in the insolvency, the respondent was freed from personal liability. The powers of the Official Assignee or Receiver to deal with the property which vests in him at the time of the order of discharge do not cease with the passing of the order of discharge. The discharge protects the insolvent and not the assets in the hands of the Official Assignee or Receiver. It does not release a co-debtor, nor does it release the surety. If the surety pays the creditor he cannot sue the debtor after the debtor has obtained his discharge, but he is entitled to prove for the amount paid. An order of discharge does not exempt the insolvent from being proceeded against for any criminal offence, whether connected with insolvency or not. An order of discharge does not operate outside India so as to prevent recovery of the debt there out of the property which has not been taken by the Official Assignee or Receiver.

DUTIES OF INSOLVENT AFTER DISCHARGE UNDER PRESIDENCY TOWNS ACT (SEC. 43)

Under the Presidency-Towns Insolvency Act, a discharged insolvent must, notwithstanding his discharge, give such assistance as the Official Assignee may require in the realisation and distribution of such of his property as is vested in the Official Assignee, and if he fails to do so, he will be guilty of 'Contempt of Court'; and the Court may also, if it thinks fit, revoke his discharge but without prejudice to the validity of any sale, disposition or payment duly made or thing duly done subsequently to the discharge, but before its revocation.

If the order of discharge is revoked the result would be the same as if there had been no discharge and the debtor had continued-insolvent throughout; but sales and other disposition of property made by the insolvent subsequent to the discharge would remain valid. There is no corresponding section in the Provincial Insolvency Act.

REVOCATION OF ORDER OF DISCHARGE UNDER PRESIDENCY TOWNS INSOLVENCY ACT

In the following three cases under the Presidency-Towns Insolvency Act an order of discharge may be revoked, namely :—
1. where the insolvent fails to assist the Official Assignee in the realisation and distribution of his property under Sec. 47 of the Act;
2. where the insolvent fails to file the statement showing particulars of his after-acquired property in cases in which he is bound to do so;
3. where an order of discharge is made conditional upon the insolvent consenting to a judgment being entered up against him in favour of the Official Assignee, and he fails to give his consent within the time prescribed.

SMALL INSOLVENCIES

Summary Administration—When a petition is presented by or against a debtor, if the Court is satisfied by affidavit or otherwise that the property is not likely to exceed in value, under the Presidency-Towns Insolvency Act, ₹ 3,000 or such other less amount as may be prescribed, and under the Provincial Insolvency Act, ₹ 500, the Court may make an order that the insolvent's estate be administered in a summary manner.

Upon such order being made:—

1. **In cases governed by the Provincial Insolvency Act,** the provisions of the Act will apply subject to the following modifications, namely :—

(a) unless the Court otherwise directs, no notice required by this Act shall be published in the Official Gazette;

(b) on the admission of a petition by a debtor, the property of the debtor shall vest in the Court as a Receiver;

(*c*) at the hearing of the petition, the Court shall inquire into the debts and assets of the debtor and determine the same by an order in writing, and it shall not be necessary to frame a schedule of creditors;

(d) the property of the debtor shall be realised with all reasonable despatch and thereafter, when practicable, distributed in a single dividend;

(e) the debtor shall apply for his discharge within six months from the date of adjudication; and

(f) such other modifications as may be prescribed with the view of saving expense and simplifying procedure, provided that the court may at any time direct that the ordinary procedure provided for in this Act shall be followed in regard to the debtor's estate and thereafter the Act shall have effect accordingly.

2. **In cases governed by the Presidency-Towns Insolvency Act**, the provisions of that Act will apply subject to the following modifications, namely—

(a) no appeal shall lie from any order of the Court, except by leave of the Court;

(b) no examination of the insolvent shall be held except on the application of a creditor or the Official Assignee;

(c) the estate shall, where practicable, be distributed in a single dividend;

(d) such other modification as may be prescribed with the view of saving expense and simplifying procedure;

Provided that nothing in this section shall permit the modification of the provisions of this Act relating to the discharge of the insolvent. The Court may at any time, if it thinks fit, revoke an order for the summary administration of an insolvent's estate.

PENALTIES

The Acts prescribe penalties for certain offences committed by an insolvent as under:—

1. An undischarged insolvent obtaining credit to the extent of ₹ 50 or upwards from any person without informing such person that he is an undischarged insolvent shall on conviction by a Magistrate be punished with imprisonment for a term which may extend to six months or with fine, or with both.

2. If a debtor, who is adjudged an insolvent—

(a) fraudulently with intent to conceal the state of his affairs or to defeat the objects of the Acts,—

(i) has destroyed or otherwise wilfully prevented or purposely withheld the production of any books, papers or writing (documents) relating to such of his affairs as are subject to investigation under the Acts, or

(ii) has kept or caused to be kept false books, or

(iii) has made false entries in or withheld entries from or wilfully altered or falsified any document relating to such of his affairs as are subject to investigation under the Acts, or

(b) if he fraudulently with intent to diminish the sum to be divided among his creditors or to give an undue preference to any of the said creditors—

(i) has discharged or concealed any debt due to or from him, or

(ii) has made away with, charged, mortgaged or concealed any part of his property of any kind whatsoever, he shall be punishable on conviction with imprisonment which may extend, under the Presidency-Towns Insolvency Act, to two years, and under the Provincial Insolvency Act, to one year.

3. If the debtor or insolvent wilfully fails to perform the duties imposed upon him by the respective Acts, or to deliver up possession to the Official Assignee or Receiver of any part of his property

which is divisible among his creditors under the Acts, and which is for the time being in his possession or under his control, he shall, under the Presidency-Town Inlovency Act, be, in addition to any other punishment to which he may be subject, guilty of Contempt of Court and may be punished accordingly, and under the Provincial Insolvency Act, be punishable on conviction with imprisonment which may extend to one year.

SUMMARY

Insolvency is a proceeding by which, when a debtor cannot pay his debts or discharge his liabilities or the persons to whom he owes money or has incurred liabilities cannot obtain satisfaction of their claims, the State, in certain circumstances takes posses-sion of his property by an officer appointed for the purpose, and such property is realised and distributed in equal proportions amongst the persons to whom the debtor owes money or has incurred pecuniary liabilities.

The consequences of insolvency are :—
1. the debtor gets protection against legal proceedings by his creditors (Protection Order),
2. his properties vest in the Court or an Official of the Court on Adjudication Order,
3. on the completion of the proceedings the insolvent is discharged and is then free to have fresh start in life,
4. on adjudication he loses his civil rights so that he cannot be appointed a magistrate, or elected a member of any body, nor can he vote.

Generally any person capable of contracting may be adjudged an insolvent; provided that he is a "debtor" and has committed an act of insolvency.

For Acts of insolvency see *ante.*

A person is adjudged an insolvent on the presentation of a petition which may be filed either by the debtor or creditor. A secured creditor cannot present a petition.

The petition may be either dismissed or admitted and in the latter case the debtor may be adjudged an insolvent by an Adjudication Order. The Adjudication Order relates back, under the Presidency-Towns Act, to the date of the first available act of insolvency and under the Provincial Insolvency Act to the date of the presentation of the insolvency petition. This is called the Doctrine of Relation Back.

An adjudication may be annulled by the Court:—
1. where the debtor ought not to have been adjudged insolvent,
2. where debts have been paid in full,
3. where debtor had presented a petition without leave and leave was necessary.

An insolvent may submit a composition in satisfaction of his debts or a scheme of arrangement of his affairs and if it is accepted by a majority in number and 3/4ths in value of the creditors, the Court will sanction it. The debtor will have right to deal with his estate as if he had not been adjudged an insolvent

If default is made in the fulfilment of any term of the scheme, the debtor will be re-adjudged insolvent and the composition or scheme annulled.

When a person is adjudged insolvent his property vests in the Official Assignee or Receiver who will realize it and distribute it among the creditors *pari passu* on proof of the debt.

The insolvent may at any time after the order of adjudication and must where time for application for discharge is fixed, apply to the Court for his discharge. The Court may, after hearing the parties, either—
1. grant an absolute order of discharge, or
2. refuse an order of discharge, or
3. suspend operation of order of discharge, or
4. grant an order of discharge subject to any conditions.

The Acts provide for certain restrictions on the powers of the Court to grant an absolute discharge.

CASES FOR RECAPITULATION

1. *A* buys cotton from *B* and pays the price to *B*. The goods are left with *B* who pledges them with *C*. *C* sells the goods as pawnee and there remains a surplus in his hands after he has paid himself the amount of the loan made by him to *B*. Afterwards *B* is adjudged insolvent and the surplus is claimed both by *A*, the buyer of the goods, and the Official Assignee. *Held*, *A*, the buyer of the goods, and not the Official Assignee, is entitled to receive the surplus. The doctrine of reputed ownership does not apply, as the goods were not in possession, order or disposition of the insolvent [*Greenting* v. *Clark* (1825) 4B & C 316].

2. *W* was adjudicated insolvent. He later earned a salary, out of which he had saved ₹ 8,525 at the date of his death. He had also incurred debts for ₹ 3,525 in the course of his employment. The supplier of goods claims payment of the full amount of ₹ 3,525 out of the Savings, but the Official Assignee denies the supplier's right to recover his debt. *Held,* the debts were payable in full out of ₹ 8,525. The Official Assignee, if the insolvent were alive, could not claim anything more than that which was over after the insolvent had provided for what was reasonably necessary having regard to his occupa-tion and station [*In re Walter* (1929) 1 Ch. 467].

3. An insolvent was granted a conditional discharge. *A*, a judgment creditor, filed a petition for the execution of a decree which he had obtained prior to adjudication, by attachment and sale of a house belonging to the insolvent's wife. *Held, A* is not entitled to sue. The wife is under no obligation to pay. By Sec. 44(2) of the Provincial Insolvency Act, on discharge the debts which the insolvent owed his creditors become unenforceable. Hence the creditors of an insolvent who has been released from all liability, are not entitled to enforce payment by sale of a previous attached house belonging to the insolvent's wife when she herself is under no personal obligation or liability to pay the debt. She does not come within any of the categories mentioned in Sec. 44(3) of the Act (the categories are : Partners, Co-Sureties, Surety). Persons jointly bound, [*Abdul Kuthus* v. *Inayathula,* 1941 Mad. 620].

4. *A* and *B* enter into a partnership for five years on the terms of *A* paying a premium of ₹ 1,000 to *B*, out of which ₹ 500 were to be paid immediately and the rest by instalments. In the second year of the term and before the whole of the premium was paid, *A* was adjudicated insolvent on the petition of *B* and a Receiver of his estate was appointed by Court. *B* claimed from the Receiver in insolvency ₹ 500, the amount unpaid, standing as one of *A*'s creditors, whereas the Receiver in a counter-action claimed from *B* a sum of ₹ 300 as money belonging to the insolvent's assets and unjustly held by *B*. *Held,* the Receiver's claim is tenable and not that of *B*. Where a partner has paid a premium on entering into partnership for a fixed term, and the firm is dissolved before the expiration of that term otherwise than by the death of a partner, he shall be entitled to return part of the premium in proportion to the unexpired term. In this case the term was 5 years and two years have passed so that ₹ 300 for the unexpired period of 3 years in the hands of B will be payable by him to the Receiver in insolvency [Sec. 51 *Akhurst* v. *Jackson* (1818) I Wils. Ch.47].

5. *A* sells a patent to *B* in consideration of *B* paying royalties to *A*. At the same time *B* advances to *A* a sum of ₹ 1,25,000 as a loan. It is agreed that *B* should retain one-half of the royalties as they become payable to *A*, from time to time, towards the satisfaction of the debt, provided that if *A* should become insolvent *B* shall have the right to retain the whole of the royalties in satisfaction of the debt. *A* becomes insolvent before the debt is fully paid. *B* cannot retain the full royalties as per stipulation; but he is entitled to one-half of the royalties as he has charge only on one-half and that transaction is protected under the Insolvency Acts.

6. A creditor takes an assignment from the debtor for the purpose of paying himself and other creditors named in the list in full, believing that they are all the creditors. But the list turns out to be incomplete. The transaction has, however, been entered into honestly by the creditor concerned. The transaction constitutes an act of insolvency and the debtor may be adjudged an insolvent. The assignment is for the benefit of the debtor's creditors generally and amounts to an act of insolvency,

if any creditor whose name did not appear on the list applies within 3 months of the assignment for his insolvency [*Re Phillips* (1900) 2 Q.B. 329].

7. *X*, a Frenchman, residing in France, had a place of business in Bombay. He, acquired property and also incurred debts. Later on, he executed in France a deed transferring the whole of his property for the benefit of his creditors. The Bombay High Court adjudicated him insolvent. The adjudication order is not valid, for an Indian Court can pass order of adjudication on a foreigner only if he commits an act of insolvency in India and within the jurisdiction of the Court.

8. A trader in embarrassed circumstances of his business, which is his only asset, converts it into a one-man company consisting really of himself, the consideration being shares which are practically worthless and an undertaking by the company to pay his debt. The act of converting his business into a company is an act of insolvency. A transfer by a debtor of whole of his property is an act of insolvency, if the necessary consequence of the transfer will be to defeat or delay his creditors. The substitution in place of all the assets by worthless shares in a company which has taken over the debtor's assets and liabilities amounts to an act of insolvency [*In re Simms,* (1930) 2 Ch.22].

9. An insolvent purchased a house and on the same day he mortgaged the property to pay the purchase money. The mortgage is binding on the Official Assignee, assuming that the transactions took place before the commencement of insolvency. The mortgage was made to pay the purchase price of the house, and there is nothing to suggest in the case that the mortgage was without consideration and taken in good faith. There is no question of fraudulent preference or delaying or defeating creditors (Sec. 55 Pres-t. Act).

10. An insolvent had before adjudication assigned chattels to be acquired by him in future as security for debt. After the discharge of the insolvent, the creditor claimed the chattels acquired by him after discharge. *Held,* he had no right to the chattels acquired by the insolvent after his discharge. The rule is that where the order of discharge is passed before the chattels come into existence, all liability of the insolvent under the contract to assign after-acquired property is extinguished and the insolvent is released from such liability [*Collyer* v. *Isaccs* (1881) 19 Ch. D. 343].

11. A has properties, movable and immovable, in Madras, Lahore, London and New York. In case of *A*'s insolvency, movable property in all the four places will vest in the Official Receiver or Official Assignee. But immovable property situated only in Madras will vest, not in all other three cities situated in foreign countries [Sec. 2(1) (d) of Prov. Ins Act.].

12. On Ist October solicitors prepared and P executed a deed of assignment of all his property for the benefit of his creditors. He paid the solicitors ₹ 1,000, of which ₹ 400 was as fees for the work done that day and the balance as fees in advance for work which they actually did in the course of the following week. On 1st December a petition was presented against *P* and on 5th December he was adjudicated insolvent. One act of insolvency proved against him was the execution by him of the aforesaid assignment deed. The Official Assignee asks for a refund of the amount of ₹ 1,000 paid to the solicitors. *Held,* the solicitors were entitled to retain ₹ 400 which was paid as fees for the work done in connection with the execution of the assignment deed, as it was protected transaction. The Official Assignee was entitled to get the balance of ₹ 600 which amount was paid in advance for work done after the execution of the assignment deed. This could not be treated as a protected transaction as the payment related to work done or costs incurred after the act of insolvency had been committed, namely, the execution of the assignment deed which was proved to be an act of insolvency [*Re Pollil* (1893) 1 Q.B. 455].

13. *X* had two loan-accounts with a bank—Account No. 1 secured by title deeds of property and Account No. 2 not so secured. During the pendency of an insolvency petition against *X*, *X* had obtained a loan from *Y,* paid off Account No. 1 and handed over to the bank the released title deeds as security for Account No. 2. The bank had no knowledge of the insolvency petition. The Official Assignee claimed the securities. *Held,* the bank was protected under Sec. 55 which provides that any payment

by the insolvent to any of his creditors or any transfer by the insolvent for valuable consideration is protected provided it was made *bonafide* before the order of adjudication was passed and the third party had no notice of the presentation of the insolvency petition. Hence, the Official Assignee will not get the securities [*Re Seymour* (1937) 1 Ch. 688].

14. An undischarged insolvent obtained a money decree against X for personal services rendered by him after the adjudication and he assigned the decree to K. In a claim by both K and the Official Assignee, X should pay the decretal amount to K, the assignee of the money decree and not to the Official Assignee. Under Presidency-Towns Insolvency Act, the after-acquired property vests in the Official Assignee only when he intervenes on behalf of the insolvent's estate. Since the Official Assignee had not intervened when the insolvent had sued X and obtained the decree, K, the assignee of the decree, is entitled to get payment. Under Provincial Insolvency Act, however, all property acquired by the insolvent after adjudication and before discharge shall forthwith vest in the Official Receiver. Therefore, if the present case were governed by the Provincial Insolvency Act, X would have been required to pay the declared amount to the Official Receiver.

15. A brother and a sister carry on business in partnership in the brother's name. The sister is a dormant partner, and the business is carried on by the brother ostensibly as his own. The Official Assignee wishes to take possession of the sister's share in the partnership stock on the ground that the insolvent brother was the reputed owner of the stock. *Held,* the Official Assignee is not entitled to take possession of the sister's share in the partnership stock. The brother was not the apparent or reputed owner of the partnership stock. He was as much the true owner of the stock as the sister was. Also, he was not in sole possession of the partnership stock. He was in possession jointly with his sister [*Reynolds* v. *Bawley* (1867) L.R.Q.B. 474].

CHAPTER

13

Arbitration

What is Arbitration—Arbitration is a method of settling disputes and differences between two or more parties by referring them to a nominated person or persons who decide the issues after hearing both sides in a quasi-judicial manner. An arbitration is an alternative to a legal action. Reference to *Panch* or the *Panchayat* is one of the natural ways of deciding many a dispute in India.[1] The law relating to arbitration in India is contained in the Arbitration Act, 1940.

Arbitration Agreement—An arbitration agreement is also known as a 'submission' or 'reference'. An arbitration agreement means an agreement in writing to submit a present dispute or a future difference to arbitration, whether an arbitrator is named or not. Though an arbitration agreement must be in writing, a fonnal document signed by the parties is not essential (*Union of India* v. *Rallia Ram,* 1963 S.C. 1685), so long as it is clear from the document that they agreed to the settlement of dispute by arbitration.[2] The agreement may be a clause in a contract, or in bought or sold notes, or in correspondence between parties.

Where there is an arbitration clause in a contract and the contract comes to an end owing to frustration or is avoided on the ground of fraud or misrepresentation, the arbitration clause may continue to be binding.[3] But if the parties were not *ad idem, i.e.,* there was not a contract at all the arbitration clause is not binding.[4] Also, if the arbitration agreement is illegal, and therefore legally non-existent, the arbitration clause which forms part of the contract is also illegal and unenforceable. Any award in such a case shall be invalid.[5]

Where all the persons interested in the matter of dispute were not parties to the arbitration agreement, and when an agreement is not consented to by all, such an agreement is invalid and cannot give arbitrator jurisdiction to decide the dispute, and the award given on the strength of such void reference is not valid and will not bind even the consenting parties.[6]

Advantages of Arbitration—A decision by arbitration has the following advantages as compared to a law suit:—

1. Arbitration is less costly than a suit in a court of law.

---

1. Chambasappa v. Balingayya, 1927 Bom. 565 (F.B.).
2. Government of India v. Jamunadhar, 1960 Pat. 19.
3. State of Bombay v. Adamjee, 1951 Cal. 147.2.
4. Tota Ram v. Birla Jute Mills Co. (1948) 2 Cal. 171; Goolbai v. Jugal Kishore, 195? Bom. 213.
5. Suwalal Jain v. Clive Mills Co., 1960 Cal. ?0.
6. Deep Narain Singh v, Dhaneshwari, 1960 Pat. 201; Chhabba Lal v. Kailu Lal. 1946 P.C. 72, Draupadibai v. Narayan Masanu Sutar, 1985 Kant 258.

2. It is much more expeditious, and saves the parties unnecessary waste of time and irritation arising from delays in court proceedings.
3. There is hardly any publicity, which cannot be avoided in a law suit.
4. It is much more simple as regards procedure.
5. The award is usually final and no appeals lie from it.

The above advantages accrue on the assumption that the arbitrator has acted impartially and has performed his duties with competence.

EFFECT OF ARBITRATION AGREEMENT OR SUBMISSION

When some persons have entered into an agreement to refer all disputes between them, either existing or future, to arbitration, they cannot institute any suit in a Court of Law relating to those matters; otherwise the very purpose of arbitration will be frustrated. It was held in *Abhiman Singh* v. *Ram Singh,* 1958 All. 437, that a party to an arbitration agreement cannot later withdraw from that agreement and reconfer jurisdiction on the court to hear the suit. Therefore, if any of the parties disregards the agreement and institutes a suit, the other party to the agreement may apply to the court for staying the suit. The court will stay the suit or proceeding, provided the following conditions are satisfied (S, 34):

1. The suit or proceeding relates to the same matter as that covered by the arbitration agreement. No stay will be granted if the suit relates to matters outside the scope of the arbitration agreement. If the suit relates partially to matters covered by the submission, the Court may or may not, at its discretion, stay the proceeding or suit. In such a case, it is not right to cut up the litigation into two actions, one to be tried by the Court and the other by arbitration.

2. It must be shown that the applicant for stay was and is still ready and willing to proceed with the arbitration and do everything necessary for the purpose.

3. It must also be shown that there is not sufficient reason why the matter should not be referred in accordance with the arbitration agreement.

4. The party asking for stay must not have filed his written statement by way of defence in the suit, sought to be stayed, or taken any other steps in the proceedings (*e.g.*, an application for extension of time to file the written statement).

5. The arbitration agreement must not have been the result of fraud.

If the Court is satisfied that the matter should be decided by arbitration and that there is a valid arbitration agreement, it will stay the suit or proceeding. The party opposing the stay shall have to convince the Court that there are strong reasons for continuing the suit or proceeding and not granting the stay. The principles as contained in Sec. 34 and as stated above were reiterated by the Supreme Court in *Anderson Wright Ltd.* v. *Morgan & Co.* 1955 S.C. 53, where the Court stays the suit, it does not dismiss it, for in case the award is remitted or set aside the stayed suit can be heard without the necessity of filing it all over again.

Who may Refer to Arbitration—An arbitration agreement is a contract. Therefore, the parties to an arbitration agreement or submission to arbitration must have capacity to enter into a contract. Capacity to make a submission is co-extensive with capacity to contract. He who cannot contract, cannot make a submission,[7] and he who is competent to make a contract, can submit a dispute to arbitration by agreement with the other party to the dispute.

1. The *Karta* or Manager of a joint Hindu family acting *bona fide* for the benefit of the family may make a submission.
2. An agent duly authorised may enter into an arbitration agreement and bind his principal.

---

7. Per Mookerjee J. in Soudamini Ghose v. Gopal C. Ghose, 281. C. 557.

3. An attorney or counsel has implied authority to refer o arbitration a case of his client, unless restricted by express directions to the contrary.

4. A trustee may, subject to the instrument of trust, refer to arbitration any debt, account, or claim relating to the trust.

5. The Official Assignee or Receiver may, by leave of th. Court, refer any dispute to arbitration, and compromise all debts, claims and liabilities.

6. *A* natural guardian of a minor or Committee of a lunatic can submit a dispute to arbitration.[8] A certified guardian can do so only with leave of the Court.[9]

7. A minor or a lunatic cannot refer disputes to arbitration.

8. An insolvent cannot refer to arbitration so as to bind his estate.

9. A partner in a firm cannot submit a dispute to arbitration without special authority of ail the other partners, or unless there is a custom or usage of trade.

10. An executor or administrator cannot refer the question of genuineness or otherwise of a will to arbitration; but an arbitrator can be asked to construe a will.

What may be referred—As a rule, disputes of civil nature and quasi-civil nature or those which can be decided by a civil suit can also be decided by arbitration. The following matters may be submitted to arbitration :

1. Any matter affecting the private rights of the parties, which can be subject-matter of a civil suit may be referred to arbitration; *e.g.*, right to hold the office of a *pujari* in a temple.

2. Matters relating to personal rights between the parties; *e.g.*, a question of marriage or maintenance which is cognizable by a Civil Court.[10]

3. Matters like the terms on which husband and wife will separate can be the subject-matter of a valid reference.

4. Disputes regarding compliment and dignity.

5. The parties may refer to arbitration the question whether judgment has been properly obtained or it is erroneous or void.

6. A time-barred claim may be referred.

7. Both questions of fact and law can be referred.

8. Disputes between an insolvent and his creditors can be referred to arbitration by the Official Assignee or Receiver, even though insolvency proceedings cannot be so referred.

What cannot be referred—The following matters cannot be referred to arbitration, namely:—

1. A suit for divorce or a suit for conjugal right.[11]

2. A dispute arising from and founded on an illegal transaction.

3. Insolvency proceedings, which are matters for the Court only.[12]

4. Questions relating to Public Charities and Charitable Trusts.[13]

5. Lunacy proceedings in the nature of inquisition are a proper subject-matter only for a Court of law.

6. Proceedings relating to the appointment of a guardian to a minor.

7. Testamentary matters relating to the validity of a will or the issue of a probate of a will can be decided only by the Probate Court and not by an arbitrator.

---

8. Har Narayan v. Sajjan Pal, 671.A. 386 (P.C.).

9. Samad Khan v. Ramzan Khan, 1938 Lah. 582.

10. Iseribai v. Pavribai, 1930 Sind 1951.

11. Mst. Kalabati v. Prabh Dayal. 45 I.C. 163; Malka v. Sardar, 1929 Lah. 394.

12. Haji Habib v. Bhikam Chand, 1954 Nag. 306.

13. Mohd. v. Ahmed (1910) 32 All. 593.

8. Execution proceedings.

9. Matters of criminal nature are the concern of the community and must be decided by a Court of law.

ARBITRATION AND VALUATION

These two terms are often confused, as they resemble each other. An arbitration agreement is not the same as a valuation. In fact, there are important differences between the two:

(a) Where parties agree to appoint a valuer and to accept his valuation, the purpose is to *avoid* a dispute, to forestall a disagreement. When the valuer makes his valuation, there is no question of dispute between the parties. On the other hand, an arbitration is always concerned with a dispute between the parties; it presupposes a dispute.

(b) An agreement for valuation cannot be enforced in the same way as a submission. A valuation has to be enforced by legal action; an award is already a legal value.

(c) A valuer merely declares the value of the subject, a commodity or land, and does not give any judgment; but an arbitrator gives his judgment in form of an award, which can be enforced at law.

(d) A valuer may act on his own knowledge and experience; as a rule, an arbitrator must hear evidence.

(e) A valuer is liable for his own negligence, an arbitrator is not.

(f) The Court cannot set aside a valuation; it may set aside an award,

(g) A submission to arbitration requires a stamped paper; an agreement for valuation does not.

Modes of Submission— A submission to arbitration may be made in any one of the following ways:—

1. By an arbitration agreement *without the intervention of the Court.* The Court is, however, approached at the time of filing the award in order that the Court may pass judgment and give a decree in terms of the award.

2. With the intervention of the Court where there is no suit pending.

3. Through the Court where a suit is pending in the Court.

PART 13-B
ARBITRATION WITHOUT INTERVENTION OF A COURT

PROVISIONS IMPLIED IN ARBITRATION AGREEMENT

Sec. 3 provides that unless a different intention is expressed in an arbitration agreement, it shall be deemed to include the provisions set out in the first schedule in so far as they are applicable to the reference. The rules, as provided in the first schedule, are as follows:—

1. Unless otherwise expressly provided, the reference shall be to a sole arbitrator.

2. If the reference is to an even number of arbitrators, the arbitrators shall appoint an umpire not later than one month from the latest date of their respective appointments.

3. The arbitrators shall make their award within four months, after entering on the reference or after having been called upon to act by notice in writing from any party to the arbitration agreement or within such extended time as the Court may allow.

4. If the arbitrators have allowed their time to expire without making an award or have delivered to any party to the arbitration agreement or the umpire a notice in writing stating that they cannot agree, the umpire shall forthwith enter on the reference in lieu of the arbitrators.

5. The umpire shall make his award within two months of entering on the reference or within such extended time as the Court may allow.

6. The parties to the reference and all persons claiming under them shall, subject to the provisions of any law for the time being in force, submit to be examined by the arbitrators or umpires on oath or affirmation in relation to the matters in difference and shall subject as aforesaid, produce before the arbitrators or umpire all books, deeds, papers, accounts, writings and documents within their possession or power respectively, which may be required or called for, and do all other things which, during the proceedings on the reference, the arbitrators or umpire may require.

7. The award shall be final and binding on the parties and persons claiming under them respectively.

8. The costs of the reference and award shall be in the discretion of the arbitrators or umpire who may direct to, and by whom, and in what manner, such costs or any parts thereof shall be paid, and may tax or settle the amount of cost to be so paid or any part thereof and may award costs to be paid as between legal practitioner and client.

THE ARBITRATOR

An arbitrator is the person appointed by mutual consent of the contending parties for the purpose of investigation and settlement of a difference or dispute submitted to him. Where two or any even number of arbitrators are appointed, the matter in dispute must be referred to the decision of another person called the umpire. The arbitrator is an extra-judicial Court of the parties' own choice. They may, therefore, appoint whomsoever they please, however incompetent or unfit, to arbitrate on their dispute. An infant or a lunatic may be appointed an arbitrator or an umpire, so may an unincorporated and fluctuating body be validly appointed arbitrators.[14] The judge in the cause may be the arbitrator, but in such a case the award is not open to appeal.[15] Even a party to the contract may be appointed an arbitrator.[16] The authority of the arbitrator commences from the moment he begins with the business of reference and not from the time of appointment.

DISQUALIFICATIONS

Personal interest of Arbitrator—Where the interest of the arbitrator in the subject-matter is known to the parties *at or before the time of appointment,* no complaint can be made by a party who has agreed to appoint him with full knowledge of such interest. Thus, a reference to one of the parties to the suit would be valid. Where secret interest or bias of the arbitrator is alleged, the Court would consider all the material facts of the situation, the position and character of the arbitrator and the possibility of his being influenced by reason of his concealed interest as well as the nature and quantum of the interest. No hard and fast rule can be laid down for the qualification of an arbitrator; but in cases of arbitration when a person is appointed by the parties to exercise judicial duties there should be *uberrimae fidei* on the part of all concerned in relation to the selection and appointment of the arbitrator;[17] and every disclosure which might in the least affect the minds of those who are proposing to submit their disputes to the arbitrament of any particular individual, as regards his selection and fitness for the post, ought to be made, so that each party may have opportunity of considering whether the reference to arbitration to that particular individual should or should not be made.[18] A fraudulent concealment of interest invalidates the award of the arbitrator. A person is disqualified from acting as an arbitrator in f dispute in relation to which he is a necessary witness.

14. Ruthven Parish v. Elgin Parish (1875) L.R. 2 H.L. Sec. 535.
15. Sayan Rain v. Kalabhi (1899) 23 Bom.752.
16. Secretary of State v. Saran Bros. 8 Luck. 98.
17. Per Maclean, C.J. in Kali v. Rajni (1905) 27 Cal. 141.
18. Ghulam Mohd. v. Gopal Das (1933) Sind 68.

REVOCATION OF AUTHORITY

The authority of an appointed arbitrator or umpire is irrevocable except with the leave of the Court, unless the contrary intention is expressed in the arbitration agreement. The Court has the discretion to grant or refuse leave, but this power is to be exercised in very exceptional circumstances and very cautiously. For example, the Court will grant leave for such revocation if the arbitrator is not acting according to the rules of natural justice, or if he acts in collusion with a party. There is no revocation of authority of an arbitrator by the death of the appointer. Death of a party does not discharge the arbitration agreement which shall be enforceable by or against the legal representatives of the deceased unless it was intimately connected with the individuality of the deceased, *e.g.*, personal office, right to sue in respect of torts not relating to or affecting property of the deceased.

Where, however, one of the parties to an arbitration agreement becomes insolvent and it is provided in such an agreement that any difference arising shall be referred to arbitration AND if the Receiver in insolvency or Official Assignee adopts the agreement, the agreement shall be enforceable by or against him so far as it relates to any such differences. But where a person who has been adjudged an insolvent had, before the commencement of the insolvency proceedings, become a party to an arbitration agreement and any matter to which the agreement applies is required to be determined in connection with, or for the purpose of, the insolvency proceedings, then if the Receiver does not adopt the contract containing a term to refer to arbitration, any other party to the agreement or the Receiver or Assignee, may apply to the Insolvency Court for an order directing that the matter in question shall be referred to arbitration in accordance with the agreement and the Court may, if it is of the opinion that, having regard to all the circumstances of the case, the matter ought to be determined by arbitration, make an order accordingly (Sec. 7).

POWERS OF A PARTY TO APPOINT A NEW OR SOLE ARBITRATOR

Sec. 9 empowers a party to appoint a new or sole arbitrator in certain circumstances, namely where an arbitration agreement provides that a reference shall be to two arbitrators, one to be appointed by each party, unless a different intention is expressed in the agreement—

(a) if either of the appointed arbitrators neglects or refuses to act, or is incapable of acting, or dies, the party who appointed him may appoint a new arbitrator in his place, or

(b) if one party fails to appoint an arbitrator, either originally or by way of substitution as aforesaid, for 15 clear days after the service by the other party of a notice in writing to make the appointment, such other party having appointed his arbitrator before giving the notice, the party who has appointed an arbitrator may appoint that arbitrator to act as sole arbitrator in the reference and his award shall be binding on both parties as if he has been appointed by consent. The Court may, however, set aside any appointment as sole arbitrator and either, on sufficient cause being shown, allow further time to the defaulting party to appoint an arbitrator or pass such orders as it thinks fit.

Where an arbitration agreement provides that a reference shall be to three arbitrators, one to be appointed by each party and the third by the two appointed arbitrators, the agreement shall have effect as if it provided for the appointment of an umpire, and not for the appointment of a third arbitrator, by the two arbitrators appointed by the parties. Where an arbitration agreement provides that a reference shall be to three arbitrators to be appointed otherwise than as mentioned above, the award of the majority shall, unless the arbitration agreement otherwise provides, prevail. Where an arbitration agreement provides for the appointment of more arbitrators than three, the award of the majority or if the arbitrators are equally divided in their decisions the award of the umpire shall, unless the arbitration agreement otherwise provides, prevail (Sec. 10).

POWER OF COURT TO APPOINT ARBITRATOR OR UMPIRE

Sec. 8 lays down the procedure for appointment by Court of arbitrators or umpire as follows:—

"8(1). In any one of the following cases:

(a) Where an arbitration agreement provides that the reference shall be to one or more arbitrators to be appointed by consent of the parties, and all the parties do not, after differences have arisen, concur in the appointment or appointments; or

(b) if any appointed arbitrator or umpire neglects or refuses to act or is incapable of acting, or dies, and arbitration agreement does show that it was intended that the vacancy should not be supplied and the parties or the arbitrator, as the case may be, do not supply the vacancy; or

(c) where the parties or the arbitrators are required to appoint an umpire and do not appoint him; any party may serve the other parties or the arbitrator, as the case may be, with a written notice to concur in the appointment or in supplying the vacancy.

2. If the appointment is not made within 15 clear days after the service of the notice, the Court may, on the application of the party who gave the notice and after giving the other parties an opportunity of being heard, appoint an arbitrator or arbitrators or umpire, as the case may be, who shall have like powers to act in the reference and to make an award as if he or they had been appointed by consent of all parties."

REMOVAL OF ARBITRATOR OR UMPIRE BY COURT

The Court may, on the application of any party to a reference, remove an arbitrator or umpire who fails to use all reasonable despatch in entering on and proceeding with the reference and making an award, or where the arbitrator or umpire has misconducted himself or the proceedings. The arbitrator or umpire so removed shall not be entitled to receive any remuneration for service (Sec. II).

POWERS AND DUTIES OF ARBITRATORS

POWERS

Sec, 13 dealing with arbitrators' powers provides as follows:

"13. The arbitrators or umpire shall, unless a different intention is expressed in the agreement, have power to—

(a) administer oath to the parties and witness appearing;

(b) state a special case for the opinion of the Court on any question of law involved, or state the award, wholly or in part, in the form of a special case of such question for the opinion of the Court;

(c) make the award conditional or in the alternative;

(d) correct in an award any clerical mistake or error arising from an accidental slip or omission;

(e) administer to any party to the arbitration interrogatories as may, in the opinion of the arbitrators or umpire, be necessary."

The arbitrator can also award costs of the reference and award. The costs of reference include costs incurred in connection with the inquiry before the arbitrators and costs incurred by the arbitrators with the consent of the parties, like fees paid to accountants for examining accounts, as well as costs of, and incidental to, any special case submitted by the arbitrators. 'Cost of the award' covers reasonable costs of counsel or solicitor employed by the arbitrators in connection with the drawing up of the award.

DUTIES

1. To act judicially—Arbitration being a method of settling a dispute between the parties, in a quasi-judicial manner, the arbitrator must act judicially and proceed by appointing a time and place for hearing of the reference of which the parties should have due notice. An arbitrator must fix a reasonable time and place for the hearing and grant such adjournments as may be necessary so that justice may be done. Omission to give notice to the parties to appear and to represent their case is legal misconduct and vitiates the award.

2. Duty to observe first principle of justice—The arbitrators have judicial functions to perform and, therefore, they must observe the fundamental rules of justice, which govern legal proceedings although they are not bound by mere rules of practice which Courts have adopted for general convenience. An arbitrator is given the latitude to deviate from technical rules of procedure at-a hearing in Court, provided he does not disregard the substance of justice. For example, an arbitrator must not receive information from one side which is not disclosed to the other, or he must not deliberately refuse a hearing or take evidence from one side behind the back of the other. He should decide according to legal rights of parties and, it is judicial misconduct to intentionally disregard the law applicable.

3. Duty to act fairly to both parties—The arbitrator must act fairly to both parties and in the proceedings throughout the reference, he must be impartial in all respects. Since he occupies a judicial position, an arbitrator should scrupulously avoid any course of action which even remotely casts a suspicion of partiality. He must not do anything for one party which he does not do for the other. Practical application of this rule lies in the proposition that the arbitrator is not to hear one party in the absence of the other, or to take evidence from one side without communicating it to the other party and giving them an opportunity to meet the same.

4. Duty not to act as an advocate or agent of a party—An arbitrator is not to act as an advocate or agent of a party which appoints him. He must conduct himself impartially as a judge and refrain from identifying himself with the party appointing him. It is no part of his duty as an arbitrator to further the interests of the person nominating him.

5. Duty to decide all matters referred—A part of an award cannot be made a rule of Court; therefore, the award should be a final decision on all matters referred to the arbitrator, unless he is empowered to make several awards. An arbitrator who does not give a party an opportunity to put his case before him, and who does not decide all matters in dispute between the parties, acts improperly and his conduct amounts to legal misconduct.

6. Duty to discharge functions personally—As a general rule an arbitrator has no power to delegate to another, not even to a co-arbitrator, the duties which he has been appointed to discharge. Delegation is permissible only in the case of ministerial acts. Judicial acts must be performed by the arbitrator, or if there are more than one arbitrator, then jointly by all the arbitrators. Ministerial acts may, however, be done singly by the arbitrators. What is ministerial act as opposed to judicial act is not always easy to ascertain, but some illustrations may be given for guidance. The ministerial acts are: mere receipt of a written statement from a party, taking assistance in technical matters, seeking legal advice, delegation of the checking of measurements to an engineer, taxation of cost by taxing officer. It is to be noted that although an arbitrator is permitted to take assistance of experts, yet the decision must ultimately be his own judgment in the matter.

7. Not to exceed his authority—An arbitrator must not exceed the terms of reference and an award in excess of jurisdiction and determining matters outside the scope of the arbitration agreement is liable to be set aside. The arbitrator is inflexibly limited to a decision of the particular matters admitted; he cannot take upon himself an authority which the arbitration agreement does not confer.

It was held by the Supreme Court in *Harikrishan Wattal* v. *Vaikunth Nath Pandya* (1973) 2 S.C. 510 that the agreement between the parties is the foundation of the jurisdiction of the arbitrator. Although the power to enlarge time is vested in the Court and not in the arbitrator, the agreement may give him the power to extend the time. Again, like any other contract, the arbitration agreement may be modified by mutual consent of the parties to it. So even after the arbitrator enters on the reference, the parties can agree to enlarge the time, even if no power to enlarge is contained in the original agreement.

The duties of an umpire are identical with the duties of an arbitrator.

THE AWARD

An award is the final judgment or decision in writing by an arbitrator or arbitrators or an umpire on all matters referred to arbitration and as between the parties and the privies, it is entitled to that respect which is due to the judgment of a Court of last resort.[19] The award must, therefore, be as final and certain as the matters in difference could bear. If it is vague and indefinite, it will be bad for uncertainty and if it leaves undecided any cardinal point it is bad for want of finality. An award given under the Arbitration Act on a private reference requires registration under Sec. 17(1) (b) of the Registration Act, if the award affects partition of immovable property exceeding the value of ₹ 100. The matter of making and filing of an award is dealt with in Sec. 14, which provides that where an award has been made by arbitrators or umpire, they shall sign it and give notice in writing of that fact to the parties, as also of the amount of fees and charges payable in respect of the arbitration and award. If requested by a party or one claiming through him, or if so directed by the Court they shall cause the award or a signed copy of it together with any depositions and documents which may have been taken or proved before them to be filed in Court. But before doing this they have the right to be paid the fees and charges due in respect of the arbitration and award, as well as costs and charges for filing the award. If the arbitrators or umpire choose to state a special case under Sec. 13(*b*), the Court after notifying the parties and hearing them, shall pronounce its opinion, which shall be added to and form part of the award.

MODIFICATION AND CORRECTION OF AWARD

The Court may by order modify or correct an award—

(*a*) where it appears mat a part of the award is upon a matter not referred to arbitration and such part can be separated from the other part and does not affect the decision on the matter referred; or

(*b*) when the award is imperfect in form, or contains any obvious error which can be amended without affecting such decision; or

(*c*) where the award contains a clerical mistake or an error arising from an accidental slip or omission (Sec. 15).

The powers of the Court to modify and correct awards extend to awards in all types of arbitrations.

REMITTANCE OF AWARD

Sec. 16 empowers the Court to remit the award or any matter referred to arbitration to the arbitrators or umpire for reconsideration on the following grounds:—

1. where the award has left undetermined any of the matters referred to arbitration and such matter cannot be separated without affecting the determination of the matters referred; or

2. where the award is so indefinite as to be incapable of execution; or

3. where an objection to the legality of the award is apparent upon the face of it.

When remitting the award the Court shall fix the time within which the arbitrator or umpire shall submit his decision to the Court. The time may be extended by the Court if necessary. If the arbitrator or umpire fails to submit the award after reconsideration within the fixed time it shall become void and ineffective. It may be noted in this connection that the award becomes void on the failure by the arbitrator or umpire to reconsider and submit it within the time fixed only if the whole award is remitted for reconsideration. But where instead of the award, "any matter referred to arbitration is remitted," the failure on the part of the arbitrator or umpire will not render the award void. Thus, if only one matter out of several left undecided was remitted, the award remains "in a manner suspended" pending the second reference.

---

19. Bhoja Hari Saha v. Beharilal Bakos (1911) 33 Cal 83; Satish Kumar v. Surinder Kumar, 1970 S.C. 833.

INTERIM AWARD

Sec. 27 of the Act permits arbitrators to make an interim award, if they think fit, subject to a contrary intention expressed in the arbitration agreement. Everything relating to an award will also apply to an interim award.

SETTING ASIDE AN AWARD

Sec. 30 provides for the setting aside of the award and lays down the grounds on which it can be set aside by the Court. The grounds are:—

1. that an arbitrator or umpire has misconducted himself or the proceedings;[20]
2. that an award has been made after the issue of an order by the Court superseding the arbitration or after arbitration proceedings have become invalid by reason of the commencement of legal proceedings upon the whole of the subject-matter of the reference between all the parties to the reference;
3. that an award has been improperly procured or is otherwise invalid.[21]

Failure to perform the essential duties cast upon the arbitrator constitutes misconduct of arbitrator and of the proceedings, and is a good ground for setting aside the award. Failure to receive evidence properly tendered amounts to misconduct.[22] The other ground is "that the award has been improperly procured." A few examples of improper procuring of an award may be given: where an arbitrator has been bribed, or has without the knowledge of a party become personally interested in the subject-matter of the reference. Also where matters, of which the arbitrator ought to have been informed, are fraudulently concealed by a party, or he is guilty of misleading or deceiving the arbitrator. The other ground for setting aside the award is that it "is otherwise invalid." Where a part of the award covered matters which were the subject of a pending suit, it was set aside on this ground.[23] It has been held by the Supreme Court in the *Union of India* v. *Shri Om Prakash,* 1976 S.C. 1745, that the words "or is otherwise invalid" in clause (*c*) of Sec. 30 are wide enough to cover all forms of invalidity including invalidity of the reference. In cases of arbitration without the intervention of the Court, a Court has no jurisdiction after appointing an arbitrator under Sec. 8(2) to proceed further to make an order referring the dispute to the arbitrator. Where such reference has been made and award is passed in pursuance of such reference, such award can be set aside as invalid on the ground that the reference was incompetent.

It may be repeated that the award is final and conclusive, and is not ordinarily liable to be set aside on the ground that either on facts or in law, it is erroneous (*Ved Prakash* v. *Ram Narain Goel,* 1977 Delhi 47). Even a mistake of law cannot vitiate the award unless the mistake is apparent on the face of the award. Again, if the error in the award relates to a matter which is distinct and separate from the rest of the award, and the invalid part is reversible from the valid part, the entire award cannot be set aside. (*The Upper Ganges Valley Electricity Supply Co. Ltd.* v. *The U.P. Electricity Board* (1973) 1S.C. 254). But the Court may make enquiry into the allegation that the arbitrator had misconducted himself and allow the party to produce evidence (*Saif-ud-din* v. *Executive Engineer,* 1977 J & K. 19).

PROCEDURE TO SET ASIDE AWARD

The procedure for setting aside the award is that any party to an arbitration agreement or any person claiming under him should apply to the Court in which the award has been filed, for all matters relating to the arbitration can be heard and decided by that Court, and no other Court. The award is

---

20. See Chhaganlal Asaram v. Jevenlal Gangabison. 1954 Nag. 263; but See A.P. Singh v. Brij Narain, 1954 All. 244.

21. Shah & Co. v. I.S.K. Singh & Co. 1954 Cal. 164.

22. Comm. Bangalore Area v. Armu, Naga & Co. 1954 Mys. 46.

23. Ram Pratap v. Durga Prasad, 1925 P.C. 239 (Cal.).

24. 3 I.A.209 at 200.

filed in any Court, except a Small Causes Court, having jurisdiction to decide the question forming the subject-matter of the reference if the same had been subject-matter of a suit. The first application, therefore, fixes the venue for all future proceedings. The application for setting aside the award may be resisted on the following grounds:

1. **Acquiescence in Irregularities**—The principle underlying this has been enunciated by the Privy Council in *Chaudhri Murtaza Hussain* v. *Mst. Bibi Bechunissa.*[24] The applicant, having a clear knowledge of the circumstances on which he might have founded an objection to the arbitrators' proceedings to make their award, did submit to the arbitration going on; that he allowed the arbitrators to deal with the case as it stood before them........; and it is too late for him, after the award has been made and filed, to insist on this objection to the filing of the award." So where a party having full chance to object, does not do so at the right moment he is said to have waived his right to object and to have acquiesced to the irregularities and thus not allowed to move for setting aside the award.

2. **Taking benefit under the Award and performance of the Award**—Motion for setting aside an award may be met by showing that the party moving has accepted benefit under the award with full knowledge of all relevant circumstances. Where the parties to an award in a boundary asked the Settlement Officer to lay pillars alone the lines settled by the arbitrators, it was held that the parties had accepted the award.[25] A party having accepted costs given to him by an award was not permitted to have the award set aside by reason of his acquiescence.[26]

3. **That the irregularity complained of has resulted in benefit to party moving to set aside the Award**—The law relating to the point has been stated by Mukerjee, J. in *Narsingh Narayan Singh* v. *Ajodhya Prasad Singh,*[27] thus "if the arbitrator has exceeded his authority, he has done so for the benefit of the defendants and they are not entitled to assail the award which is really in their favour .... It is an elementary principle that only the party prejudiced by the act of the arbitrator is entitled to object to the award by reason of it; the party in whose favour erroneous action of the arbitrator operates cannot be heard to impeach the validity of the award on this ground."

4. **Limitation**—That the application to set aside the award has not been filed within 30 days from the date of service of the notice of the filing of the award.

JUDGMENT ON AWARD

Where the Court sees no cause to remit the award or any of the matters referred to arbitration fit for reconsideration or to set aside the award, it shall, after the time for making application to set aside the award has expired, or such application having been made, after refusing it proceed to announce judgment according to the award, and give a decree in terms of the award, which will be final and no appeal shall lie from such decree (Sec. 17). The judgment and decree on award import the final stage, but the Arbitration Act, 1940, now provides that the Court may pass **interim** orders, if a party to the award has taken or is about to take steps to defeat, delay or obstruct the execution of any decree that may be passed upon the award, or where such order becomes necessary for speedy execution of the award (Sec. 18).

Court may Supersede Arbitration—Sec. 19 empowers the Court to make an order superseding arbitration in two cases; (*i*) when an award has become void because the arbitrators did not reconsider it within the time fixed by the Court after the award was remitted to them for reconsideration, or (*ii*) when the award is set aside under Sec. 30 of the Act.

Enforcement of Foreign Awards—Under the Arbitration Protocol and Convention Act of 1937, (Sec. 2): "a foreign award means an award on differences relating to matters considered as commercial under the law in force in India made after 28th July, 1924:—

---

25. Ramrunjan v. Ram Prasad, 13 C.L.R. 26.

26. Kennard v. Harris (1824) 2 B. & C. 801.

27. (1912) I.C. 118 :16 C.W.N. 256.

(a) in pursuance of an agreement for arbitration, and

(b) between parties of whom one is subject to the jurisdiction of some one of such powers as the Central Government may declare to be parties to the Convention, and

(c) in one of such territories as the Central Government being satisfied that reciprocal provisions have been made may declare to be the territory to which the Convention applies."

Section 4 states that a foreign award is enforceable in India as if it were an award on a reference made in India.

ARBITRATION WITH INTERVENTION OF COURT WHERE NO SUIT IS PENDING

Sec. 20 provides for arbitration with the intervention of a Court where there is no suit pending. The Section reads:

"20. (1) Where any persons have entered into an arbitration agreement before the institution of any suit with respect to the subject-matter of the agreement or any part of it, and where a difference has arisen to which agreement applies, they or any of them instead of proceeding under Chapter II" [arbitration without intervention of a Court, which has been discussed in preceding pages] "may apply to a Court having jurisdiction in the matter to which the agreement relates, that the agreement be filed in Court.

2. The application shall be in writing and shall be numbered and registered as a suit between one or more of the parties interested or claiming to be interested as plaintiffs and the remainder as defendant or defendants.

3. On such application being made, the Court shall direct notice thereof to be given to all parties to the agreement other than the applicant, requiring them to show cause within the time specified in the notice why the agreement should not be filed.

4. Where no sufficient cause is shown the Court shall order the agreement to be filed, and shall make an order of reference to the arbitrator appointed by the parties, whether in the agreement or otherwise, or where the parties cannot agree upon an arbitrator, to an arbitrator appointed by the Court.

5. Therefore the arbitration shall proceed in accordance with, and shall be governed by the other provisions of this Act [already discussed] so far as they can be made applicable."

ARBITRATION IN SUITS

Secs. 21 to 25 of the Act provide for decision by arbitration of any suit which is pending in a Civil Court. The parties to a suit may by mutual consent apply in writing at any time before judgment to the Court for an order of reference, whereupon the Court shall appoint an arbitrator in such manner as may be agreed upon between the parties. Then the Court shall, by order, refer to the arbitrator the matter in difference for determination specifying the time for making the award. After referring the matter to arbitration the Court shall not deal with such matter, save as allowed by the Arbitration Act. The Act makes express provision by Sec. 24 for reference to arbitration by some of the parties to the suit on the condition only that the matter in difference between the parties applying for reference can be separated from the rest of the subject-matter of the suit. On such a reference the suit shall continue so far as it relates to the parties who have not joined in the said application and to matters not contained in the said reference.

STATUTORY ARBITRATION

Some statutes provide for arbitration in disputes arising out of matters covered by them. For example, the Co-operative Societies Act lays down that certain disputes between a member and a co-operative society must be settled by arbitration and not by suit. The Industrial Disputes Act, 1947, also permits the parties to an industrial dispute to refer it to arbitration. This type of arbitration is known as

Statutory Arbitration. The statute concerned generally provides for the procedure according to which the arbitration will be conducted.

APPEALS

Sec. 39, by specifying the appealable orders, has simplified the matter of appeal. The Section reads:—

"39(1) An appeal shall lie from the following orders passed under this Act (AND FROM NO OTHERS) to the Court authorised by law to hear appeals from original decrees of the Court passing the order:—

An order—

(i)   superseding an arbitration;
(ii) on an award stated in the form of a special case;
(iii) modifying and correcting an award;
(iv) filing or refusing to file an arbitration agreement;
(v)   staying or refusing to stay proceedings where there is arbitration agreement;
(vi) staying or refusing to set aside an award;

provided that the provisions of this Section shall not apply to any order passed by a Small Causes Court."

2. No second appeal shall lie from an order passed in appeal under this Section, but nothing in this Section shall affect or take away any right to appeal to the Supreme Court."

CASES FOR RECAPITULATION

1. A party to an arbitration agreement challenges the award alleging that a question of law was wrongly referred to the arbitrator and further that the arbitrator wrongly decided the same thereby vitiating the award. *Held,* a mistake of law in making the reference to arbitration may be invoked to obtain the intervention of the Court, if it is a mistake with regard to a party's right. A mistake with regard to the terms of a general statute, *e.g.,* Hindu Women's Right to Property Act cannot be invoked to obtain intervention of the Court (*Kalepalli Venkata Rao* v. *Kalepalli Padmavalli Tayaramma,* 1944 Mad. 324). Thus if a question of general law was wrongly referred to the arbitrator, the award cannot be set aside; but if it was a mistake of law with regard to party's private right, it may be made a ground for setting aside the award.

An arbitrator's award will only be set aside on the ground of error of law if the mistake appears on the face of the award. If the arbitrator has acted within his authority the award will be upheld. An arbitrator is a judge of both the question of fact and law, and the parties cannot be allowed to show that his decision was wrong on merits. So long as the arbitrator is within the scope of his authority, his decision will be accepted as valid and binding (*GobardhanDas* v. *Lachhmi Ram,* 1954 S.C. 689). Courts of law cannot sit in appeal on an award either with regard to error of law or error on question of fact.

2. The heirs referred to arbitration a dispute regarding the distribution of property of the deceased. One of the heirs, Mr. *M* refused to join in the reference. Despite this, the awards allotted him a share of the property. A decree in terms of the award was passed with *M*'s consent. As *M* was not a party to the arbitration agreement, he was not bound by the award. *A* cannot get the benefit of the decree based on the award, if passed. The decree cannot be made effective in his favour.

It is important to note that the agreement itself was invalid and so was the award. For where all the persons interested in the dispute were not party to arbitration agreement, and when an agreement was not assented to by all, such an agreement would be invalid and would not give the arbitrator any jurisdiction to decide the dispute. Any award given on the strength of such void reference is not valid. The award passed on such invalid reference does not bind even the consenting parties. If follows that a decree cannot be given on such an invalid award (*Deep Narain Singh* v. *Dhaneshwari,* 1960 Pat. 201).

Carriers and Carriage of Goods

PART 14-A
CONTRACT OF CARRIAGE

The law relating to carriage forms part of the law of bailment and falls under the head bailment for reward. A bailment, we know, is the delivery of goods by one person to another for some purpose, upon the contract that they shall, when the purpose is accomplished, be returned or otherwise disposed of according to the direction of the person delivering them.

When the goods are handed over to a bailee for conveyance from one place to another for a remuneration, there is a Contract of Carriage and the person who undertakes to convey the goods is called the *carrier.* The person who delivers the goods is the *consignor* or *shipper.* The person to whom the goods are addressed and to whom the carrier should deliver the consignment is called the *consignee.*

CLASSIFICATION OF CARRIERS

A carrier of goods is either a common carrier or private carrier. Some carriers cany both goods and passengers, and some carry only goods, and others only passengers.

Private Carriers—A private carrier is one who *casually* or *occasionally* carries goods for others on special terms mutually agreed upon between him and the shipper, and who reserves to himself the right to reject the goods offered to him for carriage, which a common carrier cannot do. He has the responsibility of a bailee, and negligence must be proved to make him liable for loss or damage, although loss or non-delivery is *prima facie* evidence of negligence and must be rebutted. Where a private carrier carries goods or passengers under individual contracts, he is called *contract carrier.* There is a common practice in Delhi for bus owners to engage themselves on contract basis to carry students to and from schools. Where passengers are carried, either gratuitously or for payment, the carrier is liable for both his own negligence and that of his servants.

Common Carriers—*In English law,* a common carrier is one who holds himself out as being ready to carry for reward either any person, or the goods of any person, no matter who that person may be, either by land, air or water. If he reserves the right to choose as among persons or goods, he is not a common carrier.

In Indian law, the term common carrier is used in a restricted sense. The Common Carrier Act, 1865, defines a common carrier as any individual, firm, or company (other than the Government) who transports goods, as a business, for money over land or inland waterways, without discrimination between different consignors. According to this definition, the characteristics of a common carrier in India are as follows:

1. The common carrier may be an individual, a firm or company. But the Government is not included in the category. Thus, the post office is not a common carrier, though it may carry goods.

2. Only carriers of goods are common carriers. Carriers of passengers are not common carriers.
3. To be a common carrier, he may carry goods as a business for money. One who carries goods free or only occasionally and carrying of goods is not his regular business is not a common carrier.
4. A common carrier is one who is bound to carry goods of any person without discrimination, provided there is room in his vehicle, the goods are of the type he carries and meant for his accustomed destination. If he reserves the right to refuse to carry goods of some person or persons, he is not a common carrier.
5. The term common carrier is applied to the carriage of goods by land and inland waterways. It does not apply to carriage by sea or air.

Duties of a Common Carrier— The Common Carriers Act, 1865 lays down the duties of a common carrier, although rules of English law also apply to matters not covered by the Act. The duties of a common carrier are listed below.

1. To receive and carry goods from all corners, indiscriminately—that is the force of the term common;
2. To carry the goods safely;
3. To carry by his customary route or by a reasonable route, and not to deviate from it unnecessarily;
4. To obey instructions of the consignor, e.g., where the consignor is an unpaid seller and asks the carrier to hold the goods for him, the carrier must do so;
5. To deliver the goods within the agreed time or, if no time has been agreed upon, within a reasonable time, and at the stipulated place.

The common carrier may, however, refuse to carry goods under the following circumstances:
(a) If he has insufficient or no room in his vehicle.
(b) If the goods are not of the type that he professes to carry.
(c) If the goods are not meant to be carried on his customary route, or to his accustomed destination.
(d) If the goods are dangerous to carry or they would otherwise expose him to extraordinary risk;
(e) If the goods are not offered at a reasonable time or a reasonable manner.
(f) If the consignor is not prepared to pay a reasonable amount in advance.

If a common carrier, without any of the reasons mentioned above, refuses to carry the goods of a person, he can be sued for damages. If the consignee refuses to take delivery of the goods, when tendered, the carrier may deal with the goods as he may think reasonable and prudent under the circumstances. He may even recover reasonable expenses incurred by him as a result of the consignee's refusal to take delivery.

Liabilities of a Common Carrier—Under Common Law, a common carrier is an *insurer* of goods handed over to him. But there are some exceptions to this general rule:

1. He is not liable for any loss or damage arising from an act of God, which means an unforeseen accident occasioned by the elementary forces of nature beyond the control of man. If the vehicle is struck by lightning, it is an act of God, but ordinary rain does not rank as such. The carrier can and should provide a rain-proof cover.
2. He is not liable for any injury caused by the "enemies of the State," *i.e.*, foreign enemies with whom India is at war, but not rioters or strikers.
3. He is not liable for loss arising from *inherent vice* or natural deterioration of the **goods.** Examples of this are: fright in nervous animals, deterioration of fruit, evaporation of liquids and spontaneous combustion.
4. He is not liable for loss of goods *through neglect* on the part of the consignor, e.g., defective packing. Glassware or chinaware needs special care, and if the consignor fails to disclose the fact, the carrier is not liable.

Dangerous Goods—Where dangerous goods, such as explosives, acids or poisons, are consigned, it is the duty of the consignor to warn the carrier; otherwise he will be answerable for the probable consequences of his omission.

In *Bamfield* v. *Goole and Sheffield Transport Co. Ltd* (1922) 2 K.B. 742, the consignor delivered "ferro-silicon" in casks, to a common carrier, without informing the carrier that the casks contained the poisonous article. During transit the ferro-silicon gave off poison gases which caused the death of the carrier. *Held,* the consignor was liable in damages for causing the death of the carrier.

In India the liabilities of common carriers of goods are laid down in the Common Carriers Act of 1865. This Act divides goods into two categories: Scheduled and Non-Scheduled. Scheduled goods are goods of great value, such as gold and silver coins, bullion, ornaments, precious stones and pearls, time-pieces of all descriptions, trinkets, bills and hundies, currency and bank notes, stamps and stamp papers, maps, prints and works of art, writings, title-deeds, gold or silver plate or plated articles, glass, china, silk, shawls, lace, cloth and tissue embroidered with precious metals or of which such metals form part, articles of ivory, ebony or sandal wood and musical and scientific instruments.

For scheduled articles exceeding ₹ 100 in value, the carrier is liable for loss or damage only—

(i) if the value and the description of the goods are disclosed by the consignor to the carrier; or

(ii) if the loss or damage is due to a criminal act of the carrier, his agent or servant.

The carrier can charge extra for carrying scheduled articles, but he cannot limit his statutory liability by any special agreement.

As regards non-scheduled articles, a common carrier can limit his liability by special agreement with the consignor. But even in this case he will be liable for loss or damage caused by negligence or criminal acts done by himself, his agents or servants.

PART14-B
RAILWAYS AS CARRIERS

The duties and liabilities of the Railway Administration in India are laid down in the Indian Railways Act, 1890.

Duties—By virtue of Sec. 42A, the railway administration is bound (like a common carrier discussed above) to carry goods of every person who is ready and willing to pay the freight and observes the regulations regarding packing, etc. Similarly, railways are bound to carry every passenger who pays the necessary fare. Hence, the railways, as regards duties, are common carriers.

Liabilities—As regards liabilities, railways were before 1961, ordinary bailees. But since the amendment of the Act in 1961, the railways have become common carriers as regards liabilities, too'. Consequently, railways in India, both as regards duties and liabilities, are now common carriers.

While delivering goods or animals to the railway for carriage, the consignor is required to execute a forwarding note in the prescribed form indicating the nature of the goods and condition of packing and whether the goods are to be carried at railway risk or owner's risk.

Sec. 73 provides that the railways shall be liable for loss, destruction or non-delivery in transit of animals or goods entrusted to it for carriage arising from any cause except the following:—

(a) an act of God;

(b) act of war;

(c) act of public enemies;

(d) arrest, restraint or seizure under legal process;

(e) orders or restrictions imposed by the Central or a State Government;

(f) act or omission or negligence of the consignor or the agent or servant of either;

(g) natural deterioration or wastage due to inherent defect, quality or vice of the goods;

(h) latent defects;

(i) fire, explosion, or any unforeseen risk.

Even where such loss, destruction, damage, deterioration or non-delivery has arisen from any one or more of the aforesaid causes, the railway administration shall be **liable unless the administration further proves that it has used reasonable foresight and care in the carriage of the animals or goods.**

Note, this section makes the Indian Railways as common carriers.

Railway risk or owner's risk rates—Animals or goods may be carried by the railway either at railway risk rate (ordinary rate) or owner's risk rate (reduced rate). The animals and goods will be deemed to be carried at owner's risk rate unless the consignor elects in writing to pay the railway risk (*i.e.*, higher) rate, in which case he will be given a certificate to that effect.

Where the consignment is carried at owner's risk rate the railway administration will be liable only if the loss, destruction, damage, deterioration or non-delivery was due to the negligence or misconduct on the part of the railway administration or any of its servants.

The difference between the two rates is only in relation to burden of proof. Thus, where animals or goods are carried at railway risk rate, the railway administration is responsible for any loss, etc., unless it positively proves that it has taken due care and that it or any of its servants has not been negligent or guilty of misconduct. Where, on the other hand, animals or goods are carried at owner's risk rate, the onus is on the consignor to prove that the loss, etc., was due to the negligence or misconduct of the railway administration or its servants (Sec. 74).

In *Juggal Kishore* v. *Union of India,* 1965 Pat. 196, goods were consigned at owner's risk rate. Part of the consignment was lost in a running train theft. Though the train was running in the night no proper watch and ward were provided, and the guard did not check the wagon at the scheduled stoppages nor did he check the seal at the real checking stations. *Held,* the railway administration was liable on the grounds of negligence and misconduct on the part of its servants.

Passenger's Personal Luggage—The railway is not responsible for a passenger's personal luggage, unless a railway servant has booked it and given a receipt therefor. Where the luggage is carried by the passenger in his own compartment, the railway will be liable only if the loss etc. was due to the negligence or misconduct on the part of the railway administration or any of its servants (Sec. 75).

Delay or detention in transit—A railway administration shall be responsible for loss etc. of animals or goods if the owner proves that such loss, destruction, damage or deterioration was caused by delay or detention in transit. It can, however, escape liability by proving that the delay or detention arose without negligence or misconduct on its part or on the part of its servants (Sec. 76).

Deviation of route—Sec. 76A provides that where, due to a cause beyond the control of a railway administration or due to congestion in the yard or other operational reasons, animals or goods are carried over a route other than the route by which they are booked or the usual or customary route, the railway administration shall not be deemed to have committed a breach of contract of carriage.

Wrong delivery—Where a railway administration delivers the animals or goods in good faith to a person who produces the original railway receipt, it shall not be responsible on the ground that such person is not legally entitled thereto or the indorse-ment on the railway receipt is forged or otherwise defective. But if the animals or goods are delivered to a wrong person without the production of a railway receipt the railway administration shall be responsible to the rightful person.

In *Union of India* v. *Ramji Lal,* 1965 All. 184, R sent 10 harmoniums from Aligrah to Howrah for A. The railway receipt was consigned to 'Self' but bore an endorsement by R the consignor, in favour of A. The harmoniums were delivered at Howrah to one J without any endorsement by A in favour of J or any one else. J wrote on the back of the R/R the following words: 'A & Co. J proprietor.' A denied taking delivery of the consignment either himself or through an agent. R sued for damages. *Held,* he was entitled to recover the loss, as the railway had not acted in good faith.

Exoneration from responsibility—By virtue of Sec. 78, a railway administration is not responsible for any indirect or consequential damage, or for loss of particular market. It shall not be responsible for any loss, destruction, damage, deterioration or non-delivery of—

(a) any goods in respect of which false description was given;

(b) animals or goods if a fraud has been perpetrated by the consignor or the consigne or an agent of either;

(c) animals or goods proved by the railway administration to have been caused by or to have arisen from—

(i) improper loading and unloading by the consignor or the consignee or an agent of either, or

(ii) riot, civil commotion, strike, lock-out, stoppage or restraint of labour from whatever cause, whether partial or general.

Railways are liable to pay damages for injury to passengers or death when it is due to the negligence of the railway servants. The liability for the death of a passenger would not exceed ₹ one lakh per passenger. There is no liability if the passenger is guilty of contributory negligence.

Sec.76 C says that in the case of goods to be delivered by a railway administration at a siding not belonging to the administration, the railway administration shall-not be responsible for loss, destruction, damage, deterioration or non-delivery of such goods, from whatever cause arising after the wagon containing the goods has been placed at the point of interchange of wagons between the railway administration and the owner of the siding has been informed in writing that the wagon has been so placed.

Carriage over two more railway systems—Sec. 76 D provides that where any animals or goods delivered to a railway administration to be carried by railway have been booked through over the railways of two or more railway administrations or over one or more railway administration, the person tendering the animals or goods to the railway administration shall be deemed to have contracted with each one of the railway administrations or the owners of the transport systems concerned, as the case may be, and each one of the railway administrations or the transport systems shall be liable in the same manner as provided for the single railway administration.

Sec. 76 E provides that in the case of through booking of consignments over an Indian Railway and a Foreign Railway, the responsibility of the Indian Railway as a common carrier would extend only over that portion of the carriage which is over the Indian Railway.

Sec. 76 F lays down that notwithstanding anything contained in Sec. 74—(a) where the whole of a consignment of goods, or the whole of any package forming part of a consignment, carried at owner's risk is not delivered to the consignee and such non-delivery is not proved by the railway administration to have been due to fire or to any accident to the train, or (b) where in respect of any consignment of goods or of any package which had been so covered or protected that the covering or protection was not readily removable by hand, it is pointed to the railway administration on or before delivery that any part of such consignment or package had been pilfered in transit, the railway administration shall be bound to disclose to the consignor how the consignment or the package was dealt with throughout die time it was in its possession or control; but if negligence or misconduct on the part of the railway administration or any of its servants cannot be fairly inferred from such disclosure the burden of providing such negligence or misconduct shall be on the consignor.

Sec. 77 says that the railway administration shall be responsible as a bailee under Secs. 151, 152 and 161 of the Indian Contract Act for the loss, destruction, damage, deterioration or non-delivery of goods carried by railway within a period of 30 days after termination of transit; provided that where the goods are carried at owner's risk rate, the railway administraton shall not be responsible except on proof of negligence or misconduct on the part of the railway administration or of any of its servants. But after the expiry of the 30 days, the railway administration is not responsible in any case. Transit terminates on the expiry of the free time allowed (after the arrival of the consignment) for its unloading from the railway wagon without payment of demurrage.

Sec. 77A lays down the amounts beyond which the railways will not be liable for loss or damage to animals as follows:

Elephants—₹ 1,500 per head; horses—₹ 750 per head; mules, horned cattle, and camels—₹ 200 per head; and in all other cases, including birds—₹ 30 per head. The railway may, however, accept a higher liability if the consignor pays a higher charge and declares the higher value in the forwarding note. The railway is not at all responsible if the loss or damage arises from the restiveness or fright of the animal.

By virtue of Sec. 77 B parcels or packages containing articles of special value will be carried at railway risk rate without payment of any additional charge when the value of such articles does not exceed ₹ 500.

Sec. 77C provides that when any goods tendered to a railway administration to be carried by railway (*a*) are in defective condition as a consequence of which they are liable to damage, deterioration, leakage or wastage, or (*b*) are either defectively packed or packed in a manner not in accordance with the general or special order, if any, issued under Sec. 14, and the defect has been recorded by the sender or his agent in the forwarding note, then the railway administration shall not be responsible for damage, deterioration, leakage or wastage except on proof of negligence or misconduct of the railway administration or any of its servants.

PART 14-C
CARRIAGE OF GOODS BY SEA

Contract of Affreightment—The common law took substantially the same view of sea carriage as of land carriage, that is to say, the shipowner has to carry the goods safely, under the contract of carriage. The contract of carriage of goods by sea is called a contract of Affreightment. It maybe defined as a contract by which the shipowner undertakes to carry the goods of another (called the shipper) by water, or to furnish a ship for the purpose of so carrying the goods to the destination in return for a price called "freight." A contract of affreightment may take either of the two forms, namely—

(i) A contract by charter-party, or

(ii) A contract for the carriage of goods in a General Ship when the contract is evidenced by a Bill of Lading.

CHARTER-PARTY

When goods are consigned in large quantities it is usual for the consignor to hire or charter the whole of a vessel or a substantial part of it, and the document by which he does this is known as a Charter-Party. The term is also used to denote the contract by which an agreement is made. A charter-party may be defined as a contract in writing under which the shipowner agrees to place an entire ship, or a part of it, at the disposal of a shipper for the conveyance of goods on a particular voyage to a specified place or places, or for a specified time, in consideration of sum of money called the freight. The charter-party may be under seal but must be stamped.

A charter-party may operate as a demise or lease of the ship. This form amounts to a letting of the ship by the shipowner so as to put the vessel and its crew out of his control. The charterer becomes temporary owner of the ship and is resopnsible to third parties for the acts of the master and crew, *e.g.*, in tort for damage done to other ships by negligent navigation, or in contract on bills of exchange signed by the master. The charterer's responsibility for the act of the master and the crew arises from the fact that for all intents and purposes the master and crew become his servants during the time the charter lasts. This kind of charter-party does not really involve a contract of carriage, but rather a hiring of the means of carriage.

If, however, the charterer only requires the use of the full carrying capacity of the ship, as is usually the case these days, he can obtain this in another way without taking possession of the ship and control of the master and crew, and without incurring the above-mentioned liabilities. Thus, under this form the ship remains in the possession and under the control of the shipowner, and charterer merely acquires the right to put his goods on the vessel, and to have them carried to the agreed destination. The charterer can fill the entire ship with his own goods, or he may use the ship as a *general ship,* carrying goods of third parties under bills of lading. A charter-party is either a *Time* charter-party, where it is entered into for a definite period of time, or a *Voyage* charter-party, where it is only for a definite voyage.

When the goods are delivered on board the ship, a bill of lading signed by the owner or master of the ship is given to the shipper as an acknowledgement of the receipt of the goods. It is to be noted that the bill of lading issued in the case of charter-party is only a receipt of the goods, and is quite distinct from the bill of lading issued in the case of a general ship. The contract of affreightment is made up of the two documents—the charter-party containing the terms and conditions on which the goods are to be carried, and the bill of lading acknowledging the receipt of goods on board ship.

IMPLIED WARRANTIES

In all contracts of carriage by sea the following terms are implied:—
1. **Seaworthiness of the ship**—already discussed in connection with Marine Insurance.
2. The ship shall be ready to commence the voyage and shall cany out the same with all reasonable dispatch or diligence.
3. The ship shall not deviate—dealt with in Marine Insurance.
4. The shipper shall not ship dangerous goods.

FORM OF CHARTER-PARTY

The forms of charter-parties vary considerably according to the customs of the trades, but the main stipulations are now almost uniform in all charter-parties by the custom of the shipping trade. The following is the most commonly used form:—

"It is this day mutually agreed between *Messrs. King & Co.,* owners of the good ship called *SS. Peerless,* A 1 and newly coppered of etc. of the burden of 2,000 tons registered measurement or thereabouts whereby *John Blanden* is Master now at *Port Said* and *Messrs. Blank & Co. of London* merchants, that the said ship being tight, staunch and strong, and in every way fitted for the voyage, shall with all convenient speed proceed *to Liverpool* and there load in the usual and customary manner a full and 'complete cargo of lawful merchandise say *500 tons in weight* and therewith proceed to *Bombay* as ordered before sailing, or so near thereunto as she may safely get and there deliver the same in the usual manner agreeably to bills of lading; after which she shall load there, or if required proceed to one other safe port *in India* and there load always afloat in the usual and customary manner from the agents of the said charterers a full and complete cargo *of jute* or other lawful merchandise, not exceeding what she car reasonably stow and carry over and above her tackle, apparel, provisions and furniture, the cargoes being brought to and taken from alongside the vessel at the charterer's risk and expense, which the said merchants bind themselves to ship, and being so loaded shall therewith proceed to *Glasgow* as ordered on signing bills of lading abroad, or so near thereto as she may safely get, and there deliver the same in the usual and customary manner to the said charterers or their assigns, they paying freight for same at the rate of £ 5 per ton of 50 c. feet for jute delivered for the round out and home; a deduction of 3s. per ton to be made if ship be discharged and loaded at *Colombo,* other goods, if shipped, to pay in customary proportion; in consideration whereof the outward cargo to be carried freight free; payment thereof to become due and be made as follows; then *follow the terms...* Ship is to have liberty to put on board 100 tons of hides, or other dead weights and to retain it on board during the voyage. Thirty running days (Sundays and holidays excepted) are to be allowed to the said merchant if the ship is not sooner despatched for loading in *Glasgow,* and 45 like days for all purposes abroad, and ten days on demurrage over and above the said lay days and the time therein staled at £6 *per day,* paying day by day as the same shall become due. The time occupied in changing party not to count as lay days. Charterers' liability under this charter-party to cease on the cargo being loaded, the master and owner having a lien on cargo for freight and demurrage. The-master to sign bills of lading at rates of freight as may be required by the agents of the charterers without prejudice to charter-party.

"The Act of God, King's enemies, restraint of Princes and Rulers, fire and all and every other dangers and accidents of the seas, rivers, and navigation, of what nature and kind soever, throughout the voyage, being excepted".

"The vessel to be consigned to charterers' agent abroad free of commissions. On the return of the ship to *London,* she shall be addressed to *White & Co.,* brokers or their agents at any other port of discharge. Penalty for non-performance of this agreement, the estimated amount of freight."

Clauses of Charter-Party—The following are the clauses of the Charter-party:—

1. The names and descriptions of the owner and charterer, and the fact of their agreement.

2. The name of the ship and its rating in Lloyd's register, *e.g.*, Al. The correctness of its rating is a condition precedent to the charterer's liability.

3. The measurement of the ship as indicated by its registered tonnage. A registered ton equals 100 cubic feet of space, and has no reference to weight. It is a conventional way of indicating the cubic measurement of the ship.

4. The position of the ship at the date of the signing of the charter-party, *e.g.*, now at Port Said, or that she will be in a particular port by a stated date. The truth of this statement is another condition precedent.

5. The shipowners' obligation to provide a ship which is seawothy and fit for the contemplated voyage (*the said ship being tight, staunch and strong*). This only extends to seaworthiness and fitness at the commencement of the voyage. This obligation will be implied, if it is not stated, as will the other two similar matters, viz., (a) that the voyage will be commenced and carried without delay, and (b) that there shall be no unnecessary deviation.

6. **The port of loading**—The shipowner must bring the ship to the agreed or usual place of loading at the port, and give notice to the charterer that the ship is ready to load. The charterer must then bring his goods alongside the ship, and deliver them to the servants of the shipowner, who is in general responsible for proper stowage.

7. **The duty of the charterer to furnish a full and complete cargo**—This is an absolute duty, which in practice means that the charterer must pay freight on the full carrying capacity of the ship whether he utilises it or not The custom of the port of loading determines the "full and complete cargo." Sometimes some guidance is given as to what a full and complete cargo is. Where a charterer undertakes to load a "full and complete cargo" on a ship which is chartered as of a certain capacity, he is bound to load as much cargo as the ship will safely carry.[1] But where the clause as to cargo provides that a certain number of tons is to be lodged, the charterers's liability will be to load that number and not the actual of the vessel.[2]

8. **Delivery of the goods in the manner**—At the port of discharge it is the duty of the master to proceed to the place of discharge mentioned in the contract, and get the goods out of the ship's hold and put them on the ship's deck or alongside. But the consignee or charterer must provide proper appliances for taking delivery after the shipowner has put the cargo on the rail of the ship, or in such a position that the consignee can take it.

---

1. Cuthbert v. Cumming (1856) 11 Ex. 405.
2. Morris v. Levison (1876) 1.C. U.O.155.

9. **The obligation of the charterer or consignee to pay freight**—This is generally expressed at so much per ton. It is not payable until the voyage has been completed and the goods delivered, unless non-delivery is due to the consignor's fault, or to the excepted perils. By express agreement freight may be payable in advance.

10. **Lay days and demurrage**—Lay days are certain number of days allowed by the charter-party to the charterer for the purpose of loading and unloading the cargo. The lay days begin to run from the time that the charterer has received notice of the ship's arrival at the stated port and her readiness to load and unload. These days may be either "Running Days" in which case they are counted from midnight to midnight including any intervening holidays, or "Working Days" which are the days on which the work is normally done, i.e., excluding holidays. It is essential that the work of loading and unloading must be completed within the stipulated lay days, and where no time is fixed then work must be completed within a reasonable time, regard being had to the existing circumstances and the custom of the port.[3] This condition fixes the maximum period, and if the ship is loaded in a shorter time, the charterer must allow the ship to depart, and cannot insist on her laying idle at the port of loading until all the lay days have run out.[4]

Positively stated, a charterer may detain a ship for extra days beyond the agreed lay days on payment of a stated sum, known as "Demurrage." Negatively, where the charterer detains a ship for a period longer than what he is allowed as lay days, he becomes liable to pay to the owner damages called "Demurrage." That is the strict meaning of the term, which may be defined thus : *Demurrage* is a charge agreed to be paid by the charterer to the shipowner as liquidated damages for detaining the ship beyond a stipulated or a reasonable time for loading or unloading. But the term is sometimes loosely used to cover "unliquidated damages for undue detention not specially provided for in the charter-party." No demurrage is payable if the ship has been detained through the owner's fault.

11. **The duration of charterers' liability**—For the recovery of freight and expenses the shipowner has a lien on the goods, but for other claims, such as demurrage and "dead freight" for not loading a full and complete cargo, he has no such lien, unless an express agreement is made. It is usual to insert a clause called the "Cesser Clause" in the charter-party, under which the charterers' liability ceases on the cargo being loaded, and in return the shipowner receives a lien on the cargo for freight, demurrage, including dead weight. The charterers' exemption from liability is co-extensive with the lien conferred on the shipowner. So that where no lien on the cargo has been granted, to the shipowner, the Courts refuse to relieve the charterer from liability arising either before or after shipment of cargo.[5]

12. **The right of the charterer to take other peoples' goods on board under bills of lading**—This may be a desirable right for the charterer, and there will be no hardship on the shipowner, so long as the bills of lading are without prejudice to the charter-party.

13. **Excepted perils and negligence clause**—Charter-parties contain a clause exonerating the shipowner from liability for loss caused by certain perils such as "Act of God, the King's enemies, restraints of princes and rulers, fire and all and every other dangers and accidents of the seas, rivers, and navigation, of what nature and kind soever." This clause will protect the shipowner only if the said peril could not have been avoided by the exercise of reasonable care and diligence on the part of the shipowner or his servants. If the ship is unseaworthy at the commencement of the voyage and damage results, this clause will not exonerate the shipowner from responsibilities for damage.[6] Deviation without excuse cancels the excepted perils clause.

---

3. Postewaite v. Freeland (1880) 5 A.C. 599.

4. Notsment v. Bunge (1917) 1 K.B. 160.

5. Clink v. Rattford (1891) 1 Q.B. 625.

6. Gilroy v. Price (1893) A.C. 56.

7. Morrison v. Shak (1916) 2 K.B. 783.

BILL OF LADING

Particular goods or isolated parcels are despatched from one port to another in a *General Ship* and the document used for their consignment is called a *Bill of Lading*. A general ship is a ship which is owned by a person or body of persons who ply it on a particular 'line' and offer to carry the goods of all comers to places where she will call. The owner of a general ship acts as a common carrier.

A **bill of lading** has been judicially described as a document by the shipowner or by the master or other agent on his behalf which states that certain goods have been snipped on a particular ship and which purports to set out the terms on which such goods have been delivered to, and received by, the ship.[8] A bill of lading is in the first instance an *acknowledgment of the receipt of the goods specified therein*. It is also a symbol of the *right of property in the goods;* and its transfer being a symbolic delivery of the goods has by mercantile usage the same effect as actual delivery. *Thirdly,* it is the *record of the terms of the contract* on which the goods are carried. Therefore where goods are sent in a general ship the bill of lading operates at once as a receipt of goods, a document of title, and contract of carriage.

FORM OF BILL OF LADING

"Shipped in good order and condition by *William Blake* in and upon the good ship called the *Daulat-i-Sagar* where of *Ram Nath* is master for this present voyage, and now in port of Calcutta and bound for *Hong Kong,* with liberty to call at any ports on the way for coaling or other necessary purposes, 500 (five hundred) bales of raw cotton being marked and numbered as per margin and to be delivered in the like good order and condition at the aforesaid port of *Hong Kong,* the Act of God, the Union's enemies, fire, barratry of the master and crew, and all and every other dangers and accidents of the seas, rivers and navigation of whatever kind and nature soever excepted, unto *Metro & Co.,* or to his assign, he or they paying freight for the said goods ₹.. per ton delivered with primage AND average accustomed. IN WITNESS WHEREOF, the master of the said ship hath affirmed to (three) bills of lading all of his tenor and date, one of which bills being accomplished, the others to stand void.

Dated.....

Weight, value and contents unknown."

CLEAN BILL OF LADING

It will be noted that the bill of lading begins with the words "shipped in good order and condition" and the last words are "weight, value and contents unknown." Either of these statements are retained by the master according to the circumstances of each case. Where the master states that the goods are ''shipped in good order and condition," he is bound to deliver the goods in the same good condition as they were at the time of loading, ordinary depreciation on the voyage being excepted. The document in this case is called a *Clean Bill of Lading*. In the case of a clean bill of lading the shipowner will be estopped from proving that the goods were not in good order and condition at the time they were delivered on board. The retention of the expression "weight, value and contents unknown" qualifies the liability of the shipowner, as there is no admission that the goods have been "delivered in good order and condition."

THROUGH BILL OF LADING

A through bill of lading is for the carriage of goods partly in the ship of the shipowner and by land or in the ship of another shipowner for an inclusive freight. Unless the bill states contrary, the contract is regarded as made with the shipowner who issues it.

---

8. Sewell v. Burdick (1884-85) 10 A.C. 74 (105).

RECEIVED FOR SHIPMENT BILL OF LADING

This is not a proper bill of lading and operates only as receipt of goods received for shipment. We have seen above that it is only after the goods are loaded that the proper bill of lading, sometimes called "shipped bill of lading," is issued, and if "received for shipment bill" is held by the shipper, he must surrender it and obtain the "shipped bill of lading," or if he likes have the name of the ship and the date of shipment of goods noted on it, when it will become a "shipped bill of lading."

MATE'S RECEIPT

A mate's receipt is an acknowledgment of receipt of goods given for goods delivered on board a ship, by the person in charge at the time and is taken back when the bill of lading is given. Possession of the mate's receipt is *prima facie* evidence of ownership and entitles the holder to receive a bill of lading.

PRIMAGE

Primage means a small payment of the nature of a tip made to the ship's master. It is not usual now, as the freight will cover all services, and the master will prefer an inclusive salary.

AVERAGE

Average in this context means certain dues paid by the ship for beaconage etc., and shared rateably by ship and cargo, and must be distinguished from general and particular average dealt with in connection with marine insurance.

MASTER'S AUTHORITY TO SIGN BILL OF LADING

A bill of lading is usually made out in a set of three parts and signed by the master on behalf of the shipowner. One is retained by the master of the ship and the other two are given to the shipper in exchange for the mate's receipt, or without one if the goods are on board the ship. The shipper retains one with himself and despatches the other to the consignee of the goods. Where the goods are carried in a general ship the master acting as the agent of the ship owner, has power to sign the bills of lading on such terms as he may think fit. Where the ship is under charter, but it is used as a general ship by the charterer, the master can issue bills of lading to the various shippers as the agent of the charterer. Neither the shipowner nor the charterer for whom the master may be signing the bill of lading is responsible for the shipment of goods which were never received on board the ship. The bill of lading, however, creates a presumption in favour of the holder that the goods therein mentioned are properly shipped and whoever pleads that the goods were not shipped must prove the fact.[9]

The Bill of Lading Act, 1856, Sec. 3, however, provides that every bill of lading in the hands of a consignee or indorsee for valuable consideration representing goods to have been shipped on board a vessel shall be conclusive evidence of such shipment as against the master or other person signing the same, even though the goods or some part of them may not have been so shipped, unless the holder of the bill of lading at the time of receiving it had actual notice of non-shipment, the misrepresentation was wholly due to the fraud of the shipper, or the holder, or some person under whom the holder claims.

TRANSFER OF BILL OF LADING

Bill of Lading a Document of Title—As observed before, the peculiarity of the bill of lading is that it is (*i*) a document containing the terms of the contract of carriage, and (*ii*) a document of title to the goods themselves, and remains so till the goods have come into the hands of a person entitled under the bill of lading to the possession of them.[10] The consignee of the goods may sell them while they are

---

10. Grant v. Norway (1851) 10 C.B. 115.
11. Barber v. Meyerstein (1870) L.R., 4 H.I. 317.

still at sea but he cannot obviously give physical delivery of the same. In such a case the endorsement and delivery of the bill of lading operates as delivery of the cargo, for during the period of transit the bill of lading by the law merchant is universally recognised as its symbol. It has been observed in *Henderson* v. *Comptoir de Escompte de Paris,* [11] that a bill of lading is a key which in the hands of the rightful owner is intended to unlock the door of the warehouse, floating or fixed, in which the goods may chance to be.

BILL OF LADING NOT A NEGOTIABLE INSTRUMENT

Goods shipped under a bill of lading may be made deliver able to a particular person "or to order" or "assigns," in which cases he may transfer such goods to any one he pleases by indorsement and delivery of the bill of lading. Again, the goods shipped under a bill of lading may be made deliverable to a name left blank or "to bearer" in which case the holder is at liberty to fill in the blank and then the bill of lading can change hands by mere delivery. This similarity of the bill of lading to a negotiable instrument has led to the confusion of treating it as a negotiable instrument, which it is not at all. On account of some points of resemblance between the two kinds of instruments a bill of lading is also described as "quasi negotiable" or "as good as negotiable." But in the strict sense of the term a bill of lading is not a negotiable instrument. Unlike the holder of a negotiable instrument the transferee of a bill of lading takes it subject to any defects of the transferor's title. In other words, the transferee of a bill of lading even though *bona fide* and for value does not get a better title than his transferor, while the holder in due course of a negotiable instrument does get a better title than that of his transferor. A bill of lading is negotiable in the sense that it is transferable, but it is not a negotiable instrument Where, therefore, a bill of lading has been transferred by indorsenment and delivery or by delivery, the transferee acquires by the transfer all the rights to the goods shipped, and is subject to all the liabilities in respect of them.[12] Sometimes, a bill of lading is said to be negotiable in the technical sense, and not in the real sense. At any rate, it is not a negotiable instrument at all.

Sec. 1 of the Bill of Lading Act, 1856, provides:

"Every consignee of goods named in a bill of lading and every indorsee of bill of lading to whom the property in the goods therein mentioned shall pass upon or by reason of such consignment or indorsement shall have transferred to and vested in him all rights of and be subject to the same liabilities in respect of such goods as if the contract contained in the bill of lading had been made with himself."

THE RIGHT OF STOPPAGE IN TRANSIT

The right of stoppage in transit and a right to claim freight against the original shipper is not affected by the Bill of Lading Act, 1856, and Sec. 53 of the Indian Sale of Goods Act is applicable. Accordingly, if a bill of lading has been lawfully transferred to any person as buyer or owner of the goods, and that person transfers the document by way of sale to one who takes it in good faith and for valuable consideration the right of lien and stoppage in transit is defeated. But if the transfer be merely by way *of pledge,* the consignor has a right to stop the goods in transit, subject to the payment or tender to the pledgee of the amount of the advance.

DELIVERY OF GOODS

Upon payment of the proper freight, the master is under an obligation to deliver the goods to the holder of the bill of lading. Where bills of lading are drawn in a set, and different parts are handed over

11. (1873) L.R. 5 P.C. 253.
12. Sewell v. Bardick (1885) 10 A.C. 74.

to different persons, the first transferee for value is entitled to the goods. But if the master acting *bona fide* delivers the goods to the person first presenting the bill of lading forming the set, he will not be liable if it should subsequently transpire that such person was not the first transferee.

DIFFERENCE BETWEEN CHARTER-PARTY AND BILL OF LADING

(1) A bill of lading is an acknowledgment of the receipt of goods on board the ship; a charter-party is not. (2) A bill of lading is a document of title to the goods specified therein; a charter-party is not such a document. (3) A charter-party may amount to a demise, *i.e.*, a lease of the ship or a part thereof; a bill of lading conveys no such implication. The documents, however, resemble each other as they both contain the terms and conditions of the contract of affreightment.

SHIPOWNER'S LIEN

As a carrier, the shipowner has lien on the goods carried for the freight and other charges. The lien can be enforced by not parting with the goods until his dues are paid. There is no lien when the freight has been paid in advance or when freight has been agreed to be paid after delivery of the goods. This is a possesory lien.

MARITIME LIEN

A maritime hen is a right which specifically binds a ship, including its machinery, furniture, cargo and freight, for the payment of a claim based upon maritime law. It is possessed by the following persons; seamen for their wages; the holder of bottomry bond for his dues; claimants for damages in cases of collision with the ship concerned; persons who rescue ships or property from the sea. It is not a possessory lien. In cases of maritime lien the rule is that last in time ranks first in payment

PART 14-D
CARRIAGE BY AIR

The law "elating to the carriage by air is contained in the Carriage by Air Act, 1972, which replaced the Carriage by Air Act, 1934 which in turn gave effect in India to the rules contained in the Warsaw Convention signed on 12th October, 1929. The 1972 Act makes applicable to India the rules contained in the First Schedule and the Second Schedule of the Warsaw Convention as amended by the Hague Protocol. Originally the provisions of the Act applied only to the international carriage of goods and passengers by air. But as per notification No. S. O. - 186(*E*) issued by the Ministry of Tourism and Civil Aviation, the provisions of the 1972 Act, also apply to internal or domestic flights as they apply to international flights. Accordingly, the law laid down in **Indian Airlines Corporation V. Madhury Chaudhary**, 1965 Cal. 252 is nullified by this notification, and is no more the law in India.

The term "High Contracting Party" means all the parties originally signatories to the Convention, together with those who adhere thereto subsequently as and when they adhere. ·

The expression "International Carriage" means a carriage in which the place of departure and the place of destination are situated within the territories of two High Contracting Parties, or within the Territories of a Single High Contracting Party if there is an agreed stopping place within a territory subject to the sovereignty, suzerainty, mandate or authority of another power even when that power is not a party to the Convention. *The prima facie* meaning of the expression appears to be the place at which the contractual carriage begins (place of departure) and the place at which the Contractual carriage ends (place of destination). An intermediate place at which the carriage may be broken is not a "place of destination". A carriage to be performed by several successive carriers is deemed to be undivided carriage if it has been regarded by the parties as a single operation.

DOCUMENTS OF CARRIAGE BY AIR

PASSENGER TICKET

For the carriage of passengers a carrier must deliver a passenger ticket which must contain the following particulars: (1) the place and date of issue; (2) the place of departure and of destination, (3) the agreed stopping places; (4) the name and address of the carrier or carriers; (5) the statement that the carriage is subject to the liability mentioned hereinafter. The carrier may reserve the right to alter the stopping place in case of necessity.

The absence, irregularity or loss of the passenger ticket does not affect the existence or validity of the contract of carriage. But if the carrier accepts a passenger without a passenger ticket, he cannot enjoy the benefit of limiting his liability granted under the Convention.

BAGGAGE CHECK

For the carriage of baggage other than small personal objects of which a passenger takes charge himself, the carrier must deliver a baggage check. The baggage check must be made out in duplicate, one part must contain the following particulars: (1) the place and date of issue; (2) the place of departure, and of destination; (3) Ac name and address of the carrier or carriers; (4) the number of the passenger ticket; (5) a statement that delivery of the baggage will be made to the bearer of the baggage check; (6) the number and weight of the packages; (7) the amount of the value declared in accordance with Rule 22(2) of the Warsaw Convention; (8) a statement that the carriage is subject to the rules relating to liability stated hereinafter.

The absence, irregularity or loss of the baggage check does not affect the existence or the validity of the contract of carriage; but if the baggage check does not contain the particulars set out at (4), (6) and (8) above, the carrier shall not be entitled to the benefit of rules limiting liability.

AIR WAY BILL[13]

The carrier of goods has the right to demand from the consignor a document called the "Air Way Bill" and the consignor is entitled to require the carrier to accept his document. Nevertheless, the absence, irregularity or loss of this document does not affect the existence or the validity of the contract of carriage. The air way bill to be handed over with the goods must be made out by the consignor in three original parts. The first part must be marked for the "carrier", and must be signed by the consignor. The second part must be marked "for the consignee," and must be signed by the consignor and by the carrier and must accompany the goods. The third part must be signed by the carrier and handed by him to the consignor after the goods have been accepted. The carrier must sign an acceptance of the goods; his signature may be stamped and that of the consignor may be printed or stamped. If, at the request of the consignor, the carrier makes out the air way bill he shall be deemed, subject to proof to the contrary, to have done so on behalf of the consignor. The carrier of goods has the right to require the consignor to make out separate waybills when there are more than one packages.

The air way bills must contain the following particulars: (1) the place and date of its execution; (2) the place of departure and of destination; (3) the agreed stopping places; (4) the name and address of the consignor; (5) the name and address of the first carrier; (6) the name and address of the consignee; (7) the nature of the goods; (8) the number of the packages; the method of packing, and the particular marks or numbers on the packages; (9) the weight, the quantity and the volume or dimensions of the goods; (10) the apparent condition of the goods and of the packing; (11) the freight, if it has been agreed upon, the date and place of payment, and the person who is to pay it; (12) if the goods are sent for payment on delivery, the price of the goods; (13) the amount of the value declared;

---

13. In the original rules it was known as 'Air Consignment Note'.

(14) the number of parts of the consignment note; (15) the documents handed to the carrier to accompany the note; (16) the time fixed for the completion of the carriage, and a brief note of the route to be followed; (17) a statement that the carriage is subject to the rules regarding liability.

If the carrier accepts goods without an air way bill having been made out, or if the air way bill does not contain the particulars set in (1) to (8) inclusive and (17), the carrier shall not be entitled to the benefit of limiting his liability. The consignor is responsible for the correctness of the particulars and statements relating to the goods which he inserts in the air waybill. The consignor will be liable for all damage suffered by the incompleteness of the said particulars and statements. The air way bill is *prima facie* evidence of the conclusion of the contract, of the receipt of the goods and of the conditions of carriage, as well as the statements relating to the weight, dimensions, packing of the goods, and number of packages.

LIMITATION OF LIABILITY OF THE CARRIER

The carrier is liable for damage sustained in the event of the death or wounding of a passenger or any other bodily injury suffered by a passenger, if the accident which caused the damage so sustained took place on board the aircraft or in course of any of the operations of embarking or disembarking. He is also liable for loss of or damage to any registered luggage or any goods. In the carriage of passengers, the liability of the carrier for each passenger is, in the absence of a contract for higher amount, limited to 225,000 Cranes. As regards the articles of which the passenger takes charge himself, the liability of the carrier is limited to 5,000 francs per passenger. Any provision in any contract seeking to relieve the carrier from liability or to further limit liability is void and of no effect Rule 22(2) provides that in the carriage of luggage and goods, the liability of the carrier shall be limited to a sum of 230 francs per kilogram, unless the consignor has made, when the package was delivered to the carrier, a special declaration of the place and time of delivery and has also paid a supplementary or further sum if the case so required. In that case, the carrier is liable to pay a sum not exceeding the declared sum, unless that sum is proved by the carrier to be of higher value than the real or actual value at the time and place of delivery.

In the case of damage, the person entitled to delivery must complain to the carrier forthwith after the discovery of the damage, and, at the latest, within three days from date of the receipt of the luggage or within seven days from the receipt of the goods. In the case of delay in delivery of the goods the complaint must be made within 14 days from the date on which the luggage or the goods have been actually delivered or placed at the disposal of the consignee.

Rule 33 permits the carrier either to refuse to enter into any contract of carriage or to make any regulations which do not conflict with the provisions of the Convention. In *Luddith* v. *Ginger Coote Airways Ltd.* 1947 P. C. 151, Lord Wright held that a carrier by air of passengers may refuse to carry anyone save at the passenger's own risk. He can by a special contract exempt himself from liability even for negligence of his servants provided that there are no statutory conditions limiting his right, and such a contract cannot be pronounced unreasonable, invalid or illegal by a Court of Justice.

In India, the liability of internal or domestic carriers (*e.g.*, Indian Airlines) for passengers and their baggage has been fixed as follows:

  (a) death or permanent disability by accident ₹ 2 lacs per adult passenger;

  (b) death or permanent disability by accident — ₹ 1 lac for a passenger below 12 years of age;

  (c) temporary disablement preventing the injured person from attending his usual business — ₹ 200 per day or ₹ 4,000 whichever is less;

  (d) for registered baggage and cargo — ₹ 160 per kilogram;

  (e) for articles in the charge of the passenger himself ₹ 1,000 per passenger;

A carrier cannot reduce his liability but may undertake a higher liability by a special agreement.

CASES FOR RECAPITULATION

1. A reputed race-horse was entrusted by *B* to the railway for carriage from Bombay to Calcutta. As the result of loose-shunting in transit, the horse fell and broke one of his legs, and it became necessary to shoot him. *B* claims ₹ 3,000 as damages for the loss of his horse. The railway administration is liable to pay damage as the loss of the horse resulted from the negligence and misconduct of the railway servants in loose-shunting. But the amount will depend upon whether the consignor had declared the value of the horse at the time of booking and. paid the higher charge. If he had done so, he will be entitled to get ₹ 3,000, and if not, then only ₹ 750, which is the amount provided in the Act for the loss of a horse.

2. A railway company accepts goods to be carried to a place on the system of another company. The receiving company makes a contract with the consignor to carry the goods all the way to the destination. The goods are lost while in transit on the line of the second company. The receiving company is liable to pay for the loss. Under Sec. 76 D of the Railways Act, the second company (administration) will be liable to pay damages if it is an Indian company or railway administration. If the second railway were a foreign railway, then the responsibility of the Indian railway as common carrier would extend over the portion of the carriage which is over the Indian railway.

3. The risk note of a railway company provides that in consideration of the company carrying the goods at a specially reduced rate, the sender shall be precluded from holding the railway liable for loss or damages to the goods from any cause whatever. Due to the negligence of the railway servants the goods are damaged. Under Sec. 74 the railway administration shall be liable to pay damages as the damage was caused to the goods through the negligence of the railway servants, the exemption clause will be ineffective.

4. A tiger is entrusted by *X* to the railway for carriage. The cage breaks by the jolts received during the journey and the tiger escapes. It kills a bullock belonging to *Y*, but is almost immediately crushed by the engine. Under Sec. 73 the consignor is bound of supply a strong cage; and in the instant case, the cage evidently is not strong enough to bear the jolts which are a normal accompaniment of motion of a train. *X* would be liable to *Y* on the basis of tort If the tiger had escaped because of the wilful neglect of the railway, it would be responsible to *X* and also to *Y* in tort.

5. A ship was chartered for a voyage between *A* port and is port. The ship was not seaworthy and did not sail on the date specified in the charter-party. The charterer or shipper may avoid the contract if he finds the ship unseawothy before the commencement of the voyage and the defect cannot be set right within a reasonable time. If the voyage has started and he suffers any loss, he can recover it from the shipowner. If the ship does not sail on the stipulated date and the delay is such as to go to the root of the contract and makes the marine adventure different from what it originally was, the charterer can avoid the contract, or treat the contract as broken and claim damages.

6. Cement was shipped under a bill of lading which stipulated for payment of freight within three days after the ship's arrival. On arrival a fire broke out on board and the ship had to be scuttled. When the ship was raised it was found that the cement was useless. The shipowner was not guilty of any negligence, the fire being accidental and falls within the excepted perils. Consequently, he is entitled to receive the freight although goods could not be delivered. The charterer can, of course, recover the loss from the underwriters under marine insurance.

7. A ship on which dates had been loaded was sunk during the voyage and subsequently raised. The dates still retained their appearance and were of value for distillation into spirits but were no longer merchantable as dates. The policy-holder can recover for the total loss of dates, as they are so damaged as to cease to be the thing of the kind insured; they no longer answer the denomination under which they were insured, nor can they be utilised as the thing insured.

8. *P* was a passenger on a train from Delhi to Bombay. He carried two suitcases in his first class compartment under his berth. At an intermediate station the train stopped for 15 minutes. *P* left the compartment and returned to it 10 minutes later. One of his suitcases was then missing. He sued the railway administration for the loss of the suitcase and its contents which he valued at ₹ 5,000. *Held*, the railway's common carrier liability as insurer of goods does not extend to passenger's luggage carried by him in his own compartment.

9. *S* had bought a ticket at the Kanpur railway station and was rushing on the platform to catch a train when he slipped on a banana skin and got injured and missed the train. The railway administration is not liable to pay any damages to *S*.

CHAPTER
15
Securities

In this chapter we deal with different rights a person acquires in the property of another, **by way of security,** for the liability that other person has contracted. Such rights are generally designed as "Securities." The following are the principal securities:

1. Pledge or Pawn;
2. Mortgage;
3. Charge;
4. Hypothecation;
5. Lien.

Pawn or Pledge—In a pledge, the possession of the goods is delivered to the creditor (the Pledgee or Pawnee), as secutiry for the loan, but the ownership remains with the Debtor (the Pledgor or Pawnor). We have already dealt with this subject in Chapter III—Bailment and Pledge.

MORTGAGE

The law relating to mortgages of immovable property and charges is dealt with in Secs. 58 to 104 of the Transfer of Property Act, 1882.

Definition and Nature of Mortgage—The word mortgage has come to us *via* England from the French language and it means "Dead Pledge." A Mortgage is the transfer of interest in specific immovable property for the purpose of securing the payment of money advanced or to be advanced by way of loan, an existing or future debt, or the performance of an engagement which my give rise to pecuniary liability. The mortgagor as an owner of the property is possessed of all the interests in it, and when he mortgages the property to secure a loan, he only parts with an interest in that property in favour of the mortgagee. After mortgage the interest of the mortgagor is reduced by the interest which has been transferred to the mortgagee. His ownership has become less for the time being by the interest which he has parted with in favour of the mortgagee. If the mortgagor transfers this property, the transferee gets it subject to the right of the mortgagee to recover from it what is due to him.

There are three outstanding characteristics of a mortgage: (1) the termination of the mortgagee's interest upon the performance of the obligation secured by the mortgage; (2) the right of the mortgagee to enforce the mortgage by foreclosure upon the mortgagor's failure to perform; and (3) the mortgagor's right to redeem or regain the property. It should be noted that a mortgage is not a mere contract but it is the conveyance of interest in the mortgaged property, and as soon as the mortgage deed is registered, the interest in the property vests in the mortgagee.

Form of a Mortgage Contract—Where the principal money secured is ₹ 100 or upwards, a mortgage,-other than a mortgage by the deposit of title-deeds, can be effected only by a registered instrument signed by the mortgagor and attested by two witnesses. A mortgage which secures less than ₹ 100 may be made either by a registered instrument or by delivery of property. In Punjab and Delhi a mortgage can be created orally, and even when it is in writing it need not be attested. This is so because the Transfer of Property Act does not apply there.

Kinds of Mortgages—There are in all six kinds of mortgages on immovable property, namely,—(i) Simple Mortgage; (ii) Mortgage by conditional sale; (iii) Usufructuary Mortgage; (iv) English Mortgage; (v) Mortgage by deposit of title-deeds; (vi) Anomalous Mortgage.

Simple Mortgage—In a simple mortgage the mortgagor undertakes personal liability, and agrees that in the event of his failure to pay the mortgage money, the mortgagee shall have a right to cause the property to be applied so far as may be necessary by means of a decree for the sale of the property.

Mortgage by Conditional Sale—Where the mortgagor ostensibly sells the mortgaged property—
(a) on condition that in default of payment of the mortgage money on a certain date, the sale shall become absolute, or
(b) on condition that on such payment being made the sale shall become void, or
(c) on condition that on such payment being made the buyer shall transfer the property to the seller,
the transaction is called mortgage by conditional sale and the mortgagee a mortgagee by conditional sale. In this mortgage, the ostensible sale ripens into absolute proprietorship on default by the mortgagor to repay the amount, in which case the mortgagee can sue for foreclosure but not for sale. Registration is compulsory only if the consideration is ₹ 100 or more.

Usufructuary Mortgage—Where the mortgagor delivers or expressly or by implication binds himself to deliver possession of the mortgaged property to the mortgagee, and authorises him to retain such possession until payment of the mortgage money, and to receive the rents and profits accruing from the property or any part of such rents and profits, and to appropriate the same in lieu of interest, or in payment of the mortgage money, or partly in lieu of interest and partly in payment of the mortgage money, the transaction is called a usufructuary mortgage or mortgage with possession. Registration of this kind of mortgage is necessary if the mortgage money is ₹ 100 or more.

English Mortgage— Where the mortgagor binds himself to repay the mortgage money on a certain date and transfers the mortgaged property absolutely to the mortgagee but subject to a proviso that he will retransfer it to the mortgagor upon payment of the mortgage money as agreed, the transaction is called an English Mortgage. An English mortgage represents two distinct transactions, that it involves a conveyance or transfer of ownership and also the creation of personal liability of the mortgagor to repay by a certain date. Registration is compulsory where the amount secured is ₹ 100 or more.

Mortgage by Deposit of Title Deeds or Equitable Mortgage—Where a person delivers to a creditor documents of title to immovable property, (*i.e.*, sale-deeds by which the property had been acquired) with interest to create a security thereon, the transaction is called a mortgage by deposit of title-deeds or an Equitable Mortgage. The terms on which the deposit of title-deeds is made need not be reduced to writing. The usual practice is that the mortgagor delivers the title-deeds to the mortgagee and also passes a promissory note in his favour against which the mortgagee advances the money. In case of non-payment, the mortgagee can sue for sale, but he cannot foreclose the mortgaged property.

Anomalous Mortgage—A mortgage which is not of any of the kinds stated above is called an anomalous mortgage. Anomalous mortgages are of many kinds, and may arise by the combination of two or more of the above kinds or by usage in particular localities. Thus *Lekha Mukhi* mortgage prevails in Punjab. In this mortgage the land is transferred to the creditor for management who in addition to interest charges for the management In *Waldi* mortgage the mortgagee gets possession of the property but pays one-tenth of the produce to the mortgagor as the landlord's dues.

Sub-Mortgage—Where the mortgagee transfers by mortgage his interest in the mortgaged property, or creates a mortgage of a mortgage, the transaction is known as a sub-mortgage. For example, where A mortgages his house to B for ₹ 10,000 and B mortgages his mortgagee rights to C for ₹ 8,000, B creates a sub-mortgage.

Puisne Mortgage—Where a mortgagor, having mortgaged his property to secure a loan of smaller amount than the value of the property, mortgages it to another person to secure another loan, the second mortgage is called a Puisne Mortgage. For example, *A* mortgages his house worth ₹ 50,000 to B for ₹ 20,000, he creates a mortgage, and if he mortgages the house to *C* for a further sum of ₹ 20,000 and thus creates a second mortgage, *C* would be the puisne mortgagee. The puisne mortgagee can recover subject to the right of the first mortgagee to recover.

RIGHTS AND LIABILITIES OF MORTGAGOR

Rights of Redemption—By mortgaging the property the mortgagor only transfers an interest in the property and does not cease to be its owner, and, therefore, he can redeem the mortgage property by paying the mortgage plus any interest due on it, at any time after the stipulated date for repayment, but before the right is extinguished by the act of parties or by a decree of Court, or before it is barred by the Limitation Act. The mortgagor is not entitled to redeem before the mortgage money becomes due on the date fixed for repayment of the loan.

Right of Redemption or Equity of Redemption, as the term is called in English law, is the essence of a mortgage, and any provision inserted in the mortgage deed to prevent, evade or hamper redemption is void. The rule of equity that *once a mortgage always a mortgage,* prohibits a "clog" on the right of redemption. In other words, once a transaction is found to be a mortgage the Court would not permit any condition in a mortgage deed which would prevent or impede redemption on repayment of the loan for which the security was given, for if allowed, such a condition would have the effect of clogging or fettering the equity or right of redemption. A "clog" on the equity or right of redemption arises where an obligation continues during the term of the mortgage and beoynd, thus rendering the property mortgaged less available in the hands of its owner apart from the realization of the mortgage debt. Thus the right of redemption cannot be controlled by any agreement made as a part of the transaction. But after the execution of the mortgage the parties are at liberty by a fair bargain to extinguish the right of redemption by an agreement which may be independent of the original bargain.[1] A stipulation postponing redemption for a period of 40 years with a condition that in default of redemption on a particular day the mortgage would be renewed for another period of 40 years would be a dog on redemption, as the provision gave a right of redemption for one day only in 80 years and was designed to make a redemption almost impossible.[2]

Regarding the manner of redemption, it is provided that the mortgagor must pay or offer to pay to the mortgagee the mortgage money at a proper time and place and if the mortgagee accepts the tender the debt is discharged and redemption effected, or a suit for redemption should be filed. On redemption, the mortgagee must return the mortgage deed and all other documents reating to the mortgaged property. Where the mortgage is with possession of the property the mortgagee must deliver to the mortgagor the possession of the property. Where there is any increase of property after usufructuary mortgage and before redemption, the mortgagor is entitled to get back the increased property.

Partial Redemption—A mortgage, as a rule, being one and indivisible security for the debt and every part of it, the mortgagor cannot redeem piecemeal; he must redeem the whole property. Similarly, where there are more than one mortgagor, a co-mortgagor cannot redeem his portion of the mortgaged properties. But a mortgagor of an undivided share can always redeem the whole mortgage. Thus, the owner of a part of the equity of redemption can redeem the entire mortgage but not any part of it.[3] A

1. Mohd. Sher Khan v. Raja Seth Swami Dayal, 1992 P.C. 17.
2. Sarbdawan Singh v. Bijai Singh (1914) 36 A.LL. 551.
3. Bijai Singh v. Randhir Singh, 1925 All. 643.

mortgagor who has executed two or more mortgages can redeem any one or more of the mortgages, unless there is a contract to the contrary, stipulating consolidation (Sec. 61).

Implied Contract by Mortgagor—The parties are free to enter into any terms they like; where, however the contract does not contain all the terms, Sec. 65 provides for implied terms, as follows:—

In the absence of a contract to the contrary, the mortgagor shall be deemed to have contracted with the mortgagee—

(a) that the mortgagor is entitled to transfer the interest (covenant for title);

(b) that the mortgagor will assist the mortgagee to enjoy the quiet possession;

(c) that the mortgagor will pay all public charges in respect of the property;

(d) that the mortgagor covenants as to the payment of the rent due on lease, where the mortgaged property is a lease;

(e) that the mortgagor covenants as to payment of interest and principal on prior encumbrances, where the mortgage is a second or subsequent encumbrance on the property.

Mortgagor's Power to Lease—Sec. 65A permits a mortgagor in possession to lease the property and the mortgagee will be bound by the lease if—

(a) the lost rent is reserved;

(b) no premium is paid or promised;

(c) no rent is promised to be paid in advance;

(d) there is no covenant for renewal of lease;

(e) the taking effect of the lease has not been postponed beyond 6 months;

(f) in a lease of building—(i) the duration of die lease does not exceed 3 years, and (ii) there is a right of re-entry on non-payment of the rent reserved.

RIGHTS AND LIABILITIES OF MORTGAGEE

If the mortgagor does not pay the mortgage money, the mortgagee may proceed to recover from the mortgaged property or sue for recovery from the mortgagor personally. The remedies of the mortgagee against the property are:—

1. Right to bring property to sale.
2. Right to foreclose.
3. Right to the possession of the property.

Remedy by Sale—In the case of a simple mortgage or a mortgage by deposit of title-deeds (equitable mortgage), or an English mortgage, sale is the only remedy available to the mortgagee. He has to file a suit for sale of the mortgaged property and if the Court is satisfied, it would give 6 months' time to the mortgagor to pay the decretal amount. If he fails to pay, the mortgagee will get a final decree under which he can have the property sold. If the proceeds are more than the decretal amount, the balance, after payment to the mortgagee, will be paid to the mortgagor, and if the proceeds fall short then a personal decree for the balance will be given against the mortgagor.

Foreclosure—The second remedy is foreclosure, by means of a suit to get a decree that the mortgagor shall be absolutely debarred of his right to redeem the property, if the mortgagor does not pay within the period directed by the Court. After a foreclosure decree is passed the mortgagee becomes the owner of the property. This remedy is available only, in case of a mortgage by conditional sale, or in any anomalous mortgage.

Possession— A usufructuary mortgagee has a right to file a suit for possession and by use of the property he can repay himself of the debt due to him. He can retain possession until his debt is discharged out of the income of the property. Hence where possession is not given by the mortgagor, the mortgagee sues for possession.

Right to Sue for Mortgage Money—The mortgagee has a right to sue for the mortgage-money in the following cases and no other: —

(a) where the mortgagor binds himself to repay the same.

(b) where, by any cause other than the wrongful act or default of the mortgagor or mortgagee, the mortgaged property is destroyed or the security is rendered insufficient.

(c) where the mortgagee is deprived of the whole or part of his security by or in consequence of the wrong act or default of the mortgagor.

(d) where the mortgagee, being entitled to the possession of the property (usufructuary mortgage), is not put in possession of it, or where having been put into possession, is dispossessed by the mortgagor or any other person claiming under a superior title, *e.g.*, a buyer by a registered deed.

Right of Private Sale—By virtue of Sec. 69, a mortgagee can sell the property privately, without the intervention of the Court, if the loan is not paid on a certain date in the following three cases:—

(a) where the mortgage is an English mortgage and neither the mortgagor nor the mortgagee is a Hindu, Mohammedan or Buddhist; or

(b) where the mortgagee is the Government and the mortgage deed confers an express power of sale; or

(c) where the mortgage property was on the date of the execution of the mortgage situated within the towns of Bombay, Calcutta and Madras.

The sale proceeds under a private sale of the property must be utilised, *first*, in discharging prior encumbrances, if any; *secondly,* in payment of all cost, charges and expenses of the sale; *thirdly,* the surplus to be paid to the person entitled to the mortgaged property. A mortgagee having right privately to sell the property can appoint a receiver out of the income of the mortgaged property.

Liabilities of Mortgagee in Possession—A mortgagee in possession is bound—

(a) to manage the property as a person of ordinary prudence would manage his own;

(b) to use his best endeavour to collect the rents and profits thereof;

(c) to pay out of the income all Government Revenue or other charges of a public nature;

(d) not to commit any act which is destructive to the property;

(e) to keep full and accurate accounts of all income and expenditure;

(f) when mortgagor tenders or deposits the mortgage money, to account for his receipts from the property from the date of tender or deposit.

PRIORITY

The general rule of priority of different mortgagees on the same property is that the successive mortgagee is paid after the prior mortgagee has been satisfied. Thus, if two successive mortgages are created by the mortgagor on the same property, and both cannot be satisfied out of the mortgaged property, the prior mortgagee will have the first right to satisfy his whole debt and the balance, if any, will go to the subsequent mortgagee.

MARSHALLING AND DISTRIBUTION

Marshalling—By Sec. 81, if the owner of two or more properties mortgages them to one person and then mortgages more than one of those properties to another person, the subsequent mortgagee is, in the absence of a contract to the contrary, entitled to have the prior mortgage debt satisfied out of the properties not mortgaged to him, so far as same will extend, but not so as to prejudice the rights of the prior mortgagee or of any other person who has for consideration acquired an interest in any of the properties.

The rule of marshalling applies only where—

(a) the debtor is the same and contracts different debts in the same capacity;

(b) there is no contract to the contrary;

(c) the properties are separate and not fractional share of the same property;

(d) prior mortgagee's rights or of any other person who has for consideration acquired an interest in any of the properties is not prejudiced.

An illustration will make the rule of marshalling clear. *A* mortgages properties *X* and *Y* to *B*. Then he mortgages property *Y* to *C*. Suppose *B* obtains decree on his mortgage for sale of properties *X* and *Y* which form security for his mortgage. Suppose further that *B* applies in execution to the Court for sale of property *Y* which is also mortgaged to *C*, *C* would be entitled to have the prior debt of *B* satisfied out of property *X*, which is not mortgaged to *C*, and if the whole of *B*'s debt is not satisfied out of property *X* then and then alone, the property *Y* should be proceeded against

Contribution (Sec. 82)—In marshalling we determine the different rights of the competing mortgagees, while in contribution we have to determine the rights of the mortgagors *inter se* with respect to the properties mortgaged by them. The mortgagors *inter se* are liable to contribute in proportion to the value of their property which has been included in the joint mortgage.[4] A joint mortgage to secure one debt may either arise where several owners of distinct properties contract a single mortgage debt, or where a single mortgagor mortgages different properties of his to secure a single debt, and on his death, the different properties by partition are inherited by his heirs, or where a single mortgagor after having created a single mortgage on two of his properties sells the equity of redemption in any one or more to a third person. In all these three cases, there is competition between the owners of several properties mortgaged, and where any one of them has been made to pay the whole debt of the mortgage, the owner of that property can claim contribution from his co-mortgagors in proportion to the value of their respective properties. For example, where three properties, *X* worth ₹ 4,000, *Y* worth ₹ 2,000, and *Z* worth ₹ 2,000 belong to *A*, *B*, and *C* respectively and are mortgaged to *M* for a debt of ₹ 4,000 and *A*, the owner of *X* property, pays off the entire mortgage, he will be entitled to a contribution of ₹ 1,000 each from *B* and *C*, the owners of *Y* and *Z* respectively.

Subrogation—Subrogation, we know, is the right to step into the shoes of another and thus acquire all rights and to enforce them in his own name. Sec. 92 provides that a person who is interested in the discharge of a mortgage shall, on his discharging it, be entitled to all the rights and remedies which the person paid off was entitled to. In order to enjoy the right of subrogation, he should have a right to redeem his mortgage and redeem it. The common case is that of a subsequent mortgagee paying off a prior mortgage. Although a subsequent mortgagee on paying off a prior mortgage steps into the shoes of the first mortgagee, he cannot "Tack" his original security to the first so as to get a priority over the intermediary mortgagee. "Tacking" is thus prohibited by Sec. 93. Suppose *A* creates successive mortgages on his property in favour of *B*, *C* and *P*. If *D* redeems the mortgage in favour of *B*, he is subrogated to the rights of *B* and will have priority in respect of the mortgage in favour of *B* over the mortgagee *C*; but he will not be entitled to any priority with respect of his own mortgage which was third in point of time. If tacking were permitted then *C* would be squeezed out and could redeem only by paying off the first and third mortgages.

Mergers—Whether merger will take place or not will depend upon different circumstances. Where a third party purchases the equity of redemption from the mortgagor and then redeems the mortgage on the property, merger would take place unless the intention is to keep alive the mortgage. Where, however, the mortgagee or chargeholder purchases the equity of redemption no merger takes place of his mortgage rights irrespective of the fact that the purchasing mortgagee has expressly or impliedly shown an intention to keep it alive as a shield against intermediate mortgages. Suppose *A* mortgages his house worth ₹ 2,000 to *B* for ₹ 500 (first mortgage), to *C* for ₹ 600 (second mortgage) and to *D* for ₹ 700 (third mortgage), thereby parting with his interest in the house to the extent of ₹ 1,800 in favour of the three mortgagees, and retaining with himself his interest in the property (technically known as equity of redemption) amounting to ₹ 200. If he redeems the first mortgage in favour of *B*, the interest

---

4. Jai Narain v. Rashik Behari Lal, 1931 All. 546.

in the property which he had parted with in favour of *B*, reverts to him, resulting in a merger of B's interest in the ownership of *A*. In this way, *A*'s interest will be enlarged by ₹ 500, so that the value of his equity of redemption will go up to ₹ 700. Now suppose *A* owes a simple debt to *M* who obtains a decree against *A* and in execution sells the interest of *A* in the property which is purchased by *N*. *N* has purchased the equity of redemption and thus steps into the shoes of the mortgagor *A* and then redeems the mortgage in favour of *B*. Here merger of the interest of *N* and of the mortgagee interest of *B* will take place unless it is shown that his object in redeeming *B*'s mortgage is to keep it alive.[5] If in this illustration, *C*, the second mortgagee, were to purchase the equity of redemption from *A*, no merger would take place of the interest of *C* as second mortgagee of the property and of his interest as owner thereof. This is so because *C* is not a stranger and has already an interest of a mortgagee in the property, and there being a subsequent mortgagee *D*, *C*'s mortgage would be kept alive.

Mortgage of Movable Property—A mortgage of movables may be defined as a transfer, by way of security, of the general ownership of the chattel, subject to the equity of redemption of the mortgagor. No delivery of possession is necessary to complete a mortgage in English Law, except in exceptional circumstances. In England, mortgages of movables are regulated by the Bills of Sale Act, which require registration in order to render such mortgages valid. **In India,** the mortgage of movables can be made by mere parole and without transfer of possession. A mortgage of future goods, such as a crop that may be grown on a certain plot or land, is a valid transaction in India.[6] The rule is based on the maxim: Equity considers that as done which ought to be done. However, the equitable title arising in a transaction of this kind will not avail against a subsequent transferee of the property with possession, without notice of the previous title. Note, although the term mortgage is used in connection with movable property, yet, strictly speaking, it can be applied to immovable property. Therefore, to be more correct, where a mortgage is created by delivery of possession of the goods, the transaction is a **Pledge,** and where no possession is given to the lender, but only a right to recover the debt against the specific goods, the transaction is a **Hypothecation.**

PART 15-B
CHARGE

Where immovable property of one person is by the act of parties or operation of law made security for payment of money to another, and the transaction does not amount to mortgage, the latter person is said to have a charge on the property; and all the provisions herein before contained which apply to a simple mortgage shall, so far as may be, apply to such a charge (Sec. 100).

It will be seen that a charge can be created either by the acts of parties or by the operation of law, and although the property is made a security for the payment of the loan, yet the transaction does not amount to a mortgage. We may with profit distinguish between a charge and a mortgage.

Distinction between Charge and Mortgage—
1. A mortgage is a transfer of an interest in the property made by mortgage as a security for the loan, while the charge is not the transfer of interest in the property though it is security for the payment of an amount.
2. A charge may be created by act of parties or by operation of law. A mortgage can only be created by the act of parties.
3. Sec. 59, Transfer of Property Act, requires a mortgage deed to be attested by two witnesses, while a charge need not be made in writing, and if reduced to writing, it need not be attested.

---

5. Gokal Chand v. Puran Mull (1833) 10 Cal. 1035. P.C.

6. Misri Lal v. Marhar (1816) 13 Cal. 262; The law on the subject was stated by Beaman, J. in Tehbiram v. Longin D'Mello, (1916) 18 B.L.R. 587.

4. In certain mortgages, (*i.e.*, mortgages by conditional sale, and anomalous mortgages) the mortgagor can foreclose the mortgaged property, but in a charge the charge-holder cannot foreclose though he can get the property sold as in a simple mortgage.

5. From the very nature of it, a charge, as a general rule, cannot be enforced against a transferee for consideration without notice. But in a mortgage, the transferee of the mortgaged property from the mortgagor can only acquire the remaining interest of the mortgagor, and is, therefore, bound by the mortgage.[7]

6. In a charge created by act of parties the specification of the particular land or property negatives a personal liability and the remedy of the charge-holder is against the property charged only. When there is, in addition, a personal covenant and the security will become collateral to the personal covenant and the security will in that case appear to become a transfer of right of sale to support the personal covenant and as the right of sale is a right *in rem* the transaction would be a mortgage. For this reason the absence of a personal liability is the principal test that distinguishes, charge from a simple mortgage.[8]

Charge how Created—A charge can be created either by acts of parties or by operation of law.

By Act of Parties—When in a transaction for value both parties (debtor and creditor) intend that the property existing or future shall be made available as security for the payment of a debt and that creditor shall have a present right to have it made available there is a charge. The charge is always created to take effect immediately and not at some future time, although the present legal right can only be enforced at some future date. It will be noted that the creditor gets no legal right of property, either absolute or special or any legal right to possession but only gets a right to have the security made available by an order of the Court. In a suit by *A* against *B* on the basis of a promissory note, the parties, made a compromise which was embodied in the decree. It was provided that the decretal amount would be paid by easy instalments and that *B* would not dispose of, in any way, his share in the Premier Aerated Co., at Hazart Ganj, until the satisfaction of the decretal amount. *Held,* that a charge was created on *B*'s share in the property and *A* was entitled to have the amount from the property even though *B* had sold his share to a third person. Where *M* has executed a promissory note in favour of *P* and on the same date a *Beechik* was sent by *M* to *P*, in which it was stipulated that the amount due under the promissory note should come out of the deodar timber in the jungle,[9] *held,* that *P* was entitled to a charge on *M*'s timber in the jungle. A document described as *Zamanatnama* and containing a condition restricting the executant from certain property was executed to secure repayment of a loan. It was, however, not on a proper stamp for a mortgage. *Held,* that the instrument amounts to create a charge and not a mortgage.[10]

By Operation of Law—Charges created by operation of law are those which arise on account of some statutory provisions. They are not created by a voluntary action of the parties but arise as the result of some legal obligation. An unpaid vendor has a charge on the property sold. A co-mortgagor redeeming the mortgage is entitled to claim contribution and acquires a charge in respect thereof. Also, where several properties have been mortgaged by several owners to secure one debt and the property of one of the owners has contributed more than his proportionate share of the mortgage debt, that owner is entitled to a charge on the remaining properties which have not discharged their own share of the debt to contribute rateably towards the debt.[11]

---

7. Vir Bhan v. Salig Ram, 1937 Lah. 35; see also 1938 Bom. 189.
8. Benares Bank Ltd. v. Harparshad. 1936 Lah. 482.
9. Mangat Ram v. Piyare Lal, Sunder Lal, 1929 Lah. 274.
10. Virbhan v. Salig Ram, 1937 Lah. 35.
11. Mohd. Mian v. Bharat Singh. 1930 Oudh. 260.

Instances where no charge Created

1. Where the parties do not intend that there should be a present right to have the security made available, *but only that there should be a right in the future by agreement such as a licence to seize goods,* there will be no charge.

2. A covenant that the obligee can recover from the "person and property" of the debtor is too vague to create a charge on any of his properties.

3. Where at the foot of a hundi a note was added in the words: 'Hamari Delhi wa Ludhiana ki jaidad is qarza ki zimewar hogi' (our properties at Delhi and Ludhiana will be responsible for this debt), it was held that these words did not create a charge[12].

BILLS OF SALE

Bills of sale are securities under the English Law and are governed by the Bills of Sale Act, 1878, as amended up to date. A brief description of these is given below for the benefit of students who have to study them.

A bill of sale has been defined as a document whereby the property in chattels is transferred to a grantee, either absolutely or conditionally by way of mortgage, but possession of the property remains with the grantor. The term "bill of Sale" includes (1) bill of sale proper ; (2) assignment; (3) transfer; (4) declaration of trust without transfer, (5) inventory of goods with receipt thereto attached; (6) receipt for purchase money of goods; (7) powers of attorney, authorities or licences' to take possession of personal chattels as security for any debt; (8) any agreement by which a right in equity to any personal chattels, or to any charge or security thereon, shall be conferred.

The following classes of instruments do not fall within the definition of a bill of sale, namely, (1) assignments for the benefit of the grantor's creditors; (2) marriage settlements; (3) transfers or assignments of any ship or any share thereof; (4) transfers of goods in the ordinary course of business; (5) bills of sale of goods in foreign ports or at sea; (6) bills of lading, India Warrants, warehouse-keeper's certificates, delivery orders used in the ordinary course of business.

The bills of sale are governed by the Bill of Sale Act, 1878, as amended up to date. The primary aims of the Act are to protect both the grantor and the grantee where chattels remaining in the possession of the grantor form the security for a loan made by the grantee; but third parties must also be protected, as they may be induced to enter into financial relations with the possessor of the chattels on the strength of such possession. Many arrangements other than bills of sale strictly so named, may involve the retention of the goods after a charge has been created; hence the provision that a bill of sale must be registered so that it should act as constructive notice to third parties.

The term "personal chattels" under the Bills of Sale Act means goods, furniture, and other articles capable of complete transfer by delivery, and (when separately assigned or charged) fixtures or growing crops. Trade machinery is also generally so regarded. But a bill of sale cannot be given in respect of any chose-in- action (actionable claim of the Indian law).

A bill of sale may be either (*i*) *Absolute,* or (*ii*) *Conditional.*

Absolute Bill of Sale—An absolute bill of sale is the document executed for the purpose of serving as evidence of the transfer of title. It serves as a protection to the buyer, especially if the goods are to remain temporarily in possession of the seller. An absolute bill of sale need not be in any specified form, but it must show the consideration for the transaction, and must be explained to the grantor by a solicitor and witnessed by a solicitor. The grantee may insert any conditions he pleases as to when he shall be entitled to take possession. Sometimes the possessor of property may be required to submit evidence of ownership, and a bill of sale serves the purpose. For example, it is generally required that before an automobile can be registered by a new owner a bill of sale must be submitted.

---

12. Furan Chand v. Puran Chand, Official Receiver, 1923 Lah. 625.

SPECIMEN COPY OF AN ABSOLUTE BILL OF SALE

KNOW ALL MEN BY THESE PRESENTS:

That I, *John Smith of Birmingham* (England) in consideration of the sum *of Five Hundred Pound Sterling,* to me paid by *James Brown of Birmingham,* the receipt whereof is hereby acknowledged, have bargained, sold, granted, and conveyed, and by these presents do bargain, sell, grant and convey unto the said *James Brown,* his executors, and administrators, and *assigns one Fordson Tractor, Model H. No. 06543.* To have and to hold the same unto the said *James Brown,* his executors, administrators, and assigns for ever. And I for myself and for my heirs, executors, and administrators, do hereby covenant with the said *James Brown,* his executors, administrators, and assigns, that *I am* the true and lawful owner of said described goods thereby sold and have full power to sell and convey the same; that the title so conveyed, is clear, free, and unencumbered; and furthur, that *I* do warrant and will defend the same against all claim or claims of all persons whomsoever.

IN WITNESS WHEREOF,*I* have hereunto set my hand this *fourteenth day of March, 1977.*

SIGNED AND DELIVERED IN THE PRESENCE OF:

(Signed) **William Bragg.**   (Signed) **John Smith.**

(Signed) **Harry Hilton.**

Conditional Bill of Sale—A conditional bill of sale is one given as security for the payment of money, the grantor having the right to have the chattels reconveyed to him upon fulfilling the condition. Such bills of sale are governed by the Bills of Sale Act (1878) and the Amendment Act, 1882. A conditional bill of sale need not be explained by a solicitor, or witnessed by a solicitor, but it must be witnessed by at least one credible witness. It must be in the exact form given in the Schedule to the Act, and must show the consideration which must not be less than £30, also the rate of interest, the date of repayment, and any condition on fulfilment of which the bill is to be void. An inventory of the personal chattels comprised in the bill must be attached. The grantee can only seize the goods comprised in the bill of sale for one of the following conditions mentioned in the Act, namely; (1) failing to perform the covenant; (2) bankruptcy, or allowing distraint to issue for rent, rates or taxes; (3) fraudulently removing the goods; (4) failure without reasonable excuse to produce the last receipt of rent, rates or taxes after written demand; (5) allowing execution to issue. It should, however, be remembered that even after seizure the goods cannot, without consent of the grantor, be removed from the premises or sold for 5 days, and within such 5 days the grantor may apply to the Court for relief if by payment or otherwise the cause of seizure no longer exists.

Registration of Bills of Sale—Every bill of sale, whether absolute or conditional, must be registered within 7 days of execution; and re-registered every five years. If executed out of England, registration must be effected within 7 days after the time in which it would, in the ordinary course of post, arrive in England, if posted immediately after execution. There must be produced to the Registrar the original bill, with a true copy of it and every schedule or inventory attached to it; and affidavit of due execution, stating the time it was given, and a description of the residence and occupation of the grantor and all other attesting witnesses. A conditional bill of sale must have attached a schedule specifically enumerating the chattels comprised in it, and chattels afterwards acquired cannot be included, except by way of substitution. If the omission to register arises from accident or inadvertence the judge may make an order extending the time for registration.

SPECIMEN COPY OF A CONDITIONAL BILL OF SALE

THIS INDENTURE made the....... day of ....One thousand nine hundred and seventy-seven BETWEEN ....of....... of the one part and ....of ....of the other part WITNESSETH that in consideration of the sum of ....the receipt of which the said ......hereby acknowledges. He then said ......both hereby assign unto ......his executors, administrators and assigns. All and singular the several chattels and things specifically described in the schedule hereunto annexed by way of security for the payment of the sum of...... Pounds and interest thereon at the rate of.... per cent, per annum. And the said ......doth further agree and declare that he will duly pay to the said......... the principal sum aforesaid together with the interest then due by equal...... payments of ......on the ...... in each and every .... And the said ......doth also agree with the said........that he will (Insert here terms as to insurance, payment of rent or otherwise which the parties may, agree to for the maintenance or defeasance of the security); provided always that the chattels hereby assigned shall not be liable to seizure or to be taken possession of by the said ....for any cause other than those specified in Sec. 7 of the Bills of Sale Act (1878) and the Amendment Act, 1882. IN WITNESS whereof the parties to these presents have hereunto set their hands and seals the day and year first above written.

Signed and sealed by the said....

In the presence of me **(Add witness's name, address and description)**

The Schedule above referred to
(Insert here the chattels and things comprised in the bill).

It should be remembered that the form must be strictly followed, otherwise the conveyance would be void. The bill will be void if the name, address, and description of the grantor, grantee or witness are omitted; or if the receipt clause is absent, or if the copy filed discloses even a trifling error. A term introduced to enable the grantee to retain a bill of sale after payment of the debt will also avoid the bill of sale, and so also will any term which has the effect of introducing covenants not contained in the statutory form, such as, for instance, incorporating terms by reference to another document.

HYPOTHECATION

The mortgage of movable property is called hypothecation. Neither the Indian Contract Act nor the Transfer of Property Act deals with the problem of hypothecation, but it is well settled that the mortgage of movable property, although unaccompanied by delivery of possession, is called hypothecation [*Deans* v. *Richardson* (1871) 3 N.W.P. 54]. Hypothecation may be described as a transaction whereby money is borrowed by the debtor (owner of the goods) on the security of the movable property without parting with the possession of the movable property. The owner of the hypothecated goods is called the Hypothecator, and the person to whom the goods are hypothecated is called the Hypothecatee.

The rights of the hypothecatee depend on the terms of the contract between the parties. For instance, he may be given, by the terms of the contract, the right to sell the goods himself, on default of payment by the hypothecator on due date, and to realise his dues from the sale proceeds. He can always file a suit to realise his dues by sale of the goods hypothecated.[13]

The hypothecatee may lose his rights over the goods hypothecated under the following circumstances:

1. If the hypothecator, in possession of the goods sells them to *bona fide*. purchaser—for value without notice of the hypothecation—the purchaser gets a good title to the goods and the hypothecatee cannot proceed against them (*Sreeram* v. *Bammireddi,* 42 Mad. 59; 35 M. L. J. 450).

2. If the hypothecator, in possession of the goods makes a valid pledge of the goods and the pledgee has no notice of the hypothecation, the claim of the hypothecatee will be postponed to that of the pledgee (*Co-operative Hindustan Bank* v. *Surendra,* 1932 Cal. 524).

Hypothecation differs from a mortgage in two respects:

---

13. Adapted from Ranking Spicer & Pegler's Mercantile Law.

(i) Mortgage relates to immovable property and hypothecation relates to movable property; (ii) In a mortgage there is a transfer of some interest in the property to the creditor, but in hypothecation there is only an obligation to repay money, and there is no transfer of any interest.

A pledge comes nearest to hypothecation. Both deal with movable property. But even between those two there are points of distinction. In a pledge there must be delivery of possession of the goods to the pledgee, but in hypothecation the goods need not be delivered to the hypothecatee. A hypothecatee cannot sell the goods without decree of the Court; but a pledgee can sell the goods after giving reasonable notice to the pledger.

LIEN

Lien is the right of retaining goods belonging to another until a debt due to the person retaining the goods is satisfied. Lien is of three kinds; (i) Possessory Lien, (ii) Maritime Lien, and (iii) Equitable Lien. Possessory Lien is again of two kinds, viz., (a) Particular Lien and (b) General Lien.

Possessory Lien—A possessory lien is one which can be exercised only by a person in possession of goods. A *particular lien* is a right to retain goods until some claim *concerning those goods* is paid. *General lien* is a right to retain all the goods of another in the possession of a person until all the claims of the possessor are satisfied. General lien may be conferred by an agreement to that effect or by custom and usage or by the provisions of any statute. General lien exists in the case of solicitors, bankers, factors, stock-brokers, warehousekeepers, wharfingers, and insurance brokers. (For detailed discussion, refer to Chapter on Bailment).

An unpaid seller has also a lien over the goods in his possession and property to which it has passed to the buyer until the price of the goods has been paid to him. This is also a possessory lien, as it depends on the unpaid seller's possession of the goods and not on title, and unless there is possession there is no lien.

A possessory lien can be enforced by retaining possession. The lien-holder cannot sell the property except under certain special circumstances. For example, an unpaid seller may sell the goods in his possession for non-payment of price to him after giving reasonable notice to the buyer.

A possessory lien is extinguished in the following cases; (i) when possession is lost, (ii) when the money due is paid, (iii) when the claimant takes some other security and thereby, by implication, abandons the right of lien, and (iv) when the right of lien is waived.

Maritime Lien—A maritime lien is a right specifically binding a ship, her furniture, machinery, cargo and freight for the payment of a claim based upon the maritime law. The persons who have a maritime lien are: seamen for their wages; the master for wages and disbursement; the holder of a bottomry bond for his dues; claimants for damages in cases of collision with the ship concerned; salvors, *i.e.* persons who salvage or rescue ship or property from the sea. A maritime lien is not a possessory lien. It is exercised by arresting the ship in the Admiralty Court. It comes to an end by payment, release, waiver and by the destruction of the subject-matter of the lien.

Equitable Lien—An equitable lien is an equitable right conferred by law upon one man to a charge upon the movable or immovable property of another until certain specific claims have been satisfied. Thus, an unpaid vendor of immovable property has an equitable lien on the property for the whole or part of the purchase money until actual payment. An equitable lien is binding on all persons who take the property with notice of the lien. It is enforced by a suit for the sale of the property to a *bona fide* purchaser for value without notice.

A lien differs from all the other securities in that a lien is the creation of law under certain circumstances, whereas the other securities are the creation of agreement between the parties. A lien is only a defensive right and cannot be enforced by a suit or by the sale of the property over which the lien is claimed. The only right that a holder of a lien enjoys is to retain the goods until his dues are satisfied.

CHAPTER

16

Company Law

Legal Persons—Law regulates the rights and obligations of persons, and divides them into two classes—(i) *natural persons,* or (ii) *artificial persons.* Natural persons are human beings of different degrees of capacity with whom we have been dealing so far. Artificial persons are such as are created and devised by human laws for the purposes of society and government, which are called *Corporations* or *Companies.* We shall, in the present Chapter, deal with this legal person—the Corporation or Company.

Corporation—A Corporation is an artificial person, with a distinctive name, a common seal, and created by law for the purpose of preserving in perpetual succession rights which would fail if vested in a natural person. Corporations are either "Corporations Sole" or "Corporations Aggregate."

A Corporation Sole consists of one corporator or member only at any given time, who enjoys corporate personality in virtue of his capacity as occupant of some public office for the time being. Examples are found in the perpetual offices such as the Crown, the Presidentship or a Bishopric. The office is constant, only the occupant of the office changes.

A Corporation Aggregate consists of a number of individuals contemporaneously associated so that in the eye of the law they form a single person, e.g., a Municipal Corporation such as the Municipal Corporation of Delhi or Bombay or Calcutta, or a company, which is formed mainly for the purposes of trade and commerce.

Company and its Meaning—In the ordinary common parlance, a company means a group of persons associated to achieve some common objective. Our object is to deal with a company which is formed for carrying on some business and providing for limited liability of its members. Keeping this type in mind we may define a company as a *voluntary* association for profit with capital divisible into transferable shares with *limited liability, having a corporate body and common seal.* The company is an artificial legal person created by law and endowed with certain powers. It exists in the eyes or contemplation of law as though it were a natural person, separate and distinct from the persons who are its members. As the company is created by law and is not itself a human being, and so has no physical existence, it is called artificial; and since it is clothed with many of the rights of a real person, it is called a person. It is accordingly an artificial, legal person.

This concept of the company as being a separate, legal person is fundamental in understanding the rights and duties that arise in connection with companies. It means that property of the company is not owned by the members who own shares but by the company.[1] Debts of company are debts of this artificial legal person and not of the people running the company or owning shares in it. The company

---

1. R.F. Perumal v. H. John, 1960 Mad. 43.

has a right to sue and can be sued, can own property and have banking account in its own name, own money and be a creditor but you cannot shake it by the hand, or knock it down in a fit of temper.

In consequence of the company being an entity separate and distinct from its shareholders,[2] the life of a company is not measured by the life of any member. Accordingly, a company has independent life in the sense that it continues to exist without regard to the death of the individuals involved in its corporate affairs or the transfer by them of their interests in the company; even the death of all its members does not end the company. On account of this separateness between the company and its members, a shareholder can be its creditor, too. Also, a shareholder cannot be held liable for the acts of the company, even though he holds virtually the entire share capital, as may happen in what is known as a "One-man Company." Similarly, the shareholders cannot bind the company by their acts; they are not its agents. These points are brought out by the House of Lords in the celebrated case *of Salomon v. Salomon & Company Limited* (1897) A.C. 22.

In this case, one Saloman, who carried on a prosperous leather business, sold it in solvent condition for the sum of £30,000 to a company which he formed consisting of himself, his wife and a daughter and his four sons as shareholders. His wife, daughter and four sons took one £1 share each. Salomon took 20,000 £1 shares and debentures of the amount of £10,000 secured by a floating charge on the company's assets as the price of the business transferred to the company. The company ran into difficulties and had to be wound up. The total assets amounted to £6,050; its liabilities were the £10,000 secured debentures and £8,000 owing to unsecured creditors who claimed the entire assets of £6,050, on the ground that the company and Salomon were one and the same person and that the company was mere "alias" or agent for Salomon, and hence they should be paid in priority to Salomon. The House of Lords rejected this contention of the unsecured creditors and held that as soon as the company was duly incorporated, it became in the eyes of the law a separate and distinct, as well as independent person from Salomon and was not his agent or trustee for him. Salomon, though holding almost all the shares in the company, was also a secured creditor, and so must be paid his debt out of the assets of the company in priority to unsecured creditors.

This case established the legality of what were formerly well known as "One-man" Companies. Once a company was validly formed with 7 members holding at least one share each, it became a separate entity from the members even if one of them held almost all the shares as did Salomon in this case. Although Salomon continued to be all in all even after the incorporation of the company, the business ceased to be his personal business and belonged to the company, and Salomon was its agent and not the company the agent of Salomon. Lord Macnaghton added: "The company is at law a different person altogether from the subscribers... and, though it may be that after incorporation the business is precisely the same as it was before, and the same persons are managers, and the same hands receive the profits, the company is not in law the agent of the subscribers or trustee for them. Not are the subscribers, as members, liable in any shape or form, except to the extent and in the manner provided by the Act."

The legal personality and limited liability are the two important features of a company. A person by buying shares, becomes entitled to participate in the profits when the company decides to divide them,[3] and is at liberty to dispose of them whenever he likes; and if anything goes wrong with the company, his liability is limited by the nominal amount of the shares held by him. As a natural consequence of incorporation and transferability of shares, the company has perpetual succession. This means the life of the company is independent of the lives of its members, giving immortality to the company. Hence members may come and members may go, but the company goes on

---

2. Tunstall v. Steigman (1962) 2 All E.R. 417; Dhulia etc. Transport Co. v. Roychand, 1962 Bom. 337.

3. Bacha F. Giazdar v. Com. Income-Tax, Bombay, *1955* S.C. 74; Short v. Treasury Commr. (1948) 1K.B. 116.

(until dissolved).

To sum up, the principal characteristics of a company are as follows:

1. A company has a separate and distinct personality from its members which constitute it.
2. In consequence of incorporation, it is an artificial legal person, enjoying similar rights and owing similar obligations as a natural person.
3. As a corporate person the company is entitled to own and hold property as distinct from its members.
4. As a juristic person distinct from its members it has perpetual succession.
5. The shares in the share capital of the company are generally freely transferable. This makes the life of the company independent of the lives of its members.
6. The liability of its shareholders is limited to the unpaid value of the shares held by them.
7. A company, though a person having nationality and a domicile is not a citizen.[4] It cannot therefore exercise the right of franchise, not can it be punished, in its own person, by imprisonment for criminal offences, although it can be fined for the contravention of the provisions of the Companies Act.
8. As the company is not a citizen and can act only through natural persons, it has no fundamental rights under the Constitution.[5]

Lifting or Piercing the Corporate Veil—The advantage of incorporation, as explained in the previous section, particularly the concept of separate and distinct entity, are allowed to be enjoyed only by those who do not make a fraudulent and dishonest use of the company—the artificial legal person. For instance, the Court may not recognise the separate existence of a company where the only purpose for which it appears to have been formed is the evasion of taxes.[6]

The Court may also find it just to break through the corporate shell and apply the principle of what is known as lifting or piercing the corporate veil, where it may become necessary in public interest to examine the character of persons in real control of the corporate affairs. In *Daimler & Co. Ltd. v. Continental Tyre & Rubber Co.* (1916) 2 A.C. 307, the company was registered in England, but on the declaration of war between England and Germany, the persons in control of the company and resident in Germany became alien enemies. The Court disregarded the corporate fiction of separate entity of the company and declared it an enemy company.

By virtue of Sec. 45, if the number of members falls below the statutory minimum, and the company carries on business for more than 6 months, while the number is so reduced, every shareholder who is aware of these facts shall be directly and severally liable to the creditors for the debts of the company contracted during that time, the creditors being permitted to look behind the company to the owners of the shares for their satisfaction. Thus, the privilege of limited liability is lost by the shareholder.

Under Sec. 542, the legal personality of the company may also be disregarded if in the course of winding up it appears that the machinery of incorporation has been used for some fraudulent purpose, or for defrauding creditors of the company. Any persons who were knowingly parties to the carrying on of the business in that manner will be held personally liable to the full extent for all debts, etc., of the company.

B was carrying on a jewellery business. He formed and registered a company with himself and his wife as members. The company took over nothing, but a banking account was opened in its name with £160 which B put in. B went on trading exactly as he did before for the one-man company, as its managing and sole director. The company had practically no assets. On a claim to recover £875, being the value of jewellery entrusted to him, it was contended on his behalf that the goods were

---

4. State Trading Corporation of India Ltd. v. C.T.O., 1963 S.C.J. 605.

5. Tata E. & L. Co. Ltd. v. State of Bihar, 1965 S.C.40.

6. In re Sir Dinshaw Maneckjee Petit, 1927 Bom. 371.

delivered to him and the contract made with him as managing director of the limited company, and that he was not personally liable. *Held*, it was a good case to lift or pierce the corporate veil and hold B personally liable [*Hurwitz* v. *Berman* (*The Times*, Oct. 29,1932)].

Classes of Companies—Companies are of different varieties. They may be—

1. **Chartered Companies**, such as the East India Company, which are created by Charter granted by the King or Queen in exercise of an ancient prerogative vested in the Crown. A chartered company is regulated by its charter and the Companies Act does not apply to it. Such companies have no place in India since Independence.

2. **Statutory Companies**, like the Reserve Bank of India or the State Bank of India, which are created by Special Acts of Parliament or State Legislature. A statutory company is governed by the provisions of the special Act creating it. The Companies Act does not apply to such companies.

3. **Registered Companies**, which are incorporated under the Companies Act, 1956, or were registered under the previous Companies Acts therein consolidated and recognised.

A registered company may be an *unlimited company*, in which case the liability of its members would be unlimited so that they can be called upon to pay to the full extent of their fortunes in order to meet the obligations of the company. Such companies are now almost extinct, as a vast majority of them have registered themselves as limited companies.

Another class of a registered company is a *Guarantee Company*, with its capital limited by guarantee so that each member undertakes to be liable to pay the debts of the company up to a certain amount in case of winding up. Clubs, trade associations and societies for promoting social objects are examples of this type; and in the case of these companies there is no intention to make profit.

The largest in number and most important in function are Limited Liability Companies registered with a share capital divided into shares held by shareholders whose liability is limited to the face value of the shares held by them. This class of company will be almost exclusively dealt with by us.

Functionally, a registered company with limited liability may be either Private or Public, or an Association not for Profit.

Private Company—A private company is defined by Sec. 3 (l)-(iii) as a company which by its articles of association, (i) restricts the right to transfer its shares, (ii) limits the number of its members (excluding employees who are members or ex-employees who were and continue to be members) to 50, and (iii) prohibits any invitation to the public to subscribe for any of its shares and debentures. If two or more persons hold one or more shares jointly, they shall be treated as a single member.[7] The name of every private company must end with the words "Private Limited." Since the membership of private company is confined more or less to friends and relatives, it enjoys certain special privileges and exemptions.

Privileges of Private Company—A private company enjoys the following privileges and exemptions:—

1. Only two signatories to the memorandum are sufficient to form a private company.
2. It can commence allotment of shares before the minimum subscription is subscribed or paid.
3. It is not required to file a statement in lieu of prospectus as it is not allowed to issue a prospectus to the public.
4. It need not offer further shares first to the existing shareholders under Sec. 81.
5. A private company may commence business immediately after incorporation.
6. It is not required to hold the statutory meeting and file the statutory report.
7. It may issue any kinds of shares and allow disproportionate voting right.
8. A private company need have only 2 directors.

---

7. Jamail Singh v. Bakshi Singh, 1960 Punj. 555.

9. Its director can vote on a contract in which he is interested.
10. Provisions relating to loans made to directors, duration of appointments, etc., of managing director in a public company, etc., do not apply to a private company.

Loss of Privileges—A private company will lose its privileges and will be treated as a public company, if it fails to comply with the essential requirements of a private company, viz., restrictions on transfer of shares; limitation of its members to fifty; and prohibition of invitation to the public to buy its shares or debentures (Sec. 43). The Court may, however, relieve the company from the consequences of non-compliance with the aforesaid regulations, if it is of opinion that the non-compliance was accidental or inadvertent.

CIRCUMSTANCES UNDER WHICH A PRIVATE COMPANY BECOMES A PUBLIC COMPANY

Section 34A was amended by the Companies (Amendment) Act, 1988, and with effect from June 15,1988, a private Company shall be deemed to be a public company under any of the following circumstances:—

1. Where not less than 25 per cent of the paid up share capital is held by one or more public companies or deemed public companies;
2. Where the average annual turnover of a private company during the period of three consecutive financial years is ₹10 crores or more, irrespective of the paid up share capital;
3. Where not less than 25 per cent of the paid up share capital of a public company is held by a private company;
4. Where on or after June 15, 1988, a private company accepts, after invitation by advertisement, or renews, deposits from the public other than its members, directors or their relatives.

However, even after a private company has become a deemed public company, its articles may include provisions relating to matters specified in Section 3(1) (iii) and the number of its members may be less than 7 and it may have only 2 directors.

Within 3 months from the date on which a private company becomes a public company, it shall inform the Registrar that it has become a public company. Thereupon, the Registrar will delete the word "Private" from the name of the company upon the Register. The Registrar will issue a new Certificate of Incorporation without the word "Private" in the name of the company. Failure to inform the Registrar will render the company and every officer in default liable to fine up to ₹500 per day during default.

Conversion of public company into private company—A public company having share capital, and a membership within the limits imposed upon private companies by Sec.3 (1) (iii) may become a private company by passing a special resolution altering the articles to include the necessary restrictions, limitations, and prohibitions, and to delete any provisions inconsistent with the restrictions, e.g. a power to issue share warrants to bearer. The proviso to Sec. 31 now requires that approval of the Central Government must be obtained to the conversion of a public company to a private company. The name of the company must now end with the words "Private Limited."

Conversion of private company into public company—Sec. 44 lays down the procedure as follows: The company must pass a special resolution altering its articles of association in such a manner that they no longer include the provisions of Sec. 3(1) (iii) which are required to be included in the articles of a private company. On the date of the resolution the company ceases to/be a private company and becomes a public company. If the number of members is below 7, steps should be taken to raise it to at least seven, and the number of directors should be increased to three, if it is less than three. It must within 30 days file a prospectus or statement in lieu of prospectus with the Registrar. The company will also alter those regulations contained in the articles which are inconsistent with the public company.

Public Company—A public company is one which is not a private company, and whose membership is open to the public under the provisions of its articles. The minimum number required to form such a company is seven, but there is no limitation to the maximum number of members. It can offer shares and debentures to the public by advertising such offer in a prospectus. Almost all the provisions of the Act apply to it.

Distinction between Public and Private Companies—The two types of companies differ in the following respects:

1. The minimum number with which a public company can be formed is seven and in the case of a private company it is only two.

2. There is no limitation to the maximum number of members in a public company. In the case of a private company, the number of members must not exceed fifty.

3. A public company is required to have at least three directors, but a private company may have only two directors.

4. The directors of a public company have to file with the Registrar consent to act as directors, but those of a private company need not do so.

5. A public company may, and usually does, invite by the issue of prospectus the general public to subscribe to its share capital or buy its debentures, but a private company cannot do so; it must make private arrangement to raise capital.

6. The shares in a public company, as a rule, are freely transferable. In a private company, the transfer of shares can be made subject to certain restrictions as provided in its articles.

7. Total managerial remuneration in a public company cannot exceed 11 per cent of the net profits, but a private company which is not a subsidiary of a public company may pay any remuneration.

8. A public company can issue only two kinds of shares—preference and equity, but a private company may issue any kinds of shares and even with disproportionate voting rights.

Holding and Subsidiary Companies—Sec. 4 defines the terms holding company and 'subsidiary' by explaining the circumstances in which a company shall be deemed to be the subsidiary of another. If these circumstances of subsidiary relationship are found to apply then the other company is deemed to be a holding company. The section, by defining a subsidiary, brings out the meaning of a holding company.

A company is a subsidiary company of another if,—

(a) that other, (i.e., the holding or controlling company) controls the composition of its Board of Directors; or

(b) that other (the holding or controlling company)—

    (i) exercises or controls more than half of the total voting power of the existing subsidiary company in which the holders of preference shares issued before April 1,1956, have the same voting rights as equity shareholders;

    (ii) holds more than half in nominal value of the equity share capital of a subsidiary which is the holding company of another; or

(c) the subsidiary is a subsidiary of any company which is that other company's subsidiary.

If company B is a subsidiary of company A, and company C is a subsidiary of company B, then company C is a subsidiary of company A. If D is the subsidiary of C, then D will be the subsidiary of B and also of A.

Shares held (or power exercisable) in fiduciary capacity are not to be counted and do not make the latter a holding company; but shares held by a nominee are to be counted. An **Investment Company**, that is to say, a company whose principal business is the acquisition and holding of shares, stock, debentures or other securities is not a holding company merely because part of its assets consists in 50 per cent or more of the shares in another company.

Foreign Companies—A company incorporated in a country outside India and under the law of that other country is a foreign company. Every foreign company having a place of business in India is required to file with the Registrar at New Delhi and also the Registrar of the State in which such place of business is situated a certified copy of its charter, statute or memorandum and articles defining the constitution of the company in English language, the full address of the registered or principal office of the company and a list of its directors and its secretary, as well as the address of the principal place of business in India. Every foreign company must conspicuously exhibit on the outside of every office or place of business in India the name of the company, indicating whether Private Limited or Public Limited or unlimited, and where incorporated. The new sub-sec. (2) to Sec. 591 provides that where not less than 50% of the paid-up share capital (whether equity or preference or partly equity and partly preference) of a foreign company having an established place of business in India, is held by one or more citizens of India or by one or more Indian bodies corporate, such foreign company shall comply with such of the provisions of the Act as may be prescribed with regard to the business carried on by it in India.

The provisions regarding books of accounts and annual return are the same as per the Indian companies, as also regarding registration of charges. The provisions regarding prospectus are also almost the same as for an Indian company. A foreign company, which has been carrying on business in India and stops its business here, may be wound up as an unregistered company, even if it has been dissolved or has ceased to exist under the laws of country in which it was incorporated.

Government Company—(Sec. 617). A Government company means any company in which not less than 51 per cent of the paid-up share capital is held by the Central Government, or by any State Government or Governments, or partly by the Central Government and partly by one or more State Governments and includes a company which is a subsidiary of a Government company. Government companies are also subject to the provisions of the Companies Act as any other company, except if the Central Government by notification exempts any Government company from the application of any of the provisions of the Act save Secs. 618, 619 and 619A specially dealing with Government companies. Sec. 618 prohibits a Government company from having managing agent.

Sec. 619 provides for a special procedure for audit of Government companies and lays down that the auditor of a Government company shall be appointed or re-appointed by the Central Government on the advice of the Comptroller and Auditor General of India; provided no person will be appointed or re-appointed an auditor of more than 20 Government companies. The C. & A. G. can direct the manner in which the accounts are to be audited, and may even conduct a supplementary audit His report, if any, must be placed before the annual general meeting along with the auditor's report. In addition to the annual report on the working of the company, the Central Government must place before both Houses of Parliament an annual report on the working and affairs of each Government company, together with the audit report and any comments of C. & A. G. of India.

Associations not for profit—Sec. 25 permits the registration, under a licence granted by the Central Government, of associations not for profit with limited liability without using the word "limited" or words "private limited" to their names. An association not for profit is a company formed for promoting commerce, art, science, religion, charity, or any other useful object, and which does not intend to pay any dividend to its members, but to apply its profits or other income in promoting its objects. It is registered without paying any stamp duty on its memorandum and articles. On registration, the association enjoys all the privileges of a limited company, and is subject to all its obligations except those in respect of which exemption is granted by the Central Government. The Central Government may at any time revoke the licence whereupon the company loses all exemptions and privileges and must publish its name with "limited" or "Private limited." This type of company cannot alter its object clause without the previous approval in writing of the Central Government.

Prohibition of large partnerships—Illegal Associations—Sec. 11 provides that no company, association or partnership consisting of more than 20 members (10 in the case of banking business) be formed to carry on any business for gain unless it is registered as a company under the Companies Act or is formed in pursuance of some other Indian Law, or is a joint Hindu family carrying on business as such. An association or partnership contravening the above requirements is an *illegal association,* in the sense that as a body, it has no legal existence, and cannot be wound up under the Act, not even as an unregistered company.[8] It follows that an association which falls within the terms of Sec. 11, and is not registered, has no legal existence; it is a phantom. The law does not recognise it,[9] and consequently, it is an illegal association.

As an illegal association, it—

(a) cannot enter into any contract;

(b) cannot sue any member or outsider,[10] not even if the company is subsequently registered;

(c) cannot be sued by a member,[11] or any outsider, for it cannot contract any debts;

(d) cannot be wound up by order of the Court In fact the Court should not entertain a petition for its winding up, for if it did, it would be indirectly according recognition to the illegal association.

The position of its members is an unenviable one, for every one of them is individually liable in respect of all acts or contracts which he purports to do or make on behalf of the association, they cannot either individually or collectively, bring an action to enforce any contract, so made, or to recover any debt due to the association.[12] Thus, every member of an illegal association is (i) personally liable for all liabilities incurred in the carrying on of the business of or by the illegal association, and (ii) is punishable with fine lip to ₹ 1,000.

Company Law Board—A new Section 10 E has been substituted in place of the old one with a view *to* establishing an autonomous Company Law Board with wider powers. The Board will in future exercise most of the powers of the Court and the Central Government.

Meaning of Officer in default—A new Section 5 has been substituted in place of the old Section 5. The new Section provides that for the purpose of penalty or punishment the expression "officer who is in default" means an officer of the company who is knowingly guilty of the default, or who knowingly authorises or permits such default.

All the following officers of the company are covered by the expression "Officer who is in default"

(i) the managing director or managing directors;

(ii) the whole-time director or whole-time directors;

(iii) the manager;

(iv) the secretary;

(v) any person in accordance with whose directions or instructions the Board of directors of the company is accustomed to act;

(vi) any person charged by the Board of directors with the responsibility of complying with the provisions, if the person has given his consent to the Board; (vii) when a company has no managing or whole-time director, the specified directors or all directors.

PART 16-B
FORMATION OF COMPANY

The promoters (persons wishing to form a company) must file with the Registrar of the State in which the registered office of the company is to be situate—

---

8. Raghubar Dayal v. Sarafa Chamber, 1954 All. 555.

9. Madan Gopal v. Sheo Das, 1934 Lah.882.

10. Union of India v. Commercial Association, 1959, Punj. 104.

11. Badri Prasad v. Nagarmal (1959) 29 Com.Cas, 229 (S.C.).

12. Wilkinson v. Levison (1925) 42 T.LR. 97.

1. The Memorandum of Association;
2. The Articles of Association;
3. A statement of nominal capital, and where it exceeds 50 lakhs, a certificate from the Central Government permitting the issue of capital; (the Controller of Capital Issues grants this certificate);
4. A statutory declaration by an advocate or an attorney or a chartered accountant, engaged in the formation of the company, or by a director or any other officer of the company that all requirements of the Act and Rules thereunder in respect of registration have been complied with.
5. A list of persons who have consented to be directors of the company;
6. A written consent duly signed to act as directors;
7. An undertaking in writing signed by each such director to take and pay for their qualification shares, if any.

Ordinarily, both the private and public companies will file the notice of their addresses of the Registered Office; (or it may be given within 30 days after the date of incorporation).

When the necessary stamp duty and the registration fee have been paid and the Registrar is satisfied that everything is in order, he will enter the name of the company in the register of companies maintained by him and issue a **Certificate of Incorporation** which gives the company a legal existence from the date given on it This certificate is a conclusive evidence mat everything is in order as regards registration and that the company has come into being, with rights and obligations of a natural person, competent to enter into contracts.[13]

PRELIMINARY CONTRACTS

Very often a company is formed for the purpose of buying an existing business or property. The promoters of the company would naturally like to have a binding contract from the owner of the business or property, but under the Companies Act, the company can make a binding contract only after its incorporation. Consequently, according to the Companies Act, a contract made before the incorporation of the company by some person professing to act on its behalf is not binding on the company nor can the contract be ratified by the company after incorporation, for obviously a person cannot act as an agent for another who is not yet in existence.[14] Also the company cannot sue the vendor if he fails to carry out the contract. The persons purporting to enter into contract on behalf of the company remain personally liable on the contract. Because of these difficulties it has become customary for promoters to agree to the form of draft contract to be entered into by the vendor and the company after incorporation. But Secs. 15 and 19 of the Specific Relief Act have considerably alleviated the difficulty. Sec. 15 provides that when a contract is made "for the purpose of the company and such contract is warranted by the terms of incorporation" specific performance thereof may be enforced by the company though the contract is made before its incorporation. Sec. 19 of the same Act provides that when the promoters of a public company before its incorporation enter into a contract, specific performance thereof may be enforced against the company, "provided that the company has ratified and adopted the contract and the contract is warranted by the terms of incorporation." These sections are, however, inapplicable to contracts to take shares, nor will the specific performance of contracts of personal service be ordered by the Court.

PROMOTER

The "promotion" of a company is a comprehensive term denoting that process by which a company is "incorporated" or brought into existence as a corporate body, and 'floated', or established financially

---

13. Jubilee Cotton Mill Ltd. v. Lewis (1924) A.C. 958.
14. Re. English and Colonial Produce Co. (1906) 2 Ch.435.

as a going concern, by the issue of a prospectus. Anyone who assumes primary responsibility with regard to matters relating to promotion, or any of them, may be held to be a "promoter". "The term 'promoter'." said Boden L. J., "is a term not of law but of business, usually summing up in a single word a number of business operations familiar to the commercial world by which a company is generally brought into existence".[15] The word promoter is used in common parlance to denote any individual, syndicate, association, partnership, or company, which takes all necessary steps to create and mould a company and set it going.

A promoter stands in a fiduciary relation to the company it promotes and to those persons whom he induces to become shareholders in it.[16] Although a promoter is not an agent or trustee of the company before its formation, yet the responsibility of an agent and trustee is placed upon him to account for all moneys secretly obtained by him. Consequently, a promoter must act honestly, and must not make, directly or indirectly, any profit at the expense of the company he is promoting, although he may receive some remuneration for his work. The usual ways of receiving remuneration by the promoter are: (1) by selling to the company at a profit some property purchased by the promote; before he became one; (2) by taking a commission on the shares sold; (3) by taking a grant of some shares of the company;, (4) by taking a grant of a lump sum of money from the company.

Commencement of Business—A private company may commence business immediately after obtaining the certificate of incorporation.

A public company must obtain a 'certificate to commence business' from the Registrar before it can commence business. The Registrar will grant this certificate only when—

(a) the Minimum subscription has been allotted;
(b) the directors have taken up and paid for their qualification shares;
(c) the statutory declaration and the prospectus or statement in lieu of prospectus have been filed.

Any new business (as mentioned under other objects in the memorandum) can be started only after obtaining approval of the shareholders by a special resolution, and after a declaration has been filed with the Registrar, verified by one of the directors or the Secretary that the approval by special resolution has been given by the company in general meeting.

All contracts entered into between the date of incorporation and the date of the commencement of business are provisional and would bind the company only after it is entitled to commence business. If the company does not commence business within one year of its incorporation the Court may order it to be wound up.

MEMORANDUM OF ASSOCIATION

The Memorandum of Association of a company is of supreme importance in determining its powers and, in this respect, it is the charter of the company, which contains the **fundamental conditions** upon which alone the company can be incorporated. It defines as well as confines the powers of the company, so that it not only shows the object of its formation, but also the utmost scope of its operation beyond which its action cannot go. It, in a way, regulates the external affairs of the company in relation to outsiders. Its purpose is to enable shareholders, creditors and all those who deal with the company to know what its powers are and what is the range of its activities or enterprise.

The Memorandum must be printed, divided into paragraphs, numbered consecutively and signed by seven subscribers (two in the case of a private company), in the presence of a witness who shall attest the signature of each subscriber. Each subscriber must add his address, description and occupation, and the number of shares taken.

---

15. Whaley Bridge Printing Co. v. Green (1880) 5 Q.B.D. 109.

16. Lagunas Nitrate Co. v. Lagunas Syndicate (1899) 2 Ch. 392. Omnium Electric Palaces Ltd. v. Baines (1914) 1 Ch. 332.

Contents of Memorandum—Pursuant to Sec. 13, the memorandum of a company limited by shares must state the following:—

1. The name of the company, with "limited" or "private limited" as the last words;
2. The State in which the registered office of the company is to be situate;
3. The objects of the company: (a) Main; (b) Others;
4. The fact that the liability of the members is limited;
5. The proposed amount of the capital, and its division into shares of a fixed amount; and
6. The declaration of association.

Name of the Company—Sec. 20 (1) provides that no company must be registered by a name which, in the opinion of the Central Government, is undesirable. This enables the Government to reject a name without giving any reason. The Registrar will continue, as before, to refuse names identical with, or too closely resembling names already on the register as undesirable names.[17] The company must not give an impression that the company is carrying on the business of some other well established company. Under the Emblem and Names (Prevention of Improper Use) Act, 1950, the Government may declare what names and emblems are not to be used by companies in trade marks and patents. The use of the following has been prohibited under the above Act, viz., name and emblem of the U.N.O. and the W.H.O., the Indian National Flag, the Official Seal and Emblems of the Central and State Governments. Subject to the above restrictions a company may adopt any name it likes. If by inadvertence a name is selected which is similar to that of an existing company, it must be changed.

Once the name is registered, it must be painted or affixed on the outside of every office or place of business, in a conspicuous position in letters easily legible in the language in general use in the locality. It must be engraved on the seal and mentioned in all notices, advertisements, other official publications, negotiable instruments and orders for money or goods (Sec. 147).

Registered Office—Every company must have a registered office as from the date on which it commences business or the 30th day after incorporation date whichever is earlier, to which notices and all other communications can be sent.

Objects Clause—The objects clause indicates the extent of company's powers and sphere of its activities. It defines and confines the scope of company's powers, and once registered, it can only be altered as provided by the Act. The purpose of the memorandum is two-fold: *One,* to inform the members in what kind of business their capital may be used; *secondly,* to inform persons dealing with the company what its powers are.[18] A company cannot do anything beyond its powers, and any act beyond such powers in *ultra vires* and void and cannot be ratified even by the assent of the whole body of shareholders. The objects should, therefore, be clearly set forth in the memorandum. Ambiguous and general provisions will not be of any use. Although express powers are necessary a company may do anything which is incidental to and consequential upon the powers specified, and the act will not be *ultra vires.*[19] Thus a trading company has an implied power to borrow, draw and accept bills in the ordinary form, but a railway company cannot issue bills, although it may borrow money.

As the procedure laid down in Sec. 17 for the alteration of the objects clause when some new venture is contemplated is rather cumbersome and the sanction of the Company Law Board is essential, the promoters of companies have been making the objects and purposes as wide as possible. This practice often enabled directors to participate in activities which were neither the main activities nor were they ancillary thereto, but were remote in character and far removed from the main purpose. Very often, the members of the company knew nothing, or where they did know, they could not do

---

17. Madame Tussand & Sons v. Tussand (1890) 44 Ch.D.673.
18. Cotman v. Broughman (1918) A.C. 504.
19. Attorney General v. G.E. Rly. Co. (1880) 5 A.C. 473; Evan v. Bruner (1921) 1 Ch. 359.

anything. In order to enable the shareholders to have a say in the matter, and also to let the doctrine of *ultra vires* have some play, Sec. 13 of the Act was amended in 1965 so as to make it compulsory in future for the promoters to specify in clear terms the Main and Subsidiary objects of the company.[20]

Sec. 13, as amended, provides in clauses (c) and (d) as follows:—

(c) in the case of a company in existence immediately before October 15,1965, the memorandum shall state the objects of the company;

(d) in the case of a company formed after October 14, 1965, the memorandum must state —

    (i) the *main objects* of the company to be pursued by the company on its incorporation and objects incidental and ancillary to the attainment of the main objects,

    (ii) *other objects* of the company not included in subclause (i).

An amendment to Sec. 149 prohibits a company from commencing any new business (as stated under other objects) without obtaining the prior approval of the shareholders by a special resolution passed in a general meeting. In some special cases the Central Government may allow new business to be commenced even if it is approved by an ordinary resolution.

LIMITATION OF LIABILITY

A declaration that the liability of the members of the company is limited to the amounts unpaid on their shares, must be made in the memorandum. If a shareholder has paid ₹50 on a ₹100 share, he can be called upon to pay the balance of ₹50, and if another has paid ₹100, he holds a full-paid share and cannot be called upon to pay anything. But there is one **exception** to this rule, viz., that **if a company continues to carry on business for more than 6 months after the membership has fallen below 7 in the case of a public company, and 2 in the case of a private company, then all members aware of the fact are fully and severally liable for all debts contracted after the 6 months, i.e., their liability becomes unlimited.**

Capital Clause—The capital clause in the memorandum of a company, having a share capital, states the amount of capital with which it is registered, divided into shares of a certain amount This capital is called the "registered," "nominal" or "authorised" capital. The effect of this clause is that the company cannot issue more shares than are authorised by the memorandum for the time being. A public company can issue only two kinds of shares—Preference and Equity; and the shares must not give disproportionate voting rights. A private company may, however, issue any kinds of shares and with disproportionate voting rights (Sees. 85, 88,90),

Declaration of Association or the Association Clause—At the end of the memorandum of every company there is a declaration of association or an association clause which reads something like this: "We, the several persons whose names and addresses and occupations are subscribed, are desirous of being formed into a company in pursuance of this memorandum of association and respectively agree to take the number of shares in the capital of the company set opposite our respective names." Then follow the names, addresses, occupations, the number of shares each person has taken and his signature attested by a witness. Each subscriber has to take at least one share in share capital of the company. At least 7 subscribers must sign the memorandum in the case of a public company although 2 are sufficient in the case of a private company.

DOCTRINE OF "ULTRA VIRES"

We have observed, while dealing with the "objects clause," that company exists only for the purposes which are stated in its memorandum of association or which are incidental to or consequential upon

---

20. The Vivian Bose Commission, while examining the case of Dalmia Jain Airways Ltd., had recommended the mention in the memorandum of the main and other objects separately.

these specified powers, and any act done outside the expressed or implied powers is *ultra vires,* and therefore null and void.[21] An *ultra vires* act is improper because it is a violation of the law and diversion of the assets of the company to a purpose not contemplated by the members and creditors of the company. An *ultra vires* act is not binding upon the company and cannot be ratified. The company can be restrained from employing its funds for purposes other than those stated in the memorandum. Thus a company formed to carry on one trade cannot carry on another trade.[22] Where a company by its Memorandum was incorporated with the object of making, and selling railway carriages, it was held that the purchase of a concession, for erecting a railway in a foreign country was *ultra vires* the company.[23] So also an authority to a County Council to run trams does not empower it to run omnibuses. In India, by virtue of the Companies (Donations to National Funds) Act, 1951, a company by special resolution may use its funds for making donations to the Gandhi National Memorial Fund, Sardar Vallabhbhai National Memorial Fund or any other Fund for charitable purposes which have been approved by the Central Government.

As a result, however, of the rigours of the doctrine of *ultra vires,* memoranda are now very widely drawn, and frequently specify various trades and businesses which have apparently very little if any connection with the main business of the company. It is then possible for the company to extend its operations at any time without taking steps to alter the objects of the company. It is because of this that the Bhaba Commission on Company Law remarked: "As Memoranda of Association are drafted, the doctrine of *ultra vires* was an illusory protection for shareholders or pitfall for third parties dealing with the company." Now, in the case of a company formed after the commencement of the 1965 Amendment Act, the 'main' objects and 'other' objects must be separately stated; and thus, the doctrine *of ultra vires* remains very much in the picture, although alteration of the objects clause can be made to include new purposes in the memorandum.

The doctrine of *ultra vires* is, however, subject to the following exceptions: (1) If an act is *ultra vires* the powers of the directors only, e.g., their borrowing powers, the shareholders can ratify it. (2) If it is *ultra vires* the articles of the company, the articles can be altered and the error rectified. (3) If an act is within the powers of the company, but is irregularly done, consent of all the shareholders will validate the act (4) The company's rights over property will be protected, even though the property has been acquired by *ultra vires* expenditure. (5) Though the act is *ultra vires,* rights arising independently thereout are not affected thereby.[24] (6) A person borrowing money from the company under a contract which is *ultra vires* can be sued by the company. (7) Where there is an *ultra vires* borrowing by the company, or it obtains delivery of property from a third party under an *ultra vires* contract, that third party has no claim against the company on the basis of the loan, but he has a right to follow his money or property if it exists in specie, and obtain an injunction restraining the company from parting with it, provided he intervenes before the money is spent or the identity of the property is lost [*Sinclair v. Brougham* (1914) A. C. 398]. (8) The lender of money to a company under a contract which is *ultra vires,* has a right to make the directors personally liable, on the ground of implied warranty of authority, if their act amounts to an implied misrepresentation of fact. (9) If a director of a company makes payment of a certain sum of money, which is *ultra vires* the company, he can be compelled by the company to refund it but the director in his turn may claim indemnity from the person who received it knowing that it is *ultra vires.*

21. Ashbury Rail etc. Co. Ltd. v. Riche (1875) 7 H.L 688.
22. Egyptian Salt Co. v. Port Said Salt Ass. (1931) A.C. 677.
23. Ashbury Rail Case.
24. Gerrad v. James (1925) Ch. 616.

ALTERATION OF MEMORANDUM

For the purposes of alteration, the provisions contained in the memorandum are classified into two heads: *Conditions and other provisions.* The "conditions" are those provisions which are compulsory clauses, namely, the name, the place of registered office (situation), objects, limited liability and share capital. The conditions can be altered only as expressly provided by Secs. 17, 21, 94, 99, 100 and 106.

The **other provisions**, such as the terms of appointment of managing director or manager contained in the memorandum can be altered by a special resolution with the approval of the Central Government, or a clause in the memorandum fixing limit of dividends to be paid on a particular class of shares can be altered by a special resolution.[25]

ALTERATION OF CONDITIONS

Change of name—The name of the company can be changed any time by a special resolution and with the written approval of the Central Government. If the change merely involves the addition or deletion of the word "Private" on the conversion of a public company into a private company or *vice versa,* no approval of the Central Government is necessary. The change must be communicated to the Registrar by filing a printed or type-written copy of the special resolution within 30 days of the passing thereof. The Registrar will then issue a fresh certificate of incorporation, and the change of name will be effective only thereafter. The changed name should be noted in each copy of the memorandum and articles.

Change of Registered Office—The registered office may be changed any time from one place to another within the local limits of the city, town or village where it is situated, and a notice of the change be given to the Registrar within 30 days of such change.

If the office is to be removed from one city, town or village to another city, town or village within the same State, a special resolution should be passed, and a printed or type-written copy thereof filed within 30 days. Then within 30 days of the removal of the office, a notice to the Registrar should be given of the location of the new office.

Change of Registered Office from one State to another or change of Objects—The Registered office from one State to another State, or the objects of the company, can be changed by special resolution, confirmed by the Company Law Board, if the alteration is rendered necessary—

(a) to carry on its business more economically or more efficiently;
(b) to attain its main purpose by new or improved means ;
(c) to enlarge or change the location of its operations ;
(d) to carry on some business which under existing circumstances may be conveniently or advantageously combined with the business of the company;
(e) to restrict or abandon any of the objects specified in the memorandum;
(f) to sell or dispose of the whole, or any part, of the undertaking; or
(g) to amalgamate win any other company or body of persons.

The Company Law Board being satisfied that the notice of the resolution was given to all persons whose interests are likely to be affected by the alteration, including the Registrar, and having heard him and the creditors' objections, if any, may confirm the alteration wholly or in part. A certified copy of the Company Law Board's order together with a printed copy of the altered memorandum must be filed within 3 months of the date of the order with the Registrar, who will register them and issue a certificate which will be conclusive evidence that everything has been done properly (Secs. 17 -19). The alteration of the objects clause must leave the business of the company substantially what it was before with only such changes in the mode of conducting it as would enable it to be carried on more

25. In re Rampuria Cotton Mills Ltd.. 1959 Cal 253.
26. Re Cyclists Touring Club (1907) I Ch., 269.

economically or more efficiently.[26]

Where the alteration involves a transfer of the registered office from one State to another, the certified copy of the Company Law Board's order confirming the change must be filed with the Registrars of both the States who will register the same. All the records of the company will then be transferred to the Registrar of the State to which the registered office of the company has been transferred.

Alteration of Capital—Sec. 94 provides that a limited company having a share capital may, if so authorised by its articles, alter the conditions of its memorandum relating to capital by ordinary resolution in general meeting, so as:—

(a) to **increase** it by the issue of new shares of such amount as it thinks expedient;

(b) to **consolidate and divide** all or any of its share capital into shares of larger amount than its existing shares;

(c) to **convert** all or any of its fully paid up shares into stock and reconvert that stock into fully paid up shares of any denomination;

(d) to **sub-divide** its shares or any of them, into shares of smaller amount than is fixed by the memorandum. But in the sub-division the proportion between the amount paid and the amount, if any, unpaid on each reduced share shall be the same as it was in the case of the share from which the reduced share is derived;

(e) **to cancel** shares which have not been taken or promised to be taken at the time of the resolution and such cancellation will not be deemed to be reduction of share capital. The company shall give the notice of the above alterations to the Registrar within 30 days after doing so (Secs. 95 and 97).

FURTHER ISSUE OF CAPITAL

Sec. 81 has been amended to make it clear that where the Board of Directors decides to increase the subscribed capital of a company by allotment of further shares, the further shares should ordinarily be offered to existing holders of equity shares *pro rata;* but these further shares may also be offered to any persons in any manner irrespective of the existing equity shareholders if a special resolution is passed by the company in general meeting or, although no such special resolution is passed in that general meeting, if the proposal has been carried out by a majority of votes and the Central Government is satisfied on the application of the Board of Directors that the proposal is most beneficial to the company. The provisions of this section will apply when the Board proposes to increase the subscribed capital by allotment of further shares after the expiry of 2 years from the formation of the company or after the expiry of one year from the first allotment of shares whichever is earlier.

However, the provisions of Sec. 81 will not apply to a private company nor in relation to convertible loans or debentures, i.e., in relation to the increased subscribed capital caused by the conversion of debentures or loans into shares of the company, if the following two conditions are satisfied:—

(a) that the terms of issue of such debentures or loans include a term of such option and such term has been approved by the company by a special resolution; and also

(b) has been approved by the Central Government before such issue, or such terms are in conformity with the rules made by the Central Government.

But an amendment to Sec. 81(3) made in 1963 does away with the requirement of the approval by a special resolution in relation to the conversion into shares or debentures issued to or loans raised from Government in this behalf. The effect of this change is that the financial institutions, such as the L.I.C., I.F.C., N.I.D.C., may, with the prior approval of the Central Government, ask for the conversion of loans granted by them or debentures held by them into shares of the company. The conversion will be made on fair and equitable terms. Such conversion may sometimes have to be made on grounds of public policy, but a right of appeal to the High Court is given to the company if the terms of conversion proposed by the Government are not acceptable to the company. The new Sec. 94A empowers the

Central Government to administratively increase the authorised capital when conversion of debentures or loans into shares of the company is ordered by it.

Reduction of Share Capital (Secs. 100-105)—If the articles provide for reduction of capital, a company may, by a *special resolution* and on its confirmation by the Court on petition, reduce its share capital by (a) reducing or extinguishing the liability of members for uncalled capital; or (b) by writing off or cancelling any paid-up capital which is lost or unrepresented by available assets; or (c) by paying off capital which is in excess of the wants of the company; or (d) in any other way approved by the Court Reduction under (b) and (c) may be either in addition to or without extinguishing or reducing the liability of members for uncalled capital (Sec. 100). Where, however, the reduction of share capital involves diminution of liability for unpaid capital or return to any shareholder of any paid-up share capital all creditors are entitled to object to the reduction. For this purpose the Court shall settle a list of creditors and hear their objections, if any and on being satisfied that either the creditors consent to the reduction or that their debts have been discharged or secured by the company, may confirm the reduction on any terms it thinks fit. The Court may direct the company to add the words "and reduced" to its name for a fixed period and to publish the reasons for reduction for the information of the public (Secs. 101,102). Pursuant to the reduction of the capital necessary alterations must be made in the memorandum. The resolution as confirmed by the Court will be effective only after the order of the Court and minutes as approved by the Court have been filed with the Registrar who will register them and issue a certificate of registration which will be conclusive evidence that everything was in order (Sec. 103).

LIABILITY OF MEMBERS IN RESPECT OF REDUCED SHARES

Sec. 104 provides that, upon a reduction of share capital, a past or present member of the company shall not be liable, in respect of any share, to any call or contribution exceeding in amount the difference, if any, between the amount paid on the share, or the reduced amount, if any, which is deemed to have been paid thereon, as the case may be, and the amount of the share as fixed by the minute of reduction. If, however, any creditor entitled to object to the reduction of share capital is not entered on the list of creditors, by reason of his ignorance of the proceedings for reduction or of their nature and effect with respect to his debt or claim, and the company is unable to pay his debt or claim, then:—

(a) every person who was a member of the company at the date of the registration of the order for reduction and minute, shall be liable to contribute for the payment of that debt or claim an amount not exceeding the amount which he would have been liable to contribute if the company had commenced to be wound up on the day immediately before such date of registration; and

(b) if the company is wound up, the Court, on the application of such creditor and proof of his ignorance as aforesaid, may accordingly settle a list of persons so liable to contribute, and make and enforce calls and orders on the contributories settled on the list, as if they were ordinary contributories in a winding up. This section, however, does not affect the rights of contributories among themselves.

Sec. 105 provides for punishment with imprisonment extending to one year or with fine or both, if any officer of the company knowingly conceals the name of any creditor entitled to object to the reduction or misrepresents the nature or amount of claim or debt or abets such concealment or misrepresentation.

VARIATION OF SHAREHOLDERS' RIGHTS (SEC. 106)

Where the share capital of a company is divided into different classes of shares, the rights attached to the shares of any class may be varied with the consent in writing of the holders of not less than three-fourths of the issued shares of that class. This can be done by circulating the resolution among all the shareholders of that class and obtaining the consent in writing of the holders of at least three-fourths of the issued shares. The consent can also be obtained at a meeting of the holders of shares of that class by getting the consent by three-fourths majority. The variation by either procedure is possible only if provision for such variation is contained in the memorandum or articles of the company, or even without such provision, provided the variation is not prohibited by the terms of issue of the shares of that class.

Sec. 107 empowers dissentient shareholders to apply to the Court for the cancellation of the variation. Therefore, if the holders of 10 per cent of the issued shares of that class who had not assented to the variation apply to the Court within 21 days of the date of the consent or the passing of the resolution, the Court may, after hearing the interested parties, either confirm or cancel variation.[27] The company must, within 30 days of the service of the Court's order, forward a copy of the order to the Registrar.

CONVERSION OF SHARE INTO STOCK

Fully paid-up shares may, if authorised by the articles, be turned into stock by the company in general meeting, and a notice be filed within one month of the conversion. Default would mean a fine up to ₹ 50 per day during default. The register of members and the list must show the amount of stock held by each member instead of the number of shares held (Sec. 96). The shares must be issued first and fully paid-up and then converted into stock. No original issue of stock is allowed. It should be noted that stock is simply a set of shares put together, and is transferable in sums of any amount, while a share is transferable as a whole.

ARTICLES OF ASSOCIATION

A public company limited by shares may register articles of association signed by the subscribers to the memorandum, and it may adopt any or all regulations contained in Table A of First Schedule. If articles are not registered, Table A applies. An unlimited company, or a company limited by guarantee, or a private company limited by shares, must register articles, though it may adopt any of the regulations of Table A (Secs. 26, 28). The articles must be printed, divided into paragraphs, with consecutive numbers, stamped with requisite stamps and filed with the memorandum (Sec. 30). Articles of association are the regulations or bye-laws which govern the internal organisation and conduct of the company. They are subordinate to and controlled by the memorandum. The general functions of articles were clearly stated in *Ashbury Carriage Co. v. Riche*[28] where Lord Cairns said that the articles "play a part subsidiary to the memorandum of association. They accept the memorandum of association as the charter of incorporation of the company and so accepting it the articles proceed to define the duties, the rights and the powers of the governing body as between themselves and the company at large, and the mode and form in which the business of the company is to be carried on, and the mode and form in which change in the internal regulations of the company may from time to time be made." The memorandum lays down the scope or powers of the company, and the articles govern the way in which the objects of the company are to be carried out and can be framed and altered by the members. But in framing or altering the articles care must be taken to see that its regulations do not exceed the powers of the company given by the memorandum, nor are there any provisions contrary to the statute. For, neither the articles themselves nor the power of altering them can alter the constitution of the company as defined by the memorandum, nor give validity to any provision which is inconsistent with the Companies Act. For example, taking powers in articles to appoint managing director for more than 5 years, or without the written consent of the Central Government, or to buy its own shares, is void. Sec. 9 of the Act expressly provides that the provisions of the Act will override anything contrary to it contained in the memorandum, articles, agreement, resolutions, whether registered or

---

27. Hindustan Commercial Bank Ltd. v. Hindustan General Electrical Corp. Lid. 1960 Cal. 637.
28. (1875) L.R. 6 H.L. 653.

executed, and whether before or on or after April 1,1956; and that any provision repugnant to the Act will become or be void.

ALTERATION OF ARTICLES

The right to alter at any time is inherent in every registered company, Sec. 31 provides that subject to the provisions of the Act and to the conditions contained in its memorandum a company may, by *special resolution,* alter or add to its articles. This right is so important that a company cannot in any manner deprive itself of the power to alter its articles.[29] The alteration must, however, be made *bonafide* and in the best interests of the company. If the alteration is unfair or inequitable between the members of the company, it will not be allowed. For example, an alteration will not be permitted if it constitutes an oppression or fraud on the minority, or increases the liability of the members, or is made for committing breach of contracts. No alteration in the articles can be made so as to convert a public company into a private company without the approval of the Central Government.

EFFECT OF MEMORANDUM AND ARTICLES

The memorandum and articles, when registered, bind the company and its members as if they had been signed by the company and each member and contained covenants by the company and each member to observe and be bound by all provisions thereof (Sec. 36). The members are thus bound to the company and the company to the members as **members**. In *Bradford Banking Co.* v. *Briggs,*[30] the articles provided that the company shall have a first and paramount lien upon each share for debts due to the company by the shareholders. One of the shareholders deposited his shares with a bank to secure an overdraft and the bank gave notice of the deposit to the company. It was held that shares deposited with the bank were bound by the articles, and the lien that the company had under them precluded the bank from getting priority in respect of debts incurred by the shareholder before the notice was given. But the company in its turn will have no right to priority in respect of money beriming due to it after it has received notice of the deposit.[31] The new Act (Sec. 36) clearly says that the memorandum and articles shall bind the company to its members and the members to the company as if both had covenanted to observe all the provisions of the memorandum and articles. To the rule of member's liability to the company as per the articles, there is an exception as provided by Sec. 38 that an alteration of either die articles or memorandum increasing the liability of members to contribute to the share capital of the company is not binding upon any member unless he gives his consent in writing.

As between the members *inter se,* each member is bound by the articles to the other members, but that does not mean that the memorandum and articles create an express contract between the members of the company. Thus, a member of a company has no right to bring a suit in his own name against any other member or members. It is the company alone which can bring a suit against the offender so as to protect the aggrieved member. It was laid down in *Burland* v. *Earle,*[32] that in order to redress a wrong done to the company, or to receive money alleged to be due to the company, the action *should prima facie* be brought by the company. The only exception to this rule is where the persons against whom relief is sought control the majority of shares or voting power and will not allow an action to be brought in the name of the company. In that, event, 'the complaining shareholders may sue in their

---

29. Andrews v.Gass Meter Co. (1897) 1 Ch. 361.

30. (1886) 12 A.C. 29.

31. Matheran Steam Tramway Co. v. Lang (1931) Bom/ L.R. 184.

32. (1902) A.C. 83.

own names, provided they are able to show that the acts complained of are either fraudulent or *ultra vires*.

As between outsiders and the company, neither the memorandum nor the articles give any contractual rights to outsiders against the company even though their names be mentioned in these documents in connection with the arrangements that the company might have contemplated for carrying on its business.[33] In Eley's case, the articles provided that Eley should be solicitor to the company and should not be removed from office except for misconduct. Eley acted as solicitor to the company for some time, but later the company ceased to employ him. He sued the company for damages for breach of contract. It was held that he had no cause of action because the articles did not constitute any contract between the company and himself. The party suing the company must prove a contract with the company outside and independently of the articles.[34] Krishna Rao who had been appointed a secretary by the articles, was later removed from this post, whereupon he filed a suit for declaration that he was still the secretary under the articles and that the Board of Directors had no power to remove him. It was held that his appointment must be regarded as 'de hors' the articles and he must prove a contract outside and independently of the articles.

With regard to outsiders the position is that the memorandum and articles, when registered in accordance with Sec. 33 with the Registrar, become public documents, to which all persons have access. Every person who contemplates entering into a contract with a company has the means of ascertaining, and consequently is presumed to know, not only the exact powers of the company, but also the extent to which those powers have been delegated to the directors, and of any limitations placed upon the exercise of these powers. Consequently, if he enters into a contract which is beyond the powers of the company, as defined in the memorandum, or outside the limits set upon the authority of the directors, he cannot, as a general rule, acquire any rights under the contract against the company. The principle is somewhat modified by the further rule that persons dealing with a company, having satisfied themselves that the proposed transaction is not in its nature inconsistent with the memorandum and articles, are not bound to enquire into the regularity of any internal proceedings. In other words, persons contracting with the company are presumed to have knowledge of the articles, but they are entitled to assume that the provisions of the articles have been observed. This limitation is called the Doctrine of "Indoor Management" or the RULE IN ROYAL BRITISH BANK v. TURQUAND.[35] In that case, the directors of a banking company were authorised to borrow on bond such sums of money as should from time to time, by a resolution of the company in general meeting, be authorised to be borrowed. They gave a bond to Turquand without the authority of any such resolution. It was held that Turquand could sue the company on the bond, as he was entitled to assume that the necessary resolution had been passed. The Rule, however, does not protect any one who has actual or constructive notice that the person acting on behalf of the company has no authority to enter into the transaction in question. The Rule does not apply to cases of forgery, or to transactions which are void or illegal *ab initio*, nor does it bind the company to officers of the company or other persons who should know whether the regulations in the articles have been observed.

PART 16-C
PROSPECTUS

Sec. 2 (36) defines a prospectus as "any document described or issued as prospectus and includes notice, circular, advertisement or other document inviting deposits from the public or inviting offers

---

33. Eley v. Positive Life Ins. Co. (1876) I Ex. Div. 88; Ramkumar v. Sholapur Spg. & Wvg. Co. Ltd. (1934) 36 Bom. L.R. 907.

34. Krishna Rao v. Anjaneyulu, 1954 Mad, 113.

35. (1856) 6 E. A B. 327.

from the public for the subscription or purchase of any shares in, or debentures of, a body corporate." In order to be a prospectus, a document must be an invitation to make an offer to at least *one member of the public* to subscribe for shares or debentures. According to Sec. 67, an offer or invitation to any section of the *public,* whether selected as members or debentures-holders of the com-pany, or as clients of the person making the invitation, will be deemed to be an invitation to the public. But a public company may or may not make *a public issue;* but if-it does, it will be required to publish a prospectus. A prospectus issued by or on behalf of a company, or in relation to an intended company, must be *doted,* and that date shall, unless contrary is proved, be taken as the date of the publication of the prospectus (Sec. 55). Sec. 58 prohibits the issue of prospectus which includes a statement purporting to be made by an expert, unless he has given, and has not withdrawn, his consent to the issue of the prospectus with the statement in the form and context in which it is included; and a statement that he has given and has not withdrawn such consent appears in the prospectus. Any contravention of the foregoing provisions regarding an expert and his statements renders the company and every person who is knowingly a party to the issue of prospectus, liable to a fine up to ₹ 5,000 [Sec. 59(1)].

Sec. 60 requires the delivery of a copy of the prospectus to the Registrar before its publication, duly signed by every director or proposed director, or by his agent authorised in writing, and having endorsed thereon or attached thereto the following documents: the consent of any expert; and if the prospectus is issued *generally* (i.e., to persons other than existing members or debenture-holders) (i) a copy of every contract, or a memorandum giving full particulars of a contract not reduced to writing; and (ii) if in any auditor's and accountant's report adjustments of the figures have been made, then a written statement signed by the persons making the report Every prospectus on its face must state that a copy has been delivered for registration. The Registrar will not register a prospectus unless all the above things are done. Then within 90 days of the filing of the copy with Registrar, the prospectus should be issued by newspaper advertisement or otherwise. Every form of application for shares of debentures must be accompanied by a memorandum containing the prescribed features of a prospectus. The Amendment Act, 1988, now allows companies to give an abridged prospectus with the application form, but the company must furnish a copy of the prospectus to a person who asks for it Any contravention of this section renders the company and every other person party to the issue of the prospectus liable to a fine up to ₹ 5,000.

CONTENTS OF PROSPECTUS

Sec. 56 provides that a prospectus must contain the matters specified in Part I of Schedule II and set out the Reports specified in Part II of the Schedule, namely:—

1. The main objects of the company, with the names, occupations and addresses of the signatories of the memorandum and the number of shares subscribed by them, as also the number and classes of shares, if any, and the nature of interest of the holders in the property and profits of the company, together with the number of redeemable preference shares with the date and method of redemption.

2. The number of shares, if any, fixed by the articles as the qualification of a director, and the remuneration of directors for their services.

3. The names, occupations and addresses of directors, managing director and manager, together with any provision, or compensation for loss of office.

4. The minimum subscription on which the directors may proceed to allot shares, the time of the opening of the subscription lists and the amount payable on application and allotment on each share, and in the case of a second or subsequent offer of shares, the amount offered for subscription on each previous allotment made within the two preceding years, the amount actually allotted, and the amount, if any, paid on the shares so allotted.

5. The substance of any contract or arrangement giving to any person any option or preferential right to subscribe for any shares in, or debentures of, a company, together with the amounts payable and the periods during which option is to be exercised by such persons, whose names, occupations and addresses must also be given.

6. The number, description, and amount of shares and debentures which within die two preceding years have been agreed to be issued or otherwise than in cash, together with the consideration. Also, the proposed date of issue; and where some shares of the same class are to be issued at different premiums or some at discount, and others at premium, the reasons for the difference.

7. The names, occupations and addresses of vendors of any property acquired by the company and the amount paid or payable in cash, shares or debentures to the vendor and, where there are more vendors than one, or the company is a sub-buyer, the amount paid or payable to each vendor. The nature of the title or interests in such property, with short particulars.

8. The name, description, address and occupation of each promoter or officer of the company to whom any amount as commission for subscribing or agreeing to subscribe for any shares or debentures or for underwriting them is paid within the 2 preceding years together with the amount paid and the rate of underwriting commission. Any benefit paid or payable to promoter or officer.

9. The amount or estimated amount of preliminary expenses and the persons by whom any of these expenses have been paid or are payable.

10. The dates of, parties to, and general nature of every contract appointing or fixing the remuneration of a managing director, or manager whenever entered into, and also every other material contract, and the time and place when such contract be inspected.

11. Full particulars of the nature and extent of the interest if any, of every director or promoter (i) in the promotion of the company, or (ii) in any property acquired by the company within two years of the issue of the prospectus.

12. The right of voting at meetings of the company conferred by, and the rights in respect of capital and dividends attached to, the several classes of shares respectively, together with restrictions, if any, imposed by the articles on members, regarding attendance, voting or speaking at meetings, on right of transfer of shares, as well as, on the directors in respect of their powers of management.

13. If the company has been carrying on business, the length of time of such business, and if it proposes to acquire a business, the length of time such business has been carried on.

14. If any reserves of profit of the company or any of its subsidiaries have been capitalised, particulars of such capitalisation, and particulars of surplus arising from any revaluation of the assets of the company or any of its subsidiaries during the two years preceding the date of the prospectus and the manner in which such surplus has been dealt with.

15. The names and addresses of the auditors of the company and the report of the auditors in case the company had been in business regarding profits and losses and assets and liabilities, together with the rate of dividends paid for each of the five financial years immediately preceding the issue of the prospectus, giving particulars of each class of shares on which such dividends have been paid and particulars of the cases in which no dividends have been paid in respect of any class of shares for any of those years.

16. The report must deal with the profits and losses of the company for each year of the five financial years immediately preceding the issue of the prospectus and with the assets and liabilities at the last date to which the accounts of the company were made up. If the company has subsidiaries, the report shall deal with the above separately in case of each subsidiary.

17. If the proceeds, or any part of the proceeds, of the issue of the shares or debentures are or is to be applied directly or indirectly, (i) in the purchase of any business, or (ii) in the purchase of an interest in any business, which will entitle the company to an interest in the capital or profits and

losses or both in such business exceeding 50 per cent thereof, the report shall state the profits or losses of the business for each of the five financial years immediately preceding the issue of the prospectus.

18. A statement that a copy of the prospectus has been filed with the Registrar, together with the consent of the expert to file the prospectus, as well as a copy of every contract appointing or fixing the remuneration of a managing director, or manager. Also a statement that the consent of the Central Government has been obtained as required under the Control of Capital Issue Act, 1947.

Reports from experts must not be included in a prospectus unless such experts are unconnected with the formation or management of the company and unless they gave the consent. There must be reasonable ground for believing that the professed expert who made the statement, report or valuation was competent to make. He will be liable for wrong statement, report or valuation made by him and contained in the prospectus.

There must be stated at a prominent place in every prospectus issued by a company and also in every application form that it is an offence punishable with imprisonment up to 5 years to make an application for shares in a fictitious name, or otherwise induce the company to allot or register any transfer of any shares to him or any other person in a fictitious name.

In addition to these compulsory particulars, any other information may be, and usually is, volunteered. This information may relate to the terms of the issue of shares, application to deal in the shares of the company on the Stock Exchange. The intending purchaser of shares is entitled to all true disclosures in the prospectus. Everything stated therein must be correct and everything material must not be kept back. Misstatements or non-disclosures are both fatal to the contract, for a person who buys shares on the faith of a prospectus containing untrue statements or failing to disclose what ought to have been disclosed, may rescind the contract within a reasonable time and before the winding up of the company. The effect of such rescission would be that as against the company the person would give up the shares and get back his money with interest. In addition, there is a right of compensation from any director, promoter and any other person who authorised the issue of the prospectus.

The **defences** of a director or promoter are that—
1. He had withdrawn his consent to become a director before the issue of the prospectus, and it was issued without his authority or consent;
2. The issue was made without his knowledge or consent;
3. His consent was withdrawn after the issue of the prospectus and before allotment, and public notice was given;
4. He had reasonable ground to believe that the statements were true and he believed them to be true; or
5. The statement was a correct and fair summary or copy of an expert's report, or a statement made by an official or in an official document.

Apart from their civil liability to allottees, directors and other persons are criminally liable for untrue statements. Sec. 63 provides that where a prospectus contains an untrue statement, every person responsible for its issue is liable to imprisonment up to 2 years, or fine up to ₹5,000, or both, unless he proves that the statement was immaterial or that he believed it to be true and had reasonable ground for doing so. The expert is exempt from criminal liability.

STATEMENT IN LIEU OF PROSPECTUS

A public company having privately arranged for the capital subscription may not issue a prospectus; but in that event a STATEMENT IN LIEU OF PROSPECTUS must be filed with the Registrar 3 days before any allotment of any shares or debentures can be made. It should be signed by every director or proposed director and should contain similar particulars as are required in the case of a prospectus, and should fulfil similar conditions. Contravention of this provision will render the company and every director liable to a fine up to ₹ 1,000.

PUBLIC DEPOSITS

The new section 58A empowers the Central Government to frame rules in consultation with the Reserve Bank of India, prescribing the limits up to which, the manner in which and the conditions subject to which, deposits may be invited or accepted by a company, either from the public or from its members. No company shall invite any deposits except in accordance with such rules. The company must also issue an advertisement in the prescribed form, including therein a statement showing its financial position.

Every deposit received by a company at any time before the commencement of the Amendment Act, 1974, in accordance with the directions of the Reserve Bank of India, must be repaid in accordance with the terms of such deposit, unless renewed according to the new rules. It is further provided that any deposits received before the commencement of the Amendment Act and in contravention of the direction of the Reserve Bank of India, must be repaid on or before April 1, 1975, and such payment shall be made without prejudice to any action that may be taken for the contravention.

Any deposit received in contravention of the rules when framed must be paid back by the company within 30 days from the date of acceptance of such deposit, or within such further time, not exceeding 30 days, as the Central Government may, on sufficient cause being shown by the company, allow.

Additionally, where a company omits or fails to repay any deposit as required by the Act, the company shall be punishable with fine which shall not be less than twice the amount not repaid, and half of the amount of the fine, if realised, shall be paid by the Court to the depositor. Further every officer of the company who is in default shall be punishable with imprisonment up to 5 years and shall also be liable to fine.

Where a company accepts or invites any deposit in excess of the limits prescribed by the rules or in contravention of the manner or conditions prescribed under the rules, the company shall be punishable—

(i) where such contravention relates to the acceptance of any deposit, with fine which shall not be less than an amount equal to the amount of the deposits so accepted.

(ii) where such contravention relates to the invitation of any deposits, with fine which may extend to one lakh rupees but shall not be less than ₹ 5,000.

Every officer of the company who is in default shall be punishable with imprisonment up to 5 years and also with fine.

The provisions of Sec. 58 A will not apply to a banking company, nor to any other company specified by the Central Government in consultation with the Reserve Bank of India. Financial companies may also be exempted from the application of the above provisions except those relating to advertisement.

Where a company has failed to repay any deposit or part thereof, the Company Law Board may, either on its own motion or on the application of the depositor direct the company to make repayment forthwith or within any specified time. Whoever fails to comply with the order of the Company Law Board shall be punishable with imprisonment up to 3 years and shall also be liable to fine of not less than ₹50 per day during default.

Under Section 58B, provisions of the Act relating to a prospectus shall apply to advertisement inviting deposits, so that a depositor may claim compensation under Section 62 and the directors authorising the issue of a false advertisement shall be liable to imprisonment up to 2 years under Section 63.

Ordinarily, deposits are to be accepted for a period not less than six months, although to meet current liabilities they may be accepted for a period, not less than 3 months. Further, no deposits can be accepted for a period exceeding 3 years, but they can be renewed for a period not exceeding 3 years each time. The deposits accepted for a period not less than 3 months to meet current liabilities must not exceed 10 per cent of the paid up capital of the company and its free reserves. Deposits may be accepted from members, or guaranteed by directors, but the amount must not exceed 10 per cent of the paid up capital and free reserves from those together with those accepted to meet current liabilities. The amount from the public should not exceed 25 per cent of the paid up capital and free reserves.

PART 16-D
MEMBERSHIP

MEMBERS

The "members" of a registered company are the corporator or persons who for the time being constitute the company as corporate entity. Sec. 41 defines the term "member" by indicating the modes in which a person may acquire that character. The effect of that section is that a person may become a member, either (1) by subscribing to the memorandum, or (2) by agreeing in writing to become a member, and having his name entered in the company's register of members.

By subscribing the memorandum—A subscriber to the memorandum, who must take directly from the company the agreed number of shares, becomes a member the moment the registration of the company takes place, without being placed on the register of members. Allotment of a signatory's shares is unnecessary, as he is bound by virtue of his subscription to take and pay for them. He cannot refuse to take shares even on the ground of misrepresentation or on the ground that his name did not appear on the register of members. By Sec. 266, a person who, being named in the articles or prospectus as a director or proposed director, signs and files an undertaking to take his qualification shares is, as regards those shares, in the same position as if he had subscribed the memorandum for them.

Agreement and Registration—Apart from the subscribers of the memorandum, "every other person who agrees in writing to become a member, *and whose name is entered in its register of members,* shall be a member of the company-" Registration of the name of a person as a member of a company may result from one or other of the following:—

(a) **By application and allotment**—A person who applies for a certain number of shares becomes a member when shares are allotted to him, a notice of allotment is given, and his name is entered in the register of members. The application for shares may be absolute or conditional. If it is absolute, an allotment and its notice is sufficient acceptance. If it is conditional, the allotment must be made according to the terms of the application, otherwise no contract will result. In *Roman Bhai's case,* R applied for shares to be allotted to him on the condition that he was first appointed a branch manager of the company. Shares were allotted to R, but he was not appointed the branch manager. *Held,* he could repudiate the contract, and was not liable as contributory on winding up of the company.

(b) **By transfer of shares**—A person can become a member by buying shares from an existing member and by having the transfer registered and getting his name placed on the register of members.

(c) **Transmission of shares**—A person may become a member by registration if he succeeds to the estate of a deceased member. The Official Receiver or Assignee is, likewise, entitled to be a member in the place of a shareholder who is adjudged an insolvent.

(d) **By acquiescence or estoppel**—A person is deemed to be a member if he allows his name, apart from any agreement to become a member, to be on the register of members, or otherwise holds himself out or allows himself to be held out as a member. In such cases he is estopped from denying that he is registered with his consent.

TERMINATION OF MEMBERSHIP

A person ceases to be a member when his name is removed from the register of members for sufficient reason or proper cause. This may occur when (I) he transfers all his shares; (2) his shares are forfeited; (3) he makes a valid surrender of his shares; (4) his shares are sold by the company to enforce a lien; (5) he dies; (6) redeemable preference shares are redeemed; (7) his contract to take shares is rescinded; (8) he becomes insolvent and Official Assignee or Receiver disclaims the shares or transfers them; (9) share warrants in exchange of shares are issued; (10) the shares are held by the liquidator who disclaims them.

LIABILITY OF MEMBERS

In the absence of an express agreement to the contrary, a shareholder must pay the whole nominal value of his shares in cash. 'Cash' includes property, goods, services, release of debt or the surrender of a debenture, provided it is worth the money due on the shares. But a cheque until honoured is not cash. If before the full amount is paid up, the company goes into liquidation, the shareholder becomes liable as contributory to pay the balance when called upon to pay (Sec. 429). If a person has ceased to be a member within one year prior to the winding up of the company, he is liable to be included in the 'B' list (a list of past members) and pay on the shares which he held to the extent of the amount unpaid thereon, if (i) on the winding up, debts exist which were incurred while he was a member, and (ii) the members of the' A' list (a list of present members) cannot satisfy the contribution required from them in respect of their shares (Sec. 426). A person is liable as member even in spite of a valid transfer of shares by him, if the name of the transferee is not placed on the register of members, in place of transferor's name. If a person applies for shares in the name of a fictitious person or a person not in existence, or shares are allotted in that name, he will be liable to be punished with imprisonment up to 5 years (Sec. 68 A). The liability of members becomes unlimited and several even in the case of a limited company, if the number of its members falls below 7 in the case of a public company and 2 in the case of a private company and the company continues to do business for more than 6 months after the fall of number below the aforesaid figures.

REGISTER OF MEMBERS

Sec. 150 enjoins upon every company to keep a register of its members at its registered office. The register must contain the name, address and occupation of each member, the amount and number of his shares, the date of entry on the register, the amount paid on his shares and the date on which he ceased to be a member. In case of default the company and every officer permitting such default, are severally liable to fine up to ₹ 50 for every day of default. The register is a *prima facie* evidence of all its contents (Sec. 164). Unless the register of members is in such form as to constitute in itself an index, every company having more than 50 members must keep an index of the names of its members, and must within 14 days note in the index any change made in the register of members. Default results in fine up to ₹ 50 (Sec. 151). A company's register is a public document and is open to inspection by any person on certain conditions. A member can inspect it *gratis* daily for 2 hours during business hours, and other persons on payment or Re.1. The register can, however, be closed at any time on giving 7 days' previous notice by advertisement in a newspaper circulating in the district in which the registered office of the company is situated, provided that the aggregate number of days for which it is closed do not exceed 45 days in a year and 30 days at a time (Sec. 154). Contravention of this provision will render the company and every officer at fault liable to fine up to ₹ 500 for every day during which the register is so closed.

RECTIFICATION OF REGISTER

Section 111(4), as inserted by the Companies (Amendment) Act, 1988, now gives wide powers to the Company Law Board to rectify the register of members on the application of the person aggrieved, or any member of the company or the company, if—

(a) the name of any person is, without sufficient cause, entered in the register of members;

(b) the name of any member is removed from the register;

(c) default is made, or unnecessary delay takes place, in entering the name of a person as a member;

(d) a person has ceased to be a member but the company fails or delays to remove his name from the register; or

(e) the company refuses to register the transfer of shares.

The Company Law Board has wide powers and may also determine conflicting rights. Section 467 empowers the Board to rectify the register on the winding up of the company. The Company Law Board may also award damages to the aggrieved party. The rectification will date back to the date on which the mistake or default or delay was made which is being rectified.[36] If default is made in complying with the order of the Company Law Board, the company and every officer in default is punishable with fine up to ₹ 1,000 and a further fine of ₹ 100 for every day of default.

NOTICE OF TRUSTS

Sec. 153, though short, is of very great importance. It lays down: "Notice of any trust, express, implied or constructive, shall be entered on the register of members or of debenture-holders, or be receivable by the Registrar." This provision is made to relieve the company from taking any notice of equitable interests in shares, and to preclude persons claiming under equitable titles from converting the company into a trustee for them. For example, if a shareholder dies, leaving a will appointing A as executor and bequeathing shares to B, who is a minor, A will hold the shares for B until he attains his majority. In this case a "trust" is imposed on A, and he is said to be a "trustee," while B is said to be a *cestui que trust* or "beneficiary." A's name is entered on the register of members as holder of the shares, and accordingly he is the **legal** owner of the shares: all dividends are paid to him by the company and he is entitled to exercise the right of voting and other privileges attaching to the holding of the shares. But the equitable interest in the shares belongs to B, and therefore all dividends, etc., paid to A must be held by him in trust for B, or paid to him. But the company does not take notice of this relationship between A and B. A, as registered holder of the shares, is personally liable to the company for calls made on the shares; B is subject to no liability whatever to the company. If, therefore, the trustee of the shares misappropriates dividends or the proceeds of sale of shares, the company will not be under any liability to the beneficiary. Even if the company had constructive notice of the trust in respect of such shares, it would not in any way make the company liable. The true effect of the provisions of Sec. 153 is that a share may be registered in the company's register in a name other than that of its true owner. This can enable the persons who are really in control of the company to conceal their position from the shareholders and from the public and to practise fraud in regard to the management of the company. To check such a practice, Sees. 247 and 248 respectively empower the Central Government to appoint an inspector to report on the membership of a company and, where it appears to the Central Government that there is a good reason to investigate the ownership of shares or debentures of a company or a body corporate which acts or has acted as the managing agent or secretaries and treasurers of a company, to require information for that purpose from persons interested in such shares or debentures.

PUBLIC TRUSTEE

The safeguards provided by Secs. 247 and 248 do not seem to have checked the practice of indirect control of companies by moneyed and vested interests through nominees. To prevent the use of voting rights attached to shares held by trusts for the advancement of personal interests of the donors, it was considered necessary to regulate the exercise of such rights in suitable cases. To meet this need, three

---

36. Panna Lal Sud v. Jagaljit Distilling, 1952 Pepsu 2

new Secs. 153A, 153B and 153C were added in 1963. The Central Government has been empowered to appoint a Public Trustee to exercise voting rights in respect of cases where—

(a) a trust is created by instrument in writing;

(b) trust money invested in shares in or debentures of a company amounts to at least ₹ one lakh or where it exceeds ₹ one lakh and amounts to ₹ 5 lakhs or 25 per cent of the paid up capital whichever is less.

Where a Public Trustee has been appointed the trustee must inform the Public Trustee by means of a declaration that he is holding the shares or debentures as a trustee. Failure to do so will render him liable to a fine up to ₹ 5,000 and for a continued default for a further fine of ₹100 per day during default. If a trustee makes a false declaration, he is liable to be imprisoned for a term extending to 2 years and also with fine. After the declaration by the trustee, he will cease to exercise voting right and the Public Trustee will become entitled to vote at all meetings as a member or debentureholder. He will also be entitled to receive papers, etc., as if he were a member or a debentureholder.

The intention of the new provision is not to interfere with the freedom of the trustees to administer trusts or to dispose of trust funds. It is only to check the economic power of the donor. Public interest is to be the main consideration in the exercise of this power and such interest may not be involved to any appreciable extent where the trust has been created by an instrument in writing, or the value of the shares or debentures held in trust does not exceed ₹ one lakh or 25 per cent of the paid up capital.

BENAMI HOLDING OF SHARES

Every *benami* holder of shares must file in the prescribed form and within the prescribed time a declaration with the company specifying the particulars of the person who has beneficial interest in such shares. Similar declaration must also be filed by the beneficial owner within 30 days of becoming one, specifying the particulars of the *benami* holder. Failure to do so will render the party in default liable to a fine up to ₹1,000 per day during the period of default.

The company is required to make a note of such declaration in its register of members and to file a return thereof with the Registrar within 30 days of the receipt of the declaration. Failure to comply with this provision will render the company and every officer in default liable to a fine up to ₹ 100 per day during default The Central Government may appoint inspectors to investigate and report as to whether the above provisions have been complied with.

ANNUAL RETURN

Sec. 159 requires that every company, having share capital, must prepare and file, within 60 days from the day on which each of the annual general meetings is held, or, if no annual general meeting is held, from the date when the meeting ought to have been held, with the Registrar, a return containing the following particulars, as they stood on the day:[37]—(i) the address of the registered office of the company; (ii) the name of the State outside India where any part of the register of members may be kept; (iii) a summary, distinguishing wherever possible between shares issued for cash, bonus shares and shares other than in cash and specially in respect of each class of shares, the amount of nominal capital and number of shares into which it is divided, the number of shares taken from the commencement of the company up to the date of last return, the amount called up, the total amount of calls received up-to-date, and calls remaining unpaid, total amount of commissions paid, discount allowed on any shares or debentures, shares forfeited, share-warrants issued and surrendered, indebtedness of the company. A list of all members, and those who have ceased to be members since

---

36. See State of Bombay v. Bhandhan Ram, 1961 S.C. 186. The annual return must be filed whether or not the annual meeting is held.

the date of the last return or since the incorporation if it is the first list, must be filed. This list must contain full particulars of the past and present members together with the number of shares held by each existing member at the time of the return and details of transfers, if any. But, if any of the two previous returns have given the full particulars, then very short return is to be filed.

PART 16-E
SHARES

Sec. 2(46) defines a share as "a share in the share capital of a company, and includes stock except where a distinction between stock and shares is expressed or implied." Farwell J. has defined a share as " the interest of a shareholder in the company measured by a sum of money, [i.e., the nominal amount], for the purpose of liability in the first place, and of interest in the second, but also consisting of a series of mutual covenants entered into by all the shareholders *inter se.*" Shares represent equal portions into which the capital is divided, each shareholder being entitled to a portion of a company's profits corresponding to the number of shares he holds. By Sec. 82, the shares or other interest of any member in the company is movable property, transferable in the manner provided by the articles of the company; and according to the Sale of Goods Act, 1930, shares are goods. Shares are of various classes, and the most common varieties are: Preference, Equity, Deferred or Founders. A private company may issue all or any of these classes. But a public company can now issue only two kinds of shares: Preference and Equity (Sec. 86).

PREFERENCE SHARES

By virtue of Sec. 85, preference share is that part of the share capital of the company which fulfils both the following requirements, namely, that it carries preferential right in respect of dividends and also that it carries preferential right in regard to repayment of capital. Preference shares participating in surplus profits, or participating in surplus assets on a winding up are also allowed. With regard to the payment of dividends a preference share may be cumulative or non-cumulative. The *non-cumulative* or *simple preference* gives right to a fixed percentage as dividend out of the profits of each year. In case no profits are available in a year the holders get nothing, nor can they claim unpaid dividend in subsequent years. The *cumulative preference,* however, gives a right to demand the unpaid dividend in any year, during the subsequent year or years when the profits are ample. Sec. 80 permits a company to *issue redeemable preference* shares. These shares can be redeemed only if they are fully paid up and out of the profits which would be available for dividend or out of the proceeds of die issue of new shares made with the object of redemption. These shares cannot be redeemed out of the sale proceeds of any property of the company. For the purpose of redemption out of profits, Capital Redemption Reserve Fund must be created by transferring to it any amount out of profits equal to the nominal value of the shares to be redeemed. No company can now issue shares which are redeemable after ten years from the date of issue.

EQUITY SHARES

B y Sec. 85 (2) equity shares mean all shares which are not preference shares. Equity shares receive dividends out of profits as determined by the directors and declared by the members in the annual general meeting, after due allowance for depreciation and reserve, etc., has been made. If there are preference shares, the dividend is paid after the payment of dividends on preference shares as per rights given by the articles of the company, and in the case of a private company, before the payment of dividends on deferred shares, if any. To put a check on the issue of shares with small denomination carrying disproportionate voting rights, Sec. 87 provides that every member of a public limited company, holding equity share capital, shall have votes in proportion to his share of the paid-up equity capital of the company. Preference shareholders will, ordinarily, vote only on matters relating to preference capital. Sec. 88 expressly prohibits a public company from issuing any shares (not being preference shares) which carry voting rights, or rights in the company as to dividend, capital or otherwise which are disproportionate to the rights attaching to the holders of other shares (not being preference shares). Sec. 89 provides that all existing companies having such disproportionate rights must remove these rights before April 1,1957.

ALLOTMENT OF SHARES

An allotment of shares is an appropriation by the Board of Directors of a certain number of shares in response to an application. It is in effect an acceptance by the company of the offers to take shares. The Act requires certain conditions to be fulfilled before a company can proceed to allot shares. *Firstly,* a public company must file a prospectus, or statement in lieu of prospectus, before making the *first* allotment *Secondly,* it must have received in cash the amount payable on application which shall not be less than 5 per cent of the nominal amount of the share, and deposited the amount so received in a Scheduled Bank before making *any* allotment. *Thirdly,* the "minimum subscription" as provided in the prospectus must have been subscribed or applied for before *the first* allotment can be made (Secs. 69, 70). Sec. 72 now provides that no allotment shall be made of shares applied for in pursuance of the prospectus until the beginning of the 5th day after that on which the prospectus is issued (or such later time as specified in the prospectus itself)'. Similarly, an applicant cannot withdraw his application until after the expiration of the 5th day after the time of the opening of the subscription lists. These are called opening and closing days of the subscription lists. It is also provided that the day on which the subscription lists are closed must be announced and that the allotment must be made and notice of allotment given not later than the 10th day after such closing day.

Listing of Shares—Section 73, as amended by the 1988 Act, now makes listing of shares by a public company which invites the public to subscribe for shares compulsory. Accordingly, every public company with a minimum issued equity capital of ₹3 crores must, before issue of the prospectus, apply to a recognised stock exchange for the listing of the shares and debentures. If permission is not granted within 10 weeks from the date of the closing of the subscription lists, no allotment can be made, and if made, it shall be void. But where an appeal against refusal by a stock exchange has been preferred under Sec. 22 of the Securities Contracts (Regulation) Act, 1956, such allotment shall not be void until the rejection of the appeal by the Central Government.

If the application for listing has not been made or where permission for listing has not been granted, the company must forthwith repay without interest all moneys received from the applicants for shares. If such money is not repaid within 8 days after the company becomes liable to repay it the company and every director of the company who is an officer in default shall jointly and severally be liable to repay that money with interest at the following rates:

4 per cent for delay in payment of not more than 15 days;

5 per cent for delay of more than 15 days but not more than 30 days;

12 per cent for delay of more than 30 days, but not more than 60 days;

15 per cent for delay of more than 60 days.

Where permission has been granted by the recognised stock exchange or stock exchange, all moneys in excess of the application moneys on shares allotted must be repaid forthwith without interest If such money is not repaid within 8 days, then the directors shall be jointly and severally liable to pay with 12 per cent per annum interest If default is made in complying with this provision, then the company and every officer who is in default shall be liable to be fined up to ₹ 5,000, and where repayment is not made within 6 months from the expiry of the 8th day, also with imprisonment up to one year.

MINIMUM SUBSCRIPTION

Minimum subscription is the minimum amount which, in the opinion of the directors or of the signatories of the memorandum arrived at after due inquiry, must be raised by the issue of shares to provide in respect of each of the following heads and **distinguishing the amount required under each head**: (i) the purchase price of any property bought or to be bought is to be defrayed in whole or in part of the proceeds of the issue; (ii) preliminary expenses including any commission, underwriting or otherwise for subscription of shares, payable by the company; (iii) the repayment of sums borrowed to provide for the foregoing; (iv) the working capital, and (v) any other expenditure, stating the nature and purpose thereof and the estimated amount in each case. The company must also specify the amounts to be provided in respect of the matters aforesaid otherwise than out of the proceeds of the issue and the sources out of which those amounts are to be provided [Sec. 69 (1) and Sch. II (5)]. Sec. 69 (2) further provides that shares allotted for consideration other than cash are not to be included in the minimum subscription.

CONSEQUENCES OF NON-FULFILMENT OF THE ABOVE CONDITIONS

If the company for want of minimum subscription, or for the non-fulfilment of any of the aforesaid conditions, has been unable to allot any shares within 120 days after the first issue of the prospectus, it must forthwith refund without interest all moneys received from the applicants. If the money is not repaid within 130 days of the issue of the prospectus, the directors of the company shall be jointly and severally liable to repay that money with interest at the rate of 6 per cent per annum from the expiration of the 130th day. But a director who can prove that the default in the repayment was not due to any misconduct or negligence on his part may escape liability [Sec. 69 (5)].

IRREGULAR ALLOTMENT

If a company, without complying with any of the above conditions makes an allotment, the applicant may, if he so desires, avoid the allotment within 2 months after the statutory meeting, but not later than that. If a company is not required to hold a statutory meeting or if the allotment is made after such meeting, then he must avoid the transaction within 2 months of the allotment. He can claim the refund of the money within the period even if the company is being wound up. Notice of avoidance followed by prompt legal proceedings after the two months would be sufficient. Furthermore, the directors are liable to compensate the company or the allottee for any loss, damages and costs suffered by either through such irregular allotment, provided that the proceedings to recover such loss, damages or costs are commenced before the expiration of 2 years from the date of the allotment (Sec. 71).

Penalty for fraudulently inducing a person to invest money—By virtue of Sec. 68, any person who fraudulently, either by wrong statement or dishonest concealment of material facts, induces or attempts to induce another person to enter into, or to offer to enter into—

(a) an agreement to buy or dispose of shares or debentures or to underwrite them; or
(b) an agreement the purpose of which is to secure a profit to any of the parties from the yield of shares or debentures;

shall be punishable with imprisonment for a term up to 5 years, or with fine up to ₹ 10,000, or with both.

Issue and allotment of shares in Fictitious name prohibited—The new Sec. 68 A seeks to eradicate the practice of allotting shares in fictitious name or to non-existing persons. The section makes it an offence punishable with imprisonment up to 5 years to make an application for shares in a fictitious name or otherwise induce a company to allot or register a transfer of any shares to him or any other in a fictitious name. The penal provision must be inserted at a prominent place in every prospectus issued by a company and in every application form.

Return of Allotment—A return of allotment, even if it is a single share, must be filed with the Registrar within 30 days thereafter, giving complete details of the number and nominal amount of the shares, and the names, addresses and occupations of the allottees, amount paid or due on each share, copies of written contracts in respect of shares allotted for consideration other than cash, by services rendered to the company or business or property sold to it, number and nominal amount of shares so allotted, extent to which paid and the consideration. If in the return of allotment it is shown that shares have been allotted for cash when cash has not been actually received in respect of such allotment (and mere book adjustments have been made), every officer and every promoter of the company who is guilty of this shall be punishable with fine up to ₹ 5,000. No return of allotment need be filed in respect of shares reissued after forfeiture. Where a contract in respect of shares allotted for consideration other than cash, is not reduced to writing, the company must, within 30 days after the allotment, file with the Registrar the prescribed particulars of the contract duly stamped with the requisite stamp duty. Default to file the return of allotment as required by Sec. 75 will render every officer of the company liable to a fine up to ₹ 500 for every day the default continues.

Commission—A company may pay out of capital commission, including under-writing commission, to any person who subscribes or agrees to subscribe, procures or agrees to procure, subscription for any shares, or debentures of a company if the articles authorise such payment. The rate of commission must not exceed 5 per cent of the price at which the shares are issued or the rate authorised by the articles whichever is less, and in the case of debentures, 2.5 per cent of the price of the debentures or the rate authorised by the articles whichever is less. The rate must be disclosed in the prospectus. The number of shares or debentures which persons have agreed for a commission to subscribe must also be disclosed [Sec. 76(1)]. A copy of the contract for payment of commission must be delivered to the Registrar along with the prospectus or the statement in lieu of prospectus.

The Act prohibits the payment of any commission, discount or allowance under any other circumstances. But if a company has hitherto paid any "brokerage" it may continue to do so. The Act also prohibits the payment of underwriting commission on shares or debentures which have not been offered to the public but directly allotted or privately subscribed. The effect of this new provision is that underwriting commission cannot be paid to any person in respect of shares or debentures actually subscribed for at (*he* time of filing the company's prospectus or statement in lieu of prospectus.[38]

Underwriting commission and brokerage should be distinguished, as brokerage is not "commission" under Sec. 76(3). The broker undertakes to "place" shares in consideration of an agreed brokerage, and if he fails to dispose of certain shares he is not personally liable to take them, nor is he entitled to any brokerage in respect of shares not placed. The underwriter is bound to take over the shares which the public has not taken and is entitled to the whole of the agreed commission; he is an insurer against under subscription.

Issue of Shares at Premium—Sec. 78 empowers a company to issue shares at a premium subject to certain restrictions. Where a company issues shares at a premium, a sum representing the total amount or value of the premium on such shares must be transferred to an account known as the "Share Premium Account". The amount so transferred can be applied by the company only for:—

(a) paying up shares of the company to be issued to members of the company as fully paid bonus shares; or

(b) writing off the preliminary expenses of the company; or

(c) writing off the expenses or commission paid or discount allowed on any issue of shares or debentures; or

(d) in providing for the premium payable on the redemption of any redeemable preference shares or of any debentures of the company.

---

38. In re Calcutta Stock Exchange Ass. Ltd., 1957 Cal. 438.

Issue of Shares at a Discount—Sec. 79 permits a company to issue shares at a discount only on the following conditions : (i) the issue must be of a class of shares already issued; (ii) it must be authorised by a resolution passed in general meeting and sanctioned by the Company Law Board; (iii) the maximum rate of discount must not exceed 10 per cent or such higher rate as the Company Law Board may permit in any special case; (iv) not less than one year has at the date of issue elapsed since the date of which the company was entitled to commence business; and (v) the shares must be issued within 2 months of the sanction by the Company Law Board or within such extended time as that Board may allow. Every prospectus at the date of its issue must mention particulars of the discount allowed on the issue of the shares or the exact amount of the discounts as has not been written off. Fine for default is ₹ 50.

RESTRICTIONS ON SHARE ISSUE (SEC. 77)

No company can buy its own shares, unless the consequent reduction of share capital is effected and sanctioned by the Court in pursuance of Secs. 100 to 104 or of Sec. 402. Furthermore, a public company or its subsidiary must not finance the purchase by any person of its own shares or those of its holding company. A company may, however, redeem its redeemable preference shares. A banking company may lend money in the ordinary course of its business. A provision may be made by any company to enable its employees, including a salaried director, to buy fully paid shares. It may also lend an amount to an employee (excluding directors, or manager) equal to his six months' salary or wages. Contravention renders the company and every officer at fault to a fine up to ₹ 1,000.

SHARE CERTIFICATE

By Sec. 113, where shares have been allotted to an applicant, or where a valid transfer of shares had been lodged, the company (unless the conditions of issue of the shares otherwise provide) must deliver within 3 months after allotment and within 2 months after application for registration of transfer, a certificate or certificates evidencing the title of the allottee or transferee to the shares allotted or transferred. Default makes the company and every officer in default liable to a fine up to ₹ 500 for every day of default. To be a valid certificate, it must have the common seal of the company affixed to it, and must also be stamped. One or more directors must sign it. It should state the name, address and occupation of the holder, number of shares and their distinctive numbers and amounts paid (Sec. 83). It is a *prima facie* evidence of the title of the member to such shares. The amended Sec. 84 empowers a company to issue a duplicate of a certificate if such certificate is proved to have been lost or destroyed, or having been defaced or mutilated or torn, is surrendered to the company. If a company with intent to defraud renews a certificate or issues a duplicate thereof, the company shall be punishable with fine up to ₹ 10,000 and every officer of the company who is in default with imprisonment up to six months or fine up to ₹ 10,000 or with both.

SHARE WARRANT

By Sec. 114, a public (not private) company limited by shares, if authorised by its articles, may, in respect *of fully paid* shares, issue under its common seal, and with the previous approval of the Central Government, a **share warrant** stating that the bearer thereof is entitled to share therein specified. It is a negotiable instrument and mere delivery transfers the ownership of the shares. The dividends may be paid by coupons or otherwise to the holder of the warrant. Sec. 115 provides that on the issue of a share warrant, the company must strike out of its register of members the name of the member and must enter the following particulars: (i) the fact of the issue of the warrant; (ii) a statement of the shares included in the warrant, distinguishing each share by its number; and (iii) the date of the issue of the warrant. If the articles so allow the holder of the share warrant may surrender it for cancellation, whereupon his name will be entered on the register, and a share certificate will be issued in his name.

The holder of a warrant cannot qualify himself as a director. If the articles so provide, the bearer of a share warrant may be deemed to be a member of the company.

PERSONATION OF SHAREHOLDER (SEC. 116)

If any person deceitfully personates an owner of any share or interest in a company, or of any share warrant or coupon issued in pursuance of the Act, and thereby obtains or attempts to obtain any such share or interest or any such share warrant or coupon, or receives or attempts to receive any money due to such owner, he shall be punishable with imprisonment for a term extending to 3 years and shall also be liable to fine.

TRANSFER OF SHARES

One of the most important characteristics of shares is their transferability. Sec. 82 empowers every shareholder to transfer his shares in the manner prescribed by the articles of the company. The articles of a public company may and those of a private company must restrict rights to transfer. The articles may give power to the directors to refuse transfer without assigning any reasons as long as the refusal is *bonaflde*.[39] The refusal must be by a resolution of the Board of Directors. In case of refusal, it is now provided that the company must send a notice to the transferee and the transferor within 2 months from the date on which the instrument of transfer was delivered to the company. Default renders the company and every officer at fault liable to a fine up to ₹ 50 for every day of default. Any person dissatisfied with the refusal may apply to the Company Law Board for rectification of the register of members under Sec. 111, which shall, after hearing all the parties, order the registration of the transfer or reject the appeal according to the circumstances of the case. The Company Law Board may compel the company to disclose the reason for refusal to register a transfer (Sec. 111),

Where the articles do not restrict the right to transfer, a shareholder may transfer his shares to any one *sui juris,* even to a pauper, an insolvent, or even to escape liability on them, and at the last moment before winding up, provided that the transfer is real and *bonafide,* without retaining by the transferor any interest in the shares.[40] The mode of transfer is provided in Secs. 108 to 110 and 114 (3) of the Act. By virtue of Sec. 114(3), when a *share warrant to bearer* has been issued in respect of fully paid shares, the ownership of the shares is transferred by simple delivery of the share warrant, which is a negotiable instrument. On the other hand, in the case of shares in respect of which a share certificate, made out in the name of a shareholder whose name is entered on the company's register of members, has been issued, a transfer of shares is effected by a written instrument of transfer executed by the transferor and the transferee and duly stamped, specifying the name, address and occupation of transferee, which is delivered to the company for registration along with the share certificate, and if no such certificate is in existence along with the letter of allotment of the shares.

By virtue of Sec. 108, every instrument of transfer shall be in the prescribed form and shall be presented to the prescribed authority (Registrar) before it is signed by or on behalf of the transferor and before any entry is made therein, and the prescribed authority shall stamp or otherwise endorse thereon the date on which it is so presented. Thereafter the transferor and the transferee shall execute this instrument of transfer and complete it in all other respects, and then deliver to the company for registration:—

   (i) in the case of shares dealt in or quoted on a recognised stock exchange at any time before the date on which the register of members is closed in accordance with law for the first time after the date of such presentation or within 12 months from the date of such presentation, whichever is later;

---

39. B. Choulkhani v. Western India Theatres Ltd. 1957 Cal. 709 ; See also Jagdish Mills Ltd., 1955 Bom. 79.
40. Linder's Case (1910) 1 Ch. 312.

(ii) in any other case, within two months from the date of such presentation.

An instrument which is not in conformity with these provisions shall not be accepted by the company.

Unless the directors have power to refuse to register, the transfer must be registered at the earliest moment of time and the name of the transferee substituted on the register of members for that of the transferor. The application for the registration of transfer may by made either by the transferor or the transferee. Where it is made by the transferor and relates to partly paid shares, the company must give notice of application by prepaid registered post to the transferee. If the transferee does not object to the transfer within 2 weeks from the receipt of the notice, then his name should be entered on the register of members. With regard to an application by the transferee or by the transferor relating to fully paid shares, no notice is required. It should be noted that the transfer is complete and the transferee becomes liable to pay as member calls on partly paid shares only when the instrument of transfer is registered and his name entered on the register of members and not before.[41] But as between the transferor and the transferee immediately after the transfer is made, the transferee becomes the sole beneficial owner of the transferred shares. A relation of trustee and *cestui que irast* is thereby established between them. The transferor is under obligation to comply with all reasonable directions of the transferee. The transferee should, however, take active and prompt steps to get his name registered as a member on the register of the company.[42]

CERTIFICATION OF TRANSFER

When a shareholder sells part only of the shares mentioned in the share certificate, he does not deliver the share certificate to the buyer, but produces it along with the transfer instrument to an officer of the company, who "Certifies" the transfer by writing in its margin the words "Certificate lodged" and mentions the number of snares for which it is lodged. This is called "Certification" and is taken by the buyer as tantamount to delivery to himself of the shares in the "Certified transfer." In due course the company will register the transferee as the holder of shares sold to him, cancel the old certificate and prepare two certificates: one for the shares sold which will be given to the transferee and the other for the unsold shares which will be handed over to the transferor.

FORGED TRANSFER

A forged transfer even if registered by the company, is void and the alleged transferee gets no title to the shares. The company, however, does not incur any liability by putting the transferee's name on the register, unless it issues a certificate and a person suffers damage on the faith of it. The company can claim damages from the person who procures registration by forged transfer. **Transfers** made during winding up are void, unless sanctioned by the Court or the liquidator.

Blank Transfer—When a shareholder signs the transfer form without filling in the name of the transferee and the date of execution and hands it over with the share certificate to the transferee thereby enabling him to deal with the shares, he is said to have made a "transfer in "blank". When used for legitimate business purposes it has some advantages. The holder of a blank transfer can again transfer the shares without filling his name and signature to a subsequent transferee, and thus avoid the payment of stamp duty. The ultimate holder, who wants to retain the shares, can fill his name and date and get it registered in the company's books. For this ultimate transfer and registration the first transferor will be regarded the transferor even if he is dead. On such registration the last transferee will become the member of the company.

---

1. Amraoti Electric Supply Co. v. R.S. Chandak 1954 Nag. 239; Jagjit D. & A. Industries v. Shiv Ram, 1957 Pepsu 18.

2. R. Mathalone v. Bombay Life Ass. Co. 1953 S.C. 385.

Transmission of Shares—Transmission of shares takes place when the registered holder dies, or is adjudged an insolvent. Upon the death of a sole registered holder, so far as the company is concerned, the legal representatives of the deceased are the only persons having any title to the shares. All other persons have only equitable interest in the shares. The legal representatives of the deceased member can, therefore, transfer the shares or other interest in the company held by the deceased, without getting themselves registered as members, and the transferee will get good title to the shares. The shares of an insolvent vest in the Official Assignee or Receiver, either of whom may get himself registered as holder of these shares or dispose of them. They can also disclaim them.

CALLS

Shares are generally issued to the public so that a certain amount not less than 5 per cent is payable on application and another sum on allotment. The balance may be payable as and when called for. A Call is a demand by the company in pursuance of a resolution of the Board and terms of the articles on the shareholders to pay the whole or part of the balance still due on each share made at any time during the continuance of the business, or during winding up. Each shareholder is liable to pay a valid call, which can be made only after the minimum subscription is allotted and the company is entitled to commence business. A call must be made uniformly on all shares of a class, and must be for the benefit of the company. By Sec. 92, a company may, if authorised by its articles, receive advance calls and pay interest on them as also dividends (Sec. 93).

FORFEITURE OF SHARES

Shares can be forfeited for non-payment of a call only if special power in the articles is given to the directors to do so. The forfeiture must be made strictly in accordance with the regulations regarding notice, procedure and manner stated in the articles. Any irregularity will make the forfeiture void, and the shareholder may sue for annulment. The power to declare shares forfeit is in the nature of a trust and must be exercised in good faith for the benefit of the company. After a valid forfeiture the shareholder ceases to be a member of the company, but continues to be liable for any money presently payable at the time of forfeiture, if the articles so provide, and can be sued within three years of the forfeiture, as an ordinary debtor to the company. If shares are forfeited within one year of winding up of the company, he will be liable as 'B' list contributory. Forfeited shares become the property of the company and it may either cancel them or re-issue them, if articles so provide.

SURRENDER OF SHARES

The articles usually give power to the directors to accept surrender of shares: this relieves them from going through the formality of forfeiture. A surrender of partly paid shares can only be accepted when a forfeiture would be justified. The same rule applies to fully paid shares which are surrendered for cancellation. A surrender accepted to release a shareholder or in consideration paid to him is invalid, as that amounts to purchase by the company of its own shares, which is strictly prohibited by the law

DIVIDENDS

Dividend means "the sum paid and received as the quotient forming the share of the divisible sum payable to the recipient." In simple words, dividends are the profits of trading divided among the members in proportion to their shares. The mode of payment is determined by the articles. The directors are required by Sec. 217 to make a report on the balance sheet recommending the rate of dividend which may be declared in the annual general meeting, but it cannot in any event exceed the rate recommended in the report. Besides these dividends the articles may provide for the payment of *Interim Dividend;* which can be declared at any time between two annual general meetings. Until a dividend is declared, a shareholder cannot enforce its payment. But once it is declared, it becomes a debt due from the company to each shareholder, for the recovery of which he can sue the company.[43] An interim dividend is not a debt and the directors can rescind it by a resolution. Sees. 93 and 205 to 207 make special provisions for the payment of dividends.

Sec. 93 empowers a company to pay, if authorised by its articles, dividends in proportion to the amount paid on each share where a larger amount is paid up on some shares than on others. Sec. 205 has been amended to impose an obligation on managements to provide for depreciation before declaring dividends and also to pay dividends only in cash. The section, as amended, provides that no dividend can be declared or paid by a company except out of profits of the company arrived at after providing for depreciation as laid down in Sec. 350, or in respect of each item of depreciable asset, for such an amount as is arrived at by dividing 95 per cent of the original cost thereof to the company, or on any other basis approved by the Central Government.

The new Sub-Section (2A) to Sec. 205 further provides for the transfer of such percentage of its profits for the year, not exceeding 10 per cent, as may be prescribed, before declaring or paying dividend out of the profits of the current financial year. In case of inadequacy or absence of profits in any year, the company may declare dividend out of previous years' profits and transferred to reserves in accordance with rule to be framed by the Central Government. Sec. 205A requires the transfer of unpaid or unclaimed dividends within 7 days of the expiry of 42 days from the date of the declaration of the dividend to a special account with a scheduled bank to be known as "Unpaid Dividend Account of..... Co. Ltd/Co. Private Ltd." If the amount of the unpaid dividends is not transferred to such account, then the Company shall pay interest at the rate of 12 per cent per annum. Any money transferred to this account which remains unpaid or unclaimed for 3 years shall be transferred to the general revenue account of the Central Government, and claim shall be preferred to it for payment. Failure to comply with any of the above provisions will render the company and every officer in default liable to be fined up to ₹ 500 per day during the period of default.

The dividend may also be paid out of moneys provided by the Central or State Government for the payment of dividend in pursuance of a guarantee given by such Government. Although a dividend is payable only in cash, capitalisation of profits or reserves for the purpose of issuing fully paid-up bonus shares or paying up any amount for the time being unpaid on any shares held by the members of the company is allowed. Dividend must be paid only to the registered shareholder to his order or to his bankers, or to the producers of coupons in respect of share warrants (Sec. 206). Where a dividend has been declared by the company but it has not been paid (or dividend warrant has not been posted) within 42 days from the declaration of the dividend, to any shareholder entitled to payment of the dividend, every director, managing agent secretaries and treasurers, who are knowingly party to the default shall be punishable with imprisonment up to 7 days and with fine. The only exceptions to this are : (i) where dividend could not be paid by reason of some law; (ii) where the instructions of the shareholder for payment of dividend cannot be complied with; (iii) where there is a dispute as to the right to the dividend; (iv) where the dividend has been adjusted against a claim of the company; or (v) where the company's failure to pay the dividend or post the dividend warrant was not due to any fault on its part (Sec 207).

Sub-Section (2B) has been added to Section 205 and provides that a company which fails to redeem the redeemable preference shares as required by the new Section 80, inserted by the 1988 Amendment Act, must not declare any dividend on its equity shares as long as such failure continues.

PAYMENT OF INTEREST OUT OF CAPITAL

The general rule as laid down in Sec. 205 is that dividends must not be paid out of capital. An exception to this rule is, however, constituted by Sec. 208, which provides in effect that where shares

---

43. General Ass. Society v. L.I.C. of India, 1964 S.C. 892.

are issued to raise money to defray the cost of works or buildings or of plant which cannot be made profitable for a long period, the company may pay interest on the amount of capital paid up in respect of such shares, and may charge the same to capital as part of the cost of the works, buildings or plant, provided that—(i) no such payment shall be made unless it is authorised by the articles or by a special resolution, and previous sanction of the Central Government is obtained; (ii) the payment of interest shall be made only for such period as may be determined by the Central Government and in no case beyond the end of the half year following the half year of the actual completion of the plan; (iii) the rate of interest must not exceed 4 per cent pet annum or any other rate which the Central Government may permit; (iv) the payment of interest shall not operate as a reduction of the share capital.

CAPITALISATION OF PROFITS

A company, if authorised by its articles, may capitalise its profits instead of paying them off as dividends. In such a case, the company declares a dividend or "bonus" out of its undistributed profits and issues at the same time a corresponding number of new shares and then applies the dividend or bonus which belongs to the shareholders in full payment of the amount due on shares. The effect of capitalisation is that the company does not part with any of its assets, and is enabled to increase its capital, and the shareholders get their dividend in the shape of further shares which are called "Bonus Shares." Thus, capitalisation of undistributed profits is made by issuing paid-up shares to the members, thereby transferring the sum capitalised from the profit and loss account and reserve account via the bonus to the share capital. The reason why bonus is first paid out of reserve and then taken back for payment on the newly issued shares is that direct transfer from reserve to capital in payment of fully paid shares will be payment by the company to the company, which is illegal.

PART 16-F
BORROWING POWERS

MORTGAGES AND CHARGES

Every commercial or trading company is deemed to have borrowing powers; but in the case of a non-trading company its memorandum must lay down such powers to enable it to borrow. A company having power to borrow may do so to any extent within the limitations laid down by the memorandum or articles or the Act. If a company borrows beyond its powers, the borrowing is *ultra vires* the company and void. No debt is created, and any security which may have been given in respect of the borrowing is also void.[44] The lender cannot sue the company for the repayment of the loan.[45] If the borrowing is *ultra vires* the directors only, the rule in *Royal British Bank* v. *Turquand* applied, if the shareholders elect to ratify in general meeting the act of the directors.[46] In either case, if the money has not been spent by the company, the lender can get an injunction to prevent the company from parting with it, or he may sue the directors for damages for breach of warranty of authority. If the money has been used in paying off debts which could have been enforced against the company, the lender may sue the company as he steps into the shoes of the creditors who have been paid off by virtue of the principle of subrogation.

A company having borrowing powers has also the power to give security to the lender for the loan advanced by him. This may be done by charging or mortgaging any or all of the company's property. The loan may be secured by any one or more of the following ways: (i) a legal mortgage of its property; (ii) an equitable mortgage by deposit of title deeds; (iii) a mortgage of movable property;

---

44. Pooley v. Hall Colliery Co. (1869), 21 L.T. 690.
45. Sinclair v. Brougham (1914) A.C. 398.
46. Irvine v. Union Bank of Australia (1895) 3 Cal. 250, P.C.

(iv) bonds; (v) promissory notes, bills of exchange; (vi) a charge on calls made but not paid; (vii) a floating charge; (viii) a charge on a ship or any share in a ship; (ix) a charge on goodwill, on a patent or a license under a patent, on a trade mark or on a copyright, (x) by debentures or debenture stock.

DEBENTURES AND DEBENTURE STOCK

When a company desires to borrow a considerable sum of money and therefore intends to invite the general public to subscribe, it gives a form of bond known as "debenture." A **debenture** is an acknowledgment of a debt by a company to some person or persons, and is issued to the public by means of a prospectus in the same manner as shares. A **debenture stock** is borrowed capital consolidated into one mass for the sake of convenience. Instead of each lender having a separate bond, he has a certificate entitling him to a certain sum, being a portion of one large loan. It is generally secured by a trust deed.

KINDS OF DEBENTURES

Debentures, like ordinary bonds, may be unsecured by any mortgage or charge on the property of the company, and are known as "naked" debentures; or may be, and usually are, secured, and are called "secured" or "mortgage" debentures. They may be "registered," when they are made out in the name of a particular person who is registered by the company as holder, and are transferable in the same way as shares; or "bearer" which, like share warrants, are made out to bearer, and are negotiable instruments. Debentures may also be "redeemable," that is to say, issued on the terms that the company is bound to repay the amount of the debentures, either at fixed date, or upon demand; or "perpetual" or "irredeemable" debentures in which case no time is fixed in which the company is bound to pay, although it may pay back at any time it chooses; the debenture-holder cannot demand payment as long as the company is a going concern and does not make default in payment of interest. But all debentures, whether irredeemable or otherwise, become payable on the company going into liquidation. A company may also issue convertible debentures which can be converted into equity shares.

Section 117 prohibits the issue of any debentures carrying voting rights at any meeting of the company. The conditions on which debentures are issued are indorsed on the back of the bond which gives different rights to the holders. One of the conditions usually is the debenture is one of a series of a certain number, each for a like sum, say, ₹ 100, and that all the debentures of a series rank *pari passu,* i.e., all the debentures of one series are to be paid rateably, so that, if there is not enough to go round, they will all abate proportionally. If the words *"pari passu"*are not used, the debentures will be payable according to the date of issue, and if they all are issued on the same day, they will be payable according to their numerical order.

FLOATING CHARGE

A charge upon property of the company may be "fixed" or "floating." A **fixed** charge passes legal title to certain specific assets, and the company loses the right to dispose of the property. In other words, the company can transfer the property charged only subject to the charge—the charge holder must be paid first whatever is due to him. A **floating** charge is an equitable charge on the assets for the time being of a going concern. It attaches to the subjects charged in the varying conditions in which they happen to be from time to time. The governing idea of floating security is to allow a going concern to carry on its business in the ordinary course, the effect which would be to make the assets liable to constant fluctuations. Thus the company can deal with its property so charged in a manner it likes until the charge "crystallises" or "attaches." The essence of a floating charge is that the security remains dormant until it is fixed or crystallises. The floating charge crystallises: (i) when the company ceases to be a going concern; (ii) upon the commencement of the winding up; (iii) on the appointment of a Receiver at the request of a debenture-holder who has intervened. Until one of these three things happens the charge will not become fixed, and the company may even sell the undertaking if that is one of the objects specified in the memorandum. But this does not make it a future security. It is a present security which presently affects all the assets of the company expressed to be included in it. The creation of a floating charge leaves company free to create a specific mortgage of its property having priority over the floating charge. A floating charge is also postponed to the rights of the following persons if they act before the security crystallises, namely, (i) a landlord who distrains for rent, (ii) a creditor under garnishee order absolute, (iii) a decree holder who attaches goods and has them sold, (iv) a mortgagee of the same property, even where the mortgage is created after the floating charge. Furthermore, under Sec. 123, they are postponed to the preferential debts, mentioned in Sec. 530, e.g., rates, taxes, wages, salaries, etc. A supplier of goods on hire-purchase system has priority over such charge until goods are paid for in full.

TRUST DEED

The most common form of securing debentures is to execute a trust deed conveying the property of the company to trustees and declaring a trust in favour of the debenture-holders, charging the property. This deed contains elaborate provisions for the benefit of the debenture-holders and the company until the security becomes enforceable by the trustees. The advantages of having a trust deed are: (i) in the case of default by the company the trustees can take the necessary steps on behalf of all the debenture-holders; (ii) the trustees usually have power to sell and so realise the security with the aid of the Court; (iii) the legal estate is vested by the deed in the trustees and thus a subsequent mortgagee cannot get priority; and (iv) the company can be made to issue property by the covenants in the deed. Sec. 112 makes any contract void by which trustee is exempted from liability for breach of trust where he fails to act carefully and diligently as a trustee.

Debentures may be issued at a discount if the articles allow the reason being that they do not form part of the capital of the company. Similarly, interest payable on them is a debt and can be paid out of capital. All sums allowed by way of discount must be stated in every balance sheet of the company until written off. Sec. 122 provides that specific performance of a contract to give debentures may be enforced against the company, and that the company may specifically enforce against any one a contract to take up and pay for any debentures. A debenture issued in an irregular manner may be treated as an agreement to issue a debenture.

RE-ISSUE OF DEBENTURES

Unless any provision to the contrary is contained in the articles, or in the conditions of issue, or in any contract, or the company has by resolution decided to cancel the debentures, the company may re-issue its redeemable debentures which it has redeemed, either by re-issuing the same debentures or by issuing other debentures in their place [Sec. 121 (1)]. In this manner, the company can revive the debentures, i.e., give to a new debt the same security as if it were the old debt. It is as if A's debt had not been paid and he had transferred the debt and security to B. Sec. 121(2) expressly provides that on the re-issue of these debentures, the person entitled to the re-issue debenture shall have, and shall be deemed always to have had, the same rights and priorities as if the debentures had never been redeemed.

REMEDIES OF DEBENTURE-HOLDERS

A debenture-holder who wishes to release his security and get back his money, may make use of all or any of the following remedies:—

1. He may sue on behalf of himself and all other debenture-holders to obtain payment or to enforce his security by sale. The Court will appoint a **Receiver** and a manager, for the company's

business, if necessary, and declare the debentures to be a charge on the assets of the company, and order the sale of the property.

2. He may appoint a **Receiver**, if the conditions of the issue of the debentures give him power to do so. The Receiver will sell the property and the sale proceeds will be utilised for the payment of debentures.

3. He may apply to the Court for the principal and interest thereon, present a petition for the winding up of the company.

4. He may, as a creditor for the principal and interest thereon, present a petition for the winding up of the company.

5. He may have the property sold by the trustees if the debenture trust deed permits the sale.

6. If the company is insolvent, and his security is insufficient he may value his security and prove for the whole debt.

If a debenture-holder owes a debt to the company which is unable to pay its debentures in full, the debenture-holder cannot set off his debt against the liability he owes to the company. The rule of law is that a person who claims share of a fund must first pay up everything he owes to the fund.

REGISTRATION OF CHARGES

REGISTER OF DEBENTURE-HOLDERS

Sec. 152 now requires every company to keep in one or more books a register of the holders of its debentures (except bearer debentures) and to enter therein the following particulars: (i) the name, address arid occupation of each debenture-holder; (ii) debentures held by each holder distinguishing each debenture by its number, and the amount paid or agreed to be paid on these debentures; (iii) the date at which each person was entered in the register as a debenture-holder; and (iv) the date at which any person ceased to be a debenture-holder. Like a register of members, this register should have an index, is open to inspection and may be closed in the same manner. Similarly, no notice of trust is to be registered thereon (Sees. 153, 154).

COMPANY'S REGISTER OF CHARGES

Section 124 provides that for the purpose of registration and register of charges, the expression "charge" includes a mortgage. By Sec. 143, every company must keep at its registered office a register of charges in which all charges specifically affecting property of the company and all floating charges on the undertaking or on any property of the company must be entered. The register must contain a short description of the property charged; the amount of the charge; the names of the persons entitled to the charge. Sec. 136 requires every company to keep at its registered office a copy of every instrument creating any charge requiring registration. The register and the documents should be open to inspection.

REGISTER OF CHARGES KEPT BY REGISTRAR

Section 130 has been redrafted under the 1988 Amendment Act. It now makes it compulsory for every company to file with the Registrar particulars of all charges required to be registered under Section 125. The Registrar is required to maintain, in respect of each company, a register of charges and register particulars of all charges filed with him and indicated in Sections 128 and 129 stated in the following paragraphs. The pages of the register shall be consecutively numbered and each page must be signed or initialled by the Registrar. The Registrar will issue a Certificate of Registrations and return all instruments to the company. Section 133 states that the company must cause a copy of every registration to be endorsed on every debenture issued by the company, and the payment of which is secured by the charge so registered.

REGISTRATION OF CHARGES

Sec. 125 requires a company to file within 30 days of the creation of a charge with the Registrar complete particulars together with the instrument, if any, creating or evidencing the charge, or a verified copy, of certain charges, otherwise the charge shall be void against the liquidator and creditors, although the money will become presently payable. The Registrar is now given power to allow 7 more days for filing the particulars if sufficient cause for delay is shown by the company. The **charges requiring registration are as follows**:—(a) a charge for the purpose of securing any issue of debentures; (b) a charge on uncalled share capital of the company; (c) a charge on any immovable property, wherever situate, or any interest therein; (d) a charge on any book debts of the company; (e) a charge, not being a pledge, on any movable property of the company; (f) a floating charge on the undertaking or any property of the company including stock-in-trade; (g) a charge on calls made but not paid; (h) a charge on a ship or any share in a ship; (i) a charge on goodwill, on a patent or licence under a patent, on a trade mark, or on a copyright or a licence under a copyright.

The particulars required to be registered under Sec. 125 by filing with the Registrar are as follows:

(a) When the debenture-holders of the same series are made to rank *pari passu,* Sec. 128 requires the following particulars to be registered: (i) the total amount secured by the whole series; (ii) the dates of resolutions authorising the issue of the series and the date of the covering deed, if any, by which the security is created or defined; (iii) a general description of the property charged; (iv) the names of the trustees, if any, for the debenture-holders. The deed containing the charge, or a copy of the deed verified in the prescribed manner, or, if there is no such deed, one of the debentures of the series must also be filed. If any commission, allowance, or discount has been paid or made by the company to any person for subscribing, agreeing to procure any subscription for any debenture, the amount or rate per cent so paid or made must also be filed (Sec. 129).

(b) In the case of any other charge, the particulars are: (i) if the charge was created by the company, the date of creation of the charge; and if the charge was a charge existing on property acquired by the company, the date of acquisition of the property; (ii) the amount secured; (iii) short particulars of the property charged; and (iv) the persons entitled to the charge (Sec. 130).

A registration under Sec. 125 constitutes a notice to whosoever acquires a future interest on the charged assets (Sec. 126). The Registrar should enter in his register the appointment of a Receiver or Manager, if made (Sec. 137). To enable the Registrar to make an entry relating to a charge, it is primarily the duty of the **company** to send to the Registrar the particulars, but Sec. 134 empowers every person interested in the charge which requires registration to get it registered; and such person shall be entitled to recover from the company any fees properly paid by him to the Registrar (Sec. 134). Under Sec. 138, the company must intimate to the Registrar within 30 days of, when they occur any payment or satisfaction in full, or any change in the charges. The Registrar, after giving notice to the charge holder, will make an entry of satisfaction. The register of charges can be rectified by the order of the Court. Omission to register particulars of charges in the manner prescribed by the Act and described above is made punishable with fine. The company, and every officer of the company or other person who is in default shall be liable to fine up to ₹ 500 for every day of default.

PART 16-G
MEETING AND PROCEEDINGS

There are three kinds of general meetings of a company—*Statutory, Annual* and *Extraordinary*. A private company is not required to hold a statutory meeting. Every general meeting of a company requires 21 days' notice in writing.

STATUTORY MEETING

By Sec. 165, every public company limited by shares, and limited by guarantee and having a share capital, must hold a general meeting of its members, to be called "the Statutory Meeting," within a period of not less than one month nor more than 6 months from the date at which the company is entitled to commence business. At least 21 days before the day of the meeting, the Board of Directors must forward to every member a report called **"Statutory Report"** (along with the notice of the meeting). The statutory report must state: (i) the total number of shares allotted; (ii) the total amount of cash received; (iii) an abstract of the receipts and payments by the company up to a date within 7 days of the date of the report and the balance in hand; (iv) estimate of preliminary expenses, and any commission or discount paid on shares or debentures; (v) the names, addresses and occupations of the directors, auditors and also of the managing agent, secretaries and treasurers, manager and secretary, if any, of the company, the changes which have taken place in the names, etc., of the above since the date of incorporation; (vi) the particulars of any contract, or its modification, if any; (vii) the extent to which any underwriting contract has not been carried out and the reason thereof; (viii) the arrears due on calls from every director; (ix) the particulars of any commission or brokerage paid or to be paid to any director, etc.

The statutory report must be certified as correct by at least two directors, one of whom must be a managing director, if there is one. It must also be certified as correct by the auditors of the company. A certified copy must be filed with the Registrar. A list of members showing their names, addresses and occupations together with the number of shares held by each must be kept in readiness and produced at the commencement of the meeting and kept open for inspection during the meeting. The members may discuss any matter at the meeting relating to the formation of the company or arising out of the report. No resolution can, however, be passed unless notice thereof has been given. Default renders the company and every director liable to fine up to ₹ *500*. Moreover, if the meeting is not held or the report is not filed, the Registrar or a contributory may, after expiration of 14 days of the day when the meeting ought to have been held, apply for the winding up of the company. The Court may either order winding up, or give directions for the holding of the meeting and filing of the report, and order the payment of costs by any persons at fault.

ANNUAL GENERAL MEETING

The provisions of the original Sec. 166 were not effective against delay in holding of annual general meeting, because a financial year could be of more or less duration than a calendar year. The section has been redrafted to make it more effective. Now, every company must hold its first annual general meeting within 18 months from the date of its incorporation. Thereafter, it must hold in **each year,** in addition to any other meetings, an annual general meeting, so specified in the notices calling it, provided that not more than 15 months shall elapse between two annual general meetings. In case of difficulty to hold any annual general meeting (except the first meeting) the Registrar may grant an extension up to a period of not more than 3 months. This meeting must be held on a day other than a public holiday, during business hours, at the registered office of the company, or other place within the city, town or village in which the registered office of the company is situate. The Central Government may, however, exempt any class of companies from this provision. A public company or a subsidiary of a public company may by its articles fix the time for its annual general meetings and may also by a resolution passed in one annual general meeting fix the time for its subsequent annual general meetings. A private company may in like manner and also by a resolution agreed to by all the members thereof fix the time as well as the place for its annual general meeting. If default is made in holding this meeting, the Company Law Board may, on the application of any member of the company, call or direct the calling of the meeting. Also, if this meeting is not held either originally or when ordered by the Company Law Board, then the company and every officer who is in default is punishable with fine up to ₹ 5,000, and in the case of continuing default, with a further fine of ₹ 250 per day during default. The ordinary business to be transacted at this meeting is: (i) consideration and adoption of accounts and reports of the Board and auditors; (ii) appointment of directors; (iii) appointment and fixation of remuneration of auditors; (iv) declaration of dividend.

EXTRAORDINARY GENERAL MEETING

Every general meeting other than the statutory meeting and the annual general meeting is an Extraordinary General Meeting. It is usually called by the directors for transacting some special or urgent business which has to be done before the next annual general meeting. Only the special business for which it is convened can be done at this meeting. Sec. 169 provides that such meeting must be called by the Board on the requisition of members holding 10 per cent of the paid-up capital carrying voting right in respect of the matter, and where the company has no share capital, on the requisition of members holding 10 per cent of the total voting power, within 21 days of the deposit of the requisition, stating the matters for consideration at the meeting. If the Board does not hold the meeting within 45 days of the requisition, the requisitionists may hold the meeting within 3 months of the requisition. The requisitionists can recover from the company their reasonable expenses and the company can make them good from the directors at fault.

NOTICE OF MEETINGS

Every member of a company is entitled to a notice of not less than 21 days of every general meeting, and such notice must be given in writing to every member. An annual general meeting may, however, be called by giving a shorter notice, if it is consented to by all the members entitled to vote at the meeting; and any other meeting if the holders of 95 per cent of the paid-up share capital or of the total voting power consent to the shorter notice. Notice must also be given to the auditor of the company and to the legal representatives of a deceased member. In the case of a company having share capital, or where articles allow the appointment of proxy, the notice should state that a member entitled to attend and vote is entitled to appoint one or more proxies, that the proxy need not be a member of the company.

ORDINARY AND SPECIAL BUSINESS

In the case of an annual general meeting the ordinary business will be (i) the consideration of the accounts, balance sheet and reports of the Board of Directors and auditors; (ii) the declaration of dividend; (iii) the appointment of directors in the place of those retiring; and (iv) the appointment and fixing the remuneration of auditors. *All other business at any annual general meeting and any business at any other meeting will be deemed to be special.* In the case of any items of business deemed to be special, the notice of the meeting must set out all material facts concerning the business. In regard to special business, the notice should also state the nature and extent of the interest of the directors, or manager in such business.

QUORUM

A number of members of any body sufficient to transact business at a meeting is a quorum. The quorum is generally fixed by the articles, and the number of members to form this quorum must be **personally** present at the meeting. Unless the articles provide for a larger number, 5 members personally present in the case of a public company, and 2 members personally present in the case of a private company, shall be the quorum for a general meeting of the company. Unless the articles otherwise provide, if within half an hour from the time appointed for holding a meeting of the company, a quorum is not present, the meeting if called upon the requisition of members, shall stand dissolved; but in all other cases, it shall stand adjourned to the same day in the next week, at the same time and place, or as the Board may determine. If a quorum is not similarly present at the adjourned meeting, then the members present shall be a quorum (Sec. 174). Any resolution passed without a quorum is invalid, unless all the members, though smaller in number than the quorum, are personally present.

CHAIRMAN

The chairman is a necessary element of the company's meetings, and is usually appointed by the articles. But if he is not so designated, the members personally present at the meeting may elect one of themselves to be the chairman thereof on a show of hands. If a poll is demanded on the election of the chairman, it must forthwith be taken at that meeting under the chairmanship of the person elected by the show of hands (Sec. 175). The chairman must preserve order, conduct proceedings of the meetings in a regular way and take care that the sense of the house is ascertained with regard to the question before it. He must see to it that the majority do not refuse to hear the minority. The chairman may adjourn the meeting if circumstances demand, but he must act *bonafide* and should not leave the chair. If it is brought to his notice that the meeting was improperly convened and constituted, he should declare the proceedings invalid. The chairman must be a member of the company.

PROXIES

A proxy is both an instruments appointing another person to vote for the appointer as well as the person so appointed. Sec. 176 provides that a member of a company who is entitled to attend and vote at a meeting of the company may appoint another person whether a member or not as his proxy to attend and vote instead of himself. A proxy has no right to speak at the meeting. The instrument appointing a proxy must be in writing and signed by the appointer, bearing a 15 paise stamp, or with its seal in the case of a company. No company can make it compulsory for any one to lodge proxies earlier than 48 hours before the meeting. If an invitation is issued at the expense of the company asking for the appointment of a particular person as proxy for members, every officer at fault will be liable to a fine up to ₹ 1,000. During the period beginning 24 hours before the time fixed for the commencement of the meeting and ending with the conclusion of the meeting any member may inspect the proxies lodged, by giving not less than 3 days' notice in writing to the company of his intention. As regards the right to appoint a proxy, Sec. 176 states that unless the articles otherwise provide, in the case of a company having no share capital, a member cannot appoint a proxy, and in the case of a private, company, he can appoint only one proxy, and a proxy shall not be entitled to vote except on a poll. In the case of a public company or where articles permit, a member may appoint one or more proxies, according to the number of votes held by him. He can split his votes and give a few to one proxy and others to another proxy or other proxies. A proxy may be revoked before the person appointed has voted. Where the President of India or a Governor of a State is a member of a company, he may appoint any one to represent him and vote for him.

VOTING AND POLL

Voting is in the first instance by a show of hands. Since voting by show of hands does not always reflect the interest of members upon a 'value' basis, provision has been made in Sec. 179 for demanding a poll, and voting rights must be exercised in accordance with Sec. 87 which provides that every shareholder will have votes in proportion to the equity capital held by him and not according to the number of shares. Where a company has no share capital every member has one vote. Only the persons whose names appear on the register as holders of shares are entitled to vote. If a poll is demanded, then if it relates to the question of election of the chairman or adjournment of the meeting, poll must be taken forthwith; otherwise it may be taken within 48 hours of the demand. A poll may be ordered by the chairman or it may be demanded in the case of a public company having share capital, by any member or members present in person or by proxy and holding shares in the company conferring one-tenth of the total voting power in respect of the resolution, or holding shares on which a sum of not less than ₹ 50,000 has been paid up in the aggregate. In the case of private company, one member, where not more than 7 members are present, and 2 members, if more than 7 members are present, may demand a poll. A public company or its subsidiaries cannot preclude a member from voting on the ground that he has not held the shares for a certain period or any other ground except the non-payment of calls or other sums presently payable by him, or in regard to the exercise of the right of lien by the company.[47]

COMPANY LAW BOARD MAY CALL MEETING

If for any reason it is impracticable to call a meeting of a company (other than an annual general meeting), the Company Law Board may, on the application of a director, a member having a right to vote, or on its own motion order a meeting of the company to be called and conducted as the Company Law Board thinks fit, and may also give such other ancillary consequential directions as it thinks expedient. Such a meeting will be a proper meeting (Sec. 186).

RESOLUTIONS

The Act primarily recognises two types of resolutions; (i) Ordinary, and (ii) Special. To these a third type has been added as a *resolution requiring special notice* (Secs. 189, 190). The category of extraordinary resolution has been abolished; and by Sec. 651, any reference to extraordinary resolution in the articles of a company, or elsewhere, shall in future be construed as referring to a special resolution.

ORDINARY RESOLUTION

A resolution shall be an ordinary resolution when the votes in a general meeting cast in its favour are more than votes against it. The votes may be cast on a show of hands or on a poll in general meeting of which 21 days' notice has been given [Sec. 189 (1)].

SPECIAL RESOLUTION

A special resolution is one in regard to which the intention to propose the resolution as a special resolution is specifically mentioned in the notice of the general meeting, and is passed by such a majority that the number of votes cast in favour of the resolution is three times the number cast against it, either by a show of hands or on a poll in person or by proxy. In other words, three-fourths majority of the votes cast is necessary to special resolution at a general meeting of which 21 days' notice is given [Sec. 189(2)]. The Act requires sanction of members by special resolution in respect of the following matters among others:—

(1) For changing provisions of memorandum so as to (i) change its registered office from one State to another, (ii) change of the objects clause (Sec. 17); (2) for changing the name of the company (Sec. 21); (3) for altering articles (Sec. 31); (4) for reducing share capital (Sec. 100); (5) for paying interest out of capital (Sec. 208); (6) for asking for investigation (Sec. 237); (7) for making directors' liability unlimited (Sec. 323); (8) for paying for an order of winding up (Sec. 433); (9) for voluntary winding up (Sec. 484).

RESOLUTIONS REQUIRING SPECIAL NOTICE

A resolution requiring special notice may be passed by the members at a general meeting by a simple or three-fourths majority according to the provisions of the Act in respect of different matters, provided the following procedure is followed: A notice of intention to move the resolution (which

---

47. Mahaliram v. Fort C. Jute Manufacturing Co. Ltd., 1955 Cal 132.

requires special notice as provided by the Act or in the articles) should be given to the company not less than 14 days before the meeting at which it is to be moved, excluding the days on which the notice is served and the day of the meeting; and the company should give to its members notice of such resolution along with the notice of the meeting, i.e., 21 days' notice, or if it is not practicable to give such notice, it must give notice, either by advertisement in a newspaper having an appropriate circulation or in any other mode allowed by the articles, not less than 7 days before the meeting.

Special notice is required by the Act in the following matters:—

1. For a resolution at an annual general meeting appointing an auditor, a person other than a retiring one.
2. For a resolution at an annual general meeting to provide that a retiring auditor shall not be appointed.
3. For a resolution to remove a director before the expiry of his period of office.
4. For a resolution to appoint another director in place of the removed director.
5. For a resolution to appoint a person as director in place of a retiring director.

CIRCULATION OF MEMBERS' RESOLUTION (SEC. 188)

If members having 5 per cent of the total voting power of the company, or, if 100 members having the right to vote and commanding a paid-up capital of ₹ one lakh or more require the company to do so, the company must circulate any resolution of which those members give notice of intention to move at the meeting, and also circulate any statement of not more than 1,000 words with respect to any matter or resolution to be considered at the meeting, provided the resolution is deposited with the company 6 weeks before the meeting or the statement is so deposited 2 weeks before the meeting, and a reasonable sum of money to meet the cost has also been deposited. The company need not circulate a statement if the Court is satisfied on the application either of the company or any other aggrieved person that the rights so conferred are being abused to secure needless publicity for defamatory matter. A banking company need not circulate such statement, if its Board considers that its circulation will injure the interests of the company. Default of above provisions renders every officer of the company in default liable to a fine up to ₹ 5,000.

REGISTRATION OF RESOLUTIONS AND AGREEMENTS

Sec. 192 makes it compulsory for a company to file with the Registrar printed or typewritten copies of the following resolutions and agreements, within 30 days after the passing or making thereof:— (a) special resolutions; (b) resolutions which have been agreed to by all the members or class of members; (c) any resolution of the Board, or an agreement appointing or re-appointing or varying the terms of appointment of a managing director; (d) any agreement appointing or re-appointing managing agents or secretaries and treasurers; (e) all resolutions or agreements which effectively bind all members of any class of shareholders though not agreed to by all those members; (f) resolutions passed by the company according consent to the Board of any of the powers under Sec. 293(1)(a), (d) and (e), and approving the appointment of sole selling agents under Sec. 294; (g) resolutions for voluntary winding up, passed under Sec. 484(1). If default is made in filing any of the above, the company and every officer (including a liquidator) who is in default are liable to a fine up to ₹ 20 for every day of default. A copy of every such resolution or agreement shall be embodied or annexed to every copy of registered articles issued after passing thereof.

Note : Director's age limit of 65 years deleted by 1965 Act

MINUTES OF MEETINGS

Every company must keep minutes containing a fair and correct summary of all proceedings of general meetings and Board meetings in books kept for that purpose. The minutes books must have their pages consecutively numbered and the minutes must be recorded thereon within 30 days of the meeting. Each page of every such book must be initialled or signed by the chairman of the meeting. The minutes must be recorded on the pages of the minutes book, and in no case must the minutes be pasted on the pages. All appointments of officers made at any meeting must be included in the minutes. In the case of Board meetings, the minutes must also state the names of directors present and of those who may have dissented from a resolution passed at a meeting. The chairman of the meeting may exclude from the minutes any matter which he reasonably regards defamatory of any person or irrelevant or immaterial to the proceedings (Sec. 193). Where the minutes are duly kept, they are presumptive evidence that the meeting was duly called and held and all the proceedings were duly taken. The minutes books must be kept at the registered office of the company and be open to inspection in the usual manner. The minutes books of the Board meetings are not open to inspection. Sec. 197 prohibits advertising or circulating at the expense of the company any report or proceedings of general meetings, unless the minutes circulated or advertised were duly made and entered in the minutes book. Contravention of this provision renders the company and every officer in default liable to fine up to ₹ 500 for each offence.

PART 16-H

ACCOUNTS, AUDIT AND INVESTIGATION

BOOKS OF ACCOUNT (SEC. 209)

Every company must keep at its registered office proper books of account with respect to (a) all sums of money received and expended by the company and the matters in respect of which the receipt and expenditure takes place; (b) all sales and purchases of goods by the company; and (c) the assets and liabilities of the company : provided that all or any of the books of account aforesaid may be kept at such other place in India as the Board may decide, and then the company must within 7 days of the decision file with the Registrar a notice in writing giving the full address of that other place. Where, the company has a branch office, the books of account relating to transactions effected at the branch office must be kept at that office and proper summarised returns sent to the head office at intervals of not more than 3 months. The books of account shall give a true and fair view of the affairs of the company or branch office, and explain its transactions. These books shall be open to inspection by any director during business hours as also by the Registrar or an officer authorised by the Central Government. It is now provided that the books of account relating to a period of at least 8 years' immediately preceding the current year, or if the company has not been in existence for 8 years, then for the whole period of its existence, shall be preserved in good order.

Default on the part of any of the following persons to secure compliance with the above requirements renders him liable in respect of each offence to be punished with imprisonment up to 6 months, or a fine up to ₹ 1,000 or with both. The persons are: (i) managing agent or secretaries and treasurers, or managing director or manager, (ii) partners in a managing agency firm or a firm of secretaries and treasurers; (iii) every director, if they are a body corporate; (iv) every director of the company, if it has neither a managing agent nor secretaries and treasurers nor managing director nor manager. But if any person has been charged by any of the above persons to comply with the requirements of the section and he makes a default, then he will be liable to the same punishment of imprisonment to 6 months or a fine up to ₹ 1,000 or both, and the person so charging will be excused.

ANNUAL ACCOUNTS AND BALANCE SHEET

Sec. 210 requires that at every annual general meeting of the company, the Board or Directors must lay before the company a Balance Sheet and a Profit and Loss Account; and in the case of non-profit companies, an Income and Expenditure Account should be submitted. The profit and loss account should relate, in the case of the first annual general meeting, to the period beginning with the incorporation of the company and ending with a day, the interval between which and the date of the meeting does not exceed 9 months. In the case of subsequent annual general meeting, the profit and loss account should relate to the period beginning with the day immediately after the period for which the preceding profit and loss account was made, and ending with a day, the interval between which and the date of the meeting does not exceed 6 months : but where the Registrar has granted extension of time for holding the meeting by more than 6 months and the extension granted. The period to which the profit and loss account relates is known as the "Financial Year"; and the period of the financial year must not exceed 15 months, but with the special permission of the Registrar 18 months. If any director fails to take all reasonable steps to comply with the above requirements, he is, in respect of each offence, liable to imprisonment up to 6 months, or a fine up to ₹ 1,000, or both, unless some other competent person can be held liable.

CONTENTS OF BALANCE SHEET (SEC. 211)

A balance sheet is a statement of the assets and liabilities of the company conveying a full and truthful information as to the company's position. Every balance sheet and every profit and loss account of a company must give a "true and fair" view of the affairs of the company and the company's profit and loss respectively, at the end of the financial year to which they relate. The form of the balance sheet and the details to be given in the profit and loss account are set out in Schedule VI to the Act. The requirements of this section will not apply to banking, insurance and electricity companies which are governed by their respective Acts.

The Balance Sheet of **holding company** should have annexed to it the following documents relating to its subsidiary : (i) a copy of the balance sheet of the subsidiary; (ii) a copy of its profit and loss account; (iii) a copy of its directors' report; (iv) a copy of its auditors' report; (v) a statement containing the following particulars; (a) extent of holding company's interest in the subsidiary at the end of last financial year, (b) the net aggregate amount of the profits and losses of the subsidiary, whether dealt with or not in the holding company's accounts; (vi) a statement containing the following : (a) any change in holding company's interest in the subsidiary; (b) any material changes since last financial year; (vii) where the directors of the holding company are unable to obtain the necessary information for the purpose aforesaid, then a statement to that effect (Sec. 212). The financial year of the subsidiary may end on the same day or not as of the holding company, but it should not be earlier than 6 months from the day on which holding company's year ends. The duration of financial year of both must be the same (Sec. 213). A holding company may by resolution authorise its representatives to inspect the books of its subsidiaries (Sec. 214).

Except in the case of a banking company, the balance sheet and profit and loss account of a company must be signed on behalf of the Board by two directors and countersigned by the manager, or secretary, if any. If the company has a managing director, he should be one of the signing directors. The B/S and P and L A/C must be approved by the Board before they are submitted to the auditors who must in turn attach their report thereto (Secs. 215, 216). There should be attached to the balance sheet a report of the Board regarding the company's state of affairs, the amount proposed to be carried to reserves, the amount recommended for dividend and also any change which occurred during the financial year in regard to the nature of the business of the company and its subsidiaries. The report should also explain all adverse remarks of the auditor (Sec. 217).

By Sec. 219, not less than 21 days before the date of the meeting, a copy of the B/S together with the P and L A/C, auditor's and Board's reports, must be sent to (i) every member of the company, (ii) every registered debenture-holder, (iii) every trustee for debenture-holders, (iv) every person entitled to a share in consequence of the death or insolvency of a member, (v) the auditors. Even a private company has to comply with these provisions. By Sec. 220, three copies of the B/S and P and L A/C must be filed with the Registrar within 30 days after the annual general meeting. A private company will file three copies of each separately. All officers of the company must make necessary disclosures and give all necessary information for the purposes of the annual accounts to the company and its auditors. Banking and insurance companies should publish half-yearly statements in the months of February and August.

The Amendment Act, 1974 requires every company, while appointing an auditor, to obtain a certificate from the auditor to the effect that the appointment or re-appointment will be in accordance with the following limits. The limits are that from the financial year next following the commencement of the Amendment Act, no auditor shall be appointed or re-appointed, if he is at the date of appointment or re-appointment an auditor of 20 companies each of which has a paid-up share capital of less than ₹25 lakhs, and in any other case, 20 companies, out of which not more than 10 shall be companies each of which has a paid-up share capital of ₹ 25 lakhs or more. Where a person or a firm is an auditor of more than 20 companies, immediately before the commencement of the Amendment Act, he shall, within 60 days from such commencement, intimate his or its unwillingness to be re-appointed as the auditor from the financial year from such commencement, to the company or companies of which he or it is not willing to be re-appointed as the auditor. He or it will simultaneously intimate to the Registrar the names of the companies of which he or it is unwilling to be re-appointed as the auditor and forward a copy of the intimation to each of the companies referred to therein.

Where a firm is appointed as auditors, the ceiling of 20 will be per partner so that firms may not get an advantage over the individual auditors. And where any partner of a firm of auditors is also a partner in any other firm or firms of auditors, the overall ceiling in relation to such partner will also be 20, so that he may not be able to get an extra advantage by becoming a partner in more than one firm of auditors and thereby defeat the purpose of the provisions of the Act.

The new Sec. 224A provides that in the case of a company in which not less than 25 per cent of the subscribed share capital is held, whether singly or in combination, by-

(a) a public financial institution or a Government Company or Central Government or any State Government, or

(b) any financial or other institution established by any Provincial or State Act in which the State Government holds not less than 51 per cent of the subscribed share capital, or

(c) a nationalised bank or an insurance company carrying on general insurance business,

the appointment or re-appointment at each annual general meeting of an auditor or auditors shall be made *by a special resolution.* If no special resolution in appointing an auditor is passed at an annual general meeting, then the Central Government will appoint a person as an auditor of the company.

AUDIT AND AUDITORS

Every company must, at each annual general meeting, appoint an auditor or auditors to hold office from the conclusion of that meeting until the conclusion of the next annual general meeting and must, within 7 days of the appointment, give intimation thereof to the auditor so appointed; and such auditor must, within 30 days of the intimation of his appointment, inform the Registrar in writing that he has accepted the appointment or refused it. A retiring auditor must be re-appointed unless he is disqualified for appointment as auditor, or he has expressed his unwillingness to be appointed, or the company has passed a resolution against his re-appointment, or notice has been given to the company for the appointment of another person as auditor and that other person has become incapable of acting. If an auditor is not appointed or re-appointed at the annual general meeting, the company should notify the fact to the Central Government within 7 days thereafter, and thereupon the Central Government may make the appointment.[48]

The first auditors must be appointed by the Board within one month of the company's registration, and they shall hold office until the conclusion of the first annual general meeting, unless removed by the company at an earlier general meeting. An auditor (other than the first auditor) may be removed by the company in general meeting with the previous approval of the Central Government (Sec. 224). For the appointment as auditor of a person other than the retiring auditor, special notice of 14 days of the intention to move a resolution at the annual general meeting should be given to the company. On receipt of such notice, the company should immediately send a copy thereof to the retiring auditor, who is entitled to make a written representation of reasonable length, which the company should bring to the notice of the members, otherwise the auditor is entitled to have his representation read out at the meeting. If the auditor abuses this right so as to secure needless publicity for defamatory matter, the Company Law Board may, on application, prohibit the circulation of the representation (Sec. 225).

QUALIFICATIONS AND DISQUALIFICATIONS (SEC. 226)

Only a person qualified as an auditor can be appointed an auditor of any company—private or public. To be qualified a person must be a Chartered Accountant in practice, that is to say, he must be a member of the Institute of Chartered Accountants of India and must be in actual practice and must not be in full-time employment else-where. A firm whereof all partners practising in India are Chartered Accountants may be appointed in its firm name and any partner may act in firm name. But the following persons cannot be appointed as auditors of a company: (i) a limited company, (ii) any officer or employee of the company, (iii) a partner or employee of the foregoing, (iv) a person who owes the company more than ₹ 1,000, (v) directors or members holding more than 5 per cent of the subscribed capital of the above corporate bodies. If an auditor becomes disqualified in any of the above ways after his appointment as auditor, then he shall be deemed to have vacated office.

POWERS AND DUTIES

Every auditor of a company is empowered to have free and complete access at all times to the books, accounts and vouchers of the company wherever kept, and also require from the officers of the company such information and explanation as may be necessary for the performance of his duties as an auditor [Sec. 227(1)]. He is further entitled to receive notice of and to attend the general meeting of the company and be heard on any part of the business which concerns him as auditor (Sec. 231).

The auditor must make a report to the members of the company on the accounts examined by him and also every B/S and P&L A/C. The report, besides other things necessary in any particular case, must expressly state : (a) whether, in his opinion and to the best of his information and according to the explanations given to him the accounts give the information required by the Act and in the manner so required, (b) whether the balance sheet gives a true and fair view of the company's affairs as at the end of the financial year and the profit and loss account, of the P and L for its financial year, (c) whether he has obtained all the information and explanations required by him for the purposes of his audit, (d) whether, in his opinion, proper books of account as required by law have been kept by the company, and proper returns for the purposes of his audit have been received from the branches not visited by him, (e) whether the company's B/S and P and L A/C dealt with by the report are in agreement with the books of account and returns.

---

48. See Council of C.A. of India v. Jnanendra Nath, 1955, Assam 8.

Sub-section (1A) to Sec. 227 now further requires an auditor to inquire:—

(a) whether loans and advances made by the company have been properly secured and whether the terms of the loans are not prejudicial to the interests of the company or its members;

(b) whether transactions of the company which are represented merely by book entries are not prejudicial to the interests of the company;

(c) where the company is not an investment or a banking company, whether so much of the assets of the company as consist of shares, debentures and other securities have been sold at a price less than that at which they were purchased by the company;

(d) whether loans and advances made by the company have been shown as deposits;

(e) whether personal expenses have been charged to revenue account;

(f) where it is stated in the books and papers of the company that any shares have been allotted for cash whether cash has actually been received in respect of such allotment.

The Central Government may, by order, require the auditor to include in his report statement on such matters as may be specified in the order.

Where any of the matters on which the auditor is required to report are answered in the negative or with a qualification, the auditor's report must state the reason for the answer (Sec. 227). The accounts of branch offices should ordinarily be audited by qualified auditors, and where they are not so audited, the head office auditor will audit the books of the branch (Sec. 228). The auditor's report must be signed only by a qualified auditor practising in India, and in case a firm is appointed an auditor only a practising partner and not the firm (Sec. 229). The auditor's report must be read at the general meeting and be open to inspection by any member of the company (Sec. 230).

A company auditor must be honest and must exercise reasonable skill and care, otherwise he may be sued for damages. He must be a good watchdog, be alert and careful and ascertain the true position of the company's affairs by examining the books and by making inquiry. While he must exercise reasonable care, he is not bound to be a detective and approach his work with suspicion or with a foregone conclusion that there is something wrong. He is a watchdog, but not a bloodhound. He must not, however, confine himself merely to the task of arithmetical accuracy of the balance-sheet, but should ascertain by comparison with the books of the company that it was properly drawn so as to show the correct financial position.[49] The auditor is personally liable for neglecting wilfully to perform his duties imposed by law. Thus, default to comply with requirements of Sec. 229 regarding his report, makes him liable to a fine up to ₹ 1,000, and he must be sued by the company for damages.

SPECIAL AUDIT AT THE INSTANCE OF CENTRAL GOVERNMENT (SEC. 233A)

Where the Central Government is of the opinion that the affairs of any company are not being managed in accordance with sound business principles or prudent commercial practices, or the company is being managed in a manner likely to cause serious injury or damage to the interests of the trade, industry or business to which it pertains, or the financial position of the company is such as to endanger its solvency, the Central Government may at any time by order direct that a special audit of the company's accounts for such period or periods as may be specified in the order shall be conducted by the Chartered Accountant specially appointed by the Government or by the company's auditor. Such special auditor will report to the Central Government, and the latter, on receipt of the report, shall take such action as is necessary. But if the Government does not take any action on the report within 4 months from the date of its receipt, it shall send to the company a copy of the report with its comments for circulation among the members of the company. The expenses of the special audit, as determined by the Central Government, shall be paid by the company.

49. Registrar Jt, St Co.v. Hedge, 1954 Mad. 1080; In re City Equitable Fire Ins. Co. (1925) 2 Ch. 407; Controller of Insurance v. H.C. Das, 1957 Cal. 387.

Cost Audit—Proper books of accounts, in the case of companies engaged in production, processing, manufacturing or mining activities must include particulars relating to utilisation of material and labour and other items of cost, so that the auditor may be able to conduct cost audit. The records are expected to enable the auditor to report on the efficiency and character of management. The Central Government may, by order, direct that a cost audit of any of the companies following the aforesaid activities be made for obtaining a true and fair view of the state of affairs of the company. The cost auditor should be a Cost Accountant within the meaning of the Cost and Works Accountants Act, 1959. However, as long as, in the opinion of the Central Government, sufficient number of qualified Cost Accountants are not available, that Government may direct that for a specified period a Chartered Accountant possessing the prescribed qualification may also conduct cost audit.

The auditor under this section will be appointed by the Board of directors of the company with the previous approval of the Central Government. The auditor of the company cannot be appointed its cost auditor, nor a person who is disqualified to be an auditor. Further, if the cost auditor, after his appointment as such, suffers from any of disqualifications, he must cease to act as cost accountant.

The company must give all facilities and assistance to the cost auditor who will have all the powers of an auditor. The cost auditor will make his report to the Central Government and forward at the same time a copy of the report to the company. The Central Government may call for further information or explanations, and take whatever action it considers appropriate, after considering the report and explanations. The Government may direct the company to circulate the report to its members along with the notice of the annual general meeting to be held after the submission of the report. Default is made punishable with fine up to ₹ 5,000, and in case of every officer in default with imprisonment up to 3 years, or fine up to ₹5,000 or with both.

Registrar may require information (Sec. 234). Where, on perusing any document filed with him, the Registrar is of opinion that any information or explanation is necessary, he may ask the company to supply in writing such information or explanation within a specified time. On receipt of this order, the company and every officer of the company, past or present, must furnish such information or explanation. If no information is supplied or it is inadequate the Registrar may by another order call on the company to produce before him such books as he considers necessary. Default renders the company and each officer at fault liable to fine up to ₹ 500 for each offence and for continuing default ₹ 50 per day during default; and the Court may, on the application of the Registrar, order the company to comply with the orders of the Registrar. Furthermore, if the information or explanation is not furnished within the specified time, or the document submitted discloses an unsatisfactory state of affairs, or does not disclose full and fair statement of the matter, the Registrar must report to the Central Government. If it is represented to the Registrar that the business of the company is being carried on for fraudulent or unlawful purposes, he may, after hearing the company, order it to furnish similar information and explanation.

The new Sec. 234A provides that where, upon information in his possession or otherwise, the Registrar has reasonable ground to believe that books and papers of, or relating to, any company or other body corporate, or any managing director or manager of such company or other body corporate, may be destroyed, mutilated, altered, falsified or secreted, the Registrar may apply to the Magistrate of the First Class or Presidency Magistrate having jurisdiction for an order for the seizure of such books and papers. The Magistrate may, by order, authorise the Registrar to enter the place or places where the books and papers are kept, search the places and seize such books and papers as he considers necessary. The Registrar may take copies and then within 30 days of the seizure return the books and papers to the persons from whose custody he took them and inform the Magistrate accordingly. The search will be made under the Criminal Procedure Code.

INVESTIGATION

Section 235 has been recast by the 1988 Amendment Act, and now provides that the Central Government may appoint one or more competent persons as inspectors to investigate the affairs of a company on the report of the Registrar that the company has failed to supply him information or explanation under Section 234.

Again, where an application has been made by not less than 200 members or by members holding not less than one-tenth of the total voting power in the case of a company having a share capital, and from one-fifth of the total number of members, in the case of a company having no share capital the Company Law Board may, after hearing the parties, declare that the affairs of the company ought to be investigated and on such declaration being made, the Central Government must appoint one or more inspectors who will report to the Central Government.

As per Section 237, the Central Government must appoint an inspector or inspectors, if the company by special resolution, or the Court by order, declare that the affairs of the company need to be investigated. Furthermore, it may do so, if in the opinion of the Company Law Board the business of the company is being conducted with intent to defraud its creditors, members or other persons, or otherwise for a fraudulent or unlawful purpose, or the members of the company have not been given all the information with respect to its affairs.

An inspector investigating the affairs of the company may, with the previous approval of the Central Government, inspect also the affairs of other connected companies (Sec. 239). The inspector may examine on oath past or present officers and other employees and agents (including bankers, legal advisers and auditors), and where the company is or was managed by managing agent or secretaries and treasurers, require them to produce all books and documents in their custody and also to preserve them. The inspector has to report to the Central Government who must supply a copy of the report to the company, and any other body corporate, managing agent, secretaries and treasurers, and their associates, applicants for investigation, the Court, where Court ordered the appointment. Copies may also be supplied to members or creditors of the company. If it seems desirable from the report, the Central Government may petition the Court for the winding up of the company or for an order under Sec. 397 for relief in case of oppression, or under Sec. 398 for relief in case of mismanagement, or may sue persons in the name of the company or other body corporate for the recovery of damages or property or prosecute persons criminally liable.

One of the methods adopted to delay investigation into the affairs of a company was that an application for relief against oppression and mismanagement was pending before the Court or that the company had passed a special resolution for its voluntary winding up. The new Sec. 250A provides that an investigation under Secs. 235, 237, 239,247,248 or 249 may be initiated notwithstanding the pendency of such application in the Court or the passing of the special resolution for voluntary-winding up of the company.

INVESTIGATION OF OWNERSHIP OF COMPANY

The Central Government may appoint inspectors to investigate and report on the membership of any company for the purpose of determining who are the persons financially interested in its success or failure or able to control its policy. It must appoint inspectors where the Company Law Board during any proceeding orders such appointment. The inspector may also investigate whether there are any secret arrangements or understandings observed in practice. If the company has or had a managing agent, the powers of the inspector extend to the ownership and control of the managing agency company. He may also investigate (with the prior approval of the Central Government) the ownership of other connected companies. The inspector should submit his report to the Central Government who is under no obligation to supply copies thereof to any one. Also, instead of appointing inspectors to investigate the ownership of shares or debentures, or the associateship with managing agent or secretaries and treasurers, the Central Government may require an interested party to give information. Whenever any investigation is in progress, the Central Government may impose the following restrictions on any shares : (i) that no voting rights should be exercised in respect of those shares; (ii) that no payment in respect of those shares by way of dividend, capital or otherwise should be made; (iii) that there shall be no issue of similar shares; (iv) that no transfer of such shares will be made. Similar restrictions can be imposed on debentures. Contravention is punishable with imprisonment up to 6 months.

PART 16-1

MANAGEMENT OF A COMPANY

The registration of a company under the Companies Act brings into being a legal entity, capable of carrying on business and of owning and disposing of property. Yet such an impersonal creation of law must act through some human intermediary who, in practice, takes the form of the Company Directors. For its efficient management, it is essential that the persons who discharge the various managerial and other functions should be competent, honest, and legally qualified to act. The Act lays down certain general rules for preventing the management of a company by *undesirable persons*. Therefore, Sec. 202 prohibits an undischarged insolvent from acting as a director, or manager of a company, or taking part in the promotion or formation or management of any company on pain of imprisonment up to 2 years. Sec. 203 empowers the Court to make an order prohibiting a person (i) who is convicted of an offence in connection with the. promotion or management of a company, (ii) who, in the course of winding up, has been found guilty of fraud, misfeasance or breach of duty, from acting in any of the aforesaid capacities for a period of 5 years. A company must not appoint a firm or a company to or in any office of profit under it, (other than as technician or consultant). for more than 5 years at a time, but the Central Government may allow the initial employment for ten years. No company shall appoint or employ at the same time, or continue the appointment or employment at the same time, of more than one of the following categories of managerial personnel, namely:—

(a) Managing Director,
(b) Manager

DIRECTORS

Meaning of Director—A company is an artificial legal person without intelligence and will and having no physical existence. It can, therefore, act effectively only though the agency of natural persons—men or women. The supreme executive authority in the control of a company and its affairs resides by delegation in individuals known as directors who are collectively designated the Board of Directors. Sec. 2(13) reads: "director includes any person occupying the position of director, by whatever name called" and explanation (1) to Sec. 303 says: "any person in accordance with whose direction and instructions the Board of Directors of a company is accustomed to act shall be deemed to be a director of the company. A director may, therefore, be described as an individual who guides, directs, conducts, governs, manages or superintends the policy and affairs of a company by whatever name called.

Number of Directors—The articles of a company generally prescribe the number of directors that may be appointed, but a public company must have at least three directors, and a private company including a private company which is regarded as a public company under Sec. 43A, must have at least two directors (Sec. 252). Only an individual—a man or a woman—can be a director (Sec. 253).

Appointment—The directors of a company may be appointed in any of the following ways:—
(a) By articles of association as first directors;
(b) By the company in general meeting;

(c) By the Board of directors as an additional director, or to fill a casual vacancy or as an alternative director;

(d) By debenture-holders or other creditors or by workers, it articles give power so to appoint;

(e) By the Central Government;

(f) By the rule of proportional representation.

(a) **First Directors**—The first directors are usually named in the articles, but such an appointment will be valid only if each one of the proposed directors, before the registration of the articles or the publication of the prospectus, has (i) signed the memorandum for his qualification shares, or taken such shares and paid or agreed to pay for them, or signed and filed with the Registrar an undertaking to take such shares, and pay for them, or made and filed an affidavit that shares to qualify him are registered in his name. These conditions do not apply to private company (Sec. 266).

If the articles are not registered (because Table A has been adopted) or if the directors are not named in the articles, the subscribers to the Memorandum may appoint directors after the company has been registered. If the subscribers do not appoint any directors, then the subscribers to the memorandum, who are individuals, are deemed to be the directors, until the first directors are duly appointed by the members in a general meeting (Sec. 254).

(b) **Appointment by the Company**—Sec. 255 provides that not less than two-thirds of the total number of directors of a public company or of a private company which is a subsidiary of a public company must be appointed by the company in general meeting. These two-thirds of the total number of directors, unless the articles provide for the retirement of all the directors at every annual general meeting, must be subject to retirement by rotation, and at the first annual general meeting, the number nearest to one-third must retire from office, the rotation for retirement being determined by the length of office of directors, or in case all were appointed on the same date, by lots. At every subsequent meeting one-third must retire. The retiring directors are eligible for election to fill up the vacancies thus created. If the place of the retiring directors is not filled up, the meeting shall stand adjourned till the same day in the next week. If at the adjourned meeting also, the place of the retiring directors is not filled, the retiring directors shall be deemed to have been re-appointed. The general meeting may, however, resolve not to fill the vacancies (Sec. 256).

A person, other than a retiring director, who wishes to stand for directorship, or any other person who intends to propose him, must give to the company a notice in writing at least 14 days before the meeting, and the company shall then inform the members not later than 7 days before the meeting about the candidature of the person for the office of directorship (Sec. 257). *Appointment of directors of a public company or its subsidiary must be voted on individually by separate ordinary resolution.*

(c) **Appointment by Board of Directors**—By virtue of Sec. 260, the Board of Directors may, if so authorised by the articles, appoint additional directors who will hold office only up to the next annual general meeting of the company. The number of directors and additional directors together must not exceed the maximum strength for the Board by the articles.

Sec. 262 permits the Board to fill a *casual vacancy* in the office of directorship. It says that in the case of a public company or a subsidiary of a public company, if the office of any director appointed by the company in general meeting is vacated before his term of office will expire in the normal course, the resulting casual vacancy may, subject to any regulations in the articles of the company, be filled by the Board of Directors at a meeting of the Board. A person so appointed shall hold office only up to the date up to which the director in whose place is appointed would have held office.

Sec. 313 permits the Board of directors to appoint, if the articles or a resolution passed by the company in general meeting authorise, an alternate director in place of "the original director" who may have to be absent from the State for a period longer than 3 months. The alternate director will not hold office for a period longer than that permissible to the original director, and shall vacate office if and when the original director returns to the State in which meetings of the Board are held.

(d) **Appointment by debenture-holders, etc.**—The articles may under certain circumstances give power to debenture-holders or other creditors to appoint their nominee or nominees to the Board. The debentures or the trust deed may also provide that debenture-holders may nominate a director to the Board of the company. The articles may also provide for the election of a representative of the employees on the Board of directors. The directors so appointed should not exceed one-third of the total strength of the Board.

(e) **Appointment by Central Government**—The Central Government may appoint such number of directors as the Company Law Board may, by order in writing, specify as being necessary to effectively safeguard the interests of the company, or its shareholders or the public interest for a period not exceeding 3 years on any one occasion, if the Company Law Board on reference made to it by the Central Government or on an application of not less than 100 members of the company or of the members holding not less than one-tenth of the total voting power is satisfied after such inquiry as it deems fit to make, that it is necessary to make the appointment in order to prevent the affairs of the company being conducted either in a manner, which is oppressive to any members of the company or in a manner which is prejudicial to the interests of the company or the public interest.

(f) **Appointment by proportional representation**—The articles of a company may provide for the appointment of not less than two-thirds of the total number of directors of a public company or of a private company which is a subsidiary of a public company according to the principle of proportional representation, either by the single transferable vote or by a system of cumulative voting or otherwise. The appointments are to be made once in every three years.

(g) **Increase in the number of directors**—Sec. 258 allows a company to increase or decrease the number of its directors, by an ordinary resolution passed in general meeting, so long as the total number remains within the maximum and minimum limits fixed by the articles and the Act. A public company or its subsidiary can increase the number of its directors beyond the maximum so fixed only with the approval of the Central Government, although no such approval is now necessary if the increase in the number will not make the total number of directors more than twelve.

NUMBER OF DIRECTORSHIPS

A person cannot hold office at the same time as a director in more than 20 companies (excluding private companies which are not subsidiaries). If a person who is already a director of 20 companies, is appointed a director in any other company or companies, the appointment will not be effective unless within 15 days thereafter the director has vacated his office in some other company or companies so as to keep the number within the maximum allowed (Sec. 227). Any person who holds office, or acts, as a director of more than 20 public companies is liable to be fined up to ₹ 5,000 in respect of each of those companies after the first twenty (Sec. 279).

SHARE QUALIFICATIONS

The articles usually provide for a certain share qualification for election as director. Where a qualification is required by the articles, then the Act provides that (i) it must be disclosed in the prospectus; (ii) each director must take his qualification shares within 2 months after his appointment; (iii) the nominal value of the qualification shares must not exceeds ₹ 5,000 or the nominal value of one share where it exceeds ₹ 5,000; (iv) share warrants payable to bearer will not count for purposes of qualification shares (Sec. 270). If a director fails to qualify within 2 months, he vacates office, and if he acts as director after the expiry of the 2 months without taking the qualification shares, he is liable to a fine up to ₹ 50 for every day until he stops acting (Sec. 272). But the company will be bound to third parties for the acts of such directors until the defect in appointment or qualification is disclosed, although acts done after the disclosure will not bind the company. Thus, a *de facto* director is as good as a *de jure* director so far as persons having no notice of the defect are concerned (Sec. 290). But a *de facto* director cannot claim remuneration.

DISQUALIFICATIONS

By virtue of Sec. 274, the following persons cannot be appointed as directors: (1) a person found by Court to be of unsound mind; (2) an undischarged insolvent; (3) a person who has applied to be adjudged an insolvent; (4) a person who has been convicted of an offence involving moral turpitude and sentenced to 6 months' imprisonment, and a period of 5 years has not passed from the date of the expiry of the sentence; (5) a person who has failed to pay calls for 6 months; (6) a person who has been disqualified by Court under Sec. 203. A private company may, by its articles, provide additional disqualifications.

VACATION OF OFFICE

By Sec. 283, the office of a director shall become vacant, if (a) he fails to qualify within 2 months of his appointment, or ceases to hold the qualification shares; (b) he is found by the Court to be of unsound mind; (c) he applies to be adjudged insolvent; (d) he is adjudged an insolvent; (e) he is convicted by Court of any offence involving moral turpitude and is sentenced to imprisonment for 6 months or more; (f) he fails to pay nay call within 6 months from the last date fixed for the payment, unless the Central Government by notification in the Official Gazette has removed the disqualification; (g) he absents himself from three consecutive meetings of the Board of Directors, or from all meetings of the Board for continuous period of 3 months whichever is longer, without leave of absence from the Board; (h) he receives a loan from the company; (i) he fails to disclose to the Board his interest in any contract or arrangement of the company; (j) he is debarred by a Court from being a director; (k) he is removed from directorship by an ordinary resolution passed by members in general meeting after special notice; (1) if he became director by virtue of an office or as managing agent's nominee, on coming to an end of the office or the managing agency. In the case of (d), (e) and (j), the vacation of office will take effect after 30 days from the adjudication, sentence or order, or if any appeal is filed, then after 7 days from the date of disposal of the appeal. A private company may provide additional grounds in its articles for vacation of office. If a person functions as a director after the office has become vacant, he is liable to be fined up to ₹ 500 per day during the period he so functions.

REMOVAL AND RESIGNATION

A company may, by ordinary resolution after special notice, remove a director other than a director appointed by the Central Government (Sec. 408), or a director of a private company holding office for life on April 1, 1952, or in case of proportional representation. A removed director may claim compensation for loss of office, or may continue to hold the additional office. On the removal of a director another person may be appointed in the same way to hold office for the balance of the period (Sec. 284).

A director may resign his office in the manner provided by the articles, but if the articles contain no provision, he may resign at any time by giving reasonable notice, no matter whether company accepts it or not. Once a director has resigned by a proper notice, he cannot withdraw his resignation even where the company has not accepted it.[50]

Remuneration—Directors are not entitled to any remuneration apart from express provision in the articles, or a resolution of the company in general meeting.[51] Sec. 309, recognising this principle, provides that subject to the general provisions of Sec. 198 dealing with the overall managerial

---

50. Glossop v. Glossop (1907),2Ch. 370.

51. In re George Newman & Co. (1895) 1 Ch. 674.

remuneration, the remuneration of directors may be determined by the articles or by a resolution of the company, or if the articles so require, by special resolution, and the remuneration payable to such director shall be inclusive of the remuneration payable to him for services rendered by him in any other capacity. He can, however, be paid extra for services rendered which are of professional nature, and in the opinion of the Central Government, the director possesses the requisite qualifications for the practice of the profession. A director may receive remuneration by way of a fee for each meeting of the Board, or a Committee of the Board attended by him. The redrafted Sub-Sec. (4) of Sec. 309 provides that a director who is neither in the whole-time employment of the company nor a managing director may be paid remuneration (i) by way of a monthly, quarterly or annual payment with the approval of the Central Government; or (ii) by way of commission if the company by special resolution authorises such payment: provided in either case, the remuneration paid to such director, or where there are more than one such director, to all of them together shall not exceed one per cent of the net profits of the company, if the company has a managing director, a whole-time director or manager, and three per cent of the net profits of the company in any other case. Higher remuneration may, however, be paid, if the company in general meeting, with the approval of the Central Government, so authorises. Sec. 310 has been amended to do away with the approval of the Central Government, if the increase in the remuneration is only by way of fee for each meeting of the Board or a Committee thereof   attended by any such director and the amount of the fee after such increase does not exceed the prescribed rates.

A managing director or a whole-time director may be paid remuneration either by way of a monthly payment or at a specified percentage of the net profits of the company or partly by one way and partly by the other: provided that except with the approval of the Central Government such remuneration shall not exceed 5 per cent of the net profits from one such director, and if there are more than one such director 10 per cent for all of them together. A whole-time director, or a managing director, who is in receipt of any commission from the company, shall not be entitled to receive any commission or other remuneration from any subsidiary of such company. The provisions of Sec. 309 do not apply to a private company.

Board Meetings—Directors must ordinarily act at a Board meeting, unless special powers are delegated to a director or a Committee of the Board. In the case of every company, a meeting of its Board of directors must be held *at least once in every three months and at least four such meetings shall be held in every year.* The Central Government may, however, by notification exempt any class of companies (Sec. 285). A written notice of every Board meeting must be given to all directors (Sec. 286). The quorum for a Board meeting must be one-third of its total strength or two directors, whichever is higher. Any interested director will not count for quorum and must be left out of account at the time of discussion or vote on any matter in which he is interested; and if the number of the interested directors exceeds or is equal to two-thirds of the total strength, the balance of the directors present (not being less than two) will be the quorum (Sec. 287). By the amended Sec. 292, the following powers must be exercised by the Board by resolutions passed at Board meetings; (a) the power to make calls; (b) the power to issue debentures; (c) the power to borrow moneys otherwise than on debentures; (d) the power to invest the funds of the company and (e) the power to make loans. The Board may, however, by resolution passed at a meeting, delegate to any committee of directors, the managing director, the manager or any other principal officer of the company the powers specified in clauses (c), (d) and (e) on such conditions as the Board prescribe. The Board should specify the total amount up to which the delegate may borrow money under (e), invest funds under (d) and make loans and the purposes of the loan under (e). The company may in general meeting impose restrictions on the Board's powers. Receiving of deposits by a banking company in the ordinary course of its business will not be deemed borrowing, nor will any money borrowed from another banking company or the Reserve Bank or the State Bank of India be regarded borrowing.

RESTRICTIONS ON BOARD'S POWERS

In the case of a public company and its subsidiary, the Board cannot do any of the following without the consent of the company in general meeting: (a) sell, lease or otherwise dispose of company's undertaking; (b) remit, or give time for the repayment of any debt due by a director, except in the case of renewal or continuance of an advance made by a banking company to its director in the ordinary course of business; (c) invest otherwise than in trust securities the amount of compensation received by the company in respect of the compulsory acquisition, after the commencement of this Act; (d) borrow in excess of the aggregate paid-up capital plus free reserves (temporary loans from the company's bankers in the ordinary course of the business of the company being left out of account for this purpose); (e) contribute to charitable and other funds not relating to the business of the company amounts exceeding ₹ 25,000 or 5 per cent of its average net profits in the course of any financial year. If the company wants to borrow in excess of (d), it shall, by resolution in general meeting, fix the amount up to which the Board may borrow, and also fix the amount if it wishes to contribute more than ₹ 25,000 under (e). The expression "temporary loans" in (d) means loans repayable on demand or within six months from date of the loan. If the Board acts in contravention of the above, the third parties acting in good faith are protected (Sec. 293).

POLITICAL CONTRIBUTIONS

The Companies (Amendment) Act, 1985 has substituted Sec. 293A with a new section. The new Sec. 293 A permits non-Government Companies which are in existence for not less than 3 financial years, to make contributions, directly or indirectly, in any financial year, to any political party, or for political purpose to any person, any amount or amounts not exceeding 5 per cent of their average net profits of 3 immediately preceding financial years. Expenses incurred on advertisements in souvenirs will also be included in the total quantum of 5 per cent of net profits. Every company must disclose in its profit and loss account any amount or amounts contributed by it to any political party or for political purpose and also the name of the party or person to which or to whom such amount has been contributed. If a company makes any contribution in contravention of this provision, it is liable to be fined up to three times the amount so contributed. Also every officer in default is liable to be imprisoned for a term up to 3 years and be fined.

By virtue of Sec. 293 B, the Board of directors of a company may contribute any amount to National Defence Fund or any other Fund approved by the Central Government for the purpose of National Defence.

APPOINTMENT OF SOLE SELLING AGENTS

No company must appoint a sole selling agent for any area for a term exceeding 5 years at a time, the renewals for 5 years at a time being permitted. Any appointment of a sole selling agent made by the Board shall cease to be valid from the date of the meeting, if it is not approved by the company in the first general meeting held after the appointment.

Where a company has a sole selling agent, the Central Government may require the company to furnish to it such information regarding the terms and conditions of the appointment for the purpose of determining whether or not such terms and conditions are prejudicial to the interests of the company. If the company refuses or neglects to furnish any such information, the Central Government may appoint a suitable person to investigate and report. If the said Government, after the perusal of the information supplied by the company or of the report by the investigator, is of the opinion that the terms and conditions are prejudicial to the interests of the company, it may, by order, vary them and then the terms and conditions of appointment of the sole agent shall be regulated by such order. If there are more selling agents than one, the Central Government will, after following the above procedure, determine who will be the sole selling agent for any particular area and on what terms.

The new Sec. 294AA provides that where the Central Government is of opinion that the demand for the goods of any category is substantially in excess of the production or supply of such goods and that the services of sole selling agents will not be necessary to create a market for such goods, it may, by notification in the Official Gazette, prohibit the appointment of sole selling agents for specified period of time. Further, no individual, firm or body corporate having substantial interest in the company (i.e. holds shares paid-up value of which is ₹ 5 lakhs or 5 per cent) is to be appointed sole selling agent without the previous approval of the Central Government. Again, no company having a paid-up share capital of ₹ 50 lakhs or more shall appoint a sole selling agent except with the consent of the company accorded by a special resolution and the approval of the Central Government. Where a company has a sole selling agent at the date of the commencement of the Amendment Act, it must obtain consent and approval as above within 6 months from such commencement, otherwise the appoint-ment will stand terminated on the expiry of the 6 months.

COMPENSATION FOR LOSS OF OFFICE OF SOLE SELLING AGENT

A company shall not pay or be liable to pay to its sole selling agent any compensation for the loss of his office in the following cases:—

(a) where the appointment of the sole selling agent ceases to be valid because the company in general meeting has not approved it;

(b) where he resigns his office in view of the reconstruction of the company or its amalgamation with other body or bodies corporate and is appointed as the sole selling agent of the reconstructed or amalgamated company;

(c) where he resigns his office of his own accord;

(d) where he has been guilty of fraud or breach of trust in relation to, or of gross negligence in, the conduct of his duty as the sole selling agent;

(e) where he has instigated, or has taken part directly or indirectly in bringing about, the termination of the sole selling agency.

Where the compensation is payable, it must not exceed the remuneration which he would have earned if he had been in office for the residue of his term, or for 3 years, whichever is shorter (Sec. 294A).

LOANS TO DIRECTORS

Sec. 295 provides that without obtaining previous approval of the Central Government, a public company or its subsidiary cannot, directly or indirectly, lend money or guarantee or secure loans to:—

(a) a director of the company or of its holding company;

(b) a partner or relative of any such director;

(c) any firm in which any such director or relative is a partner;

(d) any private company 25 per cent or more of whose total voting power may be exercised or controlled by any such director, or two or more directors together;

(e) any body corporate, the Board or managing director, or manager whereof is accustomed to act in accordance with the directions or instructions of any director or directors of the lending company.

The above restrictions do not apply to loans by a private company; or by a banking company; or by a holding company to its subsidiary.

DISCLOSURE OF DIRECTOR'S INTEREST

Except with the consent of the Board given in advance by a resolution at a Board meeting, a director of a company, or his relative, or a firm in which such director or a relative is partner, or any partner of such a firm, or a private company in which such director is a member or a director, should not enter into any contract with the company for the sale, purchase, or supply of any goods, materials, or services, or for underwriting the company's shares or debentures. Such contracts up to ₹ 5,000 in the aggregate in any calendar year are, however, permitted if they are part of the regular trade or business of such director, etc., or the company (Sec. 297). Where a company has a paid-up share capital of one crore rupees, approval of the Central Government is also necessary. A director of a company who is in any way concerned or interested in a contract or arrangement by or on behalf of the company must disclose such interest or concern at the Board meeting at which the contract is disclosed or at the first Board meeting after the director's becoming interested. A general declaration that he is a member of a particular firm or company will be deemed to be sufficient disclosure (Sec. 299). An interested director must not participate in the discussions or vote on the particular contract. If he does vote, his vote will not count, nor will his presence count for quorum. These restrictions do not apply in the case of a private company (Sec. 300). A register must be kept in which shall be entered particulars of all contracts to which Sec. 297 or 299 applies. The members must be informed of the director's interest in any contract appointing manager, or managing director.

REGISTER OF DIRECTORS, ETC.

Every company must keep at its registered office a Register of Directors, Managing Director, Manager and Secretary, and must file a copy within 30 days of the appointment of the first directors and must notify the Registrar of any subsequent changes within 30 days of the happening thereof. The particulars in case of each of the above that the register must contain are : (a) in case of individuals, his name, usual residential address, nationality, business occupation, and details of any directorship, managership, etc.; (b) in case of corporation, its corporate name, registered office, and full name, address and nationality of its directors; (c) in case of firm, full name, address and nationality of each partner and the date of becoming partner; (d) if any directors have been nominated by a corporation, its corporate name and particulars in (a) and (b); (e) if any firm has nominated directors, their similar particulars as in (a) and (c) (Sec. 303).

In addition to the above register, a separate register called the **"Register of Director's Shareholdings,"** showing in regard to each director the number, description and amount of the shares or debentures in the company or its subsidiaries or its holding company or a subsidiary of a holding company, held by or in trust for each director or of which each director has the right to become the holder. The register must also show the date of each share or debenture transaction and the consideration thereof when the transaction is entered into after the commencement of the Act. The register must be open to inspection of members and debenture-holders immediately before the annual general meeting and at the meeting (Sec. 307). No director can now assign his office, if it is done, it will be void. These provisions apply to managers as they apply to directors.

DIRECTOR AND OFFICE OF PROFIT

Section 413 provides that no director shall hold an office of profit without the consent of the company accorded by a special resolution.

As regards a partner or relative of a director of a company, or a firm in which such director or relative of such director is a partner, or a private company of which such director is a director or member, or a director or manager of such a private company, sub-sec. (IB) as read with Notification 3, provides that if an office of profit is held by any one of them as follows:—

(a) No approval by special resolution is required if the monthly remuneration of the relative, etc. is below ₹ 3,000;

(b) A special resolution is required if the monthly remuneration ranges between ₹ 3,000 and ₹ 5,000;

(c) Central Government's approval in addition to special resolution is necessary if the monthly remuneration is to be ₹ 6,000 or more.

But the office of managing director, manager, banker, or trustee for debenture holders is exempt from the above restrictions; and they can hold office of profit.

COMPENSATION FOR LOSS OF OFFICE

No compensation for loss of office may be paid by a company to any director other than the managing or whole time directors, or directors who are managers. Even in the case of managing or whole-time director, or manager-director, no such payment will be made; (i) where the director resigns his office on reconstruction or amalgamation of the company, or for some other reason; (ii) where office has to be vacated (being fraudulent person); (iii) he has to give up directorship beyond 20; (iv) the winding up of the company is due to his negligence or mismanagement; (v) the termination of his office is brought about collusively. Where the compensation is payable, it must not exceed the remuneration which would have been earned for the unexpired residue of the term or 3 years whichever is shorter (Sec. 318). In case of transfer of undertaking of a company, a director cannot receive compensation for loss of office, but the transferee company may pay.

LEGAL POSITION OF DIRECTORS

Directors have been described by judges as 'agents,' 'trustees' or 'managing partners.' The best description seems to be the one given by Jessel, M.R., who says:[52] "...... they are commercial men managing a trading concern for the benefit of themselves and of all the shareholders in it. They stand in a fiduciary position towards the company in respect of their powers and capital under their control." Lord Selborne, L.C., said: [53] "The directors are the mere trustees or agents of the company—trustees of the company's money and property; agents in the transactions which they enter into on behalf of the company."

AS AGENTS

Directors are correctly described as agents of the company, and the ordinary rules of agency apply. The company being a legal person, the directors as agents act on its behalf. They are agents for the company with powers and duties of carrying on the, business subject to restrictions imposed by the articles and the Act. They make contracts on behalf of the company and are not personally liable, unless they contract in their own name, or fail to exclude personal liability. If they make contracts *ultra vires* the company, they will not be liable on them unless there is an implied breach of warranty of authority. If the act done is only *ultra vires* the directors, then a contract made (i) with a member is voidable, (ii) with an outsider, who had no notice of the want of authority, is binding on the company. In either case, however, it may be made valid by the acquiescence of ALL shareholders.

AS TRUSTEES

Directors are not trustees in the full sense of the term inasmuch as no property is vested in them in their capacity as directors. Trustees are persons in whom is vested the legal ownership of assets which they administer for the benefit of others, who are said to have beneficial or equitable interest in those assets, and who can enforce their interests by suing the trustees. Directors are not vested with the ownership of the company's assets: the company owns its own property. Not are the directors trustees for the individual shareholders. Nevertheless, they are in certain respects *in the position of trustees for the company*. In the first place, as Lindley, L.J., observed:[54] "Although directors are not properly speaking trustees, yet they have been considered and treated as trustees of money which comes to

---

52. Re Forest of Dean Coal Co. (1878) 10 Ch. D. 450.

53. G.E.R.L.Y. Co. v. Turner (1872) LR. 8 Ch. App. 149.

54. Re Lands Allotment Co. (1894), 1 Ch. 616.

their hands or which is actually under their control; and ever since joint-stock companies were invented directors have been held liable to make good moneys which they have misapplied, upon the same footing as if they were trustees." In the second place, directors are in the position of trustees for their company as regards the exercise of all *powers* which they are authorised to exercise on the company's behalf.[55] For example, they are trustees of their *powers* of allotting shares, making calls, accepting payment of calls in advance, passing or rejecting transfer of shares and forfeiting shares or accepting their surrender. Thirdly, a director's position partakes of the fiduciary character of trusteeship so that he is precluded from allowing the interests of the company to clash with his own interests.

DUTIES

The duties of directors are usually regulated by the company's articles, and are likely to depend upon the size and nature of the business of a company. Romer, J., observes: [56] "In discharging his duties a director must act honestly, and must exercise such degrees of skill and diligence as would amount to the reasonable care which an ordinary man might be expected to take in the circumstances on his own behalf." In other words, directors should use fair and reasonable diligence in the management of their company's affairs, and to act honestly, but as long as they fulfil these conditions, they "are not liable for want of error of judgment." A director is not bound (apart from special agreement, e.g., whole-time director) to give continuous attention to the affairs of the company. His duties are of an intermittent nature to be performed at periodical Board meetings. He may entrust, having to the exigencies of business, to some trusted official. But a director cannot assign his office.

LIABILITIES

The various liabilities of a director may be considered under the following heads:—

As shareholder—The liability of directors for payment of share money is ordinarily limited in the same way as that of the other shareholder of the company. But the memorandum of a company may make the liability of any or all the directors unlimited as provided by Secs. 322 and 323. A notice that his liability will be unlimited must be given to the director before he accepts that office.

Breach of fiduciary duty—By Sec. 71(2), any director who knowingly contravenes or permits the contravention of the statutory restrictions with respect to allotment, remains for *two years* after the allotment under a **statutory** liability to compensate the company for any loss or damage or costs incurred. Apart from statutory liability, directors as trustees are liable for breach of their fiduciary duty to the Company. The failure of directors to act within powers (*ultra vires* acts) will render them liable, and they shall have to indemnify the company for any loss or damage.[57] Apart from *ultra vires* acts, directors may incur liability to their company as for breach of trust or misfeasance, if they act *mala fide*, i.e., otherwise than *honestly for the benefit of the company.* It is on this ground that directors may be required to account for and surrender secret profits to their company. Again, quite apart from *mala fides,* directors may be liable to the company for *negligence* in the exercise of their powers, if they do not act with *such care as is reasonably expected* from them, i.e., they do not exercise reasonable diligence in the management of company's affairs and the company suffers a loss.[58] If they give all sorts of powers to the managing director and thus enable him to commit misconduct, they are negligent and liable to make good the loss. Directors are also liable for wilful wrong or wilful misconduct.

---

55. Syke's Case (1872), L.R. 13 Eq.Cas.255.
56. Re City Equitable Ins. Co. (1925), Ch. 407.
57. Re Sharp (1892), 1 Ch. 154; Eastern Shipping Co. v. Bangkee; 1924), A.C. 177.
58. Govind v. Ranganath (1930), 45 Bom. 226.

LIABILITY TO THIRD PARTY

Directors may become personally liable to allottees of shares who apply on the faith of a prospectus containing untrue statements. They may also become liable, if the money is not paid back to the applicant for shares within 130 days of the issue of the prospectus when the company fails to allot shares within 120 days. They are also liable for irregular allotments, as also when their liability has been made unlimited under Secs. 322 and 323. In the winding up of a company, directors responsible for fraudulent trading on the part of the company may, by order of the Court under Sec. 542, be made personally liable, without any limit, for all or any of the debts or liabilities of the company. Apart from the Act, directors may incur personal liabilities for breach of warranty of authority. They will also be liable for acts *ultra vires* themselves. A director acting in his own name or without excluding personal liability on a negotiable instrument may be liable.

The Act also provides for various statutory penalties for non-compliance with the provisions, and they are referred to in their appropriate places. Directors may also become criminally liable under the common law, the Indian Penal Code or the Com-panies Act. Sixteen sections of the Act provide for criminal proceedings. Offences under the Indian Penal Code generally relate to frauds, perjury, mis-appropriation or embezzlement of funds, conspiracy to defraud, etc. Most of these offences are now expressly covered by the Companies Act.

MANAGING DIRECTOR

A managing director is a director who, by virtue of an agreement with the company or of a resolution passed by the company in general or by its Board of directors, or by virtue of its memorandum or articles of association, is entrusted with substantial powers of management which would not otherwise be exerciseable by him, and includes a director occupying the position of a managing director by whatever name called. He is, however, subject to the control of the Board of directors.

An undischarged insolvent, or a person who has at any time been adjudged an insolvent, or suspends; or has at any time suspended, payment to his creditors, or makes or has made at any time a composition with them, or is, or has at any time been convicted by a Court of an offence involving moral turpitude cannot be appointed a managing director or a whole-time director of a company.

MANAGER

A manager means an individual who, subject to the superintendence, control and direction of the Board of directors, has the management of the whole, or substantially the whole, of the affairs of the company, and includes a director or any other person occupying the position of a manager, by whatever name called. No company must appoint or continue the appointment or employment of any person as its manager who (i) is an undischarged insolvent, or (ii) has at any time within the preceding 5 years been adjudged an insolvent; or (iii) suspends or has suspended payment to his creditors; or (iv) makes, or has at any time within the preceding 5 years made, a composition with them; or (v) is, or has at any time within the preceding 5 years been, convicted of an offence involving moral turpitude. The Central Government may relax this restriction in appropriate cases (Section 385).

Appointment of Managing Director or Manager—No person can be appointed a managing director or manager for more than 5 years at a time and of more than 2 companies; and the appointment to the second company must be made by a unanimous resolution of the Board.

Section 269, as amended by the Companies (Amendment) Act, 1988, provides that with effect from June 15, 1988, every public company or a subsidiary of a public company having a paid up share capital of ₹ 5 crores or more must have a managing director, whole-time director or a manager. No approval of the Central Government is necessary if such an appointment is made in accordance with the conditions specified in Part II, and shareholders' resolutions are passed in general meeting as specified in Part III of Schedule XIII. A return of appointment must be filed within 90 days from the date of such appointment.

If the conditions specified in Schedule XIII are not complied with, then an application must be made to the Central Government within 90 days of the appointment The Central Government shall not accord approval of the application for appointment, if it is satisfied that (i) the appointee is, in its opinion, not a fit or proper person to be appointed as such or such appointment is not in the public interest; or (ii) the terms and conditions of the appointment are not fair and reasonable. The Central Government may accord approval for a period lesser than the period proposed by the company. If the appointment is not approved by the Central Government, the person so appointed shall vacate his office on the date on which the decision of the Central Government is communicated to the Company. Failure to vacate office will render him liable to fine up to ₹ 500 per day during period of default.

Where the Central Government is of opinion that any appointment is made without approval in contravention of Schedule XIII, it may refer the matter to the Company Law Board. If the Company Law Board, after giving opportunity to the Company and the appointee to be heard, comes to the conclusion that the appointment has been made in contravention of the Schedule, the company shall be liable to a fine up to ₹ 5,000 and every officer in default to a fine up to ₹ 10,000 and the appointment shall be deemed to have come to an end. The person so appointed shall, in addition to a fine of ₹ 10,000 refund the entire amount of salaries, commissions and perquisites received or enjoyed by him. Further, if a company does not comply with the aforesaid provision or any direction given by the Company Law Board, every officer in default and the appointee shall be punishable with imprisonment up to 3 years and fine up to ₹ 50 for every day of default. However, all acts done by the appointee whose appointment has been terminated shall, if the acts so done are valid otherwise, be valid.

The appointment of a managing director, whole time director or manager requires approval of the Central Government in the case of a newly formed company.

SCHEDULE XIII
PART -1

Appointments — No person shall be eligible for appointment as a managing director or whole-time director or manager (hereinafter referred to as managerial person) of a company unless he satisfies the following conditions, namely : -

    (a) he had not been sentenced to imprisonment for any period, or to a fine exceeding ₹ 1,000, for the conviction of an offence under any of the following Acts :

        (i)   the Indian Stamps Act, 1899
        (ii) the Central Excise and Salt Act, 1944
        (iii) the Industries (Development and Regulation) Act, 1951
        (iv) the Prevention of Food Adultration Act, 1954
        (v) the Essential Commodities Act, 1955
        (vi) the Companies Act, 1956
        (vii) the Securities Contracts (Regulation) Act, 1956
      (viii) the Wealth Tax Act, 1957
        (ix) the Income Tax Act, 1961
        (x) the Customs Act, 1962
        (xi) the Monopolies and Restrictive Trade Practices Act, 1969
        (xii) the Foreign Exchange Regulation Act, 1973
       (xiii) the Sick Industrial Companies (Special Provisions) Act, 1985
       (xiv) the Securities and Exchange Board of India Act, 1992
       (xv) the Foreign Trade (Development and Regulation) Act, 1992

(b) he had not been detained for any period under the Conservation of Foreign Exchange and Prevention of Smuggling Activities Act, 1974.

(c) he had completed the age of 25 years and has not attained the age of 70 years or the age of retirement, if any, specified by the company, whichever is earlier.

(d) where he is managerial person in more than one company he opts to draw remuneration from only one company.

(e) he is resident in India.

Explanation. For the purpose of this Schedule resident in India includes a person who has been staying in India for a continuous period of not less than twelve months immediately preceding the date of his appointment as a managerial person and who has come to stay in India

(i) for taking up employment in India; or

(ii) for carrying on a business or vocation in India.

PART II

Remuneration

Section I. Remuneration payable by companies having profits —

Subject to the provisions of Section 198 and Section 309, a company having profits in a financial year may pay any remuneration by way of salary, dearness allowance, perquisites, commission and other allowances which shall not exceed 5 per cent of the net profits for one such managerial person or 10 per cent for all of them together.

Section II. Remuneration payable by companies having no profits or inadequate profits —

1. Notwithstanding anything contained in this PART, where in any financial year during the currency of tenure of the managerial person, a company has no profits or its profits are inadequate, it may pay remuneration to a managerial person, by way of salary, dearness allowance, perquisites and any other allowances not exceeding ceiling limit of ₹ 10,50,000 per annum or ₹ 87,500 per month calculate on the following Scale:

Where the effective Capital of Company is	*Monthly Remuneration Payable shall not exceed*
(i) less than ₹ one crore	₹ 40,000
(ii) ₹ one crore or more but less than ₹ 5 crores	₹ 57,000
(iii) ₹ 5 crores or more but less than ₹ 15 crores	₹ 72,000
(iv) ₹ 15 crores or more	₹ 87,500

2. **Perquisites.** A managerial personal shall also be eligible to the following perquisites which shall not be included in the computation of the ceiling on remuneration specified in paragraph-1 of this Section :

(a) contribution to Provident Fund, Superannuation Fund, or Annuity Fund to the extent these either singly or put together are not taxable under the Income-Tax Act, 1961 ;

(b) gratuity payable at a rate not exceeding half a month's salary for each completed year of service, and

(c) encashment of leave at the end of the tenure.

3. In addition to the perquisites specified in paragraph 2 of this Section, an expartriate managerial person (including a non-resident Indian) shall be eligible to the following perquisites which shall not be included in the computation of the ceiling on remuneration specified paragraph 1 of this Section.

(a) Children's education allowance in case of children studying in or outside India, an allowance limited to a maximum of ₹ 5000 per month per child or actual expenses incurred whichever is less. Such allowance is admissible up to a maximum of two children.

(b) Holiday passage for children studying outside India family staving abroad. Return holiday passage once in a year by economy class or once in two years by first class to children and to the members of the family from the place of their study or stay abroad to India if they are not residing in India with the managerial person.

(c) **Leave travel concession**: Return passage for self and family in accordance with the rules specified by the company where it is proposed, that the leave be spent in home country instead of any where in India.

PART III

1. The appointment and remuneration shall be subject to approval by a resolution of the shareholders in general meeting.

2. The auditor or Secretary of the Company or where the company has not appointed a Secretary, a Secretary in whole-time practice shall certify that the requirements of the Schedule have been complied with and such certificate shall be incorporated in the return filed with the Registrar undei sub-section (2) of Section 269.

Note: The remuneration paid with reference to effective capital is *Minimum Remuneration* for the purpose of Section 198 of the Companies Act; 1956, which would be admissible in the event of absence or inadequacy of net profit in any financial year, without the approval of the Central Government in individual cases.

DIRECTORS' SITTING FEE

Paid up share Capital of the Company -	*Maximum Fee per meeting attended*
(i) upto ₹ 50 lakhs,	₹ 250
(ii) over ₹ 50 lakhs but up to ₹5 crores	₹ 500
(iii) Over ₹ 5 crores but up to ₹10 crores	₹ 750
(iv) Over ₹ 10 crores	₹ 1,000

GOVERNMENT'S POWER TO FIX MANAGERIAL REMUNERATION

The new Sec. 637AA empowers the Central Government to fix, while according approval to any appointment or re-appointment or to any remuneration at such amount or percentage of profits of the company, within the maximum limit fixed by the Act, as it deems fit. But while fixing the remuneration, the Central Government shall have regard

  (i) the financial position of the company;
 (ii) the remuneration or commission drawn by the individual concerned in any other capacity, including his capacity as a sole selling agent;
(iii) the remuneration or commission drawn by him from any other company;
(iv) professional qualifications and experience of the individual concerned;
 (v) public policy relating to the removal of disparities in income.

MANAGING AGENTS

By Sec. 2(25), Managing Agent means "any individual firm or body corporate entitled; subject to the provisions of this Act, to the management of the whole, or substantially the whole, of the affairs of the company by virtue of an agreement with the company, or, by virtue of its memorandum and articles, and includes any individual, firm or body corporate occupying the position of a managing agent, by whatever name called.

RESTRICTIONS ON FORMER MANAGING AGENTS

The managing agencies and the category of secretaries and treasurers have been abolished altogether with effect from April 3,1970. No company is therefore allowed to appoint or re-appoint any managing agent or secretaries and treasurers after April 2, 1970.

A new Sec. 204A inserted by the Amendment Act, 1974, provides that during a period of 5 years from the date of the commencement of the Amendment Act, no erstwhile managing agents, secretaries and treasurers or their associates shall be appointed as secretary, consultant or adviser or to any other office, by whatever name called, without the prior approval of the company in general meeting and the Central Government. If such appointment exists on that date, it must terminate within 6 months thereof unless approved by the company in general meeting and the Central Government.

SECRETARY

Section 2(45) defines secretary as "a Company Secretary within the meaning of clause (c) of sub-section (1) of Section 2 of the Company Secretaries Act, 1980, and includes any other individual possessing the prescribed qualifications and appointed to perform the duties which may be performed by a secretary under this Act and any other ministerial or administrative duties." Only an individual can be a secretary.

Section 383 A provides that every company having a paid up share capital of ₹ 25 lakhs or more must have a whole-time secretary, and where the Board of directors of any such company, comprises only two directors, neither of them can be the secretary of the company. If the company fails to appoint a whole-time secretary, then the company and every officer in default is liable to a fine up to ₹ 50 per day during default However, a person proceeded against may offer as defence that all reasonable care was taken to comply with the provisions or the financial position of the company was such that it was beyond its capacity to engage a whole-time secretary.

Inter-Company Loans—Section 370 provides that a company may make a loan to another company only after the lending company has been authorised by a special resolution passed in its general meeting. But the proviso, as read with Notification 449(E) of April 17,1989 states that no special resolution will be necessary in the case of loans made to other companies not under the same management where the aggregate of such loans does not exceed 20 per cent of the aggregate of the subscribed capital of the lending company and its free reserves. The aggregate of the loans made by the lending company to all other companies shall not, except with the prior approval of the Central Government, exceed (i) 30 per cent of the aggregate of the subscribed capital of the lending company and its free reserves; (ii) 20 per cent of the aggregate of the subscribed capital of the lending company and its free reserves, where all such companies are under the same management as the lending company. The term "loan" includes any deposits of money made by one company with another company, not being a banking company.

Inter-Company Investments—Section 372, as amended by the 1988 Amendment Act, and as read with Notification, dated the 17th April, 1989, provides: (1) A company, whether by itself or together with its subsidiaries shall not be entitled to invest in the shares of any other company except as staled below.

The Board of directors of the investing Company may invest in any shares of any other company up to 25 per cent of the subscribed equity share capital or the aggregate of the paid up equity and preference share capital, whichever is less. And the aggregate of the investments made by the Board in all other companies shall not, except with the previous approval of the Central Government exceed (i) 30 per cent of the aggregate of the subscribed capital and free reserves of the investing company and (ii) 20 per cent of the aggregate of the subscribed capital and free reserves of the investing company, where such other companies are in the same group. The provisions of this section do not apply to investments by a holding company in its subsidiary, other than a subsidiary which is controlled by the holding company through the composition of its Board of directors.

MEANING OF RELATIVE

Sec.6 specifically states the relatives as follows: A person shall be deemed *to* be a relative of another if, and only if,—

(a) they are members of a Hindu undivided family; or

(b) they are husband and wife; or

(c) the one is related to the other in the manner indicated below.

List of Relatives:

Father, Mother (including step-mother); Son (including step-son); Son's wife; Daughter (including step-daughter); Father's father; Father's mother: Mother's mother; Mother's father, Son's son; Son's son's wife; Son's daughter; Son's daughter's husband; Daughter's husband; Daughter's son's wife; Daughter's daughter; Daughter's daughter's husband; Brother (including step-brother); Brother's wife; Sister (including step-sister); Sister's husband.

PART 16-J
COMPROMISE AND ARRANGEMENT

Arbitration—Sec. 389 of the Act, empowered a company, like an individual or a firm, to refer to arbitration, only under the Arbitration Act, 1940, any dispute between itself and any other company or person. This created difficulties with regard to foreign arbitrations; as foreign arbitral awards could not be enforced although India is one of the signatories to the New York Convention (1948) on the recognition and enforcement of foreign arbitral awards. Consequently, Sec. 389 has been deleted and Indian companies are now free to enter into such arbitration agreements as may be permitted by their memoranda and articles, and not only under the Arbitration Act, 1940.

Compromise or Arrangement—Sec. 391 confers power on a majority of creditors to come to some suitable arrangement (beneficial to all concerned) with the company which is unable immediately to meet its liabilities. Similarly, a compromise or arrangement can be made between a company and its members. The procedure is this. Where it is proposed to make a compromise or arrangement between the company and its creditors or any class of them; or between a company and its members or any class of them, an application is made to .the Court by the company or creditor or member, or where the company is being wound up, the application is made by the liquidator. The Court may order a meeting of the creditors or the members to be called and conducted according to the directions of the Court. If the majority in number representing three-fourths in value of the creditors, or the members, as the case may be, present and voting in person or by proxy, at the meeting, agree to the compromise or arrangement, the compromise or arrangement shall, if sanctioned by the Court, be binding on all the creditors, or all the members, as the case may be, and also on the company. But the court cannot make an order sanctioning a compromise or arrangement unless it is satisfied that the company or any other person, by whom an application has been made, has disclosed to the Court, by affidavit or otherwise, all material facts relating to company, such as the latest financial position of the company, the latest auditor's report on the accounts of the company, the pendency of any investigation proceedings in relation to the company under Secs 235 to 251 and the like. Furthermore, no compromise or arrangement or scheme of amalgamation of a company which is being wound up will be sanctioned by the Court unless the Court has received a report from the Company Law Board or the Registrar that the affairs of the company have not been conducted in a manner prejudicial to the interests of its members or to public interest. Similarly, no order for the dissolution of the company will be passed by the Court unless a similar report has been received from the Official Liquidator.

The new Sec. 394A makes it obligatory on the Court to give notice to the Central Government of every application made to it under Sec. 391 or 394 and take into consideration the representation made by that Government before passing any order on the proposed compromise or arrangement or scheme of amalgamation. Subject to the aforesaid requirement, the Court has wide powers in sanctioning or rejecting the scheme. It will sanction the scheme only if the scheme is *bonafide,* beneficial to all concerned, and is not a coercion on the minority.[59] Where the Court has made an order sanctioning the compromise or arrangement, it will have effect only after a certified copy of the order has been filed with the Registrar. A copy of the order must also be annexed to every copy of the memorandum of the company. Where the scheme involves reorganisation or reduction of share capital, the company must also comply with the provisions of Sees. 94 and 100.[60]

RECONSTRUCTION OR AMALGAMATION

Secs. 394 and 395 provide for facilitating arrangements for the purposes of reconstruction or amalgamation of companies. Reconstruction of a company can take place under Sec. 484 by winding up the company voluntarily, but that may take a long time and involve great expense. Secs. 391 and 394 provide for reconstruction or amalgamation without winding up. By Sec. 394, where, on an application under Sec. 391, it is shown to the Court that the scheme of arrangement has been proposed for the purpose of reconstruction of a company, or the amalgamation of two or more companies, and the scheme involves the transfer of the whole or any part of the undertaking, property or liabilities by one company (i.e., the transferor company) to another company (i.e., the transferee company), the Court may, in sanctioning the scheme (or thereafter) provide by order for all or any of the following matters: (i) the transfer to the transferee company of the whole or any part of the undertaking, property or liabilities of any transferor company; (ii) the allotment or appropriation by the transferee company of any shares, debentures, policies, or other like interests in that company; (iii) the continuation by or against the transferee company of any pending proceedings; (iv) dissolution without winding up to transferor company; (v) provisions for dissenting member; (vi) any other incidental or consequential matters. The property transferred by the order of the Court vests in the transferee company, as well as liabilities:

As stated in the previous section, no scheme of amalgamation of a company which is being wound up will be sanctioned by the Court unless the Court has received a report from the Company Law Board or the Registrar that the affairs of the company have not been conducted in a manner prejudicial to the interests of its members or against the public interest. Further, no order of dissolution of the company will be passed by the Court unless a similar report has been received from the Official Liquidator. Also, the Court must give notice to the Central Government of every application under Sec. 391 or 394 and take into consideration the representation made by that Government before passing the order on the proposed scheme of amalgamation.

Sec. 395 enables the transferee company to compulsorily acquire the shares of dissenting members and provide as follows: Where a scheme or contract involving transfer of shares or any class of shares in the transferor company to the transferee company has, within 4 months after the making of the offer in that behalf by the transferee company, been approved by the holders of not less than *nine-tenths* in value of the shares whose transfer is involved, the transferee company may, at any time within 2 months after the expiry of the said 4 months, give notice in the prescribed manner to any dissenting shareholder, that it desires to acquire his share; and when such a notice is given, the transferee company is unless, on the application made by the dissenting shareholders within one month from the date of the notice, the Court thinks fit to order otherwise, entitled and bound to acquire those shares on the terms on which the shares of the approving shareholders are to be transferred to the transferee company.

---

59. See In re Natore Kamala Bank Ltd. (1937) 1 Cal. 368; Smt. Bhagwati v. New Bank of India Ltd., 1950 E.P. 111.

60. Palace Hotels Ltd. (1912) 2 Ch. 4381.

The transferee company is required to give notice to the dissenting shareholders within one month of the transfer under the scheme or contract, and any such holder may, within 3 months of the notice to him, require the transferee company to acquire his shares, and the company should do so. The transferee company is required to notify the transferor company of the transfer to it of the shares, pay the share value to the transferor company whereupon the transferor company must register the transferee company as the holder of those shares.[61]

Take-over Bids—Sec. 395 has been amended to check malpractices in relation to 'take-over' and acquisition of shares of dissenting shareholders under a scheme or contract approved by the majority. The amendment provides for disclosure of adequate information to shareholders in a 'take-over bid' so that they can judge for themselves whether or not to accept the offer. The amended Sub-section (3) of Sec. 395 now provides that the transferor company, after registering the transferee company as the holder of the shares of the dissenting shareholders, inform, within one month of the date of such registration, and of the receipt of the amount or other consideration representing the price payable to them by the transferee company. In the meantime, the transferor company must keep the money so received in a separate account in trust for those shareholders.

Another safeguard has been provided by the addition of a new Sub-section (4A). It lays down that in relation to every offer of a scheme or contract involving the transfer of shares or any class of shares in the transferor company to the transferee company, no circular containing an offer to take over the shares of the company should be issued until a copy thereof is presented to the Registrar who will have the power to refuse to register any such circular if it does not contain all the requisite information prescribed by the Government or if it sets out any information in such a way as to give a false impression. An appeal lies to the Court against the refusal by the Registrar to register the circular. Anyone issuing an unregistered circular is liable to be fined up to ₹ 500.

Amalgamation by order of Central Government—By Sec. 396, the Central Government may, where it is satisfied that it is essential in the public interest that two or more companies should amalgamate, by notification, provide for the amalgamation of those companies into a single company. Every member or creditor of each of the companies before amalgamation shall have, as nearly as may be, the same interest in and rights against the company resulting from amalgamation as he had in the company in which he was originally a member or creditor. If his rights in the new company become less, he shall get compensation for it.

Preservation of books and papers of Amalgamated Company—A new Sec. 396 A has been added to prevent the practice of destroying incriminating accounts and records of the company which has amalgamated with another company. This section provides that books and papers of a company which has been amalgamated with, or whose shares have been acquired by, another company under the provisions relating to take-overs and acquisition of shares shall not be disposed of without the prior permission of the Central Government. The Central Government, before granting the permission, may appoint a person to examine the books and papers or any of them for the purpose of ascertaining whether they contain any evidence of the commission of an offence in connection with the promotion or formation, or, the management of the affairs, of the first mentioned company or its amalgamation or the acquisition of its shares.

PREVENTION OF OPPRESSION AND MISMANAGEMENT

Special powers have been vested in the Company Law Board for the protection of members against oppression by the majority of shareholders and for intervention in case of mismanagement of a

---

61. S. Vishwanath v. East India D. & S. Factories Ltd., 1957 Mad. 341.

company's affairs. This has been done because the cardinal rule laid down in *Foss* v. *Harbottle,* [62] that the minority is bound by the decision of the majority, is abused in many cases. Secs. 397 and 409 provide for remedial measures.

If the oppressed minority consider that to wind up the company would not relieve but on the contrary, they would be unfairly prejudiced by winding up, they may petition the Court under Sec. 397, and the Court may impose a solution on the disputants. A certain number of members (stated below) may apply to the Company Law Board for relief on the grounds that the affairs of the company are being conducted:—

(a) in a manner oppressive to any member or members, or

(b) in a manner prejudicial to the interests of the company, or

(c) in a manner prejudicial to the public interest, or

(d) that a material change has taken place in the management or control of the company and that by reason of such change it is likely that the affairs of the company will be conducted in a manner prejudicial to the interests of the company.

If the Company Law Board is satisfied that the affairs of the company are being conducted as complained of, it may pass any orders with a view to bringing to an end the matters complained of, or apprehended.

The number of members necessary to make application is (i) in the case of a company having share capital, 100 members or 10 per cent of the total number of members, whichever is less, or members holding 10 per cent of the issued capital; (ii) in the case of a company not having share capital, 20 per cent of its total number of members. The Central Government may, in appropriate cases, authorise any lesser number to apply. The Central Government is also entitled to apply to the Company Law Board for an order as above.

The Company Law Board may in its discretion make any order that it thinks fit, and in particular, it may provide for—

(i) the regulation of the company's affairs in future, and may even frame fresh regulations; (ii) the acquisition of the shares or interests of any members by other members or by the company; (iii) the consequent reduction of the share capital in case of (ii) above; (iv) termination, setting aside or modification of any agreement, howsoever arrived at, between the company and the managing agent, secretaries and treasurers, managing director, any other director, or manager; (v) termination, setting aside or modification of any agreement between the company and any other person with the latter's consent; (vi) setting aside any transfer, delivery of goods, payment, execution or other act relating to property made or done by or against the company within 3 months of the application which would amount to a fraudulent preference in the case of an individual's insolvency; (vii) any other matter for which in the opinion of the Company Law Board it is just and equitable that provision should be made (Sec. 402). No compensation is payable for loss of office resulting from the termination of agreement by the Company Law Board. Any person whose agreement of office has been terminated cannot act for the company for 5 years thereafter without the leave of the Company Law Board. In addition to the above order, heavy penalties are provided, as stated in Schedule XI.

POWERS OF CENTRAL GOVERNMENT

Sec. 408 provides another measure to prevent oppression or mismanagement as follows. On the application of 100 members or members holding 10 per cent or more of the total voting power or on its own motion, the Central Government may appoint such number of persons as the Company Law Board may specify as being necessary to effectively safeguard the interests of the company, or its

---

62. (1843) 2 Hare 461.

shareholders or the public interest as additional directors for 3 years at a time, and such directors will not be subject to retirement by rotation nor need they hold any qualification shares; and any change in the Board after such appointment will be ineffective unless confirmed by the Company Law Board; or the Government may, instead, direct the company to alter its articles so as to arrange for the election of its directors on the basis of proportional representation. Special powers are conferred by Sec. 409 on (he Central government to prevent changes in the Board in consequence of a change in the ownership of shares. The Government can stop any change in the Board, or permit the same, if not prejudicial to the interests of the company.

Advisory Committee—By deleting Secs. 410 to 415, the Advisory Commission has been abolished, and by a new Sec. 410 an Advisory Committee has been substituted for the Advisory Commission. The Advisory Committee is to consist of not more than 5 persons with suitable qualifications and will advise, whenever required, the Central Government or the Company Law Board on such matters arising out of the administration of the Companies Act as may be referred to it by the Government or Board. All cases pending before the Advisory Commission were transferred to the Central Government on October 15,1965, for disposal. As the result of this change the powers of the Central Government have been enhanced, as there is no compulsion on its part to refer any cases to the Advisory Committee as was necessary to refer certain specified cases to the Advisory Commission before it was abolished.

PART 16-K
WINDING UP

WINDING UP BY COURT

A winding up by the Court, or compulsory winding up, as it is often called, is initiated by an application by way of petition presented to the appropriate Court for winding up order. The winding up of a company with a capital of one lakh or more must take place only in the High Court; but in other cases, the High Court may transfer the application to a District Court subordinate to it.

GROUNDS FOR COMPULSORY WINDING UP

Sec. 433 provides that a company may be wounded up by the Court:
  (a) If the company may petition, resolved to be wound up by the Court.
  (b) If default is made in delivering the statutory report to the Registrar or in holding the statutory meeting.
  (c) If the company does not commence its business within a year from its incorporation, or suspends its business for a whole year.
  (d) If the number of members falls below seven (or in case of a private company, below two).
  (e) If the company is unable to pay its debts.
  (f) If the Court is of opinion that it is just and equitable that the company should be woundup.

WHO MAY PETITION

The following may petition: (1) the company; (2) creditor; (3) contributory; (4) all or any of the above parties; (5) the Registrar; (6) any person authorised by the Central Government as per Sec. 243, i.e., following upon a report of inspectors; (7) by virtue of Sec. 440, when a company is already being wound up voluntarily, the Court may order winding up by it.

A contributory can petition only on the ground (i) that the number has fallen below the statutory minimum, or (ii) at least some of the shares held by him were originally allotted to him, or have been held by him and registered in his name, for at least 6 months during the 18 months before the commencement of the winding up or have devolved upon him through the death of a former holder. A fully paid up shareholder is a contributory under Sec. 428, and may petition, even when the company may have no assets for distribution among the shareholders after the satisfaction of its liabilities.

The Registrar may, with the previous sanction of the Central Government, present a petition for winding up only on the following grounds: (i) if default is made in filing the statutory report or in holding the statutory meeting; (ii) if the company does not commence its business within a year from its incorporation or suspends it for a whole year; (iii) if it appears to him from the balance sheet or from the report of the inspectors that the company is unable to pay its debts; or (iv) where the Registrar is authorised by the Central Government under Sec. 243 to petition. The workers have the right to be heard in winding up proceedings and not to allow them to do so is contrary to the principle of natural justice (*Rational Textile Workers Union* v. *P.R. Rama Krishnan,* 1983 .S.C.75).

PROCEDURE

On hearing the petition, the Court may dismiss it, adjourn it, make an interim order, or make a compulsory order for winding up the company. Where the winding up order is made, the Official Liquidator attached to each High Court will become the liquidator. The Court will also settle the list of contributories, make calls and settle any question arising out of winding up. The creditors will be asked to provide their claims, where necessary and the liquidators will realise the assets and distribute the proceeds among the creditors, whereupon the Court may pass an order that the company be dissolved. But within two years of the dissolution, the Court may, on the application of the Liquidator or any other person interested, declare the dissolution to have been void.

VOLUNTARY WINDING UP

A company may be wound up voluntarily: (i) when the period (if any) fixed for its duration has expired or an event on the happening of which the company is to be wound up has happened *and* the company in general meeting has passed an *ordinary* resolution to wind up; or (ii) if the company passes a *special* resolution to wind up voluntarily (Sec. 484). When the resolution has been passed, notice must be given by the company within 14 days of the passing thereof by advertisement in the Official Gazette, and also in some newspapers circulating in the district where the registered office is situated.

There are **two** kinds of voluntary winding up, namely : **Members' or Creditors'.** A company may be wound up as members' voluntary winding up, if a declaration of the company's solvency is made by its directors, or where there are more than 2 directors, by the majority of directors, at the Board meeting that they are of opinion that the company has no debts, or that it will be able to pay its debts in full within 3 years from the commencement of winding up. The declaration must be supported by an affidavit of the above directors, and must be made within 5 weeks, immediately preceding the date of the resolution for winding up and must be delivered to the Registrar before that date, and should embody a statement of company's assets and liabilities. On the passing of the resolution for winding up the company must in general meeting appoint one or more liquidators and fix his or their remuneration. Any remuneration so fixed cannot be increased at all, not even by the sanction of the Court (Sec. 490). On the appointment of the liquidator, all the powers of the Board and the managing or whole-time director and manager, cease. Within 10 days of the appointment of the liquidator, the company must give notice to the Registrar.

If in a members' voluntary winding up, the liquidator is of opinion that the company will not be able to pay its debts in full within the period stated in the declaration, or if the period has expired without full payment of debts, he must forthwith call a meeting of the creditors and lay before it a statement of company's assets and liabilities. In the event of the winding up continuing for more than one year, the liquidator must call a general meeting of the company at the end of the first year of the commencement of winding up and of each succeeding year, and must lay before the meeting an account of his acts and dealings and of the conduct of winding up. When the affairs of the company are fully wound up the liquidator must make up an account and call a final meeting of the company and lay these accounts before the meeting, then within one week of this meeting send to the Registrar and the Official Liquidator a copy each of the accounts and make a return to each of them of the holding of the meeting and of the date thereof; and the Registrar will forthwith register them. The Official Liquidator will scrutinise the books and papers of company and make a report to the Court that its affairs have not been conducted in a manner prejudicial to the interests of its members or against public interest. If the report indicates that the affairs have been conducted in prejudicial manner the Court may order the Official Liquidator to make further investigation. On receipt of this report, the Court may either make an order that the company shall stand dissolved from the specified date or make such other order as the circumstances of the case brought out in the report permit.

CREDITORS' VOLUNTARY WINDING UP

Where a declaration of solvency is not made and filed with the Registrar, it is presumed that the company is insolvent. In such a case, the company must call a meeting of its creditors for the day or the day next following the day fixed for company's general meeting for passing the resolution for winding up.

Subject to the right of the preferential creditors, the assets of a company on its winding up are applied in satisfaction of its liabilities *pari passu,* and any surplus is divided among the members according to their rights (Sec. 511).

WINDING UP UNDER SUPERVISION

Where a company is being wound up voluntarily the Court may order the continuation of voluntary winding up subject to its supervision on any terms or conditions. The liquidator will continue to exercise all powers subject to any restrictions laid down by the Court.

CONSEQUENCES OF WINDING UP GENERALLY

AS TO SHAREHOLDERS

A shareholder is liable to pay full amount of shares held by him. This liability continues after winding up, but he is then described as a "contributory." By Sec. 428, a contributory is "every person liable to contribute to the assets of a company in the event of its being wound up, and includes a holder of fully paid up shares, and also any person alleged to be contributory." Contributories are either present or past, and it is the former who is liable to pay calls, and the latter can be called upon to pay only if the present contributory is unable to pay. The nature of a contributory's liability after winding up is legal and not contractual. He cannot set off his debt against his liability for calls even if there is an express agreement to do so.

AS TO CREDITORS

A company can never be adjudged insolvent, although it may have become insolvent in the sense that it is unable to pay its debts. Where a solvent company is to be wound up all claims against the company are admissible, and when they are proved, payment is made. In the case of an insolvent company, the insolvency law applies. A secured creditor may either (i) rely on the security and ignore the liquidation, or (ii) value his security and prove for the balance of his debt, or (iii) give up his security and prove for the whole amount. Unsecured creditors of an insolvent company are paid in this order: (i) preferential payments under Sec. 530, (ii) other debts *pari passu.*

Preferential Payments are as follows:
  (a) all revenues, taxes, cesses and rates are payable by the company within 12 months next before the commencement of winding up;

(b) all wages or salary of any employee due for the period not exceeding 4 months within the 12 months next before the commencement of winding up, provided the amount payable to one claimant will not exceed ₹ 1,000;

(c) all accrued holiday remuneration becoming payable to any employee on account of winding up;

(d) unless the company is being wound up voluntarily for the purpose of reconstruction, all contributions payable during the 12 months next before winding up, by the company as the employer of any persons, under Employees' State Insurance Act, 1948, or any other law for the time being in force;

(e) all sums due as compensation under Workmen's Compensation Act, 1923;

(f) all sums due to any employee from a provident fund, a pension fund, a gratuity fund or any other fund for the welfare of the employees, maintained by the company;

(g) the expenses of any investigation held under Sec. 235 or 237, in so far as they are payable by the company.

Persons who claim to be creditors must prove their debts within the time fixed by the Court, or by the voluntary liquidator.

FRAUDULENT PREFERENCE

The insolvency rules as to fraudulent preference apply to companies. The object of the Act being a *pari passu* distribution, Sec. 531 provides that every transfer of property, movable, or immovable, delivery, of goods, payment, execution or other act relating to property made, taken or done by or against a company within 6 months before the commencement of its winding up shall be deemed, in the event of its being wound up, a fraudulent preference of its creditors and be invalid accordingly.

AS TO SERVANTS AND OFFICERS

A winding up order operates as a notice of discharge to the employees and officers of the company except when the business of the company is being continued (Sec. 444). A voluntary winding up also operates as a notice of discharge.

AS TO PROCEEDINGS

After a winding up petition is presented the Court may stay all proceedings against the company. After the winding up order is passed, all proceedings against the company must cease unless the Court gives special leave for them to continue. Further, any attachment, distress, execution put in force against the assets of the company after the commencement of winding up is void (Sec. 537). In voluntary winding up also the Court may restrain proceedings against the company if it thinks fit.

AS TO COSTS

If the company, while in liquidation; brings or defends any action and is ordered to pay costs, they are paid first out of the assets of the company. The same rule applies in a voluntary winding up. Similarly, all costs, charges and expenses of liquidation are payable out of the assets of the company prior to all other claims except those of secured creditors, if any (Sec. 520).

OFFENCES ANTECEDENT TO OR IN COURSE OF WINDING UP

OFFENCES OF OFFICERS

Every past and present officer of a company which is being wound up must assist the liquidator and if he fails to do so he is liable to be punished. He is liable to be imprisoned up to 5 years, or fined or given both punishments, if he within 12 months next before winding up and at any time thereafter fraudulently or under false pretences obtains credit for or on behalf of the company which company does not pay, or pawns, pledges or disposes of any property of the company which has been obtained on credit and has not been paid for. The pawnee or pledgee is also punishable with imprisonment up to 3 years or fine or both. Similarly, a past and present officer of the company is punishable with imprisonment up to 2 years, or fine, or both, if he does not fully and truly discover to the liquidator all property of the company within his knowledge, or does not deliver up to liquidator all property, books and papers that are in his custody or under his control, or conceals any part of the company's property to the value of ₹ 100 or more or conceals any debt due to or from the company, or fraudulently removes any part of company's property, or makes any material omission in any statement relating to the affairs of the company, or fails to inform the liquidator about false debts having been proved within his knowledge, or prevents the production of any books after winding up or cancels, destroys, mutilates or falsifies any book or paper affecting or relating to the property of the company, or makes any false entry in any book or paper relating to the property of the company, or is guilty of any representation or other fraud for getting creditor's consent in relation to affairs of the company.

If with intent to defraud or deceive any person, any officer or contributory of a company in liquidation destroys, mutilates, alters, falsifies or secretes (or is privy to any of these acts) any books, papers, or securities, or makes any fraudulent entry in any register, book of account or document belonging to the company, he shall be punishable with imprisonment up to 7 years and fine (Sec. 539).

If proper books of account were not kept by a company for a period of 2 years immediately preceding the commencement of winding up, or period between incorporation and winding up, which is shorter, every officer who is in default is liable to imprisonment up to one year (Sec. 541).

If in the course of the winding up of a company, it appears that any business of the company has been carried on with intent to defraud creditors of the company, or any other persons, or for any fraudulent purpose, the Court may declare that any persons who were knowingly parties to the carrying on of the business in the manner aforesaid shall be personally responsible without any limitation of liability for all or any debts or other liabilities of the company. In addition, the persons are liable to imprisonment up to 2 years, or fine up to ₹ 5,000 or both.

MISFEASANCE PROCEEDINGS

Sec. 543 provides that where, in the course of winding up a company (whether voluntarily or by or under the supervision of the Court), it appears that any person who has taken part in the promotion or formation of the company or any past or present director, managing agent, secretaries and treasurers, manager, liquidator or officer of the company, has misapplied or retained or become liable or accountable for any money or property of the company, or has been guilty of any misfeasance or breach of trust in relation to the company, the Court may, on application of the liquidator, or of any creditor or contributory made within five years from the date of the winding up order, or of the first appointment of the liquidator, or of the misapplication, retainer, misfeasance or breach of trust, as the case may be, whichever is longer, examine into the conduct of the person, director, managing agent, secretaries and treasurers, manager, liquidator or officer aforesaid, and compel him to repay or restore the money or property or any part thereof respectively with interest at such rate as the Court thinks just, or to contribute such sum to the assets of the company by way of compensation, notwithstanding that offence is one for which the offender may be criminally liable. An auditor of the company is an officer for the above purposes, as also the secretary.

PROSECUTION OF DELINQUENTS

By Sec. 545, if in a winding up by or under the supervision of the Court, it appears that any past or present officer, or any member, has been guilty of any offence in relation to the company in respect of which he is criminally liable, the Court may direct liquidator either himself to prosecute the offender or to refer the matter to the Registrar. In voluntary winding up, the liquidator must refer the matter to the Registrar. The Registrar may, in turn, refer it to the Central Government for further inquiry. The Central Government must thereupon investigate and may apply to the Court for an order conferring on any government nominee the power to investigate the affairs of the company. After the report of the investigation is received the Central Government may direct the Registrar to prosecute the offender.

LIQUIDATORS
COMPULSORY WINDING UP

The Official Liquidator attached to each High Court will become the liquidator on a winding up order being passed. He may also be appointed as a provisional liquidator with the same powers.

Within 21 days after the winding up order, or the appointment of provisional liquidator, a statement of affairs of the company must be submitted to the Official Liquidator. The statement must show the assets and liabilities, the names, addresses of creditors and amount due to each, debts due to the company, together with the names, addresses, occupations of debtors and amounts due from each of them, and any other information required by the Official Liquidator. The statement must be supported by an affidavit by one or more directors *and* by the manager, secretary or any other chief officer of the company.

The Official Liquidator must, after the receipt of the statement, within 6 months at the latest of the order, submit to the Court a preliminary report as to the amount of capital issued, subscribed and paid up, and the estimated amount of the company's assets and liabilities if the company has failed, the causes of its failure, and whether in his opinion any further inquiry is desirable (Sec. 455).

Within 2 months of the winding up order, the Official Liquidator must convene a meeting of the creditors to find out whether they would like to appoint a "Committee of Inspection." Then within 14 days of the above meeting, he should convene a contributories' meeting for the purpose. If the committee is to be appointed, then the total number of its members will not be more than 12, made up of equal number representing creditors and contributories.

POWERS OF LIQUIDATOR

As soon as a winding up order is made, or a provisional liquidator is appointed, the liquidator will take into his custody or under his control all the property of the company and its effects and actionable claims and get the help of the Presidency Magistrate or the District Magistrate for this purpose (Sec. 456).

The liquidator may, *with the sanction of the Court,* (i) institute or defend any suit, prosecution, or the legal proceeding in the name of the company, (ii) carry on the business of the company for its beneficial winding up, (iii) sell company's property, (iv) raise money on the security of the company's assets, and (v) do all other things necessary for the winding up. He may, *without sanction of the Court,* (i) do all acts, and execute in the name of the company, all deeds, receipts and other documents, (ii) inspect the records and returns of the company on the files of the Registrar gratis, (iii) prove, rank and claim in the insolvency of any contributory and to receive dividends therefrom, (iv) draw, accept, make, endorse any negotiable instrument in the name of the company, (v) take out, on his official name, letters of administration to any deceased contributory, and do other necessary things to obtain payment, (vi) appoint an agent.

By Sec. 456, the liquidator may, with the sanction of the Court or a special resolution, according as the winding up is compulsory or voluntary, (i) pay any class of creditors in full; (ii) make compromise or arrangement with creditors; (iii) compromise with contributory or debtor.

DUTIES OF LIQUIDATOR

Sec. 460 requires the liquidator to conduct the winding up according to the direction given by resolution of creditors' or contributories' meeting or by the Committee of Inspection. He must summon meetings of creditors or contributories when requisitioned by the holder of 10 per cent of the value. His principal duty is to get in the property and pay the debts and distribute the balance among contributories. He must keep the proper books of account, minutes books, and allow inspection thereof; twice in each year present to the Court an account of his receipts and payments in duplicate, and send a copy of the audited accounts to each creditor and contributory. He must keep all the funds of the company in "the public account of India" in the Reserve Bank of India; and must not keep any such money in his private account. All papers of the company must indicate that the company is being wound up, e.g., by adding the words "In liquidation" after the name of the company.

VOLUNTARY LIQUIDATOR

The voluntary liquidator is appointed by resolution in general meeting of the company and/or of the creditors and his remuneration fixed. By Secs. 513 to 515, a body corporate cannot be appointed a voluntary liquidator; and person who gives or agrees to give or offers to any member or creditor any gratification with a view to securing his own appointment as company's liquidator, or that of some other person, will be punishable with fine up to ₹ 1,000.

Within 21 days after his appointment, the liquidator must publish in the Official Gazette and deliver to the Registrar a notice of his appointment.

POWERS AND DUTIES

A voluntary liquidator is a paid agent of the company and is liable in damages if he neglects his duties as such. He must not make any secret profits and must keep funds of the company in Scheduled Bank to the credit of a special banking account called "the Liquidation Account of.... Co. Ltd." or "Private Ltd.", or "Company." He must not deposit such money in his personal account nor must he retain with him more than ₹ 500 for more than 10 days. He will also be liable for misfeasance, if he pays any money to a person who has no claim against the company. He may, with the sanction of special resolution, in members' or of the Court in creditors', winding up or the Committee of Inspection, do what an Official Liquidator can do under clauses (i) to (iv) of Sec. 457(2) noted above. Sec. 512 further empowers him to do without the sanction of the Court everything that the Official Liquidator can do, and also exercise some of the powers of the Court, e.g., settle lists of contributories, admit claims, make calls, call general meetings, etc., and perform other functions.

DISCLAIMER BY A LIQUIDATOR

Section 535(1) empowers the liquidator, with the leave of the Court to disclaim any onerous property of the company. It provides that where any part of the property of a company in liquidation is unsaleable or is not readily saleable, the liquidator, with leave of the Court, may disclaim it in writing signed by him at any time within 12 months after the commencement of winding up. But where an application in writing is made to the liquidator by any person interested in the property, requiring him to decide whether he will disclaim or not and the liquidator has not within 28 days of the receipt of the application given notice to the applicant of his intention to disclaim, the right to disclaim is lost.

WINDING UP OF UNREGISTERED COMPANIES

Sec. 582 specifies "unregistered companies" which may be wound up by the order of the Court. By that section, an "unregistered company" does not include (and so cannot be wound up under Sec. 583), (i) a railway company incorporated by any Act of Parliament or other Indian Law or any Act of Parliament of the United Kingdom; (ii) a company registered under the Companies Act of 1956; or (iii) a company registered under previous companies law, whose registered office is in India. Except as aforesaid, any partnership, association or company consisting of more than seven members at the time of petition for winding up will be deemed to be an "unregistered company" and may be wound up by order of the Court. An 'illegal association", formed in contraven-tion of Sec. 11, cannot be wound up by order of the Court under the present Act.

Sec. 583 p.ovides that an unregistered company may be wound up by the order of the Court having jurisdiction in the State where the company has its principal place of business, and where the principal place of business is situated in more than one State, in each such State, and where the proceedings are instituted on the following grounds: (a) if the company is dissolved, or has ceased to carry on business, or is carrying on business only for the purpose of winding up; (b) if the company is unable to pay its debt; (c) if the Court is of opinion that it is just and equitable that the company should be wound up. *An unregistered company cannot be wound up voluntarily or subject to the super-vision of the Court.*

By virtue of Sec. 584, if a company, incorporated outside India carrying on business in India, ceases to carry on business in India, it may be ordered to be wound up as an "unregistered company," even if the company has been dissolved or ceases to exist by virtue of the laws of the country under which it was incorporated.

Where an unregistered company is being wound up, every person is deemed to be a contributory, who is liable to pay, or contribute to the payment of (i) any debt or liability of the company, (ii) any sum for the adjustment of the rights of members among themselves, or (iii) the costs, charges and expenses of winding up (Sec. 585).

The same provisions as are applicable in the winding up of a "company" under the Act will apply in respect of the stay of proceedings before or after the winding up. If an unregistered company has no power to sue and be sued in a common name, or if the Court for arty other reason considers it expedient, the Court may direct that all or any part of the property of all description shall vest in the Official Liquidator. The Official Liquidator may sue or defend a suit in his official name (Sec. 588). Sec. 589 makes it clear that these provisions are in addition to other provisions relating to winding up of a "company".

CASES FOR RECAPITULATION

1. A solicitor, on the instructions of promoters who became the directors of the company, prepared the Memorandum and Articles before its formation. On demand by the solicitor of his costs and charges, it was held that the company was not liable to pay, although it has taken the benefit of his work [*Re English Colonial Produce Co. Ltd.* (1906) 2 Ch. 435].

2. A loan was advanced by a director of a company, acting on behalf of the company. This director was also a director of a private company which was the managing agent of the borrower company, and the entire powers of the managing agency had been vested in him. The lender sued the company for the recovery of the loan. It was pleaded that the company was not liable to pay as no resolution had been passed by the Board of directors of the company authorising him to borrow on its behalf. *Held,* the lender is entitled to recover from the company. The act of the director in borrowing the money bound the company. It did not matter that there was no resolution of the Board of directors of the borrower company, authorising the director to borrow on behalf of the company. The lender was protected by the doctrine of Indoor Management [*Laxmi Ratan Cotton Mills Co. Ltd.* v. *J. J. Jute Mills Co. Ltd.* (1957) 27 Comp. Cas. 660).

3. The N. Company agreed with C, as agent of the Pauline Syndicate before its formation, that the company would grant a lease of a mine to the syndicate. The syndicate, after it was incorporated, discovered a seam of coal. The company refused to carry out the contract *Held,* there was no binding contract between the company and the syndicate, as at the time of agreement with C, who purported to act on behalf of the syndicate it did not come into existence by incorporation [*Natal Land, etc. Co.* v. *Pauline Colliery Syndicate, Ltd.* (1904) A.C. 120].

4. The company acquired a piece of land for the purposes of its railway. The railway line was laid and the railway run on arches. The company let the arches as workshop, etc. The neighbours objected (on account of noise and rubbish), and claimed that letting the articles was *ultra vires* the company. *Held,* the act of company was valid, as being fairly incidental to the powers of the company [*Foster* v. *London, Chatham and Dover Rail Co.* (1895) 1 Q.B.711].

5. The memorandum gave the company power to make and sell railway carriages. The directors bought a railway concession in Belgium. The article gave express power to the company to extend its business beyond the memorandum by special resolution. The company passed a special resolution to ratify the purchase. *Held,* the purchase was bad, being *ultra vires* of the company. Lord Cairns, L.C., said : "If every shareholder had been in the room, and if every shareholder had said, "that is a contract which we authorise the directors to make, it would be void. The shareholders would thereby, by unanimous consent, have been attempting to do the very thing which by the Act of Parliament they were prohibited from doing" [*Ashbury Railway Carriage and Iron Co.* v. *Riche* (1875) L.R. 7 H.L. 653].

6. A company in which the directors held a majority of the shares altered its articles so as lo give power to the directors to require any shareholder who competed with the company's business to transfer his shares at their full value to nominees of the directors. A shareholder holding a minority of shares was doing competing business with the company. *Held,* the alteration was valid, as it was made *bonafide* for the benefit of the company as a whole, and so enforceable by the majority against the minority [*Sidebottom* v. *Kershaw Lees & Co. Ltd.* (1920) 1 Ch. 154].

7. The articles gave the company a lien on all shares "not fully paid up," for calls due to the company. A was the only holder of fully paid up shares; he also owed money to the company for calls due to other shares. A died. The company altered its articles by striking out the words "not fully paid up," and thus gave itself a lien over all A's shares. *Held,* the alteration was valid and gave the company a lien on fully paid up shares of A in respect of debts before the date of alteration [*Alien* v. *Gold Reefs of West Africa, Ltd.* (1900) I Ch. 656].

8. The directors of a company prepared a document, which was in form an offer of shares to persons generally. The document was not, however, advertised, but was shown only to Nash with a view to his joining the company and becoming a director. The document omitted to state the number of shares allotted for a consideration other than cash. On discovering that almost all the shares had been allotted for a consideration other than cash, Nash claimed damages (£ 2,000) on the ground that they had issued a false prospectus. *Held,* by the House of Lords, reversing the decision of the Court of Appeal, that the document was not a prospectus because it was never "issued" to the public as a prospectus. Nash was not entitled to claim any damages or compensation [*Nash* v. *Lynde* (1929) A.C. 158].

9. An employee of the press where a prospectus was being printed read it during the printing and on the faith of the statements made therein purchased some shares in the company. The statements were false. He claimed to repudiate the contract and also compensation from the directors. The directors are not liable to him as the prospectus had not been "issued to the public", including him. [*Based on Nash* v. *Lynde*].

10. R converted his business into a company. He has business assets of the value of £1,000 and debts of the same amount. R continued to carry on the whole business of the company, and without any meeting of the Board of directors or of the company issued debentures to D for £ 5,000 under the seal of the company. The articles empowered the company to issue debentures.-The company was ordered to be wound up. *Held,* D was entitled to assume that the debentures were valid (doctrine of Indoor Management), and he thus had priority over the other creditors [*Duck* v. *Tower Galvanizing Co. Ltd.* (1901) 2K.B.314].

11. A prospectus offering debentures for subscription stated that "the annual balance available .....

after providing for depreciation and interest on the existing debenture stocks has been sufficient to pay interest on the present issue more than five times over," and after providing for all taxation, depreciation of the fleet, etc. .... the dividends on the ordinary stock, during the last 17 years have been as follows .... Every statement in the prospectus was literally true; but the prospectus did not disclose that profits had been made in the years 1918 to 1920, and that there had been losses in every year from 1921 to 1927, and that dividends had been all these years out of the reserves accumulated in the past. *Held,* the prospectus was false in a material particular in that conveyed a false impression that the company had been prospering between 1921 to 1927, whereas actually it had been suffering losses. The managing director and Chairman, Lord Kylsant, who had made the statement, was held to be criminally liable [*R.* v. *Kylsant (Lord)* (1932) 1 K.B. 442].

12. A company carrying on business in jute is empowered by the objects clause of its memorandum to do any other business not connected with jute. By a special resolution passed unanimously the company resolved to alter the objects clause to include the power to carry on additional business in rubber. The Registrar opposed the company's applica-tion to the court for confirmation of the alteration on the ground that the business sought to be added was entirely new and also alien to the existing business and that it could not be profitably, conveniently or advantageously combined with the existing business. *Held,* the Registrar's contention could not prevail and the company could alter its objects clause for including the power to carry on additional business in rubber, since the additional business is not destructive of or inconsistent with the existing business of jute [See *Parent Tyre Co. Ltd.* (1927) 2 Sh. 222; In *re Bhutoria Bros. (P) Ltd.* 1957 Cal. 593; In *re Natesar Spg. & Wvg. Mills,* 1960 Mad. 257].

13. The directors of a company are prosecuted for default in filing the balance sheet and the profit and loss account with the Registrar of Companies. Their defence is that the annual general meeting for the relevant year was not held for some reason and therefore, since the occasion for placing the same before the general meeting did not arise, they are not guilty of contravention of Sec. 220. *Held,* the directors cannot take advantage of their own default in holding the annual general meeting and were therefore guilty. The fact that no annual general meeting of the company has been held is no defence to a prosecution for not filing the balance sheet and profit and loss account [*State of Bombay* v. *Bhandhan Ram* (1961) I.S.C. 801; (1961) 31 Comp. Cas. 1; *India Nutriments Ltd.* v. *Registrar of Companies (1946)* 34 Comp. Cas. 160].

14. The directors of a company bought some of its shares from a shareholder while they were negotiating for a transaction financially advantageous to the company, and which, if successful, would have substantially raised the market value of its shares. They did not disclose this information to the shareholder when buying his shares. The erstwhile shareholder sued the directors for rescission of sale on the ground of fraud. *Held,* the purchase of shares by the directors was good and the transaction could not be set aside, as there had been no misrepresentation. The directors are trustees and agent for the company and for individual shareholders; they owed no duty to the shareholder to disclose the circumstances which would increase the value of the shares [*Percival* v. *Wright* (1902.) 2 Ch.421].

15. Two directors of P company gave guarantee to a railway company, by reason of which the railway company agreed to carry goods on credit for P company. The Board of directors of P company therefore agreed that it should indemnify the two directors by creating a charge on its uncalled capital. The articles of P company had given to the directors to secure money **only when** borrowed and also contained a provision generally authorising the Board of directors to carry on all business of the company in accordance with the memorandum and articles. The memorandum had given powers to the company to issue securities generally. *Held,* the directors had power to give this charge. The directors are the only persons who can deal with the matters thus assigned to them, and their decision cannot be overruled even by a general meeting of the company [*Re. Pyle Works* (No.2) (1891) 1 Ch.173].

16. The debentures issued by a company created a floating charge on the company's property and stock-in-trade, with the condition that the company was not to create any prior charge. The manager of the company having forgotten his commitment deposited the title deeds of the company's property with a bank by way of security for a loan obtained. The bank also happened to hold some of the company's debentures on deposit for one of its customers. In a contention between the debenture-holders and the bank as regards profits of charges it was held that the bank had priority as it had no notice, actual or constructive, of the provision in the debentures [*Re Vallert Sanitary Steam Laundry Co. Ltd.* (1903) 2 Ch. 654].

17. On March 15,1966, a company, in consideration of a past debt of ₹ 75,000 and a future advance of ₹ 25,000, issued debentures to a creditor accompanied by a floating charge over its assets. On August 20,1966, the company is wound up. *Held,* the floating charge, so far as the past debt of ₹ 75,000 is concerned, is invalid, but so far as the fresh advance of ₹ 25,000 is concerned the charge is valid—Sec. 534 [In *re Hayman Christy and Lilly, Ltd.* (1917) 1 Ch. 283].

18. A creditor having recovered judgment against a company in respect of a trade debt the Sheriff levied execution on the goods of the company which paid the amount of the debt and the costs to the Sheriff in order to avoid sale. Before the money was paid over by the Sheriff to the execution creditor, certain debenture-holders of the company who held a floating charge on its assets made their security effective by the appointment of a receiver who thereupon claimed the money in the hands of the Sheriff. *Held,* that the title of the receiver subsequently appointed under the debentures prevailed over that of the garnishor or execution creditor. Where after a judgment creditor has obtained and served on a company a garnishee order absolute, attaching debts due from the company to the judgment creditor, the company borrows money on the security of the attachment on its goods, the title of the receiver subsequently appointed under the debenture prevails over that of the garnishor [*Geisse* v. *Taylor* (1905) 2 K.B. 658].

19. The auditors of a company presented a confidential report to the directors, pointing out that the security for the loans was insufficient and that there was difficulty in realisation. They also reported that in their opinion no dividend should be paid for the year. In their report to the shareholders, they merely stated that the value of the assets depended upon realisation. The company declared a dividend of 7 per cent out of the capital and not out of income. *Held,* the auditors were guilty of misfeasance and liable to make good the amount of the dividends paid [*Re London and General Bank* (2) (1895) 2Ch.673].

20. A buys from B 4,000 shares in a company on the faith of a share certificate issued by the company. A tenders to the company a transfer from B to himself duly executed together with B's share certificate. The company discovers that the certificate in the name of B has been fraudulently obtained and refuses to register the transfer. *Held,* although the certificate is not a warranty of title upon which A can maintain an action against the company, it estops the company from disputing A's right to be registered. The company cannot deny the title of the holder to the shares as against a person who has relied and acted upon the certificate. A could claim damages from the company to the extent of the value of the shares at the time of the refusal to register [*In re Ottos Kopje Diamond Mines* (1893) 1 Ch. 618].

21. A company, without passing a resolution in its general meeting and getting sanction of the Court, allotted 500 shares at a discount to G, its chairman, and placed his name on the register of members. In the winding up of the company, G claimed that he was not liable to be made a contributory as the allotment was made in contravention of the provisions of the Companies Act and so void. *Held,* G was liable to be made a contributory. His name appeared as a member on the register of members at the time of winding up of the company, and so he was liable under Sec. 426 of the Act and his statutory liability to contribute arose on the winding up of the company. He was not thereafter entitled to raise any objection as regards the invalidity of, or irregularity in, the allotment. When the company

is in the process of being wound up, the liability of the members is *ex lege* and not *ex contractu*. Whatever liability there was under the contract, whether void or voidable, terminates and liability thereafter, when the process of winding up starts, becomes a statutory liability and attaches by reason of the fact that the person is a member of the company [*KL. Goenka* v. *S.R. Majumdar* (1958) 28 Com. Cas.536].

22. A was on the list of contributories as a member who had transferred his shares within a year before the winding up order. After a call had been made against him by the liquidator, he bought certain debts which were due from the company before he transferred his shares, and claimed a reduction in his liability under the call to the extent of those debts. *Held,* his claim was not tenable. A person who is both a contributory and a creditor of the company cannot set off his debt against his liability for calls even if there is an express agreement to do so. The debt of contributory became payable on call and could only be extinguished by payment; and that his liability was not reduced by the purchase after call of debts due by the company before the transfer of his shares [In *re Apex Film Distributors, Lid.* (1959) 3 W.L.R. 8].

23. The executors of L were the registered shareholders of 700 shares in a company. In March, 1966, they transferred these shares to M and in May, 1966, a winding up order of the company was made. M was put on A list for 4,500 shares, including these 700 shares. In February, 1967, a call of ₹ 400 per share was made on M; but he was able to pay only a small amount. In November, 1967, the liquidator put the executors of L on B list and in June, 1968, a call of ₹ 350 per share (in respect of these 700 shares only) was made on them. Evidence showed that there was a probability that amounts received from the contributories in the A list would not be sufficient to pay all the debts of the company including some debts which the company owed whilst L, and his executors were its members. *Held,* mat in the circumstances, the executors were rightly put on the B list and a call was rightly made on them to the extent that M was unable to pay the calls made on the 700 shares formerly held by the executors [*Helber* v. *Banner Re. Earned's Bank* (1971) L.R. 5 H.L. 28].

24. A lent a sum of money to a company, upon the terms that he should have a collateral security of fully paid shares in the company. The company handed over to A certificates for 10,000 shares of £1 each. The certificates stated that he was the registered holder of the shares and that they were fully paid No money had in fact been paid upon the shares which were issued from the company direct. A did not know it and believed that they were fully paid shares. Subsequently the company was wound up and A was placed on the list of contributories. *Held,* the company and its liquidator were estopped from denying that the shares were fully paid, and A could be removed from the list If the certificate states that the shares are fully paid, the company cannot afterwards allege that they are not fully paid, [*Bloomenthal* v. *Ford* (1897) A.C. 156].

25. D carried on business under the name and style of Oriental Metal Pressing Works. In 1955, a private company was incorporated under the name of Oriental Metal Pressing Works Private Ltd., and D transferred his business to this company. By an agreement between the company and D, tie was appointed the managing director of the company for life and was given the power to appoint any person to be a managing director in his place and stead. D died in 1957, leaving a will whereby he purported to appoint G, his son and one of die shareholders of the company. The Bombay High Court held the appointment as void being in contravention of Sec. 312 which prohibits assignment of his office by a director. The Supreme Court, in reversing this judgment, held that Sec. 312 makes the assignment of his office by a director void. It does not on the face of it say that an appointment by a director of another person as the director in his place would be void. In Sec. 312 the word assignment does not include or mean 'appointment'. In assignment there is a transfer of his office by a director when he holds it, whereas an appointment to an office can be made only if the office is vacant [*Oriental Metal Pressing Works (Private) Ltd.* v. *Bhasker Thakoor,* 1961 S.C. 573].

26. For the year ending 31st December, 1959, a private company doing agency business had

declared dividends and had stated that the dividends would be disbursed as soon as it received the commission due to it. The company received the commission due to it in May, 1960, but the dividends were not paid. H and K, two shareholders, made a statutory demand on the company for the payment of the dividends, and on the failure of the company to pay the dividends, H and K filed a petition for the winding up of the company. On behalf of the company it was contended that (i) when the shares held by K were transferred to B in April, 1960, the right to the dividend was transferred along with the shares; (ii) the resolution passed in 1959 to disburse dividend on receipt of the commission was invalid as it enabled payment of declared dividends conditional; (iii) the applicants would be contributories in case the company was wound up and so could not be regarded as creditors of the company. The petition was dismissed on the ground that the company being solvent an order for its winding up could not be passed. On appeal, the Division Bench of Madras High Court held the company can be wound up under Sec. 434(1)(a) even though it is solvent if it fails to meet its creditors' demand for payment. *Held,* further that a transfer of shares effected after the declaration of dividends does not convey title to the dividend to the transferee as far as the company is concerned even if the shares have been expressly transferred *cum* dividend. When the dividend is declared, it becomes a debt immediately payable by the company to registered shareholders; the company becomes their debtor. It was also held that it is open to a company to declare a dividend on the basis of its accounts. Where it is based on estimated profits which have not actually come in the form of cash to the company, it will be open to it to pay such dividends from out of other cash in its hands or even to borrow and pay them off. The declaration of dividends before actual receipt of assets was therefore valid. As dividend had become debts due to the shareholder, H and K could file a petition as creditors of the company for its winding up. The Court ordered the winding up of the company on the ground of its inability to pay its debt, but at the same time directed the order to be kept in abeyance for a period of 3 weeks in order to enable the company to pay up the dividends to-the two creditors [*Hari Prasad* v. *Amalgamated Commercial Traders Private Ltd.* (1964) (34) Comp. Cas. 209].

27. The A company has offered to buy all the shares in the B company and the holders of nine-tenths in value of the shares in the B company have agreed to the sale. The remaining shares are held by X, who objects to the sale. The A company may acquire the shares held by X compulsorily and so obtain all the shares in the B company, by giving notice to him within 4 months of the offer by the A company as provided by Sec. 395.

28. A was appointed a director of a company on April 1,1970. The company was ordered to be wound up on May 29,1970 before A had obtained his qualification shares. The liquidator has placed his name on the list of contributories in respect of the qualification shares. *Held,* A's name cannot be included in the list of contributories, as he does not hold any shares and his name does not appear on the register of members. A director is required to obtain his qualification shares any time within 2 months after his appointment. Since winding up of the company has commenced before the expiry of the 2 months and before he acquired the shares, he was not a member [*Zahir Ahmed* v. *Banaji* (1957) 27 Comp. Cas. 634].

CHAPTER 17

The Factories Act, 1948

The main object of the Factories Act, as amended in 1987, is to ensure adequate safety measures and to promote the health and welfare of workers employed in factories. The Act extends to whole of India and covers all factories as defined under it.

DEFINITIONS

Section 2 lays down that in this Act, unless there is anything repugnant in the subject or context,

(a) adult means a person who has completed his 18th year of age;

(b) **adolescent** means a person who has completed his 18th year of age but has not completed his 18th year;

(bb) calendar year means the period of 12 months beginning with the first day of January in any year;

(c) **Child** means a person who has not completed his 15th year of age;

(ca) **competent person**, in relation to any provision of this Act means a person or an institution recognised as such by the Chief Inspector for the purpose of carrying out tests, examinations and inspections required to be done in a factory under the provisions of this Act having regard to —

   (i) the qualifications and experience of the person and facilities available at his disposal; or

   (ii) the qualifications and experience of the persons employed in such institution and facilities available therein;

with regard to the conduct of such tests, examinations, and inspections and more than one person or institution can be recognised as a competent person in relation to a factory;

(cb) **hazardous process** means any process or activity in relation to an industry specified in the First Schedule where unless special care is taken, raw materials used therein or the intermediate or finished products, by-products, wastes, or effluents thereof would —

   (i) cause material impairment to the health of the persons engaged in or connected therewith, or

   (ii) results in the pollution of the general environment;

Provided that the State Government may, by notification in the Official Gazette amend the First Schedule by way of addition, omission or variation of any industry specified in the said Schedule;

(d) **young person** means a person who is either child or an adolescent

(e) day means a period of 24 hours beginning at midnight;

(f) week means a period of 7 days beginning at midnight on Saturday night or such other night as may be approved in Writing for a particular area by the Chief Inspector of Factories;

(g) **Power** means electrical energy or any other form of energy which is mechanically transmitted and is not generated by human or animal agency;

(h) Prime mover means any engine, motor or other appliance which generates or otherwise provides power;

(i) Transmission machinery means any shaft, wheel, drum, pulley, system of pulleys, coupling, clutch, driving belt or other appliance or device by which the motion of prime mover is transmitted to or received by any machinery or appliance;

(j) machinery includes prime movers, transmission machinery and all other appliances whereby power is generated, transformed, transmitted or applied;

(k) manufacturing process means any process for —

   (i) making, altering, repairing, ornamenting, finishing, packing, oiling, washing, cleaning, breaking-up, demolishing, or otherwise, treating or adapting any article or substance with a view to its use, sale, transport, delivery or disposal; or

   (ii) pumping oil, water or sewage or any other substance; or

   (iii) generating, transforming, transmitting power, or

   (iv) composing types for printing, printing by letter press, lithography, photogravure or other similar process, or book binding; or

   (v) constructing, reconstructing, repairing, refitting, finishing or breaking up ships or vessels; or

   (vi) preserving or storing any article in cold storage.

This definition is comprehensive and artificially projected beyond the natural meaning of "manufacturing process", as it includes even transporting, washing, cleaning, oiling and packing in its meaning although these do not involve any transformation as such. According to this definition, therefore, manufacturing process refers to particular business carried on and does not necessarily refer to production of some article.

The following have been held as manufacturing processes:

1. Bidi-making (*State of Bombay* v. *Ali Sahib Kashim Tamboli,* (1955) II LLJ.182);

2. Salt making from sea water (*Ardeslier* v. *Bombay State,* (1962). S. C. 29);

3. Preparation of foodstuff in Kitchen of restaurants (*New Tajmahal Cafe Ltd.* v. *Inspector of Factories* (1956) 1 LL. J. 273);

4. Pumping of petrol from underground tank and pouring into the tanks of motor vehicles (*Gateway Auto Service* v. *Director ESIC* (1980) II LL. J. 255).

5. Sun-cured tobacco leaves subjected to processes of moistening, stripping, etc. with a view to transporting to company's factory for their use in cigarette making (*V. P. Gopala Rao* v. *Public Prosecutor.* (1970) S.C. 66).

6. Peeling, washing, etc. of prawn for putting them in cold storage (*Re D'Souza* v. *Krishnan Nair* (1968) F. I. R. 469).

   (1) **Worker** means a person employed directly or through any agency (including a contractor) with or without the knowledge of the principal employer, whether for remuneration or not, in any manufacturing process, or in cleaning any part of the machinery or premises used for manufacturing process in any other kind of work incidental to, or connected with the manufacturing process or the subject of the manufacturing process, but does not include any member of the armed forces of the Union.

A person, in order to be a worker under this section, need not necessarily receive wages.[1] The concept of employment involves these ingredients: (i) the employer; (ii) the employee; and (iii) the contract of employment. The *prima facie* test for determining the relationship between the employer and employee is that the employer has the right to supervise and control the work done by the employee.[2] And the employment should be in connection with the manufacturing process which is being carried on in the factory. Therefore in *Shankar Balaji Waje* v. *State of Maharashtra,* 1962 S. C. 517, "bidi roller" was held not to be a worker under the section. P rolled bidis in appellant's factory. There was

---

1. Stale of Bombay v. Alisahib Kashim Tomboli, 1955 Bom. 209.
2. Chintaman Rao v. State of M.P., 1958 S.C. 188.

no contract of service between the appellant and P, and P was not bound to attend the factory for any fixed hours of work or period. He was free to go to the factory as he liked and leave it when he chose to do so. Leaves were supplied to him to take home for cutting. He was paid at a fixed rate on the quantity of bidis turned out. He was not bound to roll the bidis at the factory, he could do that at home. *Held,* he was not a worker, as the three criteria of employment were not fulfilled in this case,

(m) **factory** means any premises including the precincts thereof—

(i) whereon 10 or more workers are working, or were working on any day of the preceding twelve months; and in any part of which a manufacturing process is being carried with the aid of power, or is ordinarily so carried on, or

(ii) whereon 20 or more workers are working, or were working on any day of the preceding 12 months, and in any part of which a manufacturing process is being carried on without the aid of power, or ordinarily so carried on;

but does not include a mine subject to the operation of the Mines Act, 1952, or a mobile unit belonging to the armed forces of the Union, a railway running shed, or a hotel, restaurant or eating place.

Explanation I—For computing the number of workers for the purposes of this clause all the workers in different groups and relays in a day shall be taken into account.

Explanation II—For the purposes of this clause, the mere fact that an Electronic Data Processing Unit or a Computer Unit is installed in any premises or part thereof, shall not be construed to make it a factory if no manufacturing process is being carried on in such premises or part thereof.

The term factory includes premises where anything is done towards the making or finishing of an article up to the stage when it is ready to be sold. It includes everything, machine rooms, sheds not godowns, yards, open lands. A railway work shop is a factory, but a railway running shed is not a factory, nor is a mine. In *Ardesher* v. *Bombay State,* 1962, S. C. 29, it was held that the word 'premises' is a generic term meaning open land or land with buildings or buildings alone. Lands in which the process of manufacturing of salt is carried on is a factory. Precincts means a space enclosed by walls or fences. A place solely used for some purpose other than the manufacturing process does not constitute a factory. Accordingly, to constitute a factory there must be (i) premises; (ii) a manufacturing process, and (iii) ten or more workers, if the manufacturing is carried on with the aid of power or 20 or more workers if the manufacturing process is carried on without the aid of power.

(n) **Occupier** of a factory means the person who has ultimate control over the affairs of the factory: Provided that—

(i) in the case of a firm or other association of individuals any one of the individual partners or members thereof shall be deemed to be the occupier,

(ii) in the case of the company, any one of the directors shall be deemed to be the occupier;

(iii) in the case of a factory owned or controlled by the Central Government or any State Government, or any local authority, the person or persons appointed to manage the affairs of the factory by the Central Government, the State Government or the local authority, as the case may be, shall be deemed to be the occupier;

Provided further that in the case of a ship, which is being repaired, or on which, maintenance work is being carried out, in a dry dock which is available for hire—

(1) the owner of the dock shall be deemed to be the occupier for the purposes of any matter provided for, by or under (a) Sections 6,7,7A, 7B, or 11 or 12; (b) Section 17 in so far as it relates to the providing and maintenance of sufficient and suitable lighting in or around the dock;   (c) Sections 18,19,42, 46,47 or 49 in relation to the workers employed on such repair or maintenance;

(2) the owner of the ship or his agent or master or other officer-in-charge of the ship or any person who contracts with such owner, agent or master or other officer-in-charge to carry out the repair

or maintenance work shall be deemed to be occupier for the purposes of any matter provided in this proviso or chapter VI, VII, VIII or IX or Sections 108,109, or 110. In relation to (a) the workers employed directly by him or by or through any agency, and (b) the machinery, plant or premises in use for the purposes of carrying out such repair or maintenance work by such owner, agent, master or other officer-in-charge or person.

Occupier means a person who occupies the factory either by himself or his agent. He may be an owner, a lessee or a mere licensee but he must have the right to occupy the property and dictate terms of management. He must control the working of the factory. A mere servant charged with specific duties is not an occupier. A manager of a factory who resides in the portion of the premises, of die factory is not an occupier. An owner of a factory who has left the whole conduct of the affairs of his factory *to* a manager, is an occupier, in so far as he has ultimate control over the affairs of the factory (*Emperor* v. *Modi* (1930) 33 Bom. L. R. 309; *State of U.P.* v. *Modi,* 1968 All. 197). But where premises are given over to partnership in return for periodic payments and the owner has no control over them, he is not an occupier (*Stale of Maharshtra* v. *Jamnabai Purshottarn,* 1968 S. C. 53).

Power to declare different departments to be separate factories

Section 4 empowers the State Government, either on its own motion or on an application by an occupier, to direct by an order in writing and subject to such conditions as it may deem fit that for all or any of the purposes of this Act different departments or branches of a factory of the occupier specified in the application shall be treated as separate factories or that two or more factories of the occupier specified in the application shall be treated as a single factory. But no order under this Section shall be made by the State Government on its own motion unless an opportunity of being heard is given to the occupier.

Power to exempt during Public Emergency

As per Section 5, in any case of public emergency, the State Government may, by notification in the Cfficial Gazette, exempt any factory, or class or description of factories from all or any of the provisions of this Act, except Section 67^3, for such period and subject to such conditions as it may think fit. However, no exemption can be granted for a period exceeding three months at a time.

APPROVAL OF LICENSING AND REGISTRATION OF FACTORIES

Sections 6 and 7 empower Factory Inspectorate to scrutinise the plans and specifications of factory building prior to their construction or extension. Section 6 empowers the State Government to make rules requiring (a) the submission of plans of any class or description of factories to the Chief Inspector or the State Government, (b) previous permission in writing of the State Government or the Chief Inspector to be obtained for the site on which the factory is to be situated and for construction or extension of any factory, (c) for considering applications for permission, the submission of plans and specifications, (d) nature of plans and specifications and the authority to certify them, (e) registration and licensing of factories, (f) fees payable for registration and licensing and for the renewal of licences. The licence shall not be granted unless 15 days notice as specified in Section 7 has been given.

If an application is made for approval in compliance with the foregoing requirements, and no reply is received within 3 months from the date on which it is sent, the application stands automatically approved. If the application is not approved, the applicant may within 30 days of such disapproval appeal to the Central Government against the order of the State Government and to the State Government against the order of any other authority.

---

3. Section 67 states that no child who has not completed his fourteenth year shall be required or allowed to work in a factory.

Notice by Occupier—Section 7 provides that the occupier shall, at least 15 days before he begins to occupy or use any premises as a factory, send to the Chief Inspector a written notice containing—

1. The name and situation of the factory;
2. The name and address of the occupier;
3. The name and address of the owner of the premises or building;
4. The address to which communication relating to the factory should be sent.
5. The nature of manufacturing process to be carried on in the factory during the next 12 months;
6. The total rated horse power installed or to be installed in the factory which shall not include the rated horse power of any separate standby plant.
7. The name of the Manager of the factory for the purposes of this Act.
8. The number of workers likely to be employed in the factory.
9. Such other particulars as may be prescribed.

In respect of all factories, the occupier shall send a written notice to the Chief Inspector containing the aforesaid particulars within 30 days from the date of the commencement of this Act. In the case of a seasonal factory which is engaged in a manufacturing process for less than 180 days in the year, the occupier shall, before he resumes work, give such notice at least 30 days before the commencement of work.

Whenever a new manager is appointed, the occupier shall send to the Inspector a written notice and to the Chief Inspector a copy thereof, within 7 days from the date on which such person takes over charge. If no manager is appointed or the person appointed as a manager is not functioning the occupier shall be deemed to be the manager of the factory.

General Duties of the Occupier

Section 7A was inserted by the Factories (Amendment) Act, 1987 as follows:

1. Every occupier shall ensure, so far as is reasonably practicable, the health, safety and welfare of all workers while they are at work in the factory;

2. Without prejudice to the generality of the provisions of sub section (1) the matters to which such duty extends shall include:
   (a) the provision and maintenance of plant and systems of work in the factory that are safe and without risks to health;
   (b) the arrangement in the factory for ensuring safety and absence of risks to health in connection with the use, handling, storage and transport of articles arid substances;
   (c) the provision of such information, instruction, training and supervision as are necessary to ensure the health and safety of all workers at work;
   (d) the maintenance of all places of work in the factory in a condition that is safe and without risks to health and the provision and maintenance of such means of access to, and egress from, such places as are safe and without such risks;
   (e) the provision, maintenance or monitoring of such working environment in the factory for the workers that is safe, without risks to health and adequate as regards facilities and arrangements for their welfare at work;

3. Except in such cases as may be prescribed, every occupier shall prepare, and as often as may be appropriate, revise, a written statement of his general policy with respect to the health and safety of the workers at work and the organisation and arrangements for the time being in force for carrying out that policy, and to bring the statement and any revision thereof to the notice of all the workers in such manner as may be prescribed.

General Duties of Manufacturers, etc.

Section 7B, inserted by the 1987 Amendment Act provides for the general duties of manufacturers, etc., as regards articles and substances for use in factories. It states—

(1) Every person who designs, manufactures, imports or supplies any article for use in any factory shall—

(a) ensure, so far as is reasonably practicable, that the article is so designed and constructed as to be safe and without risks to the health of the workers when properly used;

(b) carry out or arrange for the carrying out of such tests and examinations as may be considered necessary for effective implementation of the provisions of clause (a);

(c) take such steps as may be necessary to ensure that adequate information will be available—

(i) in connection with the use of the article in any factory;

(ii) about the use for which it is designed and tested; and

(iii) about any conditions necessary to ensure that the article, when put to such use, will be safe, and without risks to the health of the workers;

Provided that where an article is designed or manufactured outside India, it shall be obligatory on the part of the importer to see,

(a) that the article (including plant and machinery) conforms to the same standards of such article as manufactured in India; or

(b) if the standards adopted in the country outside for the manufacture of such article are above the standards adopted in India, that the article conforms to such standards;

(2) Every person who undertakes to design or manufacture any article for use in any factory may carry out or arrange for the carrying out of necessary research with a view to the discovery and so far as is reasonably practicable the elimination or minimisation of any risk to the health or safety of workers to which design or article may give rise.

The Section further provides that if research, testing, etc.; has already been exercised or carried out, then no such research is required again. The foregoing duties relate only to things done in the course of the business carried on by him, and to matters within his control. However, the person may get relief from the exercise of above duties if he gets an undertaking in writing from the user of such article to take necessary steps that the article will be safe and without risk to the health of the workers. The term article in this section shall include plant and machinery.

THE INSPECTING STAFF

The State Government is empowered to appoint persons possessing prescribed qualifications as Inspectors and assign to them such local limits as it may think fit. The State Government may also appoint a Chief Inspector who shall, in addition to the powers conferred on him as Chief Inspector, exercise the powers of an Inspector throughout the State. The said Government may appoint Additional Chief Inspectors, Joint Chief Inspectors and Deputy Chief Inspector to assist the Chief Inspector as may be specified.

Every District Magistrate shall be ex-officio Inspector. The State Government may also appoint certain public officers to be additional Inspectors for certain areas assigned to them. The Chief Inspector is appointed for the whole State and exercises the powers of an Inspector in addition to the powers conferred on him as Chief Inspector. To be appointed in any of the capacities as stated above, a person must not be interested directly or indirectly in any factory. He shall cease to hold such office if he gets interested in any factory, after his appointment.

Powers of the Inspector (Sec. 9)

Subject to any rules made under the Act, an Inspector may exercise any of the following powers within the local limits for which he is appointed:

1. He may enter any place which is used or which he has reason to believe is used as a factory. For this purpose, he may take the assistance of any person (i) in the service of the Government or (ii) any local or public authority, or (iii) of an expert.

2. He may make examination of the premises, plant, machinery, article or substance;

3. Inquire into any accident or dangerous occurrence whether resulting in bodily injury, disability or not, and take on the spot or otherwise statements of any person which he may consider necessary for such inquiry;

4. Require the production of any prescribed register or any other document relating to the factory;

5. Seize, or take copies of, any register, record or other document or any portion thereof as he may consider necessary in respect of the offence under this Act, which he has reason to believe has been committed.

6. Direct the occupier that any premises or any part thereof, and anything lying therein, shall be left undisturbed for so long as is necessary for the purpose of any examination.

7. Take measurements and photographs and make such recording as he considers necessary for the purpose of any examination, taking with him any necessary instrument or equipment;

8. In case of any article or substance found in any factory which appears to him to be dangerous to the health or safety of the workers, direct it to be dismantled or subject it to any test and take possession of it for making examination;

9. He may exercise such other powers as may be prescribed.

However, the Inspector is not authorised to ask the proprietor or manager or occupier to produce the registers or other documents in his office; he can do so only in the factory premises. Moreover, no person shall be compelled to answer any question or give any evidence tending to incriminate himself.

CERTIFYING SURGEONS (Sec. 10)

The State Government may appoint qualified medical practitioners to be certifying surgeons for the purposes of this Act within such limits or for such factory, or class of factories as it may assign to them respectively.

A certifying surgeon must not have any connection with, or interest in the factory directly or indirectly. A certifying surgeon will exercise the following functions:

(a) the examination and certification of young persons under this Act;

(b) the examination of persons engaged in factories in such dangerous occupations or processes as may be prescribed;

(c) the exercising of such medical supervision as may be prescribed for any factory or class or description of factories, where—

   (i) cases of illness have occurred which it is reasonable to believe are due to the nature of the manufacturing process carried on or other conditions of work prevailing therein;

   (ii) young persons are, or are to be, employed in any work which is likely to cause injury to their health;

   (iii) by reason of any change in the manufacturing process carried on or in the substances used therein or by reason of the adoption of any new manufacturing processes or of any new substance for use in the manufacturing process, there is a likelihood of injury to the health of workers employed in that manufacturing process.

   (iv) any certifying surgeon may, with the approval of the State Government authorise any qualified medical practitioner to exercise any of his powers under this Act on such conditions and for such a period of time as the State Government may prescribe.

A Certifying Surgeon, will examine children and adolescents (young persons) desirous of being employed and issue certificates of age and fitness to young persons and re-examine them, if need be. The certifying surgeon shall ordinarily visit every factory within his local limits in which young persons are known to be employed at least once in three months after giving previous notice of his visit. He will by personal examination satisfy himself that the young persons employed in the factory are fit to work therein.

HEALTH

Cleanliness (Sec. 11)

(1) Every factory shall be kept clean and free from effluvia arising from any drain, privy, or other nuisance, and in particular—

(a) all the accumulated dirt and refuse on floors, staircases and passages in the factory shall be removed daily by sweeping or by any other effective method. Suitable arrangements should also be made for the disposal of such dirt or refuse. Benches in workrooms should be wiped clean;

(b) Once in every week, the floor of every workroom should be cleaned by washing using disinfectant or by some other effective method;

(c) Effective method of drainage shall be made and maintained for removing water, to the extent possible, which may have collected on the floor due to some manufacturing process;

(d) to ensure that interior walls and ceilings etc. are kept clean; they should be—

(i) whitewashed or colour washed at least once in every period of 14months;

(ii) where surface has been painted or varnished, repaint or revarnish should be done once in every 3 years; if washable, then washed in every 6 months;

(iii) where the surface is smooth and impervious, it should be cleaned once in every period of 14 months.

(e) All doors, window frames and other wooden or metallic framework and shutters shall be painted or varnished at least once in every period of 5 years.

(f) The dates on which such processes are carried out shall be entered in the prescribed register.

Disposal of Waste and Effluents (Sec. 12)

Every occupier of a factory shall make effective arrangements for the treatment of wastes and effluents due to the manufacturing process carried on in the factory so as to render them innocuous for their disposal. Such arrangements should be in accordance with the rules, if any, laid down by the State Government, or approved by the prescribed authority.

Ventilation and Temperature (Sec. 13)

Every factory should make effective and suitable provisions for securing and maintaining (i) adequate ventilation by the circulation of fresh air, and (ii) such a temperature as will secure to the workers reasonable conditions of comfort and prevent injury to health. Walls and roofs shall be of such material and so designed that such temperature shall not be exceeded but kept as low as practicable. The State Government may prescribe a standard of adequate ventilation and reasonable temperature for any factory or class of factories and direct that proper measuring instruments shall be provided and such records as may be prescribed, shall be maintained.

Dust and Fume (Sec. 14)

In a number of factories such as textiles, jute, cotton ginning and chemicals, the manufacturing process disseminate large amount of dust and fume, arrangements for the elimination of which are frequently defective. Effective measures must be taken to prevent the inhalation of dust and its accumulation in any workroom. If any exhaust appliance is necessary for this purpose, it shall be applied at a suitable point.

Furthermore, no stationary internal combustion engine shall be operated in any factory, unless the exhaust is conducted into the open air.

Artificial Humidification (Sec. 15)

The humidification of cotton textile mills in India affects the physique of workers. It is, therefore, necessary that adequate standards must be laid down to check excessive humidity which is artificially introduced in our country.

For this purpose, Section 15 provides that in respect of all factories in which the humidity of air is artificially increased, the State Government may prescribe standards of humidification, regulate the methods for artificially increasing humidity and require the recording of humidity at different intervals. The water for this purpose \hall be taken from a public supply, or other source of drinking water or shall be effectively purified before it is so used. Methods for securing adequate ventilation and cooling of the air in the workrooms should be used.

Overcrowding (Sec. 16)

Overcrowding is another factor that injures the health of workers. Section 16 provides that no room in any factory shall be overcrowded to an extent injurious to the health of the workers employed therein. In every workroom of a factory in existence on April, 1949, there must be at least 9.9 cubic metres and of a factory built after that date at least 14.2 cubic metres of space for every worker employed therein. This space measurement has to be taken up to.4.2 metres above the level of the floor of the room.

Lighting (Sec. 17)

The sense most employed in locating things is sight. Therefore, in every part of a factory where workers are working or passing, there must be provided and maintained sufficient and suitable lighting, natural or artificial, or both. All glazed windows and sky lights must always be kept clean so as to admit adequate light. Effective provision is also required to be made for the prevention of glare, either directly from a source of light or by reflection from a smooth or polished surface, and the formation of shadows which are likely to cause eye strain or accident to any worker. The State Government may lay down standards of sufficient and suitable light.

Drinking Water (Sec. 18)

In a country like India there is hardly any need to emphasize the importance of providing a liberal supply of cool and pure water. Section 18 lays down that in every factory effective arrangements must be made to provide and maintain at suitable points conveniently situated for all workers employed therein a sufficient supply of wholesome drinking water. All such points must be legibly marked "drinking water" in a language understood by a majority of workers employed in the factory, and no such point must be situated within 6 metres of any washing place, urinal or latrine unless a shorter distance is approved in writing by the Chief Inspector. Also, in every factory wherein more than 250 workers are ordinarily employed provision must be made for cooling drinking water during hot weather by effective means and for distribution thereof. The State Government may make rules for securing compliance with these provisions.

Latrines and Urinals (Sec. 19)

In every factory—

(a) sufficient latrine and urinal accommodation of prescribed type shall be provided conveniently situated and accessible to workers at all times while they are at the factory;

(b) separate enclosed accommodation shall be provided for male and female workers;

(c) such accommodation shall be adequately lighted and ventilated, and no latrine or urinal shall, unless specially exempted in writing by the Chief Inspector, communicate with any workroom except through an intervening open space or ventilated passage;

(d) all such accommodation shall be maintained in a clean and sanitary condition at all times;

(e) sweepers shall be employed whose primary duty it would be to keep clean latrines, urinals and washing places.

It is further provided that in every factory wherein more than 250 workers are ordinarily employed—

(a) all latrine and urinal accommodation shall be of prescribed sanitary type;

(b) the floors and internal walls, up to a height of 90 centimetres, of the latrines and urinals and the sanitary block shall be laid in glazed tiles or otherwise finished to provide a smooth polished impervious surface;

(c) in addition to urinal and latrine accommodation being kept clean all the time, the floors, portions of the walls and blocks so laid or finished and the sanitary pans of latrines and urinals shall be thoroughly washed and cleaned at least once in every 7 days with suitable detergents or disinfectants or with both.

The State Government may prescribe the number of latrines and urinals to be provided in any factory in proportion to the number of male and female workers ordinarily employed therein, including the obligations of workers in this regard, as it considers necessary in the interest of the health of the workers employed therein.

Spittoons (Sec. 20)

A sufficient number of spittoons are required to be provided in every factory at convenient places and kept in a clean and hygienic condition. No person must spit within the premises of a factory except in the spittoons provided for the purpose. Any one spitting in contravention of this condition shall be punishable with a fine not exceeding ₹ 5. A notice containing this provision and the penalty for its violation must be prominently displayed at suitable places in the premises. The State Government may prescibe the number of spittoons and their location in any factory.

SAFETY

There is a duty to fence a prime mover, and every moving part thereof, every part of transmission machinery and every dangerous part of any other machinery (Sec. 21). Prime mover is machinery such as an engine or motor which provides mechanical energy. Transmission machinery is one by which the motion of a prime mover is transmitted to or received by any machine.

Examination of any part of a machinery, in motion may be carried out only by a specially trained adult male worker, wearing tight-fitting clothing. No woman or young person shall be allowed to clean, lubricate or adjust any part of a prime mover or transmission machinery when in motion, or to clean, lubricate or adjust any part of any machine if the cleaning, lubrication or adjustment thereof would expose the woman or young person to risk of injury from any moving part either of that machine or of any adjacent machinery (Sec. 22). A young person must not work at dangerous machines, unless he has been fully instructed as to the dangers arising in connection with the machines and the precautions to be observed. Such person must have received sufficient training to work at the machine and should be under adequate supervision of a person having thorough knowledge and experience of the machine (Sec. 23).

Suitable and efficient mechanical appliance such as striking gear must be provided and always used to move driving belts. Suitable devices for cutting off power in emergencies from running machinery must be maintained in every workroom (Sec. 24). To reduce risk of accidents, no traversing part of a self-acting machine, and no material carried on it, must be allowed to run within a distance of 45 centimetres from any fixed structure, if the space over which it runs is one in which any person is likely to pass (Sec. 25). Sec. 26 provides for casing of machinery to prevent accident or danger. Under Sec. 27, no woman or young person must be allowed or required to work for pressing cotton where a cotton opener is at work. Every hoist and lift must be properly constructed so as to be good mechanical construction, sound material and adequate strength, and properly maintained. It must be sufficiently protected by enclosures and must be fitted with gates. It must be examined every six months by a competent person (Sec. 28).

Cranes and other lifting machinery must be sound and well constructed, and free from defects. They must be thoroughly examined at least once a year by a competent person (Sec. 29). Sec. 30

states that effective steps must be taken to ensure that the safe working peripheral speed of every revolving machine and appliance driven by power is not exceeded, and the safe rpeed must be staled on a notice to be kept near each machine where the process of grinding is carried on. To ward against the danger of explosion it is provided in Sec. 31 that if any part of any plant or machinery is operated at a pressure above atmoshperic pressure, then effective measures must be taken to ensure that the safe working pressure is not exceeded. All floors, steps, stairs, passages and gangways must be of sound construction and properly maintained and kept free from obstructions; handrails and fencing must be provided where necessary (Sec. 32). Pits, sumps, fixed vessels, tanks, openings must be securely covered or securely fenced (Sec. 33).

No person should be employed to lift, carry or move any load so heavy as to be likely to cause him injury (Sec. 34). Screens or suitable goggles must be provided for the protection of persons employed on or in immediate vicinity of mechanical or other processes which involve any danger of injury to the worker's eyesight (Sec. 35). Precautions must be taken against dangerous fumes, by manholes or other effective means of egress. No person must enter or be permitted to enter any confined space such as chamber, tank, vat, pit, pipe, flue in which dangerous fumes are likely to be present, unless it is provided with a manhole or other effective means of egress (Sec. 36). The liability exists even though the worker entered without permission (*State* v. *Chinubhai* (1958) Bom. 226). Effective enclosures of the plant or machinery, removal or preven-tion of accumulation of dust, gas, fume or vapour, exclusion or effective enclosure of all possible source of ignition must be taken, with a view to preventing any explosion which might be the result of dust, gas, fume or vapour produced through any manufacturing process (Sec. 37).

Every factory must be provided with adequate means of escape in case of fire. Doors of rooms must not be locked or fastened so that they cannot be easily and immediately opened from the inside and unless they are of the sliding type, they must open outwards. Every fire exit must be distinctly marked in a language understood by the majority of workers and in red letters of adequate size. Clearly audible means of warning in case of fire must be provided (Sec. 38). If it appears to the Inspector that any building of a factory is dangerous, he may ask the occupier or manager or both to carry out suggested repairs, or if the danger appears to be imminent, prohibit the use of the building until repaired (Sec. 40). If it appears to the Inspector that any building or part of a building in a factory is in such a state of disrepair as is likely to be detrimental to the health and welfare of workers, he may order in writing the occupier, manager or both to carry out the specified measures by a specified date (Sec. 40A). Wherein 1,000 or more workers are ordinarily employed, or wherein, in the opinion of the State Govern-ment, any manufacturing process or operation is carried on, which process or operation involves any risk of bodily injury, poisoning or disease, or any other hazard to health to the person employed in the factory, the State Government may require the occupier to employ SAFETY OFFICERS having specified qualifications (Sec. 40B).

PROVISIONS RELATING TO HAZARDOUS PROCESSES

A new Chapter IVA was added by the 1987 Amendment Act dealing with hazardous processes.

Section 41A—*Constitution of Site Appraisal Committee.* (1) The State Government may, for purposes of advising it to consider applications for grant of permission for the initial location of a factory involving a hazardous process or for the expansion of any such factory, appoint a Site Appraisal Committee consisting of—

(a) the Chief Inspector of the State who shall be its Chairman;

(b) a representative of the Central Board for the prevention and control of Water Pollution appointed by the Central Government under Section 3 of the Water (Prevention and Control of Pollution) Act, 1974;

(c) a representative of the Central Board for the Prevention and Control of Air Pollution referred to in Section 3 of the Air (Prevention and Control of Pollution) Act, 1974;

(d) a representative of the State Board appointed under Section 4 of the Water (Prevention and Control of Pollution) Act, 1974;

(e) a representative of State Board for the Prevention and Control of Air Pollution referred to in Section 5 of the Air (Prevention and Control of Pollution) Act; 1981;

(f) a representative of the Department of Environment in the State;

(g) a representative of the Meteorological Department of the Government of India;

(h) an expert in the field of occupational health; and

(i) a representative of the Town Planning Department of the State Government; and not more than five other members who may be co-opted by the State Government who shall be —

    (i) a scientist having specialised knowledge of the hazardous process which will be involved in the factory;

    (ii) a representative of the' local authority within whose jurisdiction the factory is to be established; and

    (iii) no more than three other persons as deemed fit by the State Government.

(2) The Site Appraisal Committee shall examine an application for the establishment of a factory involving hazardous process and make its recommendation to the State government within a period of 90 days of the receipt of such application in the prescribed form.

(3) Where any process relates to a factory owned or controlled by the Central Government or to a corporation or a company owned or controlled by the Central Government, the State Government shall co-opt in the Site Appraisal Committee a representative nominated by the Central Government as a member of the Committee.

(4) The Site Appraisal Committee shall have power to call for any information from the person making an application for the establishment or expansion of a factory involving hazardous process.

(5) Where the State Government has granted approval to an application for the establishment or expansion of a factory involving a hazardous process, it shall not be necessary for an applicant to obtain a further approval from the Central Board or the State Board established under the Water and Air (Prevention and Control of Pollution) Act.

Section 41B. Compulsory Disclosure of Information by the Occupier

(1) The occupier of every factory involving a hazardous process shall disclose in the manner prescribed all information regarding dangers, including health hazards, and the measures to overcome such hazards arising from the exposure to or handling of the materials or substances in the manufacture, transportation, storage, and other processes, to the wokers employed in the factory, the Chief Inspector, the local authority within whose jurisdiction the factory is situated and the general public in the vicinity.

(2) The occupier shall at the time of registering the factory involving a hazardous process, lay down a detailed policy with respect to the health and safety of the workers employed therein and intimate such policy to the Chief Inspector and the local authority and, thereafter, at such intervals as may be prescribed, inform the Chief Inspector and the local authority of any change made in the said policy.

(3) The information furnished under sub-sec. (1) shall include accurate information as to the quantity, specifications, and other characteristics of Wastes and the manner of their disposal.

(4) Every occupier shall, with the approval of the Chief Inspector, draw up an on-site emergency plan and detailed disaster control measures for his factory and make known to the workers employed therein and to the general public living in the vicinity of the factory the safety measures required to be taken in the event of an accident taking place.

(5) Every occupier of a factory shall—

(a) if such factory is engaged in a hazardous process on the commencement of the Factories (Amendment) Act, 1987 within a period of 30 days of such commencement; and

(b) if such factory proposes to engage in hazardous process at any time after such commencement, within a period of 30 days before the commencement of such process; inform the Chief Inspector of the nature and details of the process in such form and in such manner as may be prescribed.

(6) Where any occupier of a factory contravenes the provisions of sub-sec. (5), the licence issued under Section 6 to such factory shall notwithstanding any penalty to which the occupier or factory shall be subjected to under the provisions of this Act, be liable for cancellation.

(7) The occupier of a factory involving a hazardous process shall, with the previous approval of the Chief Inspector, lay down measures for the handling, usage, transportation and storage of hazardous substances inside the factory premises and the disposal of such substances outside the factory premises and publicise them in the manner prescribed among the workers and the general public living in the vicinity.

Specific Responsibility of the Occupier in relation to Hazardous Processes —Section 41C states that every occupier of a factory involving hazardous process shall—

(a) maintain accurate and up-to-date health records or, as the case may be, medical records, of the worker in the factory who are exposed to any chemical, toxic or any other harmful substances which are manufactured, stored, handled or transported and such records shall be accessible to the workers subject to such conditions as may be prescribed;

(b) appoint persons who possess qualifications and experience in handling hazardous substances and are competent to supervise such handling within the factory and to provide at the working place, all necessary facilities for protecting the workers in the manner prescribed;

Provided that where any question arises as to the qualifications and experience of a person so appointed, the decision of the Chief Inspector shall be final;

(c) provide for medical examination of every worker—

(i) before such worker is assigned to a job involving the handling of, or working with, a hazardous substance; and

(ii) while continuing in such job, and after he has ceased to work in such job at intervals not exceeding 12 months, in such manner as may be prescribed.

Power of Central Government to appoint Inquiry Committee

As per Section 41D, (1) The Central Government may, in the event of the occurrence of an extraordinary situation involving a factory engaged in a hazardous process, appoint an Inquiry Committee to inquire into the standards of health and safety observed in the factory with a view to finding out the causes of any failure or neglect in the adoption of any measures or standards prescribed for the health and safety of the workers employed in the factory or the general public affected, or likely to be affected due to such failure or neglect and the prevention and recurrence of such extraordinary situation in future in such factory or elsewhere.

(2) The Committee appointed under Sub-sec. (1) shall consist of a Chairman and two other members and the terms of reference of the Committee and tenure of office of its members shall be such as may be determined by the Central Government according to the requirements of the situation. The recommendations of the Committee shall be advisory in nature.

Emergency Standards—Sec. 41E. (1) Where the Central Government is satisfied that no standards of safety have been prescribed in respect of hazardous process or class of hazardous processes, or where the standards so prescribed are inadequate, it may direct the Director-General of Factory Advice Service and Labour Institutes or any institution specialised in matters relating to standards of safety in hazardous processes, to lay down emergency standards for enforcement of suitable standards in respect of such hazardous processes.

(2) The emergency standards laid down under Sub-sec. (1) shall, until they are incorporated in the rules made under this Act, be enforceable and have the same effect as if they had been incorporated in the rules made under this Act.

Permissible Limits of Exposure of Chemicals and Toxic Substances—Sec. 4 IF. (1) The maximum permissible threshold limits of exposure of chemical and toxic substances in manufacturing process (whether hazardous or otherwise) in any factory shall be of the value indicated in the Second Schedule.

(2) The Central Government may, at any time, for the purpose of giving effect to any scientific proof obtained from specialised institutions or experts in the field, by notification in the Official Gazette, make suitable changes in the said Schedule.

Workers' participation in Safety Management.—Sec. 41G. (1) The occupier shall, in every factory where hazardous process takes place, or where hazardous substances are used or handled set up a Safety Committee consisting of equal number of representatives of workers and management to promote cooperation between the workers and the management in maintaining proper safety and health at work and to review periodically the measures taken in this behalf;

Provided that the State Government may, by order in writing and for reasons to be recorded, exempt the occupier of any factory or class of factories from setting up such Committee.

(2) The composition of the Safety Committee, the tenure of office of its members and their rights and duties shall be such as may be prescribed.

Right of Workers to Warn about Imminent Danger. Sec. 41H.

(1) Where the workers employed in any factory engaged in a hazardous process have reasonable apprehension that there is a likelihood of imminent danger to their lives of health due to any accident, they may bring the same to the notice of the occupier, agent, manager or any other person who is incharge of the factory or the process concerned directly or through their representatives in the Safety Committee and simul-taneously bring the same to the notice of the Inspector.

(2) It shall be the duty of such occupier, agent, manager, or the person incharge of the factory or the process to take immediate remedial action if he is satisfied about the existence of such imminent danger and send a report forthwith of the action taken to the nearest Inspector.

(3) If the occupier, agent, manager, or the person incharge referred to in sub-sec. (2) is not satisfied about the existence of any imminent danger as apprehended by the workers, he shall, nevertheless, refer the matter forthwith to the nearest Inspector whose decision on the question of the existence of such imminent danger shall be final.

WELFARE

In every factory separate and adequately screened washing facilities, conveniently accessible to male and female workers must be provided and maintained. They must be adequate, suitable and kept in clean condition (Sec 42). Suitable arrangements for sitting must be provided and maintained for all workers who have to work in a standing position, in order that they may take advantage of any opportunities for rest which may occur in the course of their work (Sec. 44).

First-aid boxes or cupboards equipped with prescribed contents and not less than one in number for every ISO workers at any one time must be provided and maintained in every factory so as to be accessible during all working hours. Nothing except the prescribed contents shall be kept in first-aid boxes or cupboards. Each first-aid box or cupboard must be kept in the charge of a separate responsible person who holds a certificate in first-aid treatment recognised by the State Government who shall always be readily available during the working hours of the factory. Further, in every factory in which more than 500 workers are ordinarily employed an ambulance room of the prescribed size, containing the prescribed equipment and in the charge of such medical and nursing staff as may bre prescribed, must be provided and maintained and those facilities must laways be made readily available during working hours of the factory (Sec. 45).

The State Government may require the occupier of any factory employing more than 250 workers to provide and maintain a canteen or canteens for the use of the workers (Sec. 46). In every factory in which more than 150 workers are ordinarily employed, adequate and suitable shelters or rooms and suitable lunch rooms sufficiently lighted and ventilated, with provision for drinking water, where workers can eat meals brought by them, must be provided and maintained in a cool and clean condition for the use of the workers (Sec. 47).

In every factory wherein more than 30 women workers are ordinarily employed there must be provided and maintained a suitable room or rooms for the use of children under the age of 6 years of such women. Such rooms (creches) must provide adequate accommodation and must be adequately lighted and ventilated. They must be kept in clean and sanitary condition, and must be under the charge of women trained in the care of children and infants. The State Government may by rules require the provision of additional facilities for the care of such children, and provision of free milk or refresh-ment or both for these children. Facilities may also be required to be given to mothers to feed their children at the necessary intervals (Sec. 48).

In every factory wherein 500 or more workers are ordinarily employed, the occupier of the factory must employ in the factory the prescribed number of welfare officers. The State Government may also prescribe the duties, qualifications and conditions of service of such welfare officers (Sec. 49).

Sec. 50 empowers the State Government to exempt any factory or class or description of factories from compliance with any of these welfare provisions, provided that it prescribes alternative arrangements for the welfare of workers. It may order that the workers, representatives shall be associated with the management of the welfare arrangements for workers.

WORKING HOURS OF ADULTS

It is now generally recognised that shorter hours of labour result in increased efficiency. Secs. 51 and 54 provide that no adult worker shall be required or allowed to work in a factory for more than 48 hours in any week, or 9 hours in any day provided that, subject to the previous approval of the Chief Inspector, the daily maximum of 9 hours may be exceeded in order to facilitate the change of shift. Secs. 55 and 56 provide that the period of adult workers in a factory each day shall be so fixed that no period exceeds 5 hours and no worker shall work for more than 5 hours before he had an interval of rest for half an hour, but in special cases the period of work may be 6 hours if the Chief Inspector permits it. The spread-over on any day (i.e., the total number of hours of his stay in the factory inclusive of rest interval) shall not be more than 10½ unless it is increased by the Chief Inspector in writing for specified reasons up to 12 hours.

Weekly Holidays (Sec. 52)

No adult worker shall be required or allowed to work in a factory on the first day of the week (i.e., Sunday, hereinafter referred to as the said day), unless (a) he has or will have a holiday for a whole day on one of the three days immediately before or after the said day, and (b) the manager of the factory has, before the said day or the substituted day under clause (a), whichever is earlier, delivered a notice at the office of the Inspector of his intention to require the worker to work on the said day and of the day which is to be substituted, and displayed a notice to that effect in the factory. No substitution shall, however, be made which will result in any worker working for more than 10 days consecutively without a holiday for a whole day. The above notices may be cancelled, if necessary, by a notice delivered at the office of the Inspector and a notice displayed in the factory not later than the day before the said day or the holiday to be cancelled, whichever is earlier. Again, when any worker works on the said day and has had a holiday on one of the three days immediately before it, that said day shall, for the purpose of calculating his weekly hours of work, be included in the preceding week.

Compensatory Holidays (Sec. 53)

Where, as a result of the passing of an order or the making of a rule under the provisions of this Act exempting a factory or the workers therein from the provisions of Sec. 52 with regard to weekly holiday, a worker is deprived of any of the weekly holidays for which the holidays were due to him or within the month in which the holidays were due to him or within the two months immediately following that month, compensatory holidays of equal number to the holidays so lost.

Night Shifts (Sec. 57)

Where a worker in a factory works on a shift which extends beyond midnight, (a) for the purpose of Secs. 52 and 56, a holiday for a whole day shall mean in his case a period of 24 consecutive hours beginning when his shift ends; (b) the following day for him shall be deemed to be the period of 24 hours beginning when such shift ends, and the hours he has worked after midnight shall be counted in the previous day.

Prohibition of Overlapping Shifts (Sec. 58)

Work shall not be carried on in any factory by means of a system, of shifts so arranged that more than one relay of workers is engaged in work of the same kind at the same time. The State Government or subject to the control of the State Government, the Chief Inspector may, however, exempt any factory or class or description of factories from this provision on specified conditions.

Extra Wages for Overtime (Sec. 59)

(1) Where a worker works in a factory for more than 9 hours in any day or for more than 48 hours in any week he shall, in respect of overtime work, be entitled to wages at the rate of twice his ordinary rate of wages. The Section applies only to cases of overtime work done beyond 9 hours a day and 48 hours a week. If the normal working hours are 8 hours a day and 44 hours a week, and a worker works beyond 8 hours but not beyond 9 hours, he is not entitled to overtime rate (*The Clothing Factory, National Workers' Union Avdi, Madras* v. *Union of India,* 1990 S.C. 1383). (2) For the purpose of Sub-Sec. (1), "ordinary rate of wages" means the basic wages plus such allowances, including the cash equivalent of the advantage accruing through the concessional sale to workers of foodgrains and other articles, as the worker is for the time being entitled to, but not included a bonus and wages for overtime work, (3) Where any workers in a factory are paid on a piece-rate basis, the time rate shall be deemed to be equivalent to the daily average of their full-time earnings for the days on which they actually worked on the same or identical job during the month immediately preceding the calendar month during which the overtime work was done, and such time rates shall be deemed to be the ordinary rates of wages of those workers; provided that in the case of a worker who has not worked in the immediately preceding calendar month on the same or identical job, the time rate shall be deemed to be equivalent to the daily average of the earnings of the worker for the days on which he actually worked in the week in which the overtime work was done. For the purpose of Sub-Sec. 3, in computing the earnings for the days on which the worker actually worked such allowances, including the cash equivalent of the advantage accruing through concessional sale *to* workers of foodgrains and other articles, as the worker is for the time being entitled to, shall be included but any bonus, or wages for overtime work payable in relation to the period with reference to which the earnings are being computed shall be excluded (4) The cash equivalent of the advantage accruing through concessional sale to a worker of foodgrains and other articles shall be computed as often as may be prescribed on the basis of the maximum quantity of foodgrains and other articles admissible to a standard family, consisting of the worker, his or her spouse and two children below the age of 14 years requiring in all three adult consumption units. The State Government may prescribe the manner in which cash equivalent shall be computed and also the registers that shall be maintained in the factory for securing the compliance with the provisions of this Section.

Restriction on Double Employment (Sec. 60)

No adult worker shall be required or allowed to work in any factory on any day on which he was already been working in any other factory, save in such circumstances as may be prescribed.

Notice of Periods of Work for Adults (Sec. 61)

In every factory there shall be displayed at some conspicuous and convenient place at or near the main entrance of the factory and maintained in a clean and legible condition, a notice in English and in a language understood by the majority of workers in the factory, stating the periods of work for adults, and showing clearly everyday the periods during which adult workers may be required to work. The periods shown in the notice must be fixed beforehand in accordance with the provisions given below, and must in no case contravene any of the provisions of Sees. 51, 52, 54, 55 and 56. The periods of workers must be fixed as follows:—

1. Where all the adult workers are not required to work during the same periods, the manager shall classify them into groups according to the nature of their work indicating the number of workers in each group.

2. For each group which is required to work on a system of shifts, the manager shall fix the periods during which the group may be required to work.

3. Where any group is required to work on a system of shifts and the relays are not to be subject to pre-determined periodical changes of shifts, the manager shall fix the periods during which each relay of the group may be required to work. But if the relays are to be subject to pre-determined periodical changes of shifts, the manager shall fix periods during which any relay of the group may be required to work and the relay which will be working at any time of the day shall be known for any day.

The State Government may prescribe forms of the notice and the manner in which it shall be maintained. In the case of a factory beginning work after April 1,1949 a copy of the notice shall be sent in duplicate to the Inspector before the day on which work is begun in the factory. Further, if any change in system of work is proposed in any factory which will necessitate a change in the notice, it shall be notified to the Inspector in duplicate before the change is made, and except with the previous sanction of the Inspector, no such change shall be made until one week has elapsed since the last change.

Register of Adult Workers (Sec. 62)

The manager of every factory shall maintain a register of adult workers to be available to the Inspector at all times during working hours, or when any work is being carried on in the factory, showing (a) the name of each adult worker in the factory, (b) the nature of his work, (c) the group, if any, in which he is included, (d) where his group works on shifts, the relay to which he is allotted, and (e) such other particulars as may be prescribed: provided that, if the Inspector is of opinion that any muster roll or register maintained as part of the routine of a factory gives in respect of any or all the workers the particulars required under this Section he may, by order in writing, direct that such muster roll or register shall to the corresponding extent be maintained in place of, and be treated as, the register of adult workers in that factory. No adult worker shall be required or allowed to work in any factory unless his name and other particulars have been entered in the register of adult workers. The State Government may prescribe the form of the register, the manner in which it shall be maintained and the period for which it shall be preserved.

Section 63 provides that the hours of work must correspond with notice under Sec. 61 and register under Sec. 62. Sec. 64(1) empowers the State Government to make rules defining the persons who hold positions of supervision or management or are employed in a confidential position in a factory; and the above provisions, except the provision prohibiting the employment of women between the hours of 7 p.m. and 6 a.m. shall not apply to any person so defined; provided that any person so defined or declared shall, where the ordinary rate of wages of such person does not exceed ₹ 750 per month, be entitled to extra wages in respect of overtime work under Sec. 59.

Section 64(2) provides that the State Government may make rules in respect of adult workers in factories providing for the exemption, to such extent and subject to such conditions as may be prescribed—

(a) of workers engaged on urgent repairs, from the provisions of Sec 51, 52, 54, 55 and 56;

(b) of workers engaged in work in the nature of preparatory or complementary work which must necessarily be carried on outside the limits laid down for the general working of the factory, from the provisions of Secs. 51, 54, 55 and 56;

(c) of workers engaged in work which is necessarily so intermittent that the intervals during which they do not work while on duty ordinarily amount to more than the intervals for rest required by or under Sec. 55, from the provisions of Secs. 51, 54, 55 and 56;

(d) of workers engaged in work which for technical reasons must be carried on continuously, from the provisions of Secs. 51, 52, 54, 55 and 56;

(e) of workers in making or supplying articles of prime necessity which must be made or supplied everyday, from the provisions of Secs. 51 and 52;

(f) or workers engaged in a manufacturing process which cannot be carried on except at times dependent on the irregular action of natural forces, from the provisions of the Secs. 52 and 55;

(g) of workers engaged in a manufacturing process which cannot be carried on except during fixed seasons, from the provisions of Sec. 52.

(h) of workers engaged in engine-rooms or boiler-houses or in attending power-plant or transmission machinery from the provisions of Secs. 51 and 52;

(i) of workers engaged in the printing of newspapers, who are held up on account of the breakdown of machinery, from the provisions of Sec. 51, 54 and 56;

(j) of workers engaged in the loading or unloading of railway wagons or lorries or trucks, from the provisions of Secs. 51, 52, 54, 55 and 56;

(k) of workers engaged in any work, which is notified by the State Government in the Official Gazette as a work of national importance from the provisions of Secs. 51, 52, 54, 55 and 56.

4. In making rules under this Section, the State Government shall not exceed, except in the case of workers engaged on urgent repairs, the following limits of work inclusive of voer- time: (i) the total number of hours of work in any day shall not exceed 10; (ii) the spread-over, inclusive of intervals for rest, shall not exceed 12 hours in any one day: provided that the State Government may in respect of workers engaged in any work which for technical reasons must be carried on continuously, make rules prescrib-ing the circumstances in which, and the conditions subject to which, the restrictions imposed by (i) and (ii) shall not apply in order to enable a shift worker to work the whole or part of a subsequent shift in the absence of a worker who has failed to report for duty; (iii) the total number of hours of work in a week, including over-time, shall not exceed sixty; (iv) the total number of hours of overtime work shall not exceed 50 for any one quarter. These rules for exemption shall remain in force for not more than five years.

Explanation. "Quarter" in (ii) above means a period of 3 consecutive months beginning on the 1st of January, the 1st of April, the 1st of July or the 1st of October.

Power to make Exempting Orders (Sec. 65)—Where the State Government is satisfied that, owing to the nature of the work carried on or to other circumstances, it is unreasonable to. require the fixation in advance of the working periods, it may by written order, relax or modify the provisions of Sec. 61. It or subject to its control, the Chief Inspector, may by written order exempt any or all of the adult workers in any factory or group or class or description of factories from any or all of the provisions of Secs. 51, 52, 54 and 56 on the ground that the exemption is required to enable the factory or factories to deal with an exceptional pressure of work: provided that any such exemption shall be subject to the following conditions:

(i)   the total number of hours of work in any day shall not exceed twelve;

(ii) the spred-over, inclusive of intervals for rest shall not exceed 13 hours in any one day;

(iii) the total number of hours of work in any week, including overtime, shall not exceed sixty;

(iv) no worker shall be allowed to work overtime for more than 7 days at a stretch and the total number of hours of overtime work in any quarter shall not exceed seventy-five.

EMPLOYMENT OF WOMEN

In addition to the general provisions applicable to adult workers of both sexes a few special provisions relating to women workers have been introduced in the Act. All the different provisions of the Act have been collected here for the convenience of the reader:

1. No woman shall be allowed in any factory to clean, lubricate or adjust any part of the machinery while that is in motion, or to work between moving parts, or between fixed and moving parts of any machinery which is in motion [Sec. 22(2)].

2. No woman shall be employed in any part of a factory for pressing cotton in which a cotton-opener is at work: provided that if the feed-end of a cotton-opener is in a room separated from the delivery end by a partition extending to the roof or to such height as the Inspector may in any particular case specify in writing, women may be employed on the side of the partition where the feed-end is situated (Sec. 27).

3. In every factory wherein more than 30 women workers are ordinarily employed there shall be provided and maintained a suitable room or rooms for the use of children under the age of 6 years of such women. Facilities shall be given for the mothers of such children to feed them at the necessary intervals (Sec. 48).

4. No exemption from the provisions of Sec. 54 may be granted in respect of any woman. In other words, no woman shall be required or allowed to work more than 48 hours in any week or 9 hours in any day [Sec. 66(a)]

5. In the case of woman workers, there shall be no change of shifts except after a weekly holiday or any other holiday.

6. No woman shall be required or allowed to work in any factory except between the hours of 6 a.m. and 7 p.m. provided that the State Government may by notification in the Official Gazette, in respect of any factory or group or class or description of factories, vary the limits, but so that no such variation shall authorise the employment of any woman between the hours of 10 p.m. and 5 a.m. The State Government may, however, make rules providing for the employment of women workers during the night in fish-curing and fish-canning factories to prevent damage to, or deterioration in, any raw material. Such rules shall remain in force for a maximum period of three years at a time (Sec. 66).

7. Where under Sec. 87 the State Government declares any manufacturing process or operation in any factory as dangerous it may prohibit or restrict the employment of women in that manufacturing process or operation [Sec. 87(b)].

EMPLOYMENT OF YOUNG PERSONS

Child labour laws have been adopted in all civilised countries. They are founded on the principle that the supreme right of the State of the guardianship of children controls the natural rights of the parent when the welfare of society or of the children themselves conflicts with parental rights. The supervision and control of minors is a subject which has always been regarded as within the province of the legislative authority. How far it shall be exercised is a question of expediency which it is the province of legislature to determine. The legislature has fixed an age limit below which children shall not be employed. It has also prohibited their employment at night in one or more kinds of work, and without a medical certificate of age and fitness. The present Act lays down certain special provisions relating to children and adolescents under the above heading, but some other provisions are also introduced at different places. For the sake of continuity, all the provisions relating to children and adolescents are given here.

Prohibition of Employment of Young Children (Sec. 67)

No child who has not completed his fourteenth year shall be required or allowed to work in any factory.

Non-adult Workers to Carry Tokens (Sec. 68)

A child who has completed his fourteenth year or an adolsecent shall not be required or allowed to work in any factory unless (a) a certificate of fitness granted with reference to him under Sec. 69 is in the custdoy of the manager of the factory and (b) such child or adolescent carries while he is at work a token giving a reference to such certificate.

Certificate of Fitness (Sec. 69)

1. A certifying surgeon shall, on the application of any young person or his parent or guardian accompanied by a document signed by the manager of a factory that such person will be employed therein if certified to be fit for work in a factory, or on the application of the manager of the factory in which any young person wishes to work, examine such person and ascertain his fitness for work in a factory.

2. The certifying surgeon, after examination may grant to such young person, in the prescribed from, or may renew—

(a) a certificate of fitness to work in a factory as an adult, if he is satisfied that the young person has completed his fourteenth year, that he has attained the prescribed physical standards and that he is fit for such work;

(b) a certificate of fitness to work in a factory as an adult, if he is satisfied that the young person has completed his fifteenth year and is fit for a full day's work in a factory;

Provided that unless the certifying surgeon has personal knowledge of the place where the young person proposes to work and of the manufacturing process in which he will be employed, he shall not grant or renew a certificate under this sub-section until he has examined such place.

3. A certificate of fitness granted or renewed under Sub-sec. 2(a), shall be valid only for a period of twelve months from the date thereof; (b) may be made subject to conditions in regard to the nature of the work in which the young person may be employed, or requiring re-examination of the young person before the expiry of the period of twelve months.

4. A certifying surgeon shall revoke any certificate granted or renewed under Sub-sec. (2) if in his opinion the holder of it is no longer fit to work in the capacity stated therein in a factory.

5. Where a certifying surgeon refuses to grant or renew a certificate or a certificate of the kind requested or revokes a certificate, he shall, if so requested by any person who could have applied for the certificate or the renewal thereof, state his reasons in writing for so doing.

6. Where a certificate under this Section with reference to any young person is granted or renewed subject to such conditions as are referred to in clause (b) Sub-sec. (3), the young person shall not be required or allowed to work in any factory except in accordance with those conditions.

7. Any fee payable for a certificate under this Section shall be paid by the occupier and shall not be recoverable from the young person, his parents or guardian.

Effect of Certificate of Fitness granted to Adolescents (Sec. 70)

An adolescent who has been granted a certificate of fitness to work in a factory as an adult, and who while at work in a factory carries a token giving reference to the certificate, shall be deemed to be an adult; provided that no such adolescent who has not attained the age of 17 years shall be employed or permitted to work in a factory during night, i.e., between 10 p.m. and 7 a. m. An adolescent who has not been granted a certificate of fitness to work as an adult shall, notwithstanding his age, be deemed to be a child for all the purposes of this Act.

Working Hours for Children (Sec. 71)

(1) No child shall be employed or permitted to work in any factory (a) for more than 4½ hours on any day, and (b) during the night, i.e., a period of at least 12 consecutive hours which shall include an interval of at least 7 consecutive hours falling between 10 p.m. and 6 a.m. (2) The period of work of all children employed in a factory shall be limited to two shifts which shall not overlap or spread over more than five hours each; and each child shall be employed in only one of the relays which shall not, except with previous permission in writing of the Chief Inspector, be changed more frequently than once in a period of 30 days. (3) The provisions of Sec. 52 relating to weekly holidays apply also to child workers, and no exemption from the provisions of that section may be granted in respect of any child. (4) No child shall be required to work in any factory on any day on which he has already been working in another factory. No female child shall be required or allowed to work in any factory except between 8 a.m. and 7 p.m.

Notice of Periods of Work for Children (Sec. 72)

There shall be displayed and correctly maintained in every factory in which children are employed a notice of period of work for children in the same manner as provided for adult workers in Sec. 61. The fixation of the periods in the notice shall be made according to the procedure laid down in that Section: but such periods as shown in the notice relating to work by children must not be such as would require or allow the children to work in contravention of Sec. 71.

Register of Child Workers (Sec. 73)

The manager, of every factory in which children are employed shall maintain a register of child workers, to be available to the Inspector at all times during working hours or when any work is being carried on in a factory, showing (a) the name of each child worker in the factory, (b) the nature of his work, (c) the group, if any, in which he is included, (d) where his group works in shifts, the relay to which he is allotted, and (e) the number of his certificate of fitness granted under Sec. 69. No child worker shall be required or allowed to work in any factory unless his name and other particulars have been entered in the register 6f child workers. The State Government may prescribe the form of the register of child workers, the manner in which it shall be maintained and the period for which it shall be preserved.

Hours of Work to correspond with Notice and Register (Sec. 74)

No child shall be employed in any factory otherwise than in accordance with the notice of periods of work for children displayed in the factory and the entries made beforehand against his name in the register of child workers of the factory.

Power to require Medical Examination (Sec. 75)

Where an Inspector is of opinion (a) that any person working in a factory without a certificate of fitness is a young person, or (b) that a young person working in a factory with a certificate of fitness is no longer fit to work in the capacity stated therein, he may serve on the manager of the factory a notice requiring that such person or young person, as the case may be, shall be examined by a certifying surgeon and such person or young person shall not, if the Inspector so directs, be employed, or permitted to work, in any factory until he has been so examined and has been granted a certificate of fitness or a fresh certificate of fitness, as the case may be, under Sec. 69, or has been certified by the certifying surgeon examining him not to be a young person.

Power to make Rules (Sec. 76)—The State Government may make rules (a) specifying the forms of certificate of fitness, providing for the grant of duplicates in the event of loss of the original certificates, and fixing the fees which may be charged for such certificates and renewals thereof and such duplicates, (b) prescribing the physical standards to be attained by children and adolescents working in factories, (c) regulating the procedure of certifying surgeons, (d) specifying other duties which the certifying surgeons may be required to perform in connection with the employment of young persons in factories, and fixing the fees for such durties and the persons by whom they shall be payable.

Section 22(2) provides that no child shall be allowed in any factory to clean, lubricate or adjust any part of the machinery while that part is in motion, or to work between moving parts, or between fixed and moving parts, of my machinery which is in motion.

Section 23 lays down that no young person shall work at any machine which has been declared by the State Government as dangerous for young persons, unless he has been fully introduced as to the dangers arising in connection with the machine and the precautions to be observed and has also received sufficient training in work at the machine, or is under adequate supervision by a person who has a thorough knowledge and experience of the machine.

Section 27 provides that no child shall be employed in any part of a factory for pressing cotton in which a cotton-opener is at work: provided that if the feed-end of a cotton-opener is in a room separated from the delivery-end by a partition extending to the roof or to such height as the Inspector may in any particular case specify in writing, children may be employed on the side of the partition where the feed-end is situated. It further lays down that where the State Government declares any operation in any factory as dangerous it may prohibit or restrict the employment of adolescents or children in that operation.

Furthermore, Sec. 77 lays down that the provisions of this Act relating to young persons are in addition to, and not in derogation of the provisions of the **Employment of Children Act, 1938**. The act has been passed *to* prohibit the employment of children in certain occupations and workshops to which the Factories Act does not apply. Sec. 3 of the Employment of Children Act reads:

1. No child who has not completed his fifteenth year shall be employed or permitted to work in any occupation (a) connected with the transport of passengers, goods or mails by railway or (b) connected with a Port Authority within the limits of any port.

2. No child who has completed his fifteenth year but has not completed his seventeenth year shall be employed or permitted to work in any occupation referred to in Sub-sec.(l), unless the periods of work of such a child for any day are so fixed as to allow an interval of rest for at least twelve consecutive hours which shall include at least seven consecutive hours between 10 p.m. and 7 a.m. as may be prescribed.

Also, no child who has not completed his fourteenth year shall be employed or permitted to work in any workshop where any of the following scheduled processes are carried on, namely:—Bidi-making; carpet-weaving; cement manufacture, including bagging of cement; cloth printing, dyeing and weaving; manufacture of matches, explosives and fireworks; mica cut ting and splitting; shellac manufacture; soapmanufacture; tanning and wool cleaning. The requirements of this provision will not, however, apply to any workshop wherein any process is carried on by the occupier with the aid of his family and without employing hired labour or to any school established by, or receiving assistance or recognition from, a State Government.

A contravention of any of the provisions of this Act is made punishable with simple imprisonment which may extend to one moth or with fine up to ₹ 500 or with both.

LEAVE WITH WAGES

The Industrial Labour Conference adopted in 1936 a Convention (No. 52) whereby workers in industrial and commercial undertakings are entitled to an annual paid holiday of at least six working days after one year of service. The Indian Factories Act, 1934, was amended in 1945 to include a special section dealing with annual paid holidays in respect of all perennial factories. The present Act his introduced elaborations and deals with the question of paid holidays in a separate chapter (Sees. 78-84), which has again been recast by the Amending Acts of 1954 and 1976.

Section 78 lays down that the following provisions relating to leave with wages will not in any way prejudice the rights to which a worker may be entitled under any Other law or under the terms of any award, agreement including settlement or contract of service; and where such award, agreement including settlement or contract of service provides for a longer annual leave with wages than provided in the present Act, the quantum of leave, which the worker shall be entitled to, shall be in accordance with such award, agreement, settlement or contract of service, but in relation to matters not provided for in such award, agreement, settlement or contract of service or matters which are provided for less favourably therein, the provisions of Secs. 79 to 82, so far as may be, shall apply. The Railway rules regarding leave are more liberal than the provisions of this Act, therefore, the provisions stated here do not apply to a factory of a Railway administered by the Government.

Annual Leave with Wages (Sec. 79)

1. Every worker who has worked for a period of 240 days or more in a factory during a calendar year shall be allowed during the subsequent calendar year leave with wages for a number of days calculated at the rate of—
   (i) if an adult, one day for every 20 days of work performed by him during previous calendar year,
   (ii) if a child, one for every 15 days of work performed by him during the previous calendar year.

For the purposes of Sub-Sec. (1): (a) any days of layoff, by agreement or contract or as permissible under the standing orders; (b) in the case of a female worker maternity leave for any number of days not exceeding 2 weeks; and (c) the leave earned in the year prior to that in which this leave is enjoyed, shall be deemed to be days on which the worker has worked in a factory for the purpose of computation of 240 days or more, but he shall not earn leave for these days. Also, the leave admissible under this sub-section shall be exclusive of all holidays whether occurring during or at either end of the period of leave.

2. A worker whose service commences otherwise than on the first day of January shall be entitled to leave with wages at the rate laid down above if he has worked for two-third of the total number of days in the remainder of the calendar year.

3. If a worker is discharged or dismissed from service or quits his employment or is superannuated or dies while in service, during the course of the calendar year, he or his heir or nominee, as the case may be, shall be entitled to wages in lieu of the quantum of leave to which he was entitled immediately before his discharge, dismissal, quitting of employment, superannuation Or death calculated at the rates specified in Sub-Sec. (1) even if he had not worked for the entire period specified in Sub Secs (1) or (2) making him eligible to avail of such leave, and such payment shall be made: (i) where the worker is discharged or dismissed or quits employment, before the expiry of the second working day from the date of such discharge, dismissal or quitting; and (ii) where the worker is superannuated or dies while in service, before the expiry of 2 months from She date of such superannuation or death.

4. In calculating leave under this Section fraction of leave of half a day or more shall be treated as full day's leave, and fraction of less than half a day shall be omitted.

5. If a worker does not in any one calendar year take the whole of the leave allowed to him under Sub-Sec. (1) or Sub-Sec. (2), as the case may be, any leave not taken by him shall be added to the leave to be allowed to him in the succeeding calendar year, subject to a maximum of 30 days in the case of an adult or 40 days in the case of a child. If, however, a worker who has applied for leave with wages but has not been given such leave in accordance with any scheme laid down in Sub-Secs. (8) and (9) or in contravention of Sub-Sec. (10), he shall be entitled to carry forward leave refused without any limit.

6. A worker may at any time apply in writing to the manager of a factory not less than 15 days (30 days in case of a public utility service) before the date on which he wishes his leave to begin, to take all leave or any portion thereof allowable to him during the calendar year. A worker cannot take leave more than 3 times during a year.

7. If a worker wants to avail himself of the leave with wages due to him to cover a period of illness, he shall be granted such leave even if the application for leave is not made within the time specified in Sub-Sec. (6) and in such a case wages as admissible under Sec. 81 shall be paid not later than 15 days or in the case of a public utility service not later than 30 days, from the date of the application for leave.

8. For the purpose of ensuring the continuity of work, the occupier or manager of the factory, in agreement with the Works Committee of the factory constituted under the Industrial Disputes Act, 1947, if any, or a similar Committee or the other Committee, in agreement with the representatives of the workers therein, may lodge with the Chief Inspector a scheme in writing whereby the grant of leave allowable under this Section may be regulated.

9. Such a scheme, which shall be in force for 12 months, shall be posted in a conspicuous and convenient place in the factory and may be renewed with or without modification for a period of 12 months at a time, provided that there is an agreement as stated in (8) above.

10. No application for leave duly made as required by Sub-Sec. (6) can be refused unless the refusal is in accordance with the schemes mentioned above in Sub-Sees. (8) and (9).

11. If the employment of worker who is entitled to leave is terminated by the occupier before he has taken the entire leave to which he is entitled, or if having applied for and having not been granted such leave, the worker quits his employment before he has taken the leave, the occupier of the factory shall pay him wages for the leave not taken before the expiry of the second working day, after the termination of employment, or on or before the next pay day where the worker himself quits his employment.

12. The unavailed leave of a worker must not be taken into consideration in computing the period of any notice required to be given before discharge or dismissal.

Wages during Leave period (Sec. 80)

1. For the leave allowed to him under Sec. 78 or Sec. 79, as the case may be, a worker shall be paid at rate equal to the daily average of his total full-time earnings for the days on which he actually worked during the month immediately preceding his leave exclusive of any overtime and bonus but inclusive of deamess allowance and the cash equivalent of the advantage accruing through concessional sale to the worker of foodgrins and other articles.

2. The cash equivalent of the advantage accruing through the concessional sale to the worker of foodgrains and other articles shall be computed as often as may be prescribed, on the basis of the maximum quantity of foodgrains and other articles admissible to a standard family. A "standard family" has been defined to mean a family consisting of a worker, his or her spouse and two children below the age of 14 years, requiring in all three adult consumption units. An "adult consumption unit" means the consumption unit of a male above the age of 14 years; and of a female above the age of 14 years and that of a child below the age of 14 years shall be calculated at the rates of 8 and 5 respectiverly of one adult consumption unit.

The State Government has been empowered to make rules for the computation of the cash equivalent of tfie above-mentioned advantage and for the maintenance of registers in the factory.

Payment in Advance in Certain Cases (Sec. 81)

A worker who has been allowed leave for not less than 4 days, in the case of an adult, and 5 days in the case of a child, shall before his leave begins, be paid the wages due for the period of leave allowed.

Mode of Recovery of Unpaid Wages (Sec. 82)

Any sum required to be paid by an employer of the leave period but not paid by him shall be recoverable as delayed wages under Sec. 15 of the Payment of Wages Act, 1936.

Section 83 empowers the State Government to prescribe for the keeping by managers of factories of registers showing such particulars as may be required and requiring such registers to be made available for examination by Inspectors. Sec. 84 provides that when the State Government is satisfied that the leave rules applicable to workers in a factory provide benefits which in its opinion (taking the totality of benefits into account) are not less favourable than those provided by this Act, it may exempt, by a written order, the factory from all or any of the provisions relating to leave with wages, subject to such conditions as may be specified in the order.

Section 85 empowers the State Government to declare any place as a factory even if the number of workers employed are less than 10 if power is used and less than 20 if no power is used, provided that such a place cannot be so declared if the owner carries on a manufacturing process with the help of his family members. Any public institution having any workshop attached to it may be exempted from the application of the provisions of the Factories Act Sec. (86).

Dangerous Operations

Section 87 provides that where the State Government is of opinion that any manufacturing process or operation carried on in a factory exposes any persons employed in it to serious risk of bodily injury, poisoning or disease, it may make rules—

(a) specifying the manufacturing process or operation and declaring *it, to be* dangerous;

(b) prohibiting or restricting the employment of women, adolescents or children in the operation;

(c) providing for the medical examination of persons employed, or seeking to be employed, in the operation, and prohibiting the employment of persons not certified as fit for such employment and requiring the payment by the occupier of the factory of fees for such medical examinations;

(d) providing for the protection of all persons employed in the operation or in the vicinity of the places where it is carried on;

(e) prohibiting, restricting or controlling the use of any specified materials or proces-ses in connection with the operation;

(f) requiring the provision of additional welfare amenities and sanitary facilities and the supply of protective equipment and clothing, and laying down the standards thereof, having regard to the dangerous nature of the manufacturing process or operation;

(g) enabling the Inspector to ask the occupier or manager to take measures for removing conditions dangerous to the health of the workers.

Section 87A states (1) where it appears to the Inspector that conditions in a factory or part thereof are such as may cause serious hazard by way of injury or death to the persons employed therein or to the general public in the vicinity, he may, by order in writing to the occupier of the factory, state the particulars in respect of which he considers the factory or part thereof to be the cause of such serious hazard and prohibit such occupier from employing any person in the factory or part thereof other than the minimum number of persons necessary to attend to the minimum tasks till the hazard is removed.

2. Any order issued by the Inspector under Sub-Sec. (1) shall have effect for a period of three days unless cт tended by the Chief Inspector by a subsequent order.

3. Any person aggrieved by an order of the Inspector under Sub-Sec. (1) and Chief Inspector under Sub-Sec. (2) shall have the right to appeal to the High Court.

4. Any person whose employment has been affected by an order issued under Sub-Sec. (1) shall be entitled to wages and other benefits and it shall be the duty of the occupier to provide alternative employment to him wherever possible and in the manner prescribed.

5. The provisions of Sub-Sec. (4) shall be without prejudice to the rights of the parties under the Industrial Disputes Act, 1947.

Section 88 provides that where in any factory an accident occurs which causes death, or which results in any bodily injury preventing the worker from working for a period of 48 hours or more, the manager of the factory must send to the prescribed authority a notice of the accident. However, where a notice related to an accident causing death, the authority to whom the notice is sent shall make an inquiry into the occurrence within one month of the receipt of the notice or, if such authority is not the Inspector, cause the Inspector to make an inquiry within the said period.

Section 88 A states that where in a factory any dangerous occurrence of such nature as may be prescribed occurs, whether causing any bodily injury or disability or not, the manager of the factory shall send notice thereof to such authorities, and in such forms and within such time, as may be prescribed.

Where any worker in a factory contracts any of the scheduled diseases, the manager of the factory must send notice thereof to prescribed authorities. The medical practitioner treating such worker must send a report to the office of the Chief Inspector and if he fails to do so, he is liable to be fined up to ₹ 1000.

Safety and Occupational Health Surveys

Section 91 A provides that (1) the Chief Inspector, or the Director General of Factory Advice Service and Labour Institutes, or the Director General of Health Services, to the Government of India, or such other officer as may be authorised in this behalf by the State Government may, at any time during the normal working hours of a factory, or at any other time as is found by him to be necessary, after giving notice in writing to the occupier or manager of the factory, undertake safety and occuptional health survey and such occupier or manager shall afford all facilities for such surveys, including facilities for the examination and testing of plant and machinery and collection of samples and other data relevant to the survey.

(2) For the purpose of facilitating surveys, every worker shall, if so required by the person conducting the survey, present himself to undergo such medical examination as may be considered necessary by such person and furnish all information in his possession and relevant to the survey.

(3) Any time spent by the worker for undergoing medical examination or furnish-ing information shall, for the purpose of calculating wages and extra wages for overtime work, be deemed to be time during which such worker worked in the factory.

Explanation—For the purpose of this Section, the report, if any, submitted to the State Government by the person conducting the survey shall be deemed to be a report submitted by an Inspector under this Act

Penalties and Procedure

Section 92 provides for penalty generally for offences against the Act, and states that if there is contravention of any provision of the Act or rules thereunder, then the occupier and the manager are punishable with imprisoment up to two years or with fine up to ₹ one lakh, or with both. If the contravention is continued after conviction, then a further fine up to ₹ 1,000 per day during the period of contravention. Furthermore, where the contravention of any of the provisions relating to safety and dangerous operations has resulted in an accident causing death or serious bodily injury, the fine shall not be less than ₹ 25,000 in case of death and ₹ 5,000 in case of serious bodily injury. Under certain circumstances the owner of the building used as a factory is made liable instead of the occupier of the factory.

Section 96 A provides that whoever fails to comply with or contravenes any of the provisions of Sections 4IB, 41C or 41H or the rules made thereunder relating to hazardous processes shall be punishable with imprisonment up to 7 years and with fine up to ₹ 2 lakhs, and in case, the failure or contravention continues with additional fine up to ₹ 5,000 for every day during which such failure or contravention continues after the conviction for the first such failure or contravention. And if the failure or contraven-tion continues beyond a period of one year after the date of conviction, the offender shall be punishable with imprisonment up to ten years.

Liability and Obligations of Workers

Section 97 provides that subject to the provisions of Section 111, if any worker employed in a factory contravenes any provision of the Act or any rules or orders made thereunder, imposing any duty or liability on workers, he shall be punishable with fine up to ₹ 5000. Further, where a worker is convicted for such contravention, the occupier or manager of the factory shall not be deemed to be guilty in respect of that contraven-tion, unless it is proved, that he failed to take all reasonable measures for its prevention.

Section 111 provides that (1) no worker in a factory—

(a) shall wilfully interfere with or misuse any appliance, convenience or other things provided in a factory for the purpose of securing the health, safety or welfare of the workers therein;

(b) shall wilfully or without reasonable cause do anything likely to endanger himself or others; and

(c) shall wilfully neglect to make use of any appliances or other things provided in the factory for the purpose of securing the health or safety of the workers therein.

(2) If any worker employed in a factory contravenes any of the provisions of this section or of any rule or order made thereunder he shall be punishable with imprisonment up to 3 months, or with fine up to ₹ 100, or with both.

Rights of Workers

Section 111A lays down that every worker shall have the right to—

(i) obtain from the occupier, information relating to workers' health and safety at work;

(ii) get travel within the factory wherever possible, or to get himself sponsored by the occupier for getting trained at a training centre or institute, duly approved by the Chief Inspector, where training is imparted for workers' health and safety at work;

(iii) represent to the inspector directly or through his representative in the matter of inadequate provision for protection of his health or safety in the factory.

Exemption of Occupier or Manager from liability—Where the occupier or manager of a factory is charged with an offence punishable under this Act, he is entitled to give to the prosecutor not less than 3 clear days' notice in that behalf and state that he is really not responsible on the charge levelled against him but than some other (named) person is responsible for the offence. He may then have that person brought before the court at the time appointed for tearing the charge (Sec. 101).

Presumption as to employment—If a person is found in a factory at a time when work is actually going on, he shall, unless contrary is proved, be deemed to have been employed in the factory (Sec. 103).

No court shall take cognizance of any offence under this Act except on complaint, by or with the previous sanction in writing of, an Inspector, before a Presidency Magistrate of First Class (Sec. 105). Further, no court can take cognizance of any offence under this Act unless the complaint is made within 3 months of the date on which the alleged offence came to the knowledge of the Inspector. If the offence consists of disobeying a written order made by an Inspector, the complaint about its commission can be made within 6 months of the date on which the offence is alleged to have been committed (Sec. 106).

Section 114 states that no fee or charge shall be realised from any worker in respect of any arrangements or facilities to be provided, or any equipment or appliances to be supplied by the occupier under the provisions of this Act.

The new Sec 119 states that the provisions of the Factories Act. 1948 shall have effect notwithstanding anything inconsistent therewith contained in the Contract Labour (Regulation and Abolition) Act, 1970.

CHAPTER 18

The Workmen's Compensation Act, 1923

(No. VIII of 1923)

The Workmen's Compensation Act aims to correct the evils that existed under the Common Law. Prior to the Act if an employee in a factory was injured or killed on account of accident due to his employment he or his dependants could file a suit for damages, and could recover them only if the injury or death could be attributed to the negligence of the employer.

The position was hardly equitable as the claims could easily be defected on other grounds, such as (1) the doctrine of "Common employment", (2) *Volenti nonfit injuria,* i.e., the defence of "assumed risk", and (3) the principle of "contributory negligence". According to the doctrine of common employment, if a workman suffered injury or death through the act or omission of a fellow-worker the employer was held not liable, as the same could not be attributed to his negligence. The defence of the "assumed risk" was based upon the idea that the employee assumed the risk knowing full well the dangers of employment. It was said that when he knew of the dangers of employment, workman was himself responsible for the calamity when it arose out of such employment. The economic theory upon which this principle was based may be stated thus: The wages of the workman represent a compensation for the labour he expends and the danger of the employment. These two—the price of the labour and the price of the risk that he voluntarily assumed in doing the work—pass into the price of the product sold by the employer, thereby transferring the burden to the consumer. Since the workman does not bear the burden of the risk, but is rather paid for it, he has no right to claim any compensation for any injury arising out of his employment. The principle was so rigidly applied that even where some person to whom the employer had delegated the duty of supplying reasonably safe appliances and such person neglected his duty and thus caused the casualty, the employer could escape liability by pleading that the employee had assumed the unnecessary risk voluntarily.

The third principle was often used to escape liability, because even in a case like the above, the employer could plead that the injury was the result wholly or partly of the injured workman's own contributory negligence. In other words, if the worker had been careful the accident would not have taken place. The defences often resulted in great injustices to the worker. But under the old system, the employer also many a time suffered a great deal. Sometimes heavy damages, half of which was the opposing Counsel's booty, were awarded against him. The Compensation Act is in a way a compromise between the employer and the employee. The employer is given only a limited and fixed liability, and the worker is sure of getting something without litigation. The principle on which the Compensation Act works is that injuries to employees "are no longer the result of fault or negligence, but they are the product of the industry itself." Therefore there should be indemnity in every case where casualty is incidental to the employment, unless indeed the casualty is brought about by the injured person's own wilful negligence. The workman is not to bear the pecuniary burden, even where the casualty is the result of the negligence of the workman or his fellow-workers, as accidents are an essential feature of industrial undertakings, and the effective force in creating and managing the employment is the employer. Moreover, the work is undertaken primarily in the interest of the

514

employer and ultimately for the public, and the compensation he has to pay can easily be transferred by him to the consumer, thus placing the burden of the workman's disablement or death upon the society. Therefore, the employer must pay for an accident arising out of and in course of employment.

The Workmen's Compensation Act performs a great service to both the employer and the employee, by providing a very simple procedure for the recovery of compensa-tion. It is cheap, prompt and both the parties know how much is to be paid, as schedules for different types of casualties are provided in the Act It must however, be remembered that the Compensation Act does not take away the employee's Common Law right to claim damages which may be quite substantial, if he can prove negligence or breach of duty on the part of the employer. The workman or his dependants are at liberty to either file a suit for damages against the employer, and run the risk of the employer's escape from liability on any of the three defences, or be content with the compensation awarded under the Workmen's Compensation Act Both remedies are in no case open to the workman or his descendants. They must make their choice one way or the other.

Another very important Act—the **Employer's Liability Act** was passed in 1938. This Act declares that the defences of "common employment" and "assumed risk" cannot be raised by employers in suits for damage. Contracting out of employer's liability is also void. Sec. 3 bars defence of common employment; the new Sec. 3 A makes void any agreement concluding or limiting employer's liability; and Sec. 4 bars the defence of assumed risk. The three sections are reproduced below.

"3. Where personal injury is caused to a workman—

(a) by reason of the omission of the employer to maintain in good and safe condition any way, works, machinery or plant connected with or used in his trade or business, or by reason of any like omission on the part of any person in the service of the employer with the duty of seeing that such way, works, machinery or plant are in good and safe condition; or

(b) by reason of the negligence of any person in the service of the employer who has any superintendence entrusted to him, whilst in the exercise of such superintendence; or

(c) by reason of the negligence of any person in the service of the employer to whose orders or directions the workman at the time of the injury was bound to conform and did conform where the injury resulted from his having so conformed; or

(d) by reason of the act or omission of any person in the service of the employer done or made (i) in the normal performance of the duties of that person; or (ii) in obedience to any rule or bye-law of the employer; or (iii) in obedience to particular instructions given by any other person to whom the employer has delegated authority in that behalf.

A suit for damages in respect of the injury instituted by the workman or by any person entitled in case of his death shall not fail by reason only of the fact that the workman was at the time of the injury workman of, or in the service of, or engaged in the work of, the employer.

3A. Any provision contained in a contract of service or apprenticeship, or in an agreement collateral thereto, shall be void in so far as it would have the effect of excluding or limiting any liability of the employer in respect of personal injuries caused to the person employed or apprenticed by the negligence of the persons in common employ-ment with him.

4. In any such suit for damages, the workman shall not be deemed to have undertaken any risk attaching to the employment unless the employer proves that the risk was fully explained to and undertook by the workman and that the workman voluntarily undertook the same.

Nature and Scope of the Act

The Workmen's Compensation Act is the first measure of social security introduced in this country on all-India basis. The Act is intended to promote the public welfare, but it does not concern itself with measures of preventive nature. This is left to the Factories Act. The underlying principle, as said above, is that compensation is not a remedy for negligence on the part of the employer, but it is rather in the nature of insurance of the workman against certain risks of accident The Act is so drafted that under it men without any expert legal knowledge, the employer and his workman, will be able to decide for themselves whether in any particular case compensation is due and if so, what that compensation amounts to.

DEFINITIONS

Section 2 lays down that in this Act, unless there is anything repugnant in the subject or context:—

1. **Dependant** means any of the following relatives of a deceased workman, namely:
   (i) a widow, a minor legitimate son, unmarried legitimate daughter, or a widowed mother; and
   (ii) if wholly dependent on the earnings of the workman at the time of his death, a son or a daughter who has attained the age of 18 years and who is infirm;
   (iii) if wholly or in part dependent on the earnings of the workman at the time of his death, a widower, a parent other than a widowed mother, a minor illegitimate son, an unmarried illegitimate daughter, a daughter legitimate or illegitimate if married and a minor, or if widowed and a minor, a minor brother, an unmarried sister or a widowed sister if a minor, a widowed daughter-in-law, a minor child of pre-deceased son, a minor child of a pre-deceased daughter where no parent of the child is alive, or, where no parent of the workman is alive, a paternal grandparent.

2. **Employer** includes any body of persons whether incorporated or not and any managing agent of an employer and the legal representative of a deceased employer, and when the services of a workman are temporarily lent or let on hire to another person by the person with whom the workman has entered into a contract of service or apprenticeship, means such other person while the workman is working for him.

3. **Managing agent** means any person appointed or acting as the representative of another person for the purpose of carrying on such other person's trade or business, but does not include an individual manager subordinate to an employer. The Chief Engineer of Public Works Department is managing agent since he is in charge of the management (*Chief Engineer, P.W.D.* v. *Smt. Kausal,* 1966 M.P. 297).

4. **Minor** means a person who has net attained live age of 18 years.

5. **Partial disablement** means, where the disablement is of a temporary nature such disablement as reduces the earning capacity of a workman in any employment in which he was engaged at the time of the accident resulting in the disablement and where the disablement is of a permanent nature, such disablement as reduces his earning capacity in *every* employment which he was capable of undertaking at that time, provided that every injury specified in Part II of Table II (p. 593) shall be deemed to result in permanent partial disablement. Where an employee becomes unfit for a particular class of job but is fit for another class which is offered to him by the employer, *held* that the workman was entitled to claim compensation on the basis of partial disablement and not total disablement (*General Manager, G.I.P. Rly.* v. *Shanker,* 1950 Nag. 201). Therefore, in cases of permanent partial disablement, the Commissioner should determine whether the earning capacity of the injured workman has been reduced in *every* employment which he was capable of undertaking at the time of the accident and not merely in the particular job in which he was employed at that time (*Bhagat Singh Ram Saran* v. *Punjab State,* 1966 Punj.397).

The Act is not limited only to physical capacity of disablement, but extends to the reduction of earning capacity as well (*Sukkai* v. *Hukam Chand Jute Mills Ltd.,* 1957 Cal. 601). So in determining compensation payable for permanent partial disablement, the Court should take into account the nature of the injury, the nature of the work which the workman was capable of undertaking and its availability to him. The Court need not follow the medical opinion. The medical certificate may be dealing only with physical inability (*Maharashtra Sugar Mills Ltd.* v. *Tribhuvan,* 1966 Bom. 240).

6. **Total disablement** means such disablement, whether of a temporary or permanent nature, as incapacitates a workman for *all work* which he was capable of performing at the time of the accident resulting in such disablement provided that permanent total disablement shall be deemed to result from every injury specified in Part 1 of Table II (p. 593) or from any combination of injuries specified in Part II of Table II where the aggregate percentage of the loss of earning capacity, as specified in Part II of that Table against those injuries, amounts to 100% or more.

Also, if, after a partial permanent disablement, a workman becomes physically fit to resume his former employment and earn his former wage, but fails to secure a job because of such a disablement, he will be deemed to be totally disabled and will get compensation on the basis of total disablement A miner was permanently blinded in the right eye as a result of an accident, but was physically fit to do his former job. In spite of all his efforts he failed to secure a job either as a miner or a quarry man. He was awarded compensation on the basis of total disablement (*Tonnoch* v. *Brownieside Coal Co. Ltd.* (1929) A. C. 542). In *Pratap Narain Singh Deo* v. *Shrinivas Sahata,* 1976 S. C. 222, the Supreme Court held that where personal injury was caused to a carpenter in the course of employment and his left hand above the elbow had to be amputated, the disablement was total and not partial, since a carpenter cannot work with one hand.

7. **Wages** include any privilege or benefit which is capable of being estimated in money other than a travelling allowance or the value of any travelling concession or a contribution paid by the employer of a workman towards any person or provident fund or a sum paid to a workman to cover any special expenses entailed on him by the nature of his employment.

The wages or earnings of a workman are whatever he receives from his employer in return for his services which include not only actual cash but also money's worth. In computing wages it will be necessary to estimate the value of any concessions in such matters as house-rent, food or clothing given by the employer. It will include all those sources of extra income which are recognised by the custom of the trade or the usage and practice of the particular employment Thus "tips" may be included if they were received by the workman with the knowledge of the employer. Dearness allowance and profit sharing bonus are also included in wages (*Chitru Tanti* v. *Tata Co.* 1946 Pat. 437; *Godavri Sugar Mills Ltd.* v. *Shakuntala* 1948 Bom. 154).

8. **Workman** means any person (other than a person whose employment is of a casual nature AND who is employed otherwise than for the purpose of the employer's trade or business) who is—

(i) a railway servant as defined in Sec. 3 of the Indian Railways Act, 1890 (IX of 1890), i.e., persons who are employed by the railway administration in connection with the service of a railway, not permanently employed in any administrative, district or sub-divisional office of a railway and not employed in any such capacity as specified in Schedule II, or

(ii) employed in any such capacity as is specified in Schedule II.

whether the contract of employment was made before or after the passing of this Act and whether such contract is expressed or implied, oral or in writing; but does not include any person working in the capacity of a member of naval, military or air force; and any reference to a workman who has been injured shall, where the workman is dead, include a reference to his dependants or any of them.

The maximum limit of "monthly wages not exceeding ₹ 1000" has been removed by the Workmen's Compensation (Amendment) Act, 1984, with the result that every workman, as defined in Section 2 of the Act is eligible for compensation for personal injury; but the amount of compensation paid will be on the basis of ₹ 1000 if his monthly wages are more than ₹ 1000.

Schedule II further elaborates the above definition. It does not limit the scope of the definition of "workman", but merely illustrates it by saying that the following persons would fall within the meaning of the term workman, that is to say, any person who is—

(i) employed, otherwise than in a clerical capacity or on a railway, in connection with the operation or maintenance of a lift or vehicle propelled by steam or other mechanical power or by electricity or in connection with the loading or unloading of any such vehicle; or

(ii) employed, otherwise than in a clerical capacity in any premises wherein, or in the precincts whereof, manufacturing process, as defined in clause (k) of Sec. 2 of the Factories Act, 1948, is being carried on, or

(iii) employed for the purpose of making, altering, repairing, ornamenting, finishing or otherwise adapting for use, transport or sale any article or part of an article in any premises wherein or within the precincts whereof, on any one day of the preceding twelve months, 20 or more persons have been so employed;

For the purposes of this clause, persons employed outside such premises or precincts but in any work incidental to, or connected with, the work relating to making, altering, repairing, ornamenting, finishing or otherwise adapting for use, transport or sale any article or part of an article shall be deemed to be employed within such premises or precincts; or

(iv) Employed in the manufacture or handling of explosives in connection with the employer's trade or business; or

(v) employed in a mine as defined in clause (i) of Sec. 2 of the Mines Act, 1952, in any mining operation, or any kind of work, other than clerical work incidental to or connected with any mining operation or with the mineral obtained, or in any kind of work whatsoever below ground; or

(vi) employed as the master or as a seaman of (a) any ship which is propelled wholly or in part by steam or other mechanical power or by electricity or which is towed or intended to be towed by a ship so propelled, or (b) any ship not included in sub-clause (a) of 25 tons net tonnage or over; or (c) any sea-going ship not included in (a) or (b); or

(vii) employed for the purpose of (a) loading, unloading, fuelling, construction, repairing, demolishing, cleaning or painting any ship of which he is not the master or a member of the crew, or in the handling or transport within the limits of any port subject to the Indian Ports Act, 1908, goods which have been discharged from or are to be loaded into any vessel; or (b) warping a ship through the lock; or (c) mooring and unmooring ships at harbour wall berths or in pier; or (d) removing or replacing dry dock caissons when vessels are entering or leaving dry docks; or (e) the docking or undocking of any vessels during an emergency; or (f) preparing splicing coir springs and check wires, painting depth marks on lock-sides, removing or replacing fenders whenever necessary, landing or gangways, maintaining life-buoys up to standard or any other maintenance work of a like nature; or (g) any work on jolly-boats for bringing a ship's line to the wharf; or

(viii) employed in the construction, repair, or demolition of (a) any building which is designed to be or is or has been more than one storey in height above the ground or 12 feet or more from the ground level to the apex of the roof; or (b) any dam or embankment which is 12 feet or more in height from its lowest to its highest point, or (c) any road, bridge, or tunnel, or (d) any wharf, quay, seawell, or marine work including any moorings of ships; or

(ix) employed in setting up, repairing, maintaining or taking down any telegraph or telephone line or post or any overhead electric line or cable or post or standard or fittings and fixtures for the same; or

(x) employed, otherwise than in a clerical capacity, in the construction, working, repair or demolition of any aerial ropeway, pipeline, sewer; or

(xi) employed in the service of any fire brigade; or

(xii) employed upon a railway as defined in clause (4) of Sec. 3, and Sub-Sec. (1) of Sec. 148 of Indian Railways Act, 1890, either directly or through a sub-contractor, by a person fulfilling a contract with the railway administration.

(xiii) employed as an inspector, mail guard, sorter or van peon in the Railway Mail Service, or as a telegraphist or as a postal or railway signaller, or employed in any occupation involving outdoor work in the Indian Posts and Telegraphs Department; or

(xiv) employed, otherwise than in a clerical capacity, in connection with operations for winning natural petroleum or natural gas; or

(xv) employed in any occupation involving blasting operations; or (xvi) employed in the making of any excavation in which on any one day of the preceding twelve months more than 25 persons have been employed or explosives have been used, or whose depth, from its highest to its lowest point exceeds 12 feet; or

(xvii) employed in the operation of any ferry boats capable of carrying more' than 10 persons or;

(xviii) employed, otherwise than in a clerical capacity, on any estate which is maintained for the purpose of growing cardamom, cinchona, coffee, rubber or tea and on which on any one day in the preceding twelve months 25 or more persons have been so employed; or

(xix) employed, otherwise than in a clerical capacity, in the generating, transforming, or supplying of electrical energy or in the generating or supplying of gas; or

(xx) employed in a lighthouse as defined in clause (d) of Sec. 2 of the Indian Lighthouse Act, 1927; or

(xxi) employed in producing cinematograph pictures intended for public exhibition or in exhibiting such pictures; or

(xxii) employed in the training, keeping, or working of elephants or wild animals; or

(xxiii) employed in the tapping of palm-trees or the felling or logging of trees, or the transport of timber by inland waters, or the control or extinguishing of forest fires; or

(xxiv) employed in operations for the catching or hunting of elephants or other wild animals; or

(xxv) employed as a diver; or

(xxvi) employed in the handling or transport of goods in, or within the precincts of:—

    (a) any warehouse of other place in which goods are stored, and in which on any one day of the preceding twelve months 10 or more persons have been so employed; or

    (b) any market in which on any one day of the preceding twelve months 50 or more persons have been so employed; or

(xxvii) employed in any occupation involving the handling and manipulation of radium or X-ray apparatus, or contact with radio-active substance; or

(xxviii) employed in or in connection with construction, erection, dismantling, operation or maintenance of an aircraft as defined in Sec. 2 of the Indian Aircraft Act, 1934; or

(xxix) employed in farming by tractors or other contrivances driven by steam or other mechanical power or electricity; or

(xxx) employed, otherwise than in a clerical capacity, in the construction, working, repair or maintenance of a tube-well; or

(xxxi) employed in the maintenance, repair or renewal of electric fittings in any building; or

(xxxii) employed in a circus.

Explanation—In this Schedule "the preceding twelve months" relates in any particular case to the twelve months ending with the day on which the accident in such case occurred.

There has been a great deal of controversy as to who is an 'employee' or 'workman' within the meaning of Workmen's Compensation Act. Without going into controversial points, we may state the cardinal rule that there must be the relationship of master and servant. A servant is a person subject to the control and command of his master as to the manner in which he shall do his work, and there is a contract of employment between the two. Therefore, an independent contractor is not a workman, even where his remuneration is based upon the amount of work done. But a casual worker, employed for the purpose of the trade or business of the employer, is a workman.

WORKMEN'S COMPENSATION

Employer's Liability

Section 3 provides that if personal injury is caused to a workman by accident arising out of AND in the course of his employment, his employer shall be liable to pay compensation. Besides bodily injury, the Section provides for employer's liability to pay compensation to an employee of his if the employee contracts any of the occupational diseases as specified in Table III on page. For the purposes of the Act contracting of these occupational diseases is deemed to be an injury by accident arising out of and in the course of employment, unless the contrary is proved.

We have seen above that the Workmen's Compensation Act has abolished the Common law doctrines of negligence, contributory negligence, assumption of risk and common employment. The employee is declared to be entitled to the benefits of the Statute regardless of negligence, actual or imputed, on the part of the employer, and also notwithstanding the fact that he himself might have been guilty of negligence. Under the Act, the issue is as to whether the injury was accidental and arose out of and in the course of his employment. If the injury (1) was accidental AND (2) arose out of and in the course of his employment, he would be entitled to get compensation, otherwise not.

Meaning of Accident

The word accident is used in the Act in the popular and ordinary sense as denoting an unlooked-for mishap or an untoward event which is not expected or designed. The word is employed in contradistinction to the expression "wilful misconduct" or "wilful disobedience". Therefore, an "injury by accident" includes any injury not expected or designed by the injured workman himself, irrespective of whether or not it was brought about by the wilful act of someone else. The Statute contemplates injuries not expected or designed by the workman himself. It should be noted that the language of the Act is not "personal injury by an accident" but "personal injury by accident". This means "personal injury not by design, but accident, by some mishap unforeseen and unex-pected : accidental personal injury."

Arising out of and in the Course of the Employment

Probably, no other expression has received so much judicial consideration as the phrase *"arising out of and in the course of the employment"*. Several Judges have, with more or less success, offered explanations. A few of the explanations by eminent Judges are stated here to give an idea of the meaning of the phrase. Before, however, discussing the meaning of the expression it may be emphasized that the injury must not only arise "in the course of" but also "out of" the employment. Proof of the one without the other will not make the employer liable to pay compensation. While an accident arising out of an employment almost necessarily occurs in the course of it, the converse does not follow. An injury which occurs in the course of the employment will ordinarily arise out of the employment, but not necessarily so. To bring the case within the Compensation Act the employee must show that he was at the time of the injury engaged in the employer's business, or in furthering that business, and was not doing something for his own benefit or accommodation. As to whether an accident arose out of his employment or not would depend on the following test laid down by Lord Summer in *Lancashire and Yorkshire Rly. Co.* v. *Highley* (1971) A.C.352. The test is: Was it part of the injured person's employment to hazard, to suffer or to do that which caused his injury? If yes, the accident arose out of his employment. If no, it did not, because what was not part of the employment to hazard, to suffer, or to do, cannot well be the cause of an accident arising out of the employment. "The decision," says Lord Atkinson, "must turn on whether the workman was, when the accident which injured him occurred in the course of performing some duty arising out of his contract of service which he owed to his employer."

Ramaswami, J., in *Mackinnon Mackenzie & Co. Pvt. Ltd.* v. *Ibrahim Mohd Issak,* (1970) 1 S.C.R. 869, observed: "To come within the Act the injury by accident must arise both out of and in the course of employment. The words 'in the course of employment' mean in the course of work which the workman is employed to do and which is incidental to it. The words 'arising out of the employment' are understood to mean that during the course of the employment, injury has resulted from some risk incidental to the duties of the service, which, unless engaged in the duty owing to the master, it is reasonable to believe the workman would not otherwise have suffered. In other words, there must be a causal relationship between the accident and the employ-ment. The expression is not confined to the mere nature of the employment but applies to the employment as such—to its nature, its conditions, its obligations and its incidents. If by reason of any of these factors the workman is brought within the scene of special danger, the injury would be one which arises out of employment. To put it differently, if the accident had occurred on account of a risk which is an incident of the employment, the claim for compensation must succeed, unless, of course, the workman has exposed himself to an added peril by his own, imprudent act."

While returning from his duty a workman was crushed by an engine, *held* he met with an accident in the course of his employment (*Workman, C. & W. Shops* v. *Mahabir,* 1954 All. 132). Where a watchman in the course of his duty lifts G.I. Pipe in order to keep it in a safe place, the injuries must be taken to have been received in the course of his employment, if he is injured (*RM. Pandey* v. *A.P. I. Ltd.,* 1956 Bom. 115). A boy returning to the factory canteen after having served tea in his usual round to certain persons in the factory premises was struck by a bullet and he died the following day. *Held,* death of the boy was due to an accident arising out and in the course of his employment (*National Iron & Steel Co.* v. *Manorama,* 1953 Cal. 143).

In an English case of unusual character the same point was emphasised. Mrs. S. sued as the widow of S, an employee of the Coal Board, who was killed in a collision with T, another employee of the Board. T had finished his day's work and was bicycling across the Board's premises to collect his wages at the Board's pay office. He made a detour across a bus park on those premises and when riding between two buses knocked down the deceased, who died from the injuries he then received. *Held,* the Coal Board was liable, because when the employee was actually on his employer's premises going to the place which the employer has said was the place to which he was required to come in order to draw his wages, it would be a very unreal and strange state of affairs if he was no longer in course of his employment [*Mrs. Staton* v. *National Coal Board* (1957) 2 All. E.R. 667].

A railway employee was ordered to travel to a certain station and repair a watermain. After finishing his work he was hurrying across the platform to catch his train, when he slipped and died as a result of the fall. *Held,* the injuries arose out of and in the course of the employment. Also, if a man is engaged in doing work, and as part of that work and in the course of it does something which he might do outside, but which, nonetheless, happens in the course of and arising out of his work, and injures him or causes his death, the accident has arisen out of and in the course of employment. A workman was engaged in the dock in loading and discharging cargo from ships. He left his home for work at 5 a.m. in a perfect state of health to all appearances. At 6 a.m. he began work of loading china clay. At 9 a.m. after taking his breakfast he was lifting his hand above his head to fasten a hook to a bag for dragging it when he fell down and died. He had heart disease, but there was nothing to show that without the work this man was engaged on he would have died of this heart disease. The case fell within the Act (*Falmouth Dock and Engineering Co. Ltd.* v. *Treloar* [1933] A.C. 481). Again, if a workman does, in a negligent way, an act which is within the scope of his employment and sustains injuries, he is entitled to compensation. But if he does an act which, from its nature, is outside the scope of his employment altogehter, he takes upon himself an added risk and is not entitled to compensation for injuries sustained. The deceased was a workman in the employ of the defendant railway company. He was sent on an errand from Bombay to Kalyan, and from Kalyan back to Bombay. On his way back he was travelling by the defendant company's electric train, and stood in the open doorway. The train, going on a bridge received a jerk, and as a result of that he fell down on the lines and was killed. The company pleaded, among other things, negligence and disobedience on the part of the deceased, as, according-to them he had ignored the warning notice which stated "Don't stand near the door". The Court held otherwise and awarded compensation, on the grounds (a) that the notice was for securing safety of passengers in general, and not for that of workmen, (b) that the accident was in the course of and arose out of the employment of the deceased and he did not take greater risk than an ordinary traveller would do while travelling on one of these electric trains (*G.I.P Rly.* v. *Kashinath Chimnaji,* 1928 Bom. I).

On the other hand, where a boy employed in a boot-making business took home contrary to the orders of authroities a pair of boots for repairing them and thus to improve his own skill and while doing the repairs at home, he injured an eye with an awl, and it had to be removed, it was held that injury did not arise out of and in the course of employment (*Borley* v. *Ockenden* [1925] 2 K.B. 325). The applicant who was a piecer in a cotton mill, went out of his work and interfered with tin rollers while in motion and his *dhoti* having been caught he put out his hand to pull it and got his hand crushed. It was held that he was not entitled to compensation (*Gouri KinkarBhakat* v. *Radha Kishan Cotton Mills,* Cal. 220). To conclude, it may be stated that an accident arises out of and in the course of employment when a causal connection exists between the employment and the accident.

In *Saurashtra Salt Mfg.. Co.* v. *Bat Valu Raja,* 1958 S.C. 881, the Supreme Court has laid down a rule of law relating to the theory of notional extension, i.e., the liability or otherwise of the employer for injury to his workman away from the works. It was observed in this case that' 'as a rule, the employment of a workman does not commence until he has reached the place of employment and does not continue when he has left the place of employment, the journey to and from the place of employment being excluded. It is now well-settled, however, that this is subject to the theory of notional extension of the employer's premises so as to include an area which the workman passes.and repasses in going to and in leaving the actual place of work. There may be some reasonable extension in both time and place and a workman may be regarded as in the course of his employment even though he had not reached or had left his employer's premises. The facts and circumstances of each case will have to be examined very carefully in order to determine whether the accident arose out and in the course of the employment of a workman, keeping in view at all times this theory of notional extension."

In this case, R was employed as a workman in the salt works. While returning home after finishing his work he, along with other workers, had to go by a public path, then through a sandy area open to the public and finally across a creek through ferry boat. R, while crossing the creek in a public ferry boat, which capsized due to bad weather was drowned. On a claim for compensation it was held on the facts of the case, that the accident could not be said to have arisen out of and in the course of employment while crossing the creek inasmuch as the theory of notional extension could not extend to the point where the boat capsized. It was said that "when a workman is on a public road or a public place or on a public transport he is there as any other member of the public and is not there in the course of his employment unless the very nature of his employment makes it necessary for him to be there. A workman is not in the course of his employment from the moment he leaves his home and is on his way to his work. He certainly is in the course of his employment if he reaches the place of work or a point or an area which comes within the theory of notional extension, outside of which the employer is not liable to pay compensation for any accident happening to him."

Employer not Liable

The employer shall not be liable to pay compensation :
(a) if the incapacity or disablement does not last for more than three days; or
(b) if the injury, not resulting in death, is caused by an accident which is directly attributable to—
  (i) the workman having been at the time of the accident under the influence of drink or drugs; or

    (ii) the wilful disobedience of the workman to an order expressly given, or to a rule expressly framed for the purpose of securing the safety of workmen; or

    (iii) the wilful removal or disregard by the workman of any safety guard or other device which he knew to have been provided for the purpose of securing the safety of workmen; or

  (c) if the accident causing the injury to or death of a workman did not arise both out of and in the course of his employment; or

  (d) if the workman has instituted in a Civil Court a suit for damages in respect of the injury against the employer or any other person.

A disablement lasting for a period of 3 days or less is considered trivial and is excluded to check workers from staying away for a day or so at intervals and also claiming compensation on account of minor injuries.

Where the injury is directly attributable to the influence of drink or drugs, the employer is saved from liability. This is because the workman by his own drunkenness is deemed to add a peril to his employment and the effective cause of the accident is said to be his state of drunkenness. He is, therefore, deemed to be the cause of the injury.

Wilful disobedience is not negligence, contributory negligence or carelessness. "Wilful" imports that disobedience or misconduct is deliberate and intentional and not a thoughtless act on the spur of the moment. Even a reckless or a rash act does not save the employer from liability. Again, wilful disobedience must be of a rule or order, expressly framed for the safety of workmen by the employer, and the accident must be the direct result of such wilful disobedience.

Wilful removal or disregard by the workman of any safety appliance is now an offence under the Factories Act, 1948, and the Compensation Act deprives him of the worker's right to compensation.

Alternative rights of election of remedies are given to the workman under the Act. He cannot recover both damages and compensation. If he is injured by the personal negligence or wilful act of the employer or his agent, the worker may either claim compensation or claim damages under his right at Common Law, Therefore, it is provided that if in exercise of his right at Common Law, he files a suit for damages in a Civil Court, he has made his choice and cannot claim compensation from his employer under this Act.

Amount of Compensation (Sec. 4)

The amount of compensation payable depends on the nature of the injury. Under the Act compensation is payable for (1) Death; (2) Permanent total disablement; (3) Permanent partial disablement; and (4)[1] Temporary disablement as provided by the new section 4 and according to Schedule IV which is reproduced below as Table I.[2]

The new Section 4 provides that (1) subject to the provisions of the Act, the amount of compensation shall be as follows, namely :—

  (a) **Death**

Where death results from the injury—

an amount equal to 40 per cent of the monthly wages of the deceased workman multiplied by the relevant factor, or ₹ 20,000 whichever is more;

  (b) **Permanent Total Disablement**

Where permanent total disablement results from the injury — an amount equal to 50 percent of the monthly wages of the injured workman multiplied by the relevant factor, or ₹ 24,000 whichever is more.

---

1. By the Workmen's Compensation (Amendment) Act, 1984, the old Sec. 4 has been substituted by a new Sec. 4.

2. Note : As per the 1959 Amendment Act, every workman, whether ad lt or minor, is entitled to receive the same amount of compensation.

Explanation I— For the purpose of clauses (a) and (b) "relevant factor", in relation to a workman means the factor specified in the second column of Schedule IV, given here as Table I against the entry in the first column of that Table specifying the number of years which arc the same as the completed years of the age of the workman on his last birthday immediately preceding the date on which the compensation fell due;

Explanation II— Where the monthly wages of a workman exceed ₹ 1,000, his monthly wages for the purpose of clauses (a) and (b) shall be deemed to be ₹ 1,000 only.

(c) **Permanent Partial Disablement**

Where permanent partial disablement results from the injury —

  (i) in the case of an injury specified in Part II of Table II given below, such percentage of the compensation which would have been payable in the case of permanent total disablement as is specified therein as being the percentage of the loss of earning capacity caused by the injury; and

  (ii) in case of an injury not specified in Table II, such percentage of the permanent total disablement as is proportionate to the loss of earning capacity (as assessed by the qualified medical practitioner) permanently caused by the injury.

Explanation I—Where more injuries than one are caused by the same accident, the amount of compensation payable under this head shall be aggregated but not so in any case as to exceed the amount which would have been payable if permanent total disablement had resulted from the injuries.

Explanation II—In assessing the loss of earning capacity for the purpose of sub-clause (ii), the qualified medical practitioner shall have regard to the percentage of loss of earning capacity in relation to different injuries specified in Table II.

(d) **Temporary Disablement**

Where temporary disablement whether total or partial results from the injury—a half monthly payment of the sum equivalent to 25 per cent of the monthly wages of the workman, to be paid in accordance with the provisions of sub-section (2), as stated below:

(2) The half-monthly payment referred to in clause (d) of sub-section (1) shall be payable on the sixteenth day—

(i) from the date of disablement where such disablement lasts for a period of 28 days or more, or

(ii) after the expiry of a waiting period of three days from the date of disablement where such disablement lasts for a period of less then 28 days; and thereafter half-monthly during the disablement or during a period of 5 years, whichever period is shorter: Provided that —

(a) there shall be deducted from any lumpsum or half-monthly payments to which the workman is entitled, the amount of any payment or allowance which the workman has received from the employer by way of compensation during, the period of disablement prior to the receipt of such lumpsum or of the first half monthly payment, as the case may be; and

(b) no monthly payment shall in any case exceed the amount, if any, by which half the amount of the monthly wages of the workman before the accident exceeds half the amount of such wages which he is earning after the accident.

Explanation—Any payment or allowance which the workman has received from the employer towards his medical treatment shall not be deemed to be a payment or allowance received by him by way of compensation within the meaning of clause (a) of the provision.

(3) On the ceasing of the disablement before the date on which any half-monthly payment falls due there shall be payable in respect of the half-month a sum proportionate to the duration of the disablemet in that half-month.

TABLE I[3]

Factors for working out lumpsum equivalent of compensation amount in case of Permanent Disablement and Death

Completed years of age on the last birthday of the workman immediately preceding the date on which the compensation fell due	Factors	Completed years of age on the last birthday of the workman immediately preceding the date on which the compensation fell due	Factors
1	2	1	2
Not more than 16	228.54	Not more than 41	181.37
17	227.49	42	178.49
18	226.38	43	175.54
19	225.22	44	172.52
20	224.00	45	169.44
21	222.71	46	166.29
22	221.37	47	163.07
23	219.95	48	159.80
24	218.47	49	156.47
25	216.91	50	153.09
26	215.28	51	149.67
27	213.57	52	146.20
28	211.79	53	142.68
29	209.92	54	139.13
30	207.98	55	135.56
31	205.95	56	131.53
32	203.85	57	128.53
33	201.66	58	124.70
34	199.40	59	121.05
35	197.06	60	117.41
36	194.64	61	113.77
37	192.14	62	110.52
38	189.56	63	106.52
39	186.90	64	102.93
40	184.17	65 or more	99.37

---

3. Substituted by 1984 Amendment Act for the original Schedule IV

TABLE II[4]
[See Secs. 2(1) and 4]

Description of Injury		Percentage of loss of earning capacity
PART I		
List of injuries deemed to result in permanent total disablement		
Loss of both hands or amputation at higher site	——	100
Loss of a hand and a foot.		100
Double amputation through leg or thigh, or amputation through leg or thigh on one side and loss of other foot.	——	100
Loss of sight to such an extent as to render the claimant unable to perform any work for which eyesight is essential.	——	100
Very severe facial disfigurement.	——	100
Absolute deafness.	——	100
PART II		
List of injuries deemed to result in permanent partial disablement		
Amputation Cases—Upper limbs (either arm)		
Amputation through shoulder joint		90
Amputation below shoulder with stump less than 8" from tip of acromion		80
Amputation from 8" from tip of acromion to less than 4½ below tip of olecranon	——	70
Loss of a hand or of the thumb and four fingers of one hand or amputation from 4½ below tip of olecranon	——	60
Loss of thumb	——	30
Loss of thumb and its metacarpal bone	——	40
Loss of four fingers of one hand	——	50
Loss of three fingers of one hand	——	30
Loss of two fingers of one hand	——	20
Loss of terminal phalanx of thumb	——	20
Amputation Cases—lower, limbs		
Amputation of both feet resulting in end bearing stumps	——	90
Amputation through both feet proximal to the metatarsophalangeal joint	——	80
Loss of all toes of both feet through the metatarsophalangeal joint	——	40
Loss of all toes of both feet proximal to the proximal to interphalangeal joint	——	30
Loss of all toes of both feet distal to the proximal to interphalangeal joint	——	20
Amputation at hip	——	90

---

4. Substituted by 1959 Act for the original schedule.

Description of Injury	Percentage of loss of earning capacity
Amputation below hip with stump not exceeding 5" in length measured from tip of great trenchanter	80
Amputation below hip with stump exceeding 5" in length measured from tip of great trenchanter but not beyond middle thigh	70
Amputation below middle thigh to 3½ below knee	60
Amputation below knee with stump exceeding 3½" but not exceeding 5"	50
Amputation below knee with stump exceeding 5"	40
Amputation of one foot resulting in end-bearing	30
Amputation of one foot proximal to the metatarsophalangeal joint	30
Loss of all toes of one foot through the metatarsophalangeal joint	20
Other Injuries	
Loss of one eye, without complications, the other being normal	40
Loss of vision of one eye, without complications or disfigurement of eye-ball, the other being normal	30
Loss of—	
A—Fingers of right or left hand	
Index Finger	
Whole	14
Two phalanges	11
One phalanx	9
Guillotine amputation of tip without loss of bone	5
Middle Finger	
Whole	12
Two phalanges	9
One phalanx	7
Guillotine amputation of tip without loss of bone	4
Ring or Little Finger	
Whole	7
Two phalanges	6
One phalanx	5
Guillotine amputation of tip without loss of bone	2
B—Toes of right or left foot	
Great toe	
Through metatarsophalangeal joint	14
Part, with some loss of bone	3
Any other toe	
Through metatarsophalangeal joint	3

Description of Injury		Percentage of loss of earning capacity
Part, with some loss of bone	——	1
Two toes of one foot, excluding great toe		
Through metatarsophalangeal joint	——	5
Part, with some loss of bone	——	2
Three toes of one foot, excluding great toe		
Through metatarsophalangeal joint	——	6
Part, with some loss of bone	——	3
Four toes of one foot, excluding great toe		
Through metatarsophalangeal joint	——	9
Part, with some loss of bone	——	2

Note: Complete and permanent loss of the use of any limb or member referred to in this Table shall be deemed to be the equivalent of the less of that limb or member.

TABLE III[5]

(See Section 3)

List of Occupational Diseases

Serial No.	Occupational Disease	Employment
1	2	3
	PART A	
1.	Infectious and parasitic diseases contracted in an occupation where there is a particular risk of contamination.	(a) A work involving exposure to health or laboratory work; (b) All work involving exposure to veterinary work; (c) Work relating to handling animals, animal carcasses, part of such carcasses, or Merchandise which mayhave been contaminated by animals or animal carcasses; (d) Other work carrying a particular risk of contamination.
2.	Diseases caused by work in compressed air.	All work involving exposure to the risk concerned.
3.	Diseases caused by lead or its toxic compounds.	All work involving exposure to the risk concerned.
4.	Poisoning by nitrous fumes.	All work involving exposure to the risk concerned.
5.	Poisoning by or ganophosphorus compounds.	All work involving exposure to the risk concerned.

---

5. Inserted by the Amendment Act, 1984.

1	2	3
	PART B	
1.	Diseases caused by phosphorus or its toxic compounds	All work involving exposure to the risk concerned.
2.	Diseases caused by mercury or its toxic compounds	All work involving exposure to the risk concerned.
3.	Diseases caused by benzene or its toxic homologues	All work involving exposure to the risk concerned.
4.	Diseases caused by nitro and amido toxic derivatives of benzene or its homologues.	All work involving exposure to the risk concerned.
5.	Diseases caused by Chromium or its toxic compounds.	All work involving exposure to the risk concerned.
6.	Diseases caused by arsenic or its toxic compounds.	All work involving exposure to the risk concerned.
7.	Diseases caused by radio-active substances and ionising radiations.	All work involving exposure to the action of radio-active substances or ionising radiations.
8.	Diseases caused by the toxic halogen derivatives hydrocarbons (of the aliphatic and aromatic series).	All work involving exposure to the risk concerned.
9.	Primary epitheliomatous cancer of the skin caused by tar, pitch, bitumen, mineral oil, anthracene, or the compounds, products or residues of these substances.	All work involving exposure to the risk concerned.
10.	Diseases caused by Carbon disulphide.	All work involving exposure to the risk concerned.
11.	Diseases caused by managnese or its toxic compounds.	All work involving exposure to the risk concerned.
12.	Skin diseases caused by physical agents not included in other items.	All work involving exposure to the risk concerned.
13.	Hearing impairment caused by noise.	All work involving exposure to the risk concerned.
14.	Poisoning by dinirrophenol or a homo-logue or by substituted dinitrophenol or by the salts of such substances.	All work involving exposure to the risk concerned.
15.	Diseases caused by beryllium or its toxic compounds.	All work involving exposure to the risk concerned.
16.	Diseases caused by cadmium or its toxic compounds.	All work involving exposure to the risk concerned.
17.	Occupational asthma caused by recognised sensitising agents inherent to the work process.	All work involving exposure to the risk concerned.
18.	Diseases caused by fluorine or its toxic compounds.	All work involving exposure to the risk concerned.

1	2	3
19.	Diseases caused by nitroglycerin or other nitroacid esters.	All work involving exposure to the risk concerned.
20.	Diseases caused by alcohols and Ketones.	All work involving exposure to the risk concerned.
21.	Diseases caused by asphyxiants carbon monoxide and its toxic derivatives, hydrogen sulphide.	All work involving exposure to the risk concerned.
22.	Lung cancer and mesotheliomas caused by asbestos.	All work involving exposure to the risk concerned.
23.	Primary neoplasm of the epithelial lining of the urinary bladder or the Kidney or the ureter.	All work involving exposure to the risk concerned.
	PART C	
1.	Pneumoconioses caused by selerogenic mineral dusts (silicosis anthrao silicosis asbestosis) and silico-tuberculosis provided that silicosis is an essen-tial factor in causing the resultant incapacity or death.	All work involving exposure to the risk concerned.
2.	Bagassosis.	All work involving exposure to the risk concerned.
3.	Bronchopulmonary disease caused by cotton, flax hemp and sisal dust (Byssinosis).	All work involving exposure to the risk concerned.
4.	Extrinsic allergic alveelitis caused by the inhalation of or-ganic dusts.	All work involving exposure to the risk concerned.
5.	Bronchopulmonary diseases caused by hard metals.	All work involving exposure to the risk concerned.

Calculation of Monthly Wages (Sec. 5)

The amount payable to the employee is to be determined from the amount of his average monthly wages. What constitutes such wages is a question of fact that requires consideration to be given to numerous circumstances; such as absence from work, duration and continuity of employment, remuneration in addition to regular wages, and the existence of concurrent employments. Specific methods for ascertaining such average monthly wages are prescribed in Sec. 5, as follows.

The expression "monthly wages" means the amount of wages deemed to be payable for a month's service (whether the wages are payable *by* the month or by whatever other period or at piece rates), and are calculated as follows:—

(a) where the workman has, during a continuous period of not less than twelve months immediately preceding the accident, been in the service of the employer who is liable to pay compensation, the monthly wages of the workman shall be one-twelfth of the total wages which have fallen due for payment to him by the employer in the last twelve months of that period;

(b) where the whole of the continuous period of service immediately preceding the accident during which the workman was in the service of the employer who is liable to pay the compensation was less than one month, the monthly wages of the workman shall be deemed to be the average monthly amount which, during the twelve months immediately preceding the accident, was being earned by a workman employed on the same work by the same employer, or, if there was no workman so employed, by a workman employed on similar work in the same locality;

(c) in other cases, the monthly wages shall be 30 times the total wages earned in respect of the last continuous period of service immediately preceding the accident from the employer who is liable to pay compensation, divided by the number of days comprising such period.

Explanation—A period of service shall be deemed to be continuous which has not been interrupted by a period of absence from work exceeding 14 days.

Computation of Half-monthly Payment (Sec. 7)

Any right to receive half-monthly payments may, by agreement between the parties or if the parties cannot agree and the payments have been continued for not less than six months, *on* the application of either party to the Commissioner be redeemed by the payment of a lump sum of such an amount as may be agreed to by the parties or determined by the Commissioner, as the case may be.

The Commissioner, on the application either of the employer or of the workman accompanied by the certificate of a qualified medical practitioner that there has been a change in the conditioner the workman, may review any half-monthly payment agreed to by the parties or fixed by the Commissioner. On such review the half-monthly payment may be continued, increased, decreased, or ended, or if the accident is found to have resulted in permanent disablement, be converted to the lump sum to which the workman is entitled less any amount which he has already received by way of half-monthly payments (Sec. 6).

Distribution of Compensation (Sec. 8)

Where an adult male worker has been totally or partially disabled by an injury the employer may either pay the compensation to the worker or deposit it with the Commis-sioner, who will then pay to the worker.

Where the compensation is payable—
(a) in respect of death of a workman, or
(b) in lump sum to a woman or a person under legal disability, it must be deposited with the Commissioner, and not paid directly to the dependants of the deceased workman or to a woman or a person under legal disability, as the case may be. Provision, however, is made for small payments out of the compensation amount by the employer to the deceased workman's dependants as (i) advances not exceeding ₹ 100 in the aggregate, or (ii) for workman's funeral expenses not exceeding ₹ 50.

On the deposit of the compensation money, the Commissioner shall distribute it among the dependants of the deceased workman in any proportion as he thinks fit, or may even allot it to any one descendant. If he is satisfied that no dependant exists, the Commissioner shall repay the money to the employer by whom it was deposited. Where the amount is payable to a woman or a person under a legal disability, such sum may be invested or otherwise dealt with for the benefit of such woman or person under legal disability.

According to a recent ruling of the Supreme Court in *Pratap Narain Singh Deo* v. *Shrinivas Sahata,* 1976 S.C. 222, the employer becomes liable to pay compensation as soon as the injury is caused to the workman at the rate as provided by Sec.4. If he fails to pay and also makes no provisional payment under Sec. 4(2) but challenges the jurisdiction of the Commissioner, the employer is liable to pay interest and penalty.

For the purpose of protecting workmen from money-lenders and others Sec. 9 provides that no lump-sum or half-monthly payment payable as compensation shall in any way be capable of being assigned or charged or be liable to attachment or pass to any person other than the workman by operation of law, nor shall any claim be set off against the same.

Notice and Claim (Sec. 10)

The Commissioner shall not entertain any claim for compensation unless a notice of the accident has been given to the employer or someone on his behalf as soon as practicable after the happening thereof, and unless the claim is preferred before him (Commissioner) within two years of the occurrence of the accident or, in the case of death, within two years from the date of the death: provided that the Commissioner may entertain the claim if he is satisfied that the failure or delay to give notice or prefer the claim was due to sufficient cause. The notice must give the name and address of the person and state in ordinary simple language the cause of the injury and the date on which the accident happened.

As the notice is meant for the benefit of the employer, it will not be necessary if the accident to the knowledge of the employer or any person responsible to the employer for management, or if he waives it, or if the delay or failure does not prejudice the employer.

Fatal or Serious Accidents

Sections 10 A and 10 B provide that all cases of fatal accidents or serious bodily injury should be brought to the notice of the Commissioner within 7 days of the death or the serious bodily injury and the circumstances attending the death. Default to give notice is punishable with fine up to ₹ 500. Where a Commissioner receives information from any source that a fatal accident has occurred, he may require, by means of a registered postal notice, the deceased workman's employer to submit, within 30 days of the service of the notice, a statement giving circumstances attending the death, and indicating whether or not the employer considers himself liable to deposit compensation. If he admits liability, the employer must make the deposit within 30 days of the notice, and if he denies it, he must state the grounds for disclaiming liability. If the employer disclaims liability, the Commissioner may inform any of the dependants of the deceased that it is open to them to prefer a claim, and may give them such other further information as he thinks fit.

Medical Examination (Sec. 11)

A workman who has given notice of accident must, if the employer wishes, submit himself for medical examination by a duly qualified medical man provided and paid for by the employer. It he refuses to do so, or obstructs the examination, his right to receive compensation or to take proceedings to recover it are suspended until he complies. The exercise of this right of the employer to ask the workman to submit to medical examination is not limited to one occasion or to any period of time, so long as the exercise is not unreasonable. Whilst receiving half-monthly payment of compensation the workman must also submit to medical examination from time to time at the request of the employer, and if he refuses or obstructs the examination such periodical payments may be suspended. The medical man so examining the workman will issue a certificate as to the workman's condition and fitness for employment, specifying, if necessary, the kind of employment for which he is fit. His right to compensation shall also be suspended if he voluntarily leaves without having been so examined the vicinity of the place of his employment. If a workman whose payment of compensation was suspended dies before such medical examination, the Commissioner may direct the payment to the dependants of the deceased workman. If an injured workman has refused to be attended by a qualified medical practitioner whose services have been offered to him by the employer free of charge or having accepted such offer has deliberately disregarded the instructions of such medical man, then, unless the workman has been regularly attended by a medical practitioner, and the injury has been aggravated thereby, the injury and resulting disablement shall be deemed to be of the same nature and duration as they might reasonably have been expected to be if the workman had been regularly attended by a qualified medical man whose instructions he had followed, and compensation if any shall be payable accordingly.

Contracting Out (Sec. 12)

Any contract or agreement whether made before or after the commencement of this Act, whereby a workman relinquishes any right of compensation from the employer for personal injury arising out of and in the course of the employment shall be null and void in so far as it purports to remove or reduce the liability of any person to pay compensation under this Act.

Section 13 provides that where a third party was responsible for the accident the employer may recover from that third party any compensation he has paid to his Workman, in addition to any other damages he may be able to claim.

Where an employer, who has insured his liability for compensation under the Act, becomes an insolvent, or if the employer being a company has, gone into liquidation, the rights of the employer against the insurers shall pass to the workman; and if the insurers[1] liability is less than the liability of the employer to the workman, the workman can prove for the balance in the insolvency proceedings or liquidation. Any breach of the contract by the employer shall not operate against the workman, so long as the premia have been regularly paid (Sec. 14).

COMMISSIONER

The Act is administered on a State basis by the Commissioners for Workmen's Compensation appointed by the State Governments. In Madras, West Bengal and Bihar the duties of the Commissioner are being discharged by Labour Commissioners. The Government of Maharashtra has appointed one Commissioner of the more important areas and for other areas it has declared Sub-Judges to be *ex-officio* Commissioners. In other States either the District Magistrates or the District and Sessions Judges discharge the duties of the Commissioners under the Act.

The duties of the Commissioner include the settlement of disputed claims, disposal of compensation in case where injury results in death, or where deposit is made because the claimant is a woman or a person under legal disability, and the revision of periodical payments.

An appeal shall lie to the High Court from the orders of a Commissioner.

CHAPTER 19

The Trade Unions Act, 1926

(No. XVI of 1926)

Definitions

Trade Union means any combination, whether temporary or permanent, formed primarily for the purpose of regulating the relations between workmen and employers or between workmen and workmen, or between employers and employers, or for imposing restrictive conditions on the conduct of any trade or business, and includes any federation of two or more Trade Unions. But this definition does not cover (i) any agreement between partners as to their own business; (ii) any agreement between an employer and those employed by him as to such employment; (iii) any agreement in consideration of the sale of the goodwill of a business or of instruction in any profession, trade or handicraft.

It will be noticed that the terminology of the definition is very vague and its scope very wide. Strictly speaking the term "Trade Union" should refer only to workers' or employees' organisation. "A Trade union is essentially an organisation of employees, not of employers, nor of independent workers."

Trade dispute means any dispute between employers and workmen or between workmen and workmen, or between employers and employers which is connected with the employment or non-employment, or the terms of employment or the conditions of labour, of any person, and "workmen" means all persons employed in trade or industry whether or not in the employment of the employer with whom the trade dispute arises.

REGISTRATION

The appropriate Government is required to appoint a person as the Registrar of Trade Unions for each State. It may appoint Additional and Deputy Registrars for local areas. Such Additional or Deputy Registrars will, under the superintendence and directions of the Registrar, exercise such powers and functions as are delegated to them and shall be deemed to be Registrars for their respective local limits.

Any seven or more members of a Trade Union may subscribe their names to the rules of the Trade Union and apply to the Registrar; but before they can be granted a certificate of registration, they must comply with certain requirements in regard to rules as laid down in Sec. 6 of the Act An application made as stated above will not become invalid if not more than half the number of applicants have disassociated themselves after the date of application and before registration.

An application for registration must be accompanied by a copy of the rules of the Trade Union and must also give the following particulars :—

(a) the names, occupations and addresses of the members making the application;

(b) the name of the Trade Union and the address of its head Office; and

(c) the titles, names, age, addresses and occupations of the officers of the Trade Union.

In the case of a Trade Union in existence for more than a year before application, a statement of its assets and liabilities must also accompany the application for registra-tion (Sec. 5).

The registration will be granted only if at least one-half of the total number of its office-bearers are persons actually engaged or employed in the industry with which the Union is concerned unless exemption is granted by the appropriate Government, and the rules of the Union provide for the following matters:

1. The name of the Trade Union.
2. The whole of the objects for which the Trade Union has been established.
3. The whole of the purposes for which the general funds of the Trade Union shall be applicable, all of which purposes shall be purposes to which such funds are all fully applicable under this Act.
4. The admission of ordinary members who shall be persons actually engaged or employed in an industry with which the Trade Union is connected, and also the admission of the number of honorary or temporary members as officers required under Sec. 22 to form the executive of the Trade Union.
5. The maintenance of a list of members of the Trade Union and adequate facilities for the inspection thereof by the office-bearers and members of the Trade Union.
6. The payment of a subscription by members of the Trade Union which shall be not less than 25 paise per month per member.
7. The conditions under which any member shall be entitled to any benefit assured by the rules and under which any fine or forfeiture may be imposed on the members.
8. The manner in which the rules shall be amended, varied or rescinded.
9. The manner in which the members of the executive and the office-bearers of the Trade Union shall be appointed and removed.
10. The safe custody of the funds of the Trade Union, and annual audit in such manner as may be prescribed, of the accounts thereof, and adequate facilities for the inspection of the account books by the office-bearers and members of the Trade Union.
11. The manner in which the Trade Union may be dissolved (Sec. 6).

Name

The name to be adopted and registered must not be similar to that of any existing Trade Union (Sec. 7). Any Trade Union may, with the consent of not less than two-thirds of the total number of its members, change its name (Sec. 23). Notice in writing of every change of name, signed by the Secretary and by seven members of the Trade Union changing its name, shall be sent to the Registrar, who will register the change if the proposed name is neither identical nor resembles with the name of any existing Trade Union (Sec. 25).

Certificate of Registration

The Registrar, on being satisfied that the Trade Union has complied with all the requirements of the Act in regard to registration; shall register the Trade Union (S. 8). On registering the Trade Union, the Registrar shall issue a certificate of registration in the prescribed form which will be conclusive evidence of the fact that the said Trade Union has been duly registered (S. 9).

Cancellation of Registration

The Registrar of Trade Unions is authorised to withdraw or cancel registration of a Trade Union on the application of the Union itself, or if he is satisfied that a certificate has been obtained by fraud or mistake, or the Trade Union has ceased to exist or if any Union has wilfully and after notice from the Registrar contravened any provision of the Act, or allowed any rule to continue in force which is inconsistent with any such provision, or has rescinded any rule which is required by the Act. But before the cancellation of registration, on grounds other than application of the Union itself, the Registrar is required to give two months' previous notice stating grounds for proposed cancellation (S. 10).

Appeal

Any person aggrieved by any refusal of the Registrar to register a Union, or by cancellation of certificate can prefer an appeal to the High Court if the head office of the Union is in a Presidency Town, or to such Court as the appropriate Governments may appoint in other cases. The final appellate authority is the High Court in all cases (S. 11).

Minor Members

Any person who has attained the age of fifteen years may be a member of a registered Trade Union subject to any rules of the Trade Union to the contrary, and may, subject as aforesaid, enjoy all the rights of a member and execute all instruments and give all acquittances necessary to be executed or given under the rules.

Office Bearers

Not less than one-half of the total number of the office-bearers of every registered Trade Union 'shall be persons actually engaged or employed in an industry with which the Trade Union is connected. The appropriate Government may, however, by special or general order, exempt any Trade Union or class of Trade Unions from the application of this rule (S. 22).

But no person can be chosen as, and be, a member of the executive or any other office-bearer of a registered Trade Union if—

(a) he has not attained the age of 18 years :

(b) he has been convicted by a Court in India of any offence involving moral turpitude and sentenced to imprisonment, unless a period of 5 years has elapsed since his release (Sec. 21 A).

Registered Office

All communications and notices to a registered Trade Union may be addressed to its registered office. Any change in the address of the head office must be communicated within 14 days of such change to the Registration will record it in the register maintained by him (Sec. 12).

Incorporation

Every registered Trade Union shall be a body corporate by the name under which it is registered, and shall have perpetual succession and a common seal with power to acquire and hold movable and immovable properly and to contract, and shall by the said name sue and be sued (S. 13).

RIGHTS AND PRIVILEGES OF A REGISTERED TRADE UNION

The Act grants immunity to office-bearers and members of a registered Trade Union against criminal proceedings in respect of any agreements for the purpose of furthering any legal objects of the Union, but not in respect of an agreement to commit an offence (S. 17). Immunity has also been granted from civil suits in respect of any act done in contemplation or furtherance of trade dispute on the ground that such act induces some other persons to break a contract of employment or that it is an interference with the trade, business or employment of some other person.

A registered Union cannot be sued in respect of any tortious acts of its agents if committed without the knowledge of, or contrary to the express instructions given by the executive of the Union (S. 18). But no immunity is granted for any act of deliberate trespass.

An agreement between the members of a registered Trade Union is not void or voidable mere by reason of the fact that any of the objects of the agreement is in restraint of trade. But this does not apply to an agreement between members of a Trade Union for the sale of goods, business transactions, work, or employment (S. 19).

Minors, who have attained the age of 15 years are eligible to become members of a Trade Union, unless its rules prohibit their entrance; but they cannot become office -bearers in any case. To become an office-bearer of a Trade Union a person must have attained the age of 18 Years (S. 21).

FUNDS OF THE TRADE UNION

The Act limits the expenditure of general funds of a registered Trade Union to objects specified in Section 15, namely :—

(a) the payment of salaries, allowances and expenses to office- bearers of the Trade Union: _

(b) the payment of expenses for the administration of the Trade Union, including audit of the account of the general funds of the Union;

(c) the prosecution or defence of any legal proceedings to which the Union or any member thereof is a party, when such prosecution or defence is undertaken for the purpose of securing or protecting any right of the Trade Union as such or any right may out of the relations of any member with his employer or with a person whom the company employs;

(d) the conduct of trade disputes on behalf of the Trade Union or any member thereof;

(e) the compensation of members for loss arising out of trade disputes;

(f) allowances to members or their dependants on account of death, old age, sickness, accidents or unemployment of such members;

(g) The issue of, or the undertaking of liability under policies of assurance on the lives of members, or under policies insuring members against sickness, accident or unemployment;

(h) the provision of educational, social or religious benefits for members (includ-ing the payment of the expenses of funeral or religious ceremonies for deceased members) or for the dependants of members;

(i) the upkeep of a periodical published mainly for the purpose of discussing questions affecting employers or workmen as such;

(j) the payment, in furtherance of any of the objects on which the general funds of the Trade Union may be spent, or contributions to any cause intended to benefit workmen in general: provided that the expenditure in respect of such contributions in. any financial year shall not at any time during that year be in excess of one-fourth of the combined total of the gross income which has up to that time accrued to the general funds of the Trade Union during that year and of the balance at the credit of those funds at the commencement of the year; and

(k) subject to any condition contained in the notification, any other object notified by the appropriate government in the Official Gazette.

SEPARATE FUND FOR POLITICAL PURPOSES

Sec. 16 provides that registered Trade Union may constitute a separate fund, from contributions separately levied for or made to that fund, from which payments may be made, for the promotion of the civic and political interests of its members, in furtherance of any of the objects specified below, namely :—

(a) the payment of any expenses incurred, either directly or indirectly, by a candidate or prospective candidate for election as a member of any legislative body constituted under the Constitution of India, or of any local authority, before, during or after the election in connection with his candidature or election; or

(b) the holding of any meeting or the distribution of any literature or documents in support of any such candidate or prospective candidate; or

(c) the maintenance of any person who is member of any legislative body constituted under the Constitution of India, or of any local authority; or

(d) the registration of electors or the selection of a candidate for any legislative body constituted under the Constitution of India or of a candidate for any local authority; or

(e) the holding of political meetings of any kind, or the distribution of political literature or political documents of any kind.

No member shall be compelled to contribute to the fund constituted for political purposes; and a member who does not contribute to the said fund shall not be excluded from any benefits of the Trade Union, or placed in any respect either directly or indirectly under any disability or at any disadvantage as compared with other members of the Trade Union (except in relation to the control or management of the said fund) by reason of his not contributing to the said fund and contribution to the said fund shall not be made a condition for admission to the Trade Union.

AMALGAMATION OF TRADE UNIONS

Any two or more registered Trade Unions may become amalgamated togehter as one Trade Union with or without dissolution or division of the funds of such Trade Unions or either or any of them: provided that the votes of at least one-half of the members of each and every such Trade Union entitled to vote are recorded, and that at least 60 per cent of the votes recorded are in favour of the proposal. Notice in writing, signed by the Secretary and by seven members of each and every Trade Union which is party thereto, shall be sent to the Registrar, and where the head office of the amalgamated Trade Union is situated in a different State, to the Registrar of such State. The Registrar of the State in which the head office of the amalgamated Trade Union is situated shall, if he is satisfied that the provisions of this Act in respect of amalgamation have been complied with, register the Trade Union and the amalgamation of two or more registered Trade Unions shall not prejudice any right of any of such Trade Unions or any right of a creditor of any of them (Secs 21 -26).

BOOKS AND RETURNS

The books of account of a registered Trade Union and its list of members shall be open to inspection by any officer or member of the Trade Union at such times as may be provided for in the rules. A statement, audited in the prescribed manner, of all receipts and expenditure during the year ending on the 31st day of December shall be sent annually to the Registrar. Any changes made in the rules of the Trade Union during the year and all changes of office-bearer, during this period must also accompany this statement. A copy of every alteration made in the rules must be sent to the Registrar within 15 days of such alteration. The Registrar or any officer authorised by him by general or special order may at all reasonable tines inspect the certificate of registration, account books, registers and other documents relating to a Trade Union, at its registered office or may require their production at such place as he may specify, but that place must not be at a distance of more than 10 miles from the registered office of the Trade Union.

PENALTIES

Failure to Submit Returns (Sec. 31)

1. If default is made on the part of any registered or recognised Trade Union in giving any notice or sending any statement, return or other document as required by or under any provision of this Act, every officer or other person bound by the rules of the Trade Union to give or send the same or, if there is no such officer or person, every member of the executive of the Trade Union, shall be punishable with fine which may extend to ₹ 5 and, in the case of a continuing default, with an additional fine which may extend to ₹ 5 for each week after the first during which the default continues: provided the aggregate fine shall not exceed ₹ 50.

2. Any person who wilfully makes or causes to be made, any false entry in, or any omission from the general statement required by Sec. 28, or in or from any copy of rules or of alteration of rules sent to the Regislerr under that Section or in or from any retain referred to in Sec. 28 shall be punishable with fine which may extend to ₹ 500.

3. Sec. 32 provides that any person who with intent to deceive, gives to any member of a registered Trade Union or to any person intending or applying to become a member of such Trade Union any document purporting to be a copy of the rules of the Trade Union or of any alterations to the same which he knows, or has reason to believe, is not a correct copy of such rules or alterations as are for the time being in force, or any person who with the like intent, gives a copy of any rules of an unregistered Trade Union to any person on the pretence that such rules are the rules of a registered Trade Union, shall be punishable with fine which may extend to ₹ 200.

Sec. 33 provides that no court inferior to that of a Presidency Magistrate or a Magistrate of the first class shall try any offence under this Act.

DISSOLUTION

1. When a registered Trade Union is dissolved, notice of the dissolution signed by seven members and by the Secretary of the Trade Union shall, within 14 days of the dissolution, be sent to the Registrar, and shall be registered by him if he is satisfied that the dissolution has been effected in accordance with the rules of the Trade Union, and the dissolution shall have effect from the date of such registration.

2. Where the dissolution of a registered Trade Union has been registered and the rules of the Union do not provide for the distribution of funds of the Union on dissolution, the Registrar shall divide the funds amongst the members in such manner as may be prescribed.

Regulation 11 of the Central Trade Union Regulations, 1938, provides that where it is necessary for the Registrar to distribute the funds of a Trade Union which has been dissolved, he shall divide the funds in proportion to the amounts contributed by the members by way of subscription during their membership.

CHAPTER 20

The Payment of Wages Act, 1936

(No. IV of 1936)

Application and Scope (Sec. 1)

The Act applies only to the payment of wages to persons receiving less than ₹ 1,000 per mensem. It applies to the payment of wages to persons employed in any factory and to persons employed (otherwise than in a factory) on any railway by a railway administration or either directly or through a subcontractor, by a person fulfilling a contract with a railway administration to coal-mines and plantations, as well as to establishments in which work relating to the construction, development or maintenance of buildings, roads, bridges, canals, or relating to operations connected with navigation, irrigation or the supply of water, or relating to generation, transmission and distribution of electricity or any other form of power is carried on. The State Governments are, however, authorised to extend all or any of the provisions of the Act to any industrial establishment. But it cannot do so in relation to any industrial establishment owned by the Central Government with objects not confined to one State, without consulting the Central Government.

Definitions (Sec. 2)

For the purpose of this Act—

(a) **industrial establishment** means any tramway or motor omnibus service; air transport service; dock, wharf or jetty, inland vessel mechanically propelled; mine, quarry or oilfield; plantation; workshop or other establishment in which articles are produced, adapted or manufactured with a view to their use, transport or sale; estab-lishment in which any work relating to the construction, development or maintenance of buildings, roads, bridges or canals, or relating to operations connected with navigation, irrigation or the supply of water, or relating to the generation, transmission and distribution of electricity or any other form of power is being carried on;

(b) **wages** means all remunerations (whether by way of salary, allowance or otherwise) expressed in terms of money or capable of being so expressed which would, if the terms of employment, express or implied, were fulfilled, be payable to a person employed in respect of his employment or of work done in such employment, and include—

(a) any remuneration payable under any award or settlement between the parties or order of a Court;

(b) any remuneration to which the person employed is entitled in respect of overtime work or holidays or any leave period;

(c) any additional remuneration payable under the terms of employment (whether called a bonus or by any other name);

(d) any sum by reason of the termination of employment of the person employed is payable under any law, contract or instrument which provides for the payment of such sum, whether with or without deductions, but does not provide for the time within which the payment is to be made;

(e) any sum to which the person employed is entitled under any scheme framed under any law for the time being in force;

but does not include—

1. Any bonus (whether under a scheme of profit sharing or otherwise) which does not form part of the remuneration payable under terms of employment or which is not payable under any award or settlement between the parties or order of a Court;

2. The value of any house accommodation, or of the supply of light, water, medical attendance or other amenity or of any service excluded from the computation of wages by a general or special order of the State Government;

3. Any contribution paid by the employer to any pension or provident fund, and the interest which may have accrued thereon;

4. Any travelling allowance or the value of any travelling concession;

5. Any sum paid to the employed person to defray special expenses entailed on him by the nature of his employment; or

6. Any gratuity payable on the determination of employment in cases other than those specified in sub-clause (d).

Responsibility for Payment of Wages (Sec. 3)

The responsibility for payment of wages to workmen is primarily that of the employer. In the case of factories, the manager; in industrial establishments, the person responsible to employer for supervision and control of the establishment; and upon railways, the person nominated by the railway administration on this behalf for the local area, shall be responsible for such payment. In respect of contractors, the intention of the Act is that the contractor should be responsible for payment where he undertakes actual work for the principal employer, and is in charge of the labour and that the principal employer or his manager shall be responsible where the contractor merely contracts for the supply of labour to the employer.

Wage-periods (Sec. 4)

Every person responsible for the payment of wages must fix wage-periods in respect of which wages shall be payable, and see that no wage-period exceeds one month in any case. The penalty for contravention of this provision is fine extending to ₹ 200.

Time of Payment of Wages (Secs. 5,6)

In regard to the time of payment of wages the following rules must be observed:—

1. In the case of undertakings employing less than one thousand persons wages must be paid before the expiry of the seventh day, and in other cases before the expiry of the tenth day, after the last day of the wage-period in respect of which the wages are payable. In the case of persons employed on a dock, wharf or jetty or in mine, the balance of wages found due on completion of the final tonnage account of the ship or wagons loaded or unloaded, as the case may be, shall be paid before the expiry of the seventh day from the day of such completion.

2. A discharged worker must be paid his wages before the expiry of the second working day from the day on which his employment is terminated.

3. All payments of wages must be made on a working day (Sec. 5). Penalty for contravention is fine up to ₹ 500.

4. All wages must be paid in current coin or currency notes or in both or with the written authorisation of the employed person, wages may be paid by cheque or by crediting the wages in his bank account (Sec. 6). Penalty for contravention is fine up to ₹ 200.

Deductions which may be made from Wages (Sec. 7)

It is laid down in this Section that notwithstanding the provisions of Sec. 47(2) of the Indian Railways Act, 1890, the wages of employed person shall be paid to him without deductions of any kind except those authorised by or under this Act Sec. 47(2) of the Indian Railways Act provides for fine or forfeiture of one month's pay for breach of rules made under that Section. According to Sec. 7 of the present Act, no such deduction can be made in respect of any railway worker whose monthly wages do not amount to ₹ 1,000 or more.

Every payment made by the employed person to the employer or his agent shall be deemed to be a deduction from wages.

Any loss of wages resulting from the imposition, for good and sufficient cause, upon a person employed of any of the following penalties, namely—

   (i) the withholding of increment or promotion (including the stoppage of increment of an efficiency bar);

   (ii) the reduction to a lower post or time-scale or to a lower stage in a time-scale; or

   (iii) suspension;

shall not be deemed to be a deduction from wages in any case where the rules framed by the employer for the imposition of such penalty are in conformity with the require-ments as specified by the State Government.

Deductions from the wages of an employed person shall be made only in accordance with the provisions of this Act, and may be of the following kinds only: (1) fines; (2) for absence from duty; (3) for damages or loss; (4) for house accommodation; (5) for amenities and services; (6) on account of advances which the employer is compelled to make, including advances for travelling allowance or conveyance allowance, or for adjustment of over-payment of wages; (7) on account of payments to certain provident funds, to cooperative societies, or premium for life insurance; (8) for recovery of loans made from any fund constituted for the welfare of labour; for recovery of loans granted for house-building; (9) for income-tax payable by the employed person; (10) under an order of a Court; (11) for payment to cooperative societies; (12) made with the written authority of the worker in furtherance of any War Savings scheme approved by the State Government for the purchase of securities of the Government of India; (13) for payment of insurance prremia; (14) for recovery of losses sustained by a railway administration on account of acceptance by the employed person of counterfeit or base coins, mutilated or forged currency notes; (15) other losses sustained by a railway administration through the negligence of an employed person.

The total amount of deductions which may be made in any wage-period from the wages of any employed person shall not exceed—

   (i) in cases where such deductions are wholly or partly made for payment to cooperative societies, 75 per cent of such wages; and

   (ii) in any other case, 50 per cent of such wages.

Fines (Sec. 8)

The following rules apply to deductions by way of fines—

1. Fines can be imposed only for acts and omissions specified in notices approved by the State Government, or the Chief Inspector of Factories, in the case of factories, or the Supervisor in other cases.

2. No fine can be imposed on any employed person unless he has been given an opportunity of showing cause against the fine.

3. No fine can be imposed on any employed person who is under the age of 15 years.

4. The total amount of fine which may be imposed in any wage-period on any employed person must not exceed an amount equal to *half-an-anna* in the rupee of the wages payable to him in respect of that wage-period.

5. The fine shall be deemed to have been imposed on the day of the act or omission in respect of which it was imposed and cannot be recovered from the person by instalments or after the expiry of 60 days from the day on which it was imposed.

6. All the fines so recovered or realised must be recorded in a prescribed register and must be credited to a fine fund.

7. The proceeds of the fine fund must be utilised only for such purposes beneficial to the workers of the factory or the establishment as are approved by the prescribed authority. Penalty for contravention of any of these rules is fine up to ₹ 500.

Deductions for Absence from Duty (Sec. 9)

Deductions for absence from duty are permitted but the amount of such deductions cannot exceed the sum which the person would have been entitled to if he had worked the same number of days for which the deduction is made; provided that, subject to any rules made in this behalf by the State Government, if ten or more employed persons acting in concert absent themselves, without due notice and without reasonable cause, such deduction from any such person may include such amount not exceeding his wages for 8 days as nay by any such terms be due to the employer *in lieu* of the due notice. By an amending Act of 1937 employers are permitted to withhold wages in the case of "stay-in" strikes. Penalty for contravention is fine up to ₹ 500.

Deductions for Damage or Loss (Sec. 10)

Deductions for damage to or loss of goods expressly entrusted to the employed person for custody, or for loss of money for which he is required to account are permitted only where such damage or loss is directly attributable to his neglect or default, and only after he has been given an opportunity of showing cause against the deduction. Such deductions are not to exceed the amount of the damage or loss to the employer and must be recorded in a prescribed register. Penalty for contravention is fine up to ₹ 500.

Deduction for Services Rendered (Sec. 11)

Deductions for house accommodation and for amenities and services rendered by the employer are permitted, but only when an employed person has accepted the house accommodation, amenity or service as a term of employment or otherwise, and shall not exceed an amount equivalent to their value. Furthermore, the deductions in respect of amenities and services can be made subject only to the following conditions:

1. The approval of the Chief Inspector of Factories shall be obtained in writing to compulsory or general deductions from wages for any amenities or services provided by the employer.

2. The kind and standard of services and amenities provided shall be subject to the approval of the Chief Inspector of Factories.

3. The maximum deduction shall not exceed half the wages at any period. Penalty for the contravention of any provisions of this Section is fine up to ₹500.

The house accommodation, for which deductions are now allowed, may be supplied by the employer or by Government or by any housing board set up under law, e.g., under the Subsidised Indus trial Housing Scheme (whether the Government or the board is the employer or not) or any other authority engaged in the business of subsidising house-accommodation.

Deductions for Recovery of Advances (Sec. 12)

Deductions for recovery of advances or for adjustment of over-payments of wages can be made only on the following conditions :—

1. An advance of money made before employment must be recovered from the first payment of wages, but advances given for travelling expenses can in no case be recovered.

2. Advances of wages not already earned are subject to rules made by State Governments, which are as follows :—

(i) an advance of wages not already earned shall not, without the previous permission of an Inspector, exceed an amount equivalent to the wages earned by the employed person during the preceding two

(Mumbai four) calendar months, or if he has not been employed for that period, twice the wages he is likely to earn during the two (Mumbai four) subsequent calendar months;

(ii) the advance may be recovered in instalments by deductions from wages spread over not more than twelve (Mumbai eighteen) months. No instalment shall exceed one-third, or where the wages of any wage-period are not more than twenty rupees, one-fourth of the wages for the wage-period in respect of which the deduction is made;

(iii) the amounts of all advances sanctioned and the payments thereof shall be entered in a prescribed register;

(iv) (Mumbai only) the rate of interest charged for advances granted shall not exceed 6 per cent per annum.

Penalty for contravention is fine up to ₹ 500.

Other Deductions Permitted by the Act

The Act also permits the following deductions from the wages of an employee:
1. Deductions of income-tax payable by the employed person;
2. Deductions required to be made by order of a Court or other competent authority;
3. Deductions for contribution to and repayment of advance from any recognised or approved fund;
4. Deductions, made with the written authorisation of the employee for payment of any premium on his life insurance policy to the Life Insurance Corporation of India, or for the purchase of securities of the Government of India or of any State Government or for being deposited in any Post Office Saving Bank in furtherance of any savings scheme of any such Government;
5. Deductions, made with the written authorisation of the employed person, for contribution to the Prime Minister's National Relief Fund or to such other Fund as the Central Government may, by notification in the Official Gazette, specify.

Penalty for contravention is fine up to ₹ 500.

The administration and enforcement of the Act is the responsibility of the State Inspectors of Factories in the case of factories within their local limits, and that of the Chief Labour Commissioner (Central) in the case of persons employed on railway (other than in railway factories). The Inspector or the Labour Commissioner may, at all reasonable hours, enter on any premises, and make such examination of register or document relating to the calculation and payment of wages, and take on the spot otherwise such evidence of any person, and exercise such other powers of inspection, as he may deem necessary for carrying out the purpose of this Act (Sec. 14).

Claims for Wrongful Deductions (Sec. 15)

The State Government may either appoint a presiding officer of any Labour Court or Industrial Tribunal or a Commissioner for Workmen's Compensation or other Officer with judicial experience (Civil Judge or magistrate) to hear and decide all claims arising out of deductions from the wages, and delay in payment of wages.

Where any wrongful deductions have been made from the wages of a person, or any payment of wages has been delayed, such person himself, or any legal practitioner of any official of a registered trade union authorised in writing to act on his behalf, or any Inspector under this Act, or any other person acting with the permission or the authority may, within twelve months of the date of deduction or the date on which the payment of wages was due, apply to the authority for a direction. An application presented after the expiry of twelve months may be admitted by the authority for sufficient cause.

On admitting the application, the authority will give an opportunity to the applicant and the employer or any person responsible for the payment of wages to be heard, and on being satisfied, direct the employer or the other person to pay to the claimant the amount wrongfully withheld *plus* compensation up to ten times that sum in the case of education, and not exceeding ₹ 25 per head in the case of delay. But the payment of compensation for delayed wages will not be ordered if the delay was due to—

(a) *bona fide* error or *bona fide* dispute as to the amount payable to the employee; or
(b) the occurrence of an emergency or the existence of exceptional circumstances, such that the person responsible for the payment of the wages was unable, though exercising reasonable diligence, to make prompt payment; or
(c) the failure of the employed person to apply for or accept payment.

An amount directed to be paid by the employer to the employed person may be recovered as if it were a fine imposed by a magistrate.

The authority may refuse to entertain the application, if after giving the applicant an opportunity to be heard, the authority is satisfied that—

(a) the applicant is not entitled to present an application; or
(b) the delay in payment of wages was excusable, as provided above; or
(c) the applicant shows no sufficient cause for making a direction for payment; or
(d) the application is insufficiently stamped or is otherwise incomplete.

If the authority hearing the application is satisfied that it was either malicious or vexatious, the authority may direct the applicant to pay a penalty not exceeding ₹ 50 to the employer.

An appeal, against an order or direction of the authority, can be preferred within 30 days of such order before a court of Small Causes in a Presidency town, and before the District Court elsewhere.

Sec. 22 provides that persons coining under the Act shall be limited to its procedure in respect of the recovery of unpaid wages or wrongful deductions. In consequence, no Court shall entertain any suit for the recovery of wages or of any deduction from wages, a claim for which could be made under Sec. 15 of this Act.

The Act prohibits contracting out agreements. Sec. 23 provides that any contract or agreement, whether made before or after the commencement of this Act, whereby an employed person relinquishes any right conferred by this Act shall be null and void in so far as it purports to deprive him of such right.

Sec. 25 provides that the person responsible for the payment of wages to persons employed in a factory shall cause to be displayed in such factory a notice containing such abstracts of this Act and of the rules made thereunder in English and in the language of the majority of the persons employed in the factory, as may be prescribed. Penalty for contravention of this Section is fine extending to ₹ 200.

The Act provides penalties for the contravention of its various provisions, but Sec. 21 lays down that no prosecution can be instituted unless a successful claim has been made under the Act or unless the authority or the appellate Court considers a prosecution to be warranted.

CHAPTER
21

The Industrial Dispute Act, 1947

The Act came into force on April, 1947 and extends to the whole of India. The purpose of the Act is to provide machinery for a just and equitable settlement by adjudication by independent Tribunals, by negotiations and by conciliation of industrial disputes. The Supreme Court laid down in the case of *Workmen of Dimakuchi Tea Estate* v. *Dimakuchi Tea Estate,* 1950 S.C. 353, the following objectives of the Act, namely:—

(i) Promotion of measures for securing and preserving amity and good relations between employer and workmen.

(ii) An investigation and settlement of industrial disputes between employers and employers, employers and workmen, or workmen and workmen, with a right of representation by registered trade union or federation of trade unions or an association of employers or a federation of association of employers.

(iii) Prevention of illegal strikes and lockouts.

(iv) Relief to workmen in the matter of layoff and retrenchment

(v) Promotion of Collective bargaining.

Definitions (Sec. 2)

1. **appropriate Government** [2(a)] Means —

(i) the Central Government in relation to industrial dispute concerning any of the following:

(a) any industry carried on by or under the authority of the Central Government, or by a railway company;

(b) any such controlled industry as may be specified by the Central Government;

(c) a Dock Labour Board; or

(d) the Industrial Finance Corporation of India; or

(e) the Employees' State Insurance Corporation; or

(f) the Board of Trustees constituted under Sec. 3A of the Coal Mines Provident Fund and Miscellaneous Provisions Act, 1942;

(g) the Central Board of Trustees and State Board of Trustees constituted under Section 5 A and Section 5B, respectively of the Employees' Provident Fund and Miscellaneous Provisions Act, 1952; or

(h) the Indian Airlines and Air India Corporations; or

(i) the Life Insurance Corporation of India; or

(j) the Oil and Natural Gas Commission; or

(k) the Deposit Insurance and Credit Guarantee Corporation; or

(1) the Central Warehousing Corporation; or

(m) the Unit Trust of India, or

546

    (n) the Food Corporation of India, or

    (o) the International Airports Authority of India, or

    (p) a Regional Rural Bank established under Sec. 3 of the Regional Rural Banks Act, 1976, or

    (q) the Export Credit and Guarantee Corporation Ltd.; or

    (r) the Industrial Reconstruction Bank of India Ltd.; or

    (s) the Banking Service Commission or a banking and an insurance company, or

    (t) a mine, an oilfield, a Cantonment Board or a major Port.

    (u) In relation to any other industrial dispute, the appropriate government means the State Government within whose territory the industrial dispute arises.

2. Average Pay [Sec. 2(aaa)]

Average pay in the case of a workman means—

    (i) in the case of monthly paid workman, the average of monthly wages payable in three Complete Calendar months;

    (ii) in the case of weekly paid workman, the average of the weekly wages payable in four complete weeks;

    (iii) in the case of daily paid workman, the average of the wages for twelve full working days;

provided that any of the foregoing periods shall be period preceding the date on which the average pay becomes payable, if the workman had worked during the said period, and where such calculation cannot be made, the average pay shall be calculated as the average of the wages payable to the workman during the period he actually worked.

3. Award means an interim or final determination of any industrial dispute or any question relating thereto by any Labour Court, Industrial Tribunal or National Tribunal and includes an arbitration award made under Section 10A.

4. Banking Company means a banking company as defined in Section 5 of the Banking Regulation Act, 1949, having branches or other establishments in more than one State, and includes the Export-Import Bank of India, the Industrial Reconstruction Bank of India, the Industrial Development Bank of India, the Reserve Bank of India, the State Bank of India, and its subsidiary banks, and Nationalised Banks.

5. Board means a Board of Conciliation constituted under this Act.

6. Conciliation Officer means a conciliation officer appointed under this Act.

7. Controlled Industry means any industry the control of which by the Union has been declared by any Central Act to be expedient in the public interest.

8. Court means a Court of Inquiry Constituted under this Act.

9. Employer means

    (i) in relation to an industry carried on by or under the authority of any department of Central Government or a State Government the authority prescribed in this behalf, or where no authority is prescribed, the head of the department;

    (ii) in relation to an industry carried on by or on behalf of a local authority, the Chief Executive officer of that authority.

This definition of an employer is neither exhaustive nor inclusive. The employer in relation to industries carried on by other authority or person will be construed in the ordinary sense.

In *Hussainbhai v. Alath Factory Tebzilai Union,* 1978 S.C. 1410, the Supreme Court observed that where a worker or group of workers labour to produce goods or services and those goods and services are for' the business of another, that other is, in fact, the employer.

10. Executive, in relation to a Trade Union, means the body by whatever name called to which the management of the affairs of the Trade Union is entrusted.

11. Independent. A person shall be deemed to be independent for the purpose of his appointment
• as the Chairman or other member of a Board, Court or Tribunal, if he is unconnected with the

industrial dispute referred to such Board, Court or Tribunal or with any industry directly affected by such dispute:

Provided that no person shall cease to be independent by reason only of the fact that he is a shareholder of an incorporated company which is connected with, or likely to be affected by, such industrial dispute; but in such a case, he shall disclose to the appropriate Government the nature and extent of the shares held by him in such company.

12. **Industry**[1] means any systematic activity carried on by cooperation between an employer and his workmen (whether such workmen are Employed by such employer directly or by or through any agency, including a contractor) for the production, supply or distribution of goods or services with a view to satisfy human wants or wishes (not being wants and wishes which are merely spiritual or religious in nature), whether or not, —

(i) any capital has been invested for the purpose of carrying on such activity; or

(ii) such activity is carried on with a motive to make any gain or profit;

and includes—

(a) any activity of the Dock Labour Board established under Sec. 5 A of the Dock Workers (Regulation of Employment) Act, 1948;

(b) any activity relating to the promotion of sales or business or both carried on by an establishment,

but does not include—

(1) any agricultural operation except when such agricultural operation is carried on in an integrated manner with any other activity (being any such activity as is referred to in the foregoing provisions of this clause) and such other activity is the predominant one.

Explanation—For the purpose of this sub-clause "agricultural operation" does not include any activity carried on in a plantation as defined in clause (0 of Section 2 of the Plantations Labour Act, 1951;

the term "industry" also does not include—

(2) hospitals or dispensaries; or (3) educational, scientific research or training institutions; or (4) institutions owned or managed by organizations wholly or substantially engaged in any charitable, social or philanthropic services; or (5) Khadi or Village industries; or (6) any activity of the Government relatable to the sovereign functions of the government including all the activities carried on by the departments of the Central Government dealing with defence research, atomic energy and space; or (7) any domestic services; or (8) any activity, being a profession practised by an individual or body of individuals, if the number of persons employed by the individual or body of individuals in relation to such profession is less than ten; or (9) any activity, being an activity carried on by a cooperative society or a club or any other like body of individuals, if the number of persons employed by the cooperative society, club or other like body of individuals in relation to such activity is less than ten.

13. **Industrial dispute** means any dispute or difference between employers and employers, or between employers and workmen, or between workmen and workmen, which is connected with the employment or non-employment or the terms of employment or with the conditions of labour, of any person.

As the definition of "industrial dispute" speaks of a dispute between employer and workmen and not employer and workman, a single workman who is aggrieved by an action of the employer cannot raise an industrial dispute. Thus, before the insertion of Sec. 2A, which is also of limited application, an individual dispute could *not per se* be an industrial dispute, but it could become one if taken up by

---

1. This new definition of industry substituted by the Industrial Disputes (Amendment) Act, 1982, nullifies many decisions of the Supreme Court and High Courts.

the Trade Union or a number of workmen; it becomes an industrial dispute only when workmen as a body make common cause with the individual workman.

By virtue of Sec. 2A, when any employer discharges, dismisses, retrenches or otherwise terminates the services of an individual workman, any dispute or difference between that workman and his employer connected with, or arising out of, such discharge, dismissal retrenchment or termination shall be deemed to be an industrial dispute notwithstanding that no other workman nor any union of workmen is a party to the dispute.

As stated above, Sec. 2A has limited application. It does not declare all individual disputes to be industrial disputes. If the dispute or difference is connected with any matter other than those mentioned in the section, then it must be a collective dispute.

14. **Industrial establishment** or undertaking means an establishment or undertaking in which any industry is carried on :

Provided that where several activities are carried on in an establishment or undertaking and only one or some of such activities is or are an industry or industries, then—

  (a) If any unit of such establishment or undertaking carrying on any activity, being an industry, is severable from the other units of such establishment or under-taking, such unit shall be deemed to be a separate industrial establishment or undertaking;

  (b) If the predominant activity or each of the predominant activities carried on in such establishment or undertaking or any unit thereof is an industry and the other activity or each of the other activities carried on in such establishment or undertaking or unit thereof is not severable from and is, for the purpose of carrying on, or aiding the carrying on of, such predominant activity or activities, the entire establishment or undertaking or, as the case may be, unit thereof shall be deemed to be an industrial establishment or undertaking.

15. **Insurance Company** means a company defined in Sec. 2 of the Insurance Act, 1938 having branches or other establishments in more than one State.

Under the Insurance Act, an Insurance Company means any insurer being a company, association of partnership which may be wound up under the Companies Act, 1956, or to which the Partnership Act, 1932 applies.

16. **Khadi** has the meaning assigned to it in clause (d) of Sec .2 of the Khadi and Village Industries Commission Act, 1956.

17. **Labour Court** means a Labour Court constituted under Section 7 of the Act.

18. **Layoff** (with its grammatical variations and cognate expressions) means (a) the failure,

  (b) refusal, or

  (c) inability of the employer—

    (i) on account of shortage of coal, or

    (ii) Power, or

    (iii) raw materials, or

    (iv) the accumulation of stocks, or

    (v) the break down of machinery, or

    (vi) natural calamity, or

    (vii) for any other connected reason

to give employment to a workman whose name is borne on the muster rolls of his industrial establishment and who has not been retrenched.

A workman is deemed to be paid off for the day, if within 2 hours of the normal time, employment is not given to him.

However, if the workman instead of being given employment at the commencement of any shift for any day is asked to present himself for the purpose during the second half of the shift for the day and is given employment then be shall be deemed to have been laid off only for one half of that day.

In case, he is not given any employment even after so presenting himself, he shall not be deemed to have been laid off for the second half of the shift for the day and shall be entitled to full basic wages and dearness allowance for that part of the day.

19. **Lock-out** means the temporary closing of a place of employment, or the suspension of work, or the refusal by an employer to continue to employ any number of persons employed by him.

20. **Major Port** means a port as defined in clause (8) of Section 3 of the Indian Ports Act, 1903. As defined in this clause 'Major Port' means any port which the Central Government may by notification in the Official Gazette declare or may by any law for the time being in force have declared to be a major port.

21. **Mine** means a mine as defined in clause (f) of sub-section (1) of Section 2 of the Mines Act, 1952. As per this clause Mine means any excavation where any operation for the purpose of searching for or obtaining mineral has been or is being carried on, and includes, unless exempted by the Central Government by notification in the Official Gazette, any premises or part thereof on which any process ancillary to the getting, dressing or preparation for sale of mineral or of coke is being carried on.

22. **National Tribunal** means a National Industrial Tribunal constituted under Section 7B of the Act

23. **Public Utility Service** means—

  (i) any railway service;

  (ii) any transport service for the carriage of passengers or goods by air;

  (iii) any service in or in connection with the working of any major port or dock;

  (iv) any section of an industrial establishment, on the working of which the safety of the establishment or the workmen employed therein depends;

  (v) any postal telegraph or telephone service;

  (vi) any industry which supplies power, light or water to the public;

  (vii) any industry specified in the First Schedule which the appropriate government may, if satisfied that public emergency or public interest so requires, by notification in the Official Gazette declare to be a public utility service for the purpose of this Act, for such period as may be specified in the notification. However, the period specified is not, in the first instance, to exceed 6 months, but may be extended from time to time by any period not exceeding 6 months at any time, if in the opinion of the appropriate governments public emergency or public interest requires such extension.

The following 20 industries are mentioned in the First Schedule:

1. Transport (other than railways) for the carriage of passengers or goods by land or water. 2. Banking. 3. Cement. 4. Coal. 5. Gotten Textiles. 6. Foodstuff. 7. Iron and Steel. 8. Defence Establishments. 9. Service in Hospitals and Dispensaries. 10. Fire Brigade Service. 11. India Government Mints. 12. India Security Press. 13. Copper Mining. 14. Lead Mining IS. Zinc Mining. 16. Iron Ore Mining. 17. Service in Oil fields. 18. Service in Uranium Industry. 19. Pyrites Mining. 20. Security Paper Mill, Hoshangabad.

24. **Retrenchment** means the termination by the employer of the services of a workman for any reason whatsoever, otherwise than as a punishment inflicted by way of disciplinary action. It does not include—

  (i) voluntary retirement of the workman; voluntary resignation by the employee, is covered by the expression voluntary retirement. By accepting resignation the employer does not retrench the employee (*J.K. Cotton Spg. & Wvg. Mills. Co. Ltd.* v. *State of U.P.,* 1990 S.C. 1808), or

  (ii) retirement of the workman on reaching the age of superannuation in terms of contracts of employment, or

(iii) termination of the service of the workman as a result of the non-renewal of the contract of employment between the employer and the workman concerned, on its expiry, or of such contract being terminated under a stipulation in that behalf contained therein, or

(iv) termination of the service of a workman on the ground of continued ill-death.

25. **Settlement** means a settlement arrived at in the course of conciliation proceedings and includes a written agreement between the employer and workman arrived at otherwise than in the cause of conciliation proceedings where such agreement has been signed by the parties thereto in such manner as may be prescribed and a copy thereof has been sent to an officer authorised in this behalf by the appropriate government and the conciliation officer.

26. **Strike** means a cessation of work by a body of persons employed in any industry acting in combination or a concerted refusal, or a refusal under a common understanding of any number of persons who are or have been so employed to continue to work or to accept employment.

27. **Tribunal** means an Industrial Tribunal constituted under Section 7A and includes an Industrial Tribunal Constituted before the 10th day of March, 1957 under this Act.

Unfair Labour Practices [Sec. 2(ra)]

28. The definition of unfair Labour Practices was incorporated into the Act by the Amendment Act of 1982 and came into force with effect from 21st August, 1984. The term means any of the following practices on the part of employers and employees.

Unfair Labour Practices on the part of the employers and their Unions

The following labour practices on the part of employers and their unions are unfair, namely :-

1. To interfere with, restrain from, or coerce, workmen in the exercise of their rights to organise, form, join or assist a trade union or to engage in concerted activities for the purpose of collective bargaining or other mutual aid or protection, that is to say—
   (a) threatening workmen with discharge, dismissal, if they join trade union;
   (b) threatening a lockout or closure, if a trade union is organised;
   (c) granting wage increase to workmen at crucial periods of trade union organisation, with a view to undermining the efforts of the trade union at organisation.

2. To dominate, interfere with or contribute support, financial or otherwise, to any trade union, that is to say—
   (a) an employer taking an active interest in organising a trade union of his workmen; and
   (b) an employer showing partiality or granting favour to one of several trade unions attempting to organise his workmen or to its members where such a trade union is not a recognised trade union.

3. To establish employer-sponsored trade unions of workmen.

4. To encourage or discourage membership in any trade union by discriminating against any workman, that is to say—
   (a) discharging or punishing a workman because he urged other workmen to join or organised trade union;
   (b) discharging or dismissing a workman for taking part in any strike (not being a strike which is deemed to be an illegal strike under this Act);
   (c) changing seniority rating of a workman because of trade union activities;
   (d) refusing to promote workmen to higher posts on account of their trade union activities;
   (e) giving unmerited promotions to certain workmen with a view to creating discord amongst other workmen, or to undermine the strength of their trade union;
   (f) discharging office-bearers or active members of the trade union on accounf of their trade union activities.

5. To discharge or dismiss workmen;

(a) by way of victimisation;

(b) not in good faith, but in the colourable exercise of the employer's rights;

(c) by falsely implicating a workman in a criminal case on false evidence c. on concocted evidence;

(d) for patently fase reasons;

(e) on untrue and trumped up allegations of absence without leave;

(f) in utter disregard of the principles of natural justice in the conduct of domestic inquiry or with undue haste;

(g) for misconduct of a minor or technical character without having any regard to the nature of the particular misconduct or the past record or service of the workman, thereby leading to a disproportionate punishment.

6. To abolish the work of a regular nature being done by workmen, and to give such work to contractors as a measure of breaking a strike.

7. To transfer a workman *mala fide* from one place to another under the guise of following management policy.

8. To insist upon individual workmen who are on a legal strike to sign a good conduct bond, as a precondition to allowing them to resume work.

9. To show favouritism or partiality to one set of workers regardless of merit.

10. To employ workmen as "badlis", casuals or temporaries and to continue them as such for years, with the object of depriving them of the status and privileges of permanent workmen.

11. To discharge or discriminate against any workman for filing charges or testifying against an employer in any enquiry or proceeding relating to any industrial dispute.

12. To recruit workmen during a strike which is not an illegal strike.

13. Failure to implement award, settlement or agreement;

14. To indulge in acts of force or violence.

15. To refuse to bargain collectively, in good faith with the recognised trade unions.

16. Proposing or continuing a lockout deemed to be illegal under this Act

Unfair Trade Practices on the Part of Workmen and their Unions include:

(1) To advise or actively support or instigate any strike deemed to be illegal under this Act.

(2) To coerce workmen in the exercise of their right to self- organisation or to join a trade union or refrain from joining any trade union, that is to say—

(a) for trade union or its members to picketing in such a manner that non-striking workmen are physically debarred from entering the work place;

(b) to indulge in acts of force or violence or hold out threats of intimidation in connection with a strike against non-striking workmen or against managerial staff.

(3) For a recognised trade union to refuse to bargain collectively in good faith with the employer.

(4) To indulge in coercive activities against certification of a bargaining representative.

(5) To stage, encourage or instigate such forms of coercive actions as wilful "go slow", squating on the work premises after working hours or "gherao" of any of the members of the managerial or other staff.

(6) To stage demonstration at the residence of the managerial staff members.

(7) To incite or indulge in wilful damage to employer's property connected with the industry.

(8) To indulge in acts of force or violence or to hold out threats of intimidation against any workman with a view to prevent him from attending work.

29. **Wages** means all remuneration capable of being expressed in terms of money, which would, if the terms of employment express or implied, were fulfilled be payable to a workman in respect of his employment or work done in such employment, and includes—

(i) such allowances (including dearness allowances) as the workman is for the time being entitled to;

(ii) the value of any house accommodation, or of supply of light, water, medical attendance or other amenity or of any service or any concessional supply of foodgrains or other articles;

(iii) any travelling concession;

(iv) any commission payable on the promotion of sales or business or both.

But the term "wages" does not include—

(a) any bonus;

(b) any contribution paid or payable by the employer to any pension fund or provident fund or for the benefit of the workmen under any law for the time being in force;

(c) any gratuity payable on the termination of his service.

30. **Workman** means any person (including an apprentice) employed in any industry to do any manual, unskilled, skilled, technical, operational, clerical or supervisory work for hire or reward, whether the terms of employment be express or implied. Furthermore, for the purposes of any proceedings, under this Act in relation to an industrial dispute, workman includes any such person who has been dismissed, discharged or retrenched in connection with or as a consequence of that dispute, or whose dismissal, discharge or retrenchment has led to that dispute.

However, workman does not include—

(i) any person who is subject to the Army Act, 1950, or Air force Act, 1950, or the Navy (Disputes) Act, 1934; or

(ii) any person who is employed in the police service or as an officer or other employee of a prison; or

(iii) any person who is employed mainly in a managerial or administrative capacity; or

(iv) any person who is employed in a supervisory capacity and drawing wages exceeding ₹ 1600 per month,

(v) any supervisor who exercises, either by the nature of the duties attached to the office or by reason of the powers vested in him, functions mainly of a managerial nature.

It should be noted that the definition of workman presupposes the relationship of master and servant. Consequently, an independent contractor is not covered by the definition of workman.

AUTHORITIES UNDER THE ACT

Works Committee (Sec. 3)

In the case of an industrial establishment in which 100 or more workmen are employed or have been employed on any day in the preceding 12 months, the appropriate Government may by general or special order require the employer to constitute a Works Committee consisting of representatives of employers and workmen engaged in the establishment, the number of representatives of workmen not being less than that of the representatives of the employers, and the representatives of the workmen to be chosen from among the workmen engaged in the establishment and in consultation with their trade union, if any. The duties of the Works Committee are to promote measures for securing and preserving amity and good relations between the employer and workmen and to comment upon matters of their interest or concern, and to endeavour to compose any material difference of opinion in respect to such matters.

Conciliation Officers (Sec. 4)

The appropriate Government may by notification in the Official Gazette appoint conciliation officers for any specified area or for one or more specified industries, either permanently or for a limited period. Conciliation officers are charged with the duty of holding conciliatory proceedings for the purpose of bringing about a fair and amicable settlement of any industrial dispute.

Boards of Concilliation (Sec. 5)

The appropriate Government may, as occasion arises, by notification in the Official Gazette, constitute a Board of Conciliation for promoting the settlement of an industrial dispute. A Board shall consist of a Chairman and two or four other members. The Chairman shall be an independent person and the other members shall represent in equal number the parties to the dispute; and shall be appointed on the recommendation of the party they represent. The quorum for a meeting is two where the total number is three, and three where the number is five. A Board, having a quorum, may act notwithstanding the absence of the Chairman or any of its members, or any vacancy in its number. But if the Government informs the Board that the services of the Chairman or any other member have ceased to be available, the Board must not act until a new Chairman or member has been appointed.

Courts of Inquiry (Sec. 6)

The appropriate Government may, as occasion arises, by notification in the Official Gazette, constitute a Court of Inquiry for inquiring into any matter appearing to be connected with or relevant to an industrial dispute. Such a Court may consist of one or more independent persons, according as the Government may appoint. Where it consists of more than one member, one of them shall be appointed the Chairman. The Court having the prescribed quorum may act even if the Chairman or a member is absent; but not if the services of the Chairman have ceased to be available, and no other Chairman has been appointed. The Court shall inquire into the matters referred to it and report thereon to the appropriate Government within 6 months from the commencement of the inquiry.

Labour Courts (Sec.7)

The appropriate Government may, by notification in the Official Gazette, constitute one or more Labour Courts for the adjudication of industrial disputes relating to any of the following matters or for performing such other functions as may be assigned to them under the Act. The Labour Courts may adjudicate on a dispute relating to—

  (i) the propriety or legality of an order passed by an employer under standing orders;
  (ii) the application and interpretation of standing orders;
  (iii) discharge or dismissal of workmen including re-instatement of, or grant of relief to, workmen wrongfully dismissed;
  (iv) withdrawal of any customary concession or privilege;
  (v) illegality or otherwise of a strike or lockout; and
  (vi) all matters other than those reserved for the Industrial Tribunals.

A Labour Court shall consist of one person only to be appointed by the appropriate Government. But no person shall be appointed as Presiding Officer of a Labour Court, unless (a) he is, or has been a Judge of a High Court; or (b) he has for a period not less than 3 years been a District Judge or an Additional District Judge; or (c) he has held the office of Chairman or any other member of the Labour Appellate Tribunal, or of any Tribunal, for a period of not less than two years; or (d) he has held any judicial office in India for not less than seven years; or (e) he has been the Presiding Officer of a Labour Court constituted under any Provincial Act for not less than five years.

Industrial Tribunals (7A)

The appropriate Government may, by notification in the Official Gazette, constitute one or more Industrial Tribunals for the adjudication of industrial disputes relating to any matters specified above as in the case of Labour Courts, or the following matters, namely,—

  (i) Wages, including the period and mode of payment;
  (ii) Compensatory and other allowances;
  (iii) Hours of work and rest intervals;
  (iv) Leave with wages and holidays;

   (v) Bonus, profit sharing, provident fund and gratuity;
  (vi) Shift working otherwise than in accordance with standing orders;
 (vii) Classification by grades;
(viii) Rules of discipline;
  (ix) Ratinalisation;
   (x) Retrenchment of workmen and closure of establishment; and
  (xi) Any other matter that may be prescribed.

A Tribunal shall consist of one person only to be appointed by the appropriate Government. A person to be appointed a presiding officer of a Tribunal must be, or must have been, a Judge of a High Court; or must have held the office of the Chairman or any other member of the Labour Appellate Court, or of any Tribunal, for a period of not less than two years. The appropriate Government may also, if it so thinks fit, appoint two persons as assessors to advise the Tribunal in the proceeding before it.

National Tribunals (7B)

The Central Government may, by notification in the Official Gazette, constitute one or more National Industrial Tribunals for the adjudication of industrial disputes which, in the opinion of the Central Government, involve questions of national importance or are of such a nature that industrial establishments situated in more than one state are likely to be interested in, or affected by, such disputes. A National Tribunal shall consist of one person only to be appointed by the Central Government. To be qualified for appointment as a presiding officer of a National Tribunal, a person must be, or must have been, a Judge of a High Court, or must have held the office of the Chairman or any other member of the Labour Appellate Tribunal for at least 2 years. The Central Government may appoint two assessors to advise the National Tribunal.

Disqualifications (7C)

No person shall be appointed to, or continue in, the office of the presiding officer of a Labour Court, Industrial Tribunal or National Tribunal, if (a) he is not an independent person; or (b) he has attained the age of 65 years.

Filling of Vacancies (Sec. 8). If, for any reason a vacancy (other than a temporary absence) occurs in the office of the presiding officer of a Labour Court, Tribunal or National Tribunal or in the office of the Chairman or any other member of a Board or Court, then in the case of a National Tribunal, the Central] Government and in any other case, the appropriate Government, shall appoint another person in accordance with the provisions of this Act to fill the vacancy, and the proceedings may be continued before the Labour Court, Tribunal, National Tribunal, Board or Court, as the case may be, from the stage at which the vacancy is filled.

Section 9 provides that no order of the appropriate government or of the Centra: Government appointing any person as the Chairman or any other member of a Board or Court or as the presiding officer of a Labour Court, Tribunal or National Tribunal shall be called in question in any manner; and no act or proceeding before any Board or Court shall be called in question in any manner on the ground merely of the existence of any vacancy in or defect in the constitution of, such Board or Court Also, no settlement arrived at in the course of a conciliation proceeding shall be invalid by reason only of the fact that such settlement was arrived at after the expiry of the period fixed by the Act for submitting the report. And where the report of any settlement arrived at in the course of conciliation proceeding before a Board is signed by the Chairman and all the other members of the Board, no such settlement shall be invalid by reason only of the causal or unforeseen absence of any of the members (including the Chairman) of the Board during any stage of the proceeding.

Notice of Change (9A). Under this new provision, no employer, who proposes to effect any change in the conditions of service applicable to any workman in respect of the matters specified below, shall effect such change (a) without giving to the workman likely to be affected by such change a notice in the prescribed manner of the nature of the change to be effected; or (b) within 21 days of giving such notice: provided that no such notice shall be required for effecting any such change (i) where the change is effected in pursuance of any settlement, award or decision of the Labour Appellate Tribunal; or (ii) when the workmen likely to be affected by the change are persons to whom the Fundamental and Supplementary Rules, Civil Services (Temporary Services) Rules, Revised Leave Rules, Civil Services Regulations, Civilians in Defence Services (Classification, Control and Appeal) Rules or the Indian Railway Establishment Code or appropriate Government in the Official Gazette, apply.

Section 9B, however, provides that where the appropriate Government is of opinion that the application of the provisions of Sec. 9A to any class of industrial establishments or to any class of workmen employed therein affect the employees in relation thereto so prejudicially that such application may cause serious repercussion on the industry concerned and that public interest so requires, the appropriate Government may by notification in the Official Gazette, exempt that industrial establishment or workers from the application of the provisions.

REFERENCE OF DISPUTES TO BOARDS, COURTS OR TRIBUNALS

Section 10 lays down: (1) Where the appropriate Government is of opinion that any industrial dispute exists or is apprehended, it may at any time by order in writing,—

(a) refer the dispute to a Board for promoting a settlement thereof; or

(b) refer to any matter appearing to be connected with or relevant to the dispute to a Court of Inquiry; or

(c) refer to a Labour Court for adjudication of the dispute or any matter appearing to be connected with or relevant to the dispute, if it relates to any of the following matters:

(i)   the propriety or legality of an order passed by an employer under the standing orders;
(ii) the application and interpretation of standing orders;
(iii) discharge or dismissal of workmen including re-instatement of, or grant of relief to workmen wrongfully dismissed;
(iv) withdrawal of any customary concession or privilege;
(v)   illegality or otherwise of strike or lockout;
(vi) all matters other than those specified to be adjudicated by Industrial Tribunals;

(d) refer to a Tribunal for adjudication of the dispute or any matter appearing to be connected with or relevant to the dispute, whether it relates to any matter specified above in (c) or to any matters given hereafter, viz.,

(i)   wages, including the period and mode of payment;
(ii)   compensatory or other allowances;
(iii) hours of work and rest intervals;
(iv)   leave with wages and holidays;
(v)   bonus, profit sharing, provident fund and gratuity;
(vi)   shift working otherwise than in accordance with standing orders;
(vii) classification of grades;
(viii) rules of discipline;
(ix)   rationalisation;
(x)   retrenchment of workmen and closure of establishment; and
(xi)   any other matter that may be presented;

Provided that when the dispute relates to any of the above matters and is not likely to affect more than 100 workmen, the appropriate Government may make the reference to a Labour Court:

Provided further that when the dispute relates to a public utility service and notice under Sec. 22 has been given, the appropriate Government shall, unless it considers that the notice has been frivolously or vexatiously given or that it would be inexpedient so to do, may make a reference, notwithstanding that any other proceedings under this Act in respect of the dispute may have commenced.

1.A. When the Central Government is of opinion that any industrial dispute exists or is apprehended and the dispute involves any question of national importance or is of such a nature that the industrial establishments situated in more than one State are likely to be interested in or affected by such dispute and that the dispute should be adjudicated by a National Tribunal, then the Central Government may (whether or not it is the appropriate Government in relation to that dispute) at any time, by order in writing, refer the dispute or any matter appearing to be connected with, or relevant to, the dispute, whether it relates to any of the matters specified in (c) or (d) above, to a National Tribunal for adjudication.

2. Where the parties to an industrial dispute apply in the prescribed manner, whether jointly or separately, for a reference of the dispute to a Board, Court, Labour Court, Tribunal, or National Tribunal the appropriate Government may, if satisfied that the person applying represent the majority of each party, shall make the reference accordingly.

3. Where an industrial dispute has been referred to a Board or the Labour Court or the Tribunal or the National Tribunal under this Section the appropriate Government may by order prohibit the continuance of any strike or lockout in connection with such dispute which may be in existence on the date of the reference.

4. Where in an order referring an industrial dispute to a Labour Court, Tribunal or National Tribunal under this section or in a subsequent order, the appropriate Government has specified the points of dispute for adjudication, the Labour Court pr the Tribunal or National Tribunal as the case may be, shall confine its adjudication to those points.

5. Where a dispute concerning any establishment or establishments has been, or is to be, referred to a Labour Court, Tribunal or National Tribunal under this section and the appropriate Government is of opinion, whether on an application made to it in this behalf or otherwise, that the dispute is of such a nature that any other establishment, group or class of establishments of a similar nature is likely to be interested in, or affected by such dispute, the appropriate Government may at the time of making the reference or at any time thereafter but before submission of the award, by order in writing include in that reference such establishments whether or not at the time of such inclusion any dispute exists or is apprehended in any of those establishments.

6. Where any reference has been made under Sub-Sec. (IA) to a National Tribunal, then notwithstanding anything contained in this Act, no Labour Court or Tribunal shall have jurisdiction to adjudicate upon any matter which is under adjudication before the National Tribunal, and accordingly—

(a) if the matter under adjudication before the National Tribunal is pending in a proceeding before a Labour Court or Tribunal, the proceeding before the Labour Court or the Tribunal, as the case may be, in so far as it relates to such matter, shall be deemed to have been quashed on such reference to the National Tribunal; and

(b) it shall not be lawful for the appropriate Government to refer the matter under adjudication before the National Tribunal to any Labour Court or Tribunal for adjudication during the pendency of the proceeding in relation to such matter before the National Tribunal.

7. Where any industrial dispute, in relation to which the Central Government is not the appropriate Government, is referred to a National Tribunal, then notwithstanding anything contained in this Act, any reference in Secs. 15, 17, 19, 33A, 33B and 36A to the appropriate Government in relation to such dispute shall be construed as a reference to the Central Government but, save as aforesaid and as otherwise expressly provided in this Act, any reference in any other provision of this Act to the appropriate Government in relation to that dispute shall mean a reference to the State Government.

Voluntary reference to arbitration (10A)

1. Where any industrial dispute exists or is apprehended and the employer and the workmen agree to refer the dispute to arbitration, they may, at any time before the dispute has been referred under Sec. 10 to a Labour Court or Tribunal or National Tribunal, by a written agreement, refer the dispute to arbitration and the reference shall be to such person or persons (including the presiding officer of a Labour Court or Tribunal or National Tribunal) as an arbitrator or arbitrators as may be specified in the arbitration agreement.

1 A. Where an arbitration agreement provides for a reference of the dispute to an even number of arbitrations, the agreement must provide for the appointment of another person as umpire, who shall enter on the reference, if the arbitrators are equally divided in their opinion, and the award of the umpire shall prevail.

2. An arbitration agreement referred to in Sub-Sec. (1) shall be in such form and shall be signed by the parties thereto in such manner as may be prescribed.

3. A copy of the arbitration agreement shall be forwarded to the appropriate Government and the conciliation officer and the appropriate Government shall, within 14 days from the date of the receipt of such copy, publish the same in the Official Gazette.

4. The arbitrator or arbitrators shall investigates the dispute and submit to the appropriate Government the arbitration award signed by the arbitrator or all the arbitrators, as the case may be.

5. Nothing in the Arbitration Act, 1940 shall apply to arbitrations under this section.

PROCEDURE AND POWERS OF AUTHORITIES

Section 11 lays down the procedure and powers of the different authorities as under—

1. Subject to any rules that may be made in this behalf, an arbitrator, a Board, Court, Labour Court, Tribunal or National Tribunal shall follow such procedure as the arbitrator or other authority concerned may think fit.

2. A Conciliation Officer or a member of 9 Board or Court or the presiding officer of a Labour Court, Tribunal or National Tribunal may for the purpose of inquiry into any existing or apprehended industrial dispute, after giving reasonable notice, enter the premises occupied by any establishment to which the dispute relates.

3. Every Board, Court, Labour Court, Tribunal and National Tribunal shall have the same powers as are vested in a Civil Court under C.P.C., 1908 when trying a suit, in respect of the following matters, viz.,—(a) enforcing the attendance of any person and examining him on oath; (b) compelling the production of documents and material objects; (c) issuing commissions for the examination of witness; (d) in respect of such other matters as may be prescribed; and every inquiry by a Board, Court, Labour Court, Tribunal or National Tribunal shall be deemed to be a judicial proceeding within the meaning of Sees. 193 and 228 of the Indian Penal Code.

4. A Conciliation Officer may call for and inspect any document which he has ground for considering to be relevant to the industrial dispute or to be necessary for the purpose of verifying the implementation of any award or carrying out any duty imposed on him under this Act and for the aforesaid purposes, the Conciliation Officer shall have the same powers as are vested in a Civil Court in respect of compelling the production of documents.

5. A Court, Labour Court, Tribunal or National Tribunal may, if it so thinks fit, appoint one or more persons having special knowledge of the matter under consideration as assessor or assessors to advise it in the proceeding before it.

6. All Conciliation Officers, members of a Board or Court and the presiding officers of a Labour Court, Tribunal or National Tribunal shall be deemed to be public servants within the meaning of Sec. 21 of the Indian Penal Code.

7. Subject to any rules made under this Act, the costs of, and incidental to, any proceeding before a Labour Court, Tribunal or National Tribunal shall be in the discretion of that Labour Court, Tribunal or National Tribunal, and the Labour Court, Tribunal or National Tribunal, as the case may be, shall have full power to determine by and to whom and to what extent and subject to what conditions, if any, such costs are to be paid, and to give all necessary directions for the purpose aforesaid and such costs may, on application made to the appropriate Government by the person entitled, be recovered by the Government in the same manner as an arrears of land revenue.

8. Every Labour Court, Tribunal or National Tribunal shall be deemed to be a Court for the purpose of Secs. 480, 482 and 484 of the Criminal Procedure Code, 1948.

Duties of Conciliation Officers (Sec. 12). For the purpose of bringing about fair end amicable settlement of an industrial dispute the Conciliation Officer is required to discharge the following duties—

1. Where any industrial dispute exists or is apprehended, the Conciliation Officer may, or where the dispute relates to a public utility service and a notice under Sec. 22 has been given, shall hold conciliation proceedings. He will interview both the employer and the workmen concerned with the dispute and endeavour to bring about a settlement.

2. The Conciliation Officer shall, for the purpose of bringing about a settlement of the dispute, without delay investigate the dispute and all matters affecting the merits and the right settlement thereof and may do all such things as he thinks fit for the purpose of inducing the parties to come to a fair and amicable settlement of the dispute.

3. If a settlement of the dispute or of any of the matters in dispute is arrived at in the course of the conciliation proceedings the Conciliation Officer shall send a report thereof to the appropriate Government together with a memorandum of the settlement signed by the parties to dispute.

4. If no such settlement is arrived at the Conciliation Officer shall, as soon as practicable after the close of the investigation, send to the appropriate Government a full report setting forth the steps taken by him for ascertaining the facts and circumstances relating to the dispute and for bringing about a settlement thereof, together with a full statement of such facts and circumstances, and the reasons on account of which, in his opinion, a settlement could not be arrived at.

5. The report must be submitted within 14 days of the commencement of the conciliation proceedings or within such shorter period as may be fixed by the appropriate Government: provided that, subject to the approval of the Conciliation Officer, the time for the submission of the report may be extended by such period as may be agreed upon in writing by all the parties to the dispute.

6. If, on a consideration of the report in respect of failure of settlement, the appropriate Government is satisfied that there is a case for reference to Board, Labour Court, Tribunal or National Tribunal, it may make such reference. Where the Govern-ment does not make such a reference, it shall record and communicate to the parties concerned its reasons therefor.

Duties of Boards (Sec. 13). The duties of the Boards are similar to those of Conciliation Officers, and reference should be made to those. It has to endeavour to bring about a settlement of a dispute referred to it and to do anything to induce the parties to come to a fair and amicable settlement. Where a settlement is reached a similar report and a memorandum of settlement have to be submitted to the appropriate Government But in case of failure, the Board, apart from furnishing all the details as required in the case of a report by a conciliation Officer, is also required to give in its report its recommendations for the determination of the dispute. The time limit prescribed for submission of such reports is 2 months of the date on which the dispute was referred to it or within such shorter period as may be fixed by the appropriate Government or extended by it for not more than 2 months. All the parties to the dispute may, however, further extend the period by agreement in writing. Where a dispute, in which the Board has failed to bring about a settlement, relates to a public utility service and the Government does not refer it to a Labour Court, Tribunal or National Tribunal, though it may if it so desires, it must inform the parties concerned its reasons for not doing so.

Duties of Courts (Sec. 14). The Court of Inquiry shall inquire into the matters referred to it and report thereon to the appropriate Government ordinarily within a period of 6 months from the commencement of its inquiry.

Duties of Labour Courts, Tribunals and National Tribunal. Where an industrial dispute has been referred to Labour Court, Tribunal or National Tribunals for adjudication, it shall hold its proceedings expeditiously and shall, as soon as it is practicable on the conclusion thereof, submit its award to the appropriate Government (Sec. 15).

The report of a Board or Court shall be in writing and shall be signed by all the members of the Board or Court, as the case may be provided that a member may record a minute of dissent. The award of a Labour Court or Tribunal or National Tribunal shall be in writing and shall be signed by its presiding officer (Sec. 16.).

Every report of a Board or Court together with any minute of dissent recorded therewith, every arbitration award and every award of Labour Court, Tribunal 01 National Tribunal shall within a period of 30 days from the date of its receipt by the appropriate Government, be published in such manner as the appropriate Government thinks fit. And subject to the provisions of Sec. 17 A, the award published as stated above shall be final and shall not be called in question by any Court in any manner whatsoever (Sec. 17A).

Commencement of the Award (Sec. 17A) 1. An award (including an arbitration award) shall become enforceable on the expiry of 30 days from the date of its publication under Sec. 17: provided that (a) if the appropriate Government is of opinion, in any case where the award has been given by a Labour court or Tribunal in relation to an industrial dispute to which it is a party; or (b) if the Central Government is of opinion, in any case where the award has been given by a National Tribunal, that it shall be inexpedient on public grounds affecting national economy or social justice to give effect to the whole or any part of the award, the appropriate Government, or as the case may be, the Central Government may, by notification in the Official Gazette, declare that the award shall not become enforceable on the expiry of the said period of 30 days.

2. Where any declaration has been made in relation to an award under the proviso to Sub-Sec. (1). the appropriate Government or the Central Government may, within 90 days from the date of publication of the award under Sec. 17, make an order rejecting or modifying the award, and shall, on the first available opportunity, lay the award together with a copy of the order before the Legislature of the State, if the order has been made by the State Government, or before Parliament if the order has been made by the Central Government.

3. Where an award as rejected or modified by an order made under Sub-Sec. (2) is laid before a Legislature of a State or before Parliament, such award shall become enforceable on the expiry of 15 days from the date on which it is so laid; and where no order under Sub-Sec. (2) is made in pursuance of a declaration under the proviso to Sub-Sec. (1) the award shall become enforceable on the expiry of the period of 90 days from the date on which it is so laid.

4. Subject to the provisions of Sub-Sec. (1) and Sub-Sec. (3) regarding the enforceability of an award, the award shall come into operation with effect from such date as may be specified therein, but where no date is specified, it shall come into operation on the date when the award becomes enforceable under Sub-Sec. (1) or Sub-Sec. (3), as the case may be.

Person on whom settlements and awards are binding (Sec. 18). 1. A settlement arrived at by agreement between the employer and workmen otherwise than in the course of conciliation proceeding shall be binding on the parties to the agreement who referred the dispute to arbitration.

2. Subject to the provisions of Sub-Sec. (3), an arbitration award which has become enforceable shall be binding on the parties to the arbitration agreement.

3. A settlement arrived at in the course of conciliation proceedings under this Act or an arbitration award in a case where a notification has been issued under Sub-Sec. (3 A) of Sec. 10A or an award of a Labour Court, Tribunal or National Tribunal which has become enforceable shall be binding on—

(a) all parties to the industrial dispute; (b) all other parties summoned to appear in the proceedings as parties to the dispute, unless the Board, arbitrator, Labour Court, Tribunal or National Tribunal, as the case may be, records the opinion that they wore so summoned without proper cause; (c) where a party referred to in clause (a) or clause (b) is an employer, his heirs, successors or assigns in respect of the establishment to which the dispute relates; (d) where a party referred to in clauses (a) or (b) is composed of workers, all persons who were employed in the establishment or part of the establishment as the case may be, to which the dispute relates on the date of the dispute and all persons who subsequently become employed in that establishment or part.

Period of operation of settlements and awards (Sec. 19), A settlement shall come into operation on such date as is agreed upon by the parties to the dispute, and if no date is agreed upon, on the date on which the memorandum of the settlement is signed by the parties to the dispute. Such settlement shall be binding for such period as is agreed upon by the parties, and if no such period is agreed upon, for a period of 6 months from the date on which the memorandum of settlement is signed by the parties to the dispute, and shall continue to be binding on the parties after the expiry of the periods aforesaid, until the expiry of 2 months from the date on which a notice in writing of an intention to terminate the settlement is given by one of the parties to the other party or parties to the settlement. An award shall remain in operation for one year from the date on which it becomes enforceable under Sec. 17A, unless the appropriate Government fixes a shorter period, or extends its operation for a year at a time up to a maximum of 3 years from the date when it came into operation. If, however, any material change in the circumstances on which the award was based has taken place, the appropriate Government may refer the award to a Labour Court, if it was the Labour Court's award, or to a Tribunal if it was that of a Tribunal or of a National Tribunal for decision whether or not the award should cease to be in operation before the period so fixed.

Commencement and Conclusion of Proceedings (Sec. 20). 1. A conciliation proceeding shall be deemed to have commenced on the date on which notice of strike or lockout under Sec. 22 is received by the conciliation officer or on the date of the order referring the dispute to a Board, as the case may be.

2. A conciliation proceeding shall be deemed to have concluded—
(a) where a settlement is arrived at, when a memorandum of the settlement is signed by the parties-to the dispute;
(b) where no settlement is arrived at, when the report of the conciliation officer is received by the appropriate Government or where the report of the Board is published under Sec. 17, as the case may be; or
(c) when the reference is made to a Court, Labour Court, Tribunal or National Tribunal under Sec. 10 during the pendency of conciliation proceedings.

3. Proceedings before an arbitrator under Sec. 10A or before a Labour Court, Tribunal or National Tribunal shall be deemed to have commenced on the date of the reference of the dispute for arbitration or adjudication, on the date on which the award becomes enforceable under Sec. 17A.

STRIKES AND LOCKOUTS

Prohibition of Strikes and Lockouts (Sec. 22)

1. No person employed in a public utility service shall go on strike in breach of contract—
(a) without giving to the employer notice of strike, as hereinafter provided, within 6 weeks before striking; or

(b) within 14 days of giving such notice; or

(c) before the expiry of the date of strike specified in any such notice as aforesaid; or

(d) during the pendency of any conciliation proceedings before a conciliation officer and 7 days after the conclusion of such proceedings.

2. No employer carrying on any public utility service shall lockout any of his workmen without complying with the conditions as specified in Sub-Sec. (1).

3. But notice of a strike or lockout will not be necessary where there is already in existence a strike or lockout in the public utility service. The employer in such a case must notify such authority as may be appointed by the appropriate Government of the declaration of a strike or lockout,

General Prohibition of Strikes and Lockouts (Sec. 23)

No workman who is employed in any industrial establishment shall go on strike in breach of contract and no employer of any such workman shall declare a lockout—

(a) during the pendency of conciliation proceedings before a Board and 7 days after the conclusion thereof;

(b) during the pendency of proceedings before a Labour Court, Tribunal or National Tribunal and 2 months after the conclusion thereof;

(c) during the period in which a settlement or award is in operation in respect of any of the matters covered by it.

Illegal Strikes and Lockouts (Sec. 24)

A strike or a lockout shall be illegal if (a) it is commenced or declared in contravention of Sec. 22 or 23; (b) is continued in contravention of the prohibitory order of the Government after the dispute has been referred under Sec. 10. But where a strike or a lockout in pursuance of an industrial dispute has already commenced and is in existence at the time of the reference of the dispute to a Board, a Labour Court, Tribunal or National Tribunal, the continuance of such strike or lockout shall not be illegal, if it was not originally illegal. A lockout declared in consequence of an illegal strike or a strike in consequence of an illegal lockout shall not be deemed to be illegal. Sec. 25 prohibits the spending or application of any money by any one in furtherance or support of any illegal strike or lockout.

LAYOFF AND RETRENCHMENT

(Chapter V-A)

Section 25A provides that Secs. 25C to 25E inclusive (relating to compensation payable for layoff) shall not apply to industrial establishments to which Chapter V-B applies, or—

(a) to industrial establishments (i.e., factories, mines and plantations) on which less than fifty workmen on an average per working day have been employed in the preceding calendar month; or

(b) to industrial establishments which are of seasonal character or in which work is performed only intermittently.

Definition of Continuous Service (Sec. 25B). 1. A workman shall be said to be in continuous service for a period if he is, for that period, in uninterrupted service, including service which may be interrupted on account of sickness or authorised leave or an accident or a strike which is not illegal, or a lockout or a cessation of work which is not due to any fault on the part of the workman;

2. Where a workman is not in continuous service within the meaning of clause (1) for a period of one year or six months, he shall be deemed to be in continuous service under an employer—

(a) for a period of one year, if the workman, during a period of 12 calendar months preceding the date with reference to which calculation is to be made, has actually worked under the employer for not less than—

(i) one hundred and ninety days in the case of a workman employed below ground in mine; and

(ii) two hundred and forty days, in any other case;

(b) for a period of 6 months, if the workman, during a period of 6 calendar months preceding the date with reference to which calculation is to be made, has actually worked under the employer for not less than—

(i) ninety-five days, in the case of a workman employed below ground in a mine; and

(ii) one hundred and twenty days, in any other case.

Explanation—*For* the purposes of clause (2), the number of days on which a workman has actually worked under an employer shall include the days on which—

(i) he has been laid-off under an agreement or as permitted by standing orders, or under this Act or under any other law applicable to the industrial establishment;

(ii) he has been on leave with full wages, earned in the previous year;

(iii) he has been absent due to temporary disablement caused by accident arising out of and in the course of his employment;

(iv) in the case of a female, she has been on maternity leave; so however, that the total period of such maternity leave does not exceed 12 weeks.

Right of Workman Laid-off for Compensation (Sec. 25C)

Whenever a workman (other than a *badli* workman or a casual workman) whose name is borne on the muster rolls of an industrial establishment and who has completed not less than one year of continuous service under an employer is laid-off, whether continuously or intermittently, he shall be paid by the employer for all days during which he is so laid-off, except for such weekly holidays as may intervene, compensation which shall be equal to 50 per cent of the total of the basic wages and dearness allowance that would have been payable to him had he not been so laid-off;

Provided that if during any period of 12 months, a workman is so laid-off for more than 45 days, no such compensation shall be payable in respect of any period of the lay-off after the expiry of the first 45 days; if there is an agreement to that effect between the workman and the employer;

Provided further that it shall be lawful for the employer in any case falling within the foregoing proviso to retrench the workman in accordance with the provisions contained in Sec. 25F at any time after the expiry of the first 45 days of the layoff and when he does so, any condensation paid to the workman for having been laid off during the preceding 12 months may be set off against the compensation payable for retrenchment

Explanation—*"Badli* workman" means a workman who is employed in an industrial establishment in the place of another workman whose name is borne on the muster rolls of the establishment, but shall cease to be regarded as such for the purpose of this section, if he has completed one year of continuous service in the establishment.

Sec. 25D requires the employer to maintain a muster roll and allow workmen to make emries thereon when they present themselves for work at the establishment,-even where workmen have been laid-off.

Workmen Laid-off not Entitled to Compensation (Sec. 25E)

No compensation shall be paid to a workman who has been laid-off—

(i) if he refuses to accept any alternative employment in the same establishment from which he has been laid-off, or in any other establishment belonging to the same employer situated in the same town or village or situated within a radius of 5 miles from the establishment to which he belongs, if, in the opinion of the employer, such alternative does not call for any special skill or previous experience and can be done by the workman, provided that the wages which would normally have been paid to the workman are offered for the alternative employment also; or

(ii) if he does not present himself for work at the establishment at the appointed time during normal working hours at least once a day; or

(iii) if such laying-off is due to a strike or slowing-down of production on the part of workmen in another part of their establishment.

Conditions of Retrenchment (Sec. 25F)

No workman employed in any industry who has been in continuous service for not less than one year under an employer shall be retrenched by that employer until—

(a) the workman has been given one month's notice in writing indicating the reasons for retrenchment and the period of notice has expired, or the workman has been paid in lieu of such notice wages for the period of the notice;

(b) the workman has been paid, at the time of retrenchment, compensation which shall be equivalent to 15 days' average pay for every completed year of continuous service or any part thereof in excess of 6 months; and

(c) notice in the prescribed manner is served on the appropriate Government or such authority as may be specified by the appropriate Government by notification in the Official Gazette.

Sec. 25FF provides that where the ownership or management of an undertaking is transferred whether by agreement or by operation of law, from the employer in relation to that undertaking to a new employer, every workman who has been in continuous service for not less than one year in that undertaking immediately before such transfer shall be entitled to notice and compensation in accordance with the provisions of Sec. 25F, as if the workman had been retrenched: Provided that nothing in this Section shall apply to a workman in any case where there has been a change of employers by reason of the transfer, if—

(a) the service of the workman has not been interrupted by such transfer;

(b) the terms and conditions of service applicable to the workman after such transfer are not in any way less favourable to the workman than those applicable to him immediately before the transfer; and

(c) the new employer is, under the terms of such transfer or otherwise, legally liable to pay the workman, in the event of his retrenchment, compensation on the basis that his service has been continuous and has not been interrupted by the transfer.

Sec. 25FFA provides that (1) an employer who intends to close down an undertaking shall serve, at least 60 days before the date on which the intended closure is to become effective, a notice, in the prescribed manner, on the appropriate Government stating clearly the reasons, for the intended closure of the undertaking: Provided that nothing in this sub-section shall apply to—

(a) an undertaking in which (i) less than 50 workmen are employed, or (ii) 'were employed on an average per working day in the preceding 12 months,

(c) an undertaking set up for the construction of buildings, bridges, roads, canals, dams or for other construction work or project.

2. Notwithstanding anything contained in sub-sec. (1), the appropriate Government may, if it is satisfied that owing to such exceptional circumstances as accident in the undertaking or death of the employer or the like it is necessary so to do, by order, direct that provisions of sub-sec. (1) shall not apply in relation to such undertaking for such period as may be specified in the order.

Sec. 25FFF provides: (1) Where an undertaking is closed down by any reason whatsoever, every workman who has been in continuous service for not less than one year in that undertaking immediately before such closure, subject to the provisions of Sub-Sec. (2), be entitled to notice and compensation in accordance with the provisions of Sec. 25f, as if the workman had been retrenched: Provided that where the undertaking is closed down on account of unavoidable circumstances beyond the control of the employer, the compensation to be paid to the workman under clause (b) of Sec. 25F shall not exceed his average pay for 3 months.

Explanation. An undertaking which is closed down by reason merely of financial difficulties (including financial losses) or accumulation of undisposed of stocks or the expiry of the period of the

THE INDUSTRIAL DISPUTES ACT, 1947

565

lease or the licence granted to it where the period of the lease or the licence expires on or after April 1, 1967, shall not be deemed to have been closed down on account of unavoidable circumstances beyond the control of the employer within the meaning of the proviso to this Sub-Section.

(1 A) Notwithstanding anything contained in Sub-Sec. (1), where an undertaking engaged in mining operations is closed down by reason merely of the exhaustion of the minerals in the area in which such operations are carried on, no workman referred to in that sub-section shall be entitled to any notice or compensation in accordance with the provisions of Sec. 25F, if—

(a) the employer provides the workman with alternative employment with effect from the date of closure at the same remuneration as he was entitled to receive arid on the same terms and conditions of services as were applicable to him, immediately before the closure;

(b) the service of the workman has not been interrupted by such alternative employment; and

(c) the employer is, under the terms of such alternative employment or otherwise, legally liable to pay to the workman, in the event of his retrenchment, compensation on the basis that his service has been continuous and has not been interrupted by such alternative employment.

2. Where any undertaking set up for the construction of buildings, bridges, roads, canals, dams or other construction work is closed down on account of the completion of the work within 2 years from the date on which the undertaking has been set up, no workman employed therein shall be entitled to any compensation under clause (b) of Sec. 25F, but if the construction work is not so completed within 2 years, he shall be entitled to notice and compensation under that Section for every completed year of continuous service or any part thereof in excess of 6 months.

Procedure for Retrenchment (Sec. 25G)

Where any workman in an industrial establishment, who is a citizen of India, is to ' be retrenched and he belongs to a particular category of workmen in that establishment, in the absence of any agreement between the employer and the workman in this behalf, the employer shall ordinarily retrench the workman who was the last person to be employed in that category, unless for reasons to be recorded the employer retrenches any other workman.

Re-employment of Retrenched Workmen (Sec. 25H)

Where any workmen are retrenched and the employer proposes to take into his employ any persons, he shall, in such manner as may be prescribed, give an opportunity to the retrenched workmen who are citizens of India to offer themselves for re-employment, and the retrenched workmen who offer themselves for re-employment, and the retrenched workmen who offer themselves for re- employment, shall have preference over others. But this section cannot be applied retrospectively (*RS. Ramdayal* v. *Labour Appellate Tribunal* (1964 S.C.-567).

(Chapter V-B)[2]

Special Provisions relating to layoff, retrenchment and closure in certain establishments

Application of Chapter V-B

Sec. 25K. 1. The provisions of this chapter shall apply to an industrial estab-lishment (not being an establishment of a seasonal character or in which work is performed only intermittently) in which not less than 300 workmen were employed on an average per working day for the preceding 12 months.

2. If a question arises whether an industrial establishment is of a seasonal character or whether work is performed therein only intermittently, the decision of the appropriate Government shall be final.

---

2. Added by the Industrial Disputes (Amendment) Act, 1976.

Definitions

Sec. 24L provides that for the purpose of this chapter,—

(a) industrial establishment means—
  (i) a factory as defined in clause (m) of Sec. 2 of the Factories Act, 1948;
  (ii) a mine as defined in clause (j) of sub-Sec. (1) of Sec. 2 of the Mines Act, 1952;or
  (iii) a plantation as defined in clause (f) of Sec. 2 of the Plantations Labour Act, 1951.

(b) Notwithstanding anything contained in sub-clause (ii) of clause (1) of Sec. 2,—
  (i) in relation to any company in which not less than 51 per cent of the paid-up share capital is held by the Central Government, or
  (ii) in relation to any corporation (not being a corporation referred to in sub-clause (i) of clause (1) of Sec. (2) established by or under any law made by Parliament, the Central Government shall be the appropriate Government.

Prohibition of Layoff (Sec. 25M)[3]

(1) No workman (other than a *badli* workman or a casual workman) whose name is home on the muster rolls of an industrial establishment to which this chapter applies shall be laid off by his employer except with the prior permission of the appropriate Government or such authority as may be specified by that Government (hereinafter in this section referred to as the specified authority), obtained on an application made in this behalf, unless such layoff is due to shortage of power or to natural calamity, and in the case of mine, such layoff is due also to fire, flood, excess of inflammable gas or explosion.

(2) An application for permission under sub-section (1) shall be made by the employer in the prescribed manner stating clearly the reasons for the intended layoff and a copy of such application shall also be served simultaneously on the workmen concerned in the prescribed manner.

(3) Where the workmen (other than *badli* workmen or casual workmen) of an industrial establishment, being a mine, have been laid-off under sub-section (1) for reasons of fire, flood or excess of inflammable gas or explosion, the employer in relation to such establishment, shall within a period of 30 days from the date of commencement of such layoff, apply in the prescribed manner, to the appropriate Government or the specified authority for permission to continue the layoff.

(4) Where an application for permission under subsection (1) or sub-section (3) has been made, the appropriate Government or the specified authority, after making such inquiry as it thinks fit and after giving a reasonable opportunity of being heard to the employer, the workmen concerned and the person interested in such layoff, may, having regard to the genuineness and adequacy of the reasons for such layoff, the interests of the workmen and all other relevant factors, by order and for reasons to be recorded in writing, grant or refuse to grant such permission and a copy of such order shall be communicated to the employer and the workmen.

(5) Where an application for permission has been made and the appropriate Government or the specified authority does not communicate the *order* granting or refusing to grant permission to the employer within a period of 60 days from the date on which such application is made, the permission applied for shall be deemed to have been granted on the expiration of the said period of 60 days.

(6) An order of the appropriate Government or the specified authority granting or refusing to grant permission shall, subject to the provisions of sub-section (7) be final and binding on all the parties concerned and shall remain in force for one year from the date of such order.

(7) The appropriate Government or the specified authority may, either on its own motion or on the application made by the employer or any workman, review its order granting or refusing to grant permission under sub-section (4) or refer the matter or, as the case may be, cause it to be referred to a Tribunal for adjudication:

---

3. Substituted by the Amendment Act, 1984.

Provided that where reference has been made to a Tribunal under this sub-section, it shall pass an order within a period of 30 days from the date of such reference.

(8) Where no application for permission under sub-section (1) is made, or where no application for permission under sub-section (3) is made within the period specified therein, or where the permission for any layoff has been refused, such layoff shall be deemed to be illegal from the date on which the workmen had been laid off and the workmen shall be entitled to all the benefits under any for the time being in force as if they had not been laid off.

(9) Notwithstanding anything contained in the foregoing provisions of this Section, the appropriate Government may, if it is satisfied that owing to such exceptional circumstances as accident in the establishment or death of the employer or like, it is necessary so to dp, by order, direct that the provisions of sub-section (1), or, as the case may be, sub-section (3) shall not apply in relation to such establishment for such period as may be specified in the order.

(10) The provisions of Sec. 25C (other than the second proviso thereto) shall apply to the cases of layoff referred to in this section.

Explanation—For the purposes of this section, a workman shall not be deemed to be laid-off by an employer if such employer offers any alternative employment (which in the opinion of the employer does not call for any special skill or previous experience and can be done by the workman) in the same establishment from which he has been laid-off or in any other establishment belonging to the same employer, situate in the same town or village, or situate within such distance from the establishment to which he belongs as may be prescribed and the transfer will not involve undue hardship to the workman having regard to the facts and circumstances of his case, provided that the wages which would normally have been paid to the workman are offered for the alternative appointment also.

Conditions Precedent to Retrenchment of Workmen (Sec. 25N)[4]

(1) No workman employed in any industrial establishment to which this Chapter applies, who has been in continuous service for not less than one year under an employer shall be retrenched by that employer until—

(a) the workman has been given 3 months notice in writing indicating the reasons for retrenchment and the period of notice has expired, or the workman has been paid in lieu of such notice, wages for period of the notice; and

(b) the prior permission of the appropriate Government or such authority as may be specified by that Government by the notification in the Official Gazette (thereafter in this section referred to as the specified authority) has been obtained on an application made in this behalf.

(2) An application for permission under sub-sec. (1) shall be made by the employer in the prescribed manner stating clearly the reasons for the intended retrenchment and a copy of such application shall also be served simultaneously on the workmen concerned in the prescribed manner.

(3) When an application for permission under sub-section (1) has been made, the appropriate Government or the specified authority, after making such inquiry as it thinks fit and after giving a reasonable opportunity of being heard to the employer, the workmen concerned and the person interested in such retrenchment, may, having regard to the genuineness and adequacy of the reasons stated by the employer, the interests of the workmen and all other relevant factors, by order and for reasons to be recorded in writing, grant or refuse to grant such permission and a copy of such order shall be communicated to the employer and the workmen.

(4) When an application for permission has been made under sub-section (1) and the appropriate Government or the specified authority does not communicate the order granting or refusing to grant permission to the employer within a period of 60 days from the date on which such application is

4. Substituted by the Amendment Act, 1984.

made, the permission applied for shall be deemed to have been granted on the expiration of the said period of 60 days.

(5) An order of the appropriate Government or the specified authority granting or refusing to grant permission shall, subject to the provisions, of sub-section (6), be final and binding on all the parties concerned and shall remain in force for one year from the date of such order.

(6) The appropriate Government or the specified authority may, either on its own motion or on the application made by the employer or any workmen, review its order granting or refusing to grant permission under sub-section (3) or refer the matter or, as the case may be, or cause it to be referred, to a Tribunal for adjudication:

Provided that where a reference has been made to a Tribunal under this sub-section, it shall pass an award within a period of 30 days from the date of such reference.

(7) When no application for permission under sub-section (1) is made, or where the permission for any retrenchment has been refused, such retrenchment shall be deemed to be illegal from the date on which the notice of retrenchment was given to the workman and the workman shall be entitled to all the benefits under any law for the time being in force as if no notice had been given to him.

(8) Notwithstanding anything contained in the foregoing provisions of this section, the appropriate Government may, if it is satisfied that owing to such exceptional circumstances as accident in the establishment or death of the employer or the like, it is necessary so to do, by order, direct that the provisions of sub-section (1) shall not apply in relation to such establishment for such period as may be specified in the order.

(9) Where permission for retrenchment has been granted under sub-section (3) or where permission for retrenchment is deemed to be granted under sub-section (4) every workman who is employed in that establishment immediately before the date of applica-tion for permission under this Section shall be entitled to receive, at the time of retrenchment, compensation which shall be equivalent to 15 days average pay for every completed year of continuous service or any part thereof in excess of 6 months.

Ninety days' Notice of intention to close down undertaking (Sec. 25O)

1. An employer who intends to close down an undertaking of an industrial establishment to which this chapter applies shall serve, for previous approval at least 90 days before the date on which the intended closure is to become effective, a notice, in the prescribed manner, on the appropriate Government stating clearly the reasons for the intended closure of the undertaking:

Provided that nothing in this section shall apply to an undertaking set up for the construction of buildings, bridges, roads, canals, dams or for other construction work.

2. On receipt of a notice under sub-sec. (1) the appropriate Government may, if it is satisfied that the reasons for the intended closure of the undertaking are not adequate and sufficient or such closure is prejudicial to the public interest, by order, direct the employer not to close down such undertaking.

3. Where a notice has been served on the appropriate Government by an employer under Sec. 25FFA(1) and the period of notice has not expired at the commencement of the Amendment Act, 1976, such employer shall not close down the undertaking but shall, within a period of 15 days from such commencement apply to the appropriate Government for permission to close down the undertaking.

4. Where an application for permission has been made under Sub-Sec.(3) and the appropriate Government does not communicate the permission or the refusal to grant the permission to the employer within 2 months from the date on which the application is made, the permission applied for shall be deemed to have been granted on the expiration of the said period of 2 months.

5. When no application for permission under Sub-Sec. (1) is made, or where no application for permission under Sub-Sec. (3) is made within the period specified therein or where the permission for closure has been refused, the closure of the undertaking shall be deemed to be illegal from the date of

closure and the workman shall be entitled to all the benefits under any law for the time being in force as if no notice had been given to him.

6. Notwithstanding anything contained in Sub-Sec. (1) and Sub-Sec. (3) the appropriate Government may, if it is satisfied that owing to such exceptional circumstances as accident in the undertaking or death of the employer or the like it is necessary so to do, by order, direct that the provisions of Sub-Sec. (1) or Sub-Sec. (3) shall not apply in relation to such undertaking for such period as may be specified in the order.

7. When an undertaking is approved or permitted to be closed down under Sub-Sec. (1) or Sub-Sec. (4), every workman in the said undertaking who has been in the continuous service for not less than one year in that undertaking immediately before the date of application for permission under this section shall be entitled to notice and compensation as specified in Sec. 25N as if the said workman has been retrenched under that section.

Special Provisions as to Restarting of Undertaking closed down before Commencement of Amendment Act, 1976

Sec. 25P provides that if the appropriate Government is of opinion in respect of any undertaking of an industrial establishment to which this Chapter applies and which closed down before the Commencement of the Industrial Disputes (Amendment) Act, 1976-

(a) that such undertaking was closed down otherwise than on account of unavoidable circumstances beyond the control of the employer;

(b) that there are possibilities of restarting the undertaking;

(c) that it is necessary for the rehabilitation of the workmen employed in such undertaking before its closure or for the maintenance of supplies and services essential to the life of the community to restart the undertaking or both; and

(d) that the restarting of the undertaking will not result in hardship to the employer in relation to the undertaking.

it may, after giving an opportunity to such employer and workmen, direct, by order published in the Official Gazette, that the undertaking shall be restarted within such time (not being less than one month from the date of the order) as may be specified in the order.

Penalty for layoff and Retrenchment without Permission (Sec. 25Q)

Any employer who contravenes the provisions of Sec. 25M or Sec. 25N shall be punishable with imprisonment for a term which may extend to one month, or with fine which may extend to ₹ 1,000, or with both.

Penalty for Closure (Sec. 25R)

1. Any employer who closes down an undertaking without complying with the provisions of the Sub-Sec. (1) of Sec. 25 O shall be punishable with imprisonment up to 6 months, or with fine up to ₹ 5,000, or with both.

2. Any employer, who contravenes a direction given under Sub-Sec. (2) of Sec. 25O or Sec. 25P, shall be punishable with imprisonment up to one year, or with fine up to ₹ 2,000 for every day during which the contravention continues after the conviction.

3. Any employer who contravenes the provisions of Sub-Sec.(3) of Sec. 25O shall be punishable with imprisonment up to one month, or with fine up to ₹ 1,000, or with both.

Certain provisions of Chapter VA to apply to an Industrial Establishment to which Chapter VB applies

Sec. 25S states that the provisions of Secs. 25B, 25D, 25FF, 25G, 25H and 25J in Chapter VA shall, so far as may be, apply also in relation to an industrial establishment to which the provisions of this Chapter (i.e., Chapter VB) apply.

PENALTIES

Any workman who commences, continues, or otherwise acts in furtherance of an illegal strike is punishable v. ith imprisonment up to one month, or fine up to ₹ 50, or with both. Any employer who does the same as above in connection with an illegal lockout shall be punishable with imprisonment up to one month, or fine up to ₹ 1,000, or with both (Sec. 26). Any person who instigates or incites others to take part in, or otherwise acts in furtherance of, an illegal strike or an illegal lockout shall be punishable with imprisonment up to 6 months, or fine up to ₹ 1,000, or with both (Sec. 27). Any person who knowingly gives financial aid to illegal strikes and lockouts shall be punishable in like manner as specified in Sec. 27 (Sec.28). Any person who commits a breach of any term of any settlement or award, which is binding on him under this Act, shall be punishable with imprisonment up to 6 months, or with fine, or with both and where the breach is a continuing one, with a further fine up to ₹ 200 for every day during which the breach continues after the conviction for the first, and the court trying the offence, if it fines the offender, may direct that the whole or any part of the fine realised from him shall be paid, by way of compensation, to any person who, in its opinion, has been injured by such breach (Sec. 29). Any employer who in contravention of the provisions of Sec. 33 alters conditions of service shall be punishable with imprisonment up to 6 months, or fine up to ₹ 1,000 or with both (Sec. 31).

MISCELLANEOUS

Offences by Companies (Sec. 32)—Where a person committing an offence under this Act is a company, or other body corporate, or an association of persons (whether incorporated or not), every director, manager, secretary, agent or other officer or person concerned with the management thereof shall, unless he proves that the offence was committed without his knowledge or consent, be deemed to be guilty of such offence.

Conditions of Service, etc., to Remain Unchanged during Pendency of Proceedings (Sec. 33)

1. During the pendency of any conciliation proceeding before a Conciliation Officer or a Board or of any proceeding before an arbitrator or a Labour Court or Tribunal or National Tribunal in respect of an industrial dispute, an employer shall,—

(a) in regard to any matter connected with the dispute, not alter, to the prejudice of the workmen concerned in such dispute, the conditions of service applicable to them immediately before the commencement of such proceedings; or

(b) any misconduct connected with the dispute, not discharge or punish, whether by dismissal or otherwise, any workman concerned in this dispute, save with the express permission in writing of the authority before which the proceeding is pending.

2. During the pendency of such proceeding in respect of an industrial dispute, the employer may, in accordance with the standing orders applicable to a workman concerned in such dispute, or, where there are no such standing orders, in accordance with the terms of the contract, whether express or implied, between him and the workman,—

(a) alter, in regard to any matter not connected with the dispute the conditions of service applicable to that workman immediately before the commencement of such proceeding; or

(b) for any misconduct not connected with the dispute, discharge or punish, whether by dismissal or otherwise, that workman provided that no such workman shall be discharged or dismissed, unless he has been paid wages for one month and an application has been made by the employer to the authority before which the proceeding is pending for approval of the action taken by the employer.

3. Notwithstanding anything contained in Sub. (2), no employer shall, during the pendency of any such proceeding in respect of industrial dispute, take an action against any protected workman concerned in such dispute.

(a) by altering, to the prejudice of such protected workman, the conditions of service applicable to him immediately before the commencement of such proceedings; or

(b) by discharging or punishing, whether by dismissal or otherwise, such protected workman, save with the express permission in writing of the authority before which the proceeding is pending.

Explanation.—For the purposes of this Sub-Sec, a protected workman, in relation to an establishment, means a workman, who being a member of the executive or other office bearer of a registered trade union connected with the establishment, is recognised as such in accordance with rules made in this behalf.

4. In every establishment, the number of workmen to be recognised as protected workmen for the purposes of Sub-Sec. (3) shall be one per cent of the total number of workmen employed therein subject to a minimum of 5 protected workmen and a maximum number of 100 protected workmen and for the aforesaid purpose, the ap-propriate Government may make rules providing for the distribution of such protected workmen among various trade unions, if any, connected with the establishment and the manner in which the workmen may be chosen and recognised as protected workmen.

5. Where an employer makes an application to a Conciliation Officer, Board, an arbitrator, a Labour Court, Tribunal or National Tribunal under the proviso to Sub-Sec. (2) for approval of the action taken by him, the authority concerned shall, without delay, hear such application and pass, as expeditiously as possible, such order in relation thereto as it deems fit.

Sec. 33 A provides that if an employer contravenes the provisions of Sec. 33, any employer aggrieved by such contravention may make a complaint in writing to the Labour Court, Tribunal or National Tribunal, and the latter shall adjudicate upon the complaint as if it were a dispute.

Sec. 33B empowers the appropriate Government to withdraw by order in writing for reasons to be stated therein, any proceeding pending before a Labour Court, Tribunal or National Tribunal and to transfer the same to another Labour Court, Tribunal or National Tribunal, as the case may be, for the disposal of the proceeding. A Tribunal or National Tribunal is also authorised to transfer to a Labour Court any proceeding before itself.

Recovery of Money Due from an Employer (Sec. 33C). Where any money is due to a workman from an employer under a settlement or an award or for layoff or retrenchment, the workman himself or any other person authorised by him in writing in this behalf, or in the case of the death of the workman, his assign or heirs may, without prejudice to any other mode of recovery, make an application, within one year from the date on which the money became due to the workman, to the appropriate Government for the recovery of money due to him, and if the appropriate Government is satisfied that any money is due to him, it shall issue a certificate for that amount to the Collector who shall proceed to recover the same in the same manner as an arrear of land revenue. Where any workman is entitled to receive from the employer any benefit which is capable of being computed in terms of money, the amount may be determined by the specified Labour Court and may be recovered in the same manner as stated above.

No person refusing to take part or to continue to take part in any strike or lockout which is illegal under this Act: shall, by reason of such refusal or by reason of any step taken by him, be subject to expulsion from any trade union or society or to any fine or penalty or to deprivation of any right or benefit to which he or his legal representatives would otherwise be entitled, or be liable to be placed in any respect, either directly or indirectly, under any disability or at any disadvantage as compared with other members of the union or society, anything to the contrary in the rules of a trade union or society notwithstanding (Sec. 35).

Representation of Parties (Sec. 36). A workman who is a party to an industrial dispute shall be entitled to be represented in any proceeding under this Act by (i) any member of the executive or other office bearer of a registered trade union of which he is a member; (ii) any member of the executive or other office bearer of a federation of trade unions to which the trade union referred to in (i) is affiliated; (iii) where a worker is not member of any trade union, by any member of the executive or other office bearer of any trade union connected with, or by any other workman employed in, the industry in which the worker is employed and authorised in such manner as may be prescribed.

An employer who is a party to a dispute shall be entitled to be represented in any proceeding under this Act by (i) an officer of an association of employers of which he is a member; (ii) by an office bearer of a federation of associations of employers to which the association referred to in (i) is affiliated; (iii) where the employer is not a member of any association of employers, by an officer of any association of employers connected with, or by any other employer engaged in the industry in which the employer is engaged and authorised in such manner as may be prescribed.

No party to a dispute shall be entitled to be represented by a legal practitioner in any conciliation proceedings under this Act or in any proceedings before a Court But in any proceeding before a Labour Court, Tribunal or National Tribunal, a party to a dispute may be represented by a legal practitioner with the consent of the other parties to the proceeding and with the leave of the Labour Court, Tribunal or National Tribunal, as the case may be.

By virtue of 36A, the appropriate Government may, if in its opinion any difficulty or doubt arises as to the interprestation of any provision of an award or settlement, refer the question to such Labour Court, Tribunal or National Tribunal as it may think fit. The Labour Court, Tribunal or National Tribunal shall, after giving the parties an opportunity of being heard, decide such question and its decision shall be final and binding on all such parties. Sec. 37 provides that no suit, prosecution or othei legal proceeding shall lie against any person for anything which is in good faith done or intended to be done in pursuance of this Act or any rules made thereunder.

REPEAL OF THE INDUSTRIAL DISPUTES (APPELLATE TRIBUNAL) ACT
(No. 48 of 1950)

The above Act has been repealed by the Industrial Disputes (Amendment and Miscellaneous Provisions) Act, 1956, and consequently the Labour Appellate Tribunal has been abolished. The abolition of the Appellate Tribunal is expected to save time in the disposal of cases and also to save about ₹ 6 lakhs in expenditure.

CHAPTER 22

The Minimum Wages Act, 1948

(No. XI of 1947)

The Minimum Wages Act, 1948 empowers the Central or State Government to fix minimum rates of wages in respect of scheduled employments, after due enquiries. The present schedule includes employments in (1) any woollen carpet-making or shawl weaving establishment; (2) any rice mill, flour mill or dal mill; (3) tobacco (including bidi-making) manufactory; (4) plantation, i.e., any estate maintained for the purpose of growing cinchona, rubber, tea or coffee; (5) oil mill; (6) under any local authority; (7) on the construction or maintenance of roads or in building operations; (8) stone-break-ing or stone-crushing; (9) lac manufactory; (10) mica works; (11) public motor transport; (12) tanneries and leather manufactory; (13) manganese mines; (14) china clay mines; (15) Kyanite mines; (16) copper mines; (17) clay mines; (18) magnesite mines; and (19) agriculture including farming, dairy, horticulture, poultry, forestry or timber operations. Sec. 27 empowers the appropriate Government to add to the schedule any employment in respect of which it is of opinion that minimum rates of wages should be fixed under this Act.

Minimum rates of wages in respect of scheduled industries excepting agriculture were to be fixed within two years from the date of the commencement of the Act, and in the case of agriculture it was to be done within three years. The minimum rate of wages includes a basic rate and a special allowance adjusted to accord with the variation in the cost of living index number. The procedure for fixing minimum rates of wages is to appoint a committee to hold enquiries and publish its proposals for rates to be paid, giving two months' time for filing objections or making representations. The rate so fixed may be reviewed or revised, if necessary. Provision has been made to set up a machinery to decide claims arising out of payment of less than the minimum rates of wages. Infringement by the employer of certain provisions of the Act has been made punishable with imprisonment or fine or with both.

Interpretation (Sec. 2)

In this Act, unless there is anything repugnant in the subject or context,—

(a) adult, adolescent and child have the meanings respectively assigned to them in Sec. 2 of the Factories Act;

(b) appropriate Government in relation to any scheduled employment has the meaning assigned to it in Sec.2(a) of the Industrial Disputes Act, 1947;

(c) competent authority means the authority appointed by the appropriate Government by notification in its Official Gazette to ascertain from time to time the cost of living index number applicable to the employees employed in the Scheduled employ-ments specified in such notification;

(d) cost of living index number in relation to employees in any scheduled employment in respect of which minimum rates of wages have been fixed, means the index number ascertained and declared by the competent authority by notification in the Official Gazette to be the cost of living index number applicable to employees in such employment;

(e) employer in relation to any scheduled employment has the meaning assigned to it in the Factories Act and the Industrial Disputes Act;

(f) wages means all remuneration capable of being expressed in terms of money, which would, if the terms of the contract of employment, express or implied, were fulfilled, be payable to a person employed in respect of his employment or of work done in such employment, and includes house rent allowance, but does not include—

(i) the value of—
  (a) any house-accommodation, supply of light, water, medical attendance, or
  (b) any other amenity or any service excluded by general or special order of the appropriate Government;
(ii) any contribution paid by the employer to any Pension Fund or Provident Fund or under any scheme of social insurance;
(iii) any travelling allowance or the value of any travelling concession;
(iv) any sum paid to the person employed to defray special expenses entailed on him by the nature of his employment; or
(v) any gratuity payable on discharge.

(g) employee means any person who is employed for hire or reward to do any work, skilled or unskilled, manual or clerical, in a scheduled employment in respect of which minimum rates of wages have been fixed; and includes an out-worker to whom any articles or materials are given out by another person to be made up, cleaned, washed, altered, ornamented, finished, repaired, adapted or otherwise processed for sale for the purposes of the trade or business of that other person where the process is to be carried out either in the home of the out-worker or in some other premises not being premises under the control and management of that other person; and also includes any employee declared to be an employee by the appropriate Government; but does not include any member of the armed forces of the Union.

Fixing of Minimum Rates of Wages (Sec.3)

1. The appropriate Government shall, in the manner hereinafter provided,—

(a) fix the minimum rates of wages payable to employees employed in an employment specified in Part I and Part II of the Schedule and in an employment added under Sec. 27: provided that the appropriate Government may instead of fixing minimum rates of wages under this sub-clause for the whole State, fix such rates for a part of the State or for any specified class or classes of such employment in the whole State or part thereof; and

(b) review at such intervals as it may think fit, such intervals not exceeding 5 years, the minimum rates of wages so fixed and revise the minimum rates, if necessary: Provided that where for any reason the appropriate Government has not reviewed the minimum rates of wages fixed by it in respect of any scheduled employment within any interval of 5 years, nothing contained in this clause shall be deemed to prevent it from reviewing the minimum rates after the expiry of the said period of 5 years and revising them, if necessary, and until they are so revised the minimum rates in force immediately before the expiry of the said period of 5 years shall continue in force.

1A. Notwithstanding anything contained in Sub-Sec. (1), the appropriate Government may refrain from fixing minimum rates of wages in respect of any scheduled employment in which there are in the whole State less than, 1,000 employees engaged in such employment, but if at any time the appropriate Government comes to a finding after such inquiry as it may make or cause to be made in this behalf that the number of employees in any scheduled employment in respect of which it has refrained from fixing minimum rates of wages has risen to 1,000 or more, it shall fix minimum rates of wages payable to employees in such employment as soon as may be after such finding.

2. The appropriate Government may fix (a) minimum time rate; (b) a minimum piece rate; (c) a guaranteed time rate; (d) overtime rate.

2A. Where in respect of an industrial dispute relating to the rates of wages payable to any of the employees employed in a scheduled employment, any proceeding is pending before a Tribunal or National Tribunal or before any other like authority, or an award has been made and is in operation, any notification fixing minimum rates of wages shall not operate during pendency of proceedings and during the currency of the award.

3. In fixing or revising minimum rates of wages under this section different minimum rates of wages may be fixed for (i) different scheduled employments; (ii) different classes of work in the same scheduled employment; (iii) adults, adolescents, children and apprentices; (iv) different localities. Minimum rates of wages may be fixed by any one or more of the following wage periods; by the hour, by the day, by the month, or by any larger wage period as may be prescribed; and where such rates are fixed by the day or by the month, the manner of calculating wages for a month or for a day, as the case may be, may be indicated.

Minimum Rates of Wages (Sec. 4)

1. Any minimum rate of wages fixed or revised by the appropriate Government in respect of scheduled employments under Sec.3 may consist of—

(i) a basic rate of wages and a special allowance at a rate to be adjusted at such intervals and in such manner as the appropriate Government may direct, to accord as nearly as practicable with the variation in the cost of living index number applicable to such workers (hereinafter referred to as the "cost of living allowance"); or

(ii) a basic rate of wages with or without the cost of living allowance, and the cash value of the concessions in respect of supplies of essential commodities at concession rates, where so authorised;

(iii) an all-inclusive rate allowing for the basic rate, the cost of living allowance and the cash value of the concession, if any.

2. The cost of living allowance and the cash value of the concessions in respect of supplies of essential commodities at concession rates shall be computed by the competent authority at such intervals and in accordance with such directions as may be specified or given by the appropriate Government.

Procedure for Fixing Wages (Sec. 5)

1. In fixing minimum rates of wages in respect of any scheduled employment for the first time under this Act or in revising minimum rates of wages so fixed, the appropriate Government shall either—

(a) appoint as many committees and sub-committees as it considers necessary to hold enquiries and advise it in respect of such fixation or revision, as the case may be, or

(b) by notification in the Official Gazette publish its proposals for the information of persons likely to be affected thereby and specify a date not less than two months from the date of the notification, on which the proposal will be taken into consideration.

2. After considering the advice of the committee appointed under clause (a) of Sub-Sec. (1), or as the case may be, all representations received by it before the date specified in the notification under clause (b) of the sub-section, the appropriate Government shall, by notification in the Official Gazette, fix, or, as the case may be, revise the minimum rates of wages in respect of each scheduled employment, and unless such notification otherwise provides, it shall come into force on the expiry of three months from the date of its issue: Provided that where the appropriate Government proposes to revise the minimum rates of wages by the mode specified in clause (b) of Sub-Sec. (/) the appropriate Government shall consult the Advisory Board also.

Committees and Advisory Boards (Secs. 7-9)

For the purpose of co-ordinating the work of committees and sub-committees appointed under Sec. 5 and advising the appropriate Government generally in the matter of fixing and revising minimum rates of wages, the appropriate Government shall appoint an Advisory Board (Sec. 7). For the purpose of advising the Central and State Governments in the matters of the fixation and the revision of minimum rates of wages and other matters under this Act and for co-ordinating the work of the Advisory Boards, the Central Government shall appoint a Central Advisory Board, which shall consist of persons to be nominated by the Central Government representing employers and employees in the scheduled employments, who shall be equal in number, and inde-pendent persons not exceeding one-third of its total number of members. One of such independent persons shall be appointed the Chairman of the Board by the Central Government (Sec.8). Each of the Committees, Sub-Committees and the Advisory Board shall consist of persons to be nominated by the appropriate Government in the same manner as for the Central Advisory Board (Sec. 9).

Sec. 10 provides that the appropriate Government may, at any time, by notification in the Official Gazette, correct clerical or arithmetical mistakes in any order fixing or revising minimum rates of wages under this Act, or errors arising therein from any accidental slip or omission. Every such notification, after it is issued, shall be placed before the Advisory Board for information.

Wages in Kind (Sec. 11)

Minimum wages payable under this Act are to be paid in cash, but where it has been the custom to pay wages wholly or partly in kind, the appropriate Government may allow the continuance of this method of payment The appropriate Government may also authorise the supply of essential commodities at concession rates, if it is of the opinion that it should be done in the interest of the employees, This cash value of wages in kind and of concessions in respect of supplies shall be estimated in the prescribed manner.

Employment of Minimum Wages (Sec. 12)

The employer must pay to every employee engaged in a scheduled employment under him wages at a rate not less than the minimum rate of wages fixed by notification for that class of employees in that employment without any deductions except as may be authorised by the appropriate Government This provision will not however, affect the provisions of the Payment of Wages Act, 1936.

Section 13(1) empowers the appropriate Government to fix the number of hours of work which shall constitute a normal working day, inclusive of one or more specified intervals, and provide for a day of rest in every period of seven days and for the payment of remuneration in respect of such days of rest. If an employee is required to work on a rest day he must be paid the overtime rate, and such a rate must be paid even where a worker is required to work overtime for any length of time. If an employee, whose minimum rate of wages has been fixed under this Act by the day, works on any day for a period less than the reputed number of hours constituting a normal working day, he shall be entitled to receive wages in respect of work done by him on that day as if he had worked for a full normal working day: provided that he shall not be entitled to receive wages for the full day, if he was unwilling to work and the employer was ready to give him the work, or if there were such other circumstances which warranted such non-payment.

2. The provisions of Sub-Sec. (1) shall, in relation to the following classes of employees, apply only to such extent and subject to such conditions as may be prescribed;

(a) employees engaged on urgent work, or in any emergency which could not have been foreseen or prevented;

(b) employees engaged in work in the nature of preparatory or complementary work which must necessarily be carried on outside the limits laid down for the general working in the employment concerned;

(c) employees whose employment is essentially intermittent;

(d) employees engaged in any work which for technical reasons has to be completed before the duty is over;

(e) employees engaged in a work which could not be carried on except at times dependent on the irregular action of natural forces.

3. An employment is intermittent when it is declared to be so by the appropriate Government on the ground that the daily hours of duty of the employee, the hours of duty, normally include periods of inaction during which the employee may be on duty but is not called upon to display either physical activity or sustained attention.

Where an employee does two or more classes of work to each of which a different minimum rate of wages is applicable, the employer shall pay to such employee in respect of the time respectively occupied in each such class of work, wages at not less than the minimum rate in force in respect of each such class (Sec.16). Where an employee is employed on piece-work for which minimum time rate and not a minimum piece-rate has been fixed under this Act, the employer shall pay to such employee wages at not less than the minimum time rate (Sec. 17).

Register and Records (Sec. 18)—Every employer shall maintain such registers and records giving such particulars of employees employed by him, the work performed by them, the wages paid to them, the receipts given by them and such other particulars and in such form as may be prescribed. He shall also keep exhibited in the factory, workshop or place where the employees in the scheduled employment may be employed, or in the case of out-workers, in such factory, workshop or place as may be used for giving out work to them, notices in the prescribed form containing prescribed particulars. The appropriate Government may provide for the issue of wage books or wage slips to employees employed in any scheduled employment in respect of which minimum rates of wages have been fixed and prescribe the manner in which entries shall be made and authenticated in such wage books or wage slips by the employer or his agent.

Inspectors (Sec.19)—The appropriate Government may, by notification in the Official Gazette, appoint such persons as it thinks fit to be Inspectors for the purposes of this Act, and define the local limits within which they shall exercise their functions. Subject to any rules made in this behalf, an Inspector may within his local limits (a) enter, at all reasonable hours, with such assistants, if any, as he thinks fit, any premises or place where employees are employed or work is given out to out-workers in any scheduled employment in respect of which minimum rates of wages have been fixed, for the purpose of examining any register, record of wages or notices and require the production thereof for inspection; (b) examine any employee, (c) require any person giving out-work and any out-workers, to give any information with regard to the work and the payments made for the work; (d) seize or take copies of any register, record of wages or notices or portions thereof as he may consider relevant in respect of any offence under this Act which he has reason to believe has been committed by an employer; and (e) exercise such other power as may be prescribed.

Claims (Sec.20)—The appropriate Government may, by notification in the Official Gazette, appoint any Commissioner for Workmen's Compensation or any officer of the Central Government exercising functions as a Labour Commissioner for any region, or any officer of the State Government not below the rank of Labour Commissioner or any Judge of a Civil Court or a Magistrate to be the Authority to hear and decide for any specified area all claims arising out of payment of less than the minimum rates of wages or in respect of remuneration for days of rest or for work done on such days under Sec. 13 or of wages at the overtime rate under Sec. 14 to employees employed or paid in that area.

2. Where an employee has any claim of the nature referred to in (1) the employee himself, or any legal practitioner or any official of registered trade union authorised in writing to act on his behalf, or any Inspector, or any person acting with the permission of the Authority, may apply to such Authority for a direction under Sub-Sec. (3): provided that every such application shall be presented within six months from the date on which the minimum wages or other amount became payable, unless the Authority admits an application after this period on sufficient cause being shown.

3. When an application under Sub-Sec. (2) is entertained, the Authority shall hear the applicant and the employer or give them an opportunity of being heard, and after such further enquiry, if any, as it may consider necessary may, without prejudice to any other penalty to which the employer may be liable under this Act, direct (i) in the case of a claim arising out of payment of less than the minimum rates of wages, the payment to the employee of the amount by which the minimum wages payable to him exceed the amount actually paid, together with the payment of such compensation as the Authority may think fit, not exceeding ten times the amount of such excess in any other case, the payment of the amount due to the employee, together with the payment of such compensation as the Authority may think fit, not exceeding ten rupees, and the Authority may direct payment of such compensation in cases where the excess or the amount due is paid by the employer to the employee before the disposal of the application.

4. If the Authority hearing any application is satisfied that it was either malicious or vexatious, it may direct the applicant to pay the employer a penalty not exceeding ₹50. Every direction of the Authority under this section shall be final.

Section 21 provides that subject to such rules as may be prescribed, a single application may be presented under Sec.20 on behalf or in respect of any number of employees employed in the scheduled employment in respect of which minimum rates of wages have been fixed and in such cases the maximum compensation which may be awarded shall not exceed ten times the aggregate amount of such excess or ten rupees per head, as the case may be. The Authority may deal with any number of separate applications as a single application.

Penalties and Procedure (Sec.22)

1. Any employer who pays to any employee less than the minimum rates of wages for that employee's class of work, or less than the amount due to him under the provisions of this Act or contravenes any order or rule made under Sec. 13 shall be punishable with imprisonment for a term which may extend to six months, or with fine which may extend to ₹ 500, or with both. In imposing any fine, the Court shall take into consideration the amount of any compensation already awarded against the accused in any proceedings taken under Sec. 20.

Section 22A* provides that an employer who contravenes any provision of this Act or of any rule or order made thereunder shall, if no other penalty is provided for .such contravention by this Act, be punishable with fine up to ₹ 500.

Section 22B* lays down that no Court shall take congnizance of a complaint against any person for an offence (a) under Sec. 22 for paying less than the minimum rate of wages unless an application under Sec. 20 has been granted wholly or in part, and the appropriate Government or an official authorised by it in this behalf has sanctioned the making of the complaint, or (b) for not complying with rules or order under Sec. 13 or under Sec. 22A, except on a complaint made by, or with the sanction of, an Inspector. The complaint under Sec. 22A must be made within 6 months of the date of the offence and in other cases within one month of the offence.

Section 22C* says that if the person committing any offence under this Act is a company, every person who at the time the offence was committed, was in charge of, and was responsible to, the company for the conduct of the business of the company as well as the company shall be deemed to be guilty of the offence and shall be liable to be proceeded against and punished accordingly: provided that he shall not be liable if he proves that the offence was committed without his knowledge or he had exercised due diligence to prevent the commission of the offence. If an offence by a company has been committed with the consent or connivance of, or is attributable to any neglect on the part of any director, manager, secretary or other officer of the company, then such person shall also be guilty of that offence and liable to be punished. A company includes any body corporate, a firm or other association of individuals and a director includes a partner.

Section 22D* provides that all amounts payable by an employer to an employee under this Act must be deposited with the prescribed authority to be dealt with, if the employee has died or cannot be traced.

Section 22E* exempts from attachment any amount deposited by an employer with the appropriate Government as security for the due performance of any contract or any amount due to the employer from the Government in respect of such contract shall not be liable to attachment under any decree or order of any Court in respect of any debt or liability of the employer other than any debt or liability towards any employee employed in connection with the contract aforesaid.

Section 22F* empowers the appropriate Government to direct by notification that any or all of the provisions of the Payment of Wages Act, 1936, will apply to the wages payable to employees in such scheduled employments as may be specified in the notification; and the Inspector employed under this Act shall be deemed to be the Inspector for the purpose of the enforcement of those provisions.

Exemption of Employer from Liability (Sec.23)—Where an employer is charged with an offence against this Act, he shall be entitled, upon complaint duly made by him to have any other person, whom he charges as the actual offender, brought before the Court at the time appointed for hearing the charge; and if, after the commission of the offence has been proved, the employer proves to the satisfaction of the Court.

(a) that he has used due diligence to enforce the execution of this Act, and
(b) that the said other person committed the offence in question without his knowledge, consent or connivance, that other person shall be convicted of the offence and shall be liable to the like punishment as if he were the employer and the employer shall be discharged. The employer will be liable to be examined on oath and the evidence of the employer or his witness shall be subject to cross-examination by the other person so charged and by the prosecution.

Section 24 bars the institution of any suit for the recovery of wages which can be or could be recovered under Sec. 20 of this Act. Sec. 25 prohibits contracting out agreement in respect of minimum rate of wages payable under this Act.

Exemptions and Exceptions (Sec. 26)

1. The appropriate Government may, subject to such conditions if any as it may think fit to impose, direct that the provisions of this Act shall not apply in relation to the wages payable to disabled employees.

2. The appropriate Government may, if for special reasons it thinks so fit, by notification in the Official Gazette, direct that subject to such conditions and for such period as it may specify the provisions of this Act or any of them shall not apply to all or any class of employees employed in any scheduled employment or to any locality where there is carried on a scheduled employment.

2A. The appropriate Government may, if it is of opinion that, having regard to the terms and conditions of service applicable to any class of employees in a scheduled employment generally or in a scheduled employment in a local area, or to any establishment or a part of any establishment in a scheduled employment it is not necessary to fix minimum wages in respect of such employees of that class or in respect of employees in such establishment or such part of any establishment as are in receipt of wages exceeding such limit as may be prescribed in this behalf, direct, by notification in the Official Gazette and subject to such conditions, if any, as it may think fit to impose, that the provisions of this Act or any of them shall not apply in relation to such employees.

3. Nothing in this Act shall apply to the wages payable by an employer to a member of his family who is living with him and is dependent on him.

Explanation—In this Sub-Section a member of the employer's family shall be deemed to include

*Inserted by Amendment Act of 1957.

his or her spouse or child or parent or brother or sister.

Section 27 empowers the appropriate Government to add to the scheduled employment any other employment, whereupon the schedule shall in its application to the State be deemed to be amended accordingly. Sec. 28 empowers the Central Government to give directions to a State Government as to the carrying into execution of this Act in the State. Sec. 29 provides that the Central Government may by notification in the Official Gazette make rules prescribing the term of office of the members, the procedure to be followed in the conduct of business, the method of voting, the manner of filling up casual vacancies in the membership and the quorum necessary for the transaction of business of the Central Advisory Board. Sec. 30 empowers the appropriate Government to make similar rules in respect of committees, sub-committees, and the Advisory Board; and in relation to other cases. Sec. 31 (1) empowers an appropriate Government to validate the fixation of certain minimum rates of wages and provides that where during the period commencing on the 1st April, 1952, and ending with the commencement of the Amending Act of 1954, minimum rates of wages have been fixed by an appropriate Government as being payable to employees employed in any employment specified in Part I of the Schedule in the belief or purported belief that such rates were being fixed under Sec. 3 (1)(a)(i), such rates shall be deemed to have been fixed in accordance with law, and shall not be questioned in any Court on the ground merely of the expiry of the time: provided that nothing contained in this section shall extend, or be construed to extend to affect any person with any punishment or penalty whatsoever by reason of the payment by him by way of wages to any of his employees during the period specified in this section an amount which is less than the minimum rates of wages referred to in this section or by reason of non-compliance during the period aforesaid with any order or rule issued under Sec. 13.

2. The provisions of Sub-Sec. (1) shall apply in relation to minimum rates of wages fixed by an appropriate Government daring the period commencing on the 31st day of December, 1954, and ending with the date of the commencement of the Minimum Wages (Amendment) Act, 1957, as they apply in relation to minimum rates of wages fixed by an appropriate Government during the period commencing on the 1st day of April, 1952, and ending with the date of commencement of Minimum Wages (Amendment) Act, 1954, subject to the modification that for the words, figures, brackets and letter' 'employ-ment specified in Part I of the Schedule in the belief or purported belief that such rates were being fixed under sub-clause (i) of clause (a) of Sub-Sec. (1) of Sec.3", the words, figures, brackets and letter "employment specified in Part I or Part II of the Schedule in the belief or purported belief that such rates were being fixed under sub-clause (i) or sub-clause (ii) of clause (a) Sub-Sec. (1) of Sec.3" shall be substituted.

THE SCHEDULE

[See Secs. 2(g) and 27]

PART I

1. Employment in any woollen carpet-making or shawl weaving establishment.
2. Employment in any rice mill, flour mill and dal mill.
3. Employment in any tobacco (including *bidi*-making) manufactory.
   Employment in any plantation, that is to say, any estate which is maintained for the purpose of growing cinchona, rubber, tea or coffee.
5. Employment in any oil mill.
6. Employment under any local authority.
7. Employment on the construction or maintenance of roads or in building operations.
8. Employment in stone-breaking or stone-crushing.
9. Employment in any lac manufactory.

10. Employment in any mica works.
11. Employment in public motor transport.
12. Employment in tanneries and leather manufactory.
13. Employment in manganese mines.
14. Employment in china clay mines.
15. Employment in kyanite mines.
16. Employment in copper mines.
17. Employment in clay mines.
18. Employment in magnesite mines.

PART II

1. Employment in agriculture, that is to say, in any form of farming, including the cultivation and tillage of the soil, dairy farming, the production, cultivation, growing and harvesting of any agricultural or horticultural commodity, the raising of livestock, bees or poultry and any practice performed by a farmer or on a farm as incidental to or in conjunction with farm operations (including any forestry or timbering operations and the preparation for market and delivery to storage or to market or to carnage for transportation to market of farm produce).

The Indian Contract Act, 1872

[25th April, 1872]
(Act. No. IX of 1872)

Whereas it is expedient to define and amend certain parts of the law relating to contracts; it is hereby enacted as follows:

Preliminary

1. Short title, extent and commencement. This Act may be called the Indian Contract Act, 1872.

It extends to [the whole of India] except the State of Jammu and Kashmir; and it shall come into force on the first day of September, 1872.

Nothing herein contained shall affect the provisions of any Statute, Act or Regulation nor hereby expressly repealed, nor any usage or custom of trade, nor any incident of any contract not inconsistent with the provisions of this Act.

2. Interpretation-clause. In this Act the following words and expressions are used in the following senses, unless a contrary intention appears from the context:—

(a) When one person signifies to another his willingness to do or to abstain from doing anything, with a view to obtaining the assent of that other to such act or abstinence, he is said to make a proposal;

(b) When the person to whom the proposal is made signifies his assent thereto, the proposal is said to be accepted. A proposal, when accepted, becomes a promise;

(c) The person making the proposal is called the "promisor", and the person accepting the proposal is called the "promisee";

(d) When, at the desire of the promisor, the promisee or any other person has done or abstained from doing, or does or abstains from doing or promises to do or to abstain from doing, something, such act or abstinence or promise is called a consideration for the promise;

(e) Every promise and every set of promises, forming the consideration for each other, is an agreement;

(f) Promises which form the consideration or part of the consideration for each other are called reciprocal promises;

(g) An agreement not enforceable by law is said to be void;

(h) An agreement enforceable by law is a contract;

(i) An agreement which is enforceable by law at the option of one or more of the parties thereto, but not at the option of the other or others, is a voidable contract;

(j) A contract which ceases to be enforceable by law becomes void when it ceases to be enforceable.

CHAPTER I

Of the Communication, Acceptance, and Revocation of Proposals

3. Communication, acceptance and revocation of proposals. The communication of proposals, the acceptance of proposals, and the revocation of proposals and acceptances, respectively, are deemed to be made by any act or omission of the party proposing, accepting or revoking by which he intends to communicate such proposal, acceptance or revocation or which has the effect of communicating it.

4. Communication when complete. The communication of a proposal is complete when it comes to the knowledge of the person to whom it is made.

The communication of an acceptance is complete,—as against the proposer, when it is put in a course of transmission to him, so as to be out of the power of the acceptor; as against the acceptor, when it comes to the knowledge of the proposer.

The communication of a revocation is complete,—as against the person who makes it, when it is put into a course of transmission to the person to whom it is made, so as to be out of the power of the person who makes it; as against the person to whom it is made, when it comes to his knowledge.

Illustrations

(a) A proposes, by letter, to sell a house to B at a certain price.

The communication of the proposal is complete when B receives the letter.

(b) B accepts A's proposal by a letter sent by post.

The communication of the acceptance is complete as against A. when the letter is posted; as against B, when the letter is received by A.

(c) A revokes his proposal by telegram.

The revocation is complete as against A, when the telegram is despatched. It is complete as against B, when B receives it.

B revokes his acceptance by telegram. B's revocation is complete as against B, when the telegram is despatched, and as against A, when it reaches him.

5. Revocation of proposal and acceptance. A proposal may be revoked at any time before the communication of its acceptance is complete as against the proposer, but not afterwards.

An acceptance may be revoked at any time before the communication of the acceptance is complete as against the acceptor, but not afterwards.

Illustrations

A proposes, by a letter sent by post, to sell his house to B.

B accepts the proposal by a letter sent by post.

A may revoke his proposal at any time before or at the moment when B posts his letter of acceptance, but not afterwards.

B may revoke his acceptance at any time before or at the moment when the letter communicating it reaches A, but not afterwards.

6. Revocation how made. A proposal is revoked—

1. by the communication of notice of revocation by the proposer to the other party;
2. by the lapse of the time prescribed in such proposal for its acceptance or, if no time is so prescribed, by the lapse of a reasonable time, without communication of the acceptance;
3. by the failure of the acceptor to fulfill a condition precedent to acceptance; or
4. by the death or insanity of the proposer, if the fact of his death or insanity comes to the knowledge of the acceptor before acceptance.

7. Acceptance must be absolute. In order to convert a proposal into a promise, the acceptance must—

1. be absolute and unqualified;
2. be expressed in some usual and reasonable manner, unless the proposal prescribes the manner in which it is to be accepted. If the proposal prescribes a manner in which it is to be accepted, and the acceptance is not made in such manner, the proposer may, within a reasonable time after

the acceptance is communicated to him, insist that his proposal shall be accepted in the prescribed manner, and not otherwise; but if he fails to do so, he accepts the acceptance.

8. Acceptance by performing conditions, or receiving consideration. Performance of the conditions of a proposal, or the acceptance of any consideration for a reciprocal promise which may be offered with a proposal, is an acceptance of the proposal.

9. Promises, express and implied. In so far as the proposal or acceptance of any promise is made in words, the promise is said to be express. In so far as such proposal or acceptance is made otherwise than in words, the promise is said to be implied.

CHAPTER II

Of Contracts, Voidable Contracts and Void Agreements

10. What agreements are contracts? All agreements are contracts if they arc made by the free consent of parties competent to contract, for a lawful consideration and with a lawful object, and are not hereby expressly declared to be void.

Nothing herein contained shall affect any law in force in India and not hereby expressly repealed, by which any contract is required to be made in writing or in the presence of witnesses, or any law relating to the registration of documents.

11. Who are competent to contract? Every person is competent to contract who is of the age of majority according to the law to which he is subject, and who is of sound mind, and is not disqualified from contracting by any law to which he is subject.

12. What is a sound mind for the purposes of contracting? A person is said to be of sound mind for the purpose of making a contract, if at the time when he makes it, he is capable of undertaking it and of forming a rational judgment as to its effect upon his interests.

A person who is usually of unsound mind, but occasionally of sound mind may make a contract when he is of sound mind.

A person who is usually of sound mind, but occasionally of unsound mind, may not make a contract when he is of unsound mind.

Illustrations

(a) A patient in a lunatic asylum, who is at intervals of sound mind, may contract during those intervals.
(b) A sane man, who is delirious from fever or who is so drunk that he cannot understand the terms of a contract or form a rational judgment as to its effect on his interest, cannot contract whilst such delirium or drunkenness asts.

13. "Consent" defined. Two or more persons are said to consent when they agree upon the same thing in the same sense.

14. "Free consent" defined. Consent is said to be free when it is not caused by—
1. coercion, as defined in Sec. 15. or
2. undue influence as defined in Sec. 16, or
3. fraud, as defined in Sec. 17, or
4. misrepresentation as defined in Sec. 18, or
5. mistake, subject to the provisions of Secs. 20, 21 and 22.

Consent is said to be so caused when it would not have been given but for the existence of such coercion, undue influence, fraud, misrepresentation or mistake.

15. "Coercion" defined. "Coercion" is the committing, or threatening to commit, any act forbidden by the Indian Penal Code (XLV of 1860), or the unlawful detaining, or threatening to detain, any property, to the prejudice of any person whatever, with the intention of causing any person to enter into an agreement.

Explanation. It is immaterial whether the Indian Penal Code (XLV of 1860) is or is not in force in the place where the coercion is employed.

Illustrations

A on board of an English ship on the high seas, causes B to enter into an agreement by an act amounting to criminal intimidation under the Indian Penal Code (XLV of 1860).

A afterwards sues B for breach of contract at Kolkata.

A has employed coercion, although his act is not an offence by the law of England, and although Sec. 506 of the Indian Code (XLV of 1860) was not in force at the time or place where the act was done.

16. "Undue influence" defined.

1. A contract is said to be induced by "undue influence" where the relations subsisting between the parties are such that one of the parties is in a position to dominate the will of the other and uses that position to obtain an unfair advantage over the other.

2. In particular and without prejudice to the generality of the foregoing principle, a person is deemed to be in a position to dominate the will of another—

(a) where he holds a real or apparent authority .over the other, or where he stands in a fiduciary relation to the other; or

(b) where he makes a contract with a person whose mental capacity is temporarily or permanently affected by reason of age, illness, or mental or bodily distress.

3. Where a person who is in a position to dominate the will of another enters into a contract with him, and the transaction appears, on the face of it or on the evidence adduced, to be unconscionable, the burden of proving that such contract was not induced by undue influence shall lie upon the person in a position to dominate the will of the other.

Nothing in this sub-section shall affect the provisions of Sec. 111 of the Indian Evidence Act, 1872 (I of 1872).

Illustrations

(a) A having advanced money to his son B, during his minority, upon B's coming of age obtains, by misuse of parental influence, a bond from B for a greater amount than the sum due in respect of the advance. A employs undue influence.

(b) A, a man enfeebled by disease or age, is induced by B 's influence over him as his medical attendant to agree to pay B an unreasonable sum for his professional services. B employs undue influence.

(c) A, being in debt to B, the money-lender of his village, contracts on a fresh loan on terms which appear to be unconscionable. It lies on B to prove that the contract was not induced by undue influence.

(d) A applies to a banker for a loan at a time when there is stringency in the money market. The banker declines to make the loan except at an unusually high rate of interest. A accepts the loan on these terms. This is a transaction in the ordinary course of business, and the contract is not induced by undue influence.

17. "Fraud" defined. "Fraud" means and includes any of the following acts committed by a party to a contract, or with his connivance or by his agent, with intent to deceive another party thereto or his agent; or to induce him to enter into the contract:—

1. the suggestion, as a fact, of that which is not true by one who does not believe it to be true;

2. the active concealment of a fact by one having knowledge or belief of the fact;

3. a promise made without any intention of performing it;

4. any other act fitted to deceive;

5. any such act or omission as the law specially declares to be fraudulent.

Explanation. Mere silence as to facts likely to affect the willingness of parties would make it A's duty to tell B if the horse is unsound.
are such that, regard being had to them, it is the duty of the person keeping silence to speak, or unless his silence is, in itself, equivalent to speech.

Illustrations

(a) A sells by auction to B, a horse which A knows to be unsound. A says nothing to B about the horse's unsoundness. This is not fraud in A.

(b) B is A's daughter and has just come of age. Here the relation between the parties would make it A's duty to tell B if the horse is unsound.

(c) B says to A— "If you do not deny it. I shall assume that the horse is sound". A says nothing. Here A's silence is equivalent to speech.

(d) A and B being traders, enter upon a contract. A has private information of a change in prices which would affect B's willingness to proceed with the contract A is not bound to inform B.

18. "Misrepresentation" defined. "Misrepresentation" means and includes—

1. the positive assertion, in a manner not warranted by the information of the person making it, of that which is not true, though he believes it to be true;

2. any breach of duty which, without an intent to deceive, gains an advantage to the person committing it, or any one, claiming under him, by misleading another to his prejudice or to the prejudice of any one claiming under him;

3. causing, however innocently, a party to an agreement to make a mistake as to the substance of the thing which is the subject of the agreement.

19. Voidability of agreements without free consent. When consent to an agreement is caused by coercion ..... fraud or misrepresentation the agreement is a contract voidable at the option of the party whose consent was so caused.

A party to a contract, whose consent was caused by fraud or misrepresentation, may, if he thinks fit, insist that the contract shall be performed, and that he shall be put in the position in which he would have been' if the representations made had been true.

Exception. If such consent was caused by misrepresentation or by silence fraudulent within the meaning of Sec. 17, the contract, nevertheless, is not voidable, if the party whose consent was so caused had the means of discovering the truth with ordinary diligence.

Explanation. A fraud or misrepresentation which did not cause the consent to a contract of the party on whom such fraud was practised, or to whom such misrepresen-tation was made, does not render a contract voidable.

Illustrations

(a) A, intending to deceive B, falsely represents that five hundred maunds of indigo are made annually at A's factory, and thereby induces B to buy the factory. The contract is voidable at the option of B.

(b) A, by a misrepresentation, leads B erroneously to believe that five hundred maunds of indigo are made annually at A's factory. B examines the accounts of the factory, which show that only four hundred maunds of indigo have been made. After this B buys the factory. The contract is not voidable on account of A's misrepresentation.

(c) A fraudulently informs B that A's estate is free from incumbrance, B there-upon buys the estate. The estate is subject to a mortgage. B may either avoid the contract, or may insist on its being carried out and the mortgage-debt redeemed.

(d) B, having discovered a vein of ore on the estate of A, adopts means to conceal, and does conceal, the existence of the ore from A. Through A's ignorance B is enabled to buy the estate at an under-value. The contract is voidable at the option of A.

(e) A is entitled to succeed to an estate at the death of B. B dies; C, having received intelligence of B's death, prevents the intelligence reaching A and thus induces A to sell him his interest in the estate. The sale is voidable at the option of A.

19-A. Power to set aside contract induced by undue influence. When consent to an agreement is caused by undue influence, the agreement is a contract voidable at the option of the party whose consent was so caused.

Any such contract may be set aside either absolutely or, if the party who was entitled to avoid it has received any benefit thereunder, upon such terms and conditions as to the Court may seem just.

Illustrations

(a) A's son has forged B's name to a promissory note. B, under threat of prosecuting A's son obtains a bond from A for the amount of the forged note. If B sues on this bond, the Court may set the bond aside.

(b) A, a money-lender, advances ₹100 to B, an agriculturist, and by undue influence, induces B to execute a bond for ₹200 with interest at 6 per cent per month. The Court may set the bond aside, ordering B to repay the ₹100 with such interest as may seem just.

20. Agreement void where both parties are under mistake as to matter of fact. Where both the parties to an agreement are under a mistake as to a matter of fact essential to the agreement, the agreement is void.

Explanation. An erroneous opinion as to the value of the thing which forms the subject-matter of the agreement is not to be deemed a mistake as to a matter of act.

Illustrations

(a) A agrees to sell to B a specific cargo of goods supposed to be on its way from England to Mumbai. It turns out that before the day of the bargain, the ship conveying the cargo had been cast away and the goods lost. Neither party was aware of the facts. The agreement is void.

(b) A agrees to buy from B a certain horse. It turns out that the horse was dead at the time of the bargain, though neither party was aware of the fact the agreement is void.

(c) A, being entitled to an estate for the life of B, agrees to sell it to C, B was dead at the time of the agreement, but both parties were ignorant of the fact. The agreement is void.

21. Effect of mistakes as to law. A contract is not voidable because it was caused by mistake as to any law in force in [India]; but a mistake as to a law not in force in [India] has the same effect as a mistake of fact.

Illustration

A and B make a contract grounded on the erroneous belief that a particular debt is bared by the Indian Law of Limitation; the contract is not voidable.

22. Contract caused by mistake of one party as to matter of fact—A contract is not voidable merely because it was caused by one of the parties to it being under a mistake as to a matter of fact.

23. What considerations and objects are lawful and what not?—The consideration or object of an agreement is lawful, unless—

it is forbidden by law; or

is of such a nature that, if permitted, it would defeat the provisions of any law; or is fraudulent; or

involves or implies injury to the person or property of another; or the Court regards it as immoral, or opposed to public policy.

In each of these cases, the consideration or object of an agreement is said to be unlawful. Every agreement of which the object or consideration is unlawful is void.

Illustrations

(a) A agrees to sell his house to B for 10,000 rupees. Here B's promise to pay the sum of 10,000 rupees is the consideration for A's promise to sell the house, and A's promise to sell the house is the consideration for B's promise to pay the 10,000 rupees. These are lawful considerations.

(b) A promises to pay B 1,000 rupees at the end of six months, if C, who owes that sum to B, fails to pay it. B promises to grant time to C accordingly. Here the promise of each party is the consideration for the promise of the other party and they are lawful considerations.

(c) A promises, for a certain sum paid to him by B, to make good to B the value of his ship if it is wrecked on a certain voyage. Here A's promise is the consideration for B's payment, and B's payment is the consideration for A's promise and these ate lawful considerations.

(d) A promises to maintain B's child and B promises to pay A 1,000 rupees yearly for the purpose. Here the promise of each party is the consideration for the promise of the other party. They are lawful considerations.

(e) A, B and C enter into an agreement for the division among them of gains acquired or to be acquired, by them by fraud. The agreement is void as its object is unlawful.

(f) A promises to obtain for B an employment in the public service, and B promises to pay 1,000 rupees to A. The agreement is void, as the consideration for it is unlawful.

(g) A, being agent for a landed proprietor, agrees for money, without the knowledge of his principal, to obtain for B a lease of land belonging to his principal. The agreement between A and B is void, as it implies a fraud by concealment by A, on his principal.

(h) A promises B to drop a prosecution which he has instituted against B for robbery, and B promises to restore the value of the things taken. The agreement is void, as its object is unlawful.

(i) A's estate is sold for arrears of revenue under the provisions of an Act of the Legislature, by which the defaulter is prohibited from purchasing the estate. B, upon an understanding with A, becomes the purchaser, and agrees to convey the estate to A upon receiving from him the price which B has paid. The agreement is void, as it renders the transaction, in effect, a purchase by the defaulter, and would so defect the object of the law.

(j) A, who is B's mukhtar, promises to exercise his influence, as such, with B in favour of C and C promises to pay 1,000 rupees to A. The agreement is void, because it is immoral.

(k) A agrees to let her daughter to B for concubinage. The agreement is void because it is immoral, though the letting may not be punishable under the Indian Penal Code (XLV of 1860).

Void Agreements

24. Agreements void, if considerations and objects unlawful in part. If any part of a single consideration for one or more objects, or any one or any part of any one of several considerations for a single object, is unlawful, the agreement is void.

Illustrations

A promises to superintend, on behalf of B, a legal manufacture of Indigo, and an illegal traffic in other articles. B promises to pay to A a salary of 10,000 rupees a year. The agreement is void, the object of A's promise and the consideration for B's promise being in part unlawful.

25. Agreement without consideration void, unless it is in writing and registered, or is a promise to compensate for something done, or is a promise to pay a debt, barred by limitation law—An agreement made without consideration is void unless—

1. it is expressed in writing and registered under the law for time being in force for the registration of [documents], and is made on account of natural love and affection between parties standing in a near relation to each other, or unless.

2. it is a promise to compensate, wholly or in part, a person who has already voluntarily done something for the promisor, or something which the promisor was legally compelled to do, or unless.

3. it is a promise, made in writing and signed by the person to be charged therewith, or by his agent generally or specially authorised in that behalf, to pay wholly or in part a debt of which the creditor might have enforced payment but for the law for the limitation of suits.

In any of these cases, such an agreement is a contract.

Explanation 1—Nothing in this section shall affect the validity as between the donor and donee, of any gift actually made.

Explanation 2—An agreement to which the consent of the promisor is freely given is not void merely because the consideration is inadequate; but the inadequacy of the consideration may be taken into account by the Court in determining the question whether the consent of the promisor was freely given.

Illustrations

(a) A promises, for no consideration, to give to B ₹ 1,000. This is a void agreement.

(b) A, for natural love and affection, promises to give his son B ₹ 1,000. A puts his promise to B into writing and registers it. This is a contract.

(c) A finds B's purse and gives it to him. B promises to give A ₹ 50. This is a contract.

(d) A supports B's infant son. B promises to pay A's expenses in so doing. This is a contract.

(e) A owes B ₹ 1,000, but the debt is barred by the Limitation Act. A signs a written promise to pay B ₹ 500 on account of the debt. This is a contract.

(f) A agrees to sell a horse worth ₹ 1,000 for ₹ 10. A's consent to the agreement was freely given. The agreement is a contract notwithstanding the inadequacy of the consideration.

(g) A agrees to sell a horse worth ₹ 1,000 for ₹ 10. A denies that his consent to the agreement was freely given.

The inadequacy of the consideration is a fact which the Court should take into account in considering whether or not A's consent was freely given.

26. Agreement in restraint of marriage void—Every agreement in restraint of the marriage of any person, other than a minor, is void.

27. Agreement in restraint of trade void—Every agreement by which any one is restrained from exercising a lawful profession, trade or business of any kind, is to that extent void.

Exception 1—**Saving of agreement not to carry on business of which goodwill is sold**—One who sells the goodwill of a business may agree with the buyer to refrain from carrying on a similar business, within specified local limits, so long as the buyer, or any person deriving title to the goodwill from him, carries on a like business therein: Provided that such limits appear to the Court reasonable, regard being had to the nature of the business.

28. Agreements in restraint of legal proceedings void—Every agreement, by which any party thereto is restricted absolutely from enforcing his rights under or in respect of any contract, by the usual legal proceedings in the ordinary tribunals, or which limits the time within which he may thus enforce his rights, is void to that extent.

Exception 1—**Saving of contract to refer to arbitration dispute that may arise**—This section shall not render illegal a contract by which two or more persons agree that any dispute which may arise between them in respect of any subject or class of subjects shall be referred to arbitration, and that only the amount awarded in such arbitration shall be recoverable in respect of the dispute so referred.

Suits barred by such contracts. When such a contract has been made, a suit may be brought for its specific performance and if a suit, other than for such specific performance, or for the recovery of the amount so awarded, is brought by one party to such contract against any other such party in

respect of any subject which they have so agreed to refer, the existence of such contract shall be a bar to the suit.

Exception 2—**Saving of contract to refer questions that have already arisen**— Nor shall this Section render illegal any contract in writing, by which two or more persons agree to refer to arbitration any question between them which has already arisen, or affect any provision of any law in force for the time being as to references to arbitration.

29. Agreement void for uncertainty—Agreements, the meaning of which is not certain, or capable of being made certain, are void.

Illustrations

(a) A agrees to sell to B "a hundred tons of oil". There is nothing whatever to show what kind of oil was intended. The agreement is void for uncertainty.

(b) A agrees to sell to B one hundred tons of oil of a specified description, known as an article of commerce. There is no uncertainty here to make agreement void.

(c) A, who is a dealer in coconut oil only, agrees to sell to B, "one hundred tons of oil". The nature of A's trade affords an indication of the meaning of the words, and A has entered into a contract for the sale of one hundred tons of coconut oil.

(d) A agrees to sell to B "all the grain in my granary at Ramnagar". There is no uncertainty here to make the agreement void.

(e) A agrees to sell to B "one thousand maunds of rice at a price to be fixed by C". As the price is capable of being made certain, there is no uncertainty here to make the agreement void.

(f) A agrees to sell to B "my white horse for rupees five hundred or rupees one thousand". There is nothing to show which of the two prices was to be given. The agreement is void.

30. Agreements by way of wager void—Agreements by way of wager are void; and no suit shall be brought for recovering anything alleged to be won on any wager, or entrusted to any person to abide the result of any game or other uncertain event on which any wager is made.

Exception in favour of certain prizes for horse racing—This section shall not be deemed to render unlawful a subscription, or contribution, or agreement to subscribe or contribute, made or entered into for or toward any plate, prize or sum of money, of the value or amount of five hundred rupees or upwards, to be awarded to the winner or winners of any horse-race.

Section 294-A of the Indian Penal Code not affected—Nothing in this section shall be deemed to legalize any transaction connected with horse-racing, to which the provisions of Sec.294-A of the Indian Penal Code (XLV of 1860) apply.

CHAPTER III

Of contingent contracts

31. "Contingent contract" defined—A "contingent contract" is a contract to do or not to do something, if some event, collateral to such contract does or does not happen.

Illustration

A contracts to pay B ₹ 10.000 if B's house is burnt. This is a contingent contract.

32. Enforcement of contracts contingent on an event happening—Contingent contracts to do or not to do anything if an uncertain future event happens cannot be enforced by law unless and until that event has happened.

If the event becomes impossible such contracts become void.

Illustrations

(a) A makes a contract with B to buy B's horse if A survives C. This contract cannot be enforced in law unless and until C dies in A's life-time.

(b) A makes a contract with B to sell a horse to B at a specified price if C, to whom the horse has been offered, refuses to buy him. The contract cannot be enforced by law unless and until C refuses to buy the horse.

(c) A contracts to pay B a sum of money when B marries C. C dies without being married to B. The contract becomes void.

33. Enforcement of contracts contingent on an event not happening—Contingent contracts to do or not to do anything if an uncertain future event does not happen can be enforced when the happening of that event becomes impossible, and not before.

Illustration

A agrees to pay B a sum of money if a certain ship does not return. The ship is sunk. The contract can be enforced when the ship sinks.

34. When event on which contract is contingent to be deemed impossible, if it is the future conduct of a living person—If the future event on which a contract is contingent is the way in which a person will act at an unspecified time, the event shall be considered to become impossible when such person does anything which renders it impossible that he should so act within any definite time, or otherwise than under further contingencies.

Illustrations

A agrees to pay B a sum of money if B marries C.

C marries D. The marriage of B to C must now be considered impossible, although it is possible that D may die and that C may afterwards marry B.

35. When contracts become void which are contingent on happening of specified event within fixed time—Contingent contracts to do or not to do anything if a specified uncertain event happens within a fixed time become void if, at the expiration of the time fixed, such event has not happened, or if, before the time fixed, such event becomes impossible.

When contracts may be enforced which are contingent on specified event not happening within fixed time—Contingent contracts to do or not to do anything if a specified uncertain event does not happen within a fixed time may be enforced by law when the time fixed has expired and such event has not happened, or, before the time fixed has expired, if it becomes certain that such event will not happen.

Illustrations

(a) A promises to pay B a sum of money if a certain ship returns within a year. The contract may be enforced if the ship returns within the year, and becomes void if the ship is burnt within the year.

(b) A promises to pay B a sum of money if a certain ship does not return within a year. The contract may be enforced if the ship does not return within the year, or is burnt within the year.

36. Agreement contingent on impossible events void—Contingent agreements to do or not to do anything, if an impossible event happens, are void, whether the impossibility of the event is known or not to the parties to the agreement at the time when it is made.

Illustrations

(a) A agree to pay B 1,000 rupees if two straight lines should enclose a space. The agreement is void.

(b) A agrees to pay B 1,000 rupees if B will marry A's daughter C. C was dead at the time of the agreement. The agreement is void.

CHAPTER IV
OF THE PERFORMANCE OF CONTRACTS

Contracts which must be performed

37. Obligation of parties to contracts—The parties to a contract must either perform, or offer to perform their respective promises, unless such performance is dispensed with or excused under the provisions of this Act, or of any other law.

Promises bind the representatives of the promisors in case of the death of such promisors before performance, unless a contrary intention appears from the contract.

Illustrations

(a) A promises to deliver goods to B on a certain day on payment of ₹ 1,000. A dies before that day. A's representatives are bound to deliver the goods to B, and B is bound to pay the ₹ 1,000 to A's representatives.

(b) A promises to paint a picture for B by a certain day, at a certain price. A dies before that day. The contract cannot be enforced either by A's representatives or by B.

38. Effect of refusal to accept offer of performance—Where a promisor has made an offer of performance to the promisee, and the offer has not been accepted, the promisor is not responsible for non-performance, nor does he thereby lose his rights under the contract

Every such offer must fulfill the following conditions:—

1. it must be unconditional;
2. it must be made at proper time and place, and under such circumstances that the person to whom it is made may have a reasonable opportunity of ascertaining that the person by whom it is able and willing there and then to do the whole of what he is bound by his promise to do;
3. if the offer is an offer to deliver anything to the promisee the promisee must have a reasonable opportunity of seeing that the thing offered is the thing which the promisor is bound by his promise to deliver.

An offer to one of several joint promisees has the same legal consequences as an offer to all of them.

Illustration

A contracts to deliver to B at his warehouse, on the first March, 1873, 100 bales of cotton of a particular quality. In order to make an offer of a performance with the effect stated in this section, A must bring the cotton to B's warehouse, on the appointed day, under such circumstances that B may have a reasonable opportunity of satisfying himself that the thing offered is cotton of the quality contracted for, and that there are 100 bales.

39. Effect of refusal of party to perform promise wholly—When a party to contract has refused to perform or disabled himself from performing his promise in its entirety, the promisee may put an end to the contract, unless he has signified by words or conduct, his acquiescence in its continuance.

Illustrations

(a) A, a singer, enters into contract with B, the manager of a theatre, to sing at his theatre two nights in every week during the next two months, and B engages to pay her 100 rupees for each night's performance. On the sixth night A wilfully absents herself from the theatre. B is at liberty to put an end to the contract.

(b) A, a singer, enters into a contract with B, the manager of a theatre, to sing at his theatre two nights in every week during the next two months, and B engages to pay her at the rate of 100 rupees for each night. On the sixth night A wilfully absents herself. With the assent of B, A sings on the seventh night. B has signified his acquiescence in the continuance of the contract, and cannot now put an end to it but is entitled to compensation for damage sustained by him through A's failure to sing on the sixth night.

By whom Contracts must be performed

40. Person by whom promise is to be performed—If it appears from the nature of the case that it was the intention of the parties to any contract that any promise contained in it should be performed by the promisor himself, such promise must be performed by the promisor. In other cases, the promisor or his representative may employ a competent person to perform it.

Illustrations

(a) A promises to pay B a sum of money. A may perform this promise, either by personally paying the money to B or by causing it to be paid to B by another; and if A dies before the time appointed for payment, his representatives must perform the promise, or employ some proper person to do so.

(b) A promises to paint a picture for B. A must perform this promise personally.

41. Effect of accepting performance from the third person—When a promisee accepts performance of the promise from a third person, he cannot afterwards enforce it against the promisor.

42. Devolution of joint liabilities—When two or more persons have made a joint promise, then unless a contrary intention appears from the contract, all such persons, during their joint lives, and after the death of any of them, his representative jointly with the survivor, or survivors, and after the death of the last survivor, the representatives of all jointly, must fulfil the promise.

43. Any one of joint promisors may be compelled to perform—When two or more persons make a joint promise, the promisee may, in the absence of express agreement to the contrary, compel any [one or more] of such joint promisors to perform the whole of the promise.

Each promisor may compel contribution—Each of two or more joint promisors may compel every other joint promisor to contribute equally with himself to the performance of the promise, unless a contrary intention appears from the contract.

Sharing of loss by default in contribution—If any one of two or more joint promisors makes default in such contribution, the remaining joint promisors must bear the loss arising from such default in equal shares.

Explanation—Nothing in this section shall prevent a surety from recovering from his principal, payments made by the surety on behalf of the principal, or entitle the principal to recover anything from the surety on account of payments made by the principal.

Illustrations

(a) A, B and C jointly promise to pay D, 3,000 rupees. D may compel either A or B or C to pay him 3,000 rupees.

(b) A, B and C jointly promise to pay D the sum of 3,000 rupees. C is compelled to pay the whole. A is insolvent, but his assets are sufficient to pay one-half of his debts. C is entitled to receive 500 rupees from A's estate, and 1,250 rupees from B.

(c) A, B and C are under a joint promise to pay D, 3,000 rupees. C is unable to pay anything, and A is compelled to pay the whole. A is entitled to receive 1,500 rupees from B.

(d) A, B and C are under a joint promise to pay D, 3,000 rupees. A and B being only sureties for C, C fails to pay. A and B are compelled to pay the whole sum. They are entitled to recover it fom C.

44. Effect of release of one joint promisor—Where two or more person have made a joint promise, a release of one of such joint promisors by the promisee does not discharge the other joint promisor or joint promisors; neither does it free the joint promisor so released from responsibility to the other joint promisor or joint promisors.

45. Devolution of joint rights—When a person has made a promise to two or more persons jointly, then, unless a contrary intention appears from the contract, the right to claim performance rests, as between him and them, with them during their joint lives, and after the death of any of them, with the representative of such deceased person jointly with the survivor or survivors, and after the death of the last survivor, with the representatives of all jointly.

Illustration

A, in consideration of 5,000 rupees lent to him by B and C, promises B and C jointly to repay them that sum with interest on a day specified. The right to claim performance rests with B's representative jointly with C during C's life, and after the death of C with the representatives of B and C jointly.

Time and place for performance

46. Time for performance of promise where no application is to be made and no time is specified— Where by the contract, a promisor is to perform his promise without application by the promisee, and no time for performance is specified, the engagement must be performed within a reasonable time.

Explanation—The question "what is a reasonable time" in each particular case, a question of fact.

47. Time and place for performance of promise, where time is specified and no application to be made—Where a promise is to be performed on a certain day and the promisor has undertaken to perform it without application by the promisee, the promisor may perform it at any time during the usual hours of business on such day and at the place at which the promise ought to be performed.

Illustration

A promises to deliver goods at B's warehouse on the first January. On that day, A brings the goods at B's warehouse, but after the usual hour for closing it, and they are not received. A has not performed his promise.

48. Application for performance on certain day to be at a proper time and place—Where a promise is to be performed on a certain day, and the promisor has not undertaken to perform it without application by the promisee, it is the duty of the promisee to apply for performance at a proper place and within the usual hours of business.

Explanation—The question "what is a proper time and place" is, in each particular case, a question of fact.

49. Place for performance of promise where no application to be made and no place fixed for performance—When a promise is to be performed without application by the promisee, and no place is fixed for the performance of it, it is the duty of the promisor to apply to the promisee to appoint a reasonable place for the performance of the promise, and to perform it at such place.

Illustration

A undertakes to deliver a thousand maunds of jute to P. on a fixed day. A must apply to B to appoint a reasonable place for the purpose of receiving it, and must deliver it to him at such place.

50. Performance in manner or at time prescribed or sanctioned by promisee—The performance of any promise may be made in any manner, or at any time which the promisee prescribes or sanctions.

Illustrations

(a) B owes A 2,000 rupees. A desires B to pay the amount to A's account with C, a banker. B, who also banks with C, orders the amount to be transferred from his account to A's credit, and this is done by C. Afterwards and before A knows of the transfer, C fails. There has been a good payment by B.

(b) A and B are mutually indebted. A and B settle an account by setting off one item against another, and B pays A the balance found to be due from him upon such settlement. This amounts to a payment by A and B respectively, of the sums which they owed to each other.

(c) A owes B 2,000 rupees. B accepts some of A's goods in deduction of the debt. The delivery of the goods operates as a part payment.

(d) A desires B, who owes him ₹100, to send him a note for ₹100 by post. The debt is discharged as soon as B puts into the post a letter containing the note duly addressed to A.

Performance of Reciprocal Promises

51. Promisor not bound to perform, unless reciprocal promisee ready and willing to perform— When a contract consists of reciprocal promises to be simultaneously performed, no promisor need perform his promise unless the promisee is ready and willing to perform his reciprocal promise.

Illustrations

(a) A and B contract that A shall deliver goods to B to be paid for by B on delivery.

A need not deliver the goods, unless B is ready and willing to pay for the goods on delivery.

B need not pay for the goods unless A is ready and willing to deliver them on payment.

(b) A and B contract that A shall deliver goods to B at a price to be paid by instalments, the first instalment to be paid on delivery.

A need not deliver, unless B is ready and willing to pay the first instalment on delivery.

B need not pay the first instalment, unless A is ready and willing to deliver the goods on payment of the first instalment.

52. Order of performance of reciprocal promises—Where the order in which reciprocal promises are to be performed is expressly fixed by the contract, they shall be performed in that order; and, where the order is not expressly fixed by the contract, they shall be performed in that order which the nature of the transaction requires.

Illustrations

(a) A and B contract that A shall build a house for B at a fixed price. A's promise to build the house must be performed before B's promise to pay for it.

(b) A and B contract that A shall make over his stock-in-trade to B at a fixed price, and B promises to give security for the payment of the money. A's promise need not be performed until the security is given, for the nature of the transaction requires that A 'should have security before he delivers up his stock.

53. Liability of party preventing event on which the contract is to take effect—When a contract contains reciprocal promises, and one party to the contract prevents the other from performing his promise, the contract becomes voidable at the option of the party so prevented, and he is entitled to compensation from the other party for any loss which he may sustain in consequence of the non-performance of the contract.

Illustration

A and B contract that B shall execute certain work for A for *A* thousand rupees. B is ready and willing to execute the work accordingly, but A prevents him from doing so.

The contract is voidable at the option of B; and if he elects to rescind it, he is entitled to recover from A compensation for any loss which he has incurred by its non-performance.

54. Effect of default as to that promise which should be first performed, in contract consisting of reciprocal promises—When a contract consists of reciprocal promises, such that one of them cannot be performed, or that its performance cannot be claimed till the other has been performed, and the promisor of the promise last mentioned fails to perform it such promisor cannot claim the performance of the reciprocal promise, and must make compensation to the other party to the contract for any loss which such other party may sustain by the non-performance of the contract.

Illustrations

(a) A hires B's ship to take in and convey, from Calcutta to the Mauritius, a cargo to be provided by A, B receiving a certain freight for its conveyance. A does not provide any cargo for the ship. A cannot claim the performance of B's promise, and must make compensation to B for the loss which B sustains by the non-performance of the contract.

(b) A contracts with B to execute certain builder's work for a fixed price, B supplying the scaffolding and timber necessary for the work. B refuses to furnish any scaffolding or timber, and the work cannot be executed. A need not execute the work, and B is bound to make compensation to A for any loss caused to him by the non-performance of the contract.

(c) A contracts with B to deliver to him, at a specified price, certain merchandise on board a ship which cannot arrive for a month, and B engages to pay for the merchandise within a week from the date of the contract. B does not pay within the week. A's promise to deliver need not be performed, and B must make compensation.

(d) A promises B to sell him one hundred bales of merchandise, to be delivered next day and B promises A to pay for them within a month. A does not deliver according to his promise, B's promise to pay need not be performed, and A must make compensation.

55. Effect of failure to perform at Fixed time in contract in which time is essential—When a party to a contract promises to do a certain thing at or before a specified time, or certain things at or before specified times, and fails to do any such thing at or before the specified time, the contract, or so much of it as has not been performed, becomes voidable at the option of the promisee, if the intention of the parties was that time should be of the essence of the contract.

Effect of such failure when time is not essential—If it was not the intention of the parties that time should be of the essence of the contract, the contract does not become voidable by the failure to do such thing at or before the specified time; but the promisee is entitled to compensation from the promisor for any loss occasioned to him by such failure.

Effect of acceptance of performance at time other than that agreed upon— If, in case of contract voidable on account of the promisor's failure to perform his promise at the time agreed, the promisee accepts performance of such promise at any time other than that agreed, the promisee cannot claim compensation for any loss occasioned by the non-performance of the promise at the time agreed, unless, at the time of such acceptance, he gives notice to the promisor of his intention to do so.

56. Agreement to do impossible act—An agreement to do an act impossible in itself is void.

Contract to do act afterwards becoming impossible or unlawful—A contract to do an act which, after the contract is made, become impossible, or by reason of some event which the promisor could not prevent, unlawful becomes void when the act becomes impossible or unlawful.

Compensation for loss through non-performance of act known to be impossible or unlawful— Where one person has promised to do something which he knew, or, with reasonable diligence, might have known, and which the promisee did not know to be impossible or unlawful, such promisor must make compensation to such promisee for any loss which such promisee sustains through the non-performance of the promise.

Illustrations

(a) A agrees with B to discover treasure by magic. The agreement is void.

(b) A and B contract to marry each other. Before the time fixed for the marriage, A goes mad. The contract becomes void.

(c) A contracts to marry B being already married to C, and being forbidden by the law to which he is subject to practise polygamy. A must make compensation to B for the loss caused to her by the non-performance of his promise.

(d) A contracts to take in cargo for B at a foreign port. A's Government afterwards declares war against the country in which the port is situated. The contract becomes void when war is declared.

(e) A contracts to act at a theatre for six months in consideration of a sum paid in advance by B. On several occasions A is too ill to act. The contract to act on those occasions becomes void.

57. Reciprocal promise to do things legal, and also other things illegal—Where persons reciprocally promise, firstly, to do certain things which are legal, and, secondly, under specified circumstances to do certain other things which are illegal, the first set of promises is a contract, but the second is a void agreement.

Illustration

A and B agree that A shall sell B a house for 10,000 rupees, but that, if B uses it as a gambling house, he shall pay A 50,000 rupees for it.

The first set of reciprocal promises, namely, to sell the house and pay 10,000 rupees for it is a contract.

The second set is for an unlawful object, namely that B may use the house as a gambling house and is a void agreement.

58. Alternative promise, one branch being illegal—In the case of an alternative promise, one branch of which is legal and the other illegal, the legal branch alone can be enforced.

Illustration

A and B agree that A shall pay 1,000 rupees, for which B shall afterwards deliver to A either rice or smuggled opium.

This is a valid contract to deliver rice and a void agreement as to the opium.

Appropriation of Payments

59. Application of payment where debt to be discharged is indicated—Where a debtor owing several distinct debts to one person, makes a payment to him, either with express intimation, or under circumstances implying that the payment is to be applied to the discharge of some particular debt, the payment, if accepted, must be applied accordingly.

Illustrations

(a) A owes B, among other debts, 1,000 rupees upon a promissory note which falls due on the first June. He owes B no other debt of that amount. On the first June A pays to B 1,000 rupees. The payment is to be applied to the discharge of the promissory note.

(b) A owes to B among other debts, the sum of 567 rupees. B writes to A and demands payment of this sum. A sends to B 567 rupees. This payment is to be applied to the discharge of the debt of which B had demanded payment.

60. Application of payment where debt to be discharged is not indicated--Where the debtor has omitted to intimate and there are no other circumstances indicating to which debt the payment is to be applied, the creditor may apply it at his discretion to any lawful debt actually due and payable to him from the debtor, whether its recovery is or is not barred by the law in force for the time being as to the limitation of suits.

61. Application of payment where neither party appropriates—Where neither party makes any appropriation the payment shall be applied in discharge of the debts in order of time, whether they are or are not barred by the law in force for the time being as to the limitation of suits. If the debts are of equal standing, the payment shall be applied in discharge of each proportionably.

Contracts which need not be performed

62. Effect of novation, rescission and alteration of contract—If the parties to a contract agree to substitute a new contract for it or to rescind or alter it, the original contract need not be performed.

Illustrations

(a) A owes money to B under a contract. It is agreed between A, B and C that B shall thenceforth accept C as his debtor, instead of A. The old debt of A to B is at in end, and a new debt from C to B has been contracted.

(b) A owes B 10,000 rupees. A enters into an arrangement with B, and gives B a mortgage of his (A's) estate for 5,000 rupees in place of the debt of 10,000 rupees. This is a new contract and extinguishes the old.

(c) A owes B 1,000 rupees under a contract. B owes C 1,000 rupees. B orders A to credit C with 1,000 rupees in his books but C does not assent to the arrangement. B still owes C 1,000 rupees, and no new contract has been entered into.

63. Promisee may dispense with or remit performance of promise—Every promisee may dispense with or remit, wholly or in part, the performance of the promise made to him, or may extend the time for such performance, or may accept instead of it any satisfaction which he thinks fit.

Illustrations

(a) A promises to paint a picture for B. B afterwards forbids him to do so. A is no longer bound to perform the promise.

(b) A owes B 5,000 rupees. A pays to B and B accepts in satisfaction of the whole debt 2,000 rupees paid at the time and place at which the 5,000 rupees were payable. The whole debt is discharged.

(c) A owes B 5,000 rupees. C pays to B 1,000 rupees and B accepts them, in satisfaction of his claim on A. This payment is discharge of the whole claim.

(d) A owes B, under a contract, a sum of money, the amount of which has not been ascertained. A without ascertaining the amount gives to B, and B, in satisfaction thereof, accepts the sum of 2,000 rupees. This is a discharge of the whole debt, whatever may be its amount.

(e) A owes B 2,000 rupees, and is also indebted to other creditors. A makes an arrangement with his creditors, including B to pay them a [composition] of 50 paise in the rupee upon their respective demands. Payment to B of 1,000 rupees is a discharge of B's demand.

64. Consequences of rescission of voidable contract—When a person at whose option a contract is voidable rescinds it, the other party thereto need not perform any promise therein contained in which he is promisor. The party rescinding a voidable contract shall, if he has received any benefit thereunder from another party to such contract, restore such benefit, so far as may be, to the person from whom it was received.

65. Obligation of person who has received advantage under void agreement or contract that becomes void—When an agreement is discovered to be void or when a contract becomes void, any person who has received any advantage under such agreement or contract is bound to restore it, or to make compensation for it to the person from whom he received it.

Illustrations

(a) A pays B 1,000 rupees in consideration of B's promising to marry C, A's daughter. C is dead at the time of the promise. The agreement is void, but B must repay A the 1,000 rupees.

(b) A contracts with B to deliver to him 250 maunds of rice before the first of May. A delivers 130 maunds only before that day, and none after, B retains the 130 maunds after the first of May. He is bound to pay A for them.

(c) A, a singer, contracts with B, the manager of a theatre, to sing at his theatre for two nights in every week during the next two months, and B engages to pay her a hundred rupees for each night's performance. On the sixth night, A wilfully absents herself from the theatre, and B, in consequence, rescinds the contract. B must pay A for the five nights on which she had sung.

(d) A contracts to sing for B at a concert for 1,000 rupees, which are paid in advance. A is too ill to sing. A is not bound to make compensation to B for the loss of the profits which B would have made if A had been able to sing, but must refund to B the 1,000 rupees paid in advance.

66. Mode of communicating or revoking rescission of voidable contract—The rescission of a voidable contract may be communicated or revoked in the same manner, and subject to the same rules, as apply to the communication or revocation of a proposal.

67. Effect of neglect of promisee to afford promisor reasonable facilities for performance—If any promisee neglects or refuses to afford the promisor reasonable facilities for the performance of his promise, the promisor is excused by such neglect or refusal as to any non-performance caused thereby.

Illustration

A contracts with B to repair B's house.

B neglects or refuses to point out to A the places in which his house requires repair. A is excused for the non-performance of the contract if it is caused by such neglect or refusal,

CHAPTER V
Of certain relations resembling those created by contract

68. Claim for necessaries supplied to person incapable of contracting or on its account—If a person, incapable of entering into a conduct, or any one whom he is legally bound to support is supplied by another person with necessaries suited to his condition in life, the person who has furnished such supplies is entitled to be reimbursed from the property of such incapable person.

Illustrations

(a) A supplies B, a lunatic, with necessaries suitable to his condition in life. A is entitled to be reimbursed from B's property.
(b) A supplies the wife and children of B, a lunatic, with necessaries suitable to their condition in life. A is entitled to be reimbursed from B's property.

69. Reimbursement of person paying money due by another in payment of which he is interested—A person who is interested in the payment of money which another is bound by law, to pay, and who therefore pays it, is entitled to be reimbursed by the other.

Illustration

B holds land in Bengal, on a lease granted by A, the zamindar. The revenue payable by A to the Government being in arrear, his land is advertised for sale by the Government. Under the revenue law, the consequence of such sale will be the annul-ment of B's lease. B, to prevent the sale and the consequent annulment of his own lease, pays to the Government the sum due from A. A is bound to make good to B the amount so paid.

70. Obligation of person enjoying benefit of non-gratuitous act—Where a person lawfully does anything for another person, or delivers anything to him, not intending to do so gratuitously, and such other person enjoys the benefit thereof, the latter is bound to make compensation to the former in respect of, or to restore, the thing so done or delivered.

Illustrations

(a) A, a tradesman, leaves goods at B's house by mistake. B treats the goods as his own. He is bound to pay A for them.
(b) A saves B's property from fire. A is not entitled to compensation from B, if the circumstances show that he intended to act gratuitously.

71. Responsibility of finder of goods—A person who finds goods belonging to another and takes them into his custody, is subject to the same responsibility as a bailee.

72. Liability of person to whom money is paid, or thing delivered by mistake or under coercion— A person to whom money has been paid, or anything delivered by mistake or under coercion, must repay or return it.

Illustrations

(a) A and B jointly owe 100 rupees to C. A alone pays the amount to C, and B, not knowing this fact, pays 100 rupees over again to C. C is bound to repay the amount to B.

(b) A railway company refuses to deliver up certain goods to the consignee except upon the payment of an illegal charge for carriage. The consignee pays the sum charged in order to obtain the goods. He is entitled to recover so much of the charge as was illegally excessive.

CHAPTER VI
Of the Consequences of Breach of Contract

73. Compensation for loss or damage caused by breach of contract— When a contract has been broken, the party who suffers by such breach is entitled to receive, from the party who has broken the contract, compensation for any loss or damage caused to him thereby, which naturally arose in the usual course of things from such breach, or which the parties knew, when they made the contract, to be likely to result from the breach of it.

Such compensation is not to be given for any remote and indirect loss or damage sustained by reason of the breach.

Compensation for failure to discharge obligation resembling those created by contract—When an obligation resembling those created by contract has been incurred and has not been discharged, any person injured by the failure to discharge it is entitled to receive the same compensation from the party in default, as if such person had contracted to discharge it and had broken his contract.

Explanation—In estimating the loss or damage arising from a breach of contract, the means which existed of remedying the inconvenience caused by the non-performance of the contract must be taken into account.

Illustrations

(a) A contracts to sell and deliver 50 maunds saltpetre to B, at a certain price to be paid on delivery. A breaks his promise. B is entitled to receive from A, by way of compensation, the sum, if any, by which the contract price falls short of the price for which B might have obtained 50 maunds of saltpetre of like quality at the time when the saltpetre ought to have been delivered.

(b) A hires B's ship to go to Bombay, and there takes on board, on the first January a cargo which A is to provide and to bring it to Calcutta, the freight to be paid when earned. B's ship does not go to Bombay, but A has opportunities of procuring suitable conveyance for the cargo upon terms as advantageous as those on which he had chartered the ship. A avails himself of those opportunities, but is put to trouble and expense in doing so. A is entitled to receive compensation from B in respect of such trouble and expense.

(c) A contracts to buy of B, at a stated price, 50 maunds of rice, no time being fixed for delivery. A afterwards informs B that he will not accept the rice if tendered to him. B is entitled to receive from A, by way of compensation, the amount, if any, by which the contract price exceeds that which B can obtain for the rice at the time when A informs B that he will not accept it.

(d) A contracts to buy B's ship for 60,000 rupees, but breaks his promise. A must pay to B, by way of compensation, the excess, if any, of the contract price over the price which B can obtain for the ship at the time of the breach of promise.

(e) A, the owner of a boat, contracts with B to take a cargo of jute to Mirzapur, for sale at that place, starting on a specified day. The boat, owing to some avoidable cause, does not start at the time appointed, whereby the arrival of the cargo at Mirzapur is delayed beyond the time when it would have arrived if the boat had sailed according to the contract. Alter that date and before the arrival of the cargo, the price of jute falls. The measure of the compensation payable to B by A is the difference between the price which B could have obtained for the cargo at Mirzapur at the time when it would have arrived if the boat had sailed according to the contract, and its market price at the time when it actually arrived.

(f) A contracts to repair B's house in a certain manner, and receives payment in advance. A repairs the house, but not according to contract, B is entitled to recover from A the cost of making the repairs conform to the contract.

(g) A contracts to let his ship to B for a year, from the first of January, for a certain price. Freights rise, and on the first of January, the hire obtainable for the ship is higher than the contract price. A breaks his promise. He must pay to B, by way of compensation, a sum equal to the difference between the contract price and the price for which B could hire a similar ship for a year on and from the first of January.

(h) A contracts to supply B with a certain quality of iron at a fixed price, being a higher price than that for which A could procure and deliver the iron. B wrongfully refuses to receive the iron. B must pay to A, by way of compensation, the difference between the contract price of the iron and the sum for which A could have obtained and delivered it.

(i) A delivers to B, a common carrier, a machine to be conveyed, without delay, to A's mill, informing B that his mill is stopped for want of the machine. B unreasonably delays the delivery of the machine, and A in consequence, loses a profitable contract with the Government. A is entitled to receive from B, by way of compensation, the average amount of profit which would have been made by the working of the mill during the time that delivery of it was delayed, but not the loss sustained through the loss of the Government contract.

(j) A, having contracted with B to supply B with 1,000 tons of iron at 100 rupees a ton, to be delivered at a stated time, contracts with C for the purchase of 1,000 tons of iron at 80 rupees a ton, telling C that he does so for the purpose of performing his contract with B. C fails to perform his contract with A, who cannot procure other iron, and B, in consequence, rescinds the contract. C must pay to A 20,000 rupees, being the profit which A would have made by the performance of his contract with B.

(k) A contracts with B to make and deliver to B, by a fixed day, for a specified price a certain piece of machinery. A does not deliver the piece of machinery at the time specified, and, in consequence of this, B is obliged to procure another at a higher price than that which he was to have paid to A, and is prevented from performing a contract which B had made with a third person at the time of his contract with A (but which had not been then communicated to A), and is compelled to make compensation for breach of that contract. A must pay to B, by way of compensation, the difference between the contract price of the piece of machinery and the sum paid by B for another, but not the sum paid by B to the third person by way of compensation.

(l) A, a builder, contracts to erect and finish a house by the first of January, in order that B may give possession of it at that time to C, to whom B has contracted to let it. A is informed of the contract between B and C. A builds the house so badly that, before the first of January, it falls down and has to be rebuilt by B, who, in consequence, loses the rent which he was to have received from C, and is obliged to make compensation to C for the breach of his contract. A must make compensation to B for the cost of rebuilding the house, for the rent lost, and for the compensation made to C.

(m) A sells certain merchandise to B, warranting it to be of a particular quality, and B, in reliance upon this warranty, sells it to C with a similar warranty. The goods prove to be not according to the warranty, and B becomes liable to pay C a sum of money by way of compensation. B is entitled to be reimbursed this sum by A.

(n) A contracts to pay a sum of money to B on a day specified. A does not pay the money on that day; B in consequence of not receiving the money on that day, is unable to pay his debts, and is totally ruined. A is not liable to make good to B anything except the principal sum he contracted to pay, together with interest up to the day of payment.

(o) A contracts to deliver 50 maunds of saltpetre to B on the first of January, at a certain price. B afterwards, before the first of January, contracts to sell the saltpetre to C at a price higher than the market price of the first of January. A breaks his promise. In estimating the compensation payable by A to B, the marked price of the first of January, and not the profit which would have arisen to B from the sale to C, is to be taken into account.

(p) A contracts to sell and deliver 500 bales of cotton to B on a fixed day. A knows nothing of B's mode of conducting his business. A breaks his promise, and B, having no cotton, is obliged to close his mill. A is not responsible to B for the loss caused to B by the dosing of the mill.

(q) A contracts to sell and deliver to B, on the first of January, certain cloth which B intends to manufacture into caps of a particular kind, for which there is no demand, except at that season. The cloth is not delivered till after the appointed time, and too late to be used that year in making caps. B is entitled to receive from A, by way of compensation, the difference between the contract price of the cloth and its market price at the time of delivery, but not the profits which he expected to obtain by making caps; not the expenses which he has been put to in making preparation for the manufacture.

(r) A, a ship owner, contracts with B to convey him from Calcutta to Sydney in A's ship, sailing on the first of January, and B pays to A, by way of deposit, one-half of his passage-money. The slip does not sail on the first of January, and B, after being, in consequence, detained in Calcutta for some time, and thereby put to some expense, proceeds to Sydney in another vessel and, in consequence, arriving too late in Sydney, loses a sum of money. A is liable to repay to B his deposit, with interest, and the expense to which he is put by his detention in Calcutta, and the excess, if any, of the passage-money paid for the second ship over that agreed upon for the first, but not the sum of money which B lost by arriving in Sydney too late.

74. Compensation for breach of contract where penalty stipulated for— When a contract has been broken, if a sum is named in the contract as the amount to be paid in case of such breach, or if the contract contain any other stipulation by way of penalty, the party complaining of the breach is entitled, whether or not actual damage or loss is proved to have been caused thereby, to receive from the party who has broken the contract, reasonable compensation not exceeding the amount so named or, as the case may be, the penalty stipulated for.

Explanation—A stipulation for increased interest from the date of default may be a stipulation by way of penalty.

Exception—When any person enters into any bail-bond, recognizance or other instrument of the same nature, or, under the provisions of any law, or under the orders of the Central Government or of any State Government, gives any bond for the performance of any public duty or act in which the public are interested, he shall be liable, upon breach of the condition of any such instrument, to pay the whole sum mentioned therein.

Explanation—A person who enters into a contract with Government does not necessarily thereby undertake any public duty, or promis to do an act in which the public are interested.

Illustrations

(a) A contracts with B to pay B ₹ 1,000 if he failed to pay B ₹ 500 on a given day. A fails to pay B ₹ 500 on that day. B is entitled to recover from A such compensation, not exceeding ₹ 1,000, as the Court considers reasonable.

(b) A contracts with B that if A practises as a Surgeon within Kolkata, he will pay B ₹ 5,000. A practises as a Surgeon in Kolkata. B is entitled to such compensation, not exceeding ₹ 5,000, as the Court considers reasonable.

(c) A gives a recognizance binding him in a penalty of ₹ 500 to appear in Court on a certain day. He forfeits his recognizance. He is liable to pay the whole penalty.

(d) A gives B a bond for the repayment of ₹ 1,000 with interest at 12 per cent, at the end of six months, with a stipulation that in case of default, interest shall be payable at the rate of 75 per cent, from the date of default This is a stipulation by way of penalty, and B is only entitled to recover from A such compensation as the Court considers reasonable.

(e) A, who owes money to B, a money-lender, undertakes to repay him by delivering to him 10 maunds of grain on a certain date, and stipulates that in the event of his not delivering the stipulated amount by the stipulated date, he shall be liable to deliver 20 maunds. This is a stipulation by way of penalty and B is only entitled to reasonable compensation in case of breach.

(f) A undertakes to repay B a loan of ₹ 1,000 by five equal monthly instalments with a stipulation that, in default of payment of any instalment, the whole shall become due. This stipulation is not by way of penalty, and the contract may be enforced according to its terms.

(g) A borrows ₹100 from B and gives him a bond for ₹ 200 payable by five yearly instalments of ₹ 40, with a stipulation that, in default of payment of any instalment, the whole shall become due. This is a stipulation by way of penalty.

75. Party rightfully rescinding contract entitled to compensation—A person who rightfully rescinds a contract is entitled to compensation for any damage which he has sustained through the non-fulfilment of the contract.

Illustration

A, a singer, contracts with B, the manager of a theatre, to sing at his theatre for two nights in every week during the next two months, and B engages to pay her 100 rupees for each night's performance. On the sixth night, A wilfully absents herself from the theatre, and B, in consequence, rescinds the contract B is entitled to claim compen-sation for the damage which he has sustained through the non-fulfilment of the contract.

CHAPTER VII

Sale of Goods

Secs. 76-123 Repealed by the Indian Sale of Goods Act 1930

(III of 1930), Sec.65

CHAPTER VIII

Of Indemnity and Guarantee

124. "Contract of indemnity" defined—A contract by which one party promises to save the other from loss caused to him by the conduct of the promisor himself, or by the conduct of any other person, is called a "contract of indemnity".

Illustration

A contracts to indemnify B against the consequences of any proceedings which C may take against B in respect of a certain sum of 200 rupees. This is a contract of indemnity.

125. Rights of indemnity-holder when sued—The promisee in a contract of indemnity, acting within the scope of his authority, is entitled to recover from the promisor—

1. all damages which he may be compelled to pay in any such suit in respect of any matter to which the promise to indemnify applies;

2. all costs which he may be compelled to pay in any such suit if, in bringing or defending it, he did not contravene the order of the promisor, and acted as it would have been prudent for him to act in the absence of any contract of indemnity, or if the promiser authorised him to bring or defend the suit;

3. all sums which he may have paid under the terms of any compromise of any such suit, if the compromise was not contrary to the orders of the promisor, and was one which it would have been prudent for the promisee to make in the absence of any contract of indemnity, or if the promisor authorized him to compromise the suit.

126. "Contract of guarantee", "surety", "principal debtor" and "creditor"—A "contract of guarantee", is a contract to perform the promise, or discharge the liability, of a third person in case of his default. The person who gives the guarantee is called the "surety", the person in respect of whose default the guarantee is given is called the "principal debtor", and the person to whom the guarantee is given is called the "creditor". A guarantee may be either oral or written.

127. Consideration for guarantee—Anything done, or any promise made for the benefit of the principal debtor may be a sufficient consideration to the surety for giving the guarantee.

Illustrations

(a) B requests A to sell and deliver to him goods on credit. A agrees to do so, provided C will guarantee the payment of the goods. C promises to guarantee the payment in consideration of A's promise to deliver the goods. This is a sufficient consideration for C's promise.

(b) A sells and delivers goods to B. C afterwards requests A to forbear to sue B for the debt for a year and promises that if he does so, C will pay for them in default of payment by B. A agrees to forbear as requested. This is a sufficient consideration for C's promise.

(c) A sells and delivers goods to B. C afterwards, without consideration, agrees to pay for them in default of B. The agreement is void.

128. Surety's liability—The liability of the surety is co-extensive with that of the principal debtor, unless it is otherwise provided by the contract.

Illustration

A guarantees to B the payment of a bill of exchange by C, the acceptor. The bill is dishonoured by C. A is liable not only for the amount of the bill but also for any interest and charges which may have become due on it.

129. "Continuing guarantee"—A guarantee which extends to a series of transactions is called a "continuing guarantee".

Illustrations

(a) A, in consideration that B will employ C in collecting the rents of B's zamindari, promises B to be responsible, to the amount of 5,000 rupees, for the due collection and payment by C of those rents. This is a continuing guarantee.

(b) A guarantee payment to B, a tea-dealer, to the amount of £100, for any tea he may from time to time supply to C. B supplies C with tea to the value of £100, and C pays B for it. Afterwards B supplies C with tea to the value of £200. C fails to pay. The guarantee given by A was a continuing guarantee, and he is accordingly liable to B to the extent of £100.

(c) A guarantees payment to B of the price of five sacks of flour to be delivered by B to C and to be paid for in a month. B delivers five sacks to C. C pays for them. Afterwards B delivers four sacks to C, which C docs not pay for. The guarantee given by A was not a continuing guarantee, and accordingly he is not liable for the price of the four sacks.

130. Revocation of continuing guarantee. Continuing guarantee may at any time be revoked by the surety, as to future transactions, by notice to the creditor.

Illustrations

(a) A, in consideration of B's discounting, at A s request, bills of exchange for C guarantees to B, for twelve months, the due payment of all such bills to the extent of 5,000 rupees. B discounts bills for C to the extent of 2,000 rupees. Afterwards at the end of three months, A revokes the guarantee. This revocation discharges A from all liability to B for any subsequent discount. But A is liable to B for the 2,000 rupees, on default of C.

(b) A guarantees to B, to the extent of 10,000 rupees, that C shall pay all the bills that B shall draw upon him, B draws upon C. C accepts the bill. A gives notice of revocation. C dishonours the bill at maturity. A i* liable upon his guarantee.

131. Revocation of continuing guarantee by surety's death—The death of the surety operates, in the absence of any contract to the contrary, as a revocation of a continuing guarantee, so far as regards future transactions.

132. Liability of two persons primarily liable, not affected by arrangement between them that one shall be surety on other's default—Where two persons contract with a third person to undertake a certain liability, and also contract with each other that one of them shall be liable only on the default of the other, the third person not being a party to such contract, the liability of each of such two persons to the third person under the first contract is not affected by the existence of the second contract, although such third person may have been aware of its existence.

Illustration

A and B make a joint and several promissory note to C. A makes it, in fact as surety for B, and C knows this at the time when the note is made. The fact that A, to the knowledge of C, made the note as surety for B, is no answer to a suit by C against A upon the note.

133. Discharge of surety by variance in terms of contract—Any variance, made without the surety's consent, in the terms of the contract between the principal debtor and the creditor, discharges the surety as to transactions subsequent to the variance.

Illustrations

(a) A becomes surety to C for B 's conduct as a manager in C's bank. Afterwards, B and C contract, without A's consent, that B's salary shall be raised, and that he shall become liable for one-fourth of the losses on overdrafts. B allows a customer to overdraw, and the bank loses a sum of money. A is discharged from his suretyship by the variance made without his consent, and is not Liable to make good this loss.

(b) A guarantees C against the misconduct of B in an office to which B is appointed by C, and of which the duties are defined by an Act of the Legislature. By a consequent Act, the nature of the office is materially altered. Afterwards, B misconducts himself. A is discharged by the change from future Liability under his guarantee, though the misconduct of B is in respect of a duty not affected by the late Act.

(c) C agrees to appoint B as his clerk to sell goods at yearly salary, upon A's becoming surety to C for B's duly accounting for moneys received by him as such clerk. Afterwards, without A's knowledge or consent, C and B agree that B should be paid by a commission on the goods sold by him and not by a fixed salary. A is not liable for subsequent misconduct of B.

(d) A gives to C a continuing guarantee to the extent of 3,000 rupees for any oil supplied by C to B on credit. Afterwards B becomes embarrassed, and without the knowledge of A, B and C contract that C shall continue to supply B with oil for ready money, and that the payments shall be applied to the then existing debts between B and C. A is not liable on his guarantee for any goods supplied after this new arrangement.

(e) C contracts to lend B 5,000 rupees on the 1st March. A guarantees repayment. A pays the 5,000 rupees to B on the 1st January. A is discharged from his liability, as the contract has been varied inasmuch as C might sue B for the money before the 1st of March.

134. Discharge of surety by release or discharge of principal debtor—The surety is discharged by any contract between the creditor and the principal debtor, by which the principal debtor is released, or by any act or omission of the creditor, the legal consequence of which is the discharge of the principal debtor.

Illustrations

(a) A gives a guarantee to C for goods to be supplied by C to B. C supplies goods to B and afterwards B becomes embarrassed and contracts with his creditors (including C) to assign to them his property in consideration of their releasing him from their demands. Here A is released from his debt by the contract with C, and A is discharged form his suretyship.

(b) A contracts with B to grow a crop of indigo on A's land and to deliver it to B at a fixed rate, and C guarantees A's performance of this contract. B diverts a stream of water which is necessary for irrigation of A's land and thereby prevents him from raising the indigo. C is no longer liable on his guarantee.

(c) A contracts with B for a fixed price to build a house for B within a stipulated time, B supplying the necessary timber. C guarantees A's performance of the contract. B omits to supply the timber. C is discharged from his suretyship.

135. Discharge of surety when creditor compounds with, gives time to, or agrees not to sue, principal debtor—A contract between the creditor and the principal debtor, by which the creditor makes a composition with, or promises to give time to, or not to sue, the principal debtor, discharges the surety, unless the surety assents to such contract.

136. Surety and discharged when agreement made with third person to give time to principal debtor—Where a contract to give time to the principal debtor is made by the creditor with a third person, and not with the principal debtor, the surety is not discharged.

Illustration

C, the holder of an overdue bill of exchange drawn by A as surety for B, and accepted by B, contracts with M to give time to B. A is not discharged.

137. Creditor's forbearance to sue does not discharge surety—Mere forbearance on the part of the creditor to sue the principal debtor or to enforce any other remedy against him does not, in the absence of any provision in the guarantee to the contrary, discharge the surety.

Illustration

B owes to. C a debt guaranteed by A. The debt becomes payable. C does not sue B for a year after the debt has become payable. A is not discharged from his suretyship.

138. Release of one co-surety does not discharge others—Where there are co-sureties a release by the creditor of one of them does not discharge the others; neither does it free the surety so released from his responsibility to the other sureties.

139. Discharge of surety by creditor's act or omission impairing surety's eventual remedy—If the creditor does any act which is inconsistent with the right of the surety, or omits to do any act which his duty to the surety requires him to do, and the eventual remedy of surety himself against the principal debtor is thereby impaired, the surety is discharged.

Illustrations

(a) B contracts to build a ship for C for a given sum, to be paid by instalments as the work reaches certain stages. A becomes surety to C for B's due performance of the contract C, without the knowledge of A, prepays to B the last two instalments. A is discharged by this prepayment.

(b) C lends money to B on the security of a joint and several promissory note made in C's favour by B, and by A as surety for B, together with a bill of sale of B's furniture, which gives power to C to sell the furniture, and apply the proceeds in discharge of the note. Subsequently, C sells the furniture but owing to his misconduct and willful negligence, only a small price is realized. A is discharged from liability on the note.

(c) A puts M as apprentice to B, and gives a guarantee to B for M's fidelity. B promises on his part that he will, at least once a month, see M make up the cash. B omits to see this done as promised, and M embezzles. A is not liable to B on his guarantee.

140. Rights of surety on payment or performance—Where a guaranteed debt has become due, or default of the principal debtor to perform a guaranteed duty has taken place, the surety, upon payment or performance of all that he is liable for, is invested with all the rights which the creditor had against the principal debtor.

141. Surety's right to benefit of creditor's securities—A surety is entitled to the benefit of every security which the creditor has against the principal debtor at the time when the contract of suretyship is entered into, whether the surety knows of the existence of such security or not; and, if the creditor loses, or, without the consent of the surety, parts with such security the surety is discharged to the extent of the value of the security.

Illustrations

(a) C advances to B, his tenant, 2,000 rupees on the guarantee of A. C has also a further security for the 2,000 rupees by a mortgage of B's furniture. C cancels the mortgage. B becomes insolvent, and C sues A on his guarantee. A is discharged from liability to the amount of the value of the furniture.

(b) C, a creditor, whose advance to B is secured by a decree, receives also a guarantee for that advance from A. C afterwards takes B's goods in execution under the decree, and then, without the knowledge of A, withdraws the execution. A is discharged.

(c) A, as surety for B, makes a bond jointly with B to C, to secure a loan from C. to B. Afterwards, C obtains from B a further security for the same debt. Subsequently, C gives up the further security. A is not discharged.

142. Guarantee obtained *by* misrepresentation invalid—Any guarantee which has been obtained by means of misrepresentation made by the creditor or with his knowledge and assent, concerning a material part of the transaction, is invalid.

143. Guarantee obtained by concealment invalid—Any guarantee which the creditor has obtained by means of keeping silence as to material circumstances is invalid.

Illustrations

(a) A engages B as clerk to collect money for him. B fails to account for some of his receipts, and A in consequence calls upon him to furnish security for his duly accounting. C gives his guarantee for B's duly accounting. A does not acquaint C with B's previous conduct. B afterwards makes default. The guarantee is invalid.

(b) A guarantees to C payment for iron to be supplied by him to B to the amount of 2,000 tons. B and C have privately agreed that B should pay five rupees per ton beyond the market price, such excess to be applied in liquidation of an old debt. This agreement is concealed from A. A is not liable as a surety.

144. Guarantee on contract that creditor shall not act on it until co-surety joins—Where a person gives a guarantee upon a contract that the creditors shall not act upon it until anothe person has joined in it as co-surety, the guarantee is not valid if that another person does not join.

145. Implied promise to indemnify surety—In every contract of guarantee there is an implied promise by the principal debtor to indemnify the surety; and the surety is entitled to recover from the principal debtor whatever sum he has rightfully paid under the guarantee, but no sums which he has paid wrongfully.

Illustrations

(a) B is indebted to C, and, A is surety for the debt. C demands payment from A, and on his refusal sues him for the amount. A defends the suit, having reasonable grounds for doing so, but is compelled to pay the amount of the debt with costs. He can recover from B the amount paid by him for costs, as well as the principal debt.

(b) C lends B a sum of money, and A, at the request of B, accepts bill of exchange drawn by B upon A to secure the amount. C, the holder of the bill, demands payment of it from A and, on A's refusal to pay, sues him upon the bill. A, not having reasonable grounds for so doing, defends the suit, and has to pay the amount of the Bill and costs.

He can recover from B the amount of the bill, but not the sum paid for costs, as there was no real ground for defending the action.

(c) A guarantees to C, to the extent of 2,000 rupees, payment for rice, to be supplied by C to B. C supplies to B rice to a less amount than 2,000 rupees, but obtains from A payment of the sum of 2,000 rupees in respect of the rice supplied. A cannot recover from B more than the price of the rice actually supplied.

146. Co-sureties liable to contribute equally. Where two or more persons are co-sureties for the same debt or duty, either jointly or severally, and whether under the same or different contracts, and whether with or without the knowledge of each other, the co-sureties in the absence of any contract to the contrary, are liable, as between themselves, to pay each an equal share of the whole debt, or of that part of it which remains unpaid by the principal debtor.

Illustrations

(a) A, B and C are sureties to D for the sum of 3,000 rupees lent to E. E makes default in payment. A, B and C are liable, as between themselves, to pay 1,000 rupees each.

(b) A, B and C are sureties to D for the sum of 1,000 rupees lent to E, and there is a contract between A, B and C that A is to be responsible to the extent of one-quarter, B to the extent of one-quarter and C to the extent of one-half. E makes default in payment. As between the sureties, A is liable to pay 250 rupees, B 250 rupees and C 500 rupees.

147. Liability of co-sureties bound in different sums — Co-sureties who are bound in different sums are liable to pay equally as far as the limits of their respective obligations permit.

Illustrations

(a) A, B and C, as sureties for D, enter into three several bonds each in a different penalty, namely, A in the penalty of 10,000 rupees, B in that of 20,000 rupees, C in that of 40,000 rupees, conditioned for D's duly accounting to E. D makes default to the extent of 30,000 rupees. A, B and C are each liable to pay 10,000 rupees.

(b) A, B and C, as sureties for D, enter into three several bonds, each in a different penalty, namely, A in the penalty of 10,000 rupees, B in that of 20,000 rupees, C in that of 40,000 rupees, conditioned for D's duly accounting to E. D makes default to the extent of 40,000 rupees. A is liable to pay 10,000 rupees, and B and C 15,000 rupees each.

(c) A, B and C, as sureties for D, enter into three several bonds, each in a different penalty, namely, A in the penalty of 10,000 rupees, B in that of 20,000 rupees, C in that of 40,000 rupees, conditioned for D's duly accounting to E. D makes default to the extent of 70,000 rupees. A, B and C have to pay each the full penalty of his bond.

CHAPTER IX
Of Bailment

148. "Bailment" "bailor" and "bailee" defined — A "bailment" is the delivery of goods by one person to another for some purpose, upon a contract that they shall, when the purpose is accomplished, be returned or otherwise disposed of according to the directions of the person delivering them. The person delivering the goods is called the "bailor". The person to whom they are delivered is called the "bailee".

Explanation. If a person already in possession of the goods of another contracts to hold them as a bailee, he thereby becomes the bailee, and the owner becomes the bailor, of such goods although they may not have been delivered by way of bailment.

149. Delivery to bailee how made—The delivery to the bailee may be made by doing anything which has the effect of putting the goods in the possession of the intended bailee or any person authorised to hold them on his behalf.

150. Bailor's duty to disclose faults in goods bailed—The bailor is bound to disclose to the bailee faults in the goods bailed, of which the bailor is aware and which materially interfere with the use of them or expose the bailee to extraordinary risks; and, if he does not make such disclosure, he is responsible for damage arising to the bailee directly from such faults.

If the goods are bailed for hire, the bailor is responsible for such damage whether he was or was not aware of the existence of such faults in the goods bailed.

Illustrations

(a) A lends a horse, which he knows to be vicious, to B. He does not disclose the fact that the horse is vicious. The horse runs away. B is thrown and injured. A is responsible to B for damage sustained.

(b) A hires a carriage of B. The carriage is unsafe, though B is not aware of it, and A is injured. B is responsible to A for the injury.

151. Care to be taken by bailee. In all cases of bailment the bailee is bound to take as much care of the goods bailed to him as a man of ordinary prudence would under similar circumstances take of his own goods of the same bulk, quantity and value as the goods bailed.

152. Bailee when not liable for loss, etc., of thing bailed—The bailee, in the absence of any special contract, is not responsible for the loss, destruction or deterioration of the thing bailed, if he has taken the amount of care of it described in Sec. 151.

153. Termination of bailment by bailee's act inconsistent with conditions. A contract of bailment is voidable at the option of the bailor if the bailee does any act with regard to the goods bailed, inconsistent with the conditions of the bailment.

Illustration

A let to B, for hire, a horse for his own riding. B drives the horse in his carriage. This is, at the option of A, a termination of the bailment.

154. Liability of bailee making unauthorized use of goods bailed—If the bailee makes any use of the goods bailed, which is not according to the conditions of the bailment, he is liable to make compensation to the bailor for any damage arising to the goods from or during such use of them.

Illustrations

(a) A lends a horse to B for his own riding only. B allows C, a member of his family, to ride the horse. C rides with care, but the horse accidentally falls and is injured. B is liable to make compensation to A for the injury done to the horse.

(b) A hires a horse in Kolkata from B expressly to march to Benares. A rides with due care, but marches to Kolkata instead. The horse accidentally falls and is injured. A is liable to make compensation to B for the injury to the horse.

155. Effect of mixture, with bailor's consent, of his goods with bailee's—If the bailee, with the consent of the bailor, mixes the goods of the bailor with his own goods, the bailor and the bailee shall have an interest, in proportion to their respective shares, in the mixture thus produced.

156. Effect of mixture without bailor's consent, when the goods can be separated—If the bailee, without the consent of the bailor, mixes the goods of the bailor with his own goods, and the goods can be separated or divided, the property in the goods remains in the parties respectively; but the bailee is bound to bear the expense of separation or division, and any damage arising from the mixture.

Illustrations

A bails 100 bales of cotton marked with a particular mark to B. B, without A's consent, mixes the 100 bales with other bales of his own, bearing a different mark. A is entitled to have his 100 bales returned, and B is bound to bear all the expenses incurred in the separation of the bales and any other incidental damage.

157. Effect of mixture, without bailor's consent, when the goods cannot be separated—If the bailee, without the consent of the bailor, mixes the goods of the bailor with his own goods, in such a manner that it is impossible to separate the goods bailed from the other goods and deliver them back, the bailor is entitled to be compensated by the bailee for the loss of the goods.

Illustration

A bails a barrel of Cape flour worth ₹ 45 to B. B, without A's consent mixes the flour with country flour of his own, worth only ₹ 25 a barrel. B must compensate A for the loss of his flour.

158. Repayment by bailor of necessary expenses—Where, by the conditions of the bailment, the goods are to be kept or to be carried, or to have work done upon them by the bailee for the bailor and the bailee is to receive no remuneration, the bailor shall repay to the bailee the necessary expenses incurred by him for the purpose of the bailment.

159. Restoration of goods lent gratuitously—The lender of a thing for use may at any time require its return, if the loan was gratuitous even though he lent it for a specified time or purpose. But if, on the faith of such loan made for a specified time or purpose, the borrower has acted in such a manner that the return of the thing lent before the time agreed upon would cause him loss exceeding the benefit derived by him from the loan, the lender must, if he compels the return, indemnify the borrower for the amount in which the loss so occasioned exceeds the benefit so derived.

160. Return of goods bailed on expiration of time or accomplishment of purpose—It is the duty of the bailee to return, or deliver according to the bailor's directions the goods bailed, without demand, as soon as the time for which they were bailed has expired, or the purpose for which they were bailed has been accomplished.

161. Bailee's responsibility when goods are not duly returned—If by the default of the bailee, the goods are not returned, delivered or tendered at the proper time, he is responsible to the bailor for any loss, destruction or deterioration of the goods from that time.

162. Termination of gratuitous bailment by death—A gratuitous bailment is terminated by the death either of the bailor or of the bailee.

163. Bailor entitled to increase or profits from goods bailed—In the absenee of any contract to the contrary, the bailee is bound to deliver to the bailor, or according to his directions, any increase or profit which may have accrued from the bailed.

Illustration

A leaves a cow in the custody of B to be taken care of. The cow has a calf. B is bound to deliver the calf as well as the cow to A.

164. Bailor's responsibility to bailee—The bailor is responsible to the bailee for any loss which the bailee may sustain by reason that the bailor was not entitled to make the bailment, or to receive back the goods or to give directions respecting them.

165. Bailment by several joint owners—If several joint owners of goods bail them, the bailee may deliver them back to, or according to the directions of one joint owner without the consent of all, in the absence of any agreement to the contrary.

166. Bailee not responsible on re-delivery to bailor without title—If the bailor has no title to the goods, and the bailee, in good faith, delivers them back to, or according to the directions of, the bailor, the bailee is not responsible to the owner in respect of such delivery.

167. Right of third person claiming goods bailed—If a person, other than the bailor, claims goods bailed, he may apply to the Court to stop the delivery-of the goods to the bailor, and to decide the title to the goods.

168. Right of finder of goods; may sue for specific reward offered—The finder of goods has no right to sue the owner for compensation for trouble and expense voluntarily incurred by him to preserve the goods and to find out the owner; but he may retain the goods against the owner until he receives such compensation; and, where the owner has offered a specific reward for the return of goods lost, the finder may sue for such reward, and may retain the goods until he receives it.

169. When finder of thing commonly on sale may sell it. When a thing which is commonly the subject of sale is lost, if the owner cannot with reasonable diligence be found or if he refuses, upon demand, to pay the lawful charges of the finder, the finder may sell it—

1. When the thing is in danger of perishing or of losing the greater part of its value, or
2. When the lawful charges of the finder in respect of the thing found, amount to two-thirds of its value.

170. Bailee's particular lien—Where the bailee has, in accordance with the purpose of the bailment, rendered any service involving the exercise of labour or skill in respect of the goods bailed, he has, in the absence of a contract to the contrary, a right to retain such goods until he receives due remuneration for the services he has rendered in respect of them.

Illustrations

(a) A delivers a rough diamond to B, a jeweller, to be cut and polished, which is accordingly done. B is entitled to retain the stone till he is paid for the services he has rendered.

(b) A gives cloth to B, a tailor, to make into a coat. B promises A to deliver the coat as soon as it is finished, and to give three months' credit for the price. B is not entitled to retain coat until he is paid.

171. General lien of bankers, factors, wharfingers, attorneys and policy brokers—Bankers, factors, wharfingers, attorneys of a High Court and policy brokers may, in the absence of a contract to the contrary, retain, as a security for a general balance of account, any goods bailed to them; but not other persons have a right to retain as a security for such balance, goods bailed to them, unless there is an express contract to that effect.

Bailments of Pledges

172. "Pledge", "pawnor" and "pawnee" defined—The bailment of goods as security for payment of a debt or performance of a promise, is called "pledge". The bailor is in this case called the "pawnor". The bailee is called the "pawnee".

173. Pawnee's right of retainer—The pawnee may retain the goods pledged, not only for payment of the debt or the performance of the promise, but for the interest of the debt, and all necessary expenses incurred by him in respect of the possession or for the preservation of the goods pledged.

174. Pawnee not to retain for debt or promise other than that for which goods pledged. Presumption in case of subsequent advances—The pawnee shall not, in the absence of a contract to that effect, retain the goods pledged for any debt or promise other than the debt or promise for which they are pledged; but such contract, in the absence of anything to the contrary, shall be presumed in regard to subsequent advances made by the pawnee.

175. Pawnee's right as to extraordinary expenses incurred—The pawnee is entitled to receive from the pawnor extraordinary expenses incurred by him for the preservation of the goods pledged.

176. Pawnee's right where pawnor makes default—If the pawnor makes default in payment of the debt, or performance, at the stipulated time of the promise, in respect of which the goods were pledged, the pawnee may bring a suit against the pawnor upon the debt or promise, and retain the goods pledged as a collateral security, or he may sell the thing pledged on giving the pawnor reasonable notice of the sale.

If the proceeds of such sale are less than the amount due in respect of the debt or promise, the pawnor is still liable to pay the balance. If the proceeds of the sale are greater than the amount so due, the pawnee shall pay over the surplus to the pawnor.

177. Defaulting pawnor's right to redeem—If a time is stipulated for the payment of the debt, or performance of the promise, for which the pledge is made, and the pawnor makes default in payment of the debt or performance of the promise at the stipulated time, he may redeem the goods pledged at any subsequent time before the actual sale of them; but he must, in that case, pay, in addition, any expenses which have arisen from his default.

178. Pledge by mercantile agent—Where a mercantile agent is, with the consent of the owner, in possession of goods or the documents of title to goods, any pledge made by him, when acting in the ordinary course of business of a mercantile agent, shall be as valid as if he were expressly authorised by the owner of the goods to make the same; provided that the pawnee acts in good faith and has not at the time of the pledge noticed that pawnor has no authority to pledge.

Explanation—In this section, the expression of mercantile agent and 'documents of title' shall have the meanings assigned to them the Indian Sale of Goods Act, 1930 (III of 1930).

178-A. Pledges by person in possession under voidable contract—When the pawnor has obtained possession of the goods pledged by him under a contract voidable under Sec. 19 or Sec. 19-A, but the contract has not been rescinded at the time of the pledge, the pawnee acquires a good title to the goods, provided he acts in good faith and without notice of the pawnor's defect of title.

179. Pledge where pawnor has only a limited interest—Where a person pledges goods in which he has only a limited interest, the pledge is valid to the extent of that interest.

Suits by Bailee or Bailors against Wrong-doers

180. Suit by bailor or bailee against wrong-doer—If a third person wrongfully deprives the bailee of the use or possession of the goods bailed, or does them any injury, the bailee is entitled to use such remedies as the owner might have used in the like case if no bailment had been made; and either the bailor or the bailee may bring a suit against a third person for such deprivation or injury.

181. Apportionment of relief or compensation obtained by such suits—Whatever is obtained by way of relief or compensation if any such suit shall, as between the bailor and the bailee, be dealt with according to their respective interests.

CHAPTER X

Agency

Appointment and Authority of Agents

182. "Agent" and "principal" defined—An "agent" is a person employed to do any act for another or to represent another in dealing with third persons. The person for whom such act is done, or who is so represented, is called the "principal".

183. Who may employ agent—Any person who is of the age of majority according to the law to which he is subject, and who is of sound mind, may employ an agent.

184. Who may be an agent—As between the principal and third persons any person may become an agent, but no person who is not of the age of majority and of sound mind can become an agent, so as to be responsible to his principal according to the provisions in that behalf herein contained.

185. Consideration not necessary—No consideration is necessary to create an agency.

186. Agent's authority may be expressed or implied—The authority of an agent may be expressed or implied.

187. Definitions of express and implied authority—An authority is said to be express when it is given by words spoken or written. An authority is said to be implied when it is to be inferred from the circumstances of the case; and things spoken or written, or the ordinary course of dealing may be accounted circumstances of the case.

Illustration

A owns a shop in Serampur, living himself in Calcutta, and visiting the shop occasionally. The shop is managed by B, and he is in the habit of ordering goods from C in the name of A for the purposes of the shop, and of paying for them out of A's funds with A's knowledge. B has an implied authority from A to order goods from C in the name of A for the purposes of the shop.

188. Extent of agent's authority—An agent having an authority to do an act has authority to do every lawful thing which is necessary in order to do such act.

An agent having an authority to carry on a business has authority to do every lawful thing necessary for the purpose, or usually done in the course of conducting such business.

Illustrations

(a) A is employed by B, residing in London, to recover at Bombay a debt' due to B. A may adopt any legal process necessary for the purpose of recovering the debt and may give a valid discharge for the same.

(b) A constitutes B his agent to carry on his business of a shipbuilder. B may purchase timber and other materials, and hire workmen, for the purposes of carrying on the business.

189. Agent's authority in an emergency—An agent has, authority, in an emergency, to do all such acts for the purpose of protecting his principal from loss as would be done by a person of ordinary prudence in his own case, under similar circumstances.

Illustrations

(a) An agent for sale may have goods repaired if it be necessary.

(b) A consigns provisions to B at Calcutta, with directions to send them immediately to C at Cuttack. B may sell the provisions at Calcutta, if they will not bear journey to Cuttack without spoiling.

Sub-Agents

190. When agent cannot delegate—An agent cannot lawfully employ another to perform acts which he has *expressly* or **impliedly** undertaken to perform personally, unless by the **ordinary custom of trade a sub-agent may, or from the nature of the agency, a sub-agent must, be employed.**

191. "Sub-agent" defined—A "sub-agent" is a person employed by, and acting under the control of, the original agent in the business of the agency.

192. Representation of principal by sub-agent properly appointed—Where a sub-agent is properly appointed the principal is, so far as regards third persons, represented by the sub-agent and is bound by and responsible for his acts as if he were an agent originally appointed by the principal.

Agent's responsibility for sub-agents—The agent is responsible to the principal for the acts of the sub-agent

Sub-Agent's responsibility—The sub-agent is responsible for his acts to the agent, but not to the principal, except in case of fraud or wilful wrong.

193. Agent's responsibility for sub-agent appointed without authority— Where an agent, without having authority to do so, has appointed a person to act as a sub-agent, the agent stands towards such person in the relation of a principal to an agent, and is responsible for his acts both to the principal and to third persons, the principal is not represented by or responsible for the acts of the person so employed, nor is that person responsible to the principal.

194. Relation between principal and person duly appointed by Agent to act in business of agency— Where an agent, holding an express or implied authority to name another person to act for the principal in the business of the agency, has named another person accordingly, such person is not a sub-agent but an agent of the principal for such part of the business of the agency as is entrusted to him.

Illustrations

(a) A directs B, his solicitor, to sell his estate by auction, and to employ an auctioneer for the purpose. B names C, an auctioneer, to conduct the sale. C is not a sub-agent, but is A's agent for the conduct of the sale.

(b) A authorises B, a merchant in Calcutta, to recover the money due to A from C & Co. A instructs D, a solicitor, to take proceedings against C & Co., for the recovery of the money. D is not a sub-agent but is solicitor for A.

195. Agent's duty in naming such person—In selecting such agent for his principal, an agent is bound to exercise the same amount of discretion as a man of ordinary prudence would exercise in his own case; and if he does this he is not responsible to the principal for the acts or negligence of the agent so selected.

Illustrations

(a) A instructs B, a merchant, to buy a ship for him. B employs a ship surveyor of good reputation to choose a ship for A. The surveyor makes the choice negligently and the ship turns out to be unseaworthy and is lost. B is not, but the surveyor is responsible to A.

(b) A consigns goods to B, a merchant, for sale. B in due course, employs an auctioneer in good credit to sell the goods of A, and allows the auctioneer to receive the proceeds of the sale. The auctioneer afterwards becomes insolvent without having accounted for the proceeds. B is responsible to A for the proceeds.

Ratification

196. Right of person as to acts done for him without his authority. Effect of ratification—Where acts are done by one person on behalf of another, but without his knowledge or authority, he may elect to ratify or to disown such acts. If he ratifies them, the same effects will follow as if they had been performed by his authority.

197. Ratification may be expressed or implied—Ratification may be expressed or may be implied in the conduct of the person on whose behalf the acts are done.

Illustrations

(a) **A, without authority, buys goods for B**—Afterwards B sells them to C on his own account; B's conduct implies a ratification of the purchase made for him by A.

(b) A, without B's authority, lends B's money to C. Afterwards B accepts interest on the money from C. B's conduct implies a ratification of the loan.

198. Knowledge requisite for valid ratification—No valid ratification can be made by a person, whose knowledge of the facts of the case is materially defective.

199. Effect of ratifying unauthorized act forming part of a transaction—A person ratifying any unauthorized act done on his behalf ratifies the whole of the transaction of which such act formed a part.

200. Ratification of unauthorized act cannot injure third person—An act done by one person on behalf of another, without such other person's authority which, if done with authority, would have the effect of subjecting a third person to damages, or of terminating any right or interest of a third person, cannot, by ratification, be made to have such effect.

Illustrations

(a) A, not being authorized thereto by B, demands on behalf of B, the delivery of a chattel, the property of B, from C, who is in possession of it. This demand cannot be ratified by B, so as to make C liable for damages for his refusal to deliver.

(b) A holds a lease from B, terminable on the three months notice. C, an unauthorized person, gives notice of termination to A. The notice cannot be ratified by B, so as to be binding on A.

Revocation of authority

201. Termination of agency—An agency is terminated by the principal revoking his authority; or by the agent renouncing the business of the agency; or by the business of the agency being completed; or by either the principal or agent dying or becoming of unsound mind; or by the principal being adjudicated an insolvent under the provisions of any Act for the time in force for the relief of insolvent debtors.

202. Termination of agency where agent has an interest in subject-matter— Where the agent has himself an interest in the property which forms the subject matter of the agency cannot, in the absence of an express contract, be terminated to the prejudice of such interest.

Illustrations

(a) A gives authority to B to sell A's land, and to pay himself, out of the proceeds, the debts due to him from A. A cannot revoke this authority, nor can it be terminated by his insanity or death.

(b) A consigns 1,000 bales of cotton to B, who has made advances to him on such cotton, and desires B to sell the cotton, and to repay himself out of the price, the amount of his own advances. A cannot revoke this authority, not is it terminated by his insanity or death.

203. When principal may revoke agent's authority—The principal may, save as is otherwise provided by the last preceding section, revoke the authority given to his agent at any time before the authority has been exercised so as to bind the principal.

204. Revocation where authority has been partly exercised—The principal cannot revoke the authority given to his agent after the authority has been partly exercised so far as regards such acts and obligations as arise from acts already done in the agency.

Illustrations

(a) A authorises B to buy 1,000 bales of cotton on account of A, and to pay for it out of A's money remaining in B's hands. B buys 1,000 bales of cotton in his own name, so as to make himself personally liable for the price. A cannot revoke B's authority so far as regards payment for the cotton.

(b) A authorises B to buy 1,000 bales of cotton on account of A, and to pay for it out of A's money remaining in B's hands. B buys 1,000 bales of cotton in A's name and so as not to render himself personally liable for the price. A cannot revoke B's authority to pay for the cotton.

205. Compensation for revocation by principal, or renunciation by agent— Where there is an express or implied contract that the agency should be continued for any period of time, the principal must make compensation to the agent, or the agent to the principal as the case may be, for any previous revocation or renunciation of the agency without sufficient cause.

206. Notice of revocation or renunciation—Reasonable notice must be given of such revocation or renunciation; otherwise the damage thereby resulting to the principal or the agent, as the case may be, must be made good to the one by the other.

207. Revocation and renunciation may be expressed or implied—Revocation and renunciation may be expressed or may be implied in the conduct of the principal or agent respectively.

Illustration

A empowers B to let A's house. Afterwards A lets it himself. This is an implied revocation of B's authority.

208. When termination of agent's authority takes effect as to agent, and as to third persons—The termination of the authority of an agent does not, so far as regards the agent, take effect before it becomes known to him, or so far as regards third persons, before it becomes known to them.

Illustrations

(a) A directs B to sell goods for him, and agrees to give B five per cent commission on the price fetched by the goods. A afterwards, by letter, revokes B's authority. B, after the letter is sent, but before he receives it, sells the goods for 100 rupees. The sale is binding on A, and B is entitled to five rupees as his commission.

(b) A, at Madras, by letter directs B to sell for him some cotton lying in a warehouse in Bombay, and afterwaids, by letter, revokes his authority to sell, and directs B to send the cotton to Madras. B, after receiving the second letter, enters into a contract with C, who knows of the first letter, but not of the second, for the sale to him of the cotton. C pays B the money, with which B absconds. C's payment is good as against A.

(c) A directs B, his agent, to pay certain money to C. A dies, and D takes out probate to his will. B, after A's death, but before hearing of it, pays the money to C. The payment is good as against D, the executor.

209. Agent's duty on termination of agency by principal's death or insanity—When an agency is terminated by the principal dying or becoming of unsound mind, the agent is bound to take, on behalf of the representatives of his late principal, all reasonable steps for the protection and preservation of the interests entrusted to him.

210. Termination of sub-agent's authority—The termination of the authority of an agent causes the termination (subject to the rules herein contained regarding the termination of an agent's authority) of the authority of all sub-agents appointed by him.

Agent's Duty to Principal

211. Agent's duty in conducting principal's business—An agent is bound to conduct the-business of his principal according to the directions given by the principal, or in the absence of any such directions, according to the custom which prevails in doing business of the same kind at the place where the agent conduct such business. When the agent acts otherwise, if any loss be sustained, he must make it good to his principal and, if any profit accrues, he must account for it.

Illustrations

(a) A, an agent engaged in carrying on for B a business, in which it is the custom to invest from time to time, at interest, the moneys which may be in hand, omits to make such investment. A must make good to B the interest usually obtained by such investment.

(b) B, a broker, in whose business it is not the custom to sell on credit, sells goods of A on credit to C, whose credit at the time was very high. C, before payment, becomes insolvent B must make good the loss to A.

212. Skill and diligence required from agent—An agent is bound to conduct the business of the agency with as much skill as is generally possessed by persons engaged in similar business, unless the principal has notice of his want of skill. The agent is always bound to act with reasonable diligence, and to use such skill as he possesses; and to make compensation to his principal in respect of the direct consequen-ces of his own neglect; want of skill or misconduct, but not in respect of loss or damage which are indirectly or remotely caused by such neglect, want of skill or misconduct.

Illustrations

(a) A, a merchant in Calcutta, has an agent B, in London to whom a sum of money is paid on A's account, with orders to remit. B retains the money for a considerable time. A, in consequence of not receiving the money, becomes insolvent. B is liable for the money and interest from the day on which it ought to have been paid, according to the usual rate, and for any further direct loss—as, e.g., by variation of rate of exchange—but not further.

(b) A, an agent for the sale of goods, having authority to sell on credit, sells to B on credit, without making the proper and usual enquiries as to the solvency of B. B, at the time of such sale, is insolvent A must make compensation to his principal in respect of any loss thereby sustained.

(c) A, an insurance broker, employed by B to effect an insurance on a ship, omits to see that the usual clauses are inserted in the policy. The ship is afterwards lost In consequence of the omission of the clauses nothing can be recovered from the under-writers. B is bound to make good the loss to A.

(d) A, a merchant in England, directs B, his agent at Mumbai, who accepts the agency, to send him 100 bales of cotton by a certain ship. B, having it in his power to send the cotton, omits to do so. The ship arrives safely in England. Soon after arrival the price of cotton rises. B is bound to make good to A the profit which he might have made by the 100 bales of cotton at the time the ship.arrived; but not any profit he might have made by the subsequent rise.

213. Agent's accounts—An agent is bound to render proper accounts to his principal on demand.

214. Agent's duty to communicate with principal—It is the duty of an agent, in case of difficulty, to use all reasonable diligence in communicating with his principal, and in seeking to obtain his instructions.

215. Right of principal when agent deals, on his own account in business of agency without principal's consent—If an agent deals on his own account in the business of the agency, without first obtaining the consent of his principal and acquaint-ing him with all material circumstances which have come to his own knowledge on the subject, the principal may repudiate the transaction, if the case shows either that any material fact has been dishonestly concealed from him by the agent or that the dealings of the agent have been disadvantageous to him.

Illustrations

(a) A directs B to sell A's estate. B buys the estate for himself in the name of C. A, on discovering that B has bought the estate for himself, may repudiate the sale, if he can show that B has dishonestly concealed any material fact, or that the sale has been disadvantageous to him.

(b) A directs B to sell A's estate. B, on looking over the estate before selling it, finds a mine on the estate which is unknown to A. B informs A that he wishes to buy the estate for himself, but conceals the discovery of the mine. A allows B to buy, in ignorance of the existence of the mine. A, on discovering that B knew of the mine at the time he bought the estate, may either repudiate or adopt the sale at his option.

Note:—The Law as to the principal's right of repudiation under Sec. 215 can be summed up thus:—'Have been disadvantageous' means 'disadvantageous in fact'. 102 1C 366. The burden of proving that the transaction is not disadvantageous to the principal is on the agent. 1101C 6.

216. Principal's right to benefit gained by agent dealing on his own account in business of agency—If an agent, without the knowledge of his principal, deals in the business of the agency on his own account instead of on account of his principal, the principal is entitled to claim from the agent any benefit which may have resulted to him from the transaction.

Illustration

A directs B, his agent, to buy a certain house for him. B tells A it cannot be bought and buys the house for himself. A may, on discovering that B has bought the house, compel him to sell it to A at the price he gave for it

217. Agent's right of retainer out of sums received on principal's account. An agent may retain, out of any sums received on account of the principal in the business of the agency, all moneys due to himself in respect of advances made or expenses properly incurred by him in conducting such business and also such remunera-tion as may be payable to him for acting as agent.

218. Agent's duty to pay sums received for principal—Subject to such deductions, the agent is bound to pay to his principal all sums received on his account.

219. When agent's remuneration becomes due—In the absence of any special contract, payment for the performance of any act is not due to the agent until the completion of such Act, but an agent may detain moneys received by him on account of goods sold, although the whole of the goods consigned to him for sale may have not been sold, or although the sale may not be actually complete.

220. Agent not entitled to remuneration for business misconducted—An agent who is guilty of misconduct in the business of the agency is not entitled to any remuneration in respect of that part of the business which has been misconducted.

Illustrations

(a) A employs B to recover 1,00,000 rupees from C, and to lay it out on good security. B recovers the 1,00,000 rupees and lays out 90,000 rupees on good security, but lays out 10,000 rupees on security which he ought to have known to be bad, whereby A loses 2,000 rupees. B is entitled to remuneration for recovering the 1,00,000 rupees and for investing the 90,000 rupees. He is not entitled to any remuneration for investing the 10,000 rupees and he must make good the 2,000 rupees to A.

(b) A employs B to recover 1,000 rupees from C. Through B's misconduct the money is not recovered. B is entitled to no remuneration for his services, and must make good the loss.

221. Agent's lien on principal's property—In the absence of any contract to the contrary, agent in entitled to retain goods, papers and other property, whether movable or immovable, of the principal received by him, until the amount due to himself for commission, disbursements and services in respect of the same has been paid or accounted for to him.

Principal's Duty to Agent

222. Agent to be indemnified against consequences of lawful acts—The employer of an agent is bound to indemnify him against the consequences of all lawful acts done by such agent in exercise of authority conferred upon him.

Illustrations

(a) B, at Singapore, under instructions from A of Calcutta, contracts with C to deliver certain goods to him. A does not send the goods to B, and C sues B for breach of contract. B informs A of the suit, and A authorises him to defend the suit. B defends the suit, and is compelled to pay damages and costs, and incurs expenses. A is liable to B for such damages, costs and expenses.

(b) B, a broker at Calcutta, by the orders of A, a merchant there, contracts with C for the purchase of 10 casks of oil for A. Afterwards A refuses to receive the oil, and B sues C. B informs A, who repudiates the contract altogether. B defends, but unsuccessfully, and has to pay damages and costs and incurs expenses. A is liable to B for such damages, costs and expenses.

223. Agent to be indemnified against consequence of acts done in good faith—Where one person employs another to do an act, and the agent does the act in good faith, the employer is liable to indemnify the agent against the consequences of that act, though it causes an injury to the rights of third persons.

Illustrations

(a) A, a decree-holder and entitled to execution of B's goods, requires the officer of the Court to seize certain goods, representing them to be the goods of B. The officer seizes the goods, and is sued by C, the true owner of the goods. A is liable to indemnify the officer for the sum which he is compelled to pay to C, in consequence of obeying A's directions.

(b) B, at the request of A, sells goods in the possession of A, but which A had no right to dispose of. B does not know this, and hands over the proceeds of the sale to A. Afterwards C, the ture owner of the goods, sues B and recovers the value of the goods and costs. A is liable to indemnify B for what he has been compelled to pay to C and for B's own expenses.

224. Non-liability of employer of agent to do a criminal act—Where one person employs another to do an act which is criminal, the employer is not liable to the agent, either upon an express or an implied promise, to indemnify him against the consequences of that act.

Illustrations

(a) A employs B to beat C, and agrees to indemnify him against all consequences of the act. B thereupon beats C, and has to pay damages to C for so doing. A is not liable to indemnify B for those damages.

(b) B, the proprietor of a newspaper, publishes, at A's request, a libel (defamation in writing) upon C in the paper, and A agrees to indemnify B against the consequences of the publication, and all costs and damages of any action in respect thereof. B is sued by C and has to pay damages and also incurs expenses. A is not liable to B upon the indemnity.

225. Compensation to agent for injury caused by principal's neglect—The principal must make compensation to his agent in respect of injury caused to such agent by the principal's neglect or want of skill.

Illustrations

A employs B as a bricklayer in building a house, and puts up the scaffolding himself. The scaffolding is unskilfully put up, and B is in consequence hurt. A must make compensation to B.

Effect of agency on contract with third persons

226. Enforcement and consequences of Agent's contract—Contract entered into through an agent, and obligations arising from acts done by an agent, may be enforced in the same manner and will have the same legal consequences, as if the contracts had been entered into and the acts done by the principal in person.

Illustrations

(a) A buys goods from B, knowing that he is an agent for their sale, but not knowing who is the principal. B's principal is the person entitled to claim from A the price of the goods, and A cannot, in a suit by the principal, set off against that claim a debt due to himself from B.

(b) A, being B's agent with authority to receive money on his behalf, receives from C a sum of money due to B. C is discharged of his obligation to pay the sum in question to B.

227. Principal how far bound, when agent exceeds authority—When an agent does more than he is authorized to do, and when the part of what he does, which is within his authority, can be separated from the part which is beyond his authority, so much only of what he does as is within his authority, is binding as between him and his principal.

Illustration

A, being owner of a ship and cargo, authorises B to procure an insurance for 4,000 rupees on the ship. B procures a policy of 4,000 rupees on the ship, and another for the like sum on the cargo. A is bound to pay the premium for the policy on the ship, but not the premium for the policy on the cargo.

228. Principal not bound when excess of agent's authority is not separable— Where an agent does more than he is authorised to do, and what he does beyond the scope of his authority cannot be separated from what is within it, the principal is not bound to recognise the transaction.

Illustration

A authorises B to buy 500 sheep for him. B buys 500 sheep and 200 lambs for one sum of 6,000 rupees. A may repudiate the whole transaction.

229. Consequences of notice given to agent—Any notice given to or information obtained by the agent, provided it be given or obtained in the course of the business transacted by him for the principal, shall as between the principal and third parties, have the same legal consequences as if it had been given to or obtained by the principal.

Illustrations

(a) A is employed by B to buy from C certain goods of which C is the apparent owner and buys them accordingly. In the course of the treaty for the sale, A learns that the goods really belonged to D, but B is ignorant of that fact B is not entitled to set off a debt owing to him from C against the price of the goods.

(b) A is employed by B to buy from C goods of which C is the apparent owner. A was, before he was so employed, a servant of C, and then learnt that the goods really belonged to D, but B is ignorant of that fact. In spite of the knowledge of his agent, B may set off against the price of the goods a debt owing to him from C.

230. Agent cannot personally enforce, nor be bound by, contracts on behalf of principal—In the absence of any contract to that effect, an agent cannot personally enforce contracts entered into by him on behalf of his principal, nor is he personally bound by them.

Presumption of contract to contrary—Such a contract shall be presumed to exist in the following cases:—

1. where the contract is made by an agent for the sale or purchase of goods for a merchant resident abroad;
2. where the agent does not disclose the name of his principal;
3. where the principal, though disclosed, cannot be sued.

231. Rights of parties to a contract made by agent not disclosed—If an agent makes a contract with a person who neither knows, not has reason to suspect, that he is an agent, his principal may require the performance of the contract; but the other contracting party has, as against the principal, the same rights as he would have had as against the agent if the agent had been principal.

If the principal discloses himself before the contract is completed, the other contracting party may refuse to fulfil the contract, if he can show that if he had known who was the principal in the contract, or if he had known that the agent was not a principal, he would not have entered into the contract.

232. Performance of contract with agent supposed to be principal—Where one man makes a contract with another, neither knowing nor having reasonable ground to suspect that the other is an agent, the principal, if he requires the performance of the contract, can only obtain such performance subject to the rights and obligations subsist-ing between the agent and the other party to the contract.

Illustration

A, who owes 500 rupees to B, sells 1,000 rupees' worth of rice to B. A is acting as agent for C in the transaction, but B has no knowledge nor reasonable ground of suspicion that such is the case. C cannot compel B to take the rice without allowing him to set off A's debt.

233. Right of person dealing with agent personally liable—In cases where the agent is personally liable, a person dealing with him may hold either him or his principal, or both of them liable.

Illustration

A enters into a contract with B to sell him 100 bales of cotton, and afterwards discovers that B was acting as agent for C. A may sue either B or C, or both, for the price of the cotton.

234. Consequence of inducing agent or principal to act on belief that principal or agent will be held exclusively liable—When a person who has made a contract with an agent induces the agent to act upon the belief that the principal only will be held liable or induces the principal to act upon the belief that the agent only will be held liable, he cannot afterwards, hold liable the agent or principal respectively.

235. Liability of pretended agent—A person untruly representing himself to be the authorised agent of another, and thereby inducing a third person to deal with him as such agent, is liable, if his alleged employer does not ratify his acts, to make compensation to the other in respect of any loss or damages which he has incurred by so dealing.

236. Person falsely contracting as agent not entitled to performance—A person with whom a contract has been entered in the character of agent is not entitled to require the performance of it if he was in reality acting, not as agent, but on his own account.

237. Liability of principal inducing belief that agent's unauthorised acts were authorised—When an agent has, without authority, done acts or incurred obliga-tions to a third person on behalf of his principal, the principal is bound by such acts or obligations if he has by his words or conduct induced such third persons to believe that such acts and obligations were within the scope of the agent's sthority.

Illustrations

(a) A consigns goods to B for sale, and gives him instruction, not to sell under a fixed price. C, being ignorant of B's instructions, enters into a contract with B to buy the goods at a price lower than the reserved price. A is bound by the contract.

(b) A entrusts B with negotiable instruments endorsed in blank. B sells them to C in violation of private orders from A. The sale is good.

238. Effect, on agreement, of misrepresentation or fraud by agent—Misrepresentations made, or frauds committed, by agents acting in the course of their business for their principals, have the same effect on agreements ma'e by such agents as if such misrepresentations or frauds had been made or committed by the principals; but misrepresentations made, or frauds committed, by agents in matters which do not fall within their authority, do not affect their principals.

Illustrations

(a) A being B's agent for the sale of goods, induces C to buy them by a misrepresentation, which he was not authorised by B to make. The contract is voidable, as between B and C, at the option of C.

(b) A, the captain of B's ship, signs bills of lading without having received on board the goods mentioned therein. The bills of lading are void as between B and the pretended consignor.

CHAPTER XI

Of Partnership

Sections 239-266 Repealed by the Indian Partnership Act, 1932 (IX of 1932), Sec. 73 and Schedule II.

SCHEDULE

Enactments Repealed

[Repealed by Sec. 3 and Schedule II of the Repealing and Amending Act, 1914 (X of 1914)].

The Indian Partnershp Act, 1932

(Act. No. IX 1932)

Whereas it is expedient to define and amend the law relating to partnership: It is hereby enacted as follows:—

CHAPTER I

Preliminary

1. Short title, extent and commencement. (1) This Act may be called the Indian Partnership Act, 1932.

(2) It extends to the whole of India.

(3) It shall come into force on the 1st day of October, 1932, except Sec. 69, which shall come into force on the 1st day of October, 1933.

2. Definitions. In this Act, unless there is anything repugnant in the subject or context,—

(a) an "act of firm" means any act or omission by all the partners, or by any partner or agent of the firm which gives rise to a right enforceable by or against the firm.

(b) "business" includes every trade, occupation and profession;

(c) "prescribed" means prescribed by rules made under this Act;

(d) "third party" used in relation to a firm or to a partner therein means any person who is not a partner in the firm; and

(e) expressions used but not defined in this Act and defined in the Indian Contract Act, 1872 (IX of 1872), shall have the meanings assigned to them in that Act.

3. Application of provisions of Act IX of 1872—The unrepealed provisions of the Indian Contract Act, 1872 (IX of 1872), save in so far as they are inconsistent with the express provisions of this Act, shall continue to apply to firms.

CHAPTER II

The Nature of Partnership

4. Definition of "partnership", "partner", "firm", and "Firm name".

"Partnership" is the relation between persons who have agreed to share the profits of a business carried on by all or any of them acting for all.

Persons who have entered into partnership with one another are called individually "partners" and collectively "a firm", and the name under which their business is carried on is called the "firm name".

5. Partnership not created by status—The relation of partnership arises from contract and not from status, and, in particular, the members of a Hindu undivided family carrying on a family business as such, or a Burmese Buddhist husband and wife carrying on business as such are not partners in such business.

6. Mode of determining existence of partnership—In determining whether a group of persons is or is not a firm, or whether a person is or is not a partner in a firm, regard shall be had to the real relation between the parties, as shown by all relevant facts taken together.

Explanation 1—The sharing of profits or of gross returns arising from property by persons holding a joint or common interest in that property does not of itself make such persons partners.

Explanation 2—The receipt by a person of a share of the profits of a business, or of a payment contingent upon the earning of profits or varying with the profits earned by a business, does not of itself make him a partner with the persons carrying on the business; and, in particular, the receipt of such share or payment—

(a) by a lender of money to persons engaged or about to engage in any business,

(b) by a servant or agent as remuneration,

(c) by the widow or child of a deceased partner, as annuity, or

(d) by a previous owner or part owner of the business, as consideration for the sale of the goodwill or share thereof,

does not of itself make the receiver a partner with the person carrying on the business.

7. Partnership at will—Where no provision is made by contract between the partners for the duration of their partnership, or for the determination of their partnership, the partnership is "partnership at will".

8. Particular partnership—A person may become a partner with another person in particular adventures or undertakings.

CHAPTER III
Relations of partners to one another

9. General duties of partners—Partners are bound to carry on the business of the firm to the greatest common advantage, to be just and faithful to each other, and to render true accounts and full information of all things affecting the firm to any partner or his legal representative.

10. Duty to indemnify for loss caused by fraud—Every partner shall indemnify the firm for any loss caused to it by his fraud in the conduct of the business of the firm.

11. Determination of rights and duties of partners by contract between the partners.

1. Subject to the provisions of this Act, the mutual rights and duties of the partners of a firm may be determined by contract between the partners, and such contract may be expressed or may be implied by a course of dealing.

Such contract may be carried by consent of all the partners, and such consent may be expressed or may be implied by a course of dealing.

2. **Agreement in restraint of trade**—Notwithstanding anything contained in Sec. 27 of the Indian Contract Act, 1872 (IX of 1872), such contracts may provide that a partner shall not carry on any business other than that of the firm while he is a partner.

12. The conduct of the business—Subject to contract between the partners,—

(a) every partner has a right to take part in the conduct of the business;

(b) every partner is bound to attend diligently to his duties in the conduct of the business;

(c) any difference arising as to ordinary matters connected with the business may be decided by a majority of the partners, and every partner shall have the right to express his opinion before the matter is decided, but no change may be made in the nature of the business without the consent of all the partners; and

(d) every partner has a right to have access to and to inspect and copy any of the books of the firm.

13. Mutual rights and liabilities—Subject to contract between the partners—

(a) a partner is not entitled to receive remuneration for taking part in the conduct of the business;

(b) the partners are entitled to share equally in the profits earned, and shall contribute equally to the losses sustained by the firm;

(c) where a partner is entitled to interest on the capital subscribed by him such interest shall be payable only out of profits;

(d) a partner making for the purposes of the business any payment or advance beyond the amount of capital he has agreed to subscribe, is entitled to interest thereon at the rate of six per cent per annum;

(e) the firm shall indemnify a partner in respect of payment made and liabilities incurred by him—

   (i) in the ordinary and proper conduct of the business, and

   (ii) in doing such act, in an emergency, for the purpose of protecting the firm from loss, as would be done by a person of ordinary prudence, in his own case, under similar circumstances;

(f) a partner shall indemnify the firm for any loss caused to it by his wilful neglect in the conduct of the business of the firm.

14. The property of the firm—Subject to contract between the partners, the property of the firm includes all property and rights and interests in property originally brought into the stock of the firm, or acquired, by purchase or otherwise, by or for the firm, or for the purposes and in the business of the firm, and includes also the goodwill of the business.

Unless the contrary intention appears, property and rights and interests in property acquired with money belonging to the firm are deemed to have been acquired for the firm.

15. Application of the property of the firm—Subject to contract between the partners, the property of the firm shall be held and used by the partners exclusively for the purposes of the business.

16 Personal profits earned by partners—Subject to contract between the partners,—

(a) if a partner derives any profits for himself from any transaction of the firm, or from the use of the property or business connection of the firm or the firm name, he shall account for that profit and pay it to the firm;'

(b) if a partner carries on any business of the same nature as and competing with that of the firm, he shall account for and pay to the firm all profits made by him in that business.

17. Rights and duties of partners after a change in the firm, after the expiry of the term of the firm, and where additional undertakings are carried out—Subject to contract between the partners,—

(a) where a change occurs in the constitution of a firm, the mutual rights and duties of the partners in the reconstituted firm remain the same as they were immediately before the change; as far as may be;

(b) where a firm constituted for a fixed term continues to carry on business after the expiry of that term the mutual rights and duties of the partners remain the same as they were before the expiry, so far as they may be consistent with the incidents of partnership at will; and

(c) where a firm constituted to carry out one or more adventures or undertakings carries out other adventures or undertakings the mutual rights and duties of the partners in respect of the other adventures or undertakings are the same as those in respect of the original adventures or undertakings.

CHAPTER IV
Relations of partners to third parties

18. Partners to be agent of the firm—Subject to the provisions of this Act, a partner is the agent of the firm for the purposes of the business of the firm.

19. Implied authority of partner as agent of the firm.

1. Subject to the provision of Sec. 22, the act of a partner which is done to carry on in the usual way, business of the kind carried on by the firm, binds the firm.

The authority of a partner to bind the firm conferred by this section is called his ' 'implied authority''.

2. In the absence of usage or custom of trade to the contrary, the implied authority of a partner does not empower him to—

(a) submit a dispute relating to the business of the firm to arbitration,
(b) open a banking account on behalf of the firm in his own name,
(c) compromise or relinquish any claim or portion of a claim by the firm,
(d) withdraw a suit or proceeding filed on behalf of the firm,
(e) admit any liability in a suit or proceeding against the firm,
(f) acquire immovable property on behalf of the firm,
(g) transfer immovable property belonging to the firm, or
(h) enter into partnership on behalf of the firm.

20. Extension and restriction of partner's implied authority

—The partners in a firm may, by contract between the partners, extend or restrict the implied authority of any partner.

Notwithstanding any such restriction, any act done by a partner on behalf of the firm which falls within his implied authority binds the firm, unless the person with whom he is dealing knows of the restriction or does not know or believe that partner to be a partner.

21. Partner's authority in an emergency

—A partner has authority, in an emergency, to do all such acts for the purpose of protecting the firm from loss as would be done by a person of ordinary prudence, in his own case, acting under similar circumstances, and such acts bind the firm.

22. Mode of doing act to bind firm

—In order to bind a firm, an act or instrument done or executed by a partner or other person on behalf of the firm shall be done or executed in the firm name, or in any other manner expressing or implying intention to bind the firm.

23. Effect of admissions by partner

—An admission or representation made by a partner concerning the affairs of the firm is evidence against the firm, if it is made in the ordinary course of business.

24. Effect of notice to acting partner

—Notice to a partner who habitually acts in the business of the firm of any matter relating to the affairs of the firm operates as notice to the firm, except in the case of a fraud on the firm committed by or with the consent of that partner.

25. Liability of a partner for acts of the firm

—Every partner is liable jointly with all the other partners and also severally, for .all acts of the firm done while he is a partner.

26. Liability of the firm for wrongful acts of a partner

—Where by the wrongful act or omission of a partner in the ordinary course of the business of a firm or with the authority of his partners, loss or injury is caused to any third party or any penalty is incurred, the firm is liable therefor to the same extent as the partner.

27. Liability of firm for misapplication by partners. Where—

(a) a partner acting within his apparent authority receives money or property from a third party and misapplies it, or
(b) a firm in the course of its business receives money or property from a third party, and the money or property is misapplied by any of the partners, while it is in the custody of the firm, the firm is liable to make good the loss.

28. Holding out.

1. Any one who by words spoken or written or by conduct represents himself, or knowingly permits himself to be represented, to be a partner in a firm, is liable as a partner in that firm, to any one who has on the faith of any such representation given credit to the firm whether the person representing himself or represented to be a partner does or does not know that the representation has reached the person so giving credit.

2. Where after a partner's death the business is continued in the old firm name, the continued use of that name or of the deceased partner's name as a part thereof shall not of itself make his legal representative or his estate liable for any act of the firm done after his death.

29. Rights of transferee of a partner's interest.

1. A transfer by a partner of his interest in the firm, either absolute or by mortgage, or by the creation by him of a charge on such interest, does not entitle the transferee, during the continuance of the firm, to interfere in the conduct of the business, or to require accounts, or to inspect the books of the firm, but entitles the transferee only to receive the share of profits of the transferring partner, and the transferee shall accept the account of profit agreed to by the partners.

2. If the firm is dissolved or if the transferring partner ceases to be a partner, the transferee is entitled as against the remaining partners to receive the share of the assets of the firm to which the transferring partner is entitled, and for the purpose of ascertaining that share, to an account as from the date of dissolution.

30. Minors admitted to the benefits of partnership.

1. A person who is a minor according to the law to which he is subject may not be a partner in a firm, but with the consent of all the partners for the time being, he may be admitted to the benefits of partnership.

2. Such minor has a right to such share of the property and of the profits of the firm as may be agreed upon, and he may have access to and inspect and copy any of the accounts of the firm.

3. Such minor's share is liable for the acts of the firm, but the minor is not personally liable for any such act

4. Such minor may not sue the partners for an account or payment of his share of the property or profits of the firm, save when severing his connection with the firm, and in such case the amount of his share shall be determined by a valuation made as far as possible in accordance with the rules contained in Sec. 48.

Provided that all the partners acting together or any partner entitled to dissolve the firm upon notice to other partners may elect in such suit to dissolve the firm, and thereupon the Court shall proceed with the suit as one for dissolution and for settling accounts between the partners, and the amount of the share of the minor shall be determined along with the share of the partners.

5. At any time within six months of his attaining majority, or of his obtaining knowledge that he had been admitted to the benefits of partnership, whichever date is later, such person may give public notice that he has elected to become or that he has elected not to become a partner in the firm, and such notice shall determine his position as regards the firm:

Provided that, if he fails to give such notice, he shall become a partner in the firm on the expiry of the said six months.

6. Where any person has been admitted as a minor to the benefits of partnership in a firm, the burden of proving the fact that such person had no knowledge of such admission until a particular date after the expiry of six months of his attaining majority shall lie on the person asserting that fact

7. Where such person becomes a partner,—
  (a) his rights and liabilities as a minor continue up to the date on which he becomes a partner, but he also becomes personally liable to third parties for all acts of the firm done since he was admitted to the benefits of partnership, and
  (b) his share in the property and profits of the firm shall be the share to which he was entitled as a minor.

8. Where such person elects not to become a partner,—
  (a) his rights and liabilities shall continue to be those of a minor under this section up to the date on which he gives public notice.

(b) his share shall not be liable for any acts of the firm done after the date of the notice, and

(c) he shall be entitled to sue the partners for his share of the property and profits in accordance with Sub-Sec. (4).

9. Nothing in Sub-Secs. (7) and (8) shall affect the provisions of Sec. 28.

CHAPTER V

Incoming and outgoing partners

31. Introduction of a partner.

1. Subject to the contract between the partners and to the provisions of Sec. 30, no person shall be introduced as a partner into a firm without the consent of all the existing partners.

2. Subject to the provisions of Sec. 30, a person who is introduced as a partner into a firm does not thereby become liable for any act of the firm done before he became a partner.

32. Retirement of a partner.

1. A partner may retire—

(a) with the consent of all the other partners,

(b) in accordance with an express agreement by the partners, or

(c) where the partnership is at will, by giving notice in writing to all the other partners of his intention to retire.

2. A retiring partner may be discharged from any liability to any third party for acts of the firm done before his retirement by an agreement made by him with such third party and the partners of the reconstituted firm, and such agreement may be implied by a course, of dealing between such third party and the reconstituted firm after he had knowledge of the retirement.

3. Notwithstanding the retirement of a partner from a firm, he and the partners continue to be liable as partners to third parties for any act done by any of them which would have been an act of the firm if done before the retirement, until public notice is given of the retirement.

Provided that a retired partner is not liable to any third party who deals with the firm without knowing that he was a partner.

4. Notices under Sub-Sec. (3) may be given by the retired partner or by any partner of the reconstituted firm.

33. Expulsion of partner.

1. A partner may not be expelled from a firm by any majority of the partners, save in the exercise in good faith of powers conferred by contract between the partners.

2. The provisions of Sub-Secs. (2), (3) and (4) of Sec. 32 shall apply to an expelled partner as if he were a retired partner.

34. Insolvency of partner.

1. Where a partner in a firm is adjudicated an insolvent he ceases to be a partner on the date on which the order of adjudication is made, whether or not the firm is thereby dissolved.

2. Where under a contract between the partners the firm is not dissolved by the adjudication of a partner as an insolvent the estate of a partner so adjudicated is not liable for any act of the firm and the firm is not liable for any act of the insolvent done after the date on which the order of adjudication is made.

35. Liability of estate of deceased partner—Where under a contract between the partners the firm is not dissolved by the death of a partner, the estate of deceased partner is not liable for any act of the firm done after his death.

36. Rights of outgoing partner to carry on competing business.

1. As outgoing partner may carry on a business competing with that of the firm and he may advertise such business, but subject to contract to the contrary he may not—

(a) use the firm name
(b) represent himself as carrying on the business of the firm, or
(c) solicit the custom of persons who were dealing with the firm before he ceased to be a partner.

2. **Agreements in restraint of trade**—A partner may make an agreement with his partners that on ceasing to be a partner he will not carry on any business similar to that of the firm within a specified period or within specified local limits; and notwithstanding anything contained in Sec. 27 of the Indian Contract Act, 1872 (IX of 1872), such agreement shall be valid if the restrictions imposed are reasonable.

37. **Right of outgoing partner in certain cases to share subsequent profit—**

Where any member of a firm has died or otherwise ceased to be a partner, and the surviving or continuing partners carry on the business of the firm with the property of the firm without any final settlement of accounts as between them and the outgoing partner or his estate, then, in the absence of a contract to the contrary, the outgoing partner or his estate is entitled at the option of himself or his representatives to such share of the profits made since he ceased to be a partner as may be attributable to the use of his share of the property of the firm or to interest at the rate of six per cent per annum on the amount of his share in the property of the firm:

Provided that where by contract between the partners an option is given to surviving or continuing partners to purchase the interest of a deceased or outgoing partner, and the option is duly exercised, the estate of the deceased partner, or the outgoing partner of his estate, as the case may be, is not entitled to any further or other share of profits; but if any partner assuming to act in exercise of the option does not in all material respects comply with the terms thereof, he is liable to account under the foregoing provisions of this section.

38. **Revocation of continuing guarantee by change in firm**—A countinuing guarantee given to a firm, or to a third party in respect of the transactions of a firm, is, in the absence of agreement to the contrary, revoked as to future transaction from the date of any change in the constitution of the firm.

CHAPTER VI
Dissolution of a firm

39. **Dissolution of a firm**—The dissolution of partnership between all the partners of a firm is called the "dissolution of the firm".

40. **Dissolution by agreement**—A firm may be dissolved with the consent of all the partners or in accordance with a contract between the partners.

41. **Compulsory dissolution.** A firm is dissolved—

(a) by the adjudication of all the partners or of all the partners but one as insolvent, or
(b) by the happening of any event which makes it unlawful for the business of the firm to be carried on or for the partners to carry it on in partnership:

Provided that, where more than one separate adventure or undertaking is carried on by the firm, the illegality of one or more shall not of itself cause the dissolution of the firm in respect of its lawful adventures and undertakings.

42. **Dissolution on the happening of certain contingencies**—Subject to contract between the partners a firm is dissolved—

(a) if constituted for a fixed term, by the expiry of that term;
(b) if constituted to carry out one or more adventures or undertakings, by the completion thereof;
(c) by the death of a partner; and
(d) by the adjudication of a partner as an insolvent

43. **Dissolution by notice of partnership at will.**

1. Where the partnership is at will the firm may be dissolved by any partner giving notice in writing to all the other partners of his intention to dissolve the firm.
2. The firm is dissolved as from the date mentioned in the notice as the date of dissolution or, if no date is so mentioned, as from the date of the communication of the notice.

44. **Dissolution by the Court**—At the suit of a partner, the Court may dissolve a firm on any of the following grounds, namely:—

(a) that a partner has become of unsound mind, in which case the suit may be brought as well by the next friend of the partner who has become of unsound mind as by any other partner;

(b) that a partner, other than the partner suing, has become in any way permanently incapable of performing his duties as partner;

(c) that a partner, other than the partner suing, is guilty of conduct which is likely to affect prejudicially the carrying on of the business, regard being has to the nature of the business;

(d) that a partner, other than the partner suing wilfully or persistently commits breach of agreements relating to the management of the affairs of the firm or the conduct of its business, or otherwise so conducts himself in matters relating to the business that it is not reasonably practicable for the other partners to carry on the business in partnership with him;

(e) that a partner, other than the partner suing, has in any way transferred the whole of his interest in the firm to a third party, or has allowed his share to be charged under the provisions of rule 49 of Order XXI of the First Schedule to the Code of Civil Procedure, 1908 (V of 1908), or has allowed it to be sold in the recovery of arrears of land-revenue or of any duties recoverable as arrears of land-revenue due by the partner;

(f) that the business of the firm cannot be carried on save at a loss; or

(g) on any other ground which renders it just and equitable that the firm should be dissolved.

45. **Liability for acts of partners done after dissolution.**

1. Notwithstanding the dissolution of a firm, the partners continue to be liable as such to third parties for any act done by any of them which would have been an act of the firm if done before the dissolution, until public notice is given of the dissolution:

Provided that the estate of a partner who dies, or who is adjudicated an insolvent or of a partner who, not having been known to the person dealing with the firm to be a partner, retires from the firm is not liable under this section for acts done after the date on which he ceased to be a partner.

2. Notices under Sub-Sec. (1) may be given by any partner.

46. **Right of partners to have business wound up after dissolution**—On the dissolution of a firm every partner or his representative is entitled, as against all the other partners or their representatives, to have the property of the firm applied in payment of the debts and liabilities of the firm, and to have the surplus distributed among the partners or their representatives according to their rights.

47. **Continuing authority of partners for purposes of winding up**—After the dissolution of a firm the authority of each partner to bind the firm, and the other mutual rights and obligations of the partners, continue notwithstanding the dissolution, so far as may be necessary to wind up the affairs of the firm and to complete transactions begun but unfinished at the time of the dissolution, but not otherwise:

Provided that the firm is in no case bound by the act of a partner who has been adjudicated insolvent; but this proviso does not affect the liability of any person who has after the adjudication represented himself or knowingly permitted himself to be represented as a partner of the insolvent.

48. **Mode of settlement of accounts between partners**—In settling the accounts of a firm after dissolution, the following rules shall, subject to agreement by the partners, be observed:—

(a) Losses, including deficiencies of capital, shall be paid first out of profits, next out of capital, and, lastly, if necessary, by the partners individually in the proportion in which they were entitled to share profits.

(b) The assets of the firm, including any sums contributed by the partners to make up deficiencies of capital, shall be applied in the following manner and order:—

    (i)   in paying the debts of the firm to third parties;

    (ii)   in paying to each partner rateably what is due to him from the firm for advances as distinguished from capital;

    (iii)   in paying to each partner rateably what is due to him on account of capital; and (iv)   the residue, if any, shall be divided among the partners in the proportions in which they were entitled to share profit.

49. Payment of firm debts and of separate debts— Where there are joint debts due from the firm, and also separate debts due from any partner, the property of the firm shall be applied in the first instance in payment of the debts of the firm, and if there is any surplus, then the share of each partner shall be applied in payment of his separate debts or paid to him. The separate property of any partner shall be applied first in the payment of his separate debts and the surplus (if any) in the payment of the debts of the firm.

50. Personal profits earned after dissolution—Subject to contract between the partners, the provisions of clause (a) of Sec. 16 shall apply to transactions by any surviving partner or by the representatives of a deceased partner, undertaken after the firm is dissolved on account of the death of a partner and before its affairs have been completely wound up:

Provided that where any partner or his representative has bought the goodwill of the firm, nothing in this section shall affect his right to use the firm name.

51. Return of premium on premature dissolution—Where a partner has paid a premium on entering into partnership for a fixed term, and the firm is dissolved before the expiration of that term otherwise than by the death of a partner, he shall be entitled to repayment of the premium or of such part thereof as may be reasonable, regard being had to the terms upon which he became a partner and to the length of time during which he was a partner, unless—

(a) the dissolution is mainly due to his own misconduct, or

(b) the dissolution is in pursuance of an agreement containing no provision for the return of the premium or any part of it.

52. Rights where partnership contract is rescinded for fraud or misrepresen-tation—Where a contract creating partnership is rescinded on the ground of the fraud or misrepresentation of any of the parties thereto, the party entitled to rescind is, without prejudice to any other right, entitled—

(a) to a lien on, or a right of retention of, the surplus or the assets of the firm remaining after the debts of the firm have been paid, or any sum paid by him for the purchase of a share in the firm and for any capital contributed by him;

(b) to rank as a creditor of the firm in respect of any payment made by him towards the debts of the firm; and

(c) to be indemnified by the partner or partners guilty of the fraud or misrepresentation against all the debts of the firm.

53. Right to restrain from use of firm name or firm property—After a firm is dissolved, every partner or his representative may, in the absence of a contract between the partners to the contrary, restrain any other partner or his representative from carrying on a similar business in the firm name or from using any of the property of the firm for his own benefit until the affairs of the firm have been completely wound up:

Provided that where any partner or his representative has bought the goodwill of the firm, nothing in this section shall affect his right to use the firm name.

54. Agreements in restraint of trade—Partners may, upon or in anticipation of the dissolution of the firm, make an agreement that some or all of them will not carry on a business similar to that of the firm within a specified period or within specified local limits; and notwithstanding anything contained in Sec. 27 of the Indian Contract Act, 1872 (IX of 1872), such agreement shall be valid if the restrictions imposed are reasonable.

55. Sale of good will after dissolution.

1. In settling the accounts of a firm after dissolution, goodwill shall, subject to contract between the partners, be included in the assets, and it may be sold either separately or along with other property of the firm.

2. **Rights of buyer and seller of goodwill**—Where the goodwill of a firm is sold after dissolution, a partner may carry on a business competing with that of the buyer and he may advertise such business, but subject to agreement between him and the buyer, he may not—

(a) use the firm name,

(b) represent himself as carrying on the business of the firm, or

(c) solicit the custom of persons who were dealing with the firm before its dissolution.

3. **Agreements in restraint of trade**—Any partner may, upon the sale of goodwill of a firm, make an agreement with the buyer that such partner will not carry on any business similar to that of the firm within a specified period or within specified local limits, and notwithstanding anything contained in Sec. 27 of the Indian Contract Act, 1872 (IX of 1872), such agreement shall be valid if the restrictions imposed are reasonable.

CHAPTER VII
Registration of firms

56. Power to exempt from application of this Chapter—The State Government of any State may, by notification in the Official **Gazette,** direct that the provisions of this Chapter shall not apply to that State or to any part thereof specified in the notification.

57. Appointment of Registrars.

1. The State Government may appoint Registrars of Firms for the purposes of this Act, and may define the areas within which they shall exercise their powers and perform their duties.

2. Every Registrar shall be deemed to be a public servant within the meaning of Sec. 21 of the Indian Penal Code (XLV of 1860).

58. Application for registration.

1. The registration of a firm may be effected at any time by sending by post or delivering to the Registrar of the area in which any place of business of the firm is situated or proposed to be situated, a statement in the prescribed form and accompanied by the prescribed fee, stating—

(a) the firm name,

(b) the place or principal place of business of the firm,

(c) the names of any other places where the firm carries on business,

(d) the date when each partner joined the firm,

(e) the names in full and permanent address of the partners, and

(f) the duration of the firm.

The statement shall be signed by all the partners, or by their agents specially authorised in this behalf.

2. Each person signing the statement shall also verify it in the manner prescribed.

3. A firm name shall bot contain any of the following words, namely:— "Crown", "Emperor", "Empress", "Empire", "Imperial", "King", "Queen", "Royal", or words expressing or implying the sanction, approval or patronage of[1]............[2].............except[3] when the[4] (State) Government signifies[5] its consent to the use of such words as part of the firm name by order in writing.[6]

59. Registration—When the Registrar is satisfied that the provisions of Sec. 58 have "been duly complied with, he shall record an entry of the statement in a register called the Register of Firms, and shall file the statement.

60. Recording of alterations in firm name and principal place of business.

1. When an alteration is made in the firm name or in the location of the principal place of business of a registered firm, a statement may be sent to the Registrar accompanied by the prescribed fee, specifying the alteration and signed and verified in the manner required under Sec. 58.

2. When the Registrar is satisfied that the provisions of Sub-Sec. (1) have been duly complied with, he shall amend the entry relating to the firm in the Register of Firms in accordance with the statement, and shall file it along with the statement relating to the firm filed under Sec. 59.

61. Noting of closing and opening of branches—When a registered firm discontinues business at any place or begins to carry on business at any place, such place not being its principal place of business, any partner or agent of the firm may send intimation thereof to the Registrar, who shall make a note of such intimation in the entry relating to the firm in the Register of Firms, and shall file the intimation along with the statement relating to the firm filed under Sec. 59.

62. Noting of changes in name and addresses of partners—When any partner in a registered firm alters his name or permanent address, an intimation of the alteration may be sent by any partner or agent of the firm to the Registrar, who shall deal with it in the manner provided in Sec. 61.

63. Recording of changes in and dissolution of a firm.

1. When a change occurs in the constitution of a registered firm any incoming, continuing or outgoing partner, and when a registered firm is dissolved any person who was a partner immediately before the dissolution, or the agent of any such partner or person specially authorised in this behalf, may give notice to the Registrar of such change or dissolution, specifying the date thereof; and the Registrar shall make a record of the notice in the entry relating to the firm in the Register of Firms, and shall file the notice along with the statement relating to the firm filed under Sec. 59.

2. Recording of withdrawal of a minor—When a minor who has been admitted to the benefits of partnership in a firm attains majority and elects to become or not to become a partner, and the firm is then a registered firm, he, or his agent specially authorised in this behalf, may give notice to the Registrar that he has or has not become a partner, and the Registrar shall deal with the notice in the manner provided in Sub-Sec. (1).

64. Rectification of mistakes.

1. The Registrar shall have power at all times to rectify any mistake in order to bring the entry in the Register of Firms relating to any firm into conformity with the documents relating to that firm filed under the Chapter.

---

[1]The words "the Crown or the Central Government or any Provincial Government" rep. by the A.O. 1950.
[2]The words "or the Crown Representative" rep. by the A.P. 1948.
[3]Subs, by the A.O. 1937 for "when the G.G. in C."
[4]Subs, by the A.O. 1950 for "Provincial".
[5]Subs, by the A. O. 1937 for "his".
[6]The words "under the hand of one of the Secretaries of the Government of India", rep. by the A. O. 1937.

2. On application made by all the parties who have signed any document relating to a firm filed under this Chapter, the Registrar may rectify any mistake in such document or in the record or note thereof made in the Register of Firms.

65. Amendment of Register by order of Court—A court deciding any matter relating to a registered firm may direct that the Registrar shall make any amendment in the entry in the Register of Firms relating to such firm which is consequential upon its decision; and the Registrar shall amend the entry accordingly.

66. Inspection of Register and filed documents.

1. The Register of Firms shall be open to inspection by any person on payment of such fee as may be prescribed.
2. All statements, notices and intimations, filed under this Chapter shall be open to inspection, subject to such conditions and on payment of such fee as may be prescribed.

67. Grant of copies—The Registrar shall on application furnish to any person, on payment of such fee as may be prescribed, a copy, certified under his hand, of any entry or portion thereof in the Register of Firms.

68. Rules of evidence.

1. Any statement, intimation or notice recorded or noted in the Register of Firms shall, as against any person by whom or on whose behalf such statement, intimation or notice was signed, be conclusive proof of any fact therein stated.

2. A certified copy of an entry relating to a firm in the Register of Firms may be produced in proof of the fact of the registration of such firm, and of the contents of any statement, intimation or notice recorded or noted therein.

69. Effect of non-registration.

1. No suit to enforce a right arising from a contract or conferred by this Act shall be instituted in any Court by or on behalf of any person suing as a partner in a firm against the firm or any person alleged to be or to have been a partner in the firm unless the firm is registered and the person suing is or has been shown in the Register of Firms as a partner in the firm.

2. No suit to enforce a right arising from a contract shall be instituted in any Court by or on behalf of a firm against any third party unless the firm is registered and the persons suing are or have been shown in the Register of Firms as partners in the firm.

3. The provisions of Sub-Secs (1) and (2) shall apply also to a claim of set-off or other proceeding to enforce a right arising from a contract, but shall not affect—

(a) the enforcement of any right to sue for the dissolution of a firm or for accounts of a dissolved firm, or any right or power to realise the property of a dissolved firm, or

(b) the powers of an official assignee, receiver or Court under the Presidency-towns Insolvency Act, 1909 (II of 1909), or the Provincial Insolvenccy Act, 1920 (V of 1920), to realise the property of an insolvent partner.

4. This section shall not apply—

(a) to firms or to partners in firms which have no place of business in the territories to which this Act extends, or whose places of business in the said territories are situated in areas to which, by notification under Sec. 56, this Chapter does not apply, or

(b) to any suit or claim of set-off not exceeding one hundred rupees in value which, in the Presidency-towns, is not of a kind specified in Sec. 19 of the Presidency Small Cause Courts Act, 1882 (XV of 1882), or outside the Presidency-towns, is not of a kind specified in the Second Schedule to the Provincial Small Cause Courts Acts, 1887 (IX of 1887), or to any proceeding in execution or other proceeding incidental to or arising from any such suit or claim.

70. **Penalty for furnishing false particulars**—Any person who signs any statement, amending statement, notice or intimation under this Chapter containing any particular which he knows to be false or does not believe to be true, or containing particulars which he knows to be incomplete or does not believe to be complete, shall be punishable with imprisonment which may extend to three months, or with fine, or with both.

71. **Power to make rules.**

1. The State Government may make rules prescribing the fees which shall accompany documents sent to the Registrar of Firms, of which shall be payable for the inspection of documents in the custody of the Registrar of Firms, or for copies from the Register of Firms:

Provided that such fees shall not exceed the maximum fees specified in Schedule I.

2. The State Government may also make rules—

(a) prescribing the form of statements submitted under Sec. 58, and of the verification thereof;

(b) requiring statements, intimations and notices under Secs 60, 61, 62 and 63 to be in prescribed form, and prescribing the form thereof;

(c) prescribing the form of the Register of Firms, and the mode in which entries relating to firms are to be made therein, and the mode in which such entries are to be amended or notes made therein;

(d) regulating the procedure of the Registrar when disputes arise;

(e) regulating the filing of documents received by the Registrar;

(f) prescribing conditions for the inspection of original documents;

(g) regulating the grant of copies;

(h) regulating the elimination of registers and documents;

(i) providing for the maintenance and form of an index to the Register of Firms; and

(j) generally to carry out the purposes of this section shall be subject to the condition of previous publication.

CHAPTER VIII
Supplemental

72. **Mode of giving public notice**—A public notice under this Act is given—

(a) where it relates to the retirement or expulsion of a partner from a registered firm, or to the dissolution of a registered firm or to the election to become or not to become a partner in a registered firm by a person attaining majority who was admitted as a minor to the benefits of partnership, by notice to the Registrar of Firms under Sec. 63, and by publication in the Official Gazette and in at least one vernacular newspaper circulating in the district where the firm to which it relates has its place or principal place of business, and

(b) in any other case, by publication in the Official Gazette and in at least one vernacular newspaper circulating in the district where the firm to which it relates has its place or principal place of business.

73. **[Repeals] Rep. by the Repealing Act, 1938 (I of 1938), Sec. 2 and Schedule.**

74. **Savings**—Nothing in this Act or any repeal effected thereby shall affect or be deemed to affect—

(a) any right, title, interest, obligation or liability already acquired, accrued or incurred before the commencement of this Act, or

(b) any legal proceeding or remedy in respect of any such right, title, interest, obligation or liability, or anything done or suffered before the commencement of this Act, or

(c) anything done or suffered before the commencement of this Act, or

(d) any enactment relating to partnership not expressly repealed by this Act, or

(e) any rule of insolvency relating to partnership, or

(f) any rule of law not inconsistent with this Act.

SCHEDULE I
Maximum Fees

[Sec Sub-Sec. (1) of Sec. 7]

Document or act in respect of with the fee is payable	Maximum fee
Statement under Sec. 58	Three rupees
Statement under Sec. 60	One rupee.
Intimation under Sec. 61	One Rupee.
Intimation under Sec. 62	One Rupee.
Notice under Sec. 63	One Rupee.
Application under Sec. 64	One Rupee.
Inspection of the Register of Firms under sub-Sec. (1) of Sec. 66	Fifty Paise for inspecting one volume of the Register.
Inspection of documents relating to a firm under Sub-Sec. (2) of Sec. 66	Fifty Paise for the inspection of all documents relating to one firm.
Copies from the Register of Firms	Twenty-five Paise for each hundred words or part thereof.

SCHEDULE II. [Enactment Repealed.] Rep. by the Repealing Act, 1938 (I of 1938), Sec. 2 and Schedule.

The Sale of Goods Act, 1930

(Act. No. III of 1930)

An Act to define and amend the law relating to the sale of goods.

Whereas it is expedient to define and amend the law relating to the sale of goods; it is hereby enacted as follows:—

CHAPTER I

Preliminary

1. **Short title, extent and commencement.**

   1. This Act may be called the Indian Sale of Goods Act, 1930.

   2. It extends to the whole of India (except the State of Jammu and Kashmir).

   3. It shall come into force on the 1st day of July, 1930.

2. **Definitions**—In this Act, unless there is anything repugnant in the subject or context—

   1. "buyer" means a person who buys or agrees to buy goods;

   2. "delivery" means voluntary transfer of possession from one person to another;

   3. goods are said to be in a "deliverable state" when they are in such state that the buyer would under the contract be bound to take delivery of them;

   4. "document of title to goods" includes a bill of lading, dock warrant, warehouse keeper's certificate, wharfingers' certificate, railway receipt, warrant, or order for the delivery of goods and any other document used in the ordinary course of business as proof of the possession or control of goods, authorising or purporting to authorise, either by endorsement or by delivery, the possessor of the document to transfer or receive goods thereby represented;

   5. "fault" means wrongful act or default;

   6. "future goods" means goods to be manufactured or produced or acquired by the seller after the making of the contract of sale;

   7. "goods" means every kind of movable property other than actionable claims and money; and includes stock and shares, growing crops, and things attached to or forming part of the land which are agreed to be severed before sale or under the contract of sale;

   8. a person is said to be "insolvent" who has ceased to pay his debts in the ordinary course of business, or cannot pay his debts as they become due; whether he has committed an act of insolvency or not;

   9. "mercantile agent" means a mercantile agent having in the customary course of business as such agent authority either to sell goods, or to consign goods for the purposes of sale, or to buy goods, or to raise money on the security of goods;

   10. "price" means the money consideration for a sale of goods;

11. "property" means the general property in goods, and not merely a special property;

12. "quality of goods" includes their state or condition;

13. "seller" means a person who sells or agrees to sell goods;

14. "specific goods" means goods identified and agreed upon at the time a contract of sale is made; and

15. expressions used but bot defined in this Act and defined in the Indian Contract Act, 1872 (IX of 1872), have the meaning assigned to them in the Act.

3. **Application of provisions of Act IX of 1872**—The unrepealed provisions of the Indian Contract Act, 1872 (IX of 1872), save in so far as they are inconsistent with the express provisions of this Act, shall continue to apply to contracts for the sale of goods.

CHAPTER II

Formation of the Contract

Contract of Sale

4. **Sale and agreement to sell.**

1. A contract of sale of goods is a contract whereby the seller transfers or agrees to transfer the property in goods to the buyer for a price. There may be a contract of sale between one part—owner and another.

2. A contract of sale may be absolute or conditional.

3. Where under a contract of sale the property in the goods is transferred from the seller to the buyer, the contract is called a sale, but where the transfer of the property in the goods is to take place at a future time or subject to some condition thereafter to be fulfilled, the contract is called an agreement to sell.

4. An agreement to sell becomes a sale when the time elapses or the conditions are fulfilled subject to which the property in the goods is to be transferred.

Formalities of Contract

5. **Contract of sale how made.**

1. A contract of sale is made by an offer to buy or sell goods for a price and the acceptance of such offer. The contract may provide for the immediate delivery of the goods or immediate payment of the price or both, or for the delivery for payment by instalments or that the delivery or payment or both shall be postponed.

2. Subject to the provisions of any law for the time being in force, a contract of sale may be made in writing or by word of mouth, or partly in writing and partly by word of mouth or may be implied from the conduct of the parties.

Subject-matter of Contract

6. **Existing or future goods.**

1. The goods which form the subject of contract of sale may be either existing goods, owned or possessed by the seller, or future goods.

2. There may be a contract for the sale of goods the acquisition of which by the seller depends upon a contingency which may or may not happen.

3. Where by a contract of sale the seller purports to effect a present sale of future goods, the contract operates as an agreement to sell the goods.

7. **Goods perishing before making of contract**—Where there is a contract for the sale of specific goods, the contract is void if the goods without the knowledge of the seller have at the time when the

contract was made, perished or become so damaged as no longer to answer to their description in the contract.

8. **Goods perishing before sale but after agreement to sell**—Where there is an agreement to sell specific goods, and subsequently the goods without any fault on the part of the seller or buyer perish or become so damaged as no longer to answer to their description in the agreement before the risk passed to the buyer, the agreement is thereby avoided.

9. **Ascertainment of price.**
1. The price in a contract of sale may be fixed by the contract or may be left to be fixed in manner thereby agreed or may be determined by the course of dealing between the parties.
2. Where the price is not determined in accordance with the foregoing provisions, the buyer shall pay the seller a reasonable price. What is a reasonable price is a question of fact dependent on the circumstances of each particular case.

10. **Agreement to sell at valuation.**
1. Where there is an agreement to sell goods on the terms that the price is to be fixed by the valuation of a third party and such third party cannot or does not make such valuation, the agreement is thereby avoided;

Provided that, if the goods or any part thereof have been delivered to, and appropriated by the buyer, he shall pay a reasonable price thereof.

2. Where such third party is prevented from making the valuation by the fault of the seller or buyer, the party not in fault may maintain a suit for damages against the party in fault.

Conditions and Warranties

11. **Stipulations as to time**—Unless a different intention appears from the terms of the contract stipulations as to time of payment are not deemed to be of the essence of a contract of sale. Whether any other stipulation as to time is of the essence of the contract or not depends on the terms of the contract.

12. **Condition and warranty.**
1. A stipulation in a contract of sale with reference to goods which are the subject thereof may be a condition or a warranty.
2. A condition is a stipulation essential to the main purpose of the contract, the breach of which gives rise to a right to treat the contract as repudiated.
3. A warranty is a stipulation collateral to the main purpose of the contract, the breach of which gives rise to a claim for damages but not a right to reject the goods and treat the contract as repudiated.
4. Weather a stipulation in a contract of sale is a condition or a warranty depends in each case on the construction of the contract. A stipulation may be a condition, though called a warranty in the contract.

13. **When condition to be treated as warranty.**
1. Where a contract of sale is subject to any condition to be fulfilled by the seller, the buyer may waive the condition or elect to treat the breach of the condition as a breach of warranty and not as a ground for treating the contract as repudiated.
2. Where a contract of sale is not severable and the buyer has accepted the goods or part thereof, the breach of any condition to be fulfilled by the seller can only be treated as a breach of warranty and not as a ground for rejecting the goods and treating the contract as repudiated, unless there is a term of the contract, express or implied, to that effect.[1]

---

[1] Amended by the Sale of Goods (Amendment) Act, 1963.

3. Nothing in this section shall affect the case of any condition or warranty fulfilment of which is excused by law by reason of impossibility or otherwise.

14. **Implied undertaking as to title, etc.** In a contract of sale, unless the circumstances of the contract are such as to show a different intention there is—

(a) an implied condition on the part of the seller that, in the case of a sale, he has a right to sell the goods and that, in the case of an agreement to sell, he will have a right to sell the goods at the time when the property is to pass;

(b) an implied warranty that the buyer shall have and enjoy quiet possession of the goods;

(c) an implied warranty that the goods shall be free from any charge or encumbrance in favour of any third party not declared or known to the buyer, before or at the time when the contract is made.

15. **Sale by description**—Where there is a contract for the sale of goods by description there is an implied condition that the goods shall correspond with the description; and, if the sale is by sample as well as by description it is not sufficient that the bulk of the goods corresponds with the sample if the goods do not also correspond with the description.

16. **Implied condition as to quality or fitness**—Subject to the provisions of this Act and of any other law for the time being in force, there is no warranty or condition as to the quality or fitness for any particular purpose of goods supplied under a contract of sale, except as follows:—

1. Where the buyer, expressly or by implication, makes known to the seller the particular purpose for which the goods are required, so as to show that the buyer relies on the seller's skill or judgment, and the goods are of a description which it is in the course of the seller's business to supply (whether he is the manufacturer or producer or not), there is an implied condition that the goods shall be reasonably fit for such purpose;

Provided that, in the case of a contract for the sale of a specified article under its patent or other trade name, there is no implied condition as to its fitness for any particular purpose.

2. Where goods are bought by description from a seller who deals in goods of that description (whether he is the manufacturer or producer or not), there is an implied condition that the goods shall be of merchantable quality:

Provided that, if the buyer has examined the goods, there shall be no implied condition as regards defects which such examination ought to have revealed.

3. An implied warranty or condition as to quality or fitness for a particular purpose may be annexed by the usage of trade.

4. An express warranty or condition does not negative a warranty or condition implied by this Act, unless inconsistent therewith.

17. **Sale by sample.**

1. A contract of sale is a contract for sale by sample where there is a term in the contract, express or implied, to that effect.

2. In the case of a contract for sale by sample there is an implied condition—

(a) that the bulk shall correspond with the sample in quality;

(b) that the buyer shall have a reasonable opportunity of comparing the bulk with the sample;

(c) that the goods shall be free from any defect, rendering them unmerchantable, which would not be apparent on reasonable examination of the sample.

CHAPTER III
Effect of the Contract
Transfer of property as between seller and buyer

18. **Goods must be ascertained**—Where there is a contract for the sale of unascertained goods, no property in the goods is transferred to the buyer unless and until the goods are ascertained.

19. Property passes when intended to pass.

1. Where there is a contract for the sale of specific or ascertained goods the property in them is transferred to the buyer at such time as the parties to the contract intend it to be transferred.

2. For the purpose of ascertaining the intention of the parties regard shall be had to terms of the contract, the conduct of the parties and the circumstances of the case.

3. Unless a different intention appears, the rules contained in Sees. 20 to 24 are rules for ascertaining the intention of the parties as to the time at which the property in the goods is to pass to the buyer.

20. Specific goods in a deliverable state—Where there is an unconditional contract for the sale of specific goods in a deliverable state, the property in the goods passes to the buyer when the contract is made, and it is immaterial whether the time of payment of the price or the delivery of the goods, or both, is postponed.

21. Specific goods to be put into a deliverable state— Where there is a contract for the sale of specific goods and the seller is bound to do something to the goods for the purpose of putting them into a deliverable state, the property does not pass until such thing is done and the buyer has notice thereof.

22. Specific goods in a deliverable state, when the seller has to do anything thereto in order to ascertain price—Where there is a contract for the sale of specific goods in a deliverable state, but the seller is bound to weigh, measure, test or do some other act or thing with reference to the goods for the purpose of ascertaining the price, the property does not pass until such act or thing is done and the buyer has notice thereof.

23. Sale of unascertained goods and appropriation.

1. Where there is a contract for the sale of unascertained or future goods by description and goods of that description and in a deliverable state are unconditionally appropriated to the contract, either by the seller with the assent of the buyer or by the buyer with the assent of the seller, the property in the goods thereupon passes to the buyer. Such assent may be expressed or implied and may be given either before or after the appropriation is made.

2. **Delivery to carrier**—Where, in pursuance of the contract, the seller delivers the goods to the buyer or to a carrier or other bailee (whether named by the buyer or not) for the purpose of transmission to the buyer, and does not reserve the right of disposal, he is deemed to have unconditionally appropriated the goods to the contract.

24. Goods sent on approval or "on sale or return"—When goods are delivered to the buyer on approval or "on sale or return" or other similar terms, the property therein passes to the buyer—

(a) when he signifies his approval or acceptance to the seller or does any other act adopting the transaction;

(b) if he does not signify his approval for acceptance to the seller but retains the goods without giving notice of rejection, then, if a time has been fixed for the return of the goods, on the expiration of such time, and, if no time has been fixed, on the expiration of a reasonable time.

25. Reservation of right of disposal.

1. Where there is a contract for the sale of specific goods or where goods are subsequently appropriated to the contract, the seller may, by the terms of the contract or appropriation, reserve the right of disposal of the goods until certain conditions are fulfilled. In such case, notwithstanding the delivery of the goods to a buyer, or to a carrier or other bailee for the purpose of transaction, to the buyer, the property in the goods Joes not pass to the buyer until the conditions imposed by the seller are fulfilled.

2. Where goods are shipped or delivered to a railway administration for carriage by railway and by the bill of lading or railway receipt, as the case may be; the goods are deliverable to the order of the seller or his agent, the seller is *prima facie* deemed to reserve the right of disposal.

3. Where the seller of goods draws on the buyer for the price and transmits to the buyer the bill of exchange together with the bill of lading or, as the case may be, the railway receipt, to secure acceptance or payment of the bill of exchange, the buyer is bound to return the bill of lading or the railway receipt if he do not honour the bill of exchange and, if he wrongfully retains the bill of lading or the railway receipt, the property in the goods does not pass to him.

Explanation—In this section, the expression 'railway' and 'railway administration' shall have the meanings respectively assigned to them under the Indian Railways Act, 1890.[2]

26. **Risk *prima facie* passes with property**— Unless otherwise agreed, the goods remain at the seller's risk until the property therein is transferred to the buyer, but when the property therein is transferred to the buyer, the goods are at the buyer's risk whether delivery has been made or not:

Provided also that nothing in this section shall affect the duties or liabilities of either seller or buyer as a bailee of the goods of the other party.

Transfer of Title

27. **Sale by person not the owner**—Subject to the provisions of this Act and of any other law for the time being in force, where goods are sold by a person who is not the owner thereof and who does not sell them under the authority or with the consent of the owner, the buyer acquires no better title to the goods than the seller had unless the owner of the goods is by his conduct precluded from denying the seller's authority to sell.

Provided that, where a mercantile agent is, with consent of the owner, in possession of the goods or of a document of title to the goods, any sale made by him, when acting in the ordinary course of business of a mercantile agent, shall be as valid as if he were expressly authorised by the owner of the goods to make the same: provided that the buyer acts in good faith and has not at the time of the contract of sale notice that the seller has not authority to sell.

28. **Sale by one of joint owners**—If one of several joint owners of goods has the sole possession of them by permission of the co-owners, the property in the goods is transferred .to any person who buys them of such joint owner in good faith and has not at the time of the contract of sale notice that the seller has not authority to sell.

29. **Sale by person in possession under voidable contract**—When the seller of goods has obtained possession thereof under a contract voidable under Sec. 19 or Sec. 19A of the Indian Contract Act, 1872 (IX of 1872), but the contract has not been rescinded at the time of the sale, the buyer acquires a good title to the goods, provided he buys them in good faith and without notice of the seller's defect of title.

30. **Seller or buyer in possession after sale.**

1. Where a person, having sold goods, continues or is in possession of the goods or of the documents of title to the goods the delivery or transfer by that person or by a mercantile agent acting for him, of the goods or documents of title under any sale, pledge or other disposition thereof to any person receiving the same in good faith and without notice of the previous sale shall have the same effect as if the person making the delivery or transfer were expressly authorised by the owner of the good to make the same.

2. Where a person, having bought or agreed to buy goods, obtains with the consent of the seller, possession of the goods or the documents of title to the goods, the delivery or transfer by that person or by a mercantile agent acting for him, of the goods, or documents of title under any sale, pledge or

---

[2]Substituted by the Sale of Goods (Amendment) Act, 1963.

other disposition thereof to any person receiving the same in good faith and without notice of any lien or other right of the original seller in respect of the goods shall have effect as if such lien or right did not exist.

CHAPTER IV
Performance of Contract

31. **Duties of seller and buyer**—It is the duty of the seller to deliver the goods and of the buyer to accept and pay for them in accordance with the terms of the contract of sale.

32. **Payment and delivery are concurrent conditions**—Unless otherwise agreed, delivery of the goods and payment of the price are concurrent conditions, that is to say, the seller shall be ready and willing to give possession of the goods to the buyer in exchange for the price, and the buyer shall be ready and willing to pay the price in exchange for possession of the goods.

33. **Delivery**—Delivery of goods sold may be made by doing anything which the parties agree shall be treated as delivery or which has the effect of putting the goods in the possession of buyer or of any person authorised to hold them on his behalf.

34. **Effect of part delivery**—A delivery of part of goods, in progress of the delivery of the whole, has the same effect, for the purpose of passing the property in such goods, as a delivery of the whole; but a delivery of part of the goods, with an intention of severing it from the whole, does not operate as a delivery of the remainder.

35. **Buyer to apply for delivery**—Apart from any express contract, the seller of goods is not bound to deliver them until the buyer applies for delivery.

36. **Rules as to delivery.**

1. Whether it is for the buyer to take possession of the goods or for the seller to send them to the buyer is a question depending in each case on the contract, express or implied, between the parties. Apart from any such contract, goods sold are to be delivered at the place at which they are at the time of the sale, and goods agreed to be sold are to be delivered at the place at which they are at the time of the agreement to sell, or if not then in existence, at the place at which they are manufactured or produced.

2. Where under the contract of sale the seller is bound to send the goods to the buyer, but no time for sending them is fixed, the seller is bound to send them within a reasonable time.

3. Where the goods at time of sale are in the possession of a third person, there is no delivery by seller to buyer unless and until such third person acknowledges to the buyer that he holds the goods on his behalf:

Provided that nothing in this section shall affect the operation of issue or transfer of any document of title to goods.

4. Demand or tender of delivery may be treated as ineffectual unless made at a reasonable hour. What is a reasonable hour is a question of fact.

5. Unless otherwise agreed, the expenses of and incidental to putting the goods into a deliverable state shall be borne by the seller.

37. **Delivery of wrong quantity.**

1. Where the seller delivers to the buyer a quantity of goods less than he contracted to sell, the buyer may reject them, but if the buyer accepts the goods so delivered he shall pay for them at the contract rate.

2. Where the seller delivers to the buyer a quantity of goods larger than he contracted to sell, the buyer may accept the goods included in the contract and reject the rest, or he may reject the whole. If the buyer accepts the whole of the goods"5o delivered, he shall pay for them at the contract rate.

3. Where the seller delivers to the buyer the good he contracted to sell mixed with goods of a different description not included in the contract the buyer may accept the goods which are in accordance with the contract and reject the rest, or may reject the whole.

4. The provisions of this section are subject to any usage of trade, special agreement or course of dealing between the parties.

38. **Instalment deliveries.**

1. Unless otherwise agreed, the buyer of goods is not bound to accept delivery thereof by instalments.

2. Where there is a contract for the sale of goods to be delivered by stated instalments which are to be separately paid for, and the seller makes no delivery or defective delivery in respect of one or more instalments, or the buyer neglects or refuses to take delivery of or pay for one or more instalments it is a question in each case depending on the terms of the contract and the circumstance of the case, whether the breach of contract is a repudiation of the whole contract, or whether it is a severable breach giving rise to a claim for compensation, but not to a right to treat the whole contract as repudiated.

39. **Delivery to carrier or wharfinger.**

1. Where, in pursuance of a contract of sale, seller is authorised pr required to send the goods to the buyer, delivery of the goods to a carrier, whether named by die buyer or not, for the purpose of transmission to the buyer, or delivery of the goods to wharfinger for safe custody, is *prima facie* deemed to be delivery of the goods to the buyer.

2. Unless otherwise authorised by the buyer, the seller shall make such contract with the carrier or wharfinger on behalf of the buyer as may be reasonable having regard to the nature of the goods and the other circumstances of the case. If the seller omits so to do, and the goods are lost or damaged in course of transit or whilst in the custody of the wharfinger, the buyer may decline to treat the delivery to the carrier or wharfinger as a delivery to himself, or may hold the seller responsible in damages.

3. Unless otherwise agreed, where goods are sent by the seller to the buyer by a route involving sea transit, in circumstances in which it is unusual to insure, the seller shall give such notice to the buyer as may enable him to insure them during their sea transit, and if the seller fails so to do, the goods shall be deemed to be at his risk during such sea transit.

40. **Risk where goods delivered at distant place**—Where the seller of goods agrees to deliver them at his own risk at a place other than that where they are when sold, the buyer shall, nevertheless, unless otherwise agreed, take any risk of deterioration in the goods necessarily incident to the course of transit.

41. **Buyer's right of examining the goods.**

1. Where goods are delivered to the buyer which he has not previously examined, he is not deemed to have accepted them unless and until he has had a reasonable opportunity of examining them for the purpose of ascertaining whether they are in conformity with the contract.

2. Unless otherwise agreed, when the seller tenders delivery of goods to the buyer, he is bound, on request, to afford the buyer a reasonable opportunity of examining the goods for the purpose of ascertaining whether they are in conformity with the contract.

42. **Acceptance**—The buyer is deemed to have accepted the goods when he intimates to the seller that he has accepted them, or when the goods have been delivered to him and he does any act in relation to them which is inconsistent with the ownership of the seller, or when, after the lapse of a reasonable time, he retains the goods without intimating to the seller that he has rejected them.

43. **Buyer not bound to return rejected goods**—Unless otherwise agreed, where goods are delivered to the buyer and he refuses to accept them, having the right so to do, he is not bound to return them to the seller, but it is sufficient if he intimates to seller that he refuses to accept them.

44. **Liability of buyer for neglecting or refusing delivery of goods**—When the seller is ready and willing to deliver the goods and requests the buyer to take delivery, and the buyer does not within a reasonable time after such request take delivery of the goods, he is liable to the seller for any loss occasioned by his neglect or refusal to take delivery, and also for a reasonable charge for the care and custody of the goods :

Provided that nothing in this section shall affect the rights of the seller where the neglect or refusal of the buyer to take delivery amounts to a repudiation of the contract.

CHAPTER V
Rights of unpaid seller against the goods

45. **"Unpaid seller" defined.**

1. The seller of goods is deemed to be an "unpaid seller" within the meaning of this Act—
(a) when the whole of the price has not been paid or tendered;
(b) when a bill of exchange or other negotiable instrument has been received as conditional payment, and the condition on which it was received has not been fulfilled by reason of the dishonour of the instrument or otherwise.

2. In this Chapter, the term "seller" includes any person who is in the position of a seller, as, for instance, an agent of the seller to whom the position of lading has been endorsed, or a consignor or agent who has himself paid, or is directly responsible for, the price.

46. **Unpaid seller's rights.**

1. Subject to the provisions of this Act and of any law for the time being in force, notwithstanding that the property in the goods may have passed to the buyer, the unpaid seller of goods, as such, has by implication of law—
(a) a lien on the goods for the price while he is in possession of them;
(b) in case of the insolvency of the buyer a right of stopping the goods in transit after he has parted with the possession of them;
(c) a right of re-sale as limited by this Act

2. Where the property in goods has not passed to the buyer, the unpaid seller has, in addition to his other remedies, a right of withholding delivery similar to and co-extensive with his rights of lien and stoppage in transit where the property has passed to the buyer.

Unpaid seller's lien

47. **Seller's lien.**

1. Subject to the provisions of this Act, the unpaid seller of goods who is in possession of them is entitled to retain possession of them until payment or tender of the price in the following cases, namely:—
(a) where the goods have been sold without any stipulation as to credit;
(b) where the goods have been sold on credit, but the term of credit has expired;
(c) where the buyer becomes insolvent.

2. The seller may exercise his right of lien notwithstanding that he is in posses-sion of the goods as agent or bailee for the buyer.

48. **Part delivery**—Where an unpaid seller has made part delivery of the goods, he may exercise his right of lien on the remainder, unless such part delivery has been made under such circumstances as to show an agreement to waive the lien.

49. **Termination of lien.**

1. The unpaid seller of goods loses his lien thereon—

(a) when he delivers the goods to a carrier or other bailee for the purpose of transmission to the buyer without reserving the right of disposal of the goods;

(b) when the buyer or his agent lawfully obtains possession of the goods;

(c) by waiver thereof.

2. The unpaid seller of goods, having a lien thereon, does not lose his lien by reason only that he has obtained a decree for the price of the goods.

Stoppage in transit

50. **Right of stoppage in transit**—Subject to the provisions of this Act when the buyer of goods becomes insolvent, the unpaid seller who has parted with the possession of the goods has the right of stopping them in transit, that is to say, he may resume possession of the goods as long as they are in the course of transit, and may retain them unti i payment or tender of the price.

51. **Duration of transit.**

1. Goods are deemed to be in course of transit from the time when they are delivered to a carrier or other bailee for the purpose of transmission to the buyer, until the buyer or his agent in that behalf takes delivery of them from such carrier or other bailee.

2. If the buyer or his agent in that behalf obtains delivery of the goods before their arrival at the appointed destination the transit is at an end.

3. If, after the arrival of the goods at the appointed destination, the carrier or other bailee acknowledges to the buyer or his agent that he holds the goods on his behalf and continues in possession of them as bailee for the buyer or his agent, the transit is at an end and it is immaterial that a further destination for the goods may have been indicated by the buyer.

4. If the goods are rejected by the buyer and the carrier or other bailee continues in possession of them, the transit is not deemed to be at an end even if the seller has refused to receive them back.

5. When goods are delivered to a ship chartered by the buyer it is a question depending upon the circumstances of the particular case, whether they are in the possession of the master as a carrier or as agent of the buyer.

6. Where the carrier or other bailee wrongfully refuses to deliver the goods to the buyer or his agent in that behalf, the transit is deemed to be at an end.

7. Where part delivery of the goods has been made to the buyer or his agent in that behalf, the remainder of the goods may be stopped in transit, unless such part delivery has been given in such circumstances as to show an agreement to give up possession of the whole of the goods.

52. **How stoppage in transit is effected**

1. The unpaid seller may exercise his right of stoppage in transit either by taking actual possession of the goods or by giving notice of his claim to the carrier or other bailee in whose possession the goods are. Such notice may be given either to the person in actual possession of the goods or to his principal. In the latter case the notice, to be effectual, shall be given at such time and in such circumstances that the principal, by the exercise of reasonable diligence, may communicate it to his servant or agent in time to prevent a delivery to the buyer.

2. When notice of stoppage in transit is given by the seller to the carrier or other bailee in possession of the goods, he shall re-deliver the goods to or according to the directions of the seller. The expenses of such re-delivery shall be borne by the seller.

Transfer by buyer and seller

53. **Effect of sub-sale or pledge by buyer.**

1. Subject to the provision of this Act, the unpaid seller's right of lien or stoppage in transit is not affected by any sale or other disposition of the goods which the buyer may have made, unless the seller has assented thereto:

Provided that where a document of title to goods has been issued or lawfully transferred to any person as buyer or owner of the goods, and that person transfers the document to a person who takes the document in good faith and for consideration, then, if such last mentioned transfer was by way of sale, the unpaid seller's right of lien or stoppage in transit is defeated, and, if such last mentioned transfer was by way of pledge or other disposition for value, the unpaid seller's right of lien or stoppage in transit can only be exercised subject to the right of the transferee.

2. Where the transfer is by way of pledge, the unpaid seller may require the pledgee to have the amount secured by the pledgee satisfied in the first instance, as far as possible, out of any other goods or securities of the buyer in the hands of the pledgee and available against the buyer,

54. Sale not generally rescinded by lien or stoppage in transit

1. Subject to the provisions of this section, a contract of sale is not rescinded by the mere exercise by an unpaid seller of his right of lien or stoppage in transit.

2. Where the goods are of a perishable nature, or where the unpaid seller who exercised his right of lien or stoppage in transit gives notice to the buyer of his intention to re-sell, the unpaid seller may, if the buyer does not within a reasonable time pay or tender the price, resell the goods within a reasonable time and recover from the original buyer damages for any loss occasioned by his breach of contract, but the buyer shall not be entitled to any profit which may occur on the re-sale. If such notice is not given, the unpaid seller shall not be entitled to recover such damages and the buyer shall not be entitled to the profit, if any, on the re-sale.

3. Where an unpaid seller who exercised his right of lien or stoppage in transit re-sells the goods, the buyer acquires a good title thereto as against the original buyer notwithstanding that no notice of the re-sale has been given to the original buyer.

4. Where the seller expressly reserves a right of re-sale in case the buyer should make default, and, on the buyer making default, re-sells the goods, the original contract of sale is thereby rescinded, but without prejudice to any claim which the seller may have for damages.

CHAPTER VI

Suits for Breach of the Contract

55. Suit for price.

1. Where under a contract of the sale the property in the goods has passed to the buyer and the buyer wrongfully neglects or refuses to pay for the goods according to the terms of the contract, the seller may sue him for the price of the goods.

2. Where under a contract of sale the price is payable on a certain day irrespective of delivery and the buyer wrongfully neglects or refuses to pay such price, the seller may sue him for the price although the property in the goods has not passed and the goods have not been appropriate to the contract

56. **Damages for non-acceptance**—Where the buyer wrongfully neglects or refuses to accept and pay for the goods, the seller may sue him for damages for non-acceptance.

57. **Damages for non-delivery**—Where the seller wrongfully neglects or refuses to deliver the goods to the buyer, the buyer may sue the seller for damages for non-delivery.

58. **Specific performance**—Subject to the provisions of Chapter II of the Specific Relief Act, 1877 (I of 1877), in any suit for breach of contract to deliver specific or ascertained goods, the Court may, if it thinks-fit, on the application of the plaintiff, by its decree direct that the contract shall be performed specifically, without giving the defendant the option of retaining the goods on payment of damages. The decree may be unconditional or upon such terms and conditions as to damages, payment of the price or otherwise, as the Court may deem just, and the application of the plaintiff may be made at any time before the decree.

59. Remedy for breach of warranty.

1. Where there is a breach of warranty by the seller, or where the buyer elects or is compelled to treat any breach of a condition on the part of the seller as a breach of warranty, the buyer is not by reason only of such breach of warranty entitled to reject the goods; but he may—

(a) set up against the seller the breach of warranty in diminution or extinction of the price; or

(b) sue the seller for damages for breach of warranty.

2. The fact that a buyer has set up a breach of warranty in diminution or extinction of the price does not prevent him from suing for the same breach of warranty if he has suffered further damage.

60. Repudiation of contract before due date—Where either party to a contract of sale repudiates the contract before the date of delivery, the other may either treat the contract as subsisting and wait till the date of delivery, or he may treat the contract as rescinded and sue for damages of the breach.

61. Interest by way of damages and special damages.

1. Nothing in this Act shall affect the right of the seller or the buyer to recover interest or special damages in any case where by law interest or special damages may be recoverable, or to recover the money paid where the consideration for the payment of it has failed.

2. In the absence of a contract to the contrary, the court may award interest at such rate as it thinks fit on the amount of the price—

(a) to the seller in a suit by him for the amount of the price—from the date of the tender of the goods or from the date on which the price was payable;

(b) to the buyer in a suit by him for the refund of the price in a case of a breach of the contract on the part of the seller—from the date on which the payment was made.

CHAPTER VII

Miscellaneous

62. Exclusion of implied terms and conditions—Where any right, duty or liability would arise under a contract of sale by implication of law, it may be negatived or varied by express agreement or by the course of dealing between the parties or by usage, if the usage is such as to bind both parties to the contract.

63. Reasonable time a question of fact—Where in this Act reference is made to a reasonable time, the question what is a reasonable time is a question of fact

64. Auction Sale— In the case of sale by auction—

1. where goods are put up for sale in lots, each lot is *prima facie* deemed to be subject of a separate contract of sale;

2. the sale is complete when the auctioneer announces its completion by the fall of the hammer or in other customary manner; and, until such announcement is made, any bidder may retract his bid;

3. a right to bid may be reserved expressly by or on behalf of the seller and where such right is expressly so reserved, but not otherwise, the seller or any one person on his behalf may, subject to the provisions hereinafter contained, bid at the auction;

4. where the sale is not notified to be subject to a right to bid on behalf of the seller, it shall not be lawful for the seller to bid himself or to employ any person to bid at such sale, or for the auctioneer knowingly to take any bid from the seller or any such person; and any sale contravening this rule may be treated as fraudulent by the buyer;

5. the sale may be notified to be subject to a reserved or upset price;

6. if the seller makes use of pretended bidding to raise the price, the sale is voidable at the option of the buyer.

64-A.[3] **In contracts of sale amount of increased or decreased duty to be added or deducted.**

1. Unless a different intention appears from the terms of the contract, in the event of any tax of the nature described in Sub-Sec. (2) being imposed, increased, decreased or remitted in respect of any goods after the making of any contract for the sale or purchase of such goods without stipulation as to the payment of tax where tax was not chargeable at the time of making of the contract, or for the sale or purchase of such goods tax- paid tax was chargeable at that time,—

(a) if such imposition to increase so takes effect that the tax or increased tax, as the case may be, or any part of such tax is paid or is payable, the seller may add so much to the contract price as will be equivalent to the amount paid or payable in respect of such tax or increase of tax, and he shall be entitled to be paid and to sue for and recover such addition; and

(b) if such decrease or remission so takes effect that the decreased tax only, or no tax, as the case may be, is paid or payable, the buyer may deduct so much from the contract price as will be equivalent to the decrease of tax or remitted tax, and he shall not be liable to pay, or be sued for, or in respect of, such deduction.

2. The provisions of Sub-Sec. (1) apply to the following taxes, namely :—

(a) any duty of customs or excise on goods;

(b) any tax on the sale or purchase of goods.

65. [Repeal. Rep. by Repealing Act, 1938 (I of 1938), Sec. 2 and Schedule.]

66. Savings.

1. Nothing in this Act, or in any repeal effected thereby shall affect or be deemed to affect—

(a) any right, title, interest, obligation or liability already acquired, accrued or incurred before the commencement of this Act, or

(b) any legal proceedings or remedy in respect of any such right, title, interest, obligation or liability, or

(c) anything done or suffered before the commencement of this Act, or

(d) any enactment relating to the sale of goods which is not expressly repealed by this Act, or

(e) any rule of law not inconsistent with this Act.

2. The rules of insolvency relating to contracts for the sale of goods shall continue to apply thereto, notwithstanding anything contained in this Act.

3. The provisions of this Act relating to contracts of sale do not apply to any transaction in the form of a contract of sale which is intended to operate by way of mortgage, pledge, charge or other security.

---

[3]Substituted by the Sale of Goods (Amendment) Act, 1963.

Test Questions

CHAPTER I

1. What do you understand by the *lexmercateria*? Discuss fully.
2. Discuss the sources of Mercantile Law of England and India.
3. Comment upon the position of Mercantile Law in India before the passing of the Contract Act.
4. What do you understand by Equity? Explain the causes that led to the development of Equity.

CHAPTER II
Contract

1. "An agreement enforceable by law is a contract". Discuss the definition, bringing out clearly the essentials of a valid contract.
2. State whether there is any contract made in the following cases:
   (a) A, having accepted an invitation to dinner, fails to attend.
   (b) A, the wife of a minor, buys goods on credit from B.
   (c) A takes a seat in an omnibus.
   (d) A calls a taxi.
   (e) A tells B that C has expressed his willingness to marry her (B).
   (f) A bids at a public auction.
   (g) A puts a coin in the slot of a weighing machine.
   (h) A eats a meal at a restaurant.
3. How is an offer made, revoked, and accepted? What rules apply when an offer is made through the Post Office, over the telephone?
4. When is communication of (i) offer, (ii) acceptance, complete?
5. Explain and illustrate the distinction between specific offer, general offer and invitation to offer.
6. (a) "All contracts are agreements, but all agreements are not contracts" Elucidate,
   (b) "The law of contracts is not the whole law of agreements nor is it the whole law of obligations." Discuss.
7. (a) Explain the rule, 'offer determines mode of acceptance,' with special reference to contract by post.
   (b) 'Acceptance must be something more than a mere mental assent.' Explain and illustrate.
   (c) 'A mere mental acceptance not evidenced by words or conduct is in the eye of law no acceptance'. Comment.
   (d) 'Acceptance is to offer what a lighted match is to a train of gun-powder. It produces something which cannot be recalled or undone.' Comment.

8. (a) 'A contract is a contract from the time it is made and not from the time its performance is due.' Discuss.

   (b) Is an agreement to agree in the future a contract?

   (c) 'Performance of the condition of a proposal is an acceptance of the proposal'. Comment.

9. "The offer and acceptance bring the parties together, but the law requires some further evidence of their intention to create an obligation'. Elucidate.

10. Who can enter into contracts? What is the effect on a contract of incoinpetency to contract?

11. Discuss fully the law relating to minor's contracts.

12. Explain consideration as an element in a valid contract. State the exceptions to the rule that an agreement without consideration is void.

13. (a) 'No stranger to the consideration can take advantage of a contract although made for his benefit'. Explain by comparing English and Indian law.

    (b) Should consideration always move from the promisee?

    (c) A promise against a promise is a good consideration. Comment.

    (d) Consideration is the price for which the promise of the other is bought. Amplify.

14. (a) Discuss the rule that a stranger to a contract cannot sue and the exceptions, if any, to that rule.

    (b) 'The legal effects of a contract are confined to the contracting parties'. Discuss.

15.(a) What is (a) free consent, (b) real consent? Discuss the importance of consent in contracts.

    (b) Distinguish between (a) fraud and innocent misrepresentation, (b) coercion and undue influence.

    (c) Consider with reference to agreements the following: (i) Undue influence as an element vitiating consent, (ii) mistake as an element excluding consent.

16. Discuss the law relating to the effect of (i) mistake, (ii) undue influence, (iii) coercion, (iv) fraud, and (v) misrepresentation.

17. (a) What are contracts *Uberrimac Fidei*? Give at least three examples of such contracts.

    (b) When and to what extent is a party to a contract bound to disclose information in his possession relating to the subject-matter of the agreement or facts within his knowledge likely to influence the judgment of the other party to the contract? What is the effect of non-disclosure of such information on the contract?

18. Write notes on contracts which law will not enforce on the ground of their being illegal, immoral and against public policy. Give examples.

19. Distinguish clearly between (i) void and voidable contracts, (ii) void and illegal agreements.

20. What is an agreement by way of wager? Is such an agreement void or illegal? Is a contract of insurance a wagering contract?

21. (a) What elements are essential to make a contract a contingent one?

    (b) Discuss the law relating to assignment of contracts.

22. State the various modes in which a contract is discharged.

23. (a) What are the remedies for breach of contract?.

    (b) Explain fully the principles on which the court would award damages for a breach of contract.

    (c) Distinguish between liquidated damages and penalty.

    (d) 'If a contract is broken, the law will endeavour, so far as money can do it, to place the injured party in the same position as if the contract has been performed.' Discuss.

24. (a) What do you understand by 'anticipatory breach of contract'? What are the rights and liabilities of parties in case of anticipatory breach of contract?

(b) X agrees to supply 100 tonnes of iron to Y on March, 1991 at ₹ 50 per tonne. Subsequent to the contract the price of iron rises to ₹ 80 per tonne and on May 1,1991, X intimates to Y that he does not intend to perform his promise. Y replies that he will hold X to his promise. On June 1,1991, the Government in order to check the soaring prices of iron, prohibits the sale of more than 10 tonnes of iron and fixes the price at ₹ 60 per tonne. Discuss, the rights of X and Y on (a) May 1,1991, and (b) on July 1,1991.

25. (a) What is a quasi-contract? Enumerate the quasi-contract provided for by the Contract Act.
    (b) What *is quantum meruit?*
    (c) 'A quantum meruit although it is quasi-contract, arises out of a contract'. Comment.
    (d) What are the rights and obligations of a finder of lost goods?
26. (a) When is an agreement in restraint of trade valid, and when is it void?
    (b) Liberty to trade is not an assent which the law will permit a person to barter away except in special circumstances. Discuss.
27. (a) ' Impossibility of performance is, as a rule, not an excuse for non-performance of a contract'. Discuss.
    (b) 'The doctrine of frustration of contracts is really an aspect or part of the law of discharge of contract'. Discuss.
28. Comment on the following statements:
    (a) An attempt at deceit which does not deceive is not fraud.
    (b) Insufficiency of consideration is immaterial, but an agreement without consideration is void.
    (c) Undue influence is a subtle form of coercion.
    (d) To consummate a contract there must be mutuality as well as a meeting of the minds of the parties.
    (e) Promises bind the representatives of the promisors in case of the death of such promisors before performance.
    (f) The failure to disclose a material fact which might influence the mind of a prudent contractor does not give the right to avoid the contract, even though it is obvious that the contractor has a wrong impression that would be removed by disclosure.
    (g) A quasi-contract is not a contract at all. It is an obligation which the law creates,
    (h) The sanctity of contract is the foundation of the law of contract and the doctrine of impossibility cannot be permitted to become a device for destroying this sanctity,
    (i) Damages never do more than restore the injured party to the position he would have been in, had the promisor performed his promise,
    (j) There cannot be a contract to make a contract.
29. Attempt the following problems, giving reasons for your answers:
    (a) A agreed to let his theatre to B for a show in connection with Mayors' Fund. Before the date of the show the Hall was destroyed by fire. Advise the parties.
    (b) A engaged B to sing at his theatre on July 1,1991, for ₹ 1,000. B is prevented from performing (i) by an accident to his taxi-cab on his way to the theatre; (ii) by a sudden illness caused by an indiscretion in diet, (iii) by A's theatre being burnt down; (iv) because B went to sing for C. Discuss the rights of A and B.
    (c) To a suit on a pro-note filed by the holder in due course the drawer's defence is that he signed the pro-note under the impression that it was a release deed. The Court believes the drawer. How would the court decide the case?

(d) A, who is trying to sell an unsound horse, forges a veterinary surgeon's certificate, stating the horse to be sound and pins it on the stable door. B comes to examine the horse but does not notice the certificate. B buys the horse at a high price. Subsequently, the horse is found to be unsound. What are the remedies of B against A, if any?

(e) A contracts to pay a sum of money to B on a day specified. A does not pay the money on that date. B, in consequence of not receiving the money on that day, is unable to pay his debts, and is totally ruined. What are the rights of B in such a case?

(f) A owes B ₹ 5,000 which he has failed to pay. B promises a rebate of ₹ 1,000 if A will pay at once. A pays ₹ 4,000 in full satisfaction. Subsequently, B demands the balance of ₹ 1,000. Advise A.

(g) A's son has forged B's name on a promissory note. B, under threat of prosecuting A's son, obtains a bond from A for the amount of the forged note. B sues A on the bond. Will he succeed?

(h) M, an old man of feeble sight, endorsed a bill of exchange for ₹ 3,000 thinking it was a guarantee. Is he liable to pay the amount?

(i) A agrees with B to give a car to B's son in consideration of his marrying A's daughter. Can B's son sue on the agreement?

CHAPTER III
Indemnity and Guarantee

1. Define and distinguish contract of indemnity and contract of guarantee.

2. What is a continuing guarantee? When and how is it revoked?

3. What is the nature of surety's liability? When is he discharged from liability?

4. 'The liability of a surety is secondary. It is co-extensive with that of the principal debtor'. The Surety is a favoured debtor'. Discuss these statements.

5. State the rights of a surety against (i) the principal debtor, (ii) the creditor, (iii) co-sureties.

6. Explain with reference to the provisions of the Contract Act, the rule that between co-sureties there is equality of the burden and the benefit.

7. (a) State the case, if any, in which the surety will not be discharged in spite of variance in the contract made without his consent,

   (b) Does the release by the creditors of one of the sureties discharge the others?

8. (a) 'A contract of guarantee is not a contract *uberrimae fidei*'. Discuss.

   (b) Suretyship and partnership are sometimes described as contracts which need full disclosure of all facts likely to affect the judgment of the intending surety or partner. Comment.

9. 'A surety is undoubtedly and not unjustly an object of some favour both at law and at equity'. Explain and illustrate.

10. Attempt the following problems, giving reasons for your answers:

    (a) K contracts to lend ₹2,000 to L on April 1,1991. M guarantees repayment. K pays the amount to L on March 1,1991. Is M discharged?

    (b) B owes C a debt guaranteed by A. The debt becomes payable. C does not sue B for a year after the debt has become payable. B then becomes insolvent. Thereafter, C sues A for the debt. A pleads B's forbearance to sue B for a year as a defence. Is this a good defence?

    (c) A agrees to guarantee the advance of a sum of ₹ 1,00,000 by B to C in the security of two properties of equal Value belonging to C. The transaction, as finally carried out, was the lending by B of a sum of ₹ 50,000 to C on the security of one of the properties. To what extent, if any, is A liable to B for failure by C to discharge his liability to B?

(d) C advances to B, his tenant, ₹ 2,000 on the guarantee of A. C has also a further security for the ₹ 2,000 by a mortgage on B's furniture. C cancels the mortgage. B becomes insolvent. Has C any claim against A?

(e) A advances to B, a minor ₹ 500 on the guarantee of C. On a demand for repayment, B pleads minority. Can A recover the amount from C?

(f) A guarantees to B to the extent of ₹ 10,000 that C shall pay all the bills that B shall draw upon him. B draws upon C and C accepts the bill. A gives notice of revocation. C dishonours the bill at maturity. Is A liable on-his guarantee?

CHAPTER IV

Bailments

1. Define 'Bailment' and state the rights and responsibilities of bailor and bailee. What is a bailee's lien?

2. Define 'pledge', and state the respective rights and duties of pawnor and pawnee.

3. Explain the legal position and rights and duties of a finder of lost goods and those of a pawnee when the pawnor makes default in repayment of the loan.

4. (a) To what extent is a bailee responsible for loss arising from defective title?

   (b) State the rights of bailee against third parties.

5. Attempt the following problems, giving reasons for your answers:

   (a) A hires a carriage of B. The carriage is unsafe although B is not aware of it, and A is injured. Is B responsible to A for the injury?

   (b) If a person sells the shares pledged to him without previously giving notice to the pledger, does the buyer get any title to the shares?

   (c) A lends a horse to B for his own riding only. A allows C, a member of his family, to ride the horse. C rides with care but the horse is injured. Is B liable for the injury to the horse?

   (d) A entered a restaurant to dine. His coat was taken by a waiter and hung on a hook behind A. While A was dining the Coat was stolen. Is the restaurant proprietor liable for the loss?

   (e) A gives silk to B, a tailor, to make into a coat. B promises to deliver the coat to A as soon as it is made and to give A three months' credit for the charges. Is B entitled to retain the coat until the charges are paid?

   (f) An elephant is entrusted to railway administration for carriage. It escapes during the course of the journey and is killed. Is the railway administration liable to make good the loss?

   (g) A delivered to B certain gold ornaments for safe custody. B kept the ornaments in a locked safe and kept the key in a box in the same room. The room was on the ground floor and was locked from outside, and, therefore, was easily accessible to burglars. The ornaments were stolen. Is B liable to make good the loss?

   (h) A hires a car from B to go to Lucknow. A goes to Agra and in the course of the journey meets with an accident and the car is completely smashed. Is B entitled to claim compensation from A for the loss of the car?

   (i) A delivered books to B to be bound. A pressed B for the return of the books, but B neglected to'do so in spite of repeated demands. A fire accidentally broke out in B's premises and the books were burnt, though B was not negligent. Is B liable to compensate A for the loss?

CHAPTER V

Agency

1. 'No one can become the agent of another person except by the will of that person'. Comment.

2. Describe the various ways in which the relationship of agent and principal may arise.

3. An agency by estoppel or holding out is as good as an express agency.

4. What is the effect of agency on contracts with third parties? When is a principal bound by the unauthorised acts of his agent?

5. Explain the terms 'general agent' and 'special agent'. State the extent of liability of the principal when he appoints each of the two.

6. What is meant by agency by ratification? State the conditions that must be fulfilled before that doctrine can apply to an act of an agent.

7. If an agent acts for (a) a disclosed principal, (b) an undisclosed principal, (c) a concealed principal, state clearly the respective rights of the agent, the principal and the third parties.

8. In what circumstances may an agent appoint (a) a sub-agent (b) a substituted agent? Is the principal liable for the acts of such agents?

9. When is an agent personally bound on contracts entered into by him on behalf of the principal?

10. Discuss the rights, and duties of an agent. How may a contract of agency be terminated? When is it irrevocable?

11. Comment on the following statements:

(a) Ratification is tantamount to prior authority;

(b) An apparent or ostensible agency is as effective as an agency deliberately created. Appearance and reality are one.

(c) A principal has power to revoke the authority of the agent, but he doesn't have the right to do so.

(d) An agent is invested with the legal power to alter his principal's legal relations with third parties, the principal is under a correlative liability to have his legal relations altered.

(e) The effect of a contract made by an agent varies according to the circumstances under which the agent contracted.

12. Attempt the following problems, giving reasons for your answers:

(a) What is meant by 'Warranty of authority?' A indorsed a bill of exchange as agent for his friend B. A knew he was not B's agent but intended to do him a service. Has A any liability for his action and if so, on what ground?

(b) B tells C in the presence of, and within the hearing of, A that he (B) is A's agent in A's business and A does not contradict the statement. Subsequently, C enters into a transaction with B bonafide believing that B is A's agent. Is A liable under that contract even when in fact B is not his agent?

(c) A enters into a contract with B to sell him 100 bales of cotton and afterwards, discovers that B was acting as agent for C. Who is liable to pay A the price of the cotton?

(d) M buys goods from N, knowing that he is an agent for their sale but not knowing who is the principal who can claim the price of the goods, N or N's principal? If N's principal files a suit for the price can M claim to set off against that claim a debt due to him from N?

(e) C, a broker, was employed by A to buy cotton for him with instructions not to disclose his name. C's credit was not good enough to contract of his own responsibility and at plaintiffs request he gave him the name of the principal. In the notes C was named as the buyer. C was called upon to pay but as he was unable to pay, the plaintiff sued A. How would you decide the suit?

(f) A makes an offer to sell a machine which B accepts on behalf of C. B had no authority to accept the offer. A then gives notice to C withdrawing the offer. Subsequently C ratifies B's acceptance. Is A bound to sell the machine to C?

(g) A owes B ₹ 5,000. He sells rice worth ₹ 10,000 to B. C gives a notice to B that A was merely acting as an agent of C in that transaction and demands payment from B. Discuss the legal position of A, B and C.

(h) A consigns goods to B, a merchant, for sale. B in due course, employs an auctioneer in good credit to sell the goods of A and allows the auctioneer to receive the proceeds of the sale. The auctioneer becomes insolvent without having accounted for the proceeds. A seeks to hold B responsible for the proceeds. Can he do so?

CHAPTER VI
Partnership

1. Define partnership and distinguish it from (i) joint Hindu family firm, (ii) co-ownership, (iii) joint stock company.

2. How far is it true to say that the law of partnership is an extension of the law relating to principal and agent? Explain the doctrine of "holding out" in reference to the relation of partners to third parties.

3. (a) How would you determine whether a group of persons does or does not constitute a partnership? Discuss fully,

   (b) The sharing of profits is only a. *prime facie* evidence of partnership. Comment.

4. Explain the position of a partner is regard to (a) liabilities existing (i) prior to the time of his joining the firm, (ii) at the time of his retirement, and (b) liabilities incurred by the firm after his retirement.

5. (a) Explain the position and rights of a minor under the law of partnership.

   (b) Discuss fully the mutual rights and duties as between partners in a firm.

   (c) Explain clearly the nature and extent of the authority of a partner in a firm.

6. (a) 'The Partnership Act has effectively assured the registration of firms without making it compulsory'. Explain,

   (b) What is the effect of non-registration of a firm?

7. (a) What is an Act of the Firm? What is the extent of the liability of a partner for the acts of the firm?

   (b) Explain the relations of partners to third parties. Can a firm he liable for the wrongful act of a partner?

8. (a) What is meant by an implied authority of a partner? Indicate the cases in which a partner has no implied authority to bind the firm. Does a partner's authority in emergency differ in any way from his implied authority?

   (b) Explain the legal position of the transferee of a partner's share.

9. How and in what circumstances is (i) a partnership dissolved automatically, (ii) a trading firm dissolved compulsorily by the court?

10. (a) What are the rights and obligations of partners after dissolution of partner-ship?

    (b) How are accounts settled between partners after dissolution?

    (c) Can a partner be expelled from the firm?

11. (a) What is 'Partnership Property' and how far is it liable for a partner's separate debts?

    (b) What do you understand by 'goodwill' of a business? What becomes of the goodwill on dissolution of the firm?

12. Attempt the following problems, giving reasons for your answer:

    (a) A and B, who are partners, borrowed money from C. Eventually C sued then on the loan and obtained a decree which was not satisfied. Subsequently, C discovered, that D was a partner with A and B at the time of the loan. Discuss the rights of the parties. Would it make any difference if D were dead and his estate being administered at the time?

(b) A, B and C are partners in a firm doing business carrying goods in motor trucks. One of the drivers of a truck, while driving at a high speed on a highway, knocks down a person who dies on the spot Are A, B & C liable in damages to the legal representatives of the deceased?

(c) A, B and C carry on partnership business as bankers. A receives ₹ 5,000 from D on behalf of the partnership firm for the purpose of investing it in good securities yielding interest at 14 per cent per annum. A does not inform B and C and appropriates the money for his own use. Is the firm liable for the money? Would it make any difference to your answer if the partnership firm were a firm of attorneys?

(d) A, B and C carry on a partnership business as druggists. A orders on credit two cases of Kulu apples to be delivered to his married daughter. The order is sent on the firm's note paper, and in firm's name, and signed by A as partner. Is the firm liable to pay for the apples?

(e) A, B and C carried on partnership business under an assumed name (X & Co.). A retired and D, a new partner, joined the firm which carried on the business in its old name, 'X & Co.' A creditor filed a suit against A, B, C & D. Will he succeed?

(f) A, B and C are partners. C is a sleeping partner. C retires. Is C liable for the subsequent debts incurred by A and B?

(g) A, B and C are partners in a trading firm, A, acting on behalf of the firm, performed the following acts:

   (i) accepted a bill of exchange in the firm's name,

   (ii) borrowed ₹ 50,000 by pledging the goods of the firm,

   (iii) Purchased a building property of the value of ₹ one lakh for housing the retail store,

   (iv) withdrew a long pending suit filed on behalf of the firm and settled the matter out of court.

Discuss the validity of A's acts so far as the other partners are concerned.

(h) A and B are partners in a trading firm. They execute a deed declaring that the partnership is dissolved with effect from 31st March, 1991.They do not give public notice, and continue the business. On April 10,1901 A indorses a bill in the partnership name to C who is not aware of the dissolution. Is the firm liable on the bill?

CHAPTER VII
Sale of Goods

1. Define the term 'Sale of Goods'. What is the practical importance of knowing the exact moment when the property in goods passes from the seller to the buyer? State and illustrate the rules which determine such moment.

2. (a) "The contract of sale is consensual, bilateral and cumulative'. Elucidate,

   (b) Distinguish between 'Sale' and 'agreement to sell'. Give examples.

3. (a) What is meant by (i) ascertained and unascertained goods, (ii) specific and generic goods, (iii) existing and future goods?

   (b) In a contract for the sale of goods, state when the property in goods sold passes from the seller to the buyer.

4. What is the difference between condition and warranty in relation to sale of goods? What is meant by an implied condition? What is the rule of *caveat emptor,* and how far is it modified by implied conditions?

5. Explain and illustrate the implied conditions and warrantees, in a sale and state the consequences of a breach in each case.

6. When may a seller give a better title to the buyer than he himself has in the goods sold? What is the rule of Market Overt? Does it apply in India?

7. When is a seller deemed to be an "unpaid seller"? What are his rights against (i) the goods, (ii) the buyer personally?

8. When is a buyer deemed to have accepted the goods? What is (i) an F.O.B. contract, (ii) C.I.F. contract? Is it correct to say that a C.I F. contract is only a sale of documents?

9. State the exception, if any, to the rule that there is no implied condition as to the quality or fitness for any particular purpose of goods supplied under the contract of sale.

10. State the law which governs the sate of goods by auction.

11. Attempt the following problems, giving reasons for your answer:

(a) A of Agra ordered certain goods from B of Bombay. B sends some goods, not ordered, along with them. What should A do?

(b) A contracts to sell to B a piece of silk. B thinks that it is Assam silk. A knows that B thinks so, but knows that it is not Assam silk. A does not correct B's impression. B afterwards discovers that it is not Assam silk. Can A repudiate the contract?

(c) A sells a horse to B. When B goes with the horse he is arrested by ths police on the charge of keeping stolen property as the horse belongs to C. Is B entitled to sue A, if so, on what basis, and what damages can he recover?

(d) A sells a horse to B. The horse will be delivered to B next week and B will pay the price on delivery. A instructs his servant to keep the horse separate from other horses. The horse dies before it is delivered and before the price is paid. Who should suffer the loss?

(e) In January, 1991 C contracts to sell to D all the mangoes in C's garden during the 1991 season (1st April to 31st August), for sum of ₹ 10,000. Discuss whether the contract is a sale or agreement to sell.

(f) P makes a contract with B to sell him Java Sugar as per sample shown by P to B. Thereafter, P delivers the agreed quantity of sugar to B which corresponds to sample but is not Java Sugar. What are B's rights, if any?

(g) M sells and consigns certain goods to N. M being still unpaid, N becomes insolvent While the goods are in transit, N assigns the bill of lading for cash to S who knows that N is insolvent Can M stop the goods in transit?

(h) A purchased tinned salmon from B, a grocer and provision merchant The Salmon was poisonous and A and his wife who ate it fell ill. A recovered from his illness, but his wife died from the effects of the poison. A claimed damages against B both for his illness and for the death of his wife, which deprived him of services rendered by her. How would you decide?

(i) A bids ₹ 1,000 for a costly vase at an auction sale. The auctioneer purports to accept the bid by striking the hammer, but accidentally strikes the vase which breaks into picks. Who is to bear the loss?

(j) H entered into a hire-purchase agreement which B in relation to a piano on the condition that on paying 12 instalments of ₹ 1,000 each the property should be the property of B. After paying 10 instalments, B pawned the piano with M, who took it in good faith. A claims the piano from M. Will he succeed?

(k) M asked for a bottle of Stone's Ginger Wine at F's shop, which was licensed for the sale of wine. While M was drawing the cork, the bottle broke and M was injured. Can M claim damages for the injury?

(1) A sold a quality of seed to B who paid by cheque, which was dishonoured upon presentment A gave a delivery order to B for the goods and B re-sold the goods to C, indorsing the delivery order to him. A refused to deliver the goods to C on the plea of non-receipt of the price. Advise C.

(m) A placed an order with B & Co., requesting them to send the goods by sea. B & Co. took a bill of lading in the name of A and sent it to their own agent The goods were, however, destroyed in the course of the voyage. Examine the position of the buyer and the seller.

(n) The plaintiffs ordered goods from an English company and paid for them in advance. The goods were to be sent F.O.B. destination Bombay. The English company packed the goods into cases marked them with the buyer's name, registered them for consignment and ordered shipping space in a named ship. Before the goods were sent to the part, a receiver was appointed by the debenture- holders of the English company and he refused to deliver the goods. The plaintiffs claimed the goods, alleging that property in the goods had passed to them. Would you allow their claim?

CHAPTER VIII, IX AND X
Insurance

1. Explain the nature of a contract of insurance. Distinguish between life insurance and other kinds of insurance.

2. Explain and illustrate the fundamental principles of insurance.

3. What do you understand by insurable interest in connection with life, fire and marine insurance? When must it subsist in the case of each? Enumerate the different kinds of insurable interest recognised by law.

4. Explain the terms in connection with insurance: Contribution, re-insurance, double insurance, premium and its return, surrender value, Causa Proximo, sub-rogation, perils of the sea, cover note, bottomry and responditia.

5. (a) Discuss fully the 'implied warranties' in a contract of marine insurance.

   (b) What is meant by deviation and change of voyage? When is deviation excused?

6. Discuss the various kinds of losses under a marine policy bringing out clearly the circumstances in which the underwriter may be liable for each.

7. What is the meaning of Fire in a fire policy? Is loss caused in extinguishing a fire recoverable as a loss covered by fire? If goods, insured against fire, are sold and subsequent to the sale are destroyed by fire, to whom is the insurer liable?

8. (a) Is the contract of life insurance a contract of indemnity? Is it a wagering contract?

   (b) Can the insurer avoid liability on the ground that

      (i) the assured committed suicide,

      (ii) the age of the assured is not correct?

   (c) Can an underwriter avoid a policy on the ground of material misrepresentation if the loss is unconnected with the fact misrepresented?

9. 'Average in fire policies is quite a different thing from average in marine policies'. Explain and illustrate.

10. Discuss the law relating assignability of insurance policies, and give the procedure in cases where it is assignable.

11. Comment on the following:

    (a) Indemnity is the controlling principle of insurance law, but all insurance contracts are not perfect contracts of indemnity.

    (b) A contract of insurance is not merely a gamble on an uncertain future.

(c) Insurance is a contract on speculation.

(d) Insurance is sometimes called an aleatory contract; it is not, however, a Wagering contract.

(e) The use of the term 'warranty' in a contract of insurance should be distinguished from its use in other branches of the law of contracts.

(f) A motor insurance policy, or a fire or burglary policy is a contract of personal indemnity.

12. Attempt the following problems, giving reasons for your answers:

(a) A takes a policy on his wife's life and divorces her. She dies. Can A recover the amount of the policy?

(b) If a theft is committed during the confusion following an outbreak of fire, is the insurer liable on a fire policy to make good the loss by theft?

(c) A, B and C are three contiguous houses insured against fire. An earthquake caused A to fall and as a consequence fire broke out and spread to B where an explosion occurred whereby C was wrecked. Is the insurer liable for the loss caused to C?

(d) A, who has a policy on his life, nominates B as his nominee. B dies during A's life time. After A's death B's heirs claim the policy money. Discuss the rights of B's heirs. Will it make any difference to your answer if A had assigned the policy to B?

(e) X, a Delhi professor, insures his household goods against risk of fire. While smoking in his bed X falls asleep and the goods catch fire. X escapes with a few bums. Can X recover under the policy?

(f) A insured his house against loss by fire. Later, while insane, he killed his wife, severely injured his only son, set fire to the house and died in the fire. The son survives and sues the insurer for the fire loss. Is he entitled to recover?

(g) A fire broke out on board a ship and caused damage to some cargo belonging to A. In putting out the fire by water some cargo of B was damaged. Discuss if A or B can claim general average contribution from the owners of the other interests in the ship and cargo.

CHAPTER XI
Negotiable Instruments

1. Explain the term negotiable instrument State the chief instruments which are at present regarded as negotiable and discuss the statement 'the list of negotiable instruments is not closed, it may be added to if the necessary conditions are fulfilled.'

2. Explain clearly what is meant by 'negotiation.' How is it effected and how does it differ from an ordinary assignment. Can an overdue instrument be negotiated?

3. (a) Define promissory note and distinguish it from a bill of exchange.

   (b) What are the presumptions in respect of a negotiable instruments?

4. State the different circumstances in which a holder in due course can regard a negotiable instrument as dishonoured. What are his rights and obligations in the event of a dishonour?

5. Explain clearly the following:

   (a) Inland instrument;   (b) ambiguous instrument;

   (c) inchoate instrument;   (d) endorsement;   (e) acceptance for honour;

   (f) drawee in case of need;   (g) noting and protesting.

6. (a) Define (i) holder, (ii) holder in due course. State and explain some of the important privileges of a holder in due course.

   (b) In a suit on a pro-note, can the defendant set up the plea of total or partial failure of consideration?

7. State concisely the essential features of an instrument which make it negotiable and specify the points of difference between the negotiability and assignability of such instrument.

8. (a) In what respect does an accommodation bill differ from a trade bill?

    (b) What is meant by (i) dishonour for non-acceptance, (ii) dishonour for non-payment? State the cases in which notice of dishonour is not necessary.

    (c) The failure of consideration for a negotiable instrument is material only between immediate parties to the instrument. Comment.

9. (a) 'Any bill of exchange on which the 'bearer' or 'order' appears is and remains a negotiable bill and no words prohibiting transfer or indicating an intention that it should hot be transferred have any effect on its negotiability. Comment.

    (b) When is payment on a negotiable instrument said to be payment in due course?

10. (a) Has a holder of a cheque any remedy against the banker for wrongful dishonour of the cheque?

    (b) Discuss the law relating to crossed cheques with special reference to the liabilities of the collecting banker in respect thereof.

    (c) If a cheque is paid across the counter against a forged indorsement, has the drawer or true owner a right of action against the banker?

    (d) Explain the effect of (i) 'Not Negotiable' crossing, (ii) 'Account Payee only' crossing.

11. (a) Indicate the cases in which a banker (i) may, (ii) must, refuse to honour a customer's cheque.

    (b) Specify the conditions under which the duty and authority of a banker to pay a cheque drawn on him by a customer is determined.

12. Indicate the significance and implications of the 'marking' of a cheque as good. Does 'marking' of a post-dated cheque bind the banker who certifies it?

13. (a) What are the circumstances in which a party to a negotiable instrument is discharged? Discuss the liability of prior parties on a negotiable instrument to a subsequent holder and amongst themselves.

    (b) What are the exceptions to the rule that the effect of a material alteration of a negotiable instrument is to discharge all parties liable on it at the time of the alteration?

14. Attempt the following problems, giving reasons for your answer:

    (a) A gives a blank acceptance to one Banerji, who fills it up as a bill payable to the drawer's order and himself signs it as the drawer and the first indorser in a fictitious name 'Jogendra Singh'. Is A or Banerji liable to the holder of the bill?

    (b) A bill of exchange is drawn in favour of John Smith or order. At maturity another person of the same name is in possession of the instrument, endorses it, and presents it for payment. The acceptor .pays him. Is he discharged by such payment? Would there be any difference if the instrument were a cheque and was paid by the drawee banker in due course?

    (c) A breaks open B's Cupboard and gets hold of B's cheque book. A then forges B's signature on a cheque and obtains money on it from B's banker. A then disappears, who should bear the loss, B or the banker?

    (d) Discuss whether any of the following is a valid pro-note:

        (i) A promises to pay B or bearer the sum of ₹ 5,000 on 6 months after date,

        (ii) A promises to pay the bearer on demand the sum of ₹ 5,000; (iii) A promises to pay B or order the sum of ₹ 5,000 one month after C's death;

        (iv) A executes a writing in favour of B as follows: 'I acknowledge myself to be indebted to B in the sum of ₹ 5,000 to be paid on demand for value received'.

    (e) A, B and C are drawer, drawee and payee respectively of a cheque. If, before the cheque is presented for payment, one of them becomes insolvent, how are the others prejudiced?

    (f) B obtains A's acceptance to a bill by fraud. B indorses it to C who takes it as a holder in due course. C indorses the bill to D who knows of the fraud. Can D recover from A?

(g) A draws a bill of exchange on B payable to C or order. C indorses it in blank and negotiates it. The bill is thereafter lost and X, who finds it, forges an indorsement in blank of D and negotiates it by delivery to E. Discuss if E has any rights on the instrument and, if so, against whom?

(h) A, the holder of a bill, endorses it 'Sans Recourse' to B. B indorses it to C, C to D, D to E and E endorses it again to A. Can A recover the amount of the bill fro n B, C, D and E or any of them?

(i) A bill was left in the drawee for acceptance. The drawee having written hit acceptance upon it kept it in his possession, and two days after having heard that the drawer had failed, cancellled the acceptance and returned the bill to the holder. Was the drawee entitled to do this?

(j) A promissory note is executed by A in favour of B in consideration of C, a relation of B, for bearing to sue on a prior pro-note executed by A in favour of C. Has the note executed by A in favour of B any lawful consideration?

(k) C, the payee of a bill, indorses it in blank and delivers it to D, who specially indorses it to E, or order. E without indorsement transfers it to F. Consider the rights of F.

CHAPTER XII
Insolvency

1. Describe fully what constitutes Acts of Insolvency.
2. (a) Under what circumstances and at whose instance may a person be adjudicated an insolvent?
   (b) Who can, (ii) cannot be adjudged an insolvent?
3. (a) What is an order of adjudication? What are its effects?
   (b) 'The object of an adjudication is to free the debtor from the claims of creditors, which are to be satisfied out of the insolvent's estate, which the Court takes possession of and distributes among his creditors'. Discuss fully.
4. Write explanatory notes on the following:
   (a) Public examination of the insolvent;
   (b) Protection order and its effect;
   (c) Fraudulent Preference;
   (d) Protected Transactions;
   (e) Disclaimer of onerous property;
   (f) Doctrine of Relation Bank;
   (g) Doctrine of Reputed Ownership;
   (h) Preferential debts;
   (i) Committee of Inspection.
5. (a) Define insolvent's property. What property of the insolvent (i) is divisible, (ii) is not divisible among his creditors?
   (b) State the duties of an insolvent as to discovery and realisation of property.
6. (a) What debts are provable in insolvency? What debts are not provable?
   (b) What is the mode of distribution of property of the insolvent?
7. (a) Discuss the effect of insolvency on antecedent transactions.
   (b) When may Insolvency Court annul an order of adjudication. State the effect of the annulment order.
8. What is an order of discharge? What are its effects? State the powers of an Insolvency Court in deciding an insolvent's application for his discharge. What matters must the Court consider in deciding the application for discharge?

9. (a) State the cases in which the Court must (i) absolutely refuse the discharge, (ii) refuse to grant an absolute discharge,

   (b) What are the disabilities of an undischarged insolvent?

10. (a) 'In matters of arising out of insolvency the Official Assignee or the Official Receiver has a higher title then the insolvent'. Discuss.

    (b) 'The effect of the doctrine of reputed ownership is to take one man's property to pay another man's debts.' Discuss the statement, explaining the range and scope of the doctrine.

11. 'A debtor may not by stipulation with a creditor, provide for a different distribution of his effects in the event of his insolvency from that which the law provides'. Elucidate.

12. Attempt the following problems, giving reasons for your answers:

    (a) A gives goods to B, a commission agent, for being sold. The goods remain unsold with B, who is adjudged an insolvent. Can the Official Assignee claim the goods? Would it make any difference to your answer if the goods have been sold off before adjudication and money had hot been received by B form the buyer?

    (b) A, while in a solvent condition, makes gift of his house to his daughter B. Fifteen months thereafter he suffers heavy losses and within eighteen months of the date of the gift he is adjudged an insolvent. Can the Official Assignee get the gift set aside?

    (c) A owed a debt to B. A was adjudicated insolvent on his own petition. B's claim was not time barred at the date of the petition but became time barred before the order of adjudication was made. Is B entitled to prove his claim in insolvency?

    (d) L, the owner of a motor car, lent it to his friend M for his domestic use. Unknown to L, M used the car in his business, so that M's customers came to regard the car to belong to M. On the insolvency of. M, can the Official Assignee claim a title to the car?

    (e) A debtor pays in cash ₹5,000 which his solicitor requires to defray counsel's fees and other legal, expenses in opposing a petition for adjudication filed against him. The petition ends in an order of adjudication. Can the Official Assignee cr Official Receiver compel the solicitor to refund the money?

    (f) A trader obtains a loan under an agreement to deliver to the lender the next day goods of an equivalent value lying in his godown to secure the loan. Both the borrower and the lender put their own locks on the door of the godown. The borrower absconds the same night and is subsequently adjudged an insolvent The Official Assignee claims the goods. How would you decide?

    (g) A sells a patent to B in consideration of B paying royalties to A. At the same time B advances to A a sum of ₹ 1,25,000 as a loan. It is agreed that B should retain one-half of the royalties as they became payable to A, from time to time, towards the satisfaction of the debt, provided that if A should become insolvent B would have the right to retain the whole of the royalties in satisfaction of the debt. A becomes insolvent before the debt is fully paid. Can B retain the royalties as stipulated?

    (h) On an insolvent's application for discharge, the Insolvency Court ordered: "I do not grant an absolute discharge, but grant a conditional one, the condition being that the creditors may recover their dues, if within time, until they become irrecoverable". Examine the validity of the order.

    (i) An insolvent was granted a conditional discharge. A, a judgment creditor, filed a petition for the execution of a decree which he had obtained prior to adjudication, by attachment and sale of a house belonging to the insolvent's wife. Discuss whether A will succeed.

CHAPTER XIII
Arbitration

1. What is meant by submission to arbitration? What is the effect of such submission on an action?
2. What are the different modes of submission? What can be referred to arbitration? Who may refer it?
3. (a) Under what circumstances would the court appoint (i) an arbitrator, (ii) an unpire?
   (b) Discuss the relative advantages of the settlement of a dispute under the Arbitration Act.
4. (a) What are powers and duties of an arbitrator?
   (b) State the presumptions in relation to arbitration.
5. Explain the nature of control the Court exercises over the proceedings of an arbitrator under the Arbitration Act When may an arbitrator state a special case for the opinion of the Court?
6. (a) What powers do the Courts enjoy over awards by an arbitrator?
   (b) When may the Court (i) modify or correct, (ii) remit for reconsideration, (iii) set aside an award?
7. What are the powers of the court where arbitrator is removed or his authority is revoked?
8. Attempt the following problems giving reasons for your answers:
   (a) An arbitrator sends notice by registered post to parties to appear before him on a certain date. One of the parties fails to appear. The arbitrator records the evidence of the other party in his absence and makes an award. What are the remedies open to the party against whom the award has been given in his absence?
   (b) In a suit by P's widow for maintenance provided by P's will all the parties agreed to appoint K as the sole arbitrator for settling the dispute and to abide by his decision. The arbitrator examined the defendant in the absence of the plaintiff and perused the will without letting her have her say. Can the award be set aside?
   (c) In a dispute between A and B for the possession of a certain property, the arbitrator gave an award on the basis of a draw of lots in favour of B, who took possession of the property. A challenges the award. Decide.

CHAPTER XIV
Carriage Goods

1. Who is a 'common carrier'? How does he differ from a private carrier? What is meant by the statement that a common carrier is an insurer of goods. To what extent can a common carrier reduce his liability by special contract? Are railways in India common carriers?
2. What is a contract of affreightment? What conditions are implied in such a contract? If any one of these conditions is broken, what is the legal consequence?
3. Distinguish a Bill of Lading from a Charter Party. What are their respective functions? Is bill of Lading negotiable?
4. (a) Explain the functions of a bill of lading. How far is it regarded as a negotiable instrument?
   (b) 'A bill of lading is negotiable only in a popular sense and not in technical sense.' Comment.
5. State clearly the position of the holder of a bill of lading in respect of goods carried on a chartered ship (i) when he is both the shipper and charterer, (ii) when he is a shipper other than a charterer; (iii) when he is an indorsee from the shipper.
6. Is the indorsee of a bill of lading liable to pay (i) freight, (ii) the loss caused to the ship owing to the dangerous character of the goods, (iii) the general average contribution?

7. (a) What are the powers and duties of the master of a ship during voyage?

    (b) Of what facts are (i) Air Way bill, and (ii) a bill of lading *prima facie* evidence? Why is it advisable for a carrier of goods by air to insist on an Air Way Bill?

8. 'The law charges the common carrier thus entrusted to carry goods against all events but Acts of God and of the public enemies'. Comment and state the present position of the law regarding liabilities of railway administration for loss of or damage to goods, animal or passengers' luggage.

9. Attempt the following problems, giving reasons for your answers:

    (a) Three boxes described to contain stationary and Eversharp fountain pens and pencils (with nibs, clips and caps of gold) were put in the luggage Van and receipt obtained by L, who was travelling in a second class compartment from Bombay to Amritsar. At Delhi, L enquired whether the boxes were there, but got no information, and was told to inquire at Amritsar. At Amritsar he was told that the boxes were missing. Can L recover damages from the railways?

    (b) A consigned a marble statue valued at ₹ 9,000 wrapped in grass and gunny bags and did not declare its value at the time of tendering it to the station master. The statue was damaged in transit. Is the Railway liable?

    (c) A carrier issues a bill of lading acknowledging receipt of a box of goods. The agent for the carrier notes on the bill of lading that the weight, value, contents and quantity of the goods are known. The shipper transfers the bill of lading to a *bonafide* purchaser. When the goods are found not to be the same as described in the bill of lading the latter brings an action for damages against the carrier. Will he succeed?

    (d) An agent for a carrier issues a bill of lading acknowledging receipt of a certain perishable goods. No goods, in fact, were delivered to the carrier. The bill of lading is transferred to a *bonafide* purchaser. Thereafter, the purchaser of the bill of lading sues the carrier for failure to deliver the goods. Is he entitled to recover damages?

    (e) The goods of A disappeared somewhere between Delhi, the point of shipment, and Bombay, the point of destination. The Railway Administration disclaimed liability foi the loss on the ground that they were stolen by thieves. Was A entitled to recover?

    (f) 'One hundred barrels of oil and one hundred and six bales of palm baskets were shipped under a bill of lading which contained the clause not accountable for rust, leakage or breakage. On delivery two barrels of oil were found to be empty and sixty bales of palm were damaged with oil. The shipper sued the ship owner for damages on account of the Joss suffered.' Decide.

CHAPTER XV
Mortgages and Charges

1. Define a mortgage, a charge, and distinguish between them.

2. Briefly described the various kinds of mortgages, bringing out clearly the distinguishing features of each.

3. State the rights and liabilities of (i) mortgagor, (ii) mortgagee.

4. Explain fully (i) Equity of Redemption; (ii) Tacking; (iii) Equitable Mortgage; (iv) Marshalling of Securities; (v) Clog on the Right of Redemption; (vi) 'Once a mortgage always a mortgage'.

5. Explain and illustrate (i) Contribution, (ii) Subrogation, in connection with mortgages.

6. What is meant by 'Right of Foreclosure'? When and how can a mortgagee exercise this right? State the cases in which a mortgagee has no right to sue for mortgage money.

7. Define a Bill of Sale. Distinguish between an absolute and conditional bill of sale.

CHAPTER XVI
Company Law

1. (a) Explain the concept of corporate personality and the principle of limited liability.

   (b) Elaborate the doctrine of lifting the 'corporate veil"? How far does it ensure protection to third parties?

2. The fundamental attribute of corporate personality is that the corporation is a legal entity distinct and separate from its members. Discuss fully.

3. Describe the procedure for the incorporation of a company, and name the documents and statements that must be filed with the Registrar of Companies.

4. Define a private company and distinguish it from a public company.

5. Enumerate the advantages from legal point of view, of converting a partnership business into a private limited company.

6. Outline the procedure for converting a private company into a public company and a public company into a private company.

7. Under what circumstances does a private company become a public company?

8. Write explanatory notes on:—

   (a) Government Company;

   (b) Holding and Subsidiary Companies;

   (c) Company Limited by guarantee;

   (d) An association not for profit;

   (e) One-man company.

9. (a) Define 'Promoter'. Mention his legal position, functions, duties and liabilities,

   (b) 'Promoter is not a trustee or agent of the company but stands in a fiduciary position towards it'. Discuss.

10. Explain the law in relation to pre-incorporation contracts, and those entered into after incorporation but before the company is entitled to commence business.

11. (a) What do you understand by (i) Memorandum of Association, (ii) Articles of Association? What is the purpose of each?

    (b) Mention the clauses that a memorandum must contain. Describe the procedure for altering the memorandum.

    (c) Describe the procedure for altering the articles and state the limitations to such alteration.

12. What is the effect of memorandum and articles upon members and outsiders?

13. Explain fully and state the limitations to —

    (a) the doctrine of ultra vires;

    (b) the doctrine of indoor management.

14. How and in what circumstances may a company increase, re-organise and reduce its share capital?

15. Explain the meaning and importance of Prospectus. What legal consequences flow from misrepresentation contained in a prospectus in respect of rights and liabilities of different parties concerned?

16. Define debenture. Explain different kinds of debentures. Distinguish debentures and debenture Stock. Enumerate the charges requiring registration.

17. Distinguish between fixed charge and floating charge, and explain the nature and incidence of a floating charge. When does a floating charge become fixed or crystallise?

18. Distinguish between the various kinds of meetings of a company and different classes of resolutions.

19. What are the powers of the majority and rights of the minority shareholders?

20. (a) Write explanatory notes on investigations under Sections 235 and 237 of the Companies Act, 1956.

    (b) Explain the provisions of the Companies Act for the prevention of oppression and mismanagement.

21. State the present position of the law with regard to the appointment and removal of auditors, as well as the number of companies of which a person can be an auditor.

22. Discuss the duties and liabilities of an auditor in the light of the dictum that an auditor is "a watchdog, not a blood hound".

23. Explain the nature of a call. In what circumstances may shares be forfeited and what is the effect of forfeiture?

24. Explain the present position of the law regarding declaration and payment of dividend. What is the duty of a company with respect to unpaid or unclaimed dividends?

25. Discuss the law relating to the appointment, remuneration and removal of directors of a public company. When does the office of a director become vacant?

26. (a) 'The directors are the mere trustee and agents of the company'. Examine this statement in the light of the legal position of directors.

    (b) 'As fiduciaries, directors must not place themselves in a position in which there is a conflict between their duties to the company and their interests'. Explain and illustrate by referring to the provisions of the Companies Act.

27. Define and distinguish Managing Director and Manager. State the present position of the law regarding appointment, and remuneration of Managing Director, whole-time director and Manager.

28. Discuss the extent of the powers of a company to enter into compromise or scheme of arrangement for reconstruction or amalgamation and describe the procedure to be adopted for the purpose.

29. In what circumstances may a company be wound up by the Court? Who are entitled to petition and when? What is the effect of a winding up order?

30. Outline the procedure for voluntary winding up. What is a declaration of solvency?

31. Point out the distinction between and special features of (i) a winding up of a company by the Court, (ii) a voluntary winding up, and (iii) a winding up subject to the supervision of the Court

32. (a) Who is a contributory? What is the nature and extent of his liability?

    (b) State the constitution, functions and legal position of a Committee of Inspection.

33. 'An unpaid creditor has a right *ex debite justitiae* to a winding up order'. Elucidate and explain when a creditor is deemed to be unpaid in order to entitle him to present a petition for winding up.

34. (a) Explain the powers and duties of (i) Official Liquidator, (ii) Voluntary Liquidator.

    (b) What is the status of a liquidator? Is he an agent of the company? Is he a trustee?

35. What is meant by an 'unregistered company'? What are the circumstances under which it can be wound up? Can a foreign company or an illegal association be wound up as an unregistered company?

36. Attempt the following problems, giving reasons for your answers:

    (a) A furniture dealer entered upon a contract with a company for furnishing the offices of the company. The company went into liquidation before it became entitled to commence business. Can the furniture dealer prove in the winding up for the price of furniture supplied to the company?

    (b) The Managing Director of a company borrowed a sum of ₹ 50,000 by signing a promissory-note to be payable on 23rd August, 1990. When the pro-note was presented for payment to the company, it refused to pay on the contention that the Managing Director was not authorised to borrow without the previous sanction oi the Board of directors, which had not been granted. Would the contention of the company be upheld?

(c) A shareholder of a company, who sold his shares, executed blank transfer forms and delivered them alongwith the share certificates to the purchaser. He wrote to the company that he had sold his shares, but neither he nor the purchaser deposited the transfer forms with the company, and consequently the transfer was not registered on the register of members. On the winding up of the company, who should be placed on the list of contributories?

(d) A, the director of a public limited company borrows money from the company. Discuss the legality or otherwise of the loan (i) if it is with security, (ii) if it is without security, (iii) if the company is a banking company.

(e) A company borrows money from X beyond its powers. Has Y, a shareholder, any remedy against (i) the company, (ii) die directors of the company?

(f) In a winding up the Court makes a can of ₹5 per equity share. The company owes ₹1,000 to a shareholder, who holds 500 equity shares. How much will the shareholder have to pay in pursuance of this call?

CHAPTER XVII

Factories Act

1. Define a factory and an occupier. When is a worker liable to punishment under the Factories Act?

2. Enumerate the general duties of (i) the occupier and (ii) the manufacturer.

3. Briefly state the provisions of the Factories Act with regard to health and welfare.

4. Describe the constitution of the Site Appraisal Committee in relation to the setting up of a factory involving hazardous processes. Also state the duties of occupier of such factory.

5. Examine the provisions of the Factories Act regarding hours of work and leave with wages.

6. What restrictions are imposed by the Factories Act in the employment and work of Women and Young persons?

7. Attempt the following problems, giving reasons for your answers:

(a) In a factory, women workers were allowed by the occupier to dust and otherwise regulate their spinning frames for their own satisfaction and comfort before the fixed time. What action would be taken against the occupier?

(b) The services of a woman worker who had completed a period of four months' continuous service in a factory were terminated before she had completed the period of twelve months continuous service. To what leave is she entitled? Would it make any difference if she were a girl under the age of 15 years?

(c) A was the owner and B manager of a factory which was sold to C on March 1, 1991. Immediately after possession, C appointed D as a manager who, during a check up, discovered that a boy, ten years old, had been working in the factory since January 1,1990. D reported the fact to the Factory Inspector and discharged the boy, whereupon prosecution was launched against A, B, C and D. How would you decide the case?

CHAPTER XVIII

Workmen's Compensation

1. Distinguish between total and partial disability (disablement) of a workman under the Workman's Compensation Act, 1923.

2. When is an employer liable and not liable to pay compensation to a workman for personal injury?

3. Explain and illustrate the expression 'arising out of and in the course of employment'. Where an accident arises out of and in course of employment, can the employer plead 'common employment', 'assumed risk' or 'contributory negligence, in his defence?

4. Discuss whether the employer is liable to pay compensation in the following cases:

   (a) A workman went across the road to fetch milk for himself for tea on the promises and was run over.

   (b) An employee left the employer's promises to take meals elsewhere.

   (c) A roadman, while working on the road, was killed by lightning.

   (d) A worker working in a shed was injured by the fall of a wall which was not the property of or under the control of the employer.

   (e) A miner in the drilling work for releasing gas was forbidden to enter the gas filled part of the mine. H violated the order and was suffocated.

   (f) An electrician in a press had, in the course of his duties frequently to go into the heating room and from there to a cooling plant where the temperature was kept considerably low. One night, when he went into the cooling room, he got pneumonia and died from that disease.

   (g) A worker lost his mental balance as a result of an injury by accident and committed suicide.

CHAPTER XIX
Trade Unions

1. (a) Define Trade Union. State the rights and privileges of a registered trade union and of its members.

   (b) Does a suit lie to prevent the office bearers of a registered trade union from trespassing on the plaintiff's land (accompanied by some armed persons) and staging demonstrations thereon which are calculated to overawe and in-timidate the plaintiff and workmen?

2. Describe the procedure for the registration of a trade union and its dissolution. When may registration be cancelled?

3. When and for what purpose may a trade union create a political fund?

4. What is general fund? State the purposes for which it is created.

CHAPTER XX AND XXI
Payment of Wages, Industrial Disputes

1. Define wages under the Payment of Wages Act, 1936.

2. (a) Who is responsible for payment of wages?

   (b) Explain the provisions regarding time limit for payment of wages.

   (c) Is an employer permitted to pay wages in kind?

3. (a) Discuss the nature, conditions and extent of authorised deductions from the wages of a worker.

   (b) What amount of compensation is payable to a worker for wrongful deductions and delay in payment of wages?

4. (a) X was employed in an industrial establishment governed by the Payment of Wages Act, 1936. His total wages per month were ₹ 1200. The employer deducted from his wages an amount or ₹ 900 during one month. The deductions included fines, provident fund, water charges, light charges, festival advance instalment and cooperative society's dues. The worker seeks your advice. Advise him.

(b) The employer of a worker under the age of 15 years and earning ₹ 300 a month deducts ₹ 5 by way of fine from his wages for the month and credits the amount to a fund created for building a temple in the employer's village. The employee petitions for refund and prays for punishment to the employer. Will he succeed?

(c) The N. Railway reduced the monthly rate of pay of A, an engine driver, by ₹ 25 for unsatisfactory work. Advise A.

5. (a) Define and distinguish 'Lay-off and 'Retrenchment'. What compensation is payable under each?

   (b) Discuss whether the termination of services in the following cases amounts to retrenchment:
   (i) where the date of termination is written in appointment letter itself;
   (ii) where services are terminated during the probation period on the ground of unsuitability.

6. Explain clearly the machinery that exists under the Industrial Disputes Act for the prevention, settlement and adjudication of industrial disputes.

7. Examine the powers and duties of a conciliation officer, and an Industrial Tribunal.

8. State the provisions relating to voluntary reference of industrial disputes to arbitration.

9. (a) Distinguish between strike and lockout When are strikes and lockouts illegal under the Industrial Disputes Act?

   (b) What are the liabilities of a person inducing or financing an illegal strike?

10. Discuss the consideration taken into account by the Adjudicators or Industrial Tribunals in deciding the issue of payment of wages during a period of strike or lockout.

11. Explain the provisions of the Industrial Disputes Act relating to recovery of money due from an employer to a workman.

12. State the legal implications of the provisions of Section 25FF of the Industrial Disputes Act relating to transfer of ownership or management of an undertaking from one employer to another employer.

13. Attempt the following problems, giving reasons for your answers:

   (a) Some workmen of a transport company were dismissed and retrenched by the employer. Out of a total of 60 workmen employed by the company, 18 workmen sponsored the cause of dismissed workmen and raised a dispute. Those who sponsored the cause of dismissed workmen included 13 dismissed workers of the company. The dispute was referred by the State Government to the Labour Court Can the dispute be said to be an industrial dispute so as to justify a reference by the State Government to Labour Court?

   (b) The employees of a bank enter the premises and occupy their respective seats, but do not pick up the pens to start working. Does this amount to a strike?

   (c) As a result of faction between rival trade unions there was a stoppage of work for twelve days in a colliery, and not a single worker out of a total strength of 2,200 men attended. The employer contended that the cessation of work was a concerted refusal to work without notice and amounted to an illegal strike. Decide the case.

CHAPTER XXII

Minimum Wages

1. What is a minimum wage, a living wage? Describe the procedure for fixing minimum wages.

2. Discuss the provisions according to which the employer must pay to his employees a minimum wage. What are the consequences of failure to pay the minimum wage? When and how can an employer escape liability for an offence committed against the Act?

3. (a) Enumerate the different kinds of employment in which minimum wages must be paid.

   (b) Is an employer bound to pay the minimum wage even when the business is running at a loss?

Index

NOTES

NOTES

NOTES

NOTES